American Southwest

2nd Edition

by Lesley King & Karl Samson

Colorado & Utah coverage by Don & Barbara Laine
Las Vegas coverage by Mary Herczog

WILEY
Wiley Publishing, Inc.

Published by:

Wiley Publishing, Inc.

111 River St.
Hoboken, NJ 07030-5774

ISBN-13: 978-0-7645-9883-8
ISBN-10: 0-7645-9883-X

Editor: Marie Morris
Production Editor: M. Faunette Johnston
Cartographer: Roberta Stockwell
Photo Editor: Richard Fox
Production by Wiley Indianapolis Composition Services

For information on our other products and services or to obtain technical support, please contact our Customer Care Department within the U.S. at 800/762-2974, outside the U.S. at 317/572-3993 or fax 317/572-4002.

Wiley also publishes its books in a variety of electronic formats. Some content that appears in print may not be available in electronic formats.

Manufactured in the United States of America

5 4 3 2 1

Contents

14 The Deserts, High Plains & Sky Islands of Southern Arizona 459

15 Sedona & the Colorado River: The Best of Central & Western Arizona 483

16 The Grand Canyon & Northern Arizona 522

17 Southern Utah's National Parks 561

18 Las Vegas 584

Appendix: The Southwest in Depth   602

Index   613

List of Maps

About the Authors

Lesley S. King (New Mexico coverage, plus chapters 2, 3, 5, and appendix) grew up on a ranch in northern New Mexico, where she still returns on weekends to help work cattle. A freelance writer and photographer, she's a contributor to *New Mexico Magazine* and an avid kayaker and skier. She has written for the *New York Times*, United Airlines' *Hemispheres* magazine, *American Cowboy*, and *Audubon*. She is writer and host of *Written on the Wind*, a television documentary series. She is also the author of *Frommer's Santa Fe, Taos & Albuquerque* and *Frommer's New Mexico*.

Karl Samson (Arizona coverage) finds that the sunny winter skies of the Arizona desert are the perfect antidote to the dreary winters of his Pacific Northwest home. Each winter, he flees the rain to explore Arizona's deserts, mountains, cities, and small towns. It is the state's unique regional style, Native American cultures, abundance of contemporary art, and, of course, boundless landscapes that keep him fascinated by Arizona. Summer finds him researching his other books, including *Frommer's Washington*, *Frommer's Oregon*, and *Frommer's Seattle & Portland*.

Residents of northern New Mexico for more than 30 years, **Don** and **Barbara Laine** (Colorado and Utah coverage) have traveled extensively throughout the Rocky Mountains and the Southwest. They are the authors of *Frommer's Colorado*, *Frommer's Utah*, *Frommer's Rocky Mountain National Park*, and *Frommer's Zion & Bryce Canyon National Parks*; are the lead authors of *Frommer's National Parks of the American West*; and have contributed to *Frommer's Texas* and *Frommer's USA*. The Laines have also written *Little-Known Southwest* and *New Mexico & Arizona State Parks* (both for The Mountaineers Books).

Mary Herczog (Las Vegas coverage) lives in Los Angeles and works in the film industry. She is the author of *Frommer's New Orleans* and *Las Vegas For Dummies*, and has contributed to *Frommer's Los Angeles*. She still isn't sure when to hit and when to hold when playing blackjack.

An Invitation to the Reader

In researching this book, we discovered many wonderful places—hotels, restaurants, shops, and more. We're sure you'll find others. Please tell us about them, so we can share the information with your fellow travelers in upcoming editions. If you were disappointed with a recommendation, we'd love to know that, too. Please write to:

Frommer's American Southwest, 2nd Edition
Wiley Publishing, Inc. • 111 River St. • Hoboken, NJ 07030-5774

An Additional Note

Please be advised that travel information is subject to change at any time—and this is especially true of prices. We therefore suggest that you write or call ahead for confirmation when making your travel plans. The authors, editors, and publisher cannot be held responsible for the experiences of readers while traveling. Your safety is important to us, however, so we encourage you to stay alert and be aware of your surroundings. Keep a close eye on cameras, purses, and wallets, all favorite targets of thieves and pickpockets.

Other Great Guides for Your Trip:

Frommer's Utah

Frommer's Arizona

Frommer's Colorado

Frommer's Las Vegas

Frommer's New Mexico

Frommer's Exploring America by RV

Frommer's National Parks of the American West

Frommer's Star Ratings, Icons & Abbreviations

Every hotel, restaurant, and attraction listing in this guide has been ranked for quality, value, service, amenities, and special features using a **star-rating system.** In country, state, and regional guides, we also rate towns and regions to help you narrow down your choices and budget your time accordingly. Hotels and restaurants are rated on a scale of zero (recommended) to three stars (exceptional). Attractions, shopping, nightlife, towns, and regions are rated according to the following scale: zero stars (recommended), one star (highly recommended), two stars (very highly recommended), and three stars (must-see).

In addition to the star-rating system, we also use **seven feature icons** that point you to the great deals, in-the-know advice, and unique experiences that separate travelers from tourists. Throughout the book, look for:

Finds	Special finds—those places only insiders know about
Fun Fact	Fun facts—details that make travelers more informed and their trips more fun
Kids	Best bets for kids and advice for the whole family
Moments	Special moments—those experiences that memories are made of
Overrated	Places or experiences not worth your time or money
Tips	Insider tips—great ways to save time and money
Value	Great values—where to get the best deals

The following **abbreviations** are used for credit cards:

AE	American Express	DISC	Discover	V	Visa
DC	Diners Club	MC	MasterCard		

Frommers.com

Now that you have the guidebook to a great trip, visit our website at **www.frommers.com** for travel information on more than 3,000 destinations. With features updated regularly, we give you instant access to the most current trip-planning information available. At Frommers.com, you'll also find the best prices on airfares, accommodations, and car rentals—and you can even book travel online through our travel booking partners. At Frommers.com, you'll also find the following:

- Online updates to our most popular guidebooks
- Vacation sweepstakes and contest giveaways
- Newsletter highlighting the hottest travel trends
- Online travel message boards with featured travel discussions

What's New in the American Southwest

THE FOUR CORNERS AREA Cherrywood floors and flowing fountains create an oasis feel at the completely renovated **Casa Blanca,** 505 E. La Plata St., Farmington, NM (© **800/550-6503** or 505/327-6503; www.4cornersbandb. com). Just blocks from Main Street, the inn has large rooms, well stocked with amenities; it's a great home base to explore area ruins.

Farmington finally has a fine-dining spot. **The Bluffs,** 3450 E. Main St. (© **505/325-8155**), serves quality steaks and seafood in a comfortable wood-accented ambience. Any of the Angus beef steaks will please.

SANTA FE The **Don Gaspar Inn,** 623 Don Gaspar (© **888/986-8664** or 505/986-8664; www.dongaspar.com), is a quiet and elegant place nestled in a historic neighborhood. It's a good choice for those who want to feel as if they live in Santa Fe.

The "City Different" has a new **performance gazebo** erected on the Plaza in 2004. On summer evenings and during festivals and markets, bands play under the copper-roofed stage.

Tesuque Pueblo (9 miles north of Santa Fe on US 84/285) has a new church. The three-story **San Diego Church** replaced an older church that burned recently.

The **Castillo Gallery,** a mile into the village of Cordova, on the High Road to Taos (© **505/351-4067**), has moved next door, into a brighter and more expansive space. It's still operated by a fine husband-and-wife artist team.

TAOS The biggest news in the region is the opening of **El Monte Sagrado,** 317 Kit Carson Rd. (© **800/828-TAOS** or 505/758-3502; www.elmontesagrado. com). The ecoresort offers impeccable, imaginative accommodations surrounding a "Sacred Circle," an open grassy area. The resort offers fine food and spa treatments.

Taos is also celebrating finally having a good hotel on its plaza. **Hotel La Fonda de Taos,** 108 South Plaza (© **800/833-2211** or 505/758-2211; www.hotella fonda.com), provides comfortable, smartly decorated rooms with a dash of history.

At Taos Ski Valley, **Edelweiss Lodge & Spa,** 106 Sutton Place (© **800/I-LUV-SKI** or 505/776-2301; www.edelweiss lodgeandspa.com), has been rebuilt into an upscale condo hotel, with luxury rooms and a complete spa. The owners are especially intent on attracting summer spa guests.

The new **De La Tierra** restaurant, at El Monte Sagrado resort, 317 Kit Carson Rd. (© **800/828-TAOS** or 505/758-3502), offers regional American food in a refined atmosphere. Diners feast on food ranging from venison medallions to rosemary-skewered shrimp.

For a while, Taos was without **Joseph's Table;** the fine restaurant had closed. It reopened in an even larger space, in the Hotel La Fonda on the plaza, and still serves some of the most imaginative food in the Southwest. It's at 108A South Taos Plaza (© **505/751-4512;** www.josephs table.com).

In the quaint village of Arroyo Seco, en route to the ski area, **Gypsy 360°,** 480 NM 150, Seco Plaza (© **505/776-3166**), could just be the region's best new casual spot. Serving Asian and American dishes ranging from pad Thai to Angus burgers, the place serves recipes as fresh as the ingredients in them.

The Kit Carson Home has passed out of the hands of the **Taos Historic Museums** (© **505/758-0505**). Exhibits from the museum have moved to the **Martinez Hacienda,** Lower Ranchitos Road, Highway 240 (© **505/758-1000**). The new **Kit Carson Museum,** 113 Kit Carson Rd. (© **505/758-4945**), presents a more accurate depiction of Carson's life and times.

Another big change in the Taos museum scene is the shifting of the collection of the **Taos Art Museum** (© **505/758-2690**) from the Van Vechten Lineberry Museum (now closed) to the **Fechin House,** 227 Paseo del Pueblo Norte. Though the museum lost some space, it gained a lovely venue.

A new hot spot for those who like to browse little villages is **Arroyo Seco,** on NM 150, about 5 miles north of town en route to Taos Ski Valley. Besides the Gypsy 360° restaurant (see above), Arroyo Seco has fun shops and amazing mountain views.

Nights in Taos will never be the same now that the **Anaconda Bar,** 317 Kit Carson Rd. (© **505/758-3502**), has opened at El Monte Sagrado resort. The contemporary feel, accented by a giant anaconda snake sculpture, as well as tasty tapas and live music draw the hippest Taoseños and visitors.

ALBUQUERQUE   Albuquerque's most happening new dining spot, **Zinc Wine Bar and Bistro,** 3009 Central Ave. NE (© **505/254-ZINC**), serves inventive meals such as blackened sliced flank steak over Greek salad. It offers interesting deals, such as wine flights, which allow diners to sample a variety of wines from a particular region.

The ¡**Explora! Science Center and Children's Museum,** 1701 Mountain Rd. (© **505/224-8300**), has moved to a better location close to Old Town. The museum features hands-on scientific exhibits for kids of all ages, even 40-something ones like me.

If you plan to travel north from Albuquerque on the Jemez Mountain Trail, make reservations at the **Cañon del Rio–Riverside Inn,** 16445 Scenic Hwy. 4, Jemez Springs (© **505/829-4377;** www.canondelrio.com). Formerly the Riverdancer, this inn near the Jemez River has undergone refurbishment by new owners.

NORTHERN NEW MEXICO   While on the Las Vegas Plaza, stop in at **Tapetes de Lana,** 1814 Plaza (© **505/426-8638**), to watch weavers make scarves, ponchos, and Rio Grande–style rugs. You can buy the creations, too.

For those getting their kicks on Route 66, also known as I-40, a good place to cool your heels is the newish **La Quinta,** 1701 Will Rogers Dr. (© **800/531-5900** or 505/472-4800; www.laquinta.com), on a hill above Santa Rosa. Lots of amenities, including a hot tub in a lovely grotto, add character to the predictability of this chain hotel.

In a search for a room in Gallup where mythic but loud train sounds didn't keep me up at night, I landed at **Holiday Inn Express,** 1500 W. Maloney Ave. (© **800/ HOLIDAY** or 505/726-1000; www.hi express.com). It sits on a hill above town and offers lots of amenities.

All the Mediterranean standards such as hummus and falafel spill from the kitchen of Gallup's new **Oasis Mediterranean Restaurant & Hookah Lounge,** 100 E. 66 Ave. (© 505/722-9572), but the real treats are chicken and meat dishes bravely spiced. The setting is a gallery, where diners can see and purchase art.

SOUTHERN NEW MEXICO In **Truth or Consequences,** the restoration a few years back of a 1920s hot springs resort, now the **Sierra Grande Lodge & Spa,** 501 McAdoo St. (© 505/894-6976; www.sierragrandelodge.com), brought luxury to this odd outpost town. The lodge's restaurant now serves year-round. When it opened, it made *Condé Nast Traveler*'s list of the top 50 new restaurants in the world. The bistro warrants a stop, even if you're just cruising by T or C on I-25. The olive-crusted salmon is delectable.

Chope's Bar and Cafe, on NM 28 (© 505/233-3420), is a legendary spot 15 minutes south of Mesilla (near Las Cruces). It serves up big plates of enchiladas and chile rellenos with lots of chile and southern New Mexican attitude— *olé!*

Outside the tiny hamlet of Tularosa, **Casa de Sueños,** 35 St. Francis Dr. (© 505/585-3494), offers tasty New Mexican fare in a whimsical Mexican setting. Start with guacamole and move on to anything smothered in chile.

The village of Capitan has woken up from a long sleep and is suddenly a culinary destination. Chefs at the **Greenhouse Café,** 103 S. Lincoln St. (© 505/354-0373), serve chicken, meat, and fish dishes with veggies grown in their own greenhouse. Try the chicken stroganoff, served in puff pastry.

PHOENIX, SCOTTSDALE & THE VALLEY OF THE SUN Bargain-hunting vacationers looking for good value at a resort in Scottsdale lost a lot of options in the past year or so. No fewer than four resorts—the Holiday Inn SunSpree, Marriott's Mountain Shadows, the Radisson Scottsdale, and the Doubletree La Posada—shut their doors and drained their pools. Some are being remade as new resorts, while others are being bulldozed to make way for condominiums. Rest assured that there are still a few bargains to be had in the Phoenix area, and you'll find the best ones listed in this book.

Scottsdale's SunBurst Resort has a new name. It's now **Caleo Resort & Spa,** 4925 N. Scottsdale Rd. (© 800/528-7867; www.caleoresort.com). Rooms have been renovated, and the resort has a new outdoor dining area and a new main restaurant.

On the restaurant scene, foodies should absolutely not miss the new restaurant **Vu,** 7500 E. Doubletree Ranch Rd., Scottsdale (© 480/991-3388), at the luxurious Hyatt Regency Scottsdale Resort and Spa at Gainey Ranch.

Another great choice for a splurge dinner is **Sassi,** 10455 E. Pinnacle Peak Pkwy. (© 480/502-9095; www.sassi. biz), in north Scottsdale. The beautiful Tuscan-style villa serves the most creative Italian food in the Phoenix area.

For the best burger in Phoenix proper, head to **Delux,** 3146 E. Camelback Rd. (© 602/522-2288; www.deluxburger. com), a stylish little place on the Camelback corridor. Deluxe also has the most amazing selection of draft beers in the city.

Car-racing fans should definitely not miss the cool little **Penske Racing Museum,** 7125 E. Chauncey Lane, Scottsdale (© 480/538-4444). It has more than a dozen race cars on display, including several that have won the Indianapolis 500.

At **Taliesin West,** 12621 Frank Lloyd Wright Blvd., Scottsdale (© 480/860-8810; www.franklloydwright.org), Frank Lloyd Wright's private living quarters have been renovated and can now be visited on tours of the Taliesin West campus.

If you plan to visit Scottsdale between January and March, try to catch one of the free Native American music and dance performances on the Scottsdale Mall. Called **Native Trails,** these shows are a great way to learn about the traditional Native American cultures of Arizona.

Note that the **Hyatt Regency Scottsdale Resort and Spa at Gainey Ranch,** 7500 E. Doubletree Ranch Rd. (© 800/55-HYATT; www.scottsdale.hyatt.com), has the word "spa" in its name. That brand-new feature is definitely worth checking out.

By the time this book comes out, the new spa at the **Wigwam Golf Club & Spa,** 300 Wigwam Blvd., Litchfield Park (© 800/327-0396; www.wigwamresort.com), on the west side of the Valley, should be up and running.

THE GRAND CANYON & NORTHERN ARIZONA There's a great new old B&B in Flagstaff. The **England House Bed & Breakfast,** 614 W. Santa Fe Ave. (© 877/214-7350; www.englandhousebandb.com), is in a beautiful red sandstone Victorian house that has been lovingly restored by owners Richard and Laurel Dunn.

El Tovar Hotel, Grand Canyon Village (© 888/297-2757; www.grandcanyonlodges.com), the premier historic lodge on the South Rim of the Grand Canyon, shut down for 3 months in early 2005 and underwent a complete renovation. The rooms now look thoroughly modern, which may or may not be what you expect from a historic lodge. Regardless of the style, this is the best hotel in Grand Canyon Village.

CENTRAL ARIZONA If you want to delve into the history of Prescott, hop aboard the trolley operated by **Old West Trolley Tours** (© 928/717-0528; www.prescotttrolley.com). History buffs should also visit the new **Fort Whipple Museum** (© 928/445-3122). If you're looking to get in some exercise, try hiking or biking the new **Iron King Trail,** which passes through scenic Granite Dells.

In Sedona, the newly refurbished and updated cabins at **Don Hoel's Cabins,** 9440 N. Hwy. 89A (© 800/292-HOEL; www.hoels.com), in Oak Creek Canyon, are a good bet for families and summertime visitors to the area. The cabins are not far from the trailhead for the West Fork Trail.

SOUTHERN ARIZONA In the Santa Cruz Valley, south of Tucson, check out the newly renovated, expanded, and upgraded **Tubac Golf Resort,** 1 Otero Rd., Tubac (© 800/848-7893; www.tubacgolfresort.com). A great new restaurant in downtown Tubac, **Border House Bistro,** 12 Plaza Rd. (© 520/398-8999; www.chefw.com), serves an eclectic menu that even includes alligator tacos.

In Bisbee, a familiar face is at a restaurant that has had four names in as many years. The **Striped Stocking Restaurant & Hotel,** 1 Howell Ave., Bisbee (© 520/432-1832), is the domain of Nancy Parana, who had the restaurant here a couple of years earlier. There's something about Bisbee that keeps pulling people back.

1

The Best of the Southwest

Planning a trip to a region as large and diverse as the American Southwest involves a lot of decision making, so in this chapter we've tried to give you some direction. We've chosen what we feel is the very best the region has to offer—the places and experiences you won't want to miss. Although the sights and activities listed here are written up in more detail elsewhere in this book, this chapter should give you an overview of the highlights and get you started.

1 The Best of the Natural Southwest

- **Monument Valley Buttes at Sunset** (UT and AZ): These stark sentinels of the desert are impressive at any time, but they take on a particularly dignified aura when the setting sun casts its deep colors over them, etching their profiles against a darkening sky. Although the park generally closes before sunset, you can arrange a sunset tour—it's well worth the cost. See p. 117.

- **Rio Grande Gorge** (NM): A hike into this dramatic gorge is unforgettable. You'll first see it as you come over a rise heading toward Taos. It's a colossal slice in the earth formed during the late Cretaceous period (130 million years ago) and the early Tertiary period (about 70 million years ago). Drive about 35 miles north of Taos, near the village of Cerro, to the **Wild Rivers Recreation Area.** From the lip of the canyon, you descend through millions of years of geologic history and land inhabited by Indians since 16,000 B.C. If you're visiting during spring and early summer and like an adrenaline rush, be sure to find a professional guide and raft the Taos Box, a 17-mile stretch of class

IV white water. See "Getting Outside," in chapter 8.

- **Carlsbad Caverns National Park** (NM): One of the world's largest and most complex cave systems is in southeastern New Mexico. The 80 known caves have spectacular stalagmite and stalactite formations. Explore the Big Room on a 1-mile self-guided tour, then catch the massive bat flight from the cave entrance at sunset. See p. 314.

- **White Sands National Monument** (NM): Located 15 miles southwest of Alamogordo, White Sands National Monument preserves the best part of the world's largest gypsum dune field. For a truly unforgettable experience, camp overnight so that you can watch the sun rise on the smooth, endless dunes. See p. 299.

- **Arizona–Sonora Desert Museum** (AZ): The name is misleading—this is more zoo and botanical garden than museum. Naturalistic settings house dozens of species of desert animals, including a number of critters you wouldn't want to meet in the wild (rattlesnakes, tarantulas, scorpions, black widows, and Gila monsters). See p. 369.

The American Southwest

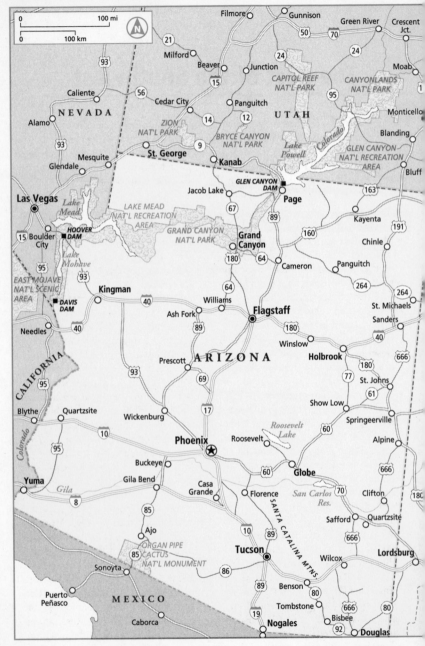

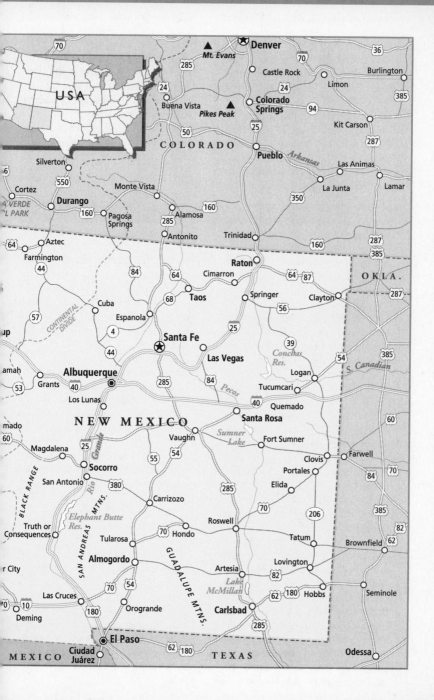

- **Saguaro National Park** (AZ): Lying both east and west of Tucson, this park preserves "forests" of saguaro cacti and is the very essence of the desert as so many people imagine it. You can hike it, bike it, or drive it. See p. 372.
- **Desert Botanical Garden** (AZ): There's no better place to learn about the plants of Arizona's Sonoran Desert and the many other deserts of the world. Displays at this Phoenix botanical garden explain plant adaptations and how indigenous tribes once used many of this region's wild plants. See p. 430.
- **Zion National Park** (UT): At the Narrows in Zion, sheer 1,000-foot-high walls enclose you in a 20-foot-wide world of hanging gardens, waterfalls, and sculpted sandstone arches, with the Virgin River beneath your feet. This is one of the park's many awe-inspiring experiences. See p. 561.

2 The Best Outdoor Activities

- **Hiking** (throughout the region): What's unique about hiking in the Southwest is the variety of terrain, from desert to alpine forest to badlands to canyons. In Utah, you can hike right past all three stone formations at Natural Bridges National Monument (p. 96) or explore the hoodoo formations in Bryce Canyon National Park (p. 567). Some of our favorite places for a hike in New Mexico are the El Malpais badlands (p. 273), the hauntingly sculpted rock formations at Abiquiu that artist Georgia O'Keeffe made famous in her paintings (p. 282), and White Sands National Monument (p. 299).

  In Arizona, a hike down into the Grand Canyon or Havasu Canyon is not for the unfit or the faint of heart, but it will take you on a journey through millions of years set in stone. This trip takes plenty of planning and requires some strenuous hiking. See "The Grand Canyon South Rim" and "A South Rim Alternative: Havasu Canyon," in chapter 16.
- **Ballooning** (NM and AZ): With the International Balloon Fiesta in Albuquerque bringing more than 750 balloons to the area, Albuquerque has become the sport's world capital. Fortunately, visitors can let loose the tethers and float free, too. Most of the operators are in Albuquerque; see p. 249 for recommendations. Ballooning is also popular in Arizona; see "Getting Outside," in chapters 12 and 13, and "Organized Tours," under "Sedona & Oak Creek Canyon," in chapter 15 for information on companies in Tucson, Phoenix, and Sedona.
- **Horseback riding** (NM and AZ): New Mexico's history is stamped with the hoof, dating from the Spanish conquistadors' introduction of horses to the New World. Riding in New Mexico still has that Old West feel, with trails that wind through wilderness, traversing passes and broad meadows. Some of the best rides are in the Pecos Wilderness and on Taos Pueblo land. See "Getting Outside," in chapters 7 and 8.

  Cowboys still ride ranges all over Arizona, and so can you if you book a stay at one of the state's many guest ranches (formerly known as dude ranches). You might even get to drive some cattle down the trail. After a long or short day in the saddle, you can soak in a hot tub, go for a swim, or play tennis before chowing down. See chapters 12, 14, and 15.

- **Mountain Biking** (NM and AZ): Almost anywhere you go in New Mexico, you'll find trails. We've hooked onto some fun old mining roads in the Black Range down south and explored sage forest on the rim of the Taos Gorge in the north. See the "Biking" sections under "Getting Outside," in each New Mexico chapter, especially chapter 8, "Taos."

  In Arizona, among the red rocks of Sedona, you can pedal through awesome scenery on some of the most memorable single-track trails in the Southwest. There's even plenty of slickrock. See "Getting Outside," under "Sedona & Oak Creek Canyon," in chapter 15.
- **River Rafting** (NM and AZ): Whether you go for 3 days or 2 weeks, no other active vacation in the region comes close to matching the excitement of a raft trip. In Arizona, nothing beats a Colorado River rafting trip through the Grand Canyon. Sure, the river is crowded with groups in the summer, but the grandeur of the canyon more than makes up for it. See "Other Ways of Seeing the Canyon," under "The Grand Canyon South Rim," in chapter 16. In New Mexico, the wild **Taos Box,** a steep-sided canyon south of the Wild Rivers Recreation Area, offers a series of class IV rapids that rarely lets up for some 17 miles, providing one of the most exciting 1-day white-water tours in the West. See "Getting Outside," in chapter 8.

3 The Best Scenic Drives

- **Monument Valley Navajo Tribal Park** (UT and AZ): This valley of sandstone buttes and mesas is one of the most photographed spots in America. It's familiar to people all over the world from countless movies, TV shows, and commercials. A 17-mile dirt road winds through the park, giving visitors close-up views of such landmarks as Elephant Butte, the Mittens, and Totem Pole. See "Monument Valley Navajo Tribal Park," in chapter 6.
- **High Road to Taos** (Santa Fe, NM): One of New Mexico's primo experiences, this road traverses the mountains from Santa Fe to Taos, passing by chile and apple farms in old Hispanic villages. Stop in Chimayo to see unique wool weaving, in Cordova to find lovely woodcarvings, and in renegade Truchas, where life remains much as it did a century ago. Most important, the route crosses the base of New Mexico's grandest peaks. See "Taking the High Road to Taos," in chapter 7.
- **Turquoise Trail** (Albuquerque, NM): Meandering through the broad Galisteo basin, this is the scenic route from Albuquerque to Santa Fe. The two-lane road runs through piñon-studded hills and old mining towns such as Madrid and Cerrillos, where 2,000 years ago Native Americans hammered turquoise and silver from the hills. Today artists and craftspeople have revived the towns. See "En Route to Santa Fe: Along the Turquoise Trail," in chapter 9.
- **Lincoln Loop** (Ruidoso, NM): Elegant art, ancient petroglyphs, and Billy the Kid memorabilia draw road warriors to this 162-mile loop in southeastern New Mexico. It begins in the mountain resort town of Ruidoso and cruises to Lincoln, where travelers can "walk in the footsteps" of the notorious punk Billy the Kid. Next it passes imaginative petroglyphs,

through the Mescalero Apache Reservation, and back to Ruidoso. See "A Scenic Drive Around the Lincoln Loop," in chapter 11.

- **The Apache Trail** (east of Phoenix, AZ): Much of this winding road, which passes just north of the Superstition Mountains, is unpaved and follows a rugged route once ridden by Apaches. This is some of the most remote country in the Phoenix area, with far-reaching desert vistas and lots to see and do along the way. See "A Side Trip from Phoenix: The Apache Trail," in chapter 13.
- **Oak Creek Canyon** (Sedona, AZ): Slicing down from the pine country outside Flagstaff to the red rocks of Sedona, Oak Creek Canyon is a cool oasis. From the scenic overlook at the top of the canyon to the swimming holes and hiking trails at the bottom, this canyon road provides a rapid change in climate and landscape. See "Sedona & Oak Creek Canyon," in chapter 15.
- **Mount Lemmon** (Tucson, AZ): The views of Tucson from the city's northern foothills are great, but the vistas from Mount Lemmon are even better. With a ski area at its summit, Mount Lemmon rises from the desert like an island emerging from the sea. Along the way, the road climbs from cactus country to cool pine forests. See "Getting Outside," in chapter 12.

4 The Best Native American Sights

- **Ute Mountain Tribal Park** (CO): These ruins differ from others in Colorado because they're on the Ute Mountain Indian Reservation, and the only way to see the reservation is on a guided tour conducted by members of the tribe. You'll see ruins and petroglyphs similar to those in Mesa Verde, but with an informed personal guide and without crowds. See p. 88.
- **Mesa Verde National Park** (CO): Home to the most impressive prehistoric cliff dwellings in the Southwest, Mesa Verde (Spanish for "green table") overwhelms you with its size and complexity. The first national park set aside to preserve works created by humans, it covers some 52,000 acres just outside Cortez. Among the most compelling sites are Spruce Tree House, Square Tower House, and Cliff Palace, a four-story, apartment-style dwelling. See "Mesa Verde National Park," in chapter 6.
- **Hovenweep National Monument** (UT): This deserted valley contains some of the most striking and most isolated archaeological sites in the Four Corners area—the remains of curious sandstone towers built more than 700 years ago by the Anasazi (ancestral Puebloans). These mysterious structures still keep archaeologists guessing. See p. 88.
- **Monument Valley Navajo Tribal Park** (UT and AZ): For most of us, Monument Valley *is* the Old West. We've seen it dozens of times in movie theaters, on TV, in magazine advertisements, and on billboards. The Old West may be gone, but many Navajos still call this home. A Navajo guide will give you the Navajo perspective on this majestic land and take you into areas not otherwise open to visitors. See p. 115.
- **Indian Pueblo Cultural Center** (Albuquerque, NM): Owned and operated as a nonprofit organization by the 19 pueblos of New Mexico, this is a fine place to begin an exploration of Native American culture. The museum is modeled after Pueblo Bonito, a spectacular 9th-century ruin in Chaco Culture National Historic

Park, and contains art and artifacts old and new. See p. 244.

- **Petroglyph National Monument** (NM): This site has 25,000 petroglyphs (prehistoric rock carvings) and a variety of hiking trails geared to differing levels of difficulty. It's right on the outskirts of Albuquerque. See p. 247.

- **Bandelier National Monument** (NM): Along with the Puye Cliff Dwellings, these ruins provide a spectacular peek into the lives of the Anasazi culture, which flourished in the area between A.D. 1100 and 1550. Less than 15 miles south of Los Alamos, the ruins spread across a peaceful canyon. The most dramatic site is a dwelling and kiva (a room used for religious activities) in a cave 140 feet above the canyon floor—reached by a climb up long pueblo-style ladders. See p. 191.

- **Pecos National Historical Park** (NM): It's hard to rank New Mexico's many ruins, but this one, sprawled on a plain about 25 miles east of Santa Fe, is one of the most impressive. It resonates with the history of the Pueblo Revolt of 1680. You'll see evidence of where the Pecos people burned the mission church before joining in the attack on Santa Fe. You'll also see where the Spanish conquistadors later compromised, allowing sacred kivas to be built next to the reconstructed mission. See p. 190.

- **Aztec Ruins National Monument** (NM): These ruins of a 500-room Native American pueblo abandoned by the Anasazi more than 200 years ago feature a completely reconstructed kiva 50 feet in diameter. See p. 129.

- **Heard Museum** (AZ): This Phoenix institution is one of the nation's premier museums devoted to Native American cultures. In addition to historical exhibits, a huge kachina collection, and an excellent store, it has annual exhibits of contemporary Native American art as well as dance performances and demonstrations of traditional skills. See p. 430.

- **Tonto National Monument** (AZ): East of Phoenix on the Apache Trail, this is one of the only easily accessible cliff dwellings in Arizona that you can still visit; you don't have to just observe from a distance. See p. 458.

- **Montezuma Castle National Monument** (AZ): Located just off I-17, this is the easiest cliff dwelling to get to in Arizona, but visitors cannot enter. Nearby Montezuma Well also has some small ruins. See p. 496.

- **Canyon de Chelly National Monument** (AZ): Small cliff dwellings up and down the length of Canyon de Chelly are visible from overlooks, while a trip into the canyon itself offers a chance to see some of these ruins up close. See p. 109.

- **Navajo National Monument** (AZ): Keet Seel and Betatakin are some of the finest examples of Anasazi cliff dwellings in the state. Although the ruins are at the end of long hikes, their size and state of preservation make the sites well worth the effort you'll expend to see them. See p. 114.

5 The Best Family Experiences

- **Albuquerque Aquarium** (NM): For those of us born and raised in the desert, this attraction quenches years of soul thirst. Exhibits focus on sea areas fed by the Rio Grande River.

You'll pass by many large tanks and within an eels' den. The culminating show is a 285,000-gallon shark tank, where many species of fish and 15 to 20 sand tiger, brown, and nurse sharks swim around looking ominous. The aquarium is part of the Albuquerque Biological Park. See p. 247.

- **Rio Grande Zoo** (NM): More than 1,200 animals of 300 species live on 60 acres of riverside bosque among ancient cottonwoods. Open-moat exhibits with animals in naturalized habitats are a treat for zoo-goers. Albuquerque's zoo has an especially fine collection of elephants, mountain lions, koalas, reptiles, and native Southwestern species. During summer, a children's petting zoo is open, and the New Mexico Symphony Orchestra performs. See p. 249.

- **Santa Fe Children's Museum** (NM): Designed for the whole family, this museum offers interactive exhibits and hands-on activities focusing on the arts, humanities, science, and technology. Most notable is a 16-foot climbing wall that kids can scale, outfitted with helmets and harnesses. The museum regularly schedules special performances and hands-on sessions with artists and scientists. Recently, *Family Life* magazine named this one of the 10 hottest children's museums in the nation. See p. 170.

- **Carlsbad Caverns National Park** (NM): Truly one of the world's natural wonders, these caverns swallow visitors as they embark on what feels like a journey to the center of the earth. Nocturnal creatures thrive, and water drips onto your body. Stalactites and stalagmites create another universe of seemingly alien life forms. Kids won't like the fact that they can't go climbing on the formations, but they'll be too fascinated to complain much. See p. 314.

- **Arizona–Sonora Desert Museum** (AZ): This Tucson attraction is actually a zoo featuring the animals of the Sonoran Desert. It has rooms full of snakes, a prairie-dog town, bighorn sheep, mountain lions, and an aviary full of hummingbirds. Kids and adults love this place. See p. 369.

- **Shootouts at the O.K. Corral** (AZ): Tombstone may be "the town too tough to die," but poor Ike Clanton and his buddies the McLaury boys have to die over and over at frequent reenactments of the famous gunfight. See p. 474.

- **The Grand Canyon Railway** (AZ): Not only is this train excursion a fun way to get to the Grand Canyon, it also lets you avoid wearisome parking problems and congestion. Shootouts and train robberies are to be expected in this corner of the Wild West. See p. 545.

- **Zion National Park** (UT): The Junior Ranger/Explorers program, available at most national parks, is particularly extensive here. Morning and afternoon activities all summer are geared toward teaching kids what makes this natural wonder so special. They'll have so much fun, they won't even notice they're learning. See p. 561.

6 The Best Luxury Hotels & Resorts

- **La Posada de Santa Fe Resort and Spa** (Santa Fe, NM; © 800/727-5276): With the feel of a meandering adobe village but the service of a fine hotel, this has become one of New Mexico's premier resorts. The resort has a Zen-Southwestern–style spa and pool and spacious spa rooms. Most units don't have views but do have outdoor patios, and most are tucked back into the quiet compound. See p. 144.

- **Hyatt Regency Tamaya Resort and Spa** (Santa Ana Pueblo, NM; © 800/

55-HYATT): Situated on Santa Ana Pueblo land, this grand resort has all a human might need to get away from the world. Three swimming pools, a 16,000-square-foot full-service spa and fitness center, and the 18-hole Twin Warriors championship golf course designed by Gary Panks make for plenty to do. Meanwhile, spacious rooms offer quiet for those who'd rather do nothing. Though the resort is surrounded by acres of countryside, it's only 15 minutes from Albuquerque and 45 minutes from Santa Fe. See p. 240.

- **Hyatt Regency Scottsdale Resort and Spa at Gainey Ranch** (Scottsdale, AZ; © **800/55-HYATT**): Contemporary desert architecture, dramatic landscaping, a water playground with its own beach, a staff that's always ready to assist you, several good restaurants that aren't overpriced, and even gondola rides—it all adds up to a lot of fun at one of the most smoothly run resorts in Arizona. See p. 402.

- **The Phoenician** (Scottsdale, AZ; © **800/888-8234**): This Xanadu of the resort world brims with marble, crystal, and art. With staff members seemingly around every corner, the hotel offers its guests impeccable service. Mary Elaine's, the resort's premier dining room, is among the finest restaurants in the state, and the views are hard to beat. See p. 403.

- **The Boulders Resort and Golden Door Spa** (Carefree, AZ; © **800/**

553-1717): Taking its name from the massive blocks of eroded granite scattered about the grounds, the Boulders is among the most exclusive and expensive resorts in the state. Pueblo architecture fits seamlessly with the landscape, and the golf course is the most breathtaking in Arizona. See p. 405.

- **Arizona Biltmore Resort & Spa** (Phoenix, AZ; © **800/950-0086**): Combining discreet service and the architectural styling of Frank Lloyd Wright, the Biltmore has long been one of Arizona's most prestigious resorts. This is a thoroughly old-money place, but it continues to keep pace with the times. See p. 407.

- **Loews Ventana Canyon Resort** (Tucson, AZ; © **800/234-5117**): With the Santa Catalina Mountains rising in the backyard and an almost-natural waterfall only steps away from the lobby, this is Tucson's most dramatic resort. Contemporary styling throughout makes constant reference to the desert setting. See p. 352.

- **Enchantment Resort** (Sedona, AZ; © **800/826-4180**): A dramatic setting in a red-rock canyon makes this the most unforgettably situated resort in the state. If you want to feel as though you're vacationing in the desert, this place fits the bill. Guest rooms are constructed in pueblo architectural style; the spa is one of Arizona's finest. See p. 506.

7 The Best B&Bs

- **Kokopelli's Cave** (Farmington, NM; © **505/326-2461**): This is an actual cave, but it's like no other cave you've ever seen. Carved deep into the side of a cliff, it's a three-room luxury apartment complete with carpet,

VCR, kitchen, and space enough for a family. Best of all is the bathroom where water pours off rocks, creating a waterfall. Golden eagles nest in the area, and ringtail cats tend to wander across the balcony. See p. 132.

- **Hacienda Antigua** (Albuquerque, NM; ☏ **800/201-2986**): This 200-year-old adobe inn, once a stagecoach stop, now offers a glimpse of the old days with refreshing modern touches. The guest rooms surround a quiet courtyard, and a pool and hot tub nestle near towering cottonwoods. The place sings of old New Mexico, with history evident in places such as La Capilla, the home's former chapel, which is now a guest room. See p. 238.

- **Casa de las Chimeneas** (Taos, NM; ☏ **877/758-4777**): This 1925 adobe home has been a model of Southwestern elegance since it opened as a B&B in 1988. The inn has lovely gardens, comfortable rooms, and a spa, as well as complete massage and facial treatments. The newest rooms have heated Saltillo tile floors, gas kiva fireplaces, and jetted tubs. The older section is delightful as well, with more of an antique feel. See p. 206.

- **The Royal Elizabeth** (Tucson, AZ; ☏ **877/670-9022**): In downtown Tucson just a block from the Temple of Music and Art, this Territorial-style historic home is filled with beautiful Victorian antiques and architectural details. Guest rooms have lots of touches not often seen in historic B&Bs, including "vintage" phones, TVs, fridges, and safes. See p. 349.

- **La Zarzuela** (Tucson; ☏ **888/848-8225**): Perched high on a hill on the west side of Tucson, this luxurious B&B boasts great views, colorful decor, and loads of outdoor spaces where guests can relax in the warmth of the desert. See p. 354.

- **Rocamadour Bed & Breakfast for (Rock) Lovers** (Prescott, AZ; ☏ **888/771-1933**): Set amid the rounded boulders of the Granite Dells just north of Prescott, this inn combines a spectacular setting with French antiques and luxurious accommodations. You won't find a more memorable setting in the state. See p. 491.

- **Briar Patch Inn** (Sedona, AZ; ☏ **888/809-3030**): Oak Creek Canyon, near Sedona, where you'll find this collection of luxurious cottages, is an oasis in the desert. Few experiences are more restorative than breakfast on the shady banks of the creek. See p. 508.

- **The Inn at 410** (Flagstaff, AZ; ☏ **800/774-2008**): This restored 1907 bungalow offers a convenient location in downtown Flagstaff, pleasant surroundings, comfortable rooms, and delicious breakfasts. Rooms feature different, distinctive themes, and eight of them have their own fireplaces. See p. 527.

- **Cochise Stronghold B&B** (Cochise County, AZ; ☏ **877/426-4141**): Surrounded by the national forest and mountainsides strewn with giant boulders, this B&B is one of the state's most remote inns. The passive solar building was built from straw bales and is not only energy-efficient but also quite beautiful. See p. 481.

8 The Best Places to Savor Southwest Flavors

- **The Compound** (Santa Fe, NM; ☏ **505/982-4353**): This reincarnation of one of Santa Fe's classic restaurants serves daring contemporary American food. Such delicacies as a seafood pan roast (black bass, halibut, and calamari) served with peas and potatoes, or seared Portuguese pork tenderloin with chorizo and crispy potatoes, will please sophisticated palates and probably simpler ones, too. See p. 154.

- **Santacafé** (Santa Fe, NM; ✆ **505/ 984-1788**): The food is Southwestern with an Asian flair, and the minimalist decor accentuates the beautiful architecture of the 18th-century Padre Gallegos House. The dishes change according to the seasons. One of my favorites is seared chile-garlic prawns served with fresh pea (or lima) and mushroom risotto. See p. 157.

- **Diane's Bakery & Cafe** (Silver City, NM; ✆ **505/538-8722**): Diane Barrett, who was once a pastry chef at La Traviata and Eldorado in Santa Fe, has brought refined flavors to the little mining town of Silver City. You'll feast on sumptuous baked goods and sophisticated meals such as rack of lamb. See p. 338.

- **Roaring Fork** (Scottsdale, AZ; ✆ **480/947-0795**): Roaring Fork's chef, Robert McGrath, has long been one of the most creative chefs in the Phoenix area. The atmosphere is lively, and everything from the bread basket and bar snacks to the entrees and desserts shows an attention to detail. See p. 418.

- **Janos/J Bar** (Tucson, AZ; ✆ **520/ 615-6100**): Serving a combination of regional and Southwestern dishes, Janos has for many years been one of Tucson's premier restaurants. It's just outside the front door of the Westin La Paloma resort, and is as formal a place as you'll find in this city. J Bar is Janos's less formal bar and grill. See p. 364 and p. 366.

- **Terra Cotta** (Tucson, AZ; ✆ **520/ 577-8100**): Café Terra Cotta was one of Arizona's pioneers in the realm of Southwestern cuisine. The beautiful, art-filled restaurant in the Tucson foothills continues to serve creative and reasonably priced meals. See p. 366.

- **Cowboy Club Grille & Spirits** (Sedona, AZ; ✆ **928/282-4200**): In the building where the Cowboy Artists of America organization was founded, this thoroughly Western restaurant is a great place to try such Arizona specialties as buffalo filet mignon, rattlesnake, and cactus fries. See p. 511.

- **The Turquoise Room** (Winslow, AZ; ✆ **928/289-2888**): Located in the little-visited town of Winslow in the restored La Posada historic hotel, this restaurant conjures up the days when the wealthy still traveled by railroad. Rarely will you find such excellent meals in such an off-the-beaten-path locale. See p. 100.

2

Planning Your Trip to the Southwest

As with any trip, a little preparation is essential before you start. This chapter provides you with a variety of planning tools, including information on when to go, how to get there, and how to get around once you're there.

1 The Regions in Brief

Four Corners   This region is the bull's-eye for this book. Containing some of the world's most cherished archaeological sites, the Four Corners area is the home to not only ancient cultures such as the Anasazi (or ancestral Puebloans), but also their modern-day descendants and other Native American people such as the Navajo and Apache. This region's other claim to fame is that it's the only place in the U.S. where four states—Colorado, Utah, New Mexico, and Arizona—meet. Each state has its own treasures. To name only a few, Colorado has Mesa Verde National Park, Utah has Monument Valley, New Mexico has Chaco Culture National Historic Park, and Arizona has Canyon de Chelly National Monument and the Hopi and Navajo reservations. These spectacular landmarks are set among painted canyons and poetic buttes, the perfect ambience to fulfill Southwestern fantasies.

Santa Fe, Taos & Albuquerque   Besides the Four Corners region, the main actor in New Mexico is its major art and cultural center, Santa Fe, with Taos and Albuquerque playing supporting roles. Santa Fe is a hip, artsy city that wears its 400-year-old mores on its sleeve. Nestled on the side of the **Sangre de Cristo Mountains,** it's an adobe showcase of centuries-old buildings that hug the earth. Many of these are artist studios and galleries set on narrow streets, ideal for desultory browsing. And then there's upstart Taos, the little arts town and ski center of just 5,000 people that lies wedged between the 13,000-foot Sangre de Cristo Mountains and the 700-foot-deep **Rio Grande Gorge.** Albuquerque is the big city, New Mexico style, a place with good restaurants and fun attractions such as a tramway to the top of the Sandia Mountains and lava flows covered with petroglyphs.

Northern New Mexico   In this region, the lush **Rocky Mountains** rise directly out of parched plateaus, with the Rio Grande nourishing rich cultures. Woven throughout this terrain are 19 settlements and numerous ruins of the Native American Pueblo culture, an incredible testament to the resilience of a proud people. The Hispanic culture also has a legacy here; its cathedrals and missions, small mountain villages, and iconographic artwork date back over 400 years. Relics of the Old West are also prevalent, in mountain towns such as Chama and on the open plains of the northeast.

Southern New Mexico   A land of wide-open spaces, this region is rich with natural wonders and Wild West and Native American history. To the east, the United States' first designated wilderness, the Gila, was once home to the Mogollon Indians; the Gila Cliff Dwellings National Monument preserves their past. The once-booming mining town of Silver City is at the heart of the region. Las Cruces, New Mexico's second-largest city, sits at the foot of the Organ Mountains, and not far east of there stand the blazing dunes of White Sands National Monument. At Carlsbad Caverns National Park, one of the nation's most elaborate cave systems offers the opportunity for underground exploration.

Tucson, Phoenix, Scottsdale & the Valley of the Sun   These cities, which form a backbone across Arizona, offer desert beauty and sophisticated lifestyles. Tucson is in the lushest part of the Sonoran Desert and has all the highlights of a major city—excellent arts and culture, and plenty more. Encircled by mountain ranges, this desert oasis offers world-class golf resorts; historical treasures with Native American, Hispanic, and Anglo roots; and some of the Southwest's best hiking in Saguaro National Park. North of Tucson, Phoenix, Scottsdale, and the Valley of the Sun sprawl across the Sonoran desert. Twenty cities and communities nestle among several mountain rages. Resorts and golf courses abound here, as do retirement communities. But the sprawl has a positive note: The area boasts world-class shopping, museums, culture such as opera, dance, and theater, and professional sports.

Southern & Eastern Arizona   Southern Arizona is a region of great contrasts, from desert lowlands to "sky islands," volcanic mountain ranges that seem to rise up from nowhere. The desert climate here attracts many retirees, and also many rare birds, which travel up from the tropics.

To the north, what's known as eastern Arizona is a world apart from these desert lands. Made up of the Mogollon Rim, an escarpment that rises some 2,000 feet off the desert floor, as well as the White Mountains, this region offers tall forests and clear streams. It's home to the Sunrise Park Resort ski area on the White Mountain Apache Indian Reservation.

Central & Western Arizona   At the center of Arizona, desert predominates. Parts of it are the desolate desert of Wile E. Coyote, but it has stunning variety. This region is home to the red-rock country of Sedona, which hosts a thriving arts scene and recreational opportunities, from hiking to hot air balloon riding. In the higher regions lie the quaint city of Prescott and the old mining town of Jerome, now an arts community. To the southwest, one of the nation's best-kept secrets lies along the Mexican border. It's Organ Pipe Cactus National Monument, with outlandish desert plant, bird, and animal life. Arizona's West Coast region has miles of waterfront—Lake Mead and Lake Mohave provide the state with plenty of watersports. It's no wonder Arizona has more motor boats per capita than any other U.S. state.

The Grand Canyon & Northern Arizona   Few sights inspire as many superlatives as does Grand Canyon National Park, which dominates this region. One of the world's natural wonders, the Grand Canyon is not only beautiful but also expansive, with numerous canyons stretching across hundreds of miles. The neighboring cities of Flagstaff, Williams, and Tusayan accommodate and feed millions of visitors each year. North of the Grand Canyon lies the state's most remote and untracked region, the Arizona Strip.

Las Vegas   In high contrast to the nature-oriented slant of the Southwest is this glittery city in the desert, noted for its art, cuisine, and shows. Yeah, right.

Most people, of course, come to gamble. In recent years this city has become a master of illusion, with hotels posing as pyramids or Italian palaces, their structures providing whole worlds of fantasy. Some find Las Vegas a fun and convenient entryway to their Southwest vacation.

Southern Utah   All five of Utah's national parks are in this region, and for good reason—it's undeniably beautiful. Ancient geologic forces, erosion, oxidation, and other natural processes have carved spectacular rock sculptures—delicate and intricate, bold and stately—and painted them in a riot of color. This is where you'll find Zion National Park, with its undulating landscapes; Bryce Canyon National Park, with its marvelous stone sculptures, called hoodoos; and the stunning red-rock country of Arches and Canyonlands National Parks. It's also the home of the bulk of Lake Powell and Glen Canyon National Recreation Area, a scenic play land for nearly every type of boater.

2 Visitor Information

Numerous agencies can assist you with planning your trip. For information on Arizona, contact the **Arizona Office of Tourism,** 1110 West Washington St., Suite 155, Phoenix, AZ 85007 (© **888/ 520-3434** or 602/364-3700; www. arizonaguide.com). The Visitors Information Center for the **New Mexico Department of Tourism** is at 491 Old Santa Fe Trail, Santa Fe, NM 87501 (© **800/545-2070** or 505/827-7400; www.newmexico.org).

For Colorado, start by contacting the **Colorado Tourism Office,** 1625 Broadway, Suite 1700, Denver, CO 80202 (© **800/COLORADO** or 303/892-3885; www.colorado.com), for a free copy of the official state vacation guide, which includes a state map and describes attractions, activities, and lodgings throughout Colorado. Another good source for Colorado information is the website of the *Denver Post,* the state's major daily newspaper (www.denverpost.com). For information on Utah as well as an official state map, contact the **Utah Tourism Office,** Council Hall/300 North State St., Salt Lake City, UT 84114 (© **800/200-1160** or 801/538-1030; www.utah.com).

For information about Las Vegas, contact the **Las Vegas Convention and Visitors Authority,** 3150 Paradise Rd., Las Vegas, NV 89109 (© **877/VISITLV** or 702/892-7575; www.visitlv.com). Another excellent information source is the **Las Vegas Chamber of Commerce,** 3720 Howard Hughes Pkwy., No. 100, Las Vegas, NV 89109 (© **702/735-1616;** www.lvchamber.com). Request the *Visitor's Guide,* which contains extensive information about accommodations, attractions, excursions, children's activities, and more. The staff can answer all your Las Vegas questions, including those about weddings and divorces.

Convention and visitors' bureaus or chambers of commerce represent cities and regions throughout the Southwest. Their addresses, telephone numbers, and Internet addresses appear in the appropriate chapters in this book.

If you're a member of **AAA,** remember that you can get a map and guidebook covering Arizona and New Mexico. You can also request the club's free *Southwestern CampBook,* which includes campgrounds in Arizona, Utah, Colorado, and New Mexico.

3 Money

Prices in the Southwest vary greatly, which is good news for both moneybags and those with holes in their pockets. You can find world-class resorts if that's your

---

Tips **Don't Stow It—Ship It**

If ease of travel is your main concern and money is no object, you can ship your luggage and sports equipment with a company that picks up, tracks, and delivers your bags (often through couriers such as Federal Express) with minimum hassle for you. Traveling luggage-free may be ultra-convenient, but it's not cheap: One-way overnight shipping can cost $100 to $200, depending on what you're sending. Specialists in door-to-door luggage delivery are **Virtual Bellhop** (www.virtualbellhop.com), **SkyCap International** (wwww.skycapinternational.com), **Luggage Express** (www.usxpluggageexpress.com), and **Sports Express** (www.sportsexpress.com).

---

bent, or a cheap roadside motel and a diner if you like to pinch pennies. If you come from a major city such as New York or London, you may find prices overall fairly inexpensive, though the major cities will be closer in price to what you're accustomed to. Exceptions are major tourist destinations such as the Grand Canyon, Zion National Park, and Carlsbad Caverns, where one or two concessionaires often have a monopoly and charge premium prices.

ATMS

The easiest and best way to get cash away from home is from an ATM (automated teller machine). The **Cirrus** (© **800/424-7787;** www.mastercard.com) and **PLUS** (© **800/843-7587;** www.visa.com) networks span the globe; look at the back of your bank card to see which network you're on, then call or check online for ATM locations at your destination. Be sure you know your personal identification number (PIN) before you leave home and be sure to find out your daily withdrawal limit before you depart. Also keep in mind that many banks impose a fee every time a card is used at a different bank's ATM, and that fee can be higher for international transactions (up to $5 or more) than for domestic ones (where they're rarely more than $1.50). On top of this, the bank from which you withdraw cash may charge its own fee. To

compare banks' ATM fees within the U.S., use www.bankrate.com. For international withdrawal fees, ask your bank.

You can also get cash advances on your credit card at an ATM. Keep in mind that credit card companies try to protect themselves from theft by limiting the funds someone can withdraw outside their home country, so call your credit card company before you leave home. And keep in mind that you'll pay interest from the moment of your withdrawal, even if you pay your monthly bills on time.

TRAVELER'S CHECKS

Traveler's checks are something of an anachronism from the days before the ATM made cash accessible at any time. Traveler's checks used to be the only sound alternative to traveling with dangerously large amounts of cash. They were as reliable as currency, but, unlike cash, could be replaced if lost or stolen.

These days, traveler's checks are less necessary because most cities have 24-hour ATMs that allow you to withdraw small amounts of cash as needed. However, keep in mind that you will likely be charged an ATM withdrawal fee if the bank is not your own, so if you're withdrawing money every day, you might be better off with traveler's checks—provided that you don't mind showing identification every time you want to cash one.

If you choose to carry traveler's checks, be sure to keep a record of their serial numbers separate from your checks in the event that they are stolen or lost. You'll get a refund faster if you know the numbers.

CREDIT CARDS

Credit cards are a safe way to carry money. They also provide a convenient record of all your expenses, and they generally offer relatively good exchange rates. You can also withdraw cash advances from your credit cards at banks or ATMs, provided you know your PIN. If you've forgotten yours, or didn't even know you had one, call the number on the back of your credit card and ask the bank to send it to you. It usually takes 5 to 7 business days, though some banks will provide the number over the phone if you tell them your mother's maiden name or some other personal information. As in the rest of the U.S., all of the major credit cards are accepted in the Southwest, though some smaller shops and restaurants may not accept credit cards at all. For tips and telephone numbers to call if your wallet is stolen or lost, go to "Lost & Found" in the "Fast Facts" section of this chapter.

4 When to Go

THE CLIMATE The climate in the Southwest is, overall, a great pleasure. Though the parched air can dry your skin, the same aridness makes the heat and cold easier to handle and promises lots of sunny days. Summers are hot throughout most of the region, though distinctly cooler at higher elevations. Winters are relatively mild in the south, harsher in the north and in the mountains. Spring and fall have pleasant temperatures, though in spring the wind blows throughout the region. Rainfall is sparse except in the higher mountains; summer afternoon thunderstorms and winter snows account for most precipitation.

WHEN TO GO The Southwest is a year-round destination, although people head to different parts at different times of year. In Phoenix, Tucson, and other parts of the desert, the high season runs from October to mid-May, with the highest hotel rates during the holidays. Wintertime is also high season in the mountain areas of northern New Mexico and southern Colorado, where skiing is popular.

Summer is high season at most national parks, particularly Grand Canyon and Carlsbad Caverns, though the latter receives much less traffic than the former. In late summer, monsoon rains cool the region in afternoons. But beware: These storms can cause flash floods that make roads briefly impassable. Avoid entering low areas if it's raining anywhere nearby.

Spring and autumn are the best times to visit the region. Temperatures are cool

New Mexico Average High/Low Temperatures in °F (°C) & Precipitation

	Jan	Apr	July	Oct	Annual Rainfall (inches)
Santa Fe	42 (6)/18 (-7)	62 (17)/33 (1)	85 (29)/56 (13)	65 (18)/38 (3)	14.0
Las Cruces	56 (13)/25 (-4)	77 (25)/41 (5)	94 (34)/65 (18)	78 (26)/44 (7)	8.6

Arizona Average High/Low Temperatures in °F (°C) & Precipitation

	Jan	Apr	July	Oct	Annual Rainfall (inches)
Flagstaff	41 (5)/14 (-10)	57 (14)/27 (-3)	81 (27)/50 (10)	63 (17)/31 (-1)	22.91
Phoenix	65 (18)/38 (3)	84 (29)/52 (11)	105 (41)/78 (26)	88 (31)/57 (14)	8.29

in the mountains and warm in the desert, without extreme temperatures on either end. Still, snow can fall in the high regions well into spring, and in fall, thunderstorms can pound the desert.

CALENDAR OF EVENTS

January

New Year's Day. King's Day transfer of canes to new officials and various dances at all eight northern New Mexico pueblos. Turtle Dance at Taos Pueblo (no photography allowed). Call © **505/793-4955** for more information. January 1.

Tostitos Fiesta Bowl Football Classic, Sun Devil Stadium, Tempe, AZ. This college bowl game usually sells out nearly a year in advance. For information, call © **800/635-5748** or 480/350-0911, or go to www.tostitosfiesta bowl.com. Early January.

Wings over Willcox, Willcox, AZ. Workshops, birding tours, and watching thousands of sandhill cranes gather in the Sulphur Springs Valley near Willcox. Call © **800/200-2272** or go to www.wingsoverwillcox.com. Third weekend in January.

Phoenix Open Golf Tournament, Scottsdale, AZ. Prestigious PGA tournament at the Tournament Players Club. Call © **602/870-4431** for details, or go to www.phoenixopen. com. Late January.

February

Flagstaff Winterfest, Flagstaff, AZ. Music, arts, sports, and special events. Call © **928/774-4505.** All month.

Parada del Sol Parade and Rodeo, Scottsdale, AZ. Crowds gather to watch the state's longest horse-drawn parade, and to attend the street dance and rodeo. Call © **480/990-3179** or go to www.scottsdalejaycees.com. Early February.

Tubac Festival of the Arts, Tubac, AZ. Exhibits by North American artists and craftspeople. Call © **520/398-2704** or go to www.tubacaz.com for more information. Early to mid-February.

Tucson Gem and Mineral Show, Tucson, AZ. Seminars, museum displays from around the world, and hundreds of dealers selling a range of rocks, from rose quartz to black diamonds. Call © **520/322-5773.** Mid-February.

O'odham Tash, Casa Grande, AZ. One of the largest annual Native American festivals in the country, attracting dozens of tribes that participate in rodeos, arts-and-crafts exhibits, and dance performances. Call © **520/836-4723.** Mid-February.

Bryce Canyon Winter Festival, Bryce, UT. A winter celebration amid the colorful rock formations of the Bryce Canyon National Park area. Call © **800/468-8660.** Mid-February.

La Fiesta de los Vaqueros, Tucson, AZ. Cowboy festival and rodeo at the Tucson Rodeo Grounds, including the Tucson Rodeo Parade. Call © **800/964-5662** or 520/741-2233, or go to www.tucsonrodeo.com. Late February.

March

Rio Grande Arts and Crafts Festival, Albuquerque, NM. A juried show featuring 200 artists and craftspeople from around the country takes place at the State Fairgrounds in Albuquerque during the second week of March. Call © **505/292-7457** for more information.

Rockhound Roundup, Deming, NM. Gems, jewelry, tools, and crafted items are displayed and sold at the Southwest New Mexico State Fairgrounds. Call © **505/544-0839.** Mid-March.

National Festival of the West, Scottsdale, AZ. This event celebrates all things cowboy, from Western movies to music. Includes a chuck-wagon cook-off, a mountain-man rendezvous, and a cowboy costume contest. Call ℂ **602/996-4387.** Mid-March.

Wak Pow Wow, Tucson, AZ. Tohono O'odham celebration at Mission San Xavier del Bac, featuring many southwestern Native American groups. Call ℂ **520/294-5727.** Mid-March.

Western Arts Festival, Cedar City, UT. Western lifestyle is the focus at this 4-day event featuring cowboy poetry, Western music, and food. Call ℂ **800/354-4849.** Mid-March.

April

Easter Weekend Celebration, At most New Mexico pueblos celebrations include masses, parades, Corn Dances, and other dances, such as the Bow and Arrow Dance at Nambé. Call ℂ **505/843-7270** for information, or go to www.indianpueblo.org. Easter weekend.

St. George Art Festival, St. George, UT. This outdoors fine art festival draws artists and visitors from all over the American West. Call ℂ **435/634-5850.** Friday and Saturday of Easter weekend.

Gathering of Nations Powwow, University Arena, Albuquerque, NM. Dance competitions, arts and crafts exhibitions, and Miss Indian World contest. Call ℂ **505/836-2810** or visit www.gatheringofnations.com for more information. Late April.

Tour of Canyonlands, Moab, UT. This annual bike race brings riders from around the country and abroad for a spectacular weekend of racing. Call ℂ **303/432-1519.**

Tucson International Mariachi Conference, Tucson, AZ. Mariachi bands from all over the world come to the Tucson Convention Center to play before standing-room-only crowds. Call ℂ **520/838-3908.** Last week of April.

May

Taos Spring Arts Festival, Taos, NM. Contemporary visual, performing, and literary arts are highlighted for 2 weeks at venues throughout Taos and Taos County. For dates and ticket info contact ℂ **800/732-TAOS** or 505/758-3873; www.taoschamber.com. Month of May.

Cinco de Mayo Fiestas, across the region. Celebrations of the restoration of the Mexican republic (from French occupation 1863–67) occur in, among other places, Phoenix, AZ (call ℂ **602/279-4669**); Tucson, AZ (ℂ **520/292-9326**); Las Cruces, NM, at Old Mesilla Plaza (ℂ **505/524-1968** or 505/541-2444); and Truth or Consequences, NM (ℂ **800/831-9487** or 505/894-3536). First weekend in May.

Taste of Santa Fe, Sweeney Convention Center, Santa Fe, NM. Sample Santa Fe's best chefs' recipes, including appetizers, entrees, and desserts. For information call ℂ **505/989-5328.** First Tuesday in May.

Sedona Chamber Music Festival, Sedona, AZ. Groups from around the world perform chamber music at various venues. Call ℂ **928/204-2415** or go to www.chambermusicsedona.org. Mid-May.

Phippen Fine Arts Show and Sale, Prescott, AZ. This is the premier Western-art sale. Call ℂ **928/778-1385** or go to www.phippenartmuseum.org. Memorial Day weekend.

Wyatt Earp Days, Tombstone, AZ. Taste the Old West with a chili cook-off, street entertainment, and gunfight reenactments in memory of the

shootout at the O.K. Corral. Call
© **800/457-3423.** Memorial Day
weekend.

Iron Horse Bicycle Classic, Durango,
CO. Mountain bikers race against a
steam train from Durango to Silver-
ton. Call © **970/259-4621** or visit the
website at www.ironhorsebicycleclas-
sic.com. Memorial Day weekend.

June

San Antonio Feast Day, NM. Corn
Dances at many of the New Mexico
pueblos. For information, call © **505/
843-7270** or go to www.indianpueblo.
org. June 13.

Rodeo de Santa Fe, Santa Fe, NM.
This 4-day event features a Western
parade, a rodeo dance, and five rodeo
performances. For tickets and information, call © **505/471-4300** or go to
www.rodeodesantafe.org. First weekend after Father's Day.

Telluride Bluegrass Festival, Telluride, CO. Features bluegrass, folk,
and country music played among
mountain splendor. Call © **303/823-
0848** or see www.planetbluegrass.com.
Late June.

Groovefest, Cedar City, UT. Blues and
bluegrass musicians entertain crowds
at the Main Street Park. The daylong
event includes barbecue and artisans
selling their work. Call © **435/867-
9800** or visit www.groovacious.com.
Late June.

Taos Solar Music Festival, Taos, NM.
Sit on the grass at Kit Carson Municipal Park and listen to major players at
this event celebrating the summer solstice. The event has a stage powered by
a solar generator and educational displays within a "Solar Village." For
information, call © **505/758-9191** or
go to www.solarmusic.com. Last weekend in June.

July

Santa Fe Opera, Santa Fe, NM. The
world-class Santa Fe Opera season runs
from the beginning of July to the end
of August. Call © **800/280-4654** or
go to www.santafeopera.org for more
information.

Annual Hopi Marketplace, Flagstaff,
AZ. Exhibit and sale of traditional arts
and crafts at the Museum of Northern
Arizona, including cultural events.
Call © **928/774-5213** or go to www.
muznaz.org. Fourth of July weekend.

Fourth of July Celebrations. Parades,
fireworks, and various other events are
held all over the region. Call the chamber of commerce in each city or town
for more information.

Prescott Frontier Days, Prescott, AZ.
The oldest rodeo in the United States
features roping and bull riding and
other celebrations. Call © **800/358-
1888** or 928/445-3103, or go to www.
worldsoldestrodeo.com. Fourth of July
week.

**Eight Northern Pueblos Artist and
Craftsman Show,** New Mexico. More
than 600 Native American artists
exhibit their work at one of the eight
northern pueblos. Traditional dances
and food booths. Call © **505/747-
1593** or go to www.indianpueblo.org
for exact dates and the location, which
varies. Mid-July.

Fiestas de Santiago y Santa Ana,
Taos, NM. The fiestas feature candlelight processions, special Masses,
music, dancing, parades, crafts, and
food booths. For information, contact
the Taos Fiesta Council (© **800/732-
8267;** www.fiestasdetaos.com). Third
weekend in July.

The Spanish Markets, Santa Fe Plaza,
Santa Fe, NM. More than 300 Hispanic artists from New Mexico and

southern Colorado exhibit and sell their work in this lively community event. For information, contact the Spanish Colonial Arts Society (𝄐 505/982-2226; www.spanishcolonial.org). Last full weekend in July.

August

Old Lincoln Days and Billy the Kid Pageant, Lincoln, NM. The main attraction is a reenactment of Billy the Kid's escape from the Lincoln jail. There's also a fiddling contest and living-history demonstrations (such as weaving and blacksmithing). Call 𝄐 505/653-4025 for more information. First weekend in August.

Southwest Wings Birding and Nature Festival, Bisbee. Lectures and field trips highlight this spirited birding event throughout southeastern Arizona and Sonora, Mexico. Call 𝄐 520/432-5421. Early August.

Intertribal Indian Ceremonial, near Gallup, NM. Thirty tribes from the United States and Mexico participate in rodeos, parades, dances, athletic competitions, and an arts and crafts show at Red Rock State Park, east of Gallup. Contact 𝄐 800/242-4282; www.gallupnm.org. Second week in August.

Bat Flight Breakfast, Carlsbad Caverns National Park, NM. A buffet breakfast is served while participants watch the bats return to the cave in the early morning. Contact 𝄐 505/785-3012; www.nps.gov/cave for details and exact date. Second Thursday of August.

Arizona Cowboy Poets' Gathering, Prescott, AZ. Traditional and contemporary cowboy poetry and even yodeling and storytelling highlight this Western event. Call 𝄐 928/445-3122 or go to www.sharlot.org. Third weekend in August.

The Indian Market, Santa Fe, NM. This is the largest all–Native American market in the country. About 1,200 artisans display their baskets, blankets, jewelry, pottery, and other arts. Sales are brisk. The market is free, but hotels are booked months in advance. Contact the Southwestern Association for Indian Art (𝄐 505/983-5220; www.swaia.org). Third weekend after the first Thursday in August.

Great American Duck Race, Deming, NM. Devised in a bar in 1979, this event has grown to include a parade, tortilla toss, outhouse race, ballooning, dances, and, of course, the duck race. Takes place on the courthouse lawn ("Duck Downs"). Call 𝄐 888/345-1125 for details. Fourth weekend in August.

September

Navajo Nation Fair, Window Rock, AZ. This large fair features traditional Navajo music and dancing, a rodeo, carnival, and parade. Call 𝄐 928/871-6478 or 928/871-6282; www.navaho nationfair.com. Early September.

New Mexico State Fair and Rodeo, State Fairgrounds, Albuquerque, NM. One of America's top state fairs, it features horse racing (with pari-mutuel betting), a nationally acclaimed rodeo, entertainment by top country artists, Native American and Spanish villages, the requisite midway livestock shows, and arts and crafts. Call 𝄐 505/265-1791 or visit www.nmstatefair.com for more information. Early September.

Telluride Film Festival, Telluride, CO. This influential international festival celebrates the art of film and has featured the premieres of some of the finest independent films. Call 𝄐 603/433-9202 or see www.telluridefilm festival.org. Labor Day weekend.

Chile Festival, Hatch, NM. New Mexicans celebrate their favorite fiery food item with a festival in the "Chile Capital of the World." Call © **505/294-6722.** Labor Day weekend.

La Fiesta de Santa Fe, Santa Fe, NM. An exuberant combination of spirit, history, and general merrymaking, La Fiesta is the oldest community celebration in the United States. Zozobra, "Old Man Gloom," a 40-foot-tall effigy of wood, canvas, and paper, is burned at dusk on Thursday to revitalize the community. For information call © **505/988-7575.** Weekend after Labor Day.

Moab Music Festival, Moab, UT. Live classical, jazz, bluegrass, and other types of music, presented in a stunning red-rock amphitheater and at other locations. Call © **435/259-7003.** Early to mid-September.

Stone Lake Fiesta, Jicarilla Reservation, 19 miles south of Dulce, NM. Apache festival with rodeo, ceremonial dances, and footrace. Contact © **505/759-4276** or www.jicarillaonline.com for more information. Mid-September.

Grand Canyon Music Festival, Grand Canyon Village, AZ. Classical music played on the South Rim of the Grand Canyon. Contact © **800/997-8285** or www.grandcanyonmusicfest.org for more information. Mid-September.

Taos Fall Festivals, Taos, NM. Events include the Fall Arts Festival, Old Taos Trade Fair, Wool Festival, and San Geronimo Day at Taos Pueblo. The arts-and-crafts festivals and cultural events are held throughout Taos and Taos County. Events, schedules, and tickets (where required) can be obtained from the Taos County Chamber of Commerce (© **800/732-8267** or 505/758-3873; www.taoschamber.com). Mid-September through late October.

Santa Fe Wine & Chile Fiesta, Santa Fe, NM. This lively celebration boasts five days of wine and food events. It takes place at many venues in downtown Santa Fe. Tickets go on sale in early July and sell out quickly. For information call © **505/438-8060** or log onto www.santafewineandchile.org. Last Wednesday through Sunday in September; the big event (Grand Food & Wine Tasting) is on the last Saturday.

Jazz on the Rocks, Sedona, AZ. Open-air jazz festival held among the red rocks. Call © **928/282-1985** or go to www.sedonajazz.com. Late September.

The Whole Enchilada Fiesta, Las Cruces, NM. The world's biggest enchilada (sometimes over 7 ft. wide) is created and eaten. Call © **505-524-1968** or visit www.lascrucescvb.org for more information. Late September or early October.

October

Arizona State Fair, Phoenix, AZ. The fair's highlights include rodeos, top-name entertainment, and ethnic food. Call © **602/252-6771** or go to www.azstatefair.com. All month.

Shiprock Navajo Fair, Shiprock, NM. The oldest and most traditional Navajo fair, it features a rodeo, dancing and singing, a parade, and arts and crafts exhibits. Contact © **800/448-1240** or www.farmingtonnm.org for details. Early October.

Albuquerque International Balloon Fiesta, Albuquerque, NM. The world's largest balloon rally, this 9-day festival brings together more than 750 colorful balloons and includes races and contests. Balloons lift off from Balloon Fiesta Park (at I-25 and Alameda Boulevard NE) on Albuquerque's northern city limits. For information, call © **800/733-9918** or visit www.

balloonfiesta.com. Second week in October.

Sedona Arts Festival, Sedona, AZ. A broad range of art shown among the grandeur of red rock country. Call ✆ **800/288-7336** or 928/204-9456. Mid-October.

Fiesta de los Chiles, Tucson, AZ. Come for lots of hot chiles, served in dishes from around the world, along with crafts and music. Call ✆ **520/326-9686** or visit www.tucsonbotanical.org. Mid- to late October.

Helldorado Days, Tombstone, AZ. Street entertainment, a carnival, a fashion show of 1880s clothing, and tribal dancers highlight this Old West celebration. Call ✆ **520/457-3291** for information. Third weekend in October.

Annual Cowboy Artists of America Exhibition, Phoenix, AZ. The Phoenix Art Museum plays host to the most prestigious and best-known Western-art show in the region. For information, call ✆ **602/257-1222** or visit www.phxart.org. Late October.

Canyonlands Fat Tire Festival, Moab, UT. Mountain-bike guided tours, hill climbs, and related events. Call ✆ **800/635-6622** or 435/259-1370. Late October to early November.

November

Thunderbird Balloon Classic, Scottsdale, AZ. More than 150 hot-air balloons fill the Arizona sky. Contact ✆ **602/840-9005;** www.thunderbird balloonandairclassic.com for more information. Early to mid-November.

Festival of the Cranes, Bosque del Apache National Wildlife Refuge, near Socorro, NM. People come from all over the world to attend this bird-watching event just 1½ hours south of Albuquerque. Call ✆ **505/835-1828.** Weekend before Thanksgiving.

Christmas on the Pecos, Carlsbad, NM. Pontoon boat rides each evening take passengers past a fascinating display of Christmas lights on riverside homes and businesses. Contact ✆ **800/ 221-1224;** www.chamber.caverns.com for more information. Thanksgiving to New Year's Eve (except Christmas Eve).

Parade of Lights, Bullfrog and Wahweap Marinas, Lake Powell, AZ. Lighted boats parade their reflections on the waters of Lake Powell. Both spectators and participants are welcome. Contact ✆ **800/528-6154** or visit www.lakepowell.com for more information. Saturday after Thanksgiving.

December

Holiday Luminaria Nights, Tucson, AZ. An enchanting display of holiday lights at the Botanical Gardens. Call ✆ **520/326-9255** for information. Early December.

Yuletide in Taos, Taos, NM. This holiday event emphasizes northern New Mexican traditions, cultures, and arts. The Taos County Chamber of Commerce (✆ **800/732-8267;** www.taos chamber.com) stages events. Thanksgiving through January 1.

Pueblo Grande Museum Indian Market, Phoenix, AZ. This creative event features more than 450 Native American artisans. Call ✆ **877/706-4408** or 602/495-0901, or visit www. pgmarket.org. Second full weekend in December.

Festival of Lights, Sedona, AZ. Thousands of luminarias are lit at dusk at the Tlaquepaque Arts and Crafts Village. Call ✆ **800/288-7336** or 928/282-4838, or go to www.tlaq. com. Mid-December.

Sundown Torchlight Procession of the Virgin, various New Mexico pueblos. Vespers at San Juan, Picuris, Tesuque, Nambé, and Taos Pueblos; Matachine Dances at Taos Pueblo; and

Buffalo Dances at Nambé Pueblo. For more information, call ℂ **505/852-4265**. December 24.

Canyon Road Farolito Walk, Santa Fe, NM. Beginning at dusk, locals and visitors bundle up and stroll Canyon Road, where *farolitos* (candle lamps) line the streets and rooftops. Musicians play and carolers sing around *luminarias* (little fires) and sip cider. Though it's not responsible for the event, the Santa Fe Convention and Visitors Bureau (ℂ **800/777-2489** or 505/955-6200; www.santafe.org) can help direct you there. Or ask your hotel concierge. December 24.

Matachines Dances and Other Dances, various New Mexico pueblos. Many New Mexico pueblos celebrate Christmas with dances. The Matachines

Dances take place at Picuris and San Juan Pueblos on Christmas morning. Contact ℂ **505/852-5265** for dance schedules for these and other pueblos. December 24 and 25.

Torchlight Procession, Taos Ski Valley, NM. Bold skiers carve down a steep run named Snakedance in the dark while carrying golden fire. For information, call ℂ **800/992-7669** or 505/776-2291 or log onto www.ski taos.org. December 24 and December 31 (followed by fireworks on New Year's Eve).

Fiesta Bowl Parade, Phoenix area, AZ. This nationally televised parade features floats and marching bands. Call ℂ **800/635-5748** or go to www. tostitosfiestabowl.com. Late December.

5 Travel Insurance

Check your existing insurance policies and credit card coverage before you buy travel insurance. You may already be covered for lost luggage, canceled tickets, or medical expenses. The cost of travel insurance varies widely, depending on the cost and length of your trip, your age and health, and the type of trip you're taking.

TRIP-CANCELLATION INSURANCE
Trip-cancellation insurance helps you get your money back if you have to back out of a trip, if you have to go home early, or if your travel supplier goes bankrupt. Allowed reasons for cancellation can range from sickness to natural disasters to the State Department declaring your destination unsafe for travel. (Insurers usually won't cover vague fears, though, as many travelers discovered who tried to cancel their trips in Oct 2001 because they were wary of flying.) In this unstable world, trip-cancellation insurance is a good buy if you're getting tickets well in advance—who knows what the state of the world, or of your airline, will be in 9

months? Insurance policy details vary, so read the fine print—and especially make sure that your airline or cruise line is on the list of carriers covered in case of bankruptcy. For information, contact one of the following insurers: **Access America** (ℂ 866/807-3982; www.accessamerica. com); **Travel Guard International** (ℂ 800/826-4919; www.travelguard. com); **Travel Insured International** (ℂ 800/243-3174; www.travelinsured. com); and **Travelex Insurance Services** (ℂ 888/457-4602; www.travelex-insur- ance.com).

MEDICAL INSURANCE   Most health insurance policies cover you if you get sick away from home—but check, particularly if you're insured by an HMO.

LOST-LUGGAGE INSURANCE   On domestic flights, checked baggage is covered up to $2,500 per ticketed passenger. On international flights (including U.S. portions of international trips), baggage is limited to approximately $9.07 per pound, up to approximately $635 per checked bag. If you plan to check items more valuable than the standard liability, see if your valuables are covered by your homeowner's policy, get baggage insurance as part of your comprehensive travel-insurance package, or buy Travel Guard's "BagTrak" product. Don't buy insurance at the airport; it's usually overpriced. Be sure to take any valuables or irreplaceable items with you in your carry-on luggage, because many valuables (including books, money, and electronics) aren't covered by airline policies.

If your luggage is lost, immediately file a lost-luggage claim at the airport, detailing the luggage contents. For most airlines, you must report delayed, damaged, or lost baggage within 4 hours of arrival. The airlines are required to deliver luggage, once found, directly to your house or destination free of charge.

6 Health & Safety

One thing that sets the Southwest apart from most other regions is its elevation. Much of the region is above 4,000 feet, and many heavily traveled areas, including the Four Corners, Grand Canyon, and Santa Fe, are at 7,000 feet or above. Getting plenty of rest, avoiding large meals, and drinking lots of nonalcoholic fluids (especially water) can help make the adjustment easier for flatlanders.

The reduced oxygen and humidity at these altitudes can bring on some unique problems, not the least of which is acute **mountain sickness.** Characterized in its early stages by headaches, shortness of breath, appetite loss or nausea, tingling in the fingers or toes, lethargy, and insomnia, it ordinarily can be treated with aspirin and a slower pace. If it persists or worsens, you must descend to a lower altitude.

Sunburn is also a concern. No matter what time of year it is, the desert sun is strong and bright, and you can burn much faster at high elevations than at sea level, because the thinner atmosphere offers less protection from the sun. Use sunscreen even when driving in your car, and wear a hat and sunglasses.

Visitors from humid climates may find the Southwest's dryness pleasant—dry heat is not as oppressive, and sweat evaporates almost immediately, cooling the skin. This is a mixed blessing, however, because many people don't feel thirsty here until they're already significantly dehydrated. Early symptoms of dehydration include headache and lethargy, and the condition may progress to include impaired concentration and irregular heartbeat. If you feel any of these symptoms, immediately find a cool place to rest and drink plenty of water. Better yet, prevent dehydration by carrying some bottled water with you and sipping it throughout the day, whether or not you feel thirsty.

Other things to be wary of are flash floods, particularly in the narrow canyons of northern Arizona and southern Utah. These may occur without warning in the desert, when the sky above you is clear but it's raining upstream. Before entering any narrow canyons in the late summer or fall, be sure to check weather conditions with the local ranger station, and avoid crossing low-lying areas during rain showers.

Most people are surprised to learn that exposure to cold causes more injuries and deaths in the region than heat and dryness do. The same clear skies that bake the desert in sunlight all day allow heat to escape rapidly at night. Evening breezes add to this effect. Hikers, in particular, must be prepared for both heat and cold, especially in the northern mountains, where snow can fall at the highest elevations in June and even July.

Finally, if you're outdoors, be on the lookout for desert creatures, particularly snakes (rattlers), Gila monsters (black-and-orange lizards), scorpions, and tarantulas. If you do encounter any of these, at all costs avoid them. Slowly move away. Don't even get close enough to take a picture (unless you have a good zoom lens).

Refer to the "Fast Facts" section under each destination for the most reliable hospitals and pharmacies in each area.

WHAT TO DO IF YOU GET SICK AWAY FROM HOME

In most cases, your existing health plan will provide the coverage you need. But double-check; you may want to buy **travel medical insurance** instead. (See the section on insurance, above.) Bring your insurance ID card with you when you travel.

If you suffer from a chronic illness, consult your doctor before your departure. For conditions like epilepsy, diabetes, or heart problems, wear a **MedicAlert identification tag** (© 888/633-4298; www.medicalert.org), which will immediately alert doctors to your condition and give them access to your records through MedicAlert's 24-hour hot line.

Pack **prescription medications** in your carry-on luggage, and carry prescription medications in their original containers, with pharmacy labels—otherwise, they won't make it through airport security. Also bring along copies of your prescriptions in case you lose your pills or run out. Don't forget an extra pair of contact lenses or prescription glasses.

STAYING SAFE

While tourist areas as a rule are safe, urban areas may not be at night. You should always stay alert. Check with your hotel's front desk staff if you are in doubt about which neighborhoods are safe. Avoid deserted areas, especially at night, and avoid public parks at night. Women should especially follow these guidelines. With purse snatchings a reality at tourist spots in the country, it's best not to carry valuables.

Remember that hotels are open to the public, and in a large hotel, security may not be able to screen everyone who enters. Always lock your room door; don't assume that once inside your hotel you are automatically safe and no longer need to be aware of your surroundings.

7 Specialized Travel Resources

TRAVELERS WITH DISABILITIES

Most disabilities shouldn't stop anyone from traveling. Throughout the region, measures have been taken to provide access for travelers with disabilities. The chamber of commerce in each town will answer questions regarding accessibility in their areas. No matter what, it is advisable to call hotels, restaurants, and attractions in advance to be sure that they are fully accessible.

The U.S. National Park Service offers a **Golden Access Passport** that gives free lifetime entrance to all properties administered by the National Park Service—national parks, monuments, historic sites, recreation areas, and national wildlife refuges—for persons who are visually impaired or permanently disabled, regardless of age. You may pick up a Golden Access Passport at any NPS entrance fee area by showing proof of medically determined disability and eligibility for receiving benefits under federal law. Besides free entry, the Golden Access Passport also offers a 50% discount on federal-use fees charged for such facilities as camping, swimming, parking, boat launching, and tours. For more information, go to www.nps.gov/fees_passes.htm or call © **888/467-2757.**

Many travel agencies offer customized tours and itineraries for travelers with disabilities. **Flying Wheels Travel** (© **507/451-5005;** www.flyingwheelstravel.com) offers escorted tours and cruises that emphasize sports and private tours in minivans with lifts. **Access-Able Travel Source** (© **303/232-2979;** www.access-able.com) offers extensive access information and advice for traveling around the world with disabilities. **Accessible Journeys** (© **800/846-4537** or 610/521-0339; www.disabilitytravel.com) caters specifically to slow walkers and wheelchair travelers and their families and friends.

Avis Rent a Car has an "Avis Access" program that offers such services as a dedicated 24-hour toll-free number (© **888/879-4273**) for customers with special travel needs; special car features such as swivel seats, spinner knobs, and hand controls; and accessible bus service.

Organizations that offer assistance to travelers with disabilities include **Moss-Rehab** (www.mossresourcenet.org), which provides a library of accessible-travel resources online; **SATH,** the Society for Accessible Travel & Hospitality (© **212/447-7284;** www.sath.org), which charges an annual fee for access to a wealth of travel resources for all types of disabilities and informed recommendations on destinations; and the **American Foundation for the Blind,** or AFB (© **800/232-5463;** www.afb.org), a referral resource for the blind or visually impaired that includes information on traveling with Seeing Eye dogs.

For more information specifically targeted to travelers with disabilities, the community website **iCan** (www.ican online.net/channels/travel/index.cfm) has destination guides and several regular columns on accessible travel. Also check out the quarterly magazine **Emerging** **Horizons** ($14.95 per year, $19.95 outside the U.S.; www.emerginghorizons.com), and *Open World* magazine, published by SATH (see above; subscription: $13 per year, $21 outside the U.S.).

Wilderness Inquiry (© **800/728-0719** or 612/676-9400; www.wilderness inquiry.org) offers trips to the Grand Canyon.

The **Information Center for New Mexicans with Disabilities** (© **800/552-8195** in New Mexico, or 505/272-8549 outside the state) has a database with lists of services ranging from restaurants and hotels to wheelchair rentals. **Access New Mexico** (www.state.nm.us/gcch/accessnm) lists accessible hotels, attractions, and restaurants throughout the state.

GAY & LESBIAN TRAVELERS

In general, gay and lesbian travelers will find they are treated just like any other visitors in the Southwest. To get in touch with the Phoenix gay community, contact the **Gay and Lesbian Community Center,** Parkway Inn, 8617 N. Black Canyon Hwy., Suite 135 (© **602/265-7283**). In Tucson, head to the **Wingspan** community center, 300 E. Sixth St. (© **520/624-1779; www.wingspan.org**). The *Observer* (© **520/622-7176;** www.tucsonobserver.com) is a local Tucson gay newspaper, available at Wingspan and at Antigone Bookstore, 411 N. Fourth Ave. (© **520/792-3715**).

Common Bond (© **505/891-3647**) provides information and outreach services for Albuquerque's gay and lesbian community as well as referrals for other New Mexico cities. Another good New Mexico resource is **www.gaynm.com**, a website that provides news, resources, and lists of events. In Colorado, contact **Gay, Lesbian, and Bisexual Community Services Center of Colorado** (© **303/733-7743;** www.coloradoglbt.org) in Denver; the organization provides information on services, events, and venues of interest to gay and lesbian visitors. The

Gay & Lesbian Community Center of Utah, 355 N. 300 West, 1st Floor, Salt Lake City (℃ **888/874-2743** or 801/ 539-8800; www.glccu.com), is a community center, coffeehouse, and information distribution point for Utah. In Las Vegas, head to **The Center,** 953 E. Sahara, Suite B-25 (℃ **702/733-9800;** www.the center-lasvegas.com), for support and information. Another source is www. lasvegaspride.org, with lists of activities for the Las Vegas area.

The following travel guides are available at most travel bookstores and gay and lesbian bookstores, or you can order them from **Giovanni's Room** bookstore, 1145 Pine St., Philadelphia, PA 19107 (℃ **215/923-2960;** www.giovannisroom. com): *Out and About* (℃ **800/929-2268;** www.outandabout.com), which offers guidebooks and a newsletter ($20 per year; 10 issues) packed with solid information on the global gay and lesbian scene; *Spartacus International Gay Guide* (Bruno Gmünder Verlag; www.spartacusworld. com/gayguide) and *Odysseus: The International Gay Travel Planner* (Odysseus Enterprises Ltd.), both good, annual English-language guidebooks focused on gay men; the *Damron* guides (www.damron.com), with separate, annual books for gay men and lesbians; and *Gay Travel A to Z: The World of Gay & Lesbian Travel Options at Your Fingertips* by Marianne Ferrari (Ferrari International; Box 35575, Phoenix, AZ 85069), a very good gay and lesbian guidebook series.

SENIOR TRAVEL

Senior travelers tend to enjoy the Southwest's mild climate. However, they are often more susceptible to changes in elevation and may experience heart or respiratory problems. Consult your physician before your trip.

Mention the fact that you're a senior when you make your travel reservations. Although all of the major U.S. airlines

except America West have canceled their senior discount and coupon book programs, many hotels still offer discounts for seniors. In most cities, people over the age of 60 qualify for reduced admission to theaters, museums, and other attractions, as well as discounted fares on public transportation.

Members of **AARP** (formerly known as the American Association of Retired Persons), 601 E St. NW, Washington, DC 20049 (℃ **888/687-2277;** www. aarp.org), get discounts on hotels, airfares, and car rentals. AARP offers members a wide range of benefits, including *AARP: The Magazine* and a monthly newsletter. Anyone over 50 can join.

The **U.S. National Park Service** offers a **Golden Age Passport** that gives seniors 62 years or older lifetime entrance to all properties administered by the National Park Service—national parks, monuments, historic sites, recreation areas, and national wildlife refuges—for a one-time processing fee of $10, which must be purchased in person at any NPS facility that charges an entrance fee. Besides free entry, a Golden Age Passport also offers a 50% discount on federal-use fees charged for such facilities as camping, swimming, parking, boat launching, and tours. For more information, go to www.nps.gov/ fees_passes.htm or call ℃ **888/467-2757.**

Many reliable agencies and organizations target the 50-plus market. **Elderhostel** (℃ **877/426-8056;** www.elder hostel.org) arranges study programs for those aged 55 and over (and a spouse or companion of any age) in the U.S. and in more than 80 countries around the world. Most courses last 5 to 7 days in the U.S. (2–4 weeks abroad), and many include airfare, accommodations in university dormitories or modest inns, meals, and tuition. **ElderTreks** (℃ **800/741-7956;** www.eldertreks.com) offers small-group tours to off-the-beaten-path or adventure-travel locations, restricted to travelers 50 and older. **INTRAV** (© **800/ 456-8100;** www.intrav.com) is a high-end tour operator that caters to the mature, discerning traveler, not specifically seniors, with trips around the world that include guided safaris, polar expeditions, private-jet adventures, and small-boat cruises down jungle rivers.

Recommended publications offering travel resources and discounts for seniors include: the quarterly magazine *Travel 50 & Beyond* (www.travel50andbeyond. com); *Travel Unlimited: Uncommon Adventures for the Mature Traveler* (Avalon); *101 Tips for Mature Travelers,* available from Grand Circle Travel (© **800/221-2610** or 617/350-7500; www.gct.com); and *Unbelievably Good Deals and Great Adventures That You Absolutely Can't Get Unless You're Over 50* (McGraw-Hill), by Joann Rattner Heilman.

FAMILY TRAVEL

If you have enough trouble getting your kids out of the house in the morning, dragging them thousands of miles away may seem like an insurmountable challenge. But family travel can be immensely rewarding, giving you new ways of seeing the world through smaller pairs of eyes.

With its robust mix of outdoorsy activities and cultural attractions, the Southwest lends itself to family vacations. That said, the drives between the activities and attractions can be rather long, and they don't always lead to the sort of juicy theme-park treats that you find in other states. Sure, you may stumble across a water park or a video arcade here and there, but the real attractions are the natural and cultural ones and the adventurous ways you can experience them: hiking along the Grand Canyon, whitewater rafting down the Rio Grande, riding a horse through the cathedrals of Monument valley, or climbing a wooden ladder up to a cliff dwelling, to name just a few.

If you're not traveling with an adventure-oriented brood, no worries. Many of the hotels and resorts listed in this book have inviting pools to laze around or onsite activities planned especially for kids. But keep in mind that the Southwest can truly offer your children a new perspective on life by exposing them to ancient ruins, zesty cuisine, and unique cultures. Throughout this book, look for the "kids" icon, which points out kid-friendly places to stay and eat, and the best adventures suited to families.

Familyhostel (© **800/733-9753;** www.learn.unh.edu/familyhostel) takes the whole family, including kids ages 8 to 15, on moderately priced domestic and international learning vacations. A team of academics guides lectures, field trips, and sightseeing.

Recommended family travel Internet sites include **Family Travel Forum** (www.familytravelforum.com), a comprehensive site that offers customized trip planning; **Family Travel Network** (www.familytravelnetwork.com), an award-winning site that offers travel features, deals, and tips; **Traveling Internationally with Your Kids** (www.travel withyourkids.com), a comprehensive site offering sound advice for long-distance and international travel with children; and **Family Travel Files** (www.thefamily travelfiles.com), which offers an online magazine and a directory of off-the-beaten-path tours and tour operators for families. For even more ideas, check out *Frommer's Las Vegas with Kids, Frommer's Family Vacations in the National Parks,* and *Frommer's Great Outdoor Guide to Arizona and New Mexico* (Wiley Publishing, Inc.). *How to Take Great Trips with Your Kids* (The Harvard Common Press) is full of good general advice that can apply to travel anywhere.

TRAVELING WITH PETS

If you're one of those soft hearts who just has to have Fido along, you're in luck. The Southwest is more and more accepting of animals as travel companions. Many of the major chain hotels, such as Motel 6 and most Best Westerns, allow pets in the rooms (though restaurants still prohibit them). Your biggest concern when traveling with a pet in the region is the heat. In fact, if you're traveling during the warm months, you'd best leave your pet at home. Though some attractions, such as Carlsbad Caverns and the Grand Canyon, have kennels available, most do not. And with all the other times you'll need to leave your pet, the risk isn't worth the joy of having your companion there. Even leaving a pet in the car to run into a fast food restaurant can be harmful.

That said, during the cooler seasons, few places are more fun to bring a pet. Hiking abounds in the region, as does space to throw a stick. In accommodations listings throughout the book, look for the note that states whether the establishment allows pets and if it charges a fee. Some websites worth checking out include www.petswelcome.com, www.pettravel.com, and www.travelpets.com.

8 Planning Your Trip Online

SURFING FOR AIRFARES

The "big three" online travel agencies, **Expedia.com, Travelocity.com,** and **Orbitz.com,** sell most of the air tickets bought on the Internet. (Canadian travelers should try expedia.ca and Travelocity.ca; U.K. residents can go to expedia.co.uk and opodo.co.uk.) Each has different business deals with the airlines and may offer different fares on the same flights, so it's wise to shop around. Expedia and Travelocity will also send you **e-mail notification** when a cheap fare becomes available to your favorite destination. Of the smaller travel agency websites, **SideStep** (www.sidestep.com) has gotten the best reviews from Frommer's authors. It's a browser add-on that purports to "search 140 sites at once," but in reality only beats competitors' fares as often as other sites do.

Also remember to check **airline websites,** especially those for low-fare carriers such as Southwest, JetBlue, or AirTran, whose fares are often misreported or simply missing from travel agency websites. Even with major airlines, you can often shave a few bucks from a fare by booking directly through the airline and avoiding a travel agency's transaction fee. But you'll get these discounts only by **booking online:** Most airlines now offer online-only fares that even their phone agents know nothing about. For the websites of airlines that fly to and from your destination, go to "Getting There," on p. 39.

Great **last-minute deals** are available through free weekly e-mail services provided directly by the airlines. Most of these are announced on Tuesday or Wednesday and must be purchased online. Most are only valid for travel that weekend, but some (such as Southwest's) can be booked weeks or months in advance. Sign up for weekly e-mail alerts at airline websites or check mega-sites that compile comprehensive lists of last-minute specials, such as **Smarter Travel** (www.smartertravel.com). For last-minute trips, **site59.com** and **lastminutetravel.com** in the U.S. and **lastminute.com** in Europe often have better air-and-hotel package deals than the major-label sites. A website listing numerous bargain sites and airlines around the world is **www.itravelnet.com**.

For much more about airfares and savvy air-travel tips and advice, pick up a copy of *Frommer's Fly Safe, Fly Smart* (Wiley Publishing, Inc.).

Frommers.com: The Complete Travel Resource

For an excellent travel-planning resource, we highly recommend **Frommers.com** (www.frommers.com), voted Best Travel Site by *PC Magazine*. We're a little biased, of course, but we guarantee that you'll find the travel tips, reviews, monthly vacation giveaways, bookstore, and online-booking capabilities thoroughly indispensable. Among the special features are our popular **Destinations** section, where you'll get expert travel tips, hotel and dining recommendations, and advice on the sights to see for more than 3,500 destinations around the globe; the **Frommers.com Newsletter,** with the latest deals, travel trends, and money-saving secrets; our **Community** area featuring **Message Boards,** where Frommer's readers post queries and share advice (sometimes even our authors show up to answer questions); and our **Photo Center,** where you can post and share vacation tips. When your research is done, the **Online Reservations System** (www.frommers.com/book_a_trip) takes you to Frommer's preferred online partners for booking your vacation at affordable prices.

SURFING FOR HOTELS

Shopping online for hotels is generally done one of two ways: through the hotel's own website, or through an independent booking agency (or a fare-service agency like Priceline). Internet hotel agencies have multiplied in mind-boggling numbers of late, competing for the business of millions of consumers surfing for accommodations around the world. This competitiveness can be a boon to consumers who have the patience and time to shop and compare the online sites for good deals—but shop they must, for prices can vary considerably from site to site. And keep in mind that hotels at the top of a site's listing may be there for no other reason than that they paid money to get the placement.

Of the "big three" sites, **Expedia** offers a long list of special deals and "virtual tours" or photos of available rooms so you can see what you're paying for (a feature that helps counter the claims that the best rooms are often held back from bargain booking websites). **Travelocity** posts unvarnished customer reviews and ranks its properties according to the AAA rating system. Also reliable are **Hotels.com** and **Quikbook.com**. An excellent free program, **TravelAxe** (www.travelaxe.net), can help you search multiple hotel sites at once, even ones you may never have heard of—and conveniently lists the total price of the room, including the taxes and service charges. Another booking site, **Travelweb** (www.travelweb.com), is partly owned by the hotels it represents (including the Hilton, Hyatt, and Starwood chains) and is therefore plugged directly into the hotels' reservations systems—unlike independent online agencies, which have to fax or e-mail reservation requests to the hotel, a good portion of which get misplaced in the shuffle. More than once, travelers have arrived at the hotel, only to be told that they have no reservation. To be fair, many of the major sites are undergoing improvements in service and ease of use, and Expedia will soon be able to plug directly into the reservations systems of many hotel chains—none of which can be bad news for consumers. In the meantime, it's a good idea to **get a confirmation number** and **make a printout** of any online booking transaction.

Though you'll note that many of the accommodations listed in this book have websites and e-mail addresses, don't be fooled into thinking that the whole place is really in the 21st century. In fact, many of the smaller establishments don't have computers at all, much less access to the Internet. And some of those that list websites have primitive connections to a chamber of commerce site where they're listed, but no real Web page of their own.

So be patient, and before you get frustrated, ditch your mouse and use the phone.

SURFING FOR RENTAL CARS

For booking rental cars online, the best deals are usually found at rental-car company websites, although all the major online travel agencies also offer rental-car reservations services. Priceline and Hotwire work well for rental cars, too; the only "mystery" is which major rental company you get, and for most travelers the difference between Hertz, Avis, and Budget is negligible.

9 Getting There

BY PLANE
Deciding where to touch down in the Southwest is a bit tricky. Where you land will depend on what part of the region you intend to focus on. For instance, Albuquerque is closest to the Four Corners region, but if you also intend to visit the Grand Canyon, you may be better off flying in and out of Phoenix, which would allow you to visit Sedona as well. However, if you intend to only visit the northernmost part of the region, you may want to fly into Las Vegas and possibly save on airfare. Meanwhile, if you want to experience some mountain country en route to the mostly desert attractions of the Southwest, you could fly into Durango. Your best bet is to take out a map, pinpoint where you want to focus your travel time, and find the closest airport. Alternately, check out the suggested itineraries described in chapter 4. You'll find airlines listed below.

Many airlines flying to both Phoenix and Tucson serve Arizona from around the United States. The Phoenix **Sky Harbor Airport** (© **602/273-3300**) is the more centrally located of the two airports and is closer to the Grand Canyon. However, if you're planning to explore the southern part of the state or are going to

visit both Phoenix and Tucson, you might want to fly into **Tucson International Airport** (© **520/573-8000**), which is smaller and charges lower taxes on its car rentals.

The following major airlines serve both Phoenix and Tucson:

- **Air Canada** © 888/247-2262; www.aircanada.ca
- **Alaska Airlines** © 800/426-0333; www.alaskaair.com
- **America West** © 800/235-9292; www.americawest.com
- **American** © 800/433-7300; www.aa.com
- **Continental** © 800/525-0280; www.continental.com
- **Delta** © 800/221-1212; www.delta.com
- **Northwest/KLM** © 800/225-2525; www.nwa.com
- **Southwest** © 800/435-9792; www.southwest.com
- **United** © 800/241-6522; www.ual.com

The following airlines serve Phoenix but not Tucson:

- **Aero México** © 800/237-6639; www.aeromexico.com
- **British Airways** © 800/247-9297; www.british-airways.com

- **Frontier** ℭ800/432-1359; www.flyfrontier.com
- **Lufthansa** ℭ800/645-3880; www.lufthansa.com
- **US Airways** ℭ800/428-4322; www.usairways.com

In addition, **Horizon** (ℭ **800/547-9308;** www.horizonair.com) serves Tucson but not Phoenix.

The **Albuquerque International Sunport** (ℭ **505/842-4366**) is the hub for travel to most parts of New Mexico. A secondary hub for southern New Mexico is **El Paso International Airport** (ℭ **915/780-4700**) in western Texas. Both airports are served by **American, America West, Continental, Delta, Frontier,** and **Southwest.** Additional airlines serving Albuquerque include **Mesa** (ℭ **800/637-2247**), **Northwest, United,** and **United Airways.**

In conjunction with United Airlines, commuter flights are offered between Santa Fe and Denver by **United Express,** which is operated by Great Lakes Aviation (ℭ **800/554-5111**).

McCarran International Airport (ℭ **702/261-5211;** www.mccarran.com) in Las Vegas, Nevada, is a good option if you plan to visit northern Arizona and southern Utah. Budget-conscious travelers may find good deals on airfares and rental cars from there.

Colorado Springs Airport (ℭ **719/550-1900**), in the southeast corner of Colorado Springs, handles over 100 flights each day, with connections to most major U.S. cities. The airport is served by **Allegiant, American, America West, Continental, Delta, Mesa, Northwest,** and **United.** Even more convenient to the region is the **Durango/La Plata County Airport** (ℭ **970/247-8143**), with direct daily nonstop service from Denver, Phoenix, and in winter, Dallas/Fort Worth. **America West Express** and **United Express** serve Durango.

Those whose destination is western Colorado can make connections to Grand Junction's **Walker Field** (ℭ **970/244-9100;** www.walkerfield.com) from Denver, Phoenix, or Salt Lake City.

There's no shortage of **discounted and promotional fares** that can result in savings of 50% or more. Watch for advertisements in your local newspaper and on TV, or call the airlines. And when you call the airlines, ask for their lowest fares, and ask if it's cheaper to book in advance, fly in midweek, or stay over a Saturday night.

GETTING THROUGH THE AIRPORT

With the federalization of airport security, security procedures at U.S. airports are more stable and consistent than ever. Generally, you'll be fine if you arrive at the airport **1 hour** before a domestic flight and **2 hours** before an international flight; if you show up late, tell an airline employee and she'll probably whisk you to the front of the line.

Bring a **current, government-issued photo ID** such as a driver's license or passport. Keep your ID at the ready to show at check-in, the security checkpoint, and sometimes even the gate. (Children under 18 do not need government-issued photo IDs for domestic flights, but they do for international flights to most countries.)

In 2003, the TSA phased out **gate check-in** at all U.S. airports. And **e-tickets** have made paper tickets nearly obsolete. Passengers with e-tickets can beat the ticket-counter lines by using airport **electronic kiosks** or even **online check-in** from your home computer. Online check-in involves logging on to your airline's website, viewing your reservation, and printing out your boarding pass—and the airline may even offer you bonus miles to do so! If you're using a kiosk at the airport, bring the credit card you used to book the ticket or your frequent-flier card. Print out your boarding pass from the kiosk and simply proceed to the security checkpoint with your pass and a photo ID. **Curbside check-in** is also a good way to avoid lines, although a few airlines still ban curbside check-in; call before you go.

Security checkpoint lines are getting shorter, but some doozies remain. If you have trouble standing for long periods of time, tell an airline employee; the airline will provide a wheelchair. Speed up security by **not wearing metal objects** such as big belt buckles. If you've got metallic body parts, a note from your doctor can prevent a long chat with the security screeners. Keep in mind that only **ticketed passengers** are allowed past security, except for folks escorting disabled passengers or children.

Federalization has stabilized **what you can carry on** and **what you can't.** The general rule is that sharp things are out, nail clippers are okay, and food and beverages must be passed through the X-ray machine—but that security screeners can't make you drink from your coffee cup. Bring food in your carry-on rather than checking it, as explosive-detection machines used on checked luggage have been known to mistake food (especially chocolate, for some reason) for bombs. Travelers in the U.S. are allowed one carry-on bag, plus a "personal item" such as a purse, briefcase, or laptop bag. Carry-on hoarders can stuff all sorts of things into a laptop bag; as long as it has a laptop in it, it's still considered a personal item. The Transportation Security Administration (TSA) has issued a list of restricted items; check its website (www.tsa.gov/public/index.jsp) for details.

Airport screeners may decide that your checked luggage needs to be searched by hand. You can now purchase luggage locks that allow screeners to open and lock a checked bag if hand-searching is necessary. Look for Travel Sentry certified locks at luggage or travel shops and Brookstone stores (you can buy them online at www.brookstone.com). For more information on the locks, visit www.travelsentry.org.

FLYING FOR LESS: TIPS FOR GETTING THE BEST AIRFARE

Passengers sharing the same airplane cabin rarely pay the same fare. Travelers who need to purchase tickets at the last minute, change their itinerary at a moment's notice, or fly one-way often get stuck paying the premium rate. Here are some ways to keep your airfare costs down:

- Passengers who can book their tickets **far in advance,** who can **stay over Saturday night,** or who **fly midweek** or **at less-trafficked hours** may pay a fraction of the full fare. If your schedule is flexible, say so, and ask if you can secure a cheaper fare by changing your flight plans.
- You can also save on airfares by keeping an eye out in local newspapers for **promotional specials** or **fare wars,** when airlines lower prices on their most popular routes. You rarely see fare wars during peak travel times, but if you can travel in the slow months, you may snag a bargain.
- Search **the Internet** for cheap fares (see "Planning Your Trip Online," earlier in this chapter).
- Join **frequent-flier clubs.** Accrue enough miles, and you'll be rewarded with free flights and elite status. You don't need to fly to build frequent-flier miles—**frequent-flier credit cards** can provide thousands of miles for doing your everyday shopping.
- For many more tips about air travel, including a rundown of the major frequent-flier credit cards, pick up a copy of *Frommer's Fly Safe, Fly Smart* (Wiley Publishing, Inc.).

Travel in the Age of Bankruptcy

Airlines go bankrupt, so protect yourself by **buying your tickets with a credit card.** The Fair Credit Billing Act guarantees that you can get your money back from the credit card company if a travel supplier goes under (and if you request the refund within 60 days of the bankruptcy). **Travel insurance** can also help, but make sure it covers "carrier default" for your specific travel provider. And be aware that if a U.S. airline goes bust mid-trip, a 2001 federal law requires other carriers to take you to your destination (albeit on a space-available basis) for a fee of no more than $25, provided you rebook within 60 days of the cancellation.

BY CAR

Three interstate highways cross the Southwest. The north-south I-25 bisects New Mexico, passing through Albuquerque and Las Cruces. The east-west I-40 follows the path of the old Route 66 through Kingman and Flagstaff, in Arizona, and Gallup, Albuquerque, and Tucumcari in New Mexico. I-10 from San Diego crosses the southern part of the region, passing through Yuma and Tucson in Arizona, and intersecting I-25 at Las Cruces, New Mexico. I-15 crosses the region at the southwest corner of Utah. These major routes help provide easy access to the many sights in the region that are on much smaller state highways and roadways.

The distance to Phoenix from Los Angeles is approximately 369 miles; from San Francisco, 778 miles; from Albuquerque, 455 miles; from Salt Lake City, 660 miles; from Las Vegas, 287 miles; and from Santa Fe, 516 miles.

Your biggest concern is weather. In winter, be sure your car has front-wheel drive or four-wheel drive and good tires, because roads can become snowpacked and icy.

BY TRAIN

Amtrak has two routes through the region. The *Southwest Chief,* which runs between Chicago and Los Angeles, passes through the region once daily in each direction, with stops in Flagstaff, Gallup, Grants, Albuquerque, Lamy (for Santa Fe), Las Vegas, Raton, Trinidad, La Junta, and Lamar. A second train, the *Sunset Limited,* skims through the southern part of the region three times weekly in each direction between Los Angeles and New Orleans, with stops in Tucson, Benson, Lordsburg, Deming, and El Paso, Texas. Greyhound/Trailways bus lines provide through-ticketing for Amtrak between Albuquerque and El Paso.

You can get a copy of Amtrak's national timetable from any Amtrak station, from travel agents, or by contacting Amtrak (© **800/USA-RAIL;** www.amtrak.com).

10 Packages for the Independent Traveler

Before you start your search for the lowest airfare, you may want to consider booking your flight as part of a travel package. Package tours are not the same thing as escorted tours. Package tours are simply a way to buy the airfare, accommodations, and other elements of your trip (such as car rentals, airport transfers, and sometimes even activities) at the same time and often at discounted prices—kind of like one-stop shopping. Tour operators buy packages in bulk and resell them to the public at a cost that usually undercuts standard rates.

One good source of package deals is the airlines themselves. Most major airlines offer air/land packages to various locations in the Southwest, including **American Airlines Vacations** (✆ 800/321-2121; www.aavacations.com), **Delta Vacations** (✆ 800/221-6666; www.delta vacations.com), **Continental Airlines Vacations** (✆ 800/301-3800; www.co vacations.com), **Southwest Airlines Vacations** (✆ 800/423-5683; www.swa vacations.com), and **United Vacations** (to Las Vegas, NV, only; ✆ 888/854-3899; www.unitedvacations.com). Several big **online travel agencies**—Expedia, Travelocity, Orbitz, Site59, and Lastminute.com—also do a brisk business in packages. If you're unsure about the pedigree of a smaller packager, check with the Better Business Bureau in the city where the company is based, or check www.bbb.org. If a packager won't tell you where it's based, don't fly with it.

Travel packages are also listed in the travel section of your local Sunday newspaper. Or check ads in the national travel magazines such as *Arthur Frommer's Budget Travel Magazine*, *Travel & Leisure*, *National Geographic Traveler*, and *Condé Nast Traveler*.

Package tours can vary by leaps and bounds. Some offer a better class of hotels than others. Some offer the same hotels for lower prices. Some offer flights on scheduled airlines, while others book charters. Some limit your choice of accommodations and travel days. You are often required to make a large payment up front. On the plus side, packages can save you money, offering group prices but allowing for independent travel. Some even let you add a few guided excursions or escorted day trips (also at prices lower than if you booked them yourself) without booking an entirely escorted tour.

Before you invest in a package tour, get some answers. Ask about the **accommodations choices** and prices for each. You'll also want to find out what **type of room** you get. If you need a certain type of room, ask for it; don't take whatever is thrown your way. Request a nonsmoking room, a quiet room, a room with a view, or whatever you fancy. Finally, look for **hidden expenses.** Ask whether the total cost includes airport departure fees and taxes, for example.

11 Getting Around

BY CAR

The broad expanses of the American Southwest make driving the best means of getting around, and they also necessitate some precautions. If you plan to drive your own vehicle to and around the region, give it a thorough road check before starting out. There are lots of wide-open desert and wilderness spaces here, and it is not fun to be stranded in the heat or cold with a vehicle that doesn't run. Check your lights, windshield wipers, horn, tires, battery, drive belts, fluid levels, alignment, and other possible trouble spots. Make sure your driver's license, vehicle registration, safety-inspection sticker, and auto-club membership (if you have one) are valid. Check with your auto insurance company to make sure you're covered when out of state, or when driving a rental car. A breakdown in the desert can be serious. Always carry water with you in the car.

Gasoline is readily available at service stations throughout the region. However, keep close tabs on your gauge, and in more remote areas fill up whenever you can. It's not unusual to drive 60 miles without seeing a gas station. Prices are cheapest in major cities and 10% to 15% more expensive in more isolated communities. All prices are subject to the same fluctuations as elsewhere in the United States.

CAR RENTALS   **Car rentals** are available in every sizable town and city in the region, always at the local airport, and usually also downtown. Major rental-car companies with offices in the Southwest include:

- **Alamo**   © 800/327-9633; www.alamo.com
- **Avis**   © 800/331-1212; www.avis.com
- **Budget**   © 800/527-0700; www.budget.com
- **Dollar**   © 800/800-4000; www.dollar.com
- **Enterprise**   © 800/736-8222; www.enterprise.com
- **Hertz**   © 800/654-3131; www.hertz.com
- **National**   © 800/227-7368; www.nationalcar.com
- **Payless**   © 800/237-2804; www.paylesscarrental.com
- **Thrifty**   © 800/367-2277; www.thrifty.com

Drivers who need wheelchair-accessible transportation should call Wheelchair Getaways of New Mexico (© **800/408-2626** or 505/247-2626; www.wheelchair-getaways.com); the company rents vans by the day, week, or month.

DRIVING RULES   Unless otherwise posted, the **speed limits** on open roads are 65 mph to 75 mph on interstate highways, 65 mph on U.S. highways, and 55 mph on state highways. The minimum age for drivers is 16. Safety belts are required for drivers and all passengers age 5 and over; children under age 5 must be in an approved child seat secured by the seat belt.

Indian reservations are considered sovereign nations, and they enforce their own laws. For instance, the Navajo reservation (the region's largest) prohibits transporting alcoholic beverages, leaving established roadways, and traveling without a seat belt. Motorcyclists must wear helmets.

EMERGENCIES   The New Mexico and Arizona State Highway and Transportation Departments provide up-to-the-hour information on road closures and conditions through their toll-free road-advisory hot lines (NM © **800/432-4269;** www.nmshtd.state.nm.us; AZ © **888/411-7623**).

Members of the **American Automobile Association (AAA)** can get free emergency road service by calling AAA's emergency number (© **800/AAA-HELP**).

MAPS   An excellent state highway map is available from the **New Mexico Department of Tourism** (see "Visitor Information," earlier in this chapter). The American Automobile Association (AAA) supplies detailed state and city maps free to members (see "Emergencies," above). Unfortunately, the Arizona Department of Transportation no longer publishes a state road map, but one is available from the Arizona Department of Tourism.

BY PLANE

This is a broad region, so if your time is short, you might want to consider flying between cities, though your options are limited. In Arizona, **America West** (© **800/235-9292;** www.americawest.com) serves Phoenix, Tucson, Flagstaff, Kingman, Prescott, Lake Havasu City, and Yuma. **Scenic Airlines** (© **800/634-6801;** www.scenic.com) flies between Las Vegas and the Grand Canyon.

In New Mexico, **Rio Grande Air** (© **877/435-9742;** www.riograndeair.com) flies between Albuquerque, Farmington, Ruidoso, and Taos; and **Mesa Airlines** (© **800/637-2247**) flies between Albuquerque, Farmington, Carlsbad, Roswell, and Hobbs.

BY TRAIN

Due to limited options, the train is not the best way of getting around the region. **Amtrak** has two routes. The *Southwest Chief,* which runs between Chicago and

Life on the Open Road: Planning an RV or Tenting Vacation

One of the best ways to explore the Southwest, especially in the warm months, is in an RV—a motor home, truck camper, or camper trailer—or a tent, if you don't mind roughing it a bit more. If you own an RV, we advise you to have the mechanical systems checked out thoroughly, keeping in mind that there are some extremely steep grades in the region; after that's done, pack up and go. If you don't have an RV or a tent, why not rent one for your trip?

There are disadvantages, of course. Tents, small trailers, and truck campers are cramped, and even the most luxurious motor homes and trailers provide somewhat close quarters. Facilities in most commercial campgrounds are less extensive than what you'd expect in moderately priced motels, and if you cook your own meals, you miss the opportunity to experience the local cuisine. All that aside, camping is just plain fun—especially in a setting as spectacular as this one.

Renting an RV   Camping to save money is possible if you limit your equipment to a tent, a pop-up tent trailer, or a small pickup-truck camper, but renting a motor home will probably end up costing as much as driving a compact car, staying in moderately priced motels, and eating in family-style restaurants. That's because motor homes go only a third (or less) as far on a gallon of gas as compact cars, and they're expensive to rent—generally between $1,000 and $1,100 per week in midsummer, when rates are highest.

If you're flying into the area and renting an RV upon arrival, choose your starting point carefully; rates vary depending on the city in which you pick up your RV. The nation's largest rental company, with an outlet in Las Vegas, is **Cruise America** (© **800/327-7799;** www.cruiseamerica.com). Request information on additional rental agencies, as well as tips on renting, from the **Recreation Vehicle Rental Association,** 3930 University Dr., Fairfax, VA 22030 (© **703/591-7130;** fax 703/591-0734; www.rvra.org).

Choosing a Campground   After you get a rig or a tent, you'll need a place to put it. Camping in the national parks, other federal lands, state parks, and many communities is discussed in the relevant sections of this book.

Members of the **American Automobile Association (AAA)** can request the club's free *Southwestern CampBook,* which includes campgrounds and RV parks in Utah, Arizona, Colorado, and New Mexico. Major bookstores carry several massive campground directories, including *Trailer Life Campgrounds, RV Parks & Services* (www.rv.net), *Woodall's Campground Directory* (www.woodalls.com), and *The Unofficial Guide to the Best RV and Tent Campground Sites in the U.S.A.* (www.frommers.com).

Los Angeles, passes through the region once daily in each direction, with stops in Flagstaff, Gallup, Grants, Albuquerque, Lamy (for Santa Fe), Las Vegas, Raton, Trinidad, La Junta, and Lamar. A second train, the *Sunset Limited,* crosses the southern part of the region three times weekly in each direction—between Los

Angeles and New Orleans—with stops in Tucson, Benson, Lordsburg, Deming, and El Paso, Texas. Greyhound/Trailways bus lines provide through-ticketing for Amtrak between Albuquerque and El Paso. If you're headed to the Grand Canyon, you can get to the town of Williams, 30 miles west of Flagstaff, on Amtrak, and transfer to the Grand Canyon Railway excursion train, which runs to Grand Canyon Village at the South Rim of the Grand Canyon. Be aware, however, that the Williams stop is on the outskirts of town; you'll have to arrange in advance to be picked up.

You can get a copy of Amtrak's national timetable from any Amtrak station, from travel agents, or by contacting Amtrak (© **800/USA-RAIL;** www. amtrak.com).

12 Tips on Accommodations

No two travelers are alike; fortunately, the Southwest has a broad enough range of accommodations to satisfy even the most eccentric adventurer. If you long to be pampered, you'll find swanky resorts, with a variety of the luxury options such as pool and exercise facilities, golf, tennis, horseback riding, and spa treatments. Of course none of it comes cheap. If you're looking to really savor the flavor of the region, you may want to opt for one of its historic hotels. They include hacienda-style inns—adobe one- or two-story structures often built around a courtyard. You'll also find some Victorian inns that have a frontier flavor. Amenities vary, from places with antique but workable plumbing and no television, to those with hot tubs and dataports in rooms.

When making your reservations during shoulder seasons, such as spring and fall, be sure to ask when hotel rates change (in the desert, for instance, they drop for the summer or go up in the fall), so you can schedule your trip to get the best rates. Remember, if you don't absolutely need all the amenities of a big resort, there are dozens of chain-motel options.

SAVING ON YOUR HOTEL ROOM

The **rack rate** is the maximum rate that a hotel charges for a room. Hardly anybody pays this price, however, except in high season or on holidays. To lower the cost of your room:

- **Ask about special rates or other discounts.** Always ask whether a room less expensive than the first one quoted is available, or whether any special rates apply to you. You may qualify for corporate, student, military, senior, or other discounts. Find out the hotel policy on children—do kids stay free in the room or is there a special rate?

- **Dial direct.** When booking a room in a chain hotel, you'll often get a better deal by calling the individual hotel's reservation desk rather than at the chain's main number.

- **Book online.** Many hotels offer Internet-only discounts, or supply rooms to Priceline, Hotwire, or Expedia at rates much lower than the ones you can get through the hotel itself. Shop around. And if you have special needs—a quiet room, a room with a view—call the hotel directly and make your needs known after you've booked online.

- **Remember the law of supply and demand.** Resort hotels are most crowded and therefore most expensive on weekends, so discounts are usually available for midweek stays. Business hotels in downtown locations are busiest during the week, so you can expect big discounts over the weekend. Many hotels have high-season and low-season prices, and booking the day after "high season" ends can mean big discounts.

- **Avoid excess charges and hidden costs.** When you book a room, ask whether the hotel charges for parking. Use your own cellphone, pay phones, or prepaid phone cards instead of dialing direct from hotel phones, which usually have exorbitant rates. And don't be tempted by the room's minibar offerings: Most hotels charge through the nose for water, soda, and snacks. Finally, ask about local taxes and service charges, which can increase the cost of a room by 15% or more. If a hotel insists upon tacking on a surprise "energy surcharge" that wasn't mentioned at check-in or a "resort fee" for amenities you didn't use, you can often make a case for getting it removed.

- **Consider the pros and cons of all-inclusive resorts and hotels.** The term "all-inclusive" means different things at different hotels. Many all-inclusive hotels include three meals daily, sports equipment, spa entry, and other amenities; others may include all or most drinks. In general, you'll save money going the "all-inclusive" way—as long as you use the facilities provided. The down side is that your choices are limited and you're stuck eating and playing in one place for the duration of your vacation.

- **Book an efficiency.** A room with a kitchenette allows you to shop for groceries and cook your own meals. This is a big money saver, especially for families on long stays.

- **Consider enrolling in hotel "frequent-stay" programs**, which reward repeat customers who accumulate enough points or credits to earn free hotel nights, airline miles, complimentary in-room amenities, or even merchandise. These are offered not only by many chain hotels and motels (Hilton HHonors, Marriott Rewards, Wyndham ByRequest, to name a few), but individual inns and B&Bs. Many chain hotels partner with other hotel chains, car-rental firms, airlines, and credit-card companies to give consumers additional ways to accumulate points in the program.

LANDING THE BEST ROOM

Somebody has to get the best room in the house. It might as well be you. You can start by joining the hotel's frequent-guest program, which may make you eligible for upgrades. A hotel-branded credit card usually gives its owner "silver" or "gold" status in frequent-guest programs for free. Always ask about a corner room. They're often larger and quieter, with more windows and light, and they often cost the same as standard rooms. When you make your reservation, ask if the hotel is renovating; if it is, request a room away from the construction. Ask about nonsmoking rooms, rooms with views, rooms with twin, queen- or king-size beds. If you're a light sleeper, request a quiet room away from vending machines, elevators, restaurants, bars, and discos. Ask for a room that has been recently renovated or redecorated.

If you aren't happy with your room when you arrive, ask for another one. Most lodgings will be willing to accommodate you.

In resort areas, particularly in warm climates, ask the following questions before you book a room:

- What's the view like? Cost-conscious travelers may be willing to pay less for a back room facing the parking lot, especially if they don't plan to spend much time in their room.

- Does the room have air-conditioning or ceiling fans? Do the windows open? If they do, and the nighttime entertainment takes place alfresco, you may want to find out when show time is over.

13 Recommended Books & Films

FICTION   Many well-known writers made their homes in the Southwest. In the 1920s, the most celebrated were **D. H. Lawrence** and **Willa Cather,** both short-term Taos residents. Lawrence's *Mornings in Mexico* and *Etruscan Places* capture the flavor of the region. Inspired by her stay in the region, Cather, a Pulitzer Prize winner famous for her depictions of the pioneer spirit, penned *Death Comes for the Archbishop.* It's a fictionalized account of the 19th-century Santa Fe bishop Jean Baptiste Lamy.

Many contemporary authors also live in and write about the region. John Nichols of Taos, whose *Milagro Beanfield War* was made into a Robert Redford movie in 1987, writes insightfully about the problems of poor Hispanic farming communities. For the past two decades, Albuquerque's Tony Hillerman has woven mysteries around Navajo tribal police in books such as *Listening Woman* and *A Thief of Time.* Of the desert environment and politics, no one wrote better than the late Edward Abbey; *The Monkey Wrench Gang* (HarperPerennial, 2000) told of an unlikely gang of ecoterrorists, which helped inspire the founding of the radical Earth First! movement. Zane Grey fans should pick up a copy of *Riders of the Purple Sage* (Pocket Books, 1974). Set in southern Utah toward the end of the 19th century, it explores polygamy and the restraints it placed on women.

NON-FICTION   Marshall Trimble and Joe Beeler's *Roadside History of Arizona* (Mountain Press Publishing, 1986) is an ideal book to take along on a driving tour of Arizona. For general histories of New Mexico, try Myra Ellen Jenkins and Albert H. Schroeder's *A Brief History of New Mexico* (University of New Mexico Press, 1974) and Marc Simmons's *New Mexico: An Interpretive History* (University of New Mexico Press, 1988). Get some Colorado history from the short, easy-to-read *Colorado: A History,* by Marshall Sprague. John Wesley Powell's 1869 diary, the first account of travels through the canyon, offers an exciting viewpoint of the Grand Canyon. You can read a recent republication of it titled *The Exploration of the Colorado River and Its Canyons* (Penguin, 1997), with an introduction by Wallace Stegner. For an interesting account of the recent human history of the canyon, read Stephen J. Pyne's *How the Canyon Became Grand* (Viking Penguin, 1999).

To catch the mood of southern Utah, read Abbey's *Desert Solitaire* (New York: Ballantine, 1968), a nonfiction work based on time Abbey spent in Arches National Monument, before it gained national-park status.

MOVIES   Hundreds of movies have been filmed in the region. One of the most notable classics is director John Ford's *Stagecoach* (1939), filmed in Monument Valley. The valley has also shown up in such non-Western films as *2001: A Space Odyssey, Thelma and Louise,* and *Forrest Gump.* Many films have been made in Tucson at what's now called Old Tucson Studios, including *Arizona, Tombstone,* John Wayne's *Rio Lobo,* Clint Eastwood's *The Outlaw Josey Wales,* Kirk Douglas's *Gunfight at the O.K. Corral,* and Paul Newman's *The Life and Times of Judge Roy Bean.* New Mexico landscapes have set the scene for Westerns such as

The Cowboys, Silverado, Young Guns, City Slickers, and *Wyatt Earp,* as well as two miniseries based on popular Larry McMurtry novels, *Lonesome Dove* and *Buffalo Girls.* The science fiction movies *Armageddon* and *Contact* were shot in New Mexico as well.

FAST FACTS: The American Southwest

American Express There are offices or representatives in Phoenix, Scottsdale, and Albuquerque. For information, call © 800/528-4800.

Area Codes The area code in Phoenix is 602. In Scottsdale, Tempe, Mesa, and the east valley, it's 480. In Glendale and the west valley, it's 623. The area code for Tucson and southeastern Arizona is 520. The rest of the state is area code 928. At press time the area code for all of New Mexico is 505, though plans are in the works to add others. The area code for southwestern Colorado is 970 and for southern Utah, 435. Las Vegas's code is 702.

ATM Networks ATMs in the region generally use the following systems: Star, Cirrus, PLUS, American Express, MasterCard, and Visa.

Business Hours The following are general hours; specific establishments' hours may vary. Banks are open Monday through Friday from 9am to 5pm (some also on Sat 9am–noon). Stores are open Monday through Saturday from 10am to 6pm and Sunday from noon to 5pm (malls usually stay open until 8 or 9pm Mon–Sat). Bars generally open around 11am and close between 1 and 2am, depending on the state.

Car Rentals See "Getting Around," earlier in this chapter.

Driving Rules See "Getting Around," earlier in this chapter.

Emergencies In most places in the region, call © 911 to report a fire, call the police, or get an ambulance. A few small towns have not adopted the emergency phone number, so if 911 doesn't work, dial 0 (zero) for the operator and state the type of emergency.

Etiquette & Customs When visiting Native American reservations or pueblos, be sure to act courteously. Don't venture beyond the areas prescribed for tourists. Always buy a photo permit before taking pictures, and ask before shooting.

Holidays See "Calendar of Events," earlier in this chapter.

Information See "Visitor Information," earlier in this chapter.

Internet Access Although you will find the occasional cybercafe around the region, they are not at all common. Your best bet, other than using access provided by your hotel or resort, is to head to the nearest public library or copy shop, such as FedEx Kinko's.

Liquor Laws The legal age for buying or consuming alcoholic beverages is 21. Each of the states in the region has its own restrictions on when and where you can buy alcohol. Arizona, New Mexico, and Colorado have pretty standard laws, which allow purchase from morning to 1 or 2am in licensed stores on most days, with some time restrictions on Sundays. Utah's laws are stricter; you can buy beer, wine, and hard liquor every day except Sunday, when the state-owned liquor stores are closed. You can buy 3.2% beer, which has less alcohol, 7 days a week. Note that some Indian reservations (including the Navajo reservation) prohibit alcohol within the reservation.

Lost & Found Be sure to tell all of your credit card companies the minute you discover your wallet has been lost or stolen, and file a report at the nearest police precinct. Your credit card company or insurer may require a police report number or record of the loss. Most credit card companies have an emergency toll-free number to call if your card is lost or stolen; they may be able to wire you a cash advance immediately or deliver an emergency credit card in a day or two. Visa's U.S. emergency number is ✆ **800/847-2911** or 410/581-9994. American Express cardholders and traveler's check holders should call ✆ **800/ 221-7282.** MasterCard holders should call ✆ **800/307-7309** or 636/722-7111. For other credit cards, call the toll-free number directory at ✆ **800/555-1212.**

If you need emergency cash over the weekend when banks and American Express offices are closed, you can have money wired to you through **Western Union** (✆ **800/325-6000**; www.westernunion.com).

Police In most places in the region, phone ✆ **911** for emergencies. A few small towns have not adopted the emergency number, so if 911 doesn't work, dial 0 (zero) for the operator and state your reason for calling.

Safety See "Health & Safety," earlier in this chapter.

Taxes Combined city and state sales taxes vary from place to place but are usually between 6% and 9% for purchases, 9% to 13% for lodging.

Time Zone The region is on Mountain Standard Time, 1 hour ahead of the West Coast and 2 hours behind the East Coast. Daylight saving time is in effect in New Mexico, Colorado, and Utah from April to October. However, Arizona does not observe daylight saving time, so time differences between Arizona and the rest of the country vary with the time of year. From the last Sunday in October until the first Sunday in April, Arizona is 1 hour later than the West Coast and 2 hours earlier than the East Coast. The rest of the year, Arizona is on the same time as the West Coast and is 3 hours earlier than the East Coast. There is an exception—the Navajo Reservation observes daylight saving time. However, the Hopi Reservation, which is completely surrounded by the Navajo Reservation, does not.

For International Visitors

Whether it's your first visit or your 10th, a trip to the United States may require an additional degree of planning. This chapter will provide you with essential information, helpful tips, and advice for the more common problems that some visitors encounter.

1 Preparing for Your Trip

ENTRY REQUIREMENTS

Check at any U.S. embassy or consulate for current information and requirements. You can also obtain a visa application and other information online at the **U.S. State Department**'s website, at **www.travel.state.gov**.

VISAS The U.S. State Department has a **Visa Waiver Program** allowing citizens of certain countries to enter the United States without a visa for stays of up to 90 days. At press time these included Andorra, Australia, Austria, Belgium, Brunei, Denmark, Finland, France, Germany, Iceland, Ireland, Italy, Japan, Liechtenstein, Luxembourg, Monaco, the Netherlands, New Zealand, Norway, Portugal, San Marino, Singapore, Slovenia, Spain, Sweden, Switzerland, and the United Kingdom. Citizens of these countries need only a valid passport and a round-trip air or cruise ticket in their possession upon arrival. If they first enter the United States, they may also visit Mexico, Canada, Bermuda, and/or the Caribbean islands and return to the United States without a visa. Further information is available from any U.S. embassy or consulate. Canadian citizens may enter the United States without visas; they need only proof of residence.

Citizens of all other countries must have (1) a valid passport that expires at least 6 months later than the scheduled end of their visit to the United States, and (2) a tourist visa, which may be obtained without charge from any U.S. consulate.

To obtain a visa, the traveler must submit a completed application form (either in person or by mail) with a 1½-inch-square photo, and must demonstrate binding ties to a residence abroad. Usually you can obtain a visa at once or within 24 hours, but it may take longer during the summer rush from June through August. If you cannot go in person, contact the nearest U.S. embassy or consulate for directions on applying by mail. Your travel agent or airline office may also be able to provide you with visa applications and instructions. The U.S. consulate or embassy that issues your visa will determine whether you will be issued a multiple- or single-entry visa and any restrictions regarding the length of your stay.

MEDICAL REQUIREMENTS Unless you're arriving from an area known to be suffering from an epidemic (particularly cholera or yellow fever), inoculations or vaccinations are not required for entry into the United States. If you have a medical condition that requires **syringe-administered medications,** carry a valid signed prescription from your physician—the government no longer allows airline passengers to pack syringes in their carry-on baggage without documented proof of medical need. If you have a disease that requires treatment with **narcotics,** you should also carry documented proof with you—smuggling narcotics aboard a plane is a serious offense that carries severe penalties in the U.S.

For **HIV-positive visitors,** requirements for entering the United States are somewhat vague and change frequently. According to the latest publication of *HIV and Immigrants: A Manual for AIDS Service Providers,* the government doesn't require a medical exam for entry into the United States, but officials may stop individuals because they look sick or because they are carrying AIDS/HIV medicine.

If an HIV-positive noncitizen applies for a nonimmigrant visa, the question on the application regarding communicable diseases is tricky no matter which way it's answered. If the applicant checks "no," INS may deny the visa on the grounds that the applicant committed fraud. If the applicant checks "yes" or if INS suspects the person is HIV-positive, it will deny the visa unless the applicant asks for a special waiver for visitors. This waiver is for people visiting the United States for a short time, to attend a conference, for instance, to visit close relatives, or to receive medical treatment. It can be a confusing situation. For up-to-the-minute information, contact **AIDSinfo** (✆ **800/448-0440,** or 301/519-6616 outside the U.S.; www.aidsinfo.nih.gov) or **Gay Men's Health Crisis** (✆ **212/367-1000;** www.gmhc.org).

DRIVER'S LICENSES Foreign driver's licenses are mostly recognized in the U.S., although you may want to get an international driver's license if your home license is not written in English.

PASSPORT INFORMATION

Safeguard your passport in an inconspicuous, inaccessible place like a money belt. Make a copy of the critical pages, including the passport number, and store it in a safe place, separate from the passport itself. If you lose your passport, visit the nearest consulate of your native country as soon as possible for a replacement. Passport applications are downloadable from the websites listed below.

Note: The International Civil Aviation Organization has recommended a policy requiring that *every* individual who travels by air have a passport. In response, many countries are now requiring that children must be issued their own passport to travel internationally, where before those under 16 or so may have been allowed to travel on a parent or guardian's passport.

FOR RESIDENTS OF CANADA

You can pick up a passport application at one of 28 regional passport offices or most travel agencies. Canadian children who travel must have their own passport. However, if you hold a valid Canadian passport issued before December 11, 2001, that bears the name of your child, the passport remains valid for you and your child until it expires. Passports cost C$85 for those 16 years and older (valid 5 years), C$35 children 3 to 15 (valid years), and C$20, children under 3 (valid 3 years). Applications, which must be accompanied by two identical passport-sized photographs and proof of Canadian citizenship, are available at travel agencies throughout Canada or from the central **Passport Office,** Department of Foreign Affairs and International Trade, Ottawa, ON K1A 0G3 (✆ **800/567-6868;** www.dfait-maeci.gc.ca/passport). Processing takes 5 to 10 days if you apply in person, or about 3 weeks by mail.

FOR RESIDENTS OF THE UNITED KINGDOM

To pick up an application for a standard 10-year passport (5-year passport for children under 16), visit the nearest Passport Office, major post office, or travel agency. You can also contact the **United Kingdom Passport Service** at ✆ **0870/571-0410** or visit its website at www.passport.gov.uk. Passports are £33 for adults and £19 for children under 16, with another £30 fee if you apply in person at a Passport Office. Processing takes about 2 weeks (1 week if you apply at the Passport Office).

FOR RESIDENTS OF IRELAND

You can apply for a 10-year passport, costing 57€, at the **Passport Office,** Setanta Centre, Molesworth Street, Dublin 2 (✆ **01/671-1633;** www.irlgov.ie/iveagh). Those under age 18 and over 65 must apply for a 12€ 3-year passport. You can also apply at 1A South Mall, Cork (✆ **021/272-525**), or over the counter at most main post offices.

FOR RESIDENTS OF AUSTRALIA

You can get an application from your local post office or any branch of Passports Australia, but you must schedule an interview at the passport office to present your application materials. Call the **Australian Passport Information Service** at ✆ **131-232,** or visit the government website at www.passports.gov.au. Passports are A$144 for adults and A$72 for those under 18.

FOR RESIDENTS OF NEW ZEALAND

You can pick up a passport application at any New Zealand Passports Office or download it from their website. Contact the **Passports Office** at ✆ **0800/225-050** in New Zealand, or 04/474-8100, or log on to www.passports.govt.nz. Passports are NZ$80 for adults and NZ$40 for children under 16.

CUSTOMS
WHAT YOU CAN BRING IN

Every visitor more than 21 years of age may bring in, free of duty, the following: (1) 1 liter of wine or hard liquor; (2) 200 cigarettes, 100 cigars (but not from Cuba), or 3 pounds of smoking tobacco; and (3) $100 worth of gifts. These exemptions are offered to travelers who spend at least 72 hours in the United States and who have not claimed them within the preceding 6 months. It is altogether forbidden to bring into the country foodstuffs (particularly fruit, cooked meats, and canned goods) and plants (vegetables, seeds, tropical plants, and the like). Foreign tourists may bring in or take out up to $10,000 in U.S. or foreign currency with no formalities; larger sums must be declared to U.S. Customs on entering or leaving, which includes filing form CM 4790. For more specific information regarding U.S. Customs and Border Protection, contact your nearest U.S. embassy or consulate, or the **U.S. Customs** office (✆ **202/927-1770;** www.customs.ustreas.gov).

WHAT YOU CAN TAKE HOME

U.K. citizens returning from a non-EU country have a customs allowance of: 200 cigarettes; 50 cigars; 250g of smoking tobacco; 2 liters of still table wine; 1 liter of spirits or strong liqueurs (over 22% volume); 2 liters of fortified wine, sparkling wine or other liqueurs; 60cc (ml) perfume; 250cc (ml) of toilet water; and £145 worth of all other goods, including gifts and souvenirs. People under 17 cannot have the tobacco or alcohol allowance. For more information, contact HM Customs & Excise at ✆ **0845/010-9000** (from outside the U.K., 020/8929-0152), or consult its website at www.hmce.gov.uk.

For a clear summary of **Canadian** rules, request the booklet *I Declare,* issued by the **Canada Customs and Revenue Agency** (✆ **800/461-9999** in Canada, or

204/983-3500; www.ccra-adrc.gc.ca). Canada allows its citizens a C$750 exemption, and you're allowed to bring back duty-free one carton of cigarettes, 1 can of tobacco, 40 imperial ounces of liquor, and 50 cigars. In addition, you're allowed to mail gifts to Canada valued at less than C$60 a day, provided they're unsolicited and don't contain alcohol or tobacco (write on the package "Unsolicited gift, under $60 value"). All valuables should be declared on the Y-38 form before departure from Canada, including serial numbers of valuables you already own, such as expensive foreign cameras. *Note:* The $750 exemption can only be used once a year and only after an absence of 7 days.

The duty-free allowance in **Australia** is A$400, or A$200 for those under 18. Citizens age 18 and over can bring in 250 cigarettes or 250 grams of loose tobacco, and 1,125 milliliters of alcohol. If you're returning with valuables you already own, such as foreign-made cameras, you should file form B263. A helpful brochure available from Australian consulates or Customs offices is *Know Before You Go.* For more information, call the **Australian Customs Service** at © 1300/363-263, or log on to www.customs.gov.au.

HEALTH INSURANCE

Although it's not required of travelers, health insurance is highly recommended. Unlike many European countries, the United States does not usually offer free or low-cost medical care to its citizens or visitors. Doctors and hospitals are expensive, and in most cases will require advance payment or proof of coverage before they render their services. Policies can cover everything from the loss or theft of your baggage and trip cancellation to the guarantee of bail in case you're arrested. Good policies will also cover the costs of an accident, repatriation, or death. See "Health & Insurance," in

chapter 2 for more information. Packages such as **Europ Assistance's "Worldwide Healthcare Plan"** are sold by European automobile clubs and travel agencies at attractive rates. **Worldwide Assistance Services, Inc.** (© 800/821-2828; www.worldwideassistance.com), is the agent for Europ Assistance in the United States.

Though lack of health insurance may prevent you from being admitted to a hospital in nonemergencies, don't worry about being left on a street corner to die: The American way is to fix you now and bill the living daylights out of you later.

INSURANCE FOR BRITISH TRAVELERS Most big travel agents offer their own insurance and will probably try to sell you their package when you book a holiday. Think before you sign. **Britain's Consumers' Association** recommends that you insist on seeing the policy and reading the fine print before buying travel insurance. **The Association of British Insurers** (© 020/7600-3333; www.abi.org.uk) gives advice by phone and publishes *Holiday Insurance,* a free guide to policy provisions and prices. You might also shop around for better deals: Try **Columbus Direct** (© 020/7375-0011; www.columbusdirect.net).

INSURANCE FOR CANADIAN TRAVELERS Canadians should check with their provincial health plan offices or call **Health Canada** (© 613/957-2991; www.hc-sc.gc.ca) to find out the extent of their coverage and what documentation and receipts they must take home in case they are treated in the United States.

MONEY

CURRENCY The U.S. monetary system is very simple: The most common **bills** are the $1 (colloquially, a "buck"), $5, $10, and $20 denominations. There are also $2 bills (seldom encountered), $50 bills, and $100 bills (the last two are usually not welcome as payment for small purchases). All the paper money was recently redesigned, making the famous faces adorning them disproportionately large. The old-style bills are still legal tender.

There are seven denominations of coins: 1¢ (1 cent, or a penny); 5¢ (5 cents, or a nickel); 10¢ (10 cents, or a dime); 25¢ (25 cents, or a quarter); 50¢ (50 cents, or a half dollar); the gold-colored "Sacagawea" coin worth $1; and, prized by collectors, the rare, older silver dollar.

Note: The "foreign-exchange bureaus" so common in Europe are rare even at airports in the United States, and nonexistent outside major cities. It's best not to change foreign money (or traveler's checks denominated in a currency other than U.S. dollars) at a small-town bank, or even a branch in a big city; in fact, leave any currency other than U.S. dollars at home—it may prove a greater nuisance to you than it's worth.

TRAVELER'S CHECKS Though traveler's checks are widely accepted, make sure that they're denominated in U.S. dollars, as foreign-currency checks are often difficult to exchange. The three traveler's checks that are most widely recognized—and least likely to be denied—are **Visa, American Express,** and **Thomas Cook.** Be sure to record the numbers of the checks, and keep that information in a separate place in case they get lost or stolen. Most businesses are pretty good about taking traveler's checks, but you're better off cashing them in at a bank (in small amounts, of course) and paying in cash. *Remember:* You'll need identification, such as a driver's license or passport, to change a traveler's check.

CREDIT CARDS & ATMs Credit cards are the most widely used form of payment in the United States: **Visa** (Barclaycard in Britain), **MasterCard** (Euro-Card in Europe, Access in Britain, Chargex in Canada), **American Express, Diners Club, Discover,** and **Carte Blanche.** There are, however, a handful of stores and restaurants that do not take credit cards, so be sure to ask in advance. Most businesses display a sticker near their entrance to let you know which cards they accept. (*Note:* Businesses may require a minimum purchase, usually around $10, to use a credit card.)

It is strongly recommended that you bring at least one major credit card. You must have a credit or charge card to rent a car. Hotels and airlines usually require a credit card imprint as a deposit against expenses, and in an emergency a credit card can be priceless.

You'll find **automated teller machines (ATMs)** on just about every block—at least in almost every town—across the country. Some ATMs will allow you to draw U.S. currency against your bank and credit cards. Check with your bank before leaving home, and remember that you will need your personal identification number (PIN) to do so. Most accept Visa, MasterCard, and American Express, as well as ATM cards from other U.S. banks. Expect to be charged up to $3 per transaction, however, if you're not using your own bank's ATM.

One way around these fees is to ask for cash back at grocery stores that accept ATM cards and don't charge usage fees. Of course, you'll have to purchase something first.

Travel Tip

Be sure to keep a copy of all your travel papers separate from your wallet or purse, and leave a copy with someone at home should you need it faxed in an emergency.

Tips **Prepare to Be Fingerprinted**

Starting in January 2004, most international visitors traveling on visas to the United States will be photographed and fingerprinted at Customs in a new program created by the Department of Homeland Security called **US-VISIT**. Non–U.S. citizens arriving at airports and on cruise ships must undergo an instant background check as part of the government's ongoing efforts to deter terrorism by verifying the identity of incoming and outgoing visitors. For more information, go to the Homeland Security website at **www.dhs.gov/dhspublic**.

ATM cards with major credit card backing, known as "debit cards," are now a commonly acceptable form of payment in most stores and restaurants. Debit cards draw money directly from your checking account. Some stores enable you to receive "cash back" on your debit card purchases as well.

SAFETY

GENERAL SUGGESTIONS Although tourist areas are generally safe, U.S. urban areas tend to be less safe than those in Europe or Japan. You should always stay alert. This is particularly true of large American cities. If you're in doubt about which neighborhoods are safe, don't hesitate to make inquiries with the hotel front desk staff or the local tourist office.

Avoid deserted areas, especially at night, and don't go into public parks after dark unless there's a concert or similar occasion that will attract a crowd.

Avoid carrying valuables with you on the street, and keep expensive cameras or electronic equipment bagged up or covered when not in use. If you're using a map, try to consult it inconspicuously—or better yet, study it before you leave your room. Hold onto your pocketbook, and place your billfold in an inside pocket. In theaters, restaurants, and other public places, keep your possessions in sight.

Always lock your room door—don't assume that once you're inside the hotel you are automatically safe and no longer need to be aware of your surroundings.

Hotels are open to the public, and in a large hotel, security may not be able to screen everyone who enters.

DRIVING SAFETY Driving safety is important, too, and carjacking is not unprecedented. Question your rental agency about personal safety and ask for a traveler-safety brochure when you pick up your car. Obtain written directions—or a map with the route clearly marked—from the agency showing how to get to your destination. (Many agencies now offer the option of renting a cellphone for the duration of your car rental; check with the rental agent when you pick up the car. Otherwise, contact **InTouch USA** at © **800/872-7626** or www.in touchusa.com for short-term cellphone rental.) And, if possible, arrive and depart during daylight hours.

If you drive off a highway and end up in a dodgy-looking neighborhood, leave the area as quickly as possible. If you have an accident, even on the highway, stay in your car with the doors locked until you assess the situation or until the police arrive. If you're bumped from behind on the street or are involved in a minor accident with no injuries, and the situation appears to be suspicious, motion to the other driver to follow you. Never get out of your car in such situations. Go directly to the nearest police station, well-lit service station, or 24-hour store.

Park in well-lit and well-traveled areas whenever possible. Always keep your car doors locked, whether the vehicle is attended or unattended. Never leave any packages or valuables in sight. If someone attempts to rob you or steal your car, don't try to resist. Report the incident to the police department immediately by calling ✆ **911.**

2 Getting to the U.S.

AIRLINE DISCOUNTS The smart traveler can find numerable ways to reduce the price of a plane ticket simply by taking time to shop around. For example, overseas visitors can take advantage of the APEX (Advance Purchase Excursion) reductions offered by all major U.S. and European carriers. For more money-saving airline advice, see "Getting There," in chapter 2. For the best rates, compare fares and be flexible with the dates and times of travel.

IMMIGRATION & CUSTOMS CLEARANCE Visitors arriving by air, no matter what the port of entry, should cultivate patience and resignation before setting foot on U.S. soil. Getting through immigration control can take as long as 2 hours on some days, especially on summer weekends, so be sure to carry this guidebook or something else to read. This is especially true in the aftermath of the September 11, 2001, terrorist attacks, when security clearances have been considerably beefed up at U.S. airports.

People traveling by air from Canada, Bermuda, and certain countries in the Caribbean can sometimes clear Customs and Immigration at the point of departure, which is much quicker.

3 Getting Around the U.S.

BY PLANE Some large airlines (for example, Northwest and Delta) offer travelers on their transatlantic or transpacific flights special discount tickets under the name **Visit USA,** allowing mostly one-way travel from one U.S. destination to another at very low prices. These discount tickets are not on sale in the United States and must be purchased abroad in conjunction with your international ticket. This system is the best, easiest, and fastest way to see the United States at low cost. You should obtain information well in advance from your travel agent or the office of the airline concerned, since the conditions attached to these discount tickets can be changed without advance notice.

BY TRAIN International visitors (excluding Canada) can also buy a **USA Rail Pass,** good for 15 or 30 days of unlimited travel on Amtrak (✆ **800/ USA-RAIL;** www.amtrak.com). The pass is available through many overseas travel agents. Prices in 2005 for a 15-day pass were $305 off-peak, $440 peak; a 30-day pass was $516 off-peak, $729 peak. With a foreign passport, you can also buy passes at some Amtrak offices in the United States, including locations in San Francisco, Los Angeles, Chicago, New York, Miami, Boston, and Washington, D.C. Reservations are generally required and should be made for each part of your trip as early as possible. Regional rail passes are also available.

BY BUS Although bus travel is often the most economical form of public transit for short hops between U.S. cities, it can also be slow and uncomfortable—certainly not an option for everyone (particularly when Amtrak, which is far more luxurious, offers similar rates). **Greyhound/Trailways** (✆ **800/231-2222;** www.greyhound.com), the sole nationwide bus line, offers an **International Ameripass** that must be purchased before coming to the United States, or by phone through the Greyhound International Office at the Port Authority Bus

Terminal in New York City (© **212/971-0492**). The pass can be obtained from foreign travel agents or through Greyhound's website (order at least 21 days before your departure to the U.S.) and costs less than the domestic version. The 2005 prices: 4 days ($169), 7 days ($229), 10 days ($279), 15 days ($339), 21 days ($399), 30 days ($459), 45 days ($509), or 60 days ($619). You can get more info on the pass at the website or by calling © **402/330-8552.** In addition, special rates are available for seniors and students.

BY CAR   Unless you plan to spend the bulk of your vacation time in a city where walking is the best and easiest way to get around (read: New York City or New Orleans), the most cost-effective, convenient, and comfortable way to travel around the United States is by car. The interstate highway system connects cities and towns all over the country; in addition to these high-speed, limited-access roadways, there's an extensive network of federal, state, and local highways and roads. Some of the national car-rental companies include **Alamo** (© 800/462-5266; www.alamo.com), **Avis** (© 800/230-4898; www.avis.com), **Budget** (© 800/527-0700; www.budget.com), **Dollar** (© 800/800-3665; www.dollar.com), **Hertz** (© 800/654-3131; www.hertz.com), **National** (© 800/227-7368; www.nationalcar.com), and **Thrifty** (© 800/847-4389; www.thrifty.com).

If you plan to rent a car in the United States, you probably won't need the services of an additional automobile organization. If you're planning to buy or borrow a car, automobile-association membership is recommended. **AAA,** the **American Automobile Association** (© **800/222-4357**), is the country's largest auto club and supplies its members with maps, insurance, and, most important, emergency road service. The cost of joining runs from $70 for singles to $95 for two members, but if you're a member of a foreign auto club with reciprocal arrangements, you can enjoy free AAA service in America.

FAST FACTS: For the International Traveler

Automobile Organizations   Auto clubs will supply maps, suggested routes, guidebooks, accident and bail-bond insurance, and emergency road service. The **American Automobile Association (AAA)** is the major auto club in the United States. If you belong to an auto club in your home country, inquire about AAA reciprocity before you leave. You may be able to join AAA even if you're not a member of a reciprocal club; to inquire, call AAA (© **800/222-4357**). AAA is actually an organization of regional auto clubs; so look under "AAA Automobile Club" in the White Pages of the telephone directory. AAA has a nationwide emergency road service telephone number (© 800/AAA-HELP).

Business Hours   Offices are usually open weekdays from 9am to 5pm. Banks are open weekdays from 9am to 3pm or later and sometimes Saturday mornings. Stores typically open between 9 and 10am and close between 5 and 6pm from Monday through Saturday. Stores in shopping complexes or malls tend to stay open late: until about 9pm on weekdays and weekends, and many malls and larger department stores are open on Sundays.

Currency & Currency Exchange See "Entry Requirements" and "Money," under "Preparing for Your Trip," earlier in this chapter.

Drinking Laws The legal age for purchase and consumption of alcoholic beverages is 21; proof of age is required and often requested at bars, nightclubs, and restaurants, so it's always a good idea to bring ID when you go out. Beer and wine often can be purchased in supermarkets, but liquor laws vary from state to state.

Do not carry open containers of alcohol in your car or any public area that isn't zoned for alcohol consumption. The police can fine you on the spot. And nothing will ruin your trip faster than getting a citation for DUI ("driving under the influence"), so don't even think about driving while intoxicated.

Electricity Like Canada, the United States uses 110 to 120 volts AC (60 cycles), compared to 220 to 240 volts AC (50 cycles) in most of Europe, Australia, and New Zealand. If your small appliances use 220 to 240 volts, you'll need a 110-volt transformer and a plug adapter with two flat parallel pins to operate them here. Downward converters that change 220–240 volts to 110–120 volts are difficult to find in the United States, so bring one with you.

Embassies & Consulates All embassies are located in the nation's capital, Washington, D.C. Some consulates are located in major U.S. cities, and most nations have a mission to the United Nations in New York City. If your country isn't listed below, call for directory information in Washington, D.C. (© 202/555-1212) or log on to **www.embassy.org/embassies**.

The embassy of **Australia** is at 1601 Massachusetts Ave. NW, Washington, DC 20036 (© **202/797-3000**; www.austemb.org). There are consulates in New York, Honolulu, Houston, Los Angeles, and San Francisco.

The embassy of **Canada** is at 501 Pennsylvania Ave. NW, Washington, DC 20001 (© **202/682-1740**; www.canadianembassy.org). Other Canadian consulates are in Buffalo (New York), Detroit, Los Angeles, New York, and Seattle.

The embassy of **Ireland** is at 2234 Massachusetts Ave. NW, Washington, DC 20008 (© **202/462-3939**; www.irelandemb.org). Irish consulates are in Boston, Chicago, New York, and San Francisco.

The embassy of **Japan** is at 2520 Massachusetts Ave. NW, Washington, DC 20008 (© **202/238-6700**; www.embjapan.org). Japanese consulates are in many cities, including Atlanta, Boston, Detroit, New York, San Francisco, and Seattle.

The embassy of **New Zealand** is at 37 Observatory Circle NW, Washington, DC 20008 (© **202/328-4800**; www.nzemb.org). New Zealand consulates are in Los Angeles, Salt Lake City, San Francisco, and Seattle.

The embassy of the **United Kingdom** is at 3100 Massachusetts Ave. NW, Washington, DC 20008 (© **202/462-1340**; www.britainusa.com). Other British consulates are in Atlanta, Boston, Chicago, Cleveland, Houston, Los Angeles, New York, San Francisco, and Seattle.

Emergencies Call © **911** to report a fire, call the police, or get an ambulance anywhere in the United States. This is a toll-free call. (No coins are required at public telephones.)

If you encounter serious problems, contact **Traveler's Aid International** (📞 **202/546-1127**; www.travelersaid.org) to help direct you to a local branch. This nationwide, nonprofit, social-service organization geared to helping travelers in difficult straits offers services that might include reuniting families separated while traveling, providing food and/or shelter to people stranded without cash, or even emotional counseling. If you're in trouble, seek them out.

Gasoline (Petrol) Petrol is known as gasoline (or simply "gas") in the United States, and petrol stations are known as both gas stations and service stations. Gasoline costs about half as much here as it does in Europe (about $2.25 per gal. at press time), and taxes are already included in the printed price. One U.S. gallon equals 3.8 liters or .85 Imperial gallons.

Holidays Banks, government offices, post offices, and many stores, restaurants, and museums are closed on the following legal national holidays: January 1 (New Year's Day), the third Monday in January (Martin Luther King Jr. Day), the third Monday in February (Presidents' Day, Washington's Birthday), the last Monday in May (Memorial Day), July 4 (Independence Day), the first Monday in September (Labor Day), the second Monday in October (Columbus Day), November 11 (Veterans' Day/Armistice Day), the fourth Thursday in November (Thanksgiving Day), and December 25 (Christmas). Also, the Tuesday following the first Monday in November is Election Day and is a federal government holiday in presidential-election years (held every 4 years; next in 2008).

Legal Aid If you are "pulled over" for a minor infraction (such as speeding), never attempt to pay the fine directly to a police officer; this could be construed as attempted bribery, a much more serious crime. Pay fines by mail, or directly into the hands of the clerk of the court. If accused of a more serious offense, say and do nothing before consulting a lawyer. Here the burden is on the state to prove a person's guilt beyond a reasonable doubt, and everyone has the right to remain silent, whether he or she is suspected of a crime or actually arrested. Once arrested, a person can make one telephone call to a party of his or her choice. Call your embassy or consulate.

Mail If you aren't sure what your address will be in the United States, mail can be sent to you, in your name, c/o General Delivery at the main post office of the city or region where you expect to be. (Call 📞 **800/275-8777** for information on the nearest post office.) The addressee must pick up mail in person and must produce proof of identity (driver's license, passport, and so on). Most post offices will hold your mail for up to 1 month, and are open Monday to Friday from 8am to 6pm and Saturday from 9am to 3pm.

Generally found at intersections, mailboxes are blue with a red-and-white stripe and carry the inscription U.S. MAIL. If your mail is addressed to a U.S. destination, don't forget to add the five-digit postal code (or zip code), after the two-letter abbreviation of the state to which the mail is addressed. This is essential to prompt delivery.

At press time, domestic postage rates were 23¢ for a postcard and 37¢ for a letter. For international mail, a first-class letter of up to one-half ounce costs 80¢ (60¢ to Canada and Mexico); a first-class postcard costs 70¢ (50¢ to Canada and Mexico); and a preprinted postal aerogramme costs 70¢.

Measurements See the chart on the inside front cover of this book for details on converting metric measurements to U.S. equivalents.

Taxes The United States has no value-added tax (VAT) or other indirect tax at the national level. Every state, county, and city has the right to levy its own local tax on all purchases, including hotel and restaurant checks, airline tickets, and so on.

Telephone, Telegraph, Telex & Fax The telephone system in the United States is run by private corporations, so rates, especially for long-distance service and operator-assisted calls, can vary widely. Generally, hotel surcharges on long-distance and local calls are astronomical, so you're usually better off using a **public pay telephone,** which you'll find clearly marked in most public buildings and private establishments as well as on the street. Convenience grocery stores and gas stations always have them. Many convenience groceries and packaging services sell **prepaid calling cards** in denominations up to $50; these can be the least expensive way to call home. Many public phones at airports now accept American Express, MasterCard, and Visa credit cards. **Local calls** made from public pay phones in most locales cost either 25¢ or 35¢. Pay phones do not accept pennies, and few will take anything larger than a quarter.

You may want to look into leasing a cellphone for the duration of your trip.

Most long-distance and international calls can be dialed directly from any phone. **For calls within the United States and to Canada,** dial 1 followed by the area code and the seven-digit number. **For other international calls,** dial 011 followed by the country code, city code, and the telephone number of the person you are calling.

Calls to area codes **800, 888, 877,** and **866** are toll-free. However, calls to numbers in area codes **700** and **900** (chat lines, bulletin boards, "dating" services, and so on) can be very expensive—usually a charge of 95¢ to $3 or more per minute, and they sometimes have minimum charges that can run as high as $15 or more.

For **reversed-charge or collect calls,** and for person-to-person calls, dial 0 (zero, not the letter O) followed by the area code and number you want; an operator will then come on the line, and you should specify that you are calling collect, or person-to-person, or both. If your operator-assisted call is international, ask for the overseas operator.

For **local directory assistance** ("information"), dial 411; for long-distance information, dial 1, then the appropriate area code and 555-1212.

Telegraph and telex services are provided primarily by Western Union. You can bring your telegram into the nearest Western Union office (there are hundreds across the country) or dictate it over the phone (© **800/325-6000**). You can also telegraph money, or have it telegraphed to you, very quickly over the

Western Union system, but this service can cost as much as 15 to 20 percent of the amount sent.

Most hotels have **fax machines** available for guest use (be sure to ask about the charge to use it). Many hotel rooms are even wired for guests' fax machines. A less expensive way to send and receive faxes may be at stores such as **The UPS Store** (formerly Mail Boxes Etc.), a national chain of retail packing service shops. (Look in the Yellow Pages directory under "Packing Services.")

There are two kinds of telephone directories in the United States. The so-called **White Pages** list private households and business subscribers in alphabetical order. The inside front cover lists emergency numbers for police, fire, ambulance, the Coast Guard, poison-control center, crime-victims hot line, and so on. The first few pages will tell you how to make long-distance and international calls, complete with country codes and area codes. Government numbers are usually printed on blue paper within the White Pages. Printed on yellow paper, the so-called **Yellow Pages** list all local services, businesses, industries, and houses of worship according to activity with an index at the front or back. (Drugstores/pharmacies and restaurants are also listed by geographic location.) The Yellow Pages also include city plans or detailed area maps, postal zip codes, and public transportation routes.

Time The continental United States is divided into **four time zones:** Eastern Standard Time (EST), Central Standard Time (CST), Mountain Standard Time (MST), and Pacific Standard Time (PST). Alaska and Hawaii have their own zones. For example, noon in New York City (EST) is 11am in Chicago (CST), 10am in Denver (MST), 9am in Los Angeles (PST), 8am in Anchorage (AST), and 7am in Honolulu (HST).

Daylight saving time is in effect from 1am on the first Sunday in April through 1am on the last Sunday in October, except in Arizona, Hawaii, and Puerto Rico. Daylight saving time moves the clock 1 hour ahead of standard time.

Tipping Tips are a very important part of certain workers' income, and gratuities are the standard way of showing appreciation for services provided. (Tipping is certainly not compulsory if the service is poor!) In hotels, tip **bellhops** at least $1 per bag ($2–$3 if you have a lot of luggage) and tip the **chamber staff** $1 to $2 per day (more if you've left a disaster area for him or her to clean up). Tip the **doorman** or **concierge** only if he or she has provided you with some specific service (for example, calling a cab for you or obtaining difficult-to-get theater tickets). Tip the **valet-parking attendant** $1 every time you get your car.

In restaurants, bars, and nightclubs, tip **service staff** 15% to 20% of the check, tip **bartenders** 10% to 15%, tip **checkroom attendants** $1 per garment, and tip **valet-parking attendants** $1 per vehicle.

As for other service personnel, tip **cab drivers** 15% of the fare; tip **skycaps** at airports at least $1 per bag ($2–$3 if you have a lot of luggage); and tip **hairdressers** and **barbers** 15% to 20%.

Toilets You won't find public toilets or "restrooms" on the streets in most U.S. cities, but they can be found in hotel lobbies, bars, restaurants, museums, department stores, railway and bus stations, and service stations. Large hotels and fast-food restaurants are probably the best bet for good, clean facilities. If possible, avoid the toilets at parks and beaches, which tend to be dirty; some may be unsafe. Restaurants and bars in resorts or heavily visited areas may reserve their restrooms for patrons. Some establishments display a notice indicating this. You can ignore this sign or, better yet, avoid arguments by paying for a cup of coffee or a soft drink, which will qualify you as a patron.

4

Suggested Itineraries

Because the Southwest is such an amazingly diverse region, planning a route through it can be overwhelming. The itineraries suggested here should help guide you to the highlights, and hopefully, your trip won't be too hectic. The most important thing to keep in mind when planning a trip to the Southwest is that this is a vast region. Distances always turn out to be much greater than they seem when you're scanning a map in the comfort of your living room. Be prepared to do a lot of driving, and you won't be too surprised by the number of miles you put on your rental car.

1 The Southwest in 1 Week

A week really isn't long enough to do justice to this vast and sprawling landscape, but if that's all the time you have, you can definitely hit the highlights. The following is just such an itinerary. You'll gaze in awe at the Grand Canyon, marvel at the play of light on the buttes and mesas of Monument Valley, ponder the mysterious cliff dwellings of Mesa Verde, and stroll the streets of Santa Fe. *Note:* If you take this trip in the summer, try to get an early start each day in order to avoid the heat. During the middle of the day, try to be in an air-conditioned car or hotel room.

Day ❶: Sedona ★★★

Fly into Phoenix. Before leaving town to head north to Sedona, stop at the Desert Botanical Garden (p. 430) or the Heard Museum (p. 430). Just be sure you make it to Sedona in time to watch the sunset from either Airport Mesa or Crescent Moon Recreation Area (p. 501).

Day ❷: Sedona to Grand Canyon National Park ★★★

In Sedona in the morning, do a **Jeep tour** (p. 503) or a hike. Then head north to the **Grand Canyon** by way of scenic **Oak Creek Canyon** (p. 497). Take US 89 from Flagstaff to the east entrance of Grand Canyon National Park. Be sure to stop at the **Cameron Trading Post** (p. 547) to see the gallery of Native American artifacts in the historic stone building. Stop at **Desert View,** just inside the park entrance, and also at **Lipan Point,** and catch the sunset over the Grand Canyon.

Day ❸: Canyon de Chelly National Monument ★★★

If you can, get up early enough to catch sunrise from one of the Grand Canyon overlooks. Then, head east out of the park to Cameron and go north to **Tuba City.** Be sure to check out the dinosaur tracks in the bedrock just west of Tuba City. Continue east through the villages of the Hopi mesas. Here, you can tour **Walpi village** (p. 103) with a guide and shop for Hopi crafts and jewelry at the many roadside crafts shops. If you got an early enough start, consider detouring a few miles from your route to visit the

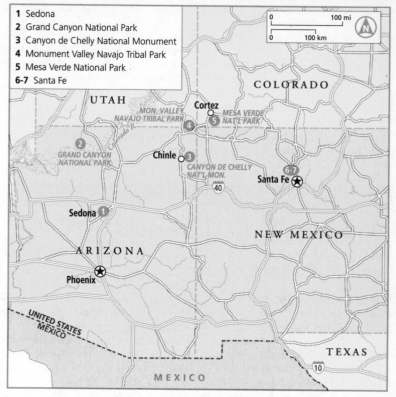

1 Sedona
2 Grand Canyon National Park
3 Canyon de Chelly National Monument
4 Monument Valley Navajo Tribal Park
5 Mesa Verde National Park
6-7 Santa Fe

Hubbell Trading Post National Historic Site (p. 100). When you reach **Canyon de Chelly National Monument** (p. 109), take one of the Rim Drives before it gets dark.

Day ❹: Canyon de Chelly to Monument Valley Navajo Tribal Park ★★★

Do a half-day truck tour of Canyon de Chelly in the morning. After lunch, drive to **Monument Valley Navajo Tribal Park** (p. 115). Make sure that you get there in time to catch the sunset. If you arrive early enough in the day, do a Jeep tour of the valley. Alternatively, go for a horseback ride; there is no more scenic spot in the Southwest to connect with your inner cowboy or cowgirl. Whether

at lunch or dinner, be sure to try some Navajo fry bread.

Day ❺: Monument Valley to Mesa Verde National Park ★★★

Today, do a morning **Jeep tour** (p. 117) of Monument Valley before heading east to Mesa Verde. En route, be sure to stop at **Four Corners Monument Navajo Tribal Park** (p. 130), the only place in the country where four states meet. At **Mesa Verde National Park** (p. 90), sign up for a ranger-led tour so you can see Balcony House, Cliff Palace, and Long House. Spend the night in Cortez.

Day ❻—❼: Santa Fe ★★★

After so many days in the desert, you'll find an oasis in Santa Fe. Spend a little time wandering the **Plaza** and visiting the **Palace of the Governors** (p. 162). If you're interested in shopping for Southwestern jewelry, peruse the offerings under the Palace of the Governors portal. Next, head to the **St. Francis Cathedral** (p. 162) and, if you have time, the **Loretto Chapel Museum** (p. 166), with its "magical" staircase. If it's summer, take in a performance at the **Santa Fe Opera** or the **Santa Fe Chamber Music Festival** (p. 182). The next day, start at the **Museum of International Folk Art** (p. 165), then visit the **Museum of Indian Arts & Culture** (p. 164). Have lunch at the **Museum Hill Café** (p. 164), and then see either the **Wheelwright Museum of the American Indian** (p. 165) or the **Museum of Spanish Colonial Art** (p. 165). Spend the late afternoon exploring and shopping along **Canyon Road** (p. 175), where you can also eat dinner.

2 The Southwest in 2 Weeks

If you have 2 weeks to explore the Southwest, consider yourself fortunate. You'll not only be able to hit the highlights, you'll be able to spend time getting to know such places as Tucson, Santa Fe, and the Grand Canyon. You'll also have time to visit some of the region's more out-of-the-way attractions, such as Carlsbad Caverns National Park and White Sands National Monument.

Day ❶–❷: Tucson ★★

Head straight for the pool at your resort—after all, lounging in the sun is one of the main reasons to visit Arizona. If you're a hiker, head to one of the trails in the foothills of the Santa Catalina Mountains. **Sabino Canyon** (p. 372) is just about the best place in the city for a quick hike. If you're more interested in culture, head to **Mission San Xavier del Bac** (p. 374), a Spanish mission church that is known as the "White Dove of the Desert." The next day, go west to the **Arizona–Sonora Desert Museum** (p. 369), which is more of a zoo than a museum. After you've hung out with the hummingbirds and communed with the coatis, drive a few miles to **Saguaro National Park** (p. 372). Be sure to check out the petroglyphs at Signal Hill.

Day ❸: White Sands National Monument ★★★

Spend the morning driving east across the Sonoran and Chihuahuan deserts. You'll see the lovely Chiricahua Mountains and the Gila National Forest en route. Stop for lunch in Las Cruces on **Old Mesilla Plaza** (p. 327). Spend the afternoon exploring **White Sands** (p. 299), the world's largest gypsum dune field, where you'll want to take the 16-mile Dunes Drive, stopping along the way to hike on the sand. Stay in the mountains at the **Lodge at Cloudcroft** (p. 299).

Day ❹: Carlsbad Caverns National Park ★★★

Today you'll drive farther, through forest and more Chihuahuan Desert to **Carlsbad Caverns National Park** (p. 314). Be sure to take the 1-mile self-guided walk down along the Natural Entrance route, following the original explorers' path deep into the earth. In the evening, visit the **Living Desert Zoo & Gardens State Park** (p. 310) to see some 50 species of (rescued) desert animals and 500 varieties of plants. Stay the night in Carlsbad.

Day ❺–❻: Santa Fe

It's a hearty drive to Santa Fe; once there, you'll enjoy the sophistication of the "City Different. "See "The Southwest in 1 Week: Day 6–7," above.

1-2 Tucson
3 White Sands National Monument
4 Carlsbad Caverns National Park
5-6 Santa Fe
7 Mesa Verde National Park
8 Monument Valley Navajo Tribal Park
9 Canyon de Chelly National Monument
10-11 Grand Canyon National Park
12-13 Sedona
14a Phoenix
14b Las Vegas

Day 7: Mesa Verde National Park ★★★

Head north on one of the region's prettiest drives, U.S. 84, to Pagosa Springs, Colorado, then across to Cortez. Spend the afternoon touring **Mesa Verde National Park** (p. 90), the largest archaeological preserve in the U.S. See "The Southwest in 1 Week: Day 5," above. Spend the night in Cortez.

Days 8: Monument Valley Navajo Tribal Park ★★★

From Mesa Verde, head to **Monument Valley Navajo Tribal Park** (p. 115). On the way, stop at **Four Corners Monument Navajo Tribal Park** (p. 130). Just be sure you reach Monument Valley early enough for a **Jeep tour** (p. 117) of the valley with a Navajo guide. Stick around to take pictures of sunset on the Mitten Buttes. This is also the best place in Arizona to go for a horseback ride. You'll feel as if you've ridden into a scene from a John Ford movie.

Day 9: Canyon de Chelly National Monument ★★★

The next day, drive to **Canyon de Chelly National Monument** (p. 109), which Navajo families still inhabit in summer, farming and raising sheep in much the same way that their ancestors did. Make a reservation in advance for a half-day **"shake-and-bake" truck tour** (p. 112) of the canyon, or hire a Navajo guide to take you into the canyon by Jeep or on horseback. Alternatively, drive one of the rim drives. The **South Rim Drive** (p. 111) is my favorite because it provides the opportunity to hike down into the canyon on the **White House Ruins** trail (p. 112).

Day ⑩–⑪: Grand Canyon National Park ★★★

From Canyon de Chelly, head south to Ganado and visit the historic **Hubbell Trading Post National Historic Site** (p. 100). Then head west across the Hopi Reservation and stop in the village of **Walpi** (p. 103). You can take a guided tour of the ancient mesa-top pueblo. Also be sure to stop at the **Cameron Trading Post** (p. 547). At the Grand Canyon, stop at **Desert View,** just inside the park entrance, and at **Lipan Point,** and catch the sunset. The next day, get up for the sunrise, then do a day hike or **mule ride** (p. 544) down into the canyon. If you plan ahead, you can even spend the night down in the canyon at **Phantom Ranch.** If you're not a hiker, spend the day exploring along **Hermit Drive,** where there are numerous overlooks.

Day ⑫–⑬: Sedona ★★★

Sedona may be touristy, but the red-rock cliffs, buttes, and mesas that surround the city make it one of the most beautiful communities in America. To get out amid the red rocks, take a **Jeep tour** (p. 503) or hike the 4- to 5-mile loop trail around **Bell Rock** and **Courthouse Rock** (p. 504). Although this trail sees a lot of hikers, it is just about the best introduction to the area's amazing hiking. Head up on **Airport Mesa** for the sunset. If you arrive too late for a Jeep tour, plan to do one the next day. On your second day in Sedona, in the morning either take a Jeep tour or visit the fascinating **V Bar V petroglyph site** (p. 501). In the afternoon, head west of town to **Palatki Ruins** (p. 500) and go for a hike in the area, perhaps up **Boynton Canyon.** Head to the **Crescent Moon Recreation Area** (p. 501) for sunset.

Day ⑭ (Option 1): Phoenix ★★

Heading south from Sedona, you can stop at the cliff dwellings at **Montezuma Castle National Monument** (p. 496). Then spend the end of your trip lounging at a resort or playing a round of golf on one of the Phoenix area's many top-rated courses. Also, before catching your flight out of town, be sure to stop at the **Heard Museum** (p. 430) or the **Desert Botanical Garden** (p. 430).

Day ⑭ (Option 2): Las Vegas ★★

If your interests lean more toward casinos and neon lights, head west to Las Vegas, where you can marvel at the nation's foremost city of excess.

3 Family Time: The Southwest for Kids & the Young at Heart in 2 Weeks

Though the Southwest lacks the major theme-park variety of attractions, it makes up for it by offering experiences that have a deeper impact. This trip takes families to the region's most notable sights, including Grand Canyon National Park and White Sands National Monument, and offers some poolside lounging and a hike through an archaeological site. While you're planning this trip, keep in mind that in the Southwest, many miles can stretch between spectacular sights. Parents who like to drive with their kids (some we know of actually do) can choose this journey. Those who find long drives with their kids difficult might want to vacation at a dude ranch or resort, or might want to focus in on one area with lots of family attractions.

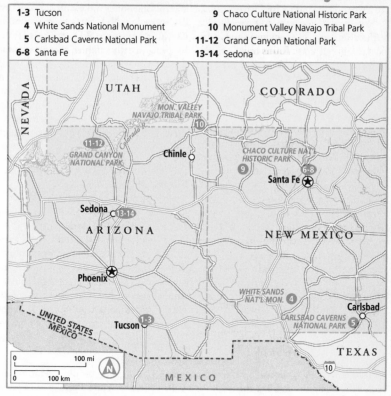

1-3	Tucson	**9**	Chaco Culture National Historic Park
4	White Sands National Monument	**10**	Monument Valley Navajo Tribal Park
5	Carlsbad Caverns National Park	**11-12**	Grand Canyon National Park
6-8	Santa Fe	**13-14**	Sedona

Day ❶–❸: Tucson ★★

Spend your first couple of days in Tucson, where you can learn all about the desert and the kids can pet snakes and tarantulas at the **Arizona–Sonora Desert Museum** (p. 369). Spend the morning at this amazing place, then after lunch head to **Old Tucson Studios** (p. 374), a one-time movie set that is now a sort of Wild West amusement park, albeit without any thrill rides. On one of your nights in town, have dinner at a cowboy steakhouse (p. 368). Alternatively, you could just spend a couple of days at a guest ranch (the Tucson area has three). On your third day in Tucson, do a day trip to **Tombstone** (p. 473). Yes, there is a Tombstone, and it's where Wyatt Earp and Doc Holliday shot it out with the bad guys at the O.K. Corral. Sure, it's touristy, but you owe it to your kids to bring them to this icon of the American west. On the way down from Tombstone, be sure to head underground at **Kartchner Caverns State Park** (p. 470). The caverns here are second only to Carlsbad Caverns for impressiveness.

Day ❹: White Sands National Monument ★★★

Head east from Tucson, stopping at **Old Mesilla Plaza** (p. 327) in Las Cruces for lunch. **White Sands National Monument** (p. 299) is a kid's dream—a giant sandbox to play in all afternoon. The world's largest gypsum dune field supplies plenty of fun hiking and sand sliding for the kids and panoramic beauty for adults. Be sure to take the 16-mile **Dunes Drive.** In the afternoon, head up to Cloudcroft, where you can cool down in the forest and enjoy a lavish night at the **Lodge at Cloudcroft** (p. 299).

Day ➎: Carlsbad Caverns National Park ★★★

Another kids' play land, **Carlsbad Caverns National Park** (p. 314) is especially appealing if you hike down into the caves from the Natural Entrance, the route the original spelunkers took. The late afternoon offers an opportunity to see gila monsters and bobcats at the **Living Desert Zoo & Gardens State Park** (p. 310). After dinner, take a stroll along or swim in the **Pecos River** (p. 310). Spend the night in Carlsbad.

Day ➏: Santa Fe ★★★

Head north, stopping to stretch your legs at the **International UFO Museum** (p. 308) in Roswell, which will challenge—or confirm—your belief in what's "out there." In the gift shop, your kids can stock up on the latest alien kitsch. Then head to Santa Fe, passing through the lovely Galisteo Basin. Wander the **Plaza** and explore the **Palace of the Governors** (p. 162) and **St. Francis Cathedral** (p. 162).

Day ➐–➑: Santa Fe ★★★

Begin at the **Museum of International Folk Art** (p. 165), which displays works from over 100 countries. Kids enjoy the hundreds of toys on display. A morsel for the parents, the **Museum of Indian Arts & Culture** (p. 164) is like a journey into another world, with vivid displays of ancient Native American life. Alternately, head to the **Santa Fe Children's Museum** (p. 170), where kids can rock climb and visit a horticulture garden. Spend the late afternoon wandering **Canyon Road** (p. 175), where parents will find world-class art and kids will find fun works such as mobiles

and rocking horses. Take your last Santa Fe day to explore New Mexico's outdoors. If it's winter, head up to **Ski Santa Fe** (p. 174). In spring or early summer, take a whitewater (or flat-water if you have small children) raft trip down the **Rio Grande** (p. 225) in Pilar. If it's summer or fall, hike in the Santa Fe National Forest. You can enjoy a **chairlift ride** (p. 173) to the Ski Santa Fe summit (panoramic views!) and then hike down.

Day ➒: Chaco Culture National Historical Park ★★★

There's plenty of space for kids to stretch their legs after the long drive to **Chaco Canyon National Historic Park** (p. 135). With its stunning desert setting and awesome ruins, the site offers opportunities to peek into dwellings and climb down into kivas. Be sure to hike up the **Pueblo Alto Trail** to see the ruins from above and get a view of the entire canyon. Spend the night in Farmington or Aztec.

Day ➓: Monument Valley Navajo Tribal Park ★★★

From Farmington, head to **Monument Valley Navajo Tribal Park** (p. 115). On the way, be sure to stop at **Four Corners Monument Navajo Tribal Park** (p. 130), the only place in the country where four states meet. Because you can stand in Colorado, Utah, Arizona, and New Mexico at once, this is one of the Southwest's premier family photo ops. Just be sure you reach Monument Valley early enough to go for a horseback ride. We recommend **Diné Trail Ride Tours** (p. 117), which leads its rides from a point deep within the valley. Alternatively, do a **Jeep tour** (p. 117). Be sure to try some fry bread or a Navajo taco while you're here.

Day ⓫–⓬: Grand Canyon National Park ★★★

From Monument Valley, head for the east entrance of **Grand Canyon National**

Park (p. 534). En route, be sure to check out the cool **dinosaur tracks** (p. 105) just west of Tuba City. **Cameron Trading Post** (p. 547) is a good place to stop for lunch. It has a huge selection of Native American crafts as well as souvenirs that will appeal to the kids. Just be sure you make it to the Grand Canyon in time for sunset. In the evening, you may be able to catch an interesting interpretive program. Spend the next day hiking a little ways into the canyon, riding a mule down into the canyon (if your kids are old enough), or exploring along Hermit Road. The historic little Hermit's Rest is a good place to get cocoa and hang out by the fireplace.

Day ⑬–⑭: Grand Canyon to Sedona ★★★

Head back out the east entrance of the park and then drive south toward Flagstaff and Sedona. You can dawdle along the way, perhaps by stopping at **Wupatki National Monument** (p. 526). From Flagstaff, drive down through Oak Creek Canyon and stop at **Slide Rock State Park** (p. 502), where you and the kids can cool off in the waters of Oak Creek and have a blast on the natural water slide. The next morning, do a Jeep tour so you can get out in the famous red rocks of Sedona. In the afternoon, head back to Slide Rock or to **Grasshopper Point** (p. 502), Oak Creek Canyon's other great swimming hole.

4 A Multisport Tour of the Southwest

Anyone who hikes, mountain bikes, or rafts knows that the Southwest's offerings for outdoors enthusiasts are unsurpassed. The Grand Canyon offers the world's greatest rafting adventure, and Moab, Utah, is legendary among mountain bikers. Hikers hold the canyonlands of southern Utah in reverent awe not only for their bizarre and beautiful rock formations but for their narrow slot canyons. In a two-week adventure, you can take in the best this region has to offer. *Note:* Because Grand Canyon rafting trips are so popular and need to be booked up to a year in advance, this itinerary is workable only if you first book your raft trip.

Day ❶–❷: Zion National Park ★★

Fly into Las Vegas and immediately head out of Sin City bound for **Zion National Park** (p. 561), a sort of paradise amid the rugged cliffs of southwestern Utah. Hiking trails abound; weather permitting, plan a day hike up the spectacular Narrows. This route follows the Virgin River, and you will get your feet wet, but it's the perfect introduction to the slot canyons of the Southwest. You can hike as far up the canyon as your stamina allows. The next day, try the **Lower Emerald Pools Trail** or the **Angel's Landing Trail.** Stay at Zion Lodge.

Day ❸: Bryce Canyon National Park ★★★

From Zion, head north to **Bryce Canyon National Park** (p. 567), which is not a canyon but rather a series of bizarrely eroded natural amphitheaters. A maze of trails meanders amid the hoodoos and forests of the national park. Spend the night at Bryce Canyon Lodge.

Day ❹–❺: Moab & Arches National Park ★★★

After 3 days of hiking in Zion and Bryce Canyon, you'll probably appreciate the chance to sit for a while as you make the long drive to Moab, the mountain-biking capital of the Southwest. In Moab, rent a bike, get your hands on a map, and head out on the slickrock trails of this wonderland of rock. In between bike rides, consider driving to **Arches National Park** (p. 576) to see some of its incredible sandstone arches.

A Multisport Tour of the Southwest

0 | 100 mi
0 | 100 km

Moab 4-5

CAPITOL REEF NAT'L PARK

CANYONLANDS NAT'L PARK

NEVADA

Panguitch

U T A H

ZION NAT'L PARK 1-2

BRYCE CANYON NAT'L PARK

3

St. George

Lake Powell

Colorado

GLEN CANYON NAT'L RECREATION AREA

Bluff

GLEN CANYON DAM 7-9

Jacob Lake

Page

MON. VALLEY NAVAJO TRIBAL PARK 6

Lake Mead

LAKE MEAD NAT'L RECREATION AREA

GRAND CANYON NAT'L PARK 10-14

Grand Canyon

HOOVER DAM

Lake Mohave

A R I Z O N A

NV | UT
CA | AZ
Area of detail

1-2 Zion National Park
3 Bryce Canyon National Park
4-5 Moab & Arches National Park
6 Monument Valley Navajo Tribal Park
7-9 Page, Lake Powell, Buckskin Gulch & Coyote Buttes
10-14 Grand Canyon National Park

Day ❻: Moab to Monument Valley

Get up early for one last bike ride in Moab. Then head south to **Monument Valley Navajo Tribal Park** (p. 115). Although this park isn't known specifically as an out-door-sports destination, the scenery is too awesome to ignore. To burn off some calories, you can hike the 3.2-mile Wildcat Trail or hire a Navajo guide to take you on a hike deeper into the park. However, if you aren't already too saddle sore from biking in Moab, you should really saddle up a palomino and ride off into the sunset. No other place in the West will give you such a feeling of having ridden right into a classic Hollywood western. Stay at **Goulding's Lodge** (p. 118) just outside the park.

Day ❼: Page & Lake Powell ★★

The next day, drive west to Page. Just before you reach town, you can stop at **Antelope Canyon** (p. 122) and hike into one of the Southwest's most pho-tographed slot canyons. It's beautiful but is also often crowded, which will give you a greater appreciation for the permit sys-tems in effect at some of the region's other slot canyons. Now for something completely different. Although the Lake Powell reservoir is best known to house-boaters and water skiers, it also offers the most spectacular **sea kayaking** in the Southwest. Rent a boat and head out to Antelope Canyon again. This time, you'll be paddling up from the mouth. If there isn't too much quicksand where the water gives way to land, you can even get out and hike up the slot canyon.

Day ❽–❾: Buckskin Gulch & Coyote Buttes ✪✪✪

Using Page as a base, spend the next 2 days exploring some of the most famous slot canyons in the Southwest. The 37-mile **Paria Canyon** (p. 124) is a 3- to 4-day trip, but you can day hike into **Buckskin Gulch,** one of its tributaries. The hike starts at the Wire Pass Trailhead about 30 miles west of Page. From this same trailhead, you can also hike into **Coyote Buttes** (p. 557), but only if you managed to get a permit, which can be difficult. If you have a permit, spend one day at Coyote Buttes and one day in Buckskin Gulch. Spend your second night in Page or at Lee's Ferry, depending on where your rafting trip starts.

Day ❿–⓮: Grand Canyon National Park ✪✪✪

Rafting the Grand Canyon (p. 555) is the adventure of a lifetime. Although it's possible to spend less than a week rafting through a portion of the canyon, such trips are in big motorized rafts that detract from the wilderness experience of floating through the canyon. If your rafting trip is a once-in-a-lifetime adventure, you owe it to yourself to make the most of the trip and go by oar-powered raft or dory. Talk about a thrill ride! If you opt for a trip that puts in at Lee's Ferry and ends at Phantom Ranch, you'll get to hike up out of the canyon at the end of your trip, adding one last great hike to an unforgettable two weeks in the Southwest. Spend your last night at one of the lodges on the park's South Rim, and the next day drive back to Las Vegas. You'll have to arrange through your rafting company to have your car shuttled to the national park.

5 Historical Delights: The Pueblo & Conquistador Trail in 2 Weeks

The Native American presence in the American Southwest stretches back as far as 3000 B.C. That history intersects with the Spanish conquistadors, whose culture has transformed over four centuries to its own unique way of life. Visitors encounter ancient ruins and artifacts, formidable mission churches and poetic Spanish villages, set against the backdrop of stunning scenery. Those who want to travel back in time will find plenty of adventure here. Though you can take this trip anytime, it's best in spring, summer, and fall.

Day ❶: Albuquerque ✪✪

Enjoy a relaxing day. Stroll **Old Town** (p. 234), wandering some of the narrow back streets in search of shops displaying Native American and Spanish artifacts. Nearby is the **Indian Pueblo Cultural Center** (p. 244), where you can get acquainted with the cultures that you'll encounter throughout the New Mexico portion of your trip. If you have the energy, head west of town to the **Petroglyph National Monument** (p. 247) to hike and watch the sunset.

Day ❷–❹: Santa Fe ✪✪✪

In the morning of day 2, drive the **Turquoise Trail** (p. 263) to Santa Fe. You'll pass through old mining towns and hills where Native Americans and others once mined turquoise. See "The Southwest in 1 Week: Day 6–7" (p. 61) for pointers on how to spend days 2 and 3. On day 4, head north to explore **Bandelier National Monument** (p. 191), or take the **High Road to Taos** (p. 192) for a visit to **Taos Pueblo** (p. 217). Your choice will depend on whether you prefer to see ancient ruins or Native Americans' current lifestyles.

Day ⑤: Acoma Pueblo ★★★

Today you'll head south and then west to **Acoma Pueblo** (p. 269). Take the bus and walking tour, but then hike down on your own to get a good sense of this mesa-top village, where people still live as their ancestors did hundreds of years ago. If you have energy and time afterward, visit **El Morro National Monument** (p. 274) to see inscriptions left by visitors for hundreds of years. Be sure to climb up to the Anasazi (ancestral Puebloan) ruins. Spend the night in Grants.

Day ⑥: Chaco Culture National Historic Park ★★★

Though it's a long, dusty drive to **Chaco Culture National Historic Park** (p. 135), the combination of a stunning setting and expansive ruins makes the park worthwhile. Chaco is the Holy Grail for Southwest history buffs. Be sure to hike up the **Pueblo Alto Trail** to get a full view of the grand kivas and amazing network of dwellings. Spend the night in Farmington at **Casa Blanca** (p. 132).

Day ⑦: Mesa Verde National Park ★★★ & Monument Valley Navajo Tribal Park ★★★

Though similar to Chaco, **Mesa Verde** (p. 90) presents a whole different style of living and architecture. Sign up for a ranger-led tour to get a close-up view of some of the best ruins. When you've finished wandering, head for **Monument Valley Navajo Tribal Park** (p. 115), arriving in time to see the sun set on Mitten Buttes. Stay the night at **Goulding's Lodge** (p. 118).

Day ⑧: Canyon de Chelly National Monument ★★★

Get an early start and drive to **Canyon de Chelly National Monument** (p. 109). See "The Southwest in 2 Weeks: Day 9."

Day ⑨: The Hopi Mesas

After leaving Canyon de Chelly, head south to Ganado and visit the historic **Hubbell Trading Post National Historic Site** (p. 100). Then head west across the Hopi Reservation and stop in the village of **Walpi** (p. 103), where you can take a guided tour of the ancient mesa-top pueblo. Also be sure to stop at **Tsakurshovi** (p. 105), a tiny crafts shop that specializes in traditional Hopi kachina dolls. Continue south to Winslow and stay at the historic **La Posada** hotel (p. 100).

Day ⑩: Sedona ★★★

Although Sedona is best known for its red-rock scenery and art galleries, the area has several small Sinagua ruins and an impressive rock art site. Get an early start and head first to **Montezuma Castle National Monument** (p. 496), a Sinagua cliff dwelling. From there, head north to **Montezuma Well** (p. 496), then continue to the **V Bar V Petroglyph Site** (p. 501), which has a small rock wall covered with fascinating petroglyphs. After a picnic on the banks of Beaver Creek or lunch in Sedona, visit the remote cliff dwellings at **Palatki Ruins** (p. 500). If you have time, visit the partially reconstructed hilltop ruins at **Tuzigoot National Monument** (p. 496) in nearby Clarkdale.

Day ⑪: Phoenix ★★

Today, head south to Phoenix and visit the **Heard Museum** (p. 430), Arizona's foremost museum of Native American art and culture. This museum can help you make sense of what you've been seeing during your trip. If you want to see more petroglyphs, visit **Deer Valley Rock Art Center** (p. 430). Alternatively, you can see a partially reconstructed Hohokam village at **Pueblo Grande Museum and Archaeological Park** (p. 431). In the evening, stroll the grounds of the **Desert Botanical Garden** (p. 430), which has an ethnobotanical garden.

Day ⑫: Bisbee & Coronado National Memorial ★

Today, head south through Tucson to the historic copper-mining town of Bisbee. It

Historical Delights: The Pueblo & Conquistador Trail in 2 Weeks

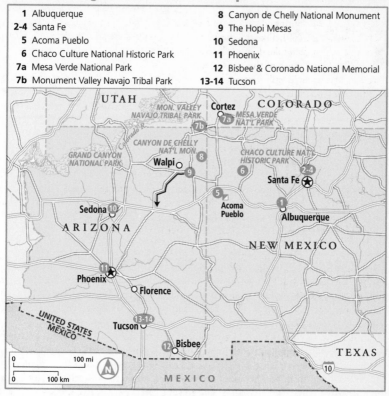

1 Albuquerque
2-4 Santa Fe
5 Acoma Pueblo
6 Chaco Culture National Historic Park
7a Mesa Verde National Park
7b Monument Valley Navajo Tribal Park

8 Canyon de Chelly National Monument
9 The Hopi Mesas
10 Sedona
11 Phoenix
12 Bisbee & Coronado National Memorial
13-14 Tucson

makes a good base for exploring the nearby **Coronado National Memorial** (p. 471). This memorial commemorates the 16th-century expedition of Spanish explorer Francisco Vásquez de Coronado. As you drive south from Phoenix to Bisbee, detour to visit **Casa Grande Ruins National Monument** (p. 458), which preserves a huge 650-year-old earth-walled Hohokam building that may have been an astronomical observatory.

Day ⑬–⑭: Tucson ★★

From Bisbee, head west on scenic back roads to the historic Spanish mission now preserved as **Tumacacori National Historical Park** (p. 462). Nearby you can tour more Spanish ruins at **Tubac Presidio State Historic Park** (p. 462). Be sure to stop at Wisdom's Café for a fruit burrito. As you drive north from Tubac, you'll come to **Mission San Xavier del Bac** (p. 374). This Spanish mission church, known as the White Dove of the Desert, is the most beautiful and best preserved of all the Spanish churches in the Southwest. The next day, stroll around the Barrio Viejo and El Presidio historic districts to get a feel for Spanish and Mexican days in Tucson. Several of the historic buildings in El Presidio neighborhood are part of the Tucson Museum of Art and are open to the public. Nearby, on the grounds of the Tucson Convention Center, you can visit the historic **Sosa-Carillo-Frémont House Museum** (p. 377).

5

The Active Vacation Planner

You may be pleasantly surprised at the range of outdoor fun available in the Southwest. From the deserts of the southern regions to the mountains and canyons of the north, diversity reigns. Whether you're interested in a short day hike or an overnight horse trip, groomed ski trails or backcountry adventures, you won't be disappointed.

For more in-depth coverage of the activities that follow, contact some of the local outfitters or organizations that appear in the "Getting Outside" sections, later in this book.

1 Bicycling

It's awesome to pedal out into the dry southwest air and see not only incredible terrain but also ancient history. Just about the entire region is conducive to the sport, making it one of the most popular places in the United States for avid cyclers, especially mountain bikers.

For road warriors, many miles of pavement traverse the area. Rides range greatly in length and difficulty; all provide beautiful scenery, and most have decent pavement with good shoulders. Check out the Show Low/Springerville Loop (see chapter 14) and Ariz. 82 east from Sonoita (see chapter 14). In northern New Mexico, try biking the Enchanted Circle (see chapter 8) and in southern New Mexico, try Silver City to Glenwood (see chapter 11). Road biking is highly recommended in Zion National Park as well (see chapter 17).

Few can think of mountain biking without Moab, Utah, coming to mind. Moab and many other parts of southern Utah hold hundreds of miles of trails, a wide variety of terrain, and spectacular scenery. In addition to the mountain biking possibilities on four-wheel-drive roads in the national parks, abundant trails on Bureau of Land Management and national forest lands are much less trafficked than national park routes. Moab's most famous trail is undoubtedly the **Slickrock Bike Trail,** a scenic but challenging 9.6-mile loop that crosses a mesa of heavily eroded pale orange Navajo sandstone just a few minutes from downtown Moab (see chapter 17 for information about Moab).

In New Mexico, bikers will find excellent trails in **Albuquerque** at the base of the Sandia Mountains (see chapter 9). In **Santa Fe,** you'll find some very rugged and steep mountain trails, most accessed off the road to Ski Santa Fe (see chapter 7). **Taos** is a rider's paradise, with lots of extreme mountain trails, as well as some that are purely scenic, such as the west rim of the Rio Grande Gorge (see chapter 8). In northwestern New Mexico, you can ride around El Malpais National Monument in the **Grants** area (see chapter 10). You can also take your bike with you to Chaco Culture National Historical Park and tour the Anasazi ruins (see chapter 6). In the southwestern region, bikes are not allowed in the Gila Wilderness, but they are permitted in other parts of

Gila National Forest; you'll find terrific trails that originate in **Silver City,** particularly the Continental Divide Trail (see chapter 11). In the southeast region, the **Cloudcroft** area has some excellent trails; there are a few that explore history as well as natural terrain, most notably the 17-mile Rim Trail (see chapter 11).

Some of the best biking in the area is in Arizona. With its wide range of climates, this sunny state offers good pedaling somewhere in the state every month of the year. In summer, the White Mountains (in the eastern part of the state; see chapter 14) and Kaibab National Forest (between Flagstaff and Grand Canyon National Park; see chapter 16) offer good mountain biking. There's also excellent biking at several Phoenix parks. My favorite trail is the Desert Classic in South Mountain Park (see chapter 13). Tucson is one of the most bicycle-friendly cities in the country. Check out the Bajada Loop Drive in the Saguaro National Park (see chapter 12). One of the best spots in the region is Sedona. Head to the Bell Rock Pathway there as well as Broken Arrow/Submarine Rock (see chapter 15).

If you don't want to strike out on your own, **Sun Mountain Bike Company,** Santa Fe (© 505/982-8986), runs bike tours from April to October to some of the most spectacular spots in northern New Mexico. Trips range from easy, scenic jaunts to more mountainous technical rides. **Backroads** (© 800/462-2848 or 510/527-1555; www.backroads.com) offers a 6-day, inn-to-inn mountain-bike trip through the red-rock country of central Arizona. **Western Spirit Cycling** (© 800/845-2453 or 435/259-8732; www.westernspirit.com) offers a number of interesting mountain-bike tours, including trips to both the North and South rims of the Grand Canyon and through the desert south of Tucson. Each trip is 5 days in duration. In Utah, you can get information on trails and outfitters, as well as rent or repair bikes, at **Slickrock Cycles,** 94 W. 415 N. Main St. (© 800/825-9791 or 435/259-1134; www.slickrock cycles.com).

Some books to check out are *Mountain Biking Utah* (Falcon Press), *Frommer's Great Outdoor Guide to Arizona & New Mexico* (Wiley Publishing, Inc.), and Sarah Bennett's *Mountain Biker's Guide to New Mexico* (Falcon Press). To research Arizona trails, pick up a copy of *Fat Tire Tales and Trails,* by Cosmic Ray.

2 Bird-Watching

Bird-watchers know that the Southwest is directly on the Central Flyway, which makes it a great spot for this activity all year long. Each region offers refuge to a wide variety of birds, including everything from doves, finches, bluebirds, and roadrunners (the New Mexico state bird) to the rare and wonderful whooping crane. The bald eagle is also frequently spotted during winter and spring migrations. A good place to pull out your binoculars is southeastern Arizona, where many species found primarily south of the border come to visit. Birding hot spots include **Ramsey Canyon Preserve** (known for its many species of hummingbirds), **Cave Creek Canyon** (nesting site for elegant trogons), **Patagonia–Sonoita Creek Preserve** (home to 22 species of fly-catchers, kingbirds, and phoebes, as well as Montezuma quails), **Buenos Aires National Wildlife Refuge** (home to masked bobwhite quail and gray hawks), and the sewage ponds outside the town of **Willcox** (known for avocets and sandhill cranes). For further information on these birding spots, see chapter 14. The **Madera Canyon National Forest Recreation Area** is another "mountain island" that attracts many of the same species seen at Ramsey Canyon and Sonoita Creek (see chapter 12). If you're into eclectic bird-watching, head to the **Vermilion Cliffs** in northern Arizona, where you'll likely catch a glimpse of the noble California condor, which the California Condor Recovery Plan has brought to the area in the hope that it can flourish there (see chapter 16). To find out which birds have been spotted lately, call the **Tucson Audubon Society's Bird Report** (✆ **520/798-1005**).

Though not quite as renowned a birding spot as southern Arizona, New Mexico does host plenty of birds. Check out the wildlife refuge centers in New Mexico, most notably the **Bosque del Apache National Wildlife Refuge,** 93 miles south of Albuquerque (✆ **505/835-1828;** see chapter 11). Others include the **Las Vegas National Wildlife Refuge,** 5 miles southeast of Las Vegas (✆ **505/425-3581;** see chapter 10), and **Bitter Lake National Wildlife Refuge,** 13 miles northeast of Roswell (✆ **505/622-6755;** see chapter 11). Some common sightings at these areas might include sandhill cranes, snow geese, a wide variety of ducks, and falcons. New Mexico is also home to an amazing variety of hummingbirds. In fact, in early 1996, the state was able to add the Cinnamon Hummingbird to its list of birds. Its sighting in Santa Teresa marked only the second sighting in the United States. If you're interested in birdwatching during your trip to New Mexico, contact the state office of the **National Audubon Society** (✆ **505/983-4609**), P.O. Box 9314, Santa Fe, NM 87504.

In Utah, head to **Escalante State Park** to find wetland birds such as grebes and herons. You might also see eagles, osprey, American kestrels and other raptors. The rare peregrine falcon sometimes nests at Zion National Park in the Weeping Rock area. Also in the park are golden eagles, hummingbirds and roadrunners. (See chapter 17.)

Serious birders who want to be sure of adding lots of rare birds to their life lists may want to visit southeastern Arizona or New Mexico on a guided tour. Contact **High Lonesome Birdtours** (✆ **800/743-2668;** www.hilonesome.com), which runs trips in southern Arizona. **WestWing Bird Watching Tours** (✆ **800/583-6928** or 505/473-2780; http://home.earthlink.net/wingswestnm) offers customized birding tours in New Mexico and Sonora, Mexico.

3 Fishing

The variety of terrain in the Southwest, from deserts to canyons to mountains, makes for a diverse and year-round fishing experience. In places such as Lees Ferry and Lake Powell, and the San Juan River and Navajo Lake, cold-water fishing and warm-water fishing are separated by yards rather than miles, thanks to dams set between these and many other rivers and lakes.

Warm-water lakes and streams are home to large- and small-mouth bass, walleye, stripers, catfish, crappie, and bluegill. In cold-water lakes and streams, look for the Rio Grande cutthroat, as well as kokanee salmon and rainbow, brown, lake, and brook trout.

Two of the best places for fishing in New Mexico are the San Juan River near Farmington, and Elephant Butte Lake, not far from Truth or Consequences. The San Juan River offers excellent trout fishing and is extremely popular with fly fishers. Elephant Butte is great for bass fishing; in fact, it is considered one of the top 10 bass fishing locations in the United States.

Arizona offers good trout fishing on the Mogollon Rim and in the White Mountains there, as well as in the Grand Canyon and the more easily accessible sections of the free-running Colorado River between Glen Canyon Dam and Lees Ferry. In fact, this latter area is among the country's most fabled stretches of trout water. Near there, Lake Powell also offers abundant lake fishing within its many finger canyons.

Colorado has many cold-water species living in lakes and streams, including seven kinds of trout (native cutthroat, rainbow, brown, brook, lake, kokanee, and white-fish), walleye, yellow perch, northern pike, tiger muskie, and bluegill. Warm-water sport fish (especially in eastern Colorado and in large rivers) include catfish, crappie, and bass (largemouth, smallmouth, white, and wiper). Both lake and stream fishing are available in the Durango area.

I recommend Ti Piper's *Fishing in New Mexico* (University of New Mexico Press). It's an excellent and wonderfully comprehensive book that describes every waterway in New Mexico in great detail. Also of note are Taylor Streit's *Guide to Fly Fishing in Arizona* and *Guide to Fly Fishing New Mexico*. They include information about regulations and descriptions of the types and varieties of fish you're likely to catch.

For information on obtaining fishing licensing, contact the **New Mexico Game and Fish Department** (© 800/862-9310 or 505/476-8000; www.wildlife.state.nm.us), the **Arizona Game and Fish Department** (© 602/942-3000; www.azgfd.com), or the **Utah Division of Wildlife Resources** (© 877/592-5169 or 435/865-6100; www.wildlife.utah.gov). The **Colorado Division of Wildlife** (© 303/297-1192; www.wildlife.state.co.us) can also help.

It is not necessary to have a fishing license in order to fish on Native American reservation land, but you must receive written permission and an official tribal document before setting out on any fishing trips. Phone numbers for individual tribes and pueblos are listed separately in the regional and city chapters later in this book.

4 Golf

Many come to this region specifically to play golf. The Southwest's hundreds of golf courses range from easy public layouts to PGA championship links that have challenged the best.

In Phoenix and Tucson, greens fees, like room rates, are seasonal. In the popular winter months, fees at resort courses range from about $90 to $250 for 18 holes, which usually includes mandatory cart rental. In summer, fees often drop more than 50%. Almost all resorts offer special golf packages as well. Municipal courses charge about $40, with cart rental an additional $20 or so. In New Mexico fees range from $20 to $145, with most averaging about $60, and with reduced rates in winter. (Cart rentals run about $15.)

North of Scottsdale in the town of Carefree, **The Boulders** (© 480/488-9009) offers some of the best playing and scenery in the state. Also in the valley, in Apache Junction, the **Gold Canyon Golf Resort** (© 800/827-5281) is an excellent course, with three of the best holes in the state. The **Wigwam Golf and Country Club** (© 623/935-3811) is legendary in the region. **The Phoenician** (© 480/423-2449) is another noteworthy resort course in the area, with a mix of traditional and desert-style holes. Though it's pricey, locals love the semiprivate **Troon North Golf Club** (© 480/585-7700), a course carved out of the raw desert. The pros head to the Stadium Course at the **Tournament Players Club (TPC) of Scottsdale** (© 480/585-4334), while the most popular municipal course is the **Papago Golf Course** (© 602/275-8428), which has an amazing 17th hole. For more information on these courses, see chapter 13.

In recent years, Tucson has gained a reputation for great golf. Among the city's resort courses, the Mountain Course at the **Ventana Canyon Golf and Racquet Club** (© 520/577-1400) is stellar. The Sunrise Course at **El Conquistador Country Club**

(© 520/544-1800) has some very memorable par-3 holes. The pros head to **Omni Tucson National Golf Resort and Spa** (© 520/575-7540), home of the Tucson Open. Tucson's best municipal course, **Randolph North** (© 520/791-4161), is the site of the city's annual LPGA tournament. For more information about all of these courses see chapter 12.

Options abound in other parts of Arizona as well. Check out the 18-hole course at **Rancho de los Caballeros** (© 928/684-2704; see chapter 15), a luxury guest ranch outside Wickenburg. For spectacular scenery, few courses compare with the **Sedona Golf Resort** (© 928/284-9355; see chapter 15). In western Arizona, along "Arizona's West Coast," check out Lake Havasu City's **London Bridge Golf Club** (© 928/855-2719), which offers a view of the London Bridge. The **Emerald Canyon Golf Course** (© 928/667-3366), a municipal course in Parker, offers unique terrain and even more dramatic views. See chapter 15 for both of these.

New Mexico provides the clear air and oft-cool climates that draw many golfers. The most challenging course in the state is the **Championship Golf Course at the University of New Mexico,** in Albuquerque (© 505/277-4546; see chapter 9). In the south, you can enjoy views, a challenging course, and cool climes even in summer at **The Links at Sierra Blanca,** in Ruidoso (© 800/854-6571 or 505/258-5330; see chapter 11). See individual chapters for many more suggestions.

If you can break away from the gambling tables long enough to play golf in Las Vegas, you'll be well rewarded. The city offers excellent courses. Three notable ones are **Bear's Best,** which offers dramatic views on a Jack Nicklaus–designed course. The **Las Vegas Paiute Golf Resort** has impeccable fairways on a challenging course, and **Dragon Ridge** offers play for many skill levels in natural desert mountain surroundings. Fees range from about $65 to $230, with summer and evening rates often half that. You can book any of these and see course overviews with photographs at www.opengolfteetimes.com, or call © 877/669-4653.

Utah and Colorado's golf courses are known for their beautiful scenery and variety of challenging terrain. They range from mountain courses set among beautiful forests to desert courses with scenic views of red rock country. The warm climate of St. George, in Utah's southwest corner, makes it a perfect location for year-round golf, and it has become the premier destination for visiting golfers—**St. George's Sunbrook Golf Course** (© 435/634-5866) is probably Utah's best. Durango has two public courses worth checking out: **Hillcrest Golf Course** (© 970/247-1499) and **Dalton Ranch & Golf Club** (© 970/247-8774). These areas of Utah and Colorado are beyond the scope of this book, so call the numbers listed above for more information.

For more information on golfing in Arizona, contact the **Arizona Golf Association,** 7226 N. 16th St., Suite 200, Phoenix, AZ 85020 (© 800/458-8484 in Arizona, or 602/944-3035; www.azgolf.org), which publishes a directory listing all the courses in the state. You can also view the directory online. *Golf Arizona,* 16508 Laser Dr., Suite 104A, Fountain Hills, AZ 85268 (© 800/942-5444; www.golf-arizona.com), also publishes a guide. In addition, you can pick up the *Tucson and Southern Arizona Golf Guide* or the *Official Arizona Golf Guide & Directory* at visitor bureaus, golf courses, and many hotels and resorts.

Golf New Mexico magazine is a good source of information, and the website lists all New Mexico golf courses (© 505/342-1563; www.golfnewmexico.com). For information on Colorado's major golf courses, contact the **Colorado Golf Resort Association** (© 303/680-9967; www.coloradogolfresorts.com). Serious golfers may want to subscribe to *The Colorado Golfer*, available at the same source, which carries information on courses throughout the state. Contact the **Utah Travel Council** (© **800/200-1160** or 801/538-1030) for a free directory of Utah's 80-plus courses.

5 Hiking

Everywhere you go in the region, you'll find opportunities for hiking. The terrain and climate vary from the heat and relative flatness of the desert to the cold, forested alpine areas. You can visit both (from 3,000–13,000 ft. in elevation) and anything in between in the same day without much trouble. Each part of the region is covered below. See later chapters for details about outfitters, guides, llama trekking services, and whom to contact for maps and other information.

In the Santa Fe area, one of the most pleasant hikes is to the top of **Santa Fe Baldy,** the **Aspen Vista Trail.** It's an easy hike through aspen forests that offers long views of New Mexico's broad eastern plains. If you're looking for something more challenging in the north-central region of the state, head up to Taos and give **Wheeler Peak** your best shot. The hike up New Mexico's highest peak is about 15 miles round-trip. If you want a much less difficult hike in the Taos area, try hiking down into **Rio Grande Gorge.** It's beautiful and can be hiked year-round. See chapter 8 for details on all of these. In the northeastern region of New Mexico, try the 1-mile loop around **Capulin Volcano.** The crater rim offers stunning views, and you can look down into the dormant caldera (see chapter 10). If you're heading to the northwestern region of the state, try hiking the **Bisti/De-Na-Zin Wilderness,** 37 miles south of Farmington. Though there are no marked trails, the hiking is easy in this area of low, eroded hills and fanciful rock formations. See chapter 6 for details. This region is also home to **El Malpais National Monument,** where you can hike into great lava tubes (see chapter 10). In the southwestern region is the **Gila National Forest,** which has more than 1,400 miles of trails with varying ranges of length and difficulty. One favorite day hike in the forest is the **Catwalk,** a moderately strenuous hike along a series of steel bridges and walkways suspended over Whitewater Canyon. See chapter 11 for details. In the southeastern region, you'll find one of New Mexico's cherished places: **White Sands National Monument.** Hiking the white-sand dunes is easy, if sometimes awkward, and the magnificence of the view is unsurpassed. See chapter 11 for more information.

Arizona also has fascinating and challenging hiking. In northern Arizona, there are good day hikes in **Grand Canyon National Park** and in the **San Francisco Peaks** north of Flagstaff (see chapter 16). Hiking is the order of the day in Sedona, where such places as **Boynton Canyon** offer red-rock beauty and ancient ruins (see chapter 15). In the Phoenix area, popular day hikes include the trails up **Camelback Mountain** and **Squaw Peak** and the many trails in **South Mountain Park** (see chapter 13). In the Tucson area, there are good hikes on **Mount Lemmon** and in **Saguaro National Park, Sabino Canyon,** and **Catalina State Park** (see chapter 12). In the southern part of the state, there are good day hikes in Chiricahua National Monument, most notably the **Heart of Rocks Loop,** which meanders through formations that could have been created by Dr. Seuss. Also in the south are the **Coronado National Forest,** the Nature Conservancy's **Ramsey Canyon Preserve** and **Patagonia–Sonoita Creek Preserve, Cochise Stronghold,** and **Organ Pipe Cactus National Monument** (see chapter 14).

The state's two most unforgettable overnight backpack trips are the hike down to Phantom Ranch at the bottom of the Grand Canyon and the hike into Havasu Canyon, a side canyon of the Grand Canyon. See chapter 16.

Hiking is the best—and sometimes only—way to see many of Utah's most beautiful and exciting areas, and the state is interlaced with hiking trails. In particular, check out **Natural Bridges National Monument,** where numerous trails take hikers through magical stone formations (see chapter 6). At Zion, the **Lower Emerald Pools Trail** takes you along emerald-colored pools, and at Bryce, the **Navajo Loop/Queen's Garden Trail** is an intermediate trail that traverses the park's magical beauty. (See chapter 17.)

The **Continental Divide Trail Alliance (CDTA)** (© 888/909-2382 or 303/838-3760; www.cdtrail.org) is building a trail—using volunteers—along the mountains of the Great Divide, from Canada to Mexico, and that means right through the middle of Colorado and New Mexico. Each year, the CDTA publishes a project schedule for the next summer, complete with volunteer needs, project description, and difficulty rating.

Guided backpacking trips of different durations and levels of difficulty are offered by the **Grand Canyon Field Institute** (© 800/858-2808 or 928/638-2485; www.grand canyon.org/fieldinstitute) and **Grand Canyon Trail Guides** (© 928/638-3194; www.grandcanyontrailguides.com). **Backroads** (© 800/462-2848 or 510/527-1555; www.backroads.com) offers a 6-day hiking/biking trip to Grand Canyon, Bryce Canyon, and Zion national parks. The highly respected **Colorado Mountain School** (© 970/586-5758; www.cmschool.com) leads climbs in various parts of Colorado. The **Friends of the Colorado Trail** (© 303/384-3729, ext. 113; www.coloradotrail.org) offers supported treks and accredited courses on the Colorado Trail.

You can choose from hundreds of other hikes. Consider purchasing a hiking book or contacting the National Park Service, National Forest Service, Bureau of Land Management, or other appropriate agencies directly. The best guides for the region are *Hiking New Mexico* (Falcon), by Laurence Parent, which outlines 70 hikes throughout the state, and *75 Hikes in New Mexico,* by Craig Martin (The Mountaineers). *Frommer's Great Outdoor Guide to Arizona & New Mexico* (Wiley Publishing, Inc.) details many favorite hikes. *Hiking Arizona,* by Stewart Aitchison and Bruce Grubbs (Falcon), outlines many excellent excursions.

6 Horseback Riding

Adventurers come from all over the world to horseback ride in the Southwest. Some of the most notable Western historic moments took place here, and many Westerns have been filmed. There's a great variety in the types of riding a person can do in the Southwest, so do some research and choose carefully.

If you're content with a nose-to-tail kind of ride, you'll be happiest riding in the mountainous regions such as the White Mountains or in more controlled environments such as through Monument Valley. But if you'd prefer to really ride—to trot and canter your horse—you'll want to go to places where the terrain allows for such riding. The Wickenburg, Arizona, area offers plenty of open-trail riding. Check out the **Kay El Bar Guest Ranch** (© 800/684-7583 or 928/684-7593; www.kayelbar.com; see chapter 15) and, in Patagonia, the **Circle Z Ranch** (© 888/854-2525 or 520/394-2525; www.circlez.com; see chapter 14). Among the more scenic spots for riding are the Grand Canyon (see chapter 16), Canyon de Chelly National Monument (see chapter 6), and the red-rock country around Sedona (see chapter 15).

Some of the most popular guided adventures in Arizona are mule rides down into the Grand Canyon. These trips vary in length from 1 to 2 days; for reservations and more information, contact **Xanterra Parks & Resorts** (② 303/297-2757; www. xanterra.com). Be advised, however, that you'll need to make mule-ride reservations many months in advance. If at the last minute (1 or 2 days before you want to ride) you decide you want to go on a mule trip into the Grand Canyon, contact the **Bright Angel Transportation Desk,** in Grand Canyon Village (② 928/638-3283), on the chance that there might be space available.

What's unique about much of New Mexico's horseback riding is its variety. You'll find a broad range of terrain, from open plains to high mountain wilderness. In the Santa Fe area, you can ride across the plains of the spectacular Galisteo Basin with **Santa Fe Detours** (② 800/338-6877 or 505/983-6565; see chapter 7). In Taos, you can explore secluded Taos Pueblo land with the **Taos Indian Horse Ranch** (② 505/ 758-3212; see chapter 8). In the northwest, try **5M Outfitters,** Chama (② 505/588-7003; see chapter 10). In the southeast, contact the **Inn of the Mountain Gods Resort & Casino,** in Carrizo Canyon (② 800/545-6040 or 505/464-4100; see chapter 11). If you're looking for a resort horseback riding experience, contact **Bishop's Lodge,** Bishop's Lodge Rd., Santa Fe (② 505/983-6377; see chapter 7). If you want an authentic cowpoke experience, call the **Double E Guest Ranch** (② 505/535-2048; see chapter 11) in the Silver City area.

Utah's most notable place to ride is Monument Valley Navajo Tribal Park. **Sacred Monument Tours** offers horseback trips ranging from 1 hour to overnight. For reservations and information, call ② 435/727-3218. (At press time, permits for riding in the area were pending updated approval; see chapter 6.) An upscale organization, **D-Spur Ranch,** offers 7- and 5-day rides through Monument Valley as well as other areas of the Southwest. See below for details.

If you'd like to saddle up and ride the mountains of Colorado, contact the **South-fork Riding Stables and Outfitters** 5 miles south of Durango (② 970/259-4871).

It's also possible to do overnight horseback rides. For information, contact **D-Spur,** 15371 E. Ojo Rd., Gold Canyon, AZ 85218 (② 602/810-7029; www.dspurranch. com), which offers overnight horseback trips in Monument Valley, the White Mountains, and the Superstition Mountains, among other places; or **Arizona Trail Tours** (② 800/477-0615 or 520/281-4122; www.aztrailtours.com), which offers trips through Coronado National Forest in southern Arizona.

7 Hot-Air Ballooning

You can't hear about the Southwest without hearing about **hot-air ballooning**—the two seem to go hand in hand. In fact, one of the region's greatest attractions is the annual Albuquerque International Balloon Fiesta in early October (see the Calendar of Events in chapter 2), which draws thousands of people from all over the world. It is possible to charter hot-air balloon rides in many parts of the region, particularly Taos and Albuquerque (see chapters 8 and 9) in New Mexico, and Tucson and Phoenix in Arizona (see chapters 12 and 13). One of the best spots for scenic floating is Sedona (see chapter 15). Most companies offer a variety of packages, from the standard flight to a more elaborate all-day affair that includes meals. For more information, see the individual chapters.

8 Houseboating

With the Colorado River turned into a long string of lakes, Arizona's "West Coast" provides excellent houseboat vacations. Although this doesn't have to be an active vacation, fishing, hiking, and swimming are usually part of a houseboat stay. Rentals are available on Lake Mead, Lake Mohave, and Lake Havasu (see chapter 15). The canyonlands scenery of Lake Powell makes it the best spot for a houseboat vacation— reserve well in advance for a summer trip. Houseboats provide all the comforts of home—toilets, showers, sleeping quarters, and full kitchens—but in somewhat tighter quarters. Some of the larger ones have facilities for up to a dozen people. You don't have to be an accomplished boater to drive one: Houseboats are easy to maneuver and can't go very fast. No boating license is required, but you'll need to reserve your house-boat well in advance, especially in summer, and send in a sizable deposit.

9 Skiing & Snowboarding

Believe it or not, the Southwest has some of the best snow skiing and snowboarding in the United States. With most alpine areas above 10,000 feet and many above 12,000 feet, several ski areas offer vertical drops of over 2,000 feet. Average annual snowfall ranges from 100 to 300 inches. Many areas, aided by vigorous snow-making efforts, open around Thanksgiving, and most open by mid-December, making this a popular vacation spot around the holidays. As a result, you'll see a definite rise in hotel room rates in and around ski areas during the holiday season. The ski season runs through March and often into the first week in April.

Some of the best skiing in the region is at **Taos Ski Valley** (© 505/776-2291; www.skitaos.org). Taos challenges skiers with plenty of vertical, and beginners can take advantage of one of the best ski schools in the country. Nearby, the resort town of **Angel Fire Resort** (© 800/633-7463 or 505/377-6401; www.angelfireresort.com) offers interesting terrain and excellent facilities. **Red River Ski Area** (© 800/331-7669 or 505/754-2223; www.redriverskiarea.com) is an excellent family mountain. See chapter 8.

Arizona has two decent-size ski areas. The **Arizona Snowbowl** (© 928/779-1951; www.arizonasnowbowl.com; see chapter 16), outside Flagstaff, is most notable, with plenty of vertical feet. **Sunrise Park Resort** (© 800/772-7669 or 928/735-7669; www.sunriseskipark.com; see chapter 14), on the Apache Reservation outside the town of McNary in the White Mountains, offers lots of runs and good snow conditions. When it's a good snow year, Tucsonans head up to **Mount Lemmon Ski Valley** (© 520/576-1321, or 520/576-1400 for snow report; see chapter 12), the southern-most ski area in the United States. All ski areas in the region offer rentals and lessons. Prices for an adult all-day ticket range from about $32 to $50.

Some of the best **cross-country skiing** in the region can be found at the Enchanted Forest near Red River and in Chama, New Mexico (see chapter 10) and outside Flagstaff, Arizona (see chapter 16). Other great areas in Arizona include Sunrise Park outside the town of McNary, at the South Rim of the Grand Canyon, in the White Mountains around Greer and Alpine, outside Payson on the Mogollon Rim, and on Mount Lemmon outside Tucson (see chapter 12). In Utah, head to Bryce Canyon National Park to ski trails along the rim (see chapter 17).

10 Tennis

Tennis is one of the most popular winter sports in the desert, and resorts all over the region have courts. Although there may be better courts, none can match the views you'll have from those at **Enchantment Resort** (© **800/826-4180** or 928/282-2900; see chapter 15) outside Sedona. Other noteworthy tennis-oriented resorts include **The Lodge at Ventana Canyon** (© **800/WYNDHAM** or 520/577-1400) and the **Hilton Tucson El Conquistador Golf & Tennis Resort** (© **800/325-7832** or 520/544-5000) in Tucson, and the **Phoenician** (© **800/888-8234** or 480/941-8200) in the Phoenix/Scottsdale area. See chapters 12 and 13 for more details.

Las Vegas is a nearly ideal spot to play tennis (except in the scorching heat of summer). One popular resort with a renowned spa and tennis facility is the **Flamingo Las Vegas** (© **800/732-2111** or 702/733-3111). The **Las Vegas Hilton** (© **888/732-7117** or 702/732-5111) also has good courts, as does the **Monte Carlo Resort & Casino** (© **800/311-8999** or 702/730-7777). See chapter 18.

Though New Mexico's high and dry climate is ideal for tennis much of the year, the sport is somewhat underdeveloped in the state. Certainly each of the major cities has municipal courts; you'll find information in the city and regional sections of this guide. If you're looking for a tennis resort experience, try **Bishop's Lodge** (© **505/983-6377**), on Bishop's Lodge Road in Santa Fe (see chapter 7).

11 Watersports

Watersports in the Southwest? Absolutely! You'll find a variety of activities, ranging from white-water rafting to pleasure boating.

WHITE-WATER RAFTING The most notable white-water rafting experience is down the Colorado River through the Grand Canyon. If it's one of your dreams, plan well ahead. Companies and trips are limited, and they tend to fill up early. For a discussion and list of companies that run trips down the canyon, see chapter 16, "The Grand Canyon & Northern Arizona." For 1-day rafting trips on the Colorado below the Grand Canyon, contact **Hualapai River Runners** (© **800/622-4409** or 928/769-2219; www.hualapaitours.com). For a half- or full-day float on the Colorado above the Grand Canyon, contact **Wilderness River Adventures** (© **800/528-6154** or 928/645-3279), which runs trips from Lees Ferry. Rafting trips are also available on the upper Salt River east of Phoenix. **Wilderness Aware Rafting** (© **800/462-7238** or 719/395-2112; www.inaraft.com), **Canyon Rio Rafting** (© **800/272-3353** or 928/774-3377; www.canyonrio.com), and **Mild to Wild Rafting** (© **800/567-6745;** www.mild2wildrafting.com) all run trips of varying lengths down this river (conditions permitting).

In Utah, the town of Moab along the **Colorado River** is rapidly becoming a major boating center. You can travel down the river in a canoe, kayak, large or small rubber raft (with or without motor), or speedy, solid jet boat. A complete list of outfitters is available at the Moab Information Center or through the **Moab Area Travel Council** (© **800/635-6622** or 435/259-8825; www.discovermoab.com).

New Mexico offers good opportunities for white-water rafting and kayaking. The waters in the Chama River and the Rio Grande are generally at their best during the spring and summer (May–July). Most notable is the 1-day trip down the Taos Box Canyon, offering an almost nonstop series of class IV rapids. Many reputable companies run the Box, including **Los Rios River Runners** (© 800/544-1181 or 505/776-8854; www.losriosriverrunners.com) and **Native Sons Adventures** (© 800/753-7559 or 505/758-9342; www.nativesonsadventures.com). In addition to calling outfitters, you can contact the **Bureau of Land Management,** 226 Cruz Alta Rd., Taos, NM 87571 (© 505/758-8851), for information.

Opportunities for **pleasure boating** are available on many of the region's lakes and reservoirs. Lake Mead, Lake Mohave, and Lake Havasu, what many call Arizona's "West Coast," offer plenty of water fun (see chapter 15). In New Mexico, Elephant Butte Lake is one of the best and most beautiful spots for boating (see chapter 11).

FLAT-WATER CANOEING & KAYAKING   Maybe these sports don't jump to mind when you think of the desert, but there are indeed calm rivers and lakes here—and they happen to be some of the best places to see wildlife. By far the most memorable place for a flat-water kayak tour is Lake Powell. **Wilderness Inquiry** (© 800/ 728-0719 or 612/676-9400; www.wildernessinquiry.org) offers several 6-day trips on the lake each spring and fall. **Arizona Kayak** (© 480/755-1924; www.arizona kayak.com) offers various canoeing and kayaking courses.

A couple of companies rent canoes and offer trips on the Colorado River south of Lake Mead. See chapter 15.

12 Special-Interest Vacations

ARCHAEOLOGY   If you like time-traveling into ancient culture, contact the **Arizona State Museum,** P.O. Box 210026, Tucson, AZ 85721 (© 520/626-8381; www.statemuseum.arizona.edu), which occasionally offers scholar-led archaeological tours, including a trip to Navajo and Hopi country.

The **Museum of Northern Arizona,** 3101 N. Fort Valley Rd., Flagstaff, AZ 86001 (© 928/774-5211, ext. 220; www.musnaz.org), offers educational backpacking, river-rafting, and van tours primarily in the Colorado Plateau in northern Arizona in a program called Ventures. Trips range from several days to more than a week.

ARCHITECTURE   Architecture buffs can get their hands dirty with continued construction of **Arcosanti,** Paolo Soleri's dream of a city that merges architecture and ecology. Located 70 miles north of Phoenix, Arcosanti offers 5-week learning-by-doing workshops. Contact Arcosanti, Attn: Workshop Coordinator, H.C. 74, Box 4136, Mayer, AZ 86333 (© 928/632-7135; www.arcosanti.org).

ART & COOKING TOURS   **Taos Art School** (© 505/758-0350; www.taosart school.org) offers a variety of imaginative art tours and hands-on courses. The Georgia O'Keeffe tour takes visitors to all the sites where the noted modern artist painted. The many hands-on experiences offer cultural bonuses, such as a potting course taught by relatives of the noted Pueblo potter Maria Martinez, as well as weaving and basketry courses. *Plein aire* (outdoor) painting and "Horses and Art" are two other popular courses.

For those interested in honing their Southwestern cooking skills, **Jane Butel's Cooking School** (© 800/472-8229 or 505/243-2622; www.janebutel.com) offers weekend and weeklong courses in Albuquerque.

CULTURAL TOURS   If Native American cultures interest you, contact **Discovery Passages,** 1161 Elk Trail, Box 630, Prescott, AZ 86303 (© 928/717-0519), which operates tours that visit the Hopi, Navajo, Apache, Tohono O'odham, Hualapai,

Yavapai, and Havasupai reservations. **Crossing Worlds Journeys & Retreats,** P.O. Box 623, Sedona, AZ 86339 (© **800/350-2693** or 928/203-0024; www. crossingworlds.com), offers tours throughout the Four Corners region, visiting the Hopi mesas as well as backcountry ruins on the Navajo Reservation.

For cultural tours in New Mexico, contact **Aventura Artistica,** P.O. Box 25671, Albuquerque, NM 87125 (© **800/808-7352;** www.newmexicotours.com), which offers small group tours focusing on New Mexico's history, culture, and natural wonders.

NATURE   If you'd like to turn a trip to the Grand Canyon into an educational experience, contact the **Grand Canyon Field Institute,** P.O. Box 399, Grand Canyon, AZ 86023 (© **800/858-2808** or 928/638-2485; www.grandcanyon.org/fieldinstitute), which offers a variety of programs from early spring to late fall. Offerings include day hikes, photography and painting classes, backpacking trips for women, llama treks, archaeology trips, and plenty of guided hikes and backpacking trips with a natural-history or ecological slant.

The **Nature Conservancy,** 1510 E. Fort Lowell Rd., Tucson, AZ 85719 (© **520/ 622-3861;** http://nature.org), and 212 E. Marcy St., Suite 200, Santa Fe, NM 87501 (© **505/988-3867**) has preserved some of the Southwest's finest land, parts of which are open to the public for hiking, bird-watching, and nature study. The organization operates educational field trips.

If you have strong hands and a soft heart, and want to help with wilderness preservation, consider a Sierra Club service trip. These trips are for the purpose of building, restoring, and maintaining hiking trails in wilderness areas. Contact the **Sierra Club Outing Department,** 85 Second St., 2nd Floor, San Francisco, CA 94105 (© **415/ 977-5500;** www.sierraclub.org). The Sierra Club also offers hiking, camping, and other adventure trips to various destinations in the Southwest.

You can join a work crew organized by the **Arizona Trail Association** (© **602/252-4794;** www.aztrail.org). Crews spend 1 to 2 days building and maintaining various portions of the Arizona Trail, which will eventually stretch from the Utah state line to the Mexico border.

The National Park Service is also looking for help. Volunteers pick up trash left in Glen Canyon National Recreation Area. Helpers spend 5 days on a houseboat called the Trash Tracker, cruising through the canyonlands of Lake Powell. Volunteers must be at least 18 years old and must provide their own food, sleeping bag, and transportation to the marina. For information, contact **Glen Canyon National Recreation Area,** P.O. Box 1507, Page, AZ 86040 (© **928/608-6404** or 928/608-6352).

See also the "Hiking" section earlier in this chapter for information about the **Continental Divide Trail Alliance (CDTA)** trail-building project.

6

The Four Corners Area

The major archaeological center of the United States, the Four Corners area—where the borders of Colorado, New Mexico, Arizona, and Utah meet—is surrounded by a vast complex of ancient villages that dominated this entire region a thousand years ago. Here among the reddish-brown rocks, abandoned canyons, and flat mesas, you'll discover another world, once ruled by the Ancestral Puebloans (also known as Anasazi), and today largely the domain of the Navajo.

Wander among the scenic splendors of Monument Valley, where the Navajo still tend their sheep and weave their rugs, and then step back in time to discover a civilization that vanished more than 7 centuries ago, leaving behind more questions than answers. The single best place to explore this ancient culture is Mesa Verde National Park. Nearby, along the Colorado–Utah border, is one of America's newest national monuments, Canyon of the Ancients, created by presidential proclamation in June of 2000.

This region is sparsely populated, and you're not going to find your favorite chain motel, fast-food restaurant, or brand of gasoline right around every corner. That's assuming you can even *find* a corner. So, many travelers discover a place they like, rent a room or campsite for a few days, and take day trips. In this chapter, we've given you a gateway town for each state and also mentioned places to stay throughout the region.

1 Cortez: Colorado's Four Corners Gateway

45 miles W of Durango, 203 miles S of Grand Junction

An important archaeological center, Cortez is surrounded by a vast complex of ancient villages that dominated the Four Corners region—where Colorado, New Mexico, Arizona, and Utah's borders meet—1,000 years ago. Mesa Verde National Park, 10 miles east, is certainly the most prominent nearby attraction, drawing hundreds of thousands of visitors annually. In addition, archaeological sites such as those at Canyons of the Ancients and Hovenweep national monuments as well as Ute Mountain Tribal Park are an easy drive from the city. Most visitors to Cortez won't be spending much time in the city, but will use it as a home base. Elevation is 6,200 feet.

ESSENTIALS

GETTING THERE By Car Cortez is located at the junction of north–south U.S. 491 and east–west U.S. 160.

As it enters Cortez from the east, U.S. 160 crosses Dolores Road (Colo. 145, which goes north to Telluride and Grand Junction), then runs due west through town for about 2 miles as Main Street. The city's main thoroughfare, Main Street intersects U.S. 491 (Broadway) at the west end of town.

By Plane   Cortez Airport, off U.S. 160 and 491, southwest of town (© **970/565-7458;** www.cityofcortez.com), is served by **Great Lakes Airlines** (© **800/554-5111** or 970/565-9510), with direct daily flights to Denver.

Budget (© **800/527-0700** or 970/564-9012) and **Enterprise** (© **800/325-8007** or 970/565-6824) provide car rentals at the airport.

VISITOR INFORMATION   Stop at the **Colorado Welcome Center at Cortez,** Cortez City Park, 928 E. Main St. (© **970/565-4048;** www.swcolo.org), open daily from 8am to 6pm in summer and from 8am to 5pm the rest of the year; or contact the **Mesa Verde Country Visitor Information Bureau,** P.O. Box HH, Cortez, CO 81321 (© **800/253-1616;** www.mesaverdecountry.com), or the **Cortez Area Chamber of Commerce,** P.O. Box 968, Cortez, CO 81321 (© **970/565-3414;** www.cortez chamber.org).

FAST FACTS   The local hospital is **Southwest Memorial Hospital,** 1311 N. Mildred Rd. (© **970/565-6666**), which has a 24-hour emergency room. The **post office** is at 35 S. Beech St.; contact the U.S. Postal Service (© **800/275-8777;** www.usps.com) for hours and additional information.

NEARBY ARCHAEOLOGICAL SITES
ANASAZI HERITAGE CENTER

When the Dolores River was dammed and the McPhee Reservoir was created in 1985, some 1,600 ancient archaeological sites were threatened. Four percent of the project costs were set aside for archaeological work, and over two million artifacts and other prehistoric items were rescued. Most are displayed in this museum. Located 10 miles north of Cortez, it is set into a hillside near the remains of 12th-century sites.

Operated by the Bureau of Land Management, the center emphasizes visitor involvement. Children and adults are invited to examine corn-grinding implements, a loom and other weaving materials, and a re-created pit house. You can touch artifacts 1,000 to 2,000 years old, examine samples through microscopes, use interactive computer programs, and engage in video lessons in archaeological techniques.

A half-mile trail leads from the museum to the **Dominguez and Escalante Ruins,** atop a low hill, with a beautiful view across the Montezuma Valley.

The center also serves as the visitor center for Canyons of the Ancients National Monument (see below). It is located at 27501 Colo. 184, Dolores (© **970/882-5600;** www.co.blm.gov/ahc). It's open March through October, daily from 9am to 5pm; November through February, daily from 9am to 4pm; and is closed Thanksgiving, Christmas, and New Year's Day. An admission fee of $3 for adults is charged March through October only; admission is free for those 17 and under. Allow 2 hours.

CANYONS OF THE ANCIENTS NATIONAL MONUMENT

Among the country's newest national monuments, Canyons of the Ancients was created by presidential proclamation in June 2000. The 164,000-acre national monument, located west of Cortez, contains thousands of archaeological sites—what some claim is the highest density of archaeological sites in the United States—including the remains of villages, cliff dwellings, sweat lodges, and petroglyphs at least 700 years old, and possibly as much as 10,000 years old.

Canyons of the Ancients includes **Lowry Pueblo,** an excavated 12th-century village that is located 26 miles from Cortez via U.S. 491, on C.R. CC, 9 miles west of

The Four Corners Region

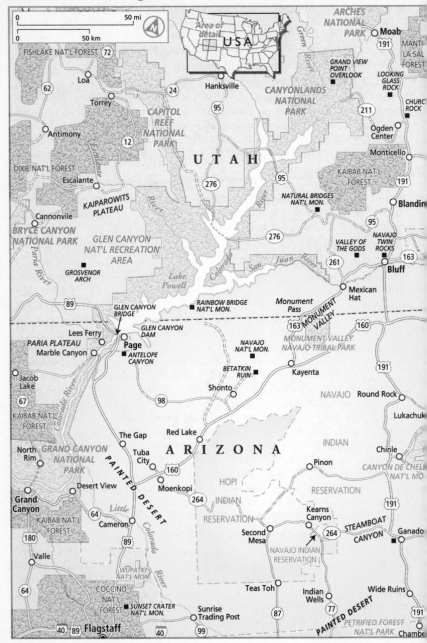

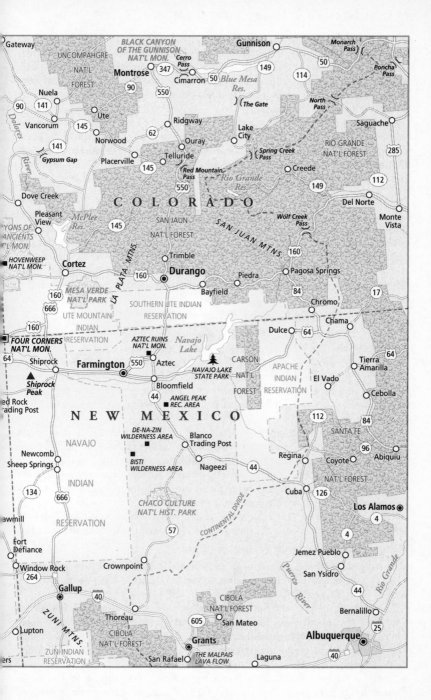

Pleasant View. This pueblo, which was likely abandoned by 1200, is believed to have housed about 100 people. It has standing walls from 40 rooms plus 9 kivas (circular underground ceremonial chambers). A short, self-guided interpretive trail leads past a kiva decorated with geometric designs and continues to the remains of a great kiva, which, at 54 feet in diameter, is among the largest ever found. There are also a picnic area, drinking water, and toilets.

Canyons of the Ancients is managed by the Bureau of Land Management, and as yet has no visitor center or even a contact station. Those wishing to explore the monument are strongly advised to contact or preferably stop first at the **Anasazi Heritage Center** (see above) for information, especially current road conditions and directions. Information is also available online at www.co.blm.gov/canm. Allow at least 2 hours.

CORTEZ CULTURAL CENTER

The center, 25 N. Market St., Cortez (© **970/565-1151;** www.cortezculturalcenter. org), includes a museum with exhibits on both prehistoric and modern American Indians, an art gallery with displays of regional art, a good gift shop offering crafts by local tribal members, and a variety of programs including American-Indian dances during the summer. From June through August the center is open daily from 10am to 10pm, and the rest of the year it is open daily from 10am to 5pm. Admission is free and you should plan to spend at least an hour. Call or check the website for the schedule of Indian dances and other programs, which are also free.

UTE MOUNTAIN TRIBAL PARK ★★

Set aside by the Ute Mountain tribe to preserve its heritage, the 125,000-acre Ute Mountain Tribal Park (P.O. Box 109, Towaoc, CO 81334; © **800/847-5485** or 970/ 565-3751 ext. 330; www.utemountainute.com/tribalpark.htm)—which abuts Mesa Verde National Park—includes wall paintings and ancient petroglyphs as well as hundreds of surface sites and cliff dwellings that are similar in size and complexity to those in Mesa Verde.

Access to the park is strictly limited to guided tours. Full- and half-day tours begin at the Ute Mountain Museum and Visitor Center at the junction of U.S. 491 and U.S. 160, 20 miles south of Cortez. Mountain-biking and backpacking trips are also offered. No food, water, lodging, gasoline, or other services are available within the park. Some climbing of ladders is necessary on the full-day tour. There's one primitive **campground** ($12 per vehicle; reservations required).

Charges for tours in your vehicle start at $20 per person for a half-day, $40 for a full day; it's $8 extra to go in the tour guide's vehicle, and reservations are required.

HOVENWEEP NATIONAL MONUMENT

Preserving some of the most striking and isolated archaeological sites in the Four Corners area, this national monument straddles the Colorado-Utah border, 40 miles west of Cortez, CO and 35 miles northeast of Bluff, UT.

Hovenweep is the Ute word for "deserted valley," appropriate because its inhabitants apparently left around 1300. The monument contains six separate sites, and is noted for mysterious, 20-foot-high sandstone towers. Archaeologists have suggested their possible function as everything from guard or signal towers, celestial observatories, and ceremonial structures to water towers or granaries.

A ranger station, with exhibits, restrooms, and drinking water, is located at the **Square Tower Site,** in the Utah section of the monument, the most impressive and best preserved of the sites. Near the Square Tower Site, the **Hovenweep Campground,** with 30 sites, is open year-round. Sites are fairly small—most appropriate for tents or small pickup truck campers—but a few sites can accommodate RVs up to 25 feet long. The campground has flush toilets, drinking water, picnic tables, and fire pits, but no showers or RV hookups. Cost is $10 per night; reservations are not accepted, but the campground rarely fills.

To get to the Square Tower Site from Cortez, take U.S. 160 south to C.R. G (McElmo Canyon Rd.), and follow signs into Utah and the monument. From Utah, follow U.S. 191 to Utah 262, between the towns of Blanding and Bluff. Head east on Utah 262 to Hatch Trading Post; then, watching for signs, follow paved roads to the monument. The other five sites are difficult to find, and you'll need to obtain detailed driving directions and check on current road conditions before setting out. Summer temperatures can reach over 100°F (38°C), and water supplies are limited—so take your own and carry a canteen, even on short walks. Bug repellent is advised, as gnats can be a nuisance in late spring.

The visitor center/ranger station is open daily from 8am to 5pm year-round, and trails are open from sunrise to sunset. Admission for up to a week costs $6 per vehicle or $3 per person on bike or foot. For advance information, contact Hovenweep National Monument, McElmo Route, Cortez, CO 81321 (© **970/562-4282** or 435/719-2100; www.nps.gov/hove).

WHERE TO STAY

Summer is the busy season here, and that's when you'll pay the highest lodging rates. Among the major chains providing comfortable, reasonably priced lodging (ranging from about $60–$150 double) in Cortez (zip code 81321) are **Best Western Sands,** 1120 E. Main St. (© 800/937-8376 or 970/565-3761); **Best Western Turquoise Inn & Suites,** 535 E. Main St. (© 800/547-3376 or 970/565-3778); **Comfort Inn,** 2321 E. Main St. (© 800/424-6423 or 970/565-3400); **Econo Lodge,** 2020 E. Main St. (© 800/553-2666 or 970/565-3474); **Super 8,** 505 E. Main St. (© 800/800-8000 or 970/565-8888); and **Travelodge,** 440 S. Broadway (© 800/578-7878 or 970/565-7778). Room tax adds about 8% to lodging bills.

Anasazi Motor Inn   This standard, well-kept motel offers spacious Southwest-decorated rooms with either one king-size bed or two queens; many of the ground-floor rooms have patios. There's also a sand volleyball court, horseshoe pits, a short walking trail, and free shuttle service to downtown.

640 S. Broadway, Cortez, CO 81321. © **800/972-6232** or 970/565-3773. Fax 970/565-1027. www.anasazimotor inn.com. 87 units. $55–$75 double. AE, DC, DISC, MC, V. Pets accepted. **Amenities:** Restaurant (American); bar; pool (outdoor heated); hot tub; airport shuttle. *In room:* A/C, TV.

Rio Grande Southern Bed & Breakfast ✪   Although the Rio Grande Southern Railroad folded in 1893 after just 2 years in business, the hotel built for its customers has endured to become a charming National Historic Landmark. You'll check in at the old front desk, climb carpeted stairs to the second floor, then pass Norman Rockwell prints and a tiny library on your way to the guest rooms. All the units here are multi-room suites, so although the individual rooms are small, you'll have plenty of room. If you're lucky, you'll be in Room 4, where Zane Gray is said to have stayed while writing *Riders of the Purple Sage.* Guest rooms are decorated with Victorian antiques and have queen-size and double beds; many have claw-foot tubs. A fine Southwestern-style breakfast is served downstairs in a small cafe. The entire property is nonsmoking.

101 S. Fifth St. (P.O. Box 516), Dolores, CO 81323. (C) **800/258-0434** or 970/882-7527. www.riograndebandb.com. 4 units. $85 double for 1-bedroom suite; $140 for 4 people in 2-bedroom suites. Rates include full breakfast. DISC, MC, V. Closed mid-Dec to Feb. *In room:* No phone.

WHERE TO DINE

Homesteaders Restaurant 🐾 AMERICAN/MEXICAN   A rustic, Old West atmosphere pervades this popular family restaurant, which is decorated with historic photos and memorabilia. The menu has a good selection of home-style American basics, such as burgers, T-bones, and top sirloins. Those wanting a bit more zip might try the Southwestern steak—top sirloin smothered with salsa, green chile, and cheese. We also suggest the barbecued baby back ribs and the old-fashioned dinners, such as thin-sliced roast beef or deep-fried catfish filet. Several Mexican standards are also offered, as well as salads and vegetarian items.

45 E. Main St. (C) **970/565-6253**. Fax 970/564-9217. www.thehomesteaders.com. Main courses $4.50–$6 lunch, $7–$17 dinner. AE, DISC, MC, V. Mon–Sat 11am–10pm; summer also Sun 5–10pm.

Main St. Brewery and Restaurant 🐾 AMERICAN   Fans slice the air under a stamped-tin ceiling, and fanciful murals splash color above subdued wood paneling. The pleasant contrasts found in the decor carry over to the menu. In addition to brew-pub staples such as fish and chips, pizza, and bratwurst, this restaurant offers steaks and prime rib—dry aged Angus beef from its own herd of Angus cattle, raised with no artificial growth stimulants or antibiotics—plus a vegetarian skewer plate and Rocky Mountain trout. The beers brewed here go well with everything. We especially recommend the hoppy, slightly bitter Pale Export and the Munich-style Pale Bock.

21 E. Main St., Cortez. (C) **970/564-9112**. Reservations not accepted. Main courses $6.95–$18. AE, MC, V. Daily 3pm–midnight.

Nero's 🐾🐾 ITALIAN/AMERICAN   Our top choice in this area when we're craving something a bit different. The innovative entrees, prepared by Culinary Institute of America chef Richard Gurd, include house specialties such as the Cowboy Steak (a charbroiled 12-ounce sirloin seasoned with a spicy rub and served with pasta or fries); our favorite, the mushroom ravioli served with an Alfredo sauce, sautéed spinach, sun-dried tomatoes, and pecans; and shrimp Alfredo—sautéed shrimp with spinach served over fettuccine with Alfredo sauce and Romano cheese. There's an excellent selection of beef, plus seafood, fowl, pork, veal, and lots of homemade pasta. A small, homey restaurant with a Southwestern art-gallery decor, Nero's also offers pleasant outdoor seating in warm weather.

303 W. Main St. (C) **970/565-7366**. http://subee.com/neros/home.html. Reservations recommended. Entrees $10–$22. AE, MC, V. Daily 5–9:30pm. Closed Sun in winter.

2 Mesa Verde National Park

125 miles E of Bluff, 390 miles SE of Salt Lake City

MESA VERDE NATIONAL PARK

Mesa Verde is the largest archaeological preserve in the United States, with some 4,000 known sites dating from A.D. 600 to 1300, including the most impressive cliff dwellings in the Southwest.

The earliest known inhabitants of Mesa Verde (Spanish for "green table") built sub-terranean pit houses on the mesa tops. During the 13th century they moved into shallow caves and constructed complex cliff dwellings. Although a massive construction project, these homes were only occupied for about a century; their residents left in about 1300 for reasons as yet undetermined.

The area was little known until ranchers Charles and Richard Wetherill chanced upon it in 1888. Looting of artifacts followed their discovery until a Denver newspaper reporter's stories aroused national interest in protecting the site. The 52,000-acre site was declared a national park in 1906—it's the only U.S. national park devoted entirely to the works of humans.

Fires have plagued the park in recent years, and burned, dead trees and blackened ground are very evident today. Two lightning-induced fires blackened about 40% of the park during the summer of 2000, closing the park for about three weeks. Officials said that although the park's piñon-juniper forests were severely burned, none of the major archaeological sites were damaged, and in fact the fires revealed some sites that they were not aware existed. Then a lightning-induced fire struck again in the summer of 2002, closing the park for about 10 days. It destroyed several employees' homes, a sewage treatment plant, and phone and power lines, and also damaged a water storage tank. Officials said that the only damage to archaeological sites was the scorching of the wall of one ruin.

JUST THE FACTS

ENTRY   The park entrance is located on U.S. 160, 10 miles east of Cortez and 6 miles west of Mancos.

FEES & REGULATIONS   Admission to the park for up to 1 week costs $10 per vehicle. Tours of Cliff Palace, Balcony House, and Long House are $2.75; ranger-guided tours of other areas are free. To protect the many archaeological sites, the Park Service has outlawed backcountry camping and off-trail hiking. It's also illegal to enter cliff dwellings without a ranger present. The Wetherill Mesa Road cannot accommodate vehicles longer than 25 feet. Cyclists must have lights to pedal through the tunnel on the entrance road.

VISITOR CENTERS & INFORMATION   **Chapin Mesa,** site of the park headquarters, museum, and a post office, is 20 miles from the park entrance on U.S. 160. The **Far View Visitor Center,** site of Far View Lodge, a restaurant, gift shop, and other facilities, is 15 miles off U.S. 160. For a park brochure, contact Mesa Verde National Park, P.O. Box 8, Mesa Verde, CO 81330-0008 (© **970/529-4465;** www.nps.gov/meve).

HOURS & SEASONS   The park is open daily year-round, but full interpretive services are available only from mid-June to Labor Day. In winter, the Mesa Top Road and museum remain open, but many other facilities are closed. The **Far View Visitor Center** is open from mid-April through mid-October only, from 8am to 5pm daily. The **Chapin Mesa Archeological Museum** is open daily from 8am to 6:30pm from mid-April through mid-October, daily from 8am to 5pm the rest of the year.

AVOIDING THE CROWDS   With close to half a million visitors annually, Mesa Verde seems packed at times, but the numbers are much lower just before and after the summer rush, usually from June 15 to August 15. Another way to beat the crowds is to make the 12-mile drive to Wetherill Mesa, which attracts only a small percentage of park visitors.

RANGER PROGRAMS   In addition to guided tours to the cliff dwellings (see below), rangers give nightly campfire programs at Morefield Campground in summer.

SEEING THE HIGHLIGHTS IN A DAY

If you have only a day to spend at the park, stop first at the Far View Visitor Center to buy tickets for a late-afternoon tour of either Cliff House or Balcony House—visitors are not allowed to tour both on the same day. Then travel to the Chapin Mesa archeological museum for a look at the history behind the sites you're about to see. From here, walk down the trail behind the museum to Spruce Tree House. Then drive the Mesa Top Loop Road. Cap your day with the guided tour.

EXPLORING THE PARK

The **Cliff Palace,** the park's largest and best-known site, is a four-story apartment complex with stepped-back roofs forming porches for the dwellings above. Accessible by guided tour only, it is reached by a quarter-mile downhill path. Its towers, walls, and kivas (large circular rooms used for ceremonies) are all set back beneath the rim of a cliff. Another ranger-led tour takes visitors up a 32-foot ladder to explore the interior of **Balcony House.** Each of these tours is given only in summer and into fall (call for exact dates). Guided tours are also offered by Far View Lodge (see "Where to Stay & Dine," below).

Two other important sites—**Step House** and **Long House,** both on Wetherill Mesa—can be visited in summer only. Rangers lead free tours to **Spruce Tree House,** another of the major cliff-dwelling complexes, only in winter, when other park facilities are closed. Visitors can also explore Spruce Tree House on their own at any time.

Although none of the trails to the Mesa Verde sites is strenuous, the 7,000-foot elevation can make the treks tiring for visitors who aren't used to the altitude. For those who want to avoid hiking and climbing, the 12-mile **Mesa Top Road** makes a number of pit houses and cliff-side overlooks easily accessible by car. **Chapin Mesa Archeological Museum** houses artifacts and specimens related to the history of the area, including other nearby sites.

OUTDOOR ACTIVITIES   Though this isn't an outdoor recreation park per se—the reason to come here is to see the cliff dwellings and other archaeological sites—you'll find yourself hiking and climbing to get to the sites. Several longer hikes into scenic Spruce Canyon let you stretch your legs and get away from the crowds. Hikers must register at the ranger's office before setting out.

CAMPING   Open from mid-April to mid-October, **Morefield Campground** (© **800/449-2288** or 970/533-1944; www.visitmesaverde.com), 4 miles south of the park entrance, has 435 sites, including 15 with full RV hookups. The campground is set in rolling hills in a grassy area with scrub oak and brush. The attractive sites are fairly well spaced, and are mostly separated by trees and other foliage. Facilities include modern restrooms, coin-operated showers (not within easy walking distance of most campsites), picnic tables, grills, and an RV dump station. Programs on the area's human and natural history and other subjects are presented nightly at the campground amphitheater from Memorial Day weekend through Labor Day weekend. Campsites cost $19, $25 with hookups. If you're hoping to snare one of the 15 full hookup sites, try getting to the park by late morning; there are almost always non-hookup sites available. There are also several commercial campgrounds along U.S. 160, just outside the park entrance.

WHERE TO STAY & DINE

There is only one lodging facility actually in the park, Far View Lodge (see below), which contains two restaurants and a bar. The company that runs the lodge also operates two other restaurants in the park—one near the campground and another near Chapin Mesa Museum. There are also numerous lodging and dining possibilities in nearby Cortez (see the previous section).

Far View Lodge   Located in the heart of Mesa Verde National Park, Far View Lodge offers not only the most convenient location for visiting the park, but also the best views of any accommodations in the area. The facility lodges guests in 17 separate buildings spread across a hilltop. Rooms aren't fancy and they're a bit on the small side, but they are well-maintained, with Southwestern decor. In fact, many of the units have recently been renovated and upgraded. New in 2003 were the "Kiva" rooms with hand-crafted furniture, one king or two queen-size beds, bathrobes, CD players, and other upscale amenities. There are no TVs, but each unit has a private balcony, and the views are magnificent in all directions.

The lodge restaurants serve three meals daily. Half-day guided tours of the park embark from the lodge daily at 9am and 1pm during the warmer months. Rates are $39 for adults, $28 for youths 5 to 17, and free for children under 5.

Mesa Verde National Park (P.O. Box 277), Mancos, CO 81328. © **800/449-2288** or 970-564-4300. Fax 970/564-4311. www.visitmesaverde.com. 150 units. Open late Apr to late Oct only. $110–$127 double. AE,DC, DISC, MC, V. Pets accepted with a deposit. **Amenities:** 2 restaurants. *In room:* Fridge (some), coffeemaker.

3 Four Corners Monument

This is the only place in the United States where you can stand in four states at once. There's a flat monument marking the spot where Utah, Colorado, New Mexico, and Arizona meet, on which visitors can perch for photos. Official seals of the four states are displayed, along with the motto FOUR STATES HERE MEET IN FREEDOM UNDER GOD. Surrounding the monument are the flags of the four states, the Navajo Nation and Ute tribes, and the United States.

There are often crafts demonstrations here, and jewelry, pottery, sand paintings, and other crafts are for sale, along with tee shirts and other souvenirs. In addition, traditional Navajo food, such as fry bread, is available, and there's a small visitor center with information on visiting the Navajo Nation.

Located a half mile northwest of U.S. 160, the monument is open daily from 7am to 8pm from March through August and 8am to 5pm the rest of the year. It's closed on Thanksgiving, Christmas, and New Year's Day. Entry costs $3 per person over age 6; free for those 6 and younger. For information, contact the **Navajo Parks and Recreation Department,** P.O. Box 2520, Window Rock, AZ 86515 (© **928/871-6647;** www.navajonationparks.org). Allow a half hour.

4 A Base Camp in Bluff: Utah's Four Corners Gateway

100 miles S of Moab, 338 miles SE of Salt Lake City

We particularly enjoy the tiny and very friendly village of Bluff, which sits near the intersection of U.S. 191 and U.S. 163, with roads leading off toward all the attractions of the Four Corners. With a population of about 300, Bluff (elevation 4,320 feet) is one of those comfortable little places with most basic services, but not a lot more. Founded by Mormon pioneers in 1880, the town's site had already been home to both Ancestral Puebloan and Navajo peoples. Local businesses distribute a free historic walking- and biking-tour guide that shows where ancient rock art and archaeological sites are located, as well as pointing out the locations of some of Bluff's handsome stone homes and other historic sites from the late 19th century.

For information on Bluff contact **The Business Owners of Bluff,** P.O. Box 220, Bluff, UT 84512 (www.bluff-utah.org). You can also get information on Bluff, as well on the other southeast Utah communities of Blanding, Monticello, Mexican Hat, and Monument Valley, from **Utah's Canyon Country,** 117 S. Main St. (P.O. Box 490), Monticello, UT 84535 (© **800/574-4386** or 435/587-3235; www.utahscanyoncountry.com). There is no visitor center in Bluff.

WHITE-WATER RAFTING & OTHER ORGANIZED TOURS

Situated along the San Juan River, Bluff is a center for river rafting. **Wild Rivers Expeditions,** Box 118, Bluff, UT 84512 (© **800/422-7654** or 435/672-2244; fax 435/672-2365; www.riversandruins.com) offers river trips on the San Juan that are both fun and educational. Boaters see dozens of American Indian sites along the river, such as the spectacular Butler Wash Petroglyph Panel—a 250-yard-long wall of petroglyphs—plus spectacular rock formations. Trips, offered from March through October, range from a full day to more than a week, with rates starting at $125 per adult and $75 per child 12 or younger, including lunch.

Guided tours into Monument Valley Navajo Tribal Park and other scenic areas and archaeological sites are offered by **Far Out Expeditions,** 7th East St. and Mulberry Ave. (P.O. Box 307), Bluff, UT 84512 (© **435/672-2294;** www.faroutexpeditions. com). Prices start at $105 for a full-day Monument Valley tour in an air-conditioned four-wheel-drive van, including lunch. The company also offers custom backcountry tours ranging from a half day to several days. Far Out Expeditions also offers a shuttle service for backpackers and river runners (call for rates), and lodging. The **Far Out Guest House,** 7th East St. and Mulberry Ave. (P.O. Box 307), Bluff, UT 84512 (© **435/672-2294;** www.faroutexpeditions.com) is a restored historic home with two bedrooms, decorated in Southwestern style. Each room has six bunk beds and a private bathroom (shower only). Both share a comfortable living room, screened porch, and fully equipped kitchen. Rates are $65 for a private room for one or two people, $75 for three or four people, $85 for five or six people, and $160 for the entire house.

Note that both of the above companies also collect per person user fees charged by the Bureau of Land Management.

MORE TO SEE & DO

About 2.2 miles west of town is **Sand Island Recreation Site,** operated by the BLM. Located along the San Juan River among cottonwoods, Russian olives, and salt cedar, this area offers boating (there's a boat ramp) and fishing. Boaters must obtain river permits in advance, and because there are usually more people wanting permits than there are permits available, a lottery is held to determine who gets the permits. Fees are charged, based on the time of year, section of river, and number of people in your party. As early as possible, preferably in December for the following summer, contact the Bureau of Land Management, 435 N. Main St. (P.O. Box 7), Monticello, UT 84535 (© **435/587-1500;** 435/587-1544 8am–noon weekdays for permits applications; www.ut.blm.gov). Nestled between the river and a high rock bluff are picnic tables, vault toilets, and graveled campsites; camping is $10 per night. Head west from the boat launch to see a number of petroglyphs, some of which can be seen easily on foot and others which require a boat to see. Unfortunately, you must have your own boat with you, as there are no nearby places to rent boats.

Goosenecks State Park, set on a rim high above the San Juan, offers spectacular views out over the twisting, turning river some 1,000 feet below. It's named for the sharp turns in the river, which meanders more than 5 miles to progress just 1 linear mile, and provides a look straight down through 300 million years of geologic history. You'll find picnic tables, trash cans, vault toilets, and an observation shelter, but no drinking water, in a gravelly open area at the end of the paved road. The park is open around the clock and admission is free; primitive camping is permitted at no charge. The park is about 23½ miles from Bluff, just off the route to Monument Valley Navajo Tribal Park. Head west on U.S. 163 for about 20 miles, turn north (right) on Utah 261 for about a mile, and then west (left) on Utah 316 for 2½ miles. For information, contact Goosenecks State Park, 600 W. 400 North, Blanding, UT 84511 (𝒞 **435/678-2238;** www.stateparks. utah.gov).

WHERE TO STAY

Lodging tax adds 9% to room bills in Bluff. Far Out Expeditions (see above) also offers accommodations in its guest house.

Desert Rose Inn 𝕏𝕏   Built in 1999, this imposing log lodge-style building houses 30 attractively decorated motel rooms, all with air-conditioning, TVs, phones, coffeemakers, combination shower/tubs, and queen or king beds. Decor is Southwestern, with log headboards, pottery-style lamps, solid-wood furnishings, and signed prints by a Hopi artist. There is also an attractive suite with a wraparound porch, king bed, and separate living room. In addition there are five pleasant cabins, a bit more rustic in appearance, each with a large walk-in shower (no tubs), two queen beds, refrigerators and microwaves, porches, and cathedral ceilings with exposed beams.

701 W. Main St. (U.S. 191). 𝒞 **888/475-7673** or 435/672-2303; fax 435/672-2217. www.desertroseinn.com. 30 units, 1 suite, 6 cabins. Winter $54–$74 double; summer $74–$94 double. $125 suite. AE, DISC, MC, V. **Amenities:** Laundry service. *In room:* A/C, satellite TV, dataport, fridge (cabins only), coffeemaker, microwave.

Recapture Lodge 〈Value〉   This property may be older, but we like its quiet, clean, and inexpensive rooms. A well-kept motel located near the center of town, Recapture Lodge has an attractive Western decor and a nature trail that follows the San Juan River along the back of the property. Rooms contain two double beds or one queen, and combination shower-tubs; several budget units, with shower only and one double bed, are also available. Guests enjoy the heated pool and hot tub.

U.S. 191 (P.O. Box 309), Bluff, Utah 84512. 𝒞 **435/672-2281.** Fax 435/672-2284. recapturelodge@hubwest.com. 28 units. Winter $36–$44 double; summer $46–$56 double. Pets welcome. AE, DISC, MC, V. **Amenities:** Solar-heated outdoor pool; hot tub; laundry service. *In room:* A/C, TV, no phone.

CAMPING

Campgrounds include **Cadillac Ranch RV Park,** U.S. 191 (P.O. Box 157), Bluff, UT 84512 (𝒞 **800/538-6195** or 435/672-2262), a down-home sort of place on the east side of town with sites around a small fishing lake, where there's no license needed and no extra charge for fishing. There are 20 RV sites—all large pull-throughs—and 10 tent sites and restrooms with showers. The campground is open year-round, but water is turned off in winter. Cost per site is $16 for tents and $18 to $19 for RVs; paddleboats can be rented at $4 per half hour.

WHERE TO DINE

Cottonwood Steakhouse ★★   Set up like a main street of an old tumbleweed town, this Old West–style restaurant knows what to do with beef. The solid fare includes a 16-ounce T-bone steak, barbecue chicken or ribs, and 12-ounce rib-eye steak, accompanied by large salads and potatoes or baked beans. Diners sit at picnic tables, both inside the restaurant and outside under cottonwood trees. Beer is available.

U.S. 191 on the west side of Bluff. ✆ 435/672-2282. Main courses $11–$22. MC, V. Open daily from 5:30pm Mar–mid-Oct. Closed mid-Oct to Feb.

Twin Rocks Cafe ★   In the shadow of the prominent Twin Rocks formation, this down-home cafe has an open, airy dining room with large windows offering views of the surrounding red rock walls. The American and Southwest selections range from half-pound burgers to fried chicken and steaks. But the most popular items by far are the regional dishes—the sheepherder's sandwich (roast beef on fry bread with cheddar cheese), Navajo taco, and Navajo fry bread. Microbrewed beers are available with meals. The cafe also serves the best breakfast in town. You can surf the Internet here, and check out the museum-quality American Indian arts and crafts at Twin Rocks Trading Post, under the same management, next door.

U.S. 191 on the east end of Bluff. ✆ 435/672-2341. Lunch and dinner main courses $6.50–$17. AE, DC, DISC, MC, V. Daily 7am–9pm in summer; reduced hours in winter.

5 Natural Bridges National Monument

60 miles NW of Bluff, 360 miles south of Salt Lake City

Utah's first National Park Service area, Natural Bridges was designated primarily to show off and protect its three outstanding natural rock bridges, carved by streams and other forms of erosion beginning some 10,000 to 15,000 years ago. You can see the bridges from roadside viewpoints, take individual hikes to each one, or hike a loop trail that connects all three.

Giant **Sipapu Bridge** is considered a "mature" bridge. It's 220 feet high, with a span of 268 feet, and is believed to be the second-largest natural bridge in the world, after Rainbow Bridge in nearby Glen Canyon National Recreation Area. **Owachomo Bridge,** which appears to be on the brink of collapse (then again, it could stand for centuries), is the smallest of the three at 106 feet high, with a span of 180 feet. **Kachina Bridge,** 210 feet high with a span of 204 feet, is the thickest of the monument's bridges at 93 feet. All three bridges were given Hopi names: Sipapu means the "gateway to the spirit world" in Hopi legend; Owachomo is Hopi for "rock mound," so called for a rounded sandstone formation atop one side of the bridge; and Kachina was named as such because rock art on the bridge resembles decorations found on traditional Hopi kachina dolls.

ESSENTIALS

Natural Bridges National Monument is about 40 miles west of Blanding, 60 miles northwest of Bluff, 43 miles north of Mexican Hat, and about 50 miles east of Glen Canyon National Recreation Area's Hite or Halls Crossing marinas.

GETTING THERE   The national monument is located in southeast Utah, off scenic Utah 95 via Utah 275. From Monument Valley, follow U.S. 163 north to Utah 261 (just past Mexican Hat); at Utah 95, go west to Utah 275 and the Monument. Beware, though—Utah 261, although a very pretty drive, has 10% grades and numerous steep switchbacks. It's not recommended for motor homes, those towing trailers, or anyone who's afraid of heights. The less adventurous and RV-bound should stick to approaching from the east, via Utah 95.

Make sure you have enough fuel for the trip to Natural Bridges; the closest gas stations are at least 40 miles away in Mexican Hat or Blanding. In fact, there are no services of any kind within 40 miles of the Monument.

INFORMATION/VISITOR CENTER   For a park brochure and other information, contact **Natural Bridges National Monument,** HC 60 Box 1, Lake Powell, UT 84533-0101 (© **435/692-1234;** www.nps.gov/nabr).

A **visitor center** at the park entrance, open daily from 8am to 5pm, has exhibits and a video program on bridge formation, the human history of the area, and the monument's plants and wildlife. Rangers are available to advise you about hiking trails and scheduled activities. The visitor center is the only place in the monument where you can get drinking water.

FEES & REGULATIONS   Entry to the monument is $6 per vehicle or $3 per person on foot, bicycle, or motorcycle. Regulations are similar to those in most areas administered by the National Park Service, with an emphasis on protecting the natural resources. Be especially careful not to damage any of the fragile archaeological sites in the monument; climbing on the natural bridges is prohibited. Overnight backpacking is not permitted within the monument, and vehicles may not be left unattended overnight. Because parking at the overlooks and trailheads is limited, anyone towing trailers or extra vehicles is asked to leave them at the visitor center parking lot. Pets must be leashed and are not allowed on trails or in buildings.

RANGER PROGRAMS   Guided hikes and walks, evening campground programs, and talks at the visitor center patio are presented from spring through fall. Schedules are posted at the visitor center.

SEEING THE HIGHLIGHTS

Natural Bridges National Monument probably won't be your major vacation destination, but you can easily spend a half or full day, or even 2 days, here. For those who want to take a quick look and get on to the other, larger national park lands in southern Utah, stop at the visitor center for a brief introduction, and then take the 9-mile (one-way) loop drive to the various natural bridge overlooks. Those with the time and the inclination might also take an easy hike down to Owachomo Bridge; it's a half-hour walk

OUTDOOR PURSUITS

Hiking is the number-one activity here. From the trailheads, you can hike separately to each of the bridges, or start at one and do a loop hike to all three. Be prepared for summer afternoon thunderstorms that can cause flash flooding. Although the possibility of encountering a rattlesnake is very small, you should still watch carefully. During the hot summers, all hikers should wear hats and other protective clothing, use sunscreen, and carry a gallon of water per person for all but the shortest walks.

The easiest hike—more of a walk—leads to **Owachomo Bridge** (0.4 mile round-trip), with an elevation gain of 180 feet. Look toward the eastern horizon to see the twin buttes named Bear's Ears. Allow a half hour.

The Sipapu and Kachina Bridge trails are both considered moderately strenuous—allocate about 1 hour for each. On the trek to **Sipapu Bridge,** you'll have a 500-foot elevation change, climbing two flights of stairs with three ladders and handrails on a 1.2-mile round-trip trail. This is the steepest trail in the park, and you'll have a splendid view of the bridge about halfway down. The hike takes about 1 hour.

The 1.5-mile round-trip hike to massive **Kachina Bridge** has a 400-foot elevation change, descending steep slickrock with handrails. Under the bridge, you'll notice a pile of rocks that fell in June 1992, slightly enlarging the bridge opening. Allow about 1 hour.

Those planning to hike the **loop to all three bridges** can start at any of the trailheads, although rangers recommend starting at Owachomo. The round-trip, including your walk back across the mesa, is 8.6 miles. Although the trails from the rim to the canyon bottom can be steep, the walk along the bottom is easy.

CAMPING

A primitive 13-site campground has pit toilets, tables, tent pads, and fire grates, but no drinking water, showers, or other facilities. It's limited to vehicles no more than 21 feet long, and only one vehicle is allowed per site. Cost is $10; sites are allotted on a first-come, first-served basis.

6 Winslow: Arizona's Four Corners Gateway

55 miles E of Flagstaff; 70 miles S of Second Mesa; 33 miles W of Holbrook

It's hard to imagine a town that could build its entire tourist fortunes on a mention in a pop song, but that is exactly what Winslow has done ever since the Eagles sang about "standin' on a corner in Winslow, Arizona," in their hit song "Take It Easy." On the corner of Second Street and Kinsley Avenue, the town has even built an official Standin' on the Corner Park (complete with a mural of a girl in a flatbed Ford).

Popular songs aside, Winslow can claim a couple of more significant attractions. Right in town is one of the Southwest's historic railroad hotels, La Posada, which is undergoing ongoing renovations that have returned it to its original glory. Twenty miles west of town is mile-wide Meteor Crater. And east of town is Homolovi Ruins State Park, which has ancient ruins as well as extensive petroglyphs.

Winslow makes a good home base for visiting some of Arizona's four corners attractions, but we've found some great places to stay scattered across the region; they're mentioned in the sections below. In particular, if you're hoping to spend some time at Canyon de Chelly National Monument, you should consider spending a night or two at one of the Chinle accommodations recommended in that section.

ESSENTIALS

GETTING THERE Winslow is on I-40 at the junction with Ariz. 87, which leads north to the Hopi mesas and south to Payson. **Amtrak** (© **800/872-7245**) trains stop in Winslow on East Second Street (at La Posada).

VISITOR INFORMATION Contact the **Winslow Chamber of Commerce,** 300 N. Park Rd. (© **928/289-2434**).

ONE BIG HOLE IN THE GROUND

Meteor Crater ★★ At 550 feet deep and 2½ miles in circumference, the Barringer Meteorite Crater is the best-preserved meteorite impact crater on earth. The meteorite, which estimates put at roughly 150 feet in diameter, was traveling at 40,000 mph when it slammed into the earth 50,000 years ago. Within seconds, more than 175 million tons of rock had been displaced, leaving a gaping crater and a devastated landscape. Today, you can stand on the rim of the crater (there are observation decks and a short

Fred Harvey & His Girls

Unless you grew up in the Southwest and can remember back to pre–World War II days, you may have never heard of Fred Harvey and the Harvey Girls. But if you spend much time in northern Arizona, you're likely to run into quite a few references to the Harvey Girls and their boss.

Fred Harvey was the Southwest's most famous mogul of railroad hospitality and an early promoter of tourism in the Grand Canyon State. Harvey, who was working for a railroad in the years shortly after the Civil War, had developed a distaste for the food served at railroad stations. He decided he could do a better job, and in 1876 opened his first Harvey House railway-station restaurant for the Santa Fe Railroad. By the time of his death in 1901, Harvey operated 47 restaurants, 30 diners, and 15 hotels across the West.

The women who worked as waitresses in the Harvey House restaurants came to be called Harvey Girls. Known for their distinctive black dresses, white aprons, and black bow ties, Harvey Girls had to adhere to very strict behavior codes and were the prim and proper women of the late-19th- and early-20th-century American West. In fact, in the late 19th century, they were considered the only real "ladies" in the West, aside from schoolteachers. So celebrated were they in their day that in the 1940s, Judy Garland starred in a Technicolor MGM musical called The Harvey Girls. Garland played a Harvey Girl who battles the evil town dance-hall queen (played by Angela Lansbury) for the soul of the local saloonkeeper.

trail) and marvel at the power, equivalent to 20 million tons of TNT, that created this otherworldly setting. In fact, so closely does this crater resemble craters on the surface of the moon that in the 1960s, NASA came here to train Apollo astronauts.

On the rim of the crater, there's a small museum that features exhibits on astrogeology and space exploration, as well as a film on meteorites. On display are a 1,400-pound meteorite and an Apollo space capsule. Throughout the day, there are 1-hour hiking tours along the rim of the crater.

20 miles west of Winslow at Exit 233 off I-40. (© 800/289-5898 or 928/289-5898. www.meteorcrater.com. Admission $12 adults, $11 seniors, $6 children 6–17. Memorial Day to Labor Day daily 7am–7pm; Labor Day to Memorial Day daily 8am–5pm. Closed Christmas.

OTHER AREA ATTRACTIONS

In downtown Winslow, near that famous corner, you'll find the little **Old Trails Museum,** 212 N. Kinsley Ave., at Second Street (© 928/289-5861), which is something of a community attic and has exhibits on Route 66 and the Harvey Girls (who once worked in the nearby La Posada hotel). From April to October, it's open Tuesday through Saturday from 1 to 5pm, and from November to March, it's open Tuesday, Thursday, and Saturday from 1 to 5pm. Admission is free.

Even if you aren't planning on staying the night at the restored **La Posada,** 303 E. Second St. (© 928/289-4366), be sure to stop by just to see this historic railway hotel. Self-guided tours are available for a $2 donation, and guided tours are arranged through Winslow's Harvey Girls association ($5 suggested donation).

On the windswept plains north of Winslow, 1¼ miles north of I-40 at Exit 257, is **Homolovi Ruins State Park** (© 928/289-4106), which preserves more than 300 Ancestral Puebloan archaeological sites, several of which have been partially excavated. Although these ruins are not nearly as impressive as those at Wupatki or Walnut Canyon, a visit here will give you a better understanding of the interrelationship of the many ancient pueblos of this region. Also in the park are numerous petroglyphs; ask for directions at the visitor center. Admission is $5 per vehicle. The ruins are open daily during daylight hours, but the visitor center is open only from 8am to 5pm. There's also a campground, charging $10 to $20 per site.

Continuing north from the state park, you'll find the little known and little visited **Little Painted Desert** ★ (© 928/524-4251), a 660-acre county park. To reach the park and its viewpoint overlooking the painted hills of this stark yet colorful landscape, continue north on Ariz. 87 from Homolovi Ruins State Park for another 12 miles. Although the trail down into the desert itself is closed, unofficially, the parks department doesn't mind if you hike down.

If you're in the market for some Route 66 memorabilia, drop by **Roadworks Gifts & Souvenirs,** 101 W. Second St. (© 928/289-5423). If you're more interested in Native American crafts, check out the **Arizona Indian Arts Cooperative,** 523 W. Second St. (© 928/289-3986), which is housed in the historic Lorenzo Hubbell Co. trading post. Also, be sure to check out the **SNOWDRIFT Art Space,** 120 W. Second St. (© 928/289-8201; www.snowdriftart.com), an art gallery opened by artist Daniel Lutzick, who was one of the people who helped get the historic La Posada hotel up and running again.

WHERE TO STAY

In addition to the following historic hotel, you'll find lots of budget chain motels in Winslow.

La Posada ★★ *Finds* What an unexpected beauty this place is! Designed by Mary Elizabeth Jane Colter, architect of many of the buildings on the South Rim of the Grand Canyon, this railroad hotel first opened in 1930. Colter gave La Posada the feel of an old Spanish hacienda, and even created a fictitious history for the building. In the lobby are numerous pieces of original furniture as well as reproductions of pieces once found in the hotel. The nicest rooms are the large units named for famous guests—Albert Einstein, Howard Hughes, Harry Truman, Charles Lindbergh, the Marx brothers. The management's artistic flair comes across in these rooms, one of which (the Howard Hughes Room) has wide plank floors, murals, a fireplace, a rustic bed and armoire, Art Deco chairs, and a kilim rug. The bathroom is a classic of black-and-white tile and original fixtures. There are also rooms with whirlpool tubs. The hotel's Turquoise Room (see "Where to Dine," below) is by far the best restaurant in the entire Four Corners region. La Posada is in the process of being slowly, but completely restored and is reason enough to overnight in Winslow.

303 E. Second St. (Rte. 66), Winslow, AZ 86047. © 928/289-4366. Fax 928/289-3873. www.laposada.org. 37 units. $89–$129 double; $149–$175 suite. AE, DC, DISC, MC, V. Pets accepted ($10 fee). **Amenities:** Restaurant (New American/Southwestern); lounge; access to nearby health club; game room; concierge. *In room:* A/C, TV, no phone.

WHERE TO DINE

The Turquoise Room ★★ *Value* NEW AMERICAN/SOUTHWESTERN When Fred Harvey began his railroad hospitality career, his objective was to provide decent meals to the traveling public. (See the box "Fred Harvey & His Girls," on p. 99.)

Here, in La Posada's reincarnated dining room, you'll get not just decent meals, but superb meals the likes of which you won't find anywhere else in northern Arizona. In summer, herbs and vegetables often come from the hotel's own gardens, and wild game is a specialty. Be sure to start your meal with the sweet corn and black bean soups, which are served side by side in the same bowl to create a sort of yin-yang symbol. On top of all this, you can watch the trains rolling by just outside the window.

At La Posada, 305 E. Second St. ⓒ **928/289-2888.** www.laposada.org. Main courses $5–$10 breakfast, $8–$11 lunch, $16–$26 dinner. AE, DISC, MC, V. Daily 7am–2pm and 5–9pm.

7 The Hopi Reservation

67 miles N of Winslow; 250 miles NE of Phoenix; 100 miles SW of Canyon de Chelly; 140 miles SE of Page/Lake Powell

The Hopi Reservation, often referred to as Hopiland or just Hopi, is completely encircled by the Navajo Reservation, and has at its center a grouping of mesas upon which the Hopi have lived for nearly 1,000 years. This remote region, with its flat-topped mesas and barren landscape, is the center of the universe for the Hopi people. Here the Hopi follow their ancient customs, and many aspects of pueblo culture remain intact. However, much of the culture is hidden from the view of visitors, and although the Hopi perform elaborate religious and social dances throughout the year, many of these dances are not open to outsiders.

The mesas are home to two of the oldest continuously inhabited villages in North America—Walpi and Old Oraibi. Although these two communities show their age and serve as a direct tie to the pueblos of the Ancestral Puebloan culture, most of the villages on the reservation are scattered collections of modern homes. These villages are not destinations unto themselves, but along Ariz. 264 there are numerous crafts shops and studios selling kachinas, baskets, pottery, and silver jewelry. The chance to buy crafts directly from the Hopi is the main reason for a visit to this area, although you can also take a guided tour of Walpi village.

Important note: When visiting the Hopi pueblos, remember that you are a guest and your privileges can be revoked at any time. Respect all posted signs at village entrances, and remember that *photographing, sketching, and recording are prohibited in the villages and at ceremonies.* Also, kivas (ceremonial rooms) and ruins are off-limits.

ESSENTIALS

GETTING THERE This is one of the state's most remote regions. Distances are great, but highways are generally in good condition. Ariz. 87 leads from Winslow to Second Mesa, and Ariz. 264 runs from Tuba City in the west to the New Mexico state line in the east.

VISITOR INFORMATION For advance information, contact the **Hopi Office of Public Relations,** P.O. Box 123, Kykotsmovi, AZ 86039 (ⓒ **928/734-3283;** www. hopi.nsn.us), or the **Hopi Cultural Preservation Office** (ⓒ **928/734-3612;** www. nau.edu/~hcpo-p).

Because each of the Hopi villages is relatively independent, you might want to contact the **community development office** of a particular village for specific information: **Bacavi** (ⓒ 928/734-9360), **Sichomovi** (ⓒ 928/737-2670), **Hotevilla** (ⓒ 928/ 734-2420), **Kykotsmovi** (ⓒ 928/734-2474), **Mishongnovi** (ⓒ 928/737-2520), **Upper Moenkopi** (ⓒ 928/283-8054), **Lower Moenkopi** (ⓒ 928/283-5212), **Shipaulovi** (ⓒ 928/737-2570), **Shungopavi** (ⓒ 928/734-7135), and **Walpi**

(© 928/737-9556). These offices are generally open Monday through Friday from 8am to 5pm.

THE VILLAGES

With the exception of Upper and Lower Moenkopi, which are near the Navajo town of Tuba City, and the recently settled Yuh Weh Loo Pah Ki community east of Keams Canyon, the Hopi villages are scattered along roughly 20 miles of Ariz. 264. Although Old Oraibi is the oldest, there are no tours of this village, and visitors are not likely to feel very welcome here. Consequently, Walpi, the only village with organized tours, is the best place for visitors to learn more about life in the Hopi villages. I mention all of the Hopi villages below to provide a bit of history and perspective on this area, but for the most part, these villages (with the exception of Walpi and Old Oraibi) are not at all picturesque. However, most do have quite a few crafts galleries and stores selling silver jewelry.

FIRST MESA   At the top of First Mesa is the village of **Walpi,** which was located lower on the slopes of the mesa until the Pueblo Revolt of 1680, when the villagers moved Walpi to the very top of the mesa so they could better defend themselves in the event of a Spanish attack. Walpi looks much like the Ancestral Puebloan villages of the Arizona canyons. Small stone houses seem to grow directly from the rock of the mesa top, and ladders jut from the roofs of kivas. The view from here stretches for hundreds of miles around.

Immediately adjacent to Walpi are the two villages of **Sichomovi,** which was founded in 1750 as a colony of Walpi, and **Hano,** which was founded by Tewa peoples who were most likely seeking refuge from the Spanish after the Pueblo Revolt. Neither of these villages has the ancient character of Walpi. At the foot of First Mesa is **Polacca,** a settlement founded in the late 1800s by Walpi villagers who wanted to be closer to the trading post and school.

SECOND MESA   Second Mesa is today the center of tourism in Hopiland, and this is where you'll find the Hopi Cultural Center. Villages on Second Mesa include **Shungopavi,** which was moved to its present site after Old Shungopavi was abandoned in 1680 following the Pueblo Revolt. Old Shungopavi is said to be the first Hopi village and was founded by the Bear Clan. Shungopavi is notable for its silver jewelry and its coiled plaques (flat baskets).

Mishongnovi, which means "place of the black man," is named for the leader of a clan that came here from the San Francisco Peaks around A.D. 1200. The original Mishongnovi village, located at the base of the mesa, was abandoned in the 1690s, and the village was reestablished at the current site atop the mesa.

Shipaulovi, which is located on the eastern edge of the mesa, was founded after the Pueblo Revolt of 1680.

THIRD MESA   Oraibi, which the Hopi claim is the oldest continuously occupied town in the United States, is located on Third Mesa. The village dates from 1150 and, according to legend, was founded by people from Old Shungopavi. A Spanish mission was established in Oraibi in 1629, and the ruins are still visible north of the village. Today, Oraibi is a mix of old stone houses and modern ones, usually of cinder block. Wander around Oraibi, and you'll likely be approached by village women and children offering to sell you various local crafts and the traditional blue-corn piki bread. You might also be invited into someone's home to see the crafts they have to offer. For this reason, Old Oraibi is the most interesting village in which to shop for local crafts.

For centuries, Oraibi was the largest of the Hopi villages, but in 1906, a schism arose from Bureau of Indian Affairs policies and many of the villagers left to form **Hotevilla.** This is considered the most conservative of the Hopi villages and has had frequent confrontations with the federal government. **Kykotsmovi,** also known as Lower Oraibi or New Oraibi, was founded in 1890 by villagers from Oraibi who wanted to be closer to the school and trading post. This village is the seat of the Hopi Tribal Government. **Bacavi** was founded in 1907 by villagers who had helped found Hotevilla but who later decided that they wanted to return to Oraibi. The people of Oraibi would not let them return, and rather than go back to Hotevilla, they founded a new village.

MOENKOPI   This village is 40 miles to the west of the Hopi mesas. Founded in 1870 by people from Oraibi, Moenkopi sits in the center of a wide green valley. Moenkopi is only a few miles from Tuba City off U.S. 160 and is divided into the villages of Upper Moenkopi and Lower Moenkopi.

EXPLORING THE WORLD OF THE HOPI

Start your visit to the Hopi pueblos at the **Hopi Cultural Center,** on Ariz. 264 in Second Mesa (© **928/734-6650**). This combination museum, motel, and restaurant is the tourism headquarters for the area. The museum is open Monday through Friday from 8am to 5pm; in summer, it's also open Saturday and Sunday from 9am to 4pm. Admission is $3 for adults and $1 for children.

The most rewarding Hopi village to visit is **Walpi** ⚘, on First Mesa. Guided tours of this tiny village are offered daily between 9:30am and 4pm (from 9am to 5pm in summer). Admission is $8 for adults and $5 for youths 6 to 17. To sign up for a tour, drive to the top of First Mesa (in Polacca, take the road that says FIRST MESA VILLAGE) and continue through the village to **Ponsi Hall Visitor Center** (© **928/737-2262**), where you'll see signs for the tours. The tours, which last 1 hour, are led by Hopis who will tell you the history of the village and explain a bit about the local culture. Similar tours are also offered by **Village of Walpi Tour Services** (© **928/737-9556**). Between April and September, these tours are offered 8am to 6pm; between October and March, tours are offered between 8am and 5pm. The cost is $5. On the third or last weekend in September, a harvest festival features 2 days of dancing.

CULTURAL TOURS

To get the most out of a visit to the Hopi mesas, it is best to book a guided tour. With a guide, you will probably learn much more about this rather insular culture than you ever could on your own. Tour companies frequently use local guides and stop at the homes of working artisans. This all adds up to a more in-depth and educational visit to one of the oldest cultures on the continent.

Gary Tso is one local guide who gives tours through his **Left-Handed Hunter Tour Co.** (© **928/734-2567;** lhhunter58@hotmail.com). Gary will take you to Walpi, Old Oraibi, a petroglyph site, and the studios of a kachina carver, a potter, and a silver- and goldsmith. All-day tours (including lunch, transportation, and entry fees) cost $205 for one person, $285 for two, $305 for three, and $365 for four. There are also half-day tours to Old Oraibi for $125 for one person, $150 for two people, $175 for three people, and $200 for four people.

Bertram Tsavadawa at **Ancient Pathways** (© **928/306-7849**) specializes in tours to Hopi petroglyph sites. These are sites that are not open to the public unless you are with a Hopi guide. Tours also visit Old Oraibi. The cost is $65 per person for a 3-hour tour and $125 for a 6-hour tour.

DANCES & CEREMONIES

The Hopi have developed the most complex religious ceremonies of any of the Southwest tribes. The masked kachina dances for which they are most famous are held from January to July. However, most kachina dances are closed to the non-Hopi public. Social dances (usually open to the public) are held August through February. If you're on the reservation during these months, ask if any dances are taking place. Who knows, you might get lucky. Snake Dances (usually closed to the non-Hopi public) are held August through December.

Kachinas, whether in the form of dolls or as masked dancers, are representative of the spirits of everything from plants and animals to ancestors and sacred places. According to legend, the kachinas lived with the Hopi long ago, but the Hopi people made the kachinas angry, causing them to leave. Before departing, though, the kachinas taught the Hopi how to perform their ceremonies.

Today, the kachina ceremonies, performed by men wearing elaborate costumes and masks, serve several purposes. Most important, they bring clouds and rain to water the all-important corn crop, but they also ensure health, happiness, long life, and harmony in the universe. As part of the kachina ceremonies, dancers often bring carved wooden kachina dolls to village children to introduce them to the various spirits.

The kachina season lasts from the winter solstice until shortly after the summer solstice. The actual dates for dances are determined by the position of the sun and usually are announced only shortly before the ceremonies are to be held.

Despite the importance of the kachina dances, it is the **Snake Dance** that has captured the attention of many non-Hopis. The Snake Dance is held every other year in Mishongnovi and Gray Spring and involves the handling of both poisonous and non-poisonous snakes. The ceremony takes place over 16 days; the actual Snake Dance is performed on the last day. When all the snakes have been danced around the plaza, they are rushed down to their homes at the bottom of the mesa to carry the Hopi prayers for rain to the spirits of the underworld.

Due to the disrespectful attitude of some past visitors, many ceremonies and dances are now closed to non-Hopis. However, a couple of Hopi villages do allow visitors to attend some of their dances. The best way to find out about attending dances is to contact the **community development office** of the individual villages (see phone numbers under "Visitor Information," above).

SHOPPING

Most visitors come to the reservation to shop for Hopi crafts. Across the reservation, there are dozens of small shops selling crafts and jewelry of different quality, and some homes, especially at the foot of First Mesa, have signs indicating that they sell crafts. Shops often sell the work of only a few individuals, so you should stop at several to get an idea of the variety of work available. Also, if you tour Walpi or wander around in Oraibi, you will likely be approached by villagers selling various crafts, including kachina dolls. The quality is not usually as high as that in shops, but then, neither are the prices.

At Keams Canyon, almost 30 miles east of the cultural center, you'll find **McGee's Indian Art Gallery** (© 928/738-2295; www.hopiart.com), which is the best place to shop for high-quality contemporary kachina dolls. This shop is adjacent to a grocery store and has been a trading post for more than 100 years.

Between First and Second mesas, watch for the signs for the **Hopi Market** (© 928/737-9434; www.hopimarket.com). This shop has a wide variety of crafts from area artisans and a great website in case you decide after you get home that you want to buy something. If you're in the market for Hopi silver jewelry, stop in at **Hopi Fine Arts** (© 928/737-2222), which is at the foot of Second Mesa at the junction of Ariz. 264 and Ariz. 87. This shop also has a good selection of kachina dolls and some beautiful coil and wicker plaque baskets.

One of the best places to get a quick education in Hopi art and crafts is **Tsakurshovi** (© 928/734-2478), a tiny shop 1½ miles east of the Hopi Cultural Center on Second Mesa. This shop has a huge selection of traditional kachina dolls, and also has lots of jewelry. The owners are very friendly and are happy to share their expertise with visitors.

If you're interested in kachina dolls, be sure to visit Oraibi's **Monongya Gallery** (© 928/734-2344), a big building right on Ariz. 264 outside of Oraibi. It usually has one of the largest selections of kachina dolls in the area. Also in Oraibi is **Hamana So-o's Arts & Crafts** (© 928/607-0176), which is in an old stone house, from which owner Sandra Hamana sells primarily artwork and crafts based on kachina images.

WHERE TO STAY & DINE

If you've brought your food along, you'll find picnic tables just east of Oraibi on top of the mesa. These tables have an amazing view!

Hopi Cultural Center Restaurant & Inn   Although it isn't much, this simple motel makes the best base for anyone planning to spend a couple of days shopping for crafts in the area. Because it is the only lodging for miles around, be sure you have a reservation before heading up for an overnight visit. Guest rooms are comfortable enough, though the grounds are quite desolate. The restaurant has a salad bar and serves American and traditional Hopi meals, including piki bread (a paper-thin bread made from blue corn) and Hopi stew with hominy, lamb, and green chile. There's also a museum.

P.O. Box 67, Second Mesa, AZ 86043. © 928/734-2401. Fax 928/734-6651. www.hopiculturalcenter.com. 33 units. Mar 15–Oct 15 $95–$100 double; Oct 16–Mar 14 $70–$75 double. Children 12 and under stay free in parent's room. AE, DC, DISC, MC, V. **Amenities:** Restaurant (American/Hopi); shopping arcade. *In room:* A/C, TV, coffeemaker.

EN ROUTE TO OR FROM THE HOPI MESAS

On the west side of the reservation, in Tuba City, is the **Tuba City Trading Post,** Main Street and Moenave Avenue. (© 928/283-5441). This octagonal trading post was built in 1906 of local stone and is designed to resemble a Navajo hogan (there's also a real hogan on the grounds). The trading post sells Native American crafts, with an emphasis on books, music, and jewelry.

On the western outskirts of Tuba City, on U.S. 160, you'll find **Van's Trading Co.** (© 928/283-5343), in the corner of a large grocery store. Van's has a dead-pawn auction on the 15th of each month at 3pm (any pawned item not reclaimed by the owner by a specified date is considered "dead pawn"). The auction provides opportunities to buy older pieces of Navajo silver-and-turquoise jewelry.

In mid-October, Tuba City is the site of the **Western Navajo Fair,** which sells Native American crafts.

West of Tuba City and just off U.S. 160, you can see **dinosaur footprints** ✿ preserved in the stone surface of the desert. There are usually a few people waiting at the site to guide visitors to the best footprints (these guides will expect a tip). The scenery out your car window is some of the strangest in the region—red-rock sandstone formations that resemble petrified sand dunes.

The **Cameron Trading Post** ✿ (© 800/ 338-7385 or 928/679-2231; ext. 415 for gallery), 16 miles south of the junction of U.S. 160 and U.S. 89, is well worth a visit. The main trading post is filled with souvenirs, but has large selections of rugs and jewelry as well. In the adjacent stone-walled gallery are museum-quality Native American artifacts (with prices to match). The trading post also includes a motel.

WHERE TO STAY

Quality Inn Navajo Nation   Located in the bustling Navajo community of Tuba City (where you'll find gas stations, fast-food restaurants, and grocery stores), this modern hotel is adjacent to the historic Tuba City Trading Post and is actually a more attractive place to stay in this region than the Hopi Cultural Center. The hotel offers comfortable rooms of average size, but the green lawns, shade trees, and old trading post (complete with hogan) are what really set this place apart. Also, the lobby has a great collection of historic photos on display.

Main St. and Moenave Ave. (P.O. Box 247), Tuba City, AZ 86045. © 800/644-8383 or 928/283-4545. Fax 928/283-4144. www.qualityinntubacity.com. 80 units. Apr–Oct $105–$140 double; Nov–Mar $85–$115 double. Children 18 and under stay free in parent's room. AE, DC, DISC, MC, V. Pets accepted ($20 deposit). **Amenities:** Restaurant (American/Mexican/Navajo); coin-op laundry. *In room:* A/C, TV, coffeemaker, iron, free local calls.

8 The Petrified Forest & Painted Desert ⋆

25 miles E of Holbrook; 90 miles E of Flagstaff; 118 miles S of Canyon de Chelly; 180 miles N of Phoenix

Petrified wood has long fascinated people, and although it can be found in almost every state, the "forest" of downed logs in northeastern Arizona is by far the most extensive. But don't head out this way expecting to see standing trees of stone, leaves and branches intact. Though there is enough petrified timber scattered across this landscape to fill a forest, it is, in fact, in the form of logs and not standing trees.

However, this area is still unique. When, in the 1850s, this vast treasure trove of petrified wood was discovered scattered like kindling across the landscape, enterprising people began exporting it wholesale to the East. Within 50 years, so much had been removed that in 1906 several areas were set aside as the Petrified Forest National Monument, which, in 1962, became a national park. A 27-mile scenic drive winds through the petrified forest (and a small corner of the Painted Desert), providing a fascinating high-desert experience.

It may be hard to believe when you drive across this arid landscape, but some 225 million years ago, this area was a vast steamy swamp. Fallen trees were washed downstream, gathered in piles in still backwaters, and eventually covered over with silt, mud, and volcanic ash. As water seeped through this soil, it dissolved the silica in the volcanic ash and redeposited this silica inside the cells of the logs. Eventually the silica recrystallized into stone to form petrified wood, with minerals such as iron, manganese, and carbon contributing the distinctive colors.

This region was later inundated with water, and thick deposits of sediment buried the logs ever deeper. Eventually the land was transformed yet again as a geologic upheaval thrust the lake bottom up above sea level. This upthrust of the land cracked the logs into the segments we see today. Wind and water gradually eroded the landscape to create the Painted Desert, and the petrified logs were once again exposed on the surface of the land.

ESSENTIALS

GETTING THERE   The north entrance to Petrified Forest National Park is 25 miles east of Holbrook on I-40. The south entrance is 20 miles east of Holbrook on U.S. 180.

FEES   The entry fee is $10 per car. The park is open daily from 8am to 5pm (from 7am to 7pm in summer).

VISITOR INFORMATION   For further information on the Petrified Forest or the Painted Desert, contact **Petrified Forest National Park** (© **928/524-6228;** www.nps.gov/pefo). For information on Holbrook and the surrounding region, contact the **Holbrook Chamber of Commerce,** 100 E. Arizona St. (© **800/524-2459** or 928/524-6558; www.ci.holbrook.az.us).

EXPLORING A UNIQUE LANDSCAPE

Petrified Forest National Park has both a north and a south entrance. If you are coming from the west, it's better to start at the southern entrance and work your way north along the park's 27-mile scenic road, which has more than 20 overlooks. This way, you'll see the most impressive displays of petrified logs early in your visit and save the Painted Desert vistas for last. If you're coming from the east, start at the northern entrance and work your way south.

The **Rainbow Forest Museum** (© **928/524-6228**) just inside the south entrance to the park is the best place to begin your tour. Here you can learn about petrified wood and get oriented. Exhibits chronicle the area's geologic and human history. There are also displays on the reptiles and dinosaurs that once inhabited this region. The museum sells maps and books and also issues free backpacking permits. It's open daily from 8am to 5pm. Adjacent to the museum is a snack bar.

The **Giant Logs self-guided trail** starts behind the museum. The trail winds across a hillside strewn with 4- to 5-foot diameter logs that certainly live up to the name. Almost directly across the parking lot from the museum is the entrance to the **Long Logs** and **Agate House** areas. On the half-mile Long Logs trail, you can see more big trees, while at Agate House, a 1.5-mile round-trip hike will lead you to the ruins of a pueblo built from colorful petrified wood.

Heading north, you'll pass by the unusual formations known as **The Flattops.** These structures were caused by the erosion of softer mineral deposits from beneath a harder and more erosion-resistant layer of sandstone. The Flattops is one of the park's wilderness areas. The **Crystal Forest** is the next stop to the north, named for the beautiful amethyst and quartz crystals once found in the cracks of petrified logs. Concern over the removal of these crystals was what led to the protection of the petrified forest. A .75-mile loop trail winds past the logs that once held the crystals.

At the **Jasper Forest Overlook,** you can see logs that include petrified roots, and a little bit farther north, at the **Agate Bridge** stop, you can see a petrified log that forms a natural agate bridge. Continuing north, you'll reach **Blue Mesa,** where pieces of petrified wood form capstones over easily eroded clay soils. As wind and water wear away at the clay beneath a piece of stone, the balance of the stone becomes more and more precarious until it eventually comes toppling down. A 1-mile loop trail here leads into the park's badlands.

Erosion has played a major role in the formation of the Painted Desert, and to the north of Blue Mesa you'll see some of the most interesting erosional features of the area. It's quite evident why these hills of sandstone and clay are known as **The Teepees.** The layers of different color are due to manganese, iron, and other minerals in the soil.

By this point, you've probably seen as much petrified wood as you'd ever care to see, so be sure to stop at **Newspaper Rock,** where instead of staring at more ancient logs, you can see a dense concentration of petroglyphs left by generations of Native

Americans. At nearby **Puerco Pueblo,** the park's largest archaeological site, you can view the remains of homes built by the people who created the park's petroglyphs. This pueblo was probably built sometime around 1400. Don't miss the petroglyphs on its back side.

North of Puerco Pueblo, the road crosses I-40. From here to the Painted Desert Visitor Center, there are eight overlooks onto the southernmost edge of the **Painted Desert.** Named for the vivid colors of the soil and stone that cover the land here, the Painted Desert is a dreamscape of pastels washed across a barren expanse of eroded hills. The colors are created by minerals dissolved in sandstone and clay soils that were deposited during different geologic periods. There's a picnic area at Chinde Point overlook. At Kachina Point, you'll find the **Painted Desert Inn,** a historic building that was closed for renovation in 2005 but which may be open again to the public by the time you visit. From here, there's access to the park's other wilderness area. The inn, which was built in 1924 and expanded by the Civilian Conservation Corps, is noteworthy for both its architecture and the Fred Kabotie murals on the interior walls. Between Kachina Point and Tawa Point, you can do an easy 1-mile round-trip hike along the rim of the Painted Desert. An even more interesting route leads down into the Painted Desert from behind the Painted Desert Inn.

Just inside the northern entrance to the park is the **Painted Desert Visitor Center** (© 928/524-6228), open daily 8am to 5pm, where you can watch a short film that explains the process by which wood becomes fossilized. Adjacent to the visitor center are a cafeteria, a bookshop, and a gas station.

OTHER REASONS TO LINGER IN HOLBROOK

Although the Petrified Forest National Park is the main reason for visiting this area, you might want to stop by downtown Holbrook's **Old West Museum,** 100 E. Arizona St. (© 928/524-6558), which also houses the Holbrook Chamber of Commerce visitor center. This old and dusty museum has exhibits on local history, but is most interesting for its old jail cells. It's open Monday through Friday from 8am to 5pm and Saturday and Sunday from 8am to 4pm; admission is free. On weekday evenings in June and July, the Holbrook Chamber sponsors Native American dances on the lawn in front.

Three miles west of town is the **International Petrified Forest/Museum of the Americas/Dinosaur Park** (© 888/830-6682 or 928/524-9178), at Exit 292 off I-40. Although this place may seem at first like just another tourist trap, it actually contains the largest collection of pre-Columbian artifacts in the Southwest, with an emphasis on Mayan and Aztec objects, along with plenty of Ancestral Puebloan and Hohokam pieces. There's also a "rock yard" full of petrified wood, dinosaur fossils, geodes, and other interesting rocks, and a 3-mile drive takes you past Triassic dig sites and more petrified wood. Oh yes, and then there are the bison and the "sand boxes" where kids can dig for fossils and artifacts. The museum is open from 8am to 6pm in summer

---

Fun Fact **Rock Talk**

Gift shops throughout this region sell petrified wood in all sizes and colors, natural and polished. This petrified wood does not come from the national park, but is collected on private land in the area. No piece of petrified wood, no matter how small, may be removed from Petrified Forest National Park.

(9am–5pm the rest of the year); admission is $10 per car. There's also a warehouse-size rock shop.

If you're interested in petroglyphs, you may want to schedule a visit to the **Rock Art Ranch** ★ (© **928/288-3260** or 928/386-5047), southwest of Holbrook on part of the old Hashknife Ranch, which was the largest ranch in the country during the late 19th century. Within the bounds of this ranch, pecked into the rock walls of Chevelon Canyon, are hundreds of Ancestral Puebloan petroglyphs. The setting, a narrow canyon that is almost invisible until you are right beside it, is enchanting, making this the finest place in the state to view petroglyphs. Tours (reservations required) are available Monday through Saturday year-round (call to get rate information and directions to the ranch).

WHERE TO STAY

Holbrook, the town nearest to Petrified Forest National Park, offers lots of budget chain motels charging very reasonable rates.

Wigwam Motel *Finds*   If you're willing to sleep on a saggy mattress for the sake of reliving a bit of Route 66 history, don't miss this collection of concrete wigwams (tepees, actually). This unique motel was built in the 1940s, when unusual architecture was springing up all along famous Route 66. The motel has been owned by the same family since it was built and still has the original rustic furniture. Old cars are kept in the parking lot for an added dose of Route 66 character.

811 W. Hopi Dr., Holbrook, AZ 86025. © **928/524-3048.** Fax 928/524-9335. www.galerie-kokopelli.com/wigwam. 15 units. $42–$48 double. MC, V. Pets accepted. *In room:* A/C, TV.

WHERE TO DINE

While there are plenty of inexpensive restaurants in Holbrook, none is particularly memorable or recommendable. Your best bet is to drive over to Winslow to the Turquoise Room at La Posada hotel.

9 Canyon de Chelly National Monument ★★★

68 miles NW of Window Rock; 222 miles NE of Flagstaff; 110 miles SE of Navajo National Monument; 110 miles SE of Monument Valley Navajo Tribal Park

It's hard to imagine narrow canyons less than 1,000 feet deep being more spectacular than the Grand Canyon, but in some ways Canyon de Chelly National Monument is just that. Gaze down from the rim at an ancient Ancestral Puebloan cliff dwelling as the whinnying of horses and clanging of goat bells drift up from far below, and you'll be struck by the continuity of human existence. For nearly 5,000 years, people have called these canyons home, and today there are not only the summer homes of Navajo farmers and sheepherders but also more than 100 prehistoric dwelling sites.

Canyon de Chelly National Monument consists of two major canyons—Canyon de Chelly (which is pronounced "canyon duh shay" and is derived from the Navajo word *tséyi,* meaning "rock canyon") and Canyon del Muerto (Spanish for "Canyon of the Dead")—and several smaller canyons. The canyons extend for more than 100 miles through the rugged slickrock landscape of northeastern Arizona, draining the seasonal snowmelt runoff from the Chuska Mountains.

In summer, Canyon de Chelly's smooth sandstone walls of rich reds and yellows contrast sharply with the deep greens of corn, pastures, and cottonwoods on the canyon floor. Vast stone amphitheaters form the caves in which the Ancestral Puebloans built their homes, and as you watch shadows and light paint an ever-changing canyon panorama, it's easy to see why the Navajo consider this sacred ground. With mysteriously abandoned cliff dwellings and breathtaking natural beauty, Canyon de Chelly is certainly as worthy of a visit as the Grand Canyon.

ESSENTIALS

GETTING THERE   From Flagstaff, the easiest route to Canyon de Chelly is I-40 to U.S. 191 to Ganado. At Ganado, drive west on Ariz. 264 and pick up U.S. 191 north to Chinle. If you're coming down from Monument Valley or Navajo National Monument, Indian Route 59, which connects U.S. 160 and U.S. 191, is an excellent road with plenty of beautiful scenery.

FEES   Monument admission is free.

VISITOR INFORMATION   Before leaving home, you can contact **Canyon de Chelly National Monument** (© **928/674-5500;** www.nps.gov/cach) for information. The visitor center is open daily, May through September from 8am to 6pm (MST) and October through April from 8am to 5pm. The monument itself is open daily from sunrise to sunset.

SPECIAL EVENTS   The annual **Central Navajo Fair** is held in Chinle in August.

EXPLORING THE CANYON

Your first stop should be the **visitor center,** in front of which is an example of a traditional crib-style hogan, a hexagonal structure of logs and earth that Navajos use as both a home and a ceremonial center. Inside the visitor center, a small museum explores the history of Canyon de Chelly, and there's often a silversmith demonstrating Navajo jewelry-making techniques. Interpretive programs are offered at the monument Memorial Day to Labor Day. Check at the visitor center for daily activities, such as campfire programs and natural-history programs, that might be scheduled.

From the visitor center, most people tour the canyon by car. Very different views of the monument's system of canyons are provided by the 15-mile North Rim and 16-mile South Rim drives. The North Rim Drive overlooks Canyon del Muerto, while the South Rim Drive overlooks Canyon de Chelly. With stops, the drive along either rim road can easily take 2 to 3 hours. If you have time for only one, make it the South Rim Drive, which provides both a dramatic view of Spider Rock and the chance to hike down into the canyon on the only trail you can explore without hiring a guide. If, on the other hand, you're more interested in the history and prehistory of this area, opt for the North Rim Drive, which overlooks several historically significant sites within the canyon.

THE NORTH RIM DRIVE

The first stop on the North Rim is the **Ledge Ruin Overlook.** On the opposite wall, about 100 feet up from the canyon floor, you can see the Ledge Ruin. This site was occupied by the Ancestral Puebloans between A.D. 1050 and 1275. Nearby, at the unmarked Dekaa Kiva Viewpoint, you can see a lone kiva (circular ceremonial building). This structure was reached by means of toeholds cut into the soft sandstone cliff wall.

The second stop is the **Antelope House Overlook,** which is the all-around most interesting overlook in the monument. Not only do you get to hike ¼ mile over the rugged rim-rock landscape, but you get to view ruins and rock art and impressive cliff walls. The Antelope House ruin takes its name from the paintings of antelopes on a nearby cliff wall, believed to date back to the 1830s. Beneath the ruins of Antelope

---

Tips Taking Photos on the Reservations

Before taking a photograph of a Navajo, always ask permission. If it's granted, a tip of $1 or more is expected. Photography is not allowed at all in Hopi villages.

House, archaeologists have found the remains of an earlier pit house dating from A.D. 693. Although most of the Ancestral Puebloan cliff dwellings were abandoned sometime after a drought began in 1276, Antelope House had already been abandoned by 1260, possibly because of damage caused by flooding. Across the wash from Antelope House, an ancient tomb, known as the Tomb of the Weaver, was discovered by archaeologists in the 1920s. The tomb contained the well-preserved body of an old man wrapped in a blanket of golden eagle feathers and accompanied by cornmeal, shelled and husked corn, pine nuts, beans, salt, and thick skeins of cotton. Also visible from this overlook is Navajo Fortress, a red-sandstone butte that the Navajo once used as a refuge from attackers. A steep trail once lead to the top of Navajo Fortress, and by using log ladders that could be pulled up into the refuge, the Navajo were able to escape their attackers.

The third stop is **Mummy Cave Overlook,** named for two mummies found in burial urns below the ruins. Archaeological evidence indicates that this giant amphitheater consisting of two caves was occupied for 1,000 years, from A.D. 300 to 1300. In the two caves and on the shelf between are 80 rooms, including three kivas. The central structure between the two caves includes an interesting three-story building characteristic of the architecture in Mesa Verde in New Mexico. Archaeologists speculate that a group of Ancestral Puebloans migrated here from New Mexico. Much of the original plasterwork is still intact and indicates that the buildings were colorfully decorated.

The fourth and last stop on the North Rim is the **Massacre Cave Overlook,** which got its name after an 1805 Spanish military expedition killed more than 115 Navajo at this site. The Navajo at the time had been raiding Spanish settlements that were encroaching on their territory. Accounts of the battle at Massacre Cave differ. One version claims there were only women, children, and old men taking shelter in the cave, but the official Spanish records claim 90 warriors and 25 women and children were killed. Also visible from this overlook is Yucca Cave, which was occupied about 1,000 years ago.

THE SOUTH RIM DRIVE

The South Rim Drive climbs slowly but steadily, and at each stop you're a little bit higher above the canyon floor. Near the mouth of the canyon is the **Tunnel Overlook,** where a short narrow canyon feeds into Chinle Wash, which is formed by streams cutting through the canyons of the national monument. *Tsegi* is a Navajo word meaning "rock canyon," and at the nearby **Tsegi Overlook,** that's just what you'll see when you gaze down from the viewpoint.

The next stop is the **Junction Overlook,** so named because it overlooks the junction of Canyon del Muerto and Canyon de Chelly. Here you can see the Junction Ruin, which has 10 rooms and a kiva. Ancestral Puebloans occupied this ruin during the great pueblo period, which lasted from around 1100 until shortly before 1300. First Ruin, which is perched precariously on a long narrow ledge, is also visible. In this ruin are 22 rooms and two kivas. Good luck picking out the two canyons in this maze of curving cliff walls.

The third stop is **White House Overlook,** from which you can see the 80-room White House Ruins, which are among the largest ruins in the canyon. These buildings were inhabited between 1040 and 1275. From this overlook, you have your only opportunity to descend into Canyon de Chelly without a guide or ranger. The **White House Ruins Trail** ★★ descends 600 feet to the canyon floor, crosses Chinle Wash, and approaches the White House Ruins. The buildings of this ruin were constructed both on the canyon floor and 50 feet up the cliff wall in a small cave. Although you cannot enter the ruins, you can get close enough to get a good look. Do not wander off this trail, and please respect the privacy of those Navajo living here. The 2.5-mile round-trip hike takes about 2 hours. Be sure to carry water.

Notice the black streaks on the sandstone walls above the White House Ruins. These streaks, known as desert varnish, are formed by seeping water, which reacts with iron in the sandstone (iron is what gives the walls their reddish hue). To create the canyon's many petroglyphs, Ancestral Puebloan artists would chip away at the desert varnish. Later, the Navajo used paints to create pictographs of animals and historic events, such as the Spanish military expedition that killed 115 Navajo at Massacre Cave. Many of these petroglyphs and pictographs can be seen if you take one of the guided tours into the canyon.

The fifth stop is **Sliding House Overlook.** These ruins were built on a narrow shelf and appear to be sliding down into the canyon. Inhabited from about 900 until 1200, Sliding House contained between 30 and 50 rooms. This overlook is already more than 700 feet above the canyon floor, with sheer walls giving the narrow canyon a very foreboding appearance.

On the last access road to the canyon rim, you'll come to the **Face Rock Overlook,** which provides yet another dizzying glimpse of the ever-deepening canyon. Here you gaze 1,000 feet down to the bottom. However, it is the next stop—**Spider Rock Overlook**—that offers the monument's most spectacular view. This viewpoint overlooks the junction of Canyon de Chelly and Monument Canyon. The monolithic pinnacle known as Spider Rock rises 800 feet from the canyon floor, its two freestanding towers forming a natural monument. Across the canyon from Spider Rock stands the similarly striking **Speaking Rock,** which is connected to the far canyon wall.

OTHER WAYS TO SEE THE CANYON

Access to the floor of Canyon de Chelly is restricted; unless you're on the White House Ruins Trail (see "The South Rim Drive," above), you must be accompanied by an authorized guide in order to enter the canyon. **Navajo guides** usually charge $20 per hour with a 3-hour minimum and will lead you into the canyon on foot or in your own four-wheel-drive vehicle. **De Chelly Tours** (℗ **928/674-3772**; dechellytours.com) charges $20 per hour, with a 3-hour minimum, to go out in your four-wheel-drive vehicle; if it supplies the vehicle, the cost goes up to $125 for three people for 3 hours. Similar tours are offered by **Canyon de Chelly Tours** (℗ **928/674-5433** or 928/674-9988; www.canyondechellytours.com), which will take you into the canyon in a jeep or a Unimog truck (a powerful 4X4 off-road vehicle). Unimog tours are $50 to $53 for adults and $30 to $32 for children 12 and under. Tours depart from the Holiday Inn parking lot. Reservations are recommended. The monument visitor center also maintains a list of guides.

Another way to see Canyon de Chelly and Canyon del Muerto is on what locals call **shake-and-bake tours** ★, via six-wheel-drive truck. In summer, these excursions really live up to the name. (In winter, the truck is enclosed to keep out the elements.)

The trucks operate out of **Thunderbird Lodge** (© **800/679-2473** or 928/674-5841; www.tbirdlodge.com) and are equipped with seats in the bed. Tours make frequent stops for photographs and to visit ruins, Navajo farms, and rock art. Half-day trips cost around $40 per person ($31 for children 12 and under), while full-day tours cost around $65 for all ages. Full-day tours, offered in spring through fall, leave at 9am and return at 5pm.

If you'd rather use a more traditional means of transportation, you can go on a guided horseback ride. Stables offering horseback tours into the canyon include **Justin's Horse Rental** (© **928/380-4617**), which charges $15 per hour per person for a horse and $15 per hour per group for a guide, with a 2-hour minimum. However, I much prefer to leave the crowds behind and drive east along South Rim Drive to **Totsonii Ranch** ⋆ (© **928/755-6209;** www.totsoniiranch.com), which is 1¼ miles past where the pavement ends. Rides from here visit a more remote part of the canyon (including the Spider Rock area) and cost the same as at Justin's.

If you're physically fit and like hiking, consider hiring a guide to lead you down into the canyon. Hikes can start at the White House Ruin trail, near the Spider Rock overlook, or from near the Antelope House overlook. These latter starting points are trails that are not open to the public without a guide and should be your top choices. The hike from Antelope House gets my vote for best option for a hike. Guides can be hired at the monument visitor center.

SHOPPING

The **Thunderbird Lodge Gift Shop,** in Chinle (© **928/674-5841**), is well worth a stop while you're in the area. It has a huge collection of rugs, as well as good selections of pottery and plenty of souvenirs. In the canyon wherever visitors gather (at ruins and petroglyph sites), you're likely to encounter craftspeople selling jewelry and other types of handiwork. These craftspeople, most of whom live in the canyon, accept cash, personal checks, and traveler's checks and sometimes credit cards.

WHERE TO STAY & DINE

Holiday Inn–Canyon de Chelly ⋆⋆   Located between the town of Chinle and the national monument entrance, this modern hotel is on the site of the old Garcia Trading Post, which has been incorporated into the restaurant and gift-shop building (although the building no longer has any historic character). All guest rooms have patios or balconies, and most face the cottonwood-shaded pool courtyard. Because there are Canyon de Chelly truck tours that leave from the parking lot here and because the restaurant serves the best food in town, this should be your top choice for a room in Chinle.

Indian Rte. 7 (P.O. Box 1889), Chinle, AZ 86503. © **800/HOLIDAY** or 928/674-5000. Fax 928/674-8264. www.holiday-inn.com/chinle-garcia. 108 units. $79–$129 double. Children under 19 stay free in parent's room; children 12 and under eat for free. AE, DC, DISC, MC, V. **Amenities:** Restaurant (American/Navajo); outdoor pool; exercise room; concierge; room service; guest laundry. *In room:* A/C, TV, dataport, fridge, coffeemaker, hair dryer, iron, high-speed Internet access.

(*Tips*   **Forget About Wine with Dinner**

Alcohol is prohibited on both Navajo and Hopi reservations. Unfortunately, however, despite this prohibition, drunk drivers are a problem on the reservation, so stay alert.

Thunderbird Lodge   Built on the site of an early trading post right at the mouth of Canyon de Chelly, the Thunderbird Lodge is the closest hotel to the national monument. The red-adobe construction of the lodge itself is reminiscent of ancient pueblos, and the presence on the property of an old stone-walled trading post gives this place lots of character. Guest rooms have both ceiling fans and air-conditioning. The old trading post now serves as a cafeteria, but there is a gift shop with a rug room on-site.

P.O. Box 548, Chinle, AZ 86503. ⓒ 800/679-2473 or 928/674-5841. Fax 928/674-5844. www.tbirdlodge.com. 73 units. Apr–Oct $101–$106 double, $145 suite; Nov–Mar $65 double, $91 suite. Children 2 and under stay free in parent's room. AE, DC, DISC, MC, V. Pets accepted. **Amenities:** Restaurant (American/Navajo); tour desk. *In room:* A/C, TV, free local calls.

CAMPGROUNDS

Adjacent to the Thunderbird Lodge is the free **Cottonwood Campground,** which has around 100 sites but does not take reservations. The campground has water and restrooms in summer. In winter you must bring your own water, and only portable toilets are available. On South Rim Drive 10 miles east of the Canyon de Chelly visitor center is another option, the private **Spider Rock Campground** (ⓒ **877/910-CAMP** or 928/674-8261; http://home.earthlink.net/~spiderrock), which charges $10 to $15 per night. This campground also has a couple of hogans for rent for $25 to $35 per night. The next nearest campgrounds are at **Tsaile Lake** and **Wheatfields Lake,** both south of the town of Tsaile on Indian Route 12. Tsaile is at the east end of the North Rim Drive.

10 Navajo National Monument ⭐

110 miles NW of Canyon de Chelly; 140 miles NE of Flagstaff; 60 miles SW of Monument Valley; 90 miles E of Page

Navajo National Monument, located 30 miles west of Kayenta and 60 miles northeast of Tuba City, encompasses three of the largest and best-preserved Ancestral Puebloan cliff dwellings in the region—Betatakin, Keet Seel, and Inscription House. It's possible to visit both Betatakin and Keet Seel, but, due to its fragility, Inscription House is closed to the public. The name Navajo National Monument is a bit misleading. Although the Navajo do inhabit the area now, the cliff dwellings were built by Kayenta Ancestral Puebloans, who were the ancestral Hopi and Pueblo peoples. The Navajo did not arrive in this area until centuries after the cliff dwelling had been abandoned.

For reasons unknown, the well-constructed cliff dwellings here were abandoned around the middle of the 13th century. Tree rings suggest that a drought in the latter part of the 13th century prevented the Ancestral Puebloans from growing sufficient crops. In Tsegi Canyon, however, there's another theory for the abandonment. The canyon was usually flooded each year by spring and summer snowmelt, which made farming quite productive, but in the mid-1200s, weather patterns changed and streams began cutting deep into the soil, forming narrow little canyons called arroyos, which lowered the water table and made farming much more difficult.

ESSENTIALS

GETTING THERE   Navajo National Monument can be reached by taking U.S. 89 north to U.S. 160 to Ariz. 564 north.

FEES   Monument admission is free.

VISITOR INFORMATION   For information, contact **Navajo National Monument** (ⓒ **928/672-2700;** www.nps.gov/nava). The visitor center is open daily from 8am to 5pm (except New Year's Day, Thanksgiving, and Christmas). The monument is open daily from sunrise to sunset.

EXPLORING THE MONUMENT

A visit to Navajo National Monument is definitely not a point-and-shoot experience. You're going to have to expend some energy if you want to see what this monument is all about. The shortest distance you'll have to walk is 1 mile, which is the round-trip from the visitor center to the Betatakin overlook. However, if you want to actually get close to these ruins, you're looking at strenuous day or overnight hikes.

Your first stop should be the **visitor center,** which has informative displays on the Ancestral Puebloan and Navajo cultures, including numerous artifacts from Tsegi Canyon. You can also watch a couple of short films or a slide show.

The only one of the monument's three ruins that can be seen easily is **Betatakin** ⭐, which means "ledge house" in Navajo. Built in a huge amphitheater-like alcove in the canyon wall, Betatakin was occupied only from 1250 to 1300, and at its height of occupation may have housed 125 people. A 1-mile round-trip paved trail from the visitor center leads to overlooks of Betatakin. The strenuous 5-mile round-trip hike to Betatakin itself is led by a ranger, takes about 5 hours, and involves descending more than 700 feet to the floor of Tsegi Canyon and later returning to the rim. Between mid-May and mid-September, these guided hikes are offered twice a day and leave the visitor center at 8:30 and 11am (MST, not Navajo Reservation time). Other times of year, tours are offered sporadically, so call to check on possible dates. Reservations can be made a day in advance. All participants should carry 1 to 2 quarts of water. Because of the danger of falling rock at the ruin site, tours no longer go inside Betatakin. This is a fascinating hike, and because the number of hikers is limited, you won't feel like you're shoulder to shoulder with a herd of tourists.

Keet Seel ⭐, which means "broken pieces of pottery" in Navajo, has a much longer history than Betatakin, with occupation beginning as early as A.D. 950 and continuing until 1300. At one point, Keet Seel may have housed 150 people. The 17-mile round-trip hike is quite strenuous. During the summer, hikers usually stay overnight at a primitive campground near the ruins, but in the winter, the hike is done as a day hike. You must carry enough water for your trip—up to 2 gallons in summer— because none is available along the trail. These hikes are offered daily between mid-May and mid-September; other months they are offered sporadically. You can apply for a summer permit 5 months in advance.

WHERE TO STAY

There is no lodge at the national monument, but there are two free campgrounds that have a total of 47 campsites. One is open year-round, and one is open from April through September. The nearest reliable motels are 30 miles away in Kayenta. See the section on Monument Valley, below, for details.

11 Monument Valley Navajo Tribal Park ⭐⭐⭐

60 miles NE of Navajo National Monument; 110 miles NW of Canyon de Chelly; 200 miles NE of Flagstaff; 150 miles E of Page

In its role as sculptor, nature has, in the north central part of the Navajo Reservation, created a garden of monoliths and spires unequaled anywhere on earth. Whether you've ever been here or not, you've almost certainly seen Monument Valley before. This otherworldly landscape has been an object of fascination for years, and since Hollywood director John Ford first came here in the 1930s, it has served as backdrop for countless movies, TV shows, and commercials.

Located 30 miles north of Kayenta and straddling the Arizona–Utah state line (you actually go into Utah to get to the park entrance), Monument Valley is a vast flat plain punctuated by natural sandstone cathedrals. These huge monoliths rise up from the sagebrush with sheer walls that capture the light of the rising and setting sun and transform it into fiery hues. Evocative names reflect the shapes the sandstone has taken under the erosive forces of nature: The Mittens, Three Sisters, Camel Butte, Elephant Butte, the Thumb, and Totem Pole.

While it may at first seem as if this strange landscape is a barren wasteland, it is actually still home to a few hardy Navajo families. The Navajo have been living in the valley for generations, herding their sheep through the sagebrush scrublands, and some families continue to reside here today. In fact, human habitation in Monument Valley dates back hundreds of years. Within the park are more than 100 Ancestral Puebloan archaeological sites, ruins, and petroglyphs dating from before A.D. 1300.

ESSENTIALS

GETTING THERE   Monument Valley Navajo Tribal Park is 200 miles northeast of Flagstaff. Take U.S. 89 north to U.S. 160 to Kayenta, which is 23 miles south of Monument Valley and 29 miles east of Navajo National Monument. Then drive north on U.S. 163.

FEES   Admission to the park is $5 per person (free for children 9 and under). *Note:* Because this is a tribal park and not a federal park, neither the National Park Service's National Park Pass nor its Golden Eagle Pass is valid here.

VISITOR INFORMATION   For information, contact **Monument Valley Navajo Nation Park** (© 435/727-5870). May through September, the park is open daily from 7am to 7pm; between October and April, it's open daily from 8am to 5pm.

EXPLORING THE PARK

This is big country, and, like the Grand Canyon, is primarily a point-and-shoot experience for most visitors. Because this is reservation land and people still live in Monument Valley, most backcountry and off-road travel are prohibited unless you're with a licensed guide. So basically, with one exception, your options for seeing the park are limited. You can take a few pictures from the overlook at the visitor center, drive the park's Valley Drive (a scenic but very rough 17-mile dirt road), take a jeep or van tour, or go on a guided hike or horseback ride. At the visitor center, you'll find a small museum, a great gift shop, a restaurant with a knockout view, and a tour desk where you can learn about companies operating jeep and hiking excursions. Adjacent to the visitor center is a campground and ¼ mile away, there's a picnic area.

Although Valley Drive is best driven in a high-clearance vehicle, plenty of people drive the loop in rental cars and other standard passenger vehicles. Take it slow and you should do fine. However, if the first stretch of rocky, rutted road convinces you to change your mind about the drive, just return to the visitor center and book a jeep or van tour and let someone else pay the repair bills. Along the loop drive, you'll pass 11 very scenic viewpoints that provide ample opportunities for photographing the valley's many natural monuments. At many of these viewpoints, you'll also encounter Navajos selling jewelry and other crafts. At John Ford's Point, so named because it was a favorite shooting location for film director John Ford, you may even get the chance to photograph a Navajo on horseback posed in front of all that spectacular scenery. He'll expect a dollar.

My, what an inefficient way to fish.

Ring toss, good. Horseshoes, bad.

Faster! Faster! Faster!

We take care of the fiddly bits, from providing over 43,000 customer reviews of hotels, to helping you find our best fares, to giving you 24/7 customer service. So you can focus on the only thing that matters. Goofing off.

travelocity
You'll never roam alone.™

Tip: If you're trying to decide whether to take a tour, here's some little-publicized information that might help you with your decision. Most tours don't just drive the 17-mile loop; they go off into a part of the valley that is closed to anyone who is not on a tour. This part of the valley is, in my opinion, the most beautiful. You'll get close-up looks at several natural arches and stop at some beautiful petroglyphs. Before booking a tour, make sure that the tour will go to this "closed" section of the valley. There are always plenty of jeep tour companies waiting for business in the park's main parking lot. If you've managed to get a room at Goulding's Lodge, which is my favorite hotel in the area and should be your first choice, then your best bet is to go out with **Goulding's Tours** (© 435/727-3231; www.gouldings.com), which has its office right at the lodge (see "Where to Stay & Dine," below), just a few miles from the park entrance. Goulding's offers 3½-hour tours ($40 for adults, $24 for children under 8) and full-day tours ($70 for adults, $51 for children). **Sacred Monument Tours** (© 435/727-3218 or 928/380-4527; www.monumentvalley.net), which charges from $30 for a 2-hour jeep tour to $75 for a 4-hour tour, is another reliable company to try.

The traditional way to explore this quintessentially Wild West landscape, however, is from the back of a horse, à la John Wayne. I recommend going out with **Diné Trail Ride Tours** (© 435/419-0135), which starts its rides from John Ford's Point, about half way around Valley Drive. Trail rides range in price from $30 for a half-hour ride to $125 for an all-day ride. This company also offers overnight rides for $135 per person and has a hogan you can stay in for $25 per person per night ($50 with meals included). Alternatively, try **Sacred Monument Tours** (© 435/727-3218 or 928/380-4527; www.monumentvalley.net), which charges from $40 to $50 for a 1-hour horseback ride up to $250 to $400 for an all-day ride. Overnight rides are $150.

Because the jeep and van tours are such a big business here, there's a steady stream of the vehicles on Valley Drive throughout the day. One way to get away from the rumble of engines, is to go out on a guided hike. These are offered by **Sacred Monument Tours** (© 435/727-3218 or 928/380-4527; www.monumentvalley.net), which charges from $75 per person for a half-day hike. **Kéyah Hózhóní Tours** (© 928/309-7440; www.monumentvalley.com) also offers hiking tours and overnight camping trips. Keep in mind that summers can be very hot here.

The exception to the no-traveling-off-road rule is the 3.2-mile **Wildcat Trail** ★★, a loop trail that circles West Mitten Butte and provides the only opportunity to get close to this picturesque butte. As you circle the butte, you'll get all kinds of different perspectives, even one that completely eliminates the "thumb." At the visitor center, you can pick up a brochure that describes the different plants you'll see as you hike this rough, but relatively easy, trail. Because this is the park's only option for unguided hiking, it is a not-to-be-missed excursion and one of the most memorable hikes in the state. In summer, be sure to carry plenty of water.

Moments Monumental Sunsets

Be sure to save some film on your camera (or storage space in your digital camera) for sunset at Monument Valley. Sure these rocks are impressive at noon, but as the sun sets and the shadows lengthen, they are positively enchanting—one of the most spectacular sites in America.

ACTIVITIES OUTSIDE THE PARK

Before leaving the area, you might want to visit **Goulding's Museum and Trading Post,** at Goulding's Lodge (see "Where to Stay & Dine," below). This old trading post was the home of the Gouldings for many years and is set up as they had it back in the 1920s and 1930s. There are also displays about the many movies that have been shot here. The trading post hours vary with the seasons; admission is by donation.

Inside Kayenta's Burger King, which is next door to the Hampton Inn, there's an interesting exhibit on the Navajo code talkers of World War II. The code talkers were Navajo soldiers who used their own language to transmit military messages, primarily in the South Pacific.

WHERE TO STAY & DINE

In addition to the lodgings listed here, you'll find several budget motels north of Monument Valley in the towns of Mexican Hat and Bluff, both of which are in Utah. When it's time for a meal, try the View Restaurant, which is in the park's visitor center and more than lives up to its name. Alternatively, try the Stagecoach Dining Room at Gouldings. The Navajo steak, served atop fry bread is great! One other thoroughly Navajo experience is to grab a quick meal at one of the dirt-floored plywood shacks that line the entrance road to Monument Valley Navajo Tribal Park. At the **Ya At Eeh Café** (no phone), you can get a Navajo cheeseburger, which is served on fry bread. Accompany it with a cup of Navajo tea, which is made from a wild plant that grows in the area.

Best Western Wetherill Inn   Located in Kayenta a mile north of the junction of U.S. 160 and U.S. 163 and 20 miles south of Monument Valley, the Wetherill Inn offers neither the convenience of Goulding's Lodge nor the amenities of the nearby Holiday Inn or Hampton Inn. The rooms, however, are comfortable enough. A cafe next door serves Navajo and American food.

1000 Main St. (P.O. Box 175), Kayenta, AZ 86033. © **800/937-8376** or 928/697-3231. Fax 928/697-3233. www. bestwestern.com/wetherillinn. 54 units. May 1–Oct 15 $98–$118 double; Oct 16–Nov 15 and Apr $73–$80 double; Nov 16–Mar 31 $60–$65 double. Children 12 and under stay free in parent's room. Rates include continental breakfast. AE, DC, DISC, MC, V. **Amenities:** Indoor pool; tour desk. *In room:* A/C, TV, dataport, coffeemaker, hair dryer, iron, free local calls, high-speed Internet access.

Goulding's Lodge ⋆   This is the only lodge actually located in Monument Valley, and should be your first choice of hotel in the area. Just be sure to make your reservation well in advance. Goulding's offers superb views from the private balconies of its large guest rooms. The restaurant serves Navajo and American dishes, and its views are enough to make any meal an event. Unfortunately, although the setting is memorable, the service can be somewhat lacking. The lodge also has a museum and a video library that includes a few films that have been shot in Monument Valley.

P.O. Box 360001, Monument Valley, UT 84536. © **435/727-3231.** Fax 435/727-3344. www.gouldings.com. 62 units. Mar 15–Nov 15 $118–$170 double; Nov 16–Mar 14 $73–$83 double. Children 6 and under stay free in parent's room. AE, DC, DISC, MC, V. Pets accepted. **Amenities:** Restaurant (American/Navajo); indoor pool; exercise room; tour desk; coin-op laundry. *In room:* A/C, TV/VCR, dataport, fridge, coffeemaker, hair dryer, iron.

Hampton Inn–Navajo Nation   In the center of Kayenta, this is the newest lodging in the area and as such should be your second choice after Goulding's. The hotel is built in a modern Santa Fe style and has spacious, comfortable guest rooms. It's adjacent to the Navajo Cultural Center and a Burger King that has an interesting display on the Navajo code talkers of World War II.

U.S. 160 (P.O. Box 1217), Kayenta, AZ 86033. ✆ 800/HAMPTON or 928/697-3170. Fax 928/697-3189. www.hampton-inn.com or www.monumentvalleyonline.com. 73 units. $59–$129 double. Rates include continental breakfast. Children under 18 stay free in parent's room. AE, DC, DISC, MC, V. Pets accepted ($20 nonrefundable deposit). **Amenities:** Restaurant (American/Navajo); small outdoor pool; room service. *In room:* A/C, TV, dataport, coffeemaker, iron.

Holiday Inn–Kayenta   This Holiday Inn, right in the center of Kayenta, is very popular with tour groups and is almost always crowded. Although the grounds are dusty and a bit run-down, the rooms are spacious and clean. I like the poolside units best. Part of the hotel's dining room is designed to look like an Ancestral Puebloan ruin, and the menu offers both American and Navajo cuisine.

U.S. 160 and U.S. 163 (P.O. Box 307), Kayenta, AZ 86033. ✆ 800/HOLIDAY or 928/697-3221. Fax 928/697-3349. www.holiday-inn.com. 163 units. Apr–Oct $109–$139 double; Nov–Mar $49–$69 double. Children under 19 stay free in parent's room. AE, DC, DISC, MC, V. **Amenities:** Restaurant (American/Navajo); small outdoor pool; exercise room; room service; coin-op laundry. *In room:* A/C, TV, dataport, coffeemaker, iron.

CAMPGROUNDS

If you're headed to Monument Valley Navajo Tribal Park, you can camp in the park at the **Mitten View Campground** (✆ 435/727-5870), which has 99 sites and charges $10 per night from April to September ($5 per night the rest of the year, when there are no facilities or running water). Another option, just outside the park, is **Goulding's Campground** (✆ 435/727-3231; www.gouldings.com), which charges $18 to $32 per night. This campground is open year-round (limited services Nov to mid-Mar) and has an indoor pool, hot showers, a playground, and a coin-op laundry.

12 Lake Powell ★★ & Page

272 miles N of Phoenix; 130 miles E of Grand Canyon North Rim; 130 miles NE of Grand Canyon South Rim

Had the early Spanish explorers of Arizona suddenly come upon Lake Powell after traipsing for months across desolate desert, they would have either taken it for a mirage or fallen to their knees and rejoiced. Imagine the Grand Canyon filled with water, and you have a pretty good picture of Lake Powell. Surrounded by hundreds of miles of parched desert, this reservoir, created by the damming of the Colorado River at Glen Canyon, seems unreal when first glimpsed. Yet real it is, and it draws everyone in the region toward its promise of relief from the heat.

Construction of the Glen Canyon Dam came about despite the angry outcry of many who felt that this canyon was even more beautiful than the Grand Canyon and should be preserved in its natural state. Preservationists lost the battle, and construction of the dam began in 1960, with completion in 1963. It took another 17 years for Lake Powell to fill to capacity. Today, the lake is a watery powerboat playground, and houseboats and water-skiers cruise where birds and waterfalls once filled the canyon with their songs and sounds. These days most people seem to agree that Lake Powell is as amazing a sight as the Grand Canyon, and it draws almost as many visitors each year as its downriver neighbor. In the past few years, however, Lake Powell has lost some of its luster as a prolonged drought in the Southwest has caused the lake's water level to drop more than 130 feet. Although this has left a bathtub-ring effect on the shores of the lake, it has exposed wide expanses of beach in the Wahweap area.

While Lake Powell is something of a man-made wonder of the world, one of the natural wonders of the world—Rainbow Bridge—can also be found on the shores of the lake. Called *nonnozhoshi*, or "the rainbow turned to stone," by the Navajo, this is the largest natural bridge on earth and stretches 275 feet across a side canyon off Lake Powell.

The town of Page, originally a camp constructed to house the workers who built the dam, has many motels and restaurants and is the main base for many visitors who come to explore Lake Powell.

ESSENTIALS

GETTING THERE   Page is connected to Flagstaff by U.S. 89. Ariz. 98 leads southeast onto the Navajo Indian Reservation and connects with U.S. 160 to Kayenta and Four Corners. The Page Airport is served by **Great Lakes Airlines** (ⓒ **800/554-5111;** www.greatlakesav.com), which flies from Phoenix. Round-trip airfare is around $120.

FEES   Admission to Glen Canyon National Recreation Area is $10 per car (good for 1 week). There is also a $16-per-week boat fee if you bring your own boat.

VISITOR INFORMATION   For further information on the Lake Powell area, contact the **Glen Canyon National Recreation Area** (ⓒ **928/608-6404;** www.nps.gov/glca); the **Page/Lake Powell Chamber of Commerce & Visitors Bureau,** 644 N. Navajo Dr., Page (ⓒ **888/261-7243** or 928/645-2741; www.pagelakepowellchamber.org); or the **John Wesley Powell Memorial Museum,** 6 N. Lake Powell Blvd., Page (ⓒ **888/597-6873** or 928/645-9496; www.powellmuseum.org). You can also go to www.powellguide.com.

GETTING AROUND   Rental cars are available at the Page Airport from **Avis** (ⓒ **800/230-4898** or 928/645-2024).

GLEN CANYON NATIONAL RECREATION AREA

Until the flooding of Glen Canyon formed Lake Powell, this area was one of the most remote regions in the contiguous 48 states. However, since the construction of Glen Canyon Dam at a spot where the Colorado River was less than a third of a mile wide, this remote and rugged landscape has become one of the country's most popular national recreation areas. Today, the lake and much of the surrounding land is designated the Glen Canyon National Recreation Area and attracts around two million visitors each year. The otherworldly setting amid the slickrock canyons of northern Arizona and southern Utah is a tapestry of colors, the blues and greens of the lake contrasting with the reds and oranges of the surrounding sandstone cliffs. This interplay of colors and vast desert landscapes easily makes Lake Powell the most beautiful of Arizona's many reservoirs.

Built to provide water for the desert communities of the Southwest and West, **Glen Canyon Dam** stands 710 feet above the bedrock and contains almost 5 million cubic yards of concrete. The dam also provides hydroelectric power, and deep within its massive wall of concrete are huge power turbines. However, most visitors are more interested in water-skiing and powerboating than they are in drinking water and power production, but since there would be no lake without the dam, any visit to this area ought to start at the **Carl Hayden Visitor Center** (ⓒ **928/608-6404**), which is located beside the dam on U.S. 89 just north of Page. Here you can tour the dam and learn about its construction. Visitor center hours are daily from 8am to 6pm between Memorial Day weekend and Labor Day weekend, and from 8am to 5pm other months.

More than 500 feet deep in some places, and bounded by nearly 2,000 miles of shoreline, **Lake Powell** is a maze of convoluted canyons where rock walls often rise hundreds of feet straight out of the water. In places, the long, winding canyons are so narrow there isn't even room to turn a motorboat around. The only way to truly appreciate this lake is from a boat, whether a houseboat, a runabout, or a sea kayak. Water-skiing, riding personal watercraft, and fishing have long been the most popular on-water activities, and consequently, you'll be hard-pressed to find a quiet corner of the lake if you happen to be a solitude-seeking sea kayaker. However, with so many miles of shoreline, you're bound to find someplace to get away from it all. Your best bet for solitude is to head up-lake from Wahweap Marina. This will get you away from the crowds and into some of the narrower reaches of the lake.

In addition to the Carl Hayden Visitor Center mentioned above, there's the **Bullfrog Visitor Center,** in Bullfrog, Utah (© **435/684-7400**). It's open April through October, daily from 8am to 5pm (closed Nov–Feb; open intermittently in Mar).

BOAT & AIR TOURS

There are few roads penetrating the Glen Canyon National Recreation Area, so the best way to appreciate this rugged region is by boat. If you don't have your own boat, you can at least see a small part of the lake on a boat tour. A variety of tours depart from **Wahweap Marina** (© **888/486-4665** or 928/645-2433; www.lakepowell.com). The paddle wheeler *Canyon King* does a 1-hour tour ($13 for adults, $10 for children) that unfortunately doesn't really show you much more of the lake than you can see from shore. The *Canyon King* also offers sunset dinner cruises ($61). A better choice for those with limited time or finances would be the **Antelope Canyon Cruise** ($29 for adults, $22 for children). To see more of the lake, opt for the full-day tour to Rainbow Bridge (see below for details).

The Glen Canyon National Recreation Area covers an immense area, much of it only partially accessible by boat. If you'd like to see more of the area than is visible from car or boat, consider taking an air tour with **Westwind Scenic Air Tours** (© **800/245-8668** or 928/645-2494; www.westwindairtours.com), which offers several tours of northern Arizona and southern Utah, including flights over Rainbow Bridge and Monument Valley. Sample rates are $103 for a 40-minute flight over Rainbow Bridge and $178 to $220 for a 90-minute flight over Monument Valley (the more expensive tour actually lands at Monument Valley and includes a 1½-hour jeep tour).

RAINBOW BRIDGE NATIONAL MONUMENT

Roughly 40 miles up Lake Powell from Wahweap Marina and Glen Canyon Dam, in a narrow side canyon of the lake, rises **Rainbow Bridge** ★★★, the world's largest natural bridge and one of the most spectacular sights in the Southwest. Preserved in Rainbow Bridge National Monument, this natural arch of sandstone stands 290 feet high and spans 275 feet. Carved by wind and water over the ages, Rainbow Bridge is an awesome reminder of the powers of erosion that have sculpted this entire region into the spectacle it is today.

Rainbow Bridge is accessible only by boat or on foot (a hike of 13 miles minimum); going by boat is by far the more popular method. **Lake Powell Resorts and Marinas** (© **888/486-4665** or 928/645-2433; www.lakepowell.com) offers full-day tours ($100 for adults, $85 for children) that not only get you to Rainbow Bridge in comfort, but also cruise through some of the most spectacular scenery on earth. Tours include a box lunch and a bit more exploring after visiting Rainbow Bridge. Currently, because the lake's water level is so low from years of drought, the boat must stop about 1¼ miles from Rainbow Bridge, so if you aren't able to walk this distance, you won't even be able to see the sandstone arch. In January 2005, winter storms damaged the trail from the lake to Rainbow Bridge, but it was expected that repairs would be made. Call to be sure.

Rainbow Bridge National Monument (© **928/608-6404;** www.nps.gov/rabr) is administered by Glen Canyon National Recreation Area. For information on hiking to Rainbow Bridge, contact the **Navajo Parks and Recreation Department,** P.O. Box 2520, Window Rock, AZ 86515 (© **928/871-6647;** www.navajonationparks.org). The hike into Rainbow Bridge is about a 25-mile round-trip hike, and a Navajo Nation permit is required to make the backpacking trip. Permits are available through the Navajo Parks and Recreation Department and at the **Cameron Visitor Center** (© **928/679-2303**), in the community of Cameron near the turnoff for the Grand Canyon and at the **LeChee Office** (© **928/698-2800**), 7 miles south of Page on Navajo Route 20.

ANTELOPE CANYON

If you've spent any time in Arizona, chances are you've noticed photos of a narrow sandstone canyon only a few feet wide. The walls of the canyon seem to glow with an inner light, and beams of sunlight slice the darkness of the deep slot canyon. Sound familiar? If you've seen such a photo, you were probably looking at Antelope Canyon (sometimes called Corkscrew Canyon). Located 2½ miles outside Page off Ariz. 98 (at milepost 299), this photogenic canyon comprises the **Antelope Canyon Navajo Tribal Park** ✦✦✦ (© **928/698-2808**), which is on the Navajo Indian Reservation and is divided into upper and lower canyons. The entry fee is $6 for adults, free for children 7 and under. From May through October, the upper canyon section of the park is open daily from 8am to 5pm and the lower canyon section is open 8am to 4pm; from November through April, hours vary and closures are common.

There are currently two options for visiting Antelope Canyon. The most convenient and reliable way is to take a 1½-hour tour with **Antelope Canyon Adventures** (© **866/645-5501** or 928/645-5501; www.jeeptour.com), or **Antelope Canyon Tours** (© **866/645-9102** or 928/645-9102; www.antelopecanyon.com), both of which charge $20 (plus Navajo permit fee) per adult for a basic tour. Photographic tours cost between $35 and $62. If you don't want to deal with crowds of tourists ogling the rocks and snapping pictures with their point-and-shoots, I recommend heading out with **Overland Canyon Tours** (© **928/608-4072;** www.overlandcanyon tours.com) to nearby Canyon X, which is much less visited than Antelope Canyon and is a good choice for serious photographers who want to avoid the crowds.

Alternatively, at both the upper and lower canyons, you'll find Navajo guides collecting park entry fees and fees for guide services. These guides charge $15 ($6 for children ages 6–12 at the lower section of the canyon). At Upper Antelope Canyon, the guide will drive you from the highway to the canyon and then pick you up again after your hike. At Lower Antelope Canyon, the guide will probably just show you the entrance to the slot canyon. You'll get more out of your experience if you go on one of the guided tours mentioned above, but you'll save a little money by visiting the canyon on your own. For more information, contact **Antelope Canyon Navajo Tours** (© **928/698-3384;** www.navajotours.com).

Just remember that if there is even the slightest chance of rain anywhere in the region, you should not venture into this canyon, which is subject to flash floods. In the past, people who have ignored bad weather predictions have been killed by such floods.

WATERSPORTS

While simply exploring the lake's maze of canyons on a narrated tour is satisfying enough for many visitors, the most popular activities are still houseboating, water-skiing, riding personal watercraft, and fishing. Five marinas (only Wahweap is in Arizona) help boaters explore the lake. At the **Wahweap Marina** (✆ **888/486-4665** or 928/645-2433; www.lakepowell.com), you can rent various types of boats, along with personal watercraft and water skis. Rates in summer range from about $138 to $611 per day depending on the type of boat. Weekly rates are also available. For information on renting houseboats, see "Where to Stay," below.

If roaring engines aren't your speed, you might want to consider exploring Lake Powell by sea kayak. While afternoon winds can sometimes make paddling difficult, mornings are often quiet. With a narrow sea kayak, you can even explore canyons too small for powerboats. Rentals are available at **Twin Finn Diving/Lake Powell Kayak Tours,** 811 Vista Ave. (✆ **928/645-3114**). Sea kayaks rent for $45 to $55 per day, and sit-on-top kayaks for $35 to $45. All-day tours are $95 to $105. Multi-day kayak tours are operated by **Hidden Canyon Kayak** (✆ **800/343-3121** or 928/645-8866; www.diamondriver.com/kayak), which charges $600 to $850 for 4- to 6-day trips.

While most of Glen Canyon National Recreation Area consists of the impounded waters of Lake Powell, the recreation area also contains a short stretch of the Colorado River that still flows swift and free. If you'd like to see this stretch of river, try a float trip from Glen Canyon Dam to Lees Ferry, operated by **Wilderness River Adventures** (✆ **800/528-6154** or 928/645-3279; www.lakepowell.com), between March and October. Half-day trips cost $62 for adults and $58 for children 12 and under. Try to reserve at least 2 weeks in advance.

If you have a boat (your own or a rental), avail yourself of some excellent year-round fishing. Smallmouth, largemouth, and striped bass, as well as walleye, catfish, crappie, and carp, are all plentiful. Because the lake lies within both Arizona and Utah, you'll need to know which state's waters you're fishing in whenever you cast your line out, and you'll need the appropriate license. (Be sure to pick up a copy of the Arizona and Utah state fishing regulations, or ask about applicable regulations at any of the marinas.) You can arrange licenses to fish the entire lake at **Lake Powell Resorts and Marinas** (✆ **928/645-2433**), which also sells bait and tackle and can provide you with advice on fishing this massive reservoir. Other marinas on the lake also sell licenses, bait, and tackle. The best season is March through November, but walleye are most often caught during the cooler months. If you'd rather try your hand at catching enormous rainbow trout, try downstream of the Glen Canyon Dam, where cold waters provide ideal conditions for trophy trout. Unfortunately, there isn't much access to this stretch of river. You'll need a trout stamp to fish for the rainbows. If you want a guide to take you where the fish are biting, contact Bill McBurney at **Ambassador Guide Service** (© **800/256-7596;** www.ambassadorguides.com).

If you're just looking for a good place for a swim near Lake Powell Resort, take the Coves Loop just west of the marina. Of the three coves, the third one, which has a sandy beach, is the best. The Chains area, another good place to jump off the rocks and otherwise lounge by the lake, is outside Page down a rough dirt road just before you reach Glen Canyon Dam. The view underwater at Lake Powell is as scenic as the view above it; to explore the underwater regions of the canyon, contact **Twin Finn Diving Center,** 811 Vista Ave. (© **928/645-3114;** www.twinfinn.com), which charges $45 a day for scuba gear and also rents snorkeling equipment.

OTHER OUTDOOR PURSUITS

If you're looking for a quick, easy hike with great views, head north on North Navajo Drive from downtown Page. At the end of this street is the main trail head for Page's **Rimview Trail.** This trail runs along the edge of Manson Mesa, upon which Page is built, and has views of Lake Powell and the entire red-rock country. The entire loop trail is 8 miles long, but if you want to do a shorter hike, I recommend the stretch of trail heading east (clockwise) from the trail head. If you happen to have your mountain bike with you, the trail is a great ride.

At Lees Ferry, a 39-mile drive from Page at the southern tip of the national recreation area, you'll find three short trails (Cathedral Wash, River, and Spencer). The 2-mile **Cathedral Wash Trail** is the most interesting of the three day hikes and follows a dry wash through a narrow canyon with unusual rock formations. The trail head is at the second turnout after turning off U.S. 89A. Be aware that this wash is subject to flash floods. The **Spencer Trail,** which begins along the River Trail, leads up to the top of a 1,500-foot cliff. Lees Ferry is also the southern trail head for famed **Paria Canyon** ★, a favorite of canyoneering backpackers. This trail is 45 miles long and follows the meandering route of a narrow slot canyon for much of its length. Most hikers start from the northern trail head, which is in Utah on U.S. 89. For more information on hiking in Paria Canyon, contact the **Arizona Strip Interpretive Association/ Interagency Visitor Center,** 345 E. Riverside Dr., St. George, UT 84770 (© **435/ 688-3246;** www.az.blm.gov/asfo/asia.htm).

The 27-hole **Lake Powell National Golf Course** ★, 400 Clubhouse Dr. (© **928/ 645-2023;** www.golflakepowell.com), is one of the most spectacular in the state. The fairways wrap around the base of the red-sandstone bluff atop which sits the town of Page. In places, eroded sandstone walls come right down to the greens. The views stretch on forever. Greens fees are $49.

OTHER AREA ATTRACTIONS

You can learn about Navajo culture at **Navajo Village Heritage Center** (© **928/660- 0304;** www.navajo-village.com), a museum and living-history center on the south side of Page off Haul Road. Programs here include demonstrations by weavers, silversmiths, and other artisans. Prices range from $35 for a 2-hour tour to $50 for a 3-hour tour (family tickets available). Both tours include dinner and traditional dances. It is sometimes possible to visit during the day and see Navajo artisans at work. Although this is definitely a tourist attraction, you will come away with a better sense of Navajo culture. Reservations are required and can be made at the Lake Powell Chamber of Commerce office (see earlier) and the John Wesley Powell Memorial Museum (see below).

John Wesley Powell Memorial Museum   In 1869, one-armed Civil War veteran John Wesley Powell, and a small band of men spent more than 3 months fighting the rapids of the Green and Colorado rivers to become the first people to travel the length of the Grand Canyon. It is for this intrepid—some said crazy—adventurer that Lake Powell is named and to whom this small museum is dedicated. Besides documenting the Powell expedition with photographs, etchings, artifacts, and dioramas, the museum displays Native American artifacts ranging from Ancestral Puebloan pottery to contemporary Navajo and Hopi crafts. The museum also acts as an information center for Page, Lake Powell, and the surrounding region.

6 N. Lake Powell Blvd. © 888/597-6873 or 928/645-9496. www.powellmuseum.org. Admission $3 adults, $2 seniors, $1 children 5–12, free for children 4 and under. Feb–Nov Mon–Fri 9am–5pm (but call to be sure). Closed Dec–Jan.

WHERE TO STAY
HOUSEBOATS
Lake Powell Resorts and Marinas ★★ Kids   Although there are plenty of hotels and motels in and near Page, the most popular accommodations here are not waterfront hotel rooms but houseboats, which function as floating vacation homes. With a houseboat, which is as easy to operate as a car, you can explore Lake Powell's beautiful red-rock country, far from any roads. No special license or prior experience is necessary, and plenty of hands-on instruction is given before you leave the marina. Because Lake Powell houseboating is extremely popular with visitors from all over the world, it's important to make reservations as far in advance as possible, especially if you plan to visit in summer.

Houseboats range in size from 44 to 75 feet, sleep anywhere from 8 to 12 people, and come complete with shower and fully equipped kitchen. The only things you really need to bring are bedding and towels. If you're coming in the summer, splurge on a boat with some sort of cooling system.

100 Lakeshore Dr. (P.O. Box 1597), Page, AZ 86040. © 888/486-4665 or 928/645-2433. Fax 928/645-1031. www.lakepowell.com. May to mid-Oct $1,666–$8,897 per week; lower rates mid-Oct to Apr. 3-, 4-, and 5-night rates also available. AE, DISC, MC, V. *In room:* Kitchen, fridge, no phone.

HOTELS & MOTELS
Best Western Arizonainn   Perched right at the edge of the mesa on which Page is built, this modern motel has a fine view across miles of desert, as do half of the guest rooms. The hotel's pool has a 100-mile view.

716 Rimview Dr. (P.O. Box 250), Page, AZ 86040. © 800/826-2718 or 928/645-2466. Fax 928/645-2053. www. bestwestern.com. 103 units. Apr–June $49–$89 double; July to mid-Oct $79–$109 double; mid-Oct to Mar $44–$54 double. Rates include continental breakfast. AE, DC, DISC, MC, V. Pets accepted ($10 fee). **Amenities:** Small outdoor pool; exercise room; Jacuzzi; coin-op laundry. *In room:* A/C, TV, dataport, coffeemaker, hair dryer, iron.

Courtyard by Marriott ★   Located at the foot of the mesa on which Page is built and adjacent to the Lake Powell National Golf Course, this is the top in-town choice. It's also the closest you'll come to a golf resort in this corner of the state. Although you'll pay a premium for views of the golf course or lake, it's a worthwhile investment. Guest rooms are larger than those at most area lodgings. Moderately priced meals are served in a casual restaurant that has a terrace overlooking the distant lake. The 18-hole golf course has great views of the surrounding landscape.

600 Clubhouse Dr. (P.O. Box 4150), Page, AZ 86040. ℂ **800/851-3855** or 928/645-5000. Fax 928/645-5004. www.courtyard.com. 153 units. $59–$129 double. Children under 18 stay free in parent's room. AE, DC, DISC, MC, V. **Amenities:** Restaurant (American); lounge; outdoor pool; 18-hole golf course; exercise room; Jacuzzi; concierge; room service; coin-op laundry. In room: A/C, TV, dataport, coffeemaker, hair dryer, iron.

Lake Powell Resort ⭐ Simply because it is right on the lake, this hotel at the sprawling Wahweap Marina 5 miles north of Page should be your first lodging choice in the area. As the biggest and busiest hotel in the area, the Lake Powell Resort features many of the amenities and activities of a resort, but it is often overwhelmed by busloads of tour groups. Consequently, don't expect very good service. Guest rooms are arranged in several long two-story wings, and every unit has either a balcony or a patio. Half of the rooms have lake views; those in the west wing have the better vantage point, as the east wing overlooks a coal-fired power plant. The Rainbow Room (see "Where to Dine," below) offers fine dining with a sweeping panorama of the lake and desert, but be prepared for a long wait for a table. Because of all the tour groups that stay here, getting a reservation can be difficult.

100 Lakeshore Dr. (P.O. Box 1597), Page, AZ 86040. ℂ **888/486-4665** or 928/645-2433. Fax 928/645-1031. www.lakepowell.com. 350 units. Apr–Oct $129–$149 double, $189–$199 suite; Nov–Mar $89–$99 double, $189 suite. Children under 18 stay free in parent's room. AE, DISC, MC, V. Pets accepted. **Amenities:** 2 restaurants (American/Southwestern, pizza); snack bar; lounge; 2 outdoor pools; Jacuzzi; watersports; boat rentals; tour desk; room service; coin-op laundry. In room: A/C, TV, fridge, coffeemaker, hair dryer.

CAMPGROUNDS

There are campgrounds at **Wahweap** (ℂ **928/645-2433**) and **Lees Ferry** (ℂ **928/355-2319**) in Arizona, and at Bullfrog, Hite, and Halls Crossing in Utah. Some scrubby trees provide a bit of shade at the Wahweap site, but the wind and sun make this a rather bleak spot in summer. Nevertheless, because of the lake's popularity, these campgrounds stay packed for much of the year. Wahweap charges $18 per night and Lees Ferry charges $10; reservations are not accepted.

WHERE TO DINE

The Dam Bar & Grille AMERICAN   This theme restaurant is a warehouse-size space designed to conjure up images of the Glen Canyon Dam. Big industrial doors are the first hint this is more than your usual small-town dining establishment. Inside, cement walls, hard hats, and a big transformer that sends out bolts of neon "electricity" will put you in a dam good mood. Sandwiches, pastas, and steaks dominate the menu, but the rotisserie chicken is my favorite dish. The lounge area is a popular local hangout, and next door is the affiliated Gunsmoke Saloon, a combination barbecue joint and nightclub.

644 N. Navajo Dr. ℂ **928/645-2161.** www.damplaza.com. Reservations recommended in summer. Main courses $7–$22. MC, V. June–Oct Mon–Sat 11:30am–10pm, Sun 4–10pm; Nov–May Sun–Thurs 4–9pm, Fri–Sat 4–10pm.

Rainbow Room AMERICAN/SOUTHWESTERN   With sweeping vistas of Lake Powell out the walls of glass, the Rainbow Room is both Page's top restaurant and its most touristy. As such, be prepared for a wait; this place regularly feeds busloads of tourists. The menu is short (due to the necessity of feeding crowds of people) but usually includes a few dishes with southwestern flavor.

At Lake Powell Resort, Lakeshore Dr. ℂ **928/645-1162.** Reservations recommended. Main courses $6–$10 lunch, $15–$19 dinner. AE, DC, DISC, MC, V. Daily 6am–2:30pm and 5–9pm.

13 Farmington & Aztec: New Mexico's Four Corners Gateways

Farmington has historic and outdoor finds that can keep you occupied for at least a day or two. A town of 36,500 residents, it sits at the junction of the San Juan, Animas, and La Plata rivers. Adorned with arched globe willow trees, it's a lush place by New Mexico standards. A system of five parks along the San Juan River and its tributaries is its pride and joy. What's most notable for me, however, is the quaint downtown area, where century-old buildings still house thriving businesses and some trading posts with great prices. It's also an industrial center (coal, oil, natural gas, and hydroelectricity) and a shopping center for people within a 100-mile radius.

For visitors, Farmington is a takeoff point for explorations of the Navajo Reservation and Chaco Culture National Historical Park. For outdoor lovers, it's the spot to head to the Bisti/De-Na-Zin Wilderness; world-class fly-fishing on the San Juan River; lovely scenery at the Angel Peak Recreation Area; and even a trip up to Durango to enjoy some rafting, kayaking, skiing, and mountain biking. The nearby towns of Aztec and Bloomfield offer a variety of attractions as well.

ESSENTIALS

GETTING THERE   From Albuquerque, take US 550 (through Cuba) from the I-25 Bernalillo exit, then head west on US 64 at Bloomfield (45 min.). From Gallup, take US 491 north to Shiprock, and then head east on US 64 (2¼ hr.). From Taos, follow US 64 all the way (4½ hr.). From Durango, Colorado, take US 500 south (1 hr.).

All commercial flights arrive at busy **Four Corners Regional Airport** on West Navajo Drive (© 505/599-1395). The principal carriers are **United Express** (© 800/241-6522), with flights from Denver and other Colorado cities; and **America West Airlines** (© 800/235-9292), with flights from Phoenix and other Arizona cities.

Car-rental agencies at Four Corners Regional Airport include **Avis** (© 800/331-1212 or 505/327-9864), **Budget** (© 505/327-7304), and **Hertz** (© 800/654-3131 or 505/327-6093).

VISITOR INFORMATION   The **Farmington Convention and Visitors Bureau,** 3041 E. Main St. (© 800/448-1240 or 505/326-7602; www.farmingtonnm.org), is the clearinghouse for tourist information for the Four Corners region. For more information, contact the **Farmington Chamber of Commerce,** 105 N. Orchard Ave. (© 505/325-0279; www.gofarmington.com).

SEEING THE SIGHTS IN THE AREA
IN FARMINGTON

Farmington Museum and Gateway Center   Small-town museums can be completely precious, and this one and its neighbor in Aztec (see below) typify a tiny part of the world, and yet the truths they reveal span continents. Here you get to see the everyday struggle of a people to support themselves within a fairly inhospitable part of the world, spanning boom and bust years of agriculture, oil and gas production, and tourism. Now located in the slick new Gateway Visitor Center, exhibits vary, utilizing over 7,000 objects. You may walk through displays of a 1930s trading post, with an old enameled scale, cloth bolts, and even a vintage box of Cracker Jacks. Next, you may get a look at the oil and gas history of the area, including a photo of the lethally named Rattlesnake Refinery, a desolate place, in operation in 1925. Excellent changing exhibits rotate through as well. While at the Gateway Center, ask about other local exhibits in other parts of the city, such as the Harvest Grove Farm and Orchards, the

E3 Children's Museum and Science Center, and the Riverside Nature Center, all located at Animas Park. A gift shop sells fun local art and some nice New Mexico–made treats.

3041 E. Main St. ⓒ **505/599-1174.** Fax 505/326-7572. www.farmingtonmuseum.org. Free admission. Mon–Sat 8am–5pm.

IN NEARBY AZTEC

VISITOR INFORMATION The **Aztec Chamber of Commerce,** 110 N. Ash St. (ⓒ **505/334-9551;** www.aztecchamber.com), is a friendly place with a wealth of information about the area.

Aztec Museum and Pioneer Village *Kids* A real treat for kids, this museum and village transport visitors back a full century to a place populated by strangely ubiquitous mannequins. The museum is crammed with memorabilia, but the outer exhibit of replicas and real buildings, with all the trimmings, is what will hold interest. You'll walk through the actual 1912 Aztec jail—nowhere you'd want to live—into the sheriff's office, where a stuffed Andy of Mayberry look-alike is strangely lethargic. The blacksmith shop has an anvil and lots of dusty, uncomfortable-looking saddles, even some oddly shaped burro shoes. The Citizens Bank has a lovely oak cage and counter, and it's run by attentive mannequin women. You'll see an authentic 1906 church and a schoolhouse where mannequins Dick and Jane lead a possibly heated discussion.

125 N. Main Ave., Aztec. ⓒ **505/334-9829.** www.aztecnm.com/museum/museum_index.htm. Admission $3 adults, $1 children 11–17, free for children 10 and under. Summer Mon–Sat 9am–5pm; winter Mon–Sat 10am–4pm.

IN NEARBY BLOOMFIELD

Salmon Ruins ★ *Kids* What really marks the 150 rooms of these ruins 11 miles west of Farmington near Bloomfield is their setting on a hillside, surrounded by lush San Juan River bosque. You'll begin in the museum, though, where a number of informative displays range from ancestral Puebloan vessels to wild plants. Like the ruins at Aztec, two strong architectural influences are visible here. First the Chacoan, who built the village around the 11th century, with walls of an intricate rubble-filled core with sandstone veneer. The more simple Mesa Verde masonry was added in the 13th century. A trail guide will lead you to each site. There is a marvelous elevated ceremonial chamber, or "tower kiva," and a Great Kiva, now a low-lying ruin, but with some engaging remains, such as the central fire pit and an antechamber possibly used by leaders for storage of ceremonial goods. There is also a photograph exhibit of Navajo pueblitos and rock art.

One of the most recently excavated ruins in the West, the site is only 30% excavated, by design. It's being saved for future generations of archaeologists, who, it's assumed, will be able to apply advanced research techniques. For now, the archaeological research center studies regional sites earmarked for natural-resource exploitation.

Built in 1990, **Heritage Park,** on an adjoining plot of land, comprises a series of reconstructed ancient and historic dwellings representing the area's cultures, from a paleoarchaic sand-dune site to an Anasazi pit house, from Apache wickiups and tepees to Navajo hogans, and an original pioneer homestead. Visitors are encouraged to enter the re-creations.

In the visitor center, you'll find a gift shop and a scholarly research library.

6131 US 64 (P.O. Box 125), Bloomfield, NM 87413. ⓒ **505/632-2013.** Fax 505/632-8633. www.salmonruins.com. Admission $3 adults, $1 children 6–16, $2 seniors, free for children under 6. Summer Mon–Fri 8am–5pm, Sat–Sun 9am–5 pm; winter Mon–Fri 8am–5pm, Sat 9am–5pm, and Sun noon–5pm.

AZTEC RUINS NATIONAL MONUMENT ★

What's most striking about these ruins is the central kiva, which visitors can enter and sit within, sensing the site's ancient history. The ruins of this 450-room Native American pueblo, left by the ancestral Puebloans 7 centuries ago, are located 14 miles northeast of Farmington, in the town of Aztec on the Animas River. Early Anglo settlers, convinced that the ruins were of Aztec origin, misnamed the site. Despite the fact that this pueblo was built long before the Aztecs of central Mexico lived, the name persisted.

The influence of the Chaco culture is strong at Aztec, as evidenced in the pre-planned architecture, the open plaza, and the fine stone masonry in the old walls. But a later occupation shows the influence of Mesa Verde (which flourished 1200–1275). This second group of settlers remodeled the old pueblo and built others nearby, using techniques less elaborate and decorative than those of the Chacoans.

Aztec Ruins is best known for its Great Kiva, the only completely reconstructed Anasazi great kiva in existence. About 50 feet in diameter, with a main floor sunken 8 feet below the surface of the surrounding ground, this circular ceremonial room rivets the imagination. It's hard not to feel spiritually impressed, and perhaps to feel the presence of people who walked here nearly 1,000 years ago. (However, be aware that doubt has been cast on the reconstruction job performed by archaeologist Earl H. Morris in 1934; some believe the structure is much taller than the original.)

Visiting Aztec Ruins National Monument will take you approximately 1 hour, even if you take the ¼-mile self-guided trail and spend some time in the visitor center, which displays some outstanding examples of Anasazi ceramics and basketry. Add another half-hour if you plan to watch the video that imaginatively documents the history of native cultures in the area.

ESSENTIALS

GETTING THERE   Aztec Ruins is approximately a half mile north of US 550 on Ruins Road (C.R. 2900) on the north edge of the city of Aztec. Ruins Road is the first street immediately west of the Animas River Bridge on Highway 516 in Aztec.

VISITOR INFORMATION   For more information, contact **Aztec Ruins National Monument,** 84 County Rd. 2900, Aztec, NM 87410-0640 (✆ **505/334-6174,** ext. 30; www.nps.gov/azru).

ADMISSION FEES & HOURS   Admission is $4 for adults; children under 17 are admitted free. The monument is open daily from 8am to 6pm Memorial Day through Labor Day and 8am to 5pm the rest of the year; it's closed Thanksgiving, Christmas, and New Year's Day.

CAMPING

Camping is not permitted at the monument. Nearby, **Bloomfield KOA** (✆ **800/562-8513** or 505/632-8339; www.koa.com), on Blanco Boulevard, offers 83 sites, 73 full hookups, tenting, cabins, laundry and grocery facilities, picnic tables, grills, and firewood. The recreation room/area has coin games, a heated swimming pool, a basketball hoop, a playground, horseshoes, volleyball, and a hot tub.

Camping is also available at **Navajo Lake State Park** (✆ **505/632-2278**).

SHOPPING

Downtown Farmington shops are generally open from 10am to 6pm Monday through Saturday. Native American arts and crafts are best purchased at trading posts, either downtown on Main or Broadway streets, or west of Farmington on US 64/550 toward Shiprock. You may want to check out the following stores.

Foutz Indian Room, 301 W. Main St. (© **505/325-9413**), has some affordable jewelry, as well as whimsical Navajo folk art such as painted carvings of pickups carrying sheep and chickens. The store also sells wool and leather to artisans.

Hogback Trading Company, 3221 US 64, Waterflow, 17 miles west of Farmington (© **505/598-5154**), has large displays of Indian jewelry, rugs, and folk art.

Navajo Trading Company, 126 E. Main St. (© **505/325-1685**), is an actual pawnshop, with lots of exquisite old jewelry, including the most incredible concho belt I've ever seen, priced at $2,500; you can peruse bracelets and necklaces while listening to clerks speaking Navajo.

GETTING OUTSIDE: NEARBY PARKS & RECREATION AREAS
SHIPROCK PEAK

This distinctive landmark, located on the Navajo Indian Reservation southwest of Shiprock, 29 miles west of Farmington via US 64, is known to the Navajo as *Tse bidá hi,* "Rock with wings." Composed of igneous rock flanked by long upright walls of solidified lava, it rises 1,700 feet off the desert floor to an elevation of 7,178 feet. There are scenic viewing points off US 491, 6 to 7 miles south of the town of Shiprock. You can get closer by taking the tribal road to the community of Red Rock, but you must have permission to get any nearer to this sacred Navajo rock. Climbing is not permitted.

The town named after the rock is a gateway to the Navajo reservation and the Four Corners region. There's a tribal visitor center here.

From Shiprock, you may want to make the 32-mile drive west on US 64 to Teec Nos Pos, Arizona, and then north on US 160, to the **Four Corners Monument.** A concrete slab here sits astride the only point in the United States where four states meet: New Mexico, Colorado, Utah, and Arizona. Kids especially like the idea of standing at the center and occupying four states at once. It's a primitive place with no visitor center, but booths sell crafts and food. With no view to speak of, some find a visit here not worth the trip or cost. For information, call © **928/871-6647.** Open daily 7am to 7pm Memorial Day to Labor Day and 8am to 5pm the rest of the year. The cost is $3 per person for adults, and $2 for kids 6 and under.

NAVAJO LAKE STATE PARK

The **San Juan River, Pine River,** and **Sims Mesa recreation sites,** all with camping, fishing, and boating, make this the most popular water-sports destination for residents of northwestern New Mexico. Trout, northern pike, largemouth bass, and catfish are caught in lake and river waters, and the surrounding hills attract hunters seeking deer and elk. A visitor center at Pine River Recreation Area has interpretive displays on natural history and on the construction and purposes of the dam.

Navajo Lake, with an area of 15,000 acres, extends from the confluence of the San Juan and Los Pinos rivers 25 miles north into Colorado. Navajo Dam, an earthen embankment, is ¾ of a mile long and 400 feet high. It provides Farmington-area cities, industries, and farms with their principal water supply. It's also the main storage reservoir for the Navajo Indian Irrigation Project, designed to irrigate 110,000 acres.

Anglers come from all over the world to fish the San Juan below the dam, a pastoral spot bordered by green hills, where golden light reflects off the water. Much of the water is designated "catch and release" and is teeming with rainbow, brown, and cutthroat trout. Experts will be heartily challenged by these fish that are attuned to the best tricks, while amateurs may want to hire a guide. For more information, see "Fishing" in chapter 5.

The park is located 40 miles east of Farmington on NM 511. For more information, call © **505/632-2278.**

ANGEL PEAK RECREATION AREA

The distinctive pinnacle of 6,991-foot Angel Peak can often be spotted from the hillsides around Farmington. The area offers a short nature trail and a variety of unusual, colorful geological formations and canyons to explore on foot. The Bureau of Land Management has developed a primitive campground with nine campsites and provided picnic tables in a few spots, but no drinking water is available here. The park is located about 35 miles south of Farmington on US 550; the last 6 miles of access, after turning off US 550, are over a graded dirt road. For more information on the park, call © **505/599-8900.**

BISTI/DE-NA-ZIN WILDERNESS

Often referred to as Bisti Badlands (pronounced bist-*eye*), this barren region may merit that name today, but it was once very different. Around 70 million years ago, large dinosaurs lived near what was then a coastal swamp, bordering a retreating inland sea. Today, their bones, and those of fish, turtles, lizards, and small mammals, are eroding slowly from the low shale hills.

Kirtland Shale, containing several bands of color, dominates the eastern part of the Wilderness and caps the mushroom-shaped formations found there. Along with the spires and fanciful shapes of rock, hikers may find petrified wood sprinkled in small chips throughout the area, or even an occasional log. Removing petrified wood, fossils, or anything else from the wilderness is prohibited.

Hiking in the Bisti is fairly easy; from the small parking lot, follow an arroyo east 2 or 3 miles into the heart of the formations, which you'll see on your right (aim for the two red hills). The De-Na-Zin Wilderness to the east requires more climbing and navigational skills. It has no designated trails, bikes and motorized vehicles are prohibited, and it has no water or significant shade. The hour just after sunset or, especially, just before sunrise is a pleasant and quite magical time to see this starkly beautiful landscape. Primitive camping is allowed, but bring plenty of water and other supplies.

Bisti/De-Na-Zin Wilderness is located just off NM 371, 37 miles south of Farmington. For more information, call the **Bureau of Land Management** at © **505/599-8900.**

WHERE TO STAY IN FARMINGTON & AZTEC
MODERATE

Best Western Inn and Suites   This is where my brother stays when he's doing business in Farmington. Built in 1976, it provides spacious rooms and good amenities, though you have to like to walk because the rooms are built around a huge quadrangle with an indoor pool in a sunny, plant-filled courtyard. Request a room at one of the four corner entrances to avoid trudging down the long hallways. Also request a room that is facing outside rather than in toward the courtyard, where noise from the pool carries. This is a good choice for winter, when you can enjoy the courtyard. Rooms are bright and decorated with Southwest accents. Beds are firm, and bathrooms are medium-size and clean. Suites have microwaves, wet bars, extra phones at desks, and sofa beds. Best of all, the hotel is just steps away from the Riverwalk, a great place to get your morning or evening exercise.

The hotel's restaurant, the Riverwalk Patio and Grille, offers a wide selection of New Mexican and Southwest Italian cuisine. Rookie's Sports Bar, which features pool tables and televised sporting events and specials, always offers a drink special.

700 Scott Ave., Farmington, NM 87401. ℭ **800/528-1234**, 800/600-5221, or 505/327-5221. Fax 505/327-1565. www.bestwestern.com. 194 units. $79–$84 double. Rates include breakfast. AE, DC, DISC, MC, V. Pets are welcome. **Amenities:** Restaurant; bar; indoor pool; exercise room; Jacuzzi; sauna; game room; car-rental desk; business center; limited room service; coin-op laundry; laundry service. *In room:* A/C, TV/VCR w/pay movies, dataport, fridge, coffeemaker, hair dryer, iron.

Step Back Inn ★ This inn offers Victorian charm in a newer building with modern conveniences. Though it's a fair-size hotel, it has a cozy inn feel and plenty of amenities. The building was designed by the same architect who built the Inn of the Anasazi in Santa Fe, and the tastefulness and functionality are apparent in the layout of the large rooms and good-size baths, as well as in the quietness, which is due to good insulation. The rooms have pretty touches such as wallpaper and early American antique replica armoires, which hold the television. Each is named after an early pioneer family of the area, some of whom are the ancestors of the hotel's owner, and each room includes a small booklet that tells their stories. The beds are firm, and the linens are good. Breakfast brings a warm, delicious cinnamon roll as large as a plate, served in a quiet tearoom.

103 W. Aztec Blvd., Aztec, NM 87410. ℭ **800/334-1255** or 505/334-1200. 39 units. May 15–Nov 1 $68–$78 double; Nov 2–May 14 $58–$68 double. Rates include cinnamon roll, juice, and coffee. AE, MC, V. *In room:* A/C, TV, hair dryer.

INEXPENSIVE

Enchantment Lodge Lots of fishers, including my mother and me when we go angling on the San Juan, enjoy this pleasant and very reasonable small roadside motel, marked by pink neon lights reminiscent of the late 1950s, when it was built. With remodeling ongoing, the simple, medium-size rooms have Southwest touches and 1950s tile in the bathrooms. A small pool offers a nice respite at the end of the day. Request a room toward the back to avoid highway noise.

1800 W. Aztec Blvd., Aztec, NM 87410. ℭ **800/847-2194** for reservations only, or 505/334-6143. Fax 505/334-9234. www.enchantmentlodge.com. 20 units. $44–$52 double. Rates include continental breakfast. AE, DC, DISC, MC, V. **Amenities:** Small outdoor pool; coin-op laundry; laundry service. *In room:* A/C, TV, fridge.

BED & BREAKFASTS

Casa Blanca ★★ *(Finds)* Recent renovation has turned this B & B into a travel destination. Located in a quiet residential neighborhood just a few blocks from the shops and restaurants of Main Street, this inn built in the 1940s was once the home of a wealthy family that traded with the Navajos. In 2004, new owners expanded it, adding patios and fountains, creating a lovely oasis. The large rooms, decorated in an elegant Southwestern style, have original artwork and plenty of amenities. Travelers with disabilities are treated especially well here (two large suites especially for them), as are business travelers (high-speed Internet and a meeting room). The full breakfast is always gourmet.

505 E. La Plata St., Farmington, NM 87401. ℭ **800/550-6503** or 505/327-6503. Fax 505/326-5680. www.4corners bandb.com. 9 units. $95–$165 double; $20 single traveler discount. Rates include full breakfast. AE, MC, V. *In room:* A/C, TV, fridge, coffeemaker, hair dryer, iron, high-speed Internet.

Kokopelli's Cave ★★ After a long day of sightseeing, I lay on a queen bed under 200 feet of sandstone, listening to Beethoven, with a sliding glass door open to a view hundreds of feet down to a river snaking across a valley. It began to rain, slow big drops that made the air smell like wet sage. It suddenly struck me: I was staying in a cave. I can't quite stress how cool an experience it was.

Here's the story: Retired geologist Bruce Black wanted to build an office in a cave, so he gave some laid-off Grants miners $20,000 to bore as deeply as they could into the side of a cliff face. This luxury apartment was the result. Through time, it worked better as a living space than a work space, and that is what it remains. Built in a semi-circle, both the entry hall and the bedroom have wide sliding glass doors leading to little balconies beyond which the cliff face drops hundreds of feet below. This really is a cliff dwelling, and you must hike a bit down to it, though good guardrails guide you.

The apartment is laid out around a broad central pillar, and the ceilings and walls are thick, undulating stone. Golden eagles nest in the area, and ring-tail cats tend to wander onto the balcony. A grill is outside, as are chairs where you can relax in the mornings and evenings. Fruit, juice, coffee, and pastries make up a self-serve breakfast.

3204 Crestridge Dr., Farmington, NM 87401. ℂ 505/326-2461. Fax 505/325-9671. www.bbonline.com/nm/kokopelli. 1 unit. $220 double; $260 for 3–4 people. Closed Dec–Feb. AE, MC, V. **Amenities:** Jacuzzi. *In room:* TV/VCR, kitchen, hair dryer, iron.

CAMPING

Downs RV Park (ℂ **800/582-6427**) has 33 sites, 31 of them with full hookups. Tenting space is also available. The park has a playground, an arcade, and a game room. It's located 5 miles west of Farmington on US 64. **Mom and Pop RV Park** (ℂ **505/327-3200**) has 36 sites, 35 of them with full hookups, tenting, a bathhouse, and a toy soldier shop. The sites are a bit desolate, around an asphalt central area, but a little grassy spot at the office has an incredible electric train set that Pop runs at certain times during the day. Mom and Pop RV Park is located at 901 Illinois Ave., in Farmington (just off US 64).

WHERE TO DINE IN FARMINGTON & AZTEC

EXPENSIVE

The Bluffs ★★ *Finds* STEAKS/SEAFOOD/SANDWICHES   Finally, Farmington has fine dining. Ten minutes east of the town center, The Bluffs serves inventive food with attention to detail. A large room is sectioned off by wooden partitions crowned with elegantly glazed glass shaped like the bluffs prominent in the surrounding area. It's a comfortable atmosphere with roomy booths and stacked sandstone accents. Service is efficient. The outdoor patio is a nice spot on not-so-hot days. For lunch, my pick is the turkey bacon club, served on ciabatta bread. The Thai beef salad is also tasty. At dinner, try your favorite steak cut of Angus beef or sesame-crusted ahi tuna. Dinners come with salad and a choice of vegetable or potato. There's a full bar here, but for a real treat, before dining, slip into the package store next door, owned by the same folks, where you'll find some very fine wines. In the restaurant, you'll pay a corking fee but still save a bundle.

3450 E. Main St. ℂ **505/325-8155**. Reservations recommended on weekend nights. Main courses $7–$11 lunch, $13–$30 dinner. AE, DISC, MC, V. Mon–Sat 11am–2pm; Mon–Thurs 5–9pm; Fri–Sat 4–10pm. Lounge daily 3–9 or 10pm.

MODERATE

3 Rivers Eatery & Brewhouse AMERICAN   After a long day of traveling, I went to this brewpub on an elegant corner in the center of downtown. One sip of their Papa Bear's Golden Honey, and I was ready to recommend the place. It's set in a big two-story brick building that once housed the Farmington Drug Store and the Farmington *Times-Hustler* newspaper. Wood floors and vintage items, such as period bottles and posters found in the renovation, complete the experience. It's a comfortable place where the owner might just sit down in one of the comfy booths with you and chat about his passion, beer brewing. I recommend the burgers, which come in a variety of flavors, from grilled onion and Swiss to jack and green chile. You'll also find barbecue pork ribs, steaks, and seafood. The waiter brought me another beer flavor to sample, Arroyo Amber Ale, which I liked as well as the first. For dessert, try the brewmaster's root beer float.

101 E. Main St., Farmington. ℂ 505/324-2187. www.threeriversbrewery.com. Main courses $5–$22 lunch and dinner. AE, DISC, MC, V. Mon–Thurs 11am–10pm; Fri–Sat 11am–11pm; Sun 11am–9pm.

INEXPENSIVE

Bagel Conspiracy BAGELS AND SANDWICHES   If you find yourself in east Farmington's strip and shopping mall never-never land and want to stop in for a quick bite, head to this spot. The interior isn't much—industrial, with a few tables and an eating counter looking out on a parking lot—but the food is fresh and tasty. Bagels are baked daily in a variety of flavors, served with a range of spreads and made into sandwiches such as an egg and cheese with bacon for breakfast or chicken salad for lunch. Wash it down with a cappuccino, an espresso, or an Italian soda.

3554 E. Main St., Suite H (in the little mall in front of Home Depot). ℂ 505/564-8888. All menu items under $6. AE, DC, DISC, MC, V. Mon–Fri 6am–5pm; Sat 7am–5pm; Sun 7am–2pm.

Main Street Bistro ★ CAFE/BAKERY   In all my travels across New Mexico I've stumbled upon a quiet quest—finding good coffee and such things as home-baked muffins and veggie sandwiches. In states with a lot of people, this would be a small task, but out here, where hundreds of miles separate gas stations, it becomes almost quixotic. Each time I find a little gem like this one, I revel in it and visit it as many times as I can while I'm in the vicinity. The place reels with imagination. The walls and floors are brightly colored, and the menu changes at the whim of the chefs. The service is friendly and decent, and the place bustles during peak hours; so if you want quiet time, go midmorning or later in the afternoon. You can't go wrong with the daily soup special, a salad, a sandwich (try the Ultimate—turkey, bacon, avocado, and sprouts), or the quiche, made fresh daily.

122 N. Main St., Aztec. ℂ 505/334-0109. All menu items under $8. DISC, MC, V. Mon–Sat 7am–4pm.

Something Special Bakery and Tea Room GOURMET HOME COOKING/ VEGETARIAN   Ask people in Farmington where to eat and they'll recommend this little shop. In a quaint Victorian home, it has wooden floors and tables and an open, friendly atmosphere. Best of all is the vine-draped, arbor-shaded patio in back. Breakfast is decadent pastries, such as a blueberry cream cheese or a spinach and feta croissant, all made with wholesome ingredients. Each day, diners have a choice of two lunch entrees, such as a vegetable quiche or a mild Thai chicken served over veggies and rice. Every day brings 20 plus dessert options, including such delicacies as blueberry/raspberry chocolate cake or a strawberry napoleon. A lighter option is the white chocolate macadamia nut cookie. Believe it or not, amid all this richness are low-fat "heart smart" menu options as well.

116 N. Auburn Ave., near Main St., Farmington. ℂ 505/325-8183. Breakfast $3–$6; lunch main course $10; desserts $5. AE, DC, DISC, MC, V. Tues–Fri 7am–2pm (lunch served 11:30am–2pm).

FARMINGTON AFTER DARK

Black River Traders, an annual outdoor historical drama, depicts 1910 trading-post life in the Four Corners region. Presented in the Lions Wilderness Park Amphitheater (off College Blvd.) against a sandstone backdrop, the drama tells of the struggle for survival by both Navajos and whites as two cultures fought to understand each other. This play, using dance and mime, was written by Mark R. Sumner. A Southwestern-style dinner is also available. The production company also presents other musicals at the amphitheater. For information and advance ticket sales, call ✆ **505/599-1148,** or you can purchase tickets at the gate. Shows are Wednesday through Saturday from late June to mid-August, with dinner at 6:30pm and the performance at 8pm.

A new night spot, **3 Rivers Tap & Game Room,** 113 E. Main St. (✆ **505/325-6605;** www.threeriversbrewery.com), is a big hit with locals. This brewpub/game room has the feel of the bar from the television show *Cheers,* with wood floors, high ceilings, and lots of laughter and brew flowing. Pool tables, foosball, and shuffleboard fill patrons' time in this nonsmoking space, while they munch on popcorn and peanuts, and, some nights, listen to live music jam. Patrons can order from the next-door brewpub/restaurant of the same name (see above).

14 Chaco Culture National Historical Park ✫✫✫

A combination of a stunning setting and well-preserved ruins makes the long drive to **Chaco Culture National Historic Park,** often referred to as Chaco Canyon, worth the trip. Whether you come from the north or south, you drive in on a dusty (and sometimes muddy) road that seems to add to the authenticity and adventure of this remote New Mexico experience.

When you finally arrive, you walk through stark desert country that seems perhaps ill suited as a center of culture. However, the ancient Anasazi people successfully farmed the lowlands and built great masonry towns, which connected with other towns over a wide-ranging network of roads crossing this desolate place.

What's most interesting here is how changes in architecture—beginning in the mid-800s, when the Anasazi started building on a larger scale than they had previously—chart the area's cultural progress. The Anasazi used the same masonry techniques that tribes had used in smaller villages in the region (walls one-stone thick, with generous use of mud mortar), but they built stone villages of multiple stories with rooms several times larger than in the previous stage of their culture. Within a century, six large pueblos were underway. This pattern of a single large pueblo with oversize rooms, surrounded by conventional villages, caught on throughout the region. New communities built along these lines sprang up. Old villages built similarly large pueblos. Eventually there were more than 75 such towns, most of them closely tied to Chaco by an extensive system of roads.

This progress led to Chaco becoming the economic center of the San Juan Basin by A.D. 1000. As many as 5,000 people may have lived in some 400 settlements in and around Chaco. As masonry techniques advanced through the years, walls rose more than four stories in height. Some of these are still visible today.

Chaco's decline after 1½ centuries of success coincided with a drought in the San Juan Basin between A.D. 1130 and 1180. Scientists still argue vehemently over why the site was abandoned and where the Chacoans went. Many believe that an influx of outsiders may have brought new rituals to the region, causing a schism among tribal members. Most agree, however, that the people drifted away to more hospitable places in the region and that their descendants live among the Pueblo people today.

This is an isolated area, and **no services** are available within or close to the park—no food, gas, auto repairs, firewood, lodging (besides the campground), or drinking water other than at the visitor center) are available. Overnight camping is permitted year-round. If you're headed towards Santa Fe after a day at the park and looking for a place to spend the night, one nice option is the **Casa del Rio–Riverside Inn,** 16445 Scenic Highway 4, Jemez Springs, NM 87025 (✆ **505/829-4377;** www.canondelrio.com).

ESSENTIALS

GETTING THERE   To get to Chaco from Santa Fe, take I-25 south to Bernalillo, then US 550 northwest. Turn off US 550 at C.R. 7900 (3 miles southeast of Nageezi and about 50 miles west of Cuba at mile 112.5). Follow the signs from US 550 to the park boundary (21 miles). This route includes 5 miles of paved road (C.R. 7900) and 16 miles of rough dirt road (C.R. 7950). This is the recommended route. Highway 57 from Blanco Trading Post is closed. The trip takes about 3½ to 4 hours. Farmington is the nearest population center, a 1½-hour drive away. The park can also be reached from Grants via I-40 west to NM 371, then north on NM 57 (with the final 19 miles ungraded dirt). This route is rough to impassable and is not recommended for RVs.

Whichever way you come, call ahead to inquire about **road conditions** (© 505/ 786-7014) before leaving the paved highways. The dirt roads can get extremely muddy and dangerous after rain or snow, and afternoon thunderstorms are common in late summer. Roads often flood when it rains.

VISITOR INFORMATION   Ranger-guided walks and campfire talks are available in the summer at the visitor center where you can get self-guided trail brochures and permits for the overnight campground (see "Camping," below). If you want information before you leave home, write to the Superintendent, Chaco Culture National Historical Park, 1808 County Rd. 7950, Nageezi, NM 87037 (© **505/786-7014;** www.nps.gov/chcu).

ADMISSION FEES & HOURS   Admission is $8 per car; a campsite is $10 extra. The visitor center is open daily 8am to 5pm. Trails are open from sunrise to sunset.

SEEING THE HIGHLIGHTS

Exploring the ruins and hiking are the most popular activities here. A series of pueblo ruins stand within 5 or 6 miles of each other on the broad, flat, treeless canyon floor. Plan to spend at least 3 to 4 hours here driving to and exploring the different pueblos. A one-way road from the visitor center loops up one side of the canyon and down the other. Parking lots are scattered along the road near the various pueblos; from most, it's only a short walk to the ruins.

You may want to focus your energy on seeing **Pueblo Bonito,** the largest prehistoric Southwest Native American dwelling ever excavated. It contains giant kivas and 800 rooms covering more than 3 acres. Also, the **Pueblo Alto Trail** is a nice hike that takes you up on the canyon rim so that you can see the ruins from above—in the afternoon, with thunderheads building, the views are spectacular. If you're a cyclist, stop at the visitor center to pick up a map outlining ridable trails.

Aerial photos show hundreds of miles of roads connecting these towns with the Chaco pueblos, one of the longest running 42 miles straight north to Salmon Ruins and the Aztec Ruins (see earlier). It is this road network that leads some scholars to believe that Chaco was the center of a unified Anasazi society.

CAMPING

Gallo Campground, located within the park, is quite popular with hikers. It's located about 1 mile east of the visitor center; fees are $10 per night. The campground has 47 sites (group sites are also available), with fire grates (bring your own wood or charcoal), central toilets, and nonpotable water. Drinking water is available only at the visitor center. The campground cannot accommodate trailers over 30 feet.

As I said above, there's no place to stock up on supplies once you start the arduous drive to the canyon, so if you're camping, make sure you're well supplied, especially with water, before you leave home base.

7

Santa Fe

With its wandering streets, flat-topped adobe buildings, and dramatic clouds, Santa Fe—the "City Different"—has always had an exotic nature. The Native Americans enlighten the area with viewpoints and lifestyles deeply tied to nature and completely contrary to the American norm. Many of the Hispanics here still live in extended families and practice a devout Catholicism; they bring a slower pace to the city and an appreciation for deep-rooted ties. Meanwhile, a strong cosmopolitan element contributes cutting-edge cuisine, world-class opera, first-run art films, and some of the finest artwork in the world, seen easily while wandering on foot from gallery to gallery, museum to museum.

The city was originally named La Villa Real de la Santa Fe de San Francisco de Asis (The Royal City of the Holy Faith of St. Francis of Assisi) by its founder, Spanish governor Don Pedro de Peralta. He built the Palace of the Governors as his capitol on the central Plaza; today it's an excellent museum of the city's 4 centuries of history and one of the major attractions in the Southwest. Under its portico,

Native Americans sell their crafts to eager tourists, as they have done for decades.

The Plaza is the focus of numerous bustling art markets and Santa Fe's early-September fiesta, celebrated annually since 1770. The fiesta commemorates the time following the years of the Pueblo revolt, when Spanish governor Don Diego de Vargas reconquered the city in 1692. The Plaza was also the terminus of the Santa Fe Trail from Missouri, and of the earlier Camino Real (Royal Road) from Mexico, when the city thrived on the wool and fur of the Chihuahua trade. Today, a new gazebo makes a fun venue for summer concerts.

The city's setting is captivating, backed by the rolling hills and the blue peaks of the Sangre de Cristo Mountains. In the summer, thunderheads build into giant swirling structures above those peaks and move over the city, dropping cool rain. In the winter, snow often covers the many flat-roofed adobe homes, creating a poetic abstraction that at every glance convinces you that the place itself is exotic art.

1 Orientation

Part of the charm of Santa Fe is that it's so easy to get around. Like most cities of Hispanic origin, it was built around the parklike central Plaza. Centuries-old adobe buildings and churches still line the narrow streets; many of them house shops, restaurants, art galleries, and museums.

Santa Fe sits high and dry at the foot of the Sangre de Cristo Range. Santa Fe Baldy rises to more than 12,600 feet, a mere 12 miles northeast of the Plaza. The city's downtown straddles the Santa Fe River, a tiny tributary of the Rio Grande that is little more than a trickle for much of the year. North is the Espanola Valley (the Santa Fe Opera grounds afford a beautiful view) and beyond that, the village of Taos, 66 miles distant (see chapter 8). South are ancient Indian turquoise mines in the Cerrillos Hills; southwest is metropolitan Albuquerque, 58 miles away (see chapter 9). To the west, across the Caja del Rio Plateau, is the Rio Grande, and beyond that, the 11,000-foot Jemez Mountains and Valle Grande, an ancient and massive volcanic caldera. Native American pueblos dot the entire Rio Grande valley; they're an hour's drive in any direction.

ARRIVING

BY PLANE   Many people fly into the Albuquerque International Sunport. If you want to save time and don't mind paying a bit more, you can fly into the **Santa Fe Municipal Airport** (© 505/955-2900), just outside the southwestern city limits on Airport Road. In conjunction with United Airlines, **United Express** (© 800/241-6522), which is operated by **Great Lakes Aviation** (© 800/473-4118), offers commuter flights from Denver, Colorado.

If you do fly into Albuquerque, you can rent a car or take a bus service. Reservations are required. **Sandia Shuttle** (© 888/775-5696 or 505/474-5696; www.sandiashuttle.com) runs almost hourly during the day to and from Santa Fe hotels; it costs $23 one-way and $43 round trip. **Santa Fe Shuttle** (© 888/833-2300 or 505/466-8500; www.shuttlesantafe.com) runs every 90 minutes to 2 hours during the day to and from Santa Fe hotels; it charges $21 one-way and $38 round trip.

From the Santa Fe Municipal Airport, **Roadrunner Shuttle** (© 505/424-3367) meets every flight and takes visitors anywhere in Santa Fe.

BY TRAIN   For information about train service to Santa Fe, see "Getting Around" in chapter 2.

BY CAR   I-25 skims past Santa Fe's southern city limits, connecting it along one continuous highway from Billings, Montana, to El Paso, Texas. I-40, the state's major east–west thoroughfare, which bisects Albuquerque, affords coast-to-coast access to Santa Fe. (From the west, motorists leave I-40 in Albuquerque and take I-25 north; from the east, travelers exit I-40 at Clines Corners and continue 52 miles to Santa Fe on US 285. *Note:* Diesel is scarce on US 285, so be sure to fill up before you leave Clines Corners.) For those coming from the northwest, the most direct route is via Durango, Colorado, on US 160, entering Santa Fe on US 84.

For information on car rentals in Santa Fe, see "Getting Around," below.

VISITOR INFORMATION

The **Santa Fe Convention and Visitors Bureau,** 201 W. Marcy St. (P.O. Box 909), Santa Fe, NM 87504-0909 (© 800/777-CITY or 505/955-6200; www.santafe.org), is in Sweeney Center at the corner of Grant Street downtown. You might also try **www.visitsantafe.com** for more information.

CITY LAYOUT

MAIN ARTERIES & STREETS   The limits of downtown Santa Fe are demarcated on three sides by the horseshoe-shaped Paseo de Peralta and on the west by St. Francis Drive, otherwise known as US 84/285. Alameda Street follows the north side of the Santa Fe River through downtown, with the State Capitol and other government buildings on the south side of the river, and most buildings of historic and tourist interest on the north, east of Guadalupe Street.

The Plaza is Santa Fe's universally accepted point of orientation. Its four diagonal walkways meet at a central fountain, around which you'll find a strange and wonderful assortment of people of all ages, nationalities, and lifestyles at nearly any hour of the day or night.

If you stand in the center of the Plaza looking north, you'll be gazing directly at the Palace of the Governors. In front of you is Palace Avenue; behind you, San Francisco Street. To your left is Lincoln Avenue, and to your right is Washington Avenue, which divides the downtown avenues into east and west. St. Francis Cathedral is the massive Romanesque structure a block east, down San Francisco Street. Alameda Street is 2 full blocks behind you.

Near the intersection of Alameda Street and Paseo de Peralta, you'll find Canyon Road running east toward the mountains. Much of this street is one-way. The best way to experience it is to walk up or down, taking time to explore shops and galleries and even have lunch or dinner.

Running southwest from the downtown area, beginning opposite the state office buildings on Galisteo Avenue, is Cerrillos Road. Once the main north-south highway connecting New Mexico's state capital with its largest city, it is now a 6-mile-long motel and fast-food strip. St. Francis Drive, which crosses Cerrillos Road 3 blocks south of Guadalupe Street, is a far less tawdry byway, linking Santa Fe with I-25, located 4 miles southwest of downtown. The Old Pecos Trail, on the east side of the city, also joins downtown and the freeway. St. Michaels Drive connects the three arteries.

FINDING AN ADDRESS   The city's layout makes it difficult to know exactly where to look for a particular address. It's best to call ahead for directions.

MAPS   Free city and state maps are available at tourist information offices. An excellent state highway map is published by the **New Mexico Department of Tourism,** 491 Old Santa Fe Trail, Lamy Building, Santa Fe, NM 87503 (© **800/733-6396** or 505/827-7307; to receive a tourism guide call © **800/777-CITY**). There's a Santa Fe visitor center in the same building. More specific county and city maps are available from the **State Highway and Transportation Department,** 1120 Cerrillos Rd., Santa Fe, NM 87504 (© **505/827-5100**). Members of AAA can obtain free maps from the **American Automobile Association office,** 1644 St. Michaels Dr. (© **505/471-6620**). Area bookstores carry other good regional maps.

2 Getting Around

The best way to see downtown Santa Fe is on foot. Free **walking-tour maps** are available at the **tourist information center** in Sweeney Center, 201 W. Marcy St. (© **800/777-CITY**). See the "What to See & Do" section later in this chapter for information on guided walking tours.

BY BUS

In 1993, Santa Fe opened **Santa Fe Trails** (© **505/955-2001**), its first public bus system. There are seven routes, and visitors can pick up a map from the Convention and Visitors Bureau. Buses operate Monday through Friday from 6am to 11pm and Saturday from 8am to 8pm. There is no service on Sunday or holidays. Call for a current schedule and fare information.

BY CAR

The following firms have offices in Santa Fe: **Avis,** Santa Fe Airport (© **505/471-5892**): **Budget,** 1946 Cerrillos Rd. (© **505/984-1596**); **Enterprise,** 2641A

Cerrillos Rd., 4450 Cerrillos Rd. (at the Auto Park), and the Santa Fe Hilton, 100 Sandoval St. (© **505/473-3600**); and **Hertz,** Santa Fe Airport (© **505/471-7189**).

If Santa Fe is your base for an extended driving exploration of New Mexico, be sure to give the vehicle you rent a thorough road check before starting out. There are a lot of wide-open desert and wilderness spaces here, so if you break down, you could be stranded for hours before someone passes by, and cellphones tend not to work in these remote areas.

Make sure your driver's license and auto club membership (if you have one) are valid before you leave home. Check with your auto-insurance company to make sure you're covered when out of state and driving a rental car.

Note: In 2002, the Santa Fe City Council imposed a law prohibiting use of cellphones while driving within the city limits and imposing strict fines. If you need to make a call, be sure to pull off the road.

Street parking is difficult to find during summer months. There's a metered parking lot near the federal courthouse, 2 blocks north of the Plaza; a city lot behind Santa Fe Village, a block south of the Plaza; and another city lot at Water and Sandoval streets. The Santa Fe Convention and Visitors Bureau, at the corner of Grant and Marcy streets, distributes a wallet-size guide to Santa Fe parking areas. The map shows both street and lot parking.

Unless otherwise posted, the speed limit on freeways is 75 mph; on most other two-lane open roads it's 60 to 65 mph. The minimum age for drivers is 16. Seat belts are required for drivers and all passengers ages 5 and over; children under 5 must use approved child seats.

Because Native American reservations enjoy a measure of self-rule, they can legally enforce their own laws. For instance, on the Navajo reservation, it is forbidden to transport alcoholic beverages, leave established roadways, or go without a seat belt. Motorcyclists must wear helmets. If you are caught breaking reservation laws, you are subject to reservation punishment—often stiff fines and, in some instances, detainment.

The **State Highway and Transportation Department's** toll-free hot line (© **800/432-4269**) provides up-to-the-hour information on road closures and conditions.

Warning: New Mexico has one of the highest per-capita rates of traffic deaths in the nation; although the number has actually been dropping in recent years, it's still a good idea to drive extra carefully!

BY TAXI

Cabs are difficult to flag from the street, but you can call for one. Expect to pay a standard fee of $2.40 for the service and an average of about $2.35 per mile. **Capital City Cab** (© **505/438-0000**) is the main company in Santa Fe.

BY BICYCLE

Riding a bicycle is an excellent way to get around town. Check with **Sun Mountain Bike Company,** 102 E. Water St., inside El Centro (© **505/982-8986**); **Bike-N-Sport,** 1829 Cerrillos Rd. (© **505/820-0809**); or **Santa Fe Mountain Sports,** 607 Cerrillos Rd. (© **505/988-3337**), for rentals.

FAST FACTS

For physician and surgeon referral and information services, call the **American Board of Medical Specialties** (© **866/275-2267**). **The Lovelace Clinic,** 440 St. Michaels Dr. (© **505/995-2400**), is open Monday to Thursday 8am to 6pm; Friday 8am to

5pm; and Saturday 8am to 3pm. **St. Vincent Hospital,** 455 St. Michaels Dr. (© **505/983-3361,** or 505/995-3934 for emergency services), is a 248-bed regional health center. Patient services include urgent and emergency-room care and ambulatory surgery. Health services are also available at the **Women's Health Services Family Care and Counseling Center** (© **505/988-8869**). **Ultimed,** 707 Paseo de Peralta (© **505/989-8707**), a new urgent care facility near the Plaza, offers comprehensive health care.

A tax of 7.31% applies to all purchases, with an additional 5% added to lodging bills.

See also "Fast Facts: The American Southwest" in chapter 2, and "Fast Facts: For the International Traveler" in chapter 3.

3 Where to Stay

It's difficult to find a bad place to stay in Santa Fe. From downtown hotels to Cerrillos Road motels, ranch-style resorts to quaint bed-and-breakfasts, the standard of accommodation is almost universally high.

You should be aware of the seasonal nature of the tourist industry in Santa Fe. Accommodations are often booked solid through the summer months, and most places raise their prices accordingly. Rates increase even more during Indian Market, the third weekend of August. During these periods, it's essential to make reservations well in advance.

DOWNTOWN

Everything within the horseshoe-shaped Paseo de Peralta and east a few blocks on either side of the Santa Fe River is considered downtown Santa Fe. All of these accommodations are within walking distance of the Plaza.

VERY EXPENSIVE

Eldorado Hotel and Spa ✦✦ Since opening in 1986, the Eldorado has been a model hotel for the city. In a large structure, the architects managed to meld Pueblo Revival style with an interesting cathedral feel, inside and out. The lobby is grand, with a high ceiling that continues into the court area and the cafe, all adorned with well over $1 million worth of Southwestern art. The spacious, quiet rooms continue the artistic motif, with a warm feel created by the kiva fireplaces in many, as well as the custom-made furniture. You'll find families, businesspeople, and conference-goers staying here. Most of the rooms have views of downtown Santa Fe, many from balconies. If you're really indulging, join the ranks of Mick Jagger, Geena Davis, and King Juan Carlos of Spain and try the penthouse five-room presidential suite. The Eldorado also manages the nearby Zona Rosa condominiums, which are two-, three-, and four-bedroom suites with full kitchens. The innovative and elegant restaurant, The Old House, serves creative American cuisine (see "Where to Dine," later in this chapter).

309 W. San Francisco St., Santa Fe, NM 87501. © **800/286-6755** or 505/988-4455. Fax 505/995-4544. www.eldoradohotel.com. 219 units. High season $279–$1,500 double; low season $169–$900 double. Ski and other packages available. AE, DC, DISC, MC, V. Valet parking $16. Pets accepted. **Amenities:** 2 restaurants (p. 156); bar; heated rooftop pool; medium-size health club (with a view); spa; Jacuzzi; his-and-hers saunas; concierge; business center; salon; room service; massage; laundry service; dry cleaning. *In room:* A/C, TV, dataport, minibar, coffeemaker, hair dryer, iron, safe.

Hilton of Santa Fe ✦ With its landmark bell tower, the Hilton encompasses a full city block and incorporates most of the historic landholdings of the 350-year-old Ortiz family estate. One block from the Plaza, it's built around a lovely courtyard pool

Reservations Services

Year-round reservation assistance is available from **Santa Fe Central Reservations** (℃ 800/745-9910), the **Accommodation Hot Line** (℃ 800/338-6877), **All Santa Fe Reservations** (℃ 877/737-7366), and **Santa Fe Stay,** which specializes in casitas (℃ 800/995-2272). **Emergency Lodging Assistance** is available free after 4pm daily (℃ 505/986-0038). All of the above are private companies and may have biases toward certain properties. Do your own research before calling.

and patio area, in a fine blend of ancient and modern styles. A renovation late in 2004 brought more style to the rooms and common areas, with handcrafted furnishings and hip Southwestern decor. Rooms vary slightly in size; my favorites are a little smaller than some but have balconies opening onto the courtyard. The Hilton also operates the Casa Ortiz de Santa Fe, luxury casitas with kitchens in a 1625 coach house adjacent to the hotel. Two restaurants on the Hilton's grounds occupy the premises of the early-18th-century Casa Ortiz.

100 Sandoval St. (P.O. Box 25104), Santa Fe, NM 87501-2131. ℃ **800/336-3676,** 800/HILTONS, or 505/988-2811. Fax 505/986-6439. www.hilton.com. 157 units. $159–$299 double; $239–$549 suite; $419–$559 casita. Extra person $20. AE, DC, DISC, MC, V. Parking $10. **Amenities:** 2 restaurants (breakfast; casual grill); bar; outdoor pool; exercise room; Jacuzzi; concierge; car-rental desk; courtesy van; business center; room service; laundry service; dry cleaning. In room: A/C, TV, dataport, coffeemaker, hair dryer, iron, safe.

Inn & Spa at Loretto ⭐ This much-photographed hotel, 2 blocks from the Plaza, was built in 1975 to resemble Taos Pueblo. Light and shadow dance on the five-level structure as the sun crosses the sky. With ongoing refinements, this hotel has become a comfortable and chic place to stay. Decor is Southwest/Montana ranch style, with faux painted walls and an interesting and cozy lobby lounge. The guest rooms and bathrooms are standard size, with the same decor as the rest of the hotel. Be aware that the Loretto likes convention traffic, so sometimes service lags for vacationers. Overall, it is fairly quiet and has nice views—especially on the northeast side, where you can see both the historic St. Francis Cathedral and the Loretto Chapel (see "More Attractions," later in this chapter). Spa Terre offers a range of treatments in intimate, Southwest-meets-Asia rooms.

211 Old Santa Fe Trail (P.O. Box 1417), Santa Fe, NM 87501. ℃ **800/727-5531** or 505/988-5531. Fax 505/984-7988. www.hotelloretto.com. 135 units. Jan–Mar $159–$265 double; Apr–June $185–$299 double; July–Oct $215–$499 double; Nov–Dec $185–$299 double. Extra person $25. Children under 18 stay free in parent's room. AE, DC, DISC, MC, V. Valet parking $15. **Amenities:** Restaurant; lounge; outdoor pool (heated year-round); spa; concierge; business center with audiovisual conferencing equipment; room service; valet laundry. In room: A/C, TV, fridge, coffeemaker, hair dryer, iron.

Inn of the Anasazi ⭐⭐⭐ This fine luxury hotel offers a feeling of grandness in a limited space. Vigas and flagstone floors create a warm and welcoming ambience that evokes the feeling of an Anasazi cliff dwelling. Oversize cacti complete the look. Accents are appropriately Navajo, in a nod to the fact that the Navajo live in the area the Anasazi (ancestral Puebloans) once inhabited. A half block off the Plaza, this hotel was built in 1991 to cater to travelers who know their hotels. On the ground floor are a living room and library with oversize furniture and replicas of Anasazi pottery and Navajo rugs. A library expansion and a new exercise room were completed in 2004. Even the smallest rooms are spacious, with pearl-finished walls and decor in cream

Downtown Santa Fe Accommodations & Dining

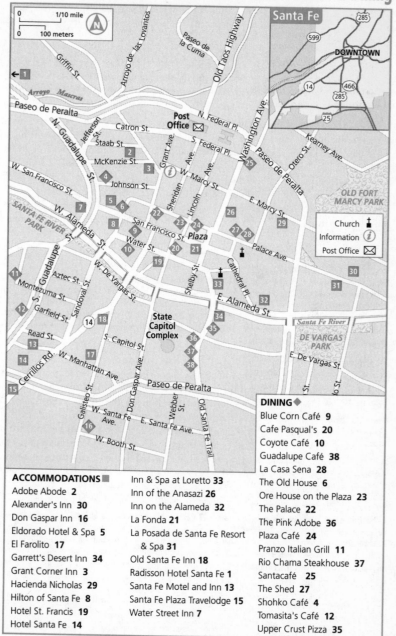

Santa Fe

DOWNTOWN

OLD FORT MARCY PARK

Church †
Information ⓘ
Post Office ✉

Plaza

State Capitol Complex

SANTA FE RIVER PARK

DE VARGAS PARK

Santa Fe River

Post Office ✉

tones accented by novelties such as iron candle sconces, original art, four-poster beds, gaslit kiva fireplaces, and humidifiers. All the rooms are quiet and comfortable, though none have dramatic views.

113 Washington Ave., Santa Fe, NM 87501. © **800/688-8100** or 505/988-3030. Fax 505/988-3277. www. innoftheanasazi.com. 57 units. Jan 5–Feb 26 $205–$405; Feb 27–Apr 28 $225–$425; Apr 29–June 23 $255–$445; June 24–Jan 4 $295–$475 double. AE, DC, DISC, MC, V. Valet parking $13. **Amenities:** Restaurant (creative Southwestern); small exercise room; concierge; room service; in-room massage; laundry service. *In room:* A/C, TV/VCR/DVD, coffeemaker, hair dryer, iron, safe.

La Fonda ✹   Whether you stay in this hotel or not, it's worth strolling through just to get a sense of how Santa Fe once was—and in some ways still is. This was the inn at the end of the Santa Fe Trail; it entertained trappers, traders, and merchants, as well as notables such as President Rutherford B. Hayes and General Ulysses S. Grant. The hotel has seen some renovation through the years, including a new wing, where you'll find deluxe suites and new meeting spaces. If you want a feel of the real Santa Fe, this is the place to stay. Overall, however, this hotel isn't the model of refinement. For that, you'd best go to the Hotel Santa Fe (see below) or other newer places. No two rooms are the same here, and while each has its own funky touch, some are more kitschy than quaint. Some have fridges, fireplaces, and private balconies. The Bell Tower Bar is the highest point in downtown Santa Fe—a great place for a cocktail and a view of the city.

100 E. San Francisco St. (P.O. Box 1209), Santa Fe, NM 87501. © **800/523-5002** or 505/982-5511. Fax 505/988-2952. www.lafondasantafe.com. 167 units. $219–$269 standard double; $239–$289 deluxe double; $349–$539 suite. Extra person $15. Children under 12 stay free in parent's room. AE, DC, DISC, MC, V. Parking $9 per day in garage. **Amenities:** Restaurant; 2 bars; outdoor pool; exercise room; spa; 2 indoor Jacuzzis; concierge; tour desk; room service; massage room and in-room massage; babysitting; laundry service; dry cleaning. *In room:* A/C, TV, dataport, coffeemaker, hair dryer, iron, safe.

La Posada de Santa Fe Resort and Spa ✹✹   If you're in the mood to stay in a little New Mexico adobe village, you'll enjoy this recently renovated luxury hotel just 3 blocks from the Plaza. Most of the hotel has pueblo-style construction; it's especially nice in the summer, when surrounded by acres of green grass. It has squeaky maple floors, vigas and *latillas,* and, in many rooms, kiva fireplaces. Most of the standard rooms are fairly small. The hotel benefited from a $23 million face-lift completed in 1999. Most notable are the Zen-Southwestern-style spa and pool and spacious spa rooms. Travelers who are wary of the whims of older adobe construction should reserve a spa room or one of the 40 other new rooms. The hotel attracts vacationers, a fair number of families, and conventioneers. Most rooms don't have views but do have outdoor patios, and most are tucked back into the quiet compound.

330 E. Palace Ave., Santa Fe, NM 87501. © **800/727-5276** or 505/986-0000. Fax 505/982-6850. www.laposada desantafe.com. 157 units. $199–$359 double; $289 and way up suite. Spa packages available. AE, DC, DISC, MC, V. Valet parking $14. **Amenities:** 2 restaurants; bar; outdoor pool; exercise room; spa with full treatments; Jacuzzi; bike rental; concierge; salon; room service; in-room massage; babysitting; dry cleaning. *In room:* A/C, TV, dataport, minibar, coffeemaker, hair dryer, iron, safe.

EXPENSIVE

Don Gaspar Inn ✹✹ *Finds*   If you'd like to pretend that you live in Santa Fe during your vacation—that you're blessed with your very own Southwestern-style home, in a historic neighborhood, full of artful touches such as Native American tapestries and a kiva fireplace—this is your inn. A 10-minute walk from the Plaza, the Don Gaspar occupies three homes, connected by brilliant gardens and brick walkways. Travelers looking for an adventure beyond a hotel stay, but without the close interaction of a

B&B, enjoy this place. Rooms vary in size, though all are plenty spacious, most with patios, some with kitchenettes. There's even a full house for rent. Though the accommodations don't have views, all are quiet. The Courtyard Casita, with a kitchenette and a sleeper couch in its own room, is nice for a small family.

623 Don Gaspar, Santa Fe, NM 87505. © 888/986-8664 or 505/986-8664. Fax 505/986-0696. www.dongaspar.com. 12 units. $115–$175 double; $145–$195 suite; $165–$295 casita or house. Rates include full breakfast. AE, MC, V. Free parking. **Amenities:** Babysitting; same-day laundry service. *In room:* A/C, TV/VCR, hair dryer, iron.

Hotel St. Francis ★   If you long for the rich fabrics, fine antiques, and slow pace of a European hotel, this is your place. The building was first constructed in the 1880s; it became fairly dilapidated but was renovated in 1986. Now elegantly redecorated, the lobby is crowned by a Victorian fireplace with hovering cherubs, a theme repeated throughout the hotel. The rooms continue the European decor, each with its own unique bent. You'll find a fishing room, a golf room, a garden room, and a music room, with each motif evoked by the furnishings: a vintage set of golf clubs here, a sheet of music in a dry flower arrangement there. The hotel, which attracts individual travelers as well as families and many Europeans, is well cared for by a concierge who speaks six languages. High tea is served in the lobby from 3 to 5:30pm daily. Request a room facing east, and you'll wake each day to a view of the mountains. Larger rooms have coffeemakers and hair dryers.

210 Don Gaspar Ave., Santa Fe, NM 87501. © 800/529-5700 or 505/983-5700. Fax 505/989-7690. www.hotel stfrancis.com. 83 units. $92–$185 double; $205–$380 suite. Children under 12 stay free in parent's room. AE, DC, DISC, MC, V. Parking $5. **Amenities:** Restaurant; bar; access to nearby health club; concierge; room service; laundry service; dry cleaning; library and gaming tables. *In room:* A/C, TV, fridge, safe.

Hotel Santa Fe ★ *Finds*   About a 10-minute walk south of the Plaza you'll find this newer three-story establishment, the only Native American–owned hotel in Santa Fe. It is a good choice for consistent, well-planned lodgings. Picuris Pueblo is the majority stockholder, and part of the pleasure of staying here is the culture the Picuris bring to your visit. This is not to say that the accommodations give any sense of the rusticity of a pueblo; the sophisticated 16-year-old hotel is decorated in Southwestern style, with a few novel touches such as an Allan Houser bronze buffalo dancer watching over the front desk and a fireplace surrounded by comfortable furniture in the lobby. The rooms are medium-size, with clean lines and comfortable beds, the decor accented with pine Taos-style furniture. Rooms on the north side get less street noise from Cerrillos Road and have better views of the mountains, but they don't have the sun shining onto their balconies. You will get a strong sense of the Native American presence on the patio during the summer, when Picuris dancers come to perform and bread bakers uncover the *horno* (oven) and prepare loaves for sale. Also of note is the more luxurious Hacienda wing.

1501 Paseo de Peralta, Santa Fe, NM 87501. © 800/825-9876 or 505/982-1200. Fax 505/984-2211. www.hotel santafe.com. 163 units. $99–$199 double; $129–$269 junior suite. Hacienda rooms and suites $199–$459. Extra person $10. Children under 18 stay free in parent's room. AE, DC, DISC, MC, V. Free parking. Pets accepted; $20 fee. **Amenities:** Restaurant; outdoor pool; Jacuzzi; concierge; car-rental desk; room service; in-room massage; babysitting; coin-op laundry; dry cleaning. *In room:* A/C, TV, dataport, minibar, iron, safe.

Inn on the Alameda ★   Across the street from the bosque-shaded Santa Fe River sits the Inn on the Alameda, a cozy stop for those who like the services of a hotel with the intimacy of an inn. Built in 1986, with additions over the years, it now rambles across four buildings. Lodgings include casita suites to the west, two three-story buildings at the center, and another one-story building that contains suites. All are pueblo-style adobe, and most were built in the late 1980s. Some of the tasteful rooms have fridges, CD players, safes, Jacuzzi tubs, and kiva fireplaces. The newer deluxe rooms and suites in the easternmost building are in the best shape. The traditional rooms are quaint, some with interesting angled bed configurations. Pet amenities include a pet-walking map.

303 E. Alameda St., Santa Fe, NM 87501. ℂ 800/289-2122 or 505/984-2121. Fax 505/986-8325. www. innonthealameda.com. 69 units. $129–$209 queen; $142–$222 king; $210–$350 suite; off-season discounts available. Rates include breakfast and afternoon wine and cheese reception. AE, DC, DISC, MC, V. Free parking. Pets accepted. **Amenities:** Bar; medium-size fitness facility; 2 open-air Jacuzzis; concierge; massage; child care by arrangement; coin-op laundry; same-day dry cleaning. *In room:* A/C, TV, dataport, hair dryer, iron.

MODERATE

Garrett's Desert Inn *(Value)* Completion of this hotel in 1957 prompted the Historic Design Review Board to implement zoning restrictions throughout downtown. Apparently, residents were appalled by the huge air conditioners adorning the roof. Though they're still unsightly, the hotel makes up for them. First, with all the focus today on retro fashions, this hotel, located 3 blocks from the Plaza, is totally in. It's a two-story concrete-block building around a broad parking lot. The hotel underwent a complete remodel in 1994, with touch-ups through the years; it has maintained some vintage touches, such as Art Deco tile in the bathrooms and plenty of space in the rooms, while being updated with larger windows, sturdy doors, and wood accents. Rooms are equipped with tile vanities, and minisuites have fridges and microwaves.

311 Old Santa Fe Trail, Santa Fe, NM 87501. ℂ 800/888-2145 or 505/982-1851. Fax 505/989-1647. www.garretts desertinn.com. 83 units. $89–$165 double or minisuite. AE, DISC, MC, V. **Amenities:** Restaurant; bar; outdoor pool; concierge; room service; in-room massage; laundry service; dry cleaning. *In room:* A/C, TV, dataport, coffeemaker, hair dryer, iron.

Old Santa Fe Inn *(Finds)* *(Kids)* Want to stay downtown and savor Santa Fe–style ambience without wearing out your plastic? This is your hotel. A multimillion-dollar renovation of a 1930s court motel created this comfortable, quiet inn just a few blocks from the Plaza. Rooms verge on small but are decorated with such lovely handcrafted colonial-style furniture that you probably won't mind. All have small Mexican-tiled bathrooms, each with an outer vanity; most have gas fireplaces. You have a choice of king, queen, or twin rooms as well as suites. Though there's no pool or hot tub, this could still be a good choice for families because it has some adjoining rooms. Breakfast is served in an atmospheric dining room next to a comfortable library.

320 Galisteo St., Santa Fe, NM 87501. ℂ 800/745-9910 or 505/995-0800. Fax 505/995-0400. www.oldsanta feinn.com. 43 units. Winter $89–$136 double, $119–$169 suite; summer $127–$149 double, $199–$249 suite. Rates include continental breakfast. AE, DC, DISC, MC, V. *In room:* A/C, TV/VCR, dataport, fridge, coffeemaker, CD player.

Santa Fe Motel and Inn If you like walking to the Plaza and restaurants but don't want to pay big bucks, this little compound is a good choice. Rooms here are larger than at the nearby Santa Fe Sage Inn and have more personality than those at the Travelodge, though they are also a little more expensive. Ask for one of the casitas in back— you'll pay more but get a little turn-of-the-20th-century charm, plus more quiet and privacy. Some have vigas, and others have skylights, fireplaces, and patios. The main part of the motel, built in 1955, is two-story Territorial style, with upstairs rooms that open onto a portal with a bit of a view. All guest rooms are decorated with a Southwestern motif and have very basic furnishings but comfortable beds. Some rooms have kitchenettes, with fridges, microwaves, stoves, coffeemakers, and toasters. Coffee is served each morning in the office, where a bulletin board lists Santa Fe activities.

510 Cerrillos Rd., Santa Fe, NM 87501. © 800/930-5002 or 505/982-1039. Fax 505/986-1275. www.santafemotel. com. 23 units. $69–$139 double. Extra person $10. Rates include continental breakfast. AE, DC, MC, V. Free parking. *In room:* A/C, TV, hair dryer, iron.

INEXPENSIVE

Santa Fe Plaza Travelodge You can count on this motel near Hotel Santa Fe (6 blocks from the Plaza) on busy Cerrillos Road for comfort, convenience, and a no-frills stay. The rooms are very clean, nicely lit, and, despite the busy location, relatively quiet. Firm mattresses and a pretty Southwestern ceiling border add to the comfort and decor.

646 Cerrillos Rd., Santa Fe, NM 87501. © 800/578-7878 or 505/982-3551. Fax 505/983-8624. www.travelodge. com. 48 units. May–Oct $65–$88 double; Nov–Apr $39–$69 double. AE, DC, DISC, MC, V. Free parking. **Amenities:** Outdoor pool. *In room:* A/C, TV, fridge, coffeemaker.

Santa Fe Sage Inn *(Value)* If you're looking for a convenient, almost-downtown location at a reasonable price, this is one of your best bets. The two-story stucco adobe motel with portals spreads through three buildings and is about a 10-minute walk from the plaza. Built in 1985, it was remodeled in 2005. The rooms aren't large but have comfortable beds. To avoid street noise, ask for a room at the back of the property. It's near McDonald's, and there's a small park in the back. An adjacent restaurant serves American and New Mexican food.

725 Cerrillos Rd., Santa Fe, NM 87501. © 866/433-0335 or 505/982-5952. Fax 505/984-8879. www.santafe sageinn.com. 160 units. $59–$129 double. Rates include continental breakfast. AE, DC, MC, V. Free parking. Pets accepted. **Amenities:** Outdoor pool. *In room:* A/C, TV, coffeemaker, iron.

NORTHSIDE

Within easy reach of the Plaza, Northside encompasses the area that lies north of the loop of Paseo de Peralta.

VERY EXPENSIVE

The Bishop's Lodge ★★ *(Kids)* More than a century ago, when Bishop Jean-Baptiste Lamy was the spiritual leader of northern New Mexico's Roman Catholic population, he often escaped clerical politics by hiking into this valley called Little Tesuque. He built a retreat and a humble chapel (now on the National Register of Historic Places) with vaulted ceilings and a hand-made altar. Today, Lamy's 1,000-acre getaway has become The Bishop's Lodge. A recent $17 million renovation spruced up the place and added a spa and 10,000 square feet of meeting space. The guest rooms, spread through many buildings, feature handcrafted furniture and regional artwork. Standard rooms are spacious, and many have balconies. Deluxe rooms feature kiva fireplaces, a combination bedroom/sitting room, and private decks or patios. The newest rooms are luxurious, and some have spectacular views of the Jemez Mountains. The Bishop's Lodge is an active resort and offers many activities.

Bishop's Lodge Rd. (P.O. Box 2367), Santa Fe, NM 87504. © 505/983-6377. Fax 505/989-8739. www.bishops lodge.com. 111 units. Summer $299–$399 double; fall and spring $249–$349 double; midwinter $189–$269 double. Extra person $15. Children under 4 stay free in parent's room. Ask about packages that include meals. AE, DC, DISC, MC, V. Free parking. **Amenities:** Restaurant; outdoor pool; tennis courts; spa; Jacuzzi; sauna; steam room; concierge; courtesy shuttle; room service; in-room massage; babysitting; laundry service. *In room:* A/C, TV, coffeemaker, safe.

MODERATE

Radisson Hotel Santa Fe ★ *(Value)* Set on a hill as you head north toward the Santa Fe Opera, this three-story hotel has recently benefited from a multimillion-dollar renovation that has made it a lovely place. The theme here is Native American, with Anasazi-style stacked sandstone throughout the lobby and dining room. The guest rooms are

Greater Santa Fe

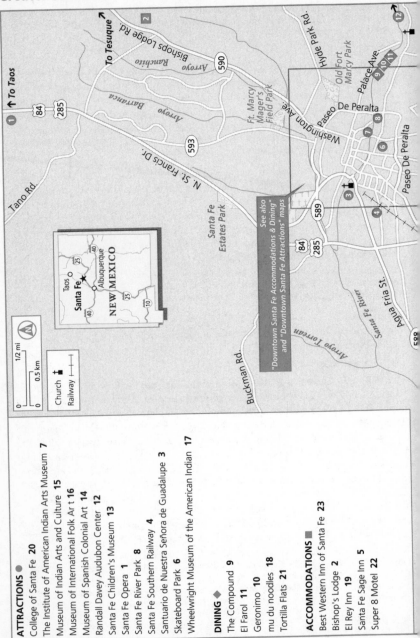

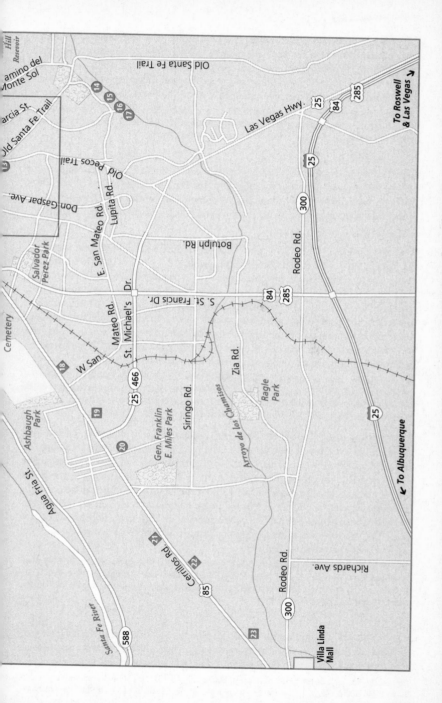

medium-size, decorated in earth tones with bold prints, some with views of the mountains, others overlooking the pool. Premium rooms are more spacious, some with large living rooms and private balconies. Each parlor suite has a Murphy bed and kiva fireplace in the living room, a big dining area, a wet bar and fridges, and a jetted bathtub. The condo units nearby have fully equipped kitchens, fireplaces, and private decks.

750 N. St. Francis Dr., Santa Fe, NM 87501. ℂ 800/333-3333 or 505/992-5800. Fax 505/992-5856. www.radisson. com. 128 units, 32 condos. $259 double; $225 suite; $309 condo. AE, DC, DISC, MC, V. Free parking. **Amenities:** Outdoor pool; free shuttle service to downtown. *In room:* A/C, TV, hair dryer, iron.

SOUTHSIDE

Santa Fe's major strip, Cerrillos Road, is US 85, the main route to and from Albuquerque and the I-25 freeway. It's about 5¼ miles from the Plaza to the Villa Linda Mall, which marks the southern boundary of the city. Most motels are on this strip, although several of them are to the east, closer to St. Francis Drive (US 84) or the Las Vegas Highway.

MODERATE

Best Western Inn of Santa Fe *Value*   This three-story hotel, a 15-minute drive from the Plaza, offers cookie-cutter rooms at a reasonable price. It was built in 1990, and renovations are ongoing. The lobby is decorated in light pastels, with nice little tables where guests can eat breakfast. The indoor Jacuzzi and pool are very clean, a good family spot to relax between outings. The somewhat narrow rooms have Aztec-motif bedspreads and blond furniture. Some doubles are more spacious, with couches. All have fairly small but functional bathrooms. Suites are larger, and some have an in-room Jacuzzi; others have two rooms, with a sofa bed in one. This is a security-conscious hotel; rooms can be entered only from interior corridors, and each room has a private safe.

3650 Cerrillos Rd., Santa Fe, NM 87505. ℂ 800/528-1234 or 505/438-3822. Fax 505/438-3795. www.best western.com. 97 units. $50–$100 double; $75–$145 suite. Children under 13 stay free in parent's room. Rates include continental breakfast. AE, DC, DISC, MC, V. Free parking. Pets accepted with prior approval. **Amenities:** Indoor pool; Jacuzzi; laundry service. *In room:* A/C, TV, coffeemaker, hair dryer, safe.

El Rey Inn ⭐ *Finds*   Staying at "The King" makes you feel as though you're traveling the old Route 66 through the Southwest. The court motel's white stucco buildings are decorated with bright trim around the doors and hand-painted Mexican tiles on the walls. Opened in the 1930s, it expanded in the 1950s, and remodeling is ongoing. No two rooms are alike. The oldest section, nearest the lobby, feels a bit cramped, though the rooms have style, with Art Deco tile in the bathrooms and vigas on the ceilings. Some have little patios. Be sure to request a room as far back as possible from Cerrillos Road. The two stories of suites around the Spanish colonial courtyard are the sweetest deal I've seen in all of Santa Fe.

1862 Cerrillos Rd. (P.O. Box 4759), Santa Fe, NM 87502. ℂ 800/521-1349 or 505/982-1931. Fax 505/989-9249. www. elreyinnsantafe.com. 85 units. $95–$165 double; $120–$225 suite. Rates include continental breakfast. AE, DC, DISC, MC, V. Free parking. **Amenities:** Outdoor pool; exercise room; Jacuzzi; sauna; coin-op laundry. *In room:* A/C, TV, fridge, coffeemaker, hair dryer, iron, safe.

INEXPENSIVE

Super 8 Motel   It's nothing flashy, but this pink stucco, boxy motel, which has received the "Pride of Super 8" award, attracts regulars who know precisely what to expect. You'll get a comfortable room with double beds, a desk, and a few other amenities.

3358 Cerrillos Rd., Santa Fe, NM 87507. ℂ 800/800-8000 or 505/471-8811. Fax 505/471-3239. www.super8.com. 96 units. $45–$80 double. Rates include continental breakfast. AE, DC, DISC, MC, V. Free parking. **Amenities:** Coin-op laundry. *In room:* A/C, TV, coffeemaker, safe.

BED & BREAKFASTS

If you prefer a homey, intimate setting to the sometimes-impersonal ambience of a large hotel, one of Santa Fe's bed-and-breakfast inns may be right for you. All those listed here are in or close to the downtown area and offer comfortable accommodations at expensive to moderate prices.

Adobe Abode ⭐   A short walk from the Plaza, in the same quiet neighborhood as the Georgia O'Keeffe Museum, this is one of Santa Fe's most imaginative B&Bs. The cozy living room is decorated with folk art. Creativity shines in each of the guest rooms, some of which are in the 1907 main house. Others, in back, are newer. The Provence Suite, decorated in sunny yellow and bright blue, offers a feel of France, while the Bronco Room is filled with cowboy paraphernalia: hats, Pendleton blankets, pioneer chests, and an entire shelf lined with children's cowboy boots. Two rooms have fireplaces, and several have private patios. Sherry, fruit, and cookies are served daily in the living room. A full breakfast of fresh fruit and a hot dish such as green chile corn soufflé is served in the country-style kitchen.

202 Chapelle St., Santa Fe, NM 87501. ℂ **505/983-3133**. Fax 505/983-3132. www.adobeabode.com. 6 units. $135–$185 double. Rates include breakfast and afternoon snacks. DISC, MC, V. Limited free parking. *In room:* A/C, TV, coffeemaker, hair dryer, iron.

El Farolito ⭐⭐   The owners of this inn, which is within walking distance of the Plaza, have created an authentic theme experience for guests in each unit. They include the Native American Room, decorated with rugs and pottery; the South-of-the-Border Room, with Mexican folk art and a full-size sofa sleeper; and the elegant Santa Fe–style Opera Room, with hand-carved, lavishly upholstered furniture. A two-room suite in the main building has a queen-size iron bed and Southwestern decor. The walls of most of the rooms were rubbed with beeswax during plastering to give them a smooth, golden finish. All rooms (except the suite) have kiva fireplaces and private patios. The common area displays works by notable New Mexico artists. Part of the inn was built before 1912, and the rest is new, but the old-world elegance carries through. Under the same stellar ownership (but a little less expensive) is the nearby **Four Kachinas Inn** ⭐ (ℂ **888/634-8782** or 505/982-2550; www.fourkachinas.com), where Southwestern-style rooms sit around a sunny courtyard.

514 Galisteo St., Santa Fe, NM 87501. ℂ **888/634-8782** or 505/988-1631. Fax 505/988-4589. www.farolito.com. 8 units. $150–$280 double or suite. Rates include expanded continental breakfast. AE, DISC, MC, V. Free parking. **Amenities:** Babysitting; valet laundry. *In room:* A/C, TV, coffeemaker, hair dryer, iron.

Grant Corner Inn ⭐⭐   This early-20th-century manor, just 2 blocks west of the Plaza and next door to the Georgia O'Keeffe Museum, offers a quiet stay with a fanciful Victorian ambience. Each room is furnished with antiques, from brass or four-poster beds to armoires and quilts, and terry robes are available for those staying in units with shared bathrooms. All rooms have ceiling fans, and some are equipped with small fridges. Each room has its own character. For example, one has a hand-painted German wardrobe closet dating from 1772 and a washbasin with brass fittings in the shape of fish; another has a private outdoor deck that catches the morning sun; another has an antique collection of dolls and stuffed animals. Breakfast here is notable. Some rooms are appropriate for children; if you're traveling as a family, say so when you make your reservation.

122 Grant Ave., Santa Fe, NM 87501. ℂ **800/964-9003**, 505/983-6678 for reservations, 505/984-9001 to contact guests. Fax 505/983-1526. www.grantcornerinn.com. 9 units, 1 hacienda. $130–$240 double. Hacienda: $145–$165 guest room rented separately; $270–$310 entire house. Extra person $20. Rates include full breakfast and afternoon

tea. AE, MC, V. Free parking. **Amenities:** Restaurant (breakfast only); Jacuzzi; concierge; tour desk; in-room massage; laundry service. *In room:* A/C, TV, hair dryer, iron.

Hacienda Nicholas ★★ This inn just a few blocks from the Plaza has a delightful Southwest hacienda feel. Rooms surround a sunny patio; my favorites are the bright Cottonwood, with a serene feel created by the muted tones of the decor, and the Sunflower, with French doors, maple floors, a kiva fireplace, and a luxurious king bed. All units have spacious bathrooms with Mexican tiles. Breakfast is served near the large fireplace in the great room or on the enclosed garden patio. Near this inn and under the same ownership, the **Madeleine** (✆ **888/877-7622** or 505/982-3465) offers a more Victorian feel; it's an 1886 Queen Anne-style home adorned with lace and stained glass. The inn doubles as an atmospheric tea room and spa called Absolute Nirvana. My favorite guest room here is the Morning Glory, with a king-size bed, a corner fireplace, and lots of sun. All rooms have terry robes.

320 E. Marcy St., Santa Fe, NM 87501. ✆ **888/284-3170** or 505/992-8385. Fax 505/982-8572. www.hacienda nicholas.com. 7 units. $125–$240 double[FB1]. AE, DISC, MC, V. Extra person $25. Rates include full breakfast and afternoon tea. **Amenities:** Concierge; activities desk. *In room:* A/C, TV/VCR, dataport, hair dryer.

Water Street Inn ★★ An award-winning adobe restoration 4 blocks from the Plaza, this friendly inn features beautiful Mexican-tile bathrooms, several kiva fireplaces and wood stoves, and antique furnishings. Each room is packed with Southwestern art and books. The afternoon happy hour, with quesadillas and margaritas, takes place in the living room or on the upstairs portal, where breakfast is also served. All rooms are decorated in Moroccan/Southwestern style. Room no. 3 provides a queen-size sofa bed to accommodate families. Room no. 4 features regional decorative touches and boasts a chaise lounge, a fur rug, built-in seating, and a corner fireplace. Four suites have elegant contemporary Southwestern furnishings and private patios with fountains. Most rooms have balconies or terraces.

427 Water St., Santa Fe, NM 87501. ✆ **800/646-6752** or 505/984-1193. Fax 505/984-6235. www.waterstreetinn. com. 12 units. $100–$250 double. Rates include continental breakfast and afternoon hors d'oeuvres and refreshments. AE, DISC, MC, V. Free parking. Children and pets accepted with prior approval. **Amenities:** Jacuzzi; concierge; room service. *In room:* A/C, TV/VCR, dataport, hair dryer.

RV PARKS & CAMPGROUNDS
RV PARKS

Several private camping areas, mainly for recreational vehicles, are within a few minutes' drive of downtown Santa Fe. Be sure to book ahead at busy times.

Los Campos RV Resort This resort has 95 spaces with full hookups, picnic tables, and a covered pavilion for use at no charge (with reservation). It's just 5 miles south of the Plaza, so it's convenient, but it is surrounded by the city.

3574 Cerrillos Rd., Santa Fe, NM 87507. ✆ **800/852-8160.** Fax 505/471-9220. $28–$33 daily; $169–$206 weekly; winter $450 monthly, summer $470 monthly. MC, V. Pets accepted. **Amenities:** Outdoor pool; concierge; coin-op laundry; restrooms; showers; grills; vending machines; free cable TV.

Rancheros de Santa Fe Campground ★ Tents, motor homes, and trailers requiring full hookups are welcome here. The park's 130 sites sit on 22 acres of piñon and juniper forest. Cabins are also available. It's about 6 miles southeast of Santa Fe and is open March 15 to October 31.

736 Old Las Vegas Hwy. (Exit 290 off I-25), Santa Fe, NM 87505. ✆ **800/426-9259** or 505/466-3482. www. rancheros.com. Tent site $17–$19; RV hookup $25–$30. DISC, MC, V. **Amenities:** Outdoor pool; coin-op laundry;

restrooms; showers; grills; cable TV hookups; grocery store; recreation room; tables; fireplaces; nature trails; playground; free nightly movies May–Sept; public telephones; propane.

Santa Fe KOA   This campground, about 11 miles northeast of Santa Fe, offers 46 RV sites and 10 tent sites set among the foothills of the Sangre de Cristo Mountains, an excellent place to enjoy northern New Mexico's pine-filled high desert. It offers full hookups, pull-through sites, and tent sites.

934 Old Las Vegas Hwy. (exit 290 or 294 off I-25), Santa Fe, NM 87505. © **800/KOA-1514** or 505/466-1419 for reservations. www.koa.com. Tent site $22–$25; RV hookup $26–$31. DISC, MC, V. **Amenities:** Coin-op laundry; restrooms; showers; store/gift shop; recreation room; playground; picnic tables; dataport; propane; dumping station.

CAMPGROUNDS

The forested sites along NM 475 on the way to Ski Santa Fe are all open from May to October. Overnight rates start at about $12.

Hyde Memorial State Park   About 8 miles from the city, this park offers a quiet retreat surrounded by pine trees. Seven RV pads with electrical pedestals and an RV dumping station are available. You can enjoy nature and hiking trails and a playground as well as a small winter skating pond.

740 Hyde Park Rd., Santa Fe, NM 87501. © **505/983-7175**. www.nmparks.com. **Amenities:** Shelters; water; tables; vault toilets.

Santa Fe National Forest ★★   Black Canyon campground, with 44 sites, is adjacent to Hyde Memorial State Park. It is one of the only campgrounds in the state for which you can make a reservation; to do so, you must go through a national reservation system (© **877/444-6777;** www.reserveusa.com). The sites sit within thick forest, with hiking trails nearby. Big Tesuque, a first-come, first-served campground with 10 rehabilitated sites, is about 12 miles from town. The sites here are closer to the road and sit at the edge of aspen forests. Both Black Canyon and Big Tesuque campgrounds, located along the Santa Fe Scenic Byway, NM 475, are equipped with vault toilets.

P.O. Box 1689, Santa Fe, NM 87504. © **505/438-7840** or 505/753-7331. www.fs.fed.us/r3/sfe. **Amenities:** Water; vault toilets.

4 Where to Dine

Santa Fe abounds in dining options, with hundreds of restaurants of all categories. Competition is steep, and spots are continually opening and closing. Locals watch closely to see which ones will survive. Some chefs create dishes that incorporate traditional Southwestern foods with ingredients not indigenous to the region; these listings classify their restaurants as "creative Southwestern." Other options include standard regional New Mexican cuisine, excellent steak and seafood, continental, European, Asian, and, of course, Mexican menus.

Especially during peak tourist seasons, dinner reservations may be essential. Reservations are always recommended at better restaurants.

DOWNTOWN

This area includes the circle defined by the Paseo de Peralta and St. Francis Drive, as well as Canyon Road. See the "Downtown Santa Fe Accommodations & Dining" map, p. 143.

EXPENSIVE

Cafe Pasqual's ★★ CREATIVE SOUTHWESTERN "You have to become the food, erase the line between it as an object and you. You have to really examine its structure, its size, its color, its strength, its weakness, know who grew it, how long it's been out of the field," says Pasqual's owner Katharine Kagel. That attitude is completely apparent in this restaurant, where murals depict voluptuous villagers playing guitars, drinking, and even flying. Needless to say, it's a festive place, though it's also excellent for a romantic dinner. Service is jovial and professional. My favorite dish for breakfast or lunch is *huevos motuleños* (two eggs over easy on blue-corn tortillas and black beans topped with sautéed bananas, feta cheese, salsa, and green chile). Soups and salads are also served at lunch, as is a delectable grilled-salmon burrito with herbed goat cheese and cucumber salsa. The frequently changing dinner menu offers grilled meats and seafood, plus vegetarian specials. Start with the Iroquois corn tamale with roasted poblano, zucchini, and asadero cheese, and move on to spinach, jack cheese, and red onion enchiladas. There's a communal table for those who would like to meet new people over a meal. Pasqual's offers imported beers and wine by the bottle or glass. Try to go at an odd hour—late morning or afternoon—or make a reservation for dinner; otherwise, you'll have to wait.

121 Don Gaspar Ave. ✆ 505/983-9340. Reservations recommended for dinner. Main courses $5.75–$13 breakfast, $6–$15 lunch, $16–$34 dinner. AE, MC, V. Year-round Mon–Sat 7am–3pm; Sun brunch 8am–2pm. Summer daily 6–10:30pm; off season Sun–Thurs 5:30–9:30pm, Fri–Sat 6–10pm.

The Compound ★★★ NEW AMERICAN This reincarnation of one of Santa Fe's classic restaurants serves some of the most flavorful and daring food in town. During warm months, a broad patio shelters diners from the city bustle. With friendly, efficient service, this is an excellent place for a romantic dinner or a relaxing lunch. Chef-owner Mark Kiffin, who spent nearly 8 years as chef at Coyote Café (see below), lets his creativity soar. You might start off with tuna tartare topped with Osetra caviar. For an entree, a signature dish is grilled beef tenderloin with Italian potatoes and foie gras hollandaise. For lunch, monkfish chorizo with watercress is outrageously tasty. Finish with bittersweet chocolate torte. A carefully selected beer and wine list accompanies the menu.

653 Canyon Rd. ✆ 505/982-4353. Reservations recommended. Main courses $12–$20 lunch, $20–$31 dinner. AE, MC, V. Mon–Fri noon–2pm; daily 6–9pm; bar opens nightly at 5pm.

Coyote Café ★★ CREATIVE SOUTHWESTERN/LATIN World-renowned chef and cookbook author Mark Miller has been "charged with single-handedly elevating the chile to haute status." That statement from the *New York Times Magazine* sums up for me the experience of eating at this trendy nouveau Southwestern restaurant about a block from the Plaza. The atmosphere is urban Southwestern, with calf-skin-covered chairs and a zoo of carved animals watching from a balcony. The exhibition kitchen has lots of brass and tile, and the waitstaff is efficient and friendly. It's the place to go for a fun night out, or you can sample the great food for lunch at a fraction of the price. Some complain that on a busy night the space is noisy. The menu changes seasonally. Start your meal with Coyote cocktails that might include a Brazilian daiquiri or margarita del Maguey. Then look for delights such as chipotle tiger prawns with griddled corn cakes or a duck tamale. Move on to braised ancho lamb shank or horseradish-crusted Maine haddock. You can order drinks from the full bar or wine by the glass. Smoking is not allowed.

Coyote Café has two adjunct establishments. In summer, the place to be seen is the **Rooftop Cantina,** which serves light Latino/Cuban fare and cocktails on a festively painted terrace. (Try the chicken skewers on sugar cane.) On the ground floor is **Cottonwoods,** offering a reasonably priced menu in a new Southwestern diner ambience.

132 Water St. © 505/983-1615. Reservations highly recommended. Main courses $19–$36 (Coyote Café), $6–$16 (Rooftop Cantina), $6–$15 (Cottonwoods). AE, DC, DISC, MC, V. Dining room: daily 6–9:30pm; daily 5:30–9pm during opera season. Rooftop Cantina: daily 11:30am–9pm.

El Farol ✪ SPANISH   This is the place to head for local ambience and old-fashioned flavor. El Farol (the lantern) is the Canyon Road artists' quarter's original neighborhood bar. The restaurant has cozy low ceilings and hand-smoothed adobe walls. It serves 35 varieties of tapas, including such delicacies as *gambas al ajillo* (shrimp with chile, garlic, Madeira, and lime) and *conejo y vino* (stewed rabbit). You can make a meal out of two or three tapas shared with friends or order a full dinner, such as paella or grilled lamb chops with cranberry salsa. Live entertainment—including jazz/swing, folk, and Latin guitar music—starts nightly at 9:30pm. In summer, two outdoor patios are open to diners.

808 Canyon Rd. © 505/983-9912. Reservations recommended. Tapas $4.50–$12; main courses $8–$15 lunch, $26–$32 dinner. DC, DISC, MC, V. Daily 11:30am–3pm and 5:30–10pm (bar until 1am weekdays, 2am Fri–Sat).

Geronimo ✪✪✪ CONTINENTAL   This elegant restaurant offers one of Santa Fe's most delectable dining experiences. It occupies an old adobe structure known as the Borrego House, built by Geronimo Lopez in 1756 and completely restored, that retains the feel of an old Santa Fe home. I especially recommend lunch, when you can get a taste of this complex food for a fraction of the dinner price. Reserve a spot on the porch and watch the action on Canyon Road. My favorite at lunch is house-smoked ruby trout salad, with crimson beluga lentils, organic grains, and sweet sesame dressing. For a dinner appetizer, try Maryland blue crab strudel and lime-toasted pepita and red onion salad. For an entree, mesquite-grilled elk tenderloin with chestnut strudel is legendary, as is grilled Maine lobster with farmer's corn and leek compote. For dessert, you won't be disappointed by the trio of crème brûlées—espresso chocolate, Chambord, and orange—or Belgian chocolate Grand Marnier cake. The menu changes seasonally, and there is an excellent wine list.

724 Canyon Rd. © 505/982-1500. Reservations recommended. Main courses $10–$19 lunch, $20–$36 dinner. AE, MC, V. Tues–Sun 11:30am–2pm; daily 6–9:30pm.

La Casa Sena ✪✪ CREATIVE SOUTHWESTERN   Combining alluring ambience and tasty food, this is one of Santa Fe's favorite restaurants, though the food isn't as precise and flavorful here as at Santacafé or The Old House. La Casa Sena sits within the Sena compound, a prime example of a Spanish hacienda, in a Territorial-style adobe house built in 1867 by Civil War hero Major José Sena. The house, which surrounds a garden courtyard, is a veritable art gallery, with museum-quality landscapes on the walls and Taos-style handcrafted furniture. The cuisine in the main dining room might be described as northern New Mexican with a Continental flair. One of my favorite lunches is flash-fried Baja sea bass tacos with mango salsa. In the evening, diners might start with a salad of garden greens and grilled mushrooms, then move to grilled lamb rack marinated with Dijon mustard and mint and accompanied by roasted root vegetables and green peppercorn sauce.

In the adjacent **La Cantina,** waiters and waitresses sing Broadway show tunes as they carry platters to the tables. La Cantina's more moderately priced menu offers the likes of cornmeal-breaded trout and grilled stuffed pork loin with peach-onion sauce. Both restaurants have exquisite desserts; try the black-and-white bittersweet chocolate terrine with raspberry sauce. The award-winning wine list features more than 850 selections. There's patio dining in summer.

125 E. Palace Ave. ℂ 505/988-9232. Reservations recommended. La Casa Sena main courses $8–$12 lunch, $21–$30 dinner; 5-course chef's tasting menu $42, with wine $58; La Cantina main courses $13–$23. AE, DC, DISC, MC, V. Mon–Sat 11:30am–3pm; Sun brunch 11am–3pm; daily 5:30–10pm.

The Old House ★★★ NEW AMERICAN/CONTINENTAL   This restaurant consistently rates as Santa Fe's best eatery in local publications' polls—and it's no wonder, with chef Martin Rios running the show. A native of Mexico, he worked his way up through some of Santa Fe's finest kitchens before embarking on a course at the Culinary Institute of America and returning to the City Different to turn The Old House into a nationally acclaimed restaurant, with a story running on PBS and a cover article in *Bon Appétit*. In a Southwestern atmosphere, rich with excellent Native American art, Rios serves quality meats, poultry, and seafood in refined sauces. The menu changes seasonally; some signature dishes remain year-round. Start with lump crab cake, with grilled portobello and butternut squash salad. Move on to my favorite, the mustard-and-pepper-crusted lamb rack, with roasted shallot potato mash and red chile–Merlot lamb jus; or sautéed Diver sea scallops with wild mushrooms, asparagus, and pumpkin seeds in a Xeres sherry reduction. My friend Michael says the crème brûlée here is the best dessert he's ever had, but my favorite is the warm-liquid-center chocolate cake. The wine list is a *Wine Spectator* award-winner.

In the Eldorado Hotel, 309 W. San Francisco St. ℂ 505/988-4455, ext. 130. Reservations recommended. Main courses $23–$30. AE, DC, DISC, MC, V. Daily 5:30–10pm. Lounge daily 4:30–10pm.

Ore House on the Plaza ★ STEAK/SEAFOOD/NEW MEXICAN   The Ore House's second-story balcony, at the southwest corner of the Plaza, is an ideal spot from which to watch the passing scene while you enjoy cocktails and hors d'oeuvres. In fact, it is *the* place to be between 4 and 6pm every afternoon. Inside, the decor is Southwestern, with plants, hanging lanterns, white walls, and booths. The menu offers fresh seafood and steaks as well as some nueva Latina dishes that incorporate interesting sauces. Daily fresh fish specials include salmon and swordfish (poached, blackened, teriyaki, or lemon), rainbow trout, lobster, and shellfish. Salmon with spinach pecan pesto has become a new favorite, and you can't go wrong with the Steak Ore House (wrapped in bacon and topped with crabmeat and béarnaise sauce). The Ore House offers vegetable platters for noncarnivores.

The bar, offering live music nightly Thursday to Sunday, serves more than 65 different margaritas. It offers a selection of domestic and imported beers and an excellent wine list. An appetizer menu is served from 2:30 to 10pm daily.

50 Lincoln Ave. ℂ 505/983-8687. Reservations recommended. Main courses $5–$13 lunch, $16–$28 dinner. AE, MC, V. Daily 11:30am–10pm (bar until midnight or later).

The Palace ★★ NEW ITALIAN   On the site of this local favorite, Santa Fe's 19th-century matriarch, Doña Tules, operated a thriving gambling hall and bordello. From the place's remains came a brass door knocker, half shaped like a horseshoe, and the other half like a saloon girl's stockinged leg; the design is now the restaurant's logo. Hearkening back to those old days, the Palace serves flavorful food in a Victorian atmosphere, with a bit of bordello flair. The restaurant changed hands in 2004 and still has a plush and comfortable feel, but with a new elegance. The owners, Cliff

Skoglund, Robert Hall, and Eric DiStefano, are well known for their magic at the acclaimed Geronimo. The Caesar salad—prepared tableside—is always good, as are the meat dishes. My favorite meals are salmon with two kinds of mushrooms, and grilled chicken breast with shrimp, leek, and scallion risotto. The pasta dishes are also tasty, as are the vegetarian options and daily specials. The wine list is long and well considered. A lovely patio and a lively bar are popular with locals. The bar schedules nightly entertainment, including dancing on Saturday after 9pm, and it has its own menu from 3pm to midnight.

142 W. Palace Ave. © **505/982-9891.** Reservations recommended. Main courses $7–$16 lunch, $16–$34 dinner. AE, DC, DISC, MC, V. Mon–Sat 11:30am–3pm; daily 6–10pm. Bar: Mon–Sat 11:30am–2am; Sun 5:30pm–midnight.

The Pink Adobe ☆ CONTINENTAL/SOUTHWESTERN   More show than flavor? Probably. This restaurant, located a few blocks off the Plaza, offers a swirl of local old-timer gaiety and food that is more imaginative than flavorful, but the Pink Adobe has remained popular since it opened in 1944. The restaurant occupies an adobe home believed to be at least 350 years old. Guests enter through a narrow side door into a series of quaint, informal dining rooms with tile or hardwood floors. Stuccoed walls display original modern art and Priscilla Hoback pottery. For lunch, I always have a chicken enchilada topped with an egg. Gypsy stew (chicken, green chile, tomatoes, and onions in sherry broth) sounds great but is on the bland side. At dinner, the Pink Adobe offers the likes of escargot and shrimp rémoulade as appetizers. The local word here is that the steak Dunigan, with sautéed mushrooms and green chile, is "the thing" to order. You can't leave without trying the hot French apple pie.

Smoking is allowed only in the Dragon Room (p. 185), the lounge across the alleyway from the restaurant. Under the same ownership, the charming bar (a real local scene) has its own menu of traditional New Mexican food. Locals come to eat hearty green chile stew.

406 Old Santa Fe Trail. © **505/983-7712.** Reservations recommended. Main courses $4.75–$9 lunch, $14–$26 dinner. AE, DC, DISC, MC, V. Mon–Fri 11:30am–2pm; daily from 5:30pm. Bar: Mon–Fri 11:30am–2am; Sat 5pm–2am; Sun 5pm–midnight.

Rio Chama Steakhouse ☆☆ STEAK/SEAFOOD   Serving up tasty steaks in a refined ranch atmosphere, this is one of Santa Fe's best newer restaurants. It's a good spot for a business lunch or a fun-filled evening, and the patio is a bright spot during warm months. Service is efficient, and there's a full bar. My favorite for lunch is the buffalo patty, much more flavorful than beef. Lunch also brings a good selection of salads and sandwiches, as well as steaks at a reasonable price. In the evening, prime rib is a big seller, as is the nightly seafood special. For dessert, try the chocolate cake.

414 Old Santa Fe Trail. © **505/955-0765.** Reservations recommended on weekend nights. Main courses $8–$22 lunch, $15–$35 dinner. AE, DC, DISC, MC, V. Daily 11am–3pm and 5–10pm; patio bar from 5pm.

Santacafé ☆☆☆ *Moments* NEW AMERICAN/CREATIVE SOUTHWESTERN   When you eat at this fine restaurant, be prepared to savor every bite. The food combines the best of many cuisines, from Asian to Southwestern, served in an elegant setting with minimalist decor that accentuates the graceful architecture of the 18th-century Padre Gallegos House, 2 blocks from the Plaza. The white walls are decorated only with deer antlers, and each room contains a fireplace. In warm months you can sit under elm trees in the charming courtyard. Be aware that on busy nights the rooms are noisy. The dishes change to take advantage of seasonal specialties, each served with precision. For a starter, try shiitake and cactus spring rolls with Southwestern ponzu. One of my favorite main courses is Alaskan halibut with English peas and saffron couscous. A heartier eater might try bacon-wrapped Black Angus filet mignon with roasted garlic mashed potatoes. There's an extensive wine list, with wine by the glass as well. Desserts, as elegant as the rest of the food, are made in-house; try warm chocolate upside-down cake with vanilla ice cream. Sunday brunch is served in summer and on Easter and Mother's Day.

231 Washington Ave. ✆ **505/984-1788.** Reservations recommended. Main courses $9–$15 lunch, $19–$40 dinner. AE, MC, V. Mon–Sat 11:30am–2pm; daily 6–10pm.

MODERATE

Pranzo Italian Grill ★★ REGIONAL ITALIAN   Housed in a renovated warehouse and decorated in warm Tuscan colors, this contemporary restaurant decorated with modern abstract art serves food prepared on an open grill. Homemade soups, salads, and creative thin-crust pizzas are among the less expensive menu items. A local favorite is cioppino, a seafood stew in a rich wine broth. *Pizza ala pesto e gamberoni* (pizza with shrimp, pesto, goat cheese, and roasted peppers) is also a consistent favorite. Steak, chicken, veal, and fresh seafood grills—heavy on the garlic—dominate the dinner menu. The bar has the Southwest's largest collection of grappas, as well as a wide selection of wines and champagnes by the glass. The rooftop terrace is lovely for seasonal moon-watching over a glass of wine.

540 Montezuma St. (Sanbusco Center). ✆ **505/984-2645.** Reservations recommended. Main courses $7–$15 lunch, $10–$24 dinner. AE, DC, DISC, MC, V. Mon–Sat 11:30am–3pm and 5pm–midnight; Sun 5–10pm.

Shohko Cafe ★ JAPANESE/SUSHI   Santa Fe's favorite sushi restaurant serves fresh fish in a 150-year-old adobe building that was once a bordello. The atmosphere is sparse and comfortable, a blending of New Mexican decor with traditional Japanese decorative touches. Up to 30 fresh varieties of raw seafood, including sushi and sashimi, are served at plain pine tables in various rooms or at the sushi bar. Request the sushi bar, where the atmosphere is coziest, and you can watch the chefs at work. My mother likes the tempura combination with veggies, shrimp, and scallops. On an odd night, I'll order salmon teriyaki, but most nights I have sushi, particularly the *anago* and spicy tuna roll. If you're daring, you might try the Santa Fe roll (with green chile, shrimp tempura, and *masago*). Wine, imported beers, and hot sake are available.

321 Johnson St. ✆ **505/983-7288.** Reservations recommended. Main courses $4.25–$17 lunch, $9–$25 dinner. AE, DISC, MC, V. Mon–Fri 11:30am–2pm; Sun–Thurs 5:30–9pm; Fri–Sat 5:30–9:30pm.

INEXPENSIVE

Blue Corn Café *Kids* NEW MEXICAN/MICROBREWERY   If you're ready for a fun and inexpensive night out, eating decent New Mexican food, this is your place. The raucous, buoyant atmosphere makes this a good place to bring kids. The overworked waitstaff may be slow, but the servers are friendly. I recommend sampling dishes from the combination menu. You can get two to five items served with your choice of rice, beans, or one of the best versions of *posole* (hominy and chile) that I've tasted. I had the chicken enchilada, which I recommend, and the chalupa, which I don't because it was soggy. You can have tacos, tamales, and rellenos, too. Kids have their own menu and crayons to keep them occupied. There are nightly specials—tasty shrimp fajitas come with nice guacamole and the usual toppings. Since this is also a brewery, you might want to sample the High Altitude Pale Ale or the Plaza Porter. My beverage choice is prickly pear iced tea (black tea with enough cactus juice to give it a zing). The Spanish flan is tasty and large enough to share. The **Blue Corn Cafe &**

Brewery (4056 Cerrillos Rd., Suite G; ☎ **505/438-1800**), on the south side of Santa Fe at the corner of Cerrillos and Rodeo roads, has similar fare and atmosphere.

133 W. Water St. ☎ 505/984-1800. Main courses $7–$18. AE, DC, DISC, MC, V. Daily 11am–10pm.

Guadalupe Cafe ★★ NEW MEXICAN   When I want New Mexican food, I go to this restaurant, and like many Santa Feans, I go there often. This casually elegant cafe is in a white stucco building with a nice-size patio for dining in warmer months. Service is generally friendly and conscientious. For breakfast, try spinach-mushroom burritos or huevos rancheros, and for lunch, chalupas or stuffed *sopaipillas*. At dinner, I'd start with fresh roasted ancho chiles (filled with a combination of Montrachet and Monterey Jack cheeses and piñon nuts, and topped with your choice of chile) and move on to the sour-cream chicken enchilada or any of the other Southwestern dishes. Order both red and green chile ("Christmas") so that you can sample some of the best sauces in town. Beware, though: The chile here can be hot, and the chef won't put it on the side. Diners can order from a selection of delicious salads. There are also traditional favorites, such as chicken-fried steak and turkey piñon meatloaf. Daily specials are available, and don't miss the chocolate-amaretto adobe pie for dessert. Beer, wine, and margaritas are served.

422 Old Santa Fe Trail. ☎ 505/982-9762. Breakfast $4.50–$9, lunch $6–$12, dinner $7–$15. DISC, MC, V. Tues–Fri 7am–2pm; Sat–Sun 8am–2pm; Tues–Sat 5:30–9pm.

Plaza Cafe ★ AMERICAN/DELI/NEW MEXICAN/GREEK   This cafe serves excellent food in a bright and friendly atmosphere right on the Plaza. I like to meet friends here, sit in a booth, eat, and laugh about life. A restaurant since the turn of the 20th century, it's been owned by the Razatos family since 1947. The decor has changed only enough to stay comfortable and clean, with red upholstered banquettes, Art Deco tile, and a soda-fountain–style service counter. Service is always quick and conscientious, and only during the heavy tourist seasons will you have to wait long for a table. Breakfasts are excellent and large, and the hamburgers and sandwiches are good. I also like the soups and New Mexican dishes, such as green-chile stew or, if you're more adventurous, pumpkin *posole*. Check out the Greek dishes, such as vegetable moussaka or beef and lamb gyros. Wash it down with an Italian soda, in flavors from vanilla to Amaretto. Alternatively, you can have a shake, a piece of coconut cream pie, or the cafe's signature dessert, *cajeta* (apple and pecan pie with Mexican caramel). Beer and wine are available.

54 Lincoln Ave. (on the Plaza). ☎ 505/982-1664. Main courses $8–$15. AE, DISC, MC, V. Daily 7am–9pm.

The Shed ★★ NEW MEXICAN   This longtime local favorite is so popular that during lunch, lines often form outside. Half a block east of the Plaza and a luncheon institution since 1953, it occupies several rooms and the patio of a rambling hacienda built in 1692. Festive folk art adorns the doorways and walls. The food is some of the best in the state, and a compliment to traditional Hispanic and Pueblo cooking. The cheese enchilada is renowned in Santa Fe. Also good are tacos and burritos, all served on blue-corn tortillas, with pinto beans on the side. The green chile soup is a local favorite. The Shed's Joshua Carswell has added vegetarian and low-fat Mexican foods to the menu, as well as a variety of soups and salads and grilled chicken and steak. The mocha cake is possibly the best dessert you'll ever eat. In addition to wine and beer, there is full bar service.

113½ E. Palace Ave. ☎ 505/982-9030. Reservations recommended; accepted only at dinner. Main courses $5.75–$10 lunch, $8–$17 dinner. AE, DC, DISC, MC, V. Mon–Sat 11am–2:30pm and 5:30–9pm.

Tomasita's Cafe ✦ NEW MEXICAN   When I was in high school, I used to eat at Tomasita's, a little dive on a back street. I always ordered a burrito, and people used to bring liquor in bags. It's now in a modern building near the train station, and its food has become renowned. The atmosphere is simple—hanging plants and wood accents— with lots of families sitting at booths or tables and a festive spillover from the bar, where many come to drink margaritas. Service is quick, even a little rushed, which is my biggest gripe. The food is still tasty, but unless you go at an odd hour, you'll wait for a table, and once you're seated, you may eat and be out again in less than an hour. The burritos are still excellent, though you may want to try chile rellenos, a house specialty. Vegetarian dishes, burgers, steaks, and daily specials are also offered.

500 S. Guadalupe St. ⓒ **505/983-5721.** Reservations not accepted, but large parties should call ahead. Lunch $5.25–$12, dinner $5.75–$13. DISC, MC, V. Mon–Sat 11am–10pm.

Upper Crust Pizza ✦ *Kids* PIZZA/ITALIAN   Upper Crust serves Santa Fe's best pizzas, in an adobe house near the old San Miguel Mission. Meals-in-a-dish include the Grecian gourmet pizza (feta and olives) and the whole-wheat vegetarian pizza (topped with sesame seeds). You can eat here or request free delivery (it takes about 30 min.) to your downtown hotel. Beer and wine are available, as are salads, calzones, sandwiches, and stromboli.

329 Old Santa Fe Trail. ⓒ **505/982-0000.** Pizzas $7.25–$16. DISC, MC, V. Summer daily 11am–midnight; winter Sun–Thurs 11am–10pm, Fri–Sat 11am–11pm.

SOUTHSIDE

Santa Fe's motel strip and other streets south of the Paseo de Peralta have their share of good, reasonably priced restaurants. See the "Greater Santa Fe" map (p. 148) for the location of the restaurants in this section.

MODERATE

mu du noodles ✦✦ PACIFIC RIM   If you're ready for a light, healthy meal with lots of flavor, head to this small restaurant about an 8-minute drive from downtown. The two rooms have plain pine tables and chairs and sparse Asian prints on the walls. The carpeted back room is cozier, and a woodsy-feeling patio is definitely worth requesting during the warmer months. The waitstaff is friendly and unimposing. I almost always order Malaysian *laksa,* thick rice noodles in a blend of coconut milk, hazelnuts, onions, and red curry, stir-fried with chicken or tofu and julienned vegetables and sprouts. If you're eating with others, you may want to order different dishes and share. The pad Thai is lighter and spicier than most, served with a chile-vinegar sauce. A list of beers, wines, and sakes is available, tailored to the menu. I'm especially fond of the ginseng ginger ale. Menu items change seasonally.

1494 Cerrillos Rd. ⓒ **505/983-1411.** Reservations accepted for parties of 3 or more only. Main courses $9–$18. AE, DC, DISC, MC, V. Mon–Sat 5:30–9pm (sometimes 10pm in summer).

INEXPENSIVE

La Choza ✦✦ NEW MEXICAN   This sister restaurant of The Shed (p. 159) offers some of the best New Mexican food in town, in a convenient location. When other restaurants are packed, you'll wait only a little while here. A warm, casual eatery with vividly painted walls, it's especially popular on cold days, when diners gather around the wood-burning stove and fireplace. Service is friendly and efficient. The menu offers enchiladas, tacos, and burritos on blue-corn tortillas, as well as green chile stew, chile con carne, and carne adovada. The portions are medium-size, so if you're hungry, start with guacamole or nachos. For years, I've ordered the cheese or chicken enchilada, two dishes I will always recommend. My new favorite, though, is the blue-corn burritos (tortillas stuffed with beans and cheese) served with *posole;* the dish can be made vegetarian if you like. For dessert, you can't leave without trying the mocha cake (chocolate cake with a mocha pudding filling, served with whipped cream). Vegetarians and children have their own menus. Beer and wine are available.

905 Alarid St. ② 505/982-0909. Main courses $7–$8.75. AE, DC, DISC, MC, V. Summer Mon–Sat 11am–9pm; winter Mon–Thurs 11am–8pm, Fri–Sat 11am–9pm.

Tortilla Flats ✦ *Kids* NEW MEXICAN   This casual restaurant takes pride in its all-natural ingredients and vegetarian offerings (the vegetarian burrito is famous around town). The atmosphere is a bit like Denny's, but the food is authentic. The blueberry pancakes are delicious, as are fajitas and eggs with a side of black beans. I also like the blue-corn enchiladas and the chimichangas. The Santa Fe Trail steak (8 oz. of prime rib-eye smothered with red or green chile and topped with grilled onions) will satisfy a big appetite. Above all, try the fresh tortillas and *sopaipillas,* prepared on the spot (you can even peek through a window into the kitchen and watch them being made). There's a full bar, and a children's menu and take-out are available.

3139 Cerrillos Rd. ② 505/471-8685. Main courses $2–$8 breakfast, $5–$10 lunch, $6–$11 dinner. DISC, MC, V. Sun–Thurs 7am–9pm (10pm in summer); Fri–Sat 7am–10pm.

5 What to See & Do

One of the oldest cities in the United States, Santa Fe has long been a center for the creative and performing arts, so it's not surprising that most of the city's major sights are related to local history and the arts. The city's Museum of New Mexico, art galleries and studios, historic churches, and cultural sights associated with local Native American and Hispanic communities all merit a visit. It would be easy to spend a full week sightseeing in the city without ever heading out to any nearby attractions. Of special note is the recently opened Georgia O'Keeffe Museum.

THE TOP ATTRACTIONS

Georgia O'Keeffe Museum ✦   The Georgia O'Keeffe Museum, inaugurated in July 1997, contains the largest collection of O'Keeffes in the world: It's currently home to 117 oil paintings, drawings, watercolors, and pastels, and more than 50 works by other artists of note. It is the only museum in the United States dedicated solely to one woman's work. You can see such killer O'Keeffes as *Jimson Weed* (1932), and *Evening Star No. VII* (1917). The rich and varied collection adorns the walls of a cathedral-like, 13,000-square-foot space—a former Baptist church with adobe walls. O'Keeffe's images are tied inextricably to local desert landscapes. She first visited New Mexico in 1917 and returned for extended periods from the '20s through the '40s.

217 Johnson St. ② 505/946-1000. www.okeeffemuseum.org. Admission $8, free for students, free for all Fri 5–8pm. July–Oct daily 10am–5pm (Fri until 8pm); Nov–June Thurs–Tues 10am–5pm (Fri until 8pm).

Museum of Fine Arts ✦   Located opposite the Palace of the Governors, this was one of the first Pueblo Revival–style buildings constructed in Santa Fe (in 1917).

The museum's permanent collection of more than 20,000 works emphasizes regional art and includes landscapes and portraits by all the Taos masters, *los Cincos Pintores* (a 1920s organization of Santa Fe artists), and contemporary artists. The museum also has a collection of photographic works by such masters as Ansel Adams, Edward Weston, and Elliot Porter. Temporary exhibits feature modern artists. Two sculpture gardens present a range of three-dimensional art, from traditional to abstract.

Graceful **St. Francis Auditorium,** patterned after the interiors of traditional Hispanic mission churches, adjoins the art museum (see "The Performing Arts," later in this chapter). A museum shop sells gifts, art books, prints, and postcards of the collection.

107 W. Palace (at Lincoln Ave.). © 505/476-5072. www.museumofnewmexico.org. Admission $7 adults, free for children under 17, free for seniors Wed, free for all Fri 5–8pm. 4-day pass (good at all 4 branches of the Museum of New Mexico and the Museum of Spanish Colonial Art) $15 adults. Tues–Sun 10am–5pm (Fri until 8pm). Closed Jan 1, Easter, Thanksgiving, Dec 25.

Palace of the Governors ★★   To fully appreciate this structure, it's important to know that this is where the only successful Native American uprising took place, in 1680. Prior to the uprising, this was the local seat of power, and after de Vargas reconquered the natives, it resumed that position. Built in 1610 as the original capitol of New Mexico, the palace has been in continuous public use longer than any other structure in the United States. A watchful eye can find remnants of the conflicts this building has seen through the years. Begin out front, where Native Americans sell jewelry, pottery, and some weavings under the portal. This is a good place to buy and a fun place to shop, especially if you visit with the artisans about their work. When you buy a piece, you may learn its history, a treasure as valuable as the item itself.

Inside, a map illustrates 400 years of New Mexico history, from the 16th-century Spanish explorations through the frontier era and modern times. A rickety stagecoach contains tools, such as farm implements and kitchen utensils, used by early Hispanic residents. There's a replica of a mid-19th-century chapel, with a simple, brightly colored altarpiece made in 1830 for a Taos church by folk artist José Rafael Aragón. What I find most interesting are the period photos scattered throughout. The building's exterior seems elaborate now, but it was once a simple flat-topped adobe with thin posts. You can see a fireplace and chimney chiseled into the adobe wall, and, in the west section of the museum, a cutaway of the adobe floor. Farther in that direction, unearthed in a recent excavation, are storage pits where the Pueblo Indians kept corn, wheat, barley, and other goods.

The palace is the flagship of the Museum of New Mexico system; the main office is at 113 Lincoln Ave. (© **505/476-5060**). The system comprises five state monuments and four Santa Fe museums: the Palace of the Governors, the Museum of Fine Arts, the Museum of International Folk Art, and the Museum of Indian Arts & Culture.

North Plaza. © 505/476-5100. www.palaceofthegovernors.org. Admission $7 adults, free for children under 17, free for all Fri. 4-day pass (good at all 4 branches of the Museum of New Mexico and the Museum of Spanish Colonial Art) $15 adults. Tues–Sun 10am–5pm. Closed Jan 1, Thanksgiving, Dec 25.

St. Francis Cathedral ★   The French design of Santa Fe's grandest religious structure makes it an architectural anomaly in the city. A block east of the Plaza, it was built between 1869 and 1886 by Archbishop Jean-Baptiste Lamy in the style of the great cathedrals of Europe. French architects designed the Romanesque building—named after Santa Fe's patron saint—and Italian masons assisted with its construction. The small adobe Our Lady of the Rosary chapel on the northeast side of the cathedral has a Spanish look. Built in 1807, it's the only portion that remains from Our Lady of the Assumption Church, founded along with Santa Fe in 1610. The new cathedral was built over and around the old church.

A wooden icon set in a niche in the wall of the north chapel, Our Lady of Peace, is the oldest representation of the Madonna in the United States. Rescued from the old

Downtown Santa Fe Attractions

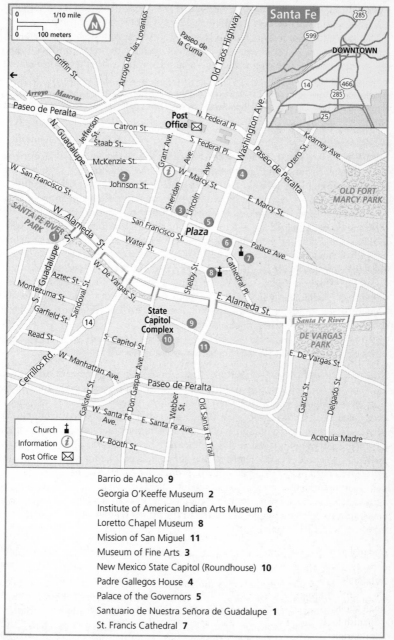

church during the 1680 Pueblo Rebellion, it was brought back by Don Diego de Vargas on his (mostly peaceful) reconquest 12 years later—thus the name.

The cathedral's front doors feature 16 carved panels of historic note and a plaque memorializing the 38 Franciscan friars who were martyred during New Mexico's early years. There's also a large bronze statue of Bishop Lamy himself; his grave is under the main altar of the cathedral.

Cathedral Place at San Francisco St. (C) 505/982-5619. Donations appreciated. Daily 7:30am–6pm. Mass Mon–Sat 7am and 5:15pm; Sun 8am, 10am, noon, and 5:15pm. Free parking in city lot next to the cathedral to attend church services.

MORE ATTRACTIONS
MUSEUMS

Institute of American Indian Arts Museum ⭐ A visit to this museum—the most comprehensive collection of contemporary Native American art in the world— offers a profound look into the lives of a people negotiating two worlds: traditional and contemporary. Here, you'll see cutting-edge art that pushes the limits of many media, from creative writing to textile manufacturing to painting. One young artist says in a video, "I feel if I see one more warrior riding off into the sunset, I'm going to throw up." Much of the work originates with artists from the Institute of American Indian Arts (IAIA), the nation's only congressionally chartered institute of higher education devoted solely to the study and practice of the artistic and cultural traditions of all American Indian and Alaskan native peoples.

Exhibits change periodically, and a permanent collection of Allan Houser's monumental sculpture is on display in the museum's Art Park. The store has a broad collection of jewelry, pottery, books, and music.

108 Cathedral Place. (C) 505/983-8900. www.iaiancad.org. Admission $4 adults, $2 seniors and students, free for children under 17. Oct–May Mon–Sat 10am–5pm, Sun noon–5pm; June–Sept daily 9am–5pm.

Museum of Indian Arts & Culture ⭐⭐ An interactive permanent exhibit here has made this one of the most exciting Native American museum experiences in the Southwest. "Here, Now and Always" takes visitors through thousands of years of Native American history. More than 70,000 pieces of basketry, pottery, clothing, carpets, and jewelry—much of it quite old—are on continual rotating display. You begin by entering through a tunnel that symbolizes the *sipapu,* the Anasazi (ancestral Puebloan) entrance into the upper worlds; the sounds of trickling water, drums, and Native American music greet you. Videos show Native Americans telling creation stories. Visitors can reflect on the lives of modern-day Native Americans by juxtaposing a traditional Pueblo kitchen with a modern kitchen. You can step into a Navajo hogan and stroll through a trading post. The rest of the museum houses a lovely pottery collection as well as changing exhibits.

Cultural Chow

If you get hungry while visiting the Museum of Indian Arts & Culture, the Museum of International Folk Art, the Wheelwright Museum of the American Indian, and the Museum of Spanish Colonial Art (all located together, southeast of the Plaza), you can now feast on more than your fingernails. The **Museum Hill Café** ((C) 505/820-1776) is open Tuesday through Saturday for beverages and snacks at 10am, and a tasty lunch from 11am to 3pm; it serves Sunday brunch from 11am to 3pm.

Look for demonstrations of traditional skills by tribal artisans and regular programs in a 70-seat multimedia theater. Call for information on year-round lectures and classes on native traditions and arts, as well as performances of Native American music and dancing by tribal groups. In February, look for an annual fiber show, and in June, a presentation on oral traditions.

The laboratory, founded in 1931 by John D. Rockefeller, Jr., is itself a point of interest. Designed by the well-known Santa Fe architect John Gaw Meem, it is an exquisite example of Pueblo Revival architecture.

710 Camino Lejo. (C) 505/476-1250. www.miaclab.org. Admission $7 adults, free for kids under 17. 4-day pass (good at all 4 branches of the Museum of New Mexico and the Museum of Spanish Colonial Art) $15. Tues–Sun 10am–5pm. Drive southeast on Old Santa Fe Trail (it turns left; if you find yourself on Old Pecos Trail, you missed the turn). Look for signs pointing right onto Camino Lejo.

Museum of International Folk Art ★★ *Kids*   This branch of the Museum of New Mexico may not seem as typically Southwestern as other Santa Fe museums, but it's the largest of its kind in the world. With a collection of some 130,000 objects from more than 100 countries, it's my favorite city museum, well worth an hour or two of perusing. It was founded in 1953 by the Chicago collector Florence Dibell Bartlett, who said, "If peoples of different countries could have the opportunity to study each other's cultures, it would be one avenue for a closer understanding between men." That's the basis on which the museum operates today. The special collections include Spanish colonial silver, traditional and contemporary New Mexican religious art, Mexican tribal costumes and majolica ceramics, Brazilian folk art, European glass, African sculptures, East Indian textiles, and the marvelous Morris Miniature Circus. Particularly delightful are numerous dioramas of people around the world at work and play in typical town, village, and home settings. Recent acquisitions include American weather vanes and quilts, Palestinian costume jewelry and amulets, and Bhutanese and Indonesian textiles. Children love to look at the hundreds of toys on display throughout the museum.

706 Camino Lejo. (C) 505/476-1200. www.moifa.org. Admission $7 adults, free for kids under 17. 4-day pass (good at all 4 branches of the Museum of New Mexico and the Museum of Spanish Colonial Art) $15. Tues–Sun 10am–5pm. The museum is about 2 miles southeast of the Plaza. Drive southeast on Old Santa Fe Trail (it turns left; if you find yourself on Old Pecos Trail, you missed the turn). Look for signs pointing right onto Camino Lejo.

Museum of Spanish Colonial Art ★   Beauty often follows in the tragic wake of imperialism. A good example of this point is Spanish colonial art, which has flourished from Europe across the Americas and even in the Philippines. This museum celebrates the art with a collection of 3,000 devotional and decorative works and utilitarian artifacts. Housed in a home built by noted architect John Gaw Meem, the museum displays *retablos* (religious paintings on wood), *bultos* (freestanding religious sculptures), furniture, metalwork, and textiles and, outside, an 18th-century wooden colonial house from Mexico.

750 Camino Lejo. (C) 505/982-2226. www.spanishcolonial.org. Admission $6 adults, free for kids under 17. 4-day pass (good at all 4 branches of the Museum of New Mexico and the Museum of Spanish Colonial Art) $15. Tues–Sun 10am–5pm. The museum is about 2 miles southeast of the Plaza. Drive southeast on Old Santa Fe Trail (it turns left; if you find yourself on Old Pecos Trail, you missed the turn). Look for signs pointing right onto Camino Lejo.

Wheelwright Museum of the American Indian ★ *Kids*   This museum resembles a Navajo hogan, with its doorway facing east (toward the rising sun) and its ceiling formed in the interlocking "whirling log" style. It was founded in 1937 by Boston scholar Mary Cabot Wheelwright, in collaboration with a Navajo medicine man, Hastiin Klah, to preserve and document Navajo ritual beliefs and practices. Klah took the designs of sand paintings used in healing ceremonies and adapted them into the woven pictographs that are a major part of the museum's treasure. In 1976, the focus was altered to include the living arts of all Native American cultures. The museum offers three or four exhibits per year. You may see a basketry exhibit, mixed-media Navajo toys, or amazing contemporary Navajo rugs. An added treat is the Case Trading Post, an arts-and-crafts shop built to resemble the typical turn-of-the-20th-century trading post found on the Navajo reservation. Docent tours of the exhibition start Monday to Wednesday and Friday at 2pm and Saturday at 11am. On Saturday and Tuesday at 10:15am and Sunday at 2pm, the Trading Post presents a lively and informative introduction to Southwestern Indian art. The museum has excellent access for travelers with disabilities.

704 Camino Lejo. © **800/607-4636** or 505/982-4636. Fax 505/989-7386. www.wheelwright.org. Donations appreciated. Mon–Sat 10am–5pm; Sun 1–5pm. Closed Jan 1, Thanksgiving, Dec 25. Drive southeast on Old Santa Fe Trail (it turns left; if you find yourself on Old Pecos Trail, you missed the turn). Look for signs pointing right onto Camino Lejo.

CHURCHES

Loretto Chapel Museum ⭐
Though no longer consecrated for worship, the Loretto Chapel is an important site. Patterned after the famous Sainte-Chapelle church in Paris, it was constructed in 1873—by the same French architects and Italian masons who were building Archbishop Lamy's cathedral—as a chapel for the Sisters of Loretto, who had established a school for young women in Santa Fe in 1852.

The chapel is especially notable for its remarkable spiral staircase: It makes two complete 360-degree turns, with no central or other visible support. The structure is steeped in legend: The building was nearly finished in 1878, when workers realized the stairs to the choir loft wouldn't fit. Hoping for a solution more attractive than a ladder, the sisters made a novena to St. Joseph and were rewarded when a mysterious carpenter appeared astride a donkey and offered to build a staircase. Armed with only a saw, a hammer, and a T-square, the master constructed this work of genius by soaking slats of wood in tubs of water to curve them and holding them together with wooden pegs. Then he disappeared without bothering to collect his fee.

207 Old Santa Fe Trail (between Alameda and Water sts.). © **505/982-0092**. www.lorettochapel.com. Admission $2.50 adults, $2 children 7–12 and seniors over 65, free for children under 7. Mon–Sat 9am–5pm; Sun 10:30am–5pm.

Mission of San Miguel
If you want to get the feel of colonial Catholicism, visit this church. Better yet, attend Mass here. Built in 1610, the church has massive adobe walls, high windows, an elegant altar screen (erected in 1798), and a 780-pound San José bell (now found inside), which was cast in Spain in 1356. If that doesn't impress you, perhaps the buffalo hide and deerskin Bible paintings used in 1630 by Franciscan missionaries to teach the Native Americans will. Anthropologists have excavated near the altar, down to the original floor that some claim was part of a 12th-century pueblo. A small store sells religious articles.

401 Old Santa Fe Trail (at E. de Vargas St.). © **505/983-3974**. Admission $1, free for children under 6. Mon–Sat 9am–5pm; Sun 10am–4pm. Opens earlier in summer. Mass Sun 5pm.

Santuario de Nuestra Señora de Guadalupe ⭐
This church, built in 1776–96 at the end of El Camino Real by Franciscan missionaries, is believed to be the oldest shrine in the United States honoring the Virgin of Guadalupe. Better known as Santuario de Guadalupe, the shrine has adobe walls that are almost 3 feet thick. The

Moments   Santa Fe Spas

If traveling, skiing, or other activities have left you weary, a great place to treat your body and mind is **Ten Thousand Waves** 🌸🌸, a Japanese-style health spa about 3 miles northeast of Santa Fe on Hyde Park Road (📞 505/982-9304; www.tenthousandwaves.com). This serene retreat, nestled in a grove of piñon, offers hot tubs, saunas, and cold plunges, plus a variety of massage and other bodywork techniques. Bathing suits are optional in both the 10-foot communal hot tub (during the day) and the women's communal tub, where you can stay as long as you want for $14. Nine private hot tubs cost $20 to $27 an hour, with discounts for seniors and children. You can also arrange therapeutic massage, hot-oil massage, in-water *watsu* massage, herbal wraps, salt glows, facials, dry-brush aromatherapy treatments, Ayurvedic treatments, and the much-praised Japanese Hot Stone Massage. If you call far enough in advance, you may be able to find lodging at **Ten Thousand Waves** as well. The spa is open Sunday, Monday, Wednesday, and Thursday from 10am to 10pm; Tuesday from 4:30 to 10pm; and Friday and Saturday from 10am to 11pm (winter hours are shorter, so be sure to call). Reservations are recommended.

Decorated in Southwestern-cum-Asian style, with clean lines and lots of elegant stone, Santa Fe's most chic spa option is **Avanu** 🌸🌸 at the La Posada de Santa Fe Resort and Spa (📞 505/986-0000). A full-service spa offering a range of treatments from massage to salt glows, it may initially seem expensive (about $95 for 50 min.), but treatments include full use of the steam room, hot tub, and grass-surrounded pool.

deep-red plaster wall behind the altar was dyed with ox blood in traditional fashion when the church was restored early in the 20th century.

It is well worth a visit to see photographs of the transformation of the building over time; its styles have ranged from flat-topped Pueblo to New England town meeting and today's northern New Mexico style. On one wall is a famous oil painting, *Our Lady of Guadalupe*, created in 1783 by the renowned Mexican artist José de Alzibar. Painted expressly for this church, it was brought from Mexico City by mule caravan.

100 S. Guadalupe St. 📞 505/988-2027. Donations appreciated. May–Oct Mon–Sat 9am–4pm; Nov–Apr Mon–Fri 9am–4pm.

OTHER ATTRACTIONS

New Mexico State Capitol (Roundhouse)   Some are surprised to learn that this is the only round capitol building in the U.S. Built in 1966, it's designed in the shape of a Zia Pueblo emblem (or sun sign, which is also the state symbol). It symbolizes the circle of life: four winds, four seasons, four directions, and four sacred obligations. Surrounding the capitol is a lush 6½-acre garden boasting more than 100 varieties of plants, including roses, plums, almonds, nectarines, Russian olive trees, and sequoias. Inside you'll find standard offices, with New Mexican art hanging on the walls. Check out the Governor's Gallery and the Capitol Art Collection. Self-guided tours are available 8am to 5pm Monday through Friday year-round; Memorial Day to Labor Day guided tours are available Monday through Saturday at 10am and 2pm.

Paseo de Peralta and Old Santa Fe Trail. © 505/986-4589. www.legis.state.nm.us. Free admission and tours. Mon–Sat 8am–5pm. Free parking.

Santa Fe Southern Railway ★ "Riding the old Santa Fe" referred to riding the Atchison, Topeka & Santa Fe railroad. The main route of the AT&SF bypassed Santa Fe, which probably forestalled some development for the capital city. A spur was run off the main line to Santa Fe in 1880, and today, an 18-mile ride along that spur offers views of some of New Mexico's most spectacular scenery.

The Santa Fe Depot is a well-preserved tribute to the Mission architecture that the railroad brought to the West in the early 1900s. Characterized by stuccoed walls, arched openings, and tile roofs, this style was part of an architectural revolution in Santa Fe when builders snubbed the traditional pueblo style.

Inside the restored coach, passengers are surrounded by aged mahogany and faded velvet seats. The train snakes through Santa Fe and onto the New Mexico plains, broad landscapes spotted with piñon and chamisa, with views of the Sandia and Ortiz mountains. Arriving in the small track town of Lamy, you get another glimpse of a Mission-style station, this one surrounded by spacious lawns where passengers picnic. Check out the sunset rides on weekends and the specialty trains throughout the year.

410 S. Guadalupe St. © 888/989-8600 or 505/989-8600. Fax 505/983-7620. www.sfsr.com. Reservations required. Tickets $28–$80 adults, $14–$65 children. Trains depart Santa Fe Depot daily 9:30am–5pm (call to check schedule).

GETTING CLOSE TO NATURE: PARKS & REFUGES

Old Fort Marcy Park Marking the 1846 site of the first U.S. military reservation in the Southwest, this park overlooks the northeast corner of downtown. Only a few mounds remain from the fort, but the Cross of the Martyrs, at the top of a winding brick walkway from Paseo de Peralta near Otero Street, is a popular spot for bird's-eye photographs. The cross was erected in 1920 by the Knights of Columbus and the Historical Society of New Mexico to commemorate the Franciscans killed during the Pueblo Rebellion of 1680. It has since played a role in numerous religious processions. It's open daily 24 hours.

617 Paseo de Peralta.

Randall Davey Audubon Center ★ Named for the late Santa Fe artist who willed his home to the National Audubon Society, this wildlife refuge occupies 135 acres at the mouth of Santa Fe Canyon. Just a few minutes' drive from the Plaza, it's an excellent escape. More than 100 species of birds and 120 types of plants live here, and varied mammals have been spotted—including black bears, mule deer, mountain lions, bobcats, raccoons, and coyotes. Trails winding through more than 100 acres of the nature sanctuary are open to day hikers, but not to dogs. There's also a natural history bookstore on site.

1800 Upper Canyon Rd. © 505/983-4609. Trail admission $1. Daily 9am–5pm. House tours (conducted by appointment and sporadically during the summer) $2 adults, $1 children under 12; call for hours. Gift shop daily 10am–4pm (call for winter hours). Free 1-hr. guided bird walk 1st Sat every month 8:30am (9am in winter).

Santa Fe River Park This is a lovely spot for an early morning jog, a midday walk beneath the trees, or a sack lunch at a picnic table. The green strip, which does not close, follows the midtown stream for about 4 miles as it meanders along Alameda from St. Francis Drive upstream beyond Camino Cabra, near its source.

Alameda St. © 505/955-2103.

COOKING, ART & PHOTOGRAPHY CLASSES

If you're looking for something to do that's a little off the beaten tourist path, you might consider taking a class.

You can master the flavors of Santa Fe with an entertaining 3-hour demonstration cooking class at the **Santa Fe School of Cooking and Market** ✿, on the upper level of the Plaza Mercado, 116 W. San Francisco St. (© **505/983-4511;** fax 505/983-7540; www.santafeschoolofcooking.com). The class teaches about the flavors and history of traditional New Mexican and contemporary Southwestern cuisines. "Cooking Light" classes are available as well. Prices range from $40 to $88 and include a meal; call for a class schedule. The adjoining market offers a variety of regional foods, cookbooks, and gift baskets.

If Southwestern art has you hooked, you can take a drawing and painting class led by Santa Fe artist Jane Shoenfeld. Students sketch such outdoor subjects as the Santa Fe landscape and adobe architecture. In case of inclement weather, classes are held in the studio. Each class lasts 3 hours, and art materials are included in the fee, which ranges from $85 to $90. Private lessons and children's classes can be arranged. All levels of experience are welcome. You can create your own personal art adventure with one of Shoenfeld's 1-day classes at Ghost Ranch in Abiquiu, or a 5-day intensive class at Ghost Ranch. Contact Jane at **Sketching Santa Fe,** P.O. Box 5912, Santa Fe, NM 87502 (© **505/986-1108;** fax 505/986-3845; www.skyfields.net).

Some of the world's most outstanding photographers convene in Santa Fe at various times during the year. They attend the **Santa Fe Photography & Digital Workshops,** P.O. Box 9916, Santa Fe, NM 87504 (© **505/983-1400;** www.santafe workshops.com), at a delightful campus in the hills on the east side of town. Most courses last a week. Food and lodging packages are available.

WINE TASTINGS

If you enjoy sampling regional wines, consider visiting the wineries within easy driving distance of Santa Fe: **Balagna Winery/Il Santo Cellars,** 223 Rio Bravo Dr., in Los Alamos (© **505/672-3678**), north on US 84/285 and then west on NM 502; **Santa Fe Vineyards,** with a retail outlet at 235 Don Gaspar Ave., in Santa Fe (© **505/982-3474**), or the vineyard itself about 20 miles north of Santa Fe on US 84/285 (© **505/753-8100**); **Madison Vineyards & Winery,** in Ribera (© **505/421-8028**), about 45 miles east of Santa Fe on I-25 north; and the **Black Mesa Winery,** 1502 Hwy. 68, in Velarde (© **800/852-6372**), north on US 84/285 to NM 68. Be sure to call ahead for hours and directions.

ESPECIALLY FOR KIDS

Don't miss taking the kids to the **Museum of International Folk Art,** where they'll love the dioramas and the toys (discussed earlier in this chapter). Also visit the tepee at the **Wheelwright Museum of the American Indian** (discussed earlier in this chapter), where storyteller Joe Hayes spins traditional Spanish *cuentos,* Native American folk tales, and Wild West tall tales on weekend evenings. **The Bishop's Lodge** has extensive children's programs during the summer. These include horseback riding, swimming, arts and crafts, and special activities, such as archery and tennis.

The **Genoveva Chavez Community Center,** 3221 Rodeo Rd. (© **505/955-4001**), is a full-service family recreation center on the south side of Santa Fe. The complex includes a 50-meter pool, a leisure pool, a therapy pool, an ice-skating rink, three gyms, a workout room, racquetball courts, and an indoor running track, as well as a spa and sauna. Call ahead for hours and more information.

Santa Fe Children's Museum ⚐ *Kids*   This museum offers interactive exhibits and hands-on activities in the arts, humanities, and science. The most notable features include a 16-foot climbing wall that kids—outfitted with helmets and harnesses—can scale, and a 1-acre Southwestern horticulture garden, complete with animals, wetlands, and a greenhouse. This fascinating area serves as an outdoor classroom for ongoing environmental educational programs. Special performances and hands-on sessions with artists and scientists are regularly scheduled. *Family Life* magazine has named this one of the 10 hottest children's museums in the nation.

1050 Old Pecos Trail. ✆ **505/989-8359.** www.santafechildrensmuseum.org. Admission $4; children under 12 must be accompanied by an adult. Wed–Sat 10am–5pm; Sun noon–5pm.

Skateboard Park *Kids*   Split-level ramps for daredevils, park benches for onlookers, and climbing structures for youngsters are located at this park near downtown.

De Vargas and Sandoval sts. ✆ **505/955-2100.** Free admission. Daily 24 hr.

6 Organized Tours

BUS TOURS

LorettoLine   For an open-air tour of the city, contact LorettoLine. Tours last 1½ hours and are offered daily from April to October. Tour times are every hour on the hour during the day from 10am to 3pm.

Hotel Loretto, 211 Old Santa Fe Trail. ✆ **505/983-3701.** Tours $12 adults, $6 children.

WALKING TOURS

Storytellers and the Southwest: A Literary Walking Tour ⚐   Barbara Harrelson, a former Smithsonian museum docent and local writer, leads 2-hour literary walking tours of downtown, exploring the history, legends, characters, and authors of the region through its landmarks and historic sites. It's a great way to absorb the unique character of Santa Fe. Tours take place by appointment.

924 Old Taos Hwy. ✆ **505/989-4561.** www.sfaol.com/books/littour.html. Apr–Oct. Tours $15 per person, 2-person minimum.

Walking Tour of Santa Fe ⚐   One of Santa Fe's best walking tours begins under the T-shirt tree at Tees & Skis, 107 Washington Ave., near the northeast corner of the Plaza. It lasts about 2½ hours. From Memorial Day to Labor Day, tours begin daily at 9:30am and 1:30pm; the rest of the year, they take place less frequently. Always reserve in advance.

54½ E. San Francisco St. (tour meets at 107 Washington Ave.). ✆ **800/338-6877** or 505/983-6565. Tours $10 adults, free for children under 12.

MISCELLANEOUS TOURS

Pathways Customized Tours ⚐   Don Dietz offers several planned tours, including a downtown Santa Fe walking tour, a full city tour, a trip to the cliff dwellings and native pueblos, a "Taos adventure," and a trip to Georgia O'Keeffe country (with a focus on the landscape that inspired the art now on view in the O'Keeffe Museum). He will try to accommodate special requests. Tours last anywhere from 2 to 9 hours, depending on the one you choose. Don has extensive knowledge of the area's culture, history, geology, and flora and fauna, and will help you make the most of your precious vacation time.

161F Calle Ojo Feliz. © 505/982-5382. www.santafepathways.com. Tours $60–$200 and up per day per couple. No credit cards.

Rain Parrish ⭐ A Navajo (or *Diné*) anthropologist, artist, and curator, Rain Parrish offers custom guide services focusing on cultural anthropology, Native American arts, and the history of the Native Americans of the Southwest. Some of her excursions are true adventures to insider locations. Options include visits to local Pueblo villages.

704 Kathryn St. © 505/984-8236. Tours for up to 2 people $130 for 4½ hr., $230 for 7 hr. Nominal fee for extra person.

Recursos de Santa Fe/Royal Road Tours This is a full-service destination management company, emphasizing custom-designed itineraries to meet the interests of any group. It specializes in the archaeology, art, literature, spirituality, architecture, environment, food, and history of the Southwest. Call or visit the website for a calendar and information about its annual writers' conferences and the international bead expo that it sponsors in Santa Fe in March of even-numbered years.

826 Camino de Monte Rey. © 505/982-9301. www.recursos.org.

Rojo Tours & Services Customized and private tours include pueblos, cliff dwellings, ruins, hot-air ballooning, backpacking, or whitewater rafting. Rojo also provides planning services for groups.

2408 Calle Bella. © 505/474-8333. Fax 505/474-2992. www.rojotours.com.

Santa Fe Detours ⭐ Santa Fe's most extensive tour-booking agency accommodates almost all travelers' tastes, from bus and rail tours to river rafting, backpacking, and cross-country skiing. The agency can also facilitate hotel reservations, from budget to high end.

54½ San Francisco. Summer tour desk: 107 Washington Ave. © 800/338-6877 or 505/983-6565. www.sfdetours.com.

Southwest Safaris ⭐⭐ This tour offers one of the most interesting Southwestern experiences available. Pilot Bruce Adams flies visitors across the Southwest while explaining millions of years of geologic history. Trips to many destinations are available, including the Grand Canyon, Monument Valley, Mesa Verde, Canyon de Chelly, and Arches/Canyonlands, as well as a trip to Capulin Volcano and the ruins at Aztec, New Mexico. Local 1- and 2-hour scenic flights are available as well, to places such as the Rio Grande Gorge, the back route in to Acoma Pueblo, and Abiquiu Valley—Georgia O'Keefe country. Tours depart from the Santa Fe Airport.

P.O. Box 945, Santa Fe, NM 87504. © 800/842-4246 or 505/988-4246. www.gouldings.com/sw_safaris. Tours $129–$699 per person.

7 Getting Outside

Set between the granite peaks of the Sangre de Cristo Mountains and the subtler volcanic Jemez Mountains, with the Rio Grande flowing through, the Santa Fe area offers outdoor enthusiasts many opportunities to play. This is the land of high desert, where temperatures vary with the elevation, allowing for a full range of activities throughout the year.

BALLOONING

New Mexico is renowned for its spectacular Balloon Fiesta, which takes place annually in Albuquerque (p. 25). If you want to take a ride, you'll probably have to go to Albuquerque or Taos, but you can book your trip in Santa Fe through **Santa Fe Detours,** 54½ E. San Francisco St. (summer tour desk: 107 Washington Ave.; © **800/ 338-6877** or 505/983-6565). Flights take place early in the day. Rates begin at around $135 per person.

BIKING

You can cycle along main roadways and paved country roads year-round in Santa Fe, but be aware that traffic is particularly heavy around the Plaza. All over town, motorists are not particularly attentive to bicyclists, so you need to be especially alert. Mountain biking interest has exploded here and is especially popular in the spring, summer, and fall; the high-desert terrain is rugged and challenging, but mountain bikers of all levels can find exhilarating rides. The Santa Fe Convention and Visitors Bureau can supply you with bike maps.

I recommend the following trails: West of Santa Fe, the **Caja del Rio** area has nice dirt roads and some light-to-moderate technical biking; the **railroad tracks south of Santa Fe** provide wide-open biking on beginner-to-intermediate technical trails; and the **Borrego Trail** up toward Santa Fe Ski Area is a challenging technical ride that links up with the **Windsor Trail,** a nationally renowned technical romp with plenty of verticality.

In Santa Fe bookstores, look for my book *Frommer's Great Outdoor Guide to Arizona and New Mexico; Mountain Biking in Northern New Mexico: Historical and Natural History Rides* by Craig Martin; and *The Mountain Biker's Guide to New Mexico* by Sarah Bennett. They are excellent guides to trails in Santa Fe, Taos, and Albuquerque, and outline tours for beginner, intermediate, and advanced riders. **Santa Fe Mountain Sports,** 606 Cerrillos Rd. (© **505/988-3337**), rents hard-tail mountain bikes ($20 for half a day and $25 for a full day) or full-suspension bikes ($35 for a full day). **Sun Mountain Bike Company,** 102 E. Water St. (© **505/ 982-8986**), rents quality front-suspension mountain bikes for $30 a day. Add $7 and the company will deliver to and pick up from your Santa Fe–area hotel. Multiday rentals are $22 per day. Both shops supply accessories such as helmets, locks, water, maps, and trail information. **Sun Mountain** also runs bike tours from April through October to some of the most spectacular spots in northern New Mexico. Trips range from an easy Glorieta Mesa tour to my favorite, the West Rim Trail, with prices from $60 to $109. All tours include bikes, transportation, and a snack.

FISHING

In the lakes and waterways around Santa Fe, anglers typically catch trout (there are five varieties in the area). Other local fish include bass, perch, and kokanee salmon. The most popular fishing holes are Cochiti and Abiquiu lakes as well as the Rio Chama, the Pecos River, and the Rio Grande. A world-renowned fly-fishing destination, the **San Juan River,** near Farmington, is worth a visit and can make for an exciting 2-day trip in combination with a tour around **Chaco Culture National Historic Park** (see chapter 6). Check with the **New Mexico Game and Fish Department** (© **800/862-9310** or 505/476-8000) for information (including maps of area waters), licenses, and fishing proclamations. **High Desert Angler,** 435 S. Guadalupe St. (© **505/988-7688**), specializes in fly-fishing gear and guide services.

GOLF

There are three courses in the Santa Fe area: the 18-hole **Santa Fe Country Club,** on Airport Road (© 505/471-2626); the often-praised 18-hole **Cochiti Lake Golf Course,** 5200 Cochiti Hwy., Cochiti Lake, about 35 miles southwest of Santa Fe on I-25 and NM 16 and 22 (© 505/465-2239); and Santa Fe's newest 18-hole course, **Marty Sanchez Links de Santa Fe,** 205 Caja del Rio (© 505/955-4400).

HIKING

It's hard to decide which of the 1,000 miles of nearby national forest trails to tackle. Four wilderness areas are nearby, most notably **Pecos Wilderness,** with 223,000 acres east of Santa Fe, and the 58,000-acre **Jemez Mountain National Recreation Area.** Information on these and other wilderness areas is available from the **Santa Fe National Forest,** P.O. Box 1689 (1474 Rodeo Rd.), Santa Fe, NM 87504 (© 505/438-7840). If you're looking for company on your trek, contact the Santa Fe branch of the **Sierra Club,** 621 Old Santa Fe Trail, Suite 10 (© 505/983-2703). You can pick up a hiking schedule in the local newsletter outside the office. Some people enjoy taking a chairlift ride to the summit of the **Santa Fe Ski Area** (© 505/982-4429; www.skisantafe.com) and hiking around up there during the summer. You might also consider purchasing *The Hiker's Guide to New Mexico* (Falcon Press) by Laurence Parent; it outlines 70 hikes throughout the state. *Frommer's Great Outdoor Guide to Arizona and New Mexico* (Wiley Publishing, Inc.), written by yours truly, details many of my favorite hikes. A popular guide with Santa Feans is *Day Hikes in the Santa Fe Area,* put out by the local branch of the Sierra Club.

The most popular hiking trails are the **Borrego Trail,** a moderate 4-mile jaunt through aspens and ponderosa pines, ending at a creek; and **Aspen Vista,** an easy 1- to 5-mile hike through aspen forest with views to the east. Both are easy to find; simply head up Hyde Park Road toward Ski Santa Fe. The Borrego Trail is 8.25 miles up, and Aspen Vista is 10 miles. In recent years an energetic crew has cut the **Dale Ball Trails** (© 505/955-2103), miles of hiking/biking trails throughout the Santa Fe foothills. The easiest access is off Hyde Park Road toward Ski Santa Fe. Drive 2 miles from Bishop's Lodge Road and watch for the trailhead on the left.

HORSEBACK RIDING

Trips ranging in length from a few hours to overnight can be arranged by **Santa Fe Detours,** 54½ E. San Francisco St. (summer tour desk: 107 Washington Ave.; © 800/ 338-6877 or 505/983-6565). You'll ride with "experienced wranglers" and can even arrange a trip that includes a cookout or brunch. Rides are also major activities at the **Bishop's Lodge** (see "Where to Stay," earlier in this chapter). The **Broken Saddle Riding Company** (© 505/424-7774) offers rides through the stunning Galisteo Basin south of Santa Fe.

HUNTING

Hunters in the Pecos Wilderness and Jemez Mountains take elk and mule deer, as well as occasional black bears and bighorn sheep. Wild turkeys and grouse are frequently bagged in the uplands, geese and ducks at lower elevations. Check with the **New Mexico Game and Fish Department** (© 800/862-9310 or 505/476-8000) for information and licenses.

RIVER RAFTING & KAYAKING

Although Taos is the real rafting center of New Mexico, several companies serve Santa Fe during the April-to-October white-water season. They include **Southwest**

Wilderness Adventures, P.O. Box 9380, Santa Fe, NM 87504 (© **505/983-7262**); **New Wave Rafting,** 70 County Rd. 84B, Santa Fe, NM 87506 (© **800/984-1444** or 505/984-1444); **Santa Fe Rafting Co.,** 1000 Cerrillos Rd., Santa Fe, NM 87505 (© **800/467-RAFT** or 505/988-4914; www.santaferafting.com); and **Wolf Whitewater,** 4626 Palo Alto SE, Albuquerque, NM 87108 (© **505/262-1099;** www.wolfwhitewater.com). You can expect the cost of a full-day trip to range from about $85 to $105.

RUNNING

Despite its elevation, Santa Fe is popular with runners, and hosts numerous competitions, including the annual **Old Santa Fe Trail Run** on Labor Day. Each Wednesday, Santa Fe runners gather at 6pm at the Plaza and set out on foot for runs in the surrounding area. This is a great opportunity for travelers to find their way and to meet some locals. **Santa Fe Striders** (www.santafestriders.org) sponsors runs.

SKIING

There's something for every ability level at **Ski Santa Fe,** about 16 miles northeast of Santa Fe on Hyde Park (Ski Basin) Road. Lots of locals ski here, particularly on weekends; if you can, go on a weekday. It's a good family area and fairly small, so it's easy to split off from and later reconnect with your party. Built on the upper reaches of 12,000-foot Tesuque Peak, the area has an average annual snowfall of 225 inches and a vertical drop of 1,650 feet. Seven lifts, including a 5,000-foot triple chair and a new quad chair, serve 39 runs and 590 acres of terrain, with a total capacity of 7,800 riders an hour. Base facilities, at 10,350 feet, center around **La Casa Mall,** with a cafeteria, lounge, ski shop, and boutique. **Totemoff's** restaurant has a midmountain patio.

The ski area is open daily from 9am to 4pm; the season often runs from Thanksgiving to early April, depending on snow conditions. Rates for all lifts are $48 for adults, $39 for teens (13–20), $35 for children and seniors, free for children less than 46 inches tall (in their ski boots), and free for seniors 72 and older. For more information, contact **Ski Santa Fe,** 2209 Brothers Rd., Suite 220 (© **505/982-4429;** www.skisantafe.com). For 24-hour reports on snow conditions, call © **505/983-9155. Ski New Mexico** (© **505/982-5300**) provides statewide reports. Ski packages are available through **Santa Fe Central Reservations** (© **800/745-9910**).

Cross-country skiers find seemingly endless miles of snow to track in the **Santa Fe National Forest** (© **505/438-7840**). A favorite place to start is at the Black Canyon campground, about 9 miles from downtown en route to the Santa Fe Ski Area. In the same area are the **Borrego Trail**, **Aspen Vista Trail**, and **Norski Trail**, all en route to the Santa Fe Ski Area as well. Other popular activities at the ski area in winter include snowshoeing, snowboarding, sledding, and inner-tubing. Snowshoe and snowboard rentals are available at a number of downtown shops and the ski area.

SWIMMING

There's a public pool at the **Fort Marcy Complex** (© **505/955-2500**) on Camino Santiago, off Bishop's Lodge Road. Admission is $1.85 for adults, $1.50 for ages 13 to 18, 75¢ for ages 8 to 12 and seniors, and 30¢ for children under 8.

TENNIS

Santa Fe has 44 public tennis courts and four major private facilities. The **City Recreation Department** (© **505/955-2100**) can help you locate indoor, outdoor, and lighted public courts.

8 Shopping

Santa Fe has a broad range of shopping, from traditional Native American crafts and Hispanic folk art to extremely innovative contemporary work. Some call Santa Fe one of the top art markets in the world. Galleries speckle the downtown area, and as an artists' thoroughfare, Canyon Road is preeminent. The greatest concentration of Native American crafts is displayed beneath the portal of the Palace of the Governors.

Any serious arts aficionado should try to attend one or more of the city's great arts festivals—the Spring Festival of the Arts in May, the Spanish Market in July, the Indian Market in August, and the Fall Festival of the Arts in October.

For a current listing of gallery openings, with recommendations for which ones to attend, purchase a copy of the monthly magazine the *Santa Fean* by Santa Fean, LLC (444 Galisteo, Santa Fe, NM 87501; www.santafean.com). Also check in the Friday "Pasatiempo" section of the local newspaper, the *New Mexican* (www.santafenew mexican.com).

Business hours vary quite a bit, but most establishments are open at least weekdays from 10am to 5pm, with mall stores open until 8 or 9pm. Most shops are open similar hours on Saturday, and many also open on Sunday afternoon during the summer. Winter hours tend to be more limited.

THE TOP GALLERIES
CONTEMPORARY ART

Adieb Khadoure Fine Art   This is a working artists' studio, featuring contemporary artists Steven Boone, Hal Larsen, Robert Anderson, and Barry Lee Darling. Their works are shown in the gallery daily from 10am to 6pm. Adieb Khadoure also sells elegant rugs, furniture, and pottery from around the world. 610 Canyon Rd. ℂ 505/820-2666.

Canyon Road Contemporary Art   This gallery represents some of the finest emerging U.S. contemporary artists as well as internationally known artists. You'll find figurative, landscape, and abstract paintings, as well as raku pottery. 403 Canyon Rd. ℂ 505/983-0433.

Hahn Ross Gallery   Owners Tom Ross and Elizabeth Hahn, a children's book illustrator and surrealist painter, respectively, specialize in representing artists who create colorful, fantasy-oriented works. I'm especially fond of the wild party scenes by Susan Contreras. Check out the sculpture garden here. 409 Canyon Rd. ℂ 505/984-8434.

La Mesa of Santa Fe ★ *Finds*   Step into this gallery and let your senses dance. Dramatically colored ceramic plates, bowls, and other kitchen items fill one room. Contemporary kachinas by Gregory Lomayesva—a real buy—line the walls, accented by steel lamps and rag rugs. An adventure. 225 Canyon Rd. ℂ 505/984-1688.

LewAllen Contemporary ★ *Finds*   This is one of my favorite galleries. You'll find bizarre and beautiful contemporary works in a range of media, from granite to clay to twigs. There are always exciting works on canvas. 129 W. Palace Ave. ℂ 505/988-8997.

Linda Durham Contemporary Art ★   The opening of this broad and bright art space in 2004 marked the return of one of Santa Fe's best galleries. Longtime gallery owner Linda Durham, who had moved her establishment 25 miles south of town, returned with a strong roster of talent, including Greg Erf and Judy Tuwaletstiwa. 1101 Paseo de Peralta. ℂ 505/466-6600.

Peyton Wright Gallery ⭐ Housed in the Historic Spiegelberg House, this excellent gallery offers contemporary, Spanish colonial, African, Russian, Native American, and pre-Columbian art and antiquities. In addition to representing such artists as Kellogg Johnson, Larry Fodor, and Darren Vigil Gray, the gallery features monthly exhibitions. 237 E. Palace Ave. ℂ 800/879-8898 or 505/989-9888.

Shidoni Foundry, Gallery, and Sculpture Gardens ⭐⭐ *Finds* This is one of the area's most exciting spots for sculptors and sculpture enthusiasts. Visitors may take a tour through the foundry to view casting processes. In addition, Shidoni Foundry includes a 5,000-square-foot contemporary gallery, a bronze gallery, and a wonderful sculpture garden. Bishop's Lodge Rd., Tesuque. ℂ 505/988-8001.

Waxlander Gallery Primarily featuring the whimsical acrylics and occasional watercolors of Phyllis Kapp, this is the place to browse if you like bold color. 622 Canyon Rd. ℂ 800/342-2202 or 505/984-2202.

NATIVE AMERICAN & OTHER INDIGENOUS ART

Andrea Fisher Fine Pottery ⭐ This expansive gallery is a wonderland of authentic Southwestern Indian pottery. You'll find real showpieces here, including the work of renowned San Ildefonso Pueblo potter Maria Martinez. 100 W. San Francisco St. ℂ 505/986-1234.

Frank Howell Gallery If you've never seen the wonderful illustrative hand of the late Frank Howell, you'll want to visit this gallery. It displays a variety of works by contemporary American Indian artists, such as Pablo Antonio Milan, as well as the Southwestern impressionism of Paula Shaw. The gallery also features sculpture, jewelry, and graphics. 103 Washington Ave. ℂ 505/984-1074.

Morning Star Gallery ⭐⭐ *Finds* This is one of my favorite places to browse. Throughout the rambling gallery are American Indian art masterpieces, all elegantly displayed. You'll see a broad range of works, from late-19th-century Navajo blankets to 1920s Zuni needlepoint jewelry. 513 Canyon Rd. ℂ 505/982-8187.

Ortega's on the Plaza A hearty shopper could spend hours here, perusing inventive turquoise and silver jewelry and especially fine strung beadwork, as well as rugs and pottery. An adjacent room showcases a wide array of clothing, all with a hip Southwestern flair. 101 W. San Francisco St. ℂ 505/988-1866.

PHOTOGRAPHY

Andrew Smith Gallery ⭐ I'm always amazed when I enter this gallery and notice works I've seen reprinted in major magazines for years. There they are, photographic prints, large and beautiful, hanging on the wall. Here, you'll see famous works by Edward Curtis, Henri Cartier-Bresson, Ansel Adams, Annie Leibovitz, and others. 203 W. San Francisco St. ℂ 505/984-1234.

Photo-Eye Gallery You're bound to be surprised each time you step into this gallery a few blocks off Canyon Road. Dealing in contemporary photography, Photo-Eye represents both internationally renowned and emerging artists. 370 Garcia St. ℂ 505/988-5152.

SPANISH & HISPANIC ART

Montez Gallery This shop is rich with New Mexican (and Mexican) art, decorations, and furnishings such as *santos* (saints), *retablos* (paintings), *bultos* (sculptures), and *trasteros* (armoires). Sena Plaza Courtyard, 125 E. Palace Ave., Suite 33. ℂ 505/982-1828.

TRADITIONAL ART

Altermann Galleries This gallery offers interesting traditional art, mostly American paintings and sculpture. It represents Remington and Russell, in addition to Taos founders, Santa Fe artists, and members of the Cowboy Artists of America and the National Academy of Western Art. The sculpture garden features whimsical bronzes of children and dogs. 225 Canyon Rd. ℂ 505/983-1590.

Gerald Peters Gallery ★★ The works in this two-story Pueblo-style building are so fine you'll feel as though you're in a museum. You'll find American painting and sculpture, featuring the art of Georgia O'Keeffe, William Wegman, and the founders of the Santa Fe and Taos artist colonies, as well as contemporary works. 1011 Paseo de Peralta. ℂ 505/954-5700.

The Mayans Gallery Ltd. Established in 1977, this is one of the oldest galleries in Santa Fe. You'll find 20th- and 21st-century American and Latin American paintings, photography, prints, and sculpture. 601 Canyon Rd. ℂ 505/983-8068.

Nedra Matteucci Galleries ★ As you approach this gallery, note the elaborately crafted stone and adobe wall that surrounds it; it's merely a taste of what's to come. The gallery specializes in American art. Inside, you'll find a lot of high-ticket works such as those of early Taos and Santa Fe painters, as well as classic American Impressionism, historical Western modernism, and contemporary landscapes and sculpture. 1075 Paseo de Peralta. ℂ 505/982-4631.

Owings-Dewey Fine Art ★ These are treasure-filled rooms. You'll find 19th-, 20th-, and 21st-century American painting and sculpture, including works by Georgia O'Keeffe, Robert Henri, Maynard Dixon, Fremont Ellis, and Andrew Dasburg, as well as antique works such as Spanish colonial *retablos, bultos,* and tin works. Don't miss the Day of the Dead exhibition around Halloween. 76 E. San Francisco St., upstairs. ℂ 505/982-6244.

Zaplin Lampert Gallery ★★ Art aficionados as well as those who just like a nice landscape will enjoy this gallery, one of Santa Fe's classics. Hanging on old adobe walls are works by some of the region's early masters, including Bert Phillips, Gene Kloss, and Gustauve Baumann. 651 Canyon Rd. ℂ 505/982-6100.

MORE SHOPPING A TO Z
BELTS

Desert Son of Santa Fe ★ *Moments* From belts to mules, everything in this narrow little shop is hand-tooled, hand-carved, and/or hand-stamped. Besides leather items, look for cowboy hats and exotic turquoise jewelry. It's a slip of a shop with lots of character, presided over by the artist herself, Mindy Adler. 725 Canyon Rd. ℂ 505/982-9499.

BOOKS

Borders With close to 200 stores nationwide, this chain provides a broad range of books, music, and videos, and it schedules in-store appearances by authors, musicians, and artists. 500 Montezuma Ave. ℂ 505/954-4707.

Collected Works Bookstore This is a good downtown book source, with carefully recommended books up front and shelves of Southwest, travel, nature, and other books. 208B W. San Francisco St. ℂ 505/988-4226.

Horizons—The Discovery Store *Kids* Here, you'll find adult and children's books, science-oriented games and toys, telescopes, binoculars, and a variety of unusual

Nouveau Shopping on the Plaza

The **Santa Fe Arcade**, 60 E. San Francisco St. (© **505/995-0219**), on the south side of the Plaza, offers three stories of shops in a sleek, glassy European-style space. It's a far cry from the Woolworth's that once lived there. Showy Western wear, fine Indian jewelry, and hip clothing fill the display windows of some 60 spaces in the mall, which opened in 2004. Local favorite **Back at the Ranch** (suite 127; © **800/962-6687** or 505/989-8110; www.backattheranch. com) has a satellite shop in the arcade, where it displays a portion of what it calls the "largest selection of handmade cowboy boots in the country." Prima Fine Jewelry's **Oro Fino** (suite 218; © **505/983-9699**) sells contemporary and Southwestern inlaid jewelry in silver, gold, and platinum.

educational items. I always find interesting gifts for my little nieces in this store. 328 S. Guadalupe St. © **505/983-1554**.

Nicholas Potter, Bookseller   This store handles rare and used books, as well as tickets to many local events. 211 E. Palace Ave. © **505/983-5434**.

CRAFTS

Davis Mather Folk Art Gallery   This shop is a wild animal adventure. You'll find New Mexican animal woodcarvings in shapes of lions, tigers, and bears, as well as other folk and Hispanic arts. 141 Lincoln Ave. © **505/983-1660**.

Nambé Outlets (Finds)   Here, you'll find cooking, serving, and decorating pieces, fashioned from an exquisite sand-cast and handcrafted alloy. These items are also available at the Nambe Outlet stores at 104 W. San Francisco St. (© **505/988-3574**) and in Taos in Yucca Plaza, 113A Paseo del Pueblo Norte (© **505/758-8221**). 924 Paseo De Peralta. © **505/988-5528**.

FASHIONS

Judy's Unique Apparel   Judy's has eclectic separates made locally and imported from around the globe. You'll find a wide variety of items here, many at surprisingly reasonable prices. 714 Canyon Rd. © **505/988-5746**.

Origins (Moments)   A little like a Guatemalan or Turkish marketplace, this store is packed with wearable art, folk art, and the work of local designers. Look for good buys on ethnic jewelry. Trunk shows offer opportunities to meet the artists. 135 W. San Francisco St. © **505/988-2323**.

Overland Sheepskin Company   The rich smell of leather will draw you in the door and possibly hold on to you until you purchase a coat, blazer, hat, or other finely made leather item. 74 E. San Francisco St. © **505/983-4727**.

FOOD

The Chile Shop   This store has too many cheap trinketlike items for me, but many find novelty items to take back home. You'll see everything from salsas to cornmeal to tortilla chips. The shop also stocks cookbooks and pottery. 109 E. Water St. © **505/983-6080**.

Cookworks   This is a fun place for browsing. You'll find inventive food products and cooking items spread across three shops. Cookworks also offers gourmet food and cooking classes. 316 S. Guadalupe St. © 505/988-7676.

Señor Murphy Candy Maker   This candy store is unlike any you'll find in other parts of the country—everything here is made with local ingredients. The chile piñon-nut brittle is a taste sensation! Señor Murphy has another shop in the Santa Fe Place mall (© **505/471-8899**). La Fonda hotel, 100 E. San Francisco St. © 505/982-0461.

FURNITURE & DECOR

Asian Adobe   One of the Santa Fe Railyard district's newest treats, this shop marries the warmth of Southwestern decor with the austere grace of Asian decor. You'll find weathered wood tables and trasteros, colorful wall hangings, and moody rugs. 530 S. Guadalupe (in the Gross Kelly Warehouse). © **505/992-6846**.

Casa Nova   In the Santa Fe Railyard district, this colorful shop offers everything from dishware to furniture, all in bold and inventive colors. Those with whimsical natures will get happily lost here. 530 S. Guadalupe St. (in the Gross Kelly Warehouse). © **505/983-8558**.

El Paso Import Company ⚹   Whenever I'm in the vicinity of this shop, I always stop in. It's packed—and I mean packed—with colorful, weathered colonial and ranchero furniture. The home furnishings and folk art are imported from Mexico. 418 Sandoval St. © 505/982-5698.

Jackalope ⚹ *Kids* *Value*   Spread over 7 acres, this is a wild place to spend a morning or an afternoon browsing through exotic furnishings from India and Mexico, as well as imported textiles, pottery, jewelry, and clothing. Kids love the new petting zoo and prairie dog village. 2820 Cerrillos Rd. © **505/471-8539**.

Southwest Spanish Craftsmen   The Spanish colonial and Spanish provincial furniture, doors, and home accessories in this store are a bit too elaborate for my taste, but if you find yourself dreaming of carved wood, this is your place. 328 S. Guadalupe St. © 505/982-1767.

Taos Furniture   Here you'll find classic Southwestern furnishings handcrafted in solid ponderosa pine—both contemporary and traditional. Prices are a little better here than in downtown shops. 219 Galisteo St. © **800/443-3448** or 505/988-1229.

GIFTS & SOUVENIRS

El Nicho *Value*   If you want to take a little piece of Santa Fe home with you, you'll likely find it at this shop. You'll find handcrafted Navajo folk art as well as jewelry and other items by local artisans, including woodcarvings (watch for the *santos*) by the renowned Ortega family. 227 Don Gaspar Ave. © 505/984-2830.

HATS

Montecristi Custom Hat Works ⚹   This fun shop hand-makes fine Panama and felt hats in a range of styles, from Australian outback to Mexican bolero. 322 McKenzie St. © **505/983-9598**. www.montecristihats.com.

JEWELRY

Packards ⚹   Opened by a notable trader, Al Packard, and later sold to new owners, this store on the Plaza is worth checking out to see some of the best jewelry available. You'll also find exquisite rugs and pottery. 61 Old Santa Fe Trail. © 505/983-9241.

Tresa Vorenberg Goldsmiths   You'll find some wildly imaginative designs in this store, which represents more than 40 artisans. All items are handcrafted, and custom commissions are welcome. 656 Canyon Rd. © 505/988-7215.

MALLS & SHOPPING CENTERS

de Vargas Center   This is Santa Fe's small, struggling mall, which has approximately 50 merchants and restaurants. Though there are fewer shops than at Santa Fe Place, this is where I shop because I don't tend to suffer the mall phobia I get in more massive places. Open Monday to Friday 10am to 7pm, Saturday 10am to 6pm, and Sunday noon to 5pm. N. Guadalupe St. and Paseo de Peralta. © 505/982-2655.

Sanbusco Market Center   Unique shops and restaurants occupy this remodeled warehouse near the old Santa Fe Railyard. Many of the shops are overpriced, but it's a fun place to window-shop. Open Monday to Saturday 10am to 6pm, Sunday noon to 5pm. 500 Montezuma St. © 505/989-9390.

Santa Fe Premium Outlets   Outlet shopping fans will enjoy this open-air mall on the south end of town. Anchors include Brooks Brothers, Jones New York, Nautica, and Coach. 8380 Cerrillos Rd. © 505/474-4000.

Santa Fe Place   Santa Fe's largest mall (formerly Villa Linda Mall) is near the southwestern city limits, not far from the I-25 on-ramp. If you're from a major city, you'll probably find shopping here very provincial. Anchors include JCPenney, Sears, Dillard's, and Mervyn's. Open Monday to Saturday 10am to 9pm, Sunday noon to 6pm. 4250 Cerrillos Rd. (at Rodeo Rd.). © 505/473-4253.

MARKETS

Farmers' Market ★ *Finds*   The farmers' market has everything from fruits, vegetables, and flowers to cheeses, cider, and salsas. Great local treats! If you're an early riser, stroll through and enjoy good coffee and excellent pastries. Open April to mid-November, Saturday and Tuesday 7am to noon. In the Santa Fe Railyard, off S. Guadalupe behind Tomasita's Cafe. © 505/983-4098.

Tesuque Flea Market ★ *Moments*   More than 500 vendors here sell everything from used cowboy boots (you might find some real beauties) to clothing, jewelry, books, and furniture, all against a big northern New Mexico view. Open March to late November, Friday to Sunday. Vendors open at about 7:30am and continue until about 6:30pm, weather permitting. US 84/285 (about 8 miles north of Santa Fe). No phone.

NATURAL ART

Mineral & Fossil Gallery of Santa Fe   You'll find ancient artwork here, from fossils to geodes in all sizes and shapes. There are also natural mineral jewelry and decorative items for the home, including lamps, wall clocks, furniture, art glass, and carvings. Mineral & Fossil also has galleries in Taos, and in Scottsdale and Sedona, Arizona. 127 W. San Francisco St. © 800/762-9777 or 505/984-1682.

Stone Forest *Finds*   Proprietor Michael Zimber travels to China and other Asian countries every year to collaborate with the stone carvers who create the fountains, sculptures, and bath fixtures that fill this inventive shop and garden not far from the Plaza. 833 Dunlap. © 505/986-8883.

POTTERY & TILES

Artesanos Imports Company ★ *Moments*   This is like a trip south of the border, with all the scents and colors you'd expect on such a journey. You'll find a wide selection of Talavera tile and pottery, as well as light fixtures and many other accessories for the home. There's even an outdoor market where you can buy fountains, sculpture items, and outdoor furniture. A second store is at 1414 Maclovia St. (© **505/471-8020**). 222 Galisteo St. © **505/983-1743**.

Santa Fe Pottery   The work of more than 120 master potters from New Mexico and the Southwest is on display here; you'll find everything from mugs to lamps. From June to December, the shop schedules a series of six one-person and group or theme shows, with an opening for each. 323 S. Guadalupe St. © **505/989-3363**.

RUGS
Seret & Sons Rugs, Furnishings, and Architectural Pieces ★   If you're like me and find Middle Eastern decor irresistible, you need to wander through this shop. You'll find kilims and Persian and Turkish rugs, as well as some of the Moorish-style ancient doors and furnishings that you see around Santa Fe. 224 Galisteo St. © **505/988-9151** or 505/983-5008.

9 Santa Fe After Dark

Santa Fe is a city committed to the arts, so it's no surprise that the nightlife scene is dominated by highbrow cultural events, beginning with the world-famous Santa Fe Opera. The club and popular music scene runs a distant second.

Information on all major cultural events is available from the **Santa Fe Convention and Visitors Bureau** (© **800/777-CITY** or 505/955-6200) or from the **City of Santa Fe Arts Commission** (© **505/955-6707**). Current listings are published each Friday in the "Pasatiempo" section of *The New Mexican* (www.santafenewmexican.com), the city's daily newspaper, and in the *Santa Fe Reporter* (www.sfreporter.com), published every Wednesday.

Nicholas Potter, Bookseller, 211 E. Palace Ave. (© **505/983-5434**), sells tickets to select events. You can also order by phone from **Ticketmaster** (© **505/883-7800**). Discount tickets may be available on the night of a performance; for example, the opera offers standing-room tickets on the day of the performance. Sales start at 10am.

A variety of free concerts, lectures, and other events are presented in the summer, cosponsored by the City of Santa Fe and the Chamber of Commerce. Many of these musical and cultural events take place on the Plaza; check in the "Pasatiempo" section for current listings and information.

THE PERFORMING ARTS
At least two dozen performing-arts groups flourish in this city of 65,000. Many of them perform year-round, but some are seasonal. The acclaimed Santa Fe Opera, for instance, has just a 2-month summer season.

Note: Many companies noted here perform at locations other than their listed addresses, so check the site of the performance you plan to attend.

MAJOR PERFORMING ARTS COMPANIES
OPERA & CLASSICAL MUSIC
Santa Fe Opera ★★★   Many rank the Santa Fe Opera second only to the Metropolitan Opera of New York in the United States. Established in 1957, it consistently attracts famed conductors, directors, and singers. At the height of the season, the company is 500 strong. It's noted for its performances of the classics, little-known works by classical European composers, and American premieres of 21st-century works. The

theater, completed for the 1998 season, sits on a wooded hilltop 7 miles north of the city, off US 84/285. It's partially open-air, with open sides. A controversial structure, the new theater replaced the original, built in 1968, but preserved the sweeping curves attuned to the contour of the surrounding terrain. On a clear night, you can see the lights of Los Alamos in the distance.

The 40-performance season runs from late June through late August. Highlights for 2005 included the opera's first Spanish work in almost 30 years, Osvaldo Golijov's *Ainadamar*, based on the life of poet and playwright Federico García Lorca. Also slated were Puccini's *Turandot*, Rossini's *Barber of Seville*, Mozart's *Lucio Silla*, and Britten's *Peter Grimes*. All performances begin at 9pm, until the last 2 weeks of the season, when performances begin at 8:30pm. A screen in front of each seat shows the libretto during the performance. The entire theater is wheelchair accessible, and there's a gift shop on the premises. P.O. Box 2408, Santa Fe, NM 87504-2408. ✆ **800/280-4654** or 505/986-5900. www.santafeopera.org. Tickets $20–$130; standing room $10; Opening Night Gala $1,000–$2,500. Backstage tours July–Aug Mon–Sat noon. Tours $5 adults, free for children 5–17.

ORCHESTRAL & CHAMBER MUSIC
Santa Fe Pro Musica Chamber Orchestra & Ensemble   This chamber ensemble performs everything from Bach to Vivaldi to contemporary masters. During Holy Week, the Santa Fe Pro Musica presents its annual Mozart and Hayden Concert at the St. Francis Cathedral. Christmas brings candlelight chamber ensemble concerts. Pro Musica's season runs September to May. 430 Manhattan, Suite 10, Santa Fe, NM 87501. ✆ **505/988-4640.** www.santafepromusica.com. Tickets $15–$50.

Santa Fe Symphony Orchestra and Chorus   This 60-piece professional orchestra has grown rapidly in stature since its founding in 1984. Matinee and evening performances of classical and popular works are presented in a subscription series at the Lensic Performing Arts Center from October to May. There's a lecture before each performance. During the spring, the orchestra presents music festivals (call for details). P.O. Box 9692, Santa Fe, NM 87504. ✆ **800/480-1319** or 505/983-1414. www.sf-symphony.org. Tickets $15–$48 (5 seating categories).

MUSIC FESTIVALS & CONCERT SERIES
Santa Fe Chamber Music Festival ★★   An extraordinary group of international artists comes to Santa Fe every summer for this festival. It runs from mid-July to mid-August in the St. Francis Auditorium and the Lensic Performing Arts Center. Performances are Monday, Tuesday, Thursday, and Friday at 8pm; Saturday evening at various times; and Sunday at 6pm. Open rehearsals, youth concerts, and pre-concert lectures are free to the public. 239 Johnson St., Suite B (P.O. Box 2227), Santa Fe, NM 87504. ✆ **505/983-2075** or 505/982-1890 for box office (after June 22). www.sfcmf.org. Tickets $15–$40.

Santa Fe Concert Association   Founded in 1937, the oldest musical organization in northern New Mexico has a September-to-May season that includes approximately 17 events. Among them are a "Great Performances" series and an "Adventures" series, both featuring renowned instrumental and vocal soloists and chamber ensembles. The association also schedules holiday concerts around Christmas. Performances are at the Lensic Performing Arts Center and the St. Francis Auditorium. 210 E. Marcy St. (P.O. Box 4626, Santa Fe, NM 87502). Tickets available through the Lensic box office (✆ **505/988-1234**), ✆ **800/905-3315** (www.tickets.com), or 505/984-8759. Tickets $16–$75.

THEATER COMPANIES

Greer Garson Theater Center   In this intimate theater, the College of Santa Fe's Performing Arts Department produces four plays annually, with six presentations of each, between October and May. The season usually consists of a comedy, a drama, a musical, and a classic. The college also sponsors studio productions and contemporary music concerts. College of Santa Fe, 1600 St. Michaels Dr., Santa Fe, NM 87505. ℂ 505/473-6511. www.csf.edu. Tickets $8–$17 adults, $5 students.

Santa Fe Playhouse   Founded in the 1920s, this is the oldest extant theater group in New Mexico. In a historic adobe theater in the Barrio de Analco, it attracts thousands for its dramas, avant-garde theater, and musical comedy. Its popular one-act melodramas call on the public to boo the sneering villain and swoon for the damsel in distress. 142 E. de Vargas St., Santa Fe, NM 87501. ℂ 505/988-4262. www.santafeplayhouse.org. Tickets "pay what you wish" to $20.

Theater Grottesco ★ *Finds*   This troupe combines the best of comedy, drama, and dance in its original productions performed each spring and summer. Expect to be romanced, shocked, intellectually stimulated, and, above all, struck silly with laughter. Look for winter shows as well. 551 W. Cordova Rd. #8400, Santa Fe, NM 87505. ℂ 505/474-8400. www.theatergrottesco.org. Tickets $7–$20.

Theaterwork Studio ★   A critic for the *Santa Fe New Mexican* called Theaterwork's performance of Chekhov's *Uncle Vanya* "the most rewarding experience I have yet had at a Santa Fe theater." That high praise is well deserved; this community theater goes out of its way to present refreshing, at times risky, plays. In an intimate theater on the south end of town, Theaterwork offers seven main-stage productions a year, a broad variety including new plays and classics by regional and national playwrights. 1336 Rufina Circle (P.O. Box 842, Santa Fe, NM 87504-0842). ℂ 505/471-1799. www.theaterwork.org. Tickets $10–$15. Call for performance times.

DANCE COMPANIES

María Benitez Teatro Flamenco ★★ *Finds*   You won't want to miss this cultural treat. True flamenco is one of the most thrilling of dance forms, displaying the inner spirit and verve of the gypsies of Spanish Andalusia, and María Benitez, trained in Spain, is a fabulous performer. The Benitez Company's "Estampa Flamenca" summer series runs nightly except Tuesday from late June to early September. The María Benitez Theater at the Radisson Hotel is modern and showy, and yet intimate enough that you're immersed in the art. Institute for Spanish Arts, P.O. Box 8418, Santa Fe, NM 87504-8418. For tickets call ℂ 888/435-2636, or the box office (June 16–Sept 3) 505/982-1237. www.mariabenitez.com. Tickets $18–$42.

THE CLUB & MUSIC SCENE

In addition to the clubs and bars listed below, numerous hotel bars and lounges feature some type of entertainment (see "Where to Stay," earlier in this chapter).

COUNTRY, JAZZ & LATIN

Cowgirl Hall of Fame   It's difficult to categorize what goes on in this bar and restaurant, but there's live entertainment nightly. Some nights it's blues guitar, other nights folk music; you might also find progressive rock, comedy, or cowboy poetry. In the summer, this is a great place to sit under the stars and listen to music. 319 S. Guadalupe St. ℂ 505/982-2565. No cover for music Sun, Mon, and Wed. Tues and Thurs–Sat $3 cover. Special performances $10.

The Major Concert & Performance Halls

Center for Contemporary Arts and Plan B Cinematheque, 1050 Old Pecos Trail (© 505/982-1338).

Lensic Performing Arts Center, 211 W. San Francisco St. (© **505/988-7050,** or 505/988-1234 box office).

St. Francis Auditorium, Museum of Fine Arts, Lincoln and Palace avenues (© **505/476-5072**).

Sweeney Convention Center, 201 W. Marcy St. (© **800/777-2489** or 505/955-6200).

Eldorado Hotel   In a grand lobby lounge full of fine art, classical guitarists and pianists perform nightly. 309 W. San Francisco St. © **505/988-4455.**

El Farol   The original neighborhood bar of the Canyon Road artists' quarter is the place to head for local ambience. Its low ceilings and dark brown walls set the scene for Santa Fe's largest and most unusual selection of tapas. Jazz, swing, folk, and ethnic musicians—some of national note—perform most nights. 808 Canyon Rd. © **505/983-9912. Cover $7.**

La Fiesta Lounge ⭐   In the notable La Fonda hotel on the Plaza, this nightclub offers excellent country bands on weekends, with old- and new-timers two-stepping across the floor. The lively lobby bar offers cocktails, an appetizer menu, and live entertainment nightly. It's a great authentic Santa Fe spot. La Fonda hotel, 110 E. San Francisco St. © **505/982-5511.**

Rodeo Nites   A real locals' spot, this club offers dancing to a variety of music, including New Mexican, Mexican, and, on weekends, country. Open Wednesday through Sunday. 2911 Cerrillos Rd. © **505/473-4138.** Cover averages $6.

ROCK & DISCO

Catamount Bar and Grille   The postcollege crowd hangs out at this bar, where there's live rock and blues music on weekends. Food is served until midnight, and there is also a billiards room. 125 E. Water St. © **505/988-7222.**

Paramount Lounge and Night Club   This hip nightspot presents an ambitious array of entertainment—from live music to comedy to weekly DJ dance nights. "Trash Disco" on Wednesday (a blend of disco hits from the '70s and more contemporary house music) is especially popular and always draws an eclectic crowd. On other nights, the dance floor transforms into a live-music venue; recent performances included J. J. Cale and Buckwheat Zydeco.

In the back of the building you'll find Bar B, a much smaller room with an intimate, martini-lounge atmosphere. Along with happy hour Monday to Friday, weekly live jazz, and changing art shows, Bar B schedules many musical acts—often "unplugged" singer-songwriters.

The **Candyman,** 851 St. Michaels Dr. (© **505/983-5906**), and the **CD Café** (© **505/986-0735**), 301 N. Guadalupe, sell tickets for Paramount Lounge events. 331 Sandoval St. © **505/982-8999.** Cover $5 for dance nights; call for music performances.

THE BAR SCENE

The Dragon Room ⭐ A number of years ago, *International Newsweek* named the Dragon Room at the Pink Adobe (see "Where to Dine," earlier in this chapter) one of the top 20 bars in the world. The reason is its spirited but comfortable ambience, which draws students, artists, politicians, and even an occasional celebrity. Dragons are carved on the front doors as well as hanging from the ceiling of the low-lit, elegant space. Live trees grow through the roof. In addition to the tempting lunch and bar menu, there's always a complimentary bowl of popcorn close at hand. 406 Old Santa Fe Trail. ② 505/983-7712.

El Paseo Bar and Grill You can almost always catch live music at this casual, unpretentious place. The crowd is somewhat younger than at most other downtown establishments, and on certain nights, the bar is completely packed. In addition to the open-mike night on Tuesday, a variety of local bands regularly crank out many types of music, from blues to rock to jazz to bluegrass. 208 Galisteo St. ② 505/992-2848. Cover $3–$5 weekends.

Evangelo's A popular downtown hangout, this bar can get raucous at times. It's an interesting place, with tropical decor and a mahogany bar. More than 60 varieties of imported beer are available, and pool tables are an added attraction. On Friday and Saturday starting at 9pm and Wednesday at 7:30pm, live bands (jazz, rock, or reggae) play. Evangelo's is extremely popular with the local crowd. Open Monday to Saturday noon to 1:30am, Sunday until midnight. 200 W. San Francisco St. ② 505/982-9014. Cover for special performances only.

Swig ⭐ *Finds* Santa Fe's most happening club stirs a splash of '60s retro in with a good shot of contemporary chic. Catering to a broad clientele, this martini bar serves classic and cutting-edge drinks along with delectable small plates of Asian food. The lounge serves until 11pm on weekdays and midnight on weekends, making it one of the few Santa Fe spots for late-night food. Open Tuesday through Saturday from 5pm to 2am. 135 W. Palace Ave., level 3. ② 505/955-0400.

Vanessie of Santa Fe ⭐ This is Santa Fe's most popular piano bar. The talented Doug Montgomery and Charles Tichenor have a loyal local following. Their repertoire ranges from Bach to Billy Joel, Gershwin to Barry Manilow. They play nightly from 8pm until closing (anywhere from midnight to 2am). There's an extra microphone, so if you're daring (or drunk), you can stand up and accompany the piano and vocals— though this is *not* a karaoke scene. National celebrities, including Harry Connick, Jr., have even joined in. Vanessie's offers a great bar menu. 434 W. San Francisco St. ② 505/ 982-9966.

10 Touring Some Pueblos Around Santa Fe

Of the eight northern pueblos, Tesuque, Pojoaque, Nambe, San Ildefonso, San Juan, and Santa Clara are within about 30 miles of Santa Fe. Picuris (San Lorenzo) is on the High Road to Taos (see section 13, later in this chapter), and Taos Pueblo (p. 217) is just outside the town of Taos.

The four pueblos described in this section can easily be visited in a single day's trip from Santa Fe, though we suggest visiting just those few that really give a feel of the ancient lifestyle: San Ildefonso, with its broad plaza; Santa Clara and its Puye Cliff Dwellings; and San Juan, home to an arts cooperative. In an easy day trip from Santa

Pueblo Etiquette

When you visit pueblos, it is important to observe certain rules of etiquette. These are personal dwellings, important historic sites, or both, and must be respected as such. Don't climb on the buildings or peek into doors or windows. Don't enter sacred grounds, such as cemeteries and kivas. If you attend a dance or ceremony, remain silent while it is taking place and refrain from applause when it's over. Many pueblos prohibit photography or sketches; others require you to pay a fee for a permit. If you don't respect the privacy of the Native Americans who live at the pueblo, you'll be asked to leave.

Fe you can take in all three, with some delicious New Mexican food in Española en route. If you're in the area at a time when you can catch certain rituals, that's when to see some of the other pueblos.

TESUQUE PUEBLO

Tesuque (Te-*soo*-keh) **Pueblo** is about 9 miles north of Santa Fe on US 84/285. You will know that you are approaching the pueblo when you see a large store near the highway. If you're driving north and you reach the unusual Camel Rock and a large roadside casino, you've missed the pueblo entrance.

The 400 pueblo dwellers at Tesuque are faithful to their traditional religion, rituals, and ceremonies. Excavations confirm that a pueblo has existed here at least since A.D. 1200; this pueblo is now on the National Register of Historic Places. When you come to the welcome sign at the pueblo, turn right, go a block, and park on the right. You'll see the plaza off to the left. There's not a lot to see; in recent years renovation has brought a new look to some of the homes around the plaza. There's a big open area where dances are held, and the **San Diego Church,** completed in 2004 on the site of an 1888 structure that had burned down. It's the fifth church on the pueblo's plaza since 1641. Visitors are asked to remain in this area.

Some Tesuque women are skilled potters; Ignacia Duran's black-and-white and red micaceous pottery and Teresa Tapia's miniatures and pots with animal figures are especially noteworthy. You'll find many crafts at a gallery on the plaza's southeast corner. The **San Diego Feast Day,** which may feature harvest, buffalo, deer, flag, or Comanche dances, is November 12.

The Tesuque Pueblo address is Route 5, Box 360T, Santa Fe, NM 87501 (© **505/ 983-2667**). Admission to the pueblo is free; however, there is a $20 charge for use of still cameras; special permission is required for movie cameras, sketching, and painting. The pueblo is open daily 9am to 5pm. **Camel Rock Casino** (© **505/984-8414**) is open Sunday to Wednesday 8am to 4am, Thursday to Saturday 24 hours; it has a snack bar on the premises.

SAN ILDEFONSO PUEBLO ★★

Pox Oge, as **San Ildefonso Pueblo** is called in its own Tewa language, means "place where the water cuts down through," possibly because of the way the Rio Grande slices through the mountains nearby. Turn left on NM 502 at Pojoaque, and drive about 6 miles to the turnoff. This pueblo has a broad, dusty plaza, with a kiva on one side, ancient dwellings on the other, and a church at the far end. It's nationally famous for its matte-finish, black-on-black pottery, developed by tribeswoman María

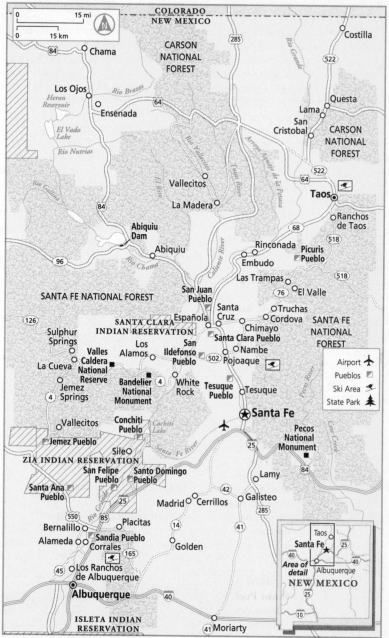

Cultural Pit Stop

Pojoaque Pueblo's Poeh Cultural Center and Museum is a good stop-off point between Santa Fe and Española. It features art and cultural programs, as well as a three-story Sun Tower. The center is at 78 Cities of Gold Rd. in Pojoaque, 15 miles north of Santa Fe (© **505/455-3334**). Admission is free. Open daily from 8am to 5pm. Sketching, cameras, and video cameras are prohibited.

Martinez in the 1920s. One of the most visited pueblos in northern New Mexico, San Ildefonso attracts more than 20,000 visitors a year.

The San Ildefonsos could best be described as rebellious; this was one of the last pueblos to succumb to the reconquest spearheaded by Don Diego de Vargas in 1692. Within view of the pueblo is the volcanic Black Mesa, a symbol of the San Ildefonso people's strength. Through the years, each time San Ildefonso felt itself threatened by enemy forces, the residents, along with members of other pueblos, would hide out up on the butte, returning to the valley only when starvation set in. Today, a visit to the pueblo is valuable mainly in order to see or buy rich black pottery. A few shops surround the plaza, and the **San Ildefonso Pueblo Museum** is tucked away in the governor's office beyond the plaza. I especially recommend visiting during ceremonial days. **San Ildefonso Feast Day,** January 23, features the buffalo and Comanche dances in alternate years. **Corn dances,** held in late August or early September, commemorate a basic element in pueblo life, the importance of fertility in all creatures and plants.

The pueblo has a 4½-acre fishing lake surrounded by *bosque;* it's open April to October. Picnicking is encouraged; look at the sites before you decide on one, because some are nicer than others. Camping is not allowed.

The pueblo's address is Route 5, Box 315A, Santa Fe, NM 87506 (© **505/455-3549**). Admission is $3 per car. The charge for using a still camera is $10; you'll pay $20 to use a video camera and $25 for sketching. If you plan to fish, the charge is $10 for adults and $8 for seniors and children under 12, but call ahead to be sure the lake is open. In summer, the pueblo is open weekdays 8am to 5pm; call for weekend hours. In the winter, it is open Monday to Friday 8am to 4:30pm. It's closed for major holidays and tribal events.

SAN JUAN PUEBLO ⊛

If you continue north on US 84/285, you will reach **San Juan Pueblo** on NM 74, a mile off NM 68, about 4 miles north of Española.

The largest (pop. 1,950) of the Tewa-speaking pueblos and headquarters of the Eight Northern Indian Pueblos Council, San Juan is on the east side of the Rio Grande. It stands opposite the 1598 site of San Gabriel, the first Spanish settlement west of the Mississippi River and the first capital of New Spain. In 1598, the Spanish, impressed with the openness and helpfulness of the people of San Juan, decided to establish a capital there (it was moved to Santa Fe 10 years later), making San Juan Pueblo the first to be subjected to Spanish colonization. The Indians were generous, providing food, clothing, shelter, and fuel—they even helped sustain the settlement when its leader, Conquistador Juan de Oñate, became preoccupied with his search for gold and neglected the needs of his people.

The Spanish subjugation of the Indians left them virtual slaves, forced to provide the Spanish with corn, venison, cloth, and labor. They were compelled to participate in Spanish religious ceremonies and to abandon their own religious practices. Indian ceremonies were not allowed; those caught participating in them were punished. In 1676, several Indians were accused of sorcery and jailed in Santa Fe. Later they were led to the plaza and flogged or hanged. This despicable incident became a turning point in Indian-Spanish relations, generating rage in the Indian community. One of the accused, a San Juan Pueblo Indian named Po'Pay, became a leader in the Great Pueblo Revolt, which led to freedom from Spanish rule for 12 years.

Past and present cohabit here. Though many of the tribe members are Catholics, most of the San Juan tribe still practices traditional religious rituals. Thus, two rectangular kivas flank the church in the main plaza, and *caciques* (pueblo priests) share power with civil authorities. The annual **San Juan Fiesta,** on June 23 and 24, features buffalo and Comanche dances. Another annual ceremony is the **turtle dance** on December 26. The **Matachine dance,** performed here Christmas Day, vividly depicts the subjugation of the Native Americans by the Catholic Spaniards.

The address of the pueblo is P.O. Box 1099, San Juan Pueblo, NM 87566 (© **505/ 852-4400** or 505/852-4210). Admission is free. Photography or sketching may be allowed with prior permission from the governor's office. For information, call the number above. Fishing and picnicking are encouraged at the **San Juan Tribal Lakes.** The charge for fishing is $8 for adults and $5 for children and seniors. The pueblo is open daily during daylight hours.

The **Eight Northern Indian Pueblos Council** (© 505/852-4265) is a sort of chamber of commerce and social-service agency.

A crafts shop, **Oke Oweenge Arts and Crafts Cooperative** (© 505/852-2372), specializes in local wares. This is a fine place to seek out San Juan's distinctive red pottery, a lustrous ceramic incised with traditional geometric symbols. Also displayed for sale are seed, turquoise, and silver jewelry; wood and stone carvings; indigenous clothing and weavings; embroidery; and paintings. Artisans often work on the premises, allowing visitors to watch. The co-op is open Monday through Saturday 9am to 4:30pm in winter, until 5pm in summer (but is closed on San Juan Feast Day, June 24). **Sunrise Crafts,** another crafts shop, is located to the right of the co-op. There you'll find one-of-a-kind handcrafted pipes, beadwork, and burned and painted gourds.

Ohkay Casino (© 505/747-1668) offers table games and slot machines, as well as live music nightly Tuesday through Saturday. It's open daily, 24 hours.

SANTA CLARA PUEBLO

Close to Española (on NM 5), **Santa Clara Pueblo,** with a population of about 1,800, is one of the largest pueblos, and it's the most special to me. I've spent a good bit of time here, writing about the Santa Clara people. You'll see the village sprawling across the river basin near the beautiful Black Mesa, rows of tract homes surrounding an adobe central area. Although it's in an incredible setting, the pueblo itself is not much to see; however, a trip through it will give you a real feel for the contemporary lives of these people. Though stories vary, the Santa Clarans teach their children that their ancestors once lived in cliff-side dwellings named Puye and migrated down to the river bottom in the 13th century. This pueblo is noted for its language program. Artisan/elders work with children to teach them their native Tewa language, on the brink of extinction because so many now speak English. This pueblo is also the home of noted potter Nancy Youngblood, who comes from a long line of famous potters and does alluring contemporary work.

Follow the main route to the old village, where you come to the visitor center, also known as the neighborhood center. There you can get directions to small shops that sell distinctive black, incised Santa Clara pottery, red burnished pottery, baskets, and other crafts. One stunning sight here is the cemetery. Stop on the west side of the church and look over the 4-foot wall. It's a primitive site, with plain wooden crosses and some graves adorned with plastic flowers.

There are corn and harvest dances on **Santa Clara Feast Day,** August 12. Information on other special days (including the corn or harvest dances, as well as children's dances) is available from the pueblo office.

The famed **Puye Cliff Dwellings** (see below) are on the Santa Clara reservation.

The pueblo's address is P.O. Box 580, Española, NM 87532 (© **505/753-7326**). Admission is free. The charge for still cameras is $5; video cameras and sketching are not allowed. The pueblo is open daily 9am to 4pm; the visitor center is open Monday to Friday 8am to 4:30pm.

PUYE CLIFF DWELLINGS ★★

Well worth visiting, the Puye Cliff Dwellings offer a view of centuries of culture so well preserved you can almost hear ancient life clamoring around you. Unfortunately, recent fires devastated the area, so Santa Clara has closed the ruins and recreation area indefinitely. Call before setting out for open times and admission information (© **505/753-7326**).

11 A Side Trip to Pecos National Historic Park

About 15 miles east of Santa Fe, I-25 meanders through **Glorieta Pass,** site of an important Civil War skirmish. In March 1862, volunteers from Colorado and New Mexico, along with Fort Union regulars, defeated a Confederate force marching on Santa Fe, thereby turning the tide of Southern encroachment in the West.

Follow NM 50 east to **Pecos** for about 7 miles. This quaint town, well off the beaten track since the interstate was constructed, is the site of a noted **Benedictine monastery.** About 26 miles north of here on NM 63 is the village of **Cowles,** gateway to the natural wonderland of the **Pecos Wilderness.** There are many camping, picnicking, and fishing locales en route.

Pecos National Historical Park (© **505/757-6414;** www.nps.gov/peco), about 2 miles south of the town of Pecos off NM 63, contains the ruins of a 15th-century pueblo and 17th- and 18th-century missions that jut up spectacularly from a high meadow. Coronado mentioned Pecos Pueblo in 1540: "It is feared through the land," he wrote. The approximately 2,000 Native Americans here farmed in irrigated fields and hunted wild game. Their pueblo had 660 rooms and many kivas. By 1620, Franciscan monks had established a church and convent. Military and natural disasters took their toll on the pueblo, and in 1838, the 20 surviving Pecos went to live with relatives at the Jemez Pueblo.

The **E. E. Fogelson Visitor Center** tells the history of the Pecos people in a well-done, chronologically organized exhibit, complete with dioramas. A 1.5-mile loop trail begins at the center and continues through Pecos Pueblo and the **Misión de Nuestra Señora de Los Angeles de Porciuncula** (as the church was formerly called). This excavated structure—170 feet long and 90 feet wide at the transept—was once the most magnificent church north of Mexico City.

Pecos National Historical Park is open Memorial Day to Labor Day, daily 8am to 6pm; the rest of the year, daily 8am to 5pm. It's closed January 1 and December 25. Admission is $3 per person over age 16.

12 Los Alamos & the Ancient Cliff Dwellings of Bandelier National Monument

Los Alamos, a town of 18,000 residents, spreads over the colorful, fingerlike mesas of the Pajarito Plateau, between the Jemez Mountains and the Rio Grande Valley. It's the home of Los Alamos National Laboratory, established here during World War II, the origin of the first atomic bomb. Still the home of a world-renowned science laboratory, the town is about 35 miles west of Santa Fe and about 65 miles southwest of Taos. From Santa Fe, take US 84/285 north approximately 16 miles to the Pojoaque junction, then turn west on NM 502. Driving time is about 50 minutes. As NM 502 enters Los Alamos from Santa Fe, it follows Trinity Drive, where accommodations, restaurants, and other services are located.

A NEARBY ATTRACTION

Bandelier National Monument ★★★   Less than 15 miles south of Los Alamos along NM 4, this National Park Service area contains stunningly preserved ruins of the ancient cliff-dwelling Anasazi (ancestral Puebloan) culture within 46 square miles of canyon-and-mesa wilderness. The national monument is named after the archaeologist Adolph Bandelier, who explored here in the 1880s. During busy summer months, head out early; there can be a line to wait for parking.

After an orientation stop at the visitor center and museum to learn about the culture that flourished here between 1100 and 1550, most visitors follow a trail along Frijoles Creek to the principal ruins. The pueblo site, including an underground kiva, has been stabilized. The biggest thrill for most folks is climbing hardy ponderosa pine ladders to visit an alcove—140 feet above the canyon floor—that was once home to prehistoric people. Tours are self-guided or led by a National Park Service ranger. Dogs are not allowed on trails.

On summer nights, rangers offer campfire talks about the history, culture, and geology of the area. The guided night walks offered on some summer evenings reveal a different, spooky aspect of the ruins and cave houses, outlined in the two-dimensional chiaroscuro of the thin light from the starry sky. During the day, nature programs are sometimes offered for adults and children. The small museum at the visitor center displays artifacts found in the area.

Elsewhere in the monument area, 70 miles of maintained trails lead to more tribal ruins, waterfalls, and wildlife habitats. A recent fire decimated parts of this area, and periodic closings allow the land to reforest.

The **Tsankawi** section, reached by an ancient 2-mile trail close to **White Rock,** has a large unexcavated ruin on a high mesa overlooking the Rio Grande Valley.

NM 4 (HCR 1, Box 1, Suite 15, Los Alamos, NM 87544-9701). © **505/672-3861**, ext 517. www.nps.gov/band. Admission $10 per vehicle. Daily dawn–dusk. No pets allowed on trails. Closed Jan 1, Dec 25.

A GREAT PICNIC SPOT

The town of White Rock, about 10 miles southeast of Los Alamos on NM 4, offers spectacular panoramas of the river valley in the direction of Santa Fe; the **White Rock Overlook** is a great picnic spot. Within Bandelier, areas have been set aside for picnicking and camping.

While you're in the area, check out the **Valles Caldera National Preserve,** past Bandelier National Monument on NM 4, beginning about 15 miles from Los Alamos. The reserve is all that remains of a volcanic caldera created by a collapse after

Home of the Atomic Bomb

Pueblo tribes lived in the rugged Los Alamos area for well over 1,000 years, and an exclusive boys' school operated atop the 7,300-foot plateau from 1918 to 1943. Then the **Los Alamos National Laboratory** was established here in secrecy, code-named Site Y of the Manhattan Project, the hush-hush wartime program that developed the world's first atomic bombs.

Project director J. Robert Oppenheimer, later succeeded by Norris E. Bradbury, worked along with thousands of scientists, engineers, and technicians in research, development, and production of those early weapons. Today, more than 10,000 people work at the Los Alamos National Laboratory, making it the largest employer in northern New Mexico. Operated from the beginning by the University of California, currently under a contract through the U.S. Department of Energy, its 2,200 individual facilities and 47 separate technical areas occupy 43 square miles of mesa-top land.

Today the lab is one of the world's foremost scientific institutions. It primarily focuses on nuclear weapons research—the Trident and Minuteman strategic warheads were designed here, for example—and has many other interdisciplinary research programs, including international nuclear safeguards and nonproliferation, space, and atmospheric studies; supercomputing; theoretical physics; biomedical and materials science; and environmental restoration.

Current plans call for Los Alamos National Laboratory to begin building a limited number of replacement plutonium pits in 2007 for use in the enduring

eruptions nearly a million years ago. When the mountain spewed ashes and dust as far away as Kansas and Nebraska, its underground magma chambers collapsed, forming this great valley—one of the largest volcanic calderas in the world. Lava domes that pushed up after the collapse obstruct a full view across the expanse, but the beauty of the place is still within grasp. Visitors have many guided options for exploring the preserve, from sleigh rides in winter to fly-fishing in summer. For more information, check out www.vallescaldera.gov.

13 Taking the High Road to Taos

Unless you're in a hurry to get from Santa Fe to Taos, the High Road—also called the Mountain Road or the King's Road—is by far the most fascinating route between the two cities. It begins in lowlands of mystically formed pink and yellow stone, passing by apple and peach orchards and chile farms in the weaving village of **Chimayo.** Then it climbs toward the highlands to the village of **Cordova,** known for its woodcarvers, and higher still to **Truchas,** a renegade arts town where Hispanic traditions and ways of life continue much as they did a century ago. Though I've described this tour from south to north, the most scenic way to see it is from north to south, on your return from Taos.

U.S. nuclear weapons stockpile. The lab has the only plutonium-processing facility in the United States that is capable of producing those components.

Bradbury Science Museum ✪ This is a great place to get acquainted with what goes on at a weapons production facility after nuclear proliferation. Los Alamos National Laboratory runs the museum, which definitely puts a positive spin on the business of producing weapons. It's a fascinating place to explore and includes more than 35 hands-on exhibits. Begin in the History Gallery, where you'll learn about the evolution of the site from the Los Alamos Ranch School days through the Manhattan Project to the present. Artifacts include a 1939 letter from Albert Einstein to President Franklin D. Roosevelt, suggesting research into uranium as a new and important source of energy. Next, move into the Research and Technology Gallery, where you can see work that's been done on the Human Genome Project, including a computer map of human DNA. You can try out a laser and learn about the workings of a particle accelerator. Meanwhile, listen for announcement of the film *The Town That Never Was*, an 18-minute presentation on this community that grew up shrouded in secrecy (shown in the auditorium). Further exploration will take you to the Defense Gallery, where you can test the heaviness of plutonium against that of other substances, see an actual 5-ton Little Boy nuclear bomb (like the one dropped on Hiroshima), and see firsthand how Los Alamos conducts worldwide surveillance of nuclear explosions.

15th St. and Central Ave. © *505/667-4444. Free admission. Tues–Fri 9am–5pm; Sat–Mon 1–5pm. Closed January 1, Thanksgiving, and December 25.*

CHIMAYO

About 28 miles north of Santa Fe on NM 76/285 is the historic weaving center of **Chimayo.** It's approximately 16 miles past the Pojoaque junction, at the junction of NM 520 and NM 76 off NM 503. In this small village, families maintain the tradition of crafting hand-woven textiles initiated by their ancestors seven generations ago, in the early 1800s. The Ortegas are one such family, and **Ortega's Weaving Shop** (© 505/351-4215) and **Galeria Ortega** (© 505/351-2288), both at the corner of NM 520 and NM 76, are fine places to take a close look at this ancient craft. A more humble spot is **Trujillo Weavings** (© 505/351-4457) on NM 76. If you're lucky enough to find the proprietors in, you might get a weaving history lesson. You can see an 80-year-old loom and a 100-year-old shuttle carved from apricot wood. The weavings you'll find are some of the best of the Rio Grande style, with rich patterns, many made from naturally dyed wool. Also on display are some fine Cordova woodcarvings.

One of the best places to shop in Chimayo, **Chimayo Trading and Mercantile** (© 505/351-4566), on Highway 76, is a richly cluttered store carrying local arts and crafts as well as select imports. It has a good selection of kachinas and Hopi corn maidens, as well as specialty items such as elaborately beaded cow skulls. Look for George Zarolinski's "smoked porcelain."

Many people come to Chimayo to visit **El Santuario de Nuestro Señor de Esquipulas (The Shrine of Our Lord of Esquipulas)** ★★, better known simply as "El Santuario de Chimayo." Ascribed with miraculous powers of healing, this church has attracted thousands of pilgrims since its construction in 1814 to 1816. Up to 30,000 people participate in the annual Good Friday pilgrimage, many of them walking from as far away as Albuquerque.

Although only the earth in the anteroom beside the altar is presumed to have the gift of healing powers, the entire shrine radiates serenity. A National Historic Landmark, the church has five beautiful *reredos* (panels of sacred paintings)—one behind the main altar and two on each side of the nave. Each year during the fourth weekend in July, the military exploits of the 9th-century Spanish saint Santiago are celebrated in a weekend fiesta, including the historic play *Los Moros y Los Cristianos (The Moors and the Christians)*.

A good place to stop for a quick bite, **Leona's Restaurante de Chimayo** (© 505/351-4569), is next door to the Santuario de Chimayo. Leona herself presides over this little taco and burrito stand with plastic tables inside and, during warm months, out. Leona has gained national fame for her flavored tortillas—such delicacies as raspberry and chocolate really are tasty. Burritos and soft tacos made with chicken, beef, or veggie-style with beans will definitely tide you over en route to Taos or Santa Fe. Open Thursday through Monday 11am to 5pm.

WHERE TO STAY & DINE IN CHIMAYO

Casa Escondida ★ On the outskirts of Chimayo, this inn offers a lovely retreat and a good home base for exploring the Sangre de Cristo Mountains and their many soulful farming villages. This hacienda-feeling place has a cozy living room with a large kiva fireplace. Decor is simple and classic, with Mission-style furniture lending a colonial feel. The breakfast room is a sunny atrium with French doors that open out in summer to a grassy yard spotted with apricot trees. Accommodations vary; my favorites are in the main house. The Sun Room catches all that passionate northern New Mexico sun on its red brick floors and private flagstone patio. It has an elegant feel and connects with a smaller room, so it's a good choice for families.

Off County Rd. 0100 (P.O. Box 142), Chimayo, NM 87522. © 800/643-7201 or 505/351-4805. Fax 505/351-2575. www.casaescondida.com. 8 units. $85–$145 double. Rates include full breakfast. MC, V. Pets accepted for a small fee; prearrangement required. **Amenities:** Jacuzzi; in-room massage; laundry service.

Restaurante Rancho de Chimayo ★ NEW MEXICAN For as long as I can remember, my family and many of my friends' families have scheduled trips to northern New Mexico to coincide with lunchtime or dinnertime at this fun restaurant. In an adobe home built by Hermenegildo Jaramillo in the 1880s, it is now a restaurant run by his descendants. Unfortunately, the restaurant has become so famous that tour buses stop here. However, the food has suffered only a little. In the warmer months, you can dine on the terraced patio. During winter, you'll be seated in one of a number of cozy rooms. The food is prepared from generations-old Jaramillo family recipes. You can't go wrong with enchiladas, served layered, northern New Mexico style, rather than rolled. For variety you might want to try the *combinación picante* (carne adovada, tamale, enchilada, beans, and *posole*). Each plate comes with two *sopaipillas*. With a little honey, who needs dessert? The full bar serves delicious margaritas.

County Rd. 98 (P.O. Box 11), Chimayo, NM 87522. © 505/351-4444. Reservations recommended. Lunch $7.50–$13, dinner $10–$15. AE, DC, DISC, MC, V. Daily 11:30am–9pm; Sat–Sun 8:30–10:30am. Closed Mon Nov–Apr.

CORDOVA

Just as Chimayo is famous for its weaving, **Cordova,** about 7 miles east on NM 76, is noted for its woodcarvers. It's easy to whiz by this village, nestled below the High Road, but don't. Just a short way through this traditional northern New Mexico town is a gem: The **Castillo Gallery** ✩ (℃ 505/351-4067), a mile into the village of Cordova, carries moody and colorful acrylic paintings by Paula Castillo, as well as her found-art welded sculptures. It also carries the work of Terry Enseñat Mulert, whose contemporary woodcarvings are treasures of the high country. En route to the Castillo, you may want to stop in at two other local carvers' galleries. The first you'll come to is that of **Sabinita Lopez Ortiz;** the second belongs to her cousin **Gloria Ortiz.** Both are descendants of the noted José Dolores Lopez. Carved from cedar wood and aspen, their works range from simple statues of saints (santos) to elaborate scenes of birds.

TRUCHAS

Robert Redford's 1988 movie *The Milagro Beanfield War* featured the town of **Truchas** (which means "trout"). A former Spanish colonial outpost built on top of an 8,000-foot mesa, 4 miles east of Cordova, it was chosen as the site for the film in part because traditional Hispanic culture is still very much in evidence. Subsistence farming is prevalent here. The scenery is spectacular: 13,101-foot Truchas Peak dominates one side of the mesa, and the broad Rio Grande Valley dominates the other.

Be sure to find your way to the **Cordovas' Handweaving Workshop** (℃ 505/689-2437). Harry Cordova, a fourth-generation weaver with a unique style, runs this tiny shop in the center of town. His works tend to be simpler than many Rio Grande weavings, utilizing mainly stripes in the designs.

Just down the road from the Cordovas' is **Hand Artes Gallery** (℃ 800/689-2441 or 505/689-2443), a definite surprise in this remote region. Here you'll find an array of contemporary as well as representational art by noted regional artists. Look for Sheila Keeffe's worldly painted panels, Susan Christie's monoprints and subtly textured paintings, and Norbert Voelkel's colorful paintings.

About 6 miles east of Truchas on NM 76 is the small town of **Las Trampas,** noted for its **San José Church,** which, with its thick walls and elegant lines, might be the most beautiful of all New Mexico churches built during the Spanish colonial period.

PICURIS (SAN LORENZO) PUEBLO

Near the regional education center of Peñasco, about 24 miles from Chimayo, near the intersection of NM 75 and NM 76, is **Picuris (San Lorenzo) Pueblo** (℃ 505/587-2519). The 375 citizens of this 15,000-acre pueblo, native Tewa speakers, consider themselves a sovereign nation: Their forebears never made a treaty with any foreign country, including the U.S. They observe a traditional form of tribal council government. A few of the original mud-and-stone houses still stand, as does a lovely church. A striking aboveground ceremonial kiva called "the Roundhouse," built at least 700 years ago, and some historic excavated kivas and storerooms are on a hill above the pueblo and are open to visitors. The **annual feast days** at San Lorenzo Church are August 9 and 10.

The people here are modern enough to have fully computerized their public showcase operations as Picuris Tribal Enterprises. Besides running the Hotel Santa Fe in the state capital, they own the **Picuris Pueblo Museum and Visitor's Center,** where weaving, beadwork, and distinctive reddish-brown clay cooking pottery are exhibited daily 9am to 6pm. Self-guided tours through the old village ruins begin at the museum and cost $5; the camera fee is $6; sketching and video camera fees are $25. The pueblo has an information center, a crafts shop, and a restaurant.

DIXON & EMBUDO

Taos is about 24 miles north of Peñasco on NM 518, but day-trippers from Santa Fe can loop back to the capital by taking NM 75 west from Picuris Pueblo. Dixon, approximately 12 miles west of Picuris, and its twin village Embudo, a mile farther on NM 68 at the Rio Grande, are home to many artists and craftspeople who exhibit their works during the annual **autumn show** sponsored by the Dixon Arts Association. If you get to Embudo at mealtime, stop in at **Embudo Station** (© **800/852-4707** or 505/852-4707), a restaurant right on the banks of the Rio Grande. From mid-April to October—the only time it's open—you can sit on the patio under giant cottonwoods and sip the restaurant's own microbrewed beer (try the green-chile ale, its most celebrated) and signature wines while watching the peaceful Rio flow by. The specialty is Southwestern food, but you'll find other tantalizing tastes as well. Try rainbow trout roasted on a cedar plank. The restaurant is generally open Tuesday to Sunday noon to 9pm, but call before making plans. It is especially known for its Jazz on Sunday, an affair that PBS once featured.

For more taste of the local grape, you can follow signs to **La Chiripada Winery** (© **505/579-4437**), whose product is surprisingly good, especially to those who don't know that New Mexico has a long winemaking history. Local pottery is also sold. The winery is open Monday to Saturday 10am to 5pm, Sunday noon to 5pm.

Two more small villages lie in the Rio Grande Valley at 6-mile intervals south of Embudo on NM 68. **Velarde** is a fruit-growing center; in season, the road here is lined with stands selling fresh fruit or crimson chile ristras and wreaths of native plants. **Alcalde** is the site of Los Luceros, an early-17th-century home that is to be refurbished as an arts and history center. The unique **Dance of the Matachines,** a Moorish ritual brought from Spain, is performed here on holidays and feast days.

ESPAÑOLA

The commercial center of Española (pop. 7,000) no longer has the railroad that led to its establishment in the 1880s, but it may have New Mexico's greatest concentration of **low riders.** These are late-model customized cars, so called because their suspension leaves them sitting quite close to the ground. The **Convento,** built to resemble a colonial cathedral, on the Española Plaza (at the junction of NM 30 and US 84), houses a variety of shops, including a trading post and an antique gallery, as well as a display room for the Historical Society. Major events include the July **Fiesta de Oñate,** commemorating the valley's founding in 1596. The **Española Valley Chamber of Commerce,** 710 Paseo de Onate, Española, NM 87532 (© **505/753-2831**), distributes information on Española and the vicinity.

If you admire the work of Georgia O'Keeffe, try to plan a short trip to **Abiquiu,** a tiny town at a bend of the Rio Chama, 14 miles south of Ghost Ranch and 22 miles north of Española on US 84. When you see the surrounding terrain, it will be clear that this was the inspiration for many of her startling landscapes. **O'Keeffe's adobe home** ⊛ (© **505/685-4539**) is open for public tours. See p. 283 for details.

WHERE TO DINE

El Paragua ⊛ NORTHERN NEW MEXICAN This restaurant is a great place to stop en route to Taos, though some Santa Feans make a special trip here. Every time

Georgia O'Keeffe & New Mexico: A Desert Romance

In June 1917, during a short visit to the Southwest, the painter Georgia O'Keeffe (1887–1986) visited New Mexico for the first time. She was immediately enchanted by the stark scenery; even after her return to the energy and chaos of New York City, her mind wandered frequently to New Mexico's arid land and undulating mesas. However, not until the arts patron and "collector of people" Mabel Dodge Luhan coaxed her 12 years later did O'Keeffe return to the multihued desert of her daydreams.

O'Keeffe was reportedly ill, both physically and emotionally, when she arrived in Santa Fe in April 1929. New Mexico seemed to soothe her spirit and heal her physical ailments almost magically. Two days after her arrival, Luhan persuaded O'Keeffe to move into her home in Taos. There she would be free to paint and socialize as she liked.

In Taos, O'Keeffe began painting what would become some of her best-known canvases—close-ups of desert flowers and objects such as cow and horse skulls. "The color up there is different . . . the blue-green of the sage and the mountains, the wildflowers in bloom," O'Keeffe once said of Taos. "It's a different kind of color from any I've ever seen—there's nothing like that in north Texas or even in Colorado." Taos transformed not only her art, but her personality as well. She bought a car and learned to drive. Sometimes, on warm days, she ran naked through the sage fields. That August, a new, rejuvenated O'Keeffe rejoined her husband, photographer Alfred Stieglitz, in New York.

The artist returned to New Mexico year after year, spending time with Luhan as well as staying at the isolated Ghost Ranch. She drove through the countryside in her snappy Ford, stopping to paint in her favorite spots along the way. Until 1949, O'Keeffe always returned to New York in the fall. That year, 3 years after Stieglitz's death, she relocated permanently to New Mexico, spending winter and spring in Abiquiu, summer and fall at Ghost Ranch. Georgia O'Keeffe died in Santa Fe in 1986.

A great way to see Ghost Ranch is on a hike that climbs above the mystical area. Take US 84 north from Española about 36 miles to Ghost Ranch and follow the road to the Ghost Ranch office. The ranch is managed by the Presbyterian Church, and the staff will supply you with a primitive map for the **Kitchen Mesa** and **Chimney Rock** hikes.

I enter El Paragua ("the umbrella"), with its red tile floors and colorful Saltillo-tile trimmings, I feel as though I've stepped into Mexico. The restaurant opened in 1958 as a small taco stand owned by two brothers. It has received praise from many sources, including *Gourmet* magazine and N. Scott Momaday, writing for the *New York Times*. You can't go wrong ordering the enchilada suprema, a chicken and cheese enchilada with onion and sour cream. Also on the menu are fajitas and a variety of seafood and steaks, including *churrasco Argentino*. Served at your table in a hot brazier, it's cooked in a green herb *salsa chimichurri*. From the full bar, you may want to try Don Luis's

Italian coffee, made with a coffee-flavored liquor called Tuaca. For equally excellent but faster food, go next door to **El Parasol** and order a chicken taco—the best ever.

603 Santa Cruz Rd., Española (off the main drag; turn east at Long John Silver's). ℂ 505/753-3211. Reservations recommended. Main courses $9–$20. AE, DISC, MC, V. Daily 11am–9pm.

OJO CALIENTE

Many locals like to rejuvenate at **Ojo Caliente Mineral Springs,** Ojo Caliente, NM 87549 (ℂ **800/222-9162** or 505/583-2233); it's on US 285, 50 miles (a 1-hr. drive) northwest of Santa Fe and 50 miles southwest of Taos. This National Historic Site was considered sacred by prehistoric tribes. When Spanish explorer Cabeza de Vaca discovered and named the springs in the 16th century, he called them "the greatest treasure that I found these strange people to possess." No other hot spring in the world has Ojo Caliente's combination of iron, soda, lithium, sodium, and arsenic. If the weather is warm enough, the outdoor mud bath is a real treat. The dressing rooms are fairly new and in good shape; however, the whole place has an earthy feel. If you're a fastidious type, you won't be comfortable here. The resort offers herbal wraps and massages, lodging, and meals. It's open daily 8am to 8pm (9pm Fri–Sat).

8

Taos

New Mexico's favorite arts town sits in a masterpiece setting. It's wedged between the towering peaks of the Rocky Mountains and the plunging chasm of the Rio Grande Gorge.

Located just 40 miles south of the Colorado border, about 70 miles north of Santa Fe, and 135 miles from Albuquerque, this town of 5,000 residents combines 1960s hippiedom (thanks to communes set up in the hills back then) with the ancient culture of Taos Pueblo (some people still live without electricity and running water, as their ancestors did 1,000 years ago). It can be an odd place, where some completely eschew materialism and live "off the grid" in half-underground houses called earthships. But there are plenty more mainstream attractions as well—Taos boasts some of the best restaurants in the state, a hot and funky arts scene, and incredible outdoors action, including world-class skiing.

Taos's history is rich. Throughout the Taos valley, ruins and artifacts attest to a Native American presence dating back 5,000 years. The Spanish first visited this area in 1540, colonizing it in 1598. In the last 2 decades of the 17th century, they put down three rebellions at the Taos Pueblo. During the 18th and 19th centuries, Taos was an important trade center: New Mexico's annual caravan to Chihuahua, Mexico, couldn't leave until after the annual midsummer **Taos Fair.** French trappers began attending the fair in 1739. Even though the Plains tribes often attacked the pueblos at other times, they attended the market festival under a temporary annual truce. By the early 1800s, Taos had become a meeting place for American mountain men, the most famous of whom, Kit Carson, made his home in Taos from 1826 to 1868.

Taos remained loyal to Mexico during the Mexican War of 1846. The town rebelled against its new U.S. landlord in 1847, even killing newly appointed Governor Charles Bent in his Taos home. Nevertheless, the town was incorporated into the Territory of New Mexico in 1850. During the Civil War, Taos fell into Confederate hands for 6 weeks; afterward, Carson and two other men raised the Union flag over Taos Plaza and guarded it day and night. Since that time, Taos has had the honor of flying the flag 24 hours a day.

Taos's population declined when the railroad bypassed it in favor of Santa Fe. In 1898 two East Coast artists—Ernest Blumenschein and Bert Phillips—discovered the dramatic, varied effects of sunlight on the natural environment of the Taos valley and depicted them on canvas. By 1912, thanks to the growing influence of the **Taos Society of Artists,** the town had gained a worldwide reputation as a cultural center. Today, it is estimated that more than 15% of the population are painters, sculptors, writers, or musicians, or otherwise earn their income from artistic pursuits.

1 Orientation

ARRIVING

BY PLANE   The **Taos Municipal Airport** (© 505/758-4995) is about 8 miles northwest of town on US 64. **Rio Grande Air** (© 877/435-9742 or 505/737-9790; www.riograndeair.com) runs daily flights between Albuquerque and Taos. Most people opt to fly into Albuquerque International Sunport, rent a car, and drive to Taos. The drive takes approximately 2½ hours. If you'd rather be picked up at Albuquerque International Sunport, call **Faust's Transportation, Inc.** (© 505/758-3410), which offers daily service, as well as taxi service between Taos and Taos Ski Valley.

BY BUS   The **Taos Bus Center** is 5 miles south of the plaza at 1386 Paseo del Pueblo Sur (© 505/758-1144). **TNM&O** (© 505/242-4998) arrives and departs from this depot several times a day. For more information on this and other bus services to and from Albuquerque and Santa Fe, see "Getting There" in chapter 2.

BY CAR   Most visitors arrive in Taos on either NM 68 or US 64. Northbound travelers should exit I-25 at Santa Fe, follow US 285 as far as San Juan Pueblo, and continue on the divided highway when it becomes NM 68. Taos is about 79 miles from the I-25 junction. Southbound travelers from Denver on I-25 should exit about 6 miles south of Raton at US 64 and follow it about 95 miles to Taos. Another major route is US 64 from the west (214 miles from Farmington).

VISITOR INFORMATION

The **Taos County Chamber of Commerce,** at the junction of NM 68 and NM 585 (P.O. Drawer I), Taos, NM 87571 (© 800/732-TAOS or 505/758-3873; www.taos chamber.com), is open in summer and fall daily 9am to 5pm, and from November to Memorial Day Monday to Saturday 9am to 5pm. It's closed on major holidays. **Carson National Forest** has an information center in the same building.

CITY LAYOUT

The **plaza** is a short block west of Taos's major intersection—where US 64 (Kit Carson Rd.) from the east joins NM 68, **Paseo del Pueblo Sur.** US 64 proceeds north from the intersection as **Paseo del Pueblo Norte. Camino de la Placita** (Placitas Rd.) circles the west side of downtown, passing within a block of the other side of the plaza. Many of the cross streets are winding lanes lined with traditional adobe homes, many of them over 100 years old.

Most of the art galleries are on or near the plaza, which was paved over with bricks several years ago, and along neighboring streets. Others are in the **Ranchos de Taos** area a few miles south of the plaza.

MAPS   To find your way around town, pick up a free map from the **Chamber of Commerce at Taos Visitor Center,** 1139 Paseo del Pueblo Sur (© 505/758-3873). Area bookstores (see "Shopping," later in this chapter) sell good, detailed city maps.

2 Getting Around

BY CAR

With offices at the Taos airport, **Enterprise** (© 800/369-4226 or 505/751-7490) is reliable and efficient. Other car-rental agencies have offices in Albuquerque. See "Getting Around," in chapter 9, for details.

Tips **Warning for Drivers**

En route to many recreation sites, reliable paved roads often give way to poorer forest roads. When you get off the main roads, you don't find gas stations or cafes. Four-wheel-drive vehicles are recommended on snow and much of the unpaved terrain of the region. If you're doing some off-road adventuring, it's wise to go with a full gas tank, extra food and water, and warm clothing—just in case. At the higher-than-10,000-foot elevations of northern New Mexico, sudden summer snowstorms are not unheard of.

PARKING   Parking can be difficult during the summer rush, when the stream of tourists' cars moving north and south through town never ceases. If you can't find parking on the street or in the plaza, check out some of the nearby roads (Kit Carson Rd., for instance); Taos has plenty of metered and unmetered lots.

ROAD CONDITIONS   The **State Highway Department** (© 800/432-4269) provides information on highway conditions throughout the state.

BY BUS & TAXI

If you're in Taos without a car, you're in luck: **Chile Line Town of Taos Transit** (© 505/751-4459) provides local bus service. It operates on the half-hour Monday to Saturday 7am to 7pm in summer, 7am to 6pm in winter, and on the hour Sunday 8am to 5pm. Two routes run southbound from Taos Pueblo and northbound from the Ranchos de Taos Post Office. Each route includes stops at the casino and various hotels in town, as well as Taos RV Park. Bus fares are 50¢ one-way, $1 round-trip, $5 for a 7-day pass, and $20 for a 31-day pass.

In addition, **Faust's Transportation** (© 505/758-3410) has a taxi service linking town hotels and Taos Ski Valley. Faust's Transportation also offers shuttle service and on-call taxi service daily from 7am to 9pm. Fares are about $8 anywhere within the city limits for up to two people ($2 per additional person).

BY BICYCLE

Bicycle rentals are available from **Gearing Up Bicycle Shop,** 129 Paseo del Pueblo Sur (© 505/751-0365). Rentals run $35 for a full day and $25 for a half day for a mountain bike with front suspension. From April to October, **Native Sons Adventures,** 1033A Paseo del Pueblo Sur (© 800/753-7559 or 505/758-9342), rents no-suspension bikes ($15 for a half day, $20 for a full day), front-suspension bikes ($25 for a half day, $35 for a full day), and full-suspension bikes ($35 for a half day, $45 for a full day). It also rents car racks for $5. Each shop supplies helmets and water bottles with rentals.

FAST FACTS

Members of the **Taos Medical Group,** on Weimer Road (© 505/758-2224), are highly respected. Also recommended is **Family Practice Associates of Taos,** 630 Paseo del Pueblo Sur, Suite 150 (© 505/758-3005). **Holy Cross Hospital,** 1397 Weimer Rd., off Paseo del Canyon (© 505/758-8883), has 24-hour emergency service. Serious cases are transferred to Santa Fe or Albuquerque.

Gross receipts tax for Taos is 7.5%. There is an additional tax of about 5% on hotel rooms.

See also "Fast Facts: The American Southwest" in chapter 2, and "Fast Facts: For the International Traveler" in chapter 3.

3 Where to Stay

A tiny town with a big tourist market, Taos has thousands of rooms in hotels, motels, condominiums, and bed-and-breakfasts. Many recently opened properties have turned Taos into a buyer's market. In the slower seasons—January through early February and April through May—when competition for travelers is steep, you may even want to try bargaining your room rate down. Most of the hotels and motels are on Paseo del Pueblo Sur and Norte, with a few scattered just east of the town center, along Kit Carson Road. Condos and bed-and-breakfasts are generally scattered throughout Taos's back streets.

During peak seasons, visitors without reservations may have difficulty finding vacant rooms. **Taos Central Reservations,** P.O. Box 1713, Taos, NM 87571 (© **800/ 821-2437**), might be able to help.

Fifteen hundred or so of Taos County's beds are in condominiums and lodges at or near Taos Ski Valley. The **Taos Valley Resort Association,** P.O. Box 85, Taos Ski Valley, NM 87525 (© **800/776-1111** or 505/776-2233; fax 505/776-8842; www. visitnewmexico.com), can book these, as well as rooms in Taos and the rest of northern New Mexico, and private home rentals.

Reservations of Taos, 1033A Paseo del Pueblo Sur, Taos, NM 87571 (© **505/751- 1292**), will help you find accommodations from bed-and-breakfasts to home rentals, hotels, RV parks, and cabins throughout Taos and the rest of northern New Mexico. It'll also help you arrange package prices for outdoor activities such as whitewater rafting, horseback riding, hot-air ballooning, snowmobiling, fishing, and skiing.

There are two high seasons in Taos: winter (the Christmas-to-Easter ski season, except for Jan, which is notoriously slow) and summer. Spring and fall are shoulder seasons, often with lower rates. The period between Easter and Memorial Day is also slow in the tourist industry here, and many proprietors of restaurants and other businesses take their annual vacations at this time. Book well ahead for ski holiday periods (especially Christmas) and for the annual arts festivals (late May to mid-June and late Sept to early Oct). A tax of 12.5% in Taos proper and 12.31% in Taos County will be added to every hotel bill.

TAOS & VICINITY
EXPENSIVE
Hotels/Motels
El Monte Sagrado ★★★ *(Moments)*   For those, like me, who are blessed (or cursed) with sensitive senses, El Monte Sagrado (the Sacred Mountain), Taos's new resort near the center of town, is pure heaven. Often while traveling I find I'm accosted by sounds, scents, even sights, but at this resort my senses rejoice. Water running over falls, clear air, and delicious food and drink lull guests into a sweet *samadhi,* or state of relaxation, while the eyes luxuriate in the impeccably decorated rooms. Themes range from the Caribbean Casita, a medium-size room with a medium-size bathroom, which evokes the feel of a tropical jungle; to the China Casita, a large two-bedroom suite with two large bathrooms, all bathed in gold, with its own patio and outdoor hot tub; to the Kamasutra Suite, with suggestive carvings throughout, a room resort owner Tom Worrell describes as "the first honeymoon suite to come with instructions." All

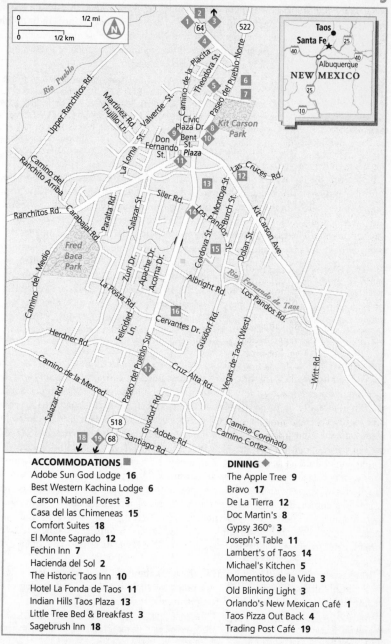

Central Taos Accommodations & Dining

0   1/2 mi
0   1/2 km

Taos
Santa Fe
NEW MEXICO
Albuquerque

Rio Pueblo
Upper Ranchitos Rd.
Martinez Rd.
Trujillo Ln.
Valverde St.
Camino de la Placita
Theodora St.
Paseo del Pueblo Norte
Camino del Ranchito Arriba
Ranchitos Rd.
Camino del Medio
Fred Baca Park
Civic Plaza Dr.
Don Fernando St.
Bent St.
Plaza
Kit Carson Park
Las Cruces Rd.
Kit Carson Ave.
La Loma St.
Paralta Rd.
Salazar St.
Siler Rd.
Los Pandos
Montoya St.
Burch St.
Dolan St.
Cordova St.
Zuni Dr.
Apache Dr.
Acoma Dr.
La Posta Rd.
Albright Rd.
Rio Fernando de Taos
Los Pandos Rd.
Felicidad Ln.
Cervantes Dr.
Gusdorf Rd.
Vegas de Taos (West)
Herdner Rd.
Camino de la Merced
Paseo del Pueblo Sur
Cruz Alta Rd.
Witt Rd.
Salazar Rd.
Gusdorf Rd.
Adobe Rd.
Santiago Rd.
Camino Coronado
Camino Cortez

ACCOMMODATIONS ■
Adobe Sun God Lodge **16**
Best Western Kachina Lodge **6**
Carson National Forest **3**
Casa del las Chimeneas **15**
Comfort Suites **18**
El Monte Sagrado **12**
Fechin Inn **7**
Hacienda del Sol **2**
The Historic Taos Inn **10**
Hotel La Fonda de Taos **11**
Indian Hills Taos Plaza **13**
Little Tree Bed & Breakfast **3**
Sagebrush Inn **18**

DINING ◆
The Apple Tree **9**
Bravo **17**
De La Tierra **12**
Doc Martin's **8**
Gypsy 360° **3**
Joseph's Table **11**
Lambert's of Taos **14**
Michael's Kitchen **5**
Momentitos de la Vida **3**
Old Blinking Light **3**
Orlando's New Mexican Café **1**
Taos Pizza Out Back **4**
Trading Post Café **19**

units are quiet and lovely, with patios or balconies and views. They surround a grassy, cottonwood-shaded "Sacred Circle," which also has trout and koi ponds. In line with Worrell's plan to preserve the environment through responsible development and sustainable technologies, the resort recycles its water and makes much of its own electricity. The intimate spa offers a full range of treatments.

317 Kit Carson Rd., Taos, NM 87571. ℂ **800/828-TAOS** or 505/758-3502. www.elmontesagrado.com. 36 units. $245–$375 1-bedroom casita; $295–$395 1-bedroom junior suite; $395–$795 1-bedroom exclusive casita; $1,095–$1,495 2-bedroom global suite. AE, DC, DISC, MC, V. **Amenities:** Restaurant (p. 210); bar (p. 231); indoor pool; well-equipped health club and spa; Jacuzzi; concierge; babysitting; laundry service. *In room:* A/C, TV, dataport, hair dryer, safe.

Fechin Inn ⭐⭐ This masterfully created luxury hotel provides comfort, quiet, and lots of amenities. Next door to Russian artist Nicolai Fechin's 1927 home (see the Taos Art Museum listing, later in this chapter), the hotel features elegantly carved wood furniture and artwork by Jeremy Morelli of Santa Fe. The hotel is next to Kit Carson Park, a short walk from the plaza. The two-story lobby is airy, with a bank of windows and French doors looking south to a portal where diners can eat breakfast in the warmer months. The spacious rooms have Southwestern decor with nice touches such as guest robes, hickory furniture, and flagstone-topped tables; some have balconies or patios. Suites have kiva fireplaces. The bathrooms are delightful, with Italian tile. There's a library where you can play chess or backgammon. An elaborate continental breakfast is available for an additional charge. In the evenings, drinks are available.

227 Paseo del Pueblo Norte, Taos, NM 87571. ℂ **800/811-2933** or 505/751-1000. Fax 505/751-7338. www.fechininn.com. 84 units. $114–$177 double; $282–$512 suite. Extra person $15. AE, DC, DISC, MC, V. Pets accepted with some restrictions; $50 fee. **Amenities:** Medium-size health club; Jacuzzi; car-rental desk; room service; massage; coin-op laundry; same-day dry cleaning and laundry service. *In room:* A/C, TV, dataport, fridge, coffeemaker, hair dryer.

The Historic Taos Inn ⭐ It's rare to see a hotel that has withstood the years with grace. The Historic Taos Inn has. You'll be surrounded by 20th-century luxury without ever forgetting that you're within the thick walls of a number of 19th-century Southwestern homes. Dr. Thomas Paul Martin, the town's first physician, purchased the complex in 1895. In 1936, a year after the doctor's death, his widow, Helen, enclosed the plaza—now the inn's darling two-story lobby—and turned it into a hotel. In 1981–82, the inn was restored; it's on both the State and National Registers of Historic Places.

The lobby doubles as the **Adobe Bar,** a popular local gathering place, with adobe *bancos* (benches) and a sunken fireplace, all surrounding a wishing well that was once the old town well. A number of rooms open onto a balcony that overlooks this area. If you like community and don't mind the sound of jazz and flamenco drifting up toward your room, these rooms are for you. However, if you appreciate solitude and silence, request one of the courtyard rooms downstairs. Rooms are unique and comfortable, decorated with Spanish colonial art, Taos-style furniture, and interesting touches; many rooms have fireplaces.

In recent years I've had complaints from guests about the temperamental nature of these old buildings. You may encounter problems such as windows not staying open or not having screens. I've also had complaints about the service.

125 Paseo del Pueblo Norte, Taos, NM 87571. ℂ **800/TAOS-INN** or 505/758-2233. Fax 505/758-5776. www.taosinn.com. 36 units. $65–$225 double. AE, DISC, MC, V. **Amenities:** Restaurant (p. 210); bar; seasonal outdoor pool; Jacuzzi; room service; coffee or refreshments in lobby. *In room:* A/C, TV, VCR on request, hair dryer, iron.

Hotel La Fonda de Taos ⭐ Finally, Taos has a recommendable hotel on the plaza. The historic property built in 1880 underwent a $3 million renovation (completed in

2001) that turned it into a comfortable, fun spot with a stellar location. The charismatic Taos figure Saki Kavaras put this hotel on the society map in the 1930s, when, most notably, British author D. H. Lawrence frequented it. His legacy is preserved in a unique D. H. Lawrence Forbidden Art Museum, where some of his risqué paintings hang—a must-see even if you don't stay here (free for guests; $3 for nonguests). Rooms are set off broad hallways, each styled in earth tones, Southwestern furnishings, and tile bathrooms. Standards are small, each with a queen-size bed. Your better bet is to reserve a plaza or deluxe plaza room, or a suite. These are larger, with king beds. My favorite rooms are 201 and 301, which overlook the plaza. Groups can rent the whole top (third) floor, which includes a full kitchen suite.

108 South Plaza, Taos, NM 87571. ℂ 800/833-2211 or 505/758-2211. Fax 505/758-8508. www.hotellafonda.com. 24 units. $99–$169 standard double; $129–$219 plaza or deluxe double; $169–$229 suite. AE, DC, DISC, MC, V. **Amenities:** Restaurant; coffee shop; bar. *In room:* A/C, TV, hair dryer, iron.

MODERATE

Best Western Kachina Lodge & Meeting Center ⭐ *Kids*   Built in the early 1960s, this lodge is on the north end of town, within walking distance of the plaza. It has a lot of charm despite the fact that it's really a motor hotel. Though it has traditionally been a good spot for families and travelers, in recent years management has begun catering so much to convention traffic that the service has suffered for others. Remodeling is ongoing in the solidly built Southwestern-style rooms—some have couches, and most have Taos-style *trasteros* (armoires) that hold the TVs. Rooms surround a grassy courtyard studded with huge blue spruce trees, allowing kids room to run. In the center is a stage where a family from Taos Pueblo builds a bonfire and dances nightly in the summer and explains the significance of the dances—a real treat.

413 Paseo del Pueblo Norte (P.O. Box NM), Taos, NM 87571. ℂ 800/522-4462 or 505/758-2275. Fax 505/758-9207. www.kachinalodge.com. 118 units. $59–$129 double. Extra person $10. Children under 12 stay free in parent's room. AE, DC, DISC, MC, V. **Amenities:** 2 restaurants; lounge; outdoor pool; salon; coin-op laundry. *In room:* A/C, TV, coffeemaker, hair dryer, iron.

Comfort Suites   New and predictable is what you'll get here. Each unit has a small living/dining area with a sleeper sofa, and a bedroom with handcrafted wood furniture and a comfortable king- or queen-size bed. If you have kids, you might want a ground-floor poolside room. The pool is warm, roomy, and adjacent to a hot tub.

1500 Paseo del Pueblo Sur (P.O. Box 1268), Taos, NM 87571. ℂ 888/751-1555 or 505/751-1555. Fax 505/751-1991. www.comfortsuites.com. 62 units. $69–$149 double. Rates include continental breakfast. AE, DC, DISC, MC, V. **Amenities:** Outdoor pool; Jacuzzi; sauna; car-rental desk; in-room massage; same-day dry cleaning. *In room:* A/C, TV, dataport, fridge, coffeemaker, hair dryer, microwave.

Sagebrush Inn ⭐   Three miles south of Taos, surrounded by acres of sage, this inn is in an adobe building that has been added on to decade after decade, creating an interesting mix of accommodations. The original structure was built in 1929. It had three floors and 12 rooms, hand-sculpted from adobe; hand-hewn vigas held the roof in place. That part remains, and the small, cozy rooms have the feel of old Taos—in fact, Georgia O'Keeffe lived and worked here for 10 months in the late 1930s. But to those more accustomed to refined style, it might feel dated.

The treasure of this place is the large grass courtyard dotted with elm trees, where visitors sit and read in the warm months. Some of the rooms added in the '50s through '70s have a tackiness not overcome by the vigas and tile work. More recent additions (to the west) are more skillful; these suites away from the hotel proper spacious and full of amenities, but they have noisy plumbing.

The lobby-cum-cantina has an Old West feel that livens at night when it becomes a venue for country-western dancing and one of Taos's most active nightspots for live music (see "Taos After Dark," later in this chapter). Traditionally, this has been a family hotel, but management is working to appeal to convention guests as well.

1508 Paseo del Pueblo Sur (P.O. Box 557), Taos, NM 87571. *(C)* 800/428-3626 or 505/758-2254. Fax 505/758-5077. www.sagebrushinn.com. 100 units. $70–$95 double; $90–$155 deluxe or small suite; $105–$185 executive suite. Extra person $10. Children under 18 stay free in parent's room. Rates include breakfast. AE, DC, DISC, MC, V. Pets accepted. **Amenities:** 2 restaurants; bar (p. 233); 2 outdoor pools; tennis courts; Jacuzzi; courtesy shuttle; business center; in-room massage; same-day dry cleaning; executive-level rooms. *In room:* A/C, TV, dataport, fridge, coffeemaker, hair dryer, iron.

INEXPENSIVE

Adobe Sun God Lodge   For a comfortable, economical stay with a northern New Mexico ambience, this is a good choice. This hotel, a 5-minute drive from the plaza, has three distinct parts spread across 1½ acres of landscaped grounds. The oldest was solidly built in 1958 and has some court-motel charm, with low ceilings and large windows. To update the rooms, the owners added tile sinks, Taos-style furniture, and new carpeting. To the south is a section built in 1988. The rooms are small but have touches that make them feel cozy, such as little *nichos* (niches) and hand-carved furnishings. In back to the east are the newest buildings, built in 1994. These are two-story structures with portal-style porches and balconies. Some rooms have kitchenettes, which include microwaves, fridges, and stoves; others have kiva fireplaces. The two suites on the northeast corner of the property are the quietest and have the best views.

919 Paseo del Pueblo Sur, Taos, NM 87571. *(C)* 800/821-2437 or 505/758-3162. Fax 505/758-1716. www.sungodlodge. com. 53 units. $49–$99 double; $69–$139 suite. AE, DISC, MC, V. Pets accepted for $10 per day. **Amenities:** Jacuzzi. *In room:* A/C, TV, dataport, coffeemaker.

Indian Hills Inn Taos Plaza *Kids*   This is a good choice if you're looking for a decent, functional night's stay close to the plaza (3 blocks away). The hotel has two sections, one built in the 1950s, and the other completed in 1996. The older section has received a major face-lift. However, for a few more dollars you can stay in the newer section, where the rooms are larger, with gas-log fireplaces, and the bathrooms are fresher, though noise can travel from nearby guest rooms. Both sections sit on a broad lawn studded with towering blue spruce trees. Picnic tables and barbecue grills provide families a respite from the restaurant scene. The hotel offers discounted golf, ski, and rafting packages, as well as Cumbres & Toltec Scenic Railroad tickets (see chapter 10).

233 Paseo del Pueblo Sur (P.O. Box 1229), Taos, NM 87571. *(C)* 800/444-2346 or 505/758-4293. www.taosnet.com/ indianhillsinn. 55 units. $49–$99 double. Group and package rates available. Rates include continental breakfast. AE, DC, DISC, MC, V. Small pets accepted with prior arrangements. **Amenities:** Outdoor pool; tour desk. *In room:* A/C, TV.

Bed & Breakfasts

Casa de las Chimeneas ★★★   This 1925 adobe home has, since its opening in 1988, been a model of Southwestern elegance. Now, with some additions, it has become a full-service luxury inn as well. The addition includes a spa with a small fitness room and sauna, as well as complete massage and facial treatments (for an additional charge). I highly recommend the Rio Grande and Territorial rooms, which are air-conditioned. Both have heated Saltillo-tile floors, gas kiva fireplaces, and Jacuzzi tubs. If you prefer a more antique-feeling room, try the delightful older section, especially the Library Suite. Each room in the inn is decorated with original works of art and has elegant bedding, a private entrance, robes, and a minifridge stocked with complimentary soft drinks, juices, and mineral water. All rooms have kiva fireplaces, and most look out on flower and herb gardens. Smoking is not permitted.

405 Cordoba Rd., at Los Pandos Rd. (5303 NDCBU), Taos, NM 87571. ⓒ 877/758-4777 or 505/758-4777. Fax 505/758-3976. www.visittaos.com. 8 units. $165–$290 double; $325 suite. Rates include breakfast and supper. AE, DC, DISC, MC, V. **Amenities:** Small exercise room; spa; Jacuzzi; sauna; concierge; car-rental desk; in-room massage; coin-op laundry; laundry service. *In room:* TV/VCR, dataport, minibar, coffeemaker, hair dryer, iron.

Hacienda del Sol ★★   What's unique about this B&B is its unobstructed view of Taos Mountain. Because the 1¼-acre property borders Taos Pueblo, the land is pristine. The inn also has a rich history. It was once owned by arts patron Mabel Dodge Luhan, and author Frank Waters wrote *The People of the Valley* here. You'll find bold splashes of color—from the gardens, where in summer tulips, pansies, and flax bloom, to the rooms, where woven bedspreads and original art lend a Mexican feel. The main house is nearly 200 years old, so it has the wonderful curves of adobe as well as thick vigas. Some guest rooms are in this section. Others range from 3 to 10 years in age. These newer rooms are finely constructed, and I almost recommend them over the others because they're a little more private and the bathrooms are more refined. All rooms have robes and CD players, most have fireplaces, three have private Jacuzzis, and three have private steam rooms. Some have minifridges.

109 Mabel Dodge Lane (P.O. Box 177), Taos, NM 87571. ⓒ 505/758-0287. Fax 505/758-5895. www.taoshacienda delsol.com. 11 units. $85–$245 double. Rates include full breakfast and evening hors d'oeuvres. AE, DISC, MC, V. **Amenities:** Jacuzzi; sauna; concierge; in-room massage. *In room:* TV, CD player, dataport, fridge, hair dryer.

Little Tree Bed & Breakfast ★★ *(Finds)*   Little Tree is one of my favorite Taos B&Bs, partly because it's in a beautiful, secluded setting, and partly because it's constructed with real adobe that's been left in its raw state, lending the place an authentic hacienda feel. Located 2 miles down a country road, about midway between Taos and the ski area, it's surrounded by sage and piñon. The charming and cozy rooms have radiant heat under the floors, queen-size beds (one has a king), nice medium-size bathrooms (one with a Jacuzzi tub), and access to the portal and courtyard garden, at the center of which is the little tree for which the inn is named. The Piñon (my favorite) and Juniper rooms have fireplaces and private entrances. The Piñon and Aspen rooms offer sunset views. The Spruce Room, Victorian in ambience, is decorated with quilts. In the main building, the living room has a traditional viga-and-*latilla* ceiling and *tierra blanca* adobe (adobe that's naturally white; if you look closely, you can see little pieces of mica and straw). Guests enjoy a scrumptious breakfast on the portal during warmer months. On arrival, guests are treated to refreshments.

County Rd. B-143 (P.O. Box 509), Taos, NM 87513. ⓒ 800/334-8467 or 505/776-8467. www.littletreebandb.com. 4 units. $105–$175 double. Rates include breakfast and afternoon snack. MC, V. *In room:* TV/VCR.

TAOS SKI VALLEY

For information on skiing and the facilities at Taos Ski Valley, see "Skiing Taos," later in this chapter.

EXPENSIVE
Hotels

Edelweiss Lodge & Spa ★★   Opened in 2005, this lodge at the base of the mountain is a remake of a 1960s classic. Now, it's a brand-new condo hotel, with the only full spa facility in Taos Ski Valley. The owners have been excellent hosts since they purchased the property in 1997, so you can count on quality lodgings. Each upscale condominium has a fireplace and full kitchen with stainless-steel appliances, and many have balconies; the hotel rooms are more standard. All have comfortable beds and medium-size bathrooms. Ski week rates include gourmet meals, lift tickets, and lessons.

106 Sutton Place, Taos Ski Valley, NM 87525. ℂ 800/I-LUV-SKI or 505/776-2301. Fax 505/776-2533. www. edelweisslodgeandspa.com. 46 units. Ski week $1,145–$1,590 per person double. per-day room rates: winter $165–$270 double, summer $100–$150 double. AE, DISC, MC, V. **Amenities:** Restaurant; bar; health club and full spa; 2 Jacuzzis; sauna; concierge; massage. *In room:* TV, fridge, coffeemaker, hair dryer.

Inn at Snakedance ★★   With all the luxuries of a full-service hotel, this inn can please most people. Skiers will appreciate the inn's location, just steps from the lift, as well as amenities such as ski storage and boot dryers. The original structure that stood on this site (part of which has been restored) was known as the Hondo Lodge. Before there was a Taos Ski Valley, Hondo Lodge served as a refuge for fishermen, hunters, and artists. Constructed from enormous pine timbers that had been cut for a copper mining operation in the 1890s, it was literally nothing more than a place for the men to bed down for the night. The Inn at Snakedance today offers comfortable guest rooms; many feature wood-burning fireplaces, and all have humidifiers. The furnishings are modern, the decor stylish, and the windows (many of which offer views) open to let in the mountain air. Some rooms adjoin, connecting a standard hotel room with a fireplace room—perfect for families. Smoking is prohibited in the guest rooms and most public areas. The Hondo Restaurant and Bar offers dining and entertainment daily during the ski season (off-season schedules vary) and sponsors wine tastings and wine dinners. The hotel also offers shuttle service to and from nearby shops and restaurants.

110 Sutton Place (P.O. Box 89), Taos Ski Valley, NM 87525. ℂ 800/322-9815 or 505/776-2277. Fax 505/776-1410. www.innsnakedance.com. 60 units. Christmas holiday $270 double; rest of ski season $225 double; value season $165 double; summer $75 double. AE, DC, DISC, MC, V. Children under 7 not accepted. Free parking at Taos Ski Valley parking lot. Closed mid-Apr to mid-June and mid-Oct to mid-Nov. **Amenities:** Restaurant; bar; exercise room; spa; Jacuzzi; sauna; massage; convenience store (with food, sundries, video rental, and alcoholic beverages). *In room:* TV, fridge, coffeemaker, hair dryer, humidifier.

Powderhorn Suites and Condominiums ★★ *(Finds)*   A cozy, homelike feel and Euro-Southwestern ambience make this inn one of the best buys in Taos Ski Valley, just a 2-minute walk from the lift. You'll find consistency and quality here, with impeccably clean medium-size rooms, mountain views, vaulted ceilings, spotless bathrooms, and comfortable beds. The larger suites have stoves, balconies, and fireplaces. Adjoining rooms are perfect for families. You can expect conscientious and expert service as well. There's no elevator, so if stairs are a problem for you, be sure to ask for a room on the ground floor.

5 Ernie Blake Rd. (P.O. Box 69), Taos Ski Valley, NM 87525. ℂ 800/776-2346 or 505/776-2341. Fax 505/776-2341 ext. 103. www.taoswebb.com/powderhorn. 17 units. Ski season $99–$165 double, $130–$200 suite, $195–$400 condo; summer $69 double, $79–$89 suite, $109–$129 condo. MC, V. Free valet parking. **Amenities:** 2 Jacuzzis; massage. *In room:* TV, dataport, kitchenette.

Condominiums

Sierra del Sol Condominiums ★   I have wonderful memories of these condominiums, which are just a 2-minute walk from the lift; family friends used to invite me to stay with them here when I was about 10. The units, built in the 1960s, with additions through the years, have been well maintained. Though they're privately owned, and therefore decorated at the whim of the owners, management does inspect them every year and make suggestions. They're smartly built and vary in size: studio, one-bedroom, and two-bedroom. The one- and two-bedroom units have big living rooms with fireplaces and porches that look out on the ski runs. The bedrooms are spacious, and some have sleeping lofts. Each unit has a full kitchen, with a dishwasher, stove, oven, and fridge. Most also have microwaves and humidifiers. Two-bedroom units sleep up to six. Grills and picnic tables on the grounds sit near a mountain river. The prices listed below give a sense of the wide range in room rates.

13 Thunderbird Rd. (P.O. Box 84), Taos Ski Valley, NM 87525. ℂ **800/523-3954** or 505/776-2981. Fax 505/776-2347. www.sierrataos.com. 32 units. Studio $70 summer; 2-bedroom condo $395 high season. AE, DISC, MC, V. Free parking. **Amenities:** 2 Jacuzzis; 2 saunas; massage; babysitting; coin-op laundry. *In room:* TV/VCR, kitchen, safe.

MODERATE

Alpine Village Suites ⭐   Alpine Village is a small village within Taos Ski Valley, a few steps from the lift. Owned by John and Barbara Cottam, the complex also houses a ski shop and a bar and restaurant. The Cottams began with seven rooms, still nice rentals, above their ski shop. Each has a sleeping loft for the agile who care to climb a ladder, as well as sunny windows. The newer section has nicely decorated rooms, with attractive touches such as Mexican furniture and inventive tile work done by locals. Like most other accommodations at Taos Ski Valley, the rooms are not especially soundproof. Fortunately, most skiers go to bed early. All rooms have stoves, microwaves, and minifridges. In the newer building, rooms have fireplaces and private balconies. Request a south-facing room for a view of the slopes. The Jacuzzi has a fireplace and a view of the slopes.

100 Thunderbird Rd. (P.O. Box 98), Taos Ski Valley, NM 87525. ℂ **800/576-2666** or 505/776-8540. Fax 505/776-8542. www.alpine-suites.com. 29 units. Ski season $70–$145 suite for 2, $265–$335 suite for up to 6; summer $65–$120 suite for 2 (includes continental breakfast). AE, DISC, MC, V. Covered valet parking $10. **Amenities:** Jacuzzi; sauna; massage. *In room:* TV/VCR, kitchenette.

Thunderbird Lodge ⭐   Owners Elisabeth and Tom Brownell's goal is to bring people together, and they accomplish it—sometimes a little too well. The Bavarian-style lodge sits on the sunny side of the ski area. The lobby has a stone fireplace, raw pine pillars, and tables accented with copper lamps. There's a sun-lit room ideal for mealtime, with a bank of windows looking out toward the notorious Al's Run and the rest of the ski village. Adjoining is a large bar/lounge with booths, a grand piano, and a fireplace, where live entertainment plays during the evenings through the winter. Guest rooms are small—some are tiny–and noise travels up and down the halls, giving these three stories a dormitory atmosphere. I suggest when making reservations that you request the widest available room; otherwise, you may feel as though you're in a train car. Across the road, the Thunderbird also has a chalet with larger rooms and a brilliant sun porch. Food is the big draw at the Thunderbird. Ski week rates include 14 gourmet meals, six lift tickets, and ski lessons.

3 Thunderbird Rd. (P.O. Box 87), Taos Ski Valley, NM 87525. ℂ **800/776-2279** or 505/776-2280. Fax 505/776-2238. www.thunderbird-taos.com. 32 units. $126–$147 per person double. Rates include breakfast and dinner. Ski week package $1,190–$1,260 per person double. AE, MC, V. Free valet parking. **Amenities:** Bar; Jacuzzi; his-and-hers saunas; game room; business center; massage; babysitting by prior arrangement; laundry service.

RV PARKS & CAMPGROUNDS

Carson National Forest   Nine national-forest camping areas lie within 20 miles of Taos; these developed areas are open from Memorial Day to Labor Day. They range from woodsy, stream-side sites on the road to Taos Ski Valley to open lowlands with lots of sage. Call the Forest Service to discuss the best location for your needs.

208 Cruz Alta Rd., Taos, NM 87571. ℂ **505/758-6200**. www.fs.fed.us/r3/carson. $7–$15/night. No credit cards.

Taos RV Park This RV park on the edge of town offers a convenient location with a city atmosphere. It has very clean bathrooms and showers. Two tepees rent for around $25 each, but beware: They're right on the main drag and may be noisy. The park is on a local bus line.

1802 NM 68, Taos, NM 87557. ℂ **800/323-6009** or 505/758-1667. Fax 505/758-1989. www.taosbudgethost.com. 33 spaces. $17 without RV hookup; $25 with RV hookup. Senior discount available. DISC, MC, V.

Taos Valley RV Park and Campground Just 2½ miles south of the plaza, this campground is surrounded by sage and offers views of the surrounding mountains. Each site has a picnic table and grill. The place has a small store, a laundry room, a playground, and tent shelters, as well as a dump station and very clean restrooms.

120 Este Rd., off NM 68 (7204 NDCBU), Taos, NM 87571. ℂ **800/999-7571** or 505/758-4469. Fax 505/758-4469. www.camptaos.com/rv. 92 spaces. $18 without RV hookup; $24–$27 with RV hookup. MC, V. Pets accepted.

4 Where to Dine

Be aware that Taos is not a late-night place; most restaurants finish serving at about 9pm. For the locations of these restaurants, see the map "Central Taos Accommodations & Dining" on p. 203.

EXPENSIVE

De La Tierra ✦✦✦ REGIONAL AMERICAN This hot spot not far from the plaza always leaves me with an exotic and buoyant sense that I attribute to its setting and cuisine. Located at the new El Monte Sagrado ecoresort, the restaurant exudes old-world Orient elegance, with a high ceiling and comfortable black silk chairs. It serves imaginative American fare with an emphasis on wild game. Service is excellent, and a master sommelier oversees the wine selections. The chef utilizes seasonal and local ingredients, including organic products when he can. For starters, I recommend the Dungeness crab cake, or, for a more exotic treat, yak satay (the meat comes from the resort owner's high-mountain animals). For a main course, I've enjoyed the venison medallions, served over garlic mashed potatoes with roasted spring mushrooms. My mother likes the rosemary skewered shrimp, served with white-corn polenta and chard. The Gardens, a more casual spot with lots of exotic plants and a lovely patio, serves tasty food during the day (try the yak cheese frittata). The Anaconda Bar serves tapas.

In the El Monte Sagrado hotel, 317 Kit Carson Rd. ℂ **800/828-TAOS** or 505/758-3502. Reservations recommended. The Gardens main courses $5–$11 breakfast, $8–$16 lunch; De La Tierra main courses $19–$34. AE, DC, DISC, MC, V. The Gardens daily 7–10am and 11am–2:30pm; De La Tierra daily 5:30–10pm.

Doc Martin's ✦ NEW AMERICAN Doc Martin's serves innovative food in a historic setting. The restaurant comprises Dr. Thomas Paul Martin's former home, office, and delivery room. In 1912, painters Bert Philips (Doc's brother-in-law) and Ernest Blumenschein hatched the concept of the Taos Society of Artists in the dining room. Art still predominates here, in both the paintings that adorn the walls and the cuisine. The food is often good but can be inconsistent. The wine list has received numerous Awards of Excellence from *Wine Spectator*. In a rich atmosphere, with bins of yellow squash, eggplants, and red peppers near the kiva fireplace, diners feast on Southwestern breakfast fare such as huevos rancheros (fried eggs on a blue-corn tortilla smothered with chile and jack cheese). Lunch might include the house specialty, the Doc chile relleno, or chipolte shrimp on corn cake. For dinner, good bets are piñon-encrusted salmon and Southwest lacquered duck served with *posole* and mango relish.

There's always a nice selection of desserts—try chocolate mousse cake or *capirotada* (New Mexican bread pudding). The Adobe bar has live jazz with no cover charge.

In the Historic Taos Inn, 125 Paseo del Pueblo Norte. ℂ **505/758-1977.** www.taosinn.com. Reservations recommended. Breakfast $5–$8, lunch $5.50–$11, dinner $14–$28, fixed-price menu $23. AE, DISC, MC, V. Mon–Sat 7:30–11am and 11:30am–2:30pm; Sun brunch 7:30am–2:30pm; daily 5:30–9pm.

Joseph's Table ★★ *Finds* NEW AMERICAN/MEDITERRANEAN   Taos funk meets European flair at this intimate restaurant on the plaza. Recently moved to the renovated Hotel La Fonda de Taos, this notable eatery now occupies a larger space, but it can still fill up. Chef-owner Joseph Wrede (*Food and Wine* once named him one of the 10 "Best New Chefs" in America) creates such delicacies as six-way duck and lovely steak au poivre, inventively prepared and served. The duck is literally cooked six different ways, ranging from roasted to sliced thinly, prosciutto style, and paired with delicate corn crème brûlée. The steak sits atop smooth mashed potatoes and is crowned with an exotic mushroom salad. The offerings are not for the faint of palate, though. Wrede likes complex flavors, so those who prefer more conservative food might opt for Lambert's (below). The servers can help guide you through the complex menu, so be sure to ask. For dessert, try such delicacies as mescal chocolate bar with lime sorbet or black-pepper-roasted pineapple bread pudding. An eclectic selection of beers and wines by the bottle and glass is available. Be aware that in winter, parts of the restaurant can be cold.

In the Hotel La Fonda de Taos, 108A South Taos Plaza. ℂ **505/751-4512.** www.josephstable.com. Reservations recommended. Main courses $8–$18 lunch, $18–$35 dinner. AE, DISC, MC, V. Apr–Nov daily 11:30am–2:30pm and 5:30–10pm; ski season daily 4:30–10pm. Sun brunch 10:30am–2:30pm year-round. Winter lunch hours vary; call ahead.

Lambert's of Taos ★★ CONTEMPORARY AMERICAN   Zeke Lambert, once the head chef at Doc Martin's, opened this fine-dining establishment in 1989 in the historic Randall Home near Los Pandos Road. A sparsely decorated place with contemporary art on the walls, it's a nice spot for a romantic evening. The service is friendly and efficient, and the meal begins with a complimentary aperitif. The house salad is nicely prepared, with butter lettuce and radicchio. Appetizers include a Mediterranean olive plate and chile-dusted rock shrimp. The restaurant's signature dish is pepper-crusted lamb. If you like strong flavors, this is your dish—very peppery, served with a red wine demi-glace and linguine. Others I've spoken to have enjoyed the grilled salmon with tomato-sage sauce. For dessert, white chocolate ice cream and Zeke's chocolate mousse with raspberry sauce are delicious. Espresso, beers, and wine are served.

309 Paseo del Pueblo Sur. ℂ **505/758-1009.** Reservations recommended. Main courses $17–$30. AE, DC, DISC, MC, V. Daily 5pm–closing (usually 9pm or so).

MODERATE

The Apple Tree ★ SOUTHWESTERN/AMERICAN   Eclectic music pervades the four adobe rooms of this restaurant, a block north of the plaza. Original paintings by Taos masters watch over the candlelit service indoors. Outside, diners sit at wooden tables on the lovely patio beneath a spreading apple tree. This restaurant is popular among locals and travelers, but it isn't my favorite. Though the chefs use fresh and tasty ingredients, the recipes often try too hard. I suggest ordering what looks simplest. The Apple Tree salad (greens sprinkled with dried cranberries, walnuts, and blue cheese, served with vinaigrette) is very good, as is the *calabasa* (squash) quesadilla. A popular dish is mango chicken enchiladas (chicken simmered with onions and spices, layered between blue corn tortillas with mango chutney, sour cream, and salsa fresca, and smothered with green chile), but beware: They're sweet. I prefer salmon Alfredo, made with sun-dried tomatoes and New Mexico goat cheese. The brunch offerings are worth sampling. Such standards as French toast and eggs Benedict are good, but the specials usually outshine them, especially the fresh fruit crepes, such as blueberry or peach, served with whipped cream. The Apple Tree has an award-winning wine list, and the desserts are prepared fresh daily.

123 Bent St. ℰ 505/758-1900. Reservations recommended. Main courses $5–$11 brunch, $6–$12 lunch, $12–$30 dinner. AE, DC, DISC, MC, V. Mon–Sat 11:30am–3pm; Sun brunch 11am–3pm; daily 5:30–9pm.

Bravo ⭐ AMERICAN/CAFE   This bustling cafe on the south end of town offers a refreshing big-city mix of atmosphere and flavors. A large communal table sits at the restaurant's heart. The menu is eclectic, offering good-size portions of very tasty food. With owner-chef Lionel Garnier's French background lending magic, the flavors are refined. Locals rave about the three-cheese pizza; my favorite is the Bravo, with roasted vegetables. Caesar salad with chicken is also popular, as is the elaborate salad bar, complete with pasta and bean concoctions. A variety of sandwiches fills out the menu, and in the evening you can order Continental dishes. During busy hours, service is slow but congenial. There's also a martini and beer bar, with specials, such as a beer sampler and enough types of martinis to make you wonder how many things you really should mix with gin or vodka. Bravo is a specialty wine and beer shop, package liquor store, and gourmet deli as well as a restaurant.

1353A Paseo del Pueblo Sur, Ranchos de Taos. ℰ 505/758-8100. Main courses $6–$12 lunch, $8–$18 dinner. AE, DISC, MC, V. Mon–Sat 11am–9pm.

Old Blinking Light ⭐ AMERICAN   This restaurant on the Ski Valley Road provides tasty American food in a casual atmosphere. Decorated with Spanish colonial furniture and an excellent art collection, this is a good place to stop after skiing. The service is friendly and efficient. To accompany the free chips and house-made salsa, order a margarita and sip it next to the patio bonfire, open evenings year-round. The menu is broad, ranging from salads and burgers to steaks, seafood, and Mexican food. I say head straight for the fajitas, especially the jumbo shrimp wrapped in bacon and stuffed with poblano peppers and jack cheese. Leave room for Old Blinking Light mud pie, made with local Taos Cow Ice Cream. Live music plays Monday and Friday nights. The wine shop and liquor store on the premises carries more than 100 wines priced under $15.

US 150, mile marker 1. ℰ 505/776-8787. Reservations recommended Fri–Mon. Main courses $9–$26. AE, MC, V. Wine shop daily noon–10pm. Restaurant daily 5–10pm.

Taos Pizza Out Back ⭐ (Kids) PASTA/GOURMET PIZZA   My kayaking buddies always go here after a day on the river. That will give you an idea of the level of informality (high), the quality of the food and beer (great), and the size of the portions (large). It's a raucous old hippie-decorated adobe restaurant, with a friendly and eager waitstaff. What to order? *PIZZA.* Sure, spicy Greek pasta is good, as is the Veggie Zone (a calzone filled with stir-fried veggies and two cheeses)—but, why? The pizzas are incredible. All come with a delicious thin crust (no sogginess here) that's folded over on the edges and sprinkled with sesame seeds. The sauce is unthinkably tasty, and the variations are broad. There's Thai chicken pizza (pineapple, peanuts, and spicy sauce); the Killer, with sun-dried tomatoes, Gorgonzola, green chile, and black olives; and my favorite, pizza Florentine (spinach, basil, sun-dried tomatoes, chicken breast, mushrooms, capers, and garlic, sautéed in white wine). Don't leave without trying either a

Dalai Lama bar (coconut, chocolate, and caramel) or the Taos Yum (a "mondo" chocolate-chip cookie with ice cream, whipped cream, and chocolate sauce).

712 Paseo del Pueblo Norte (just north of Allsup's). ℂ **505/758-3112.** Reservations recommended weekends and holidays. Pizza $12–$26, pasta and calzone $7–$12. MC, V. Summer daily 11am–10pm; winter Sun–Thurs 11am–9pm, Fri–Sat 11am–10pm.

Trading Post Café ★★ *Finds* NORTHERN ITALIAN/INTERNATIONAL   One of my tastiest writing assignments was a profile of this restaurant for the *New York Times.* Chef-owner René Mettler spent 3 hours serving course after course of dishes prepared especially for us. If you think that gastronomical orgy might color my opinion, just ask anyone in town where he most likes to eat. Even notables such as R. C. Gorman, Dennis Hopper, and Gene Hackman will likely name the Trading Post. What draws the crowds is a gallery atmosphere, where rough plastered walls washed with an orange hue are set off by sculptures, paintings, and photographs. The meals are also artistically served. "You eat with your eyes," says Mettler. If you show up without reservations, be prepared to wait for a table. Don't expect quiet romance here: The place bustles. A bar—a fun place to sit—encloses an open-exhibition kitchen. Although the focus is on the fine food, diners can feel comfortable here, even if they're trying three appetizers and skipping the main course. The outstanding Caesar salad has an interesting twist—garlic chips. If you like pasta, you'll find a nice variety on the menu. Fettuccine alla carbonara is tasty, as is seafood pasta. Heartier appetites might like New Zealand lamb chops with tomato-mint sauce. There's also a fresh fish of the day and usually some nice stews and soups, at very reasonable prices. A good list of beers and wines rounds out the experience. For dessert, try the tarts.

4179 Paseo del Pueblo Sur, Ranchos de Taos. ℂ **505/758-5089.** Reservations recommended. Menu items $6–$28. AE, DC, DISC, MC, V. Tues–Sat 11:30am–9:30pm; Sun 5–9pm.

INEXPENSIVE

Michael's Kitchen *Kids* NEW MEXICAN/AMERICAN   A couple of blocks north of the plaza, this eatery provides big portions of okay food in a relaxed atmosphere. Between its hardwood floor and viga ceiling are various knickknacks: a deer head here, a Tiffany lamp there. Seating is at booths and tables. Breakfast dishes, including a large selection of pancakes and egg preparations (with names like the "Moofy," and "Omelette Extra-ordinaire") are served all day, as are lunch sandwiches (including Philly cheese steak, tuna melt, and a veggie option). Some people like the generically (and facetiously) titled "Health Food" meal, a double order of fries with red or green chile and cheese. Dinners range from veal cordon bleu to plantation-fried chicken. For breakfast, try one of the excellent doughnuts from Michael's bakery.

304 C Paseo del Pueblo Norte. ℂ **505/758-4178.** Reservations not accepted. Main courses $3–$8 breakfast, $4–$9.50 lunch, $6–$14 dinner. AE, DISC, MC, V. Daily 7am–8:30pm. Closed major holidays.

Orlando's New Mexican Café ★ *Kids* NEW MEXICAN   Festivity reigns in this spicy little cafe on the north end of town. Serving some of northern New Mexico's best chile, this place has colorful tables set around a bustling open kitchen, and airy patio dining during warmer months. Service is friendly but minimal. Try Los Colores, the most popular dish, with three enchiladas (chicken, beef, and cheese) smothered in chile and served with beans and *posole.* Taco salad is another favorite. Portions are big. You can order a Mexican or microbrew beer, or a New Mexican or California wine.

114 Don Juan Valdez Lane (1¾ miles north of the plaza, off Paseo del Pueblo Norte). ℂ **505/751-1450.** Reservations not accepted. Main courses under $10. No credit cards. Daily 10:30am–9pm.

NORTH OF TOWN

Gypsy 360° ♦ *Finds* ASIAN/AMERICAN   This funky cafe on a side street in Arroyo Seco is as cute as the village. And the food is tasty and inventive. During the winter, diners sit in a sunny atrium or a more enclosed space, all casual with lawn-style furnishings and bright colors. In warm months, a sunny patio opens up the place. Service is accommodating though at times overworked. The food ranges from sushi to Thai to sandwiches. My Berkley Bowl salad had lots of spring greens and crisp goodies such as carrots and jicama, and the chef accommodated my request for grilled salmon on top. The pesto dressing is now my all-time favorite. My mother's Angus burger was thick and juicy, topped with crisp bacon and blue cheese; her potato salad had fresh dill. Other times I've enjoyed the noodle bowls, such as Sri Lankan red curry or pad Thai. If you're staying in Taos, this spot makes a great destination, with plenty of fun shops to peruse when your tummy's full.

480 NM 150, Seco Plaza, Arroyo Seco. © 505/776-3166. Main courses $7.50–$15. MC, V. Tues–Wed and Sat 8am–4pm; Thurs–Fri 8am–8pm; Sun 9am–3pm.

Momentitos de la Vida ♦♦ NEW AMERICAN   For years, this personable adobe building housed Casa Cordova, where, in the '60s and '70s, the jet-set après ski crowd hung out, drinking martinis. Well, as long as martinis are back in style, why not revamp this spot on the outskirts of Arroyo Seco and once again make it the place to be? That was what owner-chefs Chris and Kelly Maher had in mind for this restaurant. The atmosphere is moody; the service is refined and attentive. Though locals call the place too pricey, the food is thoughtfully prepared, with real attention to imaginative detail. You might start with a smoked trout éclair or grilled habañero prawns. One of the most popular main courses is blackened filet mignon, served with root mashed potatoes (a tasty mixture of rutabaga and parsnip), wilted greens, and asparagus. The vegan shepherd's pie is also a tasty option. In warm months, you can dine on the patio, surrounded by a plum orchard. Jazz plays fireside Friday to Sunday.

5 miles north of the intersection of NM 150 and NM 522, Arroyo Seco. © 505/776-3333. Reservations recommended on weekends. Bistro menu main courses $8–$15; dining room main courses $19–$36. AE, MC, V. Tues–Sun 5:30–10pm; bar 4:30pm–closing.

5 What to See & Do

With a history shaped by pre-Columbian civilization, Spanish colonialism, and the Wild West; outdoor activities that range from ballooning to world-class skiing; and a clustering of artists, writers, and musicians, Taos has something to offer almost everybody.

THE TOP ATTRACTIONS

Millicent Rogers Museum of Northern New Mexico ♦   This museum will give you a glimpse of some of the finest Southwestern arts and crafts anywhere, but it's small enough to avoid being overwhelming. Millicent Rogers's family founded it in 1953, after her death. Rogers was a Taos oil baroness who in 1947 began acquiring a magnificent collection of beautiful Native American arts and crafts. Included are Navajo and Pueblo jewelry, Navajo textiles, Pueblo pottery, Hopi and Zuni kachina dolls, paintings from the Rio Grande Pueblo people, and basketry from a wide variety of Southwestern tribes. The museum also presents exhibitions of Southwestern art, crafts, and design.

Since the 1970s, the scope of the museum's permanent collection has expanded to include Anglo arts and crafts and Hispanic religious and secular arts and crafts, from

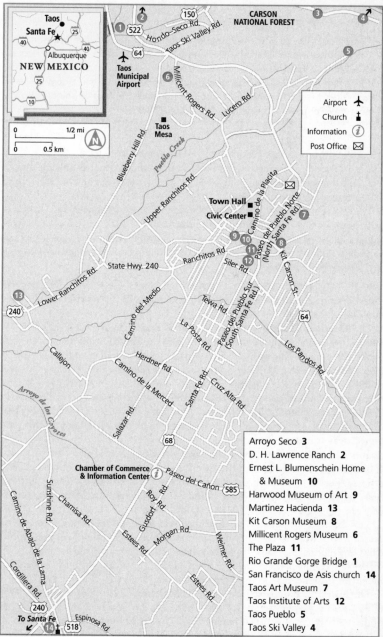

Taos Attractions

NEW MEXICO

Taos
Santa Fe
Albuquerque

CARSON
NATIONAL FOREST

Taos Municipal Airport

Taos Mesa

Pueblo Creek

Hondo-Seco Rd.

Taos Ski Valley Rd.

Millicent Rogers Rd.

Lucero Rd.

Blueberry Hill Rd.

Upper Ranchitos Rd.

Town Hall
Civic Center

Camino de la Placita

Paseo del Pueblo Norte
(North Santa Fe Rd.)

Kit Carson St.

Ranchitos Rd.

Siler Rd.

State Hwy. 240

Lower Ranchitos Rd.

Camino del Medio

Tewa Rd.

La Posta Rd.

Paseo del Pueblo Sur
(South Santa Fe Rd.)

Los Pandos Rd.

Callejon

Herdner Rd.

Camino de la Merced

Santa Fe Rd.

Cruz Alta Rd.

Salazar Rd.

Arroyo de los Coyotes

Chamber of Commerce
& Information Center

Paseo del Cañon

Roy Rd.

Sunshine Rd.

Chamisa Rd.

Gusdorf Rd.

Estees Rd.

Morgan Rd.

Weimer Rd.

Estees Rd.

Camino de Abajo de la Lama

Cordillera Rd.

To Santa Fe

Espinosa Rd.

Legend	
Airport	✈
Church	✝
Information	ⓘ
Post Office	✉

0   1/2 mi
0   0.5 km

Arroyo Seco **3**
D. H. Lawrence Ranch **2**
Ernest L. Blumenschein Home & Museum **10**
Harwood Museum of Art **9**
Martinez Hacienda **13**
Kit Carson Museum **8**
Millicent Rogers Museum **6**
The Plaza **11**
Rio Grande Gorge Bridge **1**
San Francisco de Asis church **14**
Taos Art Museum **7**
Taos Institute of Arts **12**
Taos Pueblo **5**
Taos Ski Valley **4**

Spanish and Mexican colonial to contemporary times. Included are *santos* (religious images), furniture, weavings, *colcha* embroideries, and decorative tinwork. Agricultural implements, domestic utensils, and craftspeople's tools dating from the 17th and 18th centuries are also on display.

The museum gift shop has a fine collection of superior regional art. Classes and workshops, lectures, and field trips run throughout the year.

Millicent Rogers Rd., off NM 522, 4 miles north of Taos Plaza. ☏ 505/758-2462. www.millicentrogers.org. Admission $6 adults, $5 students and seniors, $1 children 6–16, $15 families. Apr–Oct daily 10am–5pm; Nov–Mar Tues–Sun 10am–5pm. Closed Jan 1, Easter, Thanksgiving, Dec 25.

Taos Historic Museums ★★ Two historical homes, the Martinez Hacienda and Ernest Blumenschein Home, are operated as museums, affording visitors a glimpse of early Taos lifestyles.

The **Martinez Hacienda,** Lower Ranchitos Road, Highway 240 (☏ **505/758-1000**), is the only Spanish colonial hacienda in the United States that's open to the public year-round. This was the home of the merchant, trader, and *alcalde* (mayor) Don Antonio Severino Martinez, who bought it in 1804 and lived here until his death in 1827. His eldest son was Padre Antonio José Martinez, northern New Mexico's controversial spiritual leader from 1826 to 1867. Located on the west bank of the Rio Pueblo de Taos, about 2 miles southwest of the plaza, the museum is remarkably beautiful, with thick, raw adobe walls. The hacienda has no exterior windows—this was to protect against raids by Plains tribes.

Twenty-one rooms were built around two *placitas,* or interior courtyards. They give you a glimpse of the austerity of frontier lives, with only a few pieces of modest period furniture in each. You'll see bedrooms, servants' quarters, stables, a kitchen, and a large fiesta room. Exhibits tell the story of the Martinez family and life in Spanish Taos between 1598 and 1821, when Mexico gained control.

Taos Historic Museums has developed the Martinez Hacienda into a living museum with weavers, blacksmiths, and woodcarvers. Demonstrations are scheduled daily, and during the **Taos Trade Fair** (late Sept) they run virtually nonstop. The Trade Fair commemorates the era when Native Americans, Spanish settlers, and mountain men met here to trade with each other.

The **Ernest L. Blumenschein Home & Museum,** 222 Ledoux St. (☏ **505/758-0505**), 1½ blocks southwest of the plaza, re-creates the lifestyle of one of the founders of the Taos Society of Artists (founded 1915). An adobe home with garden walls and a courtyard, parts of which date from the 1790s, it became the home and studio of Blumenschein (1874–1960) and his family in 1919. Period furnishings include European antiques and handmade Taos furniture in Spanish colonial style.

Blumenschein was born and raised in Pittsburgh. In 1898, after training in New York and Paris, he and fellow painter Bert Phillips were on assignment for *Harper's* and *McClure's* magazines when a wheel of their wagon broke 30 miles north of Taos. Blumenschein drew the short straw and was obliged to bring the wheel by horseback to Taos for repair. He later recounted his initial reaction to the valley he entered: "No artist had ever recorded the New Mexico I was now seeing. No writer had ever written down the smell of this air or the feel of that morning sky. I was receiving . . . the first great unforgettable inspiration of my life. My destiny was being decided."

That spark later led to the foundation of Taos as an art colony. An extensive collection of works by early-20th-century Taos artists, including some by Blumenschein's daughter, Helen, is on display in several rooms of the home.

222 Ledoux St. ⓒ 505/758-0505 (for information about both museums). www.taoshistoricmuseums.com. Admission for each museum $5 adults, $3 children 6–16, free for children under 6, $10 families. Summer daily 9am–5pm; call for winter hours.

Taos Pueblo ★★★   It's amazing that in our frenetic world, more than 100 Taos Pueblo residents still live much as their ancestors did 1,000 years ago. When you enter the pueblo, you'll see two large buildings, both with rooms piled on top of each other, forming structures that echo the shape of Taos Mountain (which sits to the northeast). Here, some Taos residents live without electricity and running water. The remaining 2,000 residents of Taos Pueblo live in conventional homes on the pueblo's 95,000 acres.

The main buildings' distinctive flowing lines of shaped mud, with a straw-and-mud exterior plaster, are typical of Pueblo architecture throughout the Southwest. The style blends in with the surrounding land. Bright blue doors are the same shade as the sky that frames the brown buildings.

The northernmost of New Mexico's 19 pueblos, Taos Pueblo has been home to the Tiwa tribes for more than 900 years. Many residents here still practice ancestral rituals. The center of their world is nature; women use hornos to bake bread, and most still drink water that flows down from the sacred Blue Lake. Meanwhile, arts and crafts and other tourism-related businesses support the economy, along with government services, ranching, and farming. Because this is a living community, you can expect periodic closures, so your best bet is to call before venturing out.

The village looks much the same today as it did when a regiment from Coronado's expedition first came upon it in 1540. Though the Tiwa were essentially a peaceful agrarian people, they are perhaps best remembered for spearheading the only successful revolt by Native Americans in history. Launched by Popé (Poh-*pay*) in 1680, the uprising drove the Spanish from Santa Fe until 1692 and from Taos until 1698.

As you explore the pueblo, you can visit the residents' studios, sample homemade bread, look into the **San Geronimo Chapel,** and wander past the fascinating ruins of the old church and cemetery. You're expected to ask permission from individuals before taking their photos; some will ask for a small payment. Do not trespass into kivas (ceremonial rooms) and other areas marked as restricted.

The **Feast of San Geronimo** (the patron saint of Taos Pueblo), on September 29 and 30, marks the end of the harvest season. The feast day is reminiscent of an ancient trade fair for the Taos Indians, when tribes from as far south as South America and as far north as the Arctic would come and trade for wares, hides, clothing, and harvested crops. The day is filled with foot races, pole climbing done by traditional Indian clowns, and artists and craftspeople mimicking the early traders. Dances are performed the evening of September 29. Other annual events include a **turtle dance** on New Year's Day, **deer or buffalo dances** on Three Kings Day (Jan 6), and **corn dances** on Santa Cruz Day (May 3), San Antonio Day (June 13), San Juan Day (June 24), Santiago Day (July 25), and Santa Ana Day (July 26). The annual **Taos Pueblo Powwow,** a dance competition and parade that brings together tribes from throughout North America, is held the second weekend of July on tribal lands off NM 522 (see the "Calendar of Events" in chapter 2). The pueblo Christmas celebration begins on Christmas Eve, with bonfires and a procession with children's dances. On Christmas day, the **deer** or **Matachine dances** take place.

During your visit to the pueblo you will have the opportunity to purchase traditional fried and oven-baked bread as well as a variety of arts and crafts. If you would like to try traditional feast-day meals, the **Tiwa Kitchen,** near the entrance to the pueblo, is a good place. Close to Tiwa Kitchen is the **Oo-oonah Children's Art Center,** where you can see the creative works of pueblo children.

As with many of the other pueblos in New Mexico, Taos Pueblo has opened a casino. **Taos Mountain Casino (© 888/WIN-TAOS)** is on the main road to Taos Pueblo and features slot machines, blackjack, and poker.

Veterans Hwy. (P.O. Box 1846), Taos Pueblo. © 505/758-1028. www.taospueblo.com. Admission cost, as well as camera, video, and sketching fees, subject to change annually; be sure to ask about telephoto lenses and digital cameras. Photography not permitted on feast days. Daily 8am–4:30pm, with a few exceptions. Guided tours available. Closed for 45 consecutive days every year late winter or early spring (call ahead). From Paseo del Pueblo Norte, travel north 2 miles on Veterans Hwy.

MORE ATTRACTIONS

D. H. Lawrence Ranch   A trip to this ranch north of Taos leads you into odd realms of devotion for the controversial 20th-century author who lived and wrote in the area in the early 1920s. A short uphill walk from the ranch home (not open to visitors) is the D. H. Lawrence Memorial, a shedlike structure that's a bit of a forgotten place, where people have left a few mementos such as juniper berries and sticks of gum. The guest book is also interesting: One couple wrote of trying for 24 years to get here from England.

Lawrence lived in Taos on and off between 1922 and 1925. The ranch was a gift to his wife, Frieda, from the art patron Mabel Dodge Luhan. Lawrence repaid Luhan the favor by giving her the manuscript of *Sons and Lovers*. When Lawrence died in southern France in 1930 of tuberculosis, his ashes were returned here for burial. The grave of Frieda, who died in 1956, is outside the memorial. The memorial is the only public building at the ranch, which is the University of New Mexico operates as an educational and recreational retreat.

NM 522, San Cristobal. © 505/776-2245. Free admission. Daily 8am–5pm. Drive north from Taos about 15 miles on NM 522, then another 6 miles east into the forested Sangre de Cristo range on a well-marked dirt road.

Harwood Museum of Art of the University of New Mexico ★   With its high ceilings and broad wood floors, this museum is a lovely place to wander among New Mexico–inspired images. A cultural and community center since 1923, the museum displays paintings, drawings, prints, sculpture, and photographs by Taos-area artists from 1800 to the present. Featured are paintings from the early days of the art colony by members of the Taos Society of Artists, including Oscar Berninghaus, Ernest Blumenschein, Herbert Dunton, Victor Higgins, Bert Phillips, and Walter Ufer. Also included are works by Emil Bisttram, Andrew Dasburg, Agnes Martin, Larry Bell, and Thomas Benrimo.

The museum also schedules more than eight changing exhibitions a year, many of which feature works by celebrated artists currently living in Taos.

238 Ledoux St. ℭ 505/758-9826. www.harwoodmuseum.org. Admission $5. Tues–Sat 10am–5pm; Sun noon–5pm.

Kit Carson Museum
The Kit Carson Home and Museum, a block east of the plaza, is a 12-room adobe home built in 1825. Carson, the famous mountain man, Indian agent, and scout, purchased it in 1843 as a wedding gift for his young bride, Josefa Jaramillo. It remained their home until both died (exactly a month apart) in 1868. The Taos Historic Museums used to run the house as the town's general museum of Taos history. In 2003, the owners of the home, the Masonic Lodge, closed it, with the intent of reopening it as a new museum. The Kit Carson collection, however, remains in the hands of the Taos Historic Museums, and many pieces are on display at the Martinez Hacienda. In May 2005, the Masons opened a new museum that gives a more historically accurate depiction of the life of Kit Carson (who was a Mason himself). Still in the early stages, the museum will one day be an interactive affair, with a film documenting Carson's life, docents dressed in period clothing, and electronic media. Currently, visitors may want to spend a half hour getting a glimpse of what a tough and minimalist life Kit and his cronies lived.

113 Kit Carson Rd. ℭ 505/758-4945. www.kitcarsonhome.com. Admission $5 adults, $4 seniors over 65, $3 teens, $2 children under 13, $12 family of 4 or more. Daily 9am–6pm. Closed major holidays.

Rio Grande Gorge Bridge ★ (Kids)
This impressive bridge, west of the Taos airport, spans the Southwest's greatest river. At 650 feet above the canyon floor, it's one of America's highest bridges. If you can withstand the vertigo, it's interesting to come more than once, at different times of day, to observe how the changing light plays tricks with the colors of the cliff walls. A curious aside: The wedding scene in the movie *Natural Born Killers* was filmed here.

US 64, 10 miles west of Taos. Admission free. Daily 24 hr.

San Francisco de Asis church ★★
On NM 68, about 4 miles south of Taos, this famous church appears as a modern adobe sculpture with no doors or windows, an image that has often been photographed and painted. Visitors must walk through the garden on the east side to enter the two-story church and get a full perspective of its massive walls, authentic adobe plaster, and beauty.

A video presentation begins every hour on the half-hour in the church office. On the wall is an unusual painting, *The Shadow of the Cross,* by Henri Ault (1896). Under ordinary light, it portrays a barefoot Christ at the Sea of Galilee; in darkness, however, the portrait becomes luminescent, and the perfect shadow of a cross forms over the left shoulder of Jesus' silhouette. The artist reportedly was as shocked as everyone else to see this. The reason for the illusion remains a mystery. A few crafts shops surround the square.

Ranchos de Taos Plaza. ℭ 505/758-2754. Admission $3 for video and mystery painting. Mon–Sat 9am–4pm. Mass Mon–Fri 5:30pm, Sat 6pm (Mass rotates from this church to the 3 mission chapels), Sun 7am (in Spanish), 9am, and 11:30am. Closed to the public except for services 1st 2 weeks in June.

Taos Art Museum ★ (Finds)
In the home of Russian artist Nicolai Fechin (*Feh*-shin), this collection displays works of the Taos Society of Artists, which give a sense of what Taos was like in the late 19th and early 20th centuries. The rich and varied works include panoramas and images of Native American and Hispanic villagers. The setting, Fechin's home from 1927 until 1933, is unique. The historic building commemorates

his career. Born in Russia in 1881, Fechin came to the United States in 1923, already acclaimed as a master of painting, drawing, sculpture, architecture, and woodwork. In Taos, he renovated the home and embellished it with hand-carved doors, windows, gates, posts, fireplaces, and other features of a Russian country home. Fechin died in 1955.

227 Paseo del Pueblo Norte. © 505/758-2690. www.taosmuseums.org. Admission $6 adults, $3 children 6–16, free for children under 6. Summer Thurs–Sun 10am–5pm; call for winter hours.

ART CLASSES

If you'd like to pursue an artistic adventure of your own in Taos, check out the week-long classes in such subjects as writing, sculpting, painting, jewelry making, photography, clay working, and textiles at the **Taos Institute of Arts,** 108B Civic Plaza Dr. (© **800/822-7183** or 505/758-2793; www.tiataos.com). Class sizes are limited, so request information well in advance. Fees vary from class to class and usually don't include the cost of materials.

ORGANIZED TOURS

Taos Historic Walking Tours (© 505/758-4020) offers an excellent opportunity to explore the historic downtown area. Tours cost $10 and take 1½ to 2 hours. They leave from the Mabel Dodge Luhan house at 10:30am Monday to Saturday (May–Sept). No tours on Sundays and holidays. Call to make an appointment during the off season.

If you'd like a taste of Taos history and drama, call **Enchantment Dreams Walking Tours** (© 505/776-2562). Roberta Courtney Meyers, a theater artist, dramatist, and composer, will guide you through Taos's history while performing a number of characters, such as Georgia O'Keeffe and Kit Carson. Walking tours cost $20 per person.

6 Skiing Taos

DOWNHILL SKIING

Five alpine resorts are within an hour's drive of Taos; all offer complete facilities, including equipment rentals. Although exact opening and closing dates vary according to snow conditions, the season usually begins around Thanksgiving and continues into early April.

You can buy ski clothing and rent or buy ski equipment from several Taos outlets. Among them are **Cottam's Ski & Outdoor Shops** (© **800/322-8267** or 505/758-2822), with four locations (call for the one nearest you), and **Taos Ski Valley Sportswear, Ski & Boot Co.,** in Taos Ski Valley (© **505/776-2291**).

TAOS SKI VALLEY

Taos Ski Valley ★★★, P.O. Box 90, Taos Ski Valley, NM 87525 (© **505/776-2291;** www.skitaos.org), is the preeminent ski resort in the southern Rocky Mountains. A Swiss-German immigrant, Ernie Blake, founded it in 1955. According to local legend, Blake searched for 2 years in a small plane for the perfect location for a ski resort comparable to what he was accustomed to in the Alps. He found it at the abandoned mining site of Twining, high above Taos. Today, under the management of two younger generations of Blakes, the resort is internationally renowned for its light, dry powder (as much as 320 in. annually), its superb ski school, and its personal, friendly service. The quality of the snow is believed to be a product of the dry Southwestern air and abundant sunshine.

The more experienced skier can best appreciate Taos Ski Valley. It offers steep, high-alpine, high-adventure skiing. The mountain is more intricate than it might seem at first glance, and it holds many surprises and challenges—even for the expert. The *London Times* called the valley "without any argument the best ski resort in the world. Small, intimate, and endlessly challenging, Taos simply has no equal." And, if you're sick of dealing with yahoos on snowboards, you will be pleased to know that they're not permitted, at least for now.

Between the 11,819-foot summit and the 9,207-foot base are 72 trails and bowls, more than half of them designated for expert and advanced skiers. Most of the remaining trails are suitable for advanced intermediates; there is little flat terrain for novices to gain experience and mileage. However, many beginning skiers find that after spending time in lessons they can enjoy the **Kachina Bowl,** which offers spectacular views as well as wide-open slopes.

The area has an uphill capacity of 15,000 skiers per hour on its five double chairs, one triple, four quads, and one surface tow. Full-day lift tickets cost $57 for adults, $35 for children 7 to 12, $45 for teens 13 to 17, and $43 for seniors 65 to 69, and are free for seniors 70 and over and for children under 7 with an adult ticket purchase. Full rental packages are $25 for adults and $15 for children. Taos Ski Valley is open daily 9am to 4pm from Thanksgiving to around the second week of April. *Note:* Taos Ski Valley has one of the best ski schools in the country, specializing in teaching people to negotiate steep and challenging runs.

Taos Ski Valley has many lodges and condominiums, with nearly 1,500 beds. (See "Where to Stay," earlier in this chapter for details on accommodations.) All offer ski-week packages; four of them have restaurants. There are three restaurants on the mountain in addition to the many facilities of Village Center at the base. For reservations, contact the **Taos Valley Resort Association** (© **800/776-1111** or 505/776-2233; www.visitnewmexico.com).

RED RIVER SKI & SNOWBOARD AREA

Not far from Taos Ski Valley is **Red River Ski & Snowboard Area,** P.O. Box 900, Red River, NM 87558 (© **800/331-7669** for reservations, or 505/754-2223 for information; www.redriverskiarea.com). One of the bonuses of this ski area is that lodgers at Red River can walk out their doors and be on the slopes. Two other factors make this 4-decade-old, family-oriented area special: First, most of its 57 trails are geared toward the intermediate skier (though beginners and experts also have some trails); and second, snowmaking guarantees good snow early and late in the year (the equipment can work on 87% of the runs, more than any other in New Mexico). However, be aware that this human-made snow tends to be icy, and the mountain is full of inexperienced skiers, so you really have to watch your back. Locals in the area refer to this as "Little Texas" because it's so popular with Texans and Southerners. A very friendly atmosphere, with a touch of redneck attitude, prevails.

Kids Skiing with Kids

Its children's ski school has always made Taos Ski Valley an excellent location for skiing families, but with the 1994 addition of an 18,000-square-foot children's center (Kinderkäfig Center), skiing with your children in Taos is even better. Kinderkäfig offers every service imaginable, from equipment rental for children to babysitting. Call ahead for more information.

There's a 1,600-foot vertical drop here to a base elevation of 8,750 feet. Lifts include four double chairs, two triple chairs, and a surface tow, with a capacity of 7,920 skiers per hour. The cost of a ticket for all lifts is $49 for adults; $43 for teens 13 to 17; $34 for children ages 4 to 12 and seniors 60 to 69. Free for seniors 70 and over. Rental packages start at $20 for adults, $13 for children. Lifts run daily 9am to 4pm Thanksgiving to about March 28.

ANGEL FIRE RESORT

Also quite close to Taos is **Angel Fire Resort** ✦, P.O. Drawer B, Angel Fire, NM 87710 (© **800/633-7463** or 505/377-6401; www.angelfireresort.com). If you (or your kids) don't feel up to skiing steeper Taos Mountain, Angel Fire is a good choice. The 62 trails are heavily oriented to beginner and intermediate skiers and snowboarders, with a few runs for more advanced skiers and snowboarders. The mountain has undergone over $7 million in improvements in past years. This is not an old village like you'll find at Taos and Red River. Instead, it's a Vail-style resort, built in 1960, with a variety of activities other than skiing (see "Exploring the Enchanted Circle," later in this chapter). The snowmaking capabilities are excellent, and the ski school is good, though I hear it's so crowded that it's difficult to get in during spring break. Angel Fire has the only two high-speed quad lifts in New Mexico, so you can get to the top fast and have a long ski to the bottom. There are also three double lifts and one surface lift. Also here are a large snowboard park (with a banked slalom course, rails, jumps, and other obstacles) and some new hike-access advanced runs; note, however, that the hike is substantial. Cross-country skiing, snowshoeing, and snow biking are also available. All-day lift tickets cost $49 for adults, $32 for teens 13 to 17, and $26 for children 7 to 12. Kids under 7 and seniors 70 and over ski free. Open from approximately Thanksgiving to March 29 (depending on the weather) daily 9am to 4pm.

CROSS-COUNTRY SKIING

Just east of Red River, with 16 miles of groomed trails (in addition to 6 miles of trails strictly for snowshoers) in 400 acres of forestlands atop Bobcat Pass, is the **Enchanted Forest Cross Country Ski Area** (© **505/754-6112;** www.enchantedforestxc.com). Full-day trail passes, good 9am to 4:30pm, are $10 for adults; $8 for teens 13 to 17 and seniors 62 to 69; $3 for children 7 to 12; and free for children under 7 and seniors age 70 and over. In addition to cross-country ski and snowshoe rentals, the ski area also rents pulk sleds—high-tech devices in which children are pulled by their skiing parents. The ski area offers a full snack bar. Equipment rentals and lessons can be arranged either at Enchanted Forest or at **Miller's Crossing** ski shop, 417 W. Main St., Red River (© **505/754-2374**). Nordic skiers can get instruction in cross-country classic as well as freestyle skating.

Taos Mountain Outfitters, 114 S. Plaza (© **505/758-9292**), offers telemark and cross-country sales, rentals, and guide service, as does **Los Rios Whitewater Ski Shop** (© **800/544-1181** or 505/776-8854).

7 Getting Outside

Taos County's 2,200 square miles embrace a great diversity of scenic beauty, from New Mexico's highest mountain, 13,161-foot **Wheeler Peak,** to the 650-foot-deep chasm of the **Rio Grande Gorge** ✦✦. Carson National Forest, which extends to the eastern city limits of Taos and cloaks a large part of the county, contains several major ski facilities as well as hundreds of miles of hiking trails through the Sangre de Cristo range.

Recreation areas are mainly in the national forest, where pine and aspen provide refuge for abundant wildlife. Forty-eight areas (38 with campsites) are accessible by road. There are also areas on the high desert mesa, carpeted by sagebrush, cactus, and, frequently, wildflowers. Two beautiful areas within a short drive of Taos are the **Valle Vidal Recreation Area,** north of Red River, and the **Wild Rivers Recreation Area,** near Questa. For complete information, contact **Carson National Forest,** 208 Cruz Alta Rd. (© **505/758-6200**), or the **Bureau of Land Management,** 226 Cruz Alta Rd. (© **505/758-8851**).

BALLOONING

As in many other towns throughout New Mexico, hot-air ballooning is a top attraction. **Paradise Hot Air Balloon Adventure** (© **505/751-6098**) offers recreational trips over the Taos Valley and Rio Grande Gorge. The company also offers ultralight rides.

BIKING

Even if you're not an avid cyclist, it won't take long for you to realize that getting around Taos by bike is preferable to driving. You won't have the usual parking problems, and you won't have to sit in traffic as it snakes through the center of town. If you feel like exploring the surrounding area, Carson National Forest rangers recommend several biking trails in the greater Taos area. Head to the **Taos Box West Rim** for a scenic and easy ride. To reach the trail, follow NM 68 south for 17 miles to Pilar; turn west onto NM 570. Travel along the river for 6¼ miles, cross the bridge, and drive to the top of the ridge. Watch for the trail marker on your right. For a more technical and challenging ride, go to **Devisadero Loop:** From Taos, drive out of town on US 64 to the first pullout on the right, just as you enter the canyon at El Nogal Picnic Area. To ride the notorious **South Boundary Trail,** a 20-mile romp for advanced riders, contact Native Sons Adventures (below). Native Sons can arrange directions, a shuttle, and a guide, if necessary. The **U.S. Forest Service** office, 208 Cruz Alta Rd. (© **505/758-6200**), has excellent trail information. Also look for the *Taos Trails* map (created jointly by Carson National Forest, Native Sons Adventures, and Trails Illustrated) at area bookstores.

Bicycle rentals are available from the **Gearing Up Bicycle Shop,** 129 Paseo del Pueblo Sur (© **505/751-0365**); daily rentals run $35 for a mountain bike with front suspension. **Native Sons Adventures,** 1033A Paseo del Pueblo Sur (© **800/753-7559** or 505/758-9342), rents bikes ranging from regular (unsuspended) to full-suspension bikes for $15 to $35 for a half day and $20 to $45 for a full day; it also rents some car racks. All these prices include use of helmets and water bottles.

Annual touring events include Red River's **Enchanted Circle Century Bike Tour** (© **505/754-2366**) on the weekend following Labor Day.

FISHING

In many of New Mexico's waters, fishing is possible year-round, though many high lakes and streams are fishable only during the warmer months. Overall, the best fishing is in the spring and fall. The Rio Grande is a favorite fishing spot, but there is also excellent fishing in the streams around Taos. Taoseños favor the Rio Hondo, Rio Pueblo (near Tres Ritos), Rio Fernando (in Taos Canyon), Pot Creek, and Rio Chiquito. Rainbow, cutthroat, German brown trout, and kokanee (a freshwater salmon) are commonly stocked and caught. Pike and catfish have been caught in the Rio Grande as well. Jiggs, spinners, or woolly worms are recommended as lure, or worms, corn, or salmon eggs as bait; many experienced anglers prefer fly-fishing.

Licenses are required and are sold, along with tackle, at several Taos sporting-goods shops. For backcountry guides, try **Deep Creek Wilderness Outfitters and Guides,** P.O. Box 721, El Prado, NM 87529 (© **505/776-8423** or 505/776-5901), or **Taylor Streit Flyfishing Service,** 405 Camino de la Placita (© **505/751-1312;** www.streitfly fishing.com).

FITNESS FACILITIES

The **Taos Spa and Tennis Club,** 111 Dona Ana Dr., across from Sagebrush Inn (© **505/758-1980;** www.taosspa.com), is a fully equipped fitness center that rivals any you'd find in a big city. It has a variety of cardiovascular machines, bikes, and weight-training machines, as well as saunas, indoor and outdoor Jacuzzis, a steam room, and indoor and outdoor pools. Classes range from yoga to Pilates to water fitness. In addition, it has tennis and racquetball courts. Therapeutic massage, facials, and physical therapy are available daily by appointment. Children's programs include a tennis camp and swimming lessons, and babysitting is available in the morning and evening. The spa is open weekdays 5am to 9pm, weekends 7am to 8pm. Monthly and summer memberships and punch cards are available. For visitors, the daily rate is $12.

The **Northside Health and Fitness Center,** 1307 Paseo del Pueblo Norte (© **505/751-1242**), is also a full-service facility, featuring top-of-the-line Cybex equipment, free weights, and cardiovascular equipment. Aerobics classes are scheduled daily (Jazzercise classes weekly), and there are indoor/outdoor pools and four tennis courts, as well as children's and seniors' programs. Open weekdays 6am to 9pm, weekends 8am to 8pm. The daily visitors' rate is $10.

GOLF

The 18-hole golf course at the **Taos Country Club,** 54 Golf Course Dr., Ranchos de Taos (© **800/758-7375** or 505/758-7300), is open to the public. Located on Country Road 110, just 6 miles south of the plaza, it's a first-rate championship course designed for all levels of play. It has open fairways and no hidden greens. The club also features a driving range, putting and chipping green, and instruction by PGA professionals. Greens fees are seasonal and start at $48; cart and club rentals are available. The country club has a clubhouse, featuring a restaurant and full bar. It's always advisable to call ahead for tee times 1 week in advance, but it's not unusual for people to show up unannounced and manage to find a time.

The par-72, 18-hole **Angel Fire Resort Golf Course** (© **800/633-7463** or 505/377-3055) is PGA endorsed. Surrounded by stands of ponderosa pine, spruce, and aspen, at 8,500 feet, it's one of the highest regulation golf courses in the world. It also has a driving range and putting green. Carts and clubs can be rented, and the club pro provides instruction. Greens fees range from $45 to $65.

HIKING

Hundreds of miles of hiking trails cross Taos County's mountain and high-mesa country. The trails are especially well traveled in the summer and fall, although nights turn chilly and mountain weather may be fickle by September.

Free materials and advice on all **Carson National Forest** trails and recreation areas can be obtained from the **Forest Service Building,** 208 Cruz Alta Rd. (© **505/758-6200**), open weekdays 8am to 4:30pm. Detailed USGS topographical maps of backcountry areas are for sale at **Taos Mountain Outfitters,** South Plaza (© **505/758-9292**).

The 19,663-acre **Wheeler Peak Wilderness** is a wonderland of alpine tundra, encompassing New Mexico's highest peak (13,161 ft.). A favorite (though rigorous) hike to Wheeler Peak's summit (15 miles round-trip, with a 3,700-ft. elevation gain) makes for a long but fun day. The trail head is at Taos Ski Valley. For year-round hiking, head to the **Wild Rivers Recreation Area** (© 505/770-1600), near Questa (see "Exploring the Enchanted Circle," later in this chapter).

HORSEBACK RIDING

The sage meadows and pine-covered mountains around Taos make it one of the West's most romantic places to ride. **Taos Indian Horse Ranch** ★★ (© 505/758-3212), on Pueblo land off Ski Valley Road, just before Arroyo Seco, offers a variety of guided rides. Open by appointment, the ranch provides horses for all types of riders (English, Western, Australian, and bareback) and ability levels. Call ahead to reserve and for prices, which will likely run about $85 for a 2-hour trail ride.

Horseback riding is also offered by **Rio Grande Stables,** P.O. Box 2122, El Prado (© 505/776-5913; www.lajitasstables.com/taos.htm), with rides taking place during the summer months at Taos Ski Valley. Most riding outfitters offer lunch trips and overnight trips. Call for prices and details.

ICE-SKATING & SKATEBOARDING

If a latent Michelle Kwan or Brian Boitano dwells in you, try your blades at **Taos Youth Family Center,** 406 Paseo del Cañon, 2 miles south of the plaza and about ¾ mile off Paseo del Pueblo Sur (© 505/758-4160). The rink is open daily from early November thorough mid-March. Call for hours. Admission is $4, and skate rentals are available. Also at the center is an in-line skate and skateboarding park, open when there's no snow or ice. Admission is free.

LLAMA TREKKING

For a taste of the unusual, you might want to try letting a llama carry your gear and food while you walk and explore, free of any heavy burdens. They're friendly, gentle animals that have keen senses of sight and smell. Often, other animals, such as elk, deer, and mountain sheep, are attracted to the scent of the llamas and will venture near hikers. Two good outfitters are **El Paseo Llama Expeditions** ★★ (© 800/455-2627 or 505/758-3111; www.elpaseollama.com) and **Wild Earth Llama Adventures** ★★ (© 800/758-LAMA [5262] or 505/586-0174; www.llamaadventures.com). The llama expeditions are scheduled May to mid-October, and day hikes are scheduled year-round. Gourmet meals are provided. Half-day hikes cost about $60, day hikes about $79, with multiday hikes available.

RIVER RAFTING

Half- or full-day white-water rafting trips down the Rio Grande and Rio Chama originate in Taos and can be booked through a variety of outfitters in the area. The wild **Taos Box** ★★★, a steep-sided canyon south of the Wild Rivers Recreation Area, offers a series of class IV rapids that rarely let up for some 17 miles. The water drops up to 90 feet per mile, providing one of the most exciting 1-day whitewater tours in the West. May and June, when the water is rising, is a good time to go. Experience is not required, but you will be required to wear a life jacket (provided), and you should be willing to get wet.

Most of the companies listed run the **Taos Box** ($99–$109 per person) and **Pilar Racecourse** ($40–$48 per person per half day) on a daily basis.

I highly recommend **Los Rios River Runners** ⭐, P.O. Box 2734, Taos (© **800/544-1181** or 505/776-8854; www.losriosriverrunners.com). Other safe bets are **Native Sons Adventures,** 1033A Paseo del Pueblo Sur (© **800/753-7559** or 505/758-9342; www.nativesonsadventures.com); and **Far Flung Adventures,** P.O. Box 707, El Prado (© **800/359-2627** or 505/758-2628; www.farflung.com).

Safety warning: Taos is not the place to experiment if you are not an experienced rafter. Check with the **Bureau of Land Management,** 226 Cruz Alta Rd. (© **505/758-8851**), to make sure you're fully equipped to go whitewater rafting without a guide. Have the staff check your gear to ensure that it's sturdy enough—this is serious rafting!

ROCK CLIMBING

Mountain Skills, P.O. Box 206, Arroyo Seco, NM 87514 (© **505/776-2222;** www.climbingschoolusa.com), offers rock-climbing instruction for all skill levels, from beginners to more advanced climbers who would like to fine-tune their abilities or just find out about the best area climbs.

SNOWMOBILING AND ATV RIDING

Native Sons Adventures, 1033A Paseo del Pueblo Sur (© **800/753-7559** or 505/758-9342), runs fully guided tours in the Sangre de Cristo Mountains. Rates run $64 to $150. Reservations are required.

SWIMMING

The **Don Fernando Pool** (© **505/737-2622**), on Civic Plaza Drive at Camino de la Placita, opposite the new Convention Center, admits swimmers over age 8 without adult supervision.

TENNIS

Taos Spa and Tennis Club (see "Fitness Facilities," above) has four courts, and the **Northside Health and Fitness Center** (see "Fitness Facilities," above) has three tennis courts. In addition, there are four free public courts in Taos, two at **Kit Carson Park,** on Paseo del Pueblo Norte, and two at **Fred Baca Memorial Park,** on Camino del Medio, south of Ranchitos Road. **Quail Ridge Inn** (© **800/624-4448** or 505/776-2211; www.quailridgeinn.com) on Ski Valley Road has outdoor tennis courts available to those staying in Quail Ridge condos.

8 Shopping

Given the town's historical associations with the arts, it isn't surprising that many visitors come to Taos to buy fine art. Fifty or so galleries are within easy walking distance of the plaza, and a couple dozen more are a short drive from downtown. Galleries and shops are generally open daily during summer and closed Sunday during winter. Hours vary but generally run from 10am to 5 or 6pm. Some artists show their work by appointment only.

The best-known artist in modern Taos is R. C. Gorman, a Navajo from Arizona who has made his home in Taos for more than 2 decades. He is internationally acclaimed for his bright, somewhat surrealistic depictions of Navajo women. His **Navajo Gallery,** 210 Ledoux St. (© **505/758-3250**), is a showcase for his widely varied work: acrylics, lithographs, silk screens, bronzes, tapestries, hand-cast ceramic vases, etched glass, and more.

My favorite new spot to shop is the village of **Arroyo Seco** ⭐ on NM 150, about 5 miles north of Taos en route to Taos Ski Valley. Not only is there a lovely 1834 church, La Santísima Trinidad, but a few cute little shops line the winding lane through town. My favorites are the **Taos Sunflower** (© 505/776-5644), selling specialty yarns and fibers, just off the highway near the Gypsy 360° cafe, and **Arroyo Seco Mercantile** (© 505/776-8806) 488 NM 150, which is full of cowboy hats, antiques, and country home items.

ART

Act I Gallery   This gallery has a broad range of works in a variety of media. You'll find watercolors, *retablos,* furniture, paintings, Hispanic folk art, pottery, jewelry, and sculpture. 218 Paseo del Pueblo Norte. © 800/666-2933 or 505/758-7831.

Fenix Gallery   The Fenix Gallery focuses on Taos artists with national and international collections and reputations who live and work in Taos. The work is primarily non-objective and very contemporary. Some "historic" artists are represented as well. Recent expansion has doubled the gallery space. 228B N. Pueblo Rd. © 505/758-9120.

Franzetti Metalworks   This gallery's designs are surprisingly whimsical for metalwork. Much of the work is functional; you'll find laughing-horse switch plates and "froggie" earthquake detectors. 120G Bent St. © 505/758-7872.

Gallery A   The oldest gallery in town, Gallery A has contemporary and traditional paintings and sculpture, including Gene Kloss etchings, watercolors, and oils, as well as regional and national collections. 105–107 Kit Carson Rd. © 505/758-2343.

Inger Jirby Gallery ★ *Finds*   The word *expressionist* could have been created to define the work of internationally known artist Inger Jirby. Full of bold color and passionate brush strokes, Jirby's oils record the lives and landscapes of villages from the southwestern U.S. to Guatemala to Bali. This gallery, which meanders back through a 400-year-old adobe house, is a feast for the eyes and soul. 207 Ledoux St. © 505/758-7333.

Lumina of New Mexico ★★ *Finds*   Located in the historic Victor Higgins home, next to the Mabel Dodge Luhan estate, Lumina is one of the loveliest galleries in New Mexico. You'll find a large variety of fine art, including paintings, sculpture, and photography. This place is as much a tourist attraction as any of the museums and historic homes in town. Look for the wonderful paintings and sculpture of Enrico Embrilo, and take a stroll through the new 2-acre Ridhwan sculpture garden with a pond and waterfall, where you'll find large outdoor pieces from all over the United States. About 8 minutes from town is **Lumina North** in Arroyo Seco, which features 3 acres of Buddhist sculpture and a tea house. 239 Morada Rd. (off Kit Carson Rd.). © 505/758-7282. Lumina North: 11 Des Moines Rd. © 505/776-3957.

Michael McCormick Gallery ★ *Finds*   Nationally renowned artists dynamically play with Southwestern themes in the works hanging at this gallery, steps from the plaza. Especially notable are the bright portraits by Miguel Martinez and the moody architectural pieces by Margaret Nes. If the gallery's namesake is in, strike up a conversation about art or poetry. 106C Paseo del Pueblo Norte. © 800/279-0879 or 505/758-1372.

New Directions Gallery   Here you'll find a variety of contemporary abstract works such as the beautiful blown glasswork of Tony Jojola. My favorites are the impressionist works depicting northern New Mexico villages by Tom Noble. 107 North Plaza Suite B. © 800/658-6903 or 505/758-2771.

Nichols Taos Fine Art Gallery   Here you will find traditional works in all media, including Western and cowboy art. 403 Paseo del Pueblo Norte. © 505/758-2475.

Parks Gallery ★ Some of the region's finest contemporary art decks the walls of this gallery just off the plaza. The top artists here include Melissa Zink, Jim Wagner, Susan Contreres, and Erin Currier. 127 Bent St. ℂ **505/751-0343.**

Philip Bareiss Gallery The works of some 30 leading Taos artists, including sculptor and painter Ron Davis, sculptor Gray Mercer, and watercolorist Patricia Sanford, are exhibited here. 15 Rt. 150. ℂ **505/776-2284.** bareiss@taosartappraisal.com.

R. B. Ravens A trader for many years, including 21 on the Ranchos Plaza, R. B. Ravens is skilled at finding incredible period artwork. Here, you'll see (and have the chance to buy) Navajo rugs and pottery. The setting is an old home with raw pine floors and hand-sculpted adobe walls. 4146 NM 68 (across from the St. Francis Church Plaza), Ranchos de Taos. ℂ **505/758-7322.**

Shriver Gallery This gallery sells traditional paintings, drawings, etchings, and bronze sculptures. 401 Paseo del Pueblo Norte. ℂ **505/758-4994.**

BOOKS

Brodsky Bookshop This shop has an exceptional inventory of fiction, nonfiction, Southwestern and Native American–studies books, children's books, used books, cards, tapes, and CDs. 226 Paseo del Pueblo Norte. ℂ **888/223-8730** or 505/758-9468.

Moby Dickens Bookshop ★ This is one of Taos's best bookstores. You'll find children's and adults' collections of Southwest, Native American, and out-of-print books. The shop has comfortable places to sit and read. 124A Bent St. ℂ **888/442-9980** or 505/758-3050.

CRAFTS

Clay & Fiber Gallery Clay & Fiber represents more than 150 artists from around the country. Merchandise changes frequently, but you should expect to see a variety of ceramics, fiber arts, jewelry, and wearables. 201 Paseo del Pueblo Sur. ℂ **505/758-8093.**

Southwest Moccasin & Drum ★ (Kids) Home of the All One Tribe Drum, this favorite local shop carries a large variety of drums in all sizes and styles, handmade by master Native American drum makers from Taos Pueblo. The shop also has the country's second-largest selection of moccasins, as well as an impressive inventory of indigenous world instruments and tapes, sculpture, weavings, rattles, fans, fetishes, bags, decor, and many handmade one-of-a-kind items. Kids enjoy the instruments as well as other colorful goods. A percentage of the store's profits support Native American causes. 803 Paseo del Pueblo Norte. ℂ **800/447-3630** or 505/758-9332. www.swnativecrafts.com.

Taos Artisans Cooperative Gallery (Value) This seven-member cooperative gallery, owned and operated by local artists, sells local handmade jewelry, wearables, clay work, glass, leather work, and garden sculpture. You'll always find an artist in the shop. 107C Bent St. ℂ **505/758-1558.**

Taos Blue This gallery has fine Native American and contemporary handcrafts. 101A Bent St. ℂ **505/758-3561.**

Twining Weavers and Contemporary Crafts Here, you'll find an interesting mix of hand-woven wool rugs and pillows by owner Sally Bachman, as well as creations by other gallery artists in fiber, basketry, and clay. 133 Kit Carson Rd. ℂ **505/758-9000.**

Weaving Southwest Contemporary tapestries by New Mexico artists, as well as one-of-a-kind rugs, blankets, and pillows, are the woven specialties here. 216B Paseo del Pueblo Norte. ℂ **505/758-0433.**

FASHIONS

Artemisia   Wearable art in bold colors defines this little shop a block from the plaza. Goods are pricey but unique, most hand-woven or hand-sewn, all for women. 115 Bent St. © 505/737-9800.

Mariposa Boutique   Bright chile-pepper-print overalls for kids first caught my eye in this little shop. Closer scrutiny brought me to plenty of finds for myself, such as suede and rayon broomstick skirts and Mexican-style dresses, perfect for showing off turquoise jewelry. 120F Bent St. © 505/758-9028.

Overland Sheepskin Company ★ *Finds*   You can't miss the weathered barn sitting on a meadow north of town. Inside, you'll find anything you can imagine in leather: coats, gloves, hats, slippers. The coats are exquisite, from oversize ranch styles to tai-lored blazers in a variety of leathers, from sheepskin to buffalo hide. NM 522 (a few miles north of town). © 505/758-8820.

FURNITURE

Country Furnishings of Taos   Here, you'll find unique hand-painted folk-art fur-niture. The pieces are as individual as the styles of the local folk artists who make them. There are also home accessories, unusual gifts, clothing, and jewelry. 534 Paseo del Pueblo Norte. © 505/758-4633.

Lo Fino   The name means "the refined," so you know that this expansive showroom is worth taking time to wander through. You'll find a variety of home furnishings, from driftwood lamps and finely painted *trasteros* (armoires) to handcrafted traditional and contemporary Southwestern furniture. Lo Fino specializes in custom-built furni-ture. 201 Paseo del Pueblo Sur. © 505/758-0298. lofino@newmex.com.

The Taos Company   This interior-design showroom specializes in unique South-western and contemporary furniture and decorative accessories. Especially look for graceful stone fountains, iron-and-wood furniture, and custom jewelry. 124K John Dunn Plaza, Bent St. © 800/548-1141 or 505/758-1141.

GIFTS & SOUVENIRS

Chimayo Trading del Norte   Specializing in Navajo weavings, pueblo pottery, and other types of pottery, this is a fun spot to peruse on the Ranchos de Taos Plaza. Look especially for Casas Grandes pottery from Mexico. #1 Ranchos de Taos Plaza. © 505/758-0504.

El Rincón Trading Post *Finds*   This shop has a real trading-post feel. It's a wonder-ful place to find turquoise jewelry, whether you're looking for contemporary or antique. In the back of the store is a museum full of Native American and Western artifacts. 114 Kit Carson Rd. © 505/758-9188.

San Francisco de Asis Gift Shop   Local devotional art fills this funky little shop behind the San Francisco de Asis church. *Retablos* (altar paintings), rosary beads, and hand-carved wooden crosses appeal to a range of visitors, from the deeply religious to the pagan power shopper. Ranchos de Taos Plaza. © 505/758-2754.

JEWELRY

Artwares Contemporary Jewelry   The gallery owners call their contemporary jewelry "a departure from the traditional." True to this slogan, each piece offers a new twist on traditional Southwestern and Native American design, by artists such as John Hardy and Diane Malouf. 129 N. Plaza. © 800/527-8850 or 505/758-8850.

Taos Gems & Minerals   In business for over 30 years, Taos Gems & Minerals is a fine lapidary showroom. This is a great place to explore; you can buy jewelry, carvings, and antique pieces at reasonable prices. 637 Paseo del Pueblo Sur. ℗ 505/758-3910.

MUSICAL INSTRUMENTS

Taos Drum Company   Drum-making is an age-old tradition to which local artisans give continued life in Taos. The drums are made of hollowed-out logs stretched with rawhide, and they come in all different shapes, sizes, and styles. Taos Drums has the largest selection of Native American log and hand drums in the world. In addition to drums, the showroom displays Southwestern and wrought-iron furniture, cowboy art, and more than 60 styles of rawhide lampshades, as well as a constantly changing selection of South American imports, primitive folk art, ethnic crafts, Native American music tapes, books, and other information on drumming. Ask about the tour that demonstrates the drum-making process. To find Taos Drum Company, look for the tepees and drums. Off NM 68, 5 miles south of Taos Plaza. ℗ 505/758-3796.

POTTERY & TILES

Stephen Kilborn Pottery   Visiting this shop in town is a treat, but for a real adventure, go 17 miles south of Taos (toward Santa Fe) to Stephen Kilborn's studio in Pilar. It's open Monday to Saturday 10am to 5pm, Sunday noon to 4pm. There, you'll see where the pottery is made. 136A Paseo del Pueblo Norte. ℗ 800/758-0136 or 505/758-5760. www.kilbornpottery.com.

Vargas Tile Co.   Vargas Tile has a great little collection of hand-painted Mexican tiles at good prices. You'll find beautiful pots with sunflowers on them and colorful cabinet doorknobs, as well as inventive sinks. South end of town on NM 68. ℗ 505/758-5986.

9 Taos After Dark

For a small town, Taos has its share of top entertainment. The resort atmosphere and the arts community attract performers, and the city enjoys annual programs in music and literary arts. State troupes, such as the New Mexico Repertory Theater and New Mexico Symphony Orchestra, make regular visits.

Many events are scheduled by the **Taos Center for the Arts (TCA),** 133 Paseo del Pueblo Norte (℗ 505/758-2052; www.taoscenterforthearts.org), at the **Taos Community Auditorium** (℗ 505/758-2052). The TCA imports local, regional, and national performers in theater, dance, and concerts. Robert Mirabal, among others, has performed here, and *The Vagina Monologues* has been presented. Also, look for a weekly film series offered year-round.

You can obtain information on current events in the *Taos News,* published every Thursday. The **Taos County Chamber of Commerce** (℗ 800/732-TAOS or 505/758-3873; www.taoschamber.com) publishes semiannual listings of *Taos County Events,* and the annual *Taos Country Vacation Guide* lists events and happenings around town.

THE PERFORMING ARTS

Fort Burgwin   This historic site (of the 1,000-year-old Pot Creek Pueblo), located about 10 miles south of Taos, is a summer campus of Dallas's Southern Methodist University. From mid-May through mid-August, the SMU-in-Taos curriculum (including studio arts, humanities, and sciences) includes courses in music and theater. Regularly scheduled orchestral concerts, guitar and harpsichord recitals, and theater

The Major Concert & Performance Halls

Taos Civic Plaza and Convention Center, 121 Civic Plaza Dr. (© 505/758-4160). This convention space has an exhibit center that books presentations, lectures, and concerts.

Taos Community Auditorium, Kit Carson Memorial State Park (© 505/758-4677). A comfortable, small-town space, this community auditorium makes a nice venue for films, concerts, and lectures.

performances are available to the community, without charge, throughout the summer. 6580 NM 518, Ranchos de Taos. © 505/758-8322.

Music from Angel Fire   This acclaimed program of chamber music begins in mid-August with weekend concerts, and continues up to Labor Day. Based in the small resort community of Angel Fire (about 21 miles east of Taos, off US 64), it also presents numerous concerts in Taos, Las Vegas, and Raton. P.O. Box 502, Angel Fire, NM 87710. © 505/377-3233 or 505/989-4772.

Taos School of Music   Founded in 1963, this music summer school offers excellent concerts by notable artists. The school is at the Hotel St. Bernard in Taos Ski Valley. An intensive 8-week study and performance program for advanced students of violin, viola, cello, and piano runs from mid-June to mid-August. The 8-week **Chamber Music Festival,** an important adjunct of the school, offers 16 concerts and seminars for the public; performances are given by pianist Robert McDonald, the Chicago String Quartet, the Brentano String Quartet, Michael Tree, and the international young student artists. Performances are at the Taos Community Auditorium and the Hotel St. Bernard. P.O. Box 1879. © 505/776-2388. www.taosschoolofmusic.com. Chamber music concert tickets $15 adults, $10 children under 16.

THE CLUB & MUSIC SCENE

Adobe Bar   A favorite gathering place for locals and visitors, the Adobe Bar is known for its live music series (nights vary) devoted to the eclectic talents of Taos musicians. The schedule offers a little of everything—classical, jazz, folk, Hispanic, and acoustic. The Adobe Bar features a wide selection of international beers, wines by the glass, light New Mexican dining, desserts, and an espresso menu. In the Historic Taos Inn, 125 Paseo del Pueblo Norte. © 505/758-2233. Daily noon–10:30pm.

Alley Cantina ✦ *(Moments)*   This bar that touts its location as the oldest house in Taos has become the hot late-night spot. The focus is on interaction, as well as TV sports. Patrons playing shuffleboard, pool, chess, and backgammon listen to live music 4 to 5 nights a week. Burgers, fish and chips, and other informal dishes are served until 11pm. 121 Teresina Lane. © 505/758-2121. Cover for live music only.

Anaconda Bar ✦✦   Set in the new ecoresort El Monte Sagrado, this is Taos's happening night spot, with live entertainment—jazz, blues, Native American flute, or country—nightly. An anaconda sculpture snaking across the ceiling and an 11,000-gallon fish tank set the contemporary tone of the place, which serves a variety of delectable tapas. In the El Monte Sagrado hotel, 317 Kit Carson Rd. © 505/758-3502.

The Taos Area (including Enchanted Circle)

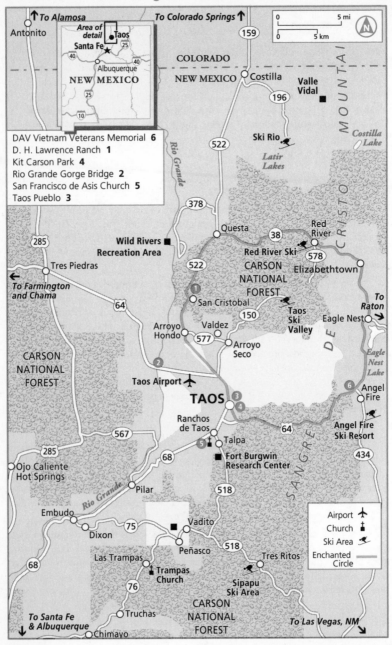

DAV Vietnam Veterans Memorial **6**
D. H. Lawrence Ranch **1**
Kit Carson Park **4**
Rio Grande Gorge Bridge **2**
San Francisco de Asis Church **5**
Taos Pueblo **3**

Moments   Exploring the Enchanted Circle

Longing for a little road trip? Few places offer more white-stripe adventure than the 90-mile loop around northern New Mexico's Enchanted Circle. The road leads through old Hispanic villages such as Arroyo Hondo and Questa. About 3 miles north of the latter, you can turn west of NM 522 onto NM 378 and travel 8 miles on a paved road to **Wild Rivers Recreation Area** (© 505/770-1600), a great place to begin a hike into the Rio Grande Gorge. Next the Enchanted Circle heads into a pass the Plains Indians once used, to the Wild West mining town of Red River, along the base of some of New Mexico's tallest peaks, to the resort village of Angel Fire, and back to Taos along the meandering Rio Fernando de Taos. Although you can drive the entire loop in 2 hours from Taos, most folks prefer to take a full day, and some take several days. If you get hungry along the way, stop for lunch at **Main Street Deli,** 316 E. Main St., Red River (© 505/754-3400), where you'll find tasty meatloaf and chicken-and-dumpling specials, as well as home-baked muffins, soups, and sub sandwiches for under $9. To drive the loop, travel north on NM 522 10 miles to Arroyo Hondo. Then drive another 13 miles to Questa. Turn right on NM 38, traveling 12 miles to Red River. Stay on NM 38 and drive 16 miles to Eagle Nest. From there you come to U.S. 64, which travels west for 12 miles to Angel Fire. The final leg is a lovely 21-mile jaunt on US 64 back to Taos.

Momentitos de la Vida ★★   This low-lit, moody bar, with thick pine tables and comfortable chairs, serves martinis and jazz in bluesy doses. Other drinks and music selections also play here, with live music on Friday and Saturday night. The restaurant-cum-club serves a bistro menu ($8.50–$14). Nonsmoking. Open Tuesday through Sunday 5–10:30pm or so (later on weekends). 4¾ miles north of the intersection of NM 150 and NM 522 (P.O. Box 505), Arroyo Seco. © 505/776-3333.

Sagebrush Inn ★   This is a real hot spot for locals. The atmosphere is Old West, with a rustic wooden dance floor and plenty of smoke. Dancers generally two-step to country music nightly, year-round, starting at 9pm. Paseo del Pueblo Sur (P.O. Box 557). © 505/758-2254.

Thunderbird Lodge   Throughout the winter, the Thunderbird offers a variety of nightly entertainment at the foot of the ski slopes. You'll also find wine tastings. Taos Ski Valley. © 505/776-2280. Cover occasionally on holidays.

9

Albuquerque

At first glance, New Mexico's largest city appears like one giant strip mall sandwiched between a spectacular mountain range, the Sandias, and the lifeblood of the state, the mighty Rio Grande. But this city offers much more than Walgreens and Wal-Mart. It's full of history, has many fun exhibits for kids and the young at heart, and boasts some of the best sunsets in the Southwest.

The railroad, which set up a major stop here in 1880, prompted much of Albuquerque's initial growth, but that economic explosion was nothing compared with what has happened since World War II. Designated a major national center for military research and production, Albuquerque became a trading center for New Mexico, whose populace spreads widely across the land. That's why the city may strike visitors as nothing more than one big strip mall. Look closely and you'll see ranchers, Native Americans, and Hispanic villagers stocking up on goods to take home.

Climbing out of the valley is **Route 66,** well worth a drive, if only to see the rust

that time has left. Old court motels, many with funky '50s signage, still line the street. One enclave on this route is the **University of New Mexico district,** with a number of hippie-ish cafes and shops.

Farther downhill, you'll come to **downtown Albuquerque.** During the day, this area is all suits and heels, but at night it boasts a hip nightlife scene.

The **Old Town** section is worth a visit. Though it's the most touristy part of town, it's also a unique Southwestern village with a beautiful and intact plaza. Also in this area are Albuquerque's aquarium and botanical gardens, as well as its zoo.

Indian pueblos in the area welcome tourists, and along with other pueblos throughout New Mexico have worked together to create the Pueblo Cultural Center, a showplace of Indian crafts of both past and present. The country's longest aerial tramway takes visitors to the top of Sandia Peak, which protects the city's eastern flank. To the west runs a series of volcanoes; the Petroglyph National Monument there is an amazing tribute to the area's ancient Native American past.

1 Orientation

ARRIVING

Albuquerque is the transportation hub for New Mexico, so getting in and out of town is easy. For more detailed information, see "Getting There" in chapter 2.

BY PLANE The **Albuquerque International Sunport** (© 505/842-4366) is in the south-central part of the city, between I-25 on the west and Kirtland Air Force Base on the east, just south of Gibson Boulevard. Most national airlines and two local ones serve the sleek, efficient airport.

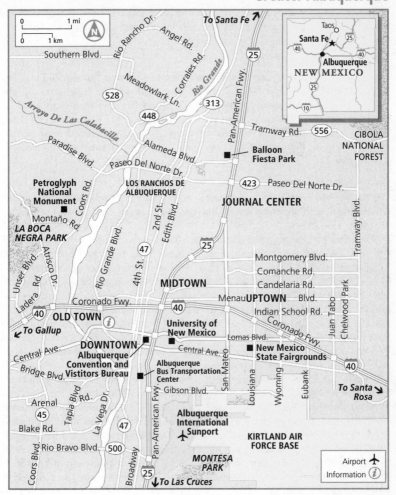

Most hotels have courtesy vans that meet guests. In addition, **Checker Airport Express** (☎ **505/765-1234**) runs to and from city hotels. **ABQ Ride** (☎ **505/243-7433**), Albuquerque's public bus system, also makes airport stops. There is efficient taxi service to and from the airport, and numerous car-rental agencies.

BY TRAIN **Amtrak**'s Southwest Chief arrives and departs daily to and from Los Angeles and Chicago. The station is at 214 First St. SW, 2 blocks south of Central Avenue (☎ **800/USA-RAIL** or 505/842-9650).

BY BUS **Greyhound/Trailways** (☎ **800/231-2222** for schedules, fares, and information) and **TNM&O** (☎ **505/243-4435**) arrive and depart from the Albuquerque Bus Transportation Center, 300 Second St. SW (at the corner of Lead, near the train station).

BY CAR   If you're driving, you'll probably arrive on either the east–west I-40 or the north-south I-25. Exits are well marked. For information and advice on driving in New Mexico, see "Getting There" in chapter 2.

VISITOR INFORMATION

The main office of the **Albuquerque Convention and Visitors Bureau,** 20 First Plaza NW (© **800/284-2282** or 505/842-9918), is open Monday to Friday 8am to 5pm. There are information centers at the airport, on the lower level at the bottom of the escalator, open daily 9:30am to 8pm; and in Old Town, at 303 Romero St. NW, Suite 107, open daily 9am to 5pm. Tape-recorded information about current local events is available from the bureau after 5pm weekdays and all day Saturday and Sunday. Call © **800/284-2282.**

CITY LAYOUT

The city's sprawl takes a while to get used to. A visitor's first impression is of a grid of arteries lined with shopping malls and fast-food eateries, with residences tucked behind on side streets.

If you look at a map of Albuquerque, you'll notice that it lies at the crossroads of I-25 and I-40. Focus on the southwest quadrant: Here, you'll find both downtown Albuquerque and Old Town, site of many tourist attractions. Lomas Boulevard and Central Avenue, the old Route 66 (US 66), flank downtown on the north and south. They come together 2 miles west of downtown, near Old Town Plaza, the historical and spiritual heart of the city. Lomas and Central continue east across I-25, staying about half a mile apart as they pass by the University of New Mexico and the New Mexico State Fairgrounds. The airport is directly south of the UNM campus, about 3 miles on Yale Boulevard. Kirtland Air Force Base—site of Sandia National Laboratories—is an equal distance south of the fairgrounds, on Louisiana Boulevard.

Roughly paralleling I-40 to the north is Menaul Boulevard, the focus of midtown and uptown shopping, as well as the hotel districts. As Albuquerque expands northward, the Journal Center business park area, about 4½ miles north of the freeway interchange, is getting more attention. East of Eubank Boulevard lie the Sandia Foothills, where the alluvial plain slants a bit more steeply toward the mountains.

When looking for an address, it is helpful to know that Central Avenue divides the city into north and south, and the railroad tracks—which run just east of First Street downtown—are the dividing line between east and west. Street names are followed by a directional: NE, NW, SE, or SW.

MAPS   The most comprehensive Albuquerque street map is distributed by the **Convention and Visitors Bureau,** 20 First Plaza NW (© **800/284-2282** or 505/842-9918).

2 Getting Around

Albuquerque is easy to get around, thanks to its wide thoroughfares, grid layout, and efficient transportation systems.

BY PUBLIC TRANSPORTATION   **ABQ Ride** (© **505/243-7433**) cloaks the city with its bus network. Call for information on routes and fares.

BY TAXI   **Yellow Cab** (© **505/247-8888**) serves the city and surrounding area 24 hours a day.

BY CAR The Yellow Pages list more than 30 car-rental agencies in Albuquerque. Among them are the following well-known national firms: **Alamo,** 3400 University Blvd. SE (© **505/842-4057**); **Avis,** at the airport (© **505/842-4080**); **Budget,** at the airport (© **505/247-3443**); **Dollar,** at the airport (© **505/842-4224**); **Hertz,** at the airport (© **505/842-4235**); **Rent-A-Wreck,** 500 Yale Blvd. SE (© **505/232-7552**); and **Thrifty,** 2039 Yale Blvd. SE (© **505/842-8733**). Those not at the airport are close by and can provide rapid airport pickup and delivery service.

Parking is generally not difficult in Albuquerque. Meters operate weekdays 8am to 6pm and are not monitored at other times. Only the large downtown hotels charge for parking. **Traffic** is a problem only at certain hours. Avoid I-25 and I-40 at the center of town around 5pm.

FAST FACTS

Call the **Greater Albuquerque Medical Association** (© **505/821-4583**) for a physician referral. The major hospitals are **Presbyterian Hospital,** 1100 Central Ave. SE (© **505/841-1234,** or 505/841-1111 for emergency services); and **University of New Mexico Hospital,** 2211 Lomas Blvd. NE (© **505/272-2111,** or 505/272-2411 for emergency services).

In Albuquerque, the hotel tax is 11.75%; it will be added to your bill. This includes gross receipts tax of 6.75%.

See also "Fast Facts: The American Southwest" in chapter 2, and "Fast Facts: For the International Traveler" in chapter 3.

3 Where to Stay

Albuquerque's hotel glut is good news to travelers looking for quality rooms at a reasonable cost. Except during peak periods—specifically, the New Mexico Arts and Crafts Fair (late June), the New Mexico State Fair (Sept), and the Albuquerque International Balloon Fiesta (early Oct)—most of the city's hotels have vacant rooms, so guests can frequently request and get a lower room rate than the one posted.

A tax of 11.75% is added to every hotel bill. All hotels and bed-and-breakfasts listed offer rooms for nonsmokers and travelers with disabilities.

DOWNTOWN/OLD TOWN

This area is the best location to stay if you want to be close to many of the major sights and attractions.

Sheraton Old Town ✦ No Albuquerque hotel is closer to top tourist attractions than the Sheraton. It's only a 5-minute walk from Old Town Plaza and two important museums. Constructed in 1975, it has undergone an estimated $4 million in renovations. Mezzanine-level windows light the adobe-toned lobby, creating an airiness that carries into the rooms. Request a south-side room, and you'll get a balcony overlooking Old Town and the pool. The medium-size rooms have handcrafted Southwestern furniture.

800 Rio Grande Blvd. NW, Albuquerque, NM 87104. © **800/237-2133** reservations only, or 505/843-6300. Fax 505/842-9863. www.sheraton.com. 188 units. $119–$169 double; $189 suite. Children stay free in parent's room. AE, DC, DISC, MC, V. Free parking. **Amenities:** 2 restaurants; outdoor pool; Jacuzzi; concierge; business center; limited room service; babysitting; valet laundry; same-day dry cleaning; executive-level rooms. *In room:* A/C, TV w/pay movies, dataport, minibar, coffeemaker, hair dryer, iron.

NEAR THE AIRPORT

Wyndham Albuquerque Hotel ★★   This 15-story hotel right at the airport provides spacious rooms with a touch of elegance. The lobby, grill, and lounge areas employ a lot of sandstone, wood, copper, and tile to lend an Anasazi feel, which extends into the rooms, each with a broad view from a balcony. Air travelers enjoy this hotel's location, but because it has good access to freeways and excellent views, it could also be a wise choice for a few days of browsing around Albuquerque. Of course, you will hear some jet noise. The Rojo Grill serves a variety of American and Southwestern dishes.

2910 Yale Blvd. SE, Albuquerque, NM 87106. *©* 800/227-1117 or 505/843-7000. Fax 505/843-6307. www. wyndham.com. 276 units. $99–$179 double. AE, DC, DISC, MC, V. Free parking. Small pets accepted with prior approval. **Amenities:** Restaurant; outdoor pool; access to golf club; 2 tennis courts; concierge; business center; coin-op laundry. *In room:* A/C, TV, dataport, coffeemaker, hair dryer, iron.

JOURNAL CENTER/NORTH CITY

North of Montgomery Boulevard, the focal point is the I-25 interchange with Osuna Road and San Mateo Boulevard. On the west side of the freeway, the giant pyramid of the Crowne Plaza dominates the Journal Center business park. East of the freeway, at San Mateo and Academy boulevards, numerous hotels, restaurants, and shopping complexes dominate. This is the closest area to the Balloon Fiesta launch site.

Albuquerque Marriott Pyramid North ★   About a 15-minute drive from Old Town and downtown, this Aztec pyramid–shaped structure provides decent rooms in an interesting environment. The 10 guest floors surround a skylit atrium. Vines drape from planter boxes on the balconies, and water falls five stories to a pool between the two glass elevators. The rooms, remodeled in 2003, are spacious, though not extraordinary, with picture windows and ample views. With lots of meeting space at the hotel, you're likely to encounter name-tagged conventioneers here. Overall, the service seems to be good enough to handle the crowds, but there are only two elevators, so guests often must wait.

5151 San Francisco Rd. NE, Albuquerque, NM 87109. *©* 800/228-9290 or 505/821-3333. Fax 505/822-8115. www. marriott.com. 310 units. $139–$184 double; $140–$275 suite. Ask about weekend and package rates. AE, DC, DISC, MC, V. Free parking. **Amenities:** Restaurant; lounge; indoor/outdoor pool; medium-size health club; Jacuzzi; sauna; concierge; business center; room service; valet laundry. *In room:* A/C, TV, dataport, coffeemaker, hair dryer, iron.

La Quinta Inn   La Quinta offers reliable rooms at a decent price. Rooms are tastefully decorated, fairly spacious, and comfortable, each with a table and chairs and a shower-only bathroom big enough to move around in. Each king room has a recliner, and two-room suites are available. If you're headed to the Balloon Fiesta, this is a good choice because it's not far from the launch site, though you'll have to reserve as much as a year in advance.

There's another La Quinta near the airport: **La Quinta Airport Inn,** 2116 Yale Blvd. SE. Make reservations for either branch through the toll-free number.

5241 San Antonio Dr. NE, Albuquerque, NM 87109. *©* 800/531-5900 or 505/821-9000. Fax 505/821-2399. www.lq.com. 130 units. $70–$76 double (higher during Balloon Fiesta). Children stay free in parent's room. AE, DC, DISC, MC, V. Free parking. Pets accepted. **Amenities:** Heated outdoor pool (May–Oct). *In room:* A/C, TV, dataport, coffeemaker, hair dryer, iron.

A BED-&-BREAKFAST NEAR OLD TOWN

Hacienda Antigua ★★ *Finds*   This 200-year-old adobe home was once the first stagecoach stop out of Old Town in Albuquerque. Now, it's one of Albuquerque's most elegant inns. The artistically landscaped courtyard, with its large cottonwood tree and abundance of greenery, offers a welcome respite for tired travelers. The rooms

Central Albuquerque Accommodations & Dining

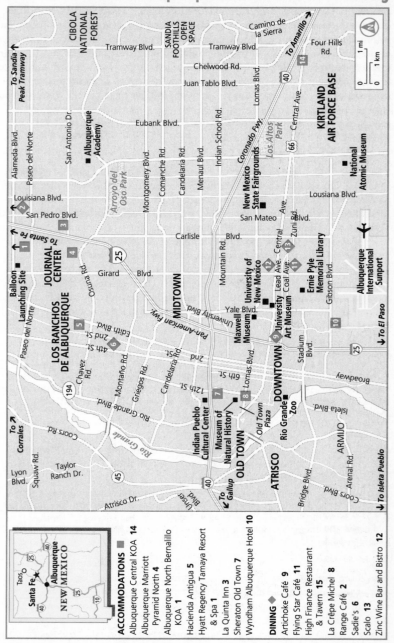

ACCOMMODATIONS ■

Albuquerque Central KOA **14**
Albuquerque Marriott Pyramid North **4**
Albuquerque North Bernalillo KOA **1**
Hacienda Antigua **5**
Hyatt Regency Tamaya Resort & Spa **3**
La Quinta Inn **3**
Sheraton Old Town **7**
Wyndham Albuquerque Hotel **10**

DINING ◆

Artichoke Café **9**
Flying Star Café **11**
High Finance Restaurant & Tavern **15**
La Crêpe Michel **8**
Range Café **2**
Sadie's **6**
Scalo **13**
Zinc Wine Bar and Bistro **12**

are gracefully and comfortably furnished with antiques. La Capilla, the home's former chapel, is furnished with a queen-size bed, a fireplace, and a carving of St. Francis (the patron saint of the garden). La Sala has a king-size bed and a large Jacuzzi, with a view of the Sandia Mountains. All the rooms are equipped with fireplaces and signature soaps. A gourmet breakfast is served in the garden during warm weather and by the fire in winter. The inn is a 20-minute drive from the airport. Light sleepers, beware—the Santa Fe Railroad runs by this inn, with one to three trains passing by each night.

6708 Tierra Dr. NW, Albuquerque, NM 87107. ☏ **800/201-2986** or 505/345-5399. Fax 505/345-3855. www. haciendantigua.com. 8 units. $129–$209 double. Extra person $25. Rates include breakfast. AE, MC, V. Free parking. Pets accepted; $30 fee. **Amenities:** Outdoor pool; Jacuzzi. *In room:* A/C, TV/VCR, coffeemaker, hair dryer.

NEAR ALBUQUERQUE

Hyatt Regency Tamaya Resort and Spa ★★★   This is the spot for a get-away-from-it-all luxury vacation. Set in the hills above the lush Rio Grande Valley on Santa Ana Pueblo, this Pueblo-style resort offers a 16,000-square-foot full-service spa and fitness center, an 18-hole championship golf course designed by Gary Panks, and views of the Sandia Mountains. Rooms are spacious, with large tile bathrooms. Request one that faces the mountains for one of the state's most spectacular vistas. Other rooms look out across a large courtyard, where the pools and hot tub are. Though the resort is surrounded by acres of quiet countryside, it's only 15 minutes from Albuquerque and 45 minutes from Santa Fe. The concierge offers trips to attractions, as well as on-site activities such as hot air balloon rides, horseback rides, and nature/cultural walks or carriage rides by the river. Plan at least one dinner at the innovative Corn Maiden.

1300 Tuyuna Trail, Santa Ana Pueblo, NM 87004. ☏ **800/55-HYATT** or 505/867-1234. www.hyatt.com. 350 units. May–Oct $200–$350 double; Nov–Apr $135–$250 double. Suite rates available upon request. Ask about spa, horseback riding, golf, and family packages. AE, DC, DISC, MC, V. Free parking. From I-25 take exit 242, following US 550 west to Tamaya Blvd.; drive 1½ miles to the resort. **Amenities:** 2 restaurants; 2 snack bars; lounge; 3 outdoor pools (heated year-round); golf course; 2 tennis courts; health club and spa; children's programs; concierge; tour desk; elaborate business center; room service; laundry; basketball court. *In room:* A/C, TV, dataport, fridge, coffeemaker, hair dryer, iron, safe.

RV PARKS

Albuquerque Central KOA   This RV park in the foothills east of Albuquerque is a good choice for those who want to be close to town. It offers lots of amenities and convenient freeway access. Cabins are available.

12400 Skyline Rd. NE, Albuquerque, NM 87123. ☏ **800/562-7781** or 505/296-2729. www.koa.com. $19–$36 tent site; $33–$51 RV site, depending on hookup; $38–$55 1-room cabin; $48–$65 2-room cabin. All prices valid for up to 2 people. Extra adult $5, child with 2 adults $3. AE, DISC, MC, V. Free parking. Pets accepted. **Amenities:** Outdoor pool (summer only); Jacuzzi; bike rentals; store; coin-op laundry; bathhouse; miniature golf; playground; wheelchair-accessible restroom.

Albuquerque North Bernalillo KOA ★   More than 1,000 cottonwood and pine trees shade this park, and in the warm months many flowers bloom. Located at the foot of the mountains, 14 miles from Albuquerque, this campground has plenty of amenities. Rates include a daily pancake breakfast. Reservations are recommended. Six camping cabins are also available.

555 Hill Rd., Bernalillo, NM 87004. ☏ **800/562-3616** or 505/867-5227. www.koa.com. $20–$22 tent site; $30–$36 RV site, depending on hookup; $35 1-bedroom cabin; $45 2-bedroom cabin. Rates include pancake breakfast and are valid for up to 2 people. Extra person $4. Children under 6 stay free with parent. AE, DISC, MC, V. Free parking. Pets accepted. **Amenities:** Restaurant; outdoor pool (summer only); store; coin-op laundry; playground; free outdoor movies.

4 Where to Dine

For the locations of these restaurants, see the map "Central Albuquerque Accommodations & Dining" on p. 239.

OLD TOWN & VICINITY

La Crêpe Michel ⭐⭐ FRENCH   For years my father raved about the crepes at this small cafe tucked away in a secluded walkway not far from the plaza. Finally, he took me there, and now I understand what all the fuss was about. Run by chef Claudie Zamet-Wilcox from France, it has a cozy, informal European feel, with checked table coverings and simple furnishings. Service is friendly and calm, which makes this a good place for a romantic meal. You can't miss with any of the crepes. The *crêpe aux fruits de mer* (with a blend of sea scallops, bay scallops, and shrimp in a velouté sauce with mushrooms) is especially nice, as is the *crêpe à la volaille* (chunks of chicken in cream sauce with mushrooms and Madeira wine). For a heartier meal, try one of the specials listed on the board on the wall, such as beef filet (tenderloin finished with either black peppercorn–brandy cream sauce or Roquefort-brandy cream sauce) or *saumon au poivre vert* (filet of salmon with green peppercorn–brandy sauce). For dessert, don't leave without having a *crêpe aux fraises* (strawberry crepe). To accompany your meal, choose from a carefully planned beer and wine menu.

400 San Felipe St. NW. ⓒ 505/242-1251. Reservations recommended on weekends. Main courses $6–$24. MC, V. Tues–Sun 11:30am–2pm; Thurs–Sat 6–9pm.

Sadie's ⭐ *Kids* NEW MEXICAN   Many New Mexicans lament the lost days when this restaurant was in a bowling alley. In fact, much of my family has refused to go to its new, larger location, fearing that it left its good food behind. Well, it hasn't. Sure, you can no longer hear the pins fall, and the main dining room is a little too big and the atmosphere a little too bright, but something is still drawing crowds: It's the food— simply some of the best in New Mexico, with tasty sauces and large portions. I recommend the enchilada, either chicken or beef. The delicious stuffed *sopaipilla* dinner is one of the signature dishes. All meals come with chips and salsa, beans, and *sopaipillas*. There's a full bar, with excellent margaritas (and TV screens for you sports lovers). A casual atmosphere where kids can be themselves makes this a nice spot for families.

6230 4th St. NW. ⓒ 505/345-5339. Main courses $7–$14. AE, DC, DISC, MC, V. Mon–Sat 11am–10pm; Sun 11am–9pm.

DOWNTOWN

Artichoke Cafe ⭐⭐ CONTINENTAL   An art gallery as well as a restaurant, this popular spot has modern paintings and sculptures set against azure walls, a hint at the innovative dining experience. Set in three rooms, with dim lighting, this is a nice romantic place. The staff is friendly and efficient, though a little slow on busy nights. I was impressed by the list of special drinks: a variety of interesting waters that included my favorite, Ame, as well as ginger beer, Jamaican iced coffee, microbrews, and an excellent list of California and French wines. You might start with an artichoke, steamed with three dipping sauces, or have roasted garlic with Montrachet goat cheese. For lunch, there are a number of salads and gourmet sandwiches, as well as dishes such as garlic and lime prawns with orzo. Check out the fresh fish specials; my favorite is wahoo on glass noodles with miso broth. From the menu, try pumpkin ravioli with butternut squash, spinach, and ricotta filling with hazelnut-sage butter sauce.

424 Central Ave. SE. ⓒ 505/243-0200. Reservations recommended. Main courses $7–$12 lunch, $13–$24 dinner. AE, DC, DISC, MC, V. Mon–Fri 11am–2:30pm; Mon 5:30–9pm; Tues–Sat 5:30–10pm; Sun 5–9pm.

THE NORTHEAST HEIGHTS

High Finance Restaurant and Tavern ✦ CONTINENTAL   People don't rave about the food at this restaurant, but they do rave about the experience of eating here. Set high above Albuquerque, at the top of the Sandia Peak Tramway, it offers a fun and romantic adventure. The decor includes lots of shiny brass, and the service is decent. You might start with sesame-fried calamari, served with greens and Thai dipping sauce. There are a number of pasta dishes, or you can try skillet-roasted ahi tuna served with spicy curry glaze. For meat lovers, there's prime rib or a filet. High Finance has a full bar. The restaurant recommends that you arrive at the Tramway base 45 minutes before your reservation.

40 Tramway Rd. NE (atop Sandia Peak). ✆ 505/243-9742. www.highfinancerestaurant.com. Reservations recommended. Main courses $8–$13 lunch, $15–$45 dinner. Tramway $10 with dinner reservations ($15 without). AE, DC, DISC, MC, V. Summer daily 11am–9pm; winter daily 11am–8pm.

UNIVERSITY & NOB HILL

Flying Star Cafe CAFE/BAKERY   The new Flying Star Cafe makes good on its promise of uptown food with down-home ingredients. This restaurant, with four locations, has been around Albuquerque awhile, under the moniker Double Rainbow, but it's been renamed and revamped into a hipper restaurant with excellent contemporary international food. **Beware:** During mealtime, this branch (the university location) gets packed and rowdy. The selections range broadly, from 16 breakfast options to homemade soups and salads to sandwiches and pasta (and pizza at the Juan Tabo and Rio Grande locations). Try the Rancher's melt (New Zealand sirloin sautéed with green chile, provolone, and horseradish on sourdough), or Buddha's bowl (sautéed vegetables in ginger sauce with tofu over jasmine rice). Flying Star also has locations at 4501 Juan Tabo Blvd. NE (✆ 505/275-8311); 8001 Menaul Blvd. NE (✆ 505/293-6911); and 4026 Rio Grande Blvd. NW (✆ 505/344-6714). They don't serve alcohol, but they do brew up plenty of espresso and cappuccino. Hours vary, but all locations serve breakfast, lunch, and dinner daily.

3416 Central Ave. SE. ✆ 505/255-6633. Reservations not accepted. All menu items under $10. AE, DISC, MC, V. Daily 6am–11pm.

Scalo ✦ INTERNATIONAL/ITALIAN   This Italian restaurant is a local favorite, but over the years frequent chef turnover has made it less reliable than it once was, and the service varies greatly as well. The place has a simple, bistro-style elegance, with white-linen-clothed tables indoors, plus outdoor tables on a covered, temperature-controlled patio. The kitchen, which makes its own pasta and breads, has recently moved to a more international menu and offers meals in small, medium, and large portions. Seasonal menus focus on New Mexico–grown produce. One signature dish is risotto-fried calamari with spicy marinara sauce. A hearty main dish is the double-cut pork chop with champagne-roasted peaches, kale, and fried shallots. The daily specials are big hits. Dessert selections change daily. There's a good wine list, from which you can sample 30 wines by the glass, and a full bar.

3500 Central Ave. SE. ✆ 505/255-8781. Reservations recommended. Main courses $6–$12 lunch, $8–$26 dinner. AE, DC, DISC, MC, V. Tues–Thurs 11:30am–10pm; Fri 11:30am–11pm; Sat 5–11pm; Sun 5–10pm.

Zinc Wine Bar and Bistro ✦✦ NEW AMERICAN   In a moody, urban atmosphere with wood floors and a high ceiling, this newest "in" place serves imaginative food meticulously prepared. The bi-level dining room with well-spaced tables can get crowded and noisy at peak hours (especially under the balcony, so avoid sitting there then). Service is congenial but inconsistent. Businesspeople and others fill the seats here, dining on such treats as blackened flank steak, Greek salad at lunch (my favorite), or portobello-crusted Alaskan halibut with chorizo sausage polenta at dinner. The restaurant offers other inventive elements, such as "wine flights," which allow diners to sample a variety of wines from a particular region for a fairly reasonable set price. Or you may opt for an excellent martini from the full bar. In the lower level, a lounge serves less formally in a wine-cellar atmosphere with live music playing 2 to 3 nights a week (open Mon–Sat 4pm–1am; food served until midnight).

3009 Central Ave. NE. ⓒ 505/254-ZINC. Reservations recommended. Main courses $7.50–$12 lunch, $14–$25 dinner. AE, DC, DISC, MC, V. Sun–Fri 11am–2:30pm; Mon–Thurs 5–10pm; Fri–Sat 5–11pm.

OUTSIDE ALBUQUERQUE

Range Café ⭐ *Kids* NEW MEXICAN/AMERICAN   This cafe on the main drag of Bernalillo, about 15 minutes north of Albuquerque, is a perfect place to stop on your way out of town. Housed in what was once an old drugstore, the restaurant has a pressed-tin ceiling and is decorated with Western touches, such as cowboy boots and whimsical art. The food ranges from enchiladas and burritos to chicken-fried steak to more elegant meals. The proprietors and chef have come from such notable restaurants as Scalo in Albuquerque (p. 242) and Prairie Star at Santa Ana Pueblo, so you can count on great food. For breakfast, try pancakes or the breakfast burrito. For lunch or dinner, I recommend Tom's meatloaf, served with roasted-garlic mashed potatoes, mushroom gravy, and sautéed vegetables. For dinner, you might try pan-seared trout with sun-dried tomato and caper butter sauce. Taos Cow ice cream is the order for dessert, or try the baked goods and specialty drinks from the full bar. No smoking is permitted. In the same locale, the Lizard Rodeo Lounge is a smoke-free, hoppin' place with Wild West decor that offers live music many nights. There's also a retail space that sells local art and New Mexico wines. Two Albuquerque branches of the restaurant are at 4200 Wyoming Blvd. NE (ⓒ **505/293-2633**), and 2200 Menaul Blvd. NE (ⓒ **505/888-1660**).

925 Camino del Pueblo (P.O. Box 1780), Bernalillo. ⓒ 505/867-1700. Reservations accepted for parties of 8 or more. Breakfast and lunch $4–$9, dinner $9–$20. AE, DISC, MC, V. Summer Sun–Thurs 7:30am–10pm, Fri–Sat 7:30am–10:30pm; winter Sun–Thurs 7:30am–9:30pm, Fri–Sat 7:30am–10pm. Closed Thanksgiving, Dec 25.

5 What to See & Do

Albuquerque's original town site, known today as Old Town, is the central point of interest for visitors. Here, grouped around the Plaza, are the venerable Church of San Felipe de Neri and numerous restaurants, art galleries, and crafts shops. Several important museums are close by. Within a few blocks is the Albuquerque Biological Park (near Central Ave. and Tingley Dr. NW).

But don't get stuck in Old Town. Elsewhere you will find the Sandia Peak Tramway, the Petroglyphs National Monument, and a number of natural attractions. Within day-trip range are several pueblos and a trio of significant monuments (see "Touring the Jemez Mountain Trail," later in this chapter).

THE TOP ATTRACTIONS

Albuquerque Museum of Art and History ⭐ *Kids*   Take an interesting journey down into the caverns of New Mexico's past in this museum on the outskirts of Old Town. Drawing on the largest U.S. collection of Spanish colonial artifacts, displays here include Don Quixote–style helmets, swords, and horse armor. You can wander through an 18th-century house compound with adobe floor and walls, and see gear used by *vaqueros,* the original cowboys who came to the area in the 16th century. A weaving exhibition allows kids to try spinning wool, and a trapping section provides them with pelts to touch. An old-style theater shows two films on Albuquerque history. In the History Hopscotch area, kids can explore an old trunk or play with antique blocks and other toys. An Old Town walking tour originates here at 11am Tuesday to Sunday during spring, summer, and fall. The upper floors house permanent art collections and, best of all, a huge exhibit space where you'll find some extraordinary shows. A gift shop sells books and jewelry and has a nice selection of Navajo dolls.

2000 Mountain Rd. NW, Albuquerque, NM 87104. ⓒ 505/243-7255. www.albuquerquemuseum.com. Admission $4 adults, $2 seniors 65 and older and children 4–12. Tues–Sun 9am–5pm. Closed major holidays.

Indian Pueblo Cultural Center ★ *Kids* Owned and operated as a nonprofit organization by the 19 pueblos of New Mexico, this is a fine place to begin an exploration of Native American culture. Located about a mile northeast of Old Town, this museum—modeled after Pueblo Bonito, a spectacular 9th-century ruin in Chaco Culture National Historic Park—consists of several parts.

Begin your exploration in the basement, where a permanent exhibit depicts the **evolution of the various pueblos** from prehistory to the present, including displays of the distinctive handcrafts of each community. Note especially how pottery differs in concept and design from pueblo to pueblo. You'll also find a small screening room where you can see films of some of New Mexico's most noted Native American artists, including San Ildefonso potter María Martinez, firing her pottery with open flames.

The **Pueblo House Children's Museum,** in a separate building, is a hands-on experience that gives children the opportunity to learn about and understand the evolution of Pueblo culture. There they can touch pot shards, play with *heishi* (shell) drills, and even don fox tails and dance.

Upstairs in the main building is an enormous **gift shop** featuring fine pottery, rugs, sand paintings, kachinas, drums, jewelry, Southwestern clothing, and souvenirs, among other things. Prices are quite reasonable.

Every weekend throughout the year, **Native American dancers** perform at 11am and 2pm in an outdoor arena surrounded by original murals. Often, artisans demonstrate their crafts there as well. During certain weeks of the year, such as during the Balloon Fiesta, dances are performed daily.

A restaurant serves traditional Native American foods. I wouldn't eat a full meal here, but it's a good place to try some Indian fry bread and a bowl of *posole.*

2401 12th St. NW, Albuquerque, NM 87104. ⓒ 800/766-4405 or 505/843-7270. www.indianpueblo.org. Admission $4 adults, $3 seniors, $1 students, free for children under 5. AE, DISC, MC, V. Daily 9am–4:30pm; restaurant 8am–3pm. Closed Jan 1, Memorial Day, July 4, Labor Day, Thanksgiving, Dec 25.

National Hispanic Cultural Center ★ Located in the historic Barelas neighborhood on the Camino Real, this gem of Albuquerque museums offers a rich cultural journey through hundreds of years of history and across the globe. It explores Hispanic culture and life with visual arts, drama, music, dance, and other programs. I most enjoyed the 11,000-square-foot gallery space, which exhibits exciting contemporary and traditional works. Look for photographs by Miguel Gandert. An interesting 2004 exhibit was *Corridos Sin Fronteras,* which re-created the historical development of the *corrida* (a song portraying an adventure) in Mexico and the Southwestern U.S. A restaurant offers New Mexican and American food. It's a good spot to sample authentic

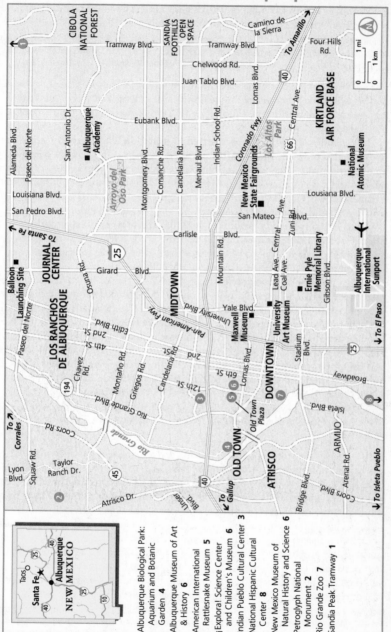

Albuquerque Biological Park: Aquarium and Botanic Garden **4**
Albuquerque Museum of Art & History **6**
American International Rattlesnake Museum **5**
¡Explora! Science Center and Children's Museum **6**
Indian Pueblo Cultural Center **3**
National Hispanic Cultural Center **8**
New Mexico Museum of Natural History and Science **6**
Petroglyph National Monument **2**
Rio Grande Zoo **7**
Sandia Peak Tramway **1**

regional dishes such as tacos and enchiladas from a buffet or off the menu. My favorite is the tortilla burger (a burger served in a flour tortilla, with all the fixin's).

1701 4th St. SW (corner of 4th St. and Av. Cesar Chavez). ℂ **505/246-2261**. Fax 505/246-2613. www.nhccnm.org. Admission Tues–Sat $3 adults, $2 seniors 60 and over, free for children under 17; Sun $1 adults and seniors. AE, DISC, MC, V. Tues–Sun 10am–5pm; restaurant 8am–3pm. Closed Jan 1, Easter, Memorial Day, Labor Day, Dec 25.

Old Town ★★ A maze of cobbled courtyard walkways leads to hidden patios and gardens where you'll find many of Old Town's 150 galleries and shops. Adobe buildings, many refurbished in the Pueblo Revival style of the 1950s, group around the tree-shaded plaza, created in 1780.

The buildings of Old Town once served as mercantile shops, grocery stores, and government offices, but the importance of Old Town as Albuquerque's commercial center declined after 1880, when the railroad came through 1¼ miles east of the plaza and businesses relocated to be closer to the trains. Old Town clung to its historical and sentimental roots, but the quarter fell into disrepair until the 1930s and 1940s, when artisans and other shop owners rediscovered it and the tourism industry burgeoned.

When Albuquerque was established in 1706, the first building erected was the **Church of San Felipe de Neri,** which faces the north side of the plaza. It's a cozy church with wonderful stained-glass windows and vivid *retablos* (religious paintings). It has been in almost continuous use for nearly 300 years.

Though you'll wade through a few trinket and T-shirt shops on the plaza, don't be fooled: Old Town is an excellent place to shop. Look for good buys from the Native Americans selling jewelry on the plaza, especially silver bracelets and strung turquoise. If you want to take something fun home and spend very little, buy a dyed corn necklace. Your best bet when wandering around Old Town is to just peek into shops, but there are a few places you'll definitely want to spend time. See "Shopping," later in this chapter, for a list of recommendations. An excellent Old Town historic walking tour originates at the Albuquerque Museum of Art and History (see above) at 11am Tuesday to Sunday during spring, summer, and fall. Plan to spend 2 to 3 hours strolling around.

Northeast of Central Ave. and Rio Grande Blvd. NW. Old Town Visitor Center: 303 Romero St. NW (across the street from the Church of San Felipe de Neri). ℂ **505/243-3215**. Visitor center daily 9am–5pm summer; 9:30am–4:30pm rest of the year.

Sandia Peak Tramway ★★ *Kids* This fun and exciting half-day or evening outing allows incredible views of Albuquerque's landscape and wildlife. The Sandia Peak Tram is a "jigback"; in other words, as one car approaches the top, the other nears the bottom. The two pass halfway through the trip, in the midst of a 1½-mile "clear span" of unsupported cable between the second tower and the upper terminal.

Several hiking trails are available on Sandia Peak, and one of them—La Luz Trail—takes you on a steep and rigorous trek from the base to the summit. The views in all directions are extraordinary. *Note:* The trails on Sandia may not be suitable for children. A popular and expensive restaurant, High Finance Restaurant and Tavern, sits at Sandia's summit (see "Where to Dine," earlier in this chapter). Special tram rates apply with dinner reservations. Note that the tram does not operate on very windy days.

10 Tramway Loop NE, Albuquerque, NM 87122. ℂ **505/856-7325**. Fax 505/856-6335. www.sandiapeak.com. Admission $15 adults, $12 seniors, $10 children 5–12, free for children under 5. Memorial Day to Labor Day daily 9am–9pm; spring and fall Thurs–Tues 9am–8pm, Wed 5–8pm; ski season Thurs–Tues 9am–8pm, Wed noon–8pm. Closed 2 weeks each spring and fall for maintenance; check website. Parking $1 daily. AE, DISC, MC, V. To reach the base of the tram, take I-25 north to Tramway Rd. (exit 234), then proceed east about 5 miles on Tramway Rd. (NM 556); or take Tramway Blvd., exit 167 (NM 556), north of I-40 approximately 8½ miles.

Cooking School

If you've fallen in love with New Mexican and Southwestern cooking during your stay (or if you did even before you arrived), you might like to sign up for cooking classes with Jane Butel, a leading Southwestern cooking authority, author of 14 cookbooks, and host of the national TV show *Jane Butel's Southwestern Kitchen*. At **Jane Butel Cooking School** ✮, at La Posada de Albuquerque, 125 Second St. NW (© **800/472-8229** or 505/243-2622; fax 505/243-8296; www.janebutel.com), you'll learn the history and techniques of Southwestern cuisine and have ample opportunity for hands-on preparation. If you choose the weeklong session, you'll start by learning about chiles and move on to native breads and dishes, appetizers, beverages, and desserts.

MORE SIGHTS TO SEE & PLACES TO BE
OTHER ATTRACTIONS
Petroglyph National Monument ✮ *Kids*   These lava flows were a hunting and gathering area for prehistoric Native Americans, who left a chronicle of their beliefs etched on the dark basalt boulders. Some 25,000 petroglyphs provide a nice outdoor adventure after a morning in a museum. You'll want to stop at the visitor center to get a map, check out the interactive computer, and, in summer, hook up with a ranger-led tour. From there, you can drive north to the Boca Negra area, where you have a choice of three trails. Mesa Point Trail (30 min.) climbs quickly up the side of a hill, offering many petroglyph sightings as well as an outstanding view of the Sandia Mountains. If you're traveling with your dog, you can bring her along on the Rinconada Trail. Hikers can have fun searching the rocks for more petroglyphs; many remain to be found. This trail, a few miles south of the visitor center, runs for miles around a huge *rincon* (corner) at the base of the lava flow. The third option, the Volcanoes Trail, offers vast views of Albuquerque. Camping is not permitted in the park; it's strictly for day use, with picnic areas, drinking water, and restrooms provided.

6001 Unser Blvd. NW (at Western Trail, 3 miles north of I-40). © **505/899-0205.** Fax 505/899-0207. www.nps.gov/petr. Admission $1 per vehicle weekdays, $2 weekends. DISC, MC, V. Visitor Center and Boca Negra area daily 8am–5pm. Closed Jan 1, Thanksgiving, Dec 25.

6 Especially for Kids

Albuquerque Biological Park: Aquarium and Botanic Garden ✮ *Kids*   For those of us born and raised in the desert, the aquarium quenches years of soul thirst. The self-guided tour begins with a beautifully produced 9-minute film that describes the course of the Rio Grande from its origin to the Gulf Coast. Then you'll move on to the touch pool, where at certain times you can touch hermit crabs and starfish. You'll pass by a replica of a salt marsh, where a gentle tidal wave moves in and out, and you'll explore the eel tank, an arched aquarium you walk through. There's a colorful coral-reef exhibit, as well as the culminating show, in a 285,000-gallon shark tank, where many species of fish and 15 to 20 sand-tiger, brown, and nurse sharks swim around, looking ominous.

In a state-of-the-art 10,000-square-foot conservatory, you'll find the botanical garden, split into two sections. The smaller one houses the desert collection and features plants from the lower Chihuahuan and Sonoran deserts, including unique species from Baja California. The larger pavilion exhibits the Mediterranean collection and includes many exotic species native to the Mediterranean climates of southern California, South Africa, Australia, and the Mediterranean Basin. Allow at least 2 hours to see both parks. There is a restaurant on the premises.

In December, the River of Lights Holiday Light Display runs Tuesday through Sunday; from June through August, you can attend Thursday evening concerts.

2601 Central Ave. NW, Albuquerque, NM 87104. ℂ 505/764-6200. www.cabq.gov/biopark. Admission $7 adults ($10 with Rio Grande Zoo admission), $3 seniors 65 and over and children under 13 ($5 with Rio Grande Zoo admission). Ticket sales stop 30 min. before closing. MC, V. June–Aug Tues–Fri 9am–5pm, Sat–Sun 9am–6pm; Sept–May Tues–Sun 9am–5pm. Closed Jan 1, Thanksgiving, Dec 25.

American International Rattlesnake Museum *Finds* *Kids*   This unique museum, just off Old Town Plaza, exhibits living specimens of common, uncommon, and very rare rattlesnakes of North, Central, and South America in naturally landscaped habitats. Oddities such as albino and patternless rattlesnakes are included, as is a display popular with youngsters: baby rattlesnakes. More than 30 species can be seen, followed by a 7-minute film. Throughout the museum are rattlesnake artifacts from early American history, Native American culture, medicine, the arts, and advertising. The gift shop sells a variety of items, all with an emphasis on rattlesnakes.

202 San Felipe St. NW. ℂ 505/242-6569. www.rattlesnakes.com. Admission $2.50 adults, $2 seniors, $1.50 children. AE, DISC, MC, V. Mon–Sat 10am–6pm; Sun noon–5pm.

¡Explora! Science Center and Children's Museum *Kids*   A center for lifelong learning, ¡Explora! houses more than 250 hands-on scientific exhibits for visitors of all ages, on topics as diverse as water, the Rio Grande, light and optics, and energy. It features exhibits utilizing technology that is creatively accessible to the public and exhibits that engage visitors in creating all kinds of art.

1701 Mountain Rd. ℂ 505/224-8300. Fax 505/224-8325. www.explora.mus.nm.us. Admission $7 adults, $5 seniors 65 and over and children 1–11, free for children under 1. Mon–Sat 10am–6pm; Sun noon–6pm.

New Mexico Museum of Natural History and Science *★★* *Kids*   This museum takes you through 12 billion years of natural history, from the formation of the universe to the present day. Begin by looking at a display of stones and gems, then stroll through the "Age of Giants" display, where you'll see dinosaur skeletons cast from the real bones. Next, you come into the Cretaceous Period and learn of the progression of flooding in the southwestern United States, beginning 100 million years ago and continuing until 66 million years ago, when New Mexico became dry. This exhibit takes you through a tropical oasis, with aquariums of alligator gars, fish that were here 100 million years ago and still exist today. Next, step into the Evolator (kids love this!), a simulated time-travel ride that moves and rumbles, taking you 1¼ miles up (or down) and through 38 million years of history. The journey continues through many interactive displays. Be sure to check out the LodeStar Astronomy Center, a sophisticated planetarium with the Virtual Voyages Simulation theater. An additional fee applies for those exhibits, as well as the DynaTheater, which surrounds you with images and sound. A gift shop sells imaginative nature games and other curios. This museum has good access for people with disabilities.

1801 Mountain Rd. NW. © 505/841-2800. http://museums.state.nm.us/nmmnh/nmmnh.html. Admission $5 adults, $4 seniors, $2 children 3–12, free for children under 3. Extra charge (about $6 adults, $3 children) for DynaTheater, Planetarium, and Virtual Voyages. Discounted combination tickets available. Daily 9am–5pm. Closed Thanksgiving, Dec 25, and Mon in Jan and Sept except major holidays.

Rio Grande Zoo ★ *Kids*   More than 1,200 animals from 300 species live on 60 acres of riverside bosque among ancient cottonwoods. Open-moat exhibits with animals in naturalized habitats are a treat for visitors. Major exhibits include polar bears, giraffes, sea lions (with underwater viewing), a bird show, and ape country. The zoo has an especially fine collection of elephants, mountain lions, koalas, reptiles, and native Southwestern species. A petting zoo is open during the summer. There are numerous snack bars on the zoo grounds, and La Ventana Gift Shop carries film and souvenirs. Also check out the seal and sea lion feeding at 10:30am and 3:30pm daily and the summer Zoo Music Concert Series.

903 10th St. SW. © 505/764-6200. www.cabq.gov/biopark/zoo. Admission $7 adults ($10 with Albuquerque Biological Park admission), $3 seniors and children 3–12 ($5 with Aquarium and Botanic Garden admission), free for children under 3. Daily 9am–4:30pm (6pm summer weekends). Closed Jan 1, Thanksgiving, Dec 25.

7 Getting Outside
BALLOONING
Visitors have a choice of several hot-air balloon operators; rates start at about $135 per person per hour. Call **Rainbow Ryders,** 11520 San Bernardino NE (© **505/823-1111**), or **World Balloon Corporation,** 1103 La Poblana NW (© **505/293-6800**). If you have your heart set on a balloon flight, reserve a time early in your trip, because flights are sometimes canceled due to bad weather. That way, if you have to reschedule, you'll have enough time to do so.

If you'd rather just watch, go to the annual **Albuquerque International Balloon Fiesta** ★★, the first and second weekends of October (see the "Calendar of Events," in chapter 2, for details).

BIKING
Albuquerque is a major bicycling hub in the summer, for both road racers and mountain bikers. For an excellent map of bicycle routes, call the **Albuquerque Parks & Recreation Department** (© **505/768-3550**) or visit **www.cabq.gov**, click on "Interactive Maps (GIS)," and then click on "Bike Paths." A great place to bike is **Sandia Peak** (© **505/242-9133**; www.sandiapeak.com) in Cíbola National Forest. You can't take your bike on the tram, but a chairlift is available for uphill or downhill transportation with a bike. Bike rentals are available at the top and bottom of the chairlift. They cost $38 for adult bikes, $28 for junior ones. The lift costs $14 and runs on weekends, plus Friday in July and August, though you'll want to call to be sure. Helmets are mandatory. The clearly marked trails range from easy to very difficult.

Down in the valley, the **bosque trail** that runs along the Rio Grande is accessible through the Rio Grande Nature Center (see "Especially for Kids," above). To the east, the **Foothills Trail** runs along the base of the mountains. It's a fun 7-mile trail that offers excellent views. Reach it by driving east from downtown on Montgomery Boulevard, past the intersection with Tramway Boulevard. Go left on Glenwood Hills Drive and head north about a half-mile before turning right onto a short road that leads to the Embudito trail head.

Northeast Cyclery, 8305 Menaul Blvd. NE (© **505/299-1210**), rents bikes for $25 per day for front-suspension mountain bikes, $35 per day for road bikes. Multiday discounts are available. Unfortunately, the shop doesn't rent children's bikes. Rentals come with helmets.

BIRD-WATCHING

Bosque del Apache National Wildlife Refuge ★★ (© **505/835-1828**) is a haven for migratory waterfowl such as snow geese and cranes. It's 90 miles south of Albuquerque on I-25, and it's well worth the drive. For details, see chapter 11.

FISHING

There are no real fishing opportunities in Albuquerque, but there is a nearby fishing area known as **Shady Lakes** (© **505/898-2568**). Nestled among cottonwood trees, it's near I-25 on Albuquerque's north side. The most common catches are rainbow trout, black bass, bluegill, and channel catfish. To reach Shady Lakes, take I-25 north to the Tramway exit. Follow Tramway Road west for a mile and then go right on NM 313 for a half-mile. **Sandia Lakes Recreational Area** (© **505/897-3971**), also on NM 313, is another popular fishing spot. It has a bait-and-tackle shop.

GOLF

The Albuquerque area has quite a few public courses. The **Championship Golf Course at the University of New Mexico,** 3601 University Blvd. SE (© **505/277-4546**), is one of the best in the Southwest; *Golf Digest* rated it one of the country's top 25 public courses. **Paradise Hills Golf Course,** 10035 Country Club Lane NW (© **505/898-7001**), is a popular 18-hole course on the west side of town. Other Albuquerque courses are **Ladera,** 3401 Ladera Dr. NW (© **505/836-4449**); **Los Altos,** 9717 Copper Ave. NE (© **505/298-1897**); **Puerto del Sol,** 1800 Girard Blvd. SE (© **505/265-5636**); and **Arroyo del Oso,** 7001 Osuna Rd. NE (© **505/884-7505**). Greens fees range from $20 to $80, with most averaging about $30. When not included, cart rentals run about $15.

If you're willing to drive a short distance, you can play at the **Santa Ana Golf Club at Santa Ana Pueblo,** 288 Prairie Star Rd., Bernalillo (© **505/867-9464**), just outside Albuquerque. The *New York Times* rated it one of the best public golf courses in the country. Club rentals are available (call for information). In addition, **Isleta Pueblo,** 4001 Hwy. 47 (© **505/869-0950**), south of Albuquerque, has an 18-hole course.

HIKING

The 1.5-million-acre **Cíbola National Forest** offers ample hiking opportunities. In town, the best hike is the **Embudito Trail,** which heads up into the foothills, with spectacular views down across Albuquerque. The 5½-mile one-way hike is moderate to difficult. Allow 1 to 8 hours, depending on how far you want to go. To get there, drive east from downtown on Montgomery Boulevard past the intersection with Tramway Boulevard. Go left on Glenwood Hills Drive and head north about a half-mile before turning right onto a short road that leads to the trail head. The premier Sandia Mountain hike is **La Luz Trail,** a strenuous journey from the Sandia foothills to the top of the Crest. It's a 15-mile round-trip jaunt, or half that if you take the Sandia Peak Tramway (see "The Top Attractions," earlier in this chapter) up or down. Allow a full day. Access is off Tramway Boulevard and Forest Service Road 333. For details, contact the **Sandia Ranger Station,** Highway 337 south toward Tijeras (© **505/281-3304**).

Getting Pampered: The Spa Scene

If you're looking to get pampered, you have a few options. **Mark Prado Salon & Spa** (© 800/363-7115) offers treatments at four locations: 1100 Juan Tabo Blvd. NE (© **505/298-2983**), 8001 Wyoming Blvd. NE (© **505/856-7700**), 3500 Central Ave. SE 7B (© **505/266-2400**), and Cottonwood Mall, 10000 Coors Blvd. NE (© **505/897-2288**).

Albuquerque's most luxurious spa experience is at the **Hyatt Regency Tamaya Resort & Spa** (p. 240). A vast array of treatments, and a sauna and steam room, are available in a refined atmosphere near the Rio Grande, 15 minutes north of Albuquerque, near the village of Bernalillo.

HORSEBACK RIDING

If you want to get in a saddle and eat some trail dust, call the **Hyatt Regency Tamaya Resort and Spa,** 1300 Tuyuna Trail, Santa Ana Pueblo (© 505/771-6037). The resort offers 2½-hour-long rides near the Rio Grande for $60 per person. Children must be over 7 years of age and over 4 feet tall. The resort is about 15 miles north of Albuquerque. From I-25, take exit 242, follow US 550 west to Tamaya Boulevard, and drive 1½ miles to the resort.

SKIING

Sandia Peak Ski Area is a good place for family skiing. There are plenty of beginner and intermediate runs. (If you're looking for more challenge or more variety, head north to Santa Fe or Taos.) The ski area has twin base-to-summit chairlifts to its upper slopes at 10,360 feet, and a 1,700-foot vertical drop. There are 30 runs above the day lodge and ski-rental shop. Four chairs and two pomas accommodate 3,400 skiers an hour. All-day lift tickets are $40 for adults, $33 for ages 13 to 20, $30 for children under 13 and seniors ages 62 to 71, and free for children 46 inches tall or less in ski boots and seniors ages 72 and over; rental packages are available. The season runs mid-December to mid-March. Contact the ski area, 10 Tramway Loop NE (© 505/242-9133), for more information, or call © 505/857-8977 for ski conditions.

Cross-country skiers can enjoy the trails of the **Sandia Wilderness** from Sandia Peak Ski Area, or they can venture an hour north to the remote **Jemez Wilderness** and its hot springs.

TENNIS

Albuquerque has 29 public parks with tennis courts. Because of the city's size, your best bet is to call the **Albuquerque Convention and Visitors Bureau** (© 800/284-2282) to find out which park is closest to your hotel.

8 Spectator Sports

BASEBALL

The **Albuquerque Isotopes** (© 505/924-2255; www.albuquerquebaseball.com) of the Pacific Coast League play 72 home games at Isotopes Park. Tickets cost $5 to $10. The park is at 1601 Av. Cesar Chavez SE. Take I-25 south to Avenida Cesar Chavez, and go east to the intersection with University Boulevard.

BASKETBALL

The **University of New Mexico** Lobos play an average of 16 home games from late November to early March. Capacity crowds cheer the team at the 17,121-seat University Arena (fondly called "The Pit") at University and Stadium boulevards. The arena was the site of the NCAA championship tournament in 1983. For tickets and information, call ℂ **505/925-LOBO** (www.golobos.com).

FOOTBALL

The **UNM** football team plays from September to November, usually with five home games, at the 30,000-seat University of New Mexico Stadium, opposite both Albuquerque Sports Stadium and University Arena at University and Stadium boulevards. For tickets and information, call ℂ **505/925-LOBO** (www.golobos.com).

HOCKEY

The **New Mexico Scorpions** (ℂ **505/881-7825**; www.scorpionshockey.com) play in the Western Professional Hockey League. Their home ice is Tingley Coliseum, New Mexico State Fairgrounds, Central Avenue and Louisiana Boulevard.

9 Shopping

Visitors seeking regional specialties will find many **local artists** and **galleries** of interest in Albuquerque, although not as many as in Santa Fe and Taos. The galleries and regional fashion designers around the plaza in Old Town make up a kind of shopping center for travelers, with more than 40 merchants represented. The Sandia Pueblo runs its own **crafts market** at the reservation, off I-25 at Tramway Road, just beyond Albuquerque's northern city limits.

Albuquerque has three of the largest **shopping malls** in New Mexico, two within 2 blocks of each other on Louisiana Boulevard just north of I-40—Coronado Center and Winrock Center. The other is the Cottonwood Mall on the west mesa, at 10000 Coors Blvd. NW (ℂ **505/899-SHOP**).

Business hours vary, but shops are generally open Monday to Saturday 10am to 6pm; a few, especially in malls and during the high tourist season, are open on Sunday.

In Albuquerque the sales tax is 6.75%.

BEST BUYS

The best buys in Albuquerque are Southwestern regional items, including **arts and crafts** of all kinds—traditional Native American and Hispanic objects as well as contemporary works. In local Native American art, look for silver and turquoise jewelry, pottery, weavings, baskets, sand paintings, and Hopi kachina dolls. Hispanic folk art—hand-crafted furniture, tinwork and *retablos,* and religious paintings—is worth seeking out. The best contemporary art is in paintings, sculpture, jewelry, ceramics, and fiber art, including weaving.

Other items of potential interest are Southwestern fashions, gourmet foods, and unique local Native American and Hispanic creations.

By far the most **galleries** are in Old Town; others are around the city, with smaller groupings in the university district and the northeast heights. Consult the brochure published by the **Albuquerque Gallery Association,** *A Select Guide to Albuquerque Galleries,* or Wingspread Communications's annual *Collector's Guide to Albuquerque,* widely distributed at shops. Once a month, usually from 5 to 9pm on the third Friday, the

Outback Shopping

While cruising the remote desert lands between Albuquerque and Santa Fe, you may want to stop in at **Traditions! A Festival Marketplace,** on I-25, exit 257 (© **505/867-9700**). The open-air mall offers shoppers the chance to sample many forms of New Mexico culture, from art to jewelry to food to entertainment. It's open daily 10am to 8pm.

Albuquerque Art Business Association (© 505/244-0362 for information) sponsors an ArtsCrawl to dozens of galleries and studios. It's a great way to meet the artists.

You'll find some interesting shops in the Nob Hill area, which is just west of the University of New Mexico and has an Art Deco feel.

Following are some shopping recommendations for the Albuquerque area.

ARTS & CRAFTS

Amapola Gallery ✿   Fifty artists and craftspeople show their talents at this lovely cooperative gallery off a cobbled courtyard. You'll find pottery, paintings, textiles, baskets, jewelry, and other items. 206 Romero St. © **505/242-4311.**

Bien Mur Indian Market Center ✿   Sandia Pueblo's crafts market, on the reservation, sells turquoise and silver jewelry, pottery, baskets, kachina dolls, hand-woven rugs, sand paintings, and other arts and crafts. The market is open Monday through Saturday from 9am to 5:30pm, Sunday from 11am to 5pm. I-25 at Tramway Rd. NE. © **800/365-5400** or 505/821-5400.

Dartmouth Street Gallery ✿   This gallery features vapor mirage works of Larry Bell, tapestries by Nancy Kozikowski, and a variety of work by 40 other contemporary artists, most from New Mexico. 3011 Monte Vista NE. © **800/474-7751** or 505/266-7751. www.dsg-art.com.

Gallery One   This gallery features folk art, jewelry, contemporary crafts, cards and paper, and natural-fiber clothing. In the Nob Hill Shopping Center, 3500 Central Ave. SE. © **505/ 268-7449.**

Hispaniae in Old Town ✿ *Finds*   Day of the Dead people and Frida Kahlo faces greet you at this wild shop with everything from kitschy Mexican tableware to fine Oaxacan woodcarvings. 410 Romero St. NW. © **505/244-1533.**

La Piñata   This shop features—what else?—piñatas, in shapes from dinosaurs to parrots to pigs, as well as paper flowers, puppets, toys, and crushable bolero hats decorated with ribbons. No. 2 Patio Market (Old Town). © **505/242-2400.**

Mariposa Gallery ✿✿ *Value*   Eclectic contemporary art, jewelry, blown glass, and sculpture fill this Nob Hill shop, with prices that even a travel writer can afford. In Nob Hill Shopping Center, 3500 Central Ave. SE. © **505/268-6828.**

Ortega's Indian Arts and Crafts   An institution in Gallup, adjacent to the Navajo Reservation, Ortega's now has a store in Albuquerque. It sells, repairs, and appraises silver and turquoise jewelry. 6600 Menaul Blvd. NE, no. 359. © **505/881-1231.**

The Pueblo Loft (at Gallery One)   Owner Kitty Trask takes pride in the fact that all items featured here are crafted by Native Americans. For almost 15 years, her slogan has been, "Every purchase is an American Indian work of art." In the Nob Hill Shopping Center, 3500 Central Ave. SE. 𝒞 505/268-8764.

R. C. Gorman Nizhoni Gallery Old Town ⭐ The painting and sculpture of famed Navajo artist Gorman, a resident of Taos, are shown here. Most works are available in limited-edition lithographs. 323 Romero NW, Suite 1. 𝒞 505/843-7666.

Schelu Gallery ⭐⭐ Inventive pottery you'll want to use in your kitchen as well as bold textiles present a sojourn in color in this Old Town shop. 306 San Felipe NW. 𝒞 800/234-7985 or 505/765-5869.

Skip Maisel's *Value* If you want a bargain in Native American arts and crafts, this is the place to shop. You'll find a broad range of quality and price here in goods such as pottery, weavings, and kachinas. *Take note:* Adorning the outside of the store are murals painted in 1933 by notable Navajo painter Harrison Begay and Pueblo painter Pablita Velarde. 510 Central Ave. SW. 𝒞 505/242-6526.

Tanner Chaney Galleries ⭐ In business since 1875, this gallery has fine jewelry, pottery, rugs, and more. 323 Romero NW, no. 4 (Old Town). 𝒞 800/444-2242 or 505/247-2242.

Weyrich Gallery (Rare Vision Art Galerie) Contemporary paintings, sculpture, textiles, jewelry, and ceramics by regional and nonregional artists are on exhibit at this spacious midtown gallery. 2935D Louisiana Blvd. at Candelaria Rd. 𝒞 505/883-7410.

Wright's Collection of Indian Art This gallery, opened in 1907, features a private museum and carries fine handmade Native American arts and crafts, both contemporary and traditional. 1100 San Mateo Blvd. NE. 𝒞 505/266-0120.

BOOKS

Barnes & Noble On the west side, just north of Cottonwood Mall, this huge bookstore offers plenty of browsing room and a Starbucks for lounging. The store is known for its large children's section and weekly story-time readings. 3701 Ellison Dr. NW #A. 𝒞 505/792-4234. Also at the Coronado Center, 6600 Menaul Blvd. NE. 𝒞 505/883-8200.

Bookworks ⭐ This store stocks both new and used books and has one of the most complete Southwestern nonfiction and fiction sections in the region. A good place to linger, the store has a coffee bar and a stage area for readings. It also carries CDs and books on tape. 4022 Rio Grande Blvd. NW. 𝒞 505/344-8139.

Borders This branch of the popular chain carries a broad range of books, music, and videos, and schedules in-store appearances by authors, musicians, and artists. Winrock Center, 2100 Louisiana Blvd. NE. 𝒞 505/884-7711.

FOOD

The Candy Lady Having made chocolate for over 20 years, the Candy Lady is especially known for 21 varieties of fudge, including jalapeño flavor. 524 Romero NW, Old Town. 𝒞 800/214-7731 or 505/243-6239.

La Mexicana This is a great place to shop if you're a die-hard fan of Mexican food. Many items are imported from Mexico, and others, such as tortillas, tamales, and pastries, are made fresh daily. 423 Atlantic Ave. SW. 𝒞 505/243-0391.

Rocky Mountain Chocolate Factory See old-fashioned candy made right before your eyes. 380 Coronado Center. 𝒞 800/658-6151 or 505/888-3399.

FURNITURE

Ernest Thompson Furniture ★   Original-design, handcrafted furniture is exhibited in the factory showroom. Thompson is a fifth-generation furniture maker who still uses traditional production techniques. 4531 Osuna Rd. NE (¼ block west of I-25 and ½ block north of Osuna Rd.). © 800/568-2344 or 505/344-1994.

Strictly Southwestern   You'll find nice, solid pine and oak Southwestern-style furniture here. Lighting, art, pottery, and other interior items are also available. 1321 Eubank Blvd. NE. © 505/292-7337.

GIFTS/SOUVENIRS

Jackalope International ★★   Wandering through this vast shopping area is like an adventure in another land—many lands, really. You'll find Mexican *trasteros* (armoires) next to Balinese puppets. The store sells sculpture, pottery, and Christmas ornaments as well. 834 US 550, Bernalillo. © 505/867-9813.

MARKETS

Flea Market   Every Saturday and Sunday, year-round, the fairgrounds play host to this market from 8am to 5pm. It's a great place to browse for turquoise and silver jewelry and locally made crafts, as well as newly manufactured inexpensive goods such as socks and T-shirts. The place has a fair atmosphere. There's no admission charge. New Mexico State Fairgrounds. For information, call the Albuquerque Convention and Visitors Bureau. © 800/284-2282.

SOUTHWESTERN APPAREL

Albuquerque Pendleton   Cuddle up in this store's large selection of blankets and shawls. 1100 San Mateo NE, suite 2 and 4. © 505/255-6444.

Western Warehouse   Family Western wear, including an enormous collection of boots, is the attraction here. This store claims to have the largest selection of work wear and work boots in New Mexico (8,000 pairs of boots altogether). 6210 San Mateo Blvd. NE. © 505/883-7161.

10 Albuquerque After Dark

Albuquerque has an active performing-arts and nightlife scene, as befits a city of 700,000 people. Also fittingly, the performing arts are multicultural, with Hispanic and (to a lesser extent) Native American productions sharing stage space with Anglo works, including theater, opera, symphony, and dance. Albuquerque attracts many national touring companies. Nightclubs cover the gamut, with rock, jazz, and country predominant.

Complete information on all major cultural events is available from the **Albuquerque Convention and Visitors Bureau** (© 800/284-2282 for recorded information after 5pm). Current listings appear in the two daily newspapers; detailed weekend arts calendars appear in the Thursday *Tribune* and the Friday *Journal*. The monthly *On the Scene* also carries entertainment listings.

Tickets for nearly all major entertainment and sporting events are available from **Ticketmaster**, 4004 Carlisle Blvd. NE (© 505/883-7800). Discount tickets are often available for midweek and matinee performances; check with individual theater or concert hall box offices.

The Major Concert & Performance Halls

Journal Pavilion, 5601 University Blvd. NE (© 505/452-5100).

Keller Hall, University of New Mexico, Cornell Street at Redondo Drive South NE (© 505/277-4569).

KiMo Theatre, 423 Central Ave. NW (© 505/768-3544).

Popejoy Hall, University of New Mexico, Cornell Street at Redondo Drive South NE (© 505/277-3824).

South Broadway Cultural Center, 1025 Broadway Blvd. SE (© 505/848-1320).

THE PERFORMING ARTS

CLASSICAL MUSIC

New Mexico Symphony Orchestra ★   The NMSO first played in 1932 and remains a strong cultural force. The symphony performs classics and pops, as well as family and neighborhood concerts. Each season a few notable artists visit; recent guests have included Yo-Yo Ma and Guillermo and Ivonne Figueroa. Concert venues are generally Popejoy Hall and the Rio Grande Zoo, both of which are accessible to people with disabilities. I recommend the outdoor concerts at the band shell at the zoo. 3301 Menaul Blvd. NE, Suite 4. © 800/251-6676 for tickets and information, or 505/881-9590. www.nmso.org.

DANCE

New Mexico Ballet Company   Founded in 1972, the state's oldest ballet company holds most of its performances at Popejoy Hall. Typically there is a fall production such as *Dracula,* a holiday one such as *The Nutcracker* or *A Christmas Carol,* and a contemporary spring production. 4200 Wyoming Blvd. NE, Suite B2 (P.O. Box 21518), Albuquerque, NM 87111. © 505/292-4245. www.nmballet.org. Tickets $20–$25 adults, $10–$20 children 12 and under.

THEATER

Albuquerque Little Theatre   Albuquerque Little Theatre has been offering a variety of productions, ranging from comedies to dramas to musicals, since 1930. It presents seven plays annually during its August-to-May season. Located across from Old Town, Albuquerque Little Theatre offers plenty of free parking. The box office is open weekdays from noon to 6pm. 224 San Pasquale Ave. SW. © 505/242-4750. www.swcp.com/~alt. Tickets $18, $16 students, $13 seniors.

La Compañia de Teatro de Albuquerque *Finds*   Productions by this company can provide a focused view into New Mexico culture. One of the few major professional Hispanic companies in the United States and Puerto Rico, La Compañía stages a series of bilingual productions (most original New Mexican works) every year from late September to May. The slate includes comedies, dramas, and musicals, along with an occasional Spanish-language play. Performances take place in the National Hispanic Cultural Center, the South Broadway Cultural Center, and other venues. P.O. Box 884, Albuquerque, NM 87103. © 505/242-7929. Tickets $12 adults, $8 students and seniors, $7 children under 18.

Musical Theatre Southwest Formerly known as the Albuquerque Civic Light Opera Association, this successful company has condensed its name and expanded its season. Six major Broadway musicals, in addition to several smaller productions, are presented each year at either Popejoy Hall or the MTS's own 890-seat Hiland Theater. The season runs year-round. Most productions are staged for three consecutive weekends, including some Sunday matinees. 4804 Central Ave. SE. ✆ **505/262-9301.** www.hiland theater.com. Tickets $15–$30 adults; $2 discount for students and seniors.

Vortex Theatre ✦ A nearly 30-year-old community theater known for its innovative productions, the Vortex is Albuquerque's "Off-Broadway" theater, presenting a range of plays from classic to original. Performances take place on Friday and Saturday at 8pm and on Sunday at 6pm. The black-box theater seats 90. 2004½ Central Ave. SE. ✆ **505/247-8600.** Tickets $10 adults, $8 students and seniors, $8 for everyone on Sun.

THE CLUB & MUSIC SCENE
COMEDY CLUBS/DINNER THEATER

Laffs Comedy Cafe Located on the west mesa, this club offers top acts from each coast, including comedians who have appeared on *The Late Show with David Letterman* and HBO. Shows are Wednesday through Sunday night. Call for times. San Mateo Blvd. and Osuna Rd., in the Fiesta del Norte Shopping Center. ✆ **505/296-5653.** www.laffscomedy.com. Cover $7; 2-drink and/or menu-item minimum purchase.

Mystery Cafe *Finds* If you're in the mood for a little interactive dinner theater, the Mystery Cafe might be just the ticket. You'll help the characters in this ever-popular, delightfully funny show solve the mystery as they serve you a four-course meal. Reservations are a must. Performances are Friday and Saturday at 7:30pm; doors open at 7pm. 2600 Louisiana Blvd. NE (at Menaul Blvd.). ✆ **505/237-1385.** www.abqmystery.com. Approximately $33.

COUNTRY MUSIC

Midnight Rodeo/Gotham The Southwest's largest nightclub, this place has bars in all corners; it even has its own shopping arcade, including a boutique and gift shop. A DJ spins records nightly; the hardwood dance floor is so big (5,500 sq. ft.) that it resembles an indoor horse track. There's also a hip-hop and techno dance bar called Gotham here. Open Wednesday through Sunday. 4901 McLeod Rd. NE (near San Mateo Blvd.). ✆ **505/888-0100.** $4 cover Fri–Sat.

ROCK/JAZZ

Brewsters Pub This downtown hot spot offers live blues, jazz, folk, or light rock in a sports bar–type setting. Sports fans can enjoy the action on a big-screen TV. Barbecue and burgers are served at lunch and dinner. Open Tuesday to Sunday. 312 Central Ave. SW (Downtown). ✆ **505/247-2533.**

Burt's Tiki Lounge This club won the weekly paper *Alibi*'s award for the best variety of drinks. Burt's Tiki Lounge offers live music Thursday to Sunday and charges no cover. 313 Gold Ave. ✆ **505/243-BURT.**

Kelly's BYOB Near the university, Kelly's is a brewpub in a renovated auto-body shop. The place has tasty pub fare, excellent brew specials, and live music Thursday to Saturday, usually with no cover. 3222 Central SE. ✆ **505/262-2739.**

Martini Grille ✦ On the eastern side of the Nob Hill district, this is the place for young professionals, who lush out on more than 30 flavors of martinis within a seductive

Batman cave atmosphere. Live entertainment plays most weekends and some weeknights. 4200 Central SE. ℂ 505/255-4111.

MORE ENTERTAINMENT

Albuquerque's best nighttime attraction is the **Sandia Peak Tramway,** with the restaurant High Finance at the summit (see "What to See & Do" and "Where to Dine," earlier in this chapter). Here, you can enjoy a view nonpareil of the Rio Grande Valley and the city lights.

If you want to include dice and slot machines in your trip to New Mexico, you're in luck. The expansive **Sandia Casino,** north of I-25 and ¼ mile east on Tramway Boulevard (ℂ 800/526-9366; www.sandiacasino.com), is an $80 million structure that sits on Sandia Pueblo land and has outstanding views of the Sandia Mountains. Built in Pueblo architectural style, the graceful casino has a 3,650-seat outdoor amphitheater, three restaurants (one, **Bien Shur,** has excellent food made by the same folks who operate the acclaimed Artichoke Cafe, p. 241), a lounge, more than 1,350 slot and video poker machines, the largest poker room in the state, and blackjack, roulette, and craps tables. It's open from 8am to 4am Sunday to Wednesday and 24 hours Thursday to Saturday. The **Isleta Gaming Palace,** 11000 Broadway SE (ℂ 800/460-5686 or 505/724-3800; www.isletacasinoresort.com), is a luxurious, air-conditioned casino (featuring blackjack, poker, slots, bingo, and keno) with a full-service restaurant, nonsmoking section, and free bus transportation on request. Open Monday to Thursday 9am to 5am; Friday to Sunday 24 hours a day.

11 Touring the Jemez Mountain Trail ⚹

Ten Native American pueblos are within an hour's drive of central Albuquerque. Two of them, Acoma and Laguna, are discussed in chapter 10. If you'd like to combine a tour of the archaeological sites and inhabited pueblos, consider driving the **Jemez Mountain Trail.** Head north on Interstate 25 to Bernalillo, where you can visit the Coronado State Monument. Continue west on US 550 to Zia Pueblo. Six miles farther on US 550 you reach NM 4, where you'll turn north and drive through orchards and along narrow cornfields of Jemez Pueblo. Farther north on NM 4, you'll find another archaeological site, the Jemez State Monument. You'll also find Jemez Springs, where you can stop for a hot soak. The road continues to the Los Alamos area, where you can see the spectacular ruins at Bandelier National Monument. From there you have the option of returning the way you came or via Santa Fe.

ZIA PUEBLO

Zia Pueblo, 135 Capitol Square Dr., Zia Pueblo, NM, 87053 (ℂ 505/867-3304), which has 720 inhabitants, blends in so perfectly with the soft tans of the stone and sand of the desertlike land around it that it's hard to see. It's like a chameleon on a tree trunk. The pueblo is best known for its famous sun symbol—now the official symbol of the state of New Mexico—adapted from a pottery design showing three rays going in each of the four directions from a sun, or circle. It is hailed in the pledge to the state flag as "a symbol of perfect friendship among united cultures."

Zia has a reputation for excellence in pottery making. Its pottery is identified by its unglazed terra-cotta coloring, traditional geometric designs, and plant and animal motifs painted on white slip. Paintings, weaving, and sculptures are also prized

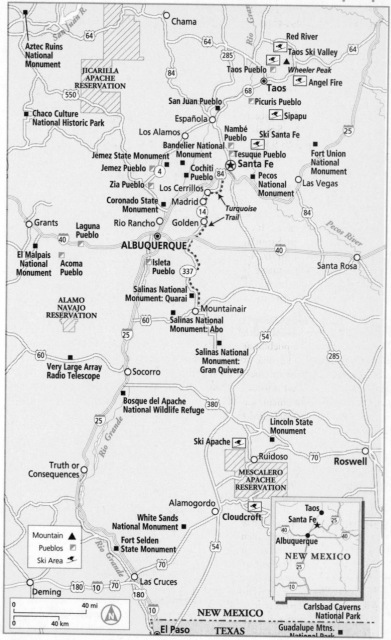

Aztec Ruins National Monument

San Juan R.

64

Chama

Rio Grande

Red River

Taos Ski Valley

64

JICARILLA APACHE RESERVATION

285

Taos Pueblo

Wheeler Peak

Angel Fire

550

Chaco Culture National Historic Park

84

San Juan Pueblo

68

Taos

Picuris Pueblo

Española

Sipapu

Los Alamos

Nambé Pueblo

Ski Santa Fe

25

Bandelier National Monument

Tesuque Pueblo

Jemez State Monument

4

Cochiti Pueblo

Santa Fe

Fort Union National Monument

Jemez Pueblo

84

Zia Pueblo

Los Cerrillos

Pecos National Monument

Las Vegas

Coronado State Monument

Madrid

Grants

Laguna Pueblo

14

Turquoise Trail

Pecos River

40

Rio Rancho

Golden

El Malpais National Monument

Acoma Pueblo

ALBUQUERQUE

40

Santa Rosa

Isleta Pueblo

337

ALAMO NAVAJO RESERVATION

Salinas National Monument: Quarai

Mountainair

60

25

Salinas National Monument: Abo

54

60

Very Large Array Radio Telescope

Socorro

Salinas National Monument: Gran Quivera

285

Bosque del Apache National Wildlife Refuge

380

Lincoln State Monument

25

Rio Grande

Ski Apache

Truth or Consequences

Ruidoso

70

Roswell

MESCALERO APACHE RESERVATION

Alamogordo

Taos

Santa Fe

White Sands National Monument

Cloudcroft

25

40

Fort Selden State Monument

54

Albuquerque

40

NEW MEXICO

25

Mountain ▲
Pueblos
Ski Area

70

Rio Grande

Deming

180

10

70

Las Cruces

180

10

0   40 mi

0   40 km

10

El Paso

NEW MEXICO

TEXAS

Carlsbad Caverns National Park

Guadalupe Mtns. National Park

259

Tips **Pueblo Etiquette: Do's & Don'ts**

Those who are not Native American are welcome to visit Indian pueblos and reservations; as a guest on tribal land, you should follow some guidelines.

Native American reservations and pueblos have their own systems of government and, therefore, their own laws and regulations. If you don't follow their laws, you will be subject to punishment as outlined by the American Indian government. The best thing that could happen is that you'd simply be asked to leave.

Stay out of cemeteries and ceremonial rooms, such as kivas, which are sacred grounds. Remember, these are not museums or tourist attractions in their own right; they are people's homes. Don't peek into doors and windows, and don't climb on top of buildings.

Most pueblos require a permit to carry a camera or to sketch or paint on location, and many prohibit photography at any time. If you want to take pictures, make a video, or sketch anything on pueblo or reservation land, find out about permits and fees in advance.

Do not wander around on your own if the residents have asked that you visit the pueblo only by guided tour. If, on a guided tour, you are asked not to take pictures of something, or are asked to stay out of a certain area, follow the guidelines. If you don't have to visit by guided tour, don't go into private buildings without being escorted by someone who lives there or who has the authority to take you inside.

Be respectful of ceremonial dances. Do not speak during dances or ceremonies, and don't applaud at the end—the participants aren't dancing for your amusement; they are dancing as part of their ceremony.

In short, be respectful and courteous and don't do anything you wouldn't do in your own mother's house.

products of the artists of the Zia community. Their work is on view at the **Zia Cultural Center** at the pueblo. A celebratory corn dance honors Our Lady of the Assumption, the patron saint, on her day, August 15.

The pueblo is about 8 miles northwest of Santa Ana Pueblo, just off US 550. It's open to visitors daily during daylight hours, and admission is free. Photography is not permitted.

JEMEZ PUEBLO

The more than 3,400 **Jemez Pueblo** natives—including descendants of the Pecos Pueblo, east of Santa Fe, abandoned in 1838—are the only remaining people to speak the Towa dialect of the Tanoan group. The Jemez are famous for their excellent dancing and feast-making; their feast days attract residents from other pueblos, turning the celebrations into multitribal fairs. Two rectangular kivas are central points for groups of dancers. However, in recent years the pueblo has been closed to visitors. Though they are allowed to visit on dance days, the pueblo has become close-mouthed about when dances occur. However, visitors can partake of the crafts at local shops along NM 4 and at the Walatowa Visitor Center (see box below). The primary craft is Jemez pottery.

A STATE MONUMENT IN THE AREA

Coronado State Monument ⭐ When the Spanish explorer Coronado traveled through this region in 1540–41 while searching for the Seven Cities of Cíbola, he wintered at a village on the west bank of the Rio Grande—probably one located on the ruins of the ancient Anasazi pueblo known as Kuaua. Those excavated ruins have been preserved in this state monument.

Hundreds of rooms can be seen, and a kiva has been restored so that visitors can descend a ladder into the enclosed space, once the site of sacred rites. Unique multi-colored murals, depicting human and animal forms, were found on successive layers of wall plaster in this and other kivas here; some examples are displayed in the monument's small archaeological museum.

485 Kuana Rd., Bernalillo (20 miles north of Albuquerque). ✆ 505/867-5351. Admission $3 adults, free for children under 17. Wed–Mon 8am–5pm. Closed Jan 1, Easter, Thanksgiving, Dec 25. Take I-25 to Bernalillo, then follow US 550 west for 1 mile.

JEMEZ SPRINGS

A visit to this village along the Jemez River can provide a relaxing retreat, an exhilarating adventure, or both. In the area are historic sites and relaxing hot springs, as well as excellent stream fishing, hiking, and cross-country skiing. You may want to combine a drive through this area with a visit to Los Alamos and Bandelier National Monument (see chapter 7).

North of town you'll come to the **Soda Dam,** a strange and beautiful mineral mass formed by travertine deposits—minerals that precipitate out of geothermal springs. Considered a sacred site by Native Americans, it has a gushing waterfall and caves. During the warm months it's a popular swimming hole.

Jemez State Monument ⭐ A stop at this small monument takes you on a journey through the history of the Jemez people. The trip begins in the museum, which tells the tale of Giusewa, "place of boiling waters," the original Tewa name of the area. Then it moves out into the mission ruins, whose story is told on small plaques that juxtapose the first impressions of the missionaries against the reality of the Jemez life.

Historic Culture with a Hint of Honey

Jemez Pueblo, home to more than 3,000, no longer welcomes visitors except on selected days. However, visitors can get a taste of the Jemez culture at the **Walatowa Visitor Center,** on NM 4, 8 miles north of the junction with US 550 (✆ 877/733-5687 or 505/834-7235; www.jemezpueblo.org). A museum and shop highlight the center, which also offers information about hiking and scenic tour routes. While in the area, you may encounter Jemez people sitting under *ramadas* (thatch-roofed lean-tos) selling home-baked native foods. If you're lucky, they may also be making fry bread, which you can smother with honey. It's one of New Mexico's more delectable treats.

> ⸨Moments⸩ **Sampling Nature's Nectars**
>
> The waters running through the Jemez area are high in mineral content. In fact, the owner of **Jemez Springs Bath House,** 62 NM 4, on Jemez Springs Plaza (ⓒ **505/829-3303;** www.jemezspringsbathhouse.com), says they are so healing, more than once she's had to run after visitors who walked off without their canes. This bathhouse was one of the first structures in what is now Jemez Springs. Built in 1870 and 1878 of river rock and mud, it has thick walls and a richly herbal scent. You soak in individual tubs in either the men's side or the women's side. In back are a series of massage rooms, and outside is a hot tub within a wooden fence. In front is a gift shop packed with interesting soaps and soulful gifts. It is open daily 10am to 8pm.

The missionaries saw the Jemez people as barbaric and set out to settle them. Part of the process involved hauling up river stones and erecting the 6-foot-thick walls of the Mission of San José de los Jemez (founded in 1621). Excavations in 1921–22 and 1935–37 unearthed this massive complex, through which you may wander. Through a broad doorway, you enter a room that once held elaborate fresco paintings; the room tapers back to the nave, with a giant bell tower above. The setting is next to a creek, with steep mountains rising behind.

18160 NM 4 (P.O. Box 143), Jemez Springs. ⓒ **505/829-3530.** Admission $3 adults, free for children under 18. Wed–Mon 8:30am–5pm. Closed Jan 1, Easter, Thanksgiving, Dec 25. From Albuquerque, take NM 550 (NM 44) to NM 4 and continue on NM 4 for about 18 miles.

WHERE TO STAY AND DINE

Cañon del Rio–Riverside Inn ⋆   "Eventually the watcher joined the river, and there was only one of us. I believe it was the river," wrote Norman Maclean in *A River Runs Through It.* That was my experience while sitting on a cottonwood-shaded bench at Cañon del Rio, on a long bow of the Jemez River, a small, fast-flowing stream lined with cottonwoods. Built in 1994, the inn has clean lines and comfortable rooms, each named after a Native American tribe. I stayed in the Hopi room, a queen unit that wasn't large but was well planned, with built-in drawers and many amenities. Each room has a sliding glass door that opens to a patio, where there's a fountain. The beds are comfortably firm, with good reading lights. The suites have private Jacuzzis and kitchens. The Great Room has a cozy, welcoming feel, with a big-screen TV. A separate house is available for rent, the only option for children at the inn. Smoking is not allowed.

16445 Scenic Hwy. 4, Jemez Springs, NM 87025. ⓒ **505/829-4377.** www.canondelrio.com. 7 units. $99–$160 double; $125–$150 house. Rates include full breakfast. AE, DISC, MC, V. **Amenities:** Jacuzzi; massage. *In room:* A/C, TV, hair dryer.

The Laughing Lizard Inn & Cafe ⋆ AMERICAN   If there were a Western version of the Whistle Stop Cafe, this would be it. It's the kind of small-town cafe that doesn't have to try to have a personality. It already has thick adobe walls, wood floors, and a wood-burning stove that give it innate charm. Added touches are brightly painted walls and funky old tables. Most dishes have a bit of an imaginative flair. Burritos come in a variety of types, such as fresh spinach with black beans, mushrooms, jack cheese, salsa, and guacamole. Pizzas feature ingredients such as pesto, sun-dried tomatoes, and feta, or more basic options with red sauce. I had a Chinese stir-fry with tofu and peanut sauce that was a little overbearing but definitely sated my appetite. No alcohol is served. Daily dessert treats include chocolate mousse and berry cobbler. The staff is friendly and accommodating.

17526 NM 4, Jemez Springs, NM 87025. ✆ 505/829-3108. www.thelaughinglizard.com. Main courses $6.50–$8.50. DISC, MC, V. June–Oct Tues–Fri 11am–8pm, Sat 11am–8:30pm, Sun 11am–6pm; Nov–May Thurs–Fri 5–8pm, Sat 11am–8pm, Sun 9am–4pm.

12 En Route to Santa Fe: Along the Turquoise Trail

Known as "The Turquoise Trail," NM 14 begins about 16 miles east of downtown Albuquerque, at I-40's Cedar Crest exit, and winds some 46 miles to Santa Fe along the east side of the Sandia Mountains. This state-designated scenic and historic route traverses the revived ghost towns of Golden, Madrid, and Cerrillos, where gold, silver, coal, and turquoise were once mined in great quantities. Modern-day settlers, mostly artists and craftspeople, have brought a renewed frontier spirit to the old mining towns.

MADRID   Madrid (pronounced *Mah*-drid) is about 12 miles north of Golden. Madrid and neighboring Cerrillos were in a fabled turquoise-mining area dating to prehistory. Gold and silver mines followed, and when they faltered, there was coal. The Turquoise Trail towns supplied fuel for the locomotives of the Santa Fe Railroad until the 1950s, when the railroad converted to diesel. Madrid used to produce 100,000 tons of coal a year, but the mine closed in 1956. Today, this is a village of artists and craftspeople seemingly stuck in the 1960s: Its funky, ramshackle houses have many counterculture residents who operate several crafts stores and import shops.

The **Old Coal Mine Museum** (✆ 505/438-3780) invites visitors to descend into a real mine that was saved when the town was abandoned. You can see the old mine's offices, steam engines, machines, and tools. It's called a living museum because blacksmiths, metalworkers, and leather workers ply their trades here in restoring parts and tools found in the mine. It's open daily; admission is $4 for adults, $3 for seniors, $1 for children 6 to 12, and free for children under 6.

Next door, the **Mine Shaft Tavern** (✆ 505/473-0743) continues its colorful career by offering a variety of burgers and presenting live music Saturday nights and Sunday afternoons; it's open for dinner Friday to Sunday, and it attracts folks from Santa Fe and Albuquerque. Next door is the **Madrid Engine House Theater** (✆ 505/438-3780), possibly the only such establishment on earth with a built-in steam locomotive on its stage. The place to eat is **Native Grill** (✆ 505/474-5555) on NM 14, in the center of town. You'll find food prepared with fresh ingredients, a broad range of choices, from pizza and burritos to a veggie bowl (steamed veggies with steak, chicken, or tofu). During the summer it's open from 11am to 6 or 7pm. In winter, it's open intermittently, so call ahead.

CERRILLOS   Cerrillos, about 3 miles north of Madrid, is a village of dirt roads that sprawls along Galisteo Creek. It appears to have changed very little since it was founded during a lead strike in 1879; the old hotel, the saloon, and even the sheriff's office look very much like parts of an Old West movie set. It's another 15 miles to Santa Fe and I-25. If, like me, you're enchanted by the Galisteo Basin, you might want to stay a night or two in nearby Galisteo at the **Galisteo Inn** (✆ 866/404-8200 or

505/466-4000; www.galisteoinn.com). Set on grassy grounds under towering cotton-wood trees, this 250-year-old hacienda has thick adobe walls and all the quiet a person could want. Rooms, all remodeled in 2004, are decorated with brightly painted walls and fun, bold-colored art. Most rooms are not sunny, but that means they stay very cool in summer. The inn serves guests full breakfast daily, and offers a prix-fixe dinner (at an extra cost) for guests and others on some nights. There's a lovely pool large enough to swim laps, a hot tub, and guided horseback riding. The inn is on NM 41, 15 miles from Cerrillos on the dirt County Road 42.

Pueblos, Reservations & the Best of Northern New Mexico

If the humdrum contemporary American life has you longing for excitement, this is the place to get your adrenaline flowing. Not only can you travel to a "foreign land"—namely Gallup, what locals call "Indian Country"—but you can also sample a history of Wild West shootouts and exploding volcanoes.

The biggest presence in the northwest is Native American culture, old and new. The Pueblo, Navajo, and Apache inhabit the area. Truly, they are the majority, and they set the pace and tone of the place. The Zuni, Acoma, and Laguna pueblos are within a short distance of I-40. **Acoma's "Sky City"** has been continually occupied for more than 9 centuries. Part of the Navajo Reservation, the largest in America, takes up a huge chunk of the northwest, and the Jicarilla Apache Reservation stretches 65 miles south from the Colorado border.

Three main towns provide launching points for adventures. **Grants** (pop. 8,900) is a boom-and-bust town on Route 66, and **Gallup** (pop. 20,000) is a mecca for silver jewelry shoppers. Outdoor adventurers head to **Chama** (pop. 1,000), where many enjoy a ride on the Cumbres & Toltec Railroad.

Two other national monuments in northwestern New Mexico also speak of the region's history. **El Morro** is a sandstone monolith known as "Inscription Rock," where travelers and explorers documented their journeys for centuries, and

El Malpais is a volcanic badland with spectacular cinder cones, ice caves, and lava tubes.

Meanwhile, the northeast is a place of wide-open plains once traversed by wagon trains on the Santa Fe Trail—a 19th-century trade route that ran from Missouri to Santa Fe. In **Cimarron** you'll see evidence of the holdings of cattle baron Lucien Maxwell, who controlled most of these prairies as his private empire in the latter half of the 19th century. Cimarron attracted nearly every gunslinger of the era, from Butch Cassidy to Clay Allison, Black Jack Ketchum to Jesse James.

Established long before its Nevada namesake, **Las Vegas** was the largest city in New Mexico at the turn of the 20th century, with a fast-growing, cosmopolitan population. Doc Holliday, Bat Masterson, and Wyatt Earp walked its wild streets in the 1880s. A decade later, it was the headquarters of Teddy Roosevelt's Rough Riders, and early in the 20th century, it was a silent film capital. Today, with a population of approximately 17,000, it is the region's largest city and the proud home of 900 historic properties. **Raton** (pop. 7,500), on I-25 in the Sangre de Cristo foothills, is the gateway to New Mexico from the north. **Clayton** (pop. 2,500), **Tucumcari** (pop. 6,831), and **Santa Rosa** (pop. 2,500) are all transportation hubs and ranching centers.

Two national monuments are particular points of interest. **Fort Union,** 24 miles north of Las Vegas, was the largest military installation in the Southwest in the 1860s and 1870s. **Capulin Volcano,** 33 miles east of Raton, last erupted 60,000 years ago; visitors can now walk inside the crater.

Drained by the Pecos and Canadian rivers, northeastern New Mexico is notable for the number of small lakes that afford opportunities for fishing, hunting, boating, camping—even scuba diving. Eleven state parks and about a half dozen designated wildlife areas are within the region.

1 Getting Outside in Northern New Mexico

BIKING Some of the best biking is in Farmington, where the "Durangatangs" come during the winter to train and ride (Durango is a mountain-biking mecca). **Bicycle Express,** 103 North Main Ave., Aztec (© **505/334-4354**), will give trail directions, as will **Cottonwood Cycles,** 4370 E. Main, Farmington (© **505/326-0429;** www.cottonwoodcycles.com). Cottonwood also rents bikes. Be sure to check out the **Lions Wilderness Park;** you'll find its renowned **Road Apple Trail** on the north end of town. Bikers are also welcome at the **Bureau of Land Management Conservation Area** just off NM 117 near **El Malpais National Monument** (see "Acoma Pueblo," below). For equipment rental in that area, try calling **Scoreboard Sporting Goods,** 107 West Coal Ave., Gallup (© **505/722-6077**), or rent something before you leave Albuquerque at **Rio Mountain Sport,** 1210 Rio Grande NW (© **505/766-9970**). At Chaco Canyon, check out the Wijiji Ruin trail, nice and easy but through beautiful country leading to an Anasazi (ancestral Puebloan) ruin. Taos also has rental shops.

BIRD-WATCHING Las Vegas National Wildlife Refuge (© **505/425-3581**), 5 miles southeast of Las Vegas, is a great place for bird-watching. Species spotted year-round include prairie falcons and hawks; during late fall and early winter, migratory birds such as sandhill cranes, snow geese, Canada geese, and bald and golden eagles frequent the refuge. In all, more than 240 species can be sighted in the area. The **Maxwell National Wildlife Refuge** (© **505/375-2331**), near Raton, also boasts a rich population of resident and migratory birds, including raptors and bald eagles.

BOATING If you're towing a boat, good places to stop are **Bluewater Lake State Park** (© **505/876-2391**), a reservoir between Gallup and Grants, and **Navajo Lake State Park** (© **505/632-2278**), about 25 miles east of Bloomfield. Both of these state parks have boat ramps, and Navajo Lake has several marinas (from which visitors can rent boats), picnic areas, a visitor center, and groceries for those who plan to make a day of it. You'll find opportunities for boating, windsurfing, and swimming throughout this northeastern region. Two of the most popular boating areas are **Storrie Lake State Park** (© **505/425-7278**), 6 miles north of Las Vegas, and **Conchas Lake State Park** (© **505/868-2270**), near Tucumcari. Storrie Lake is especially popular among **windsurfers,** who favor its consistent winds. To find information on New Mexico state parks, go to **www.nmparks.com.**

FISHING **Bluewater Lake State Park** (see "Boating," above) is one of the best places to fish in the area. In fact, some people believe it has the highest catch rate of all New Mexico lakes. Look to catch trout here. A world-renowned fishing destination, the **San Juan River** ★★, just below Navajo Dam, can be a fly-fisher's heaven and hell. For those good enough to know their flies and deduce what the large and wily

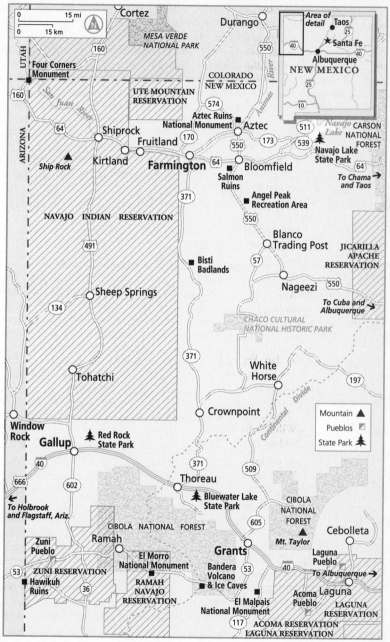

trout are eating, trophy catching is easy. For those like me who are more on the beginner end of the scale, it's a bit frustrating watching the big fish swim around your ankles while they ignore your fly. Fortunately, the scenery is outstanding enough to make up for the empty creel, and excellent guides in the area can help you fill it. **Navajo Lake State Park** (see "Boating," above) features about 150 miles of shoreline where fishers go to catch trout, bass, catfish, and pike. Navajo Lake is one of the largest lakes in New Mexico, and the park is very heavily trafficked, so if crowds aren't your thing, look for another fishing hole. Just 4 miles south of Kirtland is **Morgan Lake,** a quiet spot for largemouth bass and catfish. If you need fishing gear or want to hire a guide while in the area, contact **Duranglers on the San Juan,** 1003 NM 511, Navajo Dam (© 505/632-5952; www.duranglers.com), or the nearby **Abe's Motel and Fly Shop,** 1791 US 173, Navajo Dam (© 505/632-2194). In Farmington, contact **Dad's Boat Parts and Backyard Boutique,** 210 E. Piñon St. (© 505/326-1870), or **Zia Sporting Goods,** 500 E. Main (© 505/327-6004; www.ziasportinggoods.com). Isolated and primitive **Morphy Lake State Park** is a favorite destination for serious anglers. The lake is regularly stocked with rainbow trout. **Cimarron Canyon State Park** is also popular with fishers. Lake Alice in **Sugarite Canyon State Park,** just north of Raton at the Colorado border, is a good spot for fly-fishing.

GOLF   In this region, greens fees range from $18 to $50, with most averaging about $25; winter rates are lower. Cart rentals run about $15. A few years back, *Golf Digest* rated **Piñon Hills Golf Course,** 2101 Sunrise Pkwy., Farmington (© 505/326-6066), the best public golf course in the United States. Also in Farmington is the **Civitan Golf Course,** 2100 North Dustin (© 505/599-1194). In Kirtland (approximately 7 miles west of Farmington), your only golf option is **Riverview Golf Course,** on US 64 (© 505/598-0140). In the northeast, tee off at the following courses: **New Mexico Highlands University Golf Course,** East Mills Avenue and Country Club Drive, Las Vegas (© 505/425-7711); **Raton Municipal Golf Course,** 510 Country Club Rd., Raton (© 505/445-8113); **Pendaries Lodge and Country Club,** Rociada (© 505/425-3561; www.pendaries.net), 13 miles south of Mora and 27 miles northwest of Las Vegas; and **Tucumcari Municipal Golf Course,** Old US 66, Tucumcari (© 505/461-1849).

HIKING   This part of the state has some great hiking trails. You'll see ancient archaeological ruins in places such as Aztec Ruins and Chaco Canyon. In **Cíbola National Forest** (© 505/287-8833; www.fs.fed.us/r3/cibola), the hike to the summit of Mount Taylor is excellent. In cooler months, but not winter, try hiking around **El Malpais National Monument** (© 505/285-4641; www.nps.gov/elma). Two good hikes to try in El Malpais are the extremely taxing Zuni–Acoma Trail (if you're not in shape, don't expect to make the 15-mile round-trip hike) and the Big Lava Tubes Trail (1 mile round-trip). For quiet hiking in state parks, head to **Bluewater Lake State Park** (© 505/876-2391), **Red Rock State Park** (© 505/722-3839), or **Angel Peak Recreation Area** (© 505/599-8900). Sporting goods stores where you can get hiking gear include **REI-Albuquerque,** 1550 Mercantile Ave. NE, Albuquerque (© 505/247-1191; www.rei.com), **Frontier Sports,** 300 NE Aztec Blvd., Aztec (© 505/334-0009), and **Zia Sporting Goods,** 500 E. Main, Farmington (© 505/327-6004; www.ziasportinggoods.com). Northeastern New Mexico abounds in great places to hike, including the trails at Capulin Volcano; however, the best places are in the mountains north of Las Vegas and west of Santa Fe and Taos. **Clayton Lake, Coyote**

Creek, **Morphy Lake, Santa Rosa Lake, Sugarite Canyon,** and **Villanueva** state parks all have hiking trails, which range from fairly informal to clearly marked. For information about them, call © **888/NM-PARKS** or 505/476-3355, or visit www. emnrd.state.nm.us/nmparks. The region's premier hike takes you to the top of **Hermit's Peak,** a lovely but strenuous 8-mile round-trip foray onto a stunning precipice. Take NM 65 about 15 miles northwest of Las Vegas to the El Porvenir Campground. It's probably best to acquire equipment and supplies in Albuquerque before you set out. Try REI-Albuquerque (listed above).

HORSEBACK RIDING   You'll find lots of riding opportunities around Chama. A good bet is **5M Outfitters,** which charges approximately $60 for a half-day ride and $95 for a full day. Contact Bruce Maker, P.O. Box 361, Chama, NM 87520 (© **505/ 588-7003;** www.5moutfitters.com).

SCUBA DIVING   There couldn't possibly be scuba diving in this dry, landlocked state, could there? Yes, there is, with the best at Santa Rosa, where you'll find the **Blue Hole,** an 81-foot-deep artesian well that's a favorite of divers from around the world. The best place to rent equipment is at the **Santa Rosa Dive Center,** Blue Hole Road (© **505/472-3370**).

SKIING   Some of the best cross-country skiing in the state is in the Chama area. Lots of broad bowls make the area a favorite of backcountry enthusiasts as well as day-touring skiers. If you're up for an overnight adventure, contact **Southwest Nordic Center** (© **505/758-4761;** www.southwestnordiccenter.com). The company rents five yurts (Mongolian-style huts), four of which are in the Rio Grande National Forest near Chama. The season is from mid-November to April, depending on snow conditions. Some like to ski the old logging roads of Mount Taylor in **Cíbola National Forest** near Grants. Contact the ranger station in Grants (© **505/287-8833**) for more information. If you need to rent ski equipment, try **Chama Ski Service** (© **505/756-2492**), which also offers snow reports and trail information.

SWIMMING   Good swimming is available at **Navajo Lake State Park** (© **505/ 632-2278**). Before diving in at other lakes in state parks, make sure swimming is permitted. In the northeast, swimming is best (although chilly) at **Clayton, Conchas, Morphy, Storrie,** and **Ute lakes.** (You can find directions to and specifics about these lakes later in this chapter.) In addition, though it's an indoor rather than outdoor experience, the Olympic-size pool at the **Las Vegas Recreation Center,** 1751 North Grand Ave. (© **505/426-1739**), is an especially good place to take kids. It has a fun slide that will keep kids busy for hours. Call for more information.

2 Acoma Pueblo

30 miles SE of Grants, 90 miles SE of Gallup, 150 miles SE of Farmington

Your best base for exploring the Acoma pueblo, as well as the El Malpais and El Morro National Monuments (see section 3, below), is the town of Grants, 1¼ hours west of Albuquerque on I-40. Places to stay and dine in Grants, as well as details on the interesting New Mexico Mining Museum in Grants, appear below.

ACOMA PUEBLO ⊙⊙⊙

The spectacular Acoma Sky City, a walled adobe village perched high atop a sheer rock mesa 367 feet above the valley floor, is said to have been inhabited at least since the 11th century. It's the longest continuously occupied community in the United States.

Native history says it has been inhabited since before the time of Christ. Both the pueblo and its mission church of **San Esteban del Rey** are National Historic Landmarks. When Coronado visited in 1540, he suggested that Acoma was "the greatest stronghold in the world"; those who attempt to follow the cliff-side footpath down after their guided tour, rather than taking the bus, may agree.

About 50 to 75 Keresan-speaking Acoma (pronounced *Ack*-oo-mah) reside year-round on the 70-acre mesa top. Many others maintain ancestral homes and occupy them during ceremonial periods. The terraced three-story buildings face south for maximum exposure to the winter sun. Most of Sky City's permanent residents make their living off the throngs of tourists who flock here to see the magnificent church, built in 1639 and containing numerous masterpieces of Spanish colonial art, and to purchase the thin-walled white pottery with brown-and-black designs for which the pueblo is famous.

Many Acomas work in Grants, 15 miles west of the pueblo; in Albuquerque; or for one of Acoma's business enterprises, such as Sky City Casino. Others are cattle ranchers and farm individual family gardens.

ESSENTIALS

GETTING THERE   To reach Acoma from Grants, drive east 15 miles on I-40 to McCartys, then south 13 miles on paved tribal roads to the visitor center. From Albuquerque, drive west 65 miles to the Acoma–Sky City exit (102), then 15 miles southwest.

VISITOR INFORMATION   For additional information before you leave home, contact the pueblo at P.O. Box 309, Acoma, NM 87034 (② **800/747-0181** or 505/469-1052; www.puebloofacoma.org).

ADMISSION FEES & HOURS   Admission is $10 for adults, $9 for seniors 60 and over, $7 for children 6 to 17, and free for children under 6. Group discounts apply to parties of 15 or more, and there's also a discount for Native American visitors. The charge to take still photographs is $10; no videotaping, sketching, or painting is allowed except by special permission. The pueblo is open daily in the summer from 8am to 6pm and daily the rest of the year from 8am to 4pm.

SEEING THE HIGHLIGHTS

You absolutely cannot wander freely around Acoma Pueblo, but you can start your tour of Acoma at the **visitor center** at the base of the mesa. One-hour tours begin every 30 minutes, depending on demand; the last tour is scheduled 1 hour before closing. The pueblo is closed to visitors on Easter weekend (some years), June 24 and 29, July 10 to 13, and the first or second weekend in October. It's best to call ahead to make sure that the tour is available when you're visiting.

While waiting, peruse the excellent little **museum** of Acoma history and crafts, or buy snacks at the nearby **concession stand.** Then board the tour bus, which climbs through a rock garden of 50-foot sandstone monoliths and past precipitously dangling outhouses to the mesa's summit. With no running water or electricity in this medieval-looking village, it's a unique place. A small reservoir collects rainwater for most uses, and drinking water is transported up from below. Wood-hole ladders and mica windows are prevalent among the 300-odd adobe structures. As you tour the village, you'll have many opportunities to buy pottery and other pueblo treasures. Pottery is expensive here, but you're not going to find it any cheaper anywhere else, and if you buy it directly from the craftsperson, it's guaranteed authentic. Along the way, be sure to sample some Indian fry bread topped with honey.

DANCES & CEREMONIES

The annual San Esteban del Rey **feast day** is September 2, when a midmorning Mass, a procession, an afternoon corn dance, and an arts-and-crafts fair honor the pueblo's patron saint. The Governor's Feast is held annually in February; 4 days of Christmas festivals run from December 25 to 28. Still cameras are allowed for a $10 fee, and guided tours do not operate on the mesa during feast days.

Other **celebrations** are held in low-lying pueblo villages at Easter (in Acomita), the first weekend in May (Santa Maria feast at McCartys), and August 10 (San Lorenzo Day in Acomita).

GRANTS

If you've ever wondered what a "boom-and-bust town" looks like, come to Grants and find out. Grants first boomed with the coming of the railroad in the late 19th century, when 4,000 workers descended on the tiny farm town. When the railroad was completed, the workers left, and the town went bust. Next, Grants saw high times in the 1940s, growing carrots and sending them to the East Coast, but when packaging became more advanced, Grants lost its foothold in the market and busted again. Then came the 1950s, when a Navajo sheep rancher named Paddy Martinez discovered some strange yellow rocks near Haystack Mountain, northwest of town. The United States was in need of uranium, and his find led to the biggest boom in the area. By the early 1980s, demand for uranium had dropped, and so went the big wages and big spenders that the ore's popularity had produced. Today, the city is little more than a segment of Route 66 with some interesting old buildings.

You'll see dilapidated court motels and store signs. Note the Uranium Cafe, with a sign in the window that reads "OUR FOOD WILL BLOW YOUR MINE."

The city is the seat of expansive Cíbola County, which stretches from the Arizona border nearly to the Albuquerque area. For more information, contact the **Grants/Cíbola County Chamber of Commerce,** 100 N. Iron Ave. (P.O. Box 297), Grants, NM 87020 (© **800/748-2142** or 505/287-4802; www.grants.org). It's in the same building as the Mining Museum.

AN ATTRACTION IN GRANTS

New Mexico Mining Museum ★ *Kids*   This enormously interesting little museum primes you for the underground adventure of traveling into a re-creation of a mine shaft by showing you, on ground level, some geology, such as a fossilized dinosaur leg bone and a piece of Malpais lava. The world's only underground uranium-mining museum also gives you a sense of the context within which uranium was mined, through photos of the uranium-mining pioneers. That sets the stage for your walk into a mine-shaft–like doorway adorned with rusty metal hats. An elevator takes you down into a spooky, low-lit place with stone walls. You begin in the station where uranium was loaded and unloaded and travel down into the earth through places defined on wall plaques. While exploring, you get a sense of the dark and dirty work that mining can be. Those with claustrophobia may have to content themselves with visiting the exhibits *above* ground.

100 N. Iron Ave. (at Santa Fe Ave.). © **800/748-2142** or 505/287-4802. Fax 505/287-8224. www.grants.org/mining/mining.htm. Admission $3 adults, $2 seniors over age 60 and children 7–18; free for children under 7. Mon–Sat 9am–4pm.

WHERE TO STAY IN GRANTS

Hotels are all on or near Route 66, with major properties near I-40 interchanges, and smaller or older motels nearer downtown. Lodger's tax is 5%, and the gross receipts tax is 6.8125%, for a total tax of just under 12%. Parking is usually free.

Holiday Inn Express   Just off the interstate, this two-story motel provides large, well-conceived rooms with a comfortable atmosphere. Ground-floor rooms open both off an inner corridor and from an outside door that faces the parking lot. Rooms are spacious, with high ceilings and large bathrooms.

1496 E. Santa Fe Ave., Grants, NM 87020. ⓒ **800-HOLIDAY** or 505/285-4676. Fax 505/285-6998. www.hiexpress. com. 58 units. $90 double. Rates include continental breakfast. AE, DC, DISC, MC, V. Pets accepted. **Amenities:** Small indoor pool; Jacuzzi. *In room:* A/C, TV, dataport, coffeemaker, hair dryer, iron.

CAMPING

Grants has three decent campgrounds with both tent and RV facilities. All range in price from $9 to $14 for tent camping and $13 to $19 for full hookups. **Blue Spruce RV Park** (ⓒ **505/287-2560**) has 25 sites and 16 full hookups and is open year-round. It has enough trees to block the wind, as well as some grass. The roads and parking spaces are gravel, minimizing dust. Cable television hookups are available, as are laundry facilities and a recreation room. To reach the park, take I-40 to Exit 81 and go ¼ mile south on NM 53.

   Lavaland RV Park (ⓒ **505/287-8665;** www.lavalandrvpark.com), the closest campground to Grants, has 51 sites and 39 full hookups. Located near a lava outcropping, the site is clean, though a little desolate and dusty, with a few pine trees to block the wind. Air-conditioning and heating hookups are available, as are some free cable and telephone hookups. In addition, you'll find cabins, laundry, limited grocery facilities, picnic tables and grills, and recreation facilities. Lavaland is open year-round. From I-40, get off at exit 85 and continue 100 yards south on Access Road.

WHERE TO DINE IN GRANTS

In general, you won't find places to eat at pueblos or national monuments, so you're best off looking for a restaurant in Grants.

El Cafecito *Value* *Kids* MEXICAN/AMERICAN   This real locals' spot serves up tasty food in a relaxed atmosphere. At mealtime, the brightly lit space with Saltillo tile floors bustles with families eating huevos rancheros (eggs over tortillas, smothered in chile) for breakfast, and enchiladas, stuffed *sopaipillas,* and burgers for lunch and dinner. All meals are large and inexpensive. Kids enjoy their own menu selections.

820 E. Santa Fe Ave. ⓒ **505/285-6229.** Main courses $3–$6 breakfast, $5–$10 lunch or dinner. AE, DISC, MC, V. Mon–Fri 7am–9pm; Sat 7am–8pm.

La Ventana NEW MEXICAN/STEAKS   This is where the locals go for a big dinner or lunch out. One large room that seats about 50 people, the restaurant, in a small shopping center, boasts cheesy Southwestern decor, with a two-horse sculpture and some dancing kachinas. The place is dark, with few windows, so if you can catch Grants on a nonwindy day, opt for the patio. Service is friendly and varies in efficiency. You can't go wrong with one of the salads (such as the chicken fajita) or with the prime rib. You'll also find sandwiches such as turkey and guacamole served on seven-grain bread. There's a full bar.

110½ Geis St., Hillcrest Center. ⓒ **505/287-9393.** Reservations recommended. Main courses $4.50–$10 lunch, $8–$20 dinner. AE, DC, DISC, MC, V. Mon–Sat 11am–11pm.

3 El Malpais & El Morro National Monuments

El Malpais: 15 miles S of Grants, 75 miles SE of Gallup, 135 miles S of Farmington; El Morro: 30 miles SW of Grants, 45 miles SE of Gallup, 149 miles S of Farmington

Northwestern New Mexico has two national monuments that are must-sees for anyone touring this region: El Malpais and El Morro.

EL MALPAIS: EXPLORING THE BADLANDS ☀

Designated a national monument in 1987, El Malpais (Spanish for "badlands") is considered one of the outstanding examples of volcanic landscapes in the United States. El Malpais contains 115,000 acres of cinder cones, vast lava flows, hundreds of lava tubes, ice caves, sandstone cliffs, natural bridges and arches, Anasazi (ancestral Puebloan) ruins, ancient Native American trails, and Spanish and Anglo homesteads.

ESSENTIALS

GETTING THERE   Two roads, NM 117 and NM 53, lead to El Malpais. NM 117 has an exit off I-40 7 miles east of Grants.

VISITOR INFORMATION   Admission to El Malpais is free (unless you're visiting the privately owned Ice Caves), and it's open to visitors year-round. The **visitor center,** off Route 53 between mile markers 63 and 64, is open daily from 8:30am to 4:30pm. Here you can pick up maps of the park, leaflets on specific trails, and other details about exploring the monument. For more information, contact **El Malpais National Monument,** NPS, P.O. Box 939, Grants, NM 87020 (© **505/285-4641;** www.nps.gov/elma).

SEEING THE HIGHLIGHTS

From **Sandstone Bluffs Overlook** (10 miles south of I-40 off NM 117), many craters are visible in the lava flow, which extends for miles along the eastern flank of the Continental Divide. The most recent flows are only 1,000 years old; Native American legends tell of rivers of "fire rock." Seventeen miles south of I-40 is **La Ventana Natural Arch,** the largest accessible natural arch in New Mexico.

From NM 53, which intersects I-40 just west of Grants, visitors have access to the **Zuni-Acoma Trail,** an ancient Pueblo trade route that crosses four major lava flows in a 7½-mile (one-way) hike. A printed trail guide is available. **El Calderon,** a forested area 20 miles south of I-40, is a trail head for exploring a cinder cone, lava tubes, and a bat cave. (**Warning:** Hikers should not enter the bat cave or otherwise disturb the bats.)

The largest of all Malpais cinder cones, **Bandera Crater** is on private property 25 miles south of I-40. The National Park Service has laid plans to absorb this commercial operation, known as **Ice Caves Resort** (© **888/ICE-CAVE** or 505/783-4303; www.icecaves.com). For a fee ($8 adults, $4 children 5–12), visitors hike up the crater or walk to the edge of an ice cave. It's open daily from 8am to 7pm in summer and from 8am to 4pm in winter (generally closing 1 hr. before sunset).

Perhaps the most fascinating phenomenon of El Malpais is the lava tubes, formed when the outer surface of a lava flow cooled and solidified. When the lava river drained, it left behind tunnel-like caves. Ice caves within some of the tubes have delicate ice-crystal ceilings, ice stalactites, and floors like ice rinks.

HIKING & CAMPING

El Malpais has several hiking trails, including the above-mentioned Zuni-Acoma Trail. Most are marked with rock cairns; some are dirt trails. The best times to hike this area are spring and fall, when it's not too hot. You are pretty much on your own when exploring this area, so prepare accordingly. Carry plenty of water with you; do not drink surface water. Carrying first-aid gear is always a good idea; the lava rocks can be extremely sharp and inflict nasty cuts. Never go into a cave alone. The park service advises wearing hard hats, boots, protective clothing, and gloves, and carrying three sources of light when entering lava tubes. The weather can change suddenly, so be prepared; if lightning is around, move off the lava as quickly as possible.

Primitive camping is allowed in the park, but you must first obtain a free back-country permit from the visitor center.

EL MORRO NATIONAL MONUMENT ★

Travelers who like to look history straight in the eye are fascinated by "Inscription Rock," 43 miles west of Grants along NM 53. Looming up out of the sand and sage-brush is a bluff 200 feet high, holding some of the most captivating messages in North America. Its sandstone face displays a written record of the many who inhabited and traveled through this land, beginning with the Anasazi (ancestral Puebloans), who lived atop the formation around 1200. Carved with steel points are the signatures and comments of almost every explorer, conquistador, missionary, army officer, surveyor, and pioneer emigrant who passed this way between 1605, when Gov. Don Juan de Oñate carved the first inscription, and 1906, when it was preserved by the National Park Service. Oñate's inscription, dated April 16, 1605, was perhaps the first graffiti any European left in America.

A paved walkway makes it easy to walk to the writings, and a stone stairway leads up to other treasures. One entry reads: "Year of 1716 on the 26th of August passed by here Don Feliz Martinez, Governor and Captain General of this realm to the reduction and conquest of the Moqui." Confident of success as he was, Martinez actually got nowhere with any "conquest of the Moqui," or Hopi, peoples. After a 2-month battle, they chased him back to Santa Fe.

Another special group that passed by this way was the U.S. Camel Corps, trekking past on their way from Texas to California in 1857. The camels worked out fine in mountains and deserts, outlasting horses and mules 10 to 1, but the Civil War ended the experiment. When Peachy Breckinridge, fresh out of the Virginia Military Academy, came by with 25 camels, he noted the fact on the stone here.

El Morro was at one time as famous as the Blarney Stone of Ireland: Everybody had to stop by and make a mark. But when the Santa Fe Railroad was laid 25 miles to the north, El Morro was no longer on the main route to California, and starting in the 1870s, the tradition began to die out.

Atop Inscription Rock at the end of a short, steep trail, Anasazi (ancestral Puebloan) ruins occupy an area 200 by 300 feet. Inscription Rock's name, Atsinna, suggests that carving one's name here is a very old custom indeed: The word, in Zuni, means "writing on rock."

ESSENTIALS

GETTING THERE   El Morro is 43 miles west of Grants on NM 53.

VISITOR INFORMATION   For information, contact **El Morro National Monument,** Route 2, Box 43, Ramah, NM 87321-9603 (© **505/783-4226;** www.nps.gov/elmo). Admission to El Morro is $3 adults, free for children under 17. Self-guided trail booklets are available at the visitor center (turn off NM 53 at the El Morro sign and travel approximately ½ mile), open year-round from 9am to 5pm. Trails are also open year-round; check with the **visitor center** for hours. A **museum** at the visitor center features exhibits on the 700 years of human activity at El Morro. A 15-minute video gives a good introduction to the park. Also in the visitor center is a **bookstore** where you can pick up souvenirs and informational books. It takes between 2 and 4 hours to visit the museum and hike a couple of trails. The park is closed on January 1 and December 25.

CAMPING

Though it isn't necessary to camp here in order to see most of the park, a nine-site campground at El Morro is open from around Memorial Day to Labor Day. It costs $5 per night. No supplies are available in the park, so if you're planning on spending a night or two, be sure to arrive well equipped.

One nearby private enterprise, **El Morro RV Park,** HC 61, Box 44, Ramah, NM 87321 (© **505/783-4612;** www.elmorro-nm.com), has cabins, RV and tent camping, and a cafe.

4 Gallup: Gateway to Indian Country

62 miles NW of Grants; 118 miles NW of Albuquerque; 164 miles W of Santa Fe

For us, Gallup has always been a mysterious place—home to many Native Americans, with dust left from its Wild West days, and with an unmistakable Route 66 architectural presence, it just doesn't seem to exist in this era. The best way to get a sense of the place is by walking around downtown, through the trading posts and pawnshops and by the historic buildings. In doing so you'll get a real feel for the "Heart of Indian Country."

Gallup started when the railroad from Arizona reached this spot in 1881. At that time, the town consisted of a stagecoach stop and a saloon. Within 2 years, coal mining had created a boom, and some 22 saloons and an opera house filled the town, most of which was inhabited by immigrants from mining areas in eastern Europe, England, Wales, Germany, and Italy.

When the popularity of the railroads declined, Gallup turned briefly to the movie business. The area's red-rock canyons and lonely deserts were perfect for Westerns of the era such as *Big Carnival,* with Kirk Douglas; *Four Faces West,* with Joel McCrea; and *The Bad Man,* starring Wallace Beery, Lionel Barrymore, and Ronald Reagan. These stars and many others stayed in a Route 66 hotel built by R. E. Griffith in 1937. Today, the El Rancho Hotel and Motel is one of Gallup's most notable landmarks; it's worth strolling through (see "Where to Stay," below). Gallup's next income generator was trade and tourism. Its central location between the Navajo Reservation and the Zuni lands, as well as its proximity to the ancient ruins at Chaco, make it a crossroads for trade and travel.

Gallup's most notable special event is the **Inter-Tribal Indian Ceremonial** held every August. Native Americans converge on the town for a parade, dances, and an all-Indian rodeo east of town at Red Rock State Park. It's a busy time in Gallup, and reservations must be made way in advance. If you're not in town for the Ceremonial, try hitting Gallup on a Saturday. Many Native Americans come to town to trade, and the place gets busy. Best of all on this day is the **Flea Market,** north of town just off U.S. 666. Here you can sample fry bread, Zuni bread, and Acoma bread, eat real mutton stew, and shop for anything from jewelry to underwear. After the Flea Market, most Gallup-area residents—native and nonnative alike—go to Earl's (see "Where to Dine," below) to eat and then to Wal-Mart to shop.

ESSENTIALS

GETTING THERE   From Albuquerque, take I-40 west (2½ hr.). From Farmington, take US 64 west to Shiprock, then US 491 south (2½ hr.). From Flagstaff, Arizona, take I-40 east (3 hr.). No commercial airlines serve Gallup at this time.

VISITOR INFORMATION   The **Gallup Convention and Visitors Bureau,** 103 W. US 66, Gallup, NM 87301 (© **800/242-4282** or 505/863-3841; www. gallupnm.org), is just south of the main I-40 interchange for downtown Gallup. Or you can contact the **Gallup–McKinley County Chamber of Commerce,** 103 W. US 66, Gallup, NM 87301 (© **505/722-2228;** www.gallupchamber.com).

WHAT TO SEE & DO
EXPLORING GALLUP

Gallup has 20 buildings that are either listed on or have been nominated to the National Register of Historic Places. Some hold trading posts that are worth visiting. A good place to start your visit is at the **Santa Fe Railroad Depot,** which also houses the **Gallup Cultural Center** (for details, see "Sunset Dances," below) at East 66 Avenue and Strong Street. Built in 1923 in modified Mission style, it has been renovated into a community transportation and cultural center, with a small museum that's worth visiting, as well as a gift shop and diner. The **Rex Hotel,** 300 W. 66 Ave., constructed of locally quarried sandstone, was once known for its "ladies of the night." It's now the **Rex Museum** (© **505/863-1363**), a somewhat random display of items from the Gallup Historical Society Collection, but fun for history buffs. It's open daily but with unpredictable hours. Call before setting out.

Gallup's architectural gems include the **Chief Theater,** 228 W. Coal Ave. This structure was built in 1920; in 1936, it was completely redesigned in Pueblo-Deco style, with zigzag relief and geometric form, by R. E. "Griff" Griffith (who also built the El Rancho Hotel), brother of Hollywood producer D. W. Griffith. Now this is **City Electric Shoe Shop** (© **505/863-5252**), where the Native Americans go to buy feathers, leather, and other goods to make ceremonial clothing. It is known to locals simply as "City Electric," so called because it was the first shop in town to have an automated shoe repair machine. Also visit the 1928 **El Morro Theater,** 207 W. Coal Ave., built in Spanish colonial revival style with Spanish baroque plaster carving and bright polychromatic painting; it's where locals come to see movies and dance performances.

SHOPPING: BEST BUYS ON JEWELRY & CRAFTS

Nowhere are the jewelry and crafts of Navajo, Zuni, and Hopi tribes less expensive than in Gallup. The most intriguing places to shop are the trading posts and pawnshops, which provide a surprising range of services for their largely Native American clientele and have little in common with the pawnshops of large U.S. cities.

Navajoland **pawnbrokers** in essence are bankers, at least from the Navajo and Zuni viewpoint. Pawnshops provide safekeeping of valuable personal goods and make small-collateral loans. The trader will hold on to an item for months or even years before deeming it "dead" and putting it up for sale. Less than 5% of items ever go unredeemed, but over the years traders do accumulate a selection, so the shops are worth perusing.

If you're shopping for jewelry, look for silver concho belts, worn with jeans and Southwestern skirts; cuff bracelets; and necklaces, from traditional squash blossoms to silver beads to *heishi*, which are very fine beads worn in several strands. Earrings may be only silver, or they may be decorated with stones.

Also be on the lookout for bolo ties and belt buckles of silver or turquoise. Silver concho hatbands go great on Stetson hats. Silver or gold handcrafted earrings, sometimes decorated with turquoise, are big sellers.

Hand-woven Native American rugs may be draped on couches, hung on walls, or used on floors. Also look for pottery, kachinas, and sculpture.

Most shops are open Monday through Saturday from 9am to 5pm. For a look at everything from pawn jewelry to Pendleton robes and shawls to enamel and cast-iron kitchenware, visit **Ellis Tanner Trading Company** (© **505/863-4434**), Highway 602 Bypass, south from I-40 on Highway 602 about 2 miles; it's at the corner of Nizhoni Boulevard. **Perry Null-Tobe Turpen's Indian Trading Company,** 1710 S. Second St. (© **505/722-3806**), farther out on Second Street, is a big freestanding brick building full of jewelry, rugs, kachinas, and pottery.

SUNSET DANCES

Every evening from Memorial Day to Labor Day, dancers from a variety of area tribes sing, drum, and twirl in a stunning display of ritual from 7 to 8pm. The dances take place at the **Gallup Cultural Center,** East 66 Avenue and Strong Street (© **505/ 863-4131**). The center is open weekdays from 9am to 5pm, often with extended hours in the summer. Also at the center are a gift shop, a cafe, a museum with a permanent exhibit on regional history, and other changing art exhibits. Admission to the center and dances is free.

WHERE TO STAY IN GALLUP

Virtually every accommodation in Gallup is somewhere along Route 66, either near the I-40 interchanges or on the highway through downtown.

MODERATE

El Rancho Hotel and Motel ⭐   This historic hotel owes as much to Hollywood as to Gallup. Built in 1937 by R. E. "Griff" Griffith, brother of movie mogul D. W. Griffith, it became the place for film companies to set up headquarters when filming here. Between the 1940s and 1960s, a who's who of Hollywood stayed here. Their autographed photos line the walls of the hotel's cafe. Spencer Tracy and Katharine Hepburn stayed here during production of *The Sea of Grass;* Burt Lancaster and Lee Remick were guests when they made *The Hallelujah Trail.* The list goes on and on: Gene Autry, Lucille Ball, Jack Benny, Humphrey Bogart, James Cagney, Errol Flynn, Henry Fonda, the Marx Brothers, Ronald Reagan, Rosalind Russell, James Stewart, John Wayne, and Mae West all stayed here.

In 1986, Gallup businessman Armand Ortega, a longtime jewelry merchant, bought the run-down El Rancho and restored it to its earlier elegance. The lobby staircase rises to the mezzanine on either side of an enormous stone fireplace, and heavy ceiling beams and railings made of tree limbs give the room a hunting-lodge ambience. The hotel is on the National Register of Historic Places.

Rooms in El Rancho differ from one to the next and are named for the stars that stayed in them. Most are long and medium-size, with wagon-wheel headboards and heavy, dark-stained pine furniture. Bathrooms are small, some with showers, others with shower/tub combos. All have lovely small white hexagonal tiles. Many rooms have balconies. Two suites with kitchenettes are also available. Light sleepers should be aware that the train can be heard from all rooms in the hotel.

1000 E. 66 Ave., Gallup, NM 87301. ℂ **800/543-6351** or 505/863-9311. Fax 505/722-5917. www.elranchohotel. com. 100 units. $47–$86 double; $105 suite. AE, DISC, MC, V. Pets accepted. **Amenities:** Restaurant (below); lounge; seasonal outdoor pool; coin-op laundry. *In room:* A/C, TV.

Holiday Inn Express ✦ The challenge in Gallup is to find a quiet place to sleep. With busy train tracks running right through town, most accommodations stay noisy through the night. Sitting north of town, this is the quietest place I've found. Though highway noise persists in the night, it's not as intrusive as the train's roar and whistle. Rooms are medium-size, with high ceilings and lots of amenities. They're well maintained and have comfortable beds and fairly spacious baths. Cookies upon arrival and a hot breakfast add to the appeal. You may pay an extra $10 or $20 to stay here, but for me, a good night's sleep is easily worth that.

1500 W. Maloney Ave., Gallup, NM 87301. ℂ **800/HOLIDAY** or 505/726-1000. Fax 505/722-4954. www.hiexpress. com. 70 units. $75–$119 double. Rates include breakfast. AE, DC, DISC, MC, V. **Amenities:** Indoor pool; Jacuzzi; sauna. *In room:* A/C, TV, coffeemaker, hair dryer, iron.

CAMPING

Like the rest of the state, the Gallup area offers plenty of places to pitch a tent or hook up your RV. **USA RV Park** (ℂ **505/863-5021**) has 145 sites, 50 full hookups (cable TV costs extra), and cabins, as well as grocery and laundry facilities. Recreation facilities include video games, a seasonal heated pool, and a playground. Breakfast and dinner (not included in the lodging rates) are served outdoors. Prices range from $21 for tents to $27 for full hookups. Cabins are $35. To reach the campground, take I-40 to the US 66/Business I-40 junction (exit 16); go 1 mile east on US 66/Business I-40.

Red Rock State Park campground (ℂ **505/722-3839**) has 106 sites—50 with no hookups and 56 with water and electricity. Tent sites are available. The campground offers dry camping for $10 and camping with water and electrical hookups for $18. The sites are right against the buttes; in the spring, they will surely be dusty because there's little protection from the wind. Also here are a convenience store, picnic tables, and grills.

WHERE TO DINE IN GALLUP

Earl's *Finds* *Kids* NEW MEXICAN/AMERICAN This is where the locals come to eat, particularly on weekends, en route to and from trading in Gallup. The place fills up with a variety of customers, from college students to Navajo grandmothers. A Denny's-style diner, with comfortable booths and chairs, the restaurant allows Native Americans to sell their wares to you while you eat; however, you have the option of putting up a sign asking not to be disturbed. Often on weekends, vendors set up tables out front, so the whole place takes on a bustling bazaar atmosphere. And the food is good. I recommend the New Mexican dishes such as huevos rancheros (eggs on tortillas, smothered in chile sauce), the enchilada plate, or the smothered grande burrito. Earl's offers a kids' menu and half-portion items for smaller appetites, as well as some salads and a "baked potato meal." Open since 1947, Earl's continues to please.

1400 E. 66 Ave. ℂ **505/863-4201.** Reservations not accepted Fri–Sat. Most menu items under $10. AE, MC, V. Sat–Thurs 6am–9pm; Fri 6am–9:30pm.

El Rancho ✦ *Moments* *Kids* NEW MEXICAN/AMERICAN In the historic El Rancho Hotel (see above), this restaurant has fans all across the Southwest. They come to experience the Old West decor—with well-spaced, heavy wooden furniture and movie memorabilia on the walls—and the sense of the many movie stars who once ate here. The food is fine-diner-style, with dishes such as steak and eggs or hot cakes for breakfast, as well as regional delights, such as *atole* (hot blue-corn cereal) or a breakfast taco. At lunch you can always count on a good burger or select from a cast of sandwiches, such as the Doris Day (sirloin steak on French bread), or salads. At dinner, steaks are a big hit, as is grilled salmon, both served with soup or salad, vegetable, and choice of potato or rice. The New Mexican food is also good. Kids can select from the "little buckaroos" menu. A full bar is available.

In the El Rancho Hotel and Motel, 1000 E. 66 Ave. © 800/543-6351 or 505/863-9311. Main courses $4–$10 breakfast, $7–$9 lunch, $8–$16 dinner. AE, DISC, MC, V. Daily 6:30am–10pm.

Oasis Mediterranean Restaurant & Hookah Lounge ★ *(Finds* MEDITERRANEAN A gallery in the center of downtown provides the setting for this new restaurant, which serves some of the best food in western New Mexico. Though the setting feels a little sterile, with white floors and walls, some good art in cases is fun to peruse while you wait for your food (although the service is good). The meal starts with a medley of tasty olives, pickles, and peppers. The menu has all the Mediterranean standards—baba ghanouj and hummus for appetizers, falafel sandwiches and meat shwarmas for a light lunch or dinner, all carefully made with fresh ingredients. Rather than going with those, though, have the waitress guide you to the best choices. She recommended the chicken gallaba, which has become my favorite—richly spiced chicken with mushrooms and bell peppers, served with a choice of rice, hummus, or salad. Baklava and rice pudding are both good finishers. The restaurant also serves steaks, shrimp, and barbecued chicken. Beer and wine are available. An upstairs lounge offers "hookahs," water pipes that allow smokers to inhale flavored Palestinian tobacco smoke. Flavors range from plain to apple to strawberry and cost $7.99 per hookah.

100 E. 66 Ave. © 505/722-9572. Main courses $5–$17. AE, DISC, MC, V. Mon–Sat 11am–9pm (lounge until midnight Fri–Sat).

5 Chama: Home of the Cumbres & Toltec Scenic Railroad

59 miles NW of Taos; 91 miles NW of Santa Fe; 95 miles E of Farmington

This pioneer village of 1,250 people at the base of the 10,000-foot Cumbres Pass is New Mexico's undiscovered play land. Now, with some new additions, the town is really looking up. A park, clock-tower, and—drumroll, please—sidewalks (!) give it a friendlier tone.

Bordered by three wilderness areas, the Carson, Rio Grande, and Santa Fe national forests, the area is indeed prime for hunting, fishing, cross-country skiing, snowmobiling, snowshoeing, and hiking.

Another highlight is America's longest and highest narrow-gauge coal-fired steam line, the **Cumbres & Toltec Scenic Railroad,** which winds through valleys and mountain meadows 64 miles between Chama and Antonito, Colorado. The village of Chama boomed when the railroad arrived in 1881. A rough-and-ready frontier town, the place still maintains that flavor, with lumber and ranching making up a big part of the economy.

Landmarks to watch for are the **Brazos Cliffs** and waterfall and **Heron and El Vado lakes.** Tierra Amarilla, the Rio Arriba County seat, is 14 miles south, and is at the center—along with Los Ojos and Los Brazos—of a wool-raising and weaving tradition. Local craftspeople still weave masterpieces. Dulce, governmental seat of the Jicarilla Apache Indian Reservation, is 27 miles west.

ESSENTIALS

GETTING THERE From Santa Fe, take US 84 north (2 hr.). From Taos, take US 64 west (2½ hr.). From Farmington, take US 64 east (2¼ hr.).

VISITOR INFORMATION The **New Mexico Visitor Information Center,** P.O. Box 697, Chama, NM 87520 (ℂ **505/756-2235**), is at 2372 NM 17. It's open daily from 8am to 6pm in the summer, from 8am to 5pm in the winter. At the same address is the **Chama Valley Chamber of Commerce** (ℂ **800/477-0149** or 505/756-2306).

ALL ABOARD THE HISTORIC C&T RAILROAD

Cumbres & Toltec Scenic Railroad If you have a passion for the past and for incredible scenery, climb aboard America's longest and highest narrow-gauge steam railroad, the historic C&T. It operates on a 64-mile track between Chama and Antonito, Colorado. Built in 1880 as an extension of the Denver and Rio Grande line to serve the mining camps of the San Juan Mountains, it is perhaps the finest surviving example of what once was a vast network of remote Rocky Mountain railways.

The C&T passes through forests of pine and aspen, past striking rock formations, and over the magnificent Toltec Gorge of the Rio de los Pinos. It crests at the 10,015-foot Cumbres Pass, the highest in the United States used by scheduled passenger trains.

Halfway through the route, at Osier, Colorado, the New Mexico Express from Chama meets the Colorado Limited from Antonito. They stop to exchange greetings, engines, and through passengers. Round-trip day passengers return to their starting point after enjoying a picnic or catered lunch beside the old water tank and stock pens in Osier. Through passengers continue to Antonito and return by van. Be aware that both trips are nearly full-day events. Ask about the Parlor Car, a more luxurious alternative to coach seating. Those who find it uncomfortable to sit for long periods may instead want to opt for hiking or skiing in the area.

A walking-tour brochure, describing 23 points of interest in the Chama railroad yards, is available at the 1899 depot in Chama. The states of Colorado and New Mexico own the C&T, which is a registered National Historic Site. Special cars with lifts for people with disabilities are available with a 7-day advance reservation.

P.O. Box 789, Chama, NM 87520. ℂ **888/CUMBRES** or 505/756-2151. Fax 505/756-2694. www.cumbresandtoltec. com. All fares include lunch. Round-trip to Osier: adults $70, children under 12 $37. Through trip to Antonito, return by van (or to Antonito by van, return by train): adults $65, children $35. Reservations highly recommended. Memorial Day to mid-Oct trains leave Chama daily at 10am; vans depart for Antonito at 8am.

WHERE TO STAY IN CHAMA

Most accommodations in this area are on NM 17 or south of the US 64/84 junction, known as the "Y."

A MOTEL

River Bend Lodge Set on a bend of the Chama River, this lodging offers the best cabins in town and motel rooms. If you can reserve cabin 40, 50, or 60 at the back of the property, you'll have a sweet riverside stay. Some of these cabins are split-level, with a queen sleeping loft and a bedroom—not great for privacy, but good for a family that doesn't mind sharing space. Others are similar, but without the loft. Every cabin has a fold-out futon in the living room, an efficient little kitchen (you can request a coffeemaker or microwave), and a small bathroom. The motel rooms are medium-size, with basic furnishings.

2625 US 64/285, Chama, NM 87520. ⓒ **800/288-1371** or 505/756-2264. Fax 505/756-2664. www.chamariverbend lodge.com. 20 units. Motel $65–$78 double; cabin $89–$129 double. Extra person $10. Children under 13 stay free in parent's room. AE, DC, DISC, MC, V. Pets accepted; $10 fee. **Amenities:** Jacuzzi. *In room:* A/C, TV, fridge.

A BED & BREAKFAST

Gandy Dancer Bed & Breakfast Inn ★   In a two-story Victorian from the early railroad era (1912), this B&B offers an old-world feel with up-to-date amenities. New owners have given the place more color and a cozy atmosphere. Rooms range in size; all have medium-size bathrooms and comfortable beds. Attractive antiques make each room unique. The upstairs Caboose, with a king bed, sky-blue walls, and lots of light from all directions, is one pick of the place, but my favorite is the downstairs Main Line, a large room with a king bed and a purple iris theme. The full breakfast is well worth waking up for. Spinach quiche served with Canadian bacon and an almond French pancake from my last stay are still memorable. Ask about winter packages, which include home-cooked German dinners.

299 Maple Ave. (P.O. Box 810), Chama, NM 87520. ⓒ **800/424-6702** or 505/756-2191. Fax 505/756-2649. www.gandydancerbb.com. 7 units. Summer $95–$125 double; winter $85 double. Extra person $15. Rates include full breakfast. AE, DISC, MC, V. **Amenities:** Jacuzzi. *In room:* A/C, TV/VCR.

CAMPING

Rio Chama RV Campground (ⓒ **505/756-2303**) lies within easy walking distance of the Cumbres & Toltec Scenic Railroad depot. This shady campground with 94 sites along the Rio Chama is ideal for RVers and tenters who plan to take train rides. The campground also offers great photo opportunities of the old steam trains leaving the depot. Hot showers, a dump station, and complete hookups are available. It's open from mid-May to mid-October only. The campground is 2¼ miles north of the US 84/64 junction on NM 17.

  Twin Rivers Trailer Park (ⓒ **505/756-2218;** www.twinriversonline.net) has 50 sites and 40 full hookups; phone hookups are offered. Tenting is available, as are laundry facilities, ice, and picnic tables. River swimming and fishing are popular activities; other sports facilities include basketball, volleyball, badminton, and horseshoes. Twin Rivers is 100 yards west of the junction of NM 17 and US 84/64. It's open from April 15 to November 15.

WHERE TO DINE IN CHAMA

High Country Restaurant and Saloon ★   STEAKS/SEAFOOD/NEW MEXICAN   This is definitely a country place, with functional furniture, orange vinyl chairs, brown carpet, and a big stone fireplace. But it's *the* place innkeepers recommend, and one traveling couple I spoke to had eaten lunch and dinner here every day of their weeklong stay. The steaks are a big draw. More sophisticated appetites may like *trucha con piñon* (trout dusted in flour and cooked with pine nuts, garlic, and shallots). Meals are served with a salad and choice of potato. The New Mexican food is also good. The attached saloon has a full bar and bustles with people eating peanuts and throwing the shells on the floor. Breakfast on Sunday is country-style, with offerings such as steak and eggs and biscuits and gravy topping the menu, as well as pancakes and huevos rancheros (eggs atop tortillas smothered in chile sauce).

Main St. (¹∕₁₀ mile north of the "Y"). ⓒ **505/756-2384.** Main courses $4–$10 breakfast, $6–$12 lunch, $8–$17 dinner. AE, DISC, MC, V. Mon–Sat 11am–10pm; Sun 8am–10pm. Closed Easter, Thanksgiving, Dec 25.

Viva Vera's Mexican Kitchen NEW MEXICAN/AMERICAN   A local favorite, Vera's serves tasty sauces over rich enchiladas and burritos, followed by fluffy sopaipillas soaked with honey. Some complain that the chile is too hot, but I say bring it on. The setting is pastoral, with fields of gazing horses stretching to the river. The porch is *the* place to sit on warmer days. Inside, the restaurant has a vaulted ceiling, and typical Mexican memorabilia hangs on the walls—even sequined sombreros. The tables are well spaced, and a TV rests in the corner. Beer and wine are served, but the favorite seems to be wine margaritas, frothy and frozen, served in big glasses. For breakfast, try huevos rancheros (eggs on corn tortillas with chile sauce).

2202 NM 17. (✆ 505/756-2557. Main courses $4–$7 breakfast, $4–$12 lunch and dinner. AE, MC, V. Daily 8am–8pm.

ON THE ROAD: WHAT TO SEE & DO ON US 84 SOUTH

Note: For a map of this area, see "Excursions from Santa Fe," in chapter 7.

Distinctive yellow earth provided a name for the town of **Tierra Amarilla,** 14 miles south of Chama at the junction of US 84 and US 64. Throughout New Mexico, the name is synonymous with a continuing controversy over the land-grant rights of the descendants of the original Hispanic settlers. But the economy of this community of 1,000 is dyed in the wool—literally.

The organization *Ganados del Valle* (Livestock Growers of the Valley) is working to save the longhaired Spanish churro sheep from extinction, to introduce other unusual wool breeds to the valley, and to perpetuate a 200-year-old tradition of shepherding, spinning, weaving, and dyeing. Many of the craftspeople work in conjunction with **Tierra Wools** ✪, P.O. Box 229, Los Ojos, NM 87551 (✆ **505/588-7231;** www.handweavers.com), which has a showroom and workshop in a century-old mercantile building just north of Tierra Amarilla. One-of-a-kind blankets and men's and women's apparel are among the products displayed and sold.

East of Tierra Amarilla, the Rio Brazos cuts a canyon through the Tusas Mountains and around 11,403-foot Brazos Peak. Just north of Los Ojos, NM 512 heads east 7½ miles up the **Brazos Box Canyon.** High cliffs that rise straight from the valley floor give it a Yosemite-like appearance—which is even more apparent from an overlook on US 64, 18 miles east of Tierra Amarilla en route to Taos. **El Chorro,** an impressive waterfall at the canyon mouth, usually flows only from early May to mid-June. Several resort lodges are in the area.

About 37 miles south of Tierra Amarilla on US 84, and 3 miles north of Ghost Ranch, is **Echo Canyon Amphitheater** (✆ 505/684-2486), a U.S. Forest Service campground and picnic area. The natural "theater," hollowed out of sandstone by thousands of years of erosion, is a natural work of art, with layers of stone in colors ranging from pearl to blood red. The walls send back eerie echoes and even clips of conversations. It's a 10-minute walk from the parking area. The fee is $3. A 3-mile drive from there is **Ghost Ranch,** a collection of adobe buildings that make up a study center maintained by the United Presbyterian Church. A number of hauntingly memorable hikes originate from this place, which gets its name from the *brujas,* or witches, said to inhabit the canyons. The most notable hike is **Kitchen Mesa** (directions are available at the visitor center). World-renowned painter Georgia O'Keeffe spent time at Ghost Ranch painting these canyons and other land formations. Eventually she bought a portion of the ranch and lived in a humble adobe house there. The ranch now offers seminars, on a variety of topics, that are open to all.

The **Florence Hawley Ellis Museum of Anthropology** has interpretative exhibits of a Spanish ranch house and Native American anthropology, and the **Ruth Hall**

Paleontology Museum (both museums: ℂ **505/685-4333;** www.ghostranch.org) displays fossils of the early dinosaur named coelophysis found on the ranch. A lightly built creature, it was very fast when chasing prey. It roamed the area 250 million years ago, making it the oldest dinosaur found in New Mexico.

Georgia O'Keeffe spent most of her adult life in **Abiquiu,** a tiny town in a bend of the Rio Chama 14 miles south of the Ghost Ranch, and 22 miles north of Española, on US 84. The inspiration for O'Keeffe's startling landscapes (many of which can now be seen in the Georgia O'Keeffe Museum; p. 161) is clear in the surrounding terrain. **O'Keeffe's adobe home,** where she lived and painted until her death in 1986, is open for public tours, but reservations are required 1 to 2 months in advance (call ℂ **505/ 685-4539**). The charge is $22 for a 1-hour tour. A number of tours are given each week—on Tuesday, Thursday, and Friday—and a limited number of people are accepted per tour. Visitors are not permitted to take pictures. Fortunately, O'Keeffe's home remains as it was when she lived there. Abiquiu is on the High Road between Santa Fe and Taos (p. 199).

Many dinosaur skeletons have been found in rocks along the base of cliffs near **Abiquiu Reservoir** (ℂ **505/685-4371**), a popular boating and fishing spot formed by the Abiquiu Dam.

A good place to stay in the area is the **Abiquiu Inn,** a small country inn, restaurant, art gallery, and gift shop, half a mile north of the village of Abiquiu (ℂ **505/685- 4378**). The casitas are especially nice. Rates are $109 to $189.

A GREAT NEARBY PLACE TO STAY & DINE

Rancho de San Juan ★★   Located between Española and Ojo Caliente, this inn provides an authentic northern New Mexico desert experience with the comfort of a luxury hotel. It's the passion of architect and chef John Johnson, who's responsible for the design and cuisine, and interior designer David Heath, responsible for the elegant decor. The original part of the inn comprises four rooms around a central courtyard. Thirteen casitas have been added in the outlying hills. The original rooms are a bit small but very elegant, with European antiques and spectacular views of desert land-scapes and distant, snowcapped peaks. The Kiva suite is the most innovative, with a round bedroom and a skylight just above the bed, perfect for stargazing.

Tuesday through Saturday evenings, the inn serves a four-course prix-fixe dinner. The price is at least $45 per person, depending on the wine.

A few minutes' hike from the inn is the **Grand Chamber,** an impressive shrine that the innkeepers commissioned to be carved into a sandstone outcropping, where wed-dings and other festivities are held.

US 285 (en route to Ojo Caliente), P.O. Box 4140, Fairview Station, Española, NM 87533. ℂ 505/753-6818. www. ranchodesanjuan.com. 17 units. $175–$400 double; $25 charge for 1-night stay. AE, DISC, MC, V. **Amenities:** Restaurant; concierge; in-room massage and spa treatments; laundry service. *In room:* Stocked fridge, coffeemaker, hair dryer.

6 Las Vegas & Environs

21 miles E of Santa Fe; 59 miles SE of Taos; 141 miles NE of Albuquerque

Once known as the "gateway to New Mexico," **Las Vegas** ★★, a pleasant town in the foothills of the Sangre de Cristo Mountains, was founded by a land grant from the Mexican government in 1835. A group of 29 Spanish colonists planted crops in the area and built a central plaza, which started out as a meeting place and a defense against Indian attack but soon became a main trading center on the Santa Fe Trail. Las Vegas boomed with the advent of the Atchison, Topeka, and Santa Fe Railway in 1879; almost overnight, the town became the most important trading center and gathering place in the state. It was one of the largest towns in the Rocky Mountain West, rivaling Denver, Tucson, and El Paso in size.

Settlers who arrived by train in the late 19th century shunned the indigenous adobe architecture, favoring building styles more typical of the Midwest or New England. They put up scores of fancy Queen Anne and Victorian-style houses and hotels, and the town is noted to this day for its dazzling diversity of architectural styles. Some 900 buildings in Las Vegas are on the National Register of Historic Places.

ESSENTIALS

GETTING THERE From Santa Fe, take I-25 northeast 60 miles (1¼ hr.); from Raton, take I-25 south 105 miles (1¾ hr.); from Taos, follow NM 518 southeast 78 miles through Mora (2 hr.); from Tucumcari, follow NM 104 west 112 miles (2 hr.). **Las Vegas Municipal Airport** handles private flights and charters but has no regularly scheduled commercial service.

VISITOR INFORMATION The **Las Vegas & San Miguel County Chamber of Commerce,** 701 Grand Ave. (P.O. Box 128), Las Vegas, NM 87701 (② **800/832-5947** or 505/425-8631; www.lasvegasnm.org), is open weekdays from 9am to 5pm.

EXPLORING LAS VEGAS
THE HISTORIC DISTRICT

The chamber of commerce (see "Essentials," above) has a map of a self-guided tour of this area. What's most notable is the town's early Spanish history; some adobe buildings date from the first Spanish visits in the 16th century. In addition, you'll rarely see such a well-preserved collection of Territorial-style buildings. Most of the interesting structures are in the Plaza–Bridge Street area. In particular, don't miss the **Plaza Hotel,** 230 Old Town Plaza, the finest hotel in the New Mexico Territory in 1881. (See "Where to Stay in Las Vegas," below.)

In a 1940s-era Work Projects Administration building, the **Las Vegas City Museum and Rough Riders Memorial Collection,** 727 Grand Ave. (② **505/454-1401,** ext. 283), is a fun spot to spend about an hour. The largest contingent of Rough Riders was recruited from New Mexico to fight in the 1898 Spanish-American War. This museum chronicles their contribution to U.S. history and displays artifacts relating to the history of the city. Another exhibit documents the history of Las Vegas. Admission is free. The museum is open weekdays from 9am to noon and 1 to 4pm, and by appointment.

New to the plaza area, the **Santa Fe Trail Interpretive Center,** 127 Bridge St. (② **505/425-8803;** www.worldplaces.com/cchp/pwap.htm), offers a glimpse into efforts to restore the town's 918 historic buildings as well as information about the Santa Fe Trail. In the 1890s Winternitz Building, it's a fun stop, if you find it open. Volunteers staff the center, so hours vary.

EXPLORING THE AREA

La Cueva National Historic Site and Salman Ranch ★ *Finds* Each fall, I make a bit of a pilgrimage to this spot in a lush valley along the Mora River. Its history is rich, dating from the early 1800s, when a man named Vicente Romero began farming and

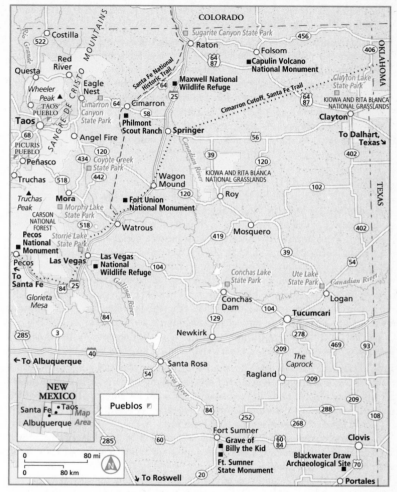

raising sheep here. He completed an elegant two-story northern New Mexico home that still stands, as well as a mill that ground flour and supplied electricity for the area (the real draw). Just north of these historic sites is the San Rafael Mission Church, with exquisite French Gothic windows. Recently restored by local people, it's now painted blue and white. The trip through these sites is worth the time during any season, but in the fall, the raspberries ripen and turn this into a must-do trip. The ranch's current owner, Frances Salman, planted 20 acres of the delectable fruit and sells it by the basket or crate, as well as in jams and over soft vanilla ice cream. Delicious.

NM 518, Buena Vista (6 miles east of Mora). ✆ **505/387-2900.** Free admission. Summer Mon–Sat 9am–5pm, Sun 10am–5pm; winter hours limited (call first).

Value Weaving Magic

You can watch weavers at work at **Tapetes de Lana** on the Las Vegas Plaza. Appropriately set in a late-1800s textile shop, this fun shop and weavers' studio offers a peek into the art as well as lovely works for sale. Hanging from antique stone walls are scarves, shawls, and Rio Grande–style rugs woven as part of a job-training program for low-income people, many of whom have mastered the art beautifully. It's located at 1814 Plaza (© **505/426-8638;** www.tapetesdelana.com) and is open Monday through Friday 8am to 5pm, Saturday 10am to 5pm. Prices are uncommonly reasonable.

FORT UNION NATIONAL MONUMENT ★

Established in 1851 to defend the Santa Fe Trail against attacks from Plains Indians, Fort Union was expanded in 1861 in anticipation of a Confederate invasion, which was subsequently thwarted at Glorieta Pass, 20 miles southeast of Santa Fe. Fort Union's location on the Santa Fe Trail made it a welcome way station for travelers, but when the railroad replaced the trail in 1879, the fort was on its way out. It was abandoned in 1891. Today, Fort Union, the largest military installation in the 19th-century Southwest, is in ruins. Though it offers little to see but adobe walls and chimneys, its very scope is impressive. Santa Fe Trail wagon ruts can still be seen nearby. Follow the 1½-mile self-guided interpretive trail that wanders through the ruins, and imagine yourself a weary 19th-century wagon traveler stopping for rest and supplies.

The national monument has a small visitor center and museum with exhibits and booklets on the fort's history. Visitors should allow 2 hours to tour the ruins.

JUST THE FACTS   To reach the site from Las Vegas, drive 18 miles north on I-25 to the Watrous exit, and then another 8 miles northwest on NM 161. Admission is $3 per person. Fort Union National Monument is open Memorial Day to Labor Day daily from 8am to 6pm; during the rest of the year, it is open daily from 8am to 4pm. It's closed January 1, Thanksgiving, and December 25.

A gift shop carries a wide selection of books on New Mexico history and women's history, and frontier military books. Camping is not available at the monument, but nearby Las Vegas has campgrounds.

For more information on the monument, contact Fort Union National Monument, P.O. Box 127, Watrous, NM 87753 (© **505/425-8025;** www.nps.gov/foun).

WHERE TO STAY IN LAS VEGAS

Most motels are on US 85 (Grand Ave.), the main north-south highway through downtown Las Vegas. (An exception is the Plaza Hotel, below.)

Inn on the Santa Fe Trail ★   Built in the 1920s as a court motel, this inn has been remodeled in hacienda style, with all rooms looking out onto the central courtyard, creating a quiet, sophisticated retreat just off busy Grand Avenue. Although it's not as historical as the Plaza Hotel (see below), the rooms are a bit more up-to-date and functional, and you can park your car right outside. Rooms are medium-size with nice accents, such as handcrafted iron light fixtures, towel racks, and hand-carved pine furniture—even *trasteros* (armoires) to conceal the televisions. The beds are comfortably firm, and each room has a table with two chairs and a desk. The bathrooms are small but very clean. Suites have sofa beds and minifridges. Be sure to read about the motel's restaurant, Blackjack's Grill, in "Where to Dine in Las Vegas," below. The outdoor pool, open seasonally, is lovely. Ask about regional cultural events that the inn helps organize.

1133 Grand Ave., Las Vegas, NM 87701. © 888/448-8438 or 505/425-6791. www.innonthesantafetrail.com. 42 units. $79 double. Rates include continental breakfast. Extra person $5. AE, DISC, MC, V. Pets accepted; $5 fee. **Amenities:** Restaurant (see below); heated outdoor pool. *In room:* A/C, TV, coffeemaker.

Plaza Hotel ★   A stay in this hotel offers a romantic peek into the past, with a view of the plaza. The windows look out on the spot where, in 1846, a ceremony led by Gen. Stephen Kearny marked the takeover of New Mexico by the United States. The inn was built in Italianate bracketed style in 1882, in the days when Western towns, newly connected with the East by train, vied with one another in constructing fancy "railroad hotels," as they were known. Considered the finest hotel in the New Mexico Territory when it was built, it underwent a $2 million renovation exactly 100 years later. Stately walnut staircases frame the lobby and conservatory (with a piano); throughout the hotel, the architecture is true to its era.

As with most renovations in northern New Mexico, don't expect to see the elegance of the Ritz. Instead, expect frontier style, with antiques a bit worn and old rugs a bit torn. Rooms vary in size, but most are average, with elegantly high ceilings, antique furnishings, comfortably firm beds, and armoires concealing the televisions. The bathrooms also range in size; most are small, with lots of original tile and up-to-date fixtures. The rooms either have windows facing out toward the plaza and surrounding streets or in toward an atrium. The inward-facing rooms are quieter but a bit claustrophobic. All rooms open onto spacious hallways with casual seating areas.

230 Plaza, Las Vegas, NM 87701. © 800/328-1882 or 505/425-3591. Fax 505/425-9659. www.plazahotel-nm.com. 36 units. $96–$116 double; $138–$146 suite. Rates include hot cooked-to-order breakfast. AE, DC, DISC, MC, V. **Amenities:** Restaurant; bar. *In room:* A/C, TV, coffeemaker, wireless Internet.

CAMPING

There's plenty of camping available in and around Las Vegas. I recommend the **Las Vegas KOA** (© **800/562-3423** or 505/454-0180; www.koa.com). It has 60 sites, 15 with full hookups, 26 with water and electricity. Laundry, grocery, ice, and recreational facilities (including a pool) are available, and there's a large gift shop. Seasonal cookouts are offered. From I-25, go 1 block southeast on US 84, then half a mile southwest on Frontage Road (also called Sheridan Rd.).

WHERE TO DINE IN LAS VEGAS

Blackjack's Grill ★★ STEAKS/SEAFOOD   Las Vegas needed a fancier restaurant for a long time, and now it has one. The main dining room at Blackjack's is small and cozy, done in brilliant colors with mood lighting. In the warmer months, diners can sit on a patio under white cloth umbrellas. As befits the area, it's a fairly informal restaurant that does fill up, so try to make reservations. Each night the chef serves some special dishes. Most are fairly traditional. I've enjoyed beef medallions in wine sauce served with garlic mashed potatoes. The pasta dishes, such as fettuccine Alfredo, can also be good. A variety of dessert specials are available. Beer and wine are served.

At the Inn on the Santa Fe Trail, 1133 Grand Ave. © 888/448-8438 or 505/425-6791. Reservations recommended. Main courses $13–$20. AE, MC, V. Daily 5–8:30pm.

El Rialto Restaurant & Lounge ★ *Kids* NEW MEXICAN   Since I was a young girl, this has been one of my favorite restaurants. In fact, my mother still asks owner Ralph Garcia to cater any big parties she has. The food is simply excellent. It's a locals' place, full of families, old Hispanic farmers, and students from the United World College. The decor is cheesy pastels, but it can be overlooked for the comfort, especially of the booths. The lounge retains the original red upholstery, which is more to my liking. Service is friendly and efficient. The chile, especially the green, is outstanding here (order anything smothered with it). My favorite is the chicken enchilada plate. The beef is good, too, and the rellenos are quite tasty. There are a variety of stuffed sopaipillas, as well as steaks, sandwiches, and a kids' menu. For dessert, I usually smother my sopaipilla with honey, though you can order pie or flan. There's a full bar and outdoor patio here.

141 Bridge St. (C) 505/454-0037. Reservations recommended. Main courses $5–$10 lunch, $7–$23 dinner. AE, DC, DISC, MC, V. Mon–Sat 10:30am–9pm.

7 Cimarron & Raton: Historic Towns on the Santa Fe Trail

Cimarron: 35 miles E of Taos, 23 miles NE of Las Vegas, 76 miles NE of Santa Fe; Raton: 67 miles NE of Taos, 93 miles NE of Las Vegas, 111 miles NE of Santa Fe

CIMARRON

Few towns in the American West have as much lore or legend attached to them as Cimarron, 41 miles southwest of Raton on US 64. Nestled against the eastern slope of the Sangre de Cristo Mountains, the town (its name is Spanish for "wild" or "untamed") achieved its greatest fame as a wild and woolly outpost on the Santa Fe Trail between the 1850s and 1880s. It was a gathering place for area ranchers, traders, gamblers, gunslingers, and other characters. Frontier personalities such as Kit Carson and Wyatt Earp, Buffalo Bill Cody and Annie Oakley, Bat Masterson and Doc Holliday, Butch Cassidy and Jesse James, painter Frederic Remington and novelist Zane Grey all passed through and stayed in Cimarron—most of them at the **St. James Hotel,** 17th Street and Collison (© **866/472-5019** or 505/376-2664). Even if you're not planning an overnight stay, it's a fun place to visit for an hour or two. The **Old Mill Museum** (© **505/376-2417**), a grand, three-story stone structure that's well worth visiting, houses an interesting collection of early photos, as well as memorabilia. It's open in May and September, Saturday from 9am to 5pm and Sunday from 1 to 5pm; Memorial Day to Labor Day, Friday through Wednesday from 9am to 5pm. It's closed October through April. Admission is $2 for adults, $1 for seniors and children. The **Cimarron Chamber of Commerce,** 104 N. Lincoln Ave. (P.O. Box 604), Cimarron, NM 87714 (© **505/376-2417;** www.cimarronnm.com), has complete information on the region. It is open in summer Thursday through Monday from 8:30am to 4:30pm; in winter Monday through Friday from 10am to 3pm.

RATON

Raton was founded in 1879 at the site of Willow Springs, a watering stop on the Santa Fe Trail. Mountain man "Uncle Dick" Wooton, a closet entrepreneur, had blasted a pass through the Rocky Mountains just north of the spring, and he began charging tolls. When the railroad bought Wooton's road, Raton developed as the railroad, mining, and ranching center for this part of the New Mexico Territory. Today it has a well-preserved historic district. The tourist information center is at the **Raton Chamber and Economic Development Council,** 100 Clayton Rd., at the corner of 2nd Street (P.O. Box 1211), Raton, NM 87740 (© **800/638-6161** or 505/445-3689; www.raton.info). The center is open daily from Memorial Day to Labor Day, 8am to 6pm, 8am to 5pm the rest of the year.

East of Raton is Capulin Mountain, home to **Capulin Volcano National Monument** ★★, which offers visitors the rare opportunity to walk inside a volcanic crater. A 2-mile road spirals up from the visitor center more than 600 feet to the crater of the 8,182-foot peak. Two self-guided trails leave from the parking area: an energetic and spectacular 1-mile hike around the crater rim, and a 100-foot descent into the crater to the ancient volcanic vent. One of the most interesting features here is the symmetry of the main cinder cone. The volcano was last active about 60,000 years ago, when it sent out the last of four lava flows. The monument is 30 miles east of Raton; take US 64/87 and go north 3 miles on NM 325. The visitor center, located at the base of the western side of the volcano, is open daily Memorial Day to Labor Day from 7:30am to 6:30pm, the rest of the year daily 8am to 4pm. An audiovisual program discusses volcanism, and park personnel will answer questions. Admission is $5 per car. For more information, contact **Capulin Volcano National Monument,** P.O. Box 40, Capulin, NM 88414 (✆ **505/278-2201;** www.nps.gov/cavo).

8 The I-40 Corridor

The 216 freeway miles on I-40 from Albuquerque to the Texas border cross featureless prairie and very few towns. But the valleys of the Pecos River (site of Santa Rosa) and the Canadian River (Tucumcari is on its banks) have several attractions, including natural lakes. There's not a lot to explore here unless you're a bird-watcher or a fisher, but both towns can make a day's stopover worthwhile.

ESSENTIALS

GETTING THERE   Travel time from Albuquerque to Tucumcari on I-40 is 2 hours, 40 minutes; to Santa Rosa, 1 hour, 45 minutes. There's no regularly scheduled commercial air service into either Tucumcari or Santa Rosa. Private planes can land at **Tucumcari Municipal Airport** (✆ **505/461-3229**).

VISITOR INFORMATION   Contact the **Tucumcari–Quay County Chamber of Commerce,** 404 W. Tucumcari Blvd. (P.O. Drawer E), Tucumcari, NM 88401 (✆ **888-664-7255** or 505/461-1694; www.tucumcarinm.com), or the **Santa Rosa City Information Center,** 486 Parker Ave., Santa Rosa, NM 88435 (✆ **505/472-3763**).

WHERE TO STAY

Major chain hotels are at I-40 interchanges in both Tucumcari and Santa Rosa. Smaller "ma and pa" motels lie along the main streets that were once segments of legendary Route 66—Tucumcari Boulevard in Tucumcari, and Will Rogers Drive in Santa Rosa.

IN TUCUMCARI

Best Western Discovery Inn   This pink Mission-style motel with large, quiet rooms provides an oasis in the somewhat barren eastern part of the state. It's off the strip but near I-40; take exit 332. The motel opened in 1985, and remodeling is ongoing. Rooms are decorated in earth tones, with comfortable beds. Bathrooms are small, but each has an outer sink/vanity and dressing room. Everything is very clean. Complimentary morning coffee is an added touch. K-Bob's restaurant is right next door.

200 E. Estrella Ave. (at I-40 exit 332), Tucumcari, NM 88401. ✆ **800/528-1234** or 505/461-4884. Fax 505/461-2463. www.bestwestern.com/discoveryinn. 107 units. May–Oct $66–$74 double; Nov–Apr $52–$58 double. AE, DC, DISC, MC, V. Pets accepted; $5 per day. **Amenities:** Seasonal outdoor pool; fitness center; Jacuzzi; coin-op laundry. In room: A/C, TV.

Camping Near Tucumcari

There are three good campgrounds around Tucumcari. **Tucumcari KOA** (© 800/ 562-1871 or 505/461-1841; www.koa.com) has 111 sites, laundry and grocery facilities, RV supplies, picnic tables, and grills. It also offers a recreation hall with video games, a heated pool, a basketball hoop, a playground, horseshoes, and shuffleboard, along with lots of elm trees for shade. From I-40, take Exit 335 off the interstate, then go ¼ mile east on South Frontage Road.

IN SANTA ROSA

La Quinta   Perched on a hill above Santa Rosa, this newer whitewashed chain hotel offers functional rooms. All are medium-size, decorated in tasteful earth tones. Each has a small bathroom with an outer sink/vanity. Beds are comfy, and each room holds a table and chairs. The place is inventively landscaped with a rock grotto patio where the hot tub sits.

1701 Will Rogers Dr., Santa Rosa, NM 88435. © 800/531-5900 or 505/472-4800. Fax 505/472-4809. www.laquinta. com. 60 units. $72–$81 double. Rates include continental breakfast. AE, DC, DISC, MC, V. **Amenities:** Indoor pool; outdoor Jacuzzi. *In room:* A/C, TV, dataport, coffeemaker, hair dryer, safe.

Camping Near Santa Rosa

The **Santa Rosa Campground** (© 505/472-3126) offers 94 sites, 33 full hookups, laundry and grocery facilities, fire rings, grills, a heated swimming pool, and a playground for the kids. Situated in a piñon and juniper forest near town, the campground has a few small elm trees on the grounds. Coming from the east on I-40, take exit 277 and go 1 mile west on Business Loop; coming from the west on I-40, take exit 275 and go ¼ mile east on Business Loop.

Also in the area is **Santa Rosa Lake State Park** (© 505/472-3110), with year-round camping at 75 sites (about a third with electric hookups) as well as grills, boating, fishing, and hiking trails. Swimming is permitted but not encouraged because of the lake's uneven bottom and lack of beaches; children are safer swimming in Park Lake in Santa Rosa.

WHERE TO DINE

Del's Family Restaurant AMERICAN/MEXICAN   The big cow atop the neon sign is not only a Route 66 landmark, it also points to the fine steaks inside. The restaurant has big windows along almost every wall, letting in plenty of daylight or neon light at night. Del's is a casual, diner-style eatery with lots of plants. Breakfast is big plates of dishes such as scrambled eggs and pancakes. At lunch, sample sandwiches and salads. Roast beef, served with a scoop of mashed potatoes and a trip to the salad bar, is a big seller at dinnertime. You can also order grilled chicken breast. The New Mexican food is good but not great. Del's is not licensed for alcoholic beverages.

1202 E. Rte. 66, Tucumcari. © 505/461-1740. Reservations not accepted. Main courses $4–$7 breakfast, $5–$9 lunch, $7–$15 dinner. MC, V. Mon–Sat 7am–9pm.

Joseph's Restaurant & Cantina ⭐ AMERICAN/NEW MEXICAN   You may want to plan your drive so that you can eat a meal at "Joe's." In business since 1956, it's a real Route 66 diner, with linoleum tables, comfortable booths, and plenty of memorabilia, from license plates to vintage RC Cola posters. The locals all eat here: You'll see Hispanic grandmothers, skinny cowboys in straw hats, and dusty farmhands just in from the fields. The varied menu offers excellent fare. Breakfast brings eggs and

Moments Route 66 Revisited: Rediscovering New Mexico's Stretch of the Mother Road

As the old Bobby Troupe hit suggests: Get your kicks on Route 66. The highway that once stretched from Chicago to California was hailed as the road to freedom. During the Great Depression, it was the way west for farmers escaping Dust Bowl poverty out on the plains. And if you found yourself in a rut in the postwar late 1940s and early '50s, all you had to do was hop in the car and head west on Route 66.

The road existed long before it gained such widespread fascination. Built in the late 1920s and paved in 1937, it was the lifeblood of communities in eight states. Nowadays, however, US 66 is as elusive as the fantasies that once carried hundreds of thousands west in search of a better life. Replaced by other roads, covered up by interstates (mostly I-40), and just plain out of use, Route 66 still exists in New Mexico, but you'll have to do a little searching and take some extra time to find it.

Motorists driving west from Texas can take a spin (make that a slow spin) on a 20-mile gravel stretch of the original highway running from Glenrio (Texas) to San Jon. From San Jon to Tucumcari, you can enjoy nearly 24 continuous paved miles of vintage 66. In Tucumcari, the historic route sliced through the center of town along what is now Tucumcari Boulevard. Santa Rosa's Will Rogers Drive is that city's 4-mile claim to the Mother Road. In Albuquerque, US 66 follows Central Avenue for 18 miles, from the 1936 State Fairgrounds, past original 1930s motels and the historic Nob Hill district, west through downtown.

One of the best spots to pretend you are a 1950s road warrior crossing the desert—whizzing past rattlesnakes, tepees, and tumbleweeds—is along NM 124, which winds 25 miles from Mesita to Acoma in northwestern New Mexico. You can next pick up old Route 66 in Grants, along 6-mile Santa Fe Avenue. In Gallup, a 9-mile segment of US 66 is lined with restaurants and hotels reminiscent of the city's days as a Western film capital from 1929 to 1964. Just outside Gallup, the historic route continues west to the Arizona border as NM 118.

For more information about Route 66, contact the **Grants/Cíbola County Chamber of Commerce** (© 800/748-2142) or the **New Mexico Department of Tourism** (© 800/545-2040).

bacon or omelets. At lunch, I've enjoyed a salad topped with juicy grilled chicken. The New Mexican dishes are large and chile-smothered, and burgers are juicy, with a variety of toppings, from the Rio Pecos topped with green chile to the Acapulco, with guacamole. Steak is a big seller at a good price. For dessert, try a piece of pie or a shake. Also on the premises are a bakery, a full-service bar, and a gift shop.

865 Will Rogers Dr., Santa Rosa. © 505/472-3361. Reservations not accepted. Main courses $4–$7 breakfast, $6–$9 lunch, $6–$12 dinner. AE, DC, DISC, MC, V. Summer daily 6am–10pm; winter daily 6am–9pm.

11

UFOs & Carlsbad Caverns: Southern New Mexico from Top to Bottom

If your idea of fun is road-tripping across exotic landscapes, delving into ancient cultures, peering into outer space, and chatting up an alien or two, southern New Mexico is your destination. Here you'll find an astonishing array of singular landscapes and unusual attractions, from the rolling gypsum sand dunes of White Sands National Monument to the underground natural cathedrals of Carlsbad Caverns National Park.

Wildness abounds at places such as the Bosque del Apache National Wildlife Refuge and the 3.3-million-acre Gila National Forest, both known for great bird-watching. Within the forest lies Gila Cliff Dwellings National Monument, home to the Mogollon people 1,000 years ago. The final frontier is also present in this region, at places such as the International UFO Museum and Research Center in Roswell, the area where aliens may have landed, and the Very Large Array, the world's most powerful radio telescope.

Between the sights lie more miles of open country than most people can imagine. Though on first glance it may appear desolate, it's actually filled with petroglyphs and lava fields, hot springs and ghost towns, places where legends such as Geronimo and Billy the Kid once roamed.

The big city in the area is Las Cruces, New Mexico's second largest, with a population of 73,600. Set at the foot of the dramatic Organ Mountains, it is an agricultural and education center. To the east lies Ruidoso, a booming resort town with good skiing in winter. To the west is Silver City, a charming mining town that's been revived in recent years. The Rio Grande slices a green swath through the center of the region, nourishing many communities along its banks.

With such long distances to cover, you'll need a reliable car to get around. Flip on the tunes, keep a close eye on the gas gauge, and enjoy the ride.

1 Getting Outside in Southern New Mexico

BIKING Several forest roads and single-track trails in this region are favorites with mountain bikers. In the Ruidoso area, near Cloudcroft, the **Rim Trail,** a 17-mile intermediate trail that offers views of the White Sands, is considered one of the top 10 trails in the nation. To reach the trail, take NM 130 from Cloudcroft to NM 6563, turn right, and look for the Rim Trail signs. The Cloudcroft area offers three other good trails: **La Luz Canyon, Silver Springs Loop,** and **Pumphouse Canyon.** For directions, contact the Cloudcroft Ranger Station (© 505/682-2551). In the Socorro area, at **Bosque del Apache National Wildlife Refuge** (© 505/835-1828), cyclists

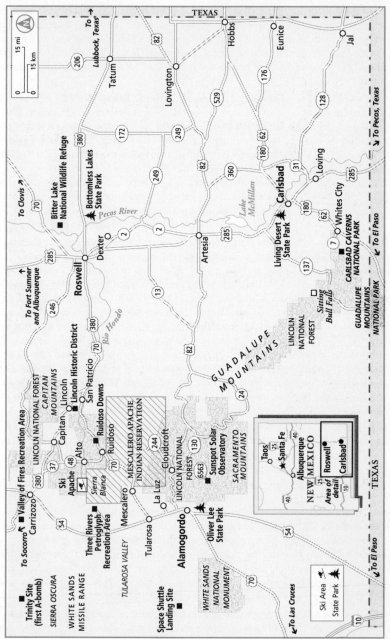

enjoy the 12-mile loop tour. Bikes are not allowed in the Gila Wilderness, but they are permitted on trails in other parts of **Gila National Forest** (© 505/388-8201; www.fs.fed.us/r3/gila). Refer to "Other Adventures in Gila National Forest," later in this chapter, for specific ride suggestions. Contact **Gila Hike and Bike** (© 505/388-3222) in Silver City for rentals and guidebooks to riding in the Gila National Forest.

BIRD-WATCHING **Bitter Lake National Wildlife Refuge** (© 505/622-6755), northeast of Roswell, is particularly good for watching migratory waterfowl, and **Bluff Springs** (© 505/682-2551), south of Cloudcroft, is popular with turkeys and hummingbirds. If you find turkey vultures particularly fascinating, **Rattlesnake Springs** (© 505/785-2232), located south of Carlsbad, is the place to go. **Bosque del Apache National Wildlife Refuge** (© 505/835-1828) is a refuge for migratory waterfowl such as snow geese and cranes. It's 16 miles south of Socorro. **North Monticello Point** (© 505/744-5421), on Elephant Butte Lake, is a great place to see pelicans, bald eagles, and a variety of waterfowl, and **Water Canyon** (© 505/854-2281), 14 miles west of Socorro in the **Cíbola National Forest,** is home to golden eagles.

BOATING Boating, water-skiing, jet-skiing, and sailing are permitted at **Carlsbad Municipal Park,** which runs through town for just over a mile along the west bank of Lake Carlsbad. The lake also has a beach that's open to swimmers. **Brantley Lake State Park** (© 505/457-2384), 15 miles north of Carlsbad, is popular with windsurfers who favor its consistent desert winds. In the Gila National Forest, both **Lake Roberts** (© 505/536-2250), about 40 miles north of Silver City on NM 15, and **Snow Lake** (© 505/533-6231), north on US 180 from Silver City and then east on NM 159, allow boating. Lake Roberts features motorboat rentals; Snow Lake permits only canoes, rowboats, and other boats without gas motors. **Elephant Butte Lake State Park** (© 505/744-5923) boasts the largest body of water in New Mexico. The lake is 43 miles long and popular with boating enthusiasts. Three ramps provide access to the lake, and there are launching areas for smaller vessels. To find information on New Mexico state parks, go to **www.nmparks.com.**

FISHING **Bonito Lake** and **Rio Ruidoso** are popular destinations for trout fishing, and **Oasis State Park** (© 505/356-5331), just north of Portales, also offers fishing. **Caballo Lake State Park** (© 505/743-3942), about 18 miles south of Truth or Consequences, offers smallmouth and largemouth bass, stripers, bluegill, crappie, catfish, and walleye fishing in its 11,500-acre lake. **Elephant Butte Lake State Park** (© 505/744-5923), also near Truth or Consequences, is another great fishing location. Look to catch white bass, black bass, catfish, walleye, crappie, and stripers here. **Lake Roberts** (© 505/536-2250), about 40 miles north of Silver City in the Gila National Forest, boasts prime rainbow trout fishing waters. A fishing license and a habitat stamp are required. You'll find fly-fishing in the **Gila River** year-round, but the best seasons are spring and fall. Mainly rainbow trout swim these waters, with catfish on the lower Gila. For more information, contact the **New Mexico Game and Fish Department** (© 505/476-8000; www.wildlife.state.nm.us).

GOLF This region has plenty of golfing opportunities. Greens fees range from $12 to $125 (the upper-end courses are in the Ruidoso area). The fee sometimes includes cart rental; when it doesn't, a cart runs about $15. In Ruidoso, **Cree Meadows Country Club,** Country Club Drive off Sudderth Drive (© 505/257-5815), is an 18-hole public course. Also in the Ruidoso area are the 18-hole public courses at the **Inn of the Mountain Gods Resort & Casino,** 287 Carrizo Canyon Rd. (© **800/545-6040** or 505/464-4100; www.innofthemountaingods.com); and the **Links at Sierra Blanca,** 105 Sierra Blanca Dr. (© **505/258-5330**). In Cloudcroft, the 9-hole **Lodge at Cloudcroft Golf Course** (© **800/395-6343** or 505/682-2566; www.thelodge resort.com) boasts an elevation of 9,200 feet; it's one of the highest courses in the world and one of the oldest in the United States. Alamogordo's **Desert Lakes Golf Course** (© **505/437-0290;** www.desertlakesgolf.com) has views of Sierra Blanca and the Sacramento Mountains. In Socorro, the 18-hole **New Mexico Tech Golf Course** (© **505/835-5335**) offers tree-lined fairways and water on more than half of its holes. The **Truth or Consequences Golf Course** (© **505/894-2603**) consists of 9 fairly traditional holes in a desert setting. A more contemporary course is in Las Cruces, at the 18-hole **Sonoma Ranch Golf Course** (© **505/521-1818;** www.sonomaranchgolf. com), which opened in 2000. Las Cruces also has the **New Mexico State University Golf Course** (© **505/646-3219;** www.nmsu.edu/~golf), built with collegiate golf in mind. With wide-spanning views and undulating terrain, this Cal Olsen–designed course has much to offer. Deming has the 18-hole **Rio Mimbres Country Club** (© **505/546-9481**). The 18-hole **Silver City Golf Course** (© **505/538-5041**) is home to the annual Billy Casper Golf Tournament, where the legend himself returns each September (usually Labor Day) to participate.

HIKING   More than 225 miles of trails weave a web through the Smokey Bear Ranger District of the **Lincoln National Forest.** From Ruidoso, favorite destinations are the White Mountain Wilderness, with nine trails, and the Capitan Mountains Wilderness, with 11 trails. **Smokey Bear Ranger District office,** 901 Mechem Dr., Ruidoso (© **505/257-4095**), has excellent and inexpensive maps of each wilderness area. Monjeau Lookout is a popular destination off Ski Run Road (NM 532). **Carlsbad Caverns National Park** has an extensive trail system as well (outside the caves, of course). There's great hiking in the **Gila National Forest** (© **505/388-8201**), which has approximately 1,500 miles of trails, ranging in length and difficulty. Your best bet for hiking in the area is to purchase a guidebook devoted entirely to hiking the Gila National Forest. Popular areas include the Crest Trail, the West Fork Trail, and the Aldo Leopold Wilderness. One favorite day hike in the forest is the Catwalk, a moderately strenuous hike along a series of steel bridges and walkways suspended over Whitewater Canyon. See "Other Adventures in Gila National Forest," later in this chapter, for more hiking suggestions. Whenever and wherever you go hiking, be sure to carry plenty of water.

HORSEBACK RIDING   Horseback riding is easily found in Ruidoso. Try the **Inn of the Mountain Gods Resort & Casino** (© **800/545-6040** or 505/464-4100; www.innofthemountaingods.com) and **Cowboy Stables** (© **505/378-8217**). The **Double E Guest Ranch** (© **505/535-2048;** www.doubleeranch.com) offers authentic ranch riding in the southwestern New Mexico desert and forest lands. Because it's also a working cattle ranch, the Double E has an authentic feel, and a guest capacity of only 12 adds to the atmosphere. Trail rides and cattle drives range across 30,000 acres, which adjoin the legendary 3-million-acre Gila Wilderness. About a half-hour from Silver City, the ranch sits on a shady bend of Bear Creek, a place that draws plenty of wildlife. The accommodations are in old ranch buildings, which range from cozy to expansive. My favorite has old saddles hanging from the rafters. These are not luxury rooms; they're real ranch lodgings. The ranch does not have a separate children's program but does accept kids.

SKIING   Southern New Mexico's premier ski resort is **Ski Apache** (© **505/257-9001** for snow reports, or 505/336-4356 for information), only 20 miles northwest of Ruidoso in the Mescalero Apache Indian Reservation. Situated on an 11,500-foot ridge of the 12,003-foot Sierra Blanca, the resort boasts a gondola, two quad chairs, five triple chairs, one double chair, a day lodge, a sport shop, a rental shop, a ski school, a first-aid center, four snack bars, and a lounge. Ski Apache has 55 trails and slopes (20% beginner, 35% intermediate, and 45% advanced), with a vertical drop of 1,900 feet and a total skier capacity of 16,500 an hour. Though its location seems remote, a lot of skiers fill this mountain during weekends and holidays. Because the mountain is owned and run by the Apaches, you can experience another culture while skiing. All-day lift tickets cost $50 for adults, $32 for children under 13. The mountain is open Thanksgiving to Easter daily from 8:45am to 4pm. Book lift-and-lodging packages through the **Inn of the Mountain Gods Resort & Casino** (© **800/545-6040** or 505/464-4100; www.innofthemountaingods.com).

SWIMMING   Swimming is permitted at **Elephant Butte Lake State Park** (© **505/744-5923**) and **Caballo Lake State Park** (© **505/743-3942**), but not at some others. Be sure to ask first.

2 Alamogordo

60 miles NE of Las Cruces; 83 miles SW of Roswell; 146 miles SE of Albuquerque

Famous for its leading role in America's space research and military technology industries, **Alamogordo** (pop. 31,000) achieved worldwide fame on July 16, 1945, when the first atomic bomb was exploded at nearby Trinity Site. Today, it is home of the New Mexico Museum of Space History, White Sands National Monument, and Holloman Air Force Base. Twenty miles east and twice as high, the resort village of **Cloudcroft** (elevation 8,650 ft.) attracts vacationers to the forested heights of the Sacramento Mountains.

ESSENTIALS
GETTING THERE   From Albuquerque, take I-25 south 87 miles to San Antonio; turn east on US 380, go 66 miles to Carrizozo; then turn south on US 54 for 58 miles (4 hr.). From Las Cruces, take US 70 northeast (1½ hr.). Note that US 70 may be closed for up to 2 hours during tests on White Sands Missile Range. From El Paso, take US 54 north (1½ hr.).

The nearest major airport is **El Paso International.** The local airport, **Alamogordo–White Sands Regional Airport,** is served by **Rio Grande Air** (© **866/880-0464** or 505/439-1275), which has flights from Albuquerque several times daily.

VISITOR INFORMATION   The **Alamogordo Chamber of Commerce** and visitor center is at 1301 N. White Sands Blvd., Alamogordo, NM 88311 (© **800/826-0294** or 505/437-6120; www.alamogordo.com).

CITY LAYOUT   Alamogordo is on the eastern edge of the Tularosa Valley, at the foot of the Sacramento Mountains. US 54 (White Sands Blvd.) is the main street, extending several miles north and south. The downtown district is 3 blocks east of White Sands Boulevard, off 10th Street.

WHAT TO SEE & DO

In addition to the attractions in Alamogordo itself, also enjoyable is the small, historic village of **La Luz**, 3 miles north of Alamogordo. It has attracted a number of resident artists and craftspeople who live, work, and display some of their products for sale. Worth seeing are the old adobe corral and the small Our Lady of Light Church.

New Mexico Museum of Space History ⚐   The museum comes in two parts: the International Space Hall of Fame and the Clyde W. Tombaugh IMAX Dome Theater. Both are on the lower slopes of the Sacramento Mountains, 2 miles east of US 54, just above New Mexico State University's Alamogordo branch campus.

The **Space Hall of Fame** occupies the "Golden Cube," a five-story building with walls of golden glass. Visitors are encouraged to start on the top floor and work their way down. En route, they recall the accomplishments of the first astronauts and cosmonauts, including America's Mercury, Gemini, and Apollo programs, and the early Soviet orbital flights. Spacecraft and a lunar exploration module are exhibited. Displays tell the history and purposes of rocketry, missiles, and satellites and provide an orientation to astronomy and other planets.

At **Tombaugh Theater,** IMAX projection and Spitz 512 Planetarium Systems create earthly and cosmic experiences on a 2,700-square-foot dome screen.

At the top of NM 2001. ✆ **877/333-6589** outside New Mexico, or 505/437-2840. Fax 505/434-2245. www.spacefame. org. Admission to International Space Hall of Fame $2.50 adults, $2.25 seniors (age 60 and older) and military, $2 children age 4–12, free for children under 4. IMAX Theater $6 adults, $5.50 seniors, $4.50 children, free for children under 4. Additional charge for double feature. Daily 9am–5pm.

TRINITY SITE

The world's first atomic bomb was exploded in this desert never-never land on July 16, 1945. It is strictly off-limits to civilians—except twice a year, on the first Saturday of April and October. A small lava monument commemorates the explosion, which left a crater ¼-mile across and 8 feet deep, and transformed the desert sand into a jade green glaze called "Trinitite" that remains today. The McDonald House, where the bomb's plutonium core was assembled 2 miles from Ground Zero, has been restored to its 1945 condition. The site is on the west slope of Sierra Oscura, 90 air miles northwest of Alamogordo. For more information, call the public affairs office of **White Sands Missile Range** (✆ **505/678-1134**).

EXPLORING THE SURROUNDING AREA

Cloudcroft ⚐ is a picturesque mountain village of 750 people high in the Sacramento Mountains, surrounded by Lincoln National Forest. Though only about 20 miles east of Alamogordo on US 82, it is twice as high, overlooking the Tularosa Valley from a dizzying elevation of almost 9,000 feet. It was founded in 1899 when railroad surveyors reached the mountain summit and built a lodge for Southern Pacific Railroad workers. Today, the Lodge is Cloudcroft's biggest attraction and biggest employer (see "Nearby Places to Stay & Dine," below). Other accommodations are also available in town, as are lots of recreational opportunities and community festivals. For information, contact the **Cloudcroft Chamber of Commerce,** P.O. Box 1290, Cloudcroft, NM 88317 (✆ **505/682-2733;** www.cloudcroft.net). It's in a log cabin in the center of town, on the south side of US 82.

For a quick bite in the village, head to **Far Side Food and Health,** 91 Glorieta Ave. (✆ **505/682-5000**). It's part health goods store, part little kitchen—and the food is excellent. Diners order at a counter and sit at small tables and comfortable chairs within the store or on a porch. Sandwiches, such as roast beef or chicken salad, are served on big slices of home-baked bread and grilled if you like. Each day has a special, such as jambalaya served with corn bread. Best of all are the pastries—cherry or apple tarts, baked fresh daily. It's open daily 11am to 3pm. If you like outdoor gear and items such as scented candles and tie-dyed clothes, stop next door at **High Altitude,** 310 Burro Ave. (© **505/682-1229**).

WHERE TO STAY IN ALAMOGORDO

All accommodations in Alamogordo are along White Sands Boulevard, the north-south highway through town.

Best Western Desert Aire   This brick-and-stucco hotel (with renovation ongoing) is the place to stay in Alamogordo. The medium-size rooms are cozy and furnished in contemporary style. You'll find firm beds and average-size, functional bathrooms. Also available are kitchenettes, which contain stoves, ovens, and microwaves. The suites are inexpensive and have 3-foot-deep Jacuzzi tubs.

1021 S. White Sands Blvd., Alamogordo, NM 88310. © **800/565-1988** or 505/437-2110. Fax 505/437-1898. www. bestwestern.com. 99 units. $58–$64 double; $65–$79 suite. Rates include continental breakfast. AE, DISC, MC, V. Pets accepted; $50 deposit. **Amenities:** Outdoor pool; Jacuzzi; sauna; game room; coin-op laundry; same-day dry cleaning. *In room:* A/C, TV, dataport, fridge, coffeemaker, hair dryer, iron.

CAMPING

Alamogordo Roadrunner (© **877/437-3003** or 505/437-3003; www.roadrunner campground.com) has laundry and grocery facilities as well as a recreation room, swimming pool, playground, shuffleboard, and planned group activities in winter. The campground is on 24th Street in Alamogordo, just east of the US 54/70/82 junction. **Oliver Lee State Park,** 15 miles southeast of Alamogordo on US 54 and Dog Canyon Road (© **505/437-8284**), is another good choice, with 44 sites, 10 full hookups, picnic tables, grills, tenting availability, a playground, and hiking trails.

WHERE TO DINE IN ALAMOGORDO

Memories Restaurant 🟊 *Finds* AMERICAN   In a 1907 Victorian home in a residential neighborhood right on the edge of historic downtown, this restaurant serves excellent food in an old-world setting. Tables sit on Brazilian-oak floors in what was once the living room and den, creating a casual, comfortable atmosphere, which is a good thing because the service is overworked and therefore slow. Many of the diners at lunch are women, who come to sample salads and croissant sandwiches; dinner customers include a more even mix of genders. Basically, the place is packed nonstop while it's open. I recommend crab salad served over avocado, or the turkey and avocado croissant sandwich. For dinner, a big seller is prime rib, which comes with salad or soup, bread, a side dish, and vegetable. Grilled shrimp is also good. Beer and wine are available.

1223 New York Ave. (corner of 13th St.). © **505/437-0077.** Reservations recommended. Main courses $5–$10 lunch, $11–$17 dinner. AE, DISC, MC, V. Mon–Sat 11am–9pm.

NEARBY PLACES TO STAY & DINE

Casa de Sueños 🟊 *Kids* NEW MEXICAN   A fun south-of-the-border stop, this new restaurant about 15 miles north of Alamogordo, outside Tularosa, serves tasty New Mexican fare with a good dose of the whimsy of Mexico. Decorated with Mexican folk paintings and a country-home mural, it exudes a fiesta atmosphere. Outside, little Christmas lights illuminate the broad patio and chili peppers decorate the tablecloths. For breakfast, try huevos rancheros (eggs over tortillas smothered in chile). A lunch buffet provides a good sampling of enchiladas and beans. To start your meal, try guacamole, made with red onions. For an entree, order anything with green chile sauce, made with fresh chiles and well seasoned. Otherwise, you might try chicken *adovado*—marinated, charbroiled chicken breast—or sample a stuffed *sopaipilla*. Vegetarian and children's selections round out the menu. You can order from a variety of beers and wines.

35 St. Francis Dr., Tularosa, NM. ℭ **505/585-3494.** Reservations recommended on weekends. Main courses $4–$8 breakfast, $7–$13 lunch and dinner. AE, DISC, MC, V. Mon–Fri 11am–9pm; Sat 9am–9pm; Sun 9am–8pm.

The Lodge at Cloudcroft ✰✰   This lodge is an antique jewel, a well-preserved relic of another era. From the grand fireplace in the lobby to the homey Victorian decor in the guest rooms, it exudes gentility and class. Its nine-hole golf course, one of the nation's highest, challenges golfers across rolling hills between 8,600 and 9,200 feet elevation and is the site of numerous regional tournaments. All rooms have views and are filled with antiques, from sideboards and lamps to mirrors and steam radiators. Each room is medium-size, and some suites have jet tubs.

Rebecca's (ℭ **505/682-2566**), the lodge's restaurant, serves three meals daily, plus a midday snack menu. Service is friendly and very efficient, and the atmosphere is elegant, with bright sunshine during the day and romantic lighting at night. I recommend the marlin with crab béarnaise sauce, served with a twice-baked potato. For dessert, try chocolate mousse pie with Oreo crust.

1 Corona Place (P.O. Box 497), Cloudcroft, NM 88317. ℭ **800/395-6343** or 505/682-2566. Fax 505/682-2715. www.thelodgeresort.com. 61 units. $109–$159 double; $169–$329 suite. AE, DC, DISC, MC, V. Pets accepted with limitations; $25 fee. **Amenities:** Restaurant; bar; heated outdoor pool; golf course; access to nearby tennis courts; exercise room; spa: Jacuzzi; sauna; bike and snowmobile rentals; fax and photocopying services; babysitting. *In room:* A/C, TV, coffeemaker; hair dryer and iron upon request.

3 White Sands National Monument ✰✰✰

15 miles SW of Alamogordo; 46 miles NE of Las Cruces; 150 miles S of Albuquerque

Arguably the most memorable natural area in this part of the Southwest, **White Sands National Monument** preserves the best part of the world's largest gypsum dune field, an area of 275 square miles of pure white gypsum sand reaching out over the floor of the Tularosa Basin in wavelike dunes. Plants and animals have evolved to adapt to the bright white environment here. Some creatures have a bleached coloration to match the whiteness all around them, and some plants have evolved means for surviving against the smothering pressures of the blowing sands.

The surrounding mountains—the Sacramentos to the east, with their forested slopes, and the serene San Andres to the west—are composed of sandstone, limestone, sedimentary rocks, and pockets of gypsum. Over millions of years, rain and melting snow dissolved the gypsum and carried it down into Lake Lucero. Here the hot sun and dry winds evaporate the water, leaving the pure white gypsum to crystallize. Then the persistent winds blow the crystals, in the form of minuscule bits of sand, in a northeastern direction, adding them to growing dunes. As each dune grows and moves farther from the lake, new ones form, rank after rank, in what seems an endless procession.

The dunes are especially enchanting at sunrise and under the light of a full moon, but you'll have to camp here to experience that extraordinary sight (see "Camping," below). If you're not camping, you'll probably want to spend only a couple of hours here. Refreshments and snacks are for sale at the visitor center, along with books, maps, posters, and other souvenirs; however, no dining or grocery facilities are available.

> ### *Tips* Safety Warnings
>
> The National Park Service emphasizes that:
> - Tunneling in this sand can be dangerous, because it collapses easily and could suffocate a person.
> - Sand-surfing down the dune slopes, although permitted, can also be hazardous. Undertake it with care, and never near an auto road.
> - Hikers can get lost in a sudden sandstorm if they stray from marked trails or areas.

ESSENTIALS

GETTING THERE   The visitor center is 15 miles southwest of Alamogordo on US 70/82. (*Note:* Due to missile testing on the adjacent White Sands Missile Range, this road sometimes closes for up to 2 hr. at a time.) The nearest major airport is **El Paso International,** 90 miles away. You can drive from there or take a commuter flight from Albuquerque to **Alamogordo–White Sands Regional Airport** (see "Essentials," under "Alamogordo," above).

VISITOR INFORMATION   For more information, contact **White Sands National Monument,** P.O. Box 1086, Holloman AFB, NM 88330-1086 (© **505/ 479-6124;** www.nps.gov/whsa). When driving in the area, tune your radio to 1610 AM for information on what's happening.

ADMISSION FEES & HOURS   Admission is $3 for adults, free for children under 17. From Memorial Day to Labor Day, the visitor center is open daily from 8am to 7pm, and Dunes Drive is open daily from 7am to 9pm. Ranger talks and sunset strolls begin nightly at 7 and 8:30pm during summer. During the rest of the year, the visitor center is open daily from 8am to 5pm, and Dunes Drive is open daily from 7am to sunset.

SEEING THE HIGHLIGHTS

The 16-mile **Dunes Drive** loops through the "heart of sands" from the visitor center. Information available at the center tells you what to look for on your drive. Sometimes the winds blow the dunes over the road, which must then be rerouted. All the dunes are in fact moving slowly to the northeast, pushed by prevailing southwest winds, some at the rate of as much as 20 feet per year.

In the center of the monument, the road itself is made of hard-packed gypsum. (*Note:* It can be especially slick after an afternoon thunderstorm, so drive cautiously!) Visitors are invited to get out of their cars at established parking areas and explore a bit; some like to climb a dune for a better view of the endless sea of sand. If you'd rather experience the park by hiking than on the long drive, try the Big Dune Trail, right near the entrance. It takes you on a 45-minute loop along the edges of the dunes and then into their whiteness, ending atop a 60-foot-tall one.

In summer, nature walks and evening programs take place in the dunes. Ranger-guided activities include orientation talks and nature walks.

4 Ruidoso *✦* & the Mescalero Apache Indian Reservation

33 miles NE of Alamagordo; 62 miles W of Roswell; 125 miles SE of Albuquerque

Ruidoso (most New Mexicans pronounce it "Ree-uh-*do*-so") is situated at 6,900 feet in the timbered Sacramento Mountains, the southernmost finger of the Rockies. It is a mountain resort town named for its site on a noisy stream and is most famous for the nearby Ruidoso Downs racetrack, where the world's richest quarter-horse race is run for a $2.5 million purse. The surrounding Lincoln National Forest attracts outdoor lovers, hikers, horseback riders, fishers, and hunters. Southern New Mexico's most important ski resort, Ski Apache, is just out of town. The nearby **Mescalero Apache Indian Reservation** includes the Inn of the Mountain Gods Resort & Casino. Not far away, the historic village of **Lincoln** recalls the Wild West days of Billy the Kid. Unless you like the bustle of a busy resort town, in the summer I suggest staying in Lincoln rather than Ruidoso. During the busiest months, the town seems to live up to its Spanish name—which translates as "noisy."

ESSENTIALS

GETTING THERE   From Albuquerque, take I-25 south 87 miles to San Antonio; turn east on US 380 and travel 74 miles; then head south on NM 37/48 (4 hr.). From Alamogordo, take US 70 northeast via Tularosa (1 hr.). From Roswell, take US 70 west (1½ hr.). No commercial airlines serve **Sierra Blanca Regional Airport** (© 505/336-8111), 17 miles north, near Alto.

VISITOR INFORMATION   The **Ruidoso Valley Chamber of Commerce** and visitor center is at 720 Sudderth Dr. For information, write to P.O. Box 698, Ruidoso, NM 88345 (© 800/253-2255 or 505/257-7395; www.ruidoso.net).

EXPLORING RUIDOSO
GALLERY HOPPING

Many noted artists—among them Peter Hurd, Henriette Wyeth, and Gordon Snidow—have made their homes in Ruidoso and surrounding Lincoln County. Dozens of other art-world hopefuls have followed, resulting in a proliferation of galleries in town. Most are open daily from 10am to 6pm. Among my favorites are **De Carol Designs,** 2616 Sudderth Dr. (© 505/257-5024); **Crucis Art Bronze Foundry and Gallery,** 524 Sudderth Dr. (© 505/257-7186); **Fenton's Gallery,** 2629 Sudderth Dr. (© 505/257-9738); **Stampede Leather,** 2331 E. Sudderth Dr. (© 505/258-4029); and **McGary Studios,** a bronze foundry at 2002 Sudderth Dr. (© 505/257-1000). **Hurd–La Rinconada** (© 505/653-4331), in San Patricio, 20 miles east of Ruidoso on US 70 (see "A Scenic Drive Around the Lincoln Loop," later in this chapter), is open Monday through Saturday from 9am to 5pm.

RUIDOSO DOWNS

In a stunning setting surrounded by green grass and pine trees, the famous **Ruidoso Downs racetrack** and **Billy the Kid Casino** (© 505/378-4431; www.ruidosodowns racing.com), 2 miles east of Ruidoso on US 70, is home to the world's richest quarter-horse race, the $2.5 million **All American Futurity,** run each year on Labor Day. Many other days of quarter horse and thoroughbred racing lead up to the big one, beginning in May and running through Labor Day. Post time is 1pm Thursday through Sunday. Grandstand admission is free; call about reserved seating prices, which range from $3.50 to $10.

The on-site casino has all the neon, noise, and smoke gamblers love. Though you'll find only slots at this casino (for more variety, head to Inn of the Mountain Gods Resort & Casino), bonuses here include simulcast racing on big-screen TVs in the bar and a well-priced buffet with tables overlooking the track. Open Saturday through Thursday from 11am to 11pm; Friday from noon to midnight.

Kids **Family Fun**

Families crave the excitement at **Funtrackers Family Fun Center** (© 505/257-3275), 101 Carrizo Canyon Rd. Spread out below a hill in town are go-cart courses for a variety of ages, bumper boats, bull-riding, and miniature golf. *Beware:* This place can be crammed with people in midsummer. Open Memorial Day to Labor Day daily from 10am to 10pm; from September to May it's open weekends only, with limited hours.

AN INTERESTING MUSEUM

The Hubbard Museum of the American West ★   This museum contains a collection of thousands of horse-related items, including saddles from all over the world, a Russian sleigh, a horse-drawn "fire engine," and an 1860 stagecoach. Several great American artists, including Frederic Remington and Charles M. Russell, are represented in the museum's permanent collection. A gift shop has some interesting books and curios.

841 W. US 70, Ruidoso Downs. © 505/378-4142. Fax 505/378-4166. www.hubbardmuseum.org. Admission $8 adults, $6 seniors and military, $3 children 6–16, free for children under 6. Daily 10am–5pm. Closed Thanksgiving, Dec 25.

RUIDOSO AFTER DARK: SPENCER THEATER FOR THE PERFORMING ARTS ★★

The dream of Alto, New Mexico, residents Dr. A. N. and Jackie Spencer, the 514-seat Spencer Theater, Sierra Blanca Airport Highway 220, 4½ miles east of NM 48 (© **888/818-7872** or 505/336-4800; www.spencertheater.com), is a model performance space that cost more than $20 million to construct. Opened in 1997, the theater has drawn such talents as the Paul Taylor Dance Company and Marvin Hamlisch. In recent years top billing has gone to the folk revival band the Brothers Four and the master illusionists the Pendragons. Free tours start at 10am Tuesday and Thursday. The theater runs two seasons year-round, and tickets cost $25 to $50.

MESCALERO APACHE INDIAN RESERVATION

Immediately south and west of Ruidoso, the Mescalero Apache Indian Reservation covers over 460,000 acres (719 sq. miles) and is home to about 2,800 members of the Mescalero, Chiricahua, and Lipan bands of Apaches. Established by order of Pres. Ulysses S. Grant in 1873, it sustains a profitable cattle-ranching industry and the Apache-run logging firm of Mescalero Forest Products.

SEEING THE HIGHLIGHTS

Even if you're not staying or dining here, visit the **Inn of the Mountain Gods Resort & Casino,** a luxury resort owned and operated by the tribe (see "Where to Stay in & Around Ruidoso," below). It's the crowning achievement of Wendell Chino, former president of the Mescalero Apache tribe.

Also on the reservation, on US 70 about 17 miles southwest of Ruidoso, is the **Mescalero Cultural Center** (© **505/671-4494**), open weekdays from 8am to 4:30pm. Photos, artifacts, clothing, crafts, and other exhibits demonstrate the history and culture of the tribe.

St. Joseph's Apache Mission ★ (© **505/464-4473**), just off US 70 in Mescalero, on a hill overlooking the reservation, is a stone Romanesque-style structure that stands 103 feet tall and has walls 4 feet thick. Built between 1920 and 1939, the grand mission church also contains an icon of the Apache Christ, with Christ depicted as a Mescalero holy man, as well as other Apache religious art. Local arts and crafts and religious items are for sale at the parish office. The church is open daily during daylight hours.

LINCOLN HISTORIC DISTRICT: A WALK IN THE FOOTSTEPS OF BILLY THE KID ★★

One of the last historic yet uncommercialized 19th-century towns remaining in the American West, the tiny community of Lincoln lies 37 miles northeast of Ruidoso on US 380, in the valley of the Rio Bonito. Only 70 people live here today, but it was once the seat of the largest county in the United States, and the focal point of the notorious Lincoln County War of 1878–1879.

Various ranching and merchant factions fought the bloody Lincoln County War over the issue of beef contracts for nearby Fort Stanton. A sharpshooting teenager named William Bonney—soon to be known as "Billy the Kid"—sided with "the good guys," escaping from the burning McSween House after his employer and colleague were shot and killed. Three years later, after shooting down a sheriff, he was captured in Lincoln and sentenced to be hanged. But he shot his way out of his jail cell in the **Old Courthouse,** now a state museum that still has a hole made by a bullet from the Kid's gun. Visitors can hear a talk on this famous escape, by request, at the Old Courthouse.

Many of the original structures from that era have been preserved and restored by the Museum of New Mexico, the Lincoln County Historical Society, and an organization called **Historic Lincoln** (© 505/653-4025), a subsidiary of the Hubbard Museum of the American West.

JUST THE FACTS At the **Visitor Center,** on NM 380 on the east side of town (© 505/653-4025), exhibits explain the role in Lincoln's history of Apaches, Hispanics, Anglo cowboys, and the black Buffalo Soldiers, and detail the Lincoln County War. A brief slide show on Lincoln history plays in an old-fashioned theater. Start your visit here and either join a tour, included in the admission cost, or pick up a brochure describing the trust's self-guided walking tour ($1). Across the courtyard is the **Luna Museum Store.**

An annual **folk pageant,** *The Last Escape of Billy the Kid,* has been presented outdoors since 1949. A highly romanticized version of the Lincoln County War, it goes up on Friday and Saturday night and Sunday afternoon during the first full weekend in August as part of the **Old Lincoln Days** celebration. The festival also includes living-history demonstrations of traditional crafts, musical programs, and food booths throughout the village.

ESSENTIALS The historic district is open year-round 8:30am to 4:30pm. Admission is $6 for adults (includes entry to seven buildings) or $3.50 per building. It's free for children under 17. For more information, write P.O. Box 36, Lincoln, NM 88338, or call © 505/653-4372.

You can jostle your way back to the 1800s on a ride in the four-horse-drawn **Lincoln County Overland Stage** ★, NM 380, mile marker 91–92, west of Lincoln (© 505/653-4954; www.stagecoach.bz). Morning and afternoon rides from about April to November take 2 hours to cover 5½ miles of an old stagecoach route from near Lincoln to Old Fort Stanton cemetery. The ride costs $25 for adults, $12 for children 3 to 16, and free for children under 3.

WHERE TO STAY IN & AROUND RUIDOSO

If you're looking for a budget stay in Ruidoso, the **Motel 6** on the outskirts of town has reliable rooms. Call © **800/466-8356** for reservations.

IN ALTO

Scarborough House ★★ (Finds)   On a ridge top 15 minutes northeast of Ruidoso, this new B&B offers rustic elegance and spectacular views. The creation of a couple from Austin, Texas, the inn has a bit of city flair. It is timber-frame construction, with high Douglas fir beams above a stacked flagstone fireplace in the great room. Guest rooms offer tasteful, imaginative sojourns, with an eye for detail. My favorite is the East Meets West room, which has an Old West rustic feel and old East Coast elegance. All rooms have fine touches, such as a locally made cedar bed or a marble bathroom sink. All have pillow-top mattresses, fine linens, and signature soaps, as well as robes, spa towels, and slippers, handy when you're heading out to the hot tub, which occupies part of the 2,000 square feet of deck space. Those decks offer views of Sierra Blanca Peak and the Capitan Mountains. Breakfast brings such delights as eggs Benedict made with roast duck confit instead of Canadian bacon and home-baked croissants. Smoking is not allowed.

110 Great View Court, Alto NM 88312. © **866/875-2592** or 505/336-4500. www.scarboroughhousebandb.com. 4 units. $119–$159 double; ask about discount packages. Rates include full breakfast and afternoon snacks. AE, DISC, MC, V. Children not accepted. **Amenities:** Jacuzzi. *In room:* A/C, TV/CD player, hair dryer.

IN TOWN

Hawthorn Suites Conference and Golf Resort ★★   Surrounded by a golf course, the most refined hotel in town is a good choice. However, if you find convention traffic daunting, you'll want to ask what's scheduled at the next-door convention center before reserving. When I visited, the hotel was quiet and serene. The grand lobby centers on an Anasazi-style stacked sandstone fireplace, creating an elegance that carries into the accommodations. The rooms are medium-size, decorated in contemporary Southwestern style, with comfortable earth tones and plenty of amenities. The large suites have sofa beds, fireplaces, and balconies. Many of the rooms have two-person Jacuzzi tubs. The hotel's golf packages are worth checking out.

107 Sierra Blanca Dr., Ruidoso, NM 88345. © **866/211-7727** or 505/258-5500. Fax 505/258-2419. www.ruidoso hawthorn.com. 120 units. $119–$179 double; $139–$239 suite. Rates include full breakfast. AE, DISC, MC, V. Take Mechem Dr. 5 min. north of Sudderth. Pets accepted. **Amenities:** Indoor pool; golf course; exercise room; Jacuzzi; massage. *In room:* A/C, TV, fridge, coffeemaker, iron, microwave.

Inn of the Mountain Gods Resort & Casino ★★   What's most impressive about this resort is its location, on a grassy slope above a mountain lake on the Mescalero Apache Indian Reservation, 3½ miles southwest of Ruidoso. It was the dream of the former tribal president, Wendell Chino, who wanted to help his people get into the recreation and tourism business. In 2004, the original resort was leveled and a new one built, much in the style of a Lake Tahoe casino, with glossy gaming rooms, restaurants, and spacious guest rooms. The rooms are tasteful, with comfortable beds and balconies with views of Sierra Blanca Peak.

The resort also has a sports bar, a night club, and a casino with more than 1,000 slot machines and 45 table games.

287 Carrizo Canyon Rd., Mescalero, NM 88340. © **800/545-6040** or 505/464-4100. www.innofthemountaingods.com. 273 units. $99–$399 double. Golf, tennis, and ski packages available. AE, DC, DISC, MC, V. **Amenities:** 2 restaurants; 2 bars; indoor pool; golf course; Jacuzzi; watersports equipment rentals; tour/activities desk; limited room service. *In room:* A/C, TV, dataport, coffeemaker, hair dryer, iron, safe.

IN LINCOLN: A HISTORIC B&B

Casa de Patrón Bed and Breakfast ⚡   The main building of Casa de Patrón, an adobe, was built around 1860 and housed Juan Patrón's old store (the home is on the National Register of Historic Places). In addition, Billy the Kid used part of the house as a hideout. Jeremy and Cleis Jordan have capitalized on the presence of that notorious punk by collecting portraits and photographs and hanging them throughout the inn's cozy sitting and dining areas.

Rooms in the old part of the house are friendly, with a homey feel created by quilts and a major collection of washboards adorning the walls. More sophisticated are the Old Trail House rooms. One has a Jacuzzi tub, the other is suitable for people with disabilities, and both have fireplaces, wet bars, and minifridges. A short walk from there are two reasonably priced casitas, ideal places for families to stay. Both have full kitchens, with stoves, ovens, microwaves, and fridges. If you stay in a casita, continental-plus breakfast is delivered to your door. If you stay in the main house or the recently added Old Trail House, Cleis and Jeremy will prepare a full breakfast, such as Dutch babies (a soufflé) served with apple compote and sausage. Although there's no air-conditioning, the thick walls of the old adobe help the place stay pretty cool.

On US 380 (P.O. Box 27), Lincoln, NM 88338. ℂ 505/653-4676. Fax 505/653-4671. www.casapatron.com. 5 units, 2 casitas. $87–$117 double; $107 casita. Rates include breakfast. MC, V. *In room:* No phone.

CAMPING

Lincoln National Forest has more than a dozen campgrounds in the region; four of them are within the immediate area. The **Smokey Bear Ranger Station,** 901 Mechem Dr., Ruidoso (ℂ **505/257-4095**), is open Memorial Day to Labor Day from 7:30am to 4:30pm Monday through Saturday, and the same hours Monday through Friday the rest of the year.

WHERE TO DINE IN & AROUND RUIDOSO
IN TOWN
Moderate
Cattle Baron Steak House ⚡ STEAK/SEAFOOD   This is the place to go if you really have an appetite. It's a casually elegant restaurant, part of a chain with six locations around the Southwest. It may not serve the best steaks and seafood you've tasted, but it provides good-quality food. Decorated in opulent Western style with lots of burgundy upholstery and brass, the place is often busy and festive, so it's not ideal for a romantic getaway. Service is efficient and friendly. For lunch, try the turkey and avocado sandwich or the teriyaki kabob. For dinner, I usually order filet mignon or shrimp scampi. A large salad bar dominates the main dining room, and a comfortable lounge sits near the entryway.

657 Sudderth Dr. ℂ 505/257-9355. Reservations recommended for parties of 6 or more. Main courses $7–$10 lunch, $8–$18 dinner. AE, DC, DISC, MC, V. Mon–Thurs 11am–10pm; Fri–Sat 11am–10:30pm; Sun 11am–9:30pm.

Inexpensive
Cafe Rio *Kids* INTERNATIONAL/PIZZA   This pizzeria-style restaurant is quite out of place in Ruidoso, offering deep-dish pizza such as you'd find in Chicago. My favorite is the Hawaiian combo, with Canadian bacon and pineapple. Some people rave about the calzones, which come with three cheeses and any of four fillings. Greek, Portuguese, and Cajun dishes are also available. You can sample from an extensive selection of domestic and imported beers, including seasonal beers. Finish with the

Moments   A Scenic Drive Around the Lincoln Loop

An enjoyable way to see many of the sights of the Ruidoso area is a 1- or 2-day 162-mile loop tour. Heading east from Ruidoso on US 70, about 18 miles past Ruidoso Downs, is the small community of **San Patricio,** where you'll find (watch for signs) the **Hurd–La Rinconada Gallery** (© 505/653-4331; www.wyethartists.com). Late artist Peter Hurd, a Roswell native, flunked out of West Point before studying with artist N. C. Wyeth, marrying Wyeth's daughter Henriette, and eventually returning with her to New Mexico. This gallery shows and sells works by Peter Hurd, Henriette Wyeth, their son Michael Hurd, Andrew Wyeth, and N. C. Wyeth. Many of the works capture the ambience of the landscape in the San Patricio area. In addition to original works, signed reproductions are available. The gallery is open Monday through Saturday from 9am to 5pm and Sunday from 10am to 4pm.

From San Patricio, continue east on US 70 for 4 miles to the community of Hondo, at the confluence of the Rio Hondo and Rio Bonito, and turn west onto US 380. From here it's about 10 miles to **Lincoln,** a fascinating little town that is also a National Historic Landmark (see "Lincoln Historic District: A Walk in the Footsteps of Billy the Kid," above). Heading west takes you to **Carrizozo,** the Lincoln County seat since 1912. The **Outpost,** 415 Central Ave. (© 505/648-9994), serves one of the best green-chile cheeseburgers in the Southwest. To continue the loop tour, turn south onto US 54 and go about 28 miles to the turnoff to **Three Rivers Petroglyph National Recreation Area** (© 505/525-4300), about 5 miles east on a paved road. Some 20,000 individual rock art images are here, carved by Mogollon peoples who lived in the area centuries ago. A trail about .75 mile long links many of the most interesting petroglyphs, and the view surrounding the area, with mountains to the east and White Sands to the southwest, is outstanding. The day use fee is $2 per vehicle. Overnight camping is $10. The U.S. Forest Service also has a campground in the area, about 5 miles east on a gravel road.

Continuing south on US 54, drive about 2 miles to Tularosa and turn east onto US 70, which you take for about 16 miles to the village of **Mescalero** on the Mescalero Apache Indian Reservation. From US 70, take the exit for the Bureau of Indian Affairs and follow the signs to the imposing **St. Joseph's Apache Mission** (see "Mescalero Apache Indian Reservation," earlier in this chapter). After you return to US 70, it's about 19 miles back to Ruidoso.

double-layer chocolate cake with chocolate espresso frosting, unless you care about sleeping that night. With its casual atmosphere, this is a great place to bring the kids.

2547 Sudderth Dr. © **505/257-7746.** Fax 505/630-1612. Reservations not accepted. Main courses $5–$10. No credit cards. Daily 11:20am–7:50pm. Closed 3 weeks after Thanksgiving and 1 month after Easter.

A NEARBY PLACE TO DINE

Flying J Ranch *Kids* CHUCK WAGON   This ranch is like a Western village, complete with staged gunfights and pony rides for the kids. Gates open at 6pm; a fairly mediocre but fun chuck-wagon dinner of barbecue beef or chicken, baked potato, beans, biscuits, applesauce cake, and coffee or lemonade is served promptly at 7:30pm. Then, at 8:20pm, the Flying J Wranglers present a fast-paced stage show with Western music and a world-champion yodeler.

NM 48, 1 mile north of Alto. © 888/458-3595 or 505/336-4330. Reservations highly recommended. $19 adults, $10 children 4–12, free for children under 4. DISC, MC, V. May–Labor Day Mon–Sat; Labor Day to mid-Oct Sat only.

NORTH OF TOWN

Greenhouse Café ★★ *Moments* NEW AMERICAN   A complete novelty, this little gem in Capitan, about 25 minutes from Ruidoso, serves fresh dishes highlighted by vegetables grown in Tom and Gail Histen's own greenhouse just up the hill. Veggies always vary, ranging from Persian garden cress to arugula to Swiss and gold chards. The setting is eclectic: a gallery displaying lovely jewelry and other art, accented by tile-topped tables and lots of plants, with a patio out back. Food ranges from vegan offerings to meatloaf lasagna. My favorite is chicken stroganoff with a light mushroom sauce, served in puff pastry. Mediterranean tilapia sits on baby spinach and grilled polenta with fresh dill. Soups, sandwiches, and salads are also delicious, as are desserts such as carrot cake or a float made with local Sierra Blanca Brewery root beer. Select wines and beers enhance the menu.

103 S. Lincoln, Capitan. © 505/354-0373. Main courses $6–$10 lunch, $14–$18 dinner. MC, V. Wed–Sat 11am–2pm and 5–9pm; Sun 9am–1pm.

5 Roswell

62 miles E of Riudiso; 83 miles NE of Alamagordo; 158 miles SE of Albuquerque

Best known as a destination for UFO enthusiasts and conspiracy theorists, Roswell has become a household name thanks to old Mulder and Scully. And even if you're not glued to your set for reruns of *The X-Files,* you may remember Roswell as the setting for major scenes from the 1996 blockbuster *Independence Day.* Government cover-ups, alien autopsies, and cigarette-smoking feds . . . come along as we venture into the UFO capital of the world.

ESSENTIALS

GETTING THERE   From Albuquerque, take I-40 east 59 miles to Clines Corners; turn south on US 285, and travel 140 miles to Roswell (4 hr.). From Las Cruces, take US 70 east (4 hr.). From Carlsbad, take US 285 north (1½ hr.).

Roswell Airport, Roswell Industrial Air Center, S. Main Street (© 505/347-5703), is served commercially by **Mesa Airlines** (© 800/MESA-AIR; www.mesa-air.com), which flies to Albuquerque almost hourly throughout the day and directly to Dallas, Texas, twice daily.

VISITOR INFORMATION   The **Roswell Chamber of Commerce** is at 131 W. 2nd St. (P.O. Box 70), Roswell, NM 88202 (© 505/623-5695; www.roswellnm.org). The Roswell Convention and Visitors Bureau is at 912 N. Main (© 888-ROSWELL or 505/624-0889; www.roswellcvb.com).

SEEING THE SIGHTS

Roswell Museum and Art Center ★   This highly acclaimed small museum is a good place to get a sense of this area before heading out to explore. Established in the 1930s through the efforts of city government, local archaeological and historical societies, and the Works Progress Administration, the museum proclaims this city's role as a center for the arts and a cradle of America's space industry.

Fun Fact The Incident at Roswell

by Su Hudson

In July 1947, something "happened" in Roswell. What was it? Debate still rages. On July 8, 1947, a local rancher named MacBrazel found unusual debris scattered across his property. The U.S. military released a statement saying the debris was wreckage from a spaceship crash. Four hours later, however, the military retracted the statement, claiming what fell from the sky was "only a weather balloon." Most of the community didn't believe the story, although some did suspect that the military was somehow involved—Robert Goddard had been working on rockets in this area since the 1930s, and the Roswell Air Base was nearby. Eyewitnesses to the account, however, maintain the debris "was not of this world."

Theorists believe that the crash actually involved two spacecraft. One disintegrated, hence the debris across the MacBrazel ranch, and the other crash-landed, hence the four alien bodies that were also claimed to have been discovered.

UFO believers have remained dissatisfied with the U.S. Air Force's weather balloon story and have insisted on an explanation for the "alien bodies." The most recent comment from the Air Force came in 1997, 2 weeks before the 50th anniversary of the "crash." The Air Force said that the most likely explanation for the unverified alien reports was that people were simply remembering and misplacing in time a number of life-size dummies dropped from the sky during a series of experiments in the 1950s.

The main place to go in Roswell to learn more about the incident is the **International UFO Museum and Research Center,** in the old Plains Theater on Main Street ((C) **505/625-9495;** www.iufomrc.org). Staffers are more than happy to discuss the crash and the alleged military cover-up. Besides displaying an hour-by-hour timeline of the "incident," the museum has photographs of bizarre and elaborate crop circles, and a videotape in which an alleged witness tells his account. The museum is open daily from 9am to 5pm; admission is free.

If you want to see one of the two possible crash sites, call **Bruce Rhodes** ((C) **505/622-0628**) to set up a private tour. The short tour is 53 miles, takes 3 hours, and costs $75 for one to three people. The long tour covers approximately 123 miles (including the debris site), takes about 5 hours, and costs $125 for one to three people.

Roswell hosts a **UFO Festival** every year during the first week in July. Some of the special events include guest speakers, the Crash and Burn Expo Race, concerts, out-of-this-world food, a laser light show, and an alien invasion at the Bottomless Lakes recreation area. For details on the event, call (C) **505/625-8607.**

The art center contains the world's finest collection of works by Peter Hurd and his wife, Henriette Wyeth, many of which depict the gentry-ranching lifestyle in this area. You'll also find works by Georgia O'Keeffe, Ernest Blumenschein, Joseph Sharp, and others famed from the early-20th-century Taos and Santa Fe art colonies. The museum has an early historical section, but its pride and joy is the **Robert Goddard Collection,** which presents engines, rocket assemblies, and specialized parts Goddard developed in the 1930s, when he lived and worked in Roswell. Goddard's workshop has been re-created for the exhibit. A special display commemorates Apollo 17, which undertook the last manned lunar landing in 1972. The Goddard Planetarium is used as a science classroom for local students and for special programs.

100 W. 11th St., Roswell, NM 88201. ℂ 505/624-6765. Fax 505/624-6765. www.roswellmuseum.org. Free admission. Mon–Sat 9am–5pm; Sun and holidays 1–5pm. Closed Jan 1, Thanksgiving, Dec 24–25.

WHERE TO STAY IN ROSWELL

Fairfield Inn & Suites by Marriott ✦   This inn at the center of town offers bright new rooms with plenty of amenities. The lobby and breakfast area have a living-room feel, and the whole place offers the convenience and good prices one can expect from the brand. Elements such as marble and tile in the bathrooms and a nice pool further enhance the place. The suites offer an interesting angled two-room configuration, with a big TV and a CD player; standard rooms are medium-size, each with a desk. All rooms have comfortable beds.

1201 N. Main St., Roswell, NM 88201. ℂ 800/228-2800 or 505/624-1300. www.marriott.com. 67 units. $84–$94 double. Rates include continental breakfast. AE, DC, DISC, MC, V. **Amenities:** Outdoor pool; exercise room; business center; coin-op laundry. *In room:* A/C, TV, dataport, coffeemaker, hair dryer, iron, microwave.

CAMPING

Town and Country RV Park, 331 W. Brasher Rd. (ℂ **800/499-4364** or 505/624-1833; www.roswell-USA.com/tandcrv), south of Roswell, is your best bet for camping, with some grass and cottonwood and elm trees for shade. The campground has 75 sites, most with full hookups. Prices range from $21 to $23. Tent campers can set up here as well. Bathrooms are clean and convenient, as is the large pool. Head south on Main Street for 3 miles and turn west on West Brasher Road.

WHERE TO DINE IN ROSWELL

Cattle Baron ✦ STEAK/SEAFOOD   This popular restaurant is always busy during mealtimes. You can usually get a table, however, and they are nicely spaced so that the noise level is minimal. It's an informal place with a wealthy ranch feel—lots of burgundy and brass. Service is fast and friendly. Many come here just to feast at the salad bar, which is one of the best I've seen; it includes many potato and pasta dishes, as well as a choice of two soups. Everything is made fresh here—the bread baked in-house, the beef hand-cut by the manager. You can't go wrong with the steaks, such as tender filet mignon wrapped in bacon. You can also get dishes such as shrimp scampi at a price that will make you glad for Roswell's provincialism. The lounge is a comfortable place to come for evening drinks, and there's a full bar.

1113 N. Main St. ℂ 505/622-2465. Reservations recommended. Main courses $5–$10 lunch, $10–$20 dinner. AE, DISC, MC, V. Mon–Thurs 11am–9:30pm; Fri–Sat 11am–10pm; Sun 11am–9pm.

6 Carlsbad & Environs

65 miles S of Roswell; 98 miles SE of Alamogordo; 139 miles E of Las Cruces

In an area once controlled by Apaches and Comanches, Carlsbad (pop. 27,800) was founded on the Pecos River in the late 1800s. Besides getting a good tourist business from Carlsbad Caverns, the town thrives on farming, with irrigated crops of cotton, hay, and pecans. The area is the largest producer of potash in the United States. The town was named for the spa in Bohemia of the same name.

The caverns (see section 7, below) are the big attraction, having drawn more than 33 million visitors since opening in 1923. A satellite community, White's City (www.whitescity.com), lies 20 miles south of Carlsbad at the park entrance junction. The family of Jack White Jr. owns all of its motels, restaurants, gift shops, and other attractions.

ESSENTIALS

GETTING THERE   From Albuquerque, take I-40 east 59 miles to Clines Corners; turn south on US 285, and travel 216 miles to Carlsbad via Roswell (6 hr.). From El Paso, take US 62/180 east (3 hr.).

Mesa Airlines (℗ **800/MESA-AIR** or 505/885-0245; www.mesa-air.com) provides commercial service, with four flights daily between Albuquerque and **Cavern City Air Terminal** (℗ **505/887-3060**), 4 miles south of the city on National Parks Highway (US 62/180). You can rent a car at the airport from **Enterprise** (℗ **505/887-3039**).

VISITOR INFORMATION   The **Carlsbad Chamber of Commerce** and the **Carlsbad Convention and Visitors Bureau,** both at 302 S. Canal St. (US 285), P.O. Box 910, Carlsbad, NM 88220 (℗ **800/221-1224** or 505/887-6516; www.carlsbad.org), are open Monday from 9am to 5pm and Tuesday through Friday from 8am to 5pm.

SEEING THE SIGHTS

Carlsbad's pride and joy is the broad Pecos River, with a 3½-mile **river walk** along the tree-shaded banks, beginning near the north end of Riverside Drive. This is a lovely place for a picnic, and if you'd like to cool off, a municipal beach at the north end has changing rooms and showers. Annual **Christmas on the Pecos** pontoon boat rides take place each evening from Thanksgiving to New Year's Eve (except Christmas Eve), past a fascinating display of Christmas lights on riverside homes and businesses. Advance reservations, available from the chamber of commerce, are required.

The **Carlsbad Museum and Art Center,** 418 W. Fox St., 1 block west of Canal Street (℗ **505/887-0276**), contains Apache relics, pioneer artifacts, and an impressive art collection. The museum's store has a small but fine selection of reasonably priced jewelry. The museum is open Monday through Saturday from 10am to 5pm; admission is free, although donations are welcome.

GETTING OUTSIDE

Recreational facilities in the Carlsbad area include some two dozen parks, several golf courses, numerous tennis courts and swimming pools, a municipal beach, and a shooting and archery range. Contact the **City of Carlsbad Recreation Department** (℗ **505/887-1191**).

Living Desert Zoo & Gardens State Park *Kids* ★   On 1,200 acres of authentic Chihuahuan Desert, this park is home to more than 50 species of desert mammals, birds, and reptiles, and almost 500 varieties of plants. Even for someone like me, who

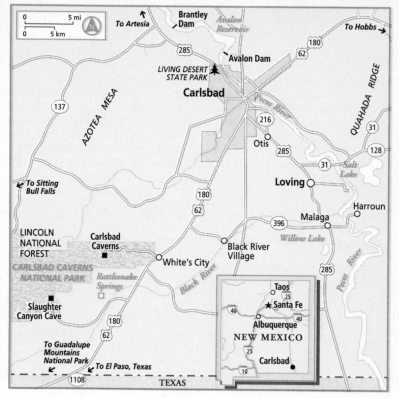

cringes at the thought of zoos, this is a pleasant 1.3-mile walk. You pass through displays with plaques pointing out vegetation such as mountain mahogany, and geologic formations such as gypsum sinkholes. In addition to the nocturnal exhibit, you're likely to see lizards and other wild creatures, as well as captive ones.

Rehabilitation programs provide for the park's animals, which have been sick or injured and are no longer able to survive in the wild. You'll see golden eagles and great horned owls among the birds of prey in the aviary, and large animals such as deer and elk in outdoor pastures. The view from the park, high atop the Ocotillo Hills on the northwest side of Carlsbad, is superb.

1504 Miehls Dr. (C) **505/887-5516.** www.livingdesert.org. Admission $5 adults, $3 children 7–12, free for children under 7. Group rates available. Memorial Day weekend to Labor Day daily 8am–8pm (last park entry by 6:30pm). Rest of year daily 9am–5pm (last park entry by 3:30pm). Gift shop closes 45 min. before zoo. Closed Dec 25. Take Miehls Dr. off US 285 west of town and proceed just over a mile.

WHERE TO STAY IN & AROUND CARLSBAD

Most properties are along the highway south toward Carlsbad Caverns National Park (see "Carlsbad Caverns National Park," below). Only the Best Western Cavern Inn is near the national park. The downside to staying there is that your restaurant and activity options are limited.

Best Western Cavern Inn If you'd like to be close to the caverns, this is the place to stay. The lobby is in an Old West storefront, and the accommodations are across the street. The staff seems to be overworked, so you may not get the service you would in Carlsbad. The motel has two main sections. The better option is the Guadalupe Inn. This section is built around a courtyard, and rooms have a rich feel, with vigas on the ceilings and nice Southwestern pine furniture. Bathrooms are roomy enough, and beds are comfortably firm. In back is a big pool surrounded by greenery. Next door, the two-story Cavern Inn consists of 1970s rooms that are large and recently remodeled, though the small bathrooms with jetted tubs could use a little sprucing up.

The White's City arcade contains a post office, a grocery store, a gift shop, the Million Dollar Museum of various antiques and paraphernalia, and Granny's Opera House, a theater for weekend melodramas scheduled intermittently.

17 Carlsbad Cavern Hwy. at NM 7 (P.O. Box 128), White's City, NM 88268. © 800/CAVERNS or 505/785-2291. Fax 505/785-2283. www.bestwestern.com. 63 units. May 15–Sept 15 $65–$115 double; Sept 16–May 14 $50–$80 double. Rates include breakfast. AE, DC, DISC, MC, V. Pets accepted; $10 fee. **Amenities:** 2 restaurants; 2 outdoor pools; tennis court; volleyball; basketball; Jacuzzi; game room; shopping arcade. *In room:* A/C, TV, dataport, coffeemaker, hair dryer, iron.

Holiday Inn ✮ A handsome Territorial-style building houses this first-rate full-service hotel in downtown Carlsbad. This is my choice of Carlsbad accommodations. It was built in 1960 and continues to undergo renovations. Rooms aren't as large as those at the Best Western Cavern Inn (see above), but they're refined, with white wooden furniture, decorated in Southwestern prints. The beds are medium-firm and comfortable; bathrooms are average size, each with an outer vanity. Large executive rooms have comfortable chairs and ottomans as well as jetted tubs. Amenities in these rooms include robes and nice soaps and shampoo.

601 S. Canal St., Carlsbad, NM 88220. © 800/HOLIDAY or 505/885-8500. Fax 505/887-5999. www.holiday-inn.com. 100 units. $86–$115 double. Rates include full breakfast. AE, DC, DISC, MC, V. Pets accepted; $25 fee. **Amenities:** Restaurant (bar and grill); outdoor pool; exercise room; Jacuzzi; sauna; playground; airport shuttle; laundry service; dry cleaning. *In room:* A/C, TV, coffeemaker, hair dryer, iron.

CAMPING

Brantley Lake State Park (© 505/457-2384) in Carlsbad has RV hookups as well as tent campsites. Picnic tables, grills, and recreational facilities are available. Boating and lake fishing are popular here. **Carlsbad RV Park and Campground,** 4301 National Parks Hwy., on the south end of town (© 888/878-7275 or 505/885-6333; www.carlsbadrvpark.com), is a large, full-service campground with a swimming pool and playground. In Artesia, try **Artesia RV Park,** Hermosa Drive (© 505/746-6184; www.artesiarvpark.com), a more moderately sized campground just south of the junction of US 82/285. Laundry facilities and a game room are available.

WHERE TO DINE IN & AROUND CARLSBAD

Blue House ✮ *Finds* CAFE/BAKERY In a quest to find good coffee in even the smallest of New Mexico towns, I now rate Carlsbad high. On a quiet residential street just north of historic downtown is this gem, in a Queen Anne–style blue house with morning-glory vines adorning the front fence. Inside, Parisian colors warm the walls, contrasting with brightly painted chairs and small round tables. The fare is simple, fresh, and imaginative; espresso, lattes, and Italian sodas are the biggest draws, along with special sandwiches and soups daily. Excellent baked goods top the breakfast menu. For lunch, try the feta spinach croissant, a deli sandwich on French country bread, or, for something sweeter, cream cheese raspberry coffee cake.

609 N. Canyon Rd. ℂ 505/628-0555. All menu items under $8. No credit cards. Mon–Sat 7:30am–3:30pm. Call to confirm hours. Take Canal St. to Church St. east, then go south on Canyon Rd.

Lucy's ⭐ MEXICAN   When you walk in the door of this busy restaurant and take in the festive Mexican decor, Lucy is likely to wave you toward the dining room and tell you to find a seat. Such is the casual nature of the place—and a sign of the good home-style food to come. Since 1974, Lucy and Justo Yanez's restaurant has been dedicated to the words of a Mexican proverb printed on the menu: *El hambre es un fuego, y la comida es fresca* (Hunger is a burning, and eating is a coolness). You'll probably want to start with a margarita or Mexican beer. The food is tasty, with Lucy's personal adaptations of old favorites, often invented by requests from regulars. "Barbara's Favorite Fix" (one beef enchilada and one chile relleno) was named after a local woman who had this meal six times a week. Everything is made by hand. I recommend the chicken fajita burrito or the combination plate. Finish with a dessert of buñelos sprinkled with cinnamon sugar. Children's plates are available; diners can choose mild or hot chile. A second Lucy's restaurant is at 4428 Lovington Hwy. in Hobbs, New Mexico.

701 S. Canal St. ℂ 505/887-7714. Reservations recommended on weekends. Main courses $3.75–$12. AE, DC, DISC, MC, V. Mon–Sat 11am–9:30pm.

Velvet Garter Saloon and Restaurant AMERICAN   This is the only restaurant in the Carlsbad Caverns area, besides the one in the base of the caverns. Despite this monopoly, the place does a pretty amazing job of preparing tasty food for a mass of travelers that pass through. The steaks are good quality and come with a trip to the salad bar, baked potato, vegetable, and bread. Your best bet may be a pasta dish. Try shrimp fettuccini Alfredo or lasagna. In the same building, Fat Jack's serves breakfast and lunch in a setting heavy with linoleum. Standards such as eggs and bacon, sandwiches, and burgers are some of the only offerings near the caverns, so the place fills

---

Finds **Dining on the Oil Fields**

If you're cruising through the town of Artesia en route to Carlsbad, this is the place to eat. In a stroke of brilliance, Artesia oil man Frank Yates, Jr., conceived the **Wellhead** ⭐, a brewpub in Artesia designed around the notion of oil wells. It's an open, friendly place, with plenty of room between tables and such touches as a 1924 flowing derrick depicted in tile, and stone core samples (from early Artesia wells) embedded in the bar. The friendly and efficient staff serves burgers and pizza, but if you'd prefer something more refined, that can be arranged. Try the Oriental salad (field greens with grilled chicken, nuts, dried cranberries, and water chestnuts) or one of the pasta or fish dishes, such as broiled salmon with lemon caper cream sauce. My favorite brew is the tasty Rough Neck Red. Check out the patio dining in summer and the TVs for sporting events.

The Wellhead, 332 West Main St. (ℂ 505/746-0640), is open Sunday through Thursday from 11am to 9pm, Friday and Saturday from 11am to 10pm. Reservations are recommended on weekends and holidays. Main courses range from $6 to $20, and most major credit cards are accepted.

up. If possible, plan to eat in Carlsbad instead. The saloon is unmistakable, with long-horns mounted over the door.

26 Carlsbad Cavern Hwy., White's City. ✆ 505/785-2291. Reservations recommended in summer. Velvet Garter main courses $10–$20; Fat Jack's main courses $5.50–$10. AE, DC, DISC, MC, V. Velvet Garter daily 4–10pm (last seating at 9:30pm); Fat Jack's winter daily 7am–4pm; summer daily 6:15am–4pm. Saloon daily 4–10pm.

CARLSBAD AFTER DARK

Fairly recently Carlsbad has gained a night scene. You have three options. The **Silver Spur,** 1829 S. Canal St. (✆ 505/887-2851), offers live country and western music most nights and free hors d'oeuvres during happy hour, as well as a big-screen TV. The **Firehouse Fire Escape,** 222 W. Fox St. (✆ 505/234-1546), has dancing in the upstairs of an old firehouse. The **Post Time Saloon,** 313 W. Fox St. (✆ 505/628-1977), is a huge place with pool tables, three bars, and a dance floor. The club offers a range of DJ mixes, including country, tejano, and karaoke.

7 Carlsbad Caverns National Park ✦✦✦

23 miles SW of Carlsbad; 81 miles S of Roswell; 150 miles NE of El Paso

One of the largest and most spectacular cave systems in the world, **Carlsbad Caverns** comprise some 100 known caves that snake through the porous limestone reef of the Guadalupe Mountains. Fantastic and grotesque formations fascinate visitors, who find every shape imaginable (and unimaginable) naturally sculpted in the underground world—from frozen waterfalls to strands of pearls, soda straws to miniature castles, draperies to ice-cream cones.

Although Native Americans had known of the caverns for centuries, they were not discovered by whites until about a century ago, when settlers were attracted by sunset flights of bats from the cave. Jim White, a guano miner, began to explore the main cave in the early 1900s and to share its wonders with tourists. By 1923, the caverns had become a national monument, upgraded to national park status in 1930.

ESSENTIALS

GETTING THERE Take US 62/180 from Carlsbad, New Mexico (see "Essentials," under "Carlsbad & Environs," earlier in this chapter), which is 23 miles to the northeast, or El Paso, Texas, which is 150 miles to the west. The scenic entrance road to the park is 7 miles long and originates at the park gate at White's City. Van service to Carlsbad Caverns National Park from White's City, south of Carlsbad, is provided by **Sun Country Tours/White's City Services** (✆ 505/785-2291).

VISITOR INFORMATION For more information about the park, contact **Carlsbad Caverns National Park,** 3225 National Parks Hwy., Carlsbad, NM 88220 (✆ 800/967-CAVE for tour reservations, 505/785-2232 for information about guided tours, or 505/785-3012 for bat flight information; www.nps.gov/cave).

ADMISSION FEES & HOURS General admission to the park is $6 for adults, $3 for children 6 to 15, and free for children under 6. Admission is good for 3 days and includes the two self-guided walking tours. Guided tours range in price from $7 to $20, depending on the type of tour, and reservations are required. The visitor center and park are open daily from Memorial Day to mid-August from 8am to 7pm; the rest of the year they're open from 8am to 5pm. They're closed December 25.

TOURING THE CAVES

Two caves, **Carlsbad Cavern** and **Slaughter Canyon Cave,** are open to the public. The National Park Service has provided facilities, including elevators, to make it easy for everyone to visit the cavern, and a kennel for pets is available. Visitors in wheelchairs are common.

In addition to the tours described below, inquire at the visitor center information desk about other ranger-guided tours, including climbing and crawling "wild" cave tours. Be sure to call days in advance, because some tours are offered only 1 day per week. Spelunkers who seek access to the park's undeveloped caves require special permission from the park superintendent.

CARLSBAD CAVERN TOURS

You can tour Carlsbad Cavern in one of three ways, depending on your schedule, interest, and level of ability. The first, and least difficult, option is to take the elevator from the visitor center down 750 feet to the start of the self-guided tour of the **Big Room.** More difficult and time-consuming, but vastly more rewarding, is the 1-mile self-guided tour along the **Natural Entrance** route, which follows the traditional explorer's route, entering the cavern through the large historic natural entrance. The paved walkway through the natural entrance winds into the depths of the cavern and leads through a series of underground rooms; this tour takes about an hour. Parts of it are steep. At its lowest point, the trail reaches 750 feet below the surface, ending finally at an underground rest area.

Visitors who take either the elevator or the Natural Entrance route begin the self-guided tour of the spectacular Big Room near the rest area. The floor of this room covers 14 acres; the tour, over a relatively level path, is 1¼ miles long and takes about an hour.

The third option is the 1½-hour ranger-guided **Kings Palace** tour, which also departs from the underground rest area. This tour descends 830 feet beneath the surface of the desert to the deepest portion of the cavern open to the public. Reservations are required, and an additional fee is charged.

> ### Carlsbad Cavern Tour Tips
> Wear flat shoes with rubber soles and heels on the slippery paths. A light sweater or jacket feels good in the constant temperature of 56°F (13°C), especially when it's 100°F (38°C) outside in the sun. The cavern is well lit, but you may want to bring along a flashlight as well. Rangers are stationed in the cave to answer questions.

SLAUGHTER CANYON CAVE TOUR

Slaughter Canyon Cave was discovered in 1937 and was mined commercially for bat guano (an excellent fertilizer) until the 1950s. It consists of a corridor 1,140 feet long, with many side passageways. The lowest point is 250 feet below the surface. The passage traversed by the ranger-guided tours is 1.75 miles, but it is more strenuous than hiking through the main cavern. There is also a strenuous 500-foot-rise hike from the parking lot to the cave mouth. The tour lasts about 2½ hours. No more than 25 people may take part in a tour, and then by reservation only. Everyone needs a flashlight (make sure you have fresh batteries), hiking boots or shoes, and a container of drinking water. To reach Slaughter Canyon Cave, take US 180 south 5 miles from White's City to a marked turnoff that leads 11 miles into a parking lot.

OTHER GUIDED TOURS

Be sure to ask about the Left Hand Tunnel, Lower Cave, Hall of the White Giant, and Spider Cave tours. These vary in degree of difficulty and adventure, from Left Hand, which is an easy half-mile lantern tour, to Spider Cave, where you can expect tight crawlways and canyonlike passages, to Hall of the White Giant, a strenuous tour that requires you to crawl long distances, squeeze through tight crevices, and climb up slippery flow-stone–lined passages. Call in advance for times of each tour. All these tours depart from the visitor center.

BAT FLIGHTS

Every sunset from May to October, a crowd gathers at the natural entrance of the cave to watch a quarter-million bats take flight for a night of insect feasting. (The bats winter in Mexico.) All day long, the Mexican free-tailed bats sleep in the cavern; at night, they all strike out on an insect hunt. A ranger program is offered around 7:30pm (verify the time at the visitor center) at the outdoor Bat Flight Amphitheater. The park sponsors a **Bat Flight Breakfast** from 5 to 7am once a year, usually on the second Thursday in August, during which visitors watch the bats return to the cavern. The cost is $6 for adults, $3 for children under 13. For information, call © **505/785-2232,** ext. 0.

OTHER PARK ACTIVITIES

Aside from the caves, the park offers a 10-mile one-way scenic loop drive through the Chihuahuan Desert to view Rattlesnake and Upper Walnut canyons. Picnickers can head for Rattlesnake Springs Picnic Area, on County Road 418 near Slaughter Canyon Cave, a water source for hundreds of years for the Native Americans, and a primo birding spot. Backcountry hikers must register at the visitor center before going out on any of the trails in the park's 46,766 acres.

8 Socorro: Gateway to Bosque del Apache & the VLA

62 miles NE of Truth or Consequences; 69 miles S of Albuquerque; 112 miles N of Las Cruces

This quiet, pleasant town of about 9,000 is an unusual mix of the 19th, 20th, and 21st centuries. Established as a mining settlement and ranching center, its downtown area is dominated by numerous mid-1800s buildings and the 17th-century San Miguel Mission. The **New Mexico Institute of Mining and Technology** (New Mexico Tech) is a major research center. Socorro is also the gateway to a vast and varied two-county region that includes the **Bosque del Apache National Wildlife Refuge,** the **Very Large Array National Radio Astronomy Observatory (VLA),** and three national forests.

ESSENTIALS

GETTING THERE   From Albuquerque, take I-25 south (1¼ hr.). From Las Cruces, take I-25 north (2¾ hr.).

VISITOR INFORMATION   The **Socorro County Chamber of Commerce,** which is also the visitor information headquarters, is at 101 Plaza (P.O. Box 743), Socorro, NM 87801 (© **505/835-0424;** www.socorro-nm.com).

EXPLORING SOCORRO

The best introduction to Socorro is a walking tour of the historic district. A brochure with a map and guidebook, available at the chamber of commerce on the **plaza,** where the tour begins, points out several historic buildings, many on the National Register

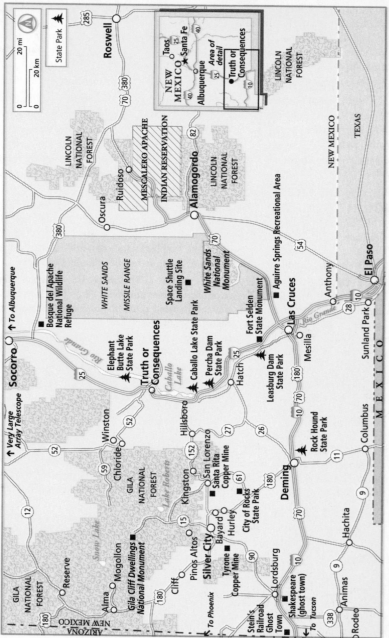

Southwestern New Mexico

of Historic Places. A decent spot to break for lunch, a snack, or just a cup of coffee is **Martha's Black Dog Coffeehouse** (© **505/838-0311**).

You'll definitely want to check out the old **Val Verde Hotel.** Although the hotel is no longer in operation, a restaurant is still open. At lunch or dinner, the **Val Verde Steak House** (see "Where to Dine in the Socorro Area," below) is a good place to stop.

OTHER ATTRACTIONS

Old San Miguel Mission ★★   Built from 1615 to 1626 but abandoned during the Pueblo Revolt of 1680, this graceful church was subsequently restored. It gained a new wing in 1853. It boasts thick adobe walls, large carved vigas (rafters), and supporting corbel arches.

403 El Camino Real NW, 2 blocks north of the plaza. © **505/835-1620.** Free admission. Summer Mon–Fri 8am–7:30pm; winter 8am–6:30pm. Mass Sat 6pm, Sun 9:30 and 11am.

SEEING THE SIGHTS NEAR SOCORRO

SOUTH OF SOCORRO   The village of **San Antonio,** the boyhood home of Conrad Hilton, is 10 miles from Socorro on I-25. During the financial panic of 1907, his merchant father, Augustus Hilton, converted part of his store into a rooming house. That gave Conrad his first exposure to the hospitality industry, and he went on to worldwide fame as a hotelier. Only ruins of the store and boardinghouse remain.

WEST OF SOCORRO   Fifty-four miles west of Socorro on US 60 is the **Very Large Array National Radio Astronomy Observatory,** or VLA. Here, 27 dish-shaped antennas, each 82 feet in diameter, spread across the plains of San Agustin, forming a single gigantic radio telescope. Many recognize the site from the 1997 movie *Contact,* starring Jodie Foster. Photographs taken with this apparatus are similar to those taken with the largest optical telescopes, except that radio telescopes are sensitive to low-frequency radio waves. All types of celestial objects are photographed, including the sun and its planets, stars, quasars, galaxies, and even the faint remains of the "big bang" that scientists believe occurred some 10 billion years ago.

You begin in the visitor center, viewing an informational film about the VLA. In the museum, you can see how radio waves can be transformed into space pictures and why this is such an effective method of exploration. On the outdoor, self-guided walking tour, you'll have a chance to get a closer look at the massive antennas. Don't miss the whispering display, where you can sample firsthand how a dish collects and transmits sound. Admission is free, and visitors are welcomed daily from 8:30am to sunset. The Socorro office is at 1003 Lopezville Rd. NW (© **505/835-7000;** www.nrao.edu).

WHERE TO STAY IN THE SOCORRO AREA

Most accommodations are along California Street, the main highway through town, or the adjacent I-25 frontage road. Most lodgings provide free parking.

Casa Blanca   The ideal situation in this part of the world is to be just a few minutes away from the Bosque del Apache. That way, you only have to get out of bed a half-hour or so before sunup in order to get to the wildlife refuge and see the morning flight (see "Oasis in the Desert: Bosque del Apache National Wildlife Refuge," below). Casa Blanca is the place to stay for this reason. The cozy Victorian farmhouse is home to proprietor Phoebe Wood, a former schoolteacher. The place has a genuine homelike quality—comfortable and well maintained. The best room is the Crane, light and airy, with a queen-size bed and private bathroom. You can eat the simple but generous continental breakfast (fruit, cereals, and home-baked muffins) early, on the way out to the Bosque, or later, upon your return. Smoking is not permitted.

13 Montoya St. (P.O. Box 31), San Antonio, NM 87832. C 505/835-3027. www.casablancabedandbreakfast.com. 3 units. $70–$90 double. Rates include continental breakfast. MC, V. Closed Memorial Day to Labor Day. Pets accepted.

Holiday Inn Express   Like most of the branches of this newer hotel chain, this two-story inn offers functional rooms and plenty of amenities. Guests can select from two types of rooms: hotel-style units opening off corridors, or motel-style ones where you park your car near your door. All rooms are medium-size with medium-firm beds and standard-size bathrooms.

1100 California Ave. NE, Socorro, NM 87801. C 888/526-4567 or 505/838-0556. Fax 505/838-0598. www.hiexpress. com. 120 units. $90 double. Rates include continental breakfast. AE, DISC, MC, V. Pets accepted; $10 fee. **Amenities:** Indoor pool; 2 exercise rooms; indoor/outdoor Jacuzzis. *In room:* A/C, TV, fridge, coffeemaker, hair dryer, iron, microwave.

CAMPING

Casey's Socorro RV Park (C **800/674-2234** or 505/835-2234) offers mountain and valley views and plenty of shade, as well as 100 sites and 30 full hookups. Tenting is available, as are picnic tables, grills, and ice. A playground and swimming pool are open year-round. To reach Casey's, take I-25 to exit 147, go 1 block west on Business I-25 and then 1 block south on West Frontage Road.

WHERE TO DINE IN THE SOCORRO AREA

El Sombrero ⋆ NEW MEXICAN   This is a real locals' place. My Socorran friends call it "the Hat" and always request the garden room, where tables surround a small fountain. This is some of the best New Mexican food around. I especially enjoy the chicken enchiladas, though my friend Dennis always orders the spinach ones. They come rolled, with beans, rice, and a sopaipilla. Most popular on the menu are beef or chicken fajitas, served with rice, beans, tortillas, and guacamole. The restaurant is known for its trademark sauces, especially poblano chile and mole, which are served over enchiladas or meats such as chicken. For dessert, try the churro, a cinnamon sugared stick with vanilla ice cream. Beer and wine are available.

210 Mesquite NE, Socorro. C 505/835-3945. Main courses $4–$11. AE, DC, DISC, MC, V. Daily 11am–9pm.

Owl Bar and Cafe AMERICAN   A low-lit tavern in a one-story adobe building 7 miles south of Socorro, the Owl was once *the* place to stop for a green-chile cheeseburger. Unfortunately, this is no longer the case. The burgers are mediocre at best, but the Owl is a decent refreshment stop. Breakfasts offer such standards as eggs and pancakes.

NM 1 and US 380, San Antonio. C 505/835-9946. Main courses $3–$8 breakfast and lunch, $6–$14 dinner. AE, DISC, MC, V. Mon–Sat 8am–9:30pm.

Val Verde Steak House ⋆ AMERICAN   Whenever my dad is traveling south, this is where he stops to eat; he has very good taste, so I often follow his recommendations. The restaurant is in the horseshoe-shaped Val Verde Hotel, a National Historic Landmark built in 1919. The California Mission–style hotel has been converted to apartments, but the public can still enjoy the old dining room. Lunch items are simple but tasty: homemade soups, salads, and sandwiches, plus steaks and seafood. A lunch buffet offers a different theme every day, from Mexican to country-style barbecue. Dinner is more elaborate, with dishes such as a 10-ounce top sirloin or an extravagant 16-ounce chateaubriand. Gourmet Southwestern dishes are also served. The nightclub is open daily until midnight, depending on the crowd, and until 1am on Friday and Saturday, when there's live music.

203 Manzanares Ave., Socorro. ⓒ 505/835-3380. Reservations recommended. Main courses $4.50–$13 lunch, $9–$39 dinner. AE, DC, DISC, MC, V. Mon–Fri 11am–2pm; Sun–Thurs 5:30–9pm; Fri–Sat 5–9:30pm. Closed July 4, Dec 25.

9 Oasis in the Desert: Bosque del Apache National Wildlife Refuge ★ ★

16 miles S of Socorro; 85 miles S of Albuquerque; 100 miles N of Las Cruces

by Ian Wilker

The barren lands on either side of I-25 south of Albuquerque hardly seem fit for rattlesnakes, much less one of the Southwest's greatest concentrations of wildlife. The plants that do find purchase in the parched washes and small canyons along the road—forbiddingly named hardies such as creosote bush, tarbush, and white thorn—serve notice that you are within the northernmost reaches of the great Chihuahuan Desert, which covers southern New Mexico and southwestern Texas and runs deep into Mexico.

To the east of the interstate is the green-margined Rio Grande. In the midst of such a blasted landscape, the river stands out as an inviting beacon to wildlife, and nowhere does it shine more brightly than at Bosque del Apache's 7,000 acres of carefully managed riparian habitat, which includes marshlands, meadows, agricultural fields, arrowweed thickets on the riverbanks, and big old-growth cottonwoods lining what were once the oxbows of the river. The refuge supports a riot of wildlife, including all the characteristic mammals and reptiles of the Southwest (mule deer, jackrabbits, and coyotes are common) and some 377 species of birds.

A visit here during the peak winter season—from November to March—is one of the most consistently thrilling wildlife spectacles in the lower 48 states, especially if you're an avid bird-watcher. You might call Bosque del Apache the LAX of the Central Flyway, one of four paths that migratory birds follow every year between their summer breeding grounds in the tundral north and wintering grounds in the southern United States, Mexico, and even as far away as South America. Many of these birds stop over here to recharge their batteries or settle down for the winter.

It is not enough to say that hundreds of species of birds are on hand. The wonder is in the sheer numbers: In early December, the refuge may harbor as many as 45,000 snow geese, 57,000 ducks of many different species, and 18,000 sandhill cranes. The huge, ungainly birds have a special majesty in flight, pinkish in the sun at dawn or dusk. Plenty of raptors are also about—numerous red-tailed hawks and northern harriers (sometimes called marsh hawks), Cooper's hawks and kestrels, and even bald and golden eagles—as well as Bosque del Apache's many year-round avian residents: pheasants and quail, wild turkeys, and much-mythologized roadrunners (*El Paisano*, in Mexican folklore). The interest of experienced birders will be whetted by the presence of Mexican mallards, Chihuahuan ravens, burrowing owls, rare grebes, beautiful longbilled American avocets, and especially whooping cranes (a very few remain from an experiment to imprint the migratory path of sandhills on whoopers). Everyone will be mesmerized by the huge societies of sandhills, ducks, and geese, going about their daily business of feeding, gabbling, quarreling, honking, and otherwise making an immense racket.

The refuge has a 12-mile auto tour loop, which you should drive very slowly; the south half of the loop travels past numerous water impoundments, where the majority of the ducks and geese hang out, and the north half has the meadows and farmland, where you'll see the roadrunners and other land birds, and where the cranes and geese feed from midmorning through the afternoon.

A few special experiences bear further explanation. Dawn is definitely the best time to be here—songbirds are far more active in the first hours of the day, and the cranes and geese take flight en masse. This last event is not to be missed. Dusk, when the birds return to the water, is also a good time. At either dawn or dusk, find your way to one of the observation decks and wait for what birders call the "fly out" (off the water to the fields) or "fly in" (from the fields to the water).

Don't despair if you can't be at the Bosque del Apache during the prime winter months; it's a special place any time of year. By April, the geese and ducks have flown north, and the refuge drains the water impoundments to allow the marsh plants to regenerate; the resulting mud flats are an ideal feeding ground for the migrating shorebirds that arrive in April and May.

If you'd like to stretch your legs a bit, check out the **Chupadera Peak Trail,** which follows a 2-mile loop or a 9.5-mile loop to a high point overlooking the refuge. Ask for directions at the visitor center.

JUST THE FACTS The Bosque del Apache National Wildlife Refuge is about a 1½-hour drive from Albuquerque. Follow I-25 for 9 miles south of Socorro, then take the San Antonio exit. At the main intersection of San Antonio, turn south onto NM 1. In 3 miles, you'll be on refuge lands, and another 4 miles will bring you to the excellent visitor center, which has a small museum with interpretive displays and a large shelf of field guides, natural histories, and other books of interest for visitors to New Mexico. The visitor center is open from 7:30am to 4pm weekdays, and from 8am to 4:30pm weekends. The refuge is open daily year-round from 1 hour before sunrise to 1 hour after sunset. Admission is $3 per vehicle. For more information, contact **Bosque del Apache National Wildlife Refuge,** P.O. Box 1246, Socorro, NM 87801 (© **505/835-1828;** www.fws.gov/southwest/refuges/newmex/bosque).

10 Truth or Consequences

58 miles N of Las Cruces; 62 miles SW of Socorro; 131 miles S of Albuquerque

Originally known as Hot Springs, after the therapeutic mineral springs bubbling up near the river, the town took the name Truth or Consequences—usually shortened to "T or C"—in 1950. That was the year that Ralph Edwards, producer of the popular radio and television program *Truth or Consequences,* began his weekly broadcast with these words: "I wish that some town in the United States liked and respected our show so much that it would like to change its name to Truth or Consequences." The reward to any city willing to do so was to become the site of the 10th-anniversary broadcast of the program, which would put it on the national map in a big way. The locals voted for the name change, which has survived three protest elections over the years.

Although the TV program was canceled decades ago, Ralph Edwards continued to return for the annual **Truth or Consequences Fiesta,** the first weekend of May. (Now that he's in his 90s, he no longer attends.) Another popular annual festival is **Geronimo Days,** the second weekend of October. Despite its festive roots, T or C seems to have an identity crisis—perhaps a consequence of giving up your name for the fame and fortune of television. The city exudes a forlorn quality, possibly due to the struggling economy. However, in recent years, a few of the bathhouses have undergone renovation, so there may be hope. Overall, you'll want to visit here to explore the strangeness of a town that traded away its identity.

ESSENTIALS

GETTING THERE   From Albuquerque, take I-25 south (2½ hr.). From Las Cruces, take I-25 north (1¼ hr.). There's no commercial flight service; those who fly themselves may contact the **Truth or Consequences Municipal Airport,** Old North Highway 85 (© **505/894-6199**).

VISITOR INFORMATION   The **visitor information center** is at the corner of Main Street (Business Loop 25) and Foch Street in downtown Truth or Consequences. Also there is the **Truth or Consequences & Sierra County Chamber of Commerce,** P.O. Drawer 31, Truth or Consequences, NM 87901 (© **505/894-3536;** www.truth orconsequencesnm.net).

CITY LAYOUT   This year-round resort town and retirement community of 7,500 spreads along the Rio Grande between the Elephant Butte and Caballo reservoirs, two of the three largest bodies of water in the state. Business Loop 25 branches off from I-25 to wind through the city, splitting into Main Street (one-way west) and South Broadway (one-way east) in the downtown area. Third Avenue connects T or C with the Elephant Butte resort community, 5 miles east.

TAKING THE WATERS AT THE HISTORIC HOT SPRINGS

The town's "original" attraction is its hot springs. The entire downtown area is over a table of odorless hot mineral water, 98°F to 115°F (37°C–46°C), that bubbles to the surface through wells or pools. The first bathhouse was built in the 1880s; most of the half-dozen historic spas operating today date from the 1930s. Generally open from morning to early evening, these spas welcome visitors for soaks and massages. Baths of 20 minutes or longer start at $5 per person.

The chamber of commerce has information on all the local spas (see "Essentials," above). Among them is **Sierra Grande Lodge & Spa,** 501 McAdoo St. (© **505/894-6976;** www.sierragrandelodge.com), where Geronimo himself is rumored to have taken a break. (See "Where to Stay in & Around Truth or Consequences," below.) **Artesian Bath House,** 312 Marr St. (© **505/894-2684**), has an RV park on the premises.

I highly recommend the **Hay-Yo-Kay Hot Springs** ☆, 300 Austin St. (© **505/894-2228;** www.hay-yo-kay.com). It has natural-flow pools (versus tubs filled with spring water). The tub rooms are private and gracefully tiled. The Long House, a cooler tub, is the largest in town and can hold up to 20 people. Hay-Yo-Kay is open in the summer Wednesday through Friday 4 to 8pm, weekends from noon to 8pm. Winter hours (Sept–May) are Wednesday through Friday 10am to 7pm, weekends from noon to 7pm. Hours on Monday holidays are from noon to 7pm. Massages and reflexology are also available.

A MUSEUM IN T OR C

Geronimo Springs Museum   Outside this museum is Geronimo's Spring, where the great Apache shaman is said to have taken his warriors to bathe their battle wounds. Turtleback Mountain, looming over the Rio Grande east of the city, is believed to have been sacred to Native Americans.

Exhibits include prehistoric Mimbres pottery (A.D. 950–1250); the Spanish Heritage Room, updated and renovated, featuring artifacts of the first families of Sierra County; and artists' work, including historical murals and sculptured bronzes. An authentic miner's cabin has been moved here from the nearby mountains. The Ralph Edwards Wing traces the history and highlights of the annual fiestas and celebrates the city's name change, including television footage from the shows filmed in T or C. The museum is geothermally heated.

211 Main St. ⓒ 505/894-6600. Admission $3 adults, $1.50 students; family rates available. DISC, MC, V. Mon–Sat 9am–5pm.

SOUTH OF TRUTH OR CONSEQUENCES   Thirty-two miles from Truth or Consequences is **Hillsboro** ⍟, another ghost town that's fast losing its ghosts to a small invasion of artists and craftspeople, antiques shops, and galleries. This town boomed after an 1877 gold strike nearby, and during its heyday it produced $6 million in silver and gold. It was the county seat from 1884 to 1938. Hillsboro's Labor Day weekend **Apple Festival** is famous throughout the state. Take I-25 south to NM 152, then go west.

WHERE TO STAY IN & AROUND TRUTH OR CONSEQUENCES

Best Western Hot Springs Inn   This freeway-exit motel lives up to the Best Western standard, with spacious, comfortable rooms in a quiet setting. All accommodations are medium-size, with up-to-date furnishings, medium-size bathrooms, and plenty of amenities. K-Bob's steakhouse is adjacent.

2270 N. Date St. (at I-25 Exit 79), Truth or Consequences, NM 87901. ⓒ 800/528-1234 or 505/894-6665. Fax 505/894-6665. www.bestwestern.com. 41 units. Winter $55–$58 double; summer $58–$64 double. AE, DC, DISC, MC, V. **Amenities:** Seasonal outdoor pool. *In room:* A/C, TV, fridge, coffeemaker.

Elephant Butte Inn ⍟   This hotel offers a comfortable stay and a unique experience. It sits above Elephant Butte Lake and has panoramic views as well as a relaxing resortlike feel. Recent years have brought a complete face-lift to the whole place. It caters to boaters, fishers, and other relaxation lovers. Rooms are standard size, furnished with medium-firm king- or queen-size beds. Bathrooms are small but functional. I recommend the lakeside view, where a big grassy lawn stretches down to tennis courts. The pool was recently remodeled and is now heated. Golf packages include greens fees at the nearby Truth or Consequences Golf Course.

NM 195 (P.O. Box 996), Elephant Butte, NM 87935. ⓒ 505/744-5431. Fax 505/744-5044. www.elephantbutte inn.com. 48 units. Mid-Sept to Apr $70–$100 double; May to early Sept $75–$105 double. AE, DC, DISC, MC, V. **Amenities:** Restaurant; outdoor pool; limited room service. *In room:* A/C, TV, coffeemaker, hair dryer, iron.

Sierra Grande Lodge & Spa ⍟⍟   This resort provides a sensual oasis in southern New Mexico. The biggest draw is the springs. Nowhere else in the state can you stay in luxury while partaking of warm, healing waters rich in minerals. The medium-size rooms in the renovated 1920s lodge have refined, handcrafted furnishings, and many have balconies. Suites have in-room Jacuzzis. A casita with its own outdoor tub is so popular it's reserved months in advance. Guests can request a DVD player.

501 McAdoo St., Truth or Consequences, NM 87901. ⓒ 505/894-6976. www.sierragrandelodge.com. 17 units. $65–$95 double Tues–Thurs, $95–$125 double Fri–Mon; $200 suite. AE, DISC, MC, V. **Amenities:** Restaurant (p. 324); 4 hot mineral baths; spa; massage. *In room:* A/C, TV, dataport, hair dryer.

CAMPING

Elephant Butte Lake State Park (*©* 505/744-5923) welcomes backpackers and RVs alike, with 200 developed campsites, 150 RV hookups, picnic tables, and access points for swimming, hiking, boating, and fishing. Kids love the playground.

Not far from Elephant Butte Lake is **Monticello Point RV Park** (*©* 505/894-6468), which offers tenting and 69 sites with full hookups. Laundry and grocery facilities are on the premises, as are restrooms with showers. To reach Monticello Point, take I-25 to exit 89 and follow signs 5½ miles east on the paved road.

Lakeside RV Park and Lodging (*©* 505/744-5996), also near Elephant Butte, has 50 sites and 2 overflow sites (all 52 are full hookups), as well as a recreation room with cable and laundry facilities. Headed south on I-25, the RV park is 4 miles southeast of the I-25/NM 195 junction (Exit 83) on NM 195. Headed north on I-25, take exit 79, go half a mile east on the paved road, 1½ miles north on NM 181, then 1½ miles east on NM 171, and finally ¼ mile south on NM 195.

Camping is also available at **Caballo Lake State Park** and **Percha Dam State Park.** For information on either park, call *©* **505/743-3942** or visit **www.nmparks.com**.

WHERE TO DINE IN & AROUND TRUTH OR CONSEQUENCES

La Cocina *Kids* NEW MEXICAN/AMERICAN   A real locals' place, this restaurant serves decent New Mexican food in a festive atmosphere. The tostadas (crispy tortillas covered with beans and meat) and chile rellenos are tasty, but my favorite is cheese enchiladas. Even better are the huge *sopaipillas*. Kids like the big booths and their own quesadillas and tacos.

1 Lakeview Dr. (at Date St.). *©* **505/894-6499.** Reservations recommended on weekends. Main courses $7–$19. DISC, MC, V. Mon–Thurs 10:30am–10pm in summer, 10:30am–9pm in winter; Fri–Sun 10:30am–10pm year-round.

Sierra Grande *★★★* NEW AMERICAN/BISTRO   Amazing! That's my reaction to finding this oasis in the middle of New Mexico's sparse Sonoran desert. When Sierra Grande opened, *Condé Nast Traveler* named it one of the world's 50 top new restaurants. Saltillo tile floors, contemporary wall sconces, and a stained-glass mural of Elephant Butte Dam give the place a warm and refreshingly sophisticated feel. The eclectic menu changes seasonally. Try delicacies such as achiote shrimp salad or crawfish cake for starters. For an entree, I've enjoyed pistachio-crusted rack of lamb served with root vegetable mashed potatoes. I've also liked olive-crusted salmon with herbed Mediterranean couscous. If you're looking for a lighter meal, you can order entrees "simply grilled." Service is attentive. On some nights, a tarot card reader will do a reading for you (for an extra fee). For dessert, try the Mexican pressed chocolate cake, with a hint of red chile. A good wine list accompanies the menu.

In the Sierra Grande Lodge & Spa, 501 McAdoo St. *©* **505/894-6976.** www.sierragrandelodge.com. Reservations recommended on summer weekends. Main courses $15–$25. AE, DISC, MC, V. Wed–Sun 5–10pm.

11 Las Cruces

60 miles SW of Alamogordo; 112 miles S of Socorro; 180 miles S of Albuquerque

Picture a valley full of weathered wooden crosses marking graves of settlers brutally murdered by Apaches, behind them mountains with peaks so jagged they resemble organ pipes. That scene led people to begin calling this city Las Cruces, meaning "the crosses." Even today, the place has a mysterious presence, its rich history haunting it still. Reminders of characters such as Billy the Kid, who was sentenced to death here, and Pancho Villa, who roamed the streets, linger throughout the area.

Established in 1849 on El Camino Real, the "royal highway" between Santa Fe and Mexico City, Las Cruces became a supply center for miners prospecting the Organ Mountains and soldiers stationed at nearby Fort Selden. Today, it is New Mexico's second-largest urban area, with 73,600 people. It is noted as an agricultural center, especially for its cotton, pecans, and chiles; as a regional transportation hub; and as the gateway to the White Sands Missile Range and other defense installations.

Las Cruces manages to survive in a desert landscape that gets only 8 inches of precipitation a year, pulling enough moisture from the Rio Grande, which runs through, to irrigate a broad swatch of valley.

ESSENTIALS

GETTING THERE From Albuquerque, take I-25 south (4 hr.). From El Paso, take I-10 north (45 min.). From Tucson, take I-25 east (5 hr.).

Las Cruces International Airport (© **505/524-2762;** www.las-cruces.org/airport), 8 miles west, has service several times daily to and from Albuquerque on **Mesa Airlines** (© **800/MESA-AIR** or 505/326-3338; www.mesa-air.com). **El Paso International Airport** (© **915/772-4271;** www.elpasointernationalairport.com), 47 miles south, has daily flights to Albuquerque, Phoenix, Dallas, and Houston, among other cities. The **Las Cruces Shuttle Service,** P.O. Box 3172, Las Cruces, NM 88003 (© **800/288-1784** or 505/525-1784; www.lascrucesshuttle.com), provides service between the El Paso airport and Las Cruces. It leaves Las Cruces 12 times daily between 5am and 9:30pm. The fare is $30 one-way or $46 round-trip, with large discounts for parties of two or more. Pickup or drop-off at places other than regular stops at major hotels costs $7. Connections can also be made three times a day from Las Cruces to Deming and Silver City.

VISITOR INFORMATION The **Las Cruces Convention and Visitors Bureau** is at 211 N. Water St., Las Cruces, NM 88001 (© **877/266-8252** or 505/541-2444; www.lascrucescvb.org). Or contact the **Greater Las Cruces Chamber of Commerce,** 760 W. Picacho St. (P.O. Drawer 519), Las Cruces, NM 88004 (© **505/524-1968;** www.lascruces.org).

WHAT TO SEE & DO IN LAS CRUCES

On a hot day, when the church bells are ringing and you're wandering the brick streets of **Mesilla** ★★, you may for a moment slip back into the late 16th century—or feel as though you have. Mexican colonists established this village on Las Cruces's southwestern flank in the late 1500s. It became the crossroads of El Camino Real and the Butterfield Overland Mail route. The Gadsden Purchase, which annexed Mesilla to the United States and fixed the current international boundaries of New Mexico and Arizona, was signed here in 1854.

Mesilla's most notorious resident, William Bonney, otherwise known as Billy the Kid, was sentenced to death at the county courthouse here. He was sent to Lincoln, New Mexico, to be hanged, but escaped before the sentence was carried out. Legendary hero Pat Garrett eventually tracked down and killed the Kid at Fort Sumner; later, Garrett was mysteriously murdered in an arroyo just outside Las Cruces. He is buried in the local Masonic cemetery.

Thick-walled adobe buildings, which once protected residents against Apache attacks, now house art galleries, restaurants, museums, and gift shops. Throughout Mesilla, colorful red-chile *ristras* (chile strung on ropes) decorate homes and businesses. On Sunday during the summer locals sell crafts and baked goods, and mariachi bands play.

PLACES OF NOTE IN MESILLA

At the **Mesilla Visitor Center,** 2340 Av. de Mesilla (© **505/647-9698**), you'll find period photos and plenty of brochures on the area, as well as clean public restrooms. Nearby is the **Gadsden Museum,** a grand old house full of memorabilia that's open only intermittently. In the back of the museum parking lot is a replica of the old Mesilla jail, a dismal storage shed with original jail doors that once helped to incarcerate Billy the Kid.

PLACES OF NOTE IN HISTORIC LAS CRUCES

Though it has a much less romantic atmosphere than Mesilla, downtown Las Cruces has a few historic buildings that make visiting worthwhile. Pick up a map of a walking tour of the area at the **Las Cruces Convention and Visitors Bureau,** 211 N. Water St.

Central to the area is the **Bicentennial Log Cabin,** Main Street and Lucero Avenue, Downtown Mall (© **505/541-2155**). The cabin, which was built around 1850 and moved to Las Cruces from the Black Range Mountains, contains authentic furnishings and artifacts. This municipal museum is open year-round by appointment.

OTHER ATTRACTIONS

Las Cruces Museum of Natural History *Kids*   This small city-funded museum offers a variety of exhibits, changed quarterly, that emphasize science and natural history. The museum features live animals of the Chihuahuan Desert, hands-on science activities, and a small native plant garden. The Cenozoic Shop carries scientific toys and books about the region. Exhibits, such as "Insects and Bugs," change every few months. In summer 2005, the exhibit was titled "Our Weakening Web."

Mesilla Valley Mall, 700 S. Telshor. © 505/522-3120. Free admission. Mon–Thurs and Sat 10am–5pm; Fri 10am–8pm; Sun 1–5pm.

New Mexico Farm and Ranch Heritage Museum   Having grown up on a New Mexico ranch, I was eager to see how this museum would present the Western lifestyle. The 47-acre interactive museum brings to life the 3,000-year history of farming, ranching, and rural living in New Mexico. It's in a huge structure that's well designed to look like a hacienda-style barn, with a U-shaped courtyard in back and exhibits on expansive grounds. The museum lacks a really exciting draw, but for someone like my brother who loves farm and ranch equipment, it would appear like Disneyland, with such relics as a 1937 John Deere tractor and a number of examples of how ranchers "make do," ingeniously combining elements such as a tractor seat with a milk barrel to come up with a chair. Most interesting are the art exhibits—in particular, pencil drawings by Robert Shufelt, which are on rotational display.

You may want to plan your visit around a meal at the Purple Sage restaurant, with upscale versions of Mexican dishes and burgers served in an elegant new Southwest atmosphere—very Santa Fe, if I do say so. Annual events at the museum are La Fiesta de San Ysidro in May and Cowboy Days on the third weekend in October.

4100 Dripping Springs Rd. (follow University Ave. east beyond the edge of town). © 505/522-4100. www.frhm.org. Admission $3 adults, $2 seniors 60 and over, $1 children 6–17, free for children under 6. Mon–Sat 9am–5pm; Sun noon–5pm.

San Albino Church ★★   This is one of the oldest churches in the Mesilla valley. The present structure was built in 1906 on the foundation of the original church, constructed in 1851. It was named for St. Albin, a medieval English bishop of North Africa, on whose day an important irrigation ditch from the Rio Grande was completed. The church bells date from the early 1870s; the pews were made in Taos of Philippine mahogany.

North side of Old Mesilla Plaza. ✆ **505/526-9349.** Free admission; donations appreciated. Usually open Mon–Sat 1–3pm (call ahead). Mass Sat 5:30pm and Sun 11am; Spanish Mass Mon–Fri 7am, Sun 8am.

SHOPPING

Shoppers should be aware that in Las Cruces, Monday is a notoriously quiet day. Some stores close for the day, so it's best to call ahead before traveling to a specific store.

For art, visit **Lundeen's Inn of the Arts,** 618 S. Alameda Blvd. (✆ **505/526-3326**), displaying the works of about 30 Southwest painters, sculptors, and potters; **Rising Sky Artworks,** 415 E. Foster (✆ **505/525-8454**), which features works in clay by local and Western artists; and the **William Bonney Gallery,** 2060 Calle de Parian, just off the southeast corner of Old Mesilla Plaza (✆ **505/526-8275**), where you'll see a variety of Southwestern art.

For books, try **Bowlin's Mesilla Book Center,** in an 1856 mercantile building on the west side of Old Mesilla Plaza (✆ **505/526-6220**).

For native crafts and jewelry, check out **Silver Assets,** 1948 Calle de Santiago (✆ **505/523-8747**), 1½ blocks east of San Albino Church in Mesilla.

Mesilla Valley Mall, 700 S. Telshor Blvd., just off the I-25 interchange with Lohman Avenue (✆ **505/522-1001**), is a full-service shopping center with well over 100 stores. The mall is open Monday through Saturday from 10am to 9pm, Sunday from noon to 6pm.

The Las Cruces area has two wineries. **Blue Teal Vineyards** (✆ **877/669-4637** or 505/524-0390; www.blueteal.com) has a tasting room next to the historic Fountain Theater, 2461 Calle de Guadalupe, south of Old Mesilla Plaza. It's open Monday through Thursday 11am to 6pm, Friday and Saturday 11am to 8pm, Sunday noon to 6pm. The tasting room at **La Viña Winery** (✆ **505/882-7632**), south of Las Cruces off NM 28, is open daily from noon to 5pm, and by appointment.

LAS CRUCES AFTER DARK

National recording artists frequently perform at NMSU's **Pan Am Center** (✆ **505/646-1420**). The **NMSU Music Department** (✆ **505/646-2421**) offers free jazz, classical, and pop concerts from August to May, and the **Las Cruces Symphony Orchestra** (✆ **505/646-3709;** www.lascrucessymphony.com) often performs here.

NMSU's **Hershel Zohn Theater** (✆ **505/646-4515;** http://theatre.nmsu.edu/astc) presents plays of the professional-and-student **American Southwest Theatre Company** from September to May. It features dramas, comedies, musicals, and original works.

The **Las Cruces Community Theatre** (✆ **505/523-1200;** www.lcctnm.org) mounts six productions a year at its own facility on the downtown mall.

In Mesilla, the **Mesilla Valley Film Society** (✆ **505/524-8287**) runs a good selection of contemporary and vintage art films at the Fountain Theatre, 2469 Calle de Guadalupe (www.fountaintheatre.org), a half-block south of the plaza. Screenings start nightly at 7:30pm and sometimes 9:45pm, and Sunday at 2:30pm and sometimes 5pm.

EXPLORING THE AREA

NORTH OF LAS CRUCES   The town of **Hatch,** 39 miles north on I-25 or 34 miles north on NM 185, calls itself the "chile capital of the world." It is the center of a 22,000-acre agricultural belt that grows and processes more chile than anywhere else in the world. The annual Hatch Chile Festival over Labor Day weekend celebrates the harvest. For information, call the **Hatch Chamber of Commerce** (✆ **505/267-5050**).

SOUTH OF LAS CRUCES **Stahmann Farms,** 10 miles south of La Mesilla on NM 28, is one of the world's largest producers of pecans. Several million pounds are harvested, mostly during November, from orchards in the bed of an ancient lake. **Stahmann's Country Store** (© **800/654-6887** or 505/526-8974; www.stahmanns. com) sells pecans, pecan candy, and other specialty foods, and has a small cafe. It's open Monday through Saturday from 9am to 6pm, Sunday from 11am to 5pm.

War Eagles Air Museum ⭐ (© **505/589-2000;** www.war-eagles-air-museum. com), at the Santa Teresa Airport, about 35 miles south of Las Cruces on I-10 (call or check the website for directions), has an extensive collection of historic aircraft from World War II and the Korean War, plus automobiles and a tank. The aircraft include a beautifully restored P-38 Lightning, P-51 Mustang, F-86 Sabre, and several Russian MIG-15s. Most of the museum's 28 planes are in flying condition and are kept inside a well-lit, 64,000-square-foot hangar. The museum is open Tuesday through Sunday from 10am to 4pm; admission is $5 for adults, $4 for senior citizens age 65 and over, free for children under 12.

EAST OF LAS CRUCES The **Organ Mountains,** so-called because they resemble the pipes of a church organ, draw inevitable comparisons to Wyoming's Grand Tetons. Organ Peak, at 9,119 feet, is the highest point in Doña Ana County.

The **Aguirre Springs Recreation Area** (© **505/525-4300**), off US 70 on the western slope of the Organ Mountains, is one of the most spectacular places I've ever camped. Operated by the Bureau of Land Management, the camping and picnic sites sit at the base of the jagged Organ Mountains. Visitors to the area can hike, camp, picnic, or ride horseback (no horse rentals on site). If you'd like to hike, don't miss the **Baylor Pass** trail, which crosses along the base of the Organ peaks, up through a pass, and over to the Las Cruces side. Though the hike is 6 miles one-way, just over 2 miles will get you to the pass, where there's a meadow with amazing views.

WHERE TO STAY IN & AROUND LAS CRUCES

La Quinta ⭐ Five minutes from Old Mesilla, this chain hotel provides comfortable, relatively quiet rooms with plenty of amenities. The well-designed rooms range from medium to large, all with desks, and medium-size bathrooms. The pool sits in a comfortable courtyard, an important addition in this warm climate. Guests eat breakfast in a bright garden room off the lobby. Though this hotel doesn't have a restaurant, a Best Western across the street does. (It's a noisier hotel without the refinement of this one, but the food is decent.)

790 Av. de Mesilla, Las Cruces, NM 88005. © **800/531-5900** or 505/524-0331. Fax 505/525-8360. www. laquinta.com. $72–$81 double. Rates include continental breakfast. AE, DISC, MC, V. Pets accepted. **Amenities:** Outdoor pool; small fitness room. *In room:* A/C, TV, coffeemaker, hair dryer, iron.

Las Cruces Hilton ⭐ South-of-the-border romance and elegance define this seven-story hotel on the east side of town, about a 15-minute drive from Mesilla, with an incredible view of the city and the Organ Mountains. The hotel was built in 1986, with remodeling ongoing. The lobby has a fountain, lots of colorful Mexican tile, and plenty of ferns. Rooms are spacious, with the same south-of-the border feel, and outfitted with sturdy pine furniture. Bathrooms are medium-size and very clean. Some rooms flank the pool and have little patios.

705 S. Telshor Blvd., Las Cruces, NM 88011. © **800/284-0616** or 505/522-4300. Fax 505/521-4707. www.hilton. com. 203 units. $89–$149 double; $125–$309 suite. Rates include full breakfast. Golf packages available. AE, DC, DISC, MC, V. **Amenities:** Restaurant; lounge; heated outdoor pool; exercise room; Jacuzzi; car rental; courtesy van; limited room service; valet laundry. *In room:* A/C, TV, dataport, coffeemaker, hair dryer, iron.

A BED & BREAKFAST

The Lundeen Inn of the Arts ⭐   This inn is a late-1890s adobe home, with white-washed walls, narrow alleys, and arched doorways. It's a complex composite of rooms stretching across 14,000 square feet of floor space. There's a wide range of rooms, each named for an artist. My favorites are in the main part of the house, set around a two-story garden room, with elegant antiques and arched windows. Most rooms are medium-size with comfortably firm beds dressed in fine linens. Bathrooms are generally small and simple. My favorite rooms are the Maria Martinez (the only room without a TV), which has wood floors and a working fireplace and gets lots of sun; and the Frederic Remington, which has a more masculine feel and a kitchenette. Other rooms have similarly equipped kitchenettes. The inn is also an art gallery, displaying the works of about 30 Southwestern painters, sculptors, and potters. Breakfast includes fresh fruit and such specialties as pumpkin waffles and huevos rancheros (eggs atop tortillas, smothered in chile sauce).

618 S. Alameda Blvd., Las Cruces, NM 88005. ⓒ 888/526-3326 or 505/526-3326. Fax 505/647-1334. www.innofthe arts.com. 18 units. $75–$85 double; $85–$105 suite. Rates include breakfast. AE, DC, DISC, MC, V. Pets accepted. **Amenities:** Secretarial service; babysitting; laundry service. *In room:* A/C, TV, hair dryer, iron.

CAMPING

Quite a few campgrounds are in or near Las Cruces. All the ones listed here include full hookups for RVs, tenting areas, and recreation areas. **Best View RV Park** (ⓒ **505/526-6555**) also offers cabins and laundry and grocery facilities. From the junction of I-10 and US 70 (exit 135), go 1½ miles east on US 70, then half a block south on Weinrich Road.

Another option is **Dalmont's RV Park** (ⓒ **505/523-2992**). If you're coming from the west, when you reach the junction of I-25 and I-10, go 2½ miles northwest on I-10 to the Main Street exit, then go 2 blocks west on Valley Drive. If you're coming from the east, at the junction of I-10 and Main Street, go ¼ mile north on Main Street and then 1 block west on Valley Drive. To reach **Siesta RV Park** (ⓒ **505/523-6816**), at the junction of I-10 and NM 28, take exit 140 and go half a mile south on NM 28. **Leasburg Dam State Park** (ⓒ **505/524-4068**) is a smaller park that also offers RV and tent camping, but it has no laundry or grocery facilities. A general country store is about 1 mile down the road, and hiking and fishing are available.

WHERE TO DINE IN & AROUND LAS CRUCES
EXPENSIVE

Double Eagle ⭐⭐ CONTINENTAL   When I was a kid, whenever we went to Las Cruces, we always made a special trip to this elegant restaurant imbued with Old West style. I'm pleased to say that it's still a quality place to dine. Built around a central courtyard, it has numerous rooms, one of which is said to be frequented by a woman's ghost. Another room has a 30-foot-long bar with Corinthian columns in gold leaf, Gay Nineties oil paintings, and 18-armed brass chandeliers hung with Baccarat crystals. The varied menu includes pasta, chicken, fish, and steak dishes. My favorite is filet mignon bordelaise, served on a French rusk with a rich red-wine sauce. Columbia River salmon, served with triple citrus–chipotle chile sauce, is also delicious. All entrees come with salad, vegetable, and choice of potato or pasta. There's a full bar, and for dessert you can end it all with Death by Chocolate Cake. The 150-year-old Territorial-style hacienda is on the National Register of Historic Places.

2355 Calle de Guadalupe, on the east side of Old Mesilla Plaza. ⓒ **505/523-6700.** Reservations recommended. Main courses $5.25–$12 lunch, $11–$27 dinner. AE, DC, DISC, MC, V. Mon–Sat 11am–10pm; Sun 11am–9pm.

MODERATE

Peppers SOUTHWESTERN   This restaurant shares a building and owners with the Double Eagle (see the previous review), but the resemblance ends there. The Eagle has age and grace; Peppers has youthful exuberance. Hispanic folk art, including traditional masks and *santos,* greets guests in the entryway, and diners can sit in a lush atrium central courtyard (a great place for a margarita) surrounded by the Double Eagle dining rooms. The cuisine is Santa Fe–style Southwestern, and the chef adds interesting touches to traditional dishes. The service tends to be slow; come only if you have time to lounge. For starters, try green chile and cheese wontons, a house specialty. The most popular dish is grilled chicken Mesilla, topped with sautéed onions and Mennonite cheese, served with guacamole and black beans. For dessert, banana enchiladas sound weird but are actually delicious crepes with ice cream and Mesilla Valley Pecan praline sauce.

2335 Calle Guadalupe, on the east side of Old Mesilla Plaza. ℂ 505/523-4999. Fax 505/523-0051. Reservations accepted for large parties only. Tapas $4–$7.50; main courses $5.25–$12 lunch, $7–$15 dinner. AE, DC, DISC, MC, V. Mon–Sat 11am–10pm; Sun noon–9pm.

INEXPENSIVE

Chope's Bar & Cafe ☆ *Finds* *Kids* NEW MEXICAN   This is one of those legendary spots, a requisite weekly pilgrimage for many. Drive 15 minutes south of Old Mesilla through pecan orchards to its door, and you'll encounter a real local scene. The dining rooms, in an old house, have tile floors, faux wood paneling, and closely set tables, usually full of families, business people, and college students. You'll feast on chile rellenos, enchiladas, and burritos. Whatever you order, make sure it's smothered with red or green chile, if you can handle the heat. If not, opt for tacos or a hamburger. Kids like the place because it's casual and they have their own menu. Service is friendly but very overworked. With your meal, order margaritas or a Mexican beer, or, if you really wish to partake, head next door to the cantina, a dark and raucous place reminiscent of a border-town bar.

NM 28 (in the center of town), La Mesa. ℂ 505/233-3420 or 505/233-9976. Main courses $4.50–$8. MC, V. Tues–Sat 11:30am–1:30pm and 5:30–8:30pm; cantina Tues–Sat 11:30am–9:30pm.

La Posta de Mesilla *Kids* MEXICAN/STEAKS   If you're on the Old Mesilla Plaza and want to eat New Mexican food for not much money, walk in here. The mid-18th-century adobe building is the only surviving stagecoach station of the Butterfield Overland Mail route from Tipton, Missouri, to San Francisco. Kit Carson, Pancho Villa, General Douglas MacArthur, and Billy the Kid were all here at one time. The entrance leads through a jungle of tall plants beneath a Plexiglas roof, past a tank of piranhas and a noisy aviary of macaws and Amazon parrots, to nine dining rooms with bright, festive decor. (Kids love this and their own menu selections.) You may want to request the atrium, where you can dine under ficus trees. The tables are basic, however, with vinyl and metal chairs, giving it a cheap air. Such is an indication of the food quality. If you want really good New Mexican food, go to Nellie's (see below). If you come here, try enchiladas, which come with a nice chile sauce. Avoid the dry rellenos and the soggy tacos. Tostadas (tortilla cups filled with beans and topped with chile and cheese) are a house specialty. There's a full-service bar.

2410 Calle de San Albino (southeast corner of Old Mesilla Plaza). ℂ 505/524-3524. Reservations recommended. Main courses $4–$13. AE, DC, DISC, MC, V. Sun and Tues–Thurs 11am–9pm; Fri–Sat 11am–9:30pm.

Nellie's ☆ NEW MEXICAN   A good indication of the quality of this restaurant that serves "chile with an attitude" is that at 10:45am on a Monday, the place was full.

I told three young guys wearing baseball caps at the next table where I was from, and one said, "This is the best damn New Mexican food in the world—too bad Santa Fe doesn't have a place this good." If I weren't so fond of my hometown, I'd have agreed. It's a small cafe with two rooms, totally unassuming, with big windows up front that let in lots of light. There's a jukebox and, on the walls, R. C. Gorman prints. Order anything on the menu and you'll be pleased. At breakfast, try eggs and bacon or huevos rancheros (eggs over tortillas, smothered with chile). For lunch or dinner, the *sopaipilla compuesta* (*sopaipilla* topped with beans, meat, lettuce, tomatoes, and cheese) is amazing. The combination plate gives you a sampling of a number of delicacies. As should be the case at any true New Mexican restaurant, you can also have menudo (beef tripe and hominy in red chile), which Nellie's calls the "breakfast of champions." I didn't dare, but I heard it, too, is tasty. No alcohol is served.

1226 W. Hadley. (©) 505/524-9982 or 505/526-6816. Reservations not accepted. Main courses $3–$7 breakfast, $5–$7.50 lunch and dinner. No credit cards. Tues–Sat 8am–4pm. Closed 1 or 2 weeks in July.

12 Deming & Lordsburg

Deming: 44 miles SE of Silver City, 52 miles W of Las Cruces, 193 miles SW of Albuquerque; Lordsburg: 52 miles W of Deming, 36 miles SW of Silver City

New Mexico's least populated corner is this one. It includes the "boot heel" of the Gadsden Purchase, which pokes 40 miles down into Mexico (a great place for backpacking). These two railroad towns, an hour apart on I-10, see a lot of traffic, but whereas **Deming** (pop. 14,500) is thriving as a ranching and retirement center, **Lordsburg** has had a steady population of about 3,000 for years. This is a popular area for rockhounds, aficionados of ghost towns, and history buffs: **Columbus,** 32 miles south of Deming, was the site of the last foreign incursion on continental American soil, by the Mexican bandit-revolutionary Pancho Villa in 1916.

ESSENTIALS

GETTING THERE   From Las Cruces, take I-10 west (1 hr. to Deming, 2 hr. to Lordsburg). From Tucson, take I-10 east (3 hr. to Lordsburg, 4 hr. to Deming).

The **Grant County Airport** (© 505/388-4554), 15 miles south of Silver City, is served by **Mesa Airlines** (© 800/MESA-AIR or 505/326-3338; www.mesa-air.com), with daily flights to Albuquerque. The **Las Cruces Shuttle Service,** P.O. Box 3172, Las Cruces, NM 88003 (© 800/288-1784 or 505/525-1784; www.lascrucesshuttle. com), runs several times daily between Deming and the El Paso airport by way of Las Cruces.

VISITOR INFORMATION   The **Deming–Luna County Chamber of Commerce** is at 800 E. Pine St. (P.O. Box 8), Deming, NM 88031 (© 800/848-4955 or 505/546-2674; www.demingchamber.com). The **Lordsburg–Hidalgo County Chamber of Commerce** is at 117 E. 2nd St., Lordsburg, NM 88045 (© 505/542-9864; www.hidalgocounty.org/lordsburgcoc).

WHAT TO SEE & DO NEAR DEMING
GETTING OUTSIDE

At **Rockhound State Park** ✦, 14 miles southeast of Deming on NM 11, visitors are encouraged to pick up and take home as much as 15 pounds of minerals—jasper, agate, quartz crystal, flow-banded rhyolite, and others. Located at the base of the Little Florida Mountains, the park is a lovely, arid, cactus-covered land with paths leading down into dry gullies and canyons. (You may have to walk a bit, because the more accessible minerals have been largely picked over.)

The campground ($10 for nonelectric hookup, $14 with electric hookup), which has shelters, restrooms, and showers, offers a distant view of mountain ranges all the way to the Mexican border. The park also has one marked hiking trail and a playground. Admission is $5 per vehicle, and the park is open year-round from dawn to dusk. For more information, call © **505/546-6182.**

Some 35 miles south of Deming is the tiny border town of **Columbus,** which looks across at Mexico. **Pancho Villa State Park** here marks the site of the last foreign invasion of American soil, in 1916. A temporary fort, where a tiny garrison was housed in tents, came under attack by 600 Mexican revolutionaries, who cut through the boundary fence at Columbus. Eighteen Americans were killed, 12 wounded; an estimated 200 Mexicans died. The Mexicans immediately retreated across the border. An American punitive expedition, headed by Gen. John J. Pershing, ventured into Mexico but got nowhere. Villa restricted his banditry to Mexico after that, until his assassination in 1923.

The state park includes ruins of the old fort and a visitor center with exhibits and a film. It's worth the trip for the strikingly beautiful desert botanical garden. The park also has campsites, restrooms, showers, an RV dump station, and a playground. The entrance fee is $5 per vehicle; the park is staffed from 8am to 5pm daily. For more information, call © **505/531-2711.**

Across the street from the state park is the old Southern Pacific Railroad Depot, which has been restored by the Columbus Historical Society and now houses the **Columbus Historical Museum** (© **505/531-2620**). It contains railroad memorabilia and exhibits on local history. Call for hours, which vary.

Three miles south across the border in Mexico is **Las Palomas, Chihuahua** (pop. 1,500). The port of entry is open 24 hours. A few desirable restaurants and tourist-oriented businesses are in Las Palomas. Mostly, though, it's a drug-trafficking town. Beware of barhopping in Palomas at night, which can be dangerous.

WHAT TO SEE & DO NEAR LORDSBURG

Visitors to Lordsburg can go **rockhounding** in this area rich in minerals of many kinds. Desert roses can be found near Summit, and agate is known to exist in many abandoned mines. Mine dumps, southwest of Hachita, contain lead, zinc, and gold; the Animas Mountains have manganese. Volcanic glass can be picked up in Coronado National Forest, and you can pan for gold in Gold Gulch.

Rodeo, 30 miles southwest on I-10 and NM 80, is the home of the **Chiricahua Gallery** (© **505/557-2225**), open Monday through Saturday from 10am to 4pm. Regional artists have joined in a nonprofit, cooperative venture to exhibit works and offer classes in a variety of media. Many choose to live on the high-desert slopes of the Chiricahua Range. The gallery is on NM 80 en route to Douglas, Arizona.

Shakespeare Ghost Town *Kids* A national historic site, Shakespeare was once the home of 3,000 miners, promoters, and dealers of various kinds. Under the name Ralston, it enjoyed a silver boom in 1870. That was followed by a notorious diamond fraud in 1872: A mine was salted with diamonds in order to raise prices on mining stock. The scheme sucked in many notables, particularly William Ralston, founder of the Bank of California. Ralston enjoyed a mining revival in 1879 under its new name,

Shakespeare. It was a town with no church, no newspaper, and no local law. Some serious fights resulted in hangings from the roof timbers in the Stage Station.

Since 1935, the Hill family has owned the town and kept it uncommercialized, with no souvenir hype or gift shops. Six original buildings and two reconstructed buildings survive in various stages of repair. Two-hour guided tours are offered on a limited basis, and reenactments and living history are staged on the fourth weekends of April, June, August, and October, if performers are available.

2½ miles south of Lordsburg (P.O. Box 253, Lordsburg, NM 88045). © 505/542-9034. www.shakespeareghostown. com. Admission $3 adults, $2 children 6–12; for shootouts and special events $4 adults, $3 children. Open 10am and 2pm on the 2nd Sun and preceding Sat of each month. Special tours by appointment. To reach Shakespeare, drive 1½ miles south from I-10 on Main St. Just before the town cemetery, turn right, proceed ½ mile, and turn right again. Follow the dirt road another ½ mile into Shakespeare.

Stein's Railroad Ghost Town *Kids*   This settlement 19 miles west of Lordsburg started as a Butterfield Stage stop and was a railroad town of about 1,000 residents from 1880 to 1955. It was so isolated that water, hauled from Doubtful Canyon, brought $1 a barrel!

Today 12 buildings remain, with 16 rooms filled with artifacts and furnishings from the 19th and early 20th centuries. Also here are a petting zoo for kids and the Steins Mercantile shop.

Exit 3, I-10 (P.O. Box 2185), Road Forks, NM 88045. © 505/542-9791. Admission $2.50 adults, free for children under 12. Daily 9am–dusk.

WHERE TO STAY
IN DEMING

Holiday Inn *ℛ*   This hotel just off I-10 brings a bit of style to dusty Deming. Though from the outside the 1974 two-story white brick structure appears basic, the rooms—with renovations ongoing—tell another story. Each is medium-size with light pine furniture and decorated in Aztec prints, with bold expressionist paintings on the walls. Bathrooms are small, but each has a vanity and dressing area. Some of the suites have Jacuzzis. Lush grass surrounds the large pool; request a poolside room, and you'll have a bit of a resort feel.

Off I-10, Exit 85 (P.O. Box 1138), Deming, NM 88031. © 800/HOLIDAY or 505/546-2661. Fax 505/546-6308. www. ichotels.com. 116 units. $50–$68 double. AE, DC, DISC, MC, V. Pets accepted. **Amenities:** Restaurant (New Mexican/American); heated outdoor pool; exercise room; Jacuzzi; limited room service; coin-op laundry; laundry service; dry cleaning. *In room:* A/C, TV, dataport, fridge, coffeemaker, hair dryer, iron.

IN LORDSBURG

Best Western Western Skies Inn   This redbrick motel built in 1990 at the I-10 interchange offers comfortable rooms on well-landscaped grounds. Remodeling is ongoing and well done. The large rooms have oak furnishings and medium-firm beds. Bathrooms are medium-size, and each has an outer vanity with a sink. Many have minifridges. The motel has a small outdoor pool, and Kranberry's Family Restaurant (see "Where to Dine in Deming & Lordsburg," below) is next door. The motel is accessible by Greyhound and Amtrak. Light sleepers beware: Trains pass by during the night.

1303 S. Main St. (at I-10 exit 22), Lordsburg, NM 88045. © 800/528-1234 or 505/542-8807. Fax 505/542-8895. www.bestwestern.com. 40 units. $62 double. AE, DC, DISC, MC, V. Pets accepted; $5–$10 fee. **Amenities:** Outdoor pool. *In room:* A/C, TV, coffeemaker, hair dryer, iron.

CAMPING IN & AROUND DEMING & LORDSBURG

City of Rocks State Park in Deming (℃ **505/536-2800**) has 52 campsites, 10 with electric hookups; tenting is available, and picnic tables and a hiking trail are nearby. **Dreamcatcher RV Park** (℃ **505/544-4004**), also in Deming (take Exit 85, Motel Dr., off I-10 and go 1 block south on Business I-10), has 92 sites, all with full hookups. It also offers free access to a nearby swimming pool and on-site laundry facilities. A larger option is **Little Vineyard RV Park** (℃ **505/546-3560**) in Deming (from I-10 take Exit 85 and go 1 mile southwest on Business I-10 toward Deming). It offers the same facilities as Dreamcatcher RV Park, with the addition of limited groceries, an indoor pool and hot tub, cable TV hookups, e-mail access, and a small RV parts store. The campground at **Rockhound State Park** (℃ **505/546-6182**) is picturesque and great for rockhounds who can't get enough of their hobby. RV sites with hookups and tenting are both available, as are shelters, restrooms, and showers.

If you'd rather camp near Lordsburg, try **Lordsburg KOA** (℃ **800/562-5772** or 505/542-8003; www.koa.com). It's in a desert setting but with shade trees, and tenting is permitted. Grocery and laundry facilities are available, in addition to a recreation room, a pool, a playground, and horseshoes. To reach the campground, take I-10 to Exit 22 and then go 1 block south; next, turn right at the Chevron station and follow the signs to the campground.

WHERE TO DINE IN DEMING & LORDSBURG

Kranberry's Family Restaurant AMERICAN/MEXICAN A friendly, casual Denny's-style family restaurant decorated with Southwestern art, Kranberry's offers American favorites. It serves eggs and pancakes for breakfast, and burgers, chicken, beef, and salads, as well as Mexican selections, for lunch and dinner. Baked goods are made on the premises daily. My favorite is corn bread, served with the soup special.

1405 S. Main St., Lordsburg. ℃ **505/542-9400**. Main courses $3–$6 breakfast, $4–$15 lunch and dinner. AE, DC, DISC, MC, V. Daily 6am–10pm.

Si Señor ⋆ MEXICAN As one local put it, this place gets packed. Locals crowd the basic downtown cafe to eat platters full of tasty New Mexican food. The plain interior has functional furniture and a few woodcarved pictures on the wall. Smoking is allowed in one section of the restaurant, but the nonsmoking section seems airy enough. At breakfast try huevos rancheros (eggs over corn tortillas, smothered in chile). The big seller at lunch and dinner is the deluxe combination, with a chile relleno, a tamale, a cheese enchilada, a taco, refried beans, Spanish rice, and red or green chile. The menu also includes salads, hamburgers, and chicken and fish dishes. All come with chips and salsa, and wine and beer are served.

200 E. Pine, Deming. ℃ **505/546-3938**. Main courses $4–$8 breakfast, $5–$10 lunch and dinner. DISC, MC, V. Mon–Sat 9am–8:30pm; Sun 9am–3pm.

---

13 Silver City: Gateway to the Gila Cliff Dwellings ⋆⋆

44 miles NW of Deming; 57 miles SW of Truth or Consequences; 170 miles SW of Albuquerque

Silver City (pop. 10,545) is an old mining town in the foothills of the Pinos Altos Range of the Mogollon Mountains, and gateway to the Gila Wilderness and the Gila Cliff Dwellings. Early Native Americans mined turquoise from these hills, and by 1804, Spanish settlers were digging for copper. In 1870, a group of prospectors discovered silver, and the rush was on. In 10 short months, newly christened Silver City grew from a single cabin to more than 80 buildings. Early visitors included Billy the Kid, Judge Roy Bean, and William Randolph Hearst.

This comparatively isolated community kept pace with every modern convenience: telephones in 1883, electric lights in 1884 (only 2 years after New York City), and a water system in 1887. Typically, the town should have busted with the crash of silver prices in 1893. But unlike many Western towns, Silver City did not become a picturesque memory. It capitalized on its high, dry climate to become today's county seat and trade center. Copper mining and processing are still the major industry.

ESSENTIALS

GETTING THERE From Albuquerque, take I-25 south, 15 miles past Truth or Consequences, then go west on NM 152 and US 180 (5 hr.). From Las Cruces, take I-10 west to Deming, then head north on US 180 (2 hr.).

Mesa Airlines (© 800/MESA-AIR or 505/326-3338; www.mesa-air.com) flies daily from Albuquerque to **Grant County Airport** (© 505/388-4554), 15 miles south of Silver City near Hurley. **Silver Stage Lines** (© 800/522-0162) offers daily shuttle service to the El Paso airport and charter service to Tucson. The **Las Cruces Shuttle Service** (© 800/288-1784 or 505/525-1784; www.lascrucesshuttle.com) runs several times daily from Silver City to the El Paso airport, by way of Las Cruces.

VISITOR INFORMATION The **Silver City–Grant County Chamber of Commerce,** 201 N. Hudson St., Silver City, NM 88061 (© 800/548-9378 or 505/538-3785; www.silvercity.org), operates a visitor information headquarters and produces extremely useful tourist publications.

WHAT TO SEE & DO IN SILVER CITY

Silver City's downtown **Historic District** ✪, the first such district to receive National Register recognition, is a must for visitors. Extensive use of brick in construction marks the downtown core: Brick clay was discovered in the area soon after the town's founding in 1870, and an 1880 ordinance prohibited frame construction within the town limits. Mansard-roofed Victorian houses, Queen Anne and Italianate residences, and commercial buildings show off the cast-iron architecture of the period. Some are still undergoing restoration.

An 1895 flood washed out Main Street and turned it into a gaping chasm, which was eventually bridged over; finally, the **Big Ditch,** as it's called, was made into a green park in the center of town. Facing downtown, in the 500 block of North Hudson Street, was a famous red-light district from the turn of the 20th century until the late 1960s.

Billy the Kid lived in Silver City as a youth. You can see his cabin site a block north of the Broadway Bridge, on the east side of the Big Ditch. The Kid (William Bonney) waited tables at the Star Hotel, at Hudson Street and Broadway. He was jailed (at 304 N. Hudson St.) in 1875 at the age of 15, after being convicted of stealing from a Chinese laundry, but he escaped—a first for the Kid. The grave of Bonney's mother, Catherine McCarty, is in Silver City Cemetery, east of town on Memory Lane, off US 180. She died of tuberculosis about a year after the family moved here in 1873.

Silver City Museum ✪ This well-presented museum of city and regional history contains collections relating to Southwestern New Mexico history, mining, Native American pottery, and early photographs. Exhibits include a southwestern New Mexico history timeline; a parlor displaying Victorian decorative arts; and a chronicle of commerce in early Silver City. A local history research library is available to visitors. The main gallery features changing exhibits. The museum is in the 1881 H. B. Ailman House, a former city hall and fire station, remarkable for its cupola and Victorian mansard roof. Ailman came to Silver City penniless in 1871, made a fortune in mining, and went on to start the Meredith and Ailman Bank. Guided walking tours of the historic district are offered on Memorial Day and Labor Day. There is also a museum store.

312 W. Broadway. ℭ 505/538-5921. Free admission. Tues–Fri 9am–4:30pm; Sat–Sun 10am–4pm. Closed Mon except Memorial Day and Labor Day.

SILVER CITY AFTER DARK

Some of southwestern New Mexico's most passionate performances are at the **Pinos Altos Melodrama Theater,** 30 Main St., Pinos Altos (ℭ **505/388-3848**), in the Pinos Altos Opera House, next to the Buckhorn Saloon. Local actors fight the forces of good and evil in such productions as *The Legend of Billy the Kid or It's Just a Little Gun Play.* Shows are on Friday and Saturday night from February to November.

EXPLORING THE AREA

NORTH OF SILVER CITY The virtual ghost town of **Pinos Altos** ⚐, straddling the Continental Divide, is 6 miles north of Silver City on NM 15. Dubbed "Tall Pines" when it was founded in the gold- and silver-rush era, it has suffered under Apache attacks and mine failures.

The adobe **Methodist-Episcopal Church** was built with William Randolph Hearst's money in 1898 and now houses the Grant County Art Guild. Also in town are the **Log Cabin Curio Shop and Museum,** in an 1866 cabin (ℭ **505/388-1882**), and the **Buckhorn Saloon and Opera House** (see "Where to Dine in & Around Silver City," below).

WEST OF SILVER CITY US 180, heading northwest from Silver City, is the gateway to Catron County and most of the Gila National Forest, including the villages of Glenwood, Reserve, and Quemado. For details on this area, see "Other Adventures in Gila National Forest," below.

WHERE TO STAY IN & AROUND SILVER CITY

Standard motels string along US 180 east of NM 90. Some of the more interesting accommodations are listed below. Most lodgings provide free parking.

Holiday Inn Express This relatively new hotel just a few miles from the center of town offers comfortable rooms. Set back from the highway, it's a quiet, family-owned spot with plenty of amenities. The rooms are medium-sized with tall ceilings, comfortable beds, desks, and medium-sized bathrooms.

1103 Superior St., Silver City, NM 88061. ℭ **800/465-4329** or 505/538-2525. www.hiexpress.com. 50 units. $80–$110 double. Rates include continental breakfast. AE, DC, DISC, MC, V. Pets accepted. **Amenities:** Small health club; Jacuzzi; laundry room. *In room:* A/C, TV, dataport, coffeemaker, hair dryer.

SMALLER INNS

Bear Mountain Lodge ⭐⭐ On 160 acres just 3½ miles northwest of downtown Silver City, this lodge, owned and operated by the Nature Conservancy, is ideal for outdoors enthusiasts, from birders to bikers. The lodge was the passion of Myra McCormick, a salty outdoorswoman who continued to run the place into her 90s. Her death saddened many of us, but her bequeathing the ranch to the Conservancy ensured its future. The 1920s guesthouse offers large rooms with maple floors and high ceilings. Each is equipped with modern amenities, including country-inn Southwestern decor and comfortable beds. Four rooms have private balconies. This is a nature lover's delight. On-site naturalist Nature Conservancy staff members are on hand to inform visitors about the flora and fauna of the area, and they also conduct guided trips (included in the room rate). Dinner is served for guests nightly for an extra fee. It's a buffet-style affair with such offerings as stuffed chicken breasts with vegetable casserole. Box lunches are also available to guests for an extra charge. What's best here is that you can count on complete quiet.

2251 Cottage San Rd., Silver City, NM 88061. (P.O. Box 1163, Silver City, NM 88062). ℂ **877/620-BEAR (2327)** or 505/538-2538. www.bearmountainlodge.com. 11 units. $115–$200 double. 2-night minimum stay. Rates include full breakfast. Horse boarding $15/night. AE, MC, V. Turn north off US 180 on Alabama St. (½ mile west of NM 90 intersection). Proceed 3 miles (Alabama becomes Cottage San Rd.) to dirt road turnoff to left; the lodge is another ½ mile. Children under 10 not accepted. **Amenities:** Hiking trails; conference and event spaces; mountain bike rental. In room: A/C, dataport, hair dryer.

Casitas de Gila ★★ If you're looking for a remote and peaceful stay in the quintessential southern New Mexico terrain, this inn is for you. On a little bluff above Bear Creek, about a half-hour from Silver City, these five *casitas* (Spanish for "small houses") represent the epitome of Southwestern style. The adobe-style dwellings are decorated with Spanish-style furniture and Mexican rugs. Medium-size guest rooms and bathrooms come well equipped with comfortably firm beds, bath supplies, and bathrobes. Each also has a kiva fireplace and a small porch with a *chiminea* (Mexican ceramic fireplace) and a grill. On hand is a hot tub with a view of the creek, canyon, and sky. The area is great for birding and hiking, and horseback riding can be arranged. Also on the property are 90 acres of hiking trails, an art gallery, and telescopes.

50 Casita Flats Rd. (P.O. Box 325), Gila, NM 88038. ℂ **877/923-4827** or 505/535-4455. Fax 505/535-4456. www.casitasdegila.com. 5 casitas. $90–$190 double. Rates include continental breakfast. AE, DISC, MC, V. **Amenities:** Jacuzzi; activities desk. In room: Dataport, kitchen, hair dryer, iron.

CAMPING

Silver City KOA (ℂ **800/562-7623** or 505/388-3351; www.koa.com) has 82 sites and 42 full hookups, and it offers groceries, laundry facilities, and a pool. The campground is 5 miles east of the NM 90/US 180 junction on US 180. **Silver City RV Park** (ℂ **505/538-2239;** www.silvercityrv.com) has 48 sites (45 with full hookups), showers, laundry facilities, and picnic tables. It's downtown on Bennett Street, behind Food Basket supermarket. Camping is also available at the Gila Cliff Dwellings (see "Gila Cliff Dwellings National Monument," below).

WHERE TO DINE IN & AROUND SILVER CITY

Buckhorn Saloon and Opera House ★ SEAFOOD/STEAKS/BURGERS Seven miles north of Silver City in Pinos Altos, the Buckhorn offers fine dining and 1860s decor. It's noted for its Western-style steaks, seafood, homemade desserts, and excellent wine list. If you have a big appetite, try the New York strip with green chile and cheese. I liked the big fried shrimp. Entrees are served with salad or soup and potatoes or rice. Live entertainment is offered nightly. The high-personality saloon offers big round tables and a great wooden bar. Many come to this saloon to have excellent burgers and hear live music (on some nights). While waiting for your food, take a moment to check out the attached opera house, where good melodrama theater is presented seasonally.

32 Main St., Pinos Altos. ℂ **505/538-9911.** Reservations highly recommended. Main courses $7–$43. MC, V. Mon–Sat 6–10pm; saloon Mon–Sat 3–10pm.

Diane's Bakery & Cafe ★★ NEW AMERICAN   This is an amazing find in a relative wasteland of taste. Diane Barrett, who was once a pastry chef at La Traviata and Eldorado in Santa Fe, has brought refined city food to this small town. At lunch, the atmosphere is bustling, usually with a slight wait for a table. At dinner, the tone is more romantic and low-key, with more nouveau specialties. The service is friendly and adequate. You can't go wrong with any of the baked goods here. At brunch, try hatch Benedict, a version of eggs Benedict made with home-baked chile cheddar toast. At lunch I suggest the *spano,* a baked spinach pastry, served with a salad; the quiche of the day is also delicious. At dinner, you may want to opt for one of the night's specials, such as grilled lamb with wild mushroom demi-glace or the chef's choice lasagna. Diane's also serves great steaks. There's a small but creative wine and beer menu. Don't leave without sampling one of the desserts, such as blueberry or apple pie.

510 N. Bullard St., Silver City. ℂ **505/538-8722.** Reservations recommended for dinner. Main courses $5–$7 lunch, $14–$25 dinner. MC, V. Tues–Sat 11am–2pm and 5:30–9pm; Sat–Sun brunch 9am–2pm.

Jalisco's *Kids* NEW MEXICAN   In an enchanting brick building in the historic district, this festive restaurant serves big portions of good food. Three dining rooms fill the old structure, which has been Latinized with arched doorways and bold Mexican street-scene calendars on the walls. The combination plates are large and popular, as are the enchiladas. There are also burgers and a children's menu. Whatever you do, be sure to order a huge, delicious *sopaipilla* for dessert. Beer and wine are served. Smoking is not allowed.

103 S. Bullard St., Silver City. ℂ **505/388-2060.** Reservations not accepted. Main courses $5–$10. DISC, MC, V. Mon–Sat 11am–8:30pm.

14 Gila Cliff Dwellings National Monument ★★

44 miles N of Silver City

It takes 1½ to 2 hours to reach the **Gila Cliff Dwellings** from Silver City, but it's definitely worth the trip. First-time visitors are inevitably awed by the remains of an ancient civilization in the mouths of caves, abandoned for 7 centuries. You reach the dwellings on a 1-mile moderate hike along which you catch your first glimpses of the ruins. This walk is an elaborate journey into the past. It winds its way into a narrow canyon, from which you spot the poetic ruins perched in six caves 180 feet up on the canyon wall, stone shiny and hard as porcelain. Then the ascent begins, up innumerable steps and rocks until you're standing face-to-face with the ancient relics. They offer a glimpse into the lives of Native Americans who lived here from the late 1270s through the early 1300s. Tree-ring dating indicates their residence didn't last longer than 30 to 40 years.

The earliest ruin that has been found in the monument is a pit house dated between A.D. 100 and 400. This dwelling below ground level was an earlier type of home occupied by the Mogollon people who grew corn and beans, hunted, and gathered wild plants for food.

What's remarkable about the journey through the cliff dwellings is the depth of some of the caves. At one point, you'll climb a ladder and pass from one cave into the next, viewing the intricate little rooms (42 total) and walls that once made up a community dwelling. Probably not more than 10 to 15 families (about 40–50 people) lived in the cliff dwellings at any one time. The inhabitants were excellent weavers and skilled potters.

Anglo settlers discovered the cliff dwellings in the early 1870s, near where the three forks of the Gila River rise. Once you leave the last cave, you'll head down again, traversing some steep steps to the canyon floor. Pets are not allowed in the monument, but they can be taken on trails in the Gila Wilderness. Be sure to pick up a trail guide at the visitor center.

ESSENTIALS

GETTING THERE   From Silver City, take NM 15 north 44 miles to the Gila Cliff Dwellings. Travel time from Silver City is approximately 2 hours. You won't find any gas stations between Silver City and Gila Cliff Dwellings, so plan accordingly. Also know that at the monument, vehicles are permitted on paved roads only.

VISITOR INFORMATION   For more information, contact **Gila Cliff Dwellings National Monument,** HC 68, Box 100, Silver City, NM 88061 (© **505/536-9461;** www.nps.gov/gicl).

ADMISSION FEES & HOURS   Admission to the monument is $3, free for children under 13. The visitor center, where you can pick up detailed brochures, is open from 8am to 5pm Memorial Day to Labor Day and from 8am to 4:30pm the rest of the year. The cliff dwellings are open from 8am to 6pm in the summer and from 9am to 4pm the rest of the year.

SEEING THE HIGHLIGHTS

The dwellings allow a rare glimpse inside the homes and lives of prehistoric Native Americans. About 75% of what you see is original, although the walls have been capped and the foundations strengthened to prevent further deterioration. It took a great deal of effort to build these homes: Mortar held the stones in place, and all the clay and water for the mortar had to be carried by hand up from the stream, because the Mogollon did not have any pack animals. The vigas for the roof were cut and shaped with stone axes or fire.

The people who lived here were farmers, as shown by the remains of beans, squash, and corn in their homes. The fields were along the valley of the west fork of the Gila River and on the mesa across the canyon. No signs of irrigation have been found.

A 1-mile loop trail, rising 175 feet from the canyon floor, provides access to the dwellings.

Near the visitor center, about a mile away, the remains of an earlier pit house (A.D. 100–400), built below ground level, and later pit houses (up to A.D. 1000), aboveground structures of adobe or wattle, have been found.

CAMPING

Camping and picnicking are encouraged in the national monument, which has four developed campgrounds. Camping is free and some sites are RV accessible, though there are no hookups. Overnight lodging is in Silver City and in the nearby town of Gila Hot Springs, which also has a grocery store, horse rentals, and guided pack trips. For information, contact the visitor center (© **505/536-9461**).

15 Other Adventures in Gila National Forest

Gila National Forest, which offers some of the most spectacular mountain scenery in the Southwest, comprises 3.3 million acres in four counties. Nearly one-fourth of that acreage (790,000 acres) is the **Gila, Aldo Leopold,** and **Blue Range wildernesses.** Its highest peak is Whitewater Baldy, at 10,892 feet. The forest encompasses six out of seven life zones, so the range of plant and wildlife is broad. You may see mule deer, elk, antelope, black bear, mountain lion, and bighorn sheep. Nearly 400 miles of streams and a few small lakes sustain populations of trout as well as bass, bluegill, and catfish. Anglers can head to Lake Roberts, Snow Lake, and Quemado Lake.

JUST THE FACTS   For more information on the national forest, contact the **U.S. Forest Service,** Forest Supervisor's Office, 3005 East Camino del Bosque, Silver City, NM 88061 (© **505/388-8201;** www.fs.fed.us).

The national forest has 29 campgrounds, all with toilets and six with drinking water. Car and backpack camping are also permitted throughout the forest.

GETTING OUTSIDE

The forest has 1,490 miles of trails for hiking and horseback riding, and, in winter, cross-country skiing. Outside the wilderness areas, trail bikes and off-road vehicles are permitted. Hiking trails in the Gila Wilderness, especially the 41-mile Middle Fork Trail, with its east end near Gila Cliff Dwellings, are among the most popular in the state and can sometimes be crowded. If you are more interested in communing with nature than with fellow hikers, you will find plenty of trails to suit you, both in and out of the officially designated wilderness areas.

Most of the trails are maintained and easy to follow. Trails along river bottoms have many stream crossings (so be prepared for hiking with wet feet) and may be washed out by summer flash floods. It's best to inquire about trail conditions before you set out. More than 50 trail heads provide roadside parking.

Some of the best hikes in the area are the Frisco Box, Pueblo Creek, Whitewater Baldy, the Catwalk and Beyond, the Middle Fork/Little Bear Loop, and the Black Range Crest Trail. The Gila National Forest contains several wilderness areas that are off-limits to mountain bikes, including the Gila, Aldo Leopold, and the Blue Range Primitive Area. However, cyclists can use quite a few trails. Some to look for are the Cleveland Mine trail, Silver City Loop, Continental Divide, Signal Peak, Pinos Altos Loop, Fort Bayard Historical Trails, and Forest Trail 100.

The **Catwalk National Recreation Trail** (© **505/539-2481**), 68 miles north of Silver City on US 180, then 5 miles east of Glenwood on NM 174, is a great break after a long drive. Kids are especially thrilled with this hike. It follows the route of a pipeline built in 1897 to carry water to the now-defunct town of Graham and its electric generator. About ¼ mile above the parking area is the beginning of a striking 250-foot metal causeway clinging to the sides of the boulder-choked Whitewater Canyon, which in spots is 20 feet wide and 250 feet deep. Along the way, you'll find water pouring through caves and waterfalls spitting off the cliff side. Farther up the canyon, a suspension bridge spans the chasm. Picnic facilities are near the parking area. There is a $3 fee per car.

12

Tucson

Encircled by mountain ranges and bookended by the two units of Saguaro National Park, Tucson is Arizona's second-largest city, and for the vacationer it has everything that Phoenix has to offer, plus a bit more. There are world-class golf resorts, excellent restaurants, art museums and galleries, an active cultural life, and, of course, plenty of great weather. Tucson also has a long history that melds Native American, Hispanic, and Anglo roots. And with a national park, a national forest, and other natural areas just beyond the city limits, Tucson is a city that celebrates its Sonoran Desert setting.

Founded by the Spanish in 1775, Tucson was built on the site of a much older Native American village, and the city's name comes from the Pima Indian word *chukeson,* which means "spring at the base of black mountain," a reference to the peak now known simply as "A Mountain." From 1867 to 1877, Tucson was the territorial capital of Arizona, but eventually the capital was moved to Phoenix. Consequently, Tucson did not develop as quickly as Phoenix and still holds fast to its Hispanic and Western heritage.

Back in the days of urban renewal, Tucson's citizens turned back the bulldozers and managed to preserve at least some of the city's old Mexican character. Likewise, today, in the face of the sort of sprawl that has given Phoenix the feel of a landlocked Los Angeles, advocates for controlled growth are fighting hard to preserve both Tucson's desert environment and the city's unique character.

The struggle to retain an identity distinct from other Southwestern cities is ongoing, and despite long, drawn-out attempts to breathe life into the city's core, the past few years have seen the loss of downtown's vibrancy as shops, galleries, and restaurants have moved out to the suburbs. However, downtown Tucson still has its art museum, convention center, and historic neighborhoods.

Despite this minor shortcoming, Tucson remains Arizona's most beautiful and most livable city. With the Santa Catalina Mountains for a backdrop, Tucson boasts one of the most dramatic settings in the Southwest, and whether you're taking in the mountain vistas from the saddle of a palomino or a table for two, we're sure you'll agree that Tucson makes a superb winter vacation destination.

1 Orientation

ARRIVING

BY PLANE   Located 6 miles south of downtown, **Tucson International Airport** (© 520/573-8000; www.tucsonairport.org) is served by the following major airlines: **Alaska/Horizon** (© 800/426-0333; www.alaskaair.com), **America West** (© 800/235-9292; www.americawest.com), **American** (© 800/433-7300; www.aa.com), **Continental** (© 800/523-3273; www.continental.com), **Delta** (© 800/221-1212;

www.delta.com), **Frontier** (© 800/432-1359; www.flyfrontier.com), **Northwest/KLM** (© 800/225-2525; www.nwa.com), **Southwest** (© 800/435-9792; www.southwest. com), and **United** (© 800/241-6522; www.ual.com).

Visitor centers in both baggage-claim areas can give you brochures and reserve a hotel room if you haven't done so already.

Many resorts and hotels in Tucson provide free or competitively priced airport shuttle service. **Arizona Stagecoach** (© **520/889-1000;** www.azstagecoach.com) operates 24-hour van service to downtown Tucson and the foothills resorts. Fares to downtown are around $18 one-way and $32 round-trip ($21 and $38 for a couple), and to the foothills resorts around $32 one-way and $55 round-trip ($40 and $71 for a couple). It takes between 45 minutes and 1 hour to reach the foothills resorts. To return to the airport, it's best to call at least a day before your scheduled departure.

You'll also find taxis waiting outside baggage claim, or you can call **Yellow Cab** (© **520/624-6611**) or **Allstate Cab** (© **520/881-2227**). The flag-drop rate at the airport is $4.50 and then $1.50 per mile. A taxi to downtown costs around $19, to the foothills resorts about $25 to $40.

Sun Tran (© **520/792-9222;** www.suntran.com), the local public transit system, operates bus service to and from the airport. The fare is $1. Route no. 6, to downtown, runs Monday through Friday from about 4:50am to 7:20pm, Saturday from about 7:15am to 6:15pm, and Sunday from about 6:20am to 5:20pm. Departures are every 30 minutes on weekdays and every hour on weekends. It takes 40 to 50 minutes to reach downtown. Route no. 11 operates on a similar schedule and travels along Alvernon Road to the midtown area.

BY CAR   I-10, the main east–west interstate across the southern United States, passes through Tucson as it swings north to Phoenix. **I-19** connects Tucson with the Mexican border at Nogales. **Ariz. 86** heads southwest into the Tohono O'Odham Indian Reservation, and **Ariz. 79** leads north toward Florence and eventually connects with **U.S. 60** into Phoenix.

If you're headed downtown, take the Congress Street exit off I-10. If you're going to one of the foothills resorts north of downtown, you'll probably want to take the Ina Road exit off I-10.

BY TRAIN   Tucson is served by **Amtrak** (© **800/872-7245;** www.amtrak.com) passenger rail service. The *Sunset Limited,* which runs between Orlando and Los Angeles, stops in Tucson. The **train station** is at 400 E. Toole Ave. (© **520/623-4442**), in the heart of downtown and within walking distance of the Tucson Convention Center, El Presidio Historic District, and a few hotels. You'll see taxis waiting to meet the train.

BY BUS   Greyhound (© **800/231-2222** or 520/792-3475; www.greyhound.com) connects Tucson to the rest of the United States through its extensive system. The bus station is downtown at 2 S. Fourth Ave., across the street from the Hotel Congress.

VISITOR INFORMATION

The **Metropolitan Tucson Convention and Visitors Bureau (MTCVB),** 100 S. Church Ave. (at Broadway), Suite 7199 (© **800/638-8350** or 520/624-1817; www. visitTucson.org), is an excellent source of information on Tucson and environs. The visitor center is open Monday through Friday from 8am to 5pm, Saturday and Sunday from 9am to 4pm.

CITY LAYOUT

MAIN ARTERIES & STREETS   Tucson is laid out on a grid that's fairly regular in the downtown areas, but becomes less orderly the farther you go from the city center. In the flatlands, major thoroughfares are spaced at 1-mile intervals, with smaller streets filling in the squares created by the major roads. In the foothills, where Tucson's most recent growth has occurred, the grid system breaks down completely because of the hilly terrain.

The main **east–west roads** are (from south to north) 22nd Street, Broadway Boulevard, Speedway Boulevard, Grant Road (with Tanque Verde Rd. as an extension), and Ina Road/Skyline Drive/Sunrise Road. The main **north–south roads** are (from west to east) Miracle Mile/Oracle Road, Stone/Sixth Avenue, Campbell Avenue, Country Club Road, Alvernon Road, and Swan Road. **I-10** cuts diagonally across the Tucson metropolitan area from northwest to southeast.

In **downtown Tucson,** Congress Street and Broadway Boulevard are the main east–west streets; Stone Avenue, Sixth Avenue, and Fourth Avenue are the main north–south streets.

FINDING AN ADDRESS   Because Tucson is laid out on a grid, finding an address is relatively easy. The zero (or starting) point for all Tucson addresses is the corner of Stone Avenue, which runs north and south, and Congress Street, which runs east and west. From this point, streets are designated either north, south, east, or west. Addresses usually, but not always, increase by 100 with each block, so that an address of 4321 E. Broadway Blvd. should be 43 blocks east of Stone Avenue. In the downtown area, many of the streets and avenues are numbered, with numbered streets running east and west and numbered avenues running north and south.

2 Getting Around

BY CAR

Unless you plan to stay by the pool or on the golf course, you'll want to rent a car. Luckily, rates are fairly economical. At press time, Alamo was charging $130 per week ($165 with taxes and surcharges included) for a compact car with unlimited mileage in Tucson. See "Getting Around" in chapter 2 for general tips on car rentals.

The following agencies have offices at Tucson International Airport as well as other locations in the area. Because taxes and surcharges add up to about 28% on car rentals at the airport, you might want to consider renting at some other location, where you can avoid paying some of these fees. Among the Tucson car-rental agencies are **Alamo** (© 800/327-9633 or 520/807-0446), **Avis** (© 800/331-1212 or 520/294-1494), **Budget** (© 800/527-0700 or 520/573-8475), **Dollar** (© 800/800-4000 or 520/573-8486), **Enterprise** (© 800/736-8222 or 520/573-5336), **Hertz** (© 800/654-3131 or 520/573-5201), and **National** (© 800/227-7368 or 520/806-4255).

Downtown Tucson is still a relatively easy place to find a parking space, and parking fees are low. There are two huge parking lots at the south side of the Tucson Convention Center, a couple of small lots on either side of the Tucson Museum of Art (one at Main Ave. and Paseo Redondo, south of El Presidio Historic District, and one at the corner of Council St. and Court Ave.), and parking garages beneath the main library (101 N. Stone Ave.) and El Presidio Park (on Alameda St.). You'll find plenty of metered parking on the smaller downtown streets. Almost all Tucson hotels and resorts provide free parking.

Lanes on several major avenues in Tucson change direction at rush hour to facilitate traffic flow, so pay attention to signs. These tell you the time and direction of traffic in the lanes.

BY PUBLIC TRANSPORTATION

BY BUS   Covering much of the Tucson metropolitan area, **Sun Tran** (☎ 520/792-9222; www.suntran.com) public buses are $1 for adults and students, 40¢ for seniors, and free for children 5 and under. Day passes are available on buses for $2.

The **Downtown-Ronstadt Transit Center,** at Congress Street and Sixth Avenue, is served by about 30 regular and express bus routes to all parts of Tucson. The bus system does not extend to such tourist attractions as the Arizona–Sonora Desert Museum, Old Tucson, Saguaro National Park, or the foothills resorts, and thus is of limited use to visitors. However, Sun Tran does provide a shuttle for sports games and special events. Call the above phone number for information.

BY TROLLEY   Although they don't go very far, the restored electric streetcars of **Old Pueblo Trolley** (☎ 520/792-1802; oldpueblotrolley.org) are a fun way to get from the Fourth Avenue shopping district to the University of Arizona. The trolleys operate on Friday from 6 to 10pm, Saturday from noon to midnight, and Sunday from noon to 6pm. The fare is $1 for adults and 50¢ for children 6 to 12. The fare on Sunday is only 25¢ for all riders. Friday and Saturday all-day passes are $2.50 for adults and $1.25 for children.

T.I.C.E.T., or Tucson Inner City Express Transit (☎ 520/747-3778), operates three free downtown-area shuttles. For visitors, the only route that is of much use is the Blue Route, which has stops near the visitor center, the Tucson Convention Center, the Tucson Children's Museum, Old Town Artisans, and the Tucson Museum of Art. Blue Route buses operate Monday through Friday and run every 10 to 20 minutes between 7am and 5:30pm.

BY TAXI

If you need a taxi, you'll have to phone for one. **AAA Yellow Cab** (☎ 520/624-6611) and **Allstate Cab** (☎ 520/881-2227) provide service throughout the city. The flag-drop rate is between $2 and $2.25, and after that it's $1.60 to $1.75 per mile. Although distances in Tucson are not as great as those in Phoenix, it's still a good 10 or more miles from the foothills resorts to downtown Tucson, so expect to pay at least $10 for any taxi ride. Most resorts have shuttle vans or can arrange taxi service to major tourist attractions.

ON FOOT

Downtown Tucson is compact and easily explored on foot, and many old streets in the downtown historic neighborhoods are narrow and much easier to appreciate if you leave your car in a parking lot. Also, although several major attractions—including the Arizona–Sonora Desert Museum, Old Tucson Studios, Saguaro National Park, and Sabino Canyon—can only be reached by car, they require quite a bit of walking once you arrive. These attractions often have uneven footing, so be sure to bring a good pair of walking shoes.

FAST FACTS

For a doctor referral, ask at your hotel or call University Health Connection (☎ 520/694-8888). For a dentist referral, call the Arizona Dental Association (☎ 800/866-2732) or Dental Referral Service (☎ 800/669-4435).

Local hospitals are the **Tucson Medical Center** at 5301 E. Grant Rd. (© **520/327-5461**) and the **University Medical Center** is at 1501 N. Campbell Ave. (© **520/694-0111**).

In addition to the 5.6% sales tax levied by the state, Tucson levies a 2% city sales tax. Car-rental taxes, surcharges, and fees add up to around 28%. The hotel tax in the Tucson area is usually 10.5% to 11.5%.

3 Where to Stay

Although Phoenix still holds the title of Resort Capital of Arizona, Tucson is not far behind, and this city's resorts boast much more spectacular settings than most comparable properties in Phoenix and Scottsdale. As far as nonresort accommodations go, Tucson has a wider variety than Phoenix—partly because several historic neighborhoods have become home to bed-and-breakfast inns. The presence of several guest ranches within a 20-minute drive of Tucson also adds to the city's diversity of accommodations. Business and budget travelers are well served with all-suite and conference hotels, as well as plenty of budget chain motels.

At the more expensive hotels and resorts, summer rates, usually in effect from May to September or October, are often less than half what they are in winter. Surprisingly, temperatures usually aren't unbearable in May or September, which makes these good times to visit if you're looking to save money. When making late spring or early fall reservations, always be sure to ask when rates are scheduled to go up or down. During the winter gem and mineral shows, the last week in January and the first 2 weeks in February, hotels around town generally charge exorbitant rates.

Most hotels offer special packages, weekend rates, various discounts (such as for AARP or AAA members), and free accommodations for children, so it helps to ask about these when you reserve. Nearly all hotels have smoke-free and wheelchair-accessible rooms.

BED & BREAKFASTS   If you're looking to stay in a B&B, several agencies can help. The **Arizona Association of Bed and Breakfast Inns** (© **800/752-1912;** www.arizona-bed-breakfast.com) has several members in Tucson. **Mi Casa Su Casa** (© **800/456-0682** or 480/990-0682; www.azres.com) will book you into one of its many home-stays (informal B&Bs) in the Tucson area or elsewhere in the state, as will **Arizona Trails Travel Services** (© **888/799-4284** or 480/837-4284; www.arizona trails.com), which also books tour and hotel reservations.

DOWNTOWN & THE UNIVERSITY AREA
EXPENSIVE

Arizona Inn ★★★   With its pink-stucco buildings and immaculately tended flower gardens, the Arizona Inn is a 14-acre oasis of tranquility in central Tucson. Gracious, welcoming, and comfortable, it's an unforgettable place to spend a vacation. Originally opened in 1930 by Isabella Greenway, Arizona's first congresswoman, the inn is still family owned and operated, and is imbued with a gracious character and Old Arizona charm you won't find elsewhere in the state. Playing a game of croquet, taking high tea in the library (complimentary), or lounging by the pool, I always feel as if this were my second home. Guest rooms vary in size and decor, but most have a mix of reproduction antiques and original pieces custom made years ago by World War I veterans with disabilities. Guest rooms also have such modern amenities as DVD

Tucson Accommodations

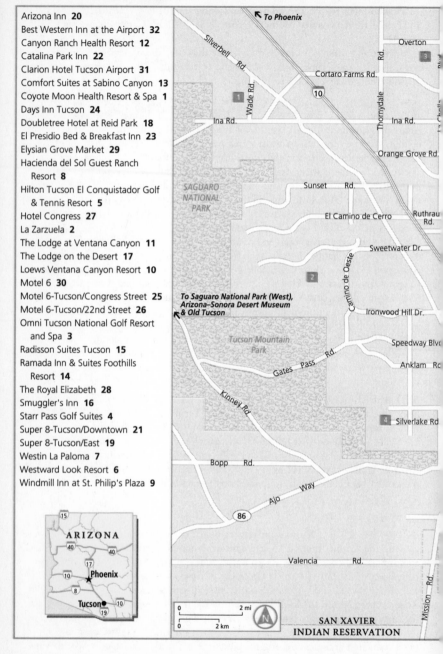

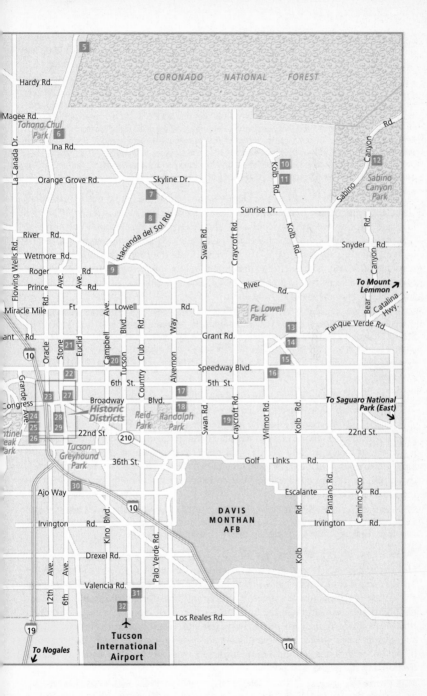

players (and access to a library of films). Some units have gas fireplaces, and most suites have private patios or enclosed sun porches. The inn's main dining room (p. 360) is a casually elegant space. Fragrant flowering trees and vines surround the small pool.

2200 E. Elm St., Tucson, AZ 85719. (©) **800/933-1093** or 520/325-1541. Fax 520/320-2182. www.arizonainn.com. 86 units. Mid-Jan to mid-Apr from $269 double, from $369 suite; mid-Apr to May from $199 double, from $259 suite; June to mid-Sept from $154 double, from $249 suite; mid-Sept to mid-Dec from $189 double, from $299 suite; mid-Dec to mid-Jan $219 double, from $329 suite. Summer rates include full breakfast and complimentary evening ice-cream fountain. Children 2 and under stay free in parent's room (10 and under during summer). AE, DC, MC, V. **Amenities:** 3 restaurants (French/American, International); 2 lounges; heated outdoor pool; 2 Har-Tru clay tennis courts; croquet; table tennis; badminton; well-equipped exercise room; access to nearby health club; saunas; bikes; concierge; business center; room service; massage; babysitting; laundry service; dry cleaning. *In room:* A/C, TV/DVD, dataport, fridge, coffeemaker, hair dryer, iron, high-speed Internet access.

The Lodge on the Desert ★★   Dating from 1936 and set amid neatly manicured lawns and gardens, the Lodge on the Desert is a classic old Arizona resort. It offers a lush and relaxing retreat that looks a lot like the Arizona Inn (though not nearly as deluxe, and without the superb service). Guest rooms are in hacienda-style adobe buildings tucked amid cacti and orange trees. Inside the rooms, you'll find a mix of contemporary and Southwestern furnishings; many units have beamed ceilings or fireplaces, and some are carpeted while others have tile floors. Although the pool is small, it has a good view of the Catalinas.

306 N. Alvernon Way, Tucson, AZ 85711. (©) **800/456-5634** or 520/325-3366. Fax 520/327-5834. www.lodgeonthe desert.com. 35 units. Mid-Jan to mid-Apr $189–$289 double, $259–$279 suite; mid-Apr to May and Oct to mid-Jan $129–$199 double, $169–$189 suite; June–Sept $89–$129 double, $119 suite. Rates include full breakfast. Children under 18 stay free in parent's room. AE, DC, DISC, MC, V. Pets accepted ($50 deposit plus $15 per night). **Amenities:** Restaurant; lounge; small outdoor pool; concierge; dry cleaning. *In room:* A/C, TV, coffeemaker, hair dryer, iron.

MODERATE

Catalina Park Inn ★★   Close to downtown and overlooking a shady park, this 1927 home has been lovingly restored by owners Mark Hall and Paul Richard. From the outside, the inn has the look of a Mediterranean villa, while many interesting and playful touches enliven the classic interior. The huge Catalina Room in the basement is one of our favorites. Not only does it conjure up the inside of an adobe, but it also has a whirlpool tub in a former cedar closet. Two upstairs rooms have balconies, while two units in a separate cottage across the garden offer more contemporary styling than the rooms in the main house.

309 E. First St., Tucson, AZ 85705. (©) **800/792-4885** or 520/792-4541. www.catalinaparkinn.com. 6 units. $136–$166 double (lower rates late spring through fall). Rates include full breakfast. AE, DISC, MC, V. No children under 10. **Amenities:** Concierge. *In room:* A/C, TV, dataport, hair dryer, iron, free local calls, wi-fi.

Doubletree Hotel at Reid Park ★★   This in-town high-rise hotel, with its pleasant orange-tree-shaded pool area, is midway between the airport and downtown Tucson, and is something of an in-town budget resort (the Randolph Park municipal golf course is right across the street). Guest rooms boast bright colors and bold contemporary designs. Although the hotel does a lot of convention business and sometimes feels crowded, the gardens are always tranquil. Guest rooms are divided between a nine-story tower that offers views of the valley (even-numbered rooms face the pool, odd-numbered rooms face the mountains) and a two-story building with patio rooms overlooking the garden and pool area.

445 S. Alvernon Way, Tucson, AZ 85711. (©) **800/222-TREE** or 520/881-4200. Fax 520/323-5225. www.dtreidpark. com. 295 units. Jan to mid-Apr $119–$229 double; mid-Apr to mid-Sept $79–$119 double; mid-Sept to Dec $99–$189

double. Children under 18 stay free in parent's room. AE, DC, DISC, MC, V. Pets accepted ($25 fee). **Amenities:** 2 restaurants; 2 lounges; outdoor pool; 3 tennis courts; large exercise room; Jacuzzi; business center; room service; massage; laundry service; dry cleaning. *In room:* A/C, TV, dataport, coffeemaker, hair dryer, iron, high-speed Internet access, wi-fi.

El Presidio Bed & Breakfast Inn ★★   Built in 1886 and lovingly restored by innkeeper Patti Toci, El Presidio is a mix of Victorian and adobe architectural styles and is in Tucson's most attractive historic district. Located only steps from the Tucson Museum of Art (p. 375), Old Town Artisans (p. 387), and El Charro Café (p. 357), this is the quintessential Tucson territorial home. There are two high-ceilinged suites in the main house, while the other two units, both with kitchenettes, are arranged around a shady courtyard at the center of which is a Mexican fountain. All are decorated with antiques and original art. Complimentary drinks, fruit, and treats are offered in the afternoon and evening.

297 N. Main Ave., Tucson, AZ 85701. © 800/349-6151 or 520/623-6151. Fax 520/623-3860. 4 units. $105–$135 double. Rates include full breakfast. 2-night minimum stay Oct–May. No credit cards. No children under 5. **Amenities:** Access to nearby health club; guest laundry. *In room:* A/C, TV, coffeemaker, hair dryer, iron.

Elysian Grove Market ★ *Finds*   Located in the Barrio Histórico just a block away from El Tiradito shrine, this former general store is now an unusual little inn filled with rustic Mexican antiques and Hispanic folk art. The two suites contain high-ceilinged living rooms that incorporate all manner of salvaged architectural details, colorful textiles, and original grocery-store fixtures. Each unit has a bedroom on the ground level and a second bedroom (rather dark but cool) down a flight of steps. Although this funky barrio B&B isn't for everyone, I love the old Mexican atmosphere and abundance of Hispanic art.

400 W. Simpson St., Tucson, AZ 85701. © 520/628-1522. 2 units. $85 double. Rates include continental/Mexican breakfast. No credit cards. Closed June–Sept. **Amenities:** Access to nearby health club; massage. *In room:* No phone.

The Royal Elizabeth ★★   Just a block away from the Temple of Music and Art in downtown, the Royal Elizabeth is an 1878 Victorian adobe home that features an unusual combination of architectural styles that makes for a uniquely Southwestern-style inn. In classic 19th-century Tucson fashion, the old home looks thoroughly unpretentious from the outside, but inside you'll find beautiful woodwork and gorgeous Victorian-era antique furnishings. Guest rooms open off a large, high-ceilinged central hall. The immediate neighborhood isn't as attractive as the El Presidio neighborhood, but the Tucson Museum of Art and several good restaurants are within walking distance.

204 S. Scott Ave., Tucson, AZ 85701. © 877/670-9022 or 520/670-9022. Fax 928/833-9974. www.royalelizabeth.com. 6 units. Sept–May $130–$180 double; June–Aug $90–$130 double. Rates include full breakfast. AE, DISC, MC, V. **Amenities:** Outdoor pool; access to nearby health club; Jacuzzi; business center; massage. *In room:* A/C, TV/VCR, dataport, fridge, hair dryer, iron, safe, free local calls, wi-fi.

INEXPENSIVE

In addition to the hotel listed below, you'll find dozens of budget chain motels along I-10 as it passes through downtown. Among the better ones are **Days Inn Tucson,** 222 S. Freeway, Exit 258 (© 520/791-7511); **Motel 6–Tucson/Congress Street,** 960 S. Freeway, Exit 258 (© 520/628-1339); **Motel 6–Tucson/22nd Street,** 1222 S. Freeway, Exit 259 (© 520/624-2516); and **Super 8–Tucson/Downtown,** 1248 N. Stone St., Exit 257 (© 520/622-6446).

Hotel Congress *Finds*   Located in the heart of downtown Tucson, the Hotel Congress, built in 1919 to serve railroad passengers, once played host to John Dillinger.

Today, it operates as a budget hotel and youth hostel. Although the place is utterly basic, the lobby has loads of Southwestern elegance. Guest rooms remain true to their historical character, with antique telephones and old radios, so don't expect anything fancy (like TVs). Most bathrooms have tubs or showers but a few have both. There's the classic little Cup Cafe off the lobby (think Edward Hopper meets Gen X), as well as a tiny Western Tap Room bar. At night, the Club Congress (p. 391) is a popular (and loud) dance club (pick up free earplugs at the front desk).

311 E. Congress St., Tucson, AZ 85701. (℃ **800/722-8848** or 520/622-8848. Fax 520/792-6366. www.hotelcongress. com. 40 units. $59–$99 double; $20–$25 per person in shared hostel rooms. AE, DC, DISC, MC, V. Pets accepted ($10 per day). **Amenities:** Restaurant; saloon; nightclub.

EAST TUCSON
EXPENSIVE
Radisson Suites Tucson ★★ *Value*   With large and very attractive rooms, this all-suite hotel is a good choice for both those who need plenty of space and those who want to be in the east-side business corridor. The five-story brick building is arranged around two long garden courtyards, one of which has a large pool and whirlpool. In fact, the pool and gardens are among the nicest at any nonresort hotel in Tucson and are the best reasons for vacationers to stay here.

6555 E. Speedway Blvd., Tucson, AZ 85710. (℃ **800/333-3333** or 520/721-7100. Fax 520/721-1991. www.radisson. com/suites_tucson. 299 suites. Feb–Apr $199–$239 double; May and Oct–Jan $89–$159 double; June–Sept $59–$89 double. Children under 18 stay free in parent's room. AE, DC, DISC, MC, V. Pets accepted ($50 fee). **Amenities:** Restaurant; large outdoor pool; exercise room; access to nearby health club; Jacuzzi; concierge; business center; room service; coin-op laundry; laundry service; dry cleaning. *In room:* A/C, TV, dataport, fridge, coffeemaker, hair dryer, iron, high-speed Internet access, wi-fi.

MODERATE
Comfort Suites at Sabino Canyon ★   Although it looks rather stark from the outside and shares a parking lot with a shopping center, this Comfort Suites is surprisingly pleasant inside. Built around four tranquil and lushly planted garden court-yards, the hotel has (for the most part) large rooms, some of which have kitchenettes. There's no restaurant, but there are plenty of good dining options nearby. This is a good economical choice close to Sabino Canyon, the Mount Lemmon Highway, and Saguaro National Park's east unit.

7007 E. Tanque Verde Rd., Tucson, AZ 85715. (℃ **800/424-6423** or 520/298-2300. Fax 520/298-6756. www.choice hotels.com. 90 units. Jan–Mar $99–$179 double; Apr to mid-May $79–$159 double; mid-May to Dec $49–$99 double. Rates include continental breakfast and evening social hour Mon–Thurs. Children 18 and under stay free in parent's room. AE, DC, DISC, MC, V. Pets accepted ($25 fee). **Amenities:** Small outdoor pool; access to nearby health club; Jacuzzi; coin-op laundry; dry cleaning. *In room:* A/C, TV, dataport, coffeemaker, hair dryer, iron.

Ramada Inn & Suites Foothills Resort ★   The best thing about this unassuming east-side chain hotel is its location right next door to Fuego, which is one of my favorite Tucson restaurants. The hotel also has an attractive courtyard pool. Standard rooms are your best bet, though there are a few second-floor suites with mountain views. Suites are large, though furniture is looking a bit worn. Book a room here and you'll also be close to Sabino Canyon, the Mount Lemmon Highway, and Saguaro National Park's east unit.

6944 E. Tanque Verde Rd., Tucson, AZ 85715. (℃ **800/2-RAMADA**, 888/546-9629, or 520/886-9595. Fax 520/721-8466. www.ramadafoothillstucson.com. 113 units. $49–$189 double; $79–$229 suite. Rates include continental breakfast and evening social hour. Children under 16 stay free in parent's room. AE, DC, DISC, MC, V. Pets accepted

($25 fee). **Amenities:** Outdoor pool; access to nearby health club; Jacuzzi; sauna; business center; coin-op laundry. *In room:* A/C, TV, dataport, fridge, coffeemaker, hair dryer, iron, safe, free local calls.

Smuggler's Inn ★ *Value* *Kids*   This comfortable, economical hotel, with its neatly trimmed lawns and tall palm trees, has the feel of a tropical oasis, and the grounds are much nicer than those at most comparably priced hotels in the area. Amid these lush surroundings are a pool and a whirlpool that lend the place the feel of a budget tropical resort. If you bring the family, the kids will have plenty of space in which to run around, and will enjoy feeding the ducks in the hotel's pond. Guest rooms are spacious, though nothing fancy.

6350 E. Speedway Blvd. (at Wilmot), Tucson, AZ 85710. © **800/525-8852** or 520/296-3292. Fax 520/722-3713. www.smugglersinn.com. 149 units. Feb–May $109–$142 double, $129–$162 suite; June–Aug $69–$89 double, $99–$118 suite; Sept–Jan $95–$129 double, $115–$149 suite. Rates include full breakfast and evening manager's reception. Children 18 and under stay free in parent's room. AE, DC, DISC, MC, V. Pets accepted ($50 fee). **Amenities:** Outdoor pool; putting green; access to nearby health club; Jacuzzi; room service; coin-op laundry; laundry service. *In room:* A/C, TV, dataport, fridge, coffeemaker, hair dryer, iron.

THE FOOTHILLS
VERY EXPENSIVE

Hilton Tucson El Conquistador Golf & Tennis Resort ★★★   Although this large resort is a bit out of the way, the view of the Santa Catalina Mountains rising up behind the property makes this northern foothills resort one of my favorites in Tucson. Sunsets are truly spectacular. Most guest rooms are built around a central courtyard with manicured lawns and a large pool that has a long water slide. Consequently, this place is a hit with families. All accommodations feature Southwestern-influenced contemporary furniture, spacious marble bathrooms, and balconies or patios. Be sure to ask for a mountain-view room.

10000 N. Oracle Rd., Tucson, AZ 85737. © **800/325-7832** or 520/544-5000. Fax 520/544-1222. www.hiltonel conquistador.com. 428 units. Jan to late May $259–$490 double, from $339 suite; late May to early Sept $119–$290 double, from $179 suite; early Sept to Dec $219–$420 double, from $299 suite. Rates do not include $10 daily service fee. Children under 18 stay free in parent's room. AE, DC, DISC, MC, V. Valet parking $11. Pets accepted ($50 deposit). **Amenities:** 5 restaurants; 2 lounges; 4 pools; 1 9-hole and 2 18-hole golf courses; 31 tennis courts; 7 racquetball courts; basketball court; volleyball court; 2 exercise rooms; spa; 5 Jacuzzis; saunas; bike rentals; children's programs; concierge; tour desk; business center; shopping arcade; room service; massage; babysitting; laundry service; dry cleaning; horseback riding. *In room:* A/C, TV, dataport, minibar, coffeemaker, hair dryer, iron, safe, high-speed Internet access, wi-fi.

The Lodge at Ventana Canyon ★★★   Golf is the name of the game at this boutique resort set within a gated country-club community at the base of the Santa Catalina Mountains. The 3rd hole of the resort's Tom Fazio–designed Mountain Course plays across a deep ravine, which makes it one of the most photographed holes in Tucson. Though small, this exclusive lodge offers plenty of big-resort amenities and places an emphasis on personal service. The accommodations are in spacious suites, most of which have walls of windows facing the Catalinas, modern mission-style furnishings, small kitchens, and large bathrooms with oversize tubs. A few units have balconies, cathedral ceilings, and spiral stairs that lead to sleeping lofts.

6200 N. Clubhouse Lane, Tucson, AZ 85750. © **800/828-5701** or 520/577-1400. Fax 520/577-4065. www.thelodgeatventanacanyon.com. 50 units. Jan to early Apr $279–$519 1-bedroom suite, $449–$719 2-bedroom suite; early Apr to mid-May $189–$419 1-bedroom suite, $359–$619 2-bedroom suite; mid-May to early Sept $99–$175 1-bedroom suite, $189–$275 2-bedroom suite; early Sept to Dec $179–$399 1-bedroom suite, $349–$599 2-bedroom suite. Rates do not include $16 nightly service charge. Children under 18 stay free in parent's room.

AE, MC, V. Pets accepted ($50 fee). **Amenities:** Restaurant; lounge; snack bar; outdoor pool; 2 acclaimed 18-hole golf courses; 12 tennis courts; exercise room; Jacuzzi; saunas; bike rentals; concierge; car-rental desk; room service; massage and spa treatments; laundry service; dry cleaning; playground. *In room:* A/C, TV, dataport, kitchen, minibar, fridge, coffeemaker, hair dryer, iron, safe, high-speed Internet access.

Loews Ventana Canyon Resort ★★★ *Kids*

For breathtaking scenery, fascinating architecture, and superb resort facilities, no other Tucson resort can compare. The Santa Catalina Mountains rise behind the property, and flagstone floors in the lobby lend a rugged but luxurious appeal. Balconies overlook city lights or mountains, and some rooms have fireplaces. Bathrooms include tubs for two. All the rooms were renovated in 2005. The Ventana Room (p. 365) is one of Tucson's finest restaurants, while the Flying V Bar & Grill (p. 392) has good food and good views. The lobby lounge serves afternoon tea before becoming an evening piano bar. In addition to numerous other amenities, there are jogging and nature trails and a playground.

7000 N. Resort Dr., Tucson, AZ 85750. © **800/234-5117** or 520/299-2020. Fax 520/299-6832. www.loewshotels. com. 398 units. Early Jan to late May $365 double, from $750 suite; late May to early Sept $150 double, from $295 suite; early Sept to early Jan $325 double, from $700 suite. Children under 18 stay free in parent's room. AE, DC, DISC, MC, V. **Amenities:** 5 restaurants; 2 lounges; 2 outdoor pools; 2 acclaimed 18-hole golf courses; 8 tennis courts; croquet court; exercise room; full-service spa; 2 Jacuzzis; saunas; bike rentals; children's programs; concierge; tour desk; courtesy shuttle; business center; salon; 24-hr. room service; massage; babysitting; laundry service; dry cleaning. *In room:* A/C, TV, dataport, minibar, hair dryer, iron, high-speed Internet access.

Omni Tucson National Golf Resort and Spa ★★★

As the name implies, golf is the driving force at this boutique resort, which is the site of the annual Tucson Open PGA golf tournament—so if you don't have your own clubs, you might feel out of place. Then again, you could just avail yourself of the superb full-service spa. Most of the spacious guest rooms cling to the edges of the golf course and have their own patios or balconies; hand-carved doors and Mexican tile bathroom counters contribute a Spanish colonial feel, while the furniture has a modern Mediterranean style. With the exception of the least expensive rooms, the accommodations here are the most luxurious in Tucson.

2727 W. Club Dr. (off Magee Rd.), Tucson, AZ 85742. © **800/528-4856** or 520/297-2271. Fax 520/297-7544. www. tucsonnational.com. 167 units. Jan–Apr $239–$339 double, $249–$399 suite; May $159–$239 double, $199–$319 suite; Jun–Aug $84–$159 double, $119–$209 suite; Sept–Dec $159–$239 double, $199–$319 suite. Rates do not include $12 nightly service charge. Children under 18 stay free in parent's room. AE, DC, DISC, MC, V. Pets accepted ($50 nonrefundable deposit). **Amenities:** 3 restaurants; 2 lounges; 2 large pools; PGA championship 27-hole golf course; 4 tennis courts; basketball court; volleyball court; health club; full-service spa; 2 Jacuzzis; bike rentals; concierge; salon; room service; massage; babysitting; laundry service; dry cleaning; concierge-level rooms. *In room:* A/C, TV, dataport, minibar, coffeemaker, hair dryer, iron, safe.

The Westin La Paloma Resort & Spa ★★★ *Kids*

If grand scale is what you're looking for, this is the place. Everything about the Westin La Paloma is big—big portico, big lobby, big pool area—and from the resort's sunset-pink Mission Revival buildings, there are big views. While adults will appreciate the resort's tennis courts, exercise facilities, and poolside lounge chairs, kids will love the 177-foot water slide. Guest rooms are in 27 low-rise buildings surrounded by desert landscaping. Couples should opt for the king rooms (ask for a mountain or golf-course view if you don't mind spending a bit more). French-inspired Southwestern cuisine is the specialty at Janos (p. 364), which is one of Tucson's finest restaurants.

3800 E. Sunrise Dr., Tucson, AZ 85718. © **800/WESTIN-1** or 520/742-6000. Fax 520/577-5878. www.westinlapaloma resort.com. 487 units. Jan to late May $249–$319 double, from $445 suite; late May to mid-Sept $99–$149 double, from $245 suite; mid-Sept to Dec $209–$279 double, from $375 suite. Rates do not include $11 daily service fee.

Children under 18 stay free in parent's room. AE, DC, DISC, MC, V. Valet parking $12. Pets accepted. **Amenities:** 5 restaurants; 2 lounges; 5 pools (1 for adults only); 27-hole golf course; 10 tennis courts; racquetball court; volleyball court; croquet lawn; health club; full-service Red Door Spa by Elizabeth Arden; 3 Jacuzzis; children's programs; concierge; car-rental desk; business center; shopping arcade; pro shops; salon; 24-hr. room service; massage; babysitting; laundry service; dry cleaning. *In room:* A/C, TV, dataport, minibar, coffeemaker, hair dryer, iron, safe, high-speed Internet access, wi-fi.

EXPENSIVE

Hacienda del Sol Guest Ranch Resort ★★ *Finds*   With its colorful Southwest styling, historic character, mature desert gardens, and ridgetop setting, Hacienda del Sol is one of Tucson's most distinctive hotels. The lodge's basic rooms, set around flower-filled courtyards, are evocative of old Mexican inns and have rustic and colorful character, with a decidedly artistic flair. If you prefer more modern, spacious accommodations, ask for a suite; if you want loads of space and the chance to stay where Katharine Hepburn and Spencer Tracy may have once stayed, ask for a casita. The Grill (p. 364) is one of Tucson's best restaurants.

5601 N. Hacienda del Sol Rd., Tucson, AZ 85718. © **800/728-6514** or 520/299-1501. www.haciendadelsol.com. 30 units. Early Jan to May $165–$255 double, $335–$345 suite, $385–$485 casita; June–Sept $89–$129 double, $155–$175 suite, $175–$275 casita; Oct to early Jan $145–$225 double, $310–$320 suite, $350–$465 casita. 2-night minimum stay weekends and holidays. Children under 5 stay free in parent's room. AE, DC, DISC, MC, V. **Amenities:** Restaurant; lounge; small outdoor pool; Jacuzzi; massage. *In room:* A/C, TV, minibar, fridge, high-speed Internet access.

Westward Look Resort ★★ *Value*   This reasonably priced resort, with the desert at its doorstep and a nature trail through the cactus, is a favorite of mine. Built in 1912 as a private estate, Westward Look is the oldest resort in Tucson and, although it doesn't have a golf course, it does have an excellent spa, riding stables, and plenty of tennis courts. The large guest rooms have a Southwestern flavor and private patios or balconies with city views. For the ultimate in Southwest luxury, opt for one of the stargazer spa suites, which have outdoor hot tubs. The Gold Room (p. 364) serves excellent Continental and Southwestern cuisine. If you aren't a golfer but do enjoy resort amenities, this is one of your best bets in Tucson. At press time, there were plans for an extensive remodel of the hotel lobby.

245 E. Ina Rd., Tucson, AZ 85704. © **800/722-2500** or 520/297-1151. Fax 520/297-9023. www.westwardlook.com. 244 units. Jan–Apr $179–$395 double; May $139–$199 double; June–Sept $89–$189 double; Oct–Dec $159–$250 double. Rates do not include $12 daily resort fee. Children under 18 stay free in parent's room. AE, DC, DISC, MC, V. Pets accepted ($50 fee). **Amenities:** 2 restaurants; lounge; 3 pools; 8 tennis courts; exercise room; full-service spa; 3 Jacuzzis; bike rentals; concierge; tour desk; car-rental desk; business center; room service; massage; laundry service; dry cleaning, executive-level rooms; horseback riding. *In room:* A/C, TV, dataport, minibar, coffeemaker, hair dryer, iron, high-speed Internet access, wi-fi.

MODERATE

Windmill Suites at St. Philip's Plaza ★ *Value*   Located on the edge of the foothills in the St. Philip's Plaza shopping center, this hotel offers both a good location and good value. There are good restaurants and upscale shops right across the parking lot. Bikes are available to guests, and out the hotel's back door is a paved pathway along the Rillito River (which is usually bone dry). Accommodations are spacious and have double vanities, wet bars, and two TVs—basically everything you need for a long, comfortable stay.

4250 N. Campbell Ave., Tucson, AZ 85718. © **800/547-4747** or 520/577-0007. Fax 520/577-0045. www.windmillinns. com. 122 units. Feb–Mar $149–$179 double; Apr–May and Oct–Jan $99–$119 double; June–Sept $69–$99 double. Rates include continental breakfast. Children under 18 stay free in parent's room. AE, DC, DISC, MC, V. Pets accepted. **Amenities:** Outdoor pool; exercise room; access to nearby health club; Jacuzzi; bikes; business center; coin-op laundry; laundry service; dry cleaning. *In room:* A/C, TV, fridge, hair dryer, iron, free local calls.

WEST OF DOWNTOWN
EXPENSIVE

La Zarzuela ★★   When I come to the desert, I want to be *in* the desert, not in the middle of the city. That's why I love this modern B&B. It sits high on a hill surrounded by saguaros and is just down a dirt road from Tucson Mountain Park, which is every bit as beautiful as Saguaro National Park. La Zarzuela has four colorfully decorated guest rooms spread out around this sprawling modern Santa Fe–style building. The pool and hot tub are built on the edge of the desert, while courtyards and patios have splashes of colorful flowers in their landscaping. It's all very Southwestern, the perfect place to stay if you want to explore the desert. For all this seclusion, the inn is surprisingly close to downtown Tucson.

P.O. Box 86030, Tucson, AZ 85754. ✆ **888/848-8225**. www.zarzuela-az.com. 5 units. $195–$250 double. Rates include full breakfast and evening wine and hors d'oeuvres. 2-night minimum. DISC, MC, V. Closed mid-June to Aug. No children under 18. **Amenities:** Outdoor pool; Jacuzzi; concierge. *In room:* A/C, fridge, coffeemaker, hair dryer.

Starr Pass Golf Suites ★★   Located 3 miles west of I-10, Starr Pass is the most economically priced golf resort in the city. It's a condominium resort, however, which means you won't find the sort of service you get at other resorts. Accommodations are in privately owned Santa Fe–style casitas rented as two-bedroom units, master suites, or standard hotel-style rooms. The master suites are more comfortable, with fireplaces, full kitchens, balconies, and a Southwestern style throughout. The smaller hotel-style rooms are a bit cramped and much less lavishly appointed. The desert-style 18-hole golf course is one of the best courses in the city. There are also hiking/biking trails on the property.

3645 W. Starr Pass Blvd., Tucson, AZ 85745. ✆ **800/503-2898** or 520/670-0500. Fax 520/670-0427. www.starrpasstucson.com. 80 units. Jan to late May $179 double, $309 suite, $429 casita; late May to Sept $89 double, $139 suite, $199 casita; Oct–Dec $119 double, $179 suite, $249 casita. Children under 18 stay free in parent's room. AE, DC, DISC, MC, V. **Amenities:** Restaurant; lounge; outdoor pool; 27-hole golf course; 2 tennis courts; exercise room; Jacuzzi; pro shop. *In room:* A/C, TV, kitchen, fridge, coffeemaker, hair dryer.

MODERATE

Casa Tierra Adobe Bed & Breakfast Inn ★   If you've come to Tucson to be in the desert, then this secluded B&B west of Saguaro National Park is well worth considering. Built to look as if it has been here since Spanish colonial days, the modern adobe home is surrounded by cactus and palo verde trees. There are great views, across a landscape full of saguaros, to the mountains, and sunsets are enough to take your breath away. Guest rooms, which have wrought-iron sleigh beds, open onto a central courtyard surrounded by a covered seating area. The two outdoor hot tubs make perfect stargazing spots, and there are a couple of telescopes on the property.

11155 W. Calle Pima, Tucson, AZ 85743. ✆ **866/254-0006** or 520/578-3058. www.casatierratucson.com. 4 units. Aug 15–June 15 $135–$195 double, $200–$325 suite. Rates include full breakfast. 2-night minimum stay. AE, DISC, MC, V. Closed June 16–Aug 14. **Amenities:** Well-equipped exercise room; Jacuzzi; concierge; massage. *In room:* A/C, dataport, kitchenette, fridge, hair dryer, iron, free local calls.

NEAR THE AIRPORT
MODERATE

Best Western Inn at the Airport   If you're the type who likes to get as much sleep as possible before rising to catch a plane, this motel right outside the airport entrance will do it for you—there's no place closer.

7060 S. Tucson Blvd., Tucson, AZ 85706. ✆ **800/772-3847** or 520/746-0271. Fax 520/889-7391. 149 units. Jan–Mar $75–$135 double; Apr–May and Sept–Oct $75–$95 double; June–Aug $59–$79 double; Nov–Dec $65–$85 double. Rates include continental breakfast. AE, DC, DISC, MC, V. Pets accepted ($25 fee). **Amenities:** Restaurant; lounge;

small outdoor pool; tennis court; Jacuzzi; business center; coin-op laundry; dry cleaning. *In room:* A/C, TV, dataport, fridge, coffeemaker, hair dryer, iron.

Clarion Hotel Tucson Airport   Just outside the airport exit, this hotel provides convenience and some great amenities, including a complimentary nightly cocktail reception and midnight snacks. Accommodations are generally quite large; the king rooms are particularly comfortable. The poolside units are convenient for swimming and lounging.

6801 S. Tucson Blvd., Tucson, AZ 85706. (℃ 800/424-6423 or 520/746-3932. Fax 520/889-9934. www.clarionhotel. com. 188 units. Jan–Mar $99–$149 double; Apr–May and Sept–Dec $79–$129 double; June–Aug $59–$89 double. Rates include full breakfast and cocktail hour. Children 18 and under stay free in parent's room. AE, DC, DISC, MC, V. **Amenities:** Restaurant; lounge; outdoor pool; exercise room; Jacuzzi; courtesy airport shuttle; business center; room service; coin-op laundry; laundry service; dry cleaning. *In room:* A/C, TV, dataport, fridge, coffeemaker, hair dryer, iron, high-speed Internet access.

INEXPENSIVE

There are numerous budget motels near the Tucson Airport. These include **Motel 6,** 1031 E. Benson Hwy., Exit 262 off I-10 (℃ **520/628-1264**), which charges $46 to $76 double, and **Super 8–Tucson/East,** 1990 S. Craycroft Rd., Exit 265 off I-10 (℃ **520/790-6021**), which charges $60 to $99 double.

SPAS

Canyon Ranch Health Resort ★★★   Canyon Ranch, one of America's premier health spas, offers the sort of complete spa experience that's available at only a handful of places around the country. On staff are doctors, nurses, psychotherapists and counselors, fitness instructors, massage therapists, and tennis and golf pros. Services offered include health and fitness assessments; health, nutrition, exercise, and stress-management evaluations; fitness classes; massage therapy; therapeutic body treatments; facials, manicures, pedicures, and haircuts; makeup consultations; cooking demonstrations; and art classes. Guests stay in a variety of spacious and very comfortable accommodations. Three gourmet, low-calorie meals are served daily.

8600 E. Rockcliff Rd., Tucson, AZ 85750. (℃ 800/742-9000 or 520/749-9000. Fax 520/749-7755. www.canyon ranch.com. 185 units. Late Sept to early June 4-night packages from $6,360 double; early June to late Sept 4-night packages from $4,240 double. Rates include all meals and a variety of spa services and programs. AE, DC, DISC, MC, V. Pets accepted. No children under 12 (with exception of infants in the care of personal nannies). **Amenities:** 2 dining rooms; 11,000-square-foot aquatic center and 3 outdoor pools; 7 tennis courts; racquetball and squash courts; 7 exercise rooms; 80,000-sq.-ft. spa complex; 8 Jacuzzis; saunas; steam rooms; bikes; concierge; courtesy airport shuttle; salon; room service; massage; guest laundry; laundry service; dry cleaning. *In room:* A/C, TV/DVD, dataport, hair dryer, iron, safe, free local calls, high-speed Internet access.

Coyote Moon Health Resort & Spa ★ *Finds*   Once a dude ranch, this property on the west side of Tucson is now the nation's first gay-and-lesbian spa resort. Coyote Moon isn't very large, so don't expect the sort of intense spa experience you'd get at Miraval or Canyon Ranch. However, guests will get all the pampering and relaxation they want with plenty of massages and other skin and body treatments available to choose from. You can take art and exercise classes and attend lectures on topics of interest to gays and lesbians. Guest rooms are all large suites, and the setting, not far from the Tucson Mountains, will give you a solid sense of being in the desert.

7501 N. Wade Rd., Tucson, AZ 85743. (℃ 877/784-7430 or 520/744-2355. Fax 520/572-4096. www.coyotemoon resort.com. 16 units. Mid-Sept to mid-May $521–$580 double; mid-May to mid-Sept $443–$492 double. Rates include 3 meals daily, 1 daily spa treatment, classes, lectures, and excursions. AE, DISC, MC, V. **Amenities:** Restaurant; outdoor pool; tennis court; exercise room; spa; Jacuzzi; concierge; courtesy airport shuttle; massage; laundry service; horseback riding. *In room:* A/C, TV, fridge, coffeemaker, hair dryer, no phone.

Miraval Life in Balance ★★★ Focusing on what it calls "life balancing," Miraval emphasizes stress management, self-discovery, and relaxation rather than facials and mud baths. To this end, activities at the all-inclusive resort include meditation, tai chi, Pilates, and yoga; more active types can go hiking, mountain biking, rock climbing, and horseback riding. Miraval offers lifestyle-management workshops, fitness/nutrition consultations, exercise classes, an "equine experience" program, massage, and skin care and facials. The spa's main pool is a gorgeous three-tiered leisure pool surrounded by waterfalls and desert landscaping. Guest rooms, many of which have views of the Santa Catalina Mountains, are done in a Southwestern style. Most of the bathrooms have showers but no tubs.

5000 E. Via Estancia Miraval, Catalina, AZ 85739. © **800/232-3969** or 520/825-4000. Fax 520/825-5163. www.miravalresort.com. 102 units. Oct to mid-May $1,150–$1,200 double, $1,570–$2,190 suite; mid-May to Sept $868–$908 double, $1,164–$1,664 suite. Rates do not include 17.5% service charge. Rates include all meals, classes, and a $110 per-person per-day spa credit. AE, DC, DISC, MC, V. No children. **Amenities:** 2 restaurants; lounge; 2 snack areas; 4 pools; 2 tennis courts; croquet court; superbly equipped exercise room; spa; 5 Jacuzzis; saunas; steam rooms; concierge; car-rental desk; business center; room service; massage; guest laundry; laundry service; dry cleaning; horseback riding. *In room:* A/C, TV/DVD, dataport, fridge, coffeemaker, hair dryer, iron, safe, high-speed Internet access, wi-fi.

GUEST RANCHES

Lazy K Bar Ranch ★ In operation as a guest ranch since 1936, the Lazy K Bar Ranch covers more than 200 acres and is adjacent to Saguaro National Park's west unit. Ranch activities include trail rides, guest rodeos, cookouts, and hay rides as well as nature talks, guided hikes, rappelling, and stargazing. Guest rooms vary in size and comfort level (some have whirlpool tubs); try for one of the newest units, which are absolutely gorgeous. Family-style meals consist of hearty American ranch food, with cookouts offered twice a week.

8401 N. Scenic Dr., Tucson, AZ 85743. © **800/321-7018** or 520/744-3050. Fax 520/744-7628. www.lazykbar.com. 24 units. Oct to mid-Dec $320–$365 double; mid-Dec to Apr $340–$385 double; May and Sept $230–$265 double. Rates include all meals and horseback riding. AE, DISC, MC, V. Closed June–Aug. Children under 2 stay free in parent's room. **Amenities:** Dining room; lounge; small outdoor pool; access to nearby health club; Jacuzzi; game room; courtesy airport shuttle (limited hours); coin-op laundry; horseback riding. *In room:* A/C, no phone.

Tanque Verde Ranch ★★ Want to spend long days in the saddle but don't want to give up resort luxuries? Then Tanque Verde Ranch, which was founded in the 1868 and still has some of its original buildings, is for you. This is far and away the most luxurious guest ranch in Tucson. The ranch borders Saguaro National Park and the Coronado National Forest, so there's plenty of room for horseback riding. There are also nature trails and a nature center, and at the end of the day, the spa provides ample opportunities to recover from too many hours in the saddle. Guest rooms are spacious and comfortable, with fireplaces and patios in many units. Some casitas are quite large and are among the most luxurious accommodations in the state. The dining room, which overlooks the Rincon Mountains, sets impressive buffets.

Tanque Verde Ranch also operates Bellota Ranch, which is located at the end of a rough dirt road, and is geared toward more experienced riders.

14301 E. Speedway Blvd., Tucson, AZ 85748. © **800/234-DUDE** or 520/296-6275. Fax 520/721-9426. www.tanqueverderanch.com. 74 units. Mid-Dec to Apr $370–$495 double; May–Sept $290–$375 double; Oct to mid-Dec $315–$405 double. Rates include all meals and ranch activities. Children 3 and under $15 extra. AE, DC, DISC, MC, V. **Amenities:** Dining room; lounge; 3 pools (indoor and outdoor); 5 tennis courts; exercise room; small full-service spa; Jacuzzi; saunas; children's programs; concierge; courtesy airport shuttle with 4-night stay; tennis pro shop; massage; babysitting; coin-op laundry; laundry service; dry cleaning; horseback riding; children's playground; hiking and biking programs. *In room:* A/C, dataport, fridge, iron.

White Stallion Ranch ★ *Kids*   Set on 3,000 acres of desert, the White Stallion Ranch is perfect for those who crave wide-open spaces. Operated since 1965 by the True family, this spread has a more authentic feel than any other guest ranch in the area. A variety of horseback rides are offered Monday through Saturday, and a petting zoo keeps kids entertained. There are also nature trails, guided nature walks and hikes, hayrides, weekly rodeos, and team cattle penning. Guest rooms vary considerably in size and comfort, from tiny, spartan single units to deluxe two-bedroom suites. Renovated rooms are worth requesting.

9251 W. Twin Peaks Rd., Tucson, AZ 85743. © **888/977-2624** or 520/297-0252. Fax 520/744-2786. www.wsranch. com. 41 units. Sept to early Oct $226–$262 double, $280–$320 suite; early Oct to mid-Dec and May–mid-June $272–$316 double, $336–$384 suite; mid-Dec to Apr $302–$366 double, $386–$444 suite. Rates do not include 15% service charge. Rates include all meals. 4- to 6-night minimum stay in winter. Children under 3 stay free in parent's room. No credit cards. Closed mid-June to Aug 31. **Amenities:** Dining room; lounge; small outdoor pool; tennis court; sports court; volleyball court; exercise room; access to nearby health club; small spa; Jacuzzi; sauna; bikes; concierge; tour desk; courtesy airport shuttle; business center; massage; coin-op laundry; horseback riding. *In room:* A/C, hair dryer, no phone.

4 Where to Dine

Variety, they say, is the spice of life, and Tucson certainly dishes up plenty of variety (and spice) when it comes to eating out. Tucson is a city that lives for spice, and in the realm of fiery foods, Mexican reigns supreme. There's historic Mexican at El Charro Café and El Minuto, *nuevo* Mexican at Café Poca Cosa and J Bar, Mexico City Mexican at La Parrilla Suiza, and family-style Mexican at Casa Molina. So if you like Mexican food, you'll find plenty of places in Tucson to get all fired up.

If Mexican leaves you cold, don't despair—there are plenty of other restaurants serving everything from the finest French cuisine to innovative American, Italian, and Southwestern food.

Foodies fond of the latest culinary trends will find plenty of spots to satisfy their cravings. Concentrations of creative restaurants can be found along East Tanque Verde Road and at foothills resorts and shopping plazas. On the other hand, if you're on a tight dining budget, you might want to look for early-bird dinners, which are particularly popular with retirees.

DOWNTOWN
MODERATE
Café Poca Cosa ★★ *Value* NUEVO MEXICAN   Created by owner/chef Suzana Davila, the food here is not just *any* Mexican food; it's imaginative and different, and the flamboyant atmosphere of red and purple walls and Mexican and Southwestern artwork is equally unusual. The cuisine consists of creations such as grilled beef with a jalapeño chile and tomatillo sauce, and chicken with a dark mole sauce made with Kahlúa, chocolate, almonds, and chiles. The staff is courteous and friendly and will recite the menu for you in both Spanish and English.

At Santa Rita Hotel, 88 E. Broadway Blvd. © **520/622-6400.** Reservations highly recommended. Main courses $9–$11 lunch, $15–$19 dinner. MC, V. Mon–Thurs 11am–9pm; Fri–Sat 11am–10pm.

El Charro Café ★ SONORAN MEXICAN   El Charro, housed in an old stone building in El Presidio Historic District, claims to be Tucson's oldest family-operated Mexican restaurant and is legendary around these parts for its unusual *carne seca,* a traditional air-dried beef that is a bit like shredded beef jerky. To see how they make carne seca, just glance up at the restaurant's roof as you approach. The large metal cage up

Tucson Dining

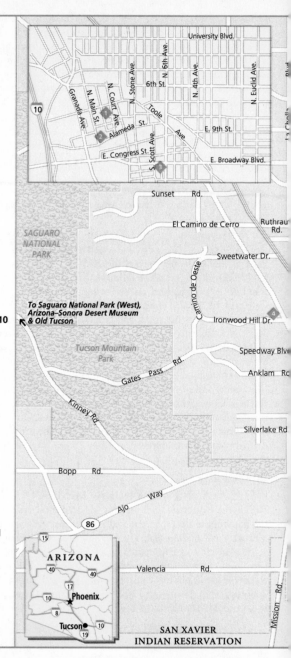

CORONADO   NATIONAL   FOREST

0   2 mi
0   2 km

Hardy Rd.

Tohono Chul Park

gee Rd.

Ina Rd.

La Canada Dr.

Orange Grove Rd.

Skyline Dr.

Kolb Rd.

Sabino Canyon Rd.

Sabino Canyon Park

River Rd.

Wetmore Rd.

Roger Rd.

Prince Rd.

oracle Mile

Hacienda del Sol Rd.

Swan Rd.

Craycroft Rd.

Sunrise Dr.

Snyder Rd.

Bear Canyon Rd.

To Mount Lemmon

Catalina Hwy.

River Rd.

Ft. Lowell Park

Tanque Verde Rd.

Flowing Wells Rd.

Oracle Rd.

Ft. Lowell Rd.

Lowell Rd.

Grant Rd.

Stone Ave.

Euclid Ave.

Campbell Ave.

Tucson Blvd.

Country Club Rd.

Alvernon Way

Speedway Blvd.

5th St.

To Saguaro National Park (East)

Grande Ave.

ngress Ave.

nel

6th St.

Broadway Blvd.

Randolph Park

Reid Park

Swan Rd.

Craycroft Rd.

Wilmot Rd.

Kolb Rd.

22nd St.

22nd St.

Tucson Greyhound Park

36th St.

Golf   Links   Rd.

Escalante

Pantano Rd.

Camino Seco Rd.

Ajo Way

DAVIS MONTHAN AFB

Irvington Rd.

Irvington Rd.

Kino Blvd.

Palo Verde Rd.

Kolb Rd.

Drexel Rd.

12th Ave.

6th Ave.

Valencia Rd.

Tucson International Airport

Los Reales Rd.

To Nogales

e inset map

there is filled with beef drying in the desert sun. You'll rarely find carne seca on a Mexican menu outside of Tucson, so indulge while you're here.

The adjacent ¡Toma! (p. 392), a colorful bar/cantina, is under the same ownership. There are other El Charro Cafes at 6310 E. Broadway (© **520/745-1922**), and at 100 W. Orange Grove (© **520/615-1922**).

311 N. Court Ave. © 520/622-1922. www.elcharrocafe.com. Reservations recommended for dinner. Main courses $6–$18. AE, DC, DISC, MC, V. Sun–Thurs 11am–9pm; Fri–Sat 11am–10pm.

INEXPENSIVE

Café à la C'Art SALADS/SANDWICHES Located in the courtyard on the grounds of the Tucson Museum of Art, this cafe serves up tasty sandwiches and makes a good lunch spot if you're downtown wandering the Presidio neighborhood or touring the museum. Try the apricot-almond chicken-salad croissant or the Cuban sandwich, which is made with roasted pork and ham. Wash it all down with some fresh lemonade and be sure to save room for dessert.

150 N. Main Ave. © 520/628-8533. Sandwiches and salads $7.50–$8.25. DISC, MC, V. Mon–Fri 11am–3pm.

El Minuto Cafe MEXICAN El Minuto, located downtown at the edge of the Barrio Histórico next to El Tiradito shrine, is a meeting ground for both Anglos and Latinos who come for the lively atmosphere and Mexican home cooking. In business since 1936, this establishment is a neighborhood landmark and a prototype that other Mexican restaurants often try to emulate. Cheese crisps (Mexican pizza) are a specialty, and enchiladas, especially *carne seca* (air-dried beef), are tasty. This is a fun place for people-watching—you'll find all types, from kids to businessmen in suits.

354 S. Main Ave. © 520/882-4145. Main courses $4.50–$13. AE, DC, DISC, MC, V. Sun–Thurs 11am–10pm; Fri–Sat 11am–11pm.

CENTRAL TUCSON & THE UNIVERSITY AREA
EXPENSIVE

Arizona Inn ★★ FRENCH/AMERICAN The dining room at the Arizona Inn, one of the state's first resorts, is consistently excellent. The pink-stucco pueblo-style buildings are surrounded by neatly manicured gardens that have matured gracefully, and it's romantic to dine in the courtyard or on the bar patio overlooking the colorful gardens. The menu changes regularly, but dishes are always well prepared. Flavors lean heavily toward classics such as vichyssoise, boeuf bourguignon, and bouillabaisse. Presentation is artistic, and fresh ingredients are emphasized. The homemade ice creams are fabulous. On weekends, you might catch some live music.

2200 E. Elm St. © 520/325-1541. Reservations recommended. Main courses $9–$17 lunch, $26–$35 dinner; tasting menu $41. AE, DC, MC, V. Daily 6:15–10am, 11:30am–2pm, and 6–10pm.

The Dish Bistro & Wine Bar ★★ NEW AMERICAN Located in the rear of the Rumrunner Wine and Cheese Co., this tiny, minimalist restaurant is brimming with urban chic. On a busy night, the space could be construed as either cozy or crowded, so if you like it more on the quiet side, come early or late. The chef has a well-deserved reputation for daring, and turns out such dishes as corn bisque with duck confit and rack of lamb with a pine nut, mint, and cilantro crust and a Moroccan sauce. Naturally, because this place is associated with a wine shop, the wine list is great; the well-informed servers will be happy to help you choose a bottle.

3200 E. Speedway Blvd. © 520/326-1714. www.dishbistro.com. Reservations highly recommended. Main courses $17–$28. AE, DC, MC, V. Tues–Thurs 5–9pm; Fri–Sat 5–10pm.

MODERATE

Cuvée World Bistro ★★ *Value* INTERNATIONAL This stylish restaurant in a small, shopping center affects a sort of Moroccan-palace decor, and if you take a seat in the lounge, you can sprawl on a banquette covered with plush pillows for a thoroughly romantic and hedonistic experience. The menu travels all over the globe for inspiration and then blends flavors and textures in deliciously creative ways. The menu changes regularly, but if you see something (perhaps wild-mushroom cakes) served over avocado pesto, order it. This pesto is so creamy and rich, it ought to be made into a spa treatment! Almost everything on the menu here sounds utterly tempting, and with prices so reasonable, you just might want to come back a few times and work your way through the list. On Friday and Saturday nights, there's live music.

3352 E. Speedway Blvd. (© **520/881-7577.** www.cuveebistro.com. Reservations recommended. Main dishes $9–$13 lunch, $15–$19 dinner. AE, DC, DISC, MC, V. Mon–Thurs 11am–10pm; Fri–Sat 11am–midnight.

Kingfisher ★ SEAFOOD If you're serious about seafood, the Kingfisher is definitely one of your best bets in Tucson. The freshest seafood, artfully blended with bright flavors and imaginative ingredients, is deftly prepared as appetizers, sandwiches, and main dishes. You may have difficulty deciding whether to begin with Umpqua Bay oysters, house-smoked trout, or scallop ceviche—so why not tackle them all and call it a meal? Meat eaters and vegetarians will also find items on the menu, and the warm cabbage salad is an absolute must. The atmosphere is upscale and lively, and the bar and late-night menu are a hit with night owls. There's also live jazz and blues on Saturday nights.

2564 E. Grant Rd. (© **520/323-7739.** www.kingfisherbarandgrill.com. Reservations recommended. Main courses $7.50–$10 lunch, $15–$22 dinner. AE, DC, DISC, MC, V. Mon–Fri 11am–midnight; Sat–Sun 5pm–midnight.

Pastiche Modern Eatery ★★ NEW AMERICAN Located in a shopping plaza that has lots of Tucson character, this high-energy bistro has for several years now been one of *the* hip places to dine in Tucson. The colorful artwork and vibrant contemporary food fairly shout *trendy,* but the restaurant manages to appeal to a broad spectrum of the population. From mushroom soufflé to spicy jerked chicken to fried jalapeño ravioli, there's enough here to keep everyone at the table happy. Light eaters can get half orders of entrees and desserts. The crowded bar is a popular watering hole that turns out some tasty margaritas.

3025 N. Campbell Ave. (© **520/325-3333.** www.pasticheme.com. Reservations recommended. Main courses $8–$24. AE, DC, DISC, MC, V. Mon–Fri 11:30am–midnight; Sat–Sun 4:30pm–midnight.

INEXPENSIVE

Beyond Bread ★ AMERICAN/BAKERY Although ostensibly a bakery, this place is more a bustling sandwich shop that also sells great breads and pastries. You can even get hot breakfasts here, but I much prefer a latte and a selection from the pastry case. The sandwich list is long, with both hot and cold varieties, and they all come on the great bread that's baked here on the premises. Most of the sandwiches are so big that you could split them between two people if you weren't too hungry.

There's another Beyond Bread over on the east side of town at Monterey Village, 6260 E. Speedway Blvd. (© **520/747-7477**).

3026 N. Campbell Ave. (© **520/322-9965.** www.beyondbread.com. No reservations. Main dishes $5–$8.75. AE, DISC, MC, V. Mon–Fri 6:30am–8pm; Sat 7am–8pm; Sun 7am–6pm.

El Cubanito Restaurant ★ CUBAN Located across the street from the University of Arizona, this place is popular with students. During spring-training season (Mar), the restaurant is also popular with Cuban baseball players. What draws everyone back to this nondescript place are the reasonably priced Cuban specialties, including various stews and a Cuban sandwich (a meat- and cheese-filled baguette pressed and warmed on the grill). The fried plantains are also worth trying, and the fruity shakes made with mango, banana, papaya, or other tropical fruits are delicious.

1150 E. Sixth St. ℂ 520/623-8020. Main courses $4.50–$9. MC, V. Mon–Sat 11am–7pm.

Feast ★ *Finds* INTERNATIONAL   This place is not only a casual sit-down restaurant but also a gourmet-to-go place and is the perfect place to pick up food for a sunset picnic dinner at Sabino Canyon Recreation Area or Saguaro National Park. The menu changes regularly, but you might find a sandwich made with roast pork and quince paste. Other possibilities might include meatloaf with chipotle mashed potatoes or red-white-and-green lasagna.

4122 E. Speedway Blvd. ℂ 520/326-9363 or 520/326-6500. www.eatatfeast.com. Main dishes $6.75–$15. AE, DISC, MC, V. Tues–Sun 11am–9pm.

Ghini's French Café ★ *Finds* FRENCH   A French cafe and breakfast spot in the middle of Tucson? *Mais oui!* This casual little spot is a real gem. The owner is from Marseille, and here reproduces plenty of favorites from the home country. At breakfast, there are flaky croissants and a Marseille-style omelet made with anchovies. Lunchtime brings interesting salads, sandwiches made from baguettes, and a good range of simple pastas. Everything is available to go.

1803 E. Prince Rd. ℂ 520/326-9095. Sandwiches and pastas $6.50–$10. AE, DC, DISC, MC, V. Tues–Sat 6:30am–3pm; Sun 8am–2pm.

Soul Feathers ★ *Finds*   I first discovered this barbecue joint when I drove past with my window down and had to find out what the wonderful smoky aroma was all about. It was slow-cooked, mesquite-smoked barbecue in the making, and I must say the baby back pork ribs here are the best I've ever had. You can also get whole barbecued chickens and beef brisket, pork loin, and chicken by the pound (think bodacious picnic fare). To find Soul Feathers, either follow your nose or look for the little pink building 5 minutes east of downtown.

1350 E. Broadway Blvd. (at Highland Ave.). ℂ 520/882-5030. Reservations not accepted. Main dishes $4–$15. AE, MC, V. Wed–Sat 11am–9pm; Sun–Tues 11am–8pm.

Yoshimatsu Healthy Japanese Food & Café ★ JAPANESE   I found out about this unusual place from a friend who had recently been to Japan and raved about this restaurant's authenticity. However, that's only part of the story. Not only is there a long menu of health-conscious Japanese dishes, but the decor in this ultra-casual place is truly outrageous, with little glass cases displaying all manner of Japanese toys and action figures. The *okonomiyaki,* sort of a Japanese pizza, is one of our favorite dishes here. For a truly bizarre treat, try the green tea milk shake! There's also a stylish little sushi bar attached to the restaurant.

2660 N. Campbell Ave. ℂ 520/320-1574. www.yoshimatsuaz.com. Main dishes $4.50–$9.50. MC, V. Sun–Thurs 11:30am–2:45pm and 5–8:45pm; Fri–Sat 11:30am–2:45pm and 5–9:45pm.

EAST TUCSON
MODERATE
Fuego ★ NEW AMERICAN/SOUTHWESTERN   In Spanish, *fuego* means "fire," and this place takes its name seriously. There are not only spicy dishes on the menu,

but actual flambéed dishes as well. The atmosphere is slightly formal but unpretentious. Waiters bustle about serving such flavorful dishes as the signature Field of Greens salad, with blue cheese, chile-roasted walnuts, and dried cranberries, or prickly-pear pork tenderloin that is so tender you can cut it with a fork. Lively yet intimate, Fuego appeals to couples, families, and retirees alike, and casual to dressy attire fits in just fine.

At Santa Fe Sq., 6958 E. Tanque Verde Rd. ℭ **520/886-1745.** www.fuegorestaurant.com. Reservations recommended. Main courses $14–$22. AE, DC, MC, V. Sun–Thurs 5–9pm; Fri–Sat 5–10pm.

INEXPENSIVE

Casa Molina MEXICAN Casa Molina, which sports a festive atmosphere, has been Tucson's favorite family-run Mexican restaurant for many years and is usually abuzz with families, groups, and couples. The margaritas are inexpensive yet tasty, and the *carne seca* (sun-dried beef) shouldn't be missed. Lighter eaters will enjoy a layered *topopo* salad made with tortillas, refried beans, chicken, lettuce, celery, avocado, tomato, and jalapeños. The food is good, and the service efficient.

Other locations include 3001 N. Campbell Ave. (ℭ **520/795-7593**) and 4240 E. Grant Rd. (ℭ **520/326-6663**).

6225 E. Speedway Blvd. (near Wilmot Rd.). ℭ **520/886-5468.** Reservations recommended. Dinners $7–$18. AE, DC, DISC, MC, V. Daily 11am–10pm.

La Parrilla Suiza MEXICO CITY MEXICAN Most Mexican food served in the United States is limited to Sonoran style, originating just south of the border. However, the cuisine of Mexico is far more varied than you might suspect from the typical restaurant menu. The meals served at La Parrilla Suiza are based on the style popular in Mexico City, where most of this chain's restaurants are located. Many menu items are sandwiched between two tortillas, much like a quesadilla, and the charcoal broiling of meats and cheeses lends the sandwiches special status. For an appetizer, we like the grilled scallions with lime.

Other locations can be found at 2720 N. Oracle Rd. (ℭ **520/624-4300**) and 4250 W. Ina Rd. (ℭ **520/572-7200**).

5602 E. Speedway Blvd. ℭ **520/747-4838.** Main courses $7–$15. AE, DISC, MC, V. Sun–Thurs 11am–10pm; Fri–Sat 11am–11pm.

Little Anthony's Diner *Kids* AMERICAN This place is primarily for kids, although lots of big kids enjoy the 1950s music and decor. The menu includes such offerings as a Jailhouse Rock burger and Chubby Checker triple-decker club sandwich. Daily specials and bottomless soft drinks make feeding the family fairly inexpensive. A video-game room will keep your kids entertained while you finish your meal. If you want to make a night of it (and you make a reservation far enough in advance), you can take in an old-fashioned melodrama next door at the Gaslight Theatre. Together, these two places make for a fun night out with the family.

7010 E. Broadway Blvd. (in back of the Gaslight Plaza). ℭ **520/296-0456.** Burgers and sandwiches $4.75–$9. MC, V. Mon–Thurs 11am–10pm; Fri 11am–11pm; Sat 10:30am–11pm; Sun 10:30am–10pm.

THE FOOTHILLS
EXPENSIVE

Anthony's in the Catalinas ★★ NEW AMERICAN/CONTINENTAL From the moment you drive up and let the valet park your car, Anthony's, housed in a modern

Italianate building overlooking the city, exudes Southwestern elegance. The waiters are smartly attired in tuxedos, and guests are nearly as well dressed. In such a rarefied atmosphere, you'd expect only the finest meal and service, and that's exactly what you get. The duck mousse and black truffle terrine is a fitting beginning, followed by the likes of chateaubriand with béarnaise sauce. Wine is not just an accompaniment but also a reason for dining out at Anthony's; at more than 100 pages, the wine list may be the most extensive in the city. Don't miss out on the next best part of a meal here (after the wine): the day's soufflé (order early).

6440 N. Campbell Ave. ℂ **520/299-1771.** www.anthonyscatalinas.com. Reservations highly recommended. Main courses $24–$41 dinner. AE, DC, DISC, MC, V. Open daily 5:30–10pm.

The Gold Room ★★ SOUTHWESTERN/CONTINENTAL With its recently updated contemporary Southwestern decor, superb views of the city far below, and expansive terrace for alfresco dining, the Gold Room is one of the best places in Tucson for a memorable Southwestern dining experience. The menu is a merger of creative contemporary fare and updated comfort foods. Think lobster martini (an appetizer, not a drink) and beef tenderloin served with house-made tater tots. The length of the wine list is staggering, and there's a welcome range of prices. Desserts are decadently rich. Although you can eat here on the cheap at lunch, the restaurant is most remarkable at night, when the cityscape of Tucson twinkles in the distance.

At the Westward Look Resort, 245 E. Ina Rd. ℂ **520/297-1151.** Reservations recommended. Main courses $13–$18 lunch, $18–$38 dinner; Sun brunch $25. AE, DC, DISC, MC, V. Mon–Sat 7am–11am, 11:30am–2pm, and 5:30–10pm; Sun 10am–1:30pm and 5:30–10pm.

The Grill ★★ REGIONAL AMERICAN Great food, historic Southwest character, views, live jazz—this place has it all, so don't visit Tucson without having a meal here. Located in a 1920s hacienda-style building at a former foothills dude ranch, the Grill is one of Tucson's best restaurants, and is known for its superb meals, classic Southwestern styling, and great views of the city. For openers, try the delicious lobster gazpacho, which comes with red-chile croutons. Despite the price, the dry-aged New York strip steak is deservedly the most popular entree on the menu and is big enough for two people to share. Sunday brunch here is a real treat. The main patio overlooks the Catalinas and the fairways of the Westin La Paloma's golf course. Thursday through Sunday, there is live music.

At the Hacienda del Sol Guest Ranch Resort, 5601 N. Hacienda del Sol Rd. ℂ **520/529-3500.** www.haciendadelsol. com. Reservations recommended. Main courses $24–$44; Sun brunch $32. AE, DC, DISC, MC, V. Mon–Sat 5:30–10pm; Sun 10am–2pm and 5:30–10pm.

Janos ★★★ SOUTHWESTERN/REGIONAL AMERICAN Janos Wilder, Tucson's most celebrated chef, is not only a world-class chef; he's a real sweetheart, too. Should you happen to bump into him while dining here, he'll make you feel as though you've been a regular at his restaurant for years. It is this conviviality, which spills over into all aspects of a meal here, that makes Janos one of my absolute favorites in the entire state. The menu changes both daily and seasonally, with such complex offerings as the not-to-be-missed lobster with papaya in champagne sauce; New York strip steak with chile hollandaise; and lamb loin with a complex spicy Southwestern rub.

At the Westin La Paloma, 3770 E. Sunrise Dr. ℂ **520/615-6100.** www.janos.com. Reservations highly recommended. Main courses $24–$45; 5-course tasting menu $75 ($110 with wines). AE, DC, MC, V. Mon–Thurs 5:30–9pm; Fri–Sat 5:30–9:30pm.

McMahon's Prime Steakhouse ✦✦ STEAKHOUSE/SEAFOOD If a perfectly done steak is what you're craving, then McMahon's is the place. This restaurant serves some of the best steaks in Tucson in an atmosphere calculated to impress. A large glass-walled wine room dominates the main dining room. You can drop a bundle on dinner here, but no more than you'd spend at such high-end restaurants as Janos or the Ventana Room. The main difference is that your choices at McMahon's are simpler: steak, seafood, or steak and seafood. You'd be wasting a night out, though, if you didn't order a steak (the aged prime beef is superb). There's a separate piano lounge and cigar bar.

2959 N. Swan Rd. ✆ 520/327-7463. www.metrorestaurants.com. Reservations recommended. Main courses $7–$16 lunch, $20–$40 dinner. AE, DC, DISC, MC, V. Mon–Fri 11:30am–10pm; Sat–Sun 5–10pm.

Ventana Room ✦✦✦ NEW AMERICAN The Ventana Room is Tucson's poshest and most classically elegant restaurant. *Ventana* means "window" in Spanish, and the views through the windows of this restaurant are every bit as memorable as the food that comes from the kitchen. For superb French-inspired cuisine and gorgeous views, this restaurant just can't be beat. Be sure you make an early dinner reservation so you can catch the sunset. Although you may have trouble concentrating on your food, do try; you wouldn't want to miss any of the subtle nuances. The tasting menus are designed to provide you with a delicious variety of flavors and textures. Ingredients are flown in from all over the world, so you never know what may show up on the menu. Neither should you allow the dessert cart to pass you by. In the restaurant's rarefied atmosphere, you'll be pampered by a bevy of waiters providing professional and unobtrusive service.

At Loews Ventana Canyon Resort, 7000 N. Resort Dr. ✆ 520/615-5494. www.ventanaroom.com. Reservations highly recommended. Jackets recommended for men. Prix-fixe menus $75–$105. AE, DC, DISC, MC, V. Tues–Thurs 6–9pm; Fri–Sat 6–10pm.

MODERATE

Bistro Zin ✦✦ REGIONAL AMERICAN Sophisticated and urbane, Bistro Zin, Tucson's premier wine bar/restaurant, affects an urban feel with its wine-colored walls decorated with black-and-white photos of jazz greats. It's all very classy and cool, and with more than 20 different wine flights available on any given day, this is the perfect place to sample wines from around the world. There's also plenty of good food to accompany the many wines. Try the grilled shrimp and the duck with drunken cherry sauce.

At Joesler Village, 1865 E. River Rd., Suite 101. ✆ 520/299-7799. www.tasteofbistrozin.com. Reservations recommended. Main courses $8–$14 lunch, $14–$28 dinner. AE, MC, V. Mon–Sat 11am–2:30pm and 5–11:30pm; Sun 5–11:30pm.

Bluefin Seafood Bistro ✦ SEAFOOD Sure, this is the middle of the desert, but there's only so much beef you can eat on a week's vacation. If you've had enough steak to start your own ranch and are craving a nice bouillabaisse, this is a good bet. Adopting a sort of New Orleans styling, Bluefin is a sister restaurant to the ever-popular Kingfisher in central Tucson. The menu is extensive; in addition to that bouillabaisse, you can get simply prepared grilled fish served with your choice of sauces. I like the rock shrimp relish. Like Kingfisher, this place stays open late.

In Casas Adobes Shopping Center, 7053 N. Oracle Rd. ✆ 520/531-8500. www.bluefinseafoodbistro.com. Reservations recommended. Main courses $8–$12 lunch, $16–$28 dinner. AE, DC, DISC, MC. V. Mon–Sat 11am–3pm and 5pm–midnight; Sun 10am–3pm and 5–9pm.

Firecracker Bistro ⭐ PAN-ASIAN With a menu that knows no boundaries and wild architectural touches that include flames issuing from torches atop the building and faux tree trunks in the bar, Firecracker is one of Tucson's hot spots. Hip decor aside, it's the large portions and reasonable prices that keep people coming back. The spicy-chicken lettuce-cup appetizers (sort of roll-your-own burritos) are a fun finger-food starter. Seafood is definitely the strong suit here, and the wok-charred chunks of salmon covered with cilantro pesto are just about the best thing on the menu.

2990 N. Swan Rd. (at Fort Lowell). © 520/318-1118. www.metrorestaurants.com. Reservations recommended. Main courses $7–$12 lunch, $13–$18 dinner. AE, DISC, MC, V. Sun–Thurs 11am–10pm; Fri–Sat 11am–10:30pm.

J Bar ⭐⭐⭐ SOUTHWESTERN The mouthwatering culinary creations of celebrity chef Janos Wilder at half-price? Sounds impossible, but that's pretty much what you'll find here at J Bar, Janos's casual bar and grill adjacent to his famed foothills restaurant. Ask for a seat out on the heated patio, and with the lights of Tucson twinkling in the distance, dig into the best nachos you'll ever taste—here made with chorizo sausage and chili con queso. No matter what you order, you'll likely find that the ingredients and flavor combinations are most memorable. Who can forget spicy jerked pork with cranberry–habañero chile pepper chutney or Yucatán-style plantain-crusted chicken with green coconut-milk curry? You won't want to miss sampling one of the *postres* (desserts).

At the Westin La Paloma, 3770 E. Sunrise Dr. © 520/615-6100. www.janos.com. Reservations highly recommended. Main courses $13–$22. AE, DC, MC, V. Mon–Thurs 5–9pm; Fri–Sat 5–9:30pm.

Tavolino Ristorante Italiano ⭐ ITALIAN Located in a shopping center at the corner of Oracle and Ina roads, this is not the Italian restaurant of your youth. Forget the red-and-white checked tablecloths; Tavolino Ristorante Italiano has a hip urban trattoria personality. Because it's small, it stays packed and boisterous. Sure there's a nice antipasto plate, but I'd opt for the eggplant stuffed with salmon mousse. For an entree, I like the lamb chops, which are pounded thin and tender. Finish your meal with an *affogato al caffe* (espresso with vanilla gelato).

In La Toscana Village Shopping Center, 7090 N. Oracle Rd. © 520/531-1913. Reservations recommended. Main courses $9.75–$19. AE, DC, MC, V. Mon–Sat 5:30–10pm.

Terra Cotta ⭐⭐ REGIONAL AMERICAN/SOUTHWESTERN Terra Cotta is Arizona's original Southwestern restaurant, and is one of my favorite places to eat in Tucson. The combination of reasonably priced creative Southwestern cooking, a casual atmosphere with loads of contemporary Southwestern appeal, and lots of local artwork make Terra Cotta truly distinctive and an Arizona classic. I always start my meals here with the rich-and-creamy garlic custard, which is served with warm salsa vinaigrette and herbed hazelnuts. The chile rellenos stuffed with smoked chicken and served on a red-pepper chipotle sauce is another of my must-haves. A large brick oven turns out creative pizzas, while salads, sandwiches, and small plates flesh out the long menu. The wine list includes a huge selection of zinfandels.

3500 E. Sunrise Dr. © 520/577-8100. www.cafeterracotta.com. Reservations recommended. Main courses $8–$13 lunch, $12–$24 dinner. AE, DC, DISC, MC, V. Daily 11:30am–10pm.

Vivace Restaurant ⭐⭐ NORTHERN ITALIAN With a beautiful Tuscan-inspired setting, this restaurant serves reasonably priced, creative dishes. The atmosphere is lively, and the food down-to-earth. For starters, we like to indulge in the luscious antipasto platter for two, containing garlic-flavored spinach, roasted red peppers, marinated arti-choke hearts, grilled asparagus, and herbed goat cheese. Pasta dishes, such as penne with sausage and roasted-pepper sauce, come nicely presented and in generous portions. But it's the crab-filled chicken breast that is most memorable. The wine list has plenty of selections, many fairly reasonably priced.

At St. Philip's Plaza, 4310 N. Campbell Ave. ✆ 520/795-7221. Reservations recommended. Main courses $8–$12 lunch, $13–$27 dinner. AE, DC, DISC, MC, V. Daily 11:30am–9pm.

Wildflower ★★ NEW AMERICAN Stylish comfort food in large portions are the order of the day at this chic and casually elegant bistro. A huge wall of glass creates minimalist drama, and large flower photographs on the walls enhance the bright and airy decor. The heaping plate of fried calamari with mizuna greens is a good bet for a starter, and entrees run the gamut from a comforting meatloaf to herb-crusted rack of lamb. Pasta and salmon both show up in various reliable guises. With so many tempt-ing, reasonably priced dishes to sample, Wildflower is a foodie's delight.

At Casas Adobes Shopping Plaza, 7037 N. Oracle Rd. (at Ina Rd.). ✆ 520/219-4230. Reservations recommended. Main courses $8–$13 lunch, $14–$27 dinner. AE, DC, DISC, MC, V. Mon–Thurs 11am–2:30pm and 5–9pm; Fri–Sat 11am–2:30pm and 5–10pm; Sun 5–9pm.

INEXPENSIVE

Candela Restaurant ★ *Finds* PERUVIAN/LATIN AMERICAN It's easy to miss this nondescript little restaurant, which is tucked into an older shopping plaza on Oracle Road south of Ina. However, keep looking. When you find it, you're in for a real treat if you enjoy trying new cuisines. As soon as you sit down, you'll be brought a basket of salty banana chips and a spicy dipping sauce. Make sure you order at least one dish with quinoa, a tiny South American grain. I love the quinoa salad here, which is made with avocados, olive oil, and balsamic vinegar. Another must-have is the *pescado sudado* (steamed fish). If you see *chichi morada* on the menu, try it. It's an unusual purple corn drink that tastes much better than it sounds.

5845 N. Oracle Rd. ✆ 520/407-0111. Reservations recommended on weekends. Main courses $3–$8 lunch, $9–$22 dinner. DISC, MC, V. Daily 11am–9pm.

HiFalutin Rapid Fire Western Grill ★ AMERICAN The first time I walked into this lively Western grill, I was absolutely hooked. The smell of burning juniper filled the restaurant, and I could almost taste the steaks. It wasn't until my second visit that I discovered the aroma was actually incense. Still, this place knows how to set the mood, and they come through with tasty comfort food with a Western twist. Get anything with the marinated flank steak and you won't be disappointed. You can get it tossed with pasta, with shrimp, and sometimes in a salad. Wash it all down with one of the great margaritas they serve and you definitely have a highfalutin kind of meal.

6780 N. Oracle Rd. ✆ 520/297-0518. Reservations recommended. Main courses $8–$21. AE, DC, DISC, MC, V. Daily 11am–9pm.

Tohono Chul Tea Room REGIONAL AMERICAN Located in a brick territorial-style building in 37-acre Tohono Chul Park (p. 373), this is one of the most tranquil restaurants in the city. Before or after lunching on grilled raspberry-chipotle chicken or tortilla soup, you can wander through the park's desert landscaping and admire the many species of cacti. The patios, surrounded by natural vegetation and plenty of

Kids Cowboy Steakhouses

Cowboy steakhouses are family restaurants that generally provide big portions of grilled steaks and barbecued ribs, as well as entertainment such as live country music. They tend to be touristy, but they're generally a big hit with the kids.

Kids and adults both love **Hidden Valley Inn**⭐, a brightly colored, false-fronted tourist cow town, as much for the filling and inexpensive meals as for the glass cases containing miniature action dioramas of humorous Western scenes. In the restaurant's very authentic dance hall, there are stage performances by magicians, Elvis impersonators, and the like. A second dining room, done up to look like a stable, is a bit less lively. There's also the Red Garter Saloon, where adults can imbibe. A lively party atmosphere reigns, and diners inevitably leave with large doggie bags. It's located at 4825 N. Sabino Canyon Rd. (© **520/299-4941;** www.hiddenvalleyinntuc.com). Main courses range from $6.50 to $23.

Located in Trail Dust Town (p. 380), a Wild West–themed shopping, dining, and family entertainment center, **Pinnacle Peak Steakhouse,** 6541 E. Tanque Verde Rd. (© **520/296-0911**), specializes in family dining in a fun cowboy atmosphere. Stroll the wooden sidewalks past the opera house and saloon to the grand old dining rooms of the restaurant. Once through the doors, you'll be surprised at the authenticity of the place, which really does resemble a dining room in Old Tombstone or Dodge City. Be prepared for crowds—this place is very popular with tour buses. Oh, and by the way, wear a necktie into this place and it will be cut off! Main courses run $6.50 to $16.

Owned by the same folks who run Tucson's Pinnacle Peak Steakhouse, **El Corral Restaurant,** at 2201 E. River Rd. (© **520/299-6092**), is another inexpensive and atmospheric steakhouse. Good prime rib and cheap prices have made this place hugely popular with retirees and families. The restaurant doesn't accept reservations, so expect long lines. Inside, the hacienda building has a genuine old-timey feeling, with flagstone floors and wood paneling that make it dark and cozy. You'll pay $9 to $16 for a complete dinner here.

potted flowers, are frequented by many species of birds. The adjacent gift shop is packed with Mexican folk art, nature-themed toys, household items, T-shirts, and books.

7366 N. Paseo del Norte (1 block west of the corner of Ina and Oracle rds. in Tohono Chul Park). © **520/797-1222.** www.tohonochulpark.org. Reservations accepted only for parties of 6 or more. Main courses $6–$11. AE, MC, V. Daily 8am–5pm.

Zona 78 ⭐ *Finds* PIZZA I'm a sucker for good pizza, and the pizza here is the best in Tucson. Maybe it's the big stone oven they use or maybe it's all the locally grown organic produce, but whatever it is, this place does it right. Try the Tuscany, covered with Italian sausage, mozzarella, black olives, fennel, roasted garlic, caramelized red onions, and mushrooms. This pie is just bursting with flavors. If you're with a crowd, order the big antipasto plate or the cheese-and-fruit plate, which has lots of great imported cheeses. If you're not that hungry, try the Tuscan bean-and-spinach soup.

78 W. River Rd. ℂ 520/888-7878. www.zona78.com. Main courses $7.25–$12. AE, DISC, MC, V. Mon–Sat 11am–11pm; Sun 4–9pm.

WEST TUCSON
MODERATE

Teresa's Mosaic Café ★ *Finds* MEXICAN   A mile or so west of I-10, this casual Mexican restaurant is hidden behind a McDonald's on the corner of Grant and Silverbell roads, but is well worth searching out for breakfast or lunch. With colorful mosaic tile tables, mirror frames, and kitchen counter, Teresa's lives up to its name. Try the chilaquiles or chorizo and eggs for breakfast, and don't pass up the fresh lemonade or *horchata* (spiced rice milk). This is an especially good spot for a meal if you're on your way to the Arizona–Sonora Desert Museum, Old Tucson, or Saguaro National Park's west unit.

2455 N. Silverbell Rd. ℂ 520/624-4512. Main courses $4.25–$13. MC, V. Mon–Sat 7:30am–9pm; Sun 7:30am–2pm.

5 Seeing the Sights

While there are plenty of interesting things to see and do all over the Tucson area, anyone interested in the desert Southwest or the cinematic Wild West should go west—to Tucson's western outskirts, that is. Here you'll find not only the west unit of Saguaro National Park (with the biggest and best stands of saguaro cactus) but also the Arizona–Sonora Desert Museum (one of Arizona's most popular attractions) and Old Tucson Studios (film site over the years for hundreds of Westerns). Together, these three attractions constitute Tucson's best and most popular day outing.

TUCSON AREA'S (MOSTLY) NATURAL WONDERS

Arizona–Sonora Desert Museum ★★★ *Kids*   Don't be fooled by the name. This is a zoo, and it's one of the best in the country. The Sonoran Desert of central and southern Arizona and parts of northern Mexico, contains within its boundaries not only arid lands but also forested mountains, springs, rivers, and streams. To reflect this diversity, exhibits here encompass the full spectrum of Sonoran Desert life—from plants to insects to fish to reptiles to mammals—and all are on display in very natural settings. Coyotes and javelinas (peccaries) seem very much at home in their compounds, which are surrounded by fences that are nearly invisible and that make it seem as though there is nothing between you and the animals. You'll also see black bears and mountain lions, tarantulas and scorpions, prairie dogs and desert bighorn sheep. Our favorite exhibit is the walk-in hummingbird aviary.

This zoological park is 14 miles west of downtown. The grounds are extensive, so wear good walking shoes; a sun hat of some sort is also advisable. Don't be surprised if you end up staying here hours longer than you had intended. If you get hungry, there are two excellent dining options—the cafeteria-style Ironwood Terraces and the more upscale Ocotillo Café.

2021 N. Kinney Rd. ℂ 520/883-2702. www.desertmuseum.org. Admission Nov–Apr $12 adults, $4 children 6–12; May–Oct $9 adults, $2 children 6–12. Oct–Feb daily 8:30am–5pm; Mar–Sept daily 7:30am–5pm (June–Aug Sat until 10pm). From downtown Tucson, go west on Speedway Blvd., which becomes Gates Pass Rd., and follow the signs.

Tucson Attractions

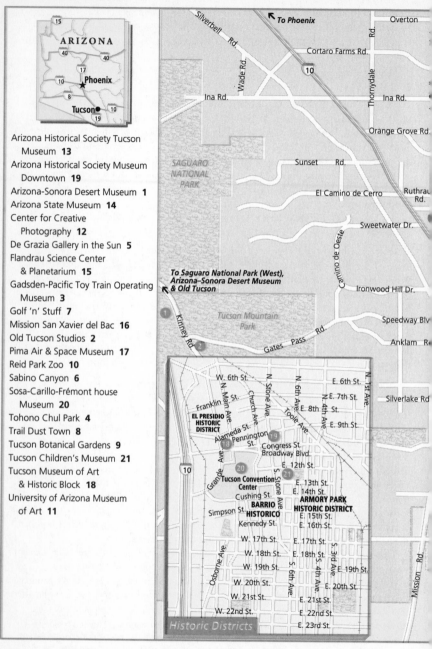

ARIZONA

40

40

17

10

8

19

Phoenix

Tucson

10

15

Silverbell Rd.

To Phoenix

Overton

Cortaro Farms Rd.

Wade Rd.

10

Thornydale

Rd.

Ina Rd.

Ina Rd.

Orange Grove Rd.

SAGUARO
NATIONAL
PARK

Sunset   Rd.

El Camino de Cerro

Ruthrau
Rd.

Sweetwater Dr.

Camino de Oeste

To Saguaro National Park (West),
Arizona–Sonora Desert Museum
& Old Tucson

Ironwood Hill Dr.

Kinney Rd.

Tucson Mountain
Park

Gates   Pass   Rd.

Speedway Blv

Anklam R

Silverlake Rd

W. 6th St.

N. Main Ave.

St.

N. Stone Ave.

Church Ave.

N. 6th Ave.

Toole Ave.

E. 6th St.

N. 4th Ave.

E. 7th St.

N. 1st Ave.

E. 8th St.

Franklin   St.

EL PRESIDIO
HISTORIC
DISTRICT

Alameda St.

Pennington
St.

E. 9th St.

Congress St.

Broadway Blvd.

E. 12th St.

10

Grande   Ave.

Tucson Convention
Center

S. Stone Ave.

E. 13th St.

E. 14th St.

ARMORY PARK
HISTORIC DISTRICT

Cushing St.

BARRIO
HISTORICO

Simpson St

E. 15th St.

Kennedy St.

E. 16th St.

W. 17th St.

E. 17th St.

Osborne Ave.

W. 18th St.

E. 18th St.

S. 3rd Ave.

S. 6th Ave.

W. 19th St.

S. 4th Ave.

E. 19th St.

W. 20th St.

E. 20th St.

Mission   Rd.

W. 21st St.

E. 21st St.

W. 22nd St.

E. 22nd St.

E. 23rd St.

Historic Districts

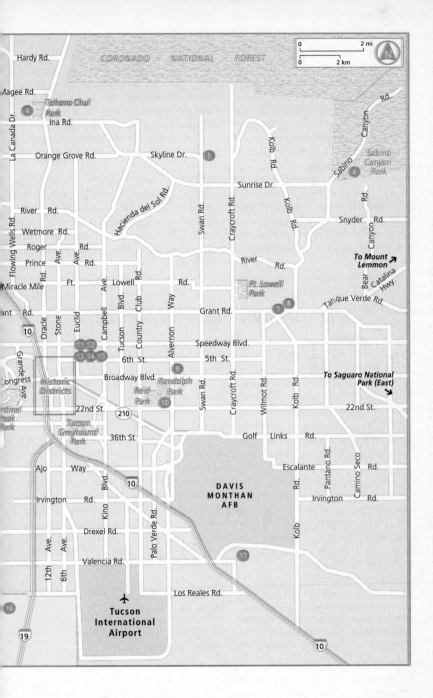

Hardy Rd.

CORONADO NATIONAL FOREST

Magee Rd.

Tohono Chul Park

La Canada Dr.

Ina Rd.

Orange Grove Rd.

Skyline Dr.

Kolb Rd.

Sabino Canyon Rd.

Sabino Canyon Park

Sunrise Dr.

Kolb Rd.

Snyder Rd.

River Rd.

Wetmore Rd.

Flowing Wells Rd.

Hacienda del Sol Rd.

Swan Rd.

Craycroft Rd.

Kolb Rd.

Bear Canyon Rd.

To Mount Lemmon

Catalina Hwy.

Roger Rd.

Prince Rd.

Miracle Mile

Ft. Lowell Rd.

River Rd.

Ft. Lowell Park

Tanque Verde Rd.

ant Rd.

10

Oracle

Stone

Euclid

Campbell Ave.

Tucson Blvd.

Country Club Rd.

Alvernon Way

Grant Rd.

6th St.

Speedway Blvd.

5th St.

Wilmot Rd.

Kolb Rd.

To Saguaro National Park (East)

Grande Ave.

ongress

Historic Districts

Broadway Blvd.

Reid Park

Randolph Park

Swan Rd.

Craycroft Rd.

22nd St.

ntinel eak ark

22nd St.

Tucson Greyhound Park

210

36th St.

Golf Links Rd.

Escalante

Pantano Rd.

Camino Seco Rd.

Ajo Way

Kino Blvd.

10

DAVIS MONTHAN AFB

Kolb Rd.

Irvington Rd.

Irvington Rd.

Drexel Rd.

Valencia Rd.

12th Ave.

6th Ave.

Palo Verde Rd.

19

Los Reales Rd.

✈ Tucson International Airport

10

Moments **Driving the Catalina Highway**

Within a span of only 25 miles, the Catalina Highway climbs roughly 1 mile in elevation from the lowland desert landscape of cacti and ocotillo bushes to forests of ponderosa pines. Passing through several different life zones, this route is the equivalent of driving from Mexico to Canada. Along the way there are numerous overlooks. There are numerous hiking trails and picnic areas along the route. For more information, contact the **Coronado National Forest Santa Catalina Ranger District,** 5700 N. Sabino Canyon Rd. (© **520/749-8700**). There's a $5 use fee.

Reid Park Zoo *Kids*   Although small and overshadowed by the Arizona–Sonora Desert Museum, the Reid Park Zoo is an important breeding center for several endangered species. Among the animals in the zoo's breeding programs are giant anteaters, white rhinoceroses, tigers, and zebras. A South American exhibit features a capybara (the largest rodent in the world), piranhas, and black jaguars. Get here early, when the animals are more active and before the crowds hit. If you've got the kids along, there's a good playground in the adjacent park.

1100 S. Randolph Way (at 22nd St. between Country Club Rd. and Alvernon Way). © 520/791-4022. www.tucson zoo.org. Admission $5 adults, $4 seniors, $2 children 2–14. Daily 9am–4pm. Closed Christmas. Bus: 7.

Sabino Canyon Recreation Area ★★   Located at the base of the Santa Catalina Mountains on the northeastern edge of the city, Sabino Canyon is a desert oasis, and, with its impressive desert scenery, hiking trails, and stream, is a fabulous place to commune with the desert for a morning or an afternoon. The chance to splash in the canyon's waterfalls and swim in natural pools (water conditions permitting) attracts many visitors, but it is just as enjoyable simply to gaze at the beauty of crystal-clear water flowing through a rocky canyon guarded by saguaro cacti. There are numerous picnic tables in the canyon, and many miles of hiking trails wind their way into the mountains from here, making it one of the best places in the city for a day hike.

A narrated tram shuttles visitors up and down the lower canyon throughout the day, and, between April and November (but not July or Aug), there are moonlight tram rides three times each month (usually the nights before the full moon). The Bear Canyon tram is used by hikers heading to the picturesque Seven Falls, which are at the end of a 2.5-mile trail and are our favorite destination within this recreation area.

Another good way to experience the park is by bicycling up the paved road during the limited hours when bikes are allowed: Sunday through Tuesday, Thursday, and Friday before 9am and after 5pm. This is a strenuous uphill ride for most of the way, but the scenery is beautiful.

5900 N. Sabino Canyon Rd. © 520/749-8700, 520/749-2861 for shuttle information, or 520/749-2327 for moonlight shuttle reservations. www.fs.fed.us/r3/Coronado. Parking $5. Sabino Canyon tram ride $7.50 adults, $3 children 3–12; Bear Canyon tram ride $3 adults, $1 children 3–12. Park daily dawn–dusk. Sabino Canyon tram rides daily 9am–4:30pm; Bear Canyon tram rides daily 9am–4pm (both trams more limited in summer). Take Grant Rd. east to Tanque Verde Rd., continuing east; at Sabino Canyon Rd., turn north and watch for the sign.

Saguaro National Park ★★★   Saguaro cacti are the quintessential symbol of the American desert and occur naturally only here in the Sonoran Desert. Sensitive to fire and frost and exceedingly slow to mature, these massive, treelike cacti grow in great profusion around Tucson but have long been threatened by both development and plant collectors. In 1933, to protect these desert giants, the federal government set aside two large tracts of land as a saguaro preserve. This preserve eventually became Saguaro National Park. The two units of the park, one on the east side of the city (Rincon Mountain District) and one on the west (Tucson Mountain District), preserve not only dense stands of saguaros, but also the many other wild inhabitants of this part of the Sonoran Desert. Both units have loop roads, nature trails, hiking trails, and picnic grounds.

The west unit of the park, because of its proximity to both the Arizona–Sonora Desert Museum and Old Tucson Studios, is the more popular area to visit (and your best choice if you're trying to do a lot in a short amount of time). This also happens to be where you'll see the most impressive stands of saguaros. Coyotes, foxes, squirrels, and javelinas all eat the sweet fruit of the saguaro, and near the west unit's Red Hills Information Center is a water hole that attracts these and other wild animals, which you're most likely to see at dawn and dusk. Be sure to take the scenic Bajada Loop Drive, where you'll find good views and several hiking trails (the Hugh Morris Trail involves a long, steep climb, but great views are the reward). To reach the west unit of the park, follow Speedway Boulevard west from downtown Tucson (it becomes Gates Pass Blvd.).

The east section of the park contains an older area of saguaro "forest" at the foot of the Rincon Mountains. This section is popular with hikers because most of it has no roads. It has a visitor center, a loop scenic drive, a picnic area, and a trail open to mountain bikes (the paved loop drive is a great road-bike ride). To reach the east unit of the park, take Speedway Boulevard east, then head south on Freeman Road to Old Spanish Trail.

Rincon Mountain District visitor center: 3693 S. Old Spanish Trail. ℂ 520/733-5153. Tucson Mountain District visitor center: 2700 N. Kinney Rd. ℂ 520/733-5158. www.nps.gov/sagu. Entry fee $10 per car, $5 per hiker or biker. Daily 7am–sunset; visitor centers daily 9am–5pm; open to hikers 24 hr. a day. Visitor centers closed Christmas.

Tohono Chul Park ★★ Although this park is fairly small, it provides an excellent introduction to the plant and animal life of the desert. You'll see a forest of cholla cacti as well as a garden of small and complex pincushion cacti. From mid-February to April, the wildflower displays here are gorgeous (if enough rain has fallen in the previous months). The park also includes an ethnobotanical garden; a garden for children that encourages them to touch, listen, and smell; a demonstration garden; natural areas; an exhibit house for art displays; a tearoom (p. 367) that's great for breakfast, lunch, or afternoon tea; and two very good gift shops. Park docents lead guided tours throughout the day, and there are also bird walks and many other special events throughout the cooler months of the year.

7366 N. Paseo del Norte (off Ina Rd. west of the intersection with Oracle Rd.). ℂ 520/742-6455. www.tohonochulpark. org. Admission $5 adults, $4 seniors, $3 students, $2 children ages 5–12; free for all on 1st Tues of every month. Grounds daily 8am–5pm (visitors may remain until sunset). Exhibit house daily 9am–5pm. Tearoom daily 8am–5pm. Buildings closed New Year's Day, July 4th, Thanksgiving, and Christmas (free admission to grounds on these days).

Moments Sunset on Signal Hill

A hike to Signal Hill, located off the Bajada Loop Drive in Saguaro National Park's west unit and only a quarter-mile walk from the parking area, will reward you with not only a grand sunset vista away from the crowds at Gates Pass, but also the sight of dozens of petroglyphs.

Tucson Botanical Gardens Set amid residential neighborhoods in midtown Tucson, these gardens are an oasis of greenery and, though small, are well worth a visit if you're interested in desert plant life, landscaping, or gardening. On the 5½-acre grounds are several small gardens that not only have visual appeal but are also historical and educational. The sensory garden stimulates all five senses, while in another garden traditional Southwestern crops are grown. Also here are a bird garden, a greenhouse with "useful" plants from tropical forests, and a gift shop.

2150 N. Alvernon Way. (🕐 520/326-9686. www.tucsonbotanical.org. Admission $5 adults, $2.50 children 6–12. Daily 8:30am–4:30pm. Closed New Year's Day, July 4th, Thanksgiving, and Christmas. Bus: 11.

HISTORIC ATTRACTIONS BOTH REAL & REEL

Mission San Xavier del Bac ★ Called the White Dove of the Desert, Mission San Xavier de Bac, an active Roman Catholic church serving the San Xavier Indian Reservation, is a blindingly white adobe building that rises from a sere, brown landscape. Considered the finest example of mission architecture in the Southwest, the beautiful church was built between 1783 and 1797 and incorporates Moorish, Byzantine, and Mexican Renaissance architectural styles. However, the church was never actually completed, which becomes apparent when the two bell towers are compared. One is topped with a dome, while the other has none.

The mission underwent an extensive restoration within the past decade, and much of the elaborate interior has taken on a new luster. Restored murals cover the walls, and behind the altar are colorful and elaborate decorations. To the left of the main altar, in a glass sarcophagus, is a statue of St. Francis Xavier, the mission's patron saint, who is believed to answer the prayers of the faithful. A visit to San Xavier's little museum provides a bit of historical perspective and a chance to explore more of the mission. To the east of the church, atop a small hill, you'll find not only an interesting view of the church but also a replica of the famous grotto in Lourdes, France. There are often food stalls selling fry bread in the parking lot in front of the church.

1950 W. San Xavier Rd. (🕐 520/294-2624. www.sanxaviermission.org. Free admission; donations accepted. Daily 7am–5pm. Take I-19 south 9 miles to Exit 92 and turn right.

Old Tucson Studios ★★ *Kids* Despite the name, this is not the historic location of the old city of Tucson—it's a Western town originally built as the set for the 1939 movie *Arizona*. In the years since, Old Tucson has been used during the filming of John Wayne's *Rio Lobo, Rio Bravo,* and *El Dorado;* Clint Eastwood's *The Outlaw Josey Wales;* Kirk Douglas's *Gunfight at the O.K. Corral;* Paul Newman's *The Life and Times of Judge Roy Bean;* and, more recently, *Tombstone* and *Geronimo.*

Today, Old Tucson is far more than just a movie set. In addition to serving as a site for film, TV, and advertising productions (call ahead to find out if any filming is scheduled), it has become a Wild West theme park with diverse family-oriented activities and entertainment. Throughout the day, there are staged shootouts in the streets, stunt demonstrations, a cancan musical revue, and other performances. Train rides, horseback and stagecoach rides, kiddie rides, restaurants, and gift shops round out the experience.

201 S. Kinney Rd. (🕐 520/883-0100. www.oldtucson.com. Admission $15 adults, $9.45 children 4–11. Daily 10am–6pm. Closed Thanksgiving and Christmas. Take Speedway Blvd. west, continuing in the same direction when it becomes Gates Pass Blvd., and turn left on S. Kinney Rd.

ART MUSEUMS

Center for Creative Photography Have you ever wished you could see an original Ansel Adams print up close, or perhaps an Edward Weston or a Richard Avedon?

You can at the Center for Creative Photography. Originally conceived by Ansel Adams, the center now holds more than 500,000 negatives, 200,000 study prints, and 60,000 master prints by more than 2,000 of the world's best photographers, making it one of the best and largest collections in the world. The center mounts excellent exhibits year-round and is also a research facility that preserves the photographic archives of various photographers, including Adams. To view images from the archives, you must make an appointment.

University of Arizona campus, 1030 N. Olive Rd. (east of Park Ave. and Speedway Blvd.). © **520/621-7968.** www.creativephotography.org. Admission by donation. Mon–Fri 9am–5pm; Sat–Sun noon–5pm. Bus: 1, 4, or 5.

De Grazia Gallery in the Sun   Southwestern artist Ettore "Ted" De Grazia was a Tucson favorite son, and his home, a sprawling, funky adobe building in the foothills, is a city landmark and now serves as a museum for this prolific artist. De Grazia is said to be the most reproduced artist in the world because many of his images of big-eyed children were used as greeting cards during the 1950s and 1960s. Today De Grazia's images tend to seem trite and maudlin, but in his day he was a very successful artist. This gallery is packed with original paintings, so it may surprise you to learn that, near the end of his life, De Grazia burned several hundred thousand dollars worth of his paintings in a protest of IRS inheritance taxes. The gift shop has lots of reproductions and other objects with De Grazia images.

6300 N. Swan Rd. © **800/545-2185** or 520/299-9191. degrazia.org. Free admission. Daily 10am–3:45pm.

Tucson Museum of Art & Historic Block ⭐   The Tucson Museum of Art is in a modern building surrounded by historic adobes and a spacious plaza frequently used to display sculptures. The *Palice Pavilion—Art of the Americas* exhibit is a highlight of the museum and is not to be missed. This exhibit consists of a large collection of pre-Columbian art that represents 3,000 years of life in Mexico and Central and South America. This collection is housed in the historic Stevens/Duffield House, which also contains Spanish colonial artifacts and Latin American folk art. The noteworthy Goodman Pavilion of Western Art comprises an extensive collection that depicts cowboys, horses, and the wide-open spaces of the American West. The museum has also preserved five historic homes on this same block, all open to the public. See "History Museums & Landmark Buildings," below, for details.

140 N. Main Ave. © **520/624-2333.** www.tucsonarts.com. Admission $5 adults, $4 seniors, $2 students, free for children 12 and under; free on 1st Sun of each month. Tues–Sat 10am–4pm; Sun noon–4pm. Closed all national holidays. All downtown-bound buses.

The University of Arizona Museum of Art ⭐⭐   With European and American works from the Renaissance to the 20th century, this collection is even more extensive

---

(*Finds* **The Conley Museum of the West**

Little more than a room at the back of the **Mark Sublette Medicine Man Gallery,** 7000 E. Tanque Verde Rd. (© **520/722-7798**), the **Conley Museum of the West** packs a lot into a tiny space. You can see not only 19th- and 20th-century pieces by some of the biggest names in Western art, but also Indian artifacts and art, Spanish colonial antiquities, and historical maps dating back to 1739. This place is a must for fans of Western art. The museum is open Monday through Saturday from 10am to 5pm and Sunday from 1 to 4pm. Admission is free.

and diverse than that of the Tucson Museum of Art. Tintoretto, Rembrandt, Picasso, O'Keeffe, Warhol, and Rothko are all represented. Another attraction, the *Retablo of Ciudad Rodrigo,* consists of 26 paintings from 15th-century Spain that were originally placed above a cathedral altar. The museum also has an extensive collection of 20th-century sculpture that includes more than 60 clay and plaster models and sketches by Jacques Lipchitz.

University of Arizona campus, Park Ave. and Speedway Blvd. © 520/621-7567. http://artmuseum.arizona.edu. Free admission. Tues–Fri 9am–5pm; Sat–Sun noon–4pm. Closed major holidays. Bus: 1, 4, or 5.

HISTORY MUSEUMS & LANDMARK BUILDINGS

In addition to the attractions listed below, downtown Tucson has a couple of historic neighborhoods that are described in the box "Architectural Highlights," below. Among the more interesting buildings are those maintained by the Tucson Museum of Art and located on the block surrounding the museum. A map and brochures are available at the museum's front desk, and free (with admission to the museum) guided tours of the historic block and Corbett House are available.

Arizona Historical Society Downtown Museum If you want to learn more about the history of Tucson, this is the museum to visit. Exhibits cover Spanish presidio days, American army days, merchants, and schools. Through the use of artifacts and old photos, these exhibits help bring the city's past to life. One of the most curious exhibits focuses on the gangster John Dillinger, who was arrested here in Tucson.

140 N. Stone Ave. © 520/770-1473. Admission $3 adults, $2 seniors and students ages 12–18, free for children under 12; free on 1st Fri of each month. Mon–Fri 10am–4pm. Closed major holidays. All downtown-bound buses.

Arizona Historical Society Second Street Museum As the state's oldest historical museum, this repository of all things Arizonan is a treasure trove for the history buff. If you've never explored a real mine, you can do the next best thing by exploring the museum's full-scale reproduction of an underground mine tunnel. You'll see an assayer's office, miner's tent, stamp mill, and blacksmith's shop in the mining exhibit. A transportation exhibit displays stagecoaches and the horseless carriages that revolutionized life in the Southwest, while temporary exhibits give a pretty good idea of what it was like back then.

949 E. Second St. © 520/628-5774. Admission $5 adults, $4 seniors and students ages 12–18, free for children under 12; free for all on the 1st Sat of each month. Mon–Sat 10am–4pm. Closed major holidays. Bus: 1 or 6.

Arizona State Museum This museum, which is the oldest anthropological museum in the Southwest, houses *Paths of Life: American Indians of the Southwest,* one of the state's most interesting exhibits on prehistoric and contemporary Native American cultures of the Southwest. The exhibit focuses on 10 different tribes from around the Southwest and northern Mexico, not only displaying a wide range of artifacts but also exploring the lifestyles and cultural traditions of Indians living in the region today. In addition, the museum showcases a collection of some 20,000 ceramic pieces. This pottery spans 2,000 years of life in the desert Southwest.

University of Arizona campus, 1013 E. University Blvd. at Park Ave. © 520/621-6302. www.statemuseum.arizona. edu. Admission $3 suggested donation. Mon–Sat 10am–5pm; Sun noon–5pm. Closed major holidays. Bus: 1 or 6.

Fort Lowell Museum Located in Fort Lowell Park on the site of a cavalry outpost that was in operation between 1873 and 1891, this museum chronicles the history of life at the fort. Some of the ruins of the original fort can still be seen. Before it was a fort, this site was a Hohokam village, and artifacts uncovered from archaeological digs are also on display. Renowned medical researcher Walter Reed, who discovered how yellow fever is transmitted, served as base surgeon here in 1876. A display focusing on medical facilities at the fort explains that, despite Hollywood's version of history, injury from Indian attacks was not the biggest medical problem during the wars with the Apaches.

2900 N. Craycroft Rd. ℭ 520/885-3832. Admission $3 adults, $2 seniors and students ages 12–18, free for children under 12. Wed–Sat 10am–4pm. Closed major holidays. Bus: 34.

Sosa-Carillo-Frémont House Museum   Located on the shady grounds of the modern Tucson Convention Center, the Sosa-Carillo-Frémont House is a classic example of Sonoran-style adobe architecture. Originally built in the 1870s, the house was rented in 1878 to territorial governor John Charles Frémont, who had led a distinguished military career as an explorer of the West. The building has been restored in the style of this period, with the living room and bedrooms opening off a large central hall known as a *zaguán*. All rooms are decorated with period antiques. The flat roof is made of pine beams called *vigas,* covered with saguaro cactus ribs, and topped by a layer of hard-packed mud. From November to March, this museum offers four different tours of historic Tucson ($10 for adults, free for children under 12) on Thursday and Saturday mornings at 10am.

151 S. Granada Ave. (in the Tucson Convention Center complex). ℭ 520/622-0956. Admission $3 adults, $2 seniors and students ages 12–18, free for children under 12; free on 1st Sat of each month. Wed–Sat 10am–4pm. Closed major holidays. All downtown-bound buses.

SCIENCE & TECHNOLOGY MUSEUMS

Biosphere 2 *Overrated*   For 2 years, beginning in September 1991, four men and four women were locked inside this airtight, 3-acre greenhouse in the desert 35 miles north of Tucson near the town of Oracle. During their tenure in Biosphere 2, they conducted experiments on how the earth, basically a giant greenhouse, manages to support all the planet's life forms. Today there are no longer any people living in Biosphere 2, and the former research facility is operated more as a tourist attraction than as a science center. Tours take visitors inside the giant greenhouse and into the mechanisms that helped keep this sealed environment going for 2 years. The strangest sight is the giant "lung" that allowed for the expansion and contraction of the air within Biosphere 2. Although the building, which sits in the middle of desert hill country, is an impressive sight, the tours are something of a letdown.

Ariz. 77, mile marker 96.5. ℭ 520/838-6200. www.bio2.com. Admission $20 ages 13 and older, $13 children 6–12. Daily 9am–4pm. Closed Thanksgiving and Christmas. Take Oracle Rd. north out of Tucson and continue north on Ariz. 77 until you see the sign.

Value **Passport to Tucson**

The **Tucson Attractions Passport** is a great way to save money on admissions to many of the city's top attractions. The passport, available at the downtown Visitors Center (100 S. Church St.; ℭ 800/638-8350 or www.visittucson.org), costs $15 and gets you two-for-one admissions to the Arizona–Sonora Desert Museum, Old Tucson Studios, Biosphere 2, the Pima Air & Space Museum, Tohono Chul Park, the Tucson Museum of Art, Kartchner Caverns, and many other attractions.

Architectural Highlights

Tucson has a long and varied cultural history, which is most easily seen by strolling through the downtown historic neighborhoods. Start your explorations in El Presidio Historic District, which is named for the Presidio of San Augustín del Tucson (1775), the Spanish garrison built here to protect the San Xavier del Bac Mission from the Apaches. For many years the presidio was the heart of Tucson, and although no original buildings are still standing, there are numerous structures from the mid–19th century. Some of our favorites are listed below.

- **La Casa Cordova,** at 175 N. Meyer Ave., dates from about 1848 and is one of the oldest buildings in Tucson. It's been restored to look as it might have in the late 1800s. Each year from November to March, this building exhibits a very elaborate *nacimiento,* a Mexican folk-art nativity scene.
- **Corbett House,** a restored Mission Revival–style building located at 180 N. Main Ave., was built in 1907. The house, which is set back behind a green lawn, is strikingly different from the older, Sonoran-style adobe homes on this block. On Tuesdays at 11am, the Tucson Museum of Art offers a guided tour.
- **Fish House,** at 120 N. Main Ave., was built in 1867 on the site of old Mexican barracks. Named for Edward Nye Fish, a local merchant, it now houses the art museum's Western-art collection.
- **Julius Kruttschnidt House,** at 297 N. Main Ave., dates from 1886 and now houses El Presidio Bed & Breakfast Inn (p. 349). Victorian trappings,

Flandrau Science Center & Planetarium   Located on the University of Arizona campus, Flandrau Planetarium is the most convenient place in Arizona to do a little stargazing through a professional telescope. As such, it should be on the itinerary of anyone coming to Tucson (unless it happens to be cloudy). The planetarium theater presents a variety of programs on the stars, and the exhibit halls contain a large mineral collection and hands-on science exhibits. However, the best reason to visit is to gaze through the planetarium's 16-inch telescope.

University of Arizona campus, 1601 E. University Blvd., at Cherry Ave. ℰ 520/621-STAR. www.flandrau.org. Admission to exhibits $3 adults, $2 children 3–13. Telescope viewing free. Planetarium $4.50–$5.50 adults, $4.50 seniors, $3.75–$4 children 3–13; children under 3 not admitted. Mon–Wed 9am–5pm; Thurs–Sat 9am–5pm and 7–9pm; Sun 1–5pm. Telescope viewing (weather permitting) Aug 15–May 15 Wed–Sat 6:40–10pm; May 16–Aug 14 Wed–Sat 7:30–10pm. Closed major holidays. Bus: 3, 9, or 15.

Pima Air & Space Museum   Located just south of Davis Monthan Air Force Base, the Pima Air & Space Museum houses one of the largest collections of historic aircraft in the world. On display are more than 250 aircraft, including an X-15 (the world's fastest aircraft), an SR-71 Blackbird, several Russian MiGs, a "Superguppy," and a B-17G "Flying Fortress." Tours are available.

The museum also offers guided tours of Davis Monthan's AMARC (Arizona Maintenance and Regeneration Center) facility, which goes by the name of the Boneyard.

including a long veranda, disguise the adobe origins of this unique and beautifully restored home.

- **Steinfeld House,** at 300 N. Main Ave., was built in 1900 in California Mission Revival style and was designed by Henry Trost, Tucson's most noted architect. It served as the original Owl's Club, a gentlemen's club for some of Tucson's most eligible turn-of-the-20th-century bachelors.

- **Owl's Club Mansion,** at 378 N. Main Ave., was built in 1902 and designed by Henry Trost in the Mission Revival style, albeit with a great deal of ornamentation. It replaced the Steinfeld House as home to the bachelors of the Owl's Club.

- Built in 1928, the **Pima County Courthouse,** located at 115 N. Church Ave., incorporates Moorish, Spanish, and Southwestern architectural features, including a colorful tiled dome.

- **Sosa-Carillo-Frémont House,** located at 151 S. Granada Ave., was built in the 1850s and later served as the home of territorial governor John C. Frémont. The restored building is open to the public and is furnished in the style of the period.

- **The Barrio Histórico District** is another worthwhile area to explore, especially the northern (and more restored) section. With 150 adobe row houses, this neighborhood contains the largest collection of 19th-century Sonoran-style adobe buildings in the United States.

Here, thousands of mothballed planes are lined up in neat rows under the Arizona sun. Tours last just under an hour and cost $6 for adults and $3 for children 12 and under. Tour reservations (© **520/618-4800**) should be made about a week in advance.

6000 E. Valencia Rd. © 520/574-0462. www.pimaair.org. Admission $9.75–$12 adults, $8.75–$9.75 seniors and military, $6–$8 children 7–12. Daily 9am–5pm. Closed Thanksgiving and Christmas. Take the Valencia Rd. exit from I-10 and drive east 2 miles to the museum.

Titan Missile Museum ★   If you've ever wondered what it would be like to have your finger on the button of a nuclear missile, here's your opportunity to find out. This deactivated intercontinental ballistic missile (ICBM) silo is now a museum—and is the only museum in the country that allows visitors to descend into a former missile silo. The huge Titan missile on display is still a terrifying sight even without its nuclear warhead. The guided tours do a great job of explaining not only the ICBM system but also what life was like for the people who worked here. Operated by the Pima Air & Space Museum, this museum is located 25 miles south of Tucson near the retirement community of Green Valley.

1580 W. Duval Mine Rd., Sahuarita (Exit 69 off I-19). © 520/625-7736. Admission $8.50 adults, $7.50 seniors, $5 children 7–12. Daily 9am–5pm. Closed Thanksgiving and Christmas. Take I-19 south to Green Valley; take Exit 69 west a half-mile to main entrance.

Kids All Aboard!

If you've got kids who idolize Thomas the Tank Engine, then you better schedule your Tucson visit for the second or fourth Sunday of the month. On those days (with a few exceptions), the **Gadsden-Pacific Division Toy Train Operating Museum,** 3975 N. Miller Ave. (© **520/888-2222**), sends out little engines that think they can. The trains chug around a variety of layouts built in different model railroad gauges. The museum is open from 12:30 to 4:30pm on the 2 days each month that it is open. Admission is free. In July and August, the museum is closed.

ESPECIALLY FOR KIDS

In addition to the museum listed below, two of the greatest places to take kids in the Tucson area are the Arizona–Sonora Desert Museum and Old Tucson Studios. Kids will also get a kick out of the Sabino Canyon tram ride, Flandrau Science Center & Planetarium, and the Pima Air & Space Museum. All are described in detail earlier in this chapter.

They'll also enjoy **Trail Dust Town,** 6541 E. Tanque Verde Rd. (© **520/296-4551**), a Wild West–themed shopping and dining center. It has a full-size carousel, a scaled-down train to ride, shootout shows, and miniature golf next door. Basically, it's a sort of scaled-down Old Tucson. Right next door is **Golf n' Stuff,** 6503 E. Tanque Verde Rd. (© **520/296-2366**), with miniature golf, bumper boats, go-karts, batting cages, laser tag, a climbing wall, and a video-game arcade.

Tucson Children's Museum   This museum, in the historic Carnegie Library in downtown Tucson, is filled with fun and educational hands-on activities. Exhibits include a bakery and farmers' market and an electricity gallery. Expect to find such perennial kid favorites as a firetruck, a police motorcycle, and dinosaur sculptures. There are featured activities daily.

200 S. Sixth Ave. © 520/792-9985. www.tucsonchildrensmuseum.org. Admission $5.50 adults, $4.50 seniors, $3.50 children 2–16; free 1 day each month (call for date). Tues–Sat 10am–5pm; Sun noon–5pm. Closed Thanksgiving and Christmas. All downtown-bound buses.

6 Organized Tours

For a look at a completely different sort of excavation, head south from Tucson 15 miles to the **ASARCO Mineral Discovery Center,** 1421 W. Pima Mine Rd., Sahuarita (© **520/625-7513;** www.mineraldiscovery.com), where you can tour a huge open-pit copper mine and learn about copper mining past and present. The center is open Tuesday through Saturday from 9am to 5pm; admission is free. One-hour mine tours are $6 for adults, $5 for seniors, and $4 for children 5 to 12. To get here, drive south from Tucson on I-19 and take Exit 80. You might want to combine this tour with a visit to the nearby Titan Missile Museum.

Want to taste raw cactus, learn about cholla-extraction devices, and hold a live tarantula or snake? Call **Sunshine Jeep Tours** (© **520/742-1943;** www.sunshine jeeptours.com), which has a two-person minimum and charges $130 for the first two people and then, after the minimum is met, charges $48 for adults, $36 for children

11 to 15, and $24 for children 6 to 10. On these tours, you'll head out across a private ranch northwest of Tucson and pass through some of the densest stands of saguaro cacti in the state.

Balloon America (© 520/299-7744; www.balloonridesusa.com) offers flights over the desert ($225) or a more adventurous trip over the foothills of the Santa Catalina Mountains ($475). The ballooning season runs October through June. **Fleur de Tucson Balloon Tours** (© 520/529-1025; www.fleurdetucson.net) offers rides over the Tucson Mountains, Saguaro National Park, and the Avra Valley. Rates are $160 to $220 per person, including brunch or hors d'oeuvres and a champagne toast.

7 Getting Outside

BICYCLING   Tucson is one of the best bicycling cities in the country, and the dirt roads and trails of the surrounding national forest and desert are perfect for mountain biking. Bikes can be rented at **Fair Wheel Bikes,** 1110 E. Sixth St. (© 520/884-9018), and go for $30 per day for road bikes and $20 per day for mountain bikes.

If you'd rather confine your pedaling to paved surfaces, there are some great options around town. The number one choice in town for cyclists in halfway decent shape is the road up **Sabino Canyon** (p. 372). Keep in mind, however, that bicycles are allowed on this road only 5 days a week and then only before 9am and after 5pm (the road is closed to bikes all day Wed and Sat). For a much easier ride, try the **Rillito River Park path,** which currently has a 1-mile paved section between Swan and Craycroft roads and a 6-mile paved section between Campbell Avenue and I-10. The trail parallels River Road and the usually dry bed of the Rillito River, and if you've got knobby tires, you can link the two paved sections or continue west past La Cholla Road after the pavement ends. Another option close to downtown is the 7-mile **Santa Cruz River Park path,** which runs along both sides of the usually dry Santa Cruz River and extends from West Grant Road to Irvington Road.

If mountain biking is more your speed, head to the west unit of Saguaro National Park (p. 372) and ride the 6-mile **Bajada Loop Drive,** an easy and scenic dirt-road loop through forests of saguaros. You can turn this into a 12-mile ride (half on paved road) by starting at the Red Hills Visitor Center.

BIRD-WATCHING   Southern Arizona has some of the best bird-watching in the country, and although the best spots are south of Tucson, there are a few places around the city that birders will enjoy seeking out. Call the **Tucson Audubon Society's Bird Report** (© 520/798-1005) to find out which birds have been spotted lately.

The year-round warm springs at **Roy P. Drachman Agua Caliente Park,** 12325 Roger Rd. (off N. Soldier Trail) are a magnet for dozens of species, including waterfowl, great blue herons, black phoebes, soras, and vermilion flycatchers. To find the park, follow Tanque Verde Road east 6 miles from the intersection with Sabino Canyon Road and turn left onto Soldier Trail. Watch for signs.

Other good places include **Sabino Canyon Recreation Area** (p. 372), the path to the waterfall at **Loews Ventana Canyon Resort** (p. 352), and the **Rillito River path** between Craycroft and Swan roads.

The very best area for bird-watching is **Madera Canyon National Forest Recreation Area** ★ (© 520/281-2296), about 40 miles south of the city in the Coronado National Forest. Avid birders flock to this canyon from around the country in hopes of spotting more than a dozen species of hummingbirds, an equal number of flycatchers, warblers, tanagers, buntings, grosbeaks, and many rare birds not found in any other state. If you're heading out for the day, arrive early—parking is very limited. To reach Madera Canyon, take the Continental Road/Madera Canyon exit off I-19; from the exit, it's another 12 miles southeast. The canyon is open daily from dawn to dusk for day use; there is a $5 day-use fee. There's also a campground ($5 per night).

GOLF   Although there aren't quite as many golf courses in Tucson as in Phoenix, this is still a golfer's town. For last-minute tee-time reservations, contact **Standby Golf** (© **800/655-5345;** www.discountteetimes.com). No fee is charged for this service.

In addition to the public and municipal links, there are numerous resort courses that allow nonguests to play. Perhaps the most famous of these are the two 18-hole courses at **Ventana Canyon Golf and Racquet Club** ✿, 6200 N. Clubhouse Lane (© **520/577-4015;** www.ventanacanyonclub.com). These Tom Fazio–designed courses offer challenging desert target–style play that is nearly legendary. The 3rd hole on the Mountain Course is one of the most photographed holes in the West. Greens fees are $109 to $209 in winter.

As famous as the Ventana Canyon courses are, it's the 27-hole **Omni Tucson National Golf Resort and Spa** ✿, 2727 W. Club Dr. (© **520/575-7540;** www. tucsonnational.com), a traditional course, that is perhaps more familiar to golfers due to the fact that it is the site of the annual Tucson Open. If you are not staying at the resort, greens fees are $200 in winter, $80 in summer.

El Conquistador Country Club, 10555 N. La Cañada Dr., Oro Valley (© **520/ 544-1800;** www.elconquistadorcc.com), with two 18-hole courses and a 9-hole course, offers stunning (and very distracting) views of the Santa Catalina Mountains. Greens fees are $90 to $120 in winter.

At **Starr Pass Country Club & Spa,** 3645 W. Starr Pass Blvd. (© **800/503-2898** or 520/670-0300; www.starrpasstucson.com), the fairways play up to the narrow Starr Pass, which was once a stagecoach route. Greens fees are $185 in winter.

There are many public courses around town. The **Arizona National,** 9777 E. Sabino Greens Dr. (© **520/749-3636;** www.arizonanationalgolfclub.com), incorporates stands of cacti and rocky outcroppings into the course layout. Greens fees are $135 to $165 in winter. **The Golf Club at Vistoso,** 955 W. Vistoso Highlands Dr. (© **877/548-1110** or 520/797-9900; www.vistosogolf.com), has a championship desert course, with fees of $99 to $159 in winter. **Heritage Highlands Golf & Country Club,** 4949 W. Heritage Club Blvd., Marana (© **520/579-7000;** www. heritagehighlands.com), is a championship desert course at the foot of the Tortolita Mountains; greens fees are $115 in winter.

Tucson Parks and Recreation operates five municipal golf courses, of which the **Randolph North** and **Dell Urich,** 600 S. Alvernon Way (© **520/791-4161**), are the premier courses. The former has been the site of Tucson's LPGA tournament. Greens fees for 18 holes at these two courses are $39 in winter. Other municipal courses include **El Rio,** 1400 W. Speedway Blvd. (© **520/791-4229**); **Silverbell,** 3600 N. Silverbell Rd. (© **520/791-5235**); and **Fred Enke,** 8251 E. Irvington Rd. (© **520/ 791-2539**). This latter course is the city's only desert-style golf course. Greens fees for 18 holes at these three courses are $34 in winter. For general information and tee-time reservations for any of the municipal courses, visit **www.tucsoncitygolf.com.**

HIKING   Tucson is nearly surrounded by mountains, most of which are protected as city and state parks, national forest, or national park, and within these public areas are hundreds of miles of hiking trails.

Saguaro National Park (© 520/733-5153) flanks Tucson on both the east and west with units accessible off Old Spanish Trail east of Tucson and past the end of Speedway Boulevard west of the city. In these areas, you can observe Sonoran Desert vegetation and wildlife and hike among the huge saguaro cacti for which the park is named. For saguaro-spotting, the west unit is the better choice. See p. 372 for details.

Tucson Mountain Park, at the west end of Speedway Boulevard, is adjacent to Saguaro National Park and preserves a similar landscape. The parking area at Gates Pass, on Speedway, is a favorite sunset spot.

Sabino Canyon (p. 372), off Sabino Canyon Road, is one of Tucson's best hiking areas, but is also the city's most popular recreation area. A cold mountain stream here cascades over waterfalls and forms pools that make great swimming holes. The 5-mile round-trip **Seven Falls Trail,** which follows Bear Canyon deep into the mountains, is the most popular hike in the recreation area. You can take a tram to the trail head or add extra miles by hiking from the main parking lot.

With the city limits pushing right out to the boundary of the Coronado National Forest, there are some very convenient hiking options in Tucson's northern foothills. The **Ventana Canyon Trail** begins at a parking area adjacent to the Loews Ventana Canyon Resort (off Sunrise Dr. west of Sabino Canyon Rd.) and leads into the Ventana Canyon Wilderness. A few miles west, there's the **Finger Rock Trail,** which starts at the top of the section of Alvernon Road accessed from Skyline Drive. There are actually a couple of trails starting here, so you can hike for miles into the desert. Over near the Westward Look Resort is the **Pima Canyon Trail,** which leads into the Ventana Canyon Wilderness and is reached off Ina Road just east of Oracle Road. Both of these trails provide classic desert canyon hikes of whatever length you feel like hiking (a dam at 3 miles on the latter trail makes a good turnaround point). Just south of the Hilton Tucson El Conquistador Golf & Tennis Resort, you'll find the **Linda Vista Trail,** which begins just off Oracle Road on Linda Vista Boulevard. This trail lies at the foot of Pusch Ridge and winds up through dense stands of prickly-pear cactus. Higher up on the trail, there are some large saguaros. Because this trail is shaded by Pusch Ridge in the morning, it's a good choice for a morning hike on a day that's going to be hot.

Catalina State Park, 11570 N. Oracle Rd. (© 520/628-5798), is set on the rugged northwest face of the Santa Catalina Mountains, between 2,500 and 3,000 feet high. Hiking trails here lead into the Pusch Ridge Wilderness; however, the park's best day hike is the 5.5-mile round-trip to **Romero Pools,** where small natural pools of water set amid the rocks are a refreshing destination on a hot day (expect plenty of other people on a weekend). This hike involves about 1,000 feet of elevation gain. Admission to the park is $6 per vehicle ($3 between Memorial Day and Labor Day). There are horseback-riding stables adjacent to the park, and within the park is an ancient Hohokam ruin.

One of the reasons Tucson is such a livable city is the presence of the cool (and, in winter, snow-covered) pine forests of 8,250-foot Mount Lemmon. Within the **Mount Lemmon Recreation Area,** at the end of the Catalina Highway, are many miles of trails, and the hearty hiker can even set out from down in the lowland desert and hike up into the alpine forests. For a more leisurely excursion, drive up onto the mountain to start your hike. In the winter, there can be snow atop Mount Lemmon. There is a $5-per-vehicle charge to use any of the sites within this recreation area. Even if you only plan to pull off at a roadside parking spot and ogle the view of the desert far below, you'll need to stop at the roadside ticket kiosk at the base of the mountain and pay your fee. For more information, contact the **Coronado National Forest Santa Catalina Ranger District,** 5700 N. Sabino Canyon Rd. (© **520/749-8700**).

HORSEBACK RIDING   In addition to renting horses and providing guided trail rides, some of the stables below offer sunset rides with cookouts. Reservations are a good idea. You can also opt to stay at a guest ranch and do as much riding as your muscles can stand.

Pusch Ridge Stables, 13700 N. Oracle Rd. (© **520/825-1664**), is adjacent to Catalina State Park and Coronado National Forest. Rates are $25 for 1 hour, $40 for 2 hours, and $30 for a sunset ride.

Over on the east side of Tucson, there's **Spanish Trail Outfitters** (© **520/749-0167**), which leads rides into the foothills of the Santa Catalina Mountains off Sabino Canyon Road. Rates are $30 for 1 hour, $50 for 2 hours, and $45 for a sunset ride.

Big Sky Rides (© **520/299-RIDE**) offers horseback rides at several locations around the area, including at Old Tucson Studios. Rates range from $30 for 1 hour to $125 for a full day with lunch. Reservations are requested.

WILDFLOWER-VIEWING   April and May are usually good times to view native wildflowers in the Tucson area. **Saguaro National Park** (p. 372) and **Sabino Canyon** (p. 372) are among the best local spots to see saguaros, other cactus species, and various wildflowers in bloom. Further afield, the wildflower displays at **Picacho Peak State Park** (p. 458), between Tucson and Casa Grande, are the most impressive in the state.

8 Spectator Sports

BASEBALL   The **Colorado Rockies** (© **520/327-9467**) pitch spring-training camp in March at Hi Corbett Field, 3400 E. Camino Campestre, in Reid Park (at South Country Club Rd. and E. 22nd St.). Tickets are $2 to $11. Both the **Chicago White Sox** and the **Arizona Diamondbacks** have their spring-training camps and exhibition games at Tucson Electric Park, 2500 E. Ajo Way (© **866/672-1343** or 520/434-1367), on the south side of the city near the airport. Tickets range from $4 to $15.

Tucson Electric Park is also where you can watch the **Tucson Sidewinders** (© **520/434-1021**; www.tucsonsidewinders.com), the AAA affiliate team of the Arizona Diamondbacks. The season runs April through August; tickets are $5 to $8.

GOLF TOURNAMENTS   The **Chrysler Classic of Tucson** (© **800/882-7660** or 520/571-0400; www.tucsonopen.pgatour.com), Tucson's main PGA tournament, is held in late February at the Omni Tucson National Golf Resort and Spa. Daily tickets are $15.

HORSE/GREYHOUND RACING   **Rillito Park Race Track,** 4502 N. First Ave. (© **520/293-5011**), was the birthplace of both the photo finish and organized quarter-horse and Arabian racing. It has now been restored for quarter-horse and thoroughbred racing. The ponies run on weekends from January to early March, and admission is $2.

9 Day Spas

If you'd prefer a massage to a round on the links, consider spending a few hours at a day spa. While full-service health spas can cost $400 to $500 or more per day, for under $100 you can avail yourself of a spa treatment or two and maybe even get to spend the day lounging by the pool at some exclusive resort. Spas in general still cater primarily to women, but most also have special programs for men.

With a 1-hour treatment at the **Elizabeth Arden Red Door Spa,** at the Westin La Paloma, 3666 E. Sunrise Dr. (© **520/742-7866;** www.reddoorspas.com), you can use the spa's facilities for the day. However, you won't find aerobics classes or a pool here. Spa packages range in price from $189 to $510.

For variety of services and gorgeous location, you just can't beat **The Spa at Loews Ventana Canyon Resort,** 7000 N. Resort Dr. (© **520/529-7830;** www.loewshotels. com). With any 50-minute body treatment, you get use of the spa's facilities and pool and can attend any fitness classes being held that day.

With six locations around the Tucson area, **Gadabout Day Spa** (www.gadabout. com) offers the opportunity to slip a relaxing visit to a spa into a busy schedule. Mud baths, facials, and massages as well as hair and nail services are available. You'll find Gadabout at the following locations: St. Philip's Plaza, 1990 E. River Rd. (© **520/ 577-2000**); 6393 E. Grant Rd. (© **520/885-0000**); 3207 E. Speedway Blvd. (© **520/325-0000**); Sunrise-Kolb, 6960 E. Sunrise Dr. (© **520/615-9700**); and 8303 N. Oracle Rd. (© **520/742-0000**). The sixth location is Gadabout Man, 2951 N. Swan Rd. (© **520/325-3300**).

10 Shopping

Although the Tucson shopping scene is overshadowed by that of Scottsdale and Phoenix, Tucson does provide a very respectable diversity of merchants. Southwestern clothing, food, crafts, furniture, and art abound (and often at reasonable prices), as do shopping centers built in a Southwestern architectural style. You'll find most of the city's large enclosed shopping malls as well as the more tasteful small shopping plazas specializing in boutiques and galleries in the northern foothills.

On Fourth Avenue, between Congress Street and Speedway Boulevard, more than 50 shops, galleries, and restaurants make up the **Fourth Avenue historic shopping and entertainment district.** The buildings here were constructed in the early 1900s, and the proximity to the University of Arizona has helped to keep this district bustling. Many of the shops cater primarily to student needs and interests. Through the underpass at the south end of Fourth Avenue is Congress Street, the heart of the **Downtown Arts District,** where there are still a few art galleries (most, however, have moved to the foothills). Both areas seem to be primarily hangouts for college students.

El Presidio Historic District around the Tucson Museum of Art is the city's center for crafts shops. This area is home to Old Town Artisans and the Tucson Museum of Art museum shop. The city's **"Lost Barrio"** section, on the corner of Southwest Park Avenue and 12th Street (a block off Broadway), is a good place to look for Mexican imports and Southwestern-style home furnishings at good prices.

ANTIQUES & COLLECTIBLES

In addition to the places listed below, a great concentration of antiques shops can be found along Grant Road between Campbell Avenue and Alvernon Way. You can pick up a map of Tucson antiques stores at the American Antique Mall.

American Antique Mall   This antiques mall has 100 dealers and is one of the largest such places in southern Arizona. For sale are all manner of collectibles and a few antiques. 3130 E. Grant Rd. © **520/326-3070.**

Eric Firestone Gallery ⭐⭐   Collectors of Stickley and other Arts and Crafts furniture will not want to miss this impressive gallery, which is located in one of the historic buildings at Joesler Village shopping plaza. In addition to the furniture, there are period paintings and accessories. At Joesler Village, 4425 N. Campbell Ave. © **520/577-7711.** www.ericfirestonegallery.com.

Michael D. Higgins   Located next door to the Eric Firestone Gallery, this little shop specializes in pre-Columbian artifacts, but also carries African, Asian, even ancient Greek and Roman pieces. At Joesler Village, 4429 N. Campbell Ave. © **520/577-8330.** www.mhiggins.com.

Primitive Arts Gallery   This is the best gallery in Tucson for pre-Columbian art, with an eclectic mix of ancient artifacts focusing on ceramics. You'll also find a smattering of other artifacts, from Greek urns to contemporary Argentinean *mate* gourds. At Broadway Village, 3026 E. Broadway. © **520/326-4852.**

ART

Most Tucson galleries have in the past few years abandoned downtown in favor of the foothills and other more affluent suburbs. The current art hot spot is the corner of Campbell Avenue and Skyline Drive, where you'll find **Sanders Galleries** and **Settlers West** (which specialize in Western art) and **Gallery Row El Cortijo** (which has several contemporary art galleries and an upscale restaurant).

Davis Dominguez Gallery   Located just a couple of blocks off Fourth Avenue in downtown Tucson, this huge gallery features some of the best and most creative contemporary art in the city. There are also a couple of other contemporary art galleries on the same block, making this the best place in Tucson to see cutting-edge art. 154 E. Sixth St. © **866/629-9759** or 520/629-9759. www.davisdominguez.com.

El Presidio Gallery   Long one of Tucson's premier galleries, El Presidio deals primarily in traditional and contemporary paintings of the Southwest, and is located in a large, modern space in El Cortijo Arts Annex. Contemporary works tend toward the large and bright and are favorites for decorating foothills homes. At El Cortijo Arts Annex, 3001 E. Skyline Dr. © **520/299-1414.** www.elpresidiogallery.com.

Etherton Gallery   For 25 years, this gallery has been presenting some of the most distinctive art to be found in Tucson, including contemporary and historic photographs. A favorite of museums and serious collectors, Etherton Gallery isn't afraid to present work with strong themes. 135 S. Sixth Ave. © **520/624-7370.** www.ethertongallery.com. Also a smaller location at the Temple of Music and Art, 330 S. Scott Ave. (© **520/624-7370**).

Jane Hamilton Fine Art   This gallery's boldly colored contemporary art really stands out, and much of the artwork reflects a desert aesthetic. At Joesler Village, 1825 E. River Rd., Suite 111. © **800/555-3051** or 520/529-4886. www.janehamiltonfineart.com.

Mark Sublette Medicine Man Gallery ⭐⭐⭐   This gallery has the finest and most tasteful traditional Western art you'll find just about anywhere in Arizona. Artists represented here include Ed Mell and Howard Post, and most of the gallery's artists have received national attention. There's an excellent selection of Native

American crafts as well; see "Native American Art, Crafts & Jewelry," below, for more details. The gallery is also the site of the Conley Museum of the West, a small collection of Western art and old maps. At Santa Fe Sq., 7000 E. Tanque Verde Rd. © 800/422-9382 or 520/722-7798. www.medicinemangallery.com.

Philabaum Contemporary Art Glass   For more than 25 years, this gallery has been exposing Tucson to the latest trends in contemporary art glass. The gallery is full of lovely and colorful pieces by Tom Philabaum and more than 100 other artists from around the country. In St. Philip's Plaza, 4280 N. Campbell Ave., Suite 105. © 520/299-1939. www.philabaumglass.com.

BOOKS

Chain bookstores in the Tucson area include **Barnes & Noble,** 5130 E. Broadway Blvd. (© **520/512-1166**), and 7325 N. La Cholla Blvd., in the Foothills Mall (© **520/742-6402**); and **Borders,** 4235 N. Oracle Rd. (© **520/292-1331**), and 5870 E. Broadway, at the Park Place Mall (© **520/584-0111**).

Bookman's   This big bookstore, housed in a former grocery store, is crammed full of used books and recordings, and has long been a favorite of Tucsonans. This store schedules everything from poetry readings to live music to belly dancing performances and classes. There are other Bookman's at 6230 E. Speedway Blvd. (© **520/748-9555**) and 3733 W. Ina Rd. (© **520/579-0303**). 1930 E. Grant Rd. © **520/325-5767.** www.bookmans.com.

Clues Unlimited   If you forgot to pack your vacation reading, drop by this fun little store. Not only can you shop for the latest Carl Hiassen, but you can say hi to Sophie, the resident pot-bellied pig. Broadway Village, 123 S. Eastbourne St. © **520/326-8533.** www.cluesunlimited.com.

Readers Oasis   A small bookstore, but packed with hand-picked titles of local and general interest. It occasionally has readings and book signings (Tucson author Barbara Kingsolver has been known to do readings here). 3400 E. Speedway Blvd., no. 114. © **520/319-7887.** www.readersoasis.com.

CRAFTS

Details & Green Shoelaces   If you enjoy highly imaginative and colorful crafts with a sense of humor, you'll get a kick out of this place. Unexpected objets d'art turn up in the form of clocks, ceramics, glass, and other media. At Plaza Palomino, 2990 N. Swan Rd. © **520/323-0222.** www.detailsart.com.

Obsidian Gallery   Contemporary crafts by nationally recognized artists fill this gallery. You'll find luminous art glass, unique and daring jewelry, imaginative ceramics, and much more. At St. Philip's Plaza, 4320 N. Campbell Ave. (at River Rd.). © **520/577-3598.** www.obsidian-gallery.com.

Old Town Artisans ⭐   Housed in a restored 1850s adobe building covering an entire city block of El Presidio Historic District, this unique shopping plaza houses half a dozen different shops brimming with traditional and contemporary Southwestern designs. 201 N. Court St. © **800/782-8072** or 520/623-6024. www.oldtownartisans.com.

Tucson Museum of Art Shop   The museum's gift shop offers a colorful and changing selection of Southwestern crafts, mostly by local and regional artists. 140 N. Main Ave. © **520/624-2333.** www.tucsonarts.com.

FASHION

See also the listing for the Beth Friedman Collection under "Jewelry," below. For cowboy and cowgirl attire, see "Western Wear," below.

Maya Palace   This shop features ethnic-inspired but very wearable women's clothing in natural fabrics. The friendly staff helps customers of all ages put together a Southwestern chic look, from casual to dressy. Shops can also be found at El Mercado de Boutiques, 6332 E. Broadway Blvd. (© **520/748-0817**), and at Casas Adobes Plaza, 7057 N. Oracle Rd. (© **520/575-8028**). At Plaza Palomino, 2960 N. Swan Rd. © **520/325-6411**. www.mayapalacetucson.com.

Rochelle K Fine Women's Apparel   With everything from the latest in the little black dress to drapey silks and casual linens, Rochelle K attracts a well-heeled clientele. You'll also find beautiful accessories and jewelry here. At Casas Adobes Plaza, 7039 N. Oracle Rd. © **520/797-2279**. www.rochellek.com.

GIFTS & SOUVENIRS

Discount Agate House ⭐   If you can't make it to Tucson for the annual gem and mineral shows, don't despair. At this cluttered shop, you can pick through shelves crammed with all manner of rare minerals and strange stones. There are even meteorites here. 3401 N. Dodge St. © **520/323-0781**. www.discountagatehouse.net.

Native Seeds/SEARCH ⭐⭐   Gardeners, cooks, and just about anyone in search of an unusual gift will likely be fascinated by this tiny shop, which is operated by a nonprofit organization dedicated to preserving biodiversity. The shelves are full of heirloom beans, corn, chiles, and other seeds from a wide variety of native desert plants. There are also gourds and inexpensive Tarahumara Indian baskets, bottled sauces and salsas made from native plants, and books about native agriculture. 526 N. Fourth Ave. © **520/622-5561**. www.nativeseeds.org.

Picánte Designs   There's a plethora of Hispanic-themed icons and accessories here, including *milagros,* Day of the Dead skeletons, Mexican crosses, jewelry, greeting cards, and folk art from around the world. This is a great place to shop for distinctive south-of-the-border kitschy gifts. 2932 E. Broadway. © **520/320-5699**.

Tohono Chul Museum Shops ⭐   The two shops here are packed with Mexican folk art, nature-themed toys, household items, T-shirts, and books; they make good stops after a visit to the surrounding Tohono Chul Park, which is landscaped with desert plants. Add a meal at the park's tearoom, and you've got a good afternoon's outing. For a description of the park, see p. 373. 7366 N. Paseo del Norte (1 block west of the corner of Ina and Oracle roads in Tohono Chul Park). © **520/742-6455**. www.tohonochulpark.org.

JEWELRY

In addition to the stores mentioned below, see the listing for the Obsidian Gallery under "Crafts," above.

Beth Friedman Collection   This shop sells a well-chosen collection of jewelry by Native American craftspeople and international designers. It also carries some extravagant cowgirl get-ups in velvet and lace as well as contemporary women's fashions. At Joesler Village, 1865 E. River Rd., Suite 121. © **520/577-6858**.

Turquoise Door   The contemporary Southwestern jewelry here is among the most stunning in the city, made with opals, diamonds, lapis lazuli, amethysts, and the ubiquitous turquoise. At St. Philip's Plaza, 4330 N. Campbell Ave. (at River Rd.). *©* **520/299-7787.** www.turquoisedoorjewelry.com.

MALLS & SHOPPING CENTERS

Built in the style of a Spanish hacienda with a courtyard and fountains, the **Plaza Palomino** shopping center, at the corner of North Swan and Fort Lowell roads, is home to some of Tucson's fun little specialty shops, galleries, and restaurants.

St. Philip's Plaza   This upscale Southwestern-style shopping center contains a couple of good restaurants, a luxury beauty salon/day spa, and numerous shops and galleries, including Bahti Indian Arts and Turquoise Door jewelry. On Sunday mornings, there is a farmers' market. Makes a great one-stop Tucson outing. 4380 N. Campbell Ave. (at River Rd.). *©* **520/529-2775.** stphilipsplaza.com.

Tucson Mall   The foothills of northern Tucson have become shopping-center central, and this is the largest of the malls. You'll find more than 200 retailers in this busy, two-story skylit complex. 4500 N. Oracle Rd. *©* **520/293-7330.** www.shoptucsonmall.com.

NATIVE AMERICAN ART, CRAFTS & JEWELRY

Bahti Indian Arts   Family-owned for more than 50 years, this store sells fine pieces—jewelry, baskets, sculpture, paintings, books, weavings, kachina dolls, Zuni fetishes, and much more. At St. Philip's Plaza, 4280 N. Campbell Ave. *©* **520/577-0290.** www.bahti.com.

Gallery West   Located right below Anthony's in the Catalinas restaurant, this tiny shop specializes in very expensive Native American artifacts (mostly pre-1940s), such as pots, Apache and Pima baskets, 19th-century Plains Indian beadwork, Navajo weavings, and kachinas. There is also plenty of both contemporary and vintage jewelry. 6420 N. Campbell Ave. (at Skyline Dr.). *©* **520/529-7002.** www.indianartwest.com.

Kaibab Courtyard Shops ★   In business since 1945, this store offers one of the best selections of Native American art and crafts in Tucson. You can find high-quality jewelry, Mexican pottery and folk arts, home furnishings, glassware, kachinas, and rugs. 2841 N. Campbell Ave. *©* **520/795-6905.**

Mark Sublette Medicine Man Gallery   This shop has the best and biggest selection of old Navajo rugs in the city, and perhaps even the entire state. There are also Mexican and other Hispanic textiles, Acoma pottery, basketry, and other Indian crafts, as well as artwork by cowboy artists. The gallery is also the site of the Conley Museum of the West. At Santa Fe Sq., 7000 E. Tanque Verde Rd. *©* **800/422-9382** or 520/722-7798. www.medicinemangallery.com.

Morning Star Traders ★★★   With hardwood floors and a museumlike atmosphere, this store features museum-quality goods: antique Navajo rugs, kachinas, furniture, and a huge selection of old Native American jewelry. This just may be the best store of its type in the entire state. 2020 E. Speedway Blvd. *©* **520/881-2112.** www.morningstartraders.com.

Silverbell Trading   Not your usual run-of-the-mill crafts store, Silverbell specializes in regional Native American artwork, such as baskets and pottery, and carries unique pieces that the shop owner hand picks. Small items such as stone Navajo corn maidens and Zuni fetishes should not be overlooked. At Casas Adobes Plaza, 7119 N. Oracle Rd. *©* **520/797-6852.**

WESTERN WEAR

Arizona Hatters Arizona Hatters carries the best names in cowboy hats, from Stetson to Bailey to Tilles, and the shop specializes in custom-fitting hats to the customer's head and face. You'll also find bolo ties, belts, and other accessories here. 2790 N. Campbell Ave. ℂ **520/292-1320.**

Western Warehouse If you want to put together your Western-wear ensemble under one roof, this is the place. It's the largest such store in Tucson and can deck you and your kids out in the latest cowboy fashions, including hats and boots. 3030 E. Speedway Blvd. ℂ **520/327-8005.**

11 Tucson After Dark

The **Downtown Arts District** is the center of all the after-dark action, with the Temple of Music and Art, the Tucson Convention Center Music Hall, and several nightclubs. The **University of Arizona campus,** only a mile away, is another hot spot for entertainment.

The free *Tucson Weekly* and the entertainment section of the *Arizona Daily Star* (which comes out each Thurs) are good sources for listings of concerts, theater and dance performances, and club offerings.

THE CLUB & MUSIC SCENE

COUNTRY

Cactus Moon Café A 20- to 40-something crowd frequents this large and glitzy nightclub, which features primarily country music, although Sundays are currently Top-40 night. 5470 E. Broadway Blvd. (on the east side of town at Craycroft Rd.). ℂ **520/748-0049.** Cover $3–$5.

Hidden Valley Inn Although primarily a family-oriented cowboy steakhouse, this sprawling place, with its faux cow-town facade, also has a fun saloon with live country music Thursday through Saturday nights. There's also a separate stage where you might catch the Sons of the Pioneers. 4825 N. Sabino Canyon Rd. ℂ **520/299-4941.** www. hiddenvalleyinntuc.com.

The Maverick The Maverick, in different incarnations and different locations around town, has long been Tucson's favorite country music dance club. Currently it's located in a modern space out in east Tucson and is open Tuesday through Saturday nights. 6622 E. Tanque Verde Rd. ℂ **520/298-0430.** No cover to $5.

DANCE CLUB

El Parador Restaurant Tropical decor and an abundance of potted plants set the mood for lively Latin dance music and Friday night salsa lessons. The music starts at 9:30pm and dance lessons start around 9pm. Saturday nights are currently '70s night. Customers range from 20- to 60-somethings, giving new meaning to the term "all ages" club. 2744 E. Broadway. ℂ **520/881-2808.**

JAZZ

To find out what's happening on the local jazz scene, call the **Tucson Jazz Society** (ℂ **520/903-1265;** www.tucsonjazz.org).

The Grill ★★ No other jazz venue in Tucson has more flavor of the Southwest than this restaurant lounge, perched high on a ridge-top overlooking the city. There's live jazz Thursday through Sunday nights. At Hacienda del Sol Guest Ranch Resort, 5601 N. Hacienda del Sol Rd. ✆ 520/529-3500. www.haciendadelsol.com.

Old Pueblo Grille With a beautiful setting in a historic home surrounded by tall palm trees, this isn't exactly your classic jazz club. However, with its outstanding selection of tequilas and live jazz Thursday through Sunday, this is the quintessential Tucson jazz spot. 60 N. Alvernon Way. ✆ 520/326-6000. No cover to $3.

MARIACHI

La Fuente ✰✰ La Fuente is the largest Mexican restaurant in Tucson and serves up good food, but what really draws the crowds is the live mariachi music. If you just want to listen and not have dinner, you can hang out in the lounge. The mariachis perform Thursday through Sunday from 6:30 to 10pm. Other nights, there is Latin jazz. 1749 N. Oracle Rd. ✆ 520/623-8659. www.lafuenterestaurant.com.

ROCK, BLUES & REGGAE

Chicago Bar Transplanted Chicagoans love to watch their home teams on the TVs at this neighborhood bar, but there's also live music nightly. Sure, blues gets played a lot, but so do reggae and rock and about everything in between. 5954 E. Speedway Blvd. ✆ 520/748-8169. www.chicagobartucson.com. Cover $5.

City Limits This big new east-side club seems to be booking a lot of the big touring bands these days and is giving Club Congress a run for its money. With a great sound system and lots of nightly specials, this place packs in the crowds. Be sure to check the calendar while you're in town. 6350 E. Tanque Verde Rd. ✆ 520/733-6262. www.ctlimits.com. Cover $5–$20.

Club Congress Just off the lobby of the restored Hotel Congress (now a budget hotel and youth hostel), Club Congress is Tucson's main alternative-music venue. There are usually a couple of nights of live music each week, and over the years such bands as Nirvana, Dick Dale, and the Goo Goo Dolls have played here. 311 E. Congress St. ✆ 520/622-8848. www.hotelcongress.com. Cover $3–$15.

The Rialto Theatre This renovated 1919 vaudeville theater, although not a nightclub, is now Tucson's main venue for performances by bands that are too big to play across the street at Club Congress (Lucinda Williams, Los Lobos, Arturo Sandoval). 318 E. Congress St. ✆ 520/798-3333. www.rialtotheatre.com. Tickets $10–$35.

THE BAR, LOUNGE & PUB SCENE

Arizona Inn If you're looking for a quiet, comfortable scene, the piano music in the Audubon Lounge at the Arizona Inn is sure to soothe your soul. The lounge, which has been restored to its original appearance, has a classic feel, and the resort's gardens are beautiful. 2200 E. Elm St. ✆ 520/325-1541.

Cascade Lounge ✰ This is Tucson's ultimate piano bar. With a view of the Catalinas, the plush lounge is perfect for romance or relaxation at the start or end of a night on the town. Several nights a week, there's live piano music or a jazz band. At Loews Ventana Canyon Resort, 7000 N. Resort Dr. ✆ 520/299-2020.

Gentle Ben's Brewing Co. Located just off the UA campus, Gentle Ben's, a big, modern place with plenty of outdoor seating, is Tucson's favorite microbrewery. The crowd is primarily college students. Food and drink specials are offered daily, and there's live music a couple of nights per week. 865 E. University Blvd. ✆ 520/624-4177. www.gentlebens.com.

Nimbus Brewing ✯   Located in a warehouse district on the south side of Tucson, this brewpub is basically the front room of Nimbus's brewing and bottling facility. The beer is good, and there's live bluegrass, rock, or jazz on a regular basis. Hard to find, and definitely a local scene. 3850 E. 44th St. (2 blocks east of Palo Verde Rd.). © 520/745-9175. www.nimbusbeer.com.

Thunder Canyon Brewery   Affiliated with the Prescott Brewing Co. in Prescott, this brewpub is your best bet in Tucson for handcrafted ales and is the most convenient brewpub for anyone staying at a foothills resort. At Foothills Mall, 7401 N. La Cholla Blvd. (at Ina Rd.). © 520/797-2652.

¡Toma! ✯   This bar, set in El Presidio Historic District and owned by the family that operates El Charro Café next door, has a fun and festive atmosphere complete with a Mexican hat fountain/sculpture in the courtyard. Drop by for cheap margaritas during happy hour (Mon–Fri 3:30–6:30pm). 311 N. Court Ave. © 520/622-1922.

COCKTAILS WITH A VIEW

In addition to those listed below, the lounge at **Anthony's in the Catalinas** has a great view. Also, at press time, **Westward Look Resort** (p. 353) had plans to completely redesign its lounge around a Mexican theme (but the gorgeous views won't change).

Desert Garden Lounge   If you'd like a close-up view of the Santa Catalina Mountains, drop by the Desert Garden Lounge (at sunset, perhaps). The large lounge has live piano music several nights a week. At the Westin La Paloma, 3800 E. Sunrise Dr. © 520/742-6000.

Flying V Bar & Grill   If you can't afford the lap of luxury, you can at least pull up a chair in it. For one of the city's best views—looking out over the golf course and Tucson far below—sit near a waterfall just outside the front door of this popular resort watering hole. At Loews Ventana Canyon Resort, 7000 N. Resort Dr. © 520/299-2020.

SPORTS BARS

Famous Sam's   With about a dozen branches around the city, Famous Sam's (www.famoussams.com) keeps a lot of Tucson's sports fans happy with its cheap prices and large portions. Other convenient locations include, 7930 E. Speedway Blvd. (© 520/290-9666), and 2320 N. Silverbell Rd. (© 520/884-7267). 1830 E. Broadway Blvd. © 520/884-0119.

GAY & LESBIAN BARS & CLUBS

To find out about other gay bars around town, pick up the *Observer,* Tucson's newspaper for the gay, lesbian, and bisexual community. You'll find it at **Antigone Books,** 411 N. Fourth Ave. (© 520/792-3715), as well as at the bars listed here.

Ain't Nobody's Bizness   Located in a small shopping plaza in midtown, this bar has long been *the* lesbian gathering spot in Tucson. There are pool tables, a dance floor, and a quiet, smoke-free room where you can duck out of the noise. 2900 E. Broadway Blvd., Suite 118. © 520/318-4838. www.aintnobodysbizness-az.com.

IBT's   Located on funky Fourth Avenue, IBT's has long been the most popular gay men's dance bar in town. The music ranges from 1980s retro to techno, and regular drag shows add to the fun. There's always an interesting crowd. 616 N. Fourth Ave. © 520/882-3053.

THE PERFORMING ARTS

Three of Tucson's major companies—the Arizona Opera Company, Ballet Arizona, and the Arizona Theatre Company—spend half their time in Phoenix. This means that

Performing-Arts Centers & Concert Halls

Tucson's largest performance venue is the **Tucson Convention Center (TCC) Music Hall,** 260 S. Church Ave. ((© **520/791-4266;** www.cityoftucson.org/tcc). It's the home of the Tucson Symphony Orchestra and where the Arizona Opera Company usually performs when it's in town.

The centerpiece of the Tucson theater scene is the **Temple of Music and Art,** 330 S. Scott Ave. ((© **520/622-2823**), a restored historic theater dating from 1927. The 605-seat Alice Holsclaw Theatre is the Temple's main stage, but there's also the 90-seat Cabaret Theatre.

University of Arizona Centennial Hall, 1020 E. University Blvd. at Park Avenue ((© **520/621-3341;** www.uapresents.org), on the UA campus, is Tucson's other main performance hall. It stages performances by touring national musical acts, international companies, and Broadway shows.

The **Center for the Arts Proscenium Theatre,** Pima Community College (West Campus), 2202 W. Anklam Rd. ((© **520/206-6986**), is another good place to check for classical music performances. It offers a wide variety of shows.

whatever gets staged in Phoenix also gets staged in Tucson. This city does, however, have its own symphony, and manages to sustain a diversified theater scene as well.

Usually, the best way to purchase tickets is directly from the company's box office. Tickets to Tucson Convention Center events (but not the symphony or the opera) and other venues around town may be available by calling the **TCC box office** (© **520/ 791-4266;** www.cityoftucson.org/tcc). **Ticketmaster** (© **520/321-1000;** www. ticketmaster.com) sells tickets to some Tucson performances.

OUTDOOR VENUES & SERIES

Tucsonans head to Reid Park's **DeMeester Outdoor Performance Center,** at Country Club Road and East 22nd Street (© **520/791-4873**), for performances under the stars. This amphitheater is the site of performances by the Tucson Community Theatre and other companies, as well as frequent musical concerts.

The **Tucson Jazz Society** (© **520/903-1265;** www.tucsonjazz.org), which manages to book a few well-known jazz musicians each year, sponsors different series at various locations around the city, including the foothills' St. Philip's Plaza. Tickets are usually between $15 and $25.

CLASSICAL MUSIC, OPERA & DANCE

Both the **Tucson Symphony Orchestra** (© **520/882-8585** or 520/792-9155; www.tucsonsymphony.org), which is the oldest continuously performing symphony in the Southwest, and the **Arizona Opera Company** (© **520/293-4336** or 520/321-1000; www.azopera.com), the state's premier opera company, perform at the Tucson Convention Center Music Hall. Symphony tickets run $15 to $46; opera tickets are $25 to $115.

THEATER

Arizona Theatre Company (ATC; © **520/622-2823;** www.aztheatreco.org), which performs at the Temple of Music and Art, splits its time between here and Phoenix and is the state's top professional theater company. Each season sees a mix of comedy, drama, and Broadway-style musical shows; tickets cost $27 to $48.

The **Invisible Theatre,** 1400 N. First Ave. (© **520/882-9721**), a tiny theater in a converted laundry building, has been home to Tucson's most experimental theater for more than 30 years (it does off-Broadway shows and musicals). Tickets go for about $18 to $24.

At the **Gaslight Theatre,** 7010 E. Broadway Blvd. (© **520/886-9428**), evil villains, stalwart heroes, and defenseless heroines pound the boards in good old-fashioned melodramas. It's all great fun for kids and adults, with plenty of pop-culture references thrown into the mix. Tickets are $16 for adults, $14 for students and seniors, and $7 for children 12 and under. Performances are held Tuesday through Sunday. Tickets sell out a month in advance, so get them as soon as possible.

13

Phoenix, Scottsdale & the Valley of the Sun

Forget the stately cacti and cowboys riding off into the sunset; think Los Angeles without the Pacific. While the nation has carefully nurtured its image of Phoenix as a desert cow town, this city in the Sonoran Desert has rocketed into the 21st century and become the sixth-largest city in the country. Sprawling across 400 square miles, the greater Phoenix metropolitan area, also known as the Valley of the Sun, is now a major metropolitan area replete with dozens of resort hotels, fabulous restaurants, excellent museums, hundreds of golf courses, world-class shopping, four pro sports teams, and a red-hot nightlife scene.

Sure, it also has traffic jams and smog, but sunshine and blue skies, day after day after day, have made this one of the most popular winter destinations in the country. Phoenicians may get the summertime blues when temperatures hit the triple digits, but from September to May, the climate here can verge on perfect—warm enough in the daytime for lounging by the pool, cool enough at night to require a jacket.

With green lawns, orange groves, swimming pools, and palm trees, it's easy to forget that Phoenix is in the middle of the desert. Water channeled in from distant reservoirs has allowed this city to flourish like a desert oasis. However, if you find yourself wondering where the desert is, you need only lift your eyes to one of the many mountains that rise up from amid the urban sprawl. It is to these cactus-covered uplands that the city's citizens retreat when they've had enough asphalt and air-conditioning. From almost anywhere in the Valley, you're no more than a 15- or 20-minute drive from a natural area where you can commune with cacti while gazing out across a bustling, modern city.

1 Orientation

ARRIVING

BY PLANE Centrally located 3 miles east of downtown Phoenix, **Sky Harbor International Airport,** 3400 E. Sky Harbor Blvd. (✆ **602/273-3300;** www.phxsky harbor.com) has three terminals, with a free 24-hour shuttle bus offering frequent service between them. For lost and found, call ✆ **602/273-3307.**

There are two entrances to the airport. The west entrance can be accessed from either the Piestewa Freeway (Ariz. 51) or 24th Street, while the east entrance can be accessed from the Hohokam Expressway (Ariz. 143), which is an extension of 44th Street. If you're headed to downtown Phoenix, leave by way of the 24th Street exit and continue west on Washington Street. If you're headed to Scottsdale, take the 44th Street exit, go north on Ariz. 143 and then east on Ariz. 202 to U.S. 101 north. For

> (*Tips* **A Name Change**
>
> In early 2003, the official name of Phoenix's Squaw Peak was changed to Piestewa Peak (pronounced Pie-*ess*-too-uh) to honor Pfc. Lori Ann Piestewa, a member of the Hopi tribe and the first female soldier to be killed in the Iraq War. Ditto for the Squaw Peak Parkway, which is now Piestewa Freeway.

Tempe or Mesa, take the 44th Street exit, go north on Ariz. 143, and then head east on Ariz. 202.

SuperShuttle (© 800/BLUE-VAN or 602/244-9000; www.supershuttle.com) offers 24-hour door-to-door van service between Sky Harbor Airport and resorts, hotels, and homes throughout the Valley. Per-person fares average $7 to $12 to the downtown and Tempe area, $16 to downtown Scottsdale, and $30 to $35 to north Scottsdale.

Taxis can be found outside all three terminals and cost only slightly more than shuttle vans. You can also call **Discount Cab** (© 602/200-2000) or **Allstate Cab** (© 602/275-8888). A taxi from the airport to downtown Phoenix will cost around $12 or $13; to Scottsdale, between $20 and $35.

Valley Metro (© 602/253-5000; www.valleymetro.org) provides public bus service throughout the Valley, with the Red Line operating between the airport and downtown Phoenix, Tempe, and Mesa. The Red Line runs daily starting between 3:30 and 5:30am and continues operating until between 10:30pm and 1am. The ride from the airport to downtown takes about 20 minutes and costs $1.25. There is no direct bus to Scottsdale, so you would first need to go to Tempe and then transfer to a northbound bus. You can pick up a copy of the *Bus Book,* a guide and route map for the Valley Metro bus system, at Central Station, at the corner of Central Avenue and Van Buren Street.

BY CAR   Phoenix is connected to Los Angeles and Tucson by I-10 and to Flagstaff via I-17. If you're headed to Scottsdale, the easiest route is to take the Red Mountain Freeway (Ariz. 202) east to U.S. 101 north. U.S. 101 loops all the way around the east, north, and west sides of the Valley. The Superstition Freeway (U.S. 60) leads to Tempe, Mesa, and Chandler.

BY TRAIN   There is no passenger rail service to Phoenix. However, **Amtrak** (© 800/872-7245; www.amtrak.com) will sell you a ticket to Phoenix, though you'll have to take a shuttle bus from either Flagstaff or Tucson. The scheduling is so horrible on these routes that you would have to be a total masochist to opt for Amtrak service to Phoenix.

VISITOR INFORMATION

You'll find **tourist information desks** in all three terminals at Sky Harbor Airport. The city's main visitor center is the **Greater Phoenix Convention & Visitors Bureau,** 50 N. Second St. (© 877/225-5749 or 602/452-6282; www.visitphoenix.com), on the corner of Adams Street in downtown Phoenix. There's also a small visitor information center at the Biltmore Fashion Park shopping center, at Camelback Road and 24th Street (© 602/452-6281).

The **Visitor Information Line** (© 602/252-5588) has recorded information about current events in Phoenix and is updated weekly.

If you're staying in Scottsdale, you can get information at the **Scottsdale Convention & Visitors Bureau Visitor Center,** Galleria Corporate Center, 4343 N. Scottsdale Rd., Suite 170 (© **866/782-1117** or 480/421-1004; www.scottsdalecvb.com).

CITY LAYOUT

MAIN ARTERIES & STREETS **U.S. Loop 101** forms a loop around the east, north, and west sides of the Valley, providing freeway access to Scottsdale from I-17 on the north side of Phoenix and from U.S. 60 in Tempe.

I-17 (Black Canyon Fwy.), which connects Phoenix with Flagstaff, is the city's main north–south freeway. This freeway curves to the east just south of downtown (where it is renamed the **Maricopa Fwy.** and merges with I-10). **I-10,** which connects Phoenix with Los Angeles and Tucson, is called the **Papago Freeway** on the west side of the Valley and as it passes north of downtown; as it curves around to pass to the west and south of the airport, it merges with I-17 and is renamed the Maricopa Freeway. At Tempe, this freeway curves around to the south and heads out of the Valley.

North of the airport, **Ariz. 202 (Red Mountain Fwy.)** heads east from I-10 and passes along the north side of Tempe, providing access to downtown Tempe, Arizona State University, Mesa, and Scottsdale (via U.S. Loop 101). On the east side of the airport, **Ariz. 143 (Hohokam Expressway)** connects Ariz. 202 with I-10.

At the interchange of I-10 and Ariz. 202, northwest of Sky Harbor Airport, **Ariz. 51 (Piestewa Fwy.)** heads north through the center of Phoenix to U.S. Loop 101 and is the best north–south route in the city.

South of the airport off I-10, **U.S. 60 (Superstition Fwy.)** heads east to Tempe, Chandler, Mesa, and Gilbert. **U.S. Loop 101** leads north from U.S. 60 (and Ariz. 202) through Scottsdale and across the north side of Phoenix to connect with I-17. U.S. 60 and U.S. 101 provide the best route from the airport to the Scottsdale resorts. U.S. Loop 101 also heads south through Chandler to connect with I-10. This section is called the Price Freeway. The section of this freeway north through Scottsdale is called the Pima Freeway.

Secondary highways in the Valley include the **Beeline Highway (Ariz. 87),** which starts at the east end of Ariz. 202 (Red Mountain Fwy.) in Mesa and leads to Payson, and **Grand Avenue (U.S. 60),** which starts downtown and leads west to Sun City and Wickenburg.

Phoenix and the surrounding cities of Mesa, Tempe, Scottsdale, and Chandler, and even those cities farther out in the Valley, are laid out in a grid pattern with major avenues and roads about every mile. For traveling east to west across Phoenix, your best choices (other than the above-mentioned freeways) are Camelback Road, Indian School Road, and McDowell Road. For traveling north and south, 44th Street, 24th Street, and Central Avenue are good choices. Hayden Road is a north–south alternative to Scottsdale Road, which gets jammed at rush hours.

FINDING AN ADDRESS **Central Avenue,** which runs north to south through downtown Phoenix, is the starting point for all east and west street numbering. **Washington Street** is the starting point for north and south numbering. North-to-south numbered *streets* are to be found on the east side of the city, while north-to-south numbered *avenues* will be found on the west. For the most part, street numbers advance by 100 with each block. Odd-numbered addresses are on the south and east sides of streets, while even-numbered addresses are on north and west sides of streets.

For example, if you're looking for 4454 East Camelback Rd., you'll find it 44 blocks east of Central Avenue between 44th and 45th streets on the north side of the street. If you're looking for 2905 North 35th Ave., you'll find it 35 blocks west of Central Avenue and 29 blocks north of Washington Street on the east side of the street. Just for general reference, Camelback marks the 5000 block north. Also, whenever getting directions, ask for the cross street closest to where you're going.

2 Getting Around

BY CAR

Phoenix and the surrounding cities that together make up the Valley of the Sun sprawl across more than 400 square miles, so it's essential to have a car. Outside downtown Phoenix, there's almost always plenty of free parking wherever you go (exceptions being Old Scottsdale and some of the more popular malls and shopping plazas). If you want to feel like a local, opt for the ubiquitous valet parking wherever possible (just be sure to keep plenty of small bills on hand for tipping the parking attendants).

Because Phoenix is a major tourist destination, good car-rental rates are often available. However, taxes and surcharges on rentals at Sky Harbor Airport now run 50% or more, which pretty much negates any deal you might get on your rate. Expect to pay around $130 to $150 per week ($210 to $235 with taxes) for a compact car in the high season. See chapter 2 for general tips on car rentals.

All major rental-car companies have rental desks at Sky Harbor Airport, although none currently have pick up and drop off right in the airport. A new Rental Car Center is scheduled to open on the airport grounds in 2006, but in the meantime, be sure to leave time in your schedule for taking a shuttle bus to and from the airport to the rental-car lot. There are also plenty of other car-rental offices in Phoenix and Scottsdale. Rental-car companies at the airport include the following: **Advantage** (© 800/777-5500 or 602/244-0450), **Alamo** (© 800/327-9633 or 602/244-0897), **Avis** (© 800/831-2847 or 602/273-3222), **Budget** (© 800/527-0700), **Dollar** (© 800/800-4000), **Enterprise** (© 800/736-8222 or 602/225-0588), **Hertz** (© 800/654-3131 or 602/267-8822), **National** (© 800/227-7368 or 602/275-4771), and **Thrifty** (© 800/847-4389 or 602/244-0311).

BY PUBLIC TRANSPORTATION

The free **Downtown Area Shuttle (DASH)** provides bus service within the downtown area Monday through Friday from 6:30am to 11pm. These buses serve regular stops every 6 to 18 minutes; they're primarily for downtown workers, but attractions along the route include the state capitol and Heritage and Science Park. In Tempe, **Free Local Area Shuttle (FLASH)** buses provide a similar service on a loop around Arizona State University. The route includes Mill Avenue and Sun Devil Stadium. For information on both DASH and FLASH, call © **602/253-5000.**

In Scottsdale, you can ride the **Scottsdale Trolley** (© **480/421-1004;** www. valleymetro.org) shuttle buses between Scottsdale Fashion Square, the Fifth Avenue shops, the Main Street Arts and Antiques district, and the Old Town district. These buses operate between November 1 and the end of May and run Monday through Saturday from 11am to 6pm (until 9pm on Thurs). Between late December and mid-April, there are also free shopping shuttles that serve many of the area's resorts, including Camelback Inn, Hyatt Regency Scottsdale Resort at Gainey Ranch, Renaissance

Scottsdale Resort, and Doubletree Paradise Valley Resort. These trolleys stop at various downtown Scottsdale shopping districts, as well as at Scottsdale Fashion Square, The Borgata, and The Shops at Gainey Village.

BY TAXI

Because distances in Phoenix are so great, the price of an average taxi ride can be quite high. However, if you don't have your own wheels or had too much to drink and the bus isn't running because it's late at night or the weekend, you won't have any choice but to call a cab. **Yellow Cab** (© **602/252-5252**) charges $2.50 for the first mile and $1.60 per mile thereafter. **Scottsdale Cab** (© **480/994-1616**) charges $2 per mile, with a $5 minimum.

FAST FACTS

The Banner Good Samaritan Medical Center, 1111 E. McDowell Rd., Phoenix (© **602/239-2000**), is one of the largest hospitals in the valley. For a doctor referral, call the Maricopa County Medical Society (© **602/252-2844**); for a dentist referral, call the Dental Referral Service (© **800/511-8663**).

State sales tax is 5.6% (plus variable local taxes). Hotel room taxes vary considerably by city but are mostly between 10% and 11%. The total taxes and surcharges when renting a car at Sky Harbor Airport add up to around 50%.

See also "Fast Facts: The American Southwest" in chapter 2, and "Fast Facts: For the International Traveler" in chapter 3.

3 Where to Stay

The Phoenix area has the greatest concentration of resorts in the continental United States. However, sunshine and spring training combine to make it hard to find a room on short notice between February and April. If you're planning to visit during these months, make your reservations as far in advance as possible. Also keep in mind that in winter, the Phoenix metro area has some of the highest room rates in the country.

With the exception of valet-parking services and parking garages at downtown convention hotels, parking is free at almost all Phoenix hotels. If there is a parking charge, I have noted it. You'll find that all hotels have nonsmoking rooms and all but the cheapest have wheelchair-accessible rooms.

Most resorts offer a variety of weekend, golf, and tennis packages, as well as off-season discounts and corporate rates (which you can often get just by asking). We've given only the official "rack rates," or walk-in rates, below, but it always pays to ask about special discounts or packages. Don't forget your AAA or AARP discounts if you belong to one of these organizations. Business hotels downtown and near the airport often lower their rates on weekends, and many hotels offer website-only specials.

BED & BREAKFASTS   Those interested in staying at a bed and breakfast instead of a luxury resort should call either **Mi Casa Su Casa** (© 800/456-0682 or 480/990-0682; www.azres.com) or **Arizona Trails Bed & Breakfast Reservation Service** (© **888/799-4284** or 480/837-4284; www.arizonatrails.com), which also books tour and hotel reservations.

SCOTTSDALE

Scottsdale is the center of the Valley's resort scene. Because Scottsdale is also the Valley's prime shopping and dining district, this is the most convenient place to stay if you're

Phoenix, Scottsdale & the Valley of the Sun Accommodations

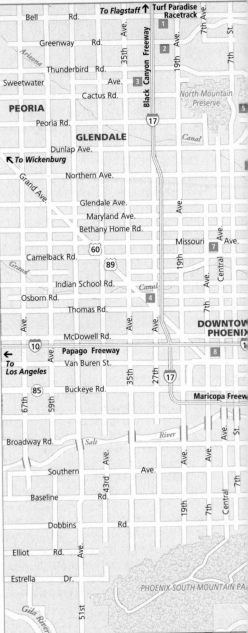

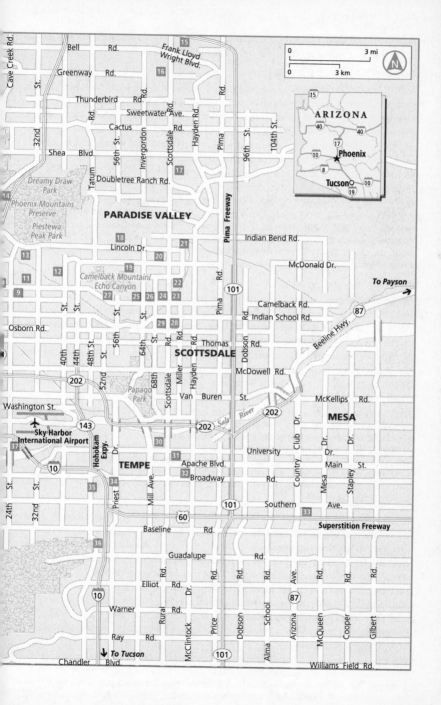

here to eat and shop. However, traffic in Scottsdale is bad, the landscape at most resorts is flat, and you don't get much of a feel for the desert.

VERY EXPENSIVE

Caleo Resort & Spa ★★   An exceptional location in the heart of the Scottsdale shopping district, dramatic Southwestern styling, and a small but well-designed pool area are the main reasons I like this little resort. Set in a lushly planted courtyard are a small lagoon-style pool, complete with sand beach and short water slide, and a second pool with flame-topped columnar waterfalls. An artificial stream and faux sandstone ruins all add up to a fun desert fantasy landscape (although not on the grand scale to be found at some area resorts). The guest rooms are quite comfortable, and there's a pretty little spa on the premises.

4925 N. Scottsdale Rd., Scottsdale, AZ 85251. © **800/528-7867** or 480/945-7666. Fax 480/946-4056. www. caleoresort.com. 204 units. Jan to late May $209 double, $399 suite; late May to early Sept $99 double, $199 suite; early Sept to Dec $189 double, $349 suite. AE, DC, DISC, MC, V. Children under 18 stay free in parent's room. **Amenities:** 2 restaurants; lounge; snack bar; 2 pools; exercise room; access to nearby health club; full-service spa; Jacuzzi; concierge; business center; room service; massage; laundry service; dry cleaning. *In room:* A/C, TV, dataport, minibar, coffeemaker, hair dryer, iron, safe, high-speed Internet access, wi-fi.

Camelback Inn, A JW Marriott Resort & Spa ★★★   Set at the foot of Mummy Mountain and overlooking Camelback Mountain, the Camelback Inn, which opened in 1936, is one of the grande dames of the Phoenix hotel scene and abounds in traditional Southwestern character. Although the two 18-hole golf courses are the main attractions for many guests, the spa is among the finest in the state. There's also an extensive pool complex that appeals to families. Guest rooms, which are spread over the sloping grounds, are decorated with Southwestern furnishings and art, and all have balconies or patios. Some rooms even have their own private pools. This is an old-money sort of place that seamlessly melds tradition with modern amenities.

5402 E. Lincoln Dr., Scottsdale, AZ 85253. © **800/24-CAMEL** or 480/948-1700. Fax 480/951-8469. www.camelbackinn. com. 453 units. Jan to early June $279–$529 double, $639–$3,000 suite; early June to early Sept $189 double, $235–$1,550 suite; early Sept to Dec $339 double, $485–$1,550 suite. Children under 18 stay free in parent's room. AE, DC, DISC, MC, V. Small pets accepted. **Amenities:** 7 restaurants; lounge; 3 pools; 2 outstanding 18-hole golf courses; pitch-and-putt green; 6 tennis courts; basketball and volleyball courts; exercise room; full-service spa; 3 Jacuzzis; bike rentals; children's programs and playground; concierge; car-rental desk; business center; salon; room service; babysitting; guest laundry and laundry service; dry cleaning. *In room:* A/C, TV, dataport, minibar, coffeemaker, hair dryer, iron, safe, high-speed Internet access, wi-fi.

Hyatt Regency Scottsdale Resort and Spa at Gainey Ranch ★★★ *Kids*   From the colonnades of palm trees to the lobby walls that slide away, this luxurious resort is designed to impress and continues to be my favorite Scottsdale resort. It's relatively close in, has interesting architecture, beautiful grounds, and, in 2005, added a big new spa. What's not to love? A 2½-acre water playground serves as the resort's focal point, and the extravagant complex of 10 swimming pools includes a water slide and a huge whirlpool spa. Guest rooms are luxurious and are designed to reflect the desert location. The resort's Native American and Environmental Learning Center provides a glimpse into Sonoran Desert culture and ecology. Children's programs make this is a super choice for families.

7500 E. Doubletree Ranch Rd., Scottsdale, AZ 85258. © **800/55-HYATT** or 480/991-3388. Fax 480/483-5550. www. scottsdale.hyatt.com. 500 units. Jan to late May $320 double, from $950 suite and casita; late May to early Sept $170 double, from $500 suite and casita; early Sept to Dec $260 double, from $860 suite and casita. Children under 18 stay free in parent's room. AE, DC, DISC, MC, V. Valet parking $20. **Amenities:** 4 restaurants; snack bar; 2 lounges; coffee bar; juice bar; 10 pools; 27-hole golf course (with lots of water hazards); 4 tennis courts; health club; full-service spa; 3 Jacuzzis; bike rentals; children's programs; concierge; car-rental desk; business center; 24-hr. room service; massage; babysitting; laundry service; dry cleaning; concierge-level rooms. *In room:* A/C, TV, dataport, minibar, coffeemaker, hair dryer, iron, safe, high-speed Internet access.

The Phoenician ★★★ *Kids*

Situated on 250 acres at the foot of Camelback Mountain, this palatial resort is one of the finest in the world. Polished marble and sparkling crystal abound in the lobby, but the valley view through a long wall of glass is what commands most guests' attention. Service here is second to none, and the character is very international. The pool complex, which has a water slide for the kids, is irresistibly seductive, and the resort's Centre for Well Being offers all the spa pampering anyone could ever want. There are also 27 challenging holes of golf. Mary Elaine's (p. 424) is Phoenix's ultimate special-occasion restaurant. The luxurious guest rooms have large patios and sunken tubs for two.

6000 E. Camelback Rd., Scottsdale, AZ 85251. © 800/888-8234 or 480/941-8200. Fax 480/947-4311. www.the phoenician.com. 654 units. Jan–May $625 double, from $1,550 suite; June to mid-Sept $295 double, from $995 suite; mid-Sept to Dec $525 double, from $1,450 suite. Children under 12 stay free in parent's room. AE, DC, DISC, MC, V. Valet parking $26. Pets under 25 lb. accepted. **Amenities:** 3 restaurants; 4 snack bars/cafes; lounge; 9 pools; 27-hole golf course; putting green; 12 tennis courts; health club and spa; Jacuzzi; bike rentals; children's programs; concierge; car-rental desk; business center; shopping arcade; salon; 24-hr. room service; massage; babysitting; laundry service; dry cleaning; executive-level rooms; lawn games. *In room:* A/C, TV, dataport, minibar, hair dryer, iron, safe, high-speed Internet access.

Renaissance Scottsdale Resort ★★ *Value*

If I were coming to Scottsdale for a romantic getaway, I would stay here. Located adjacent to the upscale Borgata shopping center (which is designed to resemble Tuscany's San Gimignano), this casual yet luxurious boutique resort feels like an isolated hideaway. Set amid shady lawns, the Renaissance Scottsdale consists of spacious, comfortable suites. More than 100 of the suites have their own private outdoor hot tubs (very romantic), and all units are done in Southwestern style. Several excellent restaurants are within walking distance.

6160 N. Scottsdale Rd., Scottsdale, AZ 85253. © 800/309-8138 or 480/991-1414. Fax 480/951-3350. www.renaissance scottsdale.com. 171 units. Jan–May $244–$289 double, $269–$349 suite; June to early Sept $89 double, $109–$129 suite; early Sept to Dec $199 double, $249–$309 suite. Children under 16 stay free in parent's room. AE, DC, DISC, MC, V. Pets accepted ($50 deposit). **Amenities:** 3 restaurants; lounge; 2 pools; putting green; 4 tennis courts; croquet court; access to nearby health club; 2 Jacuzzis; bike rentals; concierge; business center; shopping arcade; 24-hr. room service; massage; babysitting; laundry service; dry cleaning. *In room:* A/C, TV, dataport, minibar, coffeemaker, hair dryer, iron, safe.

Sanctuary on Camelback Mountain ★★★

The *JAMES* may be the hippest hotel in Scottsdale, but I still like the contemporary rooms here better than those at the *JAMES*. Located high on the northern flanks of Camelback Mountain, the lushly landscaped property has unforgettable views across the valley, especially from the restaurant and lounge. The extremely spacious guest rooms are divided between the more conservative deluxe casitas and the boldly contemporary spa casitas. With their dyed-cement floors, kidney-shaped daybeds, and streamline-moderne cabinetry, these latter units are absolutely stunning. Bathrooms are huge and some have private outdoor soaking tubs. The resort's spa is gorgeous!

5700 E. McDonald Dr., Paradise Valley, AZ 85253. © 800/245-2051 or 480/948-2100. Fax 480/483-7314. www. sanctuaryaz.com. 98 units. Late Dec to early May $415–$765 double; early May to early June and early Sept to mid-Dec $315–$665 double; early June to early Sept and mid-Dec $165–$375 double. Children under 17 stay free in parent's room. AE, DC, DISC, MC, V. Pets accepted. **Amenities:** Restaurant; lounge; 4 pools; 5 tennis courts; fitness center; full-service spa; 4 Jacuzzis; bike rentals; concierge; business center; 24-hr. room service; massage; babysitting; laundry service; dry cleaning. *In room:* A/C, TV, dataport, minibar, coffeemaker, hair dryer, iron, safe, high-speed Internet access, wi-fi.

Westin Kierland Resort & Spa ★★★ *Kids* A convenient location and distinct sense of place make this one of my favorite Phoenix-area megaresorts. Located just off Scottsdale Road adjacent to Kierland Commons shopping center, the resort features artworks by Arizona artists, numerous interpretive plaques, and historic photos that provide insights into Arizona cultural and natural history. Guest rooms all have balconies or patios, and although the bathrooms aren't all that large, this minor inconvenience is compensated for by Westin's Heavenly Beds, which are incredibly comfortable, pillow-top beds. The main pool area includes a long tubing river, a water slide, and a beach area.

6902 E. Greenway Pkwy., Scottsdale, AZ 85254. ⊘ 800/WESTIN-1 or 480/624-1000. Fax 480/624-1001. www.westin.com/kierlandresort. 735 units. Jan to early May $279–$529 double; early May to early June $189–$369 double; early June to mid-Sept $109–$269 double; mid-Sept to Dec $189–$489 double. Children under 12 stay free in parent's room. AE, DC, DISC, MC, V. Valet parking $18. Pets accepted. **Amenities:** 5 restaurants; poolside snack bar; espresso bar/ice-cream parlor; 2 lounges; 4 pools; 3 9-hole golf courses; 2 tennis courts; health club; full-service spa with 20 treatment rooms; 4 Jacuzzis; children's programs; concierge; car-rental desk; business center; 24-hr. room service; massage; babysitting; laundry service; dry cleaning; concierge-level rooms. *In room:* A/C, TV, dataport, minibar, coffeemaker, hair dryer, iron, safe, high-speed Internet access.

EXPENSIVE

Doubletree Paradise Valley Resort ★★ *Value* With its low-rise design and textured-block construction, this resort gives a bow to the pioneering architectural style of Frank Lloyd Wright, and thus stands out from comparable resorts in the area. Built around several courtyards containing swimming pools, bubbling fountains, palm trees, and gardens with desert landscaping, the property has much the look and feel of the nearby Hyatt Regency Scottsdale. It's not as grand, but the room rates are more bearable. Accommodations have a very contemporary feel, with lots of blond wood and, in some cases, high ceilings that make the rooms feel particularly spacious. With its distinctive styling and convenient location, this is an excellent choice.

5401 N. Scottsdale Rd., Scottsdale, AZ 85250. ⊘ 877/445-6677 or 480/947-5400. Fax 480/481-0209. www.paradise valleydoubletree.com. 378 units. Jan–Mar $179–$249 double, from $249 suite; Apr and Sept–Dec $99–$169 double, from $199 suite; May–Aug $65–$119 double, from $159 suite. Children under 18 stay free in parent's room. AE, DC, DISC, MC, V. Pets accepted ($75 nonrefundable deposit). **Amenities:** 2 restaurants; lounge; poolside snack bar; 2 outdoor pools; putting green; 2 tennis courts; 2 racquetball courts; health club; 2 Jacuzzis; saunas; bike rentals; children's programs; concierge; car-rental desk; business center; room service; massage; babysitting; laundry service; dry cleaning. *In room:* A/C, TV, dataport, minibar, coffeemaker, hair dryer, iron, high-speed Internet access.

JAMES Hotel ★ Move over W; here comes *JAMES*. For hipsters and fashionistas this is *the* place to stay. Designed to compete with the ultrahip W hotel chain, the *JAMES* is all sharp angles and bright walls of color outside, subdued hues and stainless steel inside. The minimalist 1950s retro style, and the huge plasma TVs and CD players make it perfectly clear that this place is designed for hip and wired young travelers. Be sure to check out the minibar, where you'll find Odwalla bars, soy chips, all the makings for martinis, and even condoms. The hotel's FiAMMA Trattoria is one of the hottest restaurants in town, and the bar is a magnet for trendy twenty-somethings (just practice saying "shaken not stirred").

7353 E. Indian School Rd., Scottsdale, AZ 85251. ⊘ 888/500-8080 or 480/308-1100. Fax 480/308-1200. www.jameshotels.com. 194 units. Jan to mid-Apr $179–$309 double; mid-Apr to May and Sept–Dec $159–$219 double; June–Aug from $159 double. AE, DC, DISC, MC, V. Pets accepted ($75 fee). **Amenities:** Restaurant; lounge; 2 outdoor pools; large, well-equipped exercise room; Jacuzzi; concierge; business center; room service; massage and spa services; laundry service; dry cleaning. *In room:* A/C, TV, dataport, minibar, coffeemaker, hair dryer, iron, safe, high-speed Internet access, wi-fi.

Scottsdale Resort & Athletic Club ★★ Fitness fanatics rejoice; this club's for you. If you can't stand the thought of giving up your workout just because you're on vacation, book a stay at this little boutique hotel (and timeshare resort) just off busy Scottsdale Road and adjacent to the Silverado Golf Course. With standard rooms and huge one- and two-bedroom "villas," this place is plenty comfortable, but the main reason I like this hotel is because it's affiliated with the Scottsdale Athletic Club, a large workout facility that emphasizes its tennis program. The basic rooms are a real steal for Scottsdale, and while the villas are quite a bit more expensive, they're gigantic and have fireplaces, DVD players, full kitchens, and washers and dryers. On top of all this, you get a view of Camelback Mountain.

8235 E. Indian Bend Rd., Scottsdale, AZ 85250. ☎ 877/343-0033 or 480/344-0600. Fax 480/344-0650. www.scottsdaleresortandathleticclub.com. 56 units. Jan–Apr $249 double, $399–$549 suite; May–Sept $119 double, $199–$279 suite; Oct–Dec $149 double, $249–$359 suite. Children under 18 stay free in parent's room. AE, DC, DISC, MC, V. **Amenities:** Restaurant; 3 pools; 11 tennis courts; health club; full-service spa; Jacuzzi; sauna; room service; dry cleaning. *In room:* A/C, TV/DVD, dataport, fridge, coffeemaker, hair dryer, iron, high-speed Internet access.

MODERATE

Days Inn Scottsdale Resort at Fashion Square Mall *Kids* *Value* This is one of the last economical hotels in the Old Town Scottsdale area, and its location adjacent to the Scottsdale Fashion Square mall makes this a great choice for shopaholics. This may be just an aging chain motel, but green lawns, tall palm trees, and a convenient location all make it worth recommending.

4710 N. Scottsdale Rd., Scottsdale, AZ 85251. ☎ 800/DAYS-INN or 480/947-5411. Fax 480/946-1324. www.scottsdaledaysinn.com. 167 units. Jan–Mar $110–$165 double; Apr–Dec $59–$165 double. Rates include continental breakfast. Children under 18 stay free in parent's room. AE, DC, DISC, MC, V. **Amenities:** Poolside bar; small outdoor pool; putting green; tennis court; Jacuzzi; car-rental desk; courtesy shopping shuttle; coin-op laundry; dry cleaning service. *In room:* A/C, TV, dataport, fridge, coffeemaker, hair dryer, iron.

INEXPENSIVE

Ramada Scottsdale on 5th Avenue *Value* For convenience and price, this motel can't be beat. It's located at the west end of the Fifth Avenue shopping district, within walking distance of some of the best shopping and dining in Scottsdale. The three-story building is arranged around a central courtyard, where you'll find the small pool. Guest rooms are large and have been fairly recently renovated.

6935 Fifth Ave., Scottsdale, AZ 85251. ☎ 800/528-7396 or 480/994-9461. Fax 480/947-1695. www.ramadascottsdale.com. 92 units. Jan–Mar $85–$95 double; Apr and Oct–Dec $65–$85 double; May–Sept $55–$65 double. Rates include continental breakfast. Children under 17 stay free in parent's room. AE, DISC, MC, V. Small pets accepted ($15 fee). **Amenities:** Small outdoor pool; exercise room; coin-op laundry; laundry service. *In room:* A/C, TV, dataport, fridge, coffeemaker, hair dryer, iron, free local calls.

NORTH SCOTTSDALE, CAREFREE & CAVE CREEK

Situated at least a 30-minute drive from downtown Scottsdale, this area boasts the newest resorts, the most spectacular hillside settings, and the best golf courses.

VERY EXPENSIVE

The Boulders Resort and Golden Door Spa ★★★ Set amid a jumble of giant boulders 45 minutes north of Old Town Scottsdale, this was the first luxury golf resort in the north Valley's rugged foothills. When not golfing, you can relax around the small pool, play tennis, relax at the resort's Golden Door Spa, or try your hand at rock climbing. The lobby is in a Santa Fe–style building with tree-trunk pillars and a flagstone floor, and the guest rooms continue the pueblo styling with stucco walls, beehive fireplaces, and beamed ceilings. For the best views, ask for one of the second-floor units. Bathrooms are large and luxuriously appointed, with tubs for two and separate showers. In addition to the resort's restaurants, there are several other dining options at the adjacent El Pedregal Festival Marketplace.

34631 N. Tom Darlington Dr. (P.O. Box 2090), Carefree, AZ 85377. © 800/553-1717, 800/WYNDHAM, or 480/488-9009. Fax 480/488-4118. www.wyndhamboulders.com. 215 units. Late Dec to May $649 double, from $1,150 villa; May to early Sept $279 double, from $800 villa; early Sept to early Dec $550 double, from $1,150 villa; early Dec to late Dec $299 double, from $800 villa (for all rates there is an additional $29–$33 nightly service charge). Children under 16 stay free in parent's room. AE, DC, DISC, MC, V. Pets accepted ($100). **Amenities:** 8 restaurants; lounge; 4 pools; 2 18-hole golf courses; 8 tennis courts; exercise room; full-service spa; 3 Jacuzzis; bike rentals; children's programs; concierge; business center; pro shop; shopping arcade; salon; room service; massage; babysitting; laundry service; dry cleaning. In room: A/C, TV, dataport, minibar, coffeemaker, hair dryer, iron, safe, high-speed Internet access.

Copperwynd Resort and Club ★★ Value   Although it's a ways from Old Town Scottsdale, this boutique hotel, high on a ridge overlooking the town of Fountain Hills, is one of the most luxurious resorts in the area. The hotel boasts some of the most picturesque mountain vistas in the Valley, which is one of the reasons I like it so much. The resort has a fabulous tennis facility, an impressive health club, and a spa. The resort's Jacuzzi, tucked into a rocky hillside, is as romantic as they come. All guest rooms have great views and feature a European deluxe decor. Balconies provide plenty of room for taking in the vista. There's an excellent restaurant on the premises.

13225 N. Eagle Ridge Dr., Fountain Hills, AZ 85268. © 877/707-7760 or 480/333-1900. www.copperwynd.com. 42 units. Late Dec to late Apr $379–$425 double, $825–$925 villa; late Apr to mid-May and late Sept to late Dec $199–$249 double, $800–$1,000 villa; mid-May to late Sept $129–$189 double, $550–$650 villa. Children under 18 stay free in parent's room. AE, DC, DISC, MC, V. **Amenities:** 2 restaurants; lounge; 2 pools; 9 tennis courts; health club and full-service spa; 3 Jacuzzis; saunas; children's programs; game room; concierge; pro shop; room service; massage; babysitting; laundry service; dry cleaning. In room: A/C, TV, dataport, fridge, coffeemaker, hair dryer, iron, safe, free local calls, high-speed Internet access, wi-fi.

Four Seasons Resort Scottsdale at Troon North ★★★   Located in the foothills of north Scottsdale adjacent to (and with privileges at) the legendary Troon North golf course, the Four Seasons is even more impressive than the nearby Boulders resort. With casita accommodations scattered across a boulder-strewn hillside, the Four Seasons boasts one of the Valley's most dramatic settings, and with a hiking trail to the nearby Pinnacle Peak Park, the resort is a good choice for anyone who wants to explore the desert on foot. Guest rooms and suites are among the most lavish you'll find in Arizona. If you can afford it, opt for one with a private plunge pool and an outdoor shower—a luxury usually found only in tropical resorts.

10600 E. Crescent Moon Dr., Scottsdale, AZ 85262. © 888/207-9696 or 480/515-5700. Fax 480/515-5599. www.fourseasons.com. 210 units. Jan to mid-May $465–$650 double, $725–$4,000 suite; mid-May to early Sept $165–$245 double, $395–$2,000 suite; early Sept to Dec $375–$550 double, $725–$4,000 suite. Children under 18 stay free in parent's room. AE, DC, DISC, MC, V. Pets accepted. **Amenities:** 3 restaurants; lounge; large 2-level pool; 2 18-hole golf courses; 2 tennis courts; large exercise room; spa; Jacuzzi; children's programs; concierge; car-rental desk; business center; 24-hr. room service; massage; babysitting; guest laundry; laundry service; dry cleaning. In room: A/C, TV/VCR, dataport, minibar, coffeemaker, hair dryer, iron, safe, high-speed Internet access.

EXPENSIVE

Carefree Resort & Villas ★   This resort on the northern edge of the Valley of the Sun is an economical alternative to the nearby Boulders resort. Located away from Scottsdale's traffic, close to the unspoiled desert, and with the Wild West cow town of Cave Creek just down the road, this resort makes a great base for exploring the desert and soaking up western character. Horseback riding, hiking, and mountain biking are all nearby, too. The rooms around the main pool were recently renovated and the big villa suites are some of the nicest and most spacious rooms in the Valley. These rooms overlook the nearby mountains and adjacent golf course.

37220 Mule Train Rd., Carefree, AZ 85377. ℂ 888/488-9034 or 480/488-5300. Fax 480/595-3719. www.carefree-resort.com. 370 units. Jan to early Apr $229–$249 double, $289–$499 suite or villa; early Apr to late May $169–$189 double, $219–$419 suite or villa; late May to mid-Sept $99–$119 double, $139–$279 suite or villa; mid-Sept to Dec $169–$189 double, $209–$349 suite or villa. Children under 18 stay free in parent's room. AE, DC, DISC, MC, V. Pets accepted ($45 fee). **Amenities:** 2 restaurants; 2 lounges; 3 pools; 5 tennis courts; exercise room; full-service spa; 2 Jacuzzis; bike rentals; car-rental desk; business center; room service; massage; laundry service; dry cleaning. *In room:* A/C, TV, dataport, coffeemaker, hair dryer, iron, free local calls, high-speed Internet access, wi-fi.

The Fairmont Scottsdale Princess ★★★ I know this faux Moorish palace belongs in Spain, not Arizona, but I still love it. With its royal palms, tiled fountains, and waterfalls, the Princess offers an exotic atmosphere unmatched in the area and will delight anyone in search of a romantic hideaway. Families will enjoy the water playground (with its two water slides) and kids' fishing pond. The resort is located a 20-minute drive from Old Town Scottsdale and is home to the FBR Open golf tournament and the city's top tennis tournament, which means the fairways and courts are top-notch. There's also the Willow Stream spa. Guest rooms, which have just been renovated, are done in an elegant Southwestern style, with spacious bathrooms. All units have private balconies.

7575 E. Princess Dr., Scottsdale, AZ 85255. ℂ 800/441-1414 or 480/585-4848. Fax 480/585-0086. www.fairmont.com. 650 units. $159–$589 double; $319–$3,800 suite. Children under 12 stay free in parent's room. AE, DC, DISC, MC, V. Pets accepted. **Amenities:** 4 restaurants; 3 lounges; 4 pools; 2 18-hole golf courses; 7 tennis courts; exercise room; full-service spa; Jacuzzi; concierge; car-rental desk; business center; golf and tennis pro shops; shopping arcade; salon; 24-hr. room service; massage; babysitting; laundry service; dry cleaning. *In room:* A/C, TV, dataport, minibar, coffeemaker, hair dryer, iron, safe.

MODERATE
Cave Creek Tumbleweed Hotel ★ Located in the heart of Cave Creek, the Valley's wildest and most western community, this older motel has rooms calculated to appeal to the country-music-loving clientele that frequent Cave Creek. Be sure to book early, because this place stays packed for much of the year. Although the guest rooms have a bit of western character, the popularity of this place is due in large part to the fun atmosphere of surrounding saloons and cowboy steakhouses. Although it's at least a 30-minute drive from here to Phoenix, the desert is a whole lot closer here than it is to Phoenix and Scottsdale's budget motels.

6333 E. Cave Creek Rd., Cave Creek, AZ 85327. ℂ 480/488-3668. www.tumbleweedhotel.com. 24 units. $99–$149 double. Children under 18 stay free in parent's room. AE, DISC, MC, V. Pets accepted ($75 refundable deposit). **Amenities:** Outdoor pool. *In room:* A/C, TV, coffeemaker.

CENTRAL PHOENIX & THE CAMELBACK CORRIDOR
This area is the heart of the upscale Phoenix shopping and restaurant scene. Old money and new money rub shoulders along the avenues here, and valet parking is de rigueur. Located roughly midway between Old Scottsdale and downtown Phoenix, this area is a good bet for those intending to split their time between the downtown Phoenix cultural and sports district and the world-class shopping and dining in Scottsdale.

VERY EXPENSIVE
Arizona Biltmore Resort & Spa ★★★ For decades this has been the favored Phoenix address of celebrities, politicians, and old money, and the distinctive cast-cement

blocks inspired by a Frank Lloyd Wright design make this a unique architectural gem. It's the historic character and timeless elegance that really set this place apart. With wide lawns, colorful flower gardens, and views of Piestewa Peak, this is a resort for outdoor lounging. While the two golf courses and expansive spa are the main draws, the children's activities center also makes this a popular choice for families. Of the several different styles of accommodations, the "resort rooms" are quite comfortable and come with balconies or patios. Those rooms in the Arizona Wing are also good choices. Afternoon tea is served in the lobby.

2400 E. Missouri Ave., Phoenix, AZ 85016. © 800/950-0086 or 602/955-6600. Fax 602/381-7600. www.arizona biltmore.com. 738 units. Jan to mid-May $425–$625 double, from $720 suite; mid-May to early Sept $195–$275 double, from $325 suite; early Sept to Dec $355–$575 double, from $635 suite. Rates do not include a $16 daily serv-ice fee. Children under 18 stay free in parent's room. AE, DC, DISC, MC, V. Pets under 20 lb. accepted in cottage rooms ($250 deposit, $50 nonrefundable). **Amenities:** 5 restaurants; lounge; 8 pools; 2 18-hole golf courses; 7 tennis courts; health club and full-service spa; 2 Jacuzzis; saunas; bike rentals; children's programs; concierge; car-rental desk; courtesy shopping shuttle; business center; room service; massage; laundry service; dry cleaning; executive-level rooms; lawn games. *In room:* A/C, TV, dataport, minibar, hair dryer, iron, safe, high-speed Internet access.

Embassy Suites Biltmore ★★ Located across the parking lot from the Biltmore Fashion Park shopping center, this hotel makes a great base if you want to be within walking distance of half a dozen good restaurants. The atrium is filled with interesting tile work, tropical greenery, waterfalls, and ponds filled with koi (colorful Japanese carp). In the atrium, you'll also find a romantic lounge with huge banquettes shaded by palm trees. Unfortunately, the rooms, all suites, are dated and a bit of a letdown, but they're certainly large. All in all, this hotel is a good value, especially when you consider that rates include both breakfast and afternoon drinks.

2630 E. Camelback Rd., Phoenix, AZ 85016. © 800/EMBASSY or 602/955-3992. Fax 602/955-6479. www.phoenix biltmore.embassysuites.com. 232 units. Jan to mid-Mar $229–$289 double; Apr to May $179–$229 double; June to early Sept $99–$159 double; early Sept to Dec $189–$259 double. Rates include full breakfast and afternoon drinks. Children under 18 stay free in parent's room. AE, DC, DISC, MC, V. Valet parking $8. Pets accepted ($25). **Amenities:** Restaurant; lounge; outdoor pool; exercise room; access to nearby health club; Jacuzzi; children's programs; concierge; courtesy car; business center; room service; massage; babysitting; coin-op laundry; laundry service; dry cleaning; executive-level rooms. *In room:* A/C, TV, dataport, fridge, coffeemaker, hair dryer, iron, wi-fi.

Hermosa Inn ★★ *Finds* This luxurious boutique hotel, once a guest ranch, is one of the few hotels in the Valley to offer any Old Southwest atmosphere, and because the Hermosa Inn is all about getting a little peace and quiet, I breathe a big sigh of relief every time I arrive here. Built in 1930 by cowboy artist Lon Megargee, the inn is situated on more than 6 acres of attractive gardens in an upscale residential neigh-borhood. The inn provides luxury, yet is completely removed from Scottsdale's hectic pace. The only other nearby place this tranquil is the Royal Palms, which is more serv-ice oriented. Rooms vary from cozy to spacious and are decorated in contemporary Western decor.

5532 N. Palo Cristi Rd., Paradise Valley, AZ 85253. © 800/241-1210 or 602/955-8614. Fax 602/955-8299. www. hermosainn.com. 35 units. Early Jan to Apr $299–$349 double, $499–$689 suite; May 1 to late May $199–$249 dou-ble, $399–$599 suite; late May to mid-Sept $110–$160 double, $310–$510 suite; mid-Sept to early Jan $250–$305 double, $450–$605 suite. Rates do not include daily hospitality fee of $11. Rates include full breakfast. Children 12 and under stay free in parent's room. AE, DC, DISC, MC, V. Take 32nd St. north from Camelback Rd., turn right on Stanford Rd., and turn left on N. Palo Cristi Rd. From Lincoln Dr., turn south on N. Palo Cristi Rd. (east of 32nd St.). Pets accepted ($50 fee). **Amenities:** Restaurant; lounge; outdoor pool; tennis court; access to nearby health club; 2 Jacuzzis; concierge; room service; massage; babysitting; laundry service; dry cleaning. *In room:* A/C, TV, dataport, minibar, coffeemaker, hair dryer, iron, safe, free local calls, high-speed Internet access, wi-fi.

The Ritz-Carlton Phoenix ★★ *Overrated* Directly across the street from the Biltmore Fashion Park shopping center, the Ritz-Carlton is the city's finest nonresort hotel and is known for providing impeccable service. The public areas are filled with European antiques, which, however, feel out of place in Phoenix. Consequently, this isn't the place to stay if you're looking for Southwest character. Still the hotel is utterly sophisticated and regularly ranks among the world's top hotels. Guest rooms got a makeover in 2004 and now have a slightly more contemporary feel. An elegant lobby lounge serves afternoon tea as well as cocktails, while a clublike lounge offers fine cigars and premium spirits.

2401 E. Camelback Rd., Phoenix, AZ 85016. ✆ **800/241-3333** or 602/468-0700. Fax 602/553-0685. www.ritzcarlton. com/hotels/phoenix. 281 units. $169–$359 double, $369–$3,000 suite. Children under 18 stay free in parent's room. AE, DC, DISC, MC, V. Valet parking $24. **Amenities:** Restaurant; 2 lounges; pool; exercise room; access to nearby health club; saunas; concierge; business center; 24-hr. room service; massage; babysitting; laundry service; dry cleaning; executive-level rooms. *In room:* A/C, TV, dataport, minibar, hair dryer, iron, safe, high-speed Internet access, wi-fi.

Royal Palms Resort and Spa ★★ This romantic, beautiful resort is located midway between Old Town Scottsdale and Biltmore Fashion Park. It was constructed more than 50 years ago by Cunard Steamship executive Delos Cooke and is done in Spanish mission style. Giving the resort the tranquil feel of a Mediterranean monastery are lush walled gardens where antique water fountains splash. The most memorable guest rooms are the deluxe casitas, each with a distinctive decor ranging from opulent contemporary to classic European. The Alvadora Spa provides a place to be pampered. This gorgeous little hideaway has the feel of a Spanish villa that was transported to Arizona. A real gem!

5200 E. Camelback Rd., Phoenix, AZ 85018. ✆ **800/672-6011** or 602/840-3610. Fax 602/840-6927. www. royalpalmsresortandspa.com. 117 units. Jan–May $385–$405 double, $425–$3,000 suite; June to mid-Sept $179–$189 double, $209–$3,000 suite; mid-Sept to Dec $355–$375 double, $385–$3,000 suite. Rates do not include daily service fee of $22. Children under 18 stay free in parent's room. AE, DC, DISC, MC, V. Pets accepted ($300 deposit, $100 nonrefundable). **Amenities:** Restaurant; poolside grill; lounge; outdoor pool with cabanas; exercise room; full-service spa; Jacuzzi; bike rentals; concierge; business center; 24-hr. room service; massage; babysitting; laundry service; dry cleaning. *In room:* A/C, TV, dataport, minibar, coffeemaker, hair dryer, iron, safe.

EXPENSIVE
Maricopa Manor Centrally located between downtown Phoenix and Scottsdale, Maricopa Manor is just a block off busy Camelback Road and has long been Phoenix's best B&B. The inn's main building, designed to resemble a Spanish manor house, was built in 1928, and the orange trees, palms, and large yard all lend an Old Phoenix atmosphere. All guest rooms are large, comfortable suites, many with Arts and Crafts touches. One suite has a sunroom and kitchen, while another has two separate sleeping areas. There are tables in the garden where you can eat your breakfast, which is delivered to your door.

15 W. Pasadena Ave., Phoenix, AZ 85013. ✆ **800/292-6403** or 602/274-6302. Fax 602/266-3904. www.maricopa manor.com. 7 units. Jan–Mar $139–$199 double; Apr and Nov–Dec $129–$179 double; May and Oct $109–$139 double; June–Sept $99–$109 double. Rates include continental breakfast. Children under 12 stay free in parent's room. AE, DC, DISC, MC, V. Pets accepted. **Amenities:** Outdoor pool; access to nearby health club; Jacuzzi; massage. *In room:* A/C, TV/VCR/DVD, dataport, fridge, coffeemaker, hair dryer, iron, free local calls, wi-fi.

MODERATE
Extended Stay Deluxe Phoenix-Biltmore ★ Billing itself as a temporary residence and offering discounts for stays of 5 days or more, this hotel consists of studio-style apartments located just north of Camelback Road and not far from Biltmore Fashion Park.

Although designed primarily for corporate business travelers on temporary assignment in the area, this lodging makes a good choice for families as well. All units have full kitchens, big bathrooms, and separate sitting areas.

5235 N. 16th St., Phoenix, AZ 85016. © **800/804-3724** or 602/265-6800. Fax 602/265-1114. www.extendedstay deluxe.com. 112 units. $74–$135 double. Children under 17 stay free in parent's room. AE, DC, DISC, MC, V. Pets accepted (fee $25 per day, $75 maximum). **Amenities:** Small outdoor pool; exercise room; Jacuzzi; coin-op laundry; dry cleaning. *In room:* A/C, TV, dataport, kitchen, coffeemaker, hair dryer, iron, high-speed Internet access.

NORTH PHOENIX

Some of the Valley's best scenery is to be found in north Phoenix, where several small mountains have been protected as parks and preserves; the two Pointe Hilton resorts claim great locations close to these parks. However, the Valley's best shopping and dining, as well as most major attractions, are all at least a 30-minute drive away.

VERY EXPENSIVE

JW Marriott Desert Ridge Resort & Spa ★★★ This is the largest resort in the state and stays crowded with conference groups, but, if you just want to spend some time in the sun drinking margaritas by the pool, it's a great option. There are 4 acres of water features and pools (including a tubing "river") and a large spa with its own lap pool. At the resort's grand entrance, desert landscaping and rows of palm trees give the resort a sense of place, and the lobby's roll-up walls let plenty of balmy desert air in during the cooler months. Guest rooms have balconies and hints of Mediterranean styling. Be sure to ask for a room with a view to the south; these rooms look out to several of Phoenix's mountain preserves.

5350 E. Marriott Blvd., Phoenix, AZ 85054. © **800/835-6206** or 480/293-5000. Fax 480/293-3600. www.jwdesert ridgeresort.com. 950 units. Jan to early Apr $449–$509 double; early Apr to early June $299–$469 double; early June to early Sept $159–$219 double; early Sept to Dec $369–$469 double; $449–$1,529 suite year-round. Children stay free in parent's room. AE, DC, DISC, MC, V. **Amenities:** 5 restaurants; 2 snack bars/cafes; 3 lounges; 5 pools; 2 18-hole golf courses; 8 tennis courts; health club; full-service spa; 3 Jacuzzis; children's programs; concierge; car-rental desk; business center; 24-hr. room service; massage; babysitting; guest laundry; laundry service; dry cleaning. *In room:* A/C, TV, dataport, minibar, coffeemaker, hair dryer, iron, safe, high-speed Internet access.

EXPENSIVE

Pointe Hilton Squaw Peak Resort ★★★ *Kids* At the foot of Piestewa Peak (formerly Squaw Peak), this lushly landscaped resort makes a big splash with its 9-acre Hole-in-the-Wall River Ranch aquatic playground, which features a tubing "river," water slide, waterfall, sports pool, and lagoon pool. An 18-hole putting course and game room also help make it a great family vacation spot. The resort is done in the Spanish villa style, and most of the guest rooms are large suites. For a family vacation, this place is hard to beat. However, I prefer the nearby Pointe Hilton Tapatio Cliffs Resort for its dramatic hillside setting and location adjacent to the hiking trails of the North Mountain Recreation Area.

7677 N. 16th St., Phoenix, AZ 85020-9832. © **800/876-4683** or 602/997-2626. Fax 602/997-2391. www.pointe hilton.com. 563 units. Jan to mid-Apr $199–$299 double, $1,300 grande suite; mid-Apr to late May and mid-Sept to Dec $109–$249 double, $1,300 grande suite; late May to mid-Sept $99–$139 double, $1,300 grande suite. Rates do not include daily resort fee of $9. Children under 18 stay free in parent's room. AE, DC, DISC, MC, V. Pets accepted. **Amenities:** 3 restaurants; 2 snack bars; 5 lounges; 8 pools; 18-hole golf course (4 miles away by shuttle); 4 tennis courts; health club (extra charge) and small spa; 6 Jacuzzis; saunas; children's programs; concierge; car-rental desk; business center; room service; massage; babysitting; laundry service; coin-op laundry; dry cleaning. *In room:* A/C, TV, dataport, minibar, coffeemaker, hair dryer, iron, high-speed Internet access.

Pointe Hilton Tapatio Cliffs Resort ★★★ If you love to lounge by the pool, then this resort is a great choice. The Falls, a 3-acre water playground, includes two pools, a 138-foot water slide, 40-foot cascades, a whirlpool tucked into an artificial grotto, and rental cabanas. If you're a hiker, you can head out on the trails of the adjacent North Mountain Recreation Area. All rooms are spacious suites with Southwest-inspired furnishings; corner units are particularly bright. This resort has steep walkways, so you need to be in good shape to stay here. The resort's Different Pointe of View restaurant has one of the finest views in the city. This resort is more adult-oriented than the Pointe Hilton Squaw Peak Resort, but is similar.

11111 N. Seventh St., Phoenix, AZ 85020. ℂ 800/876-4683 or 602/866-7500. Fax 602/993-0276. www.pointehilton. com. 585 units. Jan to mid-Apr $199–$299 double, $1,300 grande suite; mid-Apr to late May and mid-Sept to Dec $109–$249 double, $1,300 grande suite; late May to mid-Sept $99–$139 double, $1,300 grande suite. Rates do include $9 daily resort fee. Children under 18 stay free in parent's room. AE, DC, DISC, MC, V. Pets accepted. **Amenities:** 4 restaurants; 2 poolside cafes; 5 lounges; 8 pools; golf course; 2 tennis courts; fitness center (extra charge); small full-service spa; 8 Jacuzzis; sauna; steam room; seasonal children's programs; concierge; car-rental desk; business center; room service; massage; babysitting; laundry service; dry cleaning. *In room:* A/C, TV, dataport, minibar, coffeemaker, hair dryer, iron, high-speed Internet access.

MODERATE/INEXPENSIVE

Among the better moderately priced chain motels in north Phoenix are the **Best Western Inn Suites Hotel Phoenix,** 1615 E. Northern Ave., at 16th Street (ℂ **800/752-2204** or 602/997-6285), charging high-season rates of $69 to $139 double; and the **Best Western Bell Hotel,** 17211 N. Black Canyon Hwy. (ℂ **877/263-1290** or 602/993-8300), charging the same rates.

Among the better budget chain motels are the **Motel 6–Sweetwater,** 2735 W. Sweetwater Ave. (ℂ **602/942-5030**), charging $46 to $56 double; and **Super 8–Phoenix Metro/Central,** 4021 N. 27th Ave. (ℂ **602/248-8880**), charging $46 to $51.

Embassy Suites Phoenix North ★★ *Value* This resortlike hotel in north Phoenix is right off I-17, a 30- to 45-minute drive from the rest of the Valley's resorts (and good restaurants)—but if you happen to have relatives in Sun City or are planning a trip north to Sedona or the Grand Canyon, it's a good, economical choice. The lobby of the mission-style hotel has the feel of a Spanish church interior, but instead of a cloister off the lobby, there's a garden courtyard with a huge pool. The guest rooms are all suites, although furnishings are fairly basic and bathrooms small.

2577 W. Greenway Rd., Phoenix, AZ 85023. ℂ 800/EMBASSY or 602/375-1777. Fax 602/993-5693. www.embassy suites.com. 314 units. $99–$179 double. Children under 18 stay free in parent's room. Rates include full breakfast and afternoon drinks. AE, DC, DISC, MC, V. Pets accepted ($50 fee). **Amenities:** Restaurant; lounge; large pool and children's pool; tennis court; exercise room; Jacuzzi; car-rental desk; room service; laundry service; coin-op laundry; dry cleaning. *In room:* A/C, TV, dataport, fridge, coffeemaker, hair dryer, iron.

DOWNTOWN, SOUTH PHOENIX & THE AIRPORT AREA

Unless you're a sports fan or are in town for a convention, there's not much to recommend downtown Phoenix. This 9-to-5 area can feel like a ghost town at night. For the most part, south Phoenix is one of the poorest parts of the city. However, it does have a couple of exceptional resorts.

VERY EXPENSIVE

Pointe South Mountain Resort ★★★ *Kids* This sprawling resort abuts the 17,000-acre South Mountain Park, and is one of the best choices in the Valley for families. Kids will love the wave pool, tubing "river," twisty water slide, and two free-fall-style water slides. Stables at the resort allow you and the kids to ride into the sunset on South Mountain, and there are numerous children's programs, plus a kid-friendly cowboy steakhouse (Rustler's Rooste, p. 422). The guest rooms, all suites, feature contemporary Southwestern furnishings and lots of space. At press time, there were plans to double the size of the resort's spa.

7777 S. Pointe Pkwy., Phoenix, AZ 85044. © 877/800-4888 or 602/438-9000. Fax 602/431-66535. www.pointe southmtn.com. 640 units. Early Jan to Apr $259 double; May $239 double; June to early Sept $169 double; early Sept to Dec $309 double. Rates do not include $16 daily resort fee. Children under 18 stay free in parent's room. AE, DC, DISC, MC, V. **Amenities:** 6 restaurants; 3 lounges; 11 outdoor pools (including 6-acre water park); 18-hole golf course; 5 tennis courts; basketball and volleyball courts; racquetball court; health club; full-service spa; 9 Jacuzzis; children's programs; concierge; car-rental desk; business center; pro shop; room service; massage; coin-op laundry; laundry service; dry cleaning; executive-level rooms; horseback riding. *In room:* A/C, TV, dataport, minibar, coffeemaker, hair dryer, iron, high-speed Internet access, wi-fi.

Sheraton Wild Horse Pass Resort ★★★ Named for the area's wild horses, this resort is located 20 minutes south of Phoenix Sky Harbor International Airport on the Gila River Indian Reservation, and because the resort looks out across miles of desert, it has a pleasantly remote feel. Throw in horseback riding, a full-service spa featuring desert-inspired treatments, a golf course, a nature trail along a 2½-mile-long artificial river, and a pool with a water slide, and you'll find plenty to keep you busy. At press time, there were also plans to reopen Scottsdale's popular Rawhide Wild West town here on the property. The resort is owned by the Maricopa and Pima tribes, who go out of their way to share their culture with resort guests. Guest rooms have great beds, small patios, and large bathrooms with separate tubs and showers.

5594 W. Wild Horse Pass Blvd. (P.O. Box 94000), Phoenix, AZ 85070-4000. © 888/218-8989 or 602/225-0100. Fax 602/225-0300. www.wildhorsepassresort.com. 500 units. Early Jan to late May $259–$409 double, $640–$950 suite; late May to mid-Sept $110–$245 double, $600–$950 suite; mid-Sept to early Jan $229–$389 double, $600–$950 suite. Children stay free in parent's room. AE, DC, DISC, MC, V. Pets accepted. **Amenities:** 5 restaurants; snack bar; 2 lounges; 4 outdoor pools; 2 18-hole golf courses; 2 tennis courts; health club; full-service spa; 6 Jacuzzis; bike rentals; children's programs; concierge; car-rental desk; business center; shopping arcade; 24-hr. room service; massage; babysitting; laundry service; dry cleaning; horseback riding; casino. *In room:* A/C, TV, dataport, minibar, coffeemaker, hair dryer, iron, safe, high-speed Internet access.

EXPENSIVE
The Wyndham Buttes Resort ★★ Just 3 miles from Sky Harbor Airport, this resort makes the most of its craggy hilltop location, and although some people complain that the nearby freeway ruins the view, the rocky setting is quintessentially Southwestern. The only other resorts in the area with as much desert character are the far more expensive Boulders and Four Seasons. From the cactus garden, waterfall, and fishpond *inside* the lobby to the circular restaurant and free-form swimming pools, this resort is calculated to take your breath away. Guest rooms are stylishly elegant. The city-view rooms are a bit larger than the hillside-view rooms, but second-floor hillside-view rooms have patios. Unfortunately, most bathrooms have only three-quarter-size tubs. The Top of the Rock restaurant has great views.

2000 Westcourt Way, Tempe, AZ 85282. © 800/WYNDHAM or 602/225-9000. Fax 602/438-8622. www.wyndham buttes.com. 353 units. Jan to mid-Apr $189–$299 double, from $475 suite; mid-Apr to mid-May $159–$199 double, from $475 suite; mid-May to early Sept $89–$129 double, from $375 suite; early Sept to Dec $159–$269 double, from $475 suite. Children 18 and under stay free in parent's room. AE, DC, DISC, MC, V. Pets accepted ($35 fee). **Amenities:** 3 restaurants; 3 lounges; 2 pools; 4 tennis courts; volleyball courts; exercise room; health club; full-service spa; 4 Jacuzzis; sauna; bike rentals; concierge; business center; room service; massage; babysitting; dry cleaning; executive-level rooms. *In room:* A/C, TV, dataport, minibar, coffeemaker, hair dryer, iron, high-speed Internet access.

MODERATE

Hotel San Carlos ⭐   If you don't mind staying in downtown Phoenix with the convention crowds, you'll get good value at this historic hotel. Built in 1928 and listed on the National Register of Historic Places, the San Carlos provides that touch of elegance and charm missing from other downtown choices. Bedrooms are rather small by today's standards, but they were renovated in 2003. If you're up for a splurge, check out the suites, which are named for celebrities who stayed here in the hotel's heyday.

202 N. Central Ave., Phoenix, AZ 85004. © **866/253-4121** or 602/253-4121. Fax 602/253-6668. www.hotelsancarlos. com. 121 units. Jan–Apr $146–$166 double, $227 suite; May–Aug $79–$110 double, $140 suite; Sept–Dec $113–$133 double, $195 suite. Children under 18 stay free in parent's room. Rates include continental breakfast. AE, DC, DISC, MC, V. Parking $5. **Amenities:** 3 restaurants; rooftop pool; access to nearby health club; concierge; car-rental desk; laundry service; dry cleaning. *In room:* A/C, TV, dataport, coffeemaker, hair dryer, iron, wi-fi.

TEMPE, MESA & THE EAST VALLEY

Tempe, which lies just a few miles east of the airport, is home to Arizona State University, and consequently supports a lively nightlife scene. Tempe is also convenient to Papago Park, which is home to the Phoenix Zoo, the Desert Botanical Garden, a municipal golf course, and hiking and mountain-biking trails.

EXPENSIVE

Fiesta Inn Resort ⭐ *(Value)*   Reasonable rates, green lawns, palm- and eucalyptus-shaded grounds, and a location close to the airport, ASU, and Tempe's Mill Avenue make this older, casual resort one of the best deals in the Valley. Okay, so it doesn't have the desert character of The Wyndham Buttes Resort across the freeway, and it isn't as stylish as the resorts in Scottsdale, but you can't argue with the rates. The large guest rooms, although a bit dark, have an appealing retro mission styling.

2100 S. Priest Dr., Tempe, AZ 85282. © **800/528-6481** or 480/967-1441. Fax 480/967-0224. www.fiestainnresort. com. 270 units. Jan to late Apr $189 double; late Apr to May $149 double; June–Sept $100 double; Oct–Dec $165 double. AE, DISC, MC, V. Pets accepted. **Amenities:** 2 restaurants; lounge; pool; 3 tennis courts; exercise room; Jacuzzi; concierge; car-rental desk; courtesy airport shuttle; business center; room service; laundry service; dry cleaning. *In room:* A/C, TV, dataport, fridge, coffeemaker, hair dryer, iron, free local calls, high-speed Internet access.

Gold Canyon Golf Resort ⭐⭐ *(Value)*   Golfers willing to stay way out on the eastern outskirts of the Valley of the Sun (a 30- to 45-min. drive from the airport) should be thrilled by the economical room rates and great golf at this resort. Located at the foot of the Superstition Mountains, Gold Canyon is a favorite of golfers for its exceedingly scenic holes. The spacious guest rooms are housed in blindingly white pueblo-inspired buildings; some have fireplaces, while others have whirlpools. The deluxe golf-course rooms are definitely worth the higher rates. If you're here primarily to play golf and don't have a fortune to spend, this is *the* place to stay.

6100 S. Kings Ranch Rd., Gold Canyon, AZ 85218. © **800/624-6445** or 480/982-9090. Fax 480/830-5211. www. gcgr.com. 91 units. Jan–Mar $135–$185 double; Apr–Sept $89–$139 double; Oct–Dec $115–$165 double. Children under 18 stay free in parent's room. AE, DISC, MC, V. Pets accepted ($75 fee). **Amenities:** 2 restaurants; lounge; pool; 2 18-hole golf courses; exercise room; small spa; Jacuzzi; bike rentals; concierge; business center; room service; laundry service; dry cleaning. *In room:* A/C, TV, dataport, minibar, coffeemaker, hair dryer, iron.

Tempe Mission Palms Hotel ⭐⭐   With a great location on Tempe's hopping Mill Avenue and guest rooms decorated with a wild combination of bold colors and modern geometric patterns, this is the perfect choice for a fun-filled weekend in Tempe. Sure, this is a business hotel (ergonomic desk chairs), but with a rooftop pool, tennis court, and Mill Avenue's nightlife right out the front door, it's also a great choice for active travelers. Come in the spring and you won't want to leave the courtyard, which is scented by the flowers of citrus trees.

60 E. Fifth St., Tempe, AZ 85281. © 800/547-8705 or 480/894-1400. Fax 480/968-7677. www.missionpalms.com. 303 units. Jan–Apr $179–$199 double, $329 suite; May–June $129–$169 double, $269 suite; July–Aug $99–$129 double, $219 suite; Sept–Dec $149–$199 double, $299 suite. Rates do not include $6 daily hospitality fee. Children under 18 stay free in parent's room. AE, DC, DISC, MC, V. Pets accepted ($100 deposit, $25 nonrefundable). **Amenities:** Restaurant; 2 lounges; outdoor pool; tennis court; exercise room; access to nearby health club; 2 Jacuzzis; bike rentals; concierge; car-rental desk; courtesy airport shuttle; business center; room service; massage; laundry service; dry cleaning. *In room:* A/C, TV, dataport, coffeemaker, hair dryer, iron, high-speed Internet access, wi-fi.

MODERATE/INEXPENSIVE

Apache Boulevard in Tempe becomes Main Street in Mesa, and along this stretch of road there are numerous old motels charging some of the lowest rates in the Valley. However, these motels are very hit-or-miss. If you're used to staying at nonchain motels, you might want to cruise this strip and check out a few places. Otherwise, try the chain motels mentioned below.

Chain options in the Tempe area include the **Days Inn–Tempe,** 1221 E. Apache Blvd. (© **480/968-7793**), charging $59 to $120 double; and **Super 8–Tempe/Scottsdale,** 1020 E. Apache Blvd. (© **480/967-8891**), charging $59 to $109 double.

Chain options in the Mesa area include the **Motel 6–Mesa,** 336 W. Hampton Ave. (© **480/844-8899**), charging $52 to $56 double; and **Super 8–Mesa,** 6733 E. Main St. (© **480/981-6181**), charging $65 to $77 double.

WEST VALLEY

The Wigwam Golf Club & Spa ★★ Located 20 minutes west of downtown Phoenix, this property opened its doors to the public in 1929 and remains one of the nation's premier golf resorts. It's a classic, with old-school gentility, but when the money all headed to Scottsdale, this place became an elegant oasis surrounded by tract houses. Like the Arizona Biltmore and the Camelback Inn, the Wigwam Golf Club & Spa is an old-money sort of place. Most of the guest rooms are in Santa Fe–style buildings, surrounded by green lawns and colorful gardens, and all of the spacious units feature contemporary Southwestern furniture. Some units have fireplaces, but the rooms to request are those along the golf course. At press time, the resort was building a large spa and two of the golf courses were scheduled to be renovated.

300 Wigwam Blvd., Litchfield Park, AZ 85340. © 800/327-0396 or 623/935-3811. Fax 623/935-3737. www.wigwam resort.com. 331 units. Early Jan to mid-May $235–$605 double, $295–$635 suite; mid-May to early Sept $105–$275 double, $259 suite; early Sept to early Jan $195–$499 double, $245–$525 suite. Rates do not include $15 daily resort fee. Children under 17 stay free in parent's room. AE, DC, DISC, MC, V. Pets accepted ($50 deposit, $25 nonrefundable). **Amenities:** 3 restaurants; 2 lounges; 2 pools; 3 18-hole golf courses; 9 tennis courts; croquet court; health club; full-service spa; 2 Jacuzzis; bikes; children's programs; concierge; car-rental desk; 24-hr. room service; massage; babysitting; laundry service; dry cleaning; executive-level rooms. *In room:* A/C, TV, dataport, minibar, coffeemaker, hair dryer, iron, safe.

4 Where to Dine

The Valley of the Sun boasts hundreds of excellent restaurants, with most of the best dining options concentrated in the Scottsdale Road and Biltmore Corridor areas. If you want to splurge on only one expensive meal while you're here, consider a resort restaurant that offers a view of the city lights.

Good places to go trolling for a place to eat include the trendy Biltmore Fashion Park shopping center, at Camelback Road and 24th Street (© **602/955-1963**), and Old Town Scottsdale. A few of my favorites in both places are listed below.

If you happen to be visiting the Phoenix Art Museum, the Heard Museum, or the Desert Botanical Garden anytime around lunch, stay put for your noon meal. All three of these attractions have cafes serving decent, if limited, menus.

SCOTTSDALE
EXPENSIVE
Bloom ★★ (Value NEW AMERICAN   Located in the upscale Shops at Gainey Village, Bloom is affiliated with two of my favorite Tucson restaurants—Wildflower and Bistro Zin. The minimalist decor emphasizes flowers, an elegant wine bar serves a wide range of flights (tasting assortments), and the bistro-style menu has lots of great dishes in a wide range of prices. Opt for one of the wonderfully creative salads, such as fresh artichoke hearts with shaved Parmesan and white-truffle drizzle; there are also enough interesting appetizers to create a very satisfying dinner. The roast duck with whipped potatoes and drunken cherry sauce is excellent.

8877 N. Scottsdale Rd. © 480/922-5666. Reservations recommended. Main courses $8–$14 lunch, $15–$29 dinner. AE, DC, DISC, MC, V. Mon–Thurs 11am–3pm and 5–10pm; Fri–Sat 11am–3pm and 5–10:30pm; Sun 5–9:30pm.

Cowboy Ciao Wine Bar & Grill ★ SOUTHWESTERN/FUSION   Delicious food with a global influence and a fun, "cowboy chic" atmosphere make this a great place for a memorable meal. Not to be missed dishes include the exotic mushroom pan-fry and the TM soup. Keep an eye out for the porcini-crusted rib-eye steak, which sometimes shows up as a nightly special and is another good choice for mushroom fans. Cowboy Ciao is also notable for its wine list and bar, where customers can order a flight of wines. If you're feeling adventurous, try the Mexican chocolate pot de crème with chipotle cream for dessert.

7133 E. Stetson Dr. (at Sixth Ave.). © 480/WINE-111. www.cowboyciao.com. Reservations recommended. Main courses $8–$32 lunch, $20–$32 dinner. AE, DC, DISC, MC, V. Mon–Thurs 11:30am–2:30pm and 5–10pm; Fri–Sat 11:30am–2:30pm and 5–11pm; Sun 10:30am–2:30pm and 5–10pm.

Deseo ★★★ NUEVO LATINO   Jaded palates and sleepy taste buds will thank you profusely when you introduce them to the vibrant flavors on this restaurant's ceviche menu. Don't bother trying to decide between rainbow ceviche (tuna, hamachi, and salmon with white soy sauce, citrus juices, red onions, and cilantro), lobster ceviche (with lime, celery, jalapeños, yellow tomatoes, and celery sorbet), and hamachi "tiradito style" ceviche (with chili-miso sauce and pickled radish). Just order a trio. Wash everything down with a minty mojito for an unforgettable meal. Hot appetizers? Entrees? You can't go wrong, but the mahimahi is particularly memorable. Even the bread basket, with Peruvian cheese rolls and paper-thin fried plantain slices, is an absolute delight. For dessert, try the churros or rice pudding.

Westin Kierland Resort, 6902 E. Greenway Pkwy. © 480/624-1000. Main courses $27–$45. AE, DC, DISC, MC, V. Mon–Sat 6–10pm.

El Chorro Lodge ★ CONTINENTAL   Built in 1934 as a girls' school, El Chorro is a Valley landmark and one of the area's last old traditional establishments. Even if the interior is a little dowdy, at nighttime the lights twinkle on the saguaro cactus and the restaurant takes on a timeless tranquillity. The adobe building houses several

Phoenix, Scottsdale & the Valley of the Sun Dining

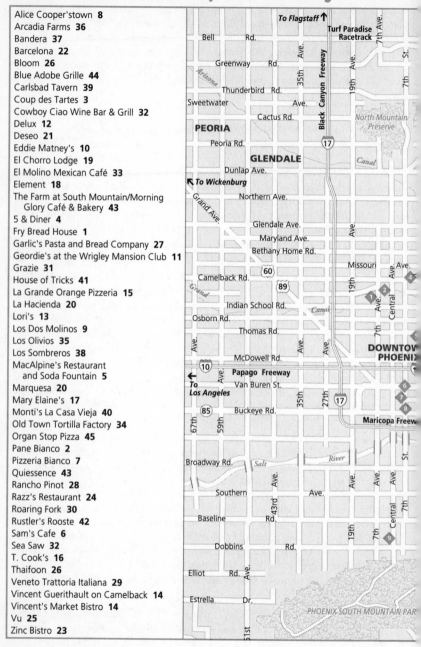

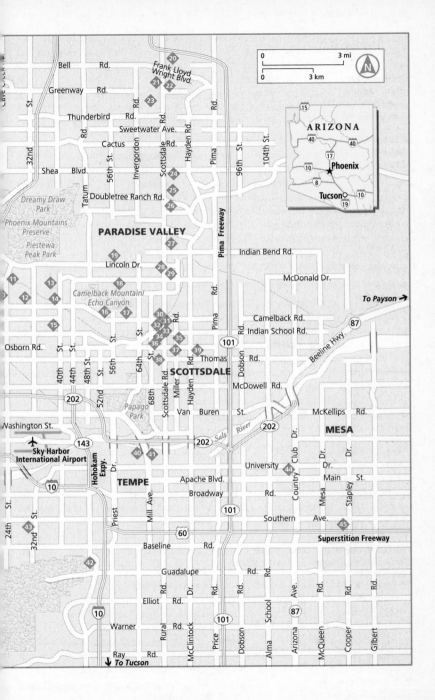

dining rooms, but the patio is the place to be, especially on cool evenings when there's a fire crackling in the patio fireplace. The menu features such classics as chateaubriand and rack of lamb. There are also several low-fat and low-salt dishes, as well as seafood options. Save room for the legendary sticky buns.

5550 E. Lincoln Dr., Paradise Valley. ✆ 480/948-5170. www.elchorro.com. Reservations recommended. Main courses $10–$20 lunch, $14–$64 dinner. AE, DC, DISC, MC, V. Mon–Thurs 11am–2pm and 5:30–10pm; Fri 11am–2pm and 5:30–11pm; Sat 5:30–11pm; Sun 9am–2pm and 5:30–10pm. Lunch and brunch served only Oct–May.

Rancho Pinot ★★ NEW AMERICAN   Rancho Pinot, hidden at the back of a non-descript shopping center adjacent to the upscale Borgata shopping plaza, combines a homey cowboy-chic decor with nonthreatening contemporary American cuisine, and has long been a favorite with Scottsdale and Phoenix residents. Look elsewhere if you're craving wildly creative flavor combinations, but if you like simple, well-prepared food, Rancho Pinot is a great choice. My favorite starter is the grilled squid salad with pre-served lemon; for an entree, you can always count on the handmade pasta or Nonni's chicken, braised with white wine, mushrooms, and herbs.

6208 N. Scottsdale Rd. (southwest corner of Scottsdale Rd. and Lincoln Dr.). ✆ 480/367-8030. Reservations rec-ommended. Main courses $18–$29. AE, DC, DISC, MC, V. Tues–Sun 5:30–10pm. Summer hours may vary.

Razz's Restaurant ★★ SOUTHWESTERN/ECLECTIC   Chef/owner Razz Kamnitzer has long been one of the most creative chefs in Scottsdale, so it may seem a bit unusual to find his superb restaurant in a nondescript old shopping center. How-ever, step through the door and you'll immediately be immersed in the conviviality that characterizes this locals' favorite. For the full-on experience, take a seat at the chef's counter where you can order a chef's sampler dinner consisting of as many or as few courses ($10–$16 per course) as you want. Razz makes the choices and you sit back and enjoy. You might wind up with spicy Indonesian noodles, foie gras–stuffed quail, or duck cakes with nopalito cactus sauce.

10315 N. Scottsdale Rd. ✆ 480/905-1308. www.razzsrestaurant.com. Reservations recommended. Main courses $20–$28. AE, DC, DISC, MC, V. Tues–Thurs 5–9pm; Fri–Sat 5–10pm.

Roaring Fork ★★ SOUTHWESTERN   This restaurant is the creation of local celeb-chef Robert McGrath, and the food is among the most creative Southwestern fare in the Valley. The bread basket alone, filled with herb-infused rolls and corn muffins accompanied by honey-chile butter, is enough to make you weep with joy. Be sure you try the sugar-and-chile-cured duck breast and the green-chile macaroni and cheese. If you can't get a table, dine in the saloon or the saloon patio. Don't miss the huckleberry margaritas.

4800 N. Scottsdale Rd. (in the Finova Building at the corner of Goldwater Blvd.). ✆ 480/947-0795. www.roaring fork.com. Reservations highly recommended. Main courses $15–$35. AE, DISC, MC, V. Mon–Sat 5–10pm; Sun 5–9pm.

Sea Saw ★★ JAPANESE   Chef Nobuo Fukuda is considered one of the best chefs in the country, but you'd never guess that this unpretentious hole-in-the-wall is home to such a celebrated chef. The menu lists only around 20 dishes, so it's almost impos-sible to go wrong here. Not one of these dishes can really be considered sushi, so don't expect items like California rolls. Instead, consider the seared tuna *tataki* or warm white fish carpaccio. The restaurant is affiliated with the adjacent Cowboy Ciao and has an overwhelmingly long wine list that includes lots of premium sakes.

7133 E. Stetson Dr. ✆ 480/481-9463. www.seasaw.net. Reservations not accepted. All plates $10–$16; tasting menu $100. AE, DC, DISC, MC, V. Sun–Thurs 5:30–10pm; Fri–Sat 5:30–11pm.

Vu ⭐⭐ NEW AMERICAN   This waterside restaurant in the beautiful Hyatt Regency resort is one of the most artistic and inspired restaurants in the Valley. The menu eschews wordy descriptions in favor of simply stating the handful of ingredients that makes up each dish. Rest assured that the result will be far from simple. Although the portions may be small and prices high, the food here is stylish, artistic, and bursting with flavors. Tasting menus are the way to go here; you'll get lots of small servings, such as succulent fried black bass served on eggplant puree with watercress oil. Calamari might come with caviar and be paired with champagne, while the Kobe beef might be served with three unusual sauces. Well worth a splurge.

Hyatt Regency Scottsdale Resort and Spa at Gainey Ranch, 7500 E. Doubletree Ranch Rd., Scottsdale, AZ 85258. ⓒ 480/991-3388. Reservations highly recommended. Main courses $24–$37; 4-course tasting menu $70 ($110 with wine). AE, DC, DISC, MC, V. Mon–Thurs 6–10pm; Fri–Sat 6–11pm.

MODERATE

Arcadia Farms ⭐ NEW AMERICAN   Long a favorite of the Scottsdale ladies-who-lunch crowd, this Old Town restaurant features a romantic setting and well-prepared contemporary fare. Try the delicious raspberry goat cheese salad with jicama and candied pecans. The warm mushroom, spinach, and goat cheese tart is another winner. Try to get a seat on the shady patio. This restaurant also operates cafes at the Desert Botanical Garden, the Heard Museum, and the Phoenix Art Museum.

7014 E. First Ave. ⓒ 480/941-5665. www.arcadiafarmscafe.com. Reservations recommended. Main courses $10–$13. MC, V. Daily 11am–3pm.

Bandera ⭐ 𝘝alue AMERICAN   Once you've gotten a whiff of the wood-roasted chickens turning on the rotisseries in Bandera's back-of-the-building, open-air stone oven, you'll know exactly what to order when you finally get seated at this perennially popular spot in Old Town. What an aroma! The succulent spit-roasted chicken is the meal to have here, and make sure you get it with some of Bandera's great mashed potatoes. Sure, you could order prime rib or clams, but you'd be a fool if you did. Stick with the chicken or maybe the barbecued ribs, and you won't go wrong.

3821 N. Scottsdale Rd. ⓒ 480/994-3524. Reservations recommended. Main courses $14–$26. AE, MC, V. Sun–Thurs 4:30–10pm; Fri–Sat 4–11pm.

Barcelona ⭐⭐ MEDITERRANEAN/NEW AMERICAN   This is the biggest and boldest of the Valley's popular supper clubs, and the building appears to have been lifted straight out of the restaurant's namesake Spanish city. There are three bar areas, including one outdoors (for smokers), and several dining areas. The menu doesn't break any new ground, but it does have surprisingly low prices for such a gorgeous setting. The main dining room faces the bandstand and converts into a dance floor late in the evening; music is primarily jazz, R&B, and Top 40. This is definitely a see-and-be-seen sort of place, with a brisk beautiful-people bar scene late at night.

There's a second Barcelona in Chandler at 900 N. 54th St. (ⓒ **480/785-9004**).

15440 Greenway-Hayden Loop. ⓒ 480/603-0370. www.barcelonadining.com. Reservations highly recommended. Main courses $12–$36. AE, DC, DISC, MC, V. Mon–Wed 11:30am–2pm and 4–10pm; Thurs–Fri 11:30am–2pm and 4–11pm; Sat 4–11pm.

Carlsbad Tavern ⭐ NEW MEXICAN   Carlsbad Tavern blends the fiery tastes of New Mexican cuisine with a hip and humorous bat-theme atmosphere (a reference to Carlsbad Caverns). The menu lists traditional New Mexican dishes such as *carne adovada* (pork simmered in a fiery red-chile sauce), as well as contemporary Southwestern specialties such as grilled chicken, andouille sausage, black beans, and pine nuts tossed with pasta in a spicy peppercorn-cream sauce. Cool off your taste buds with a prickly-pear margarita. A lagoon makes this place feel like a beach bar, while the patio fireplace is cozy on a cold night.

3313 N. Hayden Rd. (south of Osborn). ℂ 480/970-8164. www.carlsbadtavern.com. Reservations accepted for 5 or more. Main courses $7.25–$20. AE, DISC, MC, V. Mon–Sat 11am–1am; Sun 1pm–1am (limited menu daily 10 or 11pm–1am).

Old Town Tortilla Factory ✦ MEXICAN   Located in an old house surrounded by attractive patios and citrus trees that bloom in winter and spring, this moderately priced Mexican restaurant has a great atmosphere, great food, and a lively bar scene (more than 80 premium tequilas). As you enter the restaurant grounds, you might see someone making fresh tortillas. These tortillas come in a dozen different flavors. The rich tortilla soup and the tequila-lime salad make good starters. For an entree, try the pork chops crusted with ancho chile powder and raspberry sauce.

6910 E. Main St. ℂ 480/945-4567. www.oldtowntortillafactory.com. Reservations accepted only for parties of 6 or more. Main courses $11–$31. AE, DC, DISC, MC, V. Sun–Thurs 5–9:30pm; Fri–Sat 5–10:30pm.

Thaifoon ✦✦ THAI   This may not exactly be traditional Thai food, but it sure is good. Thaifoon merges a hip upscale setting with flavorful food at economical prices. In fact, the dishes here are so good, you'll likely find yourself coming back repeatedly to try others. The Thai-style coconut-mushroom soup is the best I've ever had, and the many shrimp dishes are packed with lively flavors. Don't miss the great tropical cocktails.

At The Shops at Gainey Village, 8777 N. Scottsdale Rd. ℂ 480/998-0011. www.thaifoon.com. Reservations recommended. Main courses $9–$20. AE, DC, DISC, MC, V. Daily 11am–10pm.

Veneto Trattoria Italiana ✦ VENETIAN ITALIAN   This pleasantly low-key bistro, specializing in the cuisine of Venice, serves satisfying "peasant food," including traditional pork-and-garlic sausages served with grilled polenta and braised savoy cabbage. *Baccala mantecato* (creamy fish mousse on grilled polenta, made with dried salt cod soaked overnight in milk) is absolutely heavenly. Another good bet is the salad of thinly sliced smoked beef, shaved Parmesan, and arugula. For a finale, try the *semifreddo con frutta secca,* a partially frozen meringue with dried fruits in a pool of raspberry sauce. There's a welcoming bistro ambience and outdoor seating.

6137 N. Scottsdale Rd., in Hilton Village. ℂ 480/948-9928. www.venetotrattoria.com. Reservations recommended. Main courses $8–$18 lunch, $13–$23 dinner. AE, DC, DISC, MC, V. Mon–Sat 11:30am–2:30pm and 5–10pm.

Zinc Bistro ✦✦ *Finds* FRENCH   This place is a perfect reproduction of the sort of bistro you may have loved on your last trip to Paris. Everything is authentic, from the zinc bar to the sidewalk cafe seating to the hooks under the bar for womens' purses. Try the cassoulet with duck confit, the omelet piled high with shoestring potatoes, or anything that comes with the fabulous bistro fries.

In Kierland Commons, 15034 N. Scottsdale Rd. ℂ 480/603-0922. Reservations accepted only for parties of 6 or more. Main courses $8–$15 lunch, $8–$28 dinner. AE, DC, DISC, MC, V. Sun–Thurs 11am–10pm (late-night menu until midnight); Fri–Sat 11am–midnight.

INEXPENSIVE

El Molino Mexican Café ✦ *Finds* MEXICAN   Located a bit out of the Old Town Scottsdale mainstream, this little Mexican joint is little more than a fast-food place, but it serves the best chimichangas (deep-fried burritos) in town. Try one with *machaca* (shredded and spiced beef) or the green chili meat and we're sure you'll become a convert. If fried food just doesn't do it for you, opt for a couple of green corn tamales, which are an Arizona specialty.

3554 N. Goldwater Blvd. © 480/946-4494. Reservations not accepted. Main courses. $2–$9.50. AE, DISC, MC, V. Mon–Sat 9am–8pm.

Garlic's Pasta and Bread Company AMERICAN/ITALIAN This little lunch spot is tucked into the back of the same shopping center that houses the more upscale Roy's (familiar to anyone familiar with Hawaii), and although you could conceivably grab an early dinner here, this is first and foremost a great spot for a quick lunch if you happen to be cruising Scottsdale Road at midday. Creative sandwiches are the big attraction, but there are also pasta salads, soups, and even brick-oven pizzas.

At the Scottsdale Seville shopping center, 7001 N. Scottsdale Rd. © 480/368-9699. Reservations not accepted. Main courses $6–$9. AE, MC, V. Mon–Fri 10am–5pm; Sat 11am–5pm.

Grazie ★ *Finds* PIZZA This little neighborhood pizzeria and wine bar is in downtown Scottsdale at the quiet west end of Main Street and is a little gem of a place— sophisticated and full of contemporary art. Come here to sip Italian wines, share a couple of designer pizzas from the wood-fired oven, and mix with the locals. Start your meal with the carpaccio, which is served with arugula, Parmigiano-Reggiano cheese, and a lemon vinaigrette, or a salad made with arugula, baby greens, Parmigiano-Reggiano, red onions, red bell peppers, and pine nuts. The pizzas here have paper-thin crusts, so it's easy to save room for the tiramisu.

6952 E. Main St. © 480/663-9797. Reservations recommended Fri–Sat nights. Main courses $8–$15. AE, MC, V. Daily 5–10pm.

Los Olivos ★ MEXICAN Los Olivos is a Scottsdale institution, one of the last restaurants in Old Town that dates to the days when cowboys tied up their horses on Main Street. Although the food is just standard Mexican fare, the building is a fascinating folk-art construction. The entrance is a bit like a cement cave, with strange figures rising up from the roof. Amazingly, this throwback to slower times is only steps away from the Scottsdale Museum of Contemporary Art. On Friday and Saturday nights, there's Latin dancing from 9pm until 1am.

There's another Los Olivos up in north Scottsdale, at 15544 N. Pima Rd. (© **480/ 596-9787**).

7328 Second St. © 480/946-2256. www.losolivosrestaurant.com. Reservations recommended. Main courses $4–$14. AE, DISC, MC, V. Sun–Thurs 11am–10pm; Fri–Sat 11am–11pm.

Los Sombreros ★ *Finds* MEXICAN Although this casual Mexican restaurant is in an attractive old house, it doesn't look all that special from the outside. However, the menu is surprisingly creative and veers from the standard dishes served at most Mexican restaurants. Start with the chunky homemade guacamole, which is some of the best in the city. Be sure to order the *puerco en chipotle,* succulent, slow-roasted pork in tomatillo chipotle sauce. Finish it all off with the flan, which will spoil you for any other flan anywhere else. For a real treat, get it with almond-flavored tequila.

2534 N. Scottsdale Rd. (at McKellips Rd.), Scottsdale. © 480/994-1799. Main courses $12–$17. Reservations accepted for 5 or more. AE, DC, DISC, MC, V. Sun and Tues–Thurs 5–9pm; Fri–Sat 5–10pm.

(Kids) Cowboy Steakhouses

Cowboy steakhouses are family restaurants that generally provide big portions of grilled steaks and barbecued ribs, outdoor and "saloon" dining, live country music, and various other sorts of entertainment. The biggest of these is **Pinnacle Peak Patio Steakhouse & Microbrewery** 🐾, which, despite being surrounded by some of the valley's poshest suburbs, still knows how to keep the Wild West alive. Although you can indulge in mesquite-broiled steaks with all the traditional trimmings, the real draw is all the entertainment—gunfights, cowboy bands, two-stepping, and cookouts. The restaurant is located at 10426 E. Jomax Rd. in Scottsdale (© **480/585-1599**; www.pppatio.com). Entrees cost $8 to $35.

At **Rustler's Rooste** 🐾 you can start your meal by scooting down a big slide from the bar to the main dining room. While the view north across Phoenix is entertainment enough for most people, there are also cowboy bands playing for those who like to kick up their heels. If you've got the appetite of a hardworking cowpoke, try the enormous cowboy "stuff" platter consisting of, among other things, steak kebabs, barbecued ribs, cowboy beans, fried shrimp, barbecued chicken, and skewered swordfish. You'll find Rustler's at the Pointe South Mountain Resort, 7777 S. Pointe Hwy., in Phoenix (© **602/431-6474**; www.rustlersrooste.com). Entrees range from $14 to $29.

NORTH SCOTTSDALE, CAREFREE & CAVE CREEK
VERY EXPENSIVE

Marquesa 🐾🐾🐾 MEDITERRANEAN The Marquesa, with an ambience reminiscent of an 18th-century Spanish villa, is as romantic a restaurant as you'll find in the Valley. The menu is a contemporary interpretation of Mediterranean cuisine, and though the prices are high, I can think of few better places for a special dinner. The offerings change with the seasons, but expect them to be ripe with exotic ingredients, and count on almost every dish being an intensive labor of love. Paella Valenciana, the signature dish, includes such ingredients as lobster, escargot, shrimp, and cockles, and should not be missed. The Sunday brunch is one of the best in the Valley.

At the Fairmont Scottsdale Princess, 7575 E. Princess Dr. (about 12 miles north of downtown Scottsdale). © 480/585-4848. Reservations recommended. Main courses $33–$47; brunch $70. AE, DC, DISC, MC, V. Wed–Sat 6–10pm; Sun 10am–2pm. Closed July–Sept.

Sassi 🐾🐾 ITALIAN If the precipitous plummet of the dollar against the euro has forced you to forego this year's vacation in Italy, then don't miss an opportunity to have a meal at this Tuscan villa transplanted to the Arizona desert. Every room in this beautiful, sprawling building is gorgeous and has a distinctive character of its own. You may have to eat here a few times before you decide which room you like the best. The menu is not your standard southern Italian menu, so don't go looking for spaghetti and meatballs. Instead try the wood-oven shrimp and blood-orange salad or the octopus braised in olive oil. In fact the best thing to do here is order a bunch of dishes and then share everything as any good Italian family would.

10455 E. Pinnacle Peak Pkwy., Scottsdale. © 480/502-9095. www.sassi.biz. Reservations highly recommended. Primi $10–$20; secondi $17–$32. AE, DC, DISC, MC, V. Tues–Sun 5:30–9 or 10pm.

EXPENSIVE

La Hacienda ★★ GOURMET MEXICAN As you may guess from the price range below, this is not your average taco joint. La Hacienda serves gourmet Mexican cuisine in an upscale, glamorous but rustic setting reminiscent of an early 1900s hacienda (stone-tiled floor, Mexican glassware and crockery, a beehive fireplace). Be sure to start with the *antojitos* (appetizers) platter, which might include pork flautas (a rolled-up fried tortilla), baked shrimp, crabmeat enchiladas, and a red-corn quesadilla made with squash blossoms, wild mushrooms, and goat cheese. I like the chicken in fragrant orange sauce and the quail stuffed with duck, dried fruits, and cheese. However, the rack of lamb crusted with pumpkin seeds has long been a local favorite. Live music lends a party atmosphere.

At the Fairmont Scottsdale Princess, 7575 E. Princess Dr. (about 12 miles north of downtown Scottsdale). © 480/ 585-4848. Reservations recommended. Main courses $23–$39. AE, DC, DISC, MC, V. Sept–May Thurs–Tues 5:30–10pm. Call for summer hours.

Michael's ★★ NEW AMERICAN/INTERNATIONAL Located in the classy little Citadel shopping/business plaza in north Scottsdale, this restaurant is one of the Valley's best. The setting is simple yet elegant, which allows the drama of food presentation to come to the fore. To start things off, do not miss the "silver spoons" hors d'oeuvres—tablespoons each containing three or four ingredients that burst with flavor. From there, it's on to main courses like rosemary-scented lamb chop with eggplant, goat-cheese lasagna, and tomato confit. For drinks with or without a light meal, head upstairs to the bar.

8700 E. Pinnacle Peak Rd., N. Scottsdale. © 480/515-2575. www.michaelsrestaurant.com. Reservations recommended. Main courses $8–$16 lunch, $24–$29 dinner; prix-fixe menu $55 ($90–$100 with wine). AE, DC, DISC, MC, V. Mon–Fri 11am–2pm and 6–9pm; Sat 6–9pm; Sun 10am–2pm (brunch) and 6–9pm.

Mosaic ★★★ *Finds* NEW AMERICAN The Pinnacle Peak area of north Scottsdale has seen a proliferation of high-end restaurants in recent years, and this just may be the best of a very good bunch. Okay, so dinner here is going to set you back quite a bit, but the food is superb, and if you come before the sun goes down, you can soak up some of the best desert views in the Valley. Chef/owner Deborah Knight is one of the best chefs around and likes to show off her culinary creativity with a menu that changes regularly and is always provocative and daring. How about bacon-wrapped kangaroo tenderloin or snapping turtle soup to start things out? For an entree, you might order a rosemary-and-sage grilled ostrich fillet or wild boar chops with a sauce made from dried strawberries and roses. You get the picture; this is a foodie's nirvana.

10600 E. Jomax Rd., N. Scottsdale. © 480/563-9600. www.mosaic-restaurant.com. Reservations recommended. Main courses $26–$38; tasting menu $55–$75 ($35 more with wine). AE, DC, DISC, MC, V. Tues–Sat 5:30–9 or 10pm.

MODERATE

The Original Crazy Ed's Satisfied Frog Saloon & Restaurant *Finds* AMERICAN/BARBECUE Cave Creek is the Phoenix area's favorite cow-town hangout and is filled with Wild West–themed saloons and restaurants. Crazy Ed's—affiliated with the Black Mountain Brewing Company, which produces Cave Creek Chili Beer—is my favorite. You'll find Crazy Ed's in Frontier Town, a tourist-trap cow town. This place is just plain fun, with big covered porches and sawdust on the floor. Stick to steaks and barbecue.

At Frontier Town, 6245 E. Cave Creek Rd., Cave Creek. ℂ 480/488-3317. www.satisfiedfrog.com. Reservations recommended on weekends. Main courses $8–$22 lunch, $10–$25 dinner. AE, DISC, MC, V. Sun–Thurs 11am–10pm; Fri–Sat 11am–11pm.

INEXPENSIVE

Greasewood Flat ★ *Finds* AMERICAN   Burgers and beer are the mainstays at this rustic open-air restaurant in the Pinnacle Peak area of north Scottsdale. Located down a potholed gravel road behind Reata Pass steakhouse, Greasewood Flat is a desert party spot where families, motorcycle clubs, cyclists, and horseback riders all rub shoulders. Place your order at the window and grab a seat at one of the picnic tables. While you wait for your meal, you can also peruse the old farm equipment. This place is the antithesis of Scottsdale posh, and that's exactly why we love it. Only in the Southwest could you find a place like this.

27500 N. Alma School Rd. ℂ 480/585-9430. Reservations not accepted. Main courses $3.50–$7. No credit cards. Daily 11am–1am.

CENTRAL PHOENIX & THE CAMELBACK CORRIDOR
VERY EXPENSIVE

Mary Elaine's ★★★ FRENCH   There quite simply is no place else in Arizona to compare with Mary Elaine's, and if you happen to be in town for a major wedding anniversary or milestone birthday, this is the place to celebrate. At least once in your life you have to splurge on the sort of dining experience provided here. Situated atop the posh Phoenician resort, this elegant restaurant is the pinnacle of Arizona dining not only for its haute cuisine, but also for its award-winning wine list (and master sommelier), exemplary service, and superb table settings. Chef Bradford Thompson's menu focuses on classic French cuisine with an emphasis on impeccably fresh ingredients, and foie gras, truffles, lobster, and Beluga caviar all make frequent appearances. Menus change seasonally, and there are also themed tasting menus. Try to make a reservation that allows you to take in the sunset.

At The Phoenician, 6000 E. Camelback Rd. ℂ 480/423-2530. Reservations highly recommended. Jackets required for men. Main courses $50; 3-course dinner $87; 7-course tasting menu $120 (plus $85 for matched wines). AE, DC, DISC, MC, V. Tues–Thurs 6–10pm; Fri–Sat 6–11pm.

EXPENSIVE

Coup des Tartes ★ *Finds* COUNTRY FRENCH   Chain restaurants, theme restaurants, restaurants that are all style and little substance: Sometimes in Phoenix it seems impossible to find a genuinely homey little hole-in-the-wall that serves good food. Don't despair; Coup des Tartes is just the ticket. With barely a dozen tables and no liquor license (bring your own wine; $8 corkage fee), it's about as removed from the standard Phoenix glitz as you can get without boarding a plane and leaving town. Start your meal with pâté de campagne or brie brûlée, covered with caramelized apples. The entree menu changes regularly, but the Moroccan lamb shank with couscous is so good that it's always available. The filet mignon, with the sauce of the moment, is another good choice. Of course, for dessert, you absolutely must have a tart.

4626 N. 16th St. (a couple blocks south of Camelback Rd.). ℂ 602/212-1082. Reservations recommended. Main courses $14–$30. AE, MC, V. Tues–Sat 5:30–10pm.

Eddie Matney's ✷✷ NEW AMERICAN   Eddie Matney does high-end comfort food, and he does it right. This bistro in a glass office tower at Camelback Road's most upscale corner is a popular power-lunch and business-dinner spot, but it also works well for a romantic evening out. The menu ranges far and wide for inspiration and features everything from Eddie's famous meatloaf to sesame-encrusted ahi tuna. If you're not up for a splurge, take advantage of the happy-hour appetizers in the bar, Monday through Thursday from 4 to 11pm and Friday and Saturday from 4pm to midnight.

2398 E. Camelback Rd. ✆ 602/957-3214. www.eddiematneys.com. Reservations recommended. Main courses $9–$15 lunch, $19–$29 dinner. AE, DC, DISC, MC, V. Mon–Fri 11:30am–2:30pm and 5–9:30pm; Sat 5–9:30pm.

LON's ✷✷ AMERICAN REGIONAL   Located in a beautiful old adobe hacienda built by cowboy artist Lon Megargee and surrounded by colorful gardens, this restaurant is one of the most southwestern places in the Phoenix area, and the patio, with its views of Camelback Mountain, is blissfully tranquil. At midday this place is popular with both retirees and the power-lunch set, while at dinner it bustles with a wide mix of people. Dinner entrees are reliable, though not quite as imaginative as the appetizers (I like to skip the entrees and just make a meal of appetizers). The bar is cozy and romantic.

At the Hermosa Inn, 5532 N. Palo Cristi Rd. ✆ 602/955-7878. www.lons.com. Reservations recommended. Main courses $10–$15 lunch, $19–$34 dinner. AE, DC, DISC, MC, V. Mon–Fri 11:30am–2pm and 6–10pm; Sat 6–10pm; Sun 10am–2pm (brunch) and 6–10pm.

T. Cook's ✷✷✷ MEDITERRANEAN   Ready to pop the question? On your honeymoon? Celebrating an anniversary? This is the place for you. There just isn't a more romantic restaurant in the Valley. Located within the walls of the Mediterranean-inspired Royal Palms Resort & Spa, it's surrounded by decades-old gardens and even has palm trees growing right through the roof of the dining room. The focal point of the open kitchen is a wood-fired oven that turns out a fabulous spit-roasted chicken as well as an impressive platter of paella. T. Cook's continues to make big impressions right through to the dessert course.

At the Royal Palms Resort and Spa, 5200 E. Camelback Rd. ✆ 602/808-0766. www.royalpalmshotel.com. Reservations highly recommended. Main courses $11–$16 lunch, $24–$32 dinner. AE, DC, DISC, MC, V. Mon–Sat 6–10am, 11am–2pm, and 5:30–10pm; Sun 10am–2pm (brunch) and 5–10:30pm.

Vincent Guerithault on Camelback ✷✷ SOUTHWESTERN   Vincent's is a Phoenix bastion of Southwestern cuisine and has long enjoyed a devoted local following. The menu blends Southwestern influences with classic European dishes. You could order a delicious lobster salad or sautéed beef tenderloins with Pinot Noir glaze, but if you're from outside the region, you should try the Southwestern dishes. Don't miss the duck tamale or the tequila soufflé, and for an entree, the veal sweetbreads with blue corn meal are an enduring favorite. For a casual breakfast or lunch, try the attached Vincent's Market Bistro, which is affiliated with the restaurant's Saturday farmers' market.

3930 E. Camelback Rd. ✆ 602/224-0225. www.vincentsoncamelback.com. Reservations highly recommended. Main courses $11–$16 lunch, $29–$32 dinner. AE, DC, DISC, MC, V. Main dining room Mon–Fri 11:30am–2pm and 5–10pm; Sat 5–10pm. Closed Sun–Mon June–Sept.

MODERATE

Delux ✷ BURGERS   With a sleek and stylish decor, a very limited menu (you better like burgers), and one of the best selections of draft beers in the Valley, this is the ultimate ultra-hip burger-and-beer joint. The burgers, made with flavorful Niman Ranch beef, get my vote for best burgers in the city, but it's the cute Barbie-size shopping carts full of crispy French fries that are the real reason to dine here. Talk about your guilty pleasures—it just doesn't get much better than a basket of fries and a pint of Old Rasputin imperial stout. If you're not a burger-meister, don't despair, there are great salads and a few non-beef sandwiches.

3146 E. Camelback Rd. © 602/522-2288. www.deluxburger.com. Reservations not accepted. Main courses $7–$10. AE, DISC, MC, V. Daily 11am–2am.

La Grande Orange Pizzeria ★ PIZZA   Good pizza and an off-the-beaten-tourist-path neighborhood location make this casual restaurant a good place to feel like a local. Best of all, La Grande Orange is convenient to both downtown Scottsdale and the pricey Camelback corridor. Gourmet pizzas are what this place is all about, but you should also order a Big Orange salad (arugula, fennel, oranges, avocado, almonds, and pickled onions served with goat cheese crostini). While you're here, check out the outstanding little gourmet grocery that shares the building and the Grande Orange name.

4410 N. 40th St. © 602/840-7777. Reservations not accepted. Main courses $11–$14. AE, MC, V. Mon–Thurs 5–9pm; Fri–Sat 5–10pm; Sun 4–9pm.

Vincent's Market Bistro ★★ FRENCH   Located in back of the ever-popular Vincent's restaurant, this casual place does a respectable job of conjuring up a casual back-street bistro in Paris. It's utterly quaint without being froufrou. There are tables with cast-iron bases and chairs with woven reed seats. Just inside the door, there's a table usually covered with pastries. You can sit down and have a meal here (try the coq au vin) or get some gourmet food to go. This place stays packed on Saturday mornings when Vincent's farmers' market attracts crowds of shoppers in search of gourmet snacks and fresh produce.

3930 E. Camelback Rd. © 602/224-3727. www.vincentsoncamelback.com. Main courses $7–$10; Sun brunch $25 adults, $13 children 10 and under. AE, DC, DISC, MC, V. Mon–Fri 7am–6pm, Sat–Sun 8am–3pm.

INEXPENSIVE

5 & Diner AMERICAN   If it's 2am and you just have to have a big, greasy burger and a side of fries, head for the 24-hour 5 & Diner. You can't miss it—it's the classic streamliner diner that looks as though it just materialized from New Jersey.

Other locations are in Paradise Valley at 12802 N. Tatum Blvd. (© **602/996-0033**), and in Scottsdale at Scottsdale Pavilions, 9069 E. Indian Bend Rd. (© **480/949-1957**).

5220 N. 16th St. © 602/264-5220. www.5anddiner.com. Sandwiches/plates $5.50–$15. AE, MC, V. Daily 24 hr.

Pane Bianco ★ *Finds* BAKERY/SANDWICHES   Chris Bianco, owner of downtown's immensely popular Pizzeria Bianco, has another winner on his hands with this casual counter-service bakery and sandwich shop not far from the Heard Museum. The menu consists of only four sandwiches and a couple of salads, but all the breads are baked on the premises in a wood-fired oven. The house-made mozzarella is exquisitely fresh and is served both as a caprese salad with tomatoes and basil and in a focaccia sandwich with the same ingredients. And that focaccia—the best in Phoenix.

4404 N. Central Ave. © 602/234-2100. Main courses $8. AE, MC, V. Tues–Sat 11am–3pm.

DOWNTOWN, SOUTH PHOENIX & THE AIRPORT AREA
EXPENSIVE

Quiessence ★★ *Finds* NEW AMERICAN   This place is as far from a typical Phoenix/Scottsdale dining experience as you can get without going to the airport and getting on a plane, and that's exactly why I love it. Set at the back of a shady pecan grove not far from South Mountain Park, Quiessence is surrounded by organic vegetable gardens. It is these gardens, and the freshness of the ingredients they provide, that makes the food here so wonderful, but it is the delightfully rural setting that makes Quiessence truly special. Come for lunch before going for a hike in the park (or bring a change of clothes and come for dinner after a hike). The herbed chicken here is so good you'll forget that it's actually good for you. Don't pass it up if it's on the menu. Oh, and by the way, the desserts are outrageous!

6106 S. 32nd St. (℘ **602/276-0601**. Reservations recommended. Main courses $9–$18 lunch, $14–$28 dinner. AE, MC, V. Tues–Fri 11am–2pm and 5–10pm; Sat 5–10pm.

MODERATE

Alice Cooper'stown ★ BARBECUE   Owned by Alice Cooper himself, this sports-and-rock-themed restaurant/bar is downtown's premier eat-o-tainment center. Sixteen video screens (usually showing sporting events) are the centerpiece, but there's also an abundance of memorabilia, including guitars once used by the likes of Fleetwood Mac and Eric Clapton. The waitstaff even wears Alice Cooper makeup. Barbecue is served in various permutations, including a huge barbecue sandwich. If you were an Alice Cooper fan, or hope to spot some local pro athletes, this place is a must.

101 E. Jackson St. (℘ **602/253-7337**. www.alicecooperstown.com. Reservations not accepted. Sandwiches/barbecue $7–$19. AE, DC, MC, V. Sun–Thurs 11am–10pm; Fri–Sat 11am–11pm.

Sam's Cafe ★★ *Value* SOUTHWESTERN   Sam's Cafe, one of only a handful of decent downtown restaurants, offers food that's every bit as imaginative, but not nearly as expensive, as that served at other (often overrated) Southwestern restaurants in Phoenix. Breadsticks with picante-flavored cream cheese, grilled vegetable tacos, and angel-hair pasta in a spicy jalapeño sauce with shrimp and mushrooms all have a nice balance of flavors. The downtown Sam's has a large patio that overlooks a fountain and palm garden; it stays packed with the lunchtime, after-work, and convention crowds.

There's another Sam's in Biltmore Fashion Park, 2566 E. Camelback Rd. (℘ **602/954-7100**).

At the Arizona Center, 455 N. Third St. (℘ **602/252-3545**. www.canyoncafe.com. Reservations recommended. Main courses $8–$19. AE, DISC, MC, V. Thurs–Sat 11am–10pm; Sun–Wed 11am–9pm.

INEXPENSIVE

The Farm at South Mountain/Morning Glory Café & Bakery ★ *Finds* SANDWICHES/SALADS   If being in the desert has you dreaming of shady trees and green grass, you'll enjoy this little oasis reminiscent of a deep-south pecan orchard. A rustic outbuilding has been converted to a stand-in-line lunch restaurant where you can order a focaccia sandwich or a delicious pecan turkey Waldorf salad. Breakfast means baked goods such as muffins and scones. The grassy lawn is ideal for a picnic. At the back of the farm, you'll find the breakfast cafe, and on Saturdays from 9am to 1pm, there is a farmers' market here.

6106 S. 32nd St. (℘ **602/276-6360**. Sandwiches and salads $8.95. AE, MC, V. Mid-Sept to June Tues–Sun 8am–3pm (if weather is inclement, call to be sure it's open). Closed July through mid-Sept. Take Exit 151A off I-10 and go south on 32nd St.

Fry Bread House *Finds* NATIVE AMERICAN   Fry bread is just what it sounds like—fried bread—and it's a mainstay on Indian reservations throughout the West. Although you can eat these thick, chewy slabs of fried bread plain, salted, or with honey, they also serve as the wrappers for Indian tacos, which are made with meat, beans, and lettuce. If you've already visited the Four Corners region of Arizona, then you've probably had an Indian taco. Forget them—the ones here are the best in the state. Try one with green chili. If you still have room for dessert, do not miss the fry bread with chocolate and butter.

4140 N. Seventh Ave. ☎ **602/351-2345.** Main courses $3.50–$6.50. DISC, MC, V. Mon–Thurs 10am–7pm; Fri–Sat 10am–8pm.

Los Dos Molinos ★ MEXICAN   I hope you travel with a fire extinguisher. You're gonna need it if you eat at this legendary hot spot in south Phoenix. The food here is New Mexican style, which means everything, with the exception of the margaritas, is incendiary. Actually there are a few dishes for the timid, but people who don't like their food fiery know enough to stay away from this place. So popular is the food at Los Dos Molinos that there's even one in New York. Here in the Phoenix area, there's another at 260 S. Alma School Rd., Mesa (☎ **480/969-7475**).

8646 S. Central Ave. ☎ **602/243-9113.** Reservations not accepted. Main courses $3.25–$13. AE, DC, DISC, MC, V. Tues–Fri 11am–2:30pm and 5–9pm; Sat 11am–9pm; Sun 11am–5pm.

MacAlpine's Restaurant and Soda Fountain *Finds* AMERICAN   This is the oldest operating soda fountain in the Southwest, and it hasn't changed much since its opening in 1928. Wooden booths and worn countertops show the patina of age. Big burgers and sandwiches make up the lunch offerings, and should be washed down with a lemon phosphate, chocolate malted, or egg cream. The restaurant sponsors Friday night swing dances at a nearby dance studio, so bring your dancing shoes and brush up on your Lindy.

2303 N. Seventh St. ☎ **602/262-5545.** Sandwiches/specials $4.75–$6.75. AE, DISC, MC, V. Mon–Fri 11am–2pm; Sat 11am–3pm.

Pizzeria Bianco ★ PIZZA   Even though this historic brick building is in the heart of downtown Phoenix, the atmosphere is so cozy it feels like your neighborhood local, and the wood-burning oven turns out deliciously rustic pizzas. One of my favorites is made with red onion, Parmesan, rosemary, and crushed pistachios. Don't miss the fresh mozzarella, either: Pizzeria Bianco makes its own, and it can be ordered as an appetizer or on a pizza.

At Heritage Square, 623 E. Adams St. ☎ **602/258-8300.** Reservations accepted for 6 or more. Pizzas $9–$13. AE, MC, V. Tues–Sat 5–10pm.

TEMPE, & MESA
MODERATE
Blue Adobe Grille ★★ *Finds* MEXICAN   Wedged between a Taco Bell and an aging bowling alley, this restaurant looks like just the sort of place you should drive right past. Don't! Despite appearances, this New Mexican–style restaurant serves deliciously creative Southwestern fare at very economical prices. To get an idea of what the food here is all about, order the Tres Santa Fe plate with tenderloin burrito, a shrimp enchilada, and carne adovada. Of course, there are great margaritas, but there's also a surprisingly good wine list. This place is a hangout for Chicago Cubs fans and makes a good

dinner stop on the way back from driving the Apache Trail. There's a second Blue Adobe at 10885 N. Frank Lloyd Wright Blvd., Scottsdale (© **480/314-0550**).

144 N. Country Club Dr., Mesa. © **480/962-1000.** blueadobegrille.com. Reservations recommended Fri–Sat. Main courses $9–$21. AE, DC, DISC, MC, V. Sun–Thurs 11am–9pm; Fri–Sat 11am–10pm.

House of Tricks ★★ NEW AMERICAN   Despite the name, you'll find far more treats here than tricks. Housed in a pair of old Craftsman bungalows surrounded by a garden of shady trees, this restaurant seems a world away from the bustle on nearby Mill Avenue. This is a nice spot for a romantic evening and a good place to try some innovative cuisine. The garlicky Caesar salad and house-smoked salmon with avocado, capers, and lemon cream are good bets for starters. Among the entrees, the sesame-crusted ahi tuna is a good choice. Try to get a seat on the grape-arbor-covered patio.

114 E. Seventh St., Tempe. © **480/968-1114.** www.houseoftricks.com. Reservations recommended. Main courses $6.25–$11 lunch, $16–$28 dinner. AE, DC, DISC, MC, V. Mon–Sat 11am–10pm.

Monti's La Casa Vieja ★ AMERICAN   If you're tired of the Scottsdale glitz and are looking for Old Arizona, try this place. The adobe building was constructed in 1873 (*casa vieja* means "old house" in Spanish) on the site of the Salt River ferry, which operated in the days when the river flowed year-round. Today, local families know Monti's well, and rely on the restaurant for solid meals and low prices—you can get a filet mignon for as little as $10. The dark dining rooms are filled with memorabilia of the Old West.

1 W. Rio Salado Pkwy. (at Mill Ave.), Tempe. © **480/967-7594.** www.montis.com. Reservations recommended for dinner. Main courses $9–$30. AE, DC, DISC, MC, V. Mon–Thurs 11am–10pm; Fri–Sat 11am–midnight.

Moments **Dining with a View**

Located on a hilltop adjacent to the Arizona Biltmore resort, **Geordie's at the Wrigley Mansion Club** ★★ is housed in a mansion that was built between 1929 and 1931 by chewing gum magnate William Wrigley Jr. for his wife, Ada. The views are splendid and the continental cuisine is memorable. If you go for lunch, you can take a guided tour of the mansion before or after your meal. The mansion is located at 2501 E. Telawa Trail (© **602/955-4079;** www.wrigleymansionclub.com). Main courses cost $10 to $15 at lunch; from $25 to $40 at dinner; and Sunday brunch is $33.

When you've got one of the best views around and some of the best patio dining, do you really have to serve good food? Probably not, but luckily **elements**, the stylish restaurant at the Sanctuary on Camelback Mountain resort doesn't try to slide by on looks alone. That said, the view is a big part of dinner here, so try to make a reservation so that you can catch the sunset light on Mummy Mountain. The menu changes regularly and includes influences from around the world. The restaurant is located at Sanctuary on Camelback, 5700 E. McDonald Dr., in Paradise Valley (© **480/607-2300;** www.elementsrestaurant.com). Main courses range from $11 to $24 at lunch and from $23 to $34 at dinner.

INEXPENSIVE

Organ Stop Pizza ✦ *Kids* PIZZA   The pizza here may not be the best in town, but the mighty Wurlitzer theater organ, the largest in the world, sure is memorable. This massive instrument, which contains more than 5,500 pipes, has four turbine blowers to provide the wind to create the sound, and with 40-foot ceilings in the restaurant, the acoustics are great. As you marvel at the skill of the organist, who performs songs ranging from the latest pop tunes to *The Phantom of the Opera,* you can enjoy simple pizzas, pastas, or snacks.

1149 E. Southern Ave. (at Stapley Dr.), Mesa. © 480/813-5700. www.organstoppizza.com. Pizzas and pastas $6–$16. No credit cards. Thanksgiving to mid-Apr Sun–Thurs 4–9pm, Fri–Sat 4–10pm; mid-Apr to Thanksgiving Sun–Thurs 5–9pm, Fri–Sat 5–10pm.

5 Seeing the Sights

THE DESERT & ITS NATIVE CULTURES

Deer Valley Rock Art Center ✦   Located in the Hedgepeth Hills in the northwest corner of the Valley of the Sun, the Deer Valley Rock Art Center preserves an amazing concentration of Native American petroglyphs, some of which date back 5,000 years. Although these petroglyphs may not at first seem as impressive as those at more famous sites, the sheer numbers make this a fascinating spot. The drawings, which range from simple spirals to much more complex renderings of herds of deer, are on volcanic boulders along a quarter-mile trail. An interpretive center provides background information on this site and on rock art in general. From October through April, there are guided tours Saturdays at 10am. From May through September, there are tours on Saturdays at 7:30am.

3711 W. Deer Valley Rd. © 623/582-8007. www.asu.edu/clas/anthropology/dvrac. Admission $5 adults, $3 seniors and students, $2 children 6–12. Oct–Apr Tues–Sat 9am–5pm, Sun noon–5pm; May–Sept Tues–Fri 8am–2pm, Sat 7am–5pm, Sun noon–5pm. Closed major holidays. Take the Loop 101 highway west to 27th Ave., go north to Deer Valley Rd. and go west 2½ miles to just past 35th Ave.

Desert Botanical Garden ✦✦✦   Located in Papago Park adjacent to the Phoenix Zoo, this botanic garden displays more than 20,000 desert plants from around world, and its Plants and People of the Sonoran Desert Trail is the state's best introduction to Southwestern ethnobotany (human use of plants). Along this trail you can make your own yucca-fiber brush and practice grinding corn as Native Americans once did. On the Desert Wildflower Trail, you'll find colorful wildflowers throughout much of the year. Each year in the spring, there is also usually a butterfly pavilion filled with live butterflies. If you come late in the day, you can stay until after dark and see night-blooming flowers and dramatically lit cacti. A cafe on the grounds makes a great lunch spot. In spring and fall, there are also concerts in the garden. In early December, during *Las Noches de las Luminarias,* the gardens are lit at night by luminarias (candles inside small bags).

At Papago Park, 1201 N. Galvin Pkwy. © 480/941-1225 or 480/481-8190. www.dbg.org. Admission $9 adults, $8 seniors, $5 students 13–18, $4 children 3–12. Oct–Apr daily 8am–8pm; May–Sept daily 7am–8pm. Closed July 4th and Christmas. Bus: 3.

Heard Museum ✦✦✦   The Heard Museum is one of the nation's finest museums dealing exclusively with Native American cultures and is an ideal introduction to the indigenous peoples of Arizona. From pre-Columbian to contemporary, if it's art created by Native Americans, you'll find it here. If you're interested in the native cultures of Arizona, this should be your very first stop in the state. The museum is an invaluable introduction to the state's many tribes. The newly redesigned and expanded **Home: Native Peoples of the Southwest** exhibit examines the culture of each of the major tribes of the region and is the heart and soul of the museum. In the Lincoln Gallery, you'll get an idea of the number of different kachina spirits that populate the Hopi and Zuni religions, while the Crossroads Gallery offers a fascinating look at contemporary Native American art. Guided tours are offered daily. The annual **Indian Fair and Market,** held on the first weekend in March, includes traditional dances along with arts and crafts. The museum's cafe is a good place for lunch.

The museum also operates **Heard Museum North,** at El Pedregal Festival Marketplace, 34505 N. Scottsdale Rd. (© **480/488-9817**), in Carefree. This gallery features changing exhibits and is open Monday through Saturday from 10am to 5:30pm and Sunday from noon to 5pm. Admission is $3 for adults and is free for children 12 and under.

2301 N. Central Ave. © 602/252-8848. www.heard.org. Admission $7 adults, $6 seniors, $3 children 4–12. Daily 9:30am–5pm. Closed major holidays. Bus: Blue (B), Red (R), or 0.

Pueblo Grande Museum and Archaeological Park Located near Sky Harbor Airport and downtown Phoenix, the Pueblo Grande Museum and Archaeological Park houses the ruins of an ancient Hohokam village that was one of several villages along the Salt River between A.D. 300 and 1400. Sometime around 1450, this and other villages were mysteriously abandoned. Some speculate that drought and a buildup of salts from irrigation water reduced the fertility of the soil and forced the people to seek more fertile lands. The small museum displays many of the artifacts that have been dug up on the site. Although these exhibits are actually more interesting than the ruins themselves, there are also some reconstructed and furnished Hohokam-style houses that give a good idea of how the Hohokam lived. The museum sponsors interesting workshops (some just for kids), demonstrations, and tours (including petroglyph hikes). The **Pueblo Grande Museum Indian Market,** held in mid-December at Steele Indian School Park, which is on the northeast corner of Indian School Road and Central Avenue, is the largest of its kind in the state and features more than 450 Native American artisans.

4619 E. Washington St. (between 44th and 48th sts.). © 877/706-4408 or 602/495-0901. www.pueblogrande.com. Admission $2 adults, $1.50 seniors, $1 children 6–17; free on Sun. Mon–Sat 9am–4:45pm; Sun 1–4:45pm. Closed major holidays. Bus: 1.

ART MUSEUMS

Arizona State University Art Museum at Nelson Fine Arts Center ★ Although it isn't very large, this museum is memorable for its innovative architecture and excellent temporary exhibitions. With its purplish-gray stucco facade and pyramidal shape, the stark, angular building conjures up images of sunsets on desert mountains. The entrance is down a flight of stairs that leads to a cool underground garden area. Inside are galleries for crafts, prints, contemporary art, and Latin American art, along with outdoor sculpture courts and a gift shop. The collection of American art includes works by Georgia O'Keeffe, Edward Hopper, and John James Audubon. Definitely a must for both art and architecture fans. Across the street is the **Ceramics Research Center,** 10th Street and Mill Avenue (© **480/965-2782**), and Gallery, which showcases the university's extensive collection of fine art ceramics and is open Tuesday through Saturday from 10am to

Phoenix, Scottsdale & the Valley of the Sun Attractions

ARIZONA

Phoenix

Tucson

Arizona Biltmore **8**
Arizona Capitol Museum **5**
Arizona Historical Society Museum **14**
Arizona Museum for Youth **18**
Arizona Science Center **4**
ASU Art Museum **17**
Burton Barr Library **3**
Center for Meteorite Studies **17**
Ceramics Research Center
  and Gallery **17**
Desert Botanical Garden **12**
Hall of Flame Firefighting Museum **15**
Heard Museum **1**
Historic Heritage Square **4**
McCormick-Stillman Railroad Park **10**
Mesa Southwest Museum **19**
Mystery Castle **6**
Phoenix Art Museum **2**
Phoenix Museum of History **4**
Phoenix Zoo **13**
Pueblo Grande Museum
  and Archaeological Park **16**
Scottsdale Center for the Arts **11**
Scottsdale Museum
  of Contemporary Art **11**
Taliesin West **9**
Wrigley Mansion **7**

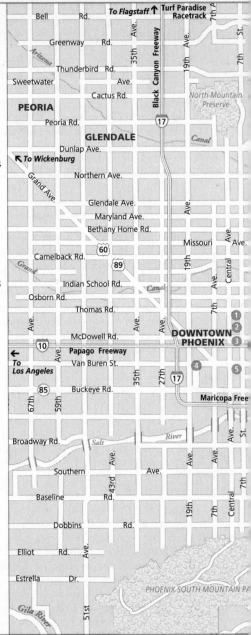

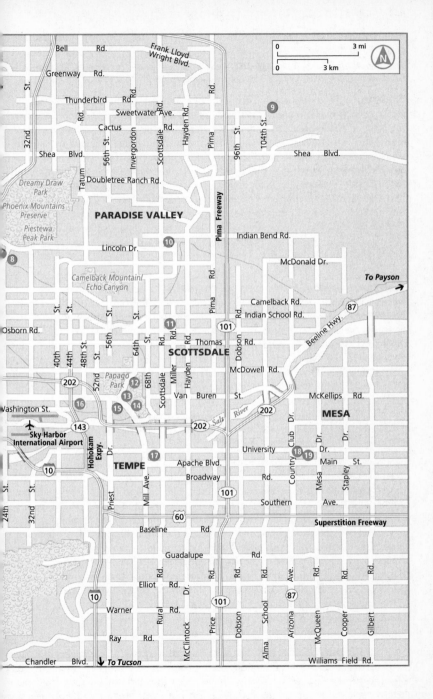

5pm. This latter center is another place not to miss. You just won't believe the amazing creativity on display.

10th St. and Mill Ave., Tempe. ℃ 480/965-2787. http://asuartmuseum.asu.edu. Free admission. Tues 10am–9pm (10am–5pm in summer); Wed–Sat 10am–5pm. Closed major holidays. Bus: Red (R), 1, 66, or 72.

Phoenix Art Museum ★★   This is one of the largest art museums in the Southwest, and within its labyrinth of halls and galleries is a respectable collection that spans the major artistic movements from the Renaissance to the present. Exhibits cover decorative arts, historic fashions, Spanish-colonial furnishings and religious art, and, of course, works by members of the Cowboy Artists of America. The collection of modern and contemporary art is particularly good, with works by Diego Rivera, Frida Kahlo, Pablo Picasso, Alexander Calder, Henry Moore, Georgia O'Keeffe, Henri Rousseau, and Auguste Rodin. The popular Thorne Miniature Collection consists of tiny rooms on a scale of 1 inch to 1 foot. Because this museum is so large, it frequently mounts traveling blockbuster exhibits. The cafe here is a good spot for lunch.

1625 N. Central Ave. (at McDowell Rd.). ℃ 602/257-1222. www.phxart.org. Admission $9 adults, $7 seniors and students, $3 children 6–17; free on Thurs. Tues–Wed and Fri–Sun 10am–5pm; Thurs 10am–9pm. Closed major holidays. Bus: Blue (B), Red (R), or 0.

Scottsdale Museum of Contemporary Art ★★   Scottsdale may be obsessed with art featuring lonesome cowboys and solemn Indians, but this boldly designed museum makes it clear that patrons of contemporary art are also welcome here. Cutting-edge art, from the abstract to the absurd, fills the galleries, with exhibits rotating every few months. In addition to the main building, there are several galleries in the adjacent Scottsdale Center for the Arts, which also has a pair of Dale Chihuly artglass installations. Don't miss James Turrell's skyspace *Knight Rise*, which is accessed from a patio off the museum shop. By the way, the museum shop is full of beautiful items that will fit in your suitcase.

7374 E. Second St., Scottsdale. ℃ 480/994-ARTS. www.smoca.org. Admission $7 adults, $5 students, free for children under 15; free on Thurs. Tues–Wed and Fri–Sat 10am–5pm; Thurs 10am–8pm; Sun noon–5pm. Closed major holidays. Bus: 41, 50, or 72. Also accessible via Scottsdale Trolley shuttle bus.

HISTORY MUSEUMS & HISTORIC LANDMARKS

Arizona Capitol Museum ★   In the years before Arizona became a state, the territorial capital moved from Prescott to Tucson, then back to Prescott, before finally settling in Phoenix. In 1898, a stately territorial capitol building was erected (with a copper roof to remind the local citizenry of the importance of that metal in the Arizona economy). Atop this copper roof was placed the statue *Winged Victory*, which still graces the old capitol building today. This building no longer serves as the actual state capitol, but has been restored to the way it appeared in 1912, the year Arizona became a state. Among the rooms on view are the senate and house chambers, as well as the governor's office. Excellent exhibits provide interesting perspectives on early Arizona events and lifestyles. There are free guided tours at 10am and 2pm.

1700 W. Washington St. ℃ 602/542-4675. www.lib.az.us/museum. Free admission. Mon–Fri 8am–5pm. Closed state holidays. Bus: 1 or DASH downtown shuttle.

Arizona Historical Society Museum in Papago Park ★   This museum, at the headquarters of the Arizona Historical Society, focuses its well-designed exhibits on the history of central Arizona. Temporary exhibits on the lives and works of the people who helped shape this region are always the highlights of a visit. An interesting permanent exhibit features life-size statues of everyday people from Arizona's past (a Mexican miner, a Chinese laborer, and so on). Quotes relate their individual stories, while props reveal what items they might have traveled with during their days in the desert.

1300 N. College Ave. (just off Curry Rd.), Tempe. © 480/929-0292. www.arizonahistoricalsociety.org. Admission $5 adults, $4 seniors and students 12–18, free for children under 12; free on first Sat of each month. Tues–Sat 10am–4pm; Sun noon–4pm. Bus: 66.

Historic Heritage Square   The city of Phoenix was founded in 1870, but today few of the city's early homes remain. However, if you have an appreciation for old houses and want a glimpse of how Phoenix once looked, stroll around this collection of historic homes, which stand on the original town site. All of the buildings are listed on the National Register of Historic Places, and although most are modest buildings from the early 20th century, there is one impressive Victorian home from the late 19th century. Today, the buildings house museums, restaurants, and gift shops. The Eastlake Victorian Rosson House, furnished with period antiques, is open for tours. The Stevens House features the Arizona Doll & Toy Museum. The Teeter House (© 602/252-4682; www.theteeterhouse.com) now serves as a Victorian tearoom (with cocktails and live jazz in the evening); the old Baird Machine Shop contains Pizzeria Bianco (see "Where to Dine," earlier in this chapter); the Thomas House is home to Bar Bianco (see "Phoenix & Scottsdale After Dark," later in this chapter); and the Silva House is the Ruby Beet Gourmet restaurant.

115 N. Sixth St., at Monroe. © 602/262-5029. www.rossonhousemuseum.org. Rosson House tours $4 adults, $3 seniors and students, $1 children 6–12. Hours vary for each building; call for information. Bus: Red (R), 0, 1, or DASH downtown shuttle.

Phoenix Museum of History   Located in the Heritage and Science Park in downtown Phoenix, this modern museum presents an interesting look at the history of a city that, to the casual visitor, might not seem to *have* any history. Interactive exhibits make this place much more interesting than your average local history museum. One unusual exhibit explores how "lungers" (tuberculosis sufferers) inadvertently helped originate the tourism industry in Arizona, while another exhibit looks at the once-popular occupation of ostrich farming.

105 N. Fifth St. © 602/253-2734. www.pmoh.org. Admission $5 adults, $3.50 seniors and students, $2.50 children 7–12, free for children 6 and under. Tues–Sat 10am–5pm. Closed major holidays. Bus: Red (R), 0, 1, or DASH downtown shuttle.

Wells Fargo History Museum   (Finds)   Yes, this museum is small, and yes, it's run by the Wells Fargo Bank, but the collection of artifacts here goes a long way toward conjuring up the Wild West so familiar from Hollywood movies. Not only is there an original Wells Fargo stagecoach on display, but there are also gold nuggets to ogle, old photos from the *real* Wild West, and plenty of artifacts and memorabilia from the days of stagecoach travel. There are also original paintings by N. C. Wyeth and bronze sculptures by Frederic Remington and Charles Russell.

100 W. Washington St. © 602/378-1852. www.wellsfargohistory.com. Free admission. Mon–Fri 9am–5pm. Bus: Red (R), 0, 1, or DASH downtown shuttle.

SCIENCE & INDUSTRY MUSEUMS

Arizona Science Center   (Kids)   So, the kids weren't impressed with the botanical garden or the Native American artifacts at the Heard Museum. Bring 'em here. They can spend the afternoon pushing buttons, turning knobs, and otherwise interacting

Architectural Highlights

Architecture buffs will find plenty to gape at in Phoenix. Here's a list of our favorite buildings.

- **Arizona Biltmore** This resort hotel, although not designed by Frank Lloyd Wright, shows the famed architect's hand in its distinctive cast-cement blocks. It also displays sculptures, furniture, and stained glass designed by Wright. To learn more about the building, reserve ahead for a tour ($10 for non-guests, free for guests). The Biltmore is located at 2400 E. Missouri Ave. (✆ **602/955-6600**).

- **Burton Barr Library** This library is among the most daring pieces of public architecture in the city, and no fan of futuristic art or science fiction should miss it. The five-story cube is partially clad in enough ribbed copper sheeting to produce roughly 17,500,000 pennies. It's located at 1221 N. Central Ave. (✆ **602/262-4636**; www.phoenixpubliclibrary.org). Free admission.

- **Mystery Castle** ✪ Built for a daughter who longed for a castle more permanent than those built in sand at the beach, Mystery Castle is a wondrous work of folk-art architecture. The 18-room fantasy has 13 fireplaces, parapets, and many other unusual touches. It's located at 800 E. Mineral Rd. (✆ **602/268-1581**). Admission $5 adults, $2 children 5–14. Closed July–Sept.

- **Taliesin West** ✪✪✪ Frank Lloyd Wright fell in love with the Arizona desert and, in 1937, built Taliesin West as a winter camp that served as his home, office, and school. Today, the buildings of Taliesin West are the headquarters of the Frank Lloyd Wright Foundation and School of Architecture. Basic tours cost $14 to $18 adults, $12 to $16 students and seniors, and $4.50 to $5 for children (ages 4–12). Prices vary by season. Expanded Insight Tours ($17–$23), behind-the-scenes tours ($25–$45), guided desert walks ($20), apprentice shelter tours ($30), and night hikes ($23–$25) are available at certain times of year. Call ahead for schedule information. The house/school is located at 12621 Frank Lloyd Wright Blvd. (at Cactus/114th St.), Scottsdale (✆ **480/860-8810** for information or 480/860-2700, ext. 494 or 495, for reservations; www.franklloydwright.org).

with all kinds of cool science exhibits. In the end, they might even learn something in spite of all the fun they had. The science center also includes a planetarium and a large-screen theater, both of which carry additional charges.

600 E. Washington St. ✆ 602/716-2000. www.azscience.org. Admission $9 adults, $7 seniors and children 3–12. Planetarium and film combination tickets also available. Daily 10am–5pm. Closed Thanksgiving and Christmas. Bus: Red (R), 0, 1, or DASH downtown shuttle.

Mesa Southwest Museum ✪✪ (Kids) This is one of the best museums in the Valley, and its wide variety of exhibits appeals to people with a range of interests. For the kids, there are animated dinosaurs on an indoor "cliff" with a roaring waterfall. Of course, there are also plenty of dinosaur skeletons. Also of interest are an exhibit on movies that have been filmed in the state, a display on Arizona mammoth kill sites, some old jail cells, and a walk-through mine mock-up with exhibits on the Lost Dutchman Mine. There's also a mock-up of a Hohokam village and an artificial cave filled with beautiful mineral specimens. This museum also operates the historic **Sirrine House,** 160 N. Center St. (© **480/644-2760**), which is open October through March on Saturdays from 10am to 5pm and on Sundays from 1 to 5pm. Admission is free.

53 N. MacDonald St. (at First St.), Mesa. © 480/644-2230. www.mesasouthwestmuseum.com. Admission $6 adults, $5 seniors and students, $3 children 3–12; free 2nd Sunday of each month. Tues–Sat 10am–5pm; Sun 1–5pm. Closed major holidays. Bus: Red (R).

PARKS & ZOOS

Perhaps the most unusual park in the Phoenix metro area centers on **Tempe Town Lake,** 620 N. Mill Ave., Tempe (© **480/350-8625;** www.tempe.gov/rio), which was created in 1999 by damming the Salt River with inflatable dams. Tempe's 2-mile-long lake offers boat rentals and tours, and lining the north and south shores are bike paths and parks. The best lake access is at Tempe Town Beach, at the foot of the Mill Avenue Bridge.

Among the city's most popular parks are its natural areas and preserves. These include Phoenix South Mountain Park, Papago Park, Phoenix Mountains Preserve (site of Piestewa Peak), North Mountain Preserve, North Mountain Recreation Area, and Camelback Mountain–Echo Canyon Recreation Area. For more information on these parks, see "Hiking," "Bicycling," and "Horseback Riding" under "Outdoor Pursuits," below.

Phoenix Zoo ★ *Kids*   Forget about polar bears and other cold-climate creatures; this zoo focuses its attention primarily on animals that come from climates similar to that of the Phoenix area (although the rainforest exhibit is an exception). Most impressive of the displays are the African savanna and the baboon colony. The Southwestern exhibits are also of interest, as are the giant Galápagos tortoises. The newest exhibit features monkeys from Central and South America. All animals are kept in naturalistic enclosures, and what with all the palm trees and tropical vegetation, the zoo sometimes manages to make you forget you're in the desert.

At Papago Park, 455 N. Galvin Pkwy. © 602/273-1341. www.phoenixzoo.org. Admission Sept–May $12 adults, $9 seniors, $5 children 3–12; June–Aug $9 adults, $7 seniors, $5 children 3–12. Early Sept to early Nov and early Jan to May daily 9am–5pm; early Nov to early Jan daily 9am–4pm; June to early Sept daily 7am–8pm. Closed Christmas. Bus: 3.

ESPECIALLY FOR KIDS

In addition to the following suggestions, kids are likely to enjoy the Arizona Science Center, the Mesa Southwest Museum, and the Phoenix Zoo—all described in detail above.

Arizona Museum for Youth   Using both traditional displays and participatory activities, this museum allows children to explore the fine arts and their own creativity. It's housed in a refurbished grocery store, and the highlight is Artville, an arts-driven kid-size town. Exhibits are geared mainly to toddlers through 12-year-olds, but all ages can work together to experience the activities.

35 N. Robson St. (between Main and First sts.), Mesa. © 480/644-2467. www.arizonamuseumforyouth.com. Admission $3.50, free for children under 2. Tues–Sun 9am–5pm. Closed all government holidays. Bus: Red (R).

Goldfield Ghost Town *Kids*   Over on the east side of the Valley, just 4 miles northeast of Apache Junction, you'll find a reconstructed 1890s gold-mining town. Although it's a bit of a tourist trap—gift shops, an ice-cream parlor, and the like—it's also home to the **Goldfield Superstition Historical Society Museum** (✆ 480/677-6463), which has interesting exhibits on the history of the area. Of particular note is the exhibit on the Lost Dutchman gold mine, perhaps the most famous mine in the country despite the fact that no one knows where it is. Goldfield Mine Tours provides guided tours of the gold mine beneath the town. The Superstition Scenic Narrow Gauge Railroad circles the town, and the **Goldfield Livery** (✆ 480/982-0133) offers horseback riding and carriage rides. If you're here at lunchtime, you can get a meal at the steakhouse/saloon.

Ariz. 88, 4 miles northeast of Apache Junction. ✆ 480/983-0333. www.goldfieldghosttown.com. Museum admission $2 adults, $1.50 seniors; train rides $5 adults, $4 seniors, $2 children 5–12; mine tours $6 adults, $5 seniors, $3 children 6–12; horseback rides $25 for 1 hr., $45 for 2 hr. Town open daily 10am–5pm; museum, tour, and ride hours vary. Closed Christmas.

Hall of Flame Firefighting Museum ★ *Kids* The world's largest firefighting museum houses a fascinating collection of vintage firetrucks. The displays date from a 1725 English hand pumper to several classic engines from the 20th century. All are beautifully restored and, mostly, fire-engine red. In all, there are more than 90 vehicles on display.

At Papago Park, 6101 E. Van Buren St. ✆ 602/275-3473. www.hallofflame.org. Admission $5.50 adults, $4 seniors, $3 students 6–17, $1.50 children 3–5, free for children under 3. Mon–Sat 9am–5pm; Sun noon–4pm. Closed New Year's Day, Thanksgiving, and Christmas. Bus: 3.

McCormick-Stillman Railroad Park If you or your kids happen to like trains, you won't want to miss this park. On the grounds are restored railroad cars and engines, two old railway depots, model railroad layouts, and, best of all, a ⁵⁄₁₂-scale model railroad that takes visitors around the park. There's also a 1929 carousel and a general store.

7301 E. Indian Bend Rd. (at Scottsdale Rd.), Scottsdale. ✆ 480/312-2312. www.therailroadpark.com. Train and carousel rides $1; museum admission $1 adults, free for children 12 and under. Hours vary with the season; call for schedule. Bus: 72.

6 Organized Tours & Excursions

The Valley of the Sun is a sprawling, often congested place, and if you're unfamiliar with the area, you may be surprised at how great the distances are. If map reading and urban navigation are not your strong points, consider taking a guided tour. There are numerous companies offering tours of both the Valley of the Sun and the rest of Arizona. However, tours of the Valley tend to include only brief stops at highlights.

BUS TOURS **Gray Line of Phoenix** (✆ 800/777-3484 or 602/437-3484; www.graylinearizona.com) is one of the largest tour companies in the Valley. It offers a 4-hour tour of Phoenix and the Valley of the Sun for $45; reservations are necessary. The tour points out such local landmarks as the state capitol, Heritage Square, Arizona State University, and Old Town Scottsdale.

HOT-AIR BALLOON RIDES The still morning air of the Valley of the Sun is perfect for hot-air ballooning, and because of the stiff competition, prices are among the lowest in the country—between $125 and $185 per person for a 1- to 1½-hour ride. Companies to try include **Over the Rainbow** (✆ 602/225-5666; www.letsgoballooning.com), **Zephyr Balloon/A Aerozona Adventure** (✆ 888/991-4260 or 480/991-4260; www.azballoon.com), and **Adventures Out West** (✆ 800/755-0935 or 480/991-3666; www.adventuresoutwest.com).

JEEP TOURS After spending a few days in Scottsdale, you'll likely start wondering where the desert is. Well, it's out there, and the easiest way to explore it is to book a jeep tour. Most hotels and resorts have particular companies they work with, so start by asking your concierge. Alternatively, you can contact one of the following companies. Most will pick you up at your hotel, take you off through the desert, and maybe even let you try panning for gold or shooting a six-gun. Depending on how many people there are in your party and where you're staying, rates range from $65 to $100 for a 4-hour tour. Companies include **Arizona Desert Mountain Jeep Tours** (© **800/567-3619** or 480/860-1777; www.azdesertmountain.com) and **Arizona Bound Tours** (© **480/994-0580;** www.arizonabound.com).

If you want to really impress your friends when you get home, you'll need to try something a little different. How about a Hummer tour? Sure, a Hummer is nothing but a jeep on steroids, but these military-issue off-road vehicles still turn heads. Contact **Desert Storm Hummer Tours** (© **866/374-8637** or 480/922-0020; www. dshummer.com), which charges $100 for a 4-hour tour, or **Stellar Adventures** (© **877/878-3552** or 602/402-0584; www.stellaradventures.com), which charges $120 for a basic 4-hour tour and $150 for its extreme tour. Both companies also offer night tours ($125) that let you spot wildlife with night-vision equipment.

7 Getting Outside

BICYCLING Although the Valley of the Sun is a sprawling place, it's mostly flat and has numerous paved bike paths, which makes bicycling a breeze as long as it isn't windy or, in the summer, too hot. In Scottsdale, **Arizona Outback Adventures,** 16447 N. 91st St. (© **866/455-1601** or 480/945-2881; www.azoutbackadventures. com) rents hybrid bikes for $35 per day and mountain bikes for $35 to $85 per day. Mountain-biking trail maps are also available. This company also does half-day and full-day guided mountain-bike tours.

Among the best mountain-biking spots in the city are Papago Park (at Van Buren St. and Galvin Pkwy.), Phoenix South Mountain Park (use the entrance off Baseline Rd. on 48th St.), and North Mountain Preserve (off Seventh St. between Dunlap Ave. and Thunderbird Rd.). With its rolling topography and wide dirt trails, Papago Park is the best place for novice mountain-bikers to get in some desert riding (and the scenery here is great). For hard-core pedalers, Phoenix South Mountain Park is the place to go. The National Trail is the ultimate death-defying ride here, but there are lots of trails for intermediate riders, including the Desert Classic Trail and the short loop trails just north of the parking area at the 48th Street entrance. North Mountain is another good place for intermediate riders.

There's also plenty of good road biking and mountain biking up in the Cave Creek area, where you can rent a bike for $40 to $50 a day at **Flat Tire Bike Shop,** 6149 Cave Creek Rd. (© **480/488-5261**). This shop also offers guided mountain-bike tours for $75 per person. If you'd like a guide for some of the best biking in the desert, contact **Desert Biking Adventures** (© **888/249-BIKE** or 602/320-4602; www. desertbikingadventures.com), which leads 2-, 3-, and 4-hour tours (and specializes in downhill rides). Prices range from $70 to $97.

If you'd rather confine your cycling to a paved surface, there's no better route than Scottsdale's **Indian Bend Wash greenbelt,** a paved path that extends for more than 10 miles along Hayden Road (from north of Shea Blvd. to Tempe). The Indian Bend Wash pathway can be accessed at many points along Hayden Road. At the south end, the path connects to paved paths on the shores of Tempe Town Lake and provides easy access to Tempe's Mill Avenue shopping district.

GOLF   With nearly 200 courses in the Valley of the Sun, golf is just about the most popular sport in Phoenix and one of the main reasons people flock here in winter. Sunshine, spectacular views, and the company of coyotes, quails, and doves make playing a round of golf here a truly memorable experience.

Despite the number of courses, it can still be difficult to get a tee time on any of the more popular courses (especially during the months of Feb, Mar, and Apr). If you're staying at a resort with a course, be sure to make your tee-time reservations at the same time you make your room reservations. If you aren't staying at a resort, you might still be able to play a round on a resort course if you can get a last-minute tee time. Try one of the tee-time reservations services below.

The only thing harder than getting a winter or spring tee time in the Valley is facing the bill at the end of your 18 holes. Greens fees at most public and resort courses range from $90 to $170, with the top courses often charging $200 to $250 or more. Municipal courses, on the other hand, charge under $40. You can save money on many courses by opting for twilight play, which usually begins between 1 and 3pm.

You can get more information on Valley of the Sun golf courses from the **Greater Phoenix Convention & Visitors Bureau,** 50 N. Second St. (© **877/225-5749** or 602/452-6282; www.visitphoenix.com).

It's a good idea to make reservations well in advance. You can avoid the hassle of booking tee times yourself by contacting **Golf Xpress** (© **888/679-8246** or 602/404-GOLF; www.azgolfxpress.com), which can make reservations farther in advance than you could if you called the golf course directly, and can sometimes get you lower greens fees as well. This company also makes hotel reservations, rents golf clubs, and provides other assistance to golfers visiting the Valley. For last-minute reservations, call **Stand-by Golf** (© **800/655-5345;** www.discountteetimes.com).

The many resort courses are the favored fairways of valley visitors. Some of our favorites are listed below:

- **The Boulders** ★★   For spectacular scenery, the two Jay Morrish–designed 18-hole courses at The Boulders, North Scottsdale Road and Carefree Highway, Carefree (© **800/553-1717** or 480/488-9009; www.thebouldersclub.com), just can't be beat. Given the option, play the South Course, and watch out as you approach the tee box on the 7th hole—it's a real heart-stopper. You'll pay $245 to $290 for a round in winter, $195 to $220 in spring.

- **Wigwam Golf and Country Club** ★   Wigwam has, count 'em, three championship 18-hole courses. The Gold Course is legendary, but even the Blue and Red courses are worth playing. The club is at Litchfield Park, on the far west side of the valley, 300 Wigwam Blvd. (© **800/909-4224** or 623/935-3811). In high season, greens fees are $135 for any of the three courses and $45 in summer.

- **Gold Canyon Golf Resort** ★   This course, way over on the east side of the valley at the foot of the Superstition Mountains, has been rated the best public course in the state. It's located at 6100 S. Kings Ranch Rd., Gold Canyon (© **800/827-5281** or 480/982-9449; www.gcgr.com). Greens fees on the Dinosaur Mountain course range from $157 to $187 in winter and from $57 to $67 in summer. The Sidewinder course is more traditional and less dramatic, but much more economical. Greens fees are $87 to $102 in winter and $42 to $47 in summer.

- **Phoenician Golf Club**   Set at the base of Camelback Mountain (6000 E. Camelback Rd.; © **800/888-8234** or 480/423-2449; www.thephoenician.com), this club has 27 holes that mix traditional and desert styles. Greens fees for non-resort guests are $110 to $180 in winter and spring, $60 to $90 in summer, and can be made up to 60 days in advance.

- **Troon North Golf Club** ★★★   Of the valley's many daily-fee courses, the two 18-hole courses at this club garner the most local accolades. This is the finest example of a desert course that you'll find anywhere in the state. It's located at 10320 E. Dynamite Blvd., Scottsdale (© **888/TROON-US** or 480/585-7700; www.troonnorthgolf.com). Greens fees are $185 to $295 in winter and spring.

- **Tournament Players Club (TPC) of Scottsdale** ★★   If you want to swing where the pros do, beg, borrow, or steal a tee time on the Tom Weiskopf and Jay Morrish–designed Stadium Course. The TPC's second 18, the Desert Course, is actually a municipal course. It's located at 17020 N. Hayden Rd. (© **888/400-4001** or 480/585-4334; www.playatpc.com). Stadium course fees top out at $228 in winter and spring, while Desert Course fees are a reasonable $57 in winter and spring.

- **Legacy Golf Resort**   If you're looking for good value in traditional or links-style courses, try the Legacy Golf Resort, Stonecreek Golf Club (6808 S. 32nd St.; © **888/828-FORE** or 602/305-5550; www.legacygolfresort.com), which is a fairly forgiving course on the south side of the valley. Greens fees are $99 to $149 in winter.

- **Dove Valley Ranch Golf Club**   If you want to take a crack at a desert-style course or two but don't want to take out a second mortgage, try this club, at 33244 N. Black Mountain Pkwy., Cave Creek (© **480/488-0009;** www.dovevalleyranch.com). Designed by Robert Trent Jones Jr., it was voted Arizona's best new public course when it opened in 1998. Greens fees are $105 to $130 in winter.

- **We-Ko-Pa Golf Club**   This course is on the Fort McDowell Yavapai Nation, and the name is Yavapai for "Four Peaks," which is the mountain range you'll be marveling at as you play. Unlike at other area courses, fairways are bounded by desert, not luxury homes, so make sure you keep your ball on the grass. The course is located off the Beeline Highway (Ariz. 87) in the northeast corner of the valley (18200 East Toh Vee Circle, Fountain Hills; © **480/836-9000;** www.wekopa.com). Greens fees are $85 to $195 in winter. Reservations are taken up to 90 days in advance.

- **Papago Golf Course**   One of the municipal courses in Phoenix, Papago offers fine views and a killer 17th hole. This is such a great course that it's used for Phoenix Open qualifying. It's located at 5595 E. Moreland St. (© **602/275-8428**), at the foot of the red sandstone Papago Buttes. In winter, greens fees are $17 to $34 to walk ($22 extra for a golf cart).

HIKING   Several mountains around Phoenix, including Camelback Mountain and Piestewa Peak, have been set aside as parks and nature preserves, and these natural areas are among the city's most popular hiking spots. The city's largest nature preserve, **South Mountain Park/Preserve** (© **602/495-0222**), covers 16,000 acres and is said to be the largest city park in the world. This park contains 58 miles of hiking, mountain-biking, and horseback-riding trails, and the views of Phoenix (whether from along the National Trail or from the parking lot at the Buena Vista Lookout) are spectacular, especially at sunset. To reach the park's main entrance, drive south on Central Avenue, which leads right into the park. Once inside the park, turn left on Summit Road and follow it to the Buena Vista Lookout, which provides a great view of the city and is the trail head for the National Trail. If you hike east on this trail for 2 miles, you'll come to an unusual little tunnel that makes a good turnaround point.

Another place to get in some relatively easy and convenient hiking is at **Papago Park,** Galvin Parkway and Van Buren Street (© 602/256-3220), home to the Desert Botanical Garden, the Phoenix Zoo, and the fascinating Hole in the Rock (a red-rock butte with a large natural opening in it). There are both paved and dirt trails within the park; the most popular hikes are around the Papago Buttes (park on W. Park Dr.) and up onto the rocks at Hole in the Rock (park past the zoo at the information center). During World War II, there was a German POW camp here.

Perhaps the most popular hike in the city is the trail to the top of **Camelback Mountain,** in **Echo Canyon Recreation Area** (© 602/256-3220), near the boundary between Phoenix and Scottsdale. This is the highest mountain in Phoenix, and the 1.25-mile Summit Trail to the top gains 1,200 feet and is very steep, yet on any given day there will be ironmen and ironwomen nonchalantly jogging up and down to stay fit. At times, it almost feels like a health-club singles scene. The views are the finest in the city. To reach the trail head, drive up 44th Street until it becomes McDonald Drive, turn right on East Echo Canyon Drive, and continue up the hill until the road ends at a parking lot, which is often full. Don't attempt this one in the heat of the day, and bring at least a quart of water.

At the east end of Camelback Mountain is the Cholla Trail, which, at 1.75 miles in length, isn't as steep as the Summit Trail (at least not until you get close to the summit, where the route gets steep, rocky, and quite difficult). The only parking for this trail is along Invergordon Road at Chaparral Road, just north of Camelback Road (along the east boundary of The Phoenician resort). Be sure to park in a legal parking space and watch the hours that parking is allowed. There's a good turnaround point about 1.5 miles up the trail, and great views down onto the fairways of the golf course at The Phoenician.

Piestewa Peak, in the **Phoenix Mountains Park and Recreation Area/Dreamy Draw Park** (© 602/262-7901), offers another aerobic workout of a hike and has views almost as spectacular as those from Camelback Mountain. The round-trip to the summit is 2.5 miles. Piestewa Peak is reached from Squaw Peak Drive off Lincoln Drive between 22nd and 23rd streets. Another section of this park, with much easier trails can be reached by taking the Northern Avenue exit of Ariz. 51 and then driving east into Dreamy Draw Park. This part of the park has a 2.25 mile paved walking and biking trail.

Of all the popular mountain trails in the Phoenix area, the trail through **Pinnacle Peak Park,** 26802 N. 102nd Way (© 480/312-0990; www.scottsdaleaz.gov/parks/pinnacle), in north Scottsdale is my favorite. The trail through the park is a 3.5-mile round-trip hike and is immensely popular with the local fitness crowd. Forget about stopping to smell the desert penstemon. If you don't keep up the pace, someone's liable to knock you off the trail into a prickly pear. If you can find a parking space (arrive before 9am on weekends) and can ignore the crowds, you'll be treated to views of rugged desert mountains (and posh desert suburbs). There are guided hikes Tuesday through Sunday at 10am. To find the park from central Scottsdale, go north on Pima Road, east on Happy Valley Road, north on Alma School Parkway, and turn left at the sign for Pinnacle Peak Patio restaurant.

For much less vigorous hiking (without the crowds), try **North Mountain Park** (✆ 602/262-7901), in North Mountain Preserve. This natural area, located on either side of Seventh Street between Dunlap Avenue and Thunderbird Road, has more flat hiking than Camelback Mountain or Piestewa Peak.

HORSEBACK RIDING Even in the urban confines of the Phoenix metro area, people like to play at being cowboys and there are plenty of places around the Valley to saddle up your palomino. Because any guided ride is going to lead you through interesting desert scenery, your best bet is to pick a stable close to where you're staying, and keep in mind that most stables require or prefer reservations.

On the south side of the city, try **Ponderosa Stables,** 10215 S. Central Ave. (✆ 602/268-1261), or **South Mountain Stables,** 10005 S. Central Ave. (✆ 602/276-8131), both of which lead rides into South Mountain Park and charge $25 for a 1-hour ride or $40 to $45 for a 2-hour ride. These stables also offer fun dinner rides ($32) to the T-Bone Steakhouse, where you buy your own dinner before riding back under the stars. If you have time for only one horseback ride while you're in Phoenix, make it this latter ride.

On the north side of the Valley, **Cave Creek Outfitters,** off Dynamite Boulevard on 144th Street (✆ 888/921-0040 or 480/471-4635; www.cavecreekoutfitters.com), offers 2-hour rides for $60 to $70.

WATER PARKS At **Waterworld Safari Water Park,** 4243 W. Pinnacle Peak Rd. (✆ 623/581-8446; www.golfland.com), you can free-fall down the Kilimanjaro speed slide or catch a gnarly wave in the wave pool. **Mesa Golfland/Sunsplash,** 155 W. Hampton Ave., Mesa (✆ 480/834-8319; www.golfland.com), has a wave pool and tunnels called black holes. **Big Surf,** 1500 N. McClintock Rd., Tempe (✆ 480/947-2477; www.golfland.com), has a wave pool, a speed slide, and more.

All three of these parks charge $21 for adults, $11 for seniors, $17 for children, $1 for children 2 and under. Waterworld Safari Water Park and Mesa Golfland/Sunsplash are open from around Memorial Day weekend to Labor Day weekend, Monday through Thursday from 10am to 8pm, Friday and Saturday from 10am to 9pm, and Sunday from 11am to 7pm. Big Surf is open from around Memorial Day to Labor Day, Monday through Saturday from 10am to 6pm and Sunday from 11am to 7pm. Mesa Golfland also has three slides that open at the start of spring break and are open Monday through Friday from 1 to 6pm, Saturday from 11am to 6pm, and Sunday from noon to 6pm. After Memorial Day, these slides are open the same hours as Sunsplash.

WHITE-WATER RAFTING & TUBING The desert may not seem like the place for white-water rafting, but up in the mountains to the northeast of Phoenix, the **Upper Salt River** still flows wild and free and offers some exciting rafting. Most years from about late February to late May, snowmelt from the White Mountains turns the Salt into a river filled with exciting Class III and IV rapids (sometimes, however, there just isn't enough water). Companies operating full-day, overnight, and multi-day rafting trips on the Upper Salt River (conditions permitting) include **Wilderness Aware Rafting** (✆ 800/462-7238; www.inaraft.com), **Canyon Rio Rafting** (✆ 800/272-3353; www.canyonrio.com), and **Mild to Wild Rafting** (✆ 800/567-6745; www.mild2wildrafting.com). Prices range from $90 to $99 for a day trip.

Tamer river trips can be had from **Salt River Tubing & Recreation** (✆ 480/984-3305; www.saltrivertubing.com), which has its headquarters 20 miles northeast of Phoenix on Power Road at the intersection of Usery Pass Road in Tonto National

Forest. For $13, the company will rent you a large inner tube and shuttle you by bus upriver for the float down. The inner-tubing season runs from mid-May to September.

8 Spectator Sports

Phoenix is nuts for pro sports and is one of the few cities in the country with teams for all four of the major sports (baseball, basketball, football, and hockey). Add to this baseball's spring training, professional women's basketball, two major golf tournaments, tennis tournaments, the annual Fiesta Bowl college football classic, and ASU football, basketball, and baseball, and you have enough action to keep even the most rabid sports fans happy. The all-around best month to visit is March, when you could feasibly catch baseball's spring training, the Suns, the Coyotes, and ASU basketball and baseball, as well as the Safeway International LPGA Tournament.

Call **Ticketmaster** (℃ 480/784-4444; www.ticketmaster.com) for tickets to most of the events below. For sold-out events, try **Tickets Unlimited** (℃ 800/289-8497 or 602/840-2340; www.ticketsunlimitedinc.com) or **Ticket Exchange** (℃ 800/800-9811 or 602/254-4444).

BASEBALL   Back in 2001, the **Arizona Diamondbacks** (℃ 888/777-4664 or 602/514-8400; diamondbacks.com) surprised most of the nation by beating the New York Yankees in the last inning of the last game of the World Series. Such an edge-of-the-seat upset makes for rabidly loyal fans for this team, which plays in downtown Phoenix at Bank One Ballpark (BOB). The ballpark's retractable roof allows for comfortable play during the blistering summers, and makes this one of only a few enclosed baseball stadiums with natural grass. Tickets to ball games are available through the Bank One Ballpark ticket office and cost between $8 and $116. On the day of a game, you can also stand in line at Gate K in hopes of getting one of the few $1 day-of-game tickets. The best seats are in sections J and Q. If you'd like to get a behind-the-scenes look at BOB, you can take a guided tour. Tours cost $6 for adults, $4 for seniors and children ages 7 to 12, and $2 for children ages 4 to 6.

For decades, baseball's spring training season has been immensely popular, especially with fans from northern teams, and don't think that the Cactus League's preseason exhibition games are any less popular just because the Diamondbacks are World Series winners and play all summer. **Spring-training games** may rank second only to golf in popularity with winter visitors to the Valley. Nine major league baseball teams have spring-training camps around the Valley in the month of March, and exhibition games are scheduled at seven different stadiums. Tickets cost $5 to $24. Get a schedule from a visitor center, check the *Arizona Republic* while you're in town, or contact the Cactus League (℃ 866/705-4816; www.cactus-league.com) or visit www.cactusleagueinfo.com. Games often sell out, especially on weekends, so be sure to order tickets in advance. The spring-training schedule for 2006 should be out by November 2005.

Teams training in the Valley include the **Los Angeles Angels of Anaheim,** Tempe Diablo Stadium, 2200 W. Alameda Dr. (48th St. and Broadway Rd.), Tempe (℃ 602/438-9300 or 480/784-4444 for tickets; www.angelsbaseball.com); the **Chicago Cubs,** HoHoKam Park, 1235 N. Center St., Mesa (℃ 800/905-3315 for tickets or 480/964-4467; www.cubspringtraining.com); the **Kansas City Royals,** Surprise Recreation Campus, 15960 N. Bullard Ave., Surprise (℃ 623/594-5600 or 480/784-4444 for tickets; www.kansascityroyals.com); the **Milwaukee Brewers,** Maryvale Baseball

Park, 3600 N. 51st Ave., Phoenix (© 800/933-7890 for tickets or 623/245-5500; www.milwaukeebrewers.com); the **Oakland Athletics,** Phoenix Municipal Stadium, 5999 E. Van Buren St., Phoenix (© 800/225-2277 or 602/392-0217 for tickets; www.oaklandathletics.com); the **San Diego Padres,** Peoria Sports Complex, 16101 N. 83rd Ave., Peoria (© 623/878-4337 or 480/784-4444 for tickets; www. padres.com); the **San Francisco Giants,** Scottsdale Stadium, 7408 E. Osborn Rd., Scottsdale (© 800/225-2277 for tickets or 480/990-7972; www.sfgiants.com); the **Seattle Mariners,** Peoria Sports Complex, 16101 N. 83rd Ave., Peoria (© 623/ 878-4337 or 480/784-4444 for tickets; www.seattlemariners.com); and the **Texas Rangers,** Surprise Recreation Campus, 15960 N. Bullard Ave., Surprise (© 623/594-5600 or 480/784-4444 for tickets; www.texasrangers.com).

BASKETBALL   The NBA's **Phoenix Suns** play at the America West Arena, 201 E. Jefferson St. (© 800/4-NBA-TIX or 602/379-SUNS; www.suns.com). Tickets cost $13 to $103. Suns tickets are hard to come by; if you haven't planned ahead, try contacting the box office the day before or the day of a game to see if tickets have been returned. Otherwise, you'll have to try a ticket agency and pay a premium.

Phoenix also has a WNBA team, the **Phoenix Mercury** (© 602/252-9622 or 602/ 514-8333; www.phoenixmercury.com), which plays at the America West Arena between late May and mid-August. Tickets cost $11 to $128.

FOOTBALL   The **Arizona Cardinals** (© 800/999-1402, 602/379-0102, or 623/ 266-5000; www.azcardinals.com) are in the process of building a new stadium in the west valley city of Glendale. However, until the new stadium is completed in 2006, the Cardinals will continue to play at Arizona State University's Sun Devil Stadium. Tickets cost $15 (day-of-game only) to $150 and go on sale around mid-July. Most are $30 to $68.

While the Cardinals get to use Sun Devil Stadium, this field really belongs to Arizona State University's **Sun Devils** (© 480/965-2381; www.thesundevils.com). Tickets range from $15 to $90. The stadium is home to the Fiesta Bowl Football Classic.

GOLF TOURNAMENTS   It's not surprising that, with more than 200 golf courses and ideal golfing weather throughout the fall, winter, and spring, the Valley of the Sun hosts some major golf tournaments. Late January's **FBR Open Golf Tournament** (© 602/870-4431; www.fbropen.com) is the by far the biggest. Held at the Tournament Players Club (TPC) of Scottsdale, it attracts more spectators than any other golf tournament in the world (more than 500,000 each year). The 18th hole has standing room for 40,000. Tickets start at $25.

Each March, the **Safeway International LPGA Tournament** (© 877/983-3300 or 602/495-4653; www.safewaygolf.com), held at the Superstition Mountain Golf & Country Club, 3976 S. Ponderosa Dr., lures nearly 100 of the top women golfers from around the world. Daily tickets are $20; weekly tickets are $50.

HORSE/GREYHOUND RACING   **Turf Paradise,** 1501 W. Bell Rd. (© 602/ 942-1101; www.turfparadise.com), is Phoenix's horse-racing track. The season runs from October to late May. Admission ranges from $2 to $5.

The **Phoenix Greyhound Park,** 3801 E. Washington St. (© 602/273-7181; www.phoenixgreyhoundpark.com), is a fully enclosed, air-conditioned facility offering seating in various grandstands, lounges, and restaurants. There's racing throughout the year; tickets are free to $3.

A Day at the Spa

If you can't or don't want to spend the money to stay at a top resort and avail yourself of the spa, you may still be able to indulge. Most resorts open their spas to the public, and for the cost of a body treatment or massage, you can spend the day at the spa, taking classes, working out in an exercise room, or lounging by the pool.

If you want truly spectacular surroundings and bragging rights, head north to the **Golden Door Spa at the Boulders,** 34631 N. Tom Darlington Dr., Carefree (© **800/553-1717** or 480/595-3500; www.goldendoorspas.com). This spa has tremendous name recognition, but it's not our favorite. The turquoise wrap, the spa's signature treatment, is a real desert experience.

Willow Stream–The Spa at Fairmont, 7575 E. Princess Dr. (© **800/441-1414** or 480/585-4848; www.fairmont.com), is our favorite valley spa. Designed to conjure up images of the journey to northern Arizona's Havasu Canyon, it includes a rooftop swimming pool and a large hot tub in a grotto below the pool.

Located high on the flanks of Mummy Mountain, the **Spa at Camelback Inn,** 5402 E. Lincoln Dr., Scottsdale (© **800/922-2635** or 480/596-7040; www.camelbackspa.com), is a deliciously tranquil place and has long been one of the valley's premiere spas. You just can't beat this spa for convenience and variety of treatments.

The **Centre for Well Being,** at the Phoenician, 6000 E. Camelback Rd., Scottsdale (© **800/843-2392** or 480/423-2452; www.centreforwellbeing. com), is one of the valley's most prestigious spas. Treatments include a botanical hydrating wrap and a Turkish body scrub.

The historic setting and convenient location of the **Arizona Biltmore Spa,** 2400 E. Missouri Ave. (© **602/381-7632;** www.arizonabiltmore.com), make this facility an excellent choice if you're spending time along the Camelback Corridor. The spa menu includes dozens of different treatments, such as massages with lavender and a cactus flower body wrap.

RODEOS, POLO & HORSE SHOWS Cowboys, cowgirls, and other horsey types will find plenty of the four-legged critters going through their paces most weeks at **WestWorld of Scottsdale,** 16601 N. Pima Rd., Scottsdale (© **480/312-6802;** www.scottsdaleaz.gov/westworld). With its hundreds of stables, numerous equestrian arenas, and a polo field, this complex provides an amazing variety of entertainment and sporting events. There are rodeos, polo matches, horse shows, horseback rides, and horseback-riding instruction.

TENNIS TOURNAMENTS Each February, top international men's tennis players compete at the **Tennis Channel Open** (© **480/922-0222;** www.scottsdaletennis. com), at the Fairmont Scottsdale Princess, 7575 E. Princess Dr., Scottsdale. Tickets run from $14 to $72 (tickets to later rounds are more expensive) and are available through Ticketmaster outlets (see above).

9 Shopping

For the most part, shopping in the Valley means malls. They're everywhere, and they're air-conditioned, which, we're sure you'll agree, makes shopping in the desert far more enjoyable when it's 110°F (43°C) outside.

Scottsdale and the Biltmore District of Phoenix (along Camelback Rd.) are the Valley's main upscale shopping areas, with several high-end shopping centers and malls. The various distinct shopping districts of downtown Scottsdale are among the few outdoor shopping areas in the Valley and are home to hundreds of boutiques, galleries, jewelry stores, Native American crafts stores, and souvenir shops. The Western atmosphere of Old Town Scottsdale is partly real and partly a figment of the local merchants' imaginations, but nevertheless it's the most popular tourist shopping area in the Valley. With dozens of galleries in the Main Street Arts and Antiques District and the nearby Marshall Way Contemporary Arts District, it also happens to be the heart of the Valley's art market.

For locals, Scottsdale's shopping scene has been moving steadily northward. Kierland Commons and the Shops at Gainey Village are both north of Old Town Scottsdale on North Scottsdale Road.

Shopping hours are usually Monday through Saturday from 10am to 6pm and Sunday from noon to 5pm; malls usually stay open until 9pm Monday through Saturday.

ANTIQUES & COLLECTIBLES

With more than 80 antiques shops and specialty stores, downtown Glendale (northwest of downtown Phoenix) is the Valley's main antiques district. You'll find the greatest concentration of antiques stores just off Grand Avenue between 56th and 59th avenues. Five or more times a year, the **Phoenix Fairgrounds Antique Market** (© **623/587-7488** or 602/717-7337; www.azantiqueshow.com), Arizona's largest collectors' show, is held at the Arizona State Fairgrounds, 19th Avenue and McDowell Road.

Antique Trove If you love browsing through packed antiques malls searching for your favorite collectibles, then this should be your first stop in the Valley. It's one of the biggest antiques malls in the area. 2020 N. Scottsdale Rd., Scottsdale. © **480/947-6074.** www.antiquetrove.com.

Arizona West Galleries ★★ Nowhere else in Scottsdale will you find such an amazing collection of cowboy collectibles and Western antiques. There are antique saddles and chaps, old rifles and six-shooters, sheriffs' badges, spurs, and the like. 7149 E. Main St., Scottsdale. © **480/994-3752.**

Bishop Gallery for Art & Antiques ★ This cramped shop is wonderfully eclectic, featuring everything from Asian antiques to unusual original art. Definitely worth a browse. 7164 Main St., Scottsdale. © **480/949-9062.**

ART

In the Southwest, only Santa Fe is a more important art market than Scottsdale, and along the streets of Scottsdale's Main Street Arts and Antiques District and the Marshall Way Contemporary Arts District, you'll see dozens of galleries selling everything from monumental bronzes to contemporary art created from found objects. On Main Street, you'll find primarily cowboy art, both traditional and contemporary, while on North Marshall Way, you'll discover much more imaginative and daring contemporary art.

In addition to the galleries listed here, you'll usually find a huge tent full of art along Scottsdale Road in north Scottsdale. The annual **Celebration of Fine Art** (© **480/443-7695;** www.celebrateart.com) takes place each year between mid-January and late March. Not only will you get to see the work of 100 artists, but on any given day, you'll also find dozens of the artists at work on the premises. Admission is $7 for adults and $6 for seniors. Call or check the website for this year's location and hours of operation.

Bentley Projects   Housed in a huge old warehouse south of the Bank One Ballpark in downtown Phoenix, this massive gallery is one the city's most cutting edge contemporary art spaces. You probably aren't in the market for a 12-feet-tall Jim Dine bronze statue of Venus, but if you'd like to see one, stop by this gallery. 215 E. Grant St., Phoenix. © 602/340-9200. www.bentleygallery.com.

Cervini Haas Gallery   This is Scottsdale's premier gallery of fine contemporary crafts, including furniture, ceramics, and jewelry. The works on display here often push the envelope of what's possible in any given medium. 4222 N. Marshall Way, Scottsdale. © 480/429-6116. www.cervinihaas.com.

Lisa Sette Gallery   If you aren't a fan of cowboy or Native American art, don't despair. Instead, drop by this gallery, which always mounts eclectic and fascinating shows, often melding 19th- and 21st-century aesthetics. 4142 N. Marshall Way, Scottsdale. © 480/990-7342. www.lisasettegallery.com.

Overland Gallery of Fine Art ★★   Traditional Western and Russian Impressionist paintings form the backbone of this gallery's fine collection. These are museum-quality works (prices sometimes approach $100,000) and definitely worth a look. However, the gallery also shows the angular Southwest landscapes of Ed Mell. 7155 Main St., Scottsdale. © 800/920-0220 or 480/947-1934. www.overlandgallery.com.

Roberts Gallery   The feathered masks and sculptures of Virgil Walker are highlights, and if you have an appreciation for fine detail work, you'll likely be fascinated by these pieces. Walker's annual show is held on Thanksgiving weekend. El Pedregal Festival Marketplace, 34505 N. Scottsdale Rd., Carefree. © 480/488-1088.

Wilde Meyer Gallery   Brightly colored and playful are the norm at this gallery, which represents Linda Carter-Holman, a Southwestern favorite who does cowgirl-inspired paintings. There's also a Wilde Meyer gallery in the Shops at Gainey Village, 8777 N. Scottsdale Rd. (© 480/488-3200). 4142 N. Marshall Way, Scottsdale. © 480/945-2323.

BOOKS

Major chain bookstores in the area include **Borders,** at Biltmore Fashion Park, 2402 E. Camelback Rd., Phoenix (© 602/957-6660), 699 S. Mill Ave., Tempe (© 480/921-8659), and 4555 E. Cactus Rd., Phoenix (© 602/953-9699); and **Barnes & Noble,** at 10235 N. Metro Parkway E., Phoenix (© 602/678-0088), in Kierland Commons, N. Scottsdale Rd. and Greenway Rd., Scottsdale (© 480/948-8551), and 10500 N. 90th St., Scottsdale (© 480/391-0048).

The Poisoned Pen   The store name should give you a clue as to what sort of bookstore this is: it specializes in mysteries. 4014 N. Goldwater Blvd., Suite 101, Scottsdale. © 888/560-9919 or 480/947-2974. www.poisonedpen.com.

FASHION

In addition to the options mentioned below, there are lots of great shops in malls all over the city. Favorite destinations for upscale fashions include Biltmore Fashion Park, the Borgata of Scottsdale, El Pedregal Festival Marketplace, and Scottsdale Fashion Square. See "Malls & Shopping Centers," below, for details.

For cowboy and cowgirl attire, see "Western Wear," below.

Barbwire Western Couture   If you, or perhaps your daughter, are looking for the latest in over-the-top cowgirl chic fashions, look no further. Barbwire is, well, cutting edge when it comes to clothes and accessories inspired by both the Wild West and rock 'n' roll. 15425 N. Scottsdale Rd., Suite 230, Scottsdale. ✆ 480/443-9473. www.barbwire.com.

Carole Dolighan   The hand-painted, hand-woven dresses, skirts, and blouses here abound in rich colors. Each is unique. At the Borgata, 6166 N. Scottsdale Rd., Scottsdale. ✆ 480/922-0616.

Objects   This eclectic shop carries hand-painted, wearable art both casual and dressy, along with unique artist-made jewelry, contemporary furnishings, and all kinds of delightful and unusual items for home decor. In The Shops at Gainey Village, 8787 N. Scottsdale Rd., Scottsdale. ✆ 480/994-4720. www.objectsgallery.com.

GIFTS & SOUVENIRS

Bischoff's Shades of the West   This is a one-stop shop for all things Southwestern. From T-shirts to regional foodstuffs, this sprawling store has it all, with good selections of candles, Mexican crafts, and wrought-iron cabinet hardware that can give your kitchen a Western look. 7247 Main St., Scottsdale. ✆ 480/945-3289. www.shadesofthewest.com.

Scottsdale Center for the Arts Gift Shop ★   This gift shop on the downtown Scottsdale mall has a wonderful selection of fun, contemporary, and artistic gifts, including lots of jewelry. There's also another gift shop next door at the Scottsdale Museum of Contemporary Art. 7380 E. Second St., Scottsdale. ✆ 480/874-4652.

Two Plates Full   I love wandering through this shop just to marvel at all the bright colors and fun designs. Featuring functional art and crafts, home accessories, and jewelry this place is a great place to shop for unique gifts. In The Borgata, 6166 N. Scottsdale Rd., Scottsdale. ✆ **480/443-3241.** www.twoplatesfull.com.

JEWELRY

Cornelis Hollander   Although this shop is much smaller and not nearly as dramatic as that of the nearby Jewelry by Gauthier store, the designs are just as cutting edge. Whether you're looking for classic chic or trendy modern designs, you'll find plenty to interest you here. There's a second store in north Scottsdale at 32607 N. Scottsdale Rd. (✆ **480/575-5583**). 4151 N. Marshall Way, Scottsdale. ✆ **480/423-5000.** www.cornelishollander.com.

Gauthier   This elegant store sells the designs of the phenomenally talented Scott Gauthier. The stylishly modern pieces use precious stones and are miniature works of art. There's a second, much smaller, shop in Kierland Commons, 15034 N. Scottsdale Rd. (✆ **480/443-4030**). 4211 N. Marshall Way, Scottsdale. ✆ **888/411-3232** or 480/941-1707. www.jewelrybygauthier.com.

Molina Boutique   If you can spend as much on a necklace as you can on a Mercedes, then this is *the* place to shop for your baubles. Although you don't need an appointment, it's highly recommended. You'll then get personalized service as you peruse the Tiffany exclusives and high-end European jewelry. 3134 E. Camelback Rd. ✆ 602/955-2055. www.molinafinejewelers.com.

MALLS & SHOPPING CENTERS

Biltmore Fashion Park ★   This open-air shopping plaza with garden courtyards is *the* place to be if shopping is your obsession. Storefronts bear the names of exclusive boutiques such as Gucci and Cartier. Saks Fifth Avenue and Macy's are the two anchors. There are also more than a dozen moderately priced restaurants here. This shopping center was undergoing a major face-lift in 2005, and the upgrades may not yet be complete by the time you visit. 2502 E. Camelback Rd. (at 24th St.). ✆ **602/955-8400**. www.westcor.com.

The Borgata of Scottsdale ★★   Designed to resemble a medieval Italian village complete with turrets, stone walls, and ramparts, the Borgata is far and away the most architecturally interesting mall in the Valley. It contains about 50 upscale boutiques, galleries, and restaurants. On Friday afternoons, there's live jazz. 6166 N. Scottsdale Rd. ✆ **602/953-6311**. www.borgata.com.

El Pedregal Festival Marketplace ★★   Adjacent to the Boulders resort 30 minutes north of Old Scottsdale, El Pedregal is the most self-consciously Southwestern shopping center in the Valley, and it's worth the long drive out just to see the neo–Santa Fe architecture. The shops offer high-end merchandise, fashions, and art. The Heard Museum also has a branch here. 34505 N. Scottsdale Rd., Carefree. ✆ **480/488-1072**. www.elpedregal.com.

Kierland Commons ★★   The urban-village concept of a shopping center—narrow streets, sidewalks, and residences mixed in with retail space—has taken off all over the country, and here in Scottsdale, the concept has taken on Texas-size proportions. However, despite the grand scale of this shopping center, it still has a great feel. You'll find Tommy Bahama, Ann Taylor Loft, Crate & Barrel, and even a few shops you may never have heard of before. N. Scottsdale Rd. and Greenway Rd. ✆ **480/348-1577**. www.kierland commons.com.

Scottsdale Fashion Square   Scottsdale has long been the Valley's shopping mecca, and for years this huge mall has been the reason why. It now houses five major department stores—Nordstrom, Dillard's, Neiman Marcus, Macy's, and Robinsons-May—and smaller stores such as Eddie Bauer, J. Crew, and Louis Vuitton. E. Camelback and Scottsdale roads, Scottsdale. ✆ **480/949-0202** or 480/990-7800. www.westcor.com.

The Shops at Gainey Village   This upscale shopping center is much smaller than Kierland Commons farther up Scottsdale Road, but is no less impressive, especially after dark when lights illuminate the tall palm trees. In addition to several women's clothing stores, there are a couple of great restaurants. N. Scottsdale and Doubletree Ranch roads. ✆ **480/948-5586**. www.theshopsatgaineyvillage.com.

NATIVE AMERICAN ARTS, CRAFTS & JEWELRY

Bischoff's at the Park ★★   This museum-like store and gallery is affiliated with another Bischoff's right across the street (see "Gifts & Souvenirs," above). However, this outpost carries higher-end jewelry, Western-style home furnishings and clothing, ceramics, sculptures, contemporary paintings, and books and music with a regional theme. 3925 N. Brown Ave., Scottsdale. ✆ **480/946-6155**. www.shadesofthewest.com.

Faust Gallery ★   Old Native American baskets and pottery, as well as old and new Navajo rugs, are the specialties at this interesting shop. It also sells Native American and Southwestern art, including ceramics, paintings, bronzes, and unusual sculptures. 7103 E. Main St., Scottsdale. ✆ **480/946-6345**. www.faustgallery.com.

Gilbert Ortega Museum Gallery   You'll find Gilbert Ortega shops all over the Valley, but this is the biggest and best. As the name implies, there are museum displays throughout the store. Jewelry is the main attraction, but there are also baskets, sculptures, pottery, rugs, paintings, and kachinas. 3925 N. Scottsdale Rd. ℂ 480/990-1808.

Heard Museum Gift Shop   The Heard Museum (see "Seeing the Sights," earlier in this chapter) has an astonishing collection of well-crafted and very expensive Native American jewelry, art, and crafts of all kinds. This is the best place in the Valley to shop for Native American arts and crafts; you can be absolutely assured of the quality. Because the store doesn't have to charge sales tax, you'll save a bit of money. At the Heard Museum, 2301 N. Central Ave. ℂ 602/252-8344. www.heard.org.

John C. Hill Antique Indian Art ★★   While shops selling Native American art and artifacts abound in Scottsdale, few offer the high quality available in this tiny shop. Not only does the store have one of the finest selections of Navajo rugs in the Valley, including quite a few older rugs, but there are also kachinas, superb Navajo and Zuni silver-and-turquoise jewelry, baskets, and pottery. 6962 E. First Ave., Scottsdale. ℂ 480/946-2910. www.johnhillgallery.com.

Old Territorial Shop ★★   This is the oldest Indian arts-and-crafts store on Main Street and offers good values on jewelry, concha belts, kachinas, fetishes, pottery, and Navajo rugs. 7077 W. Main St., Scottsdale. ℂ 480/945-5432. www.oldterritorialshop.com.

River Trading Post   If you are interesting in getting into collecting Native American art or artifacts, this is a good place to get in the ground floor. Quality is high and prices are relatively low. Not only are there high-quality Navajo rugs, but there are also museum-quality pieces of ancient Southwestern pottery. 7140 E. First Ave., Scottsdale. ℂ 480/444-0001. www.rivertradingpost.com.

WESTERN WEAR

Az-Tex Hat Company   This small shop in Old Scottsdale offers custom shaping and fitting of both felt and woven hats. 3903 N. Scottsdale Rd., Scottsdale. ℂ 800/972-2116 or 480/481-9900. www.aztexhats.com.

Out West ★   All things Western are available at this eclectic shop, and the fashions are both beautiful and fun (although fancy and pricey). 7003 E. Cave Creek Rd., Cave Creek. ℂ 480/488-0180. www.outwestmercantile.com.

Saba's Western Stores   Since 1927, this store has been outfitting Scottsdale's cowboys and cowgirls, visiting dude ranchers, and anyone else who wants to adopt the look of the Wild West. Call for other locations around Phoenix. 7254 Main St., Scottsdale. ℂ 877/342-1835 or 480/949-7404. www.sabaswesternwear.com.

Sheplers Western Wear   Sheplers is sort of a department store of cowboy duds. If you can't find it here, it just ain't available in these parts. Other locations include 8999 E. Indian Bend Rd., Scottsdale (ℂ 480/948-1933); and 2643 E. Broadway Rd., Mesa (ℂ 480/827-8244). 9201 N. 29th Ave. ℂ 602/870-8085. www.sheplers.com.

10 Phoenix After Dark

Although much of the nightlife scene is centered on Old Scottsdale, Tempe's Mill Avenue, and downtown Phoenix, you'll find things going on all over.

The weekly *Phoenix New Times* tends to have the most comprehensive listings for clubs and concert halls. *The Rep Entertainment Guide* in the Thursday edition of the

Arizona Republic also lists upcoming events and performances. *Get Out,* published by the *Tribune,* is another tabloid-format arts-and-entertainment publication that is available free around Scottsdale, Phoenix, and Tempe. Other publications to check for abbreviated listings are *Valley Guide, Key to the Valley, Where Phoenix/Scottsdale,* and *Quick Guide Arizona,* all of which are free and can usually be found at hotels and resorts.

Tickets to many concerts, theater performances, and sporting events are available through **Ticketmaster** (© 480/784-4444; www.ticketmaster.com), which has outlets at Wherehouse Records, Tower Records, Robinsons-May department stores, and Fry's Marketplace stores. For sold-out shows, check with your hotel concierge, or try **Tickets Unlimited** (© 800/289-8497 or 602/840-2340; www.ticketsunlimitedinc.com).

THE CLUB & MUSIC SCENE

Packed into a couple of dozen blocks surrounding Old Town Scottsdale, near the corner of Camelback and Scottsdale roads, there are dozens of trendy dance clubs and chic bars. This is where the wealthy fashionistas (and the wannabes) come to party. The crowd is young, affluent, and attractive. Cruise along **Stetson Drive,** which is divided into two sections (east and west of Scottsdale Rd.) to find the latest hot spots.

Although Scottsdale is the nexus of nightclubbing for the fashion conscious, the Valley has plenty of other clubs and bars for those who don't wear Prada. Other nightlife districts include Tempe's Mill Avenue and downtown Phoenix.

Mill Avenue in Tempe is a good place to wander around until you hear your favorite type of music. The crowd tends to be young and rowdy.

Downtown Phoenix is home to Symphony Hall, the Herberger Theater Center, and several sports bars. However, much of the action revolves around games and concerts at the America West Arena and Bank One Ballpark (BOB).

Clubs come and go quickly, so to find out what's hot, get a copy of the *New Times.* Bars and clubs are allowed to serve alcohol until 2am.

COUNTRY

Handlebar-J This Scottsdale landmark is about as genuine a cowboy bar as you'll find in Phoenix, and cowpokes often stop by when they come in from the ranch. You'll hear live git-down two-steppin' nightly; free dance lessons are given Wednesdays, Thursdays, and Sundays. 7116 Becker Lane, Scottsdale. © 480/948-0110. www.handlebarj.com. No cover to $5.

Rusty Spur Saloon A small, rowdy, drinkin' and dancin' place frequented by tourists, this bar is a lot of fun, with peanut shells all over the floor, dollar bills stapled to the walls, and live country music afternoons and at night. If you're a cowboy or cowgirl at heart, this is the place to party when you're in Scottsdale. 7245 E. Main St., Old Scottsdale. © 480/425-7787. www.rustyspursaloon.com.

DANCE CLUBS & DISCOS

Axis/Radius If you're looking to do a bit of celebrity-spotting, Axis is one of the best places in town to keep your eye out. For several years now, this has been one of Scottsdale's hottest dance clubs and liveliest singles scenes. The two-story glass box is a boldly contemporary space with an awesome sound system. 7340 E. Indian Plaza (2 blocks east of Scottsdale Rd. and 1 block south of Camelback Rd.), Scottsdale. © 480/970-1112. www.axis-radius.com. Cover $7–$10.

Barcelona This is Scottsdale's premier supper club, and after the dinner crowd gives up its tables, Barcelona becomes one of the city's top dance spots. The well-heeled crowd ranges primarily from 30s to 50s. 15440 Greenway-Hayden Loop. ℂ 480/603-0370. www.barcelonadining.com. No cover to $10.

Myst   Always packed to the walls with the Valley's beautiful people, Myst is currently *the* place to see and be seen. The atmosphere is lavishly ostentatious, with various themed rooms. There's even a pool room called the Ballroom. The club is only open Wednesday, Friday, and Saturday. 7340 E. Shoeman Lane, Scottsdale. ℂ 480/970-5000. www.mystaz.com. Cover $10.

Pepin   Fridays and Saturdays, a DJ plays Latin dance music from 10pm on at this small Spanish restaurant located in the Scottsdale Mall. Thursday through Saturday evenings, there are also live flamenco performances. 7363 Scottsdale Mall, Scottsdale. ℂ 480/990-9026. www.pepinrestaurant.com. Cover $7.

ROCK, JAZZ & BLUES

Char's Has the Blues   You wouldn't think to look at this little cottage, but it really does have those mean-and-dirty, low-down blues. All of the best blues brothers and sisters from around the city and around the country make the scene here. 4631 N. Seventh Ave., 4 blocks south of Camelback Rd. ℂ 602/230-0205. www.charshastheblues.com. No cover to $10.

The Rhythm Room   This blues club, long the Valley's most popular, books quite a few national acts as well as the best of the local scene, and has a dance floor if you want to move to the beat. 1019 E. Indian School Rd. ℂ 602/265-4842. www.rhythmroom.com. No cover to $25.

THE BAR, LOUNGE & PUB SCENE

AZ88   Located across the park from the Scottsdale Center for the Arts, this sophisticated bar/restaurant has a cool ambience that's just right for a cocktail before or after a performance. There's also a great patio area. 7353 Scottsdale Mall, Scottsdale. ℂ 480/994-5576.

Bar Bianco ✮   Located downtown on Heritage Square, this little wine bar is in a restored historic home and is affiliated with Pizzeria Bianco, the tiny and ever-popular designer pizza place right next door. With candles burning in every room, this is a very romantic place for a drink. 609 E. Adams St. ℂ 602/528-3699.

Durant's   In business for decades, Durant's has long been downtown Phoenix's favorite after-work watering hole with the old guard and has caught on with the young martini-drinking crowd as well. 2611 N. Central Ave. ℂ 602/264-5967. www.durantsfinefoods.com.

Four Peaks Brewing Company   Consistently voted the best brewpub in Phoenix, this Tempe establishment, housed in a former creamery, brews good beers and serves decent pub grub. A favorite of ASU students. There's a second brewpub in north Scottsdale at the corner of Hayden Road and Frank Lloyd Wright Boulevard (ℂ 480/991-1795). 1340 E. Eighth St., Tempe. ℂ 480/303-9967. www.fourpeaks.com.

Hyatt Regency Scottsdale Lobby Bar ✮✮   The open-air lounge just below the main lobby of this posh Scottsdale resort sets a romantic stage for nightly live music (often flamenco or Caribbean steel drum music). Wood fires burn in patio fire pits, and the terraced gardens offer plenty of dark spots for a bit of romance. Be sure to try the house's fruit-infused vodkas. 7500 E. Doubletree Ranch Rd., Scottsdale. ℂ 480/991-3388.

Jbar   Currently this is absolutely the hottest bar in Scottsdale, the sort of place Paris Hilton frequents when she's in town. So, dress the part, look the part, or don't even attempt to make the scene here. Remember, "shaken not stirred." In JAMES Hotel, 7353 E. Indian School Rd., Scottsdale. ℂ 480/308-1100.

Six ✸ There are those who frequent this posh bar just to see the look on new-comers' faces when they see the high-tech unisex bathrooms—the glass is transparent until you go inside! Regardless of why you come, you'll find one of the coolest and most stylish drinking establishments in the state. 7316 E. Stetson Dr., Scottsdale. ✆ **480/663-6620.**

T. Cook's ✸✸ If you aren't planning on having dinner at this opulent Mediterranean restaurant, at least stop by for a cocktail in the bar. With its mix of Spanish-colonial and 1950s tropical furnishings, this is as romantic a lounge as you'll find anywhere in the Valley. You can also snuggle with your sweetie out on the patio by the fireplace. At the Royal Palms Resort & Spa, 5200 E. Camelback Rd. ✆ **602/808-0766.**

WINE BARS

Cave Creek Coffee Co. & Wine Purveyors Located way up north in the cow town of Cave Creek, this hip coffeehouse doubles as a lively wine bar that also happens to book some great music. Past performers have included Kelly Joe Phelps, Michelle Shocked, Richie Havens, and Leo Kottke. 6033 E. Cave Creek Rd., Cave Creek. ✆ **480/488-0603.** www.cavecreekcoffee.com. Cover $15–$28.

Kazimierz World Wine Bar ✸ Sort of a spacious speak-easy crossed with a wine cellar, this unmarked place, associated with the nearby Cowboy Ciao restaurant, offers the same wide selection of wines available at the restaurant. There's live jazz and dozens of wines by the glass, but be forewarned, the cigarette smoke can be thick. 7137 E. Stetson Dr., Scottsdale. ✆ **480/946-3004.** www.kazbar.net.

Postino ✸✸ This immensely popular wine bar is in the heart of the Arcadia neighborhood south of Camelback Road. Casual yet stylish, the bar has garage-style doors that roll up to expose the restaurant to the outdoors. Choose from a great selection of wines by the glass and a limited menu of European-inspired appetizers. 3939 E. Campbell Ave. ✆ **602/852-3939.**

COCKTAILS WITH A VIEW

The Valley of the Sun has more than its fair share of spectacular views. Unfortunately, most of them are from expensive restaurants. All these restaurants have lounges, though, where for the price of a drink you can sit back and ogle a crimson sunset and the purple mountains' majesty. Among the best choices are **Different Pointe of View,** at the Pointe Hilton Tapatio Cliffs Resort; **Rustler's Rooste,** at the Pointe South Mountain Resort; and **Top of the Rock,** at The Wyndham Buttes Resort.

The Squaw Peak Bar Can't afford the lifestyles of the rich and famous? Try just pulling up a comfortable chair and faking it for a while. For the cost of a couple of drinks, you can sink into a seat here at the Biltmore's main lounge and watch the sunset test its color palette on Piestewa Peak (formerly Squaw Peak). Alternatively, you can slide into a seat near the piano and let the waves of mellow jazz wash over you. At the Arizona Biltmore Resort & Spa, 2400 E. Missouri Ave. ✆ **602/955-6600.**

Thirsty Camel Whether you've already made your millions or are still working your way up the corporate ladder, you owe it to yourself to spend a little time in the lap of luxury. You may never drink in more ostentatious surroundings than here at Charles Keating's Xanadu. The view is one of the best in the city. At The Phoenician, 6000 E. Camelback Rd. ✆ **480/941-8200.**

SPORTS BARS

Alice Cooper'stown   Sports and rock mix it up at this downtown restaurant/bar run by, you guessed it, Alice Cooper. The Bank One Ballpark is only a block away. See p. 427 for more information. 101 E. Jackson St. ℂ 602/253-7337. www.alicecooperstown.com.

Don & Charlie's   Although this is primarily a steakhouse, it also has the best sports bar in Scottsdale. What makes Don & Charlie's such a great sports bar is not the size or number of its TVs, but rather all the sports memorabilia on the walls. 7501 E. Camelback Rd. ℂ 480/990-0900. www.donandcharlies.com.

Majerle's Sports Grill   If you're a Phoenix Suns fan, you won't want to miss this sports bar located only a couple of blocks from the America West Arena, where the Suns play. Suns memorabilia covers the walls. 24 N. Second St. ℂ 602/253-0118. www.majerles.com.

GAY & LESBIAN BARS & CLUBS

Ain't Nobody's Bizness   Located in a small shopping plaza, this is the city's most popular lesbian bar. On weekends, the dance floor is usually packed. 3031 E. Indian School Rd. ℂ 602/224-9977. www.aintnobodysbizness-az.com.

Amsterdam   This classy spot is known across the Valley for its great martinis. There's usually a female impersonator one night of the week, and other nights, there's live music or DJ dance music. 718 N. Central Ave. ℂ 602/258-6122. www.amsterdambar.com.

THE PERFORMING ARTS

Downtown Phoenix claims the Valley's greatest concentration of performance halls, but there are major performing-arts venues scattered across the Valley. Calling these many valley venues home are such major companies as the Phoenix Symphony, Scottsdale Symphony Orchestra, Arizona Opera Company, Ballet Arizona, Center Dance Ensemble, Actors Theatre of Phoenix, and Arizona Theatre Company. Adding to the performances held by these companies are the wide variety of touring companies that make stops here throughout the year.

OUTDOOR VENUES & SERIES

The city's top outdoor venue is the **Cricket Pavilion,** a half-mile north of I-10 between 79th and 83rd avenues (ℂ 602/254-7200; http://cricket-pavilion.com). This 20,000-seat amphitheater is open year-round and hosts everything from Broadway musicals to rock concerts.

The **Mesa Amphitheater,** at University Drive and Center Road, Mesa (ℂ 480/644-2560; www.mesaamp.com), is a much smaller amphitheater that holds a wide variety of concerts in spring and summer, and occasionally other times of year as well.

Throughout the year, the **Scottsdale Center for the Arts,** 7380 E. Second St., Scottsdale (ℂ 480/994-ARTS; www.scottsdaleperformingarts.org), stages outdoor performances in the adjacent Scottsdale Amphitheater on the Scottsdale Civic Center Mall. The Sunday A'fair series (Oct–Apr) holds free concerts ranging from acoustic blues to zydeco from noon to 4:30pm on selected Sundays of each month.

The Music in the Garden concerts at the **Desert Botanical Garden,** 1201 N. Galvin Pkwy. in Papago Park (ℂ 480/941-1225; www.dbg.org), are held on Sundays between January and March. The season includes an eclectic array of musical styles. Tickets are $16 and include admission to the gardens. Sunday brunch is served for an additional charge. There are also Friday night jazz concerts. Up on the north side of

Major Performing-Arts Centers

Symphony Hall, 225 E. Adams St. ((C) 602/262-7272), is home to the Phoenix Symphony and the Arizona Opera Company. It also hosts touring Broadway shows and various other concerts and theatrical productions.

The **Orpheum Theatre,** 203 W. Adams St. ((C) 602/262-7272), is an elegant, historic Spanish-colonial baroque theater built in 1929.

Celebrity Theatre, 440 N. 32nd St. ((C) 602/267-1600; www.celebritytheatre. com), seems to be booking lots of great acts these days, such as James Brown, The Temptations, and Wynonna.

The **Dodge Theatre,** 400 W. Washington St. ((C) 602/379-2888; www. dodgetheatre.com), which seats from 2,000 to 5,000 people, books top names in entertainment as well as Broadway shows and international touring companies.

The Frank Lloyd Wright–designed **Grady Gammage Auditorium,** Mill Avenue and Apache Boulevard, Tempe ((C) 480/965-3434; www.asugammage. com), on the Arizona State University campus, hosts everything from barbershop quartets to touring Broadway shows.

The **Scottsdale Center for the Arts,** 7380 E. Second St., Scottsdale ((C) 480/ 994-ARTS; www.scottsdaleperformingarts.org), hosts a variety of performances and series, ranging from alternative dance to classical music.

the Valley, just outside Carefree, **El Pedregal Festival Marketplace,** 34505 N. Scottsdale Rd., Scottsdale ((C) 480/488-1072; www.elpedregal.com) stages occasional jazz, blues, and rock concerts and sometimes has free concerts on weekends.

Outdoor concerts are also held at various parks and plazas around the Valley during the warmer months. Check local papers for listings.

CLASSICAL MUSIC, OPERA & DANCE

The **Phoenix Symphony** ((C) 800/776-9080 or 602/495-1999; www.phoenix symphony.org), the Southwest's leading symphony orchestra, performs at Symphony Hall (tickets mostly run $20–$55), while the **Scottsdale Symphony Orchestra** ((C) 480/ 945-8071; www.scotsymph.org) performs at the Scottsdale Center for the Arts (tickets go for $17–$20).

Opera buffs may want to see what the **Arizona Opera Company** ((C) 602/266-7464; www.azopera.org) has scheduled. This company stages up to five operas, both familiar and more obscure, and splits its time between Phoenix and Tucson. Tickets cost $25 to $115. Performances are held at Symphony Hall.

Ballet Arizona ((C) 888/3-BALLET or 602/381-1096; www.balletaz.org) performs at the Orpheum and stages both classical and contemporary ballets; tickets run $12 to $102. The **Center Dance Ensemble** ((C) 602/252-8497; www.centerdance.com), the city's contemporary dance company, stages several productions a year at the Herberger Theater Center. Tickets cost $20. Between September and April, **Southwest Arts & Entertainment** ((C) 800/905-3315 or 602/262-7272; www.southwestae.com) brings acclaimed dance companies and music acts from around the world to Phoenix, with performances staged primarily at the Orpheum. Tickets range from $20 to $45.

THEATER

Downtown, the **Herberger Theater Center,** 222 E. Monroe St. (© **602/254-7399;** www.herbergertheater.org) is the city's main venue for live theater. Its two Broadway-style theaters together host hundreds of performances each year, including productions by the **Actors Theatre of Phoenix (ATP)** and the **Arizona Theatre Company (ATC).** ATP (© **602/253-6701;** www.atphx.org) tends to stage smaller, lesser-known off-Broadway-type works; tickets go for $20 to $44. ATC (© **602/256-6995;** www.arizonatheatre.org) is the state theater company of Arizona and splits its performances between Phoenix and Tucson. Productions range from world premieres to recent Tony award–winners to classics. Tickets run $20 to $61.

The **Phoenix Theatre,** 100 E. McDowell Rd. (© **602/254-2151;** www.phxtheatre.org), is located in the Phoenix Art Museum building. Musicals are the mainstays here; tickets are $20 to $34. The **Broadway in Arizona** series (© **480/965-3434;** www.broadwayacrossamerica.com/tempe), focusing mostly on comedies and musicals, is held at the Gammage Auditorium in Tempe. Tickets cost roughly $22 to $80, with the occasional higher prices for a real blockbuster show.

11 A Side Trip from Phoenix: The Apache Trail ★★

There isn't a whole lot of desert or history left in Phoenix, but only an hour's drive to the east you'll find quite a bit of both. The **Apache Trail,** a narrow, winding, partially gravel road that snakes its way around the north side of the Superstition Mountains, offers some of the most scenic desert driving in central Arizona. Along the way are ghost towns and legends, saguaros and century plants, ancient ruins and artificial lakes. Pick and choose the stops that appeal to you, and be sure to get an early start. The gravel section of the road is well graded and is passable for regular passenger cars.

If you'd rather leave the driving to someone else, consider **Apache Trail Tours** (© **480/982-7661;** www.apachetrailtours.com), which offers guided half-day and full-day tours along the Apache Trail. Tours range in price from $70 to $165.

To start this drive, head east on U.S. 60 to the town of Apache Junction, and then go north on Ariz. 88. About 4 miles out of town, you'll come to **Goldfield Ghost Town,** a reconstructed gold-mining town (see "Especially for Kids" under "Seeing the Sights," earlier in this chapter). Leave yourself plenty of time if you plan to stop here.

Not far from Goldfield is **Lost Dutchman State Park** (© **480/982-4485**), where you can hike into the rugged Superstition Mountains. Springtime wildflower displays here can be absolutely gorgeous. Park admission is $5 per vehicle ($3 during the summer); a campground charges $12 to $25 per site.

Continuing northeast, you'll reach **Canyon Lake,** set in a deep canyon flanked by colorful cliffs and rugged rock formations. You can go for a swim at the Acacia Picnic Area or the nearby Boulder Picnic Area, which is in a pretty side cove. You can also take a cruise on the *Dolly* steamboat (© **480/827-9144;** www.dollysteamboat.com). A 90-minute jaunt on this reproduction paddle wheeler costs $15 for adults and $8.50 for children 6 to 12. Lunch and dinner cruises are also available, and there's a lakeside restaurant at the boat landing. But if you're at all hungry, try to hold out for nearby **Tortilla Flat** (© **480/984-1776;** www.tortillaflataz.com), an old stagecoach stop with a restaurant, saloon, and general store. Don't miss the prickly-pear ice cream.

A few miles past Tortilla Flat, the pavement ends and the truly spectacular desert scenery begins. Among the rocky ridges, arroyos, and canyons of this stretch of road,

En Route to Tucson

Driving southeast from Phoenix for about 60 miles will bring you to the Casa Grande and Coolidge area, where you can learn about the Hohokam people who once inhabited this region, and, in spring, see desert wildflowers.

Casa Grande Ruins National Monument ★★, located outside Coolidge, preserves one of the most unusual Indian ruins in the state; an earth-walled structure built 650 years ago by the Hohokam people. Instead of using adobe bricks or stones, the people who built this structure used layers of hard-packed soil. Located 1 mile north of Coolidge on Ariz. 87 (© **520/723-3172;** www.nps.gov/cagr). Admission is $3.

Alternatively, if you're heading to Tucson by way of I-10, consider a stop at **Picacho Peak State Park** ★★, 35 miles northwest of Tucson at exit 219 (© **520/466-3183;** www.pr.state.az.us). Picacho Peak, which rises 1,500 feet above the desert, is a visual landmark for miles around. Hiking trails around the peak and up to the summit are especially popular in spring, when the wildflowers bloom. Admission is $6 per car ($3 in summer) for up to 4 adults; campsites in the park cost $10 to $22.

you'll see saguaro cacti and century plants (a type of agave that dies after sending up its flower stalk, which can reach heights of 15 ft.).

Shortly before reaching pavement again, you'll see **Theodore Roosevelt Dam.** This dam, built in 1911, forms Roosevelt Lake and is the largest masonry dam in the world. However, a face-lift a few years ago hid the original masonry construction; it now looks much like any other concrete dam in the state.

Continuing on Ariz. 88, you'll next come to **Tonto National Monument** ★ (© **928/ 467-2241;** www.nps.gov/tont), which preserves some of the southernmost cliff dwellings in Arizona. These pueblos were occupied between about 1300 and 1450 by the Salado people and are some of the few remaining traces of this tribe. The lower ruins are a half-mile up a steep trail, and getting to the upper ruins requires a 3-mile round-trip hike. The lower ruins are open daily year-round; the upper ruins are open November through April on guided tours (reservations required well in advance). The park is open daily from 8am to 5pm (you must begin the lower ruin trail by 4pm); admission is $3.

Keep going on Ariz. 88 to the copper-mining town of **Globe.** Be sure to visit **Besh-Ba-Gowah Archaeological Park** ★ (© **928/425-0320**), on the eastern outskirts of town. Several rooms at this Salado Indian pueblo site are set up to reflect the way they might have looked when they were first occupied about 700 years ago. The grounds are open daily from 9am to 6pm but the museum closes at 5pm (admission $3 adults, $2 seniors, free children 12 and under). To get here, head out of Globe on South Broad Street to Jesse Hayes Road.

From Globe, head west on U.S. 60. Three miles west of Superior, you'll come to **Boyce Thompson Arboretum** ★★, 37615 U.S. 60 (© **520/689-2811;** http:// arboretum.ag.arizona.edu), dedicated to researching and propagating desert plants. As you hike the nature trails of this 320-acre garden, watch for the two bizarre boojum trees. The arboretum is open daily from 8am to 5pm; admission is $7.50 for adults and $3 for children 5 to 12.

14

The Deserts, High Plains & Sky Islands of Southern Arizona

In the southeastern corner of Arizona, the mile-high grasslands, punctuated by forested mountain ranges, have long supported vast ranches where cattle range across wide-open plains. It was also here that much of America's now-legendary Western history took place. Wyatt Earp and the Clantons shot it out at Tombstone's O.K. Corral, Doc Holliday played his cards, and Cochise and Geronimo staged the last Indian rebellions. Cavalries charged, and prospectors wandered the wilderness in search of the mother lode. Today, ghost towns litter the landscape of southeastern Arizona, but the past is kept alive by people searching for a glimpse of the Wild West.

The combination of low deserts, high plains, and even higher mountains has given this region a fascinating diversity of landscapes. Giant saguaros cover the slopes of the Sonoran Desert throughout much of southern Arizona, and in the western parts of this region, organ pipe cacti reach the northern limit of their range. In the cool mountains, cacti give way to pines, and passing clouds bring snow and rain. Narrow canyons and broad valleys, fed by the rain and snowmelt, provide habitat for hundreds of species of birds and other wildlife. This is the northernmost range for many birds usually found only south of the border. Consequently, southeastern Arizona has become one of the nation's most important bird-watching spots.

1 Organ Pipe Cactus National Monument ★★

135 miles S of Phoenix; 140 miles W of Tucson; 185 miles SE of Yuma

Located roughly midway between Yuma and Tucson, Organ Pipe Cactus National Monument is a preserve for the rare cactus for which the monument is named. The organ pipe cactus resembles the saguaro cactus in many ways, but instead of forming a single main trunk, organ pipes have many trunks, some 20 feet tall, that resemble—you guessed it—organ pipes.

This is a rugged region with few towns or services. The only motels in the area are in the small town of Ajo. This former company town was built around a now-abandoned copper mine, and the downtown plaza, with its tall palm trees and arched and covered walkways, has the look and feel of a Mexican town square. Be sure to gas up your car before leaving Ajo.

ESSENTIALS

GETTING THERE   From Tucson, take Ariz. 86 west to Why and turn south on Ariz. 85. From Yuma, take I-8 east to Gila Bend and drive south on Ariz. 85.

FEES The park entry fee is $8 per car.

VISITOR INFORMATION For information, contact **Organ Pipe Cactus National Monument** (© 520/387-6849; www.nps.gov/orpi). The visitor center is open daily from 8am to 5pm, although the park itself is open 24 hours a day.

EXPLORING THE MONUMENT

Two well-graded gravel roads lead through different sections of this large national monument. The Puerto Blanco Drive is currently a 5-mile route leading only to the Red Tanks trail head. The Ajo Mountain Drive is a 21-mile one-way loop drive. Guides available at the park's visitor center explain natural features of the landscape along both drives. There are also a number of hiking trails along the roads. In the winter, there are guided tours of the Ajo Mountain Drive.

WHERE TO STAY

There are two campgrounds within the park (although nonvehicle camping is allowed in the backcountry with a permit). Campsites are $8 in the primitive **Alamo Campground** and $12 in the more developed **Twin Peaks Campground.** The nearest lodgings are in Ajo, where there are several old and very basic motels as well as a B&B. There are also plenty of budget chain motels in the town of Gila Bend, 70 miles north of the monument.

Guest House Inn Bed & Breakfast Built in 1925 as a guesthouse for mining executives, this B&B has attractive gardens in the front yard and a mesquite thicket off to one side. Guest rooms are simply furnished with reproduction antique and southwestern furnishings. There are also sunrooms on both the north and the south sides of the house.

700 Guest House Rd., Ajo, AZ 85321. © 520/387-6133. www.guesthouseinn.biz. 4 units. $89 double. Rates include full breakfast. DC, MC, V. *In room:* A/C, fridge, hair dryer, iron.

2 Tubac ✶✶ & Buenos Aires National Wildlife Refuge ✶

45 miles S of Tucson; 21 miles N of Nogales; 84 miles W of Sierra Vista

Located in the fertile valley of the Santa Cruz River 45 miles south of Tucson, Tubac is one of Arizona's largest arts communities. The concentration of shops, artist studios, and galleries makes Tubac one of southern Arizona's most popular destinations, and a small retirement community is beginning to develop.

After visiting Tubac Presidio State Historic Park and Tumacacori National Historical Park to learn about the area's history, you'll probably want to spend some time browsing through the shops. Keep in mind, however, that many of the local artists leave town in summer, prompting many local shops to close on weekdays in the summer. The shops are open daily during the busy season of October through May.

ESSENTIALS

GETTING THERE The Santa Cruz Valley towns of Amado, Tubac, and Tumacacori are all due south of Tucson on I-19.

VISITOR INFORMATION For information on Tubac and Tumacacori, contact the **Tubac Chamber of Commerce** (© 520/398-2704; www.tubacaz.com) or the **Tubac-Santa Cruz Visitor Center,** 4 Plaza Rd. (© 520/398-0007; www.toursanta cruz.com).

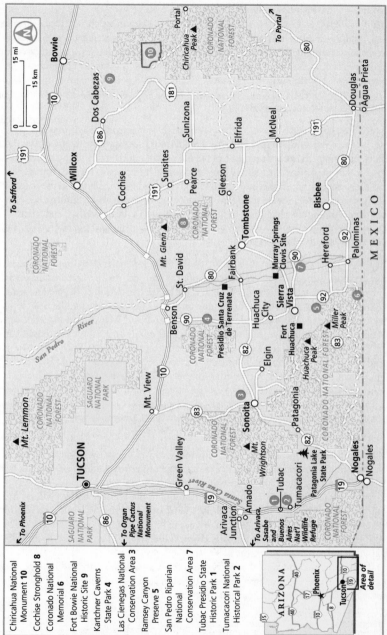

ART & HISTORY IN THE SANTA CRUZ VALLEY

Tubac Center of the Arts ⭐ Tubac is an arts community, and this Spanish colonial building serves as its center for cultural activities. Throughout the season, there are workshops, traveling exhibitions, juried shows, an annual crafts show, and theater and music performances. The quality of the art at these shows is generally better than what's found in most of the surrounding stores. There is also a good little gift shop here.

9 Plaza Rd. ℂ 520/398-2371. www.tubacarts.org. Suggested donation $2. Mon–Sat 10am–4:30pm; Sun 1–4:30pm. Closed mid-May to Labor Day and major holidays.

Tubac Presidio State Historic Park Although Tumacacori mission was founded in 1691, it was not until 1752 that Tubac Presidio was established in response to a Pima Indian uprising. Today, little remains of the old presidio (fort), but this small park does a good job of presenting the region's Spanish colonial history. Also on the grounds is the old Tubac School, which was built in 1885 and is the oldest schoolhouse in the state. Living-history presentations are staged from October through March on Sundays between 1 and 4pm. Among the characters you'll meet are Spanish soldiers, settlers, and friars.

Presidio Dr. ℂ 520/398-2252. Admission $3 adults ($2 between Memorial Day and Labor Day), free for children under 14. Daily 8am–5pm. Closed Christmas.

Tumacacori National Historical Park ⭐ Founded in 1691 by Jesuit missionary and explorer Father Eusebio Francisco Kino, the San José de Tumacacori mission was one of the first Anglo settlements in what is today Arizona. Much of the old adobe mission church still stands. A small museum contains exhibits on mission life and the history of the region. On weekends between September and May, Native American and Mexican craftspeople give demonstrations of indigenous arts. January through April, on the nights of the full moon, the monument stays open until 9pm and there are guided tours available. Every Wednesday between September and April, there are also special living history tours to two sister missions—San Cayetano de Calabazas and Los Santos Ángeles de Guevavi. These tours are by reservation and cost $10 per person.

1891 E. Frontage Rd. ℂ 520/398-2341. www.nps.gov/tuma. Admission $3 adults, free for children 16 and under. Daily 8am–5pm. Closed Thanksgiving and Christmas. Take I-19 to Exit 29; Tumacacori is 3 miles south of Tubac.

SHOPPING

While tourist brochures like to tout Tubac as an artists' community, the town is more of a Southwest souvenir mecca. There are a few genuine art galleries here, but you have to look hard amid the many tourist shops to find the real gems.

Some of the better fine art in the area is found at the **Karin Newby Gallery,** Mercado de Baca, 19 Tubac Rd. (ℂ **888/398-9662** or 520/398-9662; www.karinnewby gallery.com). For traditional Western art, some by members of the prestigious Cowboy Artists of America, visit the **Big Horn Galleries,** 37 Tubac Rd. (ℂ **520/398-9209;** www.bighorngalleries.com).

If you're in the market for jewelry, be sure to visit **Blackstar,** E. Frontage Road (ℂ **520/398-0451**), in nearby Amado (at Exit 48 off I-19). This small jewelry store specializes in locally mined opal and other exotic gemstones.

Near Tumacacori National Historical Park, you'll find all things hot (chiles, hot sauces, salsas, spices) arranged on the shelves of one of the more genuine Tubac-area institutions, the **Santa Cruz Chile and Spice Company,** 1868 E. Frontage Rd. (ℂ 520/398-2591; www.santacruzchili.com), a combination store and packing plant. The shop is open Monday through Saturday from 8am to 5pm.

BUENOS AIRES NATIONAL WILDLIFE REFUGE ⭐

If you're a bird-watcher, you'll definitely want to make the trip over to **Buenos Aires National Wildlife Refuge,** P.O. Box 109, Sasabe, AZ 85633 (📞 **520/823-4251;** www.fws.gov/southwest/refuges/arizona/buenosaires/index.html), about 28 miles from Tubac. To get here, head north from Tubac on I-19 to Arivaca Junction, then drive west on a winding two-lane road. The refuge begins just outside the small community of Arivaca.

Your first stop should be at **Arivaca Cienega,** a quarter of a mile east of Arivaca. *Cienega* is Spanish for "marsh," and that is exactly what you will find here. The marsh's seven springs provide year-round water and consequently attract an amazing variety of bird life. This is one of the few places in the United States where you can see a gray hawk, and vermilion flycatchers are quite common. Other good birding spots within the refuge include **Arivaca Creek,** 2 miles west of Arivaca, and **Aguirre Lake,** a half-mile north of the refuge headquarters and visitor center, which is off Ariz. 286 north of Sasabe.

The **visitor center** is a good place to spot one of the refuge's rarest birds, the masked bobwhite quail. Other birds you might spot outside the visitor center include Bendire's thrashers, Chihuahuan ravens, canyon towhees, and green-tailed towhees. The visitor center is open daily from 7:30am to 4pm. In the town of Arivaca, the **Arivaca Information Office** is open from 8am to 4pm when volunteers are available to staff it.

Other wildlife in the refuge includes pronghorn antelopes, javelinas, coatimundis, white-tailed deer, mule deer, and coyotes. Guided birding and other tours are offered weekends November through April. Call for details; some walks require reservations.

If you're looking for a strenuous hike, try the **Mustang Trail,** which has its trail head 2 miles west of Arivaca. The trail climbs up from Arivaca Creek into the surrounding dry hills and makes for a 5-mile round-trip hike.

GETTING OUTSIDE

Linking Tubac with Tumacacori is the 8-mile **de Anza Trail.** This trail is part of the **Juan Bautista de Anza National Historic Trail,** which stretches from Nogales to San Francisco and commemorates the overland journey of the Spanish captain who, in 1775 and 1776, led a small band of colonists overland to California. These settlers founded what is now the city of San Francisco. Today, bird-watching is the most popular activity along the trail. History buffs will also get to see an excavation of part of the Spanish colonial settlement of Tubac. The most convenient trail head is beside Tubac Presidio State Historic Park. **Rex Ranch** (📞 **520/398-2914**) offers horseback rides for $25 per hour.

If golf is more your speed, you can play a round at the **Tubac Golf Resort** (📞 **520/398-2211**), just north of Tubac off East Frontage Road. Greens fees range from $30 to $89.

WHERE TO STAY
IN AMADO

The Inn at Amado Territory Ranch ⭐   This modern inn just off I-19 in the crossroads of Amado is built in the territorial style, and captures the feel of an old Arizona ranch house. Guest rooms are outfitted in a mix of Mexican rustic furnishings and reproduction East Coast antiques, much in the style that homes would have been furnished in Arizona 100 years ago. Rooms on the second floor feature balconies with views across the farm fields of the Santa Cruz Valley, while those on the ground floor have patios. The Amado Café is right next door.

3001 E. Frontage Rd. (P.O. Box 81), Amado, AZ 85645. ☎ 888/398-8684 or 520/398-8684. Fax 520/398-8186. www.amado-territory-inn.com. 9 units. Nov–June $120–$135 double; July–Oct $95–$105 double. Rates include full breakfast. AE, DISC, MC, V. No children under 12. *In room:* A/C, no phone.

The Rex Ranch ★ *Finds* With its classic Southwestern styling and location adjacent to the de Anza Trail, this place is truly a hidden getaway. Just getting to this remote property is something of an adventure, since you have to drive *through* the Santa Cruz River to reach it. Although not all of the guest rooms are as attractively decorated as the public areas, the new rooms and the more recently renovated rooms are quite comfortable. Primarily a conference center and economical health spa, the ranch offers a wide variety of spa treatments and massages. The attractive little dining room is one of this area's best restaurants (see Cantina Romantica under "Where to Dine," below).

131 Amado Montosa Rd. (P.O. Box 636), Amado, AZ 85645. ☎ 888/REX-RANCH or 520/398-2914. Fax 520/398-8229. www.rexranch.com. 35 units. Oct–May $145–$245 double; June–Sept $125–$225 double. Rates include continental breakfast. AE, DC, DISC, MC, V. **Amenities:** Restaurant (Southwestern/New American); outdoor pool; spa; Jacuzzi; mountain-bike rentals; concierge; massage; horseback riding. *In room:* A/C, fridge, coffeemaker, no phone.

IN TUBAC

Tubac Golf Resort ★★ *Value* This economical golf resort is built on the Otero Ranch, which dates back to 1789 and is the oldest Spanish land-grant ranch in the Southwest. With its green fairways, this resort is a lush oasis amid the dry hills of the Santa Cruz Valley. Tubac Golf Resort has more a classic Southwestern feel than most of the Tucson golf resorts, and because it is fairly small, it has a low-key feel that I like. The red-tile roofs and brick archways throughout the resort help conjure up the Spanish heritage, while guest rooms are spacious and modern and situated in buildings set amid expansive lawns. Casitas have patios, beamed ceilings, and beehive fireplaces; newer rooms are worth requesting. If you're looking for a secluded getaway, this is a great choice. Oh, yes, and watch out for the cows on the golf course; they were added to return a little old-time character to the resort.

1 Otero Rd. (P.O. Box 1297), Tubac, AZ 85646. ☎ 800/848-7893 or 520/398-2211. Fax 520/398-9261. www.tubac golfresort.com. 70 units. $95–$195 double; $125–$310 suite. Children under 12 stay free in parent's room. AE, DISC, MC, V. Pets accepted ($25 fee). **Amenities:** 2 restaurants (Continental, American); lounge; outdoor pool; 18-hole golf course; tennis court; exercise room; Jacuzzi; bike rental; business center; shopping arcade; room service; massage; babysitting; coin-op laundry; laundry service. *In room:* A/C, TV, dataport, fridge, coffeemaker, hair dryer, iron.

WHERE TO DINE

In addition to the restaurants mentioned below, the **Tubac Golf Resort** (see "Where to Stay," above) has a good restaurant.

IN AMADO

Amado Café MEDITERRANEAN/AMERICAN There aren't a lot of dining options out here, making this restaurant, in a handsome territorial-style building, a real asset to the community. The best part of the experience is sitting out back on the rustic flagstone patio, listening to the gurgling fountain, and contemplating the view of the mountains in the distance. The menu includes sandwiches, salads, and more filling fare such as prime rib. The Greek dishes, including a Greek salad and stuffed grape leaves, are good bets.

3001 E. Frontage Rd. (Exit 48 off I-19), Amado. ☎ 520/398-9211. Main courses $7–$15 lunch, $12–$20 dinner. AE, DISC, MC, V. Tues–Sat 11:30am–2pm and 5–8pm; Sun 11:30am–2pm.

Cantina Romantica ★★ SOUTHWESTERN/NEW AMERICAN Located in a historic adobe hacienda at The Rex Ranch resort (see "Where to Stay," above), 6 miles

Starry, Starry Nights

Southern Arizona's clear skies and the absence of lights in the surrounding desert make the night sky here as brilliant as anywhere on earth. This fact has not gone unnoticed by the world's astronomers—southern Arizona has come to be known as the Astronomy Capital of the World.

Many observatories are open to the public but you'll need to make tour reservations well in advance. In addition to the ones listed below, the **Flandrau Science Center & Planetarium** (p. 378) in Tucson offers public viewings. In Flagstaff, there are public viewing programs at the **Lowell Observatory** (p. 525).

The **Smithsonian Institution Fred Lawrence Whipple Observatory,** located atop 8,550-foot Mount Hopkins, is the largest observatory operated by the Smithsonian Astrophysical Observatory. Tours last about 6 hours. No food is available here, so be sure to bring a picnic lunch. It's located on Mount Hopkins Road, near Amado (© **520/670-5707**). Tours are offered March through November Monday, Wednesday, and Friday and cost $7 for adults, $2.50 for children 6 to 12; no children under 6 allowed. Reservations are required and should be made 4 to 6 weeks in advance.

Located in the Quinlan Mountains atop 6,875-foot Kitt Peak, **Kitt Peak National Observatory** ✸ is the largest and most famous astronomical observatory in the region. This is the area's only major observatory to offer public nighttime viewing. Day visitors must be content with a visitor center (open daily 9am to 3:45pm), museum, and guided tour. Tours are held at 10am, 11:30am, and 1:30pm. Suggested donation is $2 per person. The observatory is 56 miles southwest of Tucson off Ariz. 86 (© **520/318-8726;** www.noao.edu/kpno). Nighttime stargazing (reservations required; call 4–8 weeks in advance) costs $36 adults; $31 students, seniors, and children under 18.

The **Mount Graham International Observatory** atop Mount Graham near the town of Safford offers 7-hour tours that include lunch, but do not include actual viewing through the telescopes at the observatory. There are, however, telescopes for public viewings on Friday and Saturday nights at Safford's **Gov Aker Observatory at Safford's Discovery Park,** 1651 W. Discovery Park Blvd. (© **888/837-1841** or 928/428-6260; www.discoverypark. com). Mount Graham International Observatory tours are $40 (reservations required); Discovery Park admission is $5 adults, $3 children 6 to 12.

Situated on the grounds of the privately owned Vega-Bray Observatory, an amateur observatory with six telescopes and a planetarium, **Skywatcher's Inn** ✸ is one of the most unusual lodgings in the state. The inn provides guests with not only a bed for the night, but also a chance to observe the night sky and the sun through the observatory's telescopes. Viewing programs range from $95 to $130 per night. The inn is located 4 miles outside Benson; call for directions (© **520/586-7906;** www.skywatchersinn.com). Rates are $85 to $185 double.

north of Tubac, Cantina Romantica is a culinary oasis in this neck of the woods. The menu has a metropolitan flair, and includes the likes of chicken picatta and New York steak with caramelized onions and Gorgonzola cheese. The setting is rustic and colorful, and the restaurant is reached by driving *through* the Santa Cruz River. Because the route to the restaurant is so unusual and because the Rex Ranch is so colorful, you should be sure to schedule an early dinner so you can enjoy the sights.

131 Amado Montosa Rd., Amado. © 520/398-2914. Reservations recommended. Main courses $15–$24. AE, DC, DISC, MC, V. Wed–Sun noon–2pm and 5:30–9pm. Call ahead during extreme heat in summer; restaurant may be closed.

IN TUBAC & TUMACACORI

Border House Bistro ★ *Finds* This fun little restaurant in the heart of Tubac, has a mesquite-wood oven and turns out some fun pizzas, including one made with alligator. Looking for something a little less exotic? Try the delicious creamy pumpkin soup. At lunch, the Argentine steak sandwich is a good bet. The striped ravioli with three cheeses is another tasty dish. If you're feeling really hungry, go for the steak with Mexican ranchero sauce or the roasted salmon.

12 Plaza Rd., #A. © 520/398-8999. www.chefw.com. Reservations not necessary. Main courses $9–$15. DISC, MC, V. Tues–Sat 11am–3pm and 5–9pm; Sun 11am–3pm.

Wisdom's Cafe *Finds* MEXICAN Located between Tubac and Tumacacori, this roadside diner is a Santa Cruz Valley institution, in business since 1944. With a cement floor and walls hung with old cowboy stuff, Wisdom's Cafe feels a bit like a cross between a cave and an old barn. The menu is short but includes some twists on standard Mexican fare, including tostadas, tacos, and enchiladas made with turkey. Don't eat too much, though, or you won't have room for this restaurant's main draw— huge fruit burros that are basically Mexican fruit pies. To find this place, just watch for the giant chicken statues out front.

1931 E. Frontage Rd., Tumacacori. © 520/398-2397. Main dishes $5–$9. AE, DISC, MC, V. Mon–Sat noon–3pm and 5–8pm.

3 Patagonia ★★ & Sonoita ★

Patagonia: 18 miles NW of Nogales; 60 miles SE of Tucson; 171 miles SE of Phoenix; 50 miles SW of Tombstone

A mild climate, numerous good restaurants, bed-and-breakfast inns, and a handful of wineries have turned the small communities of Patagonia and Sonoita into a favorite weekend getaway for Tucsonans. Sonoita Creek, one of the only perennial streams in southern Arizona, attracts an amazing variety of bird life.

Patagonia and Sonoita are only about 12 miles apart, but they have decidedly different characters. Patagonia is a sleepy little hamlet with tree-shaded streets, quite a few old adobe buildings, and a big park in the middle of town. The Nature Conservancy preserve on the edge of town makes Patagonia popular with bird-watchers. Sonoita, on the other hand, sits out on the windswept high plains and is really just a highway crossroads, not a real town. The landscape around Sonoita, however, is filled with expensive new homes on small ranches, and not far away are the vineyards of Arizona's wine country.

ESSENTIALS

GETTING THERE Sonoita is at the junction of Ariz. 83 and Ariz. 82. Patagonia is 12 miles southwest of Sonoita on Ariz. 82.

VISITOR INFORMATION   The **Patagonia Visitor Information Center,** 307 McKeown Ave. (© **888/794-0060** or 520/394-0060; www.patagoniaaz.com), inside Mariposa Books in the center of Patagonia, is open daily from 10am to 5pm.

BIRD-WATCHING & WINE TASTING

The **Patagonia–Sonoita Creek Preserve** (© **520/394-2400;** www.nature.org) is owned by the Nature Conservancy and protects 1½ miles of Sonoita Creek riparian (riverside) habitat, which is important to migratory birds. More than 300 species of birds have been spotted at the preserve, including 22 species of flycatchers, kingbirds, phoebes, and the Montezuma quail. A forest of cottonwood trees, some of which are 100 feet tall, lines the creek and is one of the best remaining examples of such a forest in southern Arizona. To reach the sanctuary, which is just outside Patagonia on a dirt road that parallels Ariz. 82, turn west on Fourth Avenue and then south on Pennsylvania Street, cross the creek and continue about 1 mile. From April to September, hours are Wednesday through Sunday from 6:30am to 4pm; from October to March, hours are Wednesday through Sunday from 7:30am to 4pm. Admission is $5 ($3 for Nature Conservancy members). On Saturdays at 9am, there are naturalist-guided walks through the preserve; reservations aren't required.

On your way to or from the Nature Conservancy Preserve, be sure to drop by **Paton's Birder's Haven,** which is basically the backyard of Marion Paton. Numerous hummingbird feeders and a variety of other feeders attract an amazing range of birds to the yard, making this a favorite stop of avid birders who are touring the region. If you're heading out to the Nature Conservancy preserve, just watch for the BIRDER'S HAVEN sign at 477 Pennsylvania Rd. after you cross the creek.

Avid birders will also want to visit **Las Cienegas National Conservation Area** (© **520/258-7200;** www.az.blm.gov/nca/lascienegas/lascieneg.htm), which has grasslands, wetlands, and oak forests. This is a good place to look for the rarely seen gray hawk. Access is off the east side of Ariz. 83, about 7 miles north of Sonoita.

Patagonia Lake State Park (© **520/287-6965**), about 7 miles south of Patagonia off Ariz. 82, is a popular boating and fishing lake formed by damming Sonoita Creek. The lake is 2½ miles long and stocked in winter with rainbow trout. Other times of year, people fish for bass, crappie, bluegill, and catfish. Park facilities include a picnic ground, campground, and swimming beach. There is also good bird-watching here— elegant trogons, which are among the most beautiful of southern Arizona's rare birds, have been spotted. The park day-use fee is $7 to $8. Campsites are $12 to $25. Adjacent to the park, you'll find the **Sonoita Creek State Natural Area** (© **520/287-2791**), a 5,000-acre preserve along the banks of Sonoita Creek. Although the natural area is still in the process of building trails, there is a visitor center. During much of the year, the natural area operates boat tours ($3 per person) several mornings each week. These tours focus on the birds and history of the area. Call the number above for information and reservations.

Sonoita proper is little more than a crossroads with a few shops and restaurants. Surrounding the community are miles of rolling grasslands that are primarily cattle ranches, and acres of vineyards that have made Sonoita Arizona's own little wine country. Just west of the village of Elgin, about 10 miles east of Sonoita, you'll find **Callaghan Vineyards,** 336 Elgin Rd. (© **520/455-5322;** www.callaghanvineyards.com), which is open for tastings Friday through Sunday from 11am to 3pm. This winery produces some of the best wine in the state. The two other area wineries don't do nearly as good a job, but you can be the judge yourself. In the ghost town of Elgin, there's the **Village of Elgin Winery** (© 520/455-9309; www.elginwines.com), which is open daily from 10am to 5pm. Three miles south of Elgin, you'll find **Sonoita Vineyards,** on Canelo Road (© 520/455-5893; www.sonoitavineyards.com), which is open daily from 10am to 4pm. The above tasting-room hours are subject to change, so you might want to call ahead.

WHERE TO STAY
IN SONOITA

La Hacienda de Sonoita ⭐ Located on the east side of Sonoita and not too far out of town, this hacienda-style B&B has unobstructed views that stretch to the distant mountain ranges surrounding these high plains. The inn is built around a central courtyard, which has a bubbling fountain and covered porches. There's also another covered porch that looks out to the eastern views. The decor in the guest rooms ranges from rancho deluxe to cowboy chic. My personal favorite is the Grand Canyon Room.

34 Swanson Rd. (P.O. Box 408), Sonoita, AZ 85637. © 520/455-5308. Fax 520/455-5309. www.haciendasonoita.com. 4 units. $110–$130 double. Children under 12 stay free in parent's room. AE, DISC, MC, V. *In room:* A/C, no phone.

Sonoita Inn Housed in a barnlike building, the Sonoita Inn plays up the area's ranching history. The building was originally constructed by the owner of the famed Triple Crown–winning thoroughbred Secretariat. The lobby, with its wooden floors, huge fireplace, and ranch brands for decoration, is cool and dark (a welcome escape on hot summer days). Guest rooms feature Indian rugs and 1950s-inspired bedspreads for a retro cowboy touch. Although it's right on Sonoita's main road, the fascinating decor more than makes up for the less-than-quiet location. The Mountain View Room on the second floor has the best view. A popular steakhouse is adjacent to the inn.

At intersection of Ariz. 82 and Ariz. 83, P.O. Box 99, Sonoita, AZ 85637. © 800/696-1006 or 520/455-5935. Fax 520/455-5069. www.sonoitainn.com. 18 units. $79–$120 double. Rates include deluxe continental breakfast. AE, DISC, MC, V. Pets accepted ($25 per night). *In room:* A/C, TV/VCR.

WHERE TO DINE
IN PATAGONIA

For good coffee and pastries, check out **Gathering Grounds,** 319 McKeown Ave. (© 520/394-2097), which also serves ice cream and has a deli. Looking for a bit of night life? Don't miss **La Mision de San Miguel,** 335 McKeown St. (© 520/394-0123; www.lamisionpatagonia.com), a Mexican-inspired bar with live music and dancing on Saturday nights.

Velvet Elvis Pizza Company ITALIAN The faux-finished walls at this casual hangout ooze artiness, while paeans to pop culture include shrines to both the Virgin Mary and Elvis. The menu features a variety of pizzas heaped with veggies, cheeses, and meats, but if you can remember to plan a day in advance, you should call in an order for the Inca quinoa pizza. Add an organic salad and accompany it with some fresh juice, microbrew, espresso, or organic wine.

292 Naugle Ave. © 520/394-2102. www.velvetelvispizza.com. Pizzas $6.50–$21. MC, V. Thurs–Sun 11:30am–8:30pm.

IN SONOITA

Grab good breads and pastries, hot breakfasts, and sandwiches at the **Grasslands Bakery/Café,** 3119 Ariz. 83 (© 520/455-4770; www.grasslandsbakery.com), which is an outpost of organic foods. The bakery is open Wednesday through Friday from 10am to 3pm, Saturday and Sunday from 8am to 3pm.

Café Sonoita ☆ AMERICAN   A tiny place with just a handful of tables, this cafe serves the best food in the area and has long been a favorite with locals. The menu, which changes daily, is limited but surprisingly creative. Ingredients are always fresh, and there are local wines to accompany the meals. Although you can get straightforward traditional fare such as steaks and prime rib, the best reason to eat here is for the more creative dishes, including the duck in cherry sauce (which shows up frequently). This place could hold its own in Tucson or Phoenix; don't miss it.

3280 Ariz. 82 (at the east end of town). ☎ 520/455-5278. Reservations accepted only for large parties. Main courses $6.25–$15. MC, V. Wed–Thurs 5–8pm; Fri–Sat 11am–2:30pm and 5–8pm.

The Steak Out ☆ STEAKHOUSE   This big barn of a place is where local ranchers and everyone else for miles around head when they want a good steak. A classic cowboy atmosphere prevails: There's even a mounted buffalo head just inside the front door. The restaurant's name and the scent of a mesquite fire should be all the hints you need about what to order—a grilled steak, preferably the exceedingly tender filet mignon. Wash it down with a margarita and you've got the perfect cowboy dinner.

At intersection of Ariz. 82 and Ariz. 83. ☎ 520/455-5205. Reservations recommended. Main courses $8–$33. AE, DISC, MC, V. Mon–Thurs 5–9pm; Fri 5–10pm; Sat 11am–10pm; Sun 11am–9pm.

4 Sierra Vista & the San Pedro Valley ☆

70 miles SE of Tucson; 189 miles SE of Phoenix; 33 miles SW of Tombstone; 33 miles W of Bisbee

Located at an elevation of 4,620 feet above sea level, Sierra Vista is blessed with the perfect climate—never too hot, never too cold. This fact more than anything else has contributed in recent years to Sierra Vista becoming one of the fastest-growing cities in Arizona. The city is wedged between the Huachuca Mountains and the valley of the San Pedro River, making it a good base for exploring the region's natural attractions.

Within a few miles' drive of town are the San Pedro Riparian National Conservation Area, Coronado National Memorial, and the Nature Conservancy's Ramsey Canyon Preserve. No other area of the United States attracts more attention from birders, who come in hopes of spotting some of the 300 species that have been sighted in southeastern Arizona. About 25 miles north of town is Kartchner Caverns State Park, the region's biggest attraction, located 9 miles south of Benson.

ESSENTIALS

GETTING THERE   Sierra Vista is at the junction of Ariz. 90 and Ariz. 92 about 35 miles south of I-10.

VISITOR INFORMATION   The **Sierra Vista Convention & Visitors Bureau,** 3020 Tacoma St. (☎ **800/288-3861** or 520/417-6960; www.visitsierravista.com), can provide information on the area. To find the visitor center if you're coming from the north, take the Ariz. 90 Bypass, turn right on Coronado Drive, left on Tacoma Street, and continue to the Oscar Yrun Community Center.

ATTRACTIONS AROUND BENSON

The Western town movie set of **Mescal** (☎ 520/883-0100) is operated by Old Tucson Studios and has been used for years in the making of Westerns, as well as TV shows and commercials. Hour-long walking tours of Mescal provide a feel for the many movies that have been shot here. For fans of old Westerns, this is a must. Tours are available Tuesday, Thursday, and Saturday between 10am and 2pm and cost $8. Roughly 35 miles east of Tucson, take Exit 297 off I-10, then head north for 3 miles on Mescal Road. When the pavement ends, head west for ½ miles on the dirt road to the town, which is visible on the hill ahead.

Kartchner Caverns State Park ★★   These caverns are among the largest and most beautiful in the country. Because they are wet caverns, stalactites, stalagmites, soda straws, and other cave formations are still growing. Within the caverns are two huge rooms, each larger than a football field with ceilings more than 100 feet high. These two rooms can be visited on two separate tours. On the shorter Rotunda/ Throne Room Tour, you will see, in the Rotunda Room, thousands of delicate soda straws in the Rotunda Room and a 58-foot-tall column in the Throne Room. The second, and longer tour, visits the Big Room and leads past many strange and rare cave formations. Within the park, there are also several miles of above-ground hiking trails. A campground charging $22 per night provides a convenient place to stay in the area.

Because the caverns are a popular attraction and tours are limited, try to make a reservation in advance, especially if you want to visit on a weekend. However, it is sometimes possible to get same-day tickets if you happen to be passing by.

Off Ariz. 90, 9 miles south of Benson. ℂ 520/586-CAVE. www.azstateparks.com. Admission $5 per car; cave tours $19–$23 adults, $9.95–$13 children 7–13. Park open daily 7:30am–6pm; cave tours approximately every 20 min. 8am–5pm. Closed Christmas.

BIRDING HOT SPOTS & OTHER NATURAL AREAS

Bird-watching has become big business over the past few years, with birders' B&Bs, bird refuges, and even birding festivals. Each year in August, the **Southwest Wings Birding Festival** (ℂ 520/432-5421; www.swwings.org) is held in Bisbee, about 30 miles east of Sierra Vista.

If you'd like to join a guided bird walk along the San Pedro River or up Carr Canyon in the Huachuca Mountains, an owl-watching night hike, or a hummingbird banding session, contact the **Southeastern Arizona Bird Observatory** (ℂ 520/432-1388; www.sabo.org), which also has a public bird-viewing area at its headquarters 2 miles north of the Mule Mountain Tunnel on Ariz. 80 north of Bisbee (watch for Hidden Meadow Lane). Most activities take place between April and September and cost $15 to $60. Workshops and tours are also offered.

Serious birders might want to visit this area on a guided tour. Your best bet is **Mark Pretti Nature Tours** (ℂ 520/803-6889; www.markprettinaturetours.com), run by the former resident naturalist at Ramsey Canyon Preserve. A half-day birding tour costs $100 and a full-day tour costs $150 to $200. Three-day ($450–$550) and 8-day ($1,150) trips are also offered. **High Lonesome Birdtours** (ℂ 800/743-2668 or 520/458-9446; www.hilonesome.com), another local tour company, charges about $950 per person for a 4-day birding trip.

Moments **Hummingbird Heaven**

In summer, hummingbird lovers should take a drive up Miller Canyon (south of Ramsey Canyon) to **Beatty's Miller Canyon Guest Ranch and Orchard,** 2173 E. Miller Canyon Rd., Hereford (ℂ 520/378-2728; www.beattysguestranch.com), where a public hummingbird-viewing area is set up. Fifteen species of hummers have been sighted here.

Coronado National Memorial   About 20 miles south of Sierra Vista is a 5,000-acre memorial dedicated to Francisco Vásquez de Coronado, the first European to explore this region. In 1540, Coronado, leading more than 700 people, left Compostela, Mexico, in search of the fabled Seven Cities of Cíbola, said to be rich in gold and jewels. Sometime between 1540 and 1542, Coronado led his band of weary men and women up the valley of the San Pedro River, which this monument overlooks. At the visitor center, you can learn about Coronado's fruitless quest for riches and check out the wildlife observation area. Outside the visitor center, a trail leads .75 mile to 600-foot-long Coronado Cave. (You'll need to bring your own flashlight and get a permit at the visitor center if you want to explore this cave.) After stopping at the visitor center, drive up to 6,575-foot Montezuma Pass, which provides far-reaching views of Sonora, Mexico, to the south, the San Pedro River to the east, and several mountain ranges and valleys to the west. Along the .8-mile round-trip Coronado Peak Trail, you'll also have good views of the valley and can read quotations from the journals of Coronado's followers. There are also some longer trails where you'll see few other hikers.

4101 E. Montezuma Canyon Rd., Hereford. ✆ 520/366-5515. www.nps.gov/coro. Free admission. Daily 8am–5pm. Closed Thanksgiving and Christmas. Take Ariz. 92 south from Sierra Vista to S. Coronado Memorial Drive and continue 5 miles to the Visitor Center.

Ramsey Canyon Preserve ⋆   Each year, beginning in late spring, a buzzing fills the air in Ramsey Canyon, but it's not the buzzing of the bees. This preserve is home to 14 species of hummingbirds, and it is the whirring of these diminutive birds' wings that fills the air. Wear bright-red clothing when you visit, and you're certain to attract the little avian dive bombers, which will mistake you for the world's largest flower. Situated in a wooded gorge in the Huachuca Mountains, this Nature Conservancy preserve covers only 380 acres. However, because Ramsey Creek, which flows through the canyon, is a year-round stream, it attracts a wide variety of wildlife, including bears, bobcats, and nearly 200 species of birds. A short nature trail leads through the canyon, and a second trail leads higher up the canyon. April and May are the busiest times here, while May and August are the best times to see hummingbirds. Guided walks are offered March through October.

27 Ramsey Canyon Rd., off Ariz. 92, 5 miles south of Sierra Vista. ✆ 520/378-2785. www.nature.org. Admission $5 ($3 for Nature Conservancy members). Mar–Oct daily 8am–5pm; Nov–Feb daily 9am–4pm. Closed New Year's Day, Thanksgiving, and Christmas.

San Pedro Riparian National Conservation Area ⋆   Located 8 miles east of Sierra Vista, this conservation area is one of Arizona's rare examples of a natural riverside habitat. Over the past 100 years, 90% of the region's free-flowing year-round rivers and streams have disappeared due to human use of desert waters. These rivers and streams once provided water and protection to myriad plants, animals, and even humans. Fossil findings from this area indicate that people were living along this river 11,000 years ago. At that time, this area was a swamp, not a desert, but today, the San Pedro River is all that remains of this ancient wetland. Due to an earthquake a century ago, much of the San Pedro's water now flows underground. Still the water attracts wildlife, especially birds, and the conservation area is very popular with birders, who have a chance of spotting more than 300 species here.

For bird-watching, the best place is the system of trails at the Ariz. 90 crossing of the San Pedro. Here you will find the **San Pedro House** (✆ **520/508-4445**), a 1930s ranch that is operated as a visitor center and bookstore. It's open daily from 9:30am to 4:30pm. Throughout the year, there are guided walks and hikes, bird walks, bird-banding sessions, and other events. Check with the San Pedro House for a calendar.

Ariz. 90. Ⓒ **520/458-3559**. www.az.blm.gov/nca/spnca/spnca-info.htm. Free admission. Parking areas open sunrise to sunset.

WHERE TO STAY
IN BENSON
Holiday Inn Express ⭐ If you're looking for lodging close to Kartchner Caverns, try this off-ramp budget hotel in Benson. The hotel's lobby is done in Santa Fe style with flagstone floors and rustic Southwestern furniture. Guest rooms are strictly hotel modern, but they are roomy.

630 South Village Loop, Benson, AZ 85602. Ⓒ **888/263-2283** or 520/586-8800. Fax 520/586-1370. www.bensonaz. hiexpress.com. 62 units. $79–$159 double. Rates include continental breakfast. Children under 18 stay free in parent's room. AE, DC, DISC, MC, V. **Amenities:** Outdoor pool; exercise room; coin-op laundry. *In room:* A/C, TV, dataport, fridge, coffeemaker, hair dryer, iron, free local calls, high-speed Internet access, wi-fi.

IN HEREFORD
Casa de San Pedro ⭐ Built with bird-watching tour groups in mind, this modern inn is set on the west side of the San Pedro River on 10 acres of land. While the setting doesn't have the historic character of the San Pedro River Inn (see below), it is much more up-to-date, with large, comfortable hotel-style guest rooms. Built in the territorial style around a courtyard garden, the inn has a large common room where birders gather to swap stories. Birding, cultural, and history tours are also offered by the inn. This is by far the most upscale inn in the region, and our favorite.

8933 S. Yell Lane, Hereford, AZ 85615. Ⓒ **888/257-2050** or 520/366-1300. Fax 520/366-0701. www.bedandbirds. com. 10 units. $129–$155 double. Rates include full breakfast. AE, DISC, MC, V. No children under 12. Pets accepted ($100 deposit). **Amenities:** Outdoor pool; Jacuzzi; concierge; business center; guest laundry. *In room:* A/C, hair dryer, free local calls, Internet access, wi-fi.

Ramsey Canyon Inn Bed & Breakfast ⭐ Adjacent to the Nature Conservancy's Ramsey Canyon Preserve, this inn is the most convenient choice in the area for avid birders to see the canyon's famous hummingbirds. The property straddles Ramsey Creek, with guest rooms in the main house and apartments in small cabins reached by a footbridge over the creek. A large country breakfast is served in the morning. Book early.

29 Ramsey Canyon Dr., Hereford, AZ 85615. Ⓒ **520/378-3010**. www.ramseycanyoninn.com. 9 units. $130–$150 double; $150–$225 suite. Room rates include full breakfast. MC, V. No children under 16 in inn; OK in apartments. *In room:* No phone.

San Pedro River Inn With the character of a small guest ranch, this family-friendly inn is a casual place that will please avid birders who prefer Old Arizona character. Located on the east side of the San Pedro Riparian National Conservation Area, the four simply furnished cottages may not be fancy, but the setting, beneath huge old cottonwood trees, is memorable. There are also trails that lead to the riparian forest along the banks of the San Pedro, and innkeeper Michael Marsden leads guests on free bird walks. Guided birding tours farther afield can also be arranged.

8326 S. Hereford Rd., Hereford, AZ 85615. Ⓒ **877/366-5532** or 520/366-5532. www.sanpedroriverinn.com. 4 units. $105 double. Rates include continental breakfast. 2-night minimum weekends, holidays, and peak season. No credit cards. **Amenities:** Guest laundry. *In room:* TV/VCR, kitchen, fridge, coffeemaker, free local calls.

CAMPING
There are two Coronado National Forest campgrounds—14-site **Reef Townsite** and 8-site **Ramsey Vista**—up the winding Carr Canyon Road south of Sierra Vista off Ariz. 92. Both charge $5 per night. For information, contact the Coronado National

Forest Sierra Vista Ranger District, 5990 S. Hwy. 92, Hereford, AZ 85615 (© **520/ 378-0311;** www.fs.fed.us/r3/coronado).

WHERE TO DINE

The Mesquite Tree STEAKHOUSE   This casual steakhouse south of town (and not far from the mouth of Ramsey Canyon) has long been a favorite of locals. It's funky and dark, but the prices can't be beat. Although you can get a variety of chicken and fish dishes done in a variety of traditional Continental styles, most people come here for the steaks. Try the Vargas rib-eye, which is smothered with green chiles, jack cheese, and enchilada sauce—a real border-country original. When the weather is warm, try to get a seat on the patio.

S. Ariz. 92 and Carr Canyon Rd. © **520/378-2758.** www.mesquitetreerestaurant.com. Reservations recommended. Main courses $8.50–$20. AE, DISC, MC, V. Tues–Sat 5–9pm; Sun 5–8pm.

The Outside Inn ✪ STEAKHOUSE/SEAFOOD/ITALIAN   Much more formal than the nearby Mesquite Tree, the Outside Inn has long been Sierra Vista's top special-occasion restaurant. Housed in a cottagelike building south of town and just north of the turnoff for Ramsey Canyon, the Outside Inn may not be in the most picturesque of surroundings, but the food is definitely among the best you'll find in the area. In the main dining room or out on the patio, you can enjoy such fare as blackened mahi-mahi or crab-stuffed giant Guaymas shrimp.

4907 S. Ariz. 92. © **520/378-4645.** Reservations recommended. Main courses $6–$9 lunch, $15–$20 dinner. AE, MC, V. Mon–Fri 11am–1:30pm and 5–9pm; Sat 5–9pm.

5 Tombstone ⭐

70 miles SE of Tucson; 181 miles SE of Phoenix; 24 miles N of Bisbee

It was on these very streets, outside a livery stable known as the O.K. Corral, that Wyatt Earp, his brothers Virgil and Morgan, and their friend Doc Holliday took on the outlaws Ike Clanton and Frank and Tom McLaury on October 26, 1881. Today, Tombstone, "the town too tough to die," is one of Arizona's most popular attractions.

Tombstone got its start as a mining town, and between 1880 and 1887, an estimated $37 million worth of silver was mined here. Such wealth created a sturdy little town, and as the Cochise County seat of the time, Tombstone boasted a number of imposing buildings, including the county courthouse, which is now a state park. In 1887, an underground river flooded the silver mines, which were never reopened. With the demise of the mines, the boom came to an end and the population rapidly dwindled.

Today, Tombstone's historic district consists of both original buildings that went up after the town's second fire and newer structures built in keeping with the architectural styles of the late 19th century. Most house souvenir shops and restaurants, which should give you some indication that this place is a classic tourist trap, but kids (and adults raised on Louis L'Amour and John Wayne) love it, especially when the famous shootout is reenacted.

ESSENTIALS

GETTING THERE   From Tucson, take I-10 east to Benson, from which Ariz. 80 heads south to Tombstone. From Sierra Vista, take Ariz. 90 north to Ariz. 82 heading east.

VISITOR INFORMATION The **Tombstone Chamber of Commerce** (© 888/457-3929 or 520/457-9317; www.tombstone.org) operates a visitor center at the corner of Allen and Fourth streets.

GUNSLINGERS & SALOONS: IN SEARCH OF THE WILD WEST

As portrayed in novels, movies, and TV shows, the shootout has come to epitomize the Wild West, and nowhere is this great American phenomenon more glorified than in Tombstone, where the star attraction is the famous **O.K. Corral,** 308 E. Allen St. (© **520/457-3456;** www.ok-corral.com), site of a 30-second gun battle that has taken on mythic proportions over the years. Inside the corral, you'll find not only displays on the shootout, but also an exhibit on Tombstone prostitutes and another focusing on local photographer C. S. Fly. Next door is **Tombstone's Historama,** a kitschy multimedia affair that's narrated by Vincent Price and rehashes the well-known history of Tombstone's "bad old days." The O.K. Corral and Tombstone Historama are open daily from 9am to 5pm and admission is $5.50; for $7.50, you can visit both attractions and take in a shootout reenactment. Here at the O.K. Corral, you can also get a genuine tintype photo taken by photographer Randy Templin (© **520/456-1102**). Very few photographers in the country still know how to produce tintype photos, which makes this little photography studio a unique attraction here in Tombstone.

When the smoke cleared in 1881, three men lay dead. They were later carted off to the **Boot Hill Graveyard** (© **800/457-9344** or 520/457-9344), on the north edge of town. The cemetery is open to the public and is entered through a gift shop on Ariz. 80. The graves of Clanton and the McLaury brothers, as well as those of others who died in gunfights or by hanging, are well marked. Entertaining epitaphs grace the grave markers; among the most famous is that of Lester Moore—"Here lies Lester Moore, 4 slugs from a 44, No Les, no more." The cemetery is open daily from 7:30am to 6:30pm in summer (7:30am to 5:30pm in other months); admission is free.

When the residents of Tombstone weren't shooting each other in the streets, they were likely to be found in the saloons and bawdy houses that lined Allen Street. Most famous was the **Bird Cage Theatre** (© **800/457-3423** or 520/457-3421) so named for the cagelike cribs (what most people would think of as box seats) that are suspended from the ceiling. These velvet-draped cages were used by prostitutes to ply their trade. For old Tombstone atmosphere, this place is hard to beat. Admission is $6 for adults, $5.50 for seniors, and $5 for children 8 to 18; the theater is open daily from 8am to 6pm.

If you want to down a cold beer, Tombstone has a couple of very lively saloons. The **Crystal Palace,** at Allen and Fifth streets (© **520/457-3611**), was built in 1879 and has been completely restored. This is one of the favorite hangouts for the town's costumed actors and other would-be cowboys and cowgirls. **Big Nose Kate's,** 417 E. Allen St. (© **520/457-3107**), is an equally entertaining spot full of Wild West characters and characters.

Tombstone has long been a tourist town, and its streets are lined with souvenir shops selling wind chimes, Beanie Babies, and other less-than-wild souvenirs. There are also several small museums scattered around town. At the **Rose Tree Inn Museum,** at Fourth and Toughnut streets (© **520/457-3326**), you can see the world's largest rose tree. Inside are antique furnishings from Tombstone's heyday in the 1880s. The museum is open daily from 9am to 5pm (closed Thanksgiving and Christmas). Admission is $3 (free for children 14 and under).

Tombstone Courthouse State Park, at 219 Toughnut St. (℗ **520/457-3311**), is the most imposing building in town and provides a much less sensational local history. Built in 1882, the courthouse is now a state historic park and museum containing artifacts, photos, and newspaper clippings that chronicle Tombstone's lively past. In the courtyard, you can still see the gallows that once ended the lives of outlaws. The courthouse is open daily from 8am to 5pm; the entrance fee is $4 ($3 between Memorial Day and Labor Day) and children under 14 are free.

Don't leave town without visiting the **Tombstone Western Heritage Museum,** Ariz. 80 and Sixth St. (℗ **520/457-3800**), a privately owned museum that is filled with Tombstone artifacts. Included in this impressive collection are artifacts that once belonged to Wyatt and Virgil Earp, plus rare photos of the Earps and the outlaws of Tombstone. The museum is open Monday through Saturday from 9am to 5pm and Sunday from 12:30 to 5pm; admission is $5 for adults and $3 for children 12 to 18.

WHERE TO STAY

Holiday Inn Express ⭐ On the northern outskirts of Tombstone, right next door to the older Best Western, this is the newest and most reliable hotel in Tombstone. The decor draws on a bit of Southwestern styling and Spanish colonial styling, but basically this is just a modern motel.

1001 N. Ariz. 80 (P.O. Box 1730), Tombstone, AZ 85638. ℗ 800/465-4329 or 520/457-9507. Fax 520/457-9506. www. holidayinntombstone.com. 60 units. $59–$139 double. Rates include deluxe continental breakfast. Children under 18 stay free in parent's room. AE, DC, DISC, MC, V. Pets accepted ($20 fee). **Amenities:** Outdoor pool; Jacuzzi; coin-op laundry. *In room:* A/C, TV, dataport, fridge, coffeemaker, hair dryer, iron, free local calls, high-speed Internet access.

Tombstone Boarding House Housed in two whitewashed 1880s adobe buildings, this inn is in a quiet residential neighborhood only 2 blocks from busy Allen Street. The main house was originally the home of Tombstone's first bank manager, while the guest rooms are in an old boardinghouse. Accommodations are comfortable and clean, with country decor. Hardwood floors and antiques lend a period feel. See "Where to Dine," below, for information on the inn's Lamplight Room restaurant.

108 N. Fourth St., Tombstone, AZ 85638. ℗ 877/225-1319 or 520/457-3716. www.tombstoneboardinghouse.com. 6 units. $69–$89 double. Rates include full breakfast. AE, DISC, MC, V. **Amenities:** Restaurant (Continental). *In room:* No phone.

WHERE TO DINE

Big Nose Kate's Saloon SANDWICHES Okay, so the food here isn't all that memorable, but the atmosphere sure is. Big Nose Kate's dates back to 1880 and is primarily a saloon. As such, it stays packed with visitors who have come to revel in Tombstone's outlaw past. So, while you sip your beer, why not order a sandwich and call it lunch? You might even catch some live country music.

417 E. Allen St. ℗ 520/457-3107. Most items $6.50–$11. MC, V. Daily 11am–8pm.

The Lamplight Room ⭐ CONTINENTAL Located a few blocks off busy Allen Street, this restaurant serves the best food in Tombstone. The Lamplight Room is in the living room of an old 1880s home, which also lends this place more character than that of any of the other restaurants in town. The menu is short and includes such dishes as chicken cordon bleu and roasted pork loin. On Friday and Saturday nights, there's live classical guitar music.

At the Tombstone Boarding House, 108 N. Fourth St. ℗ 520/457-3716. Reservations recommended. Main courses $8–$17. AE, DISC, MC, V. Tues–Thurs 11:30am–8pm; Fri–Sat 11:30am–9pm; Sun 11:30am–7pm.

6 Bisbee ★ ★

94 miles SE of Tucson; 205 miles SE of Phoenix; 24 miles NW of Douglas

Arizona has a wealth of ghost towns that boomed on mining profits and then quickly went bust when the mines played out, but none is as impressive as Bisbee, which is built into the steep slopes of Tombstone Canyon on the south side of the Mule Mountains. Between 1880 and 1975, Bisbee's mines produced more than $6 billion worth of metals. When the Phelps Dodge Company shut down its copper mines here, Bisbee nearly went the way of other abandoned mining towns, but because it's the Cochise County seat, it was saved from disappearing into the desert dust.

Bisbee's glory days date from the late 19th and early 20th centuries, and because the town stopped growing in the early part of the 20th century, it is now one of the best-preserved historic towns anywhere in the Southwest. Old brick buildings line narrow winding streets, and miners' shacks sprawl across the hillsides above downtown. Many artists call the town home, and aging hippies and other urban refugees have for many years been dropping out of the rat race to restore Bisbee's old buildings and open small inns, restaurants, and galleries. Between the rough edges left over from its mining days and this new cosmopolitan atmosphere, Bisbee is one of Arizona's most interesting towns. However, be aware that Bisbee is not for everyone. It appeals mostly to young, hip travelers who don't expect much from their accommodations and who like to stay up late partying. The rumble of motorcycles is a constant on Bisbee's streets, especially on weekends.

ESSENTIALS

GETTING THERE   Bisbee is on Ariz. 80, which begins at I-10 in the town of Benson, 45 miles east of Tucson.

VISITOR INFORMATION   Contact the **Bisbee Visitor Center,** 2 Copper Queen Plaza. (© **866/2-BISBEE** or 520/432-3554; www.discoverbisbee.com).

EXPLORING THE TOWN

At the Bisbee Chamber of Commerce visitor center, right in the middle of town, pick up walking-tour brochures that will lead you past the most important buildings and sites.

Don't miss the **Bisbee Mining and Historical Museum** ★, 5 Copper Queen Plaza (© **520/432-7071;** www.bisbeemuseum.org), housed in the 1897 Copper Queen Consolidated Mining Company office building. This small but comprehensive museum features exhibits on the history of Bisbee. It's open daily from 10am to 4pm; admission is $4 for adults, $3.50 for seniors, and $1 children 16 and under.

For another look at early life in Bisbee, visit the **Muheim Heritage House,** 207 Youngblood Hill (© **520/432-7698**), which is reached by walking up Brewery Gulch. The house was built between 1902 and 1915 and has an unusual semicircular porch. The interior is decorated with period furniture. It's open Friday through Tuesday from 10am to 4pm; admission is $4 for adults.

O.K. Street, which parallels Brewery Gulch but is high on the hill on the southern edge of town, is a good place to walk for views of Bisbee. At the top of O.K. Street, there's a path that takes you up to a hill above town for an even better panorama of Bisbee's jumble of old buildings. Atop this hill are numerous small colorfully painted shrines built into the rocks and filled with candles, plastic flowers, and pictures of the Virgin Mary. It's a steep climb on a rocky, very uneven path, but the views and the fascinating little shrines make it worth the effort.

Mining made this town what it is, so you should be sure to head underground on a tour to find out what it was like to be a miner here in Bisbee. **Queen Mine Tours** ★ (© 866/432-2071 or 520/432-2071) takes visitors down into one of the town's old copper mines. Tours are offered daily between 9am and 3:30pm and cost $12 for adults, $5 for children 4 to 15. The ticket office and mine are just south of the Old Bisbee business district at the Ariz. 80 interchange.

For a good overview of Bisbee and its history, hop aboard the **Warren Bisbee Railway** (© 520/940-7212 or 520/432-7020; www.bisbeetrolley.com), which is actually a trolley-style bus that loops through the town. Tours operate several times a day and cost $10 for adults and $7 for children. You'll find the trolley bus parked at the Copper Queen Plaza at the bottom of town. For an exploration of some of the steeper and narrower streets of Bisbee, take a 90-minute tour ($35) of old Bisbee with **Lavender Jeep Tours** (© 520/432-5369). Several other tours are also available.

Bisbee has lots of interesting stores and galleries, and shopping is the main recreational activity here. To get a look at some of the quality jewelry created from minerals mined in the area, stop by **Czar Jewelry,** 13 Main St. (© 520/432-3027). Another good place to shop for jewelry is **Bisbee Blue,** at the Lavender Pit View Point on Ariz. 80 (© 520/432-5511), an exclusive dealer of the famous Bisbee Blue turquoise.

At the **Johnson Gallery,** 28 Main St. (© 520/432-2126), you'll find an outstanding selection of Native American crafts, including Navajo rugs and jewelry, Hopi kachinas and pottery, and lots of Zuni fetishes. **Bisbee Clay,** 30 Main St. (© 520/432-1916), has beautiful pottery, both functional and decorative, in unusual designs and colors.

To protect your face from the burning rays of the sun (and make a fashion statement), visit **Optimo Custom Hat Works,** 47 Main St. (© 888/FINE-HAT or 520/432-4544; www.optimohatworks.com), which sells and custom-fits Panama straw hats as well as felt hats. (By the way, Panama hats actually come from Ecuador.)

WHERE TO STAY

Canyon Rose Suites ★ *Value*   Located on the second floor of a commercial building just off Bisbee's main street, this property offers spacious suites with full kitchens, which makes it a good bet for longer stays. All units have hardwood floors and high ceilings, and the works by local artists and the mix of contemporary and rustic furnishings give the place plenty of Bisbee character. Constructed on a steep, narrow street, the building housing this lodging has an unusual covered sidewalk, making it one of the more distinctive commercial buildings in town.

27 Subway at Shearer St. (P.O. Box 1915), Bisbee, AZ 85603-2915. © 866/296-7673 or 520/432-5098. www.canyon rose.com. 7 units. $75–$200 double. Children under 12 stay free in parent's room. AE, DISC, MC, V. **Amenities:** Access to nearby health club; guest laundry. *In room:* A/C, TV/VCR, kitchen, fridge, coffeemaker, hair dryer, iron, free local calls, wi-fi.

Copper Queen Hotel   Built in 1902 by the Copper Queen Mining Company and right at the center of town, this is Bisbee's grande dame. The atmosphere is casual yet quite authentic. Behind the check-in desk, there's an old oak rolltop desk and a safe that has been here for years. Spacious halls lead to guest rooms that are furnished with antiques but that vary considerably in size (the smallest being quite cramped). The hotel has been undergoing renovations for several years; be sure to ask for one of the renovated units, which are up-to-date and attractively furnished. The restaurant serves decent food, and out front is a terrace for alfresco dining. And what would a mining-town hotel be without its saloon?

11 Howell Ave. (P.O. Drawer CQ5), Bisbee, AZ 85603. © 800/247-5829 or 520/432-2216. www.copperqueen.com. 48 units. $93–$170 double. Children under 17 stay free in parent's room. AE, DC, MC, V. **Amenities:** Restaurant (American); lounge; small outdoor pool. *In room:* A/C, TV.

Shady Dell RV Park *Finds* Yes, this really is an RV park, but you'll find neither shade nor dell at this roadside location just south of the Lavender Pit mine. What you will find are nine vintage trailers, a 1947 Airporter bus done in retro-tiki style, and a 1947 Chris Craft yacht. All have been lovingly restored. Although the trailers don't have their own private bathrooms (there's a bathhouse in the middle of the RV park), they do have all kinds of vintage décor and furnishings—even tapes and records of period music and radio shows. In the trailers that have vintage TVs, there are VCRs and videotapes of old movies. After numerous write-ups in national publications, the Shady Dell has become so famous that reservations need to be made far in advance. **Dot's Diner** (© 520/432-1112), a 1957 vintage diner, is also on the premises.

1 Douglas Rd., Bisbee, AZ 85603. © 520/432-3567. www.theshadydell.com. 11 units. $40–$125 per trailer (for 1–2 people). MC, V. No children under 10. **Amenities:** Restaurant; coin-op laundry. *In room:* A/C, kitchen, fridge, coffeemaker, no phone.

The Striped Stocking Restaurant & Hotel ★ In a restored historic building, this hotel offers simply furnished rooms, some with decent views over the rooftops of town to the nearby hills. For the best views and great light, ask for a south- or west-facing room. Most units are fairly spacious, and large windows and high ceilings make them feel even more so. The hotel's location on Brewery Gulch, home to several bars, means you can expect a bit of noise on weekend nights.

1 Howell Ave. (P.O. Drawer DB), Bisbee, AZ 85603. © 520/432-1832. Fax 520/432-1834. www.stripedstocking.com. 5 units. $95–$105 double. DISC, MC, V. **Amenities:** Restaurant; lounge. *In room:* A/C, TV, dataport, wi-fi.

WHERE TO DINE

Big Sky Café, 203 Tombstone Canyon Rd. (© 520/432-5025), is a hip little place that serves great panini and the best breakfasts in town. It's open Wednesday through Saturday from 7am to 2:30pm and Sunday from 7am to 1pm. **Café Cornucopia,** 14 Main St. (© 520/432-4820), offers fresh juices, smoothies, and sandwiches. It's open Thursday through Monday from 10am to 5pm. For good coffee and a mining theme, check out the **Bisbee Coffee Co.,** Copper Queen Plaza, Main Street (© 520/432-7879). For burgers in a vintage diner, drop by **Dot's Diner,** at the Shady Dell RV Park, described above (©) 520/432-1112). This fabulously retro place is open Monday, Thursday, and Friday from 7am to 2pm, and Saturday and Sunday from 7am to 3pm.

Café Roka ★★ CONTEMPORARY Wow! The food at Café Roka is reason enough to visit Bisbee. Casual and hip, this place is a real find in such an out-of-the-way town and offers good value as well as delicious and imaginatively prepared food. Meals include salad, soup, sorbet intermezzo, and entrée. The grilled salmon with a Gorgonzola crust and artichoke-and-portobello lasagna are two of our favorites. Flourless chocolate cake with raspberry sauce is an exquisite ending. Local artists display their works, and on some evenings jazz musicians perform.

35 Main St. © 520/432-5153. www.caferoka.com. Reservations highly recommended. Main courses $14–$24. AE, MC, V. Wed–Sat 5–9pm (Thurs–Sat 5–9pm in winter).

The Striped Stocking Restaurant ★★ NEW AMERICAN Just a couple of doors down from the Copper Queen Hotel, this elegant little restaurant is currently being run by long-time Bisbee restaurateur Nancy Parana, who knows just what visitors and locals want in a Bisbee restaurant. For an appetizer, be sure to try the shrimp cakes, which, though small, are very flavorful. Just because you won't see it on very many other menus, you should try the daily-special pastie. This British pastry is stuffed with whatever filling strikes the chef's fancy that night. Feeling particularly hungry? Opt for the inch-thick double-cut pork chop, which is served on a bed of potatoes and seasonal vegetables.

1 Howell Ave. © 520/432-1832. www.stripedstocking.com. Reservations recommended. Main courses $12–$19. DISC, MC, V. Tues–Sat 5–9pm.

7 Exploring the Rest of Cochise County ⟨★⟩

Willcox: 81 miles E of Tucson; 192 miles SE of Phoenix; 74 miles N of Douglas

Although the towns of Bisbee, Tombstone, and Sierra Vista all lie within Cochise County, much of the county is taken up by the vast Sulphur Springs Valley, which is bounded by multiple mountain ranges. It is across this wide-open landscape that Apache chiefs Cochise and Geronimo once rode. Gazing out across this country today, it is easy to understand why the Apaches fought so hard to keep white settlers out.

While the Chiricahua and Dragoon mountains, which flank the Sulphur Springs Valley on the east and west respectively, are relatively unknown outside the region, they offer some of the Southwest's most spectacular scenery. Massive boulders litter the mountainsides, creating fascinating landscapes. The Chiricahua Mountains are also a favorite destination of bird-watchers, for it is here that the colorfully plumed elegant trogon reaches the northern limit of its range.

ESSENTIALS

GETTING THERE Willcox is on I-10, with Ariz. 186 heading southeast toward Chiricahua National Monument.

VISITOR INFORMATION The **Willcox Chamber of Commerce and Agriculture,** 1500 N. Circle I Rd. (© **800/200-2272** or 520/384-2272; www.willcoxchamber. com), can provide information.

SOUTHWEST OF WILLCOX
SCENIC LANDSCAPES

South of the community of Dragoon, which is now known for its pistachio farms, you'll find **Cochise Stronghold** ⟨★⟩ (www.cochisestronghold.com). During the Apache uprisings of the late 19th century, the Apache leader Cochise used this rugged section of the Dragoon Mountains as his hideout and managed to elude capture for years. The granite boulders and pine forests made it impossible for the army to track him and his followers. Cochise eventually died and was buried at an unknown spot somewhere within the area now called Cochise Stronghold. This rugged jumble of giant boulders is reached by a rough gravel road, at the end of which you'll find a campground, a picnic area, and hiking trails. For a short, easy walk, follow the .4-mile Nature Trail. For a longer and more strenuous hike, head up the Cochise Trail. The Stronghold Divide makes a good destination for a 6-mile round-trip hike. For more information, contact the **Coronado National Forest Douglas Ranger District,** 3081 N. Leslie Canyon Rd., Douglas (© **520/364-3468;** www.fs.fed.us/r3/coronado). There is a $3 day-use fee per vehicle at Cochise Stronghold.

A MEMORABLE MUSEUM IN AN UNLIKELY LOCALE

Amerind Foundation Museum ★★   Established in 1937, the Amerind Foundation is dedicated to the study, preservation, and interpretation of prehistoric and historic Indian cultures. To that end, the foundation has compiled the nation's finest private collection of archaeological artifacts and contemporary pieces. There are exhibits on the dances and religious ceremonies of the major Southwestern tribes, including the Navajo, Hopi, and Apache, and archaeological artifacts amassed from the numerous Amerind Foundation excavations over the years. Fascinating ethnology exhibits include amazingly intricate beadwork from the Plains tribes, old Zuni fetishes, Pima willow baskets, old kachina dolls, 100 years of Southwestern tribal pottery, and Navajo weavings. The art gallery displays works by 19th- and 20th-century American artists, such as Frederic Remington, whose paintings focused on the West.

Dragoon. ✆ **520/586-3666.** www.amerind.org. Admission $5 adults, $4 seniors, $3 children 12–18. Oct–May daily 10am–4pm; June–Sept Wed–Sun 10am–4pm. Closed major holidays. Located 64 miles east of Tucson between Benson and Willcox; take the Dragoon Rd. exit (Exit 318) from I-10 and continue 1 mile east.

EAST OF WILLCOX

Chiricahua National Monument ★★   These gravity-defying rock formations—called "the land of the standing-up rocks" by the Apache and the "wonderland of rocks" by the pioneers—are the equal of any of Arizona's many amazing rocky landmarks. Rank upon rank of monolithic giants seem to have been turned to stone as they marched across the forested Chiricahua Mountains. If you're in good physical condition, don't miss the chance to hike the 7.5-mile round-trip **Heart of Rocks Trail** ★★, which can be accessed from the visitor center or the Echo Canyon or Massai Point parking areas. This trail leads through the most spectacular scenery in the monument. A shorter loop is also possible. Within the monument are a visitor center, a campground, a picnic area, miles of hiking trails, and a scenic drive with views of many of the most unusual rock formations.

Ariz. 186, 36 miles southeast of Willcox. ✆ **520/824-3560.** www.nps.gov/chir. Admission $5 adults. Visitor center daily 8am–4:30pm. Closed Christmas.

Fort Bowie National Historic Site ★   Fort Bowie was established in 1862 to ensure the passage of slow-moving stagecoaches traversing Apache Pass. Later, it was from Fort Bowie that federal troops battled Geronimo until the Apache chief finally surrendered in 1886. Today, there's little left of Fort Bowie but some crumbling adobe walls, but the hike along the old stage route to the ruins conjures up the ghosts of Geronimo and the Indian Wars.

3203 S. Old Fort Bowie Rd. (off Ariz. 186). ✆ **520/847-2500.** www.nps.gov/fobo. Free admission. Visitor center daily 8am–4:30pm; grounds daily dawn–dusk. Closed Christmas. From Willcox, drive southeast on Ariz. 186; after about 20 miles, watch for signs; it's another 8 miles up a dirt road to the trail head. Alternatively, drive east from Willcox to Bowie and go 13 miles south on Apache Pass Rd. From the trail head, it's a 1.5-mile hike to the fort.

NEAR DOUGLAS

Slaughter Ranch Museum ★ *Finds*   Down a dusty gravel road outside the town of Douglas lies a little-known Southwestern landmark: the Slaughter Ranch. In 1884, former Texas Ranger John Slaughter bought the San Bernardino Valley and turned it into one of the finest cattle ranches in the West. Slaughter later went on to become the sheriff of Cochise County and helped rid the region of the unsavory characters. Today, the ranch is a National Historic Landmark and has been restored to its late-19th-century appearance. Surrounding the ranch buildings are wide lawns and a large pond that together attract a variety of birds, making this one of Arizona's best winter birding spots.

6153 Geronimo Trail, about 14 miles east of Douglas. © 520/558-2474. www.slaughterranch.com. Admission $5 adults, free for children under 14. Wed–Sun 10am–3pm. Closed Christmas and New Year's Day. From Douglas, go east on 15th St., which runs into Geronimo Trail; continue east 14 miles.

BIRDING HOT SPOTS

At the **Willcox Chamber of Commerce,** 1500 N. Circle I Rd. (© 800/200-2272 or 520/384-2272; www.willcoxchamber.com), you can pick up several birding maps and checklists for the region.

To the east of Chiricahua National Monument, on the far side of the Chiricahuas, lies **Cave Creek Canyon** ★, one of the most important bird-watching spots in the United States. It's here that the colorful elegant trogon reaches the northern limit of its range. Other rare birds that have been spotted here include sulfur-bellied flycatchers and Lucy's, Virginia's, and black-throated gray warblers. Stop by the visitor center for information on the best birding spots in the area. Cave Creek Canyon is just outside the community of Portal.

The **Cochise Lakes** ★ (actually the Willcox sewage ponds) are another great bird-watching spot. Birders can see a wide variety of waterfowl and shorebirds, including avocets and ibises. To find the ponds, head south out of Willcox on Ariz. 186, turn right onto Rex Allen Jr. Drive at the sign for the Twin Lakes golf course, and go past the golf course.

Between October and March, as many as 30,000 sandhill cranes gather in the Sulphur Springs Valley south of Willcox, and in January, the town holds the **Wings Over Willcox** festival, a celebration of these majestic birds. During these months, you can see these majestic birds at the **Apache Station Wildlife Viewing Area** southwest of Willcox on U.S. 191 near the Apache Station electric generating plant and the community of Cochise. The Sulphur Springs Valley is also well known for its large wintering population of raptors.

Near Douglas, the **Slaughter Ranch,** which has a large pond, and the adjacent **San Bernardino National Wildlife Refuge** are good birding spots in both summer and winter. (See the description of the Slaughter Ranch Museum, above, for directions.)

WHERE TO STAY
NEAR WILLCOX

Cochise Stronghold B&B ★ *(Finds* Set on 15 acres of private land within Coronado National Forest's Cochise Stronghold area, this remote and beautiful inn is one of my favorite B&Bs in the state. The inn is a straw-bale, passive solar home with two housekeeping suites, and it makes a superb base for hikes amid the area's fascinating rock formations and for excursions farther afield in Cochise County. Owners John and Nancy Yates are a great source of information both on solar-home design and on the preservation of the desert environment. In-room breakfast options include Southwestern dishes such as mesquite-cornmeal pancakes that are made with flour produced by grinding mesquite-bean pods. For a more rustic experience, there is also a tepee.

2126 W. Windancer Trail (P.O. Box 232), Pearce, AZ 85625. © 877/426-4141 or 520/826-4141. www.cochise strongholdbb.com. Oct–Apr $159–$199 double, $89 tepee. Rates include full breakfast. 2-night minimum stay. AE, DISC, MC, V. Amenities: Jacuzzi; massage. *In room (but not in tepee):* A/C, TV/VCR, kitchenette, fridge, coffeemaker, hair dryer, free local calls.

Sunglow Guest Ranch ★★ *Value* Located in the western foothills of the Chiricahua Mountains roughly 40 miles southeast of Willcox, this remote ranch is surrounded by Coronado National Forest and is one of the most idyllic spots in the state. There's a small lake, and rising behind the lake are the peaks of the Chiricahuas. There's great bird-watching both on the ranch and in the nearby hills, and guests can rent mountain bikes. The guest rooms are quite large and decor includes rustic Mexican furnishings. More than half the units have wood-burning fireplaces. This guest ranch is different from others around the state in that it doesn't offer horseback riding, but it does sometimes have telescopes set up for stargazing. There's a beautiful little dining hall/cafe built in classic Western-ranch style that serves some of the best food available in this corner of the state.

14066 S. Sunglow Rd., Pearce, AZ 85625. ☎ 866/786-4569 or 520/824-3334. www.sunglowranch.com. 9 units. $234–$350 double. Rates include breakfast, afternoon tea day of check-in, and dinner. Children 5 and under stay free in parent's room. AE, DISC, MC, V. Pets accepted ($10 per night). **Amenities:** Dining room; bike rentals. *In room:* No phone.

IN PORTAL

Portal Peak Lodge, Portal Store & Cafe This motel-like lodge, located behind the general store/cafe in the hamlet of Portal, has fairly modern guest rooms that face one another across a wooden deck. Meals are available in the adjacent cafe. If you're seeking predictable accommodations in a remote location, you'll find them here.

2358 Rock House Rd. (P.O. Box 16282), Portal, AZ 85632. ☎ 520/558-2223. Fax 520/558-2473. www.portalpeak lodge.com. 16 units. $75–$85 double. AE, DC, DISC, MC, V. **Amenities:** Restaurant (American). *In room:* A/C, TV, coffeemaker.

Southwestern Research Station, The American Museum of Natural History ★ *Finds* Located far up in Cave Creek Canyon, this is a field research station that takes guests when the accommodations are not filled by scientists doing research. As such, it is the best place in the area for serious bird-watchers, who will find the company of researchers a fascinating addition to a visit. Guests stay in simply furnished cabins scattered around the research center. Spring and fall are the easiest times to get reservations and the best times for bird-watching.

P.O. Box 16553, Portal, AZ 85632. ☎ 520/558-2396. Fax 520/558-2396. http://research.amnh.org/swrs. 15 units. Mar–Oct $141 double (rate includes all meals); Nov–Feb $60–$80 double (no meals provided). Children under 4 stay free in parent's room. DISC, MC, V. **Amenities:** Dining room; outdoor pool; volleyball court; guest laundry. *In room:* No phone.

CAMPGROUNDS

There's a 22-site campground charging $12 per night at **Chiricahua National Monument** (described above), on Ariz. 186 (☎ 520/824-3560), and along the road to Portal not far from the national monument, there are several small national forest campgrounds charging $10 for a site. At **Cochise Stronghold,** which is 35 miles southwest of Willcox off U.S. 191, there is a 10-site campground charging $10 per night. For information on the national forest campgrounds, contact the Coronado National Forest Douglas Ranger District (☎ 520/364-3468; www.fs.fed.us/r3/coronado/douglas). Reservations are not accepted for any of these campgrounds.

15

Sedona & the Colorado River: The Best of Central & Western Arizona

Between Phoenix and the Grand Canyon lies one of the most beautiful landscapes on earth—the red-rock country of Sedona. Decades ago, Hollywood came to Sedona to shoot Westerns; then came the artists and the retirees and the New Agers. Now it seems Hollywood is back, but this time the stars are building huge homes in the hills.

Central Arizona isn't just red rock and retirees, though. It also has the former territorial capital of Prescott, historic sites, ancient Indian ruins, an old mining town turned artists' community, even a few good old-fashioned dude ranches (now called "guest ranches") out Wickenburg way. There are, of course, thousands of acres of cactus-studded desert, but there are also high mountains, cool pine forests, and a fertile river valley. And north of Sedona's red rocks is Oak Creek

Canyon, a tree-shaded cleft in the rocks with one of the state's most scenic stretches of highway running through it.

Also included in this chapter is Arizona's "west coast," 340 miles of Colorado River waters, most of which are impounded in three huge reservoirs—Lake Mead, Lake Mohave, and Lake Havasu—that provide the water and electricity to sprawling Southwestern boom-towns like Phoenix and Las Vegas.

As with any warm coastline, Arizona's West Coast is lined with lakefront resorts, hotels, RV parks, and campgrounds. Of course, watersports of all types are extremely popular here. For the most part, however, it's a destination for desert residents, so you won't find any hotels or resorts even remotely as upscale or expensive as those in Phoenix, Tucson, or Sedona.

1 Wickenburg

53 miles NW of Phoenix; 61 miles S of Prescott; 128 miles SE of Kingman

Once known as the dude-ranch capital of the world, the town of Wickenburg, located in the desert northwest of Phoenix, attracted celebrities and families from all over the country. Today, although the area has only a handful of dude (or guest) ranches still in business, Wickenburg clings to its Wild West image. If you've come to the Southwest searching for the West the way it used to be, Wickenburg is a good place to look.

ESSENTIALS

GETTING THERE From Phoenix, take I-17 north to Ariz. 74 west and then continue west on U.S. 60. From Prescott, take Ariz. 89. If you're coming from the west, take U.S. 60 from I-10. U.S. 93 comes down from I-40 in northwestern Arizona.

VISITOR INFORMATION Contact the **Wickenburg Chamber of Commerce,** 216 N. Frontier St. (© **928/684-5479;** www.outwickenburgway.com). Their visitor center is open Monday through Friday from 9am to 5pm, Saturday and Sunday from 10am to 3pm.

EXPLORING THE AREA
A WALK AROUND TOWN

While Wickenburg's main attractions remain the guest ranches outside of town, a walk around downtown also provides a glimpse of the Old West. Most of the buildings here were built between 1890 and the 1920s (although a few are older), and although not all of them look their age, there is just enough Western character to make a stroll worthwhile (if it's not too hot).

Two of the town's most unusual attractions aren't buildings at all. The **Jail Tree,** behind the Circle K convenience store at the corner of Wickenburg Way and Tegner Street, is an old mesquite tree that served as the local hoosegow. Outlaws were simply chained to the tree. Their families would often come to visit and have a picnic in the shade of the tree. The second, equally curious, town attraction is the **Wishing Well,** which stands beside the bridge over the Hassayampa. Legend has it that anyone who drinks from the Hassayampa River will never tell the truth again. How it became a wishing well is unclear.

MUSEUMS & MINES

Desert Caballeros Western Museum ★★ Wickenburg thrives on its Western heritage, and inside this museum you'll find an outstanding collection of Western art depicting life on the range, including works by Albert Bierstadt, Charles Russell, Thomas Moran, Frederick Remington, Maynard Dixon, and other members of the Cowboy Artists of America. The Hays "Spirit of the Cowboy" collection is an impressive display of historical cowboy gear that alone makes this museum worth a stop.

21 N. Frontier St. © 928/684-2272. www.westernmuseum.org. Admission $6 adults, $4.50 seniors, $1 children 6–16. Mon–Sat 10am–5pm; Sun noon–4pm. Closed Mon Jul–Aug, New Year's Day, Easter, July 4th, Thanksgiving, and Christmas.

Robson's Arizona Mining World Boasting the world's largest collection of antique mining equipment, this private museum is a must for anyone fascinated by Arizona's rich mining history. Located on the site of an old mining camp and with the feel of a ghost town, this museum consists of more than 30 buildings filled with antiques and displays. You can pan for gold or hike through the desert to see ancient petroglyphs. Also on the property, you'll find Litsch's Bed & Breakfast (charging $85–$105 double; no credit cards accepted) and a restaurant.

Ariz. 71, 28 miles west of Wickenburg. © 928/685-2609. www.robsonsminingworld.com. Admission $5 adults, $4.50 seniors, free for children under 10. Oct–Apr Mon–Fri 10am–4pm, Sat–Sun 9am–5pm. Closed May–Sept. Head west out of Wickenburg on U.S. 60 and, after 24 miles, turn north on Ariz. 71.

A BIRDER'S PARADISE

Hassayampa River Preserve ★ At one time the Arizona desert was laced with rivers that flowed for most, if not all, of the year. In the past 100 years, however, these rivers, and the riparian habitats they once supported, have disappeared at an alarming rate. Riparian areas support trees and plants that require more water than is usually available in the desert, and this lush growth provides food and shelter for hundreds of species of birds, mammals, and reptiles.

Central Arizona

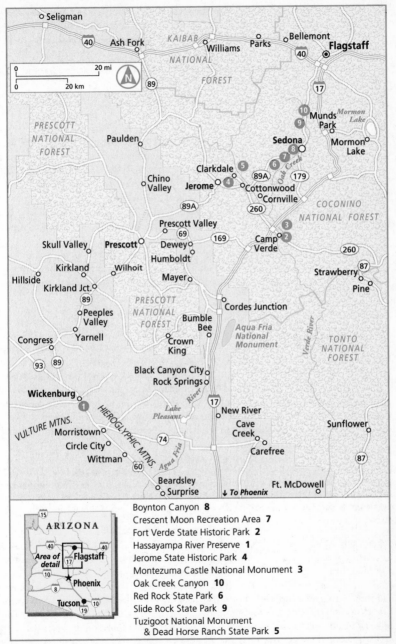

Boynton Canyon **8**
Crescent Moon Recreation Area **7**
Fort Verde State Historic Park **2**
Hassayampa River Preserve **1**
Jerome State Historic Park **4**
Montezuma Castle National Monument **3**
Oak Creek Canyon **10**
Red Rock State Park **6**
Slide Rock State Park **9**
Tuzigoot National Monument
   & Dead Horse Ranch State Park **5**

The Nature Conservancy owns and manages the Hassayampa River Preserve, which is now one of the state's most important bird-watching sites (more than 230 species of birds have been spotted here). Nature trails lead along the river beneath cottonwoods and willows and past the spring-fed Palm Lake.

49614 U.S. 60 (3 miles southeast of Wickenburg on U.S. 60). © 928/684-2772. www.nature.org. Suggested donation $5 ($3 for Nature Conservancy members). Mid-Sept to mid-May Wed–Sun 8am–5pm; mid-May to mid-Sept Fri–Sun 8am–5pm. Closed Thanksgiving, day after Thanksgiving, Christmas eve, Christmas, New Year's Eve, New Year's Day.

GETTING OUTSIDE

If you're in the area for more than a day or just can't spend another minute in the saddle, you can go out on a jeep tour and explore the desert backcountry, visit Vulture Peak, see some petroglyphs, or check out old mines. Call **B.C. Jeep Tours** (© **928/ 684-7901** or 928/684-4982), which charges $50. However, if you've got time for only one jeep tour on your Southwest vacation, make it in Sedona.

Los Caballeros Golf Club, 1551 S. Vulture Mine Rd. (© **928/684-2704**), has been rated one of the best courses in the state. Greens fees are $135 in the cooler months.

Hikers have a couple of interesting options. Southwest of town at the end of Vulture Mine Road (off U.S. 60), you can climb Vulture Peak, a steep climb best done in the cooler months. The views from up top (or even just the saddle near the top) are well worth the effort.

WHERE TO STAY

Flying E Ranch ⭐ *Kids*   This is a working cattle ranch with 20,000 high, wide, and handsome acres for you and the cattle to roam. Family owned since 1952, the Flying E attracts plenty of repeat business, with families finding it a particularly appealing and down-home kind of place. The main lodge features a spacious lounge where guests like to gather by the fireplace. Accommodations vary in size, but all have Western-style furnishings and either twin or king-size beds. Three family-style meals are served in the wood-paneled dining room, but there's no bar, so you'll need to bring your own liquor. Also available are breakfast cookouts, lunch rides, and evening chuck-wagon dinners.

2801 W. Wickenburg Way, Wickenburg, AZ 85390. © **888/684-2650** or 928/684-2690. Fax 928/684-5304. www. flyingeranch.com. 17 units. $264–$336 double. Rates include all meals. 2- to 4-night minimum stay. MC, V. Closed May–Oct. Drive 4 miles west of town on U.S. 60. **Amenities:** Dining room; outdoor pool; tennis court; exercise room; Jacuzzi; sauna; massage; horseback riding (extra $30–$40 per person per day); horseshoes; lawn games; hayrides; guest rodeos. *In room:* A/C, TV, fridge.

Kay El Bar Guest Ranch ⭐   This is the smallest and oldest of the Wickenburg guest ranches, and its adobe buildings, built between 1914 and 1925, are listed on the National Register of Historic Places. The well-maintained ranch is quintessentially Wild West in style, and the setting, on the bank of the (usually dry) Hassayampa River, lends the ranch a surprisingly lush feel compared with the arid surrounding landscape. While the cottage and the Casa Grande room are the most spacious, the smaller rooms in the adobe main lodge have original Monterey-style furnishings and other classic 1950s dude-ranch decor. I like this place because it's so small you feel like you're on a friend's ranch.

Rincon Rd., off U.S. 93 (P.O. Box 2480), Wickenburg, AZ 85358. © **800/684-7583** or 928/684-7593. Fax 928/684-4497. www.kayelbar.com. 11 units. $325 double; $700 cottage for 4. Rates do not include 15% service charge. Rates include all meals and horseback riding. 2- to 4-night minimum stay. Children 3 and under stay free in parent's room.

MC, V. Closed May to mid-Oct. **Amenities:** Dining room; lounge; small outdoor pool; Jacuzzi; massage; horseback riding. *In room:* Hair dryer, no phone.

Rancho de los Caballeros ★★
Located on 20,000 acres 2 miles west of Wickenburg, Rancho de los Caballeros is part of an exclusive country club–resort community and as such feels more like a resort than a guest ranch. However, the main lodge itself, with its flagstone floor, copper fireplace, and colorfully painted furniture, has a very Southwestern feel. Peace and quiet are the keynotes of a visit here, and most guests focus on golf (the golf course is one of the best in the state) and horseback riding. In addition, the ranch offers skeet and trap shooting and guided nature walks. Bedrooms are filled with handcrafted furnishings, exposed-beam ceilings, Indian rugs, and, in some, tile floors and fireplaces. While breakfast and lunch are quite casual, dinner is more formal, with proper attire required.

1551 S. Vulture Mine Rd. (off U.S. 60 west of town), Wickenburg, AZ 85390. © **800/684-5030** or 928/684-5484. Fax 928/684-9565. www.SunC.com. 76 units. Late Oct to mid-Dec and late Apr to early May $370–$424 double, $460 suite; mid-Dec to late Apr $426–$496 double, $558 suite. Rates do not include 15% gratuity charge. Rates include all meals. Riding and golf packages available. Children under 5 stay free in parent's room. No credit cards. Closed early May to late Oct. **Amenities:** Dining room; lounge; small outdoor pool; 18-hole golf course; 4 tennis courts; exercise room; bike rentals; children's programs; concierge; business center; massage; babysitting; laundry service; horseback riding ($35–$60 per ride). *In room:* A/C, TV, dataport, fridge, hair dryer, iron.

WHERE TO DINE
House of Berlin GERMAN/CONTINENTAL
Wickenburg may seem like an unusual place for an authentic German restaurant, but that's exactly what you'll find right downtown. The place is small and casual and serves a mix of German and other Continental dishes. Local favorites include the Wiener schnitzel and sauerbraten.

169 E. Wickenburg Way. © **928/684-5044.** Main courses $6.50–$12 lunch, $11–$16 dinner. MC, V. Tues 5–9pm; Wed–Sun 11:30am–2pm and 5–9pm.

2 Prescott
100 miles N of Phoenix; 60 miles SW of Sedona; 87 miles SW of Flagstaff

Prescott, the former territorial capital, is an anomaly; it doesn't seem like Arizona at all. With its stately courthouse on a tree-shaded square, its well-preserved historic downtown business district, and its old Victorian homes, Prescott wears the air of the quintessential American small town. Prescott has just about everything a small town should have: an 1890s saloon (The Palace), an old cattlemen's hotel (Hassayampa Inn), a burger shop (Kendall's), and a brewpub (Prescott Brewing Company). Add to this several small museums, a couple of other historic hotels, the strange and beautiful landscape of the Granite Dells, and the nearby Prescott National Forest, and you have a town that appeals to visitors with a diverse range of interests.

Prescott has become an upscale retirement community, as much for its historic heritage as for its mild year-round climate. In summer, Prescott is also a popular weekend getaway for Phoenicians; it is usually 20° cooler here than it is in Phoenix.

ESSENTIALS
GETTING THERE   Prescott is at the junction of Ariz. 89, Ariz. 89A, and Ariz. 69. If you're coming from Phoenix, take the Cordes Junction exit (Exit 262) from I-17. From Flagstaff, the most direct route is I-17 to Ariz. 169 to Ariz. 69. From Sedona, just take Ariz. 89A all the way.

America West (© 800/235-9292) offers regularly scheduled flights between Prescott's Ernest A. Love Airport, on U.S. 89, and Phoenix's Sky Harbor Airport. **Shuttle "U"** (© 800/304-6114 or 928/442-1000; www.shuttleu.com) provides service to Prescott from Sky Harbor Airport for $26 one-way, $47 round-trip.

VISITOR INFORMATION The **Prescott Chamber of Commerce** is at 117 W. Goodwin St. (© 800/266-7534 or 928/445-2000; www.prescott.org). The visitor center is open Monday through Friday from 9am to 5pm and Saturday and Sunday from 10am to 2pm.

GETTING AROUND For car rentals, call **Enterprise** (© 800/736-8222) or **Hertz** (© 800/654-3131).

EXPLORING THE TOWN

A walk around **Courthouse Plaza** should be your introduction to Prescott. The stately old courthouse in the middle of the tree-shaded plaza sets the tone for the whole town. The building, far too large for a small regional town such as this, dates from the days when Prescott was the capital of the Arizona territory. Under the big shade trees, you'll find several bronze statues of cowboys and soldiers.

Surrounding the courthouse and extending north for a block is Prescott's **historic business district.** Stroll around admiring the brick buildings, and you'll realize that Prescott was once a very important place. Duck into an old saloon or the lobby of one of the historic hotels, and you'll understand that the town was also part of the Wild West.

To learn more about the history of Prescott, contact **Melissa Ruffner** at **Prescott Historical Tours** (© 928/445-4567). Ms. Ruffner does her tours in Victorian costume and passes out copies of her book on the territorial history of Arizona. Tours cost $40 per couple. Another good way to learn about Prescott's history is aboard the trolley run by **Old West Trolley Tours** (© 928/717-0528; www.prescotttrolley.com). Tours cost $10 for adults and $5 for children 12 and under and leave from the corner of Gurley Street and Cortez Street on Courthouse Square. Trolley tickets also give you discounts off tickets to several Prescott museums.

Fort Whipple Museum Located north of town off U.S. 89 on the grounds of what is now a Veterans Administration hospital, this museum focuses on the history of this fort, which was active from 1863 to 1922 and has many stately officers' homes. Don't miss the display about Fiorello LaGuardia's time at the fort.

Veterans Administration campus, Bldg. 11, 500 N. Hwy. 89. © 928/445-3122. Free admission. Mon–Fri 10am–2pm.

Phippen Museum ★ If you're a fan of classic Western art, you won't want to miss this small museum. Located on a hill a few miles north of town, the Phippen exhibits works by both established Western artists and newcomers and is named after the first president of the prestigious Cowboy Artists of America organization. Also on display are artifacts and photos that help place the artwork in the context of the region's history. More than 100 Arizona artists are represented in the museum store. The **Phippen Museum Western Art Show & Sale** is held each year on Memorial Day weekend.

4701 U.S. 89 N. © 928/778-1385. www.phippenartmuseum.org. Admission $5 adults, $4 seniors, free for children under 12. Tues–Sat 10am–4pm; Sun 1–4pm.

Sharlot Hall Museum ★ In 1882, at the age of 12, Sharlot Hall traveled to the Arizona territory with her parents. As an adult, she began collecting artifacts from Arizona's pioneer days, and from 1909 to 1911, she was the territorial historian. In 1928, she opened this museum in Prescott's Old Governor's Mansion, a log home built in 1864. In addition to the "mansion," which is furnished much as it might have been when it was built, there are several other interesting buildings that can be toured. The Frémont House was built in 1875 for the fifth territorial governor. Its traditional wood-frame construction shows how quickly Prescott grew from a remote logging and mining camp into a civilized little town. The 1877 Bashford House reflects the Victorian architecture that was popular throughout the country around the end of the 19th century. The Sharlot Hall Building houses exhibits on Native American cultures and territorial Arizona. Every year in early summer, artisans, craftspeople, and costumed exhibitors participate in the **Folk Arts Fair.**

415 W. Gurley St. ℂ 928/445-3122. www.sharlot.org. Admission $5 adults. May–Sept Mon–Sat 10am–5pm, Sun noon–4pm; Oct–Apr Mon–Sat 10am–4pm, Sun noon–4pm. Closed New Year's Day, Thanksgiving, and Christmas.

The Smoki Museum   This interesting little museum, which houses a collection of Native American artifacts in a historic stone building, is named for the fictitious Smoki tribe. The tribe was dreamed up in 1921 by a group of non-Indians who wanted to inject some new life into Prescott's July 4th celebrations. Despite its phony origins, the museum contains genuine artifacts and basketry from many different tribes, mainly Southwestern. The museum also sponsors interesting lectures on Native American topics.

147 N. Arizona St. ℂ 928/445-1230. www.smokimuseum.org. Admission $4 adults, $3 seniors, $2 students. Apr–Dec Mon–Sat 10am–4pm, Sun 1–4pm; Jan–Mar Fri–Sat and Mon 10am–4pm, Sun 1–4pm.

GETTING OUTSIDE

Prescott is situated on the edge of a wide expanse of high plains with the pine forests of **Prescott National Forest** at its back. There are hiking and mountain-biking trails, several lakes, and campgrounds within the national forest. My favorite hiking and biking areas are Thumb Butte (west of town) and the Granite Mountain Wilderness (northwest of town).

Thumb Butte, a rocky outcropping that towers over the forest just west of town, is Prescott's most readily recognizable natural landmark. A 1.2-mile trail leads nearly to the top of this butte, and from the saddle near the summit, there's a panoramic vista of the entire region. The trail itself is very steep, but paved much of the way. The summit of the butte is a popular rock-climbing spot. An alternative return trail makes a loop hike possible. To reach the trail head, drive west out of town on Gurley Street, which becomes Thumb Butte Road. Follow the road until you see the National Forest signs, after which there's a parking lot, picnic area, and trail head. There is a $2 parking fee here.

The Granite Basin Recreation Area provides access to the **Granite Mountain Wilderness.** Trails lead beneath the cliffs of Granite Mountain, where you might spot peregrine falcons. For the best views, hike 1.5 miles to Blair Pass and then on up the Granite Mountain trail as far as you feel like going. To reach this area, take Gurley Street west from downtown, turn right on Grove Avenue, and follow it around to Iron Springs Road, which will take you northwest out of town to the signed road for the Granite Basin Recreation Area (less than 8 miles from downtown). There is a $2 parking fee here.

Both of the above areas also offer mountain-biking trails. Although the scenery isn't as spectacular as in the Sedona area, the trails are great. You can rent a bike and get maps and specific trail recommendations at **Ironclad Bicycles,** 710 White Spar Rd.

(© **928/776-1755;** www.ironcladbicycles.com), which charges $20 to $50 per day for mountain bikes.

For maps and information on these and other hikes and bike rides in the area, stop by the **Bradshaw Ranger Station,** 344 S. Cortez St. (© **928/443-8000;** www.fs.fed. us/r3/prescott).

North of town 5 miles on Ariz. 89 is an unusual and scenic area known as the **Granite Dells.** Jumbled hills of rounded granite suddenly jut up from the landscape, creating a maze of huge boulders and smooth rock. In the middle of this dramatic landscape lies **Watson Lake,** the waters of which push their way in among the boulders to create one of the prettiest lakes in the state. On the highway side of the lake, you'll find **Watson Lake Park,** which has picnic tables and great views. Spring through the fall (weather permitting) on Saturday and Sunday between 10am and 4pm, you can rent **canoes and kayaks** ($10 per hour) at the lake. Reservations aren't accepted, but you can call **Prescott Outdoors** (© **928/925-1410;** www.prescott outdoors.com), to make sure they'll be at the lake with their boats.

For hiking in the Watson Lake area, I recommend heading to the **Peavine Trail.** To find the trail head, turn east onto Prescott Lake Parkway, which is between Prescott and the Granite Dells, and then turn left onto Sun Dog Ranch Road. This rails-to-trails path extends for several miles through the middle of the Granite Dells and is the best way to fully appreciate the Dells (you'll be away from both people and the highway). Although this is a fascinating, easy hike, it also makes a great, equally easy, mountain-bike ride that can be extended 7.5 miles on the newly opened Iron King Trail.

A couple of miles west of Watson Lake on Willow Creek Road, you can hike in **Willow Creek Park,** where several miles of trails lead through grasslands and groves of huge cottonwood trees adjacent to Willow Lake. The trails eventually lead to the edge of the Granite Dells. There's great bird-watching in the trees in this park, and there are even great blue heron and cormorant rookeries.

If you want to explore the area on horseback, try **Granite Mountain Stables** (© **928/771-9551**), which offers guided trail rides in the Prescott National Forest. A 1-hour ride is $35.

Reasonably priced golf is available at the **Antelope Hills Golf Course,** 1 Perkins Dr. (© **800/972-6818** or 928/776-7888; www.antelopehillsgolf.com). Greens fees range from $40 to $55.

SHOPPING

Downtown Prescott is filled with antiques stores, especially along North Cortez Street. In the Hotel St. Michael's shopping arcade, check out **Hotel Trading,** 110 S. Montezuma St. (© **928/778-7276**), which carries some genuine Native American artifacts at reasonable prices. Owner Ernie Lister also makes silver jewelry in the 19th-century Navajo style. On this same block are both the **Arts Prescott Cooperative Gallery,** 134 S. Montezuma St. (© **928/776-7717;** www.artsprescott.com), a cooperative of local artists, and **Van Gogh's Ear,** 156B S. Montezuma St. (© **928/776-1080**), which was founded by a splinter group from the co-op and actually has higher-quality art and crafts. Also on this block, you'll find the **Newman Gallery,** 106-A S. Montezuma St. (© **928/442-9167;** www.newmangallery.net), which features the colorful Western-inspired pop-culture imagery of artist Dave Newman.

WHERE TO STAY

EXPENSIVE

Hassayampa Inn ⭐   Built as a luxury hotel in 1927, the Hassayampa Inn, which is listed on the National Register of Historic Places, evokes the time when Prescott was the bustling territorial capital. In the lobby, exposed ceiling beams, wrought-iron chandeliers, and arched doorways all reflect the place's Southwestern heritage. Although guest rooms tend to be very small, each is unique and features either original furnishings or antiques. Any hotel employee will be happy to tell you the story of the ill-fated honeymooners whose ghosts supposedly haunt the place.

122 E. Gurley St., Prescott, AZ 86301. ℂ 800/322-1927 or 928/778-9434. www.hassayampainn.com. 67 units. $99–$189 double; $159–$299 suite. Children under 12 stay free in parent's room. AE, DC, DISC, MC, V. **Amenities:** Restaurant; lounge; exercise room; room service; laundry service; dry cleaning. *In room:* A/C, TV, dataport, hair dryer, iron.

MODERATE

Hotel Vendome ⭐   Not quite as luxurious as the Hassayampa, yet not as basic as the St. Michael, the Vendome is a good middle-price choice for those who want to stay in a historic hotel. Built in 1917 as a lodging house, the restored brick building is only 2 blocks from the action of Whiskey Row, but far enough away that you can get a good night's sleep. Guest rooms are outfitted with new furnishings, but some of the bathrooms still contain original claw-foot tubs. Naturally, this hotel, like several others in town, has its own resident ghost.

230 S. Cortez St., Prescott, AZ 86303. ℂ 888/468-3583 or 928/776-0900. Fax 928/771-0395. www.vendomehotel. com. 21 units. $89–$129 double; $129–$169 2-bedroom unit. Rates include continental breakfast. Children under 16 stay free in parent's room. AE, DISC, MC, V. **Amenities:** Lounge; access to nearby health club. *In room:* A/C, TV, dataport, hair dryer, iron, free local calls.

Rocamadour Bed & Breakfast for (Rock) Lovers ⭐⭐   The Granite Dells, just north of Prescott, is the area's most unforgettable feature. Should you wish to stay amid these jumbled boulders, there's no better choice than Rocamadour. Mike and Twila Coffey honed their innkeeping skills as owners of a 40-room château in France, and antique furnishings from that château can now be found throughout this inn. The most elegant pieces are in the Chambre Trucy, which also boasts an amazing underlit whirlpool tub. One cottage is built into the boulders and has a large whirlpool tub on its deck. The unique setting, engaging innkeepers, and thoughtful details everywhere you turn make this one of the state's must-stay inns.

3386 N. Hwy. 89, Prescott, AZ 86301. ℂ 888/771-1933 or 928/771-1933. 3 units. $139–$149 double; $189 suite. AE, DC, DISC, MC, V. Rates include full breakfast. *In room:* A/C, TV/VCR.

INEXPENSIVE

Hotel St. Michael (Value)   Located right on Whiskey Row, this restored hotel, complete with resident ghost and the oldest elevator in Prescott, offers a historic setting at budget prices (don't expect the best of mattresses or most stylish furnishings). All rooms are different; some have bathtubs but no showers. The casual Whiskey Row Bistro, where breakfast is served, overlooks Courthouse Plaza.

205 W. Gurley St., Prescott, AZ 86301. ℂ 800/678-3757 or 928/776-1999. Fax 928/776-7318. www.hotelst michael.net. 72 units. $59–$89 double; $99–$109 suite. Rates include full breakfast. AE, DISC, MC, V. **Amenities:** Restaurant; shopping arcade. *In room:* A/C, TV.

WHERE TO DINE
MODERATE

Murphy's ⊛ AMERICAN Murphy's, housed in an 1890 mercantile building that is on the National Register of Historic Places, has long been one of Prescott's favorite special-occasion restaurants. Sparkling leaded-glass doors usher diners into a high-ceilinged room with fans revolving slowly overhead. Many of the shop's original shelves can still be seen in the lounge area, and the restaurant does a good job of creating a historic ambience. The best bets on the menu are the mesquite-broiled meats, but the fish specials can also be good. You can save a bit of money by dining early and ordering one of the sunset dinners.

201 N. Cortez St. ℂ 928/445-4044. www.murphysrestaurants.com. Reservations recommended. Main courses $7–$15 lunch, $15–$30 dinner. AE, DISC, MC, V. Sun–Thurs 11am–10pm; Fri–Sat 11am–11pm.

129½ ⊛ NEW AMERICAN Prescott, a classic small-town-America sort of place, may seem an odd location for a classic New York–style jazz club, but this restaurant has it down. It may not be in a basement and it isn't smoky, but everything else has just the right feel. Best of all, the restaurant also has great food. Steaks are the specialty and can be had with an assortment of delicious sauces, such as pinot and green peppercorn, rosemary cream, and shiitake and portobello mushroom (I like the pinot-and-green-peppercorn sauce).

129½ N. Cortez St. ℂ 928/443-9292. Reservations recommended. Main courses $15–$27. AE, DISC, MC, V. Tues–Thurs 11am–2pm and 5–9:30pm; Fri 11am–2pm and 5–10pm; Sat 5–10pm.

The Palace *Finds* SOUTHWESTERN/STEAKHOUSE/SEAFOOD The Palace is the oldest saloon in Arizona (in business for more than 120 years), and looks just the way it might have at the start of the 20th century. The generous steaks are your best bet here. If you bump into someone carrying a shotgun, don't panic! It's probably just the owner, who likes to dress the part of a Wild West saloonkeeper. Dinner shows are held every other Monday. There's live music Friday and Saturday nights, and on Sunday afternoons, there's a honky-tonk piano player.

120 S. Montezuma St. ℂ 928/541-1996. www.historicpalace.com. Reservations suggested on weekends. Main courses $7–$11 lunch, $13–$27 dinner. AE, DISC, MC, V. Sun–Thurs 11am–9:30pm; Fri–Sat 11am–10:30pm.

The Rose Restaurant ⊛⊛ CONTINENTAL This is Prescott's best restaurant and is a must for anyone staying in town. Chef Linda Rose brings a distinctive creative flair to her cooking and year after year continues to satisfy locals and visitors alike. Although the manicotti is a not-to-be-missed house specialty, the veal dishes can also be outstanding, and the pasta with scallops and Italian sausage is a curious combination of flavors that works well. The wine list includes plenty of reasonably priced options.

234 S. Cortez St. ℂ 928/777-8308. Reservations recommended. Main courses $16–$33. AE, DC, DISC, MC, V. Wed–Sun 5–9pm.

INEXPENSIVE

Prescott Brewing Company AMERICAN/PUB FARE Popular primarily with a younger crowd, this brewpub keeps a good selection of its own beers on tap, but its cheap and filling meals are just as sought after. Fajitas are a specialty, along with such pub standards as fish and chips, bangers and mash, and not-so-standard spent-grain beer-dough pizzas and vegetarian dishes.

130 W. Gurley St. ℂ 928/771-2795. www.prescottbrewingcompany.com. Main courses $6.50–$19. AE, DISC, MC, V. Sun–Thurs 11am–10pm; Fri–Sat 11am–11pm (pub stays open 2 hr. after kitchen closes).

PRESCOTT AFTER DARK

Back in the days when Prescott was the territorial capital and a booming mining town, it supported dozens of rowdy saloons, most of which were concentrated along Montezuma Street on the west side of Courthouse Plaza. This section of town was known as **Whiskey Row,** and legend has it there was a tunnel from the courthouse to one of the saloons so lawmakers wouldn't have to be seen ducking into the saloons during regular business hours. On July 14, 1900, a fire consumed most of Whiskey Row. However, concerned cowboys and miners managed to drag the tremendously heavy bar of the Palace saloon across the street before it was damaged.

Today, Whiskey Row still has a few noisy saloons with genuine Wild West flavor. However, within a few blocks of Whiskey Row, you can hear country, folk, jazz, and rock at a surprisingly diverse assortment of bars, restaurants, and clubs.

If you want to see what this street's saloons looked like back in the old days, drop by **The Palace,** 120 S. Montezuma St. (© **928/541-1996;** www.historicpalace.com), which still has a classic bar up front.

If you want to drink where the ranchers drink and not where the hired hands carouse, head upstairs to the **Jersey Lilly Saloon,** 116 S. Montezuma St. (© **928/ 541-7854**), which attracts a more well-heeled clientele than the street-level saloons. On weekends, there is live music in a wide range of styles.

3 Jerome

35 miles NE of Prescott; 28 miles W of Sedona; 130 miles N of Phoenix

Few towns anywhere in the Southwest make more of an impression on visitors than Jerome, a historic mining town that clings to the slopes of Cleopatra Hill high on Mingus Mountain. The town is divided into two sections that are separated by an elevation change of 1,500 vertical feet, with the upper part of town 2,000 feet above the Verde Valley. On a clear day, the view from Jerome is stupendous—it's possible to see for more than 50 miles, with the red rocks of Sedona, the Mogollon Rim, and the San Francisco Peaks visible in the distance. Add to the unforgettable views the abundance of interesting shops and galleries and the winding narrow streets, and you have a town that should not be missed.

ESSENTIALS

GETTING THERE   Jerome is on Ariz. 89A roughly halfway between Sedona and Prescott. Coming from Phoenix, take Ariz. 260 from Camp Verde.

VISITOR INFORMATION   Contact the **Jerome Chamber of Commerce** (© **928/ 634-2900;** www.jeromechamber.com) for information. It's usually open daily from 10am to 2pm.

EXPLORING THE TOWN

Wandering the streets, soaking up the atmosphere, and shopping are the main pastimes in Jerome. Before you launch yourself on a shopping tour, you can learn about the town's past at the **Jerome State Historic Park,** off Ariz. 89A on Douglas Road in the lower section of town (© **928/634-5381**). Located in a mansion built in 1916 as a home for mine owner "Rawhide Jimmy" Douglas and as a hotel for visiting mining executives, the Jerome State Historic Park contains exhibits on mining as well as a few of the mansion's original furnishings. Set on a hill above Douglas's Little Daisy Mine, the mansion overlooks Jerome and, dizzyingly far below, the Verde Valley. Constructed of adobe bricks made on the site, the mansion once contained a wine cellar, billiards room, marble shower, steam heat, and central vacuum system. Admission is $3, and the park is open daily (except Christmas) from 8am to 5pm.

To learn more about Jerome's history, stop in at the **Jerome Historical Society's Mine Museum,** 200 Main St. (✆ **928/634-5477;** www.jeromehistoricalsociety.org), which has some small and old-fashioned displays on mining. It's open daily from 9am to 4:30pm; admission is $2 for adults, $1 for seniors, and free for children 12 and under. For that classic mining-town tourist-trap experience, follow the signs up the hill from downtown Jerome to the **Gold King Mine** (✆ **928/634-0053;** www.gold kingmine.net), where you can see lots of old, rusting mining equipment and maybe even catch a demonstration. The mine is open 9am to 5pm daily.

Most visitors come to Jerome for the shops, which offer an eclectic blend of contemporary art, chic jewelry, one-of-a-kind handmade fashions, unusual imports and gifts, and the inevitable tacky souvenirs and ice cream (alas, no place stays undiscovered for long anymore; at least there's no McDonald's).

WHERE TO STAY

Connor Hotel of Jerome Housed in a renovated historic hotel, this lodging has spacious rooms with large windows; views of the valley, however, are limited. Although a few of the rooms are located directly above the hotel's popular bar, which can be quite noisy on weekends, most rooms are quiet enough to provide a good night's rest. Better yet, come on a weekday when the Harley-Davidson poseur crowd from the Scottsdale area isn't thundering through the streets on their hogs.

164 Main St. (P.O. Box 1177), Jerome, AZ 86331. ✆ **800/523-3554** or 928/634-5006. www.connorhotel.com. 12 units. $85–$125 double. Children under 12 stay free in parent's room. AE, DISC, MC, V. Pets accepted. **Amenities:** Bar. *In room:* A/C, TV, dataport, fridge, coffeemaker, hair dryer, iron, free local calls.

The Surgeon's House ★ Built in 1917 as the home of Jerome's resident surgeon, this Mediterranean-style building has a jaw-dropping view of the Verde Valley and is surrounded by beautiful gardens. All units are suites, but the old chauffeur's quarters, located in a separate cottage across the gardens, is the one to request. This unconventionally designed room has a wall of glass opposite the bed (so you can take in the view from under the covers), an old tub in one corner, and a wall of glass blocks around the toilet. The rooms in the main house are much more traditional, filled with antiques that conjure up Jerome's heyday.

101 Hill St. (P.O. Box 998), Jerome, AZ 86331. ✆ **800/639-1452** or 928/639-1452. www.surgeonshouse.com. 4 units. $100–$150 suite. Rates include full breakfast. DISC, MC, V. Pets accepted ($25 per night). **Amenities:** Massage. *In room:* A/C.

WHERE TO DINE

The Asylum ★ *Finds* ECLECTIC As the name would imply, this restaurant (inside a former hospital building high above downtown Jerome) is a bit out of the ordinary. The bedpan full of candy at the front desk and the odd little notes in the menu will also make it absolutely clear that this place doesn't take much, other than good food, seriously. I like the distinctly Southwestern dishes, including the prickly-pear barbecued pork tenderloin with tomatillo salsa, and an unusual butternut-squash soup made with a cinnamon-lime cream sauce. Cocktails all get wacky loony-bin names, and there's also a superb, award-winning wine list.

200 Hill St. ✆ **928/639-3197.** Reservations recommended. Main courses $7.50–$13 lunch, $14–$26 dinner. DISC, MC, V. Daily 11am–3pm and 5–9pm.

Flatiron Café BREAKFAST/LIGHT MEALS   The tiny Flatiron Café is a simple breakfast-and-lunch spot in, you guessed it, Jerome's version of a flatiron building. The limited menu includes the likes of lox and bagels, a breakfast quesadilla, black-bean hummus, smoked-salmon quesadillas, fresh juices, and espresso drinks. It looks as though you could hardly squeeze in here, but there's more seating across the street. Definitely not your usual ghost-town lunch counter.

416 Main St. (at Hull Ave.). © 928/634-2733. Most items $7–$9. MC, V. Daily 8:30am–3pm.

4 The Verde Valley

Camp Verde: 20 miles E of Jerome; 30 miles S of Sedona; 95 miles N of Phoenix

Named by early Spanish explorers who were impressed by the sight of such a verdant valley in an otherwise brown desert landscape, the Verde Valley has long been a magnet for both wildlife and people. Today, the valley is one of Arizona's richest agricultural and ranching regions and is quickly gaining popularity with retirees. Cottonwood and Clarkdale are old copper-smelting towns, while Camp Verde was an army post back in the days of the Indian Wars. All three towns have some interesting historical buildings, but it is the valley's two national monuments—Tuzigoot and Montezuma Castle—that are the main attractions.

Long before the first European explorers entered the Verde Valley, the Sinagua people were living by the river and irrigating their fields with its waters. Sinagua ruins can still be seen at Tuzigoot and Montezuma Castle. By the time the first pioneers began settling in this region, the Sinaguas had long since disappeared, but Apaches had claimed the valley as part of their territory. Hundreds of years of Verde Valley history and prehistory can be viewed at sites such as Fort Verde State Park and the national monuments. This valley is also the site of the state's most scenic railroad excursion.

ESSENTIALS

GETTING THERE   Camp Verde is just off I-17 at the junction with Ariz. 260. The latter highway leads northwest through the Verde Valley for 12 miles to Cottonwood.

VISITOR INFORMATION   Contact the **Cottonwood Chamber of Commerce,** 1010 S. Main St., Cottonwood (© **928/634-7593;** http://cottonwood.verdevalley.com).

FESTIVALS   Avid birders may want to plan their visit to coincide with the annual **Verde Valley Birding & Nature Festival** (© **928/634-8437;** www.birdyverde.org), which is held the last weekend in April.

A RAILWAY EXCURSION

Verde Canyon Railroad   When the town of Jerome was busily mining copper, a railway was built to link the booming town with the territorial capital at nearby Prescott. Because of the rugged mountains between Jerome and Prescott, the railroad was forced to take a longer but less difficult route north along the Verde River before turning south toward Prescott. Today, you can ride these same tracks aboard the Verde Canyon Railroad. The route through the canyon traverses both the remains of a copper smelter and unspoiled desert that is inaccessible by car and is part of the Prescott National Forest. The views of the rocky canyon walls and green waters of the Verde River are quite dramatic, and if you look closely along the way, you'll see ancient Sinagua cliff dwellings. In late winter and early spring, nesting bald eagles can also be spotted. Of the two excursion train rides in Arizona, this is by far the more scenic (although the Grand Canyon Railway certainly has a more impressive destination). Live music and a very informative narration make the ride entertaining as well.

300 N. Broadway, Clarkdale. ⓒ 800/320-0718 or 928/639-0010. www.verdecanyonrr.com. Tickets $40 adults, $36 seniors, $25 children 2–12; first-class tickets $60. Call or visit the website for schedule and reservations.

NATIONAL MONUMENTS & STATE PARKS

Dead Horse Ranch State Park You'll find this state park on the outskirts of Cottonwood, not far from Tuzigoot National Monument. Set on the banks of the Verde River, the park offers picnicking, fishing, swimming, hiking, mountain biking, and camping. Trails wind through the riparian forests along the banks of the river and visit marshes that offer good bird-watching. The ranch was named in the 1940s, when the children of a family looking to buy it told their parents they wanted to buy the ranch with the dead horse by the side of the road.

675 Dead Horse Ranch Rd., Cottonwood. ⓒ 928/634-5283. Admission $6 per car. Daily 8am–8pm. From Main St. on the east side of Cottonwood, drive north on N. 10th St.

Fort Verde State Historic Park Just south of Montezuma Castle and Montezuma Well, in the town of Camp Verde, you'll find Fort Verde State Historic Park. Established in 1871, Fort Verde was the third military post in the Verde Valley and was occupied until 1891. The military had first come to the Verde Valley in 1865 at the request of settlers who wanted protection from the local Tonto Apache and Yavapai. The tribes, traditionally hunters and gatherers, had been forced to raid the settlers' fields for food after their normal economy was disrupted by the sudden influx of whites and Mexicans into the area.

The state park preserves three officers' quarters, an administration building, and some ruins. The buildings that have been fully restored house exhibits on the history of the fort and what life was like here in the 19th century.

125 Holloman St., Camp Verde. ⓒ 928/567-3275. www.azstateparks.com. Admission $2 adults, free for children under 14. Daily 8am–5pm. Closed Christmas.

Montezuma Castle National Monument ⭐ This Sinagua ruin is one of the best-preserved cliff dwellings in Arizona. The site consists of two impressive stone pueblos that were, for some unknown reason, abandoned by the Sinagua people when they disappeared without a trace in the early 14th century.

The more intriguing of the two ruins is set in a shallow cave 100 feet up a cliff overlooking Beaver Creek. Construction on this five-story, 20-room village began in the early 12th century. Another structure, containing 45 rooms on a total of six levels, stands at the base of the cliff. This latter dwelling, which has been subjected to rains and floods over the years, is not nearly as well preserved as the cliff dwelling.

Montezuma Well, located 11 miles north of Montezuma Castle (although still part of the national monument), is a spring-fed sinkhole that was a true oasis in the desert for native peoples. This sunken pond was formed when a cavern in the area's porous limestone bedrock collapsed. Underground springs quickly filled the sinkhole, which today contains a pond measuring over 360 feet across and 65 feet deep. Sinagua structures are clustered in and near the sinkhole.

Exit 289 off I-17. ⓒ 928/567-3322. www.nps.gov/moca. Admission $3 adults, free for children 16 and under; no charge to visit Montezuma Well. Memorial Day weekend to Labor Day weekend daily 8am–6pm; other months daily 8am–5pm.

Tuzigoot National Monument Perched atop a hill overlooking the Verde River, this small, stone-walled pueblo was built by the Sinagua people and was inhabited between 1125 and 1400. The Sinagua, whose name is Spanish for "without water," were traditionally dry-land farmers relying entirely on rainfall to water their crops.

An interpretive trail leads through the Tuzigoot ruins, explaining different aspects of Sinaguan life, and inside the visitor center is a small museum displaying many of the artifacts unearthed here. Desert plants, many of which were used by the Sinagua, are identified along the trail.

Just outside Clarkdale off Ariz. 89A. © **928/634-5564.** www.nps.gov/tuzi. Admission $3 adults, free for children 16 and under. Memorial Day weekend to Labor Day weekend daily 8am–6pm; other months daily 8am–5pm. Closed Christmas.

WHERE TO STAY

Hacienda de la Mariposa ★★ *(Finds)*   This modern Santa Fe–style inn is set on the banks of Beaver Creek and is just up the road from Montezuma Castle National Monument. Guest rooms contain rustic Mexican furnishings, gas beehive-style fireplaces, small private patios, and lots of character. Bathrooms feature skylights and whirlpool tubs. With a patio overlooking the creek, the Mariposa Creekside room is my favorite. The little Casita de Milagros, a sort of cottage/massage room that serves as a gathering spot for guests, has a huge amethyst geode set into the ceiling. In a walled garden out back, you'll find a swimming pool only steps from the creek.

3875 Stagecoach Rd. (P.O. Box 1224), Camp Verde, AZ 86322. © **888/520-9095** or 928/567-1490. Fax 928/567-1436. www.lamariposa-az.com. 5 units. $195–$235 double. AE, DISC, MC, V. No children. **Amenities:** Outdoor pool; Jacuzzi; massage. *In room:* A/C, TV/VCR, coffeemaker, hair dryer, free local calls.

WHERE TO DINE

Blazin' M Ranch Chuckwagon Suppers *(Kids)* AMERICAN   Located adjacent to Dead Horse State Park, the Blazin' M Ranch is classic Southwest-style family entertainment—steaks and beans accompanied by cowboy music and comedy. This place is geared primarily toward the young 'uns, with pony rides, farm animals, and a little cow town for the kids to explore. One of the highlights is the gallery of animated wood carvings, which features humorous Western scenes.

Off 10th St., Cottonwood. © **800/937-8643** or 928/634-0334. www.blazinm.com. Reservations recommended. Dinner $23 adults, $21 seniors, $13 children ages 4–12. AE, DISC, MC, V. Wed–Sat gates open at 5pm, dinner at 6:30pm, show at 7:30pm. Closed Jan and Aug.

Old Town Café *(Finds)* CAFE   The almond croissants at this European-style cafe in downtown Cottonwood are among the best we've ever had. If that isn't recommendation enough for you, there are also good salads and sandwiches, such as a grilled panini of smoked turkey, spinach, and tomatoes.

1025 "A" N. Main St., Cottonwood. © **928/634-5980.** Salads and sandwiches $5.75–$8.50. No credit cards. Tues–Sat 8am–3pm.

5 Sedona & Oak Creek Canyon ★ ★

56 miles NE of Prescott; 116 miles N of Phoenix; 106 miles S of the Grand Canyon

There is not a town anywhere in the Southwest with a more beautiful setting than Sedona. On the outskirts of town, red-rock buttes, eroded canyon walls, and mesas rise into blue skies. Off in the distance, the Mogollon Rim looms, its forests of juniper and ponderosa pine dark against the rocks. With a wide band of rosy sandstone predominating in this area, Sedona has come to be known as red-rock country, and each evening at sunset, the rocks put on an unforgettable light show that is reason enough for a visit. All this may sound perfectly idyllic, but if you lower your eyes from the red rocks, you'll see the flip side of Sedona—a sprawl of housing developments and strip malls. However, not even the proliferation of timeshare sales offices disguised as "visitor information centers" can mar the beauty of the backdrop.

With national forest surrounding the city (and even fingers of forest extending into what would otherwise be the city limits), Sedona also has some of the best outdoor access of any city in the Southwest. All around town, alongside highways and down side streets in suburban neighborhoods, there are trail heads. Trek down any one of these trails and you leave the city behind and enter the world of the red rocks.

Located at the mouth of Oak Creek Canyon, Sedona was first settled by pioneers in 1877 and named for the first postmaster's wife. Word of Sedona's beauty did not begin to spread until Hollywood filmmakers began using the region's red rock as backdrop to their Western films. Next came artists, lured by the landscapes and desert light (it was here in Sedona that the Cowboy Artists of America organization was formed). Although still much touted as an artists' community, Sedona's art scene these days is geared more toward tourists than toward collectors of fine art.

With its drop-dead gorgeous scenery, dozens of motels and resorts, and plethora of good restaurants, Sedona makes an excellent base for exploring central Arizona. Several ancient Indian ruins (including an impressive cliff dwelling), the "ghost town" of Jerome, and the scenic Verde Canyon Railroad are all within easy driving distance, and even the Grand Canyon is but a long day trip away.

ESSENTIALS

GETTING THERE   Sedona is on Ariz. 179 at the mouth of Oak Creek Canyon. From Phoenix, take I-17 to Ariz. 179 north. From Flagstaff, head south on I-17 until you see the turnoff for Ariz. 89A and Sedona. Ariz. 89A also connects Sedona with Prescott.

Sedona Phoenix Shuttle (© **800/448-7988** in Arizona, or 928/282-2066; www. sedona-phoenix-shuttle.com) operates several trips daily between Phoenix's Sky Harbor Airport and Sedona. The fare is $40 one-way, $75 round-trip.

VISITOR INFORMATION   The **Sedona–Oak Creek Canyon Chamber of Commerce Visitor Center/Uptown Gateway Visitor Center,** 331 Forest Rd. (© **800/288-7336** or 928/282-7722; www.visitsedona.com), operates a visitor center at the corner of Ariz. 89A and Forest Road near uptown Sedona. The visitor center is open Monday through Saturday from 8:30am to 5pm and Sundays and holidays from 9am to 3pm.

You can also get information, as well as a Red Rock Pass for parking at area trail heads, at the **South Gateway Visitor Center,** Tequa Plaza, 7000 Ariz. 179, Village of Oak Creek (© **928/284-5323**), which is open daily from 8:30am to 5pm; or the **North Gateway Visitor Center,** Oak Creek Vista Overlook, Ariz. 89A (© **928/282-4119**), which is open March 1 through November 1, weather permitting, daily from 8:30am to 5pm.

GETTING AROUND   Whether traveling by car or on foot, you'll need to cultivate patience when trying to cross major roads in Sedona. Traffic here, especially on weekends, is some of the worst in the state. Also be prepared for slow traffic on roads that have good views; drivers are often distracted by the red rocks. You may hear or see references to the **"Y,"** which refers to the intersection of Ariz. 179 and Ariz. 89A between the Tlaquepaque shopping plaza and uptown Sedona.

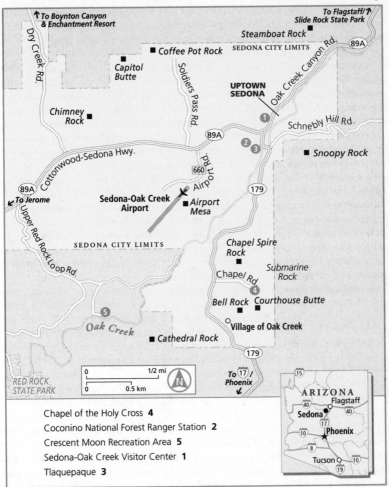

Chapel of the Holy Cross **4**
Coconino National Forest Ranger Station **2**
Crescent Moon Recreation Area **5**
Sedona-Oak Creek Visitor Center **1**
Tlaquepaque **3**

Rental cars are available through **Enterprise** (✆ 800/736-8222). You can also rent a jeep from **Farrabee Jeep Rentals of Sedona** (✆ 928/282-8700; www.farabeejeep rentals.com), which charges $125 to $185 a day. If a jeep isn't rugged enough for you, you can rent a Harley from **Red Rock Motorcycles,** 1350 W. Hwy. 89A (✆ **888/ 200-HOGS** or 928/204-0795). Bikes go for between $170 and $190 per day, with 6-hour rentals available as well.

EXPLORING RED-ROCK COUNTRY

The Grand Canyon may be Arizona's biggest attraction, but there's actually far more to do in Sedona. If you aren't an active type, there's the option of just gazing in awe at the rugged cliffs, needlelike pinnacles, and isolated buttes that rise from the green forest floor at the mouth of Oak Creek Canyon. Want to see more? Head out into the red rocks on a jeep tour or drift over the red rocks in a hot-air balloon. Want a closer look? Go for a hike, rent a mountain bike, go horseback riding. (See "Organized Tours" and "Getting Outside," below, for details.)

Although **Schnebly Hill Road,** which climbs into the red rocks east of Sedona, is a rough dirt road, it's a must for superb views of Sedona. This road is best driven in a high-clearance vehicle or SUV, but depending on how recently it has been maintained, it can be passable in a regular car. To reach this scenic road, head south out of Sedona on Ariz. 179, turn left after you cross the bridge over Oak Creek, and head up the road, which starts out paved but soon turns to dirt. The road climbs into the hills above town, every turn yielding a new and breathtaking view, and eventually reaches the top of the Mogollon Rim. At the rim is the Schnebly Hill overlook, offering the very best view in the area. If you don't feel comfortable doing this drive in your own vehicle, consider booking a jeep tour that heads up this way.

Just south of Sedona, on the east side of Ariz. 179, you'll see the aptly named **Bell Rock.** There's a parking area at the foot of this formation, and trails lead up to the top. Adjacent to Bell Rock is **Courthouse Butte,** and to the west stands **Cathedral Rock.** From the Chapel of the Holy Cross (see "Attractions & Activities Around Town," below) on Chapel Road, you can see **Eagle Head Rock** (from the front door of the chapel, look three-quarters of the way up the mountain to see the eagle's head), the **Twin Nuns** (two pinnacles standing side by side), and **Mother and Child Rock** (to the left of the Twin Nuns).

If you head west out of Sedona on Ariz. 89A and turn left onto Airport Road, you'll drive up onto **Airport Mesa,** which commands an unobstructed panorama of Sedona and the red rocks. About halfway up the mesa is a small parking area from which trails radiate. The views from here are among the best in the region, and the trails are very easy.

Boynton Canyon, located 8 miles west of the "Y," is a narrow red-rock canyon and is one of the most beautiful spots in the Sedona area. This canyon is also the site of the deluxe Enchantment resort, but hundreds of years before there were luxury casita suites here, there were Sinagua cliff dwellings. Several of these cliff dwellings can still be spotted high on the canyon walls. **Boynton Canyon Trail** leads 3 miles up into this canyon from a trail head parking area just outside the gates of Enchantment. To get to the trail head, drive west out of Sedona on Ariz. 89A, turn right on Dry Creek Road, take a left at the first **T** intersection, and a right at the second **T.**

On the way to Boynton Canyon, look north from Ariz. 89A, and you'll see **Coffee Pot Rock,** also known as Rooster Rock, rising 1,800 feet above Sedona. Three pinnacles, known as the **Three Golden Chiefs** by the Yavapai tribe, stand beside Coffee Pot Rock. As you drive up Dry Creek Road, on your right you'll see **Capitol Butte,** which resembles the U.S. Capitol.

To the west of Boynton Canyon, you can visit the well-preserved Sinagua cliff dwellings at **Palatki Ruins.** However, you now need a reservation to park at this site (call ✆ **928/282-3854** to make reservations). To reach the ruins, follow the directions to Boynton Canyon, but instead of turning right at the second **T** intersection, turn left onto unpaved Boynton Pass Road (Forest Rd. 152), which is one of the most scenic roads in the area. Follow this road to another **T** intersection and go right onto FR 525, then veer right onto FR 795, which dead-ends at the ruins. You can also get here by taking Ariz. 89A west from Sedona to FR 525, a gravel road leading north to FR 795. To visit Palatki, you'll need a Red Rock Pass (see "The High Cost of Red-Rock Views," below); ruins are usually open daily from 9:30am to 3:30pm. The dirt roads

> ## Value The High Cost of Red-Rock Views
>
> A Red Rock Pass will allow you to visit Palatki Ruins and the V Bar V Heritage Site (site of petroglyphs) and park at any national forest trailhead parking areas. The cost is $5 for a 1-day pass, $15 for a 7-day pass, and $20 for a 12-month pass. Passes are good for everyone in your vehicle. If you plan to be in the area for more than a week and also want to visit Grasshopper Point (a swimming hole), Banjo Bill (a picnic area), Call of the Canyon (the West Fork Oak Creek trail head), and Crescent Moon (Sedona's top photo-op site), you'll want to buy a Red Rock Grand Pass, for $40. These sites each charge a $5 to $7 admission, so if you aren't planning on going to all of them, the pass won't save you anything. For more information on the Red Rock Pass, visit www.red rockcountry.org.

around here become impassable to regular cars when they're wet, so don't try coming out here if the roads are at all muddy.

South of Ariz. 89A and a bit west of the turnoff for Boynton Canyon is Upper Red Rock Loop Road, which leads to **Crescent Moon Recreation Area,** a National Forest Service recreation area that has become a must-see for visitors to Sedona. Its popularity stems from a beautiful photograph of Oak Creek with **Cathedral Rock** in the background—an image that has been reproduced countless times in Sedona promotional literature and on postcards. Hiking trails lead up to Cathedral Rock. Admission is $7 per vehicle May through October and $5 November through April (unless you have previously purchased a Red Rock Grand Pass; see "The High Cost of Red-Rock Views," above). For more information, contact the Red Rock Ranger Station (see below).

If you continue on Upper Red Rock Loop Road, it becomes gravel for a while before becoming Lower Red Rock Loop Road and reaching **Red Rock State Park,** 4050 Red Rock Loop Rd. (© **928/282-6907**), which flanks Oak Creek. The views here take in many of the rocks listed above, and you have the additional bonus of being right on the creek (though swimming and wading are prohibited). Park admission is $6 per car. The park offers lots of guided walks and interpretive programs.

South of Sedona, near the junction of I-17 and Ariz. 179, you can visit one of the finest petroglyph sites in Arizona. The rock art at the **V Bar V Heritage Site** covers a small cliff face and includes images of herons and turtles. To get here, take the dirt road that leads east for 2⅔ miles from the junction of I-17 and Ariz. 179 to the Beaver Creek Campground. The entrance to the petroglyph site is just past the campground. From the parking area, it's about a half-mile walk to the petroglyphs, which are open Friday through Monday from 9:30am to 3:30pm. To visit this site, you'll need a Red Rock Pass or other valid pass. For information, contact the **Red Rock Ranger District** (© **928/282-4119**).

OAK CREEK CANYON

The **Mogollon Rim** (pronounced "*mug*-ee-un" by the locals) is a 2,000-foot escarpment cutting diagonally across central Arizona and on into New Mexico. At the top of the Mogollon Rim are the ponderosa pine forests of the high mountains, while at the bottom the lowland deserts begin. Of the many canyons cutting down from the rim, Oak Creek Canyon is the most beautiful (and one of the few that has a paved road down through it). Ariz. 89A runs through the canyon from Flagstaff to Sedona, winding its way down from the rim and paralleling Oak Creek. Along the way are overlooks, parks, picnic areas, campgrounds, cabin resorts, and small inns.

If you have a choice of how first to view Oak Creek Canyon, approach it from the north. Your first stop after traveling south from Flagstaff will be the **Oak Creek Canyon Vista,** which provides a view far down the valley to Sedona and beyond. The overlook is at the edge of the Mogollon Rim, and the road suddenly drops in tight switchbacks just south of here.

Although the top of the Mogollon Rim is a ponderosa pine forest and the bottom a desert, Oak Creek Canyon supports a forest of sycamores and other deciduous trees. There is no better time to drive scenic Ariz. 89A than between late September and mid-October, when the canyon is ablaze with red and yellow leaves.

In the desert, swimming holes are powerful magnets during the hot summer months, and consequently **Slide Rock State Park,** 6871 N. U.S. 89A (© **928/282-3034;** www.azstateparks.com), located 7 miles north of Sedona, is the most popular spot in all of Oak Creek Canyon. What pulls in the crowds of families and teenagers is the park's natural water slide and great little swimming hole. On hot days, the park is jammed with people splashing in the water and sliding over the algae-covered sandstone bottom of Oak Creek. Sunbathing and fishing are other popular pastimes. The park is open daily; admission is $8 per vehicle ($10 during the summer). There's another popular swimming area at **Grasshopper Point,** several miles closer to Sedona. Admission is $7 per vehicle, unless you have previously purchased a Red Rock Grand Pass (see "The High Cost of Red-Rock Views," above, for details).

Within Oak Creek Canyon, several hikes of different lengths are possible. By far the most spectacular and popular is the 6-mile round-trip up the **West Fork of Oak Creek.** This is a classic canyon-country hike with steep canyon walls rising up from the creek. At some points, the canyon is no more than 20 feet wide with walls rising up more than 200 feet. You can also extend the hike many more miles up the canyon for an overnight backpacking trip. The trail head for the West Fork of Oak Creek hike is 9.5 miles up Oak Creek Canyon from Sedona at the Call of the Canyon Recreation Area, which charges a $7 day-use fee per vehicle unless you have already purchased a Red Rock Grand Pass.

Stop by the Sedona–Oak Creek Chamber of Commerce for a free map of area hikes. The **Coconino National Forest's Red Rock Ranger Station,** 250 Brewer Road (© **928/282-4119;** www.fs.fed.us/r3/coconino), just west of the "Y," is an even better source of hiking information. It's open Monday through Friday from 8am to 4:30pm.

ATTRACTIONS & ACTIVITIES AROUND TOWN

Sedona's most notable architectural landmark is the **Chapel of the Holy Cross,** 780 Chapel Rd. (© **928/282-4069**), a small church built right into the red rock on the south side of town. The chapel sits high above the road just off Ariz. 179. With its contemporary styling, it is one of the most architecturally important modern churches in the country. Marguerite Brunswig Staude, a devout Catholic painter, sculptor, and designer, had the inspiration for the chapel in 1932, but it wasn't until 1957 that her dream was finally realized. The chapel's design is dominated by a simple cross forming the wall that faces the street. The cross and the starkly beautiful chapel seem to grow directly from the rock, allowing the red rock's natural beauty to speak for itself. It's open Monday through Saturday from 9am to 5pm and Sunday from 10am to 5pm.

The **Sedona Arts Center,** 15 Art Barn Rd. at Ariz. 89A (© **888/954-4442** or 928/ 282-3809; www.sedonaartscenter.com), near the north end of uptown Sedona, serves both as a gallery for work by local and regional artists and as a theater for plays and music performances.

To learn a bit about the local history, stop by the **Sedona Heritage Museum,** 735 Jordan Rd. (© **928/282-7038;** www.sedonamuseum.org), in Jordan Historical Park. The museum, which is housed in a historic home, is furnished with antiques and contains exhibits on the many movies that have been filmed in the area. The farm was once an apple orchard, and there's still apple-processing equipment in the barn. Hours are daily from 11am to 3pm; admission is $3.

Although Sedona isn't yet a resort spa destination on par with Phoenix or Tucson, it does have a few spas that might add just the right bit of pampering to your vacation. **Therapy on the Rocks,** 676 N. Hwy. 89A (© **928/282-3002;** www.myofascial release.com) is a longtime local favorite that offers massage, myofascial release, and great views of the red rocks. The **Red Rock Spa & Healing Center,** Creekside Plaza, 251 Hwy. 179 (© **928/203-9933;** www.redrockhealing.com), is just up the hill from Tlaquepaque shopping plaza and offers a variety of massages, wraps, scrubs, and facials. In the Village of Oak Creek, the **Hilton Spa,** at the Hilton Sedona Resort, 10 Ridge View Dr. (© **928/284-6975;** www.hiltonsedonaspa.com), offers a variety of treatments (try the Painted Desert clay wrap or Sedona stone massage). There are also exercise and yoga classes, a pool, and tennis and racquetball courts.

ORGANIZED TOURS

For an overview of Sedona, take a tour on the **Sedona Trolley** (© **928/282-4211;** www.sedonatrolley.com), which leaves several times daily on two separate tours. One tour visits Tlaquepaque shopping plaza, the Chapel of the Holy Cross, and several art galleries, while the other goes out through west Sedona to Boynton Canyon and Enchantment Resort. Tours are $10 for adults ($18 for both tours) and $5 for children 12 and under ($9 for both tours).

The red-rock country surrounding Sedona is the city's greatest natural attraction, and there's no better way to explore it than by four-wheel-drive vehicle on a jeep tour. These tours will get you out onto rugged roads and 4×4 trails with spectacular views. The unchallenged leader in Sedona jeep tours is **Pink Jeep Tours,** 204 N. Hwy. 89A (© **800/873-3662** or 928/282-5000; www.pinkjeep.com), which has been heading deep into the Coconino National Forest since 1958. It offers tours ranging in length from 1½ to 4 hours, however, the 2-hour "Broken Arrow" tour ($65) is the most adventurous and is the tour I recommend.

How about a chance to play cowboy? **A Day in the West,** 252 N. Hwy. 89A (© **800/9-SEDONA** or 928/282-4320; www.adayinthewest.com), has its own private ranch for some of its jeep tours and horseback rides. There are cowboy cookouts, too. Prices range from $45 to $145.

If you'd like to have a very knowledgeable local tour guide show you around places you're interested in seeing at your pace, I recommend getting in touch with Steve "Benny" Benedict at **Touch the Earth Adventures** (© **928/203-9132;** www.earth tours.com). Benny likes to take clients to spots that even many locals don't know about. And, if you want to go on a good vortex tour or an off-the-beaten-path guided hike, get in touch with Dennis Andres of **Meta Adventures** (© **928/204-2201;** www. metaadventures.com). Plan to pay $450 to $550 per couple for a full day of touring with either of these excellent guides. Shorter outings are also available.

For a tour of the Sedona area from a Native American perspective, contact **Way of the Ancients** (© 866/204-9243 or 928/204-9243; www.wayoftheancients.com), which offers 5-hour tours that cost $59. There are also excursions to the Hopi mesas ($125).

As spectacular as Sedona is from the ground, it is even more so from the air. **Arizona Helicopter Adventures** (© 800/282-5141 or 928/282-0904; www.azheli.com) offers short flights to different parts of this colorful region. Prices start at around $58 per person for a 12-minute flight. **Sky Safari Air Tours** (© 888/TOO-RIDE or 928/204-5939; www.sedonaairtours.com) offers a variety of flights in small planes. A 15-minute air tour will run you $49 per person, while a 30-minute tour will cost $79. Flights as far afield as the Grand Canyon and Canyon de Chelly can also be arranged.

My favorite Sedona air tours are those offered by **Red Rock Biplane Tours** (© 888/TOO-RIDE or 928/204-5939; www.sedonaairtours.com), which operates modern Waco open-cockpit biplanes. With the wind in your hair, you'll feel as though you've entered the world of *The English Patient.* Tours lasting 10 to 45 minutes are offered; a 20-minute tour costs $79 per person.

If something a bit slower is more your speed, how about drifting over the sculpted red buttes of Sedona in a hot-air balloon? **Northern Light Balloon Expeditions** (© 800/230-6222 or 928/282-2274; www.northernlightballoon.com) charges $170 per person; **Red Rock Balloon Adventures** (© 800/258-3754 or 928/284-0040; www.redrockballoons.com) charges $185 per person; while **Sky High Balloon Adventures** (© 800/551-7597 or 928/204-1395; www.skyhighballoons.com), which floats over the Verde Valley and includes a "splash-and-dash" descent to the river, charges $170 per person.

GETTING OUTSIDE

Hiking is the most popular outdoor activity in the Sedona area, with dozens of trails leading off into the red rocks. The most convenient trail is along the **Bell Rock Pathway,** which begins alongside Ariz. 179 just north of the Village of Oak Creek. The trail winds around the base of Bell Rock and accesses many other trails that lead up its sloping sides. It's about 5 miles to go all the way around Bell Rock. Unfortunately, it's a very popular hiking area and is always crowded.

You'll see fewer tourists if you head to the .75-mile **Cathedral Rock Trail,** which is also located between the Village of Oak Creek and uptown Sedona. The trail follows cairns (piles of rocks) up the slickrock slopes on the north side of Cathedral Rock. (To reach this trail, turn off Ariz. 179 at the sign for the Back o' Beyond housing development and watch for the trail head at the end of the paved road.) For convenience and solitude, you can't beat the **Mystic Trail,** which begins at an unmarked roadside pull-off on Chapel Road halfway between Ariz. 179 and the Chapel of the Holy Cross. This is an easy out-and-back trail that runs between a couple of housing developments, but once you're on the trail, you'll feel all alone.

Among the most popular trails in the Sedona area are those that lead into **Boynton Canyon** (site of Enchantment Resort). Here you'll glimpse ancient Native American ruins built into the red-rock cliffs. The scenery is stupendous, but the great numbers of other hikers on the trail detract considerably from the experience, and the parking lot fills up early. The 1.5-mile **Vultee Arch Trail,** which leads to an impressive sandstone arch, is another great hike. The turnoff for the trail head is 2 miles up Dry Creek Road and then another 3½ miles on a very rough dirt road. The **Devil's Bridge Trail,** which starts on the same dirt road, is a little easier to get to and leads to the largest natural sandstone arch in the area. This one is a 1.8-mile round-trip hike.

For the hands-down best views in Sedona, hike all or part of the **Airport Mesa Trail,** a 3.5-mile loop that circles Airport Mesa. With virtually no elevation gain, this is an easy hike. You'll find the trail head about halfway to the top of Airport Mesa on Airport Road. Try this one as early in the day as possible; by midday, the parking lot is usually full and it stays that way right through sunset.

For more information on hiking in Oak Creek Canyon (site of the famous West Fork of Oak Creek Trail), see "Oak Creek Canyon," above. For more information on all these hikes, contact the **Coconino National Forest's Red Rock Ranger Station,** 250 Brewer Rd. (© **928/282-4119;** www.fs.fed.us/r3/coconino), which is located just west of the junction of Ariz. 89A and Ariz. 179.

Sedona is rapidly becoming one of the Southwest's meccas for mountain biking. One of my favorite places to ride is around the base of Bell Rock. Starting at the trail head parking area just north of the Village of Oak Creek, you'll find the easy Bell Rock Path but also numerous more challenging trails.

Another great ride starts above uptown Sedona, where you can take the Jim Thompson Trail to Midgely Bridge or the network of trails that head toward Soldier Pass. The riding here is moderate and the views are superb. To reach these trails, take Jordan Road to a left onto Park Ridge Road, and follow this road to where it ends at a dirt trail head parking area. You can rent bikes from **Sedona Sports,** Creekside Plaza (below the "Y"), 251 N. Hwy. 179 (© **866/204-2377** or 928/282-1317; www.sedona sports.com), or **Mountain Bike Heaven,** 1695 W. Hwy. 89A (© **928/282-1312;** www.mountainbikeheaven.com). Rates are around $35 to $50 per day. **Sedona Bike & Bean,** 6020 Hwy. 179, Village of Oak Creek (© **928/284-0210;** www.bike-bean. com), across the street from the popular Bell Rock Pathway and its adjacent mountain-bike trails, rents bikes (and serves coffee). Bikes go for $29 to $40 for a full day.

Trail Horse Adventures (© **800/723-3538** or 928/282-7252; www.trailhorse adventures.com) offers guided horseback trail rides. A 2-hour ride (that includes creek crossings) will cost you $70. There are also breakfast, lunch, and sunset rides. **Sedona Red Rock Jeep Tours,** 270 N. Hwy. 89A (© **800/848-7728** or 928/282-6826; www.redrockjeep.com), also offers horseback rides ($75 for 2 hr.).

Oak Creek is well-known in Arizona as an excellent trout stream, and fly-fishing is quite popular here. The creek is stocked with trout during the summer. For supplies and local advice, drop by **On the Creek Sedona Outfitters,** 274 Apple Ave., Suite B (© **877/533-9973** or 928/203-9973). This shop also offers a guide service. If you want to take the family fishing, try the **Rainbow Trout Farm,** 3500 N. Ariz. 89A (© **928/282-5799**), 4 miles north of Sedona.

Sedona has surprisingly few golf courses, but they offer superb views to distract you from your game. The **Oakcreek Country Club,** 690 Bell Rock Blvd. (© **888/703-9489** or 928/284-1660; www.oakcreekcountryclub.com), south of town off Ariz. 179, has stunning views from the course. Greens fees are $59 to $99. The **Sedona Golf Resort** ★★, 35 Ridge Trail Dr. (© **877/733-9885** or 928/284-9355; www.sedona golfresort.com), south of town on Ariz. 179, offers similarly excellent views of the red rocks. Greens fees are $59 to $115.

SHOPPING

Ever since the Cowboy Artists of America organization was founded in Sedona back in 1965 (at what is now the Cowboy Club restaurant), this town has had a reputation as an artists' community. Today, with dozens of galleries around town, it's obvious that art is one of the driving forces behind the local economy. Most of Sedona's galleries specialize in traditional Western, contemporary Southwestern, and Native American art, and in some galleries, you'll see works by members of the Cowboy Artists of America. You'll find the greatest concentration of galleries and shops in the uptown area of Sedona (along Ariz. 89A just north of the "Y") and at Tlaquepaque.

With more than 40 stores and restaurants, **Tlaquepaque** (© 928/282-4838; www.tlaq.com), on Ariz. 179 at the bridge over Oak Creek on the south side of Sedona, bills itself as Sedona's arts-and-crafts village and is designed to resemble a Mexican village. (It was named after a famous arts-and-crafts neighborhood in the suburbs of Guadalajara.) The maze of narrow alleys, courtyards, fountains, and even a chapel and a bell tower are worth a visit even if you aren't in a buying mood. Most of the shops here sell high-end art. I wish all shopping centers were such fascinating places. **Hillside Sedona,** just south of Tlaquepaque, is another shopping center dedicated to art galleries and upscale retail shops. It's at 671 Hwy. 179 (© 928/282-4500; www.hillsidesedona.com).

WHERE TO STAY

Sedona is one of the most popular destinations in the Southwest, with dozens of hotels and motels around town. However, across the board, accommodations here tend to be overpriced for what you get. My advice is to save money elsewhere on your trip and make Sedona the place where you splurge on a room with a view.

VERY EXPENSIVE

El Portal Sedona ★★ You just can't help but fall in love with this amazing inn. Owner Steve Segner and his wife, Connie, have done everything right and the overall experience here makes this one of the very best lodgings in the state. Located adjacent to the Tlaquepaque shopping center and built of hand-formed adobe blocks, El Portal, with its pleasant central courtyard, is designed to resemble a 200-year-old hacienda and is a monument to fine craftsmanship. The inn is filled with antiques, including not only the furniture, but also the door knobs, hinges, and even air-conditioning vents. Each of the large guest rooms has its own distinctive character, from Arts and Crafts to cowboy chic (rustic log furniture). All but one room have whirlpool tubs, and many rooms have private balconies with red-rock views. Exquisite breakfasts and weekend dinners are served.

95 Portal Lane, Sedona, AZ 86336. © 800/313-0017. Fax 928/203-9401. www.innsedona.com. 12 units. $225–$495 double. Rates include afternoon hors d'oeuvres. 2-night minimum on weekends and holidays. AE, DISC, MC, V. Pets accepted ($35 fee). No children under 10. **Amenities:** Restaurant (New American); access to nearby health club and adjacent resort pool; bikes; concierge; massage; laundry service; guided hikes. *In room:* A/C, TV/DVD, dataport, fridge, hair dryer, iron, free local calls, high-speed Internet access, wi-fi.

Enchantment Resort ★★★ Located at the mouth of Boynton Canyon, this resort more than lives up to its name. The setting is breathtaking, the pueblo-style architecture blends in with the landscape, and the affiliated Mii amo spa is one of the finest in the state. The individual casitas can be booked as two-bedroom suites, one-bedroom suites, or single rooms, but it's worth reserving a suite (ask for one of the newer units) just so you can enjoy the casita living rooms, which feature high beamed ceilings and beehive fireplaces. All the rooms, however, have patios with dramatic views. Both the Yavapai Restaurant (p. 513) and a less formal bar and grill offer tables outdoors; lunch on the terrace should not be missed.

The Mii amo spa is actually a separate entity within the resort and has its own restaurant, guest rooms, and rates (see separate review, below). Enchantment Resort guests do, however, have access to the spa facilities.

525 Boynton Canyon Rd., Sedona, AZ 86336. ⓒ **800/826-4180** or 928/282-2900. Fax 928/282-9249. www.enchantment resort.com. 220 units. $295–$425 double; $395–$525 junior suite; $625–$855 1-bedroom suite; $875–$2,005 2-bedroom suite. AE, DC, DISC, MC, V. **Amenities:** 3 restaurants (New American, regional Southwestern, spa cuisine); lounge; 7 pools; par-3 golf course; putting green; 7 tennis courts; croquet court; full-service spa; Jacuzzi; bike rentals; children's programs; concierge; business center; room service; massage; babysitting; guest laundry; laundry service; dry cleaning. *In room:* A/C, TV, dataport, minibar, coffeemaker, hair dryer, iron, safe, high-speed Internet access.

Mii amo, a destination spa at Enchantment ★★★   This full-service health spa inside the gates of the exclusive Enchantment Resort boasts the best location in the state. Designed to resemble a modern Santa Fe–style pueblo from the outside, the spa backs up to red-rock cliffs and is shaded by cottonwood trees. Though small, Mii amo is well designed, with indoor and outdoor pools and outdoor massage cabanas at the foot of the cliffs. Guest rooms, which open onto a courtyard, have a bold, contemporary styling (mixed with Indonesian art and artifacts) that makes them some of the finest accommodations in the state. All units have private patios and gas fireplaces. No other spa in Arizona has a more Southwestern feel.

525 Boynton Canyon Rd., Sedona, AZ 86336. ⓒ **888/749-2137** or 928/203-8500. Fax 928/203-8599. www.miiamo.com. 16 units. 3-night packages: Apr–May and Sept–Oct $1,950–$2,890 per person; Nov–Feb $1,650–$2,550 per person; Mar and June–Aug $1,830–$2,730 per person. Rates include 3 meals per day and 6 spa treatments. AE, DC, DISC, MC, V. **Amenities:** Restaurant (New American/spa cuisine); 2 pools (indoor and outdoor); exercise room; full-service spa with 24 treatment rooms and wide variety of body treatments; 3 Jacuzzis; bike rentals; concierge; room service; laundry service; dry cleaning. *In room:* A/C, TV, dataport, minibar, coffeemaker, hair dryer, iron, safe.

EXPENSIVE

Adobe Village Graham Inn ★★   A garden full of bronze statues of children greets you when you pull up to this luxurious inn in the Village of Oak Creek, 6 miles south of uptown Sedona. The inn lies almost at the foot of Bell Rock and features a variety of themed accommodations. The villas, the Sundance room, and the Sedona suite are the most impressive rooms here. My favorite is the Purple Lizard villa, which opts for a colorful Taos-style interior and an amazing rustic canopy bed. The Wilderness villa resembles a luxurious log cabin. The Lonesome Dove villa is a sort of upscale cowboy cabin with a fireplace, potbelly stove, and round hot tub in a "barrel." Can you say *romantic?* This inn also operates the Adobe Grand Villas in West Sedona.

150 Canyon Circle Dr., Sedona, AZ 86351. ⓒ **800/228-1425** or 928/284-1425. Fax 928/284-0767. www.sedonas finest.com. 11 units. $189–$319 double; $349–$558 suite; $369–$469 casita. Rates include full breakfast. AE, DISC, MC, V. **Amenities:** Outdoor pool; Jacuzzi; bikes; concierge; business center; room service; massage. *In room:* A/C, TV/VCR, dataport, coffeemaker, hair dryer, iron, free local calls.

Amara Creekside Resort ★★   This stylish boutique hotel offers the best of both worlds here in Sedona, with views of the red rocks and frontage on an Oak Creek swimming hole. The minimalist decor and Zen-inspired style are a welcome addition to the Sedona hotel scene. From the outside, the hotel fits right in with the red-rock surroundings, while inside, bold splashes of color contrast with black-and-white photos. Guest rooms all have balconies or patios, wonderful pillow-top beds, and furnishings in black and red. The resort's dining room draws on interesting flavor influences from around the globe. Try to arrange for a sunset dinner while you're here.

310 N. Hwy. 89A, Sedona, AZ 86336. ⓒ **866/455-6610** or 928/282-4828. Fax 928/282-4825. www.amararesort.com. 100 units. $149–$239 double; $189–$489 suite. Children 18 and under stay free in parent's room. AE, DC, DISC, MC, V. **Amenities:** Restaurant (New American); lounge; outdoor saltwater pool; exercise room; Jacuzzi; concierge; business center; room service; massages and spa treatments; babysitting; laundry service; dry cleaning. *In room:* A/C, TV/DVD, dataport, minibar, coffeemaker, hair dryer, iron, high-speed Internet access, wi-fi.

Briar Patch Inn ★★ *(Value)*   If you're searching for tranquillity or a romantic retreat amid the cool shade of Oak Creek Canyon, this is the place. Located 3 miles north of Sedona on the banks of Oak Creek, this inn's cottages are surrounded by beautiful grounds where bird songs and the babbling creek set the mood. The cottages date from the 1940s, but have been attractively updated (some with flagstone floors), and a Western/rustic Mexican style now predominates. Most units have fireplaces and kitchenettes. There are also swimming holes and a stone gazebo for massages. The only drawback is the lack of red-rock views from the tree-shaded location.

3190 N. Hwy. 89A, Sedona, AZ 86336. © **888/809-3030** or 928/282-2342. Fax 928/282-2399. www.briarpatch inn.com. 18 units. $179–$345 double. Rates include full breakfast. Children under 4 stay free in parent's room. AE, MC, V. **Amenities:** Access to nearby health club; concierge; massage; babysitting. *In room:* A/C, fridge, coffeemaker, hair dryer, iron, no phone.

Canyon Villa ★★   Located in the Village of Oak Creek, 6 miles south of Sedona, this bed-and-breakfast offers luxurious accommodations and spectacular views of the red rocks. All rooms but one have views, as do the pool area, living room, and dining room. Guest rooms are varied in style—Victorian, Santa Fe, country, rustic—but no matter what the decor, the furnishings are impeccable. All rooms have balconies or patios, and several have fireplaces. Breakfast is a lavish affair meant to be lingered over, and in the afternoon there's an elaborate spread of appetizers.

125 Canyon Circle Dr., Sedona, AZ 86351. © **800/453-1166** or 928/284-1226. Fax 928/284-2114. www.canyon villa.com. 11 units. $189–$304 double. Rates include full breakfast. AE, DC, DISC, MC, V. No children under 11. **Amenities:** Pool; concierge. *In room:* A/C, TV, hair dryer, iron, free local calls, wi-fi.

Garland's Oak Creek Lodge ★ *(Finds)*   Located 8 miles north of Sedona in the heart of Oak Creek Canyon, this lodge is often filled with returning guests who reserve a year in advance (last-minute cancellations do occur, so don't despair). What makes the lodge so special? Maybe it's that you have to drive *through* Oak Creek to get to your log cabin. Maybe it's the beautiful gardens or the slow, relaxing atmosphere of an old-time summer getaway. The well-maintained cabins, most of which have air-conditioning, are rustic but comfortable; the larger ones have their own fireplaces. Meals include organic fruits and vegetables grown on the property, and there's a yoga pavilion overlooking the creek.

P.O. Box 152, Sedona, AZ 86339. © **928/282-3343**. www.garlandslodge.com. 16 units. $200–$235 double (plus 15% service charge). Rates include breakfast and dinner. 2-night minimum. Children under 2 stay free in parent's room. MC, V. Closed mid-Nov to Mar and Sun year-round. **Amenities:** Dining room; lounge; tennis court; access to nearby health club; concierge; massage; babysitting. *In room:* No phone.

Hilton Sedona Resort & Spa ★★   This resort boasts not only one of the most breathtaking golf courses in the state, but also the best pool area north of Phoenix. While golf is the driving force behind most stays here, anyone looking for an active vacation will find plenty to keep themselves busy. Guest rooms are suites of varying sizes, with fireplaces and balconies or patios. The resort's restaurant plays up its views of the golf course and red rocks. About the only drawback to this place is that it's quite a ways outside of uptown Sedona itself (actually south of the Village of Oak Creek).

90 Ridge Trail Dr., Sedona, AZ 86351. © **800/HILTONS** or 928/284-4040. Fax 928/284-6940. www.hiltonsedona.com. 219 units. Mar–June $159–$269 double; July–Sept $129–$239 double; Oct to mid-Nov $159–$269 double; mid-Nov to Feb $129–$239 double. Children under 18 stay free in parent's room. AE, DC, DISC, MC, V. Pets accepted ($50 non-refundable deposit). **Amenities:** Restaurant (Southwestern/American); lounge; 3 pools; 18-hole golf course; 3 tennis courts; full-service spa; 3 Jacuzzis; sauna; children's programs; concierge; business center; room service; massage; babysitting; guest laundry; laundry service; dry cleaning. *In room:* A/C, TV, dataport, minibar, coffeemaker, hair dryer, iron, safe, high-speed Internet access.

L'Auberge de Sedona ★★   Shaded by towering sycamore trees and with colorful flower gardens surrounding its many cottages, the resort is a sort of French country retreat in the middle of the desert. L'Auberge's cottages, which look like rustic log cabins from the outside have a classic styling truly worthy of a luxury French country inn (leather couches, gorgeous beds, plush towels, wood-burning fireplaces). Although there are rooms in the main lodge, the much larger cottages are definitely worth the extra cost. The restaurant, which carries on the French theme in both its decor and menu, has a creekside terrace during the summer.

301 L'Auberge Lane (P.O. Box B), Sedona, AZ 86339. ✆ **800/272-6777** or 928/282-1661. Fax 928/282-2885. www. lauberge.com. 58 units. $169–$375 double; $225–$459 cottage; $345–$595 2-bedroom cottage. Children under 12 stay free in parent's room. AE, DC, DISC, MC, V. Pets accepted ($75 fee). **Amenities:** Restaurant (French); access to nearby health club; Jacuzzi; concierge; room service; babysitting; dry cleaning. *In room:* A/C, TV, dataport, minibar, coffeemaker, hair dryer, iron, safe, high-speed Internet access.

The Lodge at Sedona ★   Set amid pine trees a block off Ariz. 89A in west Sedona, this large inn is decorated in the Arts and Crafts style, which makes it one of the more distinctive inns in Sedona. The best rooms are those on the ground floor. These tend to be large, and several are suites. Second floor rooms are more economical and tend to be fairly small. Suites are only slightly more expensive than deluxe rooms, which makes the suites the best choices here. If you want views, book one of the small upstairs rooms or the Desert Trail, Copper Canyon, or Whispering Winds suite. Breakfasts are five-course affairs that will often tide you over until dinner, and on Saturday nights, gourmet dinners are available.

125 Kallof Place, Sedona, AZ 86336. ✆ **800/619-4467** or 928/204-1942. Fax 928/204-2128. www.lodgeatsedona. com. 14 units. $160–$325 double. Rates include full breakfast. 2-night minimum on weekends. DISC, MC, V. Pets accepted ($200 deposit plus $35 per night). **Amenities:** Access to nearby health club; concierge; business center; massage; dry cleaning. *In room:* A/C, hair dryer, iron, no phone.

Saddle Rock Ranch ★   The stunning views alone make this one of Sedona's top lodging choices, but in addition, you get classic Western ranch styling in a 1926-vintage home that once belonged to Barry Goldwater. Walls of stone and adobe, huge exposed beams, and plenty of windows to take in the scenery are enough to enchant guests even before they reach their rooms. In one room you'll find Victorian elegance, in another an English canopy bed and stone fireplace. Dressing areas and private gardens add to the charm. The third room is a separate little cottage with a pine bed, flagstone floors, and a beamed ceiling. The pool and whirlpool have one of the best views in town. A trail leads up to Airport Mesa.

255 Rock Ridge Dr., Sedona, AZ 86336. ✆ **866/282-7640** or 928/282-7640. Fax 928/282-7640. www.saddlerock ranch.com. 3 units. $159–$209 double. Rates include full breakfast. MC, V. No children under 14. **Amenities:** Small outdoor pool; access to nearby health club; Jacuzzi; concierge; laundry service. *In room:* A/C, TV/VCR, hair dryer.

MODERATE

Best Western Inn of Sedona ★   Located about midway between uptown and west Sedona, this hotel has great views of the red rocks from its wide terraces and outdoor pool. Unfortunately, although the guest rooms are comfortable enough, not all of them have views. However, the modern Southwestern decor and the setting, surrounded by native landscaping and located beyond the tourist mainstream, make this an appealing choice.

1200 W. Hwy. 89A, Sedona, AZ 86336. ✆ **800/292-6344** or 928/282-3072. Fax 928/282-7218. www.innofsedona. com. 110 units. $139–$189 double. Rates include continental breakfast. Children 12 and under stay free in parent's room. AE, DC, DISC, MC, V. Pets accepted ($10 fee). **Amenities:** Small outdoor pool; exercise room; Jacuzzi; concierge; dry cleaning. *In room:* A/C, TV, dataport, fridge, coffeemaker, hair dryer, iron, free local calls.

Forest Houses ⭐ *Finds*   Set at the upper end of Oak Creek Canyon and built right on the banks of the creek, these rustic houses and apartments date back to the 1940s. Built by a stone sculptor, they feature artistic touches that set them apart from your average cabins. About half of the houses are built right on the creek, and some seem to grow straight from the rocks in the streambed. Terraces let you fully enjoy the setting. One of my favorite units is the two-bedroom Cloud House, with stone floors, peeled-log woodwork, and a loft. This property is certainly not for everyone (no phones, no TVs, and you have to drive through the creek to get here), but those who discover the Forest Houses often come back year after year.

9275 N. Hwy. 89A, Sedona, AZ 86336. ⓒ **928/282-2999.** www.foresthousesresort.com. 15 units. $90–$145 double. 2- to 4-night minimum stay. AE, MC, V. Pets accepted ($20 deposit). Closed Jan to mid-Mar. *In room:* Kitchen, no phone.

The Orchards Inn of Sedona ⭐⭐   Located in the heart of uptown Sedona and affiliated with the L'Auberge de Sedona (see review, above), this hotel claims an enviable location on a hillside above Oak Creek, with some of the best views in Sedona. Despite the name, this is much more of a hotel than an inn, and the rooms have a very tasteful and comfortable classic style. Don't be discouraged when you drive up to the front door; though the hotel is located amid the uptown tourist crowds, it seems miles away once you check into your room and gaze out at the red rocks.

254 Hwy. 89A, Sedona, AZ 86336. ⓒ **800/272-6777** or 928/282-1661. Fax 928/282-7818. www.orchardsinn.com. 41 units. Jan–Feb and late Nov to mid-Dec $125 double, $165 suite; Mar to late Nov and late Dec $145 double, $195 suite. Children under 12 stay free in parent's room. AE, DC, DISC, MC, V. **Amenities:** Restaurant (Regional American); small outdoor pool; access to nearby health club; Jacuzzi; concierge; room service; babysitting; dry cleaning. *In room:* A/C, TV, dataport, fridge, coffeemaker, hair dryer, iron, safe, high-speed Internet access.

INEXPENSIVE

Cedars Resort on Oak Creek   Located right at the "Y" and within walking distance of uptown Sedona, this motel has fabulous views across Oak Creek to the towering red rocks. Guest rooms are large and have been recently refurbished. For the best views, ask for a king-size room. A long stairway leads down to the creek.

20 W. Hwy. 89A (P.O. Box 292), Sedona, AZ 86339. ⓒ **800/874-2072** or 928/282-7010. Fax 928/282-5372. www. sedonacedarsresort.com. 38 units. $99–$139 double. Rates include continental breakfast. Children 12 and under stay free in parent's room. AE, DC, DISC, MC, V. **Amenities:** Small outdoor pool; exercise room; access to nearby health club; Jacuzzi; concierge; massage; coin-op laundry. *In room:* A/C, TV, dataport, fridge, coffeemaker, hair dryer, iron, free local calls, wi-fi.

Don Hoel's Cabins ⭐ *Kids*   If you're looking for an economically priced place to stay in the heart of Oak Creek Canyon, check out these recently updated and upgraded cabins. With their brown-and-green color scheme, the cabins feel like they belong in a national park. Although the cabins are located across the road from Oak Creek, the property includes 700 feet of private creek bank, which is particularly popular for trout fishing. With its playground, volleyball court, and outdoor Ping-Pong table, this is a good choice for families. Cabins have barbecue grills and picnic tables.

9440 N. Hwy. 89A, Sedona, AZ 86336. ⓒ **800/292-HOEL** or 928/282-3560. Fax 928/282-3654. www.hoels.com. 19 units. $100–$135 cabin for 2. 2-night minimum on weekends, 3-night minimum on certain holidays. Rates include continental breakfast. AE, MC, V. Closed Jan 1 to first weekend in Feb. **Amenities:** Playground. *In room:* Fridge, coffeemaker, no phone.

Matterhorn Inn   Located in the heart of the uptown shopping district, this choice is convenient to restaurants and shops, and all guest rooms have excellent views of the red-rock canyon walls. Although the Matterhorn is set above a row of shops fronting on busy Ariz. 89A, if you lie in bed and keep your eyes on the rocks, you'd never know there was so much going on below you. This place is a great value for Sedona.

230 Apple Ave., Sedona, AZ 86336. ℂ 800/372-8207 or 928/282-7176. www.matterhorninn.com. 23 units. Mid-Feb to Nov $79–$139 double; Dec to mid-Feb $69–$119 double. Children under 5 stay free in parent's room. AE, MC, V. Pets accepted ($10 per day). **Amenities:** Small outdoor pool; access to nearby health club; Jacuzzi. *In room:* A/C, TV, dataport, fridge, coffeemaker, hair dryer, iron, free local calls, wi-fi.

Rose Tree Inn *Finds* This little inn, only a block from Sedona's uptown shopping district, is tucked amid pretty gardens on a quiet street. The property consists of an eclectic cluster of older buildings that have all been renovated. Each unit is furnished differently—one Victorian, one Southwestern, two with gas fireplaces. Four guest rooms have kitchenettes, making them good choices for families or for longer stays. The Rose Tree Inn also handles bookings for a pair of modern little apartments a block away. Called the Rooms Upstairs, these apartments are an economical way to make yourself at home here in Sedona.

376 Cedar St., Sedona, AZ 86336. ℂ 888/282-2065 or 928/282-2065. www.rosetreeinn.com. 5 units. $89–$135 double. Children under 16 stay free in parent's room. AE, MC, V. **Amenities:** Concierge; guest laundry. *In room:* A/C, TV/VCR, coffeemaker, hair dryer, iron, free local calls, wi-fi.

Sky Ranch Lodge This motel is located atop Airport Mesa and has the most stupendous vista in town. From here you can see the entire red-rock country, with Sedona filling the valley below. Although the rooms are fairly standard motel issue, some have such features as gas fireplaces, barn-wood walls, and balconies. Only the non-view units fall into the inexpensive category, but those great views are just steps away. The more expensive rooms with views aren't really worth the price.

Airport Rd. (P.O. Box 2579), Sedona, AZ 86339. ℂ 888/708-6400 or 928/282-6400. Fax 928/282-7682. www.sky ranchlodge.com. 94 units. $75–$189 double. AE, MC, V. Pets accepted ($10 per night). **Amenities:** Small outdoor pool; Jacuzzi; coin-op laundry. *In room:* A/C, TV, dataport.

CAMPGROUNDS

Within Oak Creek Canyon along Ariz. 89A, there are five National Forest Service campgrounds. **Manzanita,** 6 miles north of town, is both the largest and the most pleasant (and the only one open in winter). Other Oak Creek Canyon campgrounds include **Bootlegger,** 9 miles north of town; **Cave Springs,** 12 miles north of town; and **Pine Flat,** 13 miles north of town. All of these campgrounds charge $16 per night. The **Beaver Creek Campground,** 3 miles east of I-17 on FR 618, which is an extension of Ariz. 179 (take Exit 298 off I-17), is a pleasant spot near the V-Bar-V Heritage Site. Campsites here are $12 per night. For more information on area campgrounds, contact the **Coconino National Forest's Red Rock Ranger Station,** 250 Brewer Rd. (ℂ **928/282-4119;** www.fs.fed.us/r3/coconino), on Brewer Road just west of the junction of Ariz. 89A and Ariz. 179. Reservations can be made for Pine Flat and Cave Spring Creek campgrounds by contacting the **National Recreation Reservation Center** (ℂ 877/444-6777 or 518/885-3639; www.reserveusa.com).

WHERE TO DINE
EXPENSIVE
Cowboy Club Grille & Spirits ☆ SOUTHWESTERN With its big booths, huge steer horns over the bar, and cowboy gear adorning the walls, this restaurant looks like a glorified cowboy steakhouse, but the menu isn't the sort any real cowboy would

likely have anything to do with. Start out with fried cactus strips with black-bean gravy or perhaps a rattlesnake brochette. For an entree, be sure to try the buffalo sirloin, served with a flavorful sauce. At lunch, try the buffalo burger or a smoked buffalo sandwich. Service is relaxed and friendly. It was in this building in 1965 that the Cowboy Artists of America organization was formed. The adjacent Silver Saddle Room is a more upscale spin on the same concept, with similar menu prices.

241 N. Hwy. 89A. ✆ **928/282-4200.** www.cowboyclub.com. Reservations recommended. Main courses $9–$19 lunch, $10–$35 dinner. AE, DISC, MC, V. Daily 11am–4pm and 5–10pm.

El Portal Sedona ★★ NEW AMERICAN/SOUTHWESTERN   Although El Portal is primarily a deluxe inn, it also serves superb dinners on Friday and Saturday nights. These dinners provide anyone who is not staying at this inn a chance to lounge around in the courtyard and living room/dining room and get a sense for what it is like to stay here. The menu is short and usually includes about a half-dozen entrees and an equal number of appetizers and salads. If the baked brie with roasted garlic and raspberry chipotle sauce is on the menu, don't even think of resisting. Grilled sea bass with roasted poblano chiles and sweet onions in chardonnay-lemon-cilantro broth and spice-encrusted duck breast with shallot-cherry–pinot noir sauce are just two examples of the sorts of entrees you can expect. Be sure to accompany your dinner with a bottle of wine from Sedona's own Echo Canyon Winery.

95 Portal Lane. ✆ **928/203-4942.** www.innsedona.com. Reservations required. 4-course prix-fixe menu $45–$49. AE, DISC, MC, V. Fri–Sat 5:30–8pm.

The Heartline Cafe ★★ SOUTHWESTERN/INTERNATIONAL   The heartline, from Zuni mythology, is a symbol of health and longevity; it is also a symbol for the healthful, creative food served here. Attention to detail and imaginative flavor combinations are the order of the day. To start with, don't miss the tea-smoked chicken dumplings with spicy peanut sauce or the Gorgonzola torte with caramelized pear. Memorable entrees include pecan-crusted local trout with Dijon cream sauce. Those searching out variety in vegetarian choices will find it here. The beautiful courtyard and traditionally elegant interior are good places to savor a meal accompanied by a selection from the reasonably priced wine list.

1610 W. Hwy. 89A. ✆ **928/282-0785.** www.heartlinecafe.com. Reservations recommended. Main courses $8–$15 lunch, $15–$27 dinner. AE, DISC, MC, V. Mon–Thurs 11am–2:30pm and 5–9pm; Fri–Sat 11am–2:30pm and 5–9:30pm.

René at Tlaquepaque ★ CONTINENTAL/AMERICAN   Although a formal dining experience and traditional French fare may seem out of place in a town that celebrates its cowboy heritage, René's makes fine dining seem as natural as mesquite-grilled steak and cowboy beans. Located in Tlaquepaque, the city's upscale south-of-the-border-themed shopping center, this restaurant is a great place for a special meal. You might start off with escargots or the salad of spinach and wild mushroom, followed by the house specialty, rack of lamb. More adventurous diners may want to try the excellent tenderloin of venison with whiskey–juniper berry sauce. Finish with a flambéed dessert and selections from the after-dinner drink cart.

At Tlaquepaque, 336 Ariz. 179, Suite 118. ✆ **928/282-9225.** www.rene-sedona.com. Reservations recommended. Main courses $9–$16 lunch, $20–$40 dinner. AE, MC, V. Sun–Thurs 11:30am to 2:30pm and 5:30–8:30pm; Fri–Sat 11:30am–3pm and 5:30–9pm.

Shugrue's Hillside Grill ★★ NEW AMERICAN/CONTINENTAL   Located at the back of the Hillside Sedona shopping plaza, this is the most upscale outpost in a small chain of popular Arizona restaurants. Although the prices are high at dinner, if you come before the sun sets, you'll be treated to unforgettable views out the walls of glass. The extensive menu includes influences from around the world. For a starter, try the blackened shrimp saganaki. There are plenty of good steak and fish entrees. For dessert, don't miss the bread pudding if it happens to be on the menu that evening.

671 Hwy. 179. ⓒ **928/282-5300.** www.shugrues.com. Reservations highly recommended. Main courses $8–$18 lunch, $10–$32 dinner. AE, DC, MC, V. Sun–Thurs 11:30am–3pm and 5–9pm; Fri–Sat 11:30am–3pm and 5–10pm.

Yavapai Restaurant ⚝ SOUTHWESTERN   The Yavapai Restaurant, at the exclusive Enchantment Resort, has the best views and most memorable setting of any restaurant in the Sedona area. It is also one of the town's most formal restaurants, which doesn't quite fit with the rugged setting, but is in keeping with Enchantment's exclusive character. The menu changes regularly to take advantage of seasonal ingredients, but keep an eye out for venison dishes and veal chops with the sauce of the moment. There's just something about the setting that makes these dishes seem just that much better. Because the scenery is every bit as important as the food here, make sure you make dinner reservations to take in the sunset on the red rocks.

At Enchantment Resort, 525 Boynton Canyon Rd. ⓒ **928/204-6000.** Reservations required. Main courses $12–$18 lunch, $24–$38 dinner; Sun brunch $33. AE, DISC, MC, V. Mon–Sat 6:30–11am, 11:30am–2:30pm, and 5:30–9:30pm; Sun 10:30am–2:30pm.

MODERATE

Cucina Rústica ⚝⚝ MEDITERRANEAN/SOUTHWESTERN   With its various distinct dining rooms and numerous antique doors, this sister restaurant to west Sedona's wonderful Dahl & DiLuca (see review, below), feels like a luxurious villa. One dining room has a central dome that is lit by what appear to be thousands of stars. For a genuine starlit dinner, ask for a seat on the patio. Start with the *bruschetta pomodoro*, a tomato and basil appetizer that tastes like a bite of summer, then move on to the *gamberi del capitano*. These grilled prawns, wrapped in radicchio and prosciutto, are among the best prawns I've ever had—positively ambrosial.

7000 Hwy. 179, Village of Oak Creek. ⓒ **928/284-3010.** Reservations recommended. Main courses $12–$26. AE, DC, DISC, MC, V. Daily 5–9 or 10pm.

Dahl & DiLuca ⚝⚝ ROMAN ITALIAN   A faux Tuscan villa interior, complete with a bar in a grotto, makes this the most romantic restaurant in Sedona, and the excellent Italian food makes it that much more unforgettable. Be sure to start with some of the *pane romano,* which, as far as we're concerned, is the best garlic bread west of New York's Little Italy. Pasta predominates here, and portions are big. I like the linguine with calamari and mushrooms. The kitchen also serves up a panoply of deftly prepared veal, seafood, chicken, and vegetarian dishes. The eggplant Parmesan and portobello *alla griglia* are real standouts. Genial and efficient service, reasonably priced wines, and nightly live music make this place even more enjoyable.

2321 W. Hwy. 89A (in west Sedona diagonally across from the Safeway Plaza). ⓒ **928/282-5219.** www.dahl-diluca. com. Reservations recommended. Main courses $11–$27. AE, DC, DISC, MC, V. Daily 5–9 or 10pm.

Fournos Restaurant ⚝ *Finds* MEDITERRANEAN   In contrast to the glitz and modern Southwest decor of so many of Sedona's restaurants, Fournos is a refreshingly casual place run by the husband-and-wife team of Shirley and Demetrios Fournos. In the kitchen, chef Demetrios cooks up a storm, preparing such dishes as shrimp flambéed in ouzo and baked with feta; lamb Cephalonian with herbs and potatoes; and poached fish Mykonos with a sauce of yogurt, onions, mayonnaise, and butter. Other specialties are rack of lamb and lamb Wellington. To make a reservation, stop by and put your name on the white board out front.

3000 W. Hwy. 89A. ℭ 928/282-3331. Reservations highly recommended. Main courses $16–$20. AE, DISC, MC, V. Thurs–Sat seatings at 6 and 8pm.

INEXPENSIVE

The Hideaway Restaurant ITALIAN/DELI   This casual family restaurant is as popular with locals as it is with visitors. Basic pizzas, subs, sandwiches, salads, and pastas are the choices here, and both the salad dressings and sausages are made on the premises. However, most people come for the knockout views. From the shady porch, you can see the creek below and the red rocks rising across the canyon. Lunch or an early sunset dinner are your best bets. The *paisano* (Sicilian sausage soup and a sandwich) lunch and antipasto salad are both good choices.

Country Sq., Ariz. 179. ℭ 928/282-4204. Reservations accepted only for parties of 10 or more. Main courses $6–$15. AE, DC, DISC, MC, V. Daily 11am–9pm.

Javelina Cantina ✦ MEXICAN   Although Javelina Cantina is part of a chain of Arizona restaurants, the formula works, and few diners leave disappointed. Sure, the restaurant is touristy, but it has good Mexican food, a lively atmosphere, decent views, and a convenient location in the Hillside shops. The grilled fish tacos are tasty, as is the pork adobo sandwich. Other dishes worth trying include the salmon tostadas and the enchiladas made with potatoes, spinach, and cheese. There are also plenty of different margaritas and tequilas to accompany your meal. Expect a wait.

At Hillside Sedona shopping plaza, 671 Hwy. 179. ℭ 928/282-1313. www.javelinacantina.com. Reservations recommended. Main courses $7.50–$17. AE, DC, MC, V. Daily 11:30am–9:30pm.

Pizza Picazzo ✦ PIZZA   For down-home pizza in an upscale setting, nothing in Sedona can compare with this artistic pizza place. Throw in an attractive walled patio dining area and a view of Coffee Pot Rock, and you have one of the best values in town. There are good by-the-slice lunch specials, and during happy hour, there are half-price appetizers. Try the Southwestern pizza, which is made with salsa, spicy chicken or beef, pepper jack cheese, and black beans. Or how about a bacon cheeseburger pizza? Great setting, great view, great pizza, and best of all, by eating here you can avoid the crowds in uptown Sedona.

1855 W. Hwy. 89A. ℭ 928/282-4140. www.pizzapicazzo.com. Reservations only for parties of 10 or more. Pizzas $11–$22. AE, DC, MC, V. Sun–Thurs 11am–10pm; Fri–Sat 11am–11pm.

Red Planet Diner ✦ *Kids* INTERNATIONAL   With its flying saucer fountain out front and its totally cosmic decor, this casual diner is a UFO-spotters dream come true. Sip a mother-ship "vorttini" while you chow down on Flash Gordon chili, moon loaf, a Roswell burger, or any of the other out-of-this-world dishes. The walls are plastered with photos of UFOs and images from old sci-fi movies. Sometimes, however, it feels as if aliens have kidnapped your wait person.

1655 W. Hwy. 89A. ℭ 928/282-6070. Main courses $8–$15. AE, DC, DISC, MC, V. Daily 11am–11pm.

SEDONA AFTER DARK

If you're searching for good microbrewed beer, head to the **Oak Creek Brewing Co.,** 2050 Yavapai Dr. (ℭ **928/204-1300;** oakcreekbrew.com), north of Ariz. 89A off

Coffee Pot Drive. There's also the affiliated **Oak Creek Brewery and Grill** (© 928/ 282-3300; www.oakcreekpub.com) in the Tlaquepaque shopping center. If you're looking for some live music, check out west Sedona's **Highway Café,** 1405 W. Hwy. 89A (© 928/282-2300). Down in the Village of Oak Creek, you can do a little dancing at the **Full Moon Saloon,** 7000 Hwy. 179 (© 928/284-1872), which is located in the Tequa Plaza shopping center and has live music several nights a week.

6 Lake Mead National Recreation Area

70 miles NW of Kingman; 256 miles NW of Phoenix; 30 miles SE of Las Vegas, NV

This watersports playground straddles the border between Arizona and Nevada, boasting two reservoirs and a scenic, free-flowing stretch of the Colorado River. Throughout the year, anglers fish for striped bass, rainbow trout, channel catfish, and other sport fish, while during the hot summer months, lakes Mead and Mohave attract tens of thousands of water-skiers and personal watercraft riders.

The larger reservoir, Lake Mead, was created by the Hoover Dam, which was constructed between 1931 and 1935. By supplying huge amounts of electricity and water to Arizona and California, the dam set the stage for the phenomenal growth the region experienced in the second half of the 20th century.

ESSENTIALS

GETTING THERE   U.S. 93, which runs between Las Vegas and Kingman, crosses over Hoover Dam, and traffic backups at the dam can be horrendous. Several small secondary roads lead to various marinas on the lake. There are also many miles of unpaved roads within the recreation area. If you have a high-clearance or four-wheel-drive vehicle, these roads can take you to some of the least visited shores of the two lakes.

VISITOR INFORMATION   For information, contact the **Lake Mead National Recreation Area,** 601 Nevada Hwy., Boulder City, NV 89005 (© 702/293-8907; www.nps.gov/lame), or stop by the **Alan Bible Visitor Center** (© 702/293-8990), between Hoover Dam and Boulder City. The visitor center is open daily from 8:30am to 4:30pm.

DAM, LAKE & RIVER TOURS

Standing 726 feet tall, from bedrock to the roadway atop it, and tapering from a thickness of 660 feet at its base to only 45 feet at the top, **Hoover Dam** (© 866/291-TOUR or 702/294-3517; www.usbr.gov/lc/hooverdam) is the tallest concrete dam in the Western Hemisphere. Behind this massive dam lie the waters of **Lake Mead,** which at 110 miles long and with a shoreline of more than 550 miles is the largest artificial lake in the United States. U.S. 93 runs right across the top of the dam, and a visitor center chronicles the dam's construction. It's open daily from 9am to 5pm (closed Thanksgiving and Christmas). Guided tours cost $10 for adults, $8 for seniors, and $5 for children 7 to 16. Parking is an additional $5. Including a tour, it takes about 2 hours to visit the dam.

If you'd like to tour the lake and the dam, call **Lake Mead Cruises** (© 702/293-6180; www.lakemeadcruises.com) to book passage on the *Desert Princess* paddle-wheeler. These cruises leave from Lake Mead Cruises Landing, off Lakeshore Drive on the Nevada side of Hoover Dam. Day tours last 1½ hours and cost $20 for adults and $9 for children 2 to 11. Other options include dinner cruises ($44 for adults, $21 for

Western Arizona

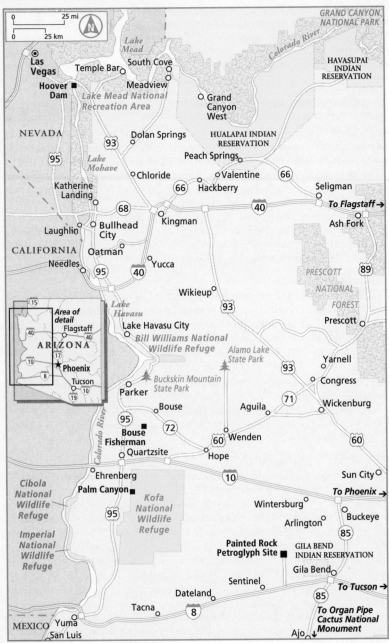

children), breakfast cruises ($33 for adults, $15 for children), and weekend dinner-and-dancing cruises ($54).

One of the most interesting ways to see remote parts of Lake Mohave is by sea kayak. **Desert River Outfitters,** 2649 U.S. 95, Suite 23 (© **888/KAYAK-33;** www.desertriveroutfitters.com), will rent you a boat and shuttle you and your gear to and from put-ins and take-outs. The trip through Black Canyon ($55 per person with a six-person minimum) starts at the base of Hoover Dam and is the most interesting route. (*Note:* This trip requires advance planning because a permit is necessary.) Other routes are also available. Raft trips through Black Canyon are offered by **Black Canyon River Adventures** (© **800/455-3490** or 702/294-1414; www.blackcanyon adventures.com). The 1-day rafting trips are an easy float through a scenic canyon and cost $73 for adults, $70 for children ages 13 to 15, and $45 for children ages 5 to 12. This is a great way to see this remote stretch of river.

GETTING OUTSIDE

Swimming, fishing, water-skiing, and powerboating are the most popular activities in Lake Mead National Recreation Area. On Arizona shores, there are swimming beaches at Lake Mohave's Katherine Landing (outside Bullhead City) and Lake Mead's Temple Bar (north of Kingman off U.S. 93). Picnic areas can be found at these two areas as well as Willow Beach on Lake Mohave and more than half a dozen spots on the Nevada side of Lake Mead.

In Arizona, marinas can be found at Katherine Landing on Lake Mohave (just outside Bullhead City), near the north end of Lake Mohave at Willow Beach (best access for trout angling), and at Temple Bar on Lake Mead. There's also a boat ramp at South Cove, north of the community of Meadview at the east end of Lake Mead. On the Nevada side of Lake Mohave, there's a marina at Cottonwood Cove, and on the Nevada side of Lake Mead, you'll find marinas at Boulder Beach, Las Vegas Bay, Callville Bay, and Echo Bay. These marinas offer motels, restaurants, general stores, campgrounds, and boat rentals. At both **Temple Bar** (© **800/752-9669** or 928/767-3211) and **Lake Mohave Resort** (© **800/752-9669** or 928/754-3245), you can rent ski boats, fishing boats, and patio boats for between $90 ($110 at Lake Mead Resort) and $260 per day. Personal watercraft are available for $110 for 2 hours or $285 a day.

WHERE TO STAY

Seven Crown Resorts rents houseboats (see below) and runs some good motels in the area. Lake Mohave Resort has huge rooms that are great for families ($35–$240 double), and Temple Bar Resort, although basically just a motel, has a wonderful remote setting with a beach right in front, great fishing nearby, and 40 miles of prime skiing waters extending from the resort. For more information, contact Seven Crown Resorts (© 800/752-9669; www.sevencrown.com).

HOUSEBOATS

Seven Crown Resorts 🖈 *Kids*   There's no better way to explore Lake Mead than on one of these floating vacation homes. You can cruise for miles, tie up at a deserted cove, and enjoy a wilderness adventure with all the comforts of home. Houseboats come complete with full kitchens, air-conditioning, and space to sleep up to 13 people. Bear in mind that the scenery here on Lake Mead isn't nearly as spectacular as that on Lake Powell, Arizona's other major houseboating lake.

P.O. Box 16247, Irvine, CA 92623-6247. © **800/752-9669.** www.sevencrown.com. $1,250–$3,050 per week. DISC, MC, V. Pets accepted. *In room:* A/C, kitchen, fridge, no phone.

CAMPING

In Arizona, there are campgrounds at Katherine Landing on Lake Mohave and at Temple Bar on Lake Mead. Both of these campgrounds have been heavily planted with trees, so they provide some semblance of shade during the hot, but popular, summer months. In Nevada, you'll find campgrounds at Cottonwood Cove on Lake Mohave and at Boulder Beach, Las Vegas Bay, Callville Bay, and Echo Bay on Lake Mead. Campsites at all campgrounds are $10 per night. For more information, contact **Lake Mead National Recreation Area** (© **702/293-8907,** 702/293-8990, or, in Arizona, 928/754-3272; www.nps.gov/lame).

7 Lake Havasu & the London Bridge

60 miles S of Bullhead City; 150 miles S of Las Vegas, NV; 200 miles NW of Phoenix

London Bridge is falling down, falling down, falling down. At least it was, until Robert McCulloch, founder of Lake Havasu City, hit upon the brilliant idea of buying the bridge and having it shipped to his undertouristed little planned community in the Arizona desert. Some 35 years later, London Bridge attracts tourists by the millions.

Lake Havasu was formed in 1938 by the building of the Parker Dam, but it wasn't until 1963 that McCulloch founded the town of Lake Havasu City. In the town's early years, not too many people were keen on spending time in this remote corner of the desert, where summer temperatures are often over 110°F (43°C). It was then that McCulloch began looking for ways to attract more people to his little "city" on the lake. His solution proved to be a stroke of genius.

Today, Lake Havasu City attracts an odd mix of visitors. In winter, the town is filled with retirees. On weekends, during the summer, and over spring break, however, Lake Havasu City is popular with Arizona college students and the water-ski and personal-watercraft crowds. Expect lots of noise on weekends and holidays.

ESSENTIALS

GETTING THERE   From Phoenix, take I-10 west to Ariz. 95 north. From Las Vegas, take U.S. 95 south to I-40 east to Ariz. 95 south.

America West (© **800/235-9292**) has regular flights to Lake Havasu City from Phoenix. The **Havasu/Vegas Express** (© **800/459-4884** or 928/453-4884; www.havasu shuttle.com) operates a shuttle van between Lake Havasu City and Las Vegas. Fares are $53 one-way and $93 round-trip.

VISITOR INFORMATION   For more information on this area, contact the **Lake Havasu Tourism Bureau,** English Village (© **800/242-8278** or 928/453-3444; www.golakehavasu.com), which is at the foot of the London Bridge.

GETTING AROUND   For car rentals, try **Avis** (© **800/831-2847** or 928/764-3001), **Enterprise** (© **800/325-8007** or 928/453-0033), or **Hertz** (© **800/654-3131** or 928/764-3994).

LONDON BRIDGE

Back in the mid-1960s, when London Bridge was sinking into the Thames River due to heavy car and truck traffic, the British government decided to sell the bridge. Robert McCulloch and his partner paid nearly $2.5 million for it and had it shipped 10,000 miles to Lake Havasu City. Reconstruction of the bridge was begun in 1968, and the grand reopening was held in 1971.

At the base of the bridge sits **English Village,** which is done up in proper English style and has shops, restaurants, and a waterfront promenade. You'll find several cruise boats and boat-rental docks here, as well as the chamber of commerce's visitor center.

Unfortunately, the London Bridge is not very impressive as bridges go, and the tacky commercialization of its surroundings makes it something of a letdown for many visitors. On top of that, over the years the jolly olde England styling that once predominated around here has been supplanted by a Mexican beach-bar aesthetic designed to appeal to partying college students on spring break.

LAND, LAKE & RIVER TOURS

Several companies offer boat tours on Lake Havasu. **Bluewater Jetboat Tours** (© 888/855-7171 or 928/855-7171; www.coloradoriverjetboattours.com) runs jetboat tours that leave from the London Bridge and spend 2½ hours cruising up the Colorado River to the Topock Gorge, a scenic area 25 miles from Lake Havasu City. The cost is $35 for adults, $32 for seniors, and $18 for children 10 to 16.

You can also go out on the *Dixie Belle* (© 866/332-9231 or 928/453-6776), a small replica paddle-wheel riverboat. Cruises are $13 for adults and $7 for children 5 to 12.

To explore the desert surrounding Lake Havasu City, arrange an off-road adventure in a six-wheel-drive Pinzgauer truck with **Outback Off-Road Adventures** (© 928/680-6151; www.outbackadventures.us), which charges $65 for a half-day tour and $165 for a full-day tour.

GETTING OUTSIDE

GOLF   **London Bridge Golf Club,** 2400 Club House Dr. (© 928/855-2719), with two 18-hole courses, is the area's premier course. High-season greens fees (with cart) top out at $89 on the West Course and $59 on the East Course. The **Havasu Island Golf Course,** 1040 McCulloch Blvd. (© 928/855-5585), is a 4,012-yard, par-61 executive course with lots of water hazards. Greens fees are $22 if you walk and $31 if you ride. The 9-hole **Bridgewater Links,** 1477 Queen's Bay Rd. (© 928/855-4777; www.londonbridgeresort.com), at the London Bridge Resort, is the most accessible and easiest of the area courses. Greens fees for 9 holes are $16 if you walk and $21 if you ride.

Moments   Canoeing the Colorado

Paddling down a desert river is an unusual and unforgettable experience. Both outfitters listed here provide boats, paddles, life jackets, maps, and shuttles to put-in and take-out points, but usually no guide. **Western Arizona Canoe and Kayak Outfitter** (© 888/881-5038 or 928/715-6414; www.azwacko.com) offers self-guided kayak or canoe trips through the beautiful and rugged Topock Gorge, where you can see ancient petroglyphs and possibly bighorn sheep. Trips take 5 to 6 hours, and the cost is $45 per person. **Jerkwater Canoe Company** (© 800/421-7803 or 928/768-7753; www.jerkwater.com) offers a similar Topock Gorge excursion and also arranges other canoe and kayak trips of varying lengths. Jerkwater's Topock Gorge self-guided 5- to 6-hour trip is $40 per person in a canoe or $55 per person in a kayak.

Golfers won't want to miss the **Emerald Canyon Golf Course** ⭐, 7351 Riverside Dr., Parker (© **928/667-3366**), about 30 miles south of Lake Havasu City. This municipal course is the most spectacular in the region and plays through rugged canyons and past red-rock cliffs, from which there are views of the Colorado River. Expect to pay $30 to $50 for greens fees in the cooler months. Also in Parker is the golf course at the **Havasu Springs Resort,** 2581 Ariz. 95 (© **928/667-3361**), which some people claim is the hardest little 9-hole, par-3 course in the state. It's atop a rocky outcropping with steep drop-offs all around. If you aren't staying here, greens fees are only $10 for 9 holes and $15 for 18 holes.

WATERSPORTS   While the London Bridge is what made Lake Havasu City, these days watersports on 45-mile-long Lake Havasu are the area's real draw.

London Bridge Beach, the best in-town beach, is located in a county park behind the Island Inn, off West McCulloch Boulevard. It features a sandy beach and lots of palm trees. Just south of the London Bridge on the "mainland" side, you'll find the large **Rotary Community Park** and the **Lake Havasu Aquatic Center,** 100 Park Ave. (© **928/453-2687**), which has an indoor wave pool and 254-foot water slide. There are more beaches at **Lake Havasu State Park** (© **928/855-2784**), 2 miles north of the London Bridge, and **Cattail Cove State Park** (© **928/855-1223**), 15 miles south of Lake Havasu City. Both state parks charge a $9 day-use fee.

At the **Adventure Center,** in English Village (© **928/453-4386**), you can rent pedal boats for $16 an hour. In this same area, you can also go for a ride on the **London Bridge Gondola** (© **928/486-1891;** www.londonbridgegondola.com); the gondolier even sings in Italian as you cruise beneath the London Bridge. Rides prices range from $13 to $30.

You can rent boats from **Fun Time Boat Rentals,** 1685 Industrial Blvd. (© **800/ 680-1003** or 928/680-1003; www.funtimerentals.com), which also has a rental facility in English Village beside the bridge. Pontoon boats cost $300 per day, and ski boats are also available.

WHERE TO STAY
HOTELS & MOTELS

Agave Inn ⭐⭐ *Finds*   Located at the foot of the London Bridge, this boutique hotel is by far the hippest hotel between Scottsdale and Las Vegas. Guest rooms are reminiscent of those at W hotels, although here you get much more room at a much lower price. Rooms are large and have balconies, and most overlook the bridge or the water. Platform beds, stylish lamps, and a sort of Scandinavian modern aesthetic make this the most distinctive hotel on this side of the state. Room no. 305, a corner room, has a great view of the bridge and is my favorite in the hotel.

1420 McCulloch Blvd N., Lake Havasu City, AZ 86403. © **866/854-2833** or 928/854-2833. Fax 928/854-1130. www.agaveinn.com. 17 units. $119–$359 suite. AE, DISC, MC, V. **Amenities:** Restaurant (Mexican); exercise room. *In room:* A/C, TV, dataport, fridge, coffeemaker, hair dryer, iron, free local calls, high-speed Internet access.

Island Inn Hotel   The Island Inn is across the London Bridge from downtown and has one of the nicest hotel settings in Lake Havasu City. Although it's not right on the water, it is close to one of the area's best public beaches. Guest rooms are large and have seen a lot of wear and tear. Ask for a room with a balcony; units on the upper floors have the better views (and higher prices).

1300 W. McCulloch Blvd., Lake Havasu City, AZ 86403. © **800/243-9955** or 928/680-0606. Fax 928/680-4218. www.havasumotels.com. 117 units. Mar–Oct $65–$209 double; Nov–Feb $39–$85 double. Children under 16 stay free in parent's room. AE, DISC, MC, V. Pets accepted ($10 nonrefundable deposit). **Amenities:** Restaurant; lounge; outdoor pool; Jacuzzi, coin-op laundry. *In room:* A/C, TV, dataport, fridge.

CAMPING

There are two state park campgrounds in the Lake Havasu City area. **Lake Havasu State Park** (© 928/855-2784) is 2 miles north of the London Bridge on London Bridge Road, while **Cattail Cove State Park** (© 928/855-1223) is 15 miles south of Lake Havasu City off Ariz. 95. The former campground charges $14 to $25 per night per vehicle, while the latter charges $19 to $25 per site. Reservations are not accepted. In addition to sites in these campgrounds, there are also boat-in campsites within Lake Havasu and Cattail Cove state parks.

WHERE TO DINE

Javelina Cantina MEXICAN   At the foot of the London Bridge on the island side, this large, modern Mexican restaurant is affiliated with Shugrue's on the other side of the street. There's a great view of the bridge from a large patio area that is kept heated in winter. The bar has an excellent selection of tequilas, and margaritas are a specialty here. Accompany your libations with tortilla soup, fish tacos, or a salad made with blackened scallops, papaya, pecans, blue cheese, and other ingredients.

1420 McCulloch Blvd. © **928/855-8226.** Main courses $7–$15. AE, DISC, MC, V. Sun–Thurs 11am–10pm; Fri–Sat 11am–11pm.

Shugrue's *Kids* STEAKHOUSE/SEAFOOD   Just across the London Bridge from the English Village shopping complex, Shugrue's seems to be popular as much for its view of the London Bridge as for its food. Offerings include seafood, prime rib, burgers, sandwiches, and a short list of pastas. This place is a favorite of retirees and families, especially for its inexpensive sunset dinners (Sun–Thurs 5–6:30pm). There's also a children's menu. The adjacent affiliated Barley Brothers Brewpub has the same good view of the bridge, and serves a menu calculated to appeal to a younger clientele.

At the Island Mall, 1425 McCulloch Blvd. © **928/453-1400.** www.shugrues.com. Reservations recommended. Main courses $8–$12 lunch, $18–$28 dinner. AE, DC, DISC, MC, V. Daily 11am–3pm and 4:30–9:30pm.

16

The Grand Canyon & Northern Arizona

The Grand Canyon attracts millions of visitors from all over the world each year. The pastel layers of rock weaving through the canyon's rugged ramparts, the interplay of shadows and light, the wind in the pines, and the croaking of ravens on the rim—these are the sights and sounds that transfix the hordes of visitors who gaze awestruck into the canyon's seemingly infinite depths.

Yet other parts of northern Arizona contain worthwhile, and less crowded, attractions. Only 60 miles south of the canyon stand the San Francisco Peaks, the tallest of which, Humphreys Peak, rises to 12,643 feet. These peaks, sacred to the Hopi and Navajo, are ancient volcanoes that today are popular with skiers, hikers, and mountain bikers.

Amid northern Arizona's miles of windswept plains and ponderosa pine forests stands the city of Flagstaff, home to Northern Arizona University. Born of the railroads and named for a flagpole, Flagstaff is now the main jumping-off point for trips to the Grand Canyon.

1 Flagstaff ✴✴

150 miles N of Phoenix; 32 miles E of Williams; 80 miles S of Grand Canyon Village

With its wide variety of accommodations and restaurants, the great outdoors at the edge of town, three national monuments nearby, one of the state's finest museums, and a university that supports a lively cultural community, Flagstaff makes an ideal base for exploring much of northern Arizona.

The San Francisco Peaks, just north of the city, are the site of the Arizona Snowbowl ski area, one of the state's main winter playgrounds. In summer, miles of trails through these same mountains attract hikers and mountain bikers. Of the area's national monuments, two preserve ancient Indian ruins and one an otherworldly landscape of volcanic cinder cones.

It was as a railroad town that Flagstaff made its fortunes, and the historic downtown offers a glimpse of the days when the city's fortunes rode the rails. The railroad still runs right through the middle of Flagstaff, much to the dismay of many visitors, who find that most of the city's inexpensive motels are too close to the busy tracks to allow them to get a good night's sleep.

ESSENTIALS

GETTING THERE Flagstaff is on I-40, one of the main east–west interstates in the United States. I-17 starts here and heads south to Phoenix. Ariz. 89A connects Flagstaff to Sedona by way of Oak Creek Canyon. U.S. 180 connects Flagstaff with the South Rim of the Grand Canyon, and U.S. 89 connects the city with Page.

The Grand Canyon & Northern Arizona

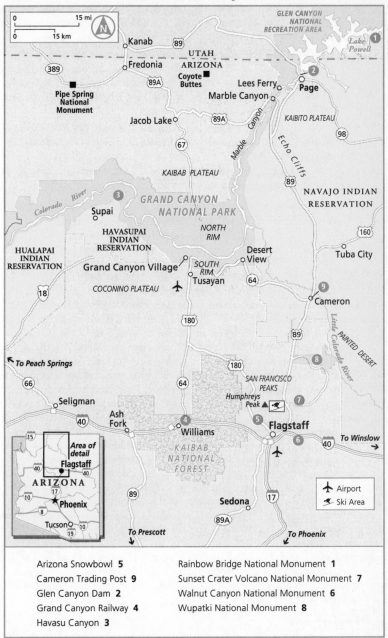

Arizona Snowbowl **5**

Cameron Trading Post **9**

Glen Canyon Dam **2**

Grand Canyon Railway **4**

Havasu Canyon **3**

Rainbow Bridge National Monument **1**

Sunset Crater Volcano National Monument **7**

Walnut Canyon National Monument **6**

Wupatki National Monument **8**

Pulliam Airport, 3 miles south of Flagstaff off I-17, is served by **America West** (© **800/235-9292**) from Phoenix. **Amtrak** (© **800/872-7245**) offers service to Flagstaff from Chicago and Los Angeles. The train station is at 1 E. Rte. 66.

VISITOR INFORMATION   Contact the **Flagstaff Visitor Center,** 1 E. Rte. 66 (© **800/842-7293** or 928/774-9541; www.flagstaffarizona.org). June through Labor Day weekend, the visitor center is open Monday through Saturday from 8am to 7pm and Sunday from 9am to 5pm; the rest of the year, it's open Monday through Saturday from 8am to 6pm and Sunday from 9am to 4pm.

GETTING AROUND   Car rentals are available from **Avis** (© 800/831-2847), **Budget** (© 800/527-0700), **Enterprise** (© 800/736-8222), **Hertz** (© 800/654-3131), and **National** (© 800/227-7368).

Call **Friendly Cab** (© 928/774-4444) if you need a taxi. **Mountain Line Transit** (© 928/779-6624) provides public bus transit around the city; the fare is $1.

GETTING OUTSIDE

Flagstaff is northern Arizona's center for outdoor activities. Chief among them is skiing at **Arizona Snowbowl** (© **928/779-1951;** www.arizonasnowbowl.com), on the slopes of Mount Agassiz, from which you can see all the way to the North Rim of the Grand Canyon. Conditions are, however, very unreliable, and the ski area can be shut down for weeks on end due to lack of snow. All-day lift tickets are $42 for adults, $24 for children 8 to 12, $22 for seniors, and free for children under 8 and seniors over 69. In summer, you can ride a chairlift almost to the summit of Mount Agassiz and enjoy the expansive views across seemingly all of northern Arizona. The round-trip lift-ticket price is $10 for adults, $8 for seniors, and $6 for children 8 to 12. To get here, take U.S. 180 north from Flagstaff for 7 miles and turn right onto Snow Bowl Road.

When there's no snow on the ground, there are plenty of trails for hiking throughout the San Francisco Peaks, and many national forest trails are open to mountain bikes. If you've got the stamina, do the **Humphreys Peak Trail,** which climbs 3,000 feet in 4.5 miles. The views from the 12,633-foot summit, the highest point in Arizona, are stupendous. To reach the trail head, take U.S. 180 north out of Flagstaff for 7 miles, turn right on Snow Bowl Road, and continue to the parking area by the ski lodge.

If you'd like a short hike with a big payoff, hike to **Red Mountain.** This hike is only about 2.5 miles round-trip, but leads to a fascinating red-walled cinder cone that long ago collapsed to reveal its strange interior walls. To find the trail head, drive north from Flagstaff toward the Grand Canyon on U.S. 180. At milepost 24, watch for a forest road leading west for about a quarter mile to the trail-head parking area.

For information on other hikes in the Coconino National Forest, contact the **Peaks Ranger District,** 5075 N. Hwy. 89, Flagstaff (© **928/526-0866;** www.fs.fed.us/r3/coconino).

Flying Heart Ranch (© **928/526-2788**), located 4½ miles north of I-40 on U.S. 89, leads **horseback rides** up into the foothills of the San Francisco Peaks and out through the juniper and piñon forests of the lower elevations. Prices range from $25 for a 1-hour ride to $45 for 2 hours.

SEEING THE SIGHTS

Downtown Flagstaff along Route 66, San Francisco Street, Aspen Avenue, and Birch Avenue is the city's **historic district.** These old brick buildings are now filled with shops selling Native American crafts, works by local artists and artisans, Route 66 souvenirs, and various other Arizona mementos such as rocks, minerals, and crystals.

Don't miss **Jonathan Day's Indian Arts,** 21 San Francisco St. (© **928/779-6099;** www.traditionalhopikachinas.com), a small shop with what just might be the best selection of traditional Hopi kachinas in the state.

MUSEUMS, PARKS & CULTURAL ACTIVITIES

Lowell Observatory ★
This historic observatory is located atop Mars Hill and is one of the oldest astronomical observatories in the Southwest. Founded in 1894 by Percival Lowell, the observatory was where Lowell studied the planet Mars and made the calculations that led him to predict the existence of Pluto. It wasn't until 13 years after Lowell's death that Pluto was finally discovered almost exactly where he had predicted it would be.

The facility consists of several observatories, a visitor center with numerous fun and educational exhibits, and outdoor displays. The main attraction is the chance to observe the stars and planets through the observatory's 24-inch telescope. The telescope domes are not heated, so if you come up to stargaze, be sure to dress appropriately.

1400 W. Mars Hill Rd. © 928/774-3358. www.lowell.edu. Admission $5 adults, $4 seniors, $2 children 5–17. Mar–Oct daily 9am–5pm (tours on the hour 10am–4pm); Nov–Feb daily noon–5pm (tours on the hour 1–4pm). Telescope viewings: June–Aug Mon–Sat 8pm; Sept–May Wed and Fri–Sat 7:30pm. Closed Jan 1, Easter, Thanksgiving, Dec 24–25, Dec 31.

Museum of Northern Arizona ★★
At this small but surprisingly thorough museum, you'll learn, through state-of-the-art exhibits, about the archaeology, ethnology, geology, biology, and fine arts of the region. The cornerstone of the museum is an exhibit that explores life on the Colorado Plateau from 15,000 B.C. to the present. Among the other displays are a life-size kiva ceremonial room and a small but interesting collection of kachinas. The large gift shop is full of contemporary Native American arts and crafts.

3101 N. Fort Valley Rd. (3 miles north of downtown Flagstaff on U.S. 180). © 928/774-5213. www.musnaz.org. Admission $5 adults, $4 seniors, $3 students, $2 children 7–17. Daily 9am–5pm. Closed New Year's Day, Thanksgiving, and Christmas.

Riordan Mansion State Historic Park ★
Built in 1904 for local timber barons Michael and Timothy Riordan, this 13,000-square-foot mansion—Arizona's finest example of an Arts and Crafts–era building—is actually two houses connected by a large central hall. Each brother and his family occupied half of the house (they had the rooflines constructed differently so that visitors could tell the two sides apart). Although the mansion looks like a log cabin, it's actually only faced with log slabs. Inside, mission-style furnishings and touches of Art Nouveau styling make it clear that this family was keeping up with the times. The west wing of the mansion holds displays on, among other things, Stickley furniture. Guided tours provide a glimpse into the lives of two of Flagstaff's most influential pioneers.

409 W. Riordan Rd. (off Milton Rd./Ariz. 89A, just north of the junction of I-40 and I-17). © 928/779-4395. www.azstateparks.com. Admission $6 adults, $2.50 children 7–13. May–Oct daily 8:30am–5pm; Nov–Apr daily 10:30am–5pm. Guided tours on the hour. Closed Christmas.

Sunset Crater Volcano National Monument ★
Dotting the landscape northeast of Flagstaff are more than 400 volcanic craters, of which Sunset Crater Volcano is the youngest. Taking its name from the sunset colors of the cinders near its summit, Sunset Crater Volcano stands 1,000 feet tall and began forming in A.D. 1064. Over a period of 100 years, the volcano erupted repeatedly, and eventually covered an area of 800 square miles with ash, lava, and cinders. A 1-mile interpretive trail passes through

a desolate landscape of lava flows, cinders, and ash as it skirts the base of this volcano. If you want to climb to the top of a cinder cone, take the 1-mile Lenox Crater Trail. In the visitor center (at the west entrance to the monument), you can learn more about the formation of Sunset Crater and about volcanoes in general. Near the visitor center is the small Bonito Campground, which is open from late May to mid-October.

14 miles north of Flagstaff off U.S. 89. ✆ **928/526-0502**. www.nps.gov/sucr. Admission $5 adults, free for children 16 and under (admission also valid for Wupatki National Monument). Daily sunrise to sunset; visitor center June–Aug daily 8am–6pm, Sept–Nov and Mar–May 8am–5pm, Dec–Feb 9am–5pm. Closed Christmas.

Walnut Canyon National Monument ✪

The remains of 300 small 13th-century Sinagua cliff dwellings can be seen in the undercut layers of limestone in this 400-foot-deep wooded canyon east of Flagstaff. These cliff dwellings, though not the most impressive in the state, are worth a visit for the chance to poke around inside the well-preserved rooms. The Sinagua were the same people who built and then abandoned the stone pueblos in Wupatki National Monument, and it is theorized that when the land to the north lost its fertility, the Sinagua began migrating southward, settling for 150 years in Walnut Canyon.

A self-guided trail leads from the visitor center on the canyon rim down 185 feet to a section of the canyon wall where 25 cliff dwellings can be viewed up close (some can even be entered). Bring binoculars so you can scan the canyon walls for other cliff dwellings. From Memorial Day to Labor Day on Tuesdays, Saturdays, and Sundays, there are guided hikes into the monument's backcountry (reservations required). There's also a picnic area near the visitor center.

7½ miles east of Flagstaff on Walnut Canyon Rd. (take Exit 204 off I-40). ✆ **928/526-3367**. www.nps.gov/waca. Admission $5 adults, free for children 16 and under. June–Aug daily 8am–6pm; Sept–Nov and Mar–May daily 8am–5pm; Dec–Feb daily 9am–5pm; trail closes 1 hr. earlier. Closed Christmas.

Wupatki National Monument ✪✪

The landscape northeast of Flagstaff is desolate and windswept, a sparsely populated region carpeted with volcanic ash deposited in the 11th century. It comes as quite a surprise, then, to learn that this area contains hundreds of Native American habitation sites. The most impressive ruins are those left by the Sinagua (the name means "without water" in Spanish), who inhabited this area from around A.D. 1100 until shortly after 1200. The Sinagua people built small villages of stone similar to the pueblos on the nearby Hopi Reservation, and today the ruins of these ancient villages can be seen in this national monument.

The largest of the pueblos is Wupatki Ruin, in the southeastern part of the monument. Here the Sinagua built a sprawling three-story pueblo containing nearly 100 rooms. They also constructed what is believed to be a ball court, which, although quite different in design from the courts of the Aztec and Maya, suggests that a similar game may have been played in this region. Another circular stone structure just below the main ruins may have been an amphitheater or dance plaza.

The most unusual feature of Wupatki, however, is a natural phenomenon: a blowhole, which may have been the reason this pueblo was constructed here. A network of small underground tunnels and chambers acts as a giant barometer, blowing air through the blowhole when the underground air is under greater pressure than the outside air. On hot days, cool air rushes out of the blowhole with amazing force.

36 miles north of Flagstaff off U.S. 89. ✆ **928/679-2365**. www.nps.gov/wupa. Admission $5 adults, free for children 16 and under. Daily sunrise to sunset. Visitor center June–Aug daily 8am–6pm; Mar–May and Sept–Nov daily 8am–5pm; Dec–Feb 9am–5pm. Closed Christmas.

WHERE TO STAY

EXPENSIVE

England House Bed & Breakfast ★★   This B&B just 3 blocks from Flagstaff's historic downtown is a beautiful two-story Victorian red sandstone house built in 1902. This old house, which opened as an inn in 2004, was lovingly restored by owners Richard and Laurel Dunn, who are devoted to details. Consequently, this inn has a delightful period authenticity. The three large guest rooms are on the second floor and are furnished with 1870s French antiques. There's also a small guest room, called the Pantry (though it isn't really *that* small) on the ground floor. Breakfasts are served in a bright sunroom just off the kitchen.

614 W. Santa Fe Ave., Flagstaff, AZ 86001. © **877/214-7350** or 928/214-7350. Fax 928/226-0011. www.england housebandb.com. 4 units. $95–$195 double. Rates include full breakfast. DISC, MC, V. No children. **Amenities:** Concierge. *In room:* Hair dryer, iron, no phone.

The Inn at 410 ★★   Situated only 2 blocks from downtown Flagstaff, this restored 1907 Craftsman home is one of the best B&Bs in Arizona. Guests can lounge and enjoy afternoon tea on the front porch, in the comfortable dining room, or out on the pleasant garden patio. Each guest room features a distinctive theme; my favorites are the Dakota and the Southwest suites, which conjure up the inn's Western heritage. All rooms have fireplaces, and three have two-person whirlpool tubs. Some of the guest rooms are in an adjacent building, and these rooms are just as nice as those in the main house. Breakfasts are delicious.

410 N. Leroux St., Flagstaff, AZ 86001. © **800/774-2008** or 928/774-0088. Fax 928/774-6354. www.inn410.com. 9 units. $150–$210 double. 2-night minimum on weekends Apr–Oct. Rates include full breakfast. MC, V. No children under 5. **Amenities:** Access to nearby health club; concierge; business center. *In room:* A/C, TV/DVD/VCR, fridge, coffeemaker, hair dryer, iron, wi-fi, no phone.

MODERATE

Arizona Sled Dog Inn ★★ *Finds*   Located on the edge of the forest south of the city, the Sled Dog is a contemporary building with lots of wood details. Guest rooms are modern lodge rustic, comfortable and uncluttered. At the end of an active day, the hot tub out back is always welcome, and don't be surprised if you wake up to see elk grazing right outside your window. The inn takes its name from the fact that the owners have a kennel full of Siberian huskies.

10155 Mountainaire Rd., Flagstaff, AZ 86001. © **800/754-0664** or 928/525-6212. www.sleddoginn.com. 10 units. $105–$149 double; $170–$225 suite. Rates include full breakfast. AE, DISC, MC, V. No children under 5. **Amenities:** Jacuzzi; sauna; bike rentals. *In room:* A/C, no phone.

Little America Hotel ★ *Value*   Set on 500 acres of pine forest and with a trail that winds for 2 miles through the property, this surprisingly luxurious and economical hotel on the east side of Flagstaff sits beneath shady pines behind a truck stop. The decor is dated but fun, with a sort of French Provincial style predominating. Rooms vary in size, but all have small private balconies.

2515 E. Butler Ave., Flagstaff, AZ 86004. © **800/865-1410** or 928/779-7900. Fax 928/779-7983. www.littleamerica. com. 247 units. $79–$129 double; $89–$139 suite. Children 12 and under stay free in parent's room. AE, DC, DISC, MC, V. Take Exit 198 off I-40. **Amenities:** 3 restaurants (American, Continental, deli); lounge; outdoor pool; croquet court; exercise room; Jacuzzi; children's playground; concierge; car-rental desk; business center; room service; massage; coin-op laundry; laundry service; dry cleaning. *In room:* A/C, TV, dataport, fridge, coffeemaker, hair dryer, iron, high-speed Internet access.

Radisson Woodlands Hotel Flagstaff ★★   With its elegant marble-floored lobby, the Woodlands Hotel is easily the most upscale lodging in Flagstaff. A white baby grand, crystal chandelier, traditional European furnishings, and contemporary sculpture all add to the unexpected luxury in the public spaces, as do intricately carved pieces of furniture and architectural details from different Asian countries. Guest rooms are comfortable.

1175 W. Rte. 66, Flagstaff, AZ 86001. © **800/333-3333** or 928/773-8888. Fax 928/773-0597. www.radisson.com/ flagstaff.az. 183 units. $84–$139 double; $104–$159 suites. AE, DC, DISC, MC, V. **Amenities:** 2 restaurants (Japanese, Continental); lounge; outdoor pool; exercise room; indoor and outdoor Jacuzzis; sauna; steam room; business center; room service; coin-op laundry; laundry service; dry cleaning. *In room:* A/C, TV, dataport, coffeemaker, hair dryer, iron, high-speed Internet access, wi-fi.

INEXPENSIVE

Historic Hotel Monte Vista   This hotel is definitely not for everyone. Although it is historic, it is also a bit run-down and appeals primarily to young travelers who appreciate the low rates and the nightclub just off the lobby. So why stay here? Well, in its day, the Monte Vista hosted the likes of Clark Gable, John Wayne, Carole Lombard, and Gary Cooper. Plus, this place is haunted (ask at the front desk about the resident ghosts). Originally opened in 1927, the Monte Vista now has creatively decorated rooms that vary in size and decor. The hotel has plenty of old-fashioned flair, but you should check out a room first to see if this is your kind of place.

100 N. San Francisco St., Flagstaff, AZ 86001. © **800/545-3068** or 928/779-6971. Fax 928/779-2904. www.hotel montevista.com. 50 units, 4 with shared bathrooms. $50–$65 double with shared bathroom; $80–$95 double with private bathroom; $90–$140 suite. Lower rates in winter. AE, DISC, MC, V. Pets accepted ($25 deposit). **Amenities:** Restaurant (Thai); lounge; massage; coin-op laundry. *In room:* TV, hair dryer.

WHERE TO DINE
EXPENSIVE

Cottage Place Restaurant ★★ CONTINENTAL/NEW AMERICAN   Despite the casual appearance of this unpretentious little cottage on the south side of the railroad tracks, dining here is a formal affair. The menu, which tends toward the rich side, is primarily Continental, with Southwestern and Middle Eastern influences as well. The house specialties are chateaubriand and rack of lamb (both served for two); there are always several choices for vegetarians as well. The appetizer sampler, with herb-stuffed mushrooms, charbroiled shrimp, and *tiropitas* (cheese-stuffed phyllo pastries), is a winner. There's a long, award-winning wine list.

126 W. Cottage Ave. © **928/774-8431.** www.cottageplace.com. Reservations recommended. 3-course meals $21–$31. AE, MC, V. Tues–Sun 5–9:30pm.

MODERATE

Jackson's Grill at the Springs ★★ NEW AMERICAN   Set on the outskirts of Flagstaff overlooking a horse pasture, this modern American bistro boasts the most attractive setting of any restaurant in town. The food here is also excellent, which makes this place well worth the 10-minute drive from downtown Flagstaff. Start with the spinach salad, which is made with blue cheese, candied pecans, and roasted beets, or the Chinese lettuce wraps filled with spicy chicken. The spit-roasted entrees are among the best bets here. If you're traveling between Flagstaff and Sedona late in the day, this makes a great place for dinner.

7055 S. Hwy. 89A. © **928/213-9350.** Reservations recommended on weekends. Main courses $12–$33. AE, DC, DISC, MC, V. Sun–Thurs 5–9pm; Fri–Sat 5–9:30pm (in summer open for lunch 11:30am–3pm).

Moments **White Buffalo**

As you drive north to the Grand Canyon on U.S. 180, about 20 miles north of Flagstaff, be sure to watch for **Spirit Mountain Ranch,** mile marker 236.5 (© **928/ 606-2779;** www.sacredwhitebuffalo.com), which is home to six white buffalo. These animals are considered sacred by Native Americans. The buffalo can be visited daily (hours vary with the seasons) and admission is $5.

Josephine's ★★ REGIONAL AMERICAN   Housed in a restored Craftsman bungalow with a beautiful stone fireplace and a wide front porch for summer dining, this restaurant combines a historical setting with excellent food that draws on a wide range of influences. For these reasons, this is my favorite downtown Flagstaff restaurant. The thinly sliced ancho-marinated steak is a real winner. At lunch, try the pecan-crusted fish tacos or the crab-cake po' boy sandwich. There's a good selection of reasonably priced wines also. Be sure to save room for the molten chocolate cake or the unusual half-baked peanut butter–chocolate-chip cookie.

503 N. Humphrey's St. © **928/779-3400.** Reservations recommended. Main courses $7.50–$11 lunch, $17–$25 dinner. AE, DISC, MC, V. Mon–Fri 11am–2:30pm and 5–9pm; Sat 5–9pm.

Pasto ★ ITALIAN   Located in downtown Flagstaff, Pasto has a lively urban feel. The food is some of the best in town and is always reliable. Casual yet sophisticated, Pasto is less formal than The Cottage Place or Josephine's, so if you don't feel like getting dressed up after a day at the canyon, try here. Located in downtown Flagstaff, this place can get pretty boisterous on the weekends. As the restaurant's name implies, the menu includes a good assortment of pastas. Try the prosciutto-wrapped shrimp or the lamb osso buco.

19 E. Aspen St. © **928/779-1937.** www.pastorestaurant.com. Reservations recommended. Main courses $13–$24. AE, DISC, MC, V. Mon–Thurs 11am–2pm and 5–9pm; Fri 11am–2pm and 5–9:30pm; Sat 5–9:30pm; Sun 5–9pm.

INEXPENSIVE

Beaver Street Brewery *Value* BURGERS/PIZZA   This big microbrewery, cafe, and billiards parlor on the south side of the railroad tracks serves up several good brews, and it also does great pizzas and salads. The Beaver Street pizza, made with roasted-garlic pesto, sun-dried tomatoes, fresh basil, and goat cheese, is particularly tasty. Robust salads include a Mongolian beef version with sesame-ginger dressing. This place stays packed with college students, but a good pint of ale helps any wait pass quickly, especially if you can grab a seat by the woodstove.

11 S. Beaver St. © **928/779-0079.** www.beaverstreetbrewery.com. Main courses $8–$11. AE, DISC, MC, V. Daily 11:30am–10pm (limited bar menu until midnight).

Macy's European Coffee House & Bakery COFFEEHOUSE/BAKERY   Good espresso and baked goodies draw people in here the first time, but there are also decent vegetarian pasta dishes, soups, salads, and other college-town standbys. This is Flagstaff's counterculture hangout, attracting both students and professors. For the true Macy's experience, order one of the huge lattes and a scone or other pastry.

14 S. Beaver St. © **928/774-2243.** Meals $4.50–$7. No credit cards. Daily 6am–10pm.

2 Williams

32 miles W of Flagstaff; 58 miles S of the Grand Canyon; 220 miles E of Las Vegas, NV

Although it's almost 60 miles south of the Grand Canyon, Williams is the closest real town to the national park. Consequently, it has dozens of motels catering to those unable to get a room in or just outside the park. Founded in 1880 as a railroading and logging town, Williams also has a bit of Western history to boast about. Old brick commercial buildings dating from the late 19th century line the main street, while modest Victorian homes sit on the tree-shaded streets that spread south from the railroad tracks. Williams was the last town on historic Route 66 to be bypassed by I-40, and the town plays up its Route 66 heritage.

Most important for many visitors, however, is that Williams is where you'll find the Grand Canyon Railway depot. The excursion train that departs from here not only provides a fun ride on the rails but also serves as an alternative to dealing with traffic congestion in Grand Canyon National Park.

Named for famed mountain man Bill Williams, the town sits at the edge of a ponderosa pine forest atop the Mogollon Rim, and surrounding Williams is the Kaibab National Forest. Within the forest and not far out of town are good fishing lakes, hiking and mountain-biking trails, and a small downhill ski area.

ESSENTIALS

GETTING THERE   Williams is on I-40 just west of the junction with Ariz. 64, which leads north to the South Rim of the Grand Canyon.

Amtrak (© **800/872-7245**) has service to Williams on its *Southwest Chief* line. There's no station, though—the train stops on the outskirts of town. However, a shuttle van from the Grand Canyon Railway Hotel will pick you up and drive you into town, and since most people coming to Williams by train are continuing on to the Grand Canyon on the Grand Canyon Railway, this arrangement works well.

For information on the **Grand Canyon Railway** excursion trains to Grand Canyon Village, see "Exploring the Area," below.

VISITOR INFORMATION   For information on the Williams area, including details on hiking, mountain biking, and fishing, contact the **City of Williams/Forest Service Visitor Center,** 200 W. Railroad Ave. (© **800/863-0546** or 928/635-4707; www. williamschamber.com). The visitor center, which includes some interesting historical displays, is open daily from 8am to 5pm (until 6:30pm in the summer). The shop carries books on the Grand Canyon and trail maps for the adjacent national forest.

EXPLORING THE AREA: ROUTE 66 & BEYOND

These days, most people coming to Williams are here to board the **Grand Canyon Railway** ★★, Grand Canyon Railway Depot, 233 N. Grand Canyon Blvd. (© **800/ 843-8724** or 928/773-1976; www.thetrain.com), which operates vintage steam and diesel locomotives and 1920s coaches between Williams and Grand Canyon Village. Round-trip fares (not including tax or the national park entrance fee) range from $60 to $155 for adults, $35 to $130 for children 11 to 16, and $25 to $85 for children 2 to 10. Although this is primarily a day-excursion train, it's possible to ride up 1 day and return on a different day—just let the reservations clerk know. If you stay overnight, you'll want to be sure you have a reservation at one of the hotels right in Grand Canyon Village; otherwise, you'll have to take a shuttle bus or taxi to your hotel.

Route 66 fans will want to drive Williams's main street, which, not surprisingly, is named Route 66. Along this stretch of the old highway, you can check out the town's vintage buildings, many of which now house shops selling Route 66 souvenirs. There are also a few antiques stores selling Route 66 collectibles.

WHERE TO STAY
MODERATE
Grand Canyon Railway Hotel ★★   This hotel is operated by the Grand Canyon Railway and combines modern comforts with the style of a classic Western railroad hotel. The high-ceilinged lobby features a large flagstone fireplace and original paintings of the Grand Canyon. The very comfortable guest rooms feature Southwestern styling; ask for a unit in the new wing (which is where you'll find the fitness room, pool, and hot tub). The hotel's elegant lounge, which features a 100-year-old English bar, serves simple meals, and there's a cafeteria-style restaurant adjacent.

233 N. Grand Canyon Blvd., Williams, AZ 86046. ℂ 800/843-8724 or 928/635-4010. Fax 928/773-1610. www.the train.com. 298 units. Apr to mid-Oct and holidays $139 double; mid-Oct to Mar $89 double. Railroad/hotel packages available (Apr to mid-Oct and holidays $139 per person; mid-Oct to Mar $109 per person). AE, DISC, MC, V. **Amenities:** Restaurant; lounge; indoor pool; exercise room; Jacuzzi; tour desk. *In room:* A/C, TV, dataport, hair dryer, free local calls.

INEXPENSIVE
In addition to the following choices, there are numerous budget chain motels in Williams.

The Canyon Motel ★ *Finds*   You'll find this updated 1940s Route 66 motor lodge on the eastern outskirts of Williams, tucked against the trees. While the setting and new rooms in duplex flagstone cottages are nice enough, the real attractions are the railroad cars parked in the front yard—you can stay in a caboose or a Pullman car. I prefer the caboose rooms, which have a more authentic feel. An indoor pool, horseshoe pit, swing set, board games, a fire ring, propane barbecues, and a nature trail provide plenty of entertainment for the whole family. There's also a deluxe RV park here.

1900 E. Rodeo Rd., Williams, AZ 86046. ℂ 800/482-3955 or 928/635-9371. Fax 928/635-4138. www.thecanyon motel.com. 23 units. $40–$79 double; $100–$120 caboose; $45–$95 Pullman double. Rates include continental breakfast. DISC, MC, V. Pets accepted. **Amenities:** Small indoor pool. *In room:* TV, fridge, coffeemaker, no phone.

The Red Garter Bed & Bakery ★ *Finds*   The Wild West lives again at this restored 1897 bordello. Located across the street from the Grand Canyon Railway terminal at the top of a steep flight of stairs, this B&B sports high ceilings, attractive wood trim, and reproduction period furnishings. On the walls in a couple of rooms, there's even graffiti written by bordello visitors in the early 20th century. All the great historic atmosphere makes this my favorite place to stay in Williams.

137 W. Railroad Ave., Williams, AZ 86046. ℂ 800/328-1484 or 928/635-1484. www.redgarter.com. 4 units. $120–$140 double. Lower rates off season. Rates include continental breakfast. DISC, MC, V. **Amenities:** Bakery. *In room:* TV, no phone.

CAMPING
There are several campgrounds near Williams in the Kaibab National Forest. They include **Cataract Lake,** 2 miles northwest of Williams on Cataract Lake Road, with 18 sites; **Dogtown Lake,** 8 miles south of Williams off Fourth Street/County Road 73, with 51 sites; **Kaibab Lake,** 4 miles northeast of Williams off Ariz. 64, with 72 sites; and **Whitehorse Lake,** 19 miles southeast of Williams off Fourth Street/County Road 73, with 105 sites. All campgrounds are first-come, first-served, and charge $10 to $12 per night.

WHERE TO DINE

Cruiser's Café 66 AMERICAN   If you're looking for a taste of old-fashioned Route 66 atmosphere, this is the place. Partly housed in a 1930s gas station, this place is full of Route 66 memorabilia, and just inside the front door is a stuffed bison with a saddle on its back. The menu runs the gamut from steaks and spicy wings to pizza and calzones, but I like to dig into the smoked baby back ribs or the platter of fajitas.

233 W. Rte. 66. © 928/635-2445. Main courses $7–$20. AE, DISC, MC, V. Daily 4–9:30pm.

Rod's Steak House STEAKHOUSE/SEAFOOD   For a good dinner in Williams, just look for the red neon steer at the east end of town. The menu here may be short, but the food is reliable. Prime rib au jus, the house specialty, comes in three different weights to fit your hunger. If you're not in the mood for steak, opt for barbecued ribs, trout, chicken, or shrimp.

301 E. Rte. 66. © 928/635-2671. www.rods-steakhouse.com. Reservations recommended. Main courses $4–$11 lunch, $10–$30 dinner. AE, DISC, MC, V. Mon–Sat 11am–9:30pm.

Get Your Kicks on Route 66

About 65 miles west of Flagstaff begins the longest remaining stretch of old Route 66. Extending for 160 miles from Ash Fork to Topock, this lonely black-top passes through some of the most remote country in Arizona. In the community of Seligman, at the east end of this stretch of the highway, you'll find **Delgadillo's Snow Cap Drive-In** (© 928/422-3291), where owner John Delgadillo serves up fast food and quick wit amid outrageous decor. Next door at **Angel & Vilma Delgadillo's Route 66 Gift Shop & Visitor's Center,** 217 E. Rte. 66 (© 928/422-3352; www.route66giftshop.com), owned by John's uncle Angel, you'll be entertained by one of Route 66's most famous residents and an avid fan of the old highway. The walls of Angel's old one-chair barbershop are covered with photos and business cards of happy customers. Today, Angel's place is a Route 66 information center and souvenir shop.

After leaving Seligman, the highway passes through such waysides as Peach Springs, Truxton, Valentine, and Hackberry. In Hackberry, be sure to stop at the **Old Route 66 Visitor Center & General Store** (© 928/769-2605), which is filled with Route 66 memorabilia as well as old stuff from the 1950s and 1960s. Before reaching Peach Springs, you'll come to **Grand Canyon Caverns,** once a near-mandatory stop for families traveling Route 66.

After driving through the wilderness west of Seligman, Kingman feels like a veritable metropolis. Today, there are dozens of modern motels in Kingman. Across the street from **Mr. D'z Route 66 Diner** is the restored powerhouse, which dates from 1907 and is home to the **Historic Route 66 Association of Arizona** (© 928/753-5001; www.azrt66.com), the **Route 66 Museum** (© 928/753-3195; www.kingmantourism.org/route66museum), and the Kingman Area Chamber of Commerce Visitor Center.

The last stretch of Route 66 in Arizona heads southwest out of Kingman through the rugged Sacramento Mountains and passes through **Oatman.**

3 The Grand Canyon South Rim ★★★

60 miles N of Williams; 80 miles NE of Flagstaff; 230 miles N of Phoenix; 340 miles N of Tucson

Whether you merely stand on the rim gazing in awe, spend several days hiking deep in the canyon, or ride the roller-coaster rapids of the Colorado River, a trip to the Grand Canyon is an unforgettable experience. A mile deep, 277 miles long, and up to 18 miles wide, the canyon is so large that it is positively overwhelming in its grandeur, truly one of the great wonders of the world.

Layers of sandstone, limestone, shale, and schist give the canyon its colors, and the interplay of shadows and light from dawn to dusk creates an ever-changing palette of hues and textures. Written in these bands of stone are more than 2 billion years of history. Geologists believe it has taken between 3 million and 6 million years for the Colorado River to carve the Grand Canyon, but the canyon's history extends much further back in time.

Millions of years ago, vast seas covered this region. Sediments carried by sea water were deposited and, over millions of years, turned into limestone and sandstone. According to one theory, when the ancient seabed was thrust upward to form the Kaibab Plateau, the Colorado River began its work of cutting through the plateau. Today, 21 sedimentary layers, the oldest of which is more than a billion years old, can be seen in the canyon. Beneath all these layers, at the very bottom, is a stratum of rock so old that it has metamorphosed, under great pressure and heat, from soft shale to a much harder stone. Called Vishnu schist, this layer is the oldest rock in the Grand Canyon and dates from 2 billion years ago.

In the more recent past, the Grand Canyon has been home to several Native American cultures, including the Ancestral Puebloans (Anasazi), who are best known for their cliff dwellings in the Four Corners region. About 150 years after the Ancestral Puebloans and Coconino peoples abandoned the canyon in the 13th century, another tribe, the Cerbat, moved into the area. Today, the Hualapai and Havasupai tribes, descendants of the Cerbat people, still live in and near the Grand Canyon on the south side of the Colorado River. On the North Rim lived the Southern Paiute, and in the west, the Navajo.

However, there have been those in the recent past who regarded the canyon as mere wasted space, suitable only for filling with water. Upstream of the Grand Canyon stands Glen Canyon Dam, which forms Lake Powell, while downstream lies Lake Mead, created by Hoover Dam. The same thing could have happened to the Grand Canyon, but luckily the forces for preservation prevailed. Today, the Grand Canyon is the last major undammed stretch of the Colorado River.

All this popularity has taken its toll; with roughly four million people visiting the park each year, traffic during the summer months has become almost as bad at the South Rim as it is during rush hour in any major city, and finding a parking space is a challenge. But don't let these inconveniences dissuade you from visiting. Despite the crowds, the Grand Canyon still more than lives up to its name and is one of the most memorable sights on earth.

ESSENTIALS
GETTING THERE
BY CAR   Parking problems and traffic congestion have become the norm at Grand Canyon Village during the popular summer months (and are becoming common in spring and fall as well). If at all possible, travel into the park by some means other than

car (see below for alternatives). There are plenty of scenic overlooks, hiking trails, restaurants, and lodges in the village area, and depending on the time of year, free shuttle buses operate along both the West Rim Drive and the East Rim Drive.

If you do drive, be sure you have plenty of gasoline in your car before setting out for the canyon; there are few service stations in this remote part of the state. The South Rim of the Grand Canyon is 60 miles north of Williams and I-40 on Ariz. 64 and U.S. 180. Flagstaff, the nearest city of any size, is 80 miles away. From Flagstaff, it's possible to take U.S. 180 directly to the South Rim or U.S. 89 to Ariz. 64 and the east entrance to the park.

BY PLANE   The Grand Canyon Airport is in Tusayan, 6 miles south of Grand Canyon Village. **Scenic Airlines** (© 800/634-6801; www.scenic.com), flies from Las Vegas and charges $205 to $305 round-trip. Alternatively, you can fly into Flagstaff and then arrange another mode of transportation the rest of the way to the national park (see "Flagstaff," earlier in this chapter, for details).

BY TRAIN   The **Grand Canyon Railway** operates excursion trains between Williams and the South Rim of the Grand Canyon. See "Williams," earlier in this chapter, for details.

For long-distance connections, **Amtrak** (© 800/872-7245; www.amtrak.com) provides service to Flagstaff and Williams. From Flagstaff, it's then possible to take a bus directly to Grand Canyon Village. From Williams, you can take the Grand Canyon Railway excursion train to Grand Canyon Village. *Note:* The Amtrak stop in Williams is undeveloped and is on the outskirts of town. If you plan to take an Amtrak train to Williams, a shuttle from the Grand Canyon Railway Hotel will pick you up where the Amtrak train drops you off.

BY BUS   Bus service between Phoenix, Flagstaff, and Grand Canyon Village is provided by **Open Road Tours** (© 800/766-7117 or 602/997-6474; www.openroad tours.com). Adult fares are $39 one-way or $70 round-trip ($27 and $46 for children) between Phoenix and Flagstaff and $25 one-way or $50 round-trip ($20 and $40 for children) between Flagstaff and the Grand Canyon.

VISITOR INFORMATION

You can get advance information on the Grand Canyon by contacting **Grand Canyon National Park,** P.O. Box 129, Grand Canyon, AZ 86023 (© **928/638-7888;** www. nps.gov/grca).

When you arrive at the park, stop by the **Canyon View Visitor Center,** at Canyon View Information Plaza, 6 miles from the south entrance. Here you'll find exhibits, an information desk, and a shop selling maps, books, and videos. The center is open daily 9am to 5pm. Unfortunately, the information plaza has no adjacent parking, so you'll have to park where you can and then walk or take a free shuttle bus. The nearest places to park are at Mather Point, Market Plaza, park headquarters, and Yavapai Observation Station. From Grand Canyon Village, you'll want to catch the Village Route bus. From Yaki Point, take the Kaibab Trail Route bus. *The Guide,* a small newspaper full of useful information about the park, is available at both South Rim park entrances.

ORIENTATION

Grand Canyon Village is built on the South Rim of the canyon and divided roughly into two sections. At the east end of the village are the Canyon View Information

Plaza, Yavapai Lodge, Trailer Village, and Mather Campground. At the west end are El Tovar Hotel and Bright Angel, Kachina, Thunderbird, and Maswik lodges, as well as several restaurants, the train depot, and the trail head for the Bright Angel Trail.

FEES

The entry fee for Grand Canyon National Park is $20 per car (or $10 per person if you happen to be coming in on foot or by bicycle). Your admission ticket is good for 7 days (don't lose it, or you'll have to pay again).

GETTING AROUND

As mentioned earlier, the Grand Canyon Village area can be extremely congested, especially in summer. If possible, you may want to use one of the transportation options below to avoid the park's traffic jams and parking problems. To give you an idea, in summer you can expect at least a 20- to 30-minute wait at the South Rim entrance gate just to get into the park. You can cut the waiting time here by acquiring either a National Parks Pass, a Golden Eagle Pass, a Golden Age Pass, or a Golden Access Pass before arriving. With pass in hand, you can use the express lane.

For **accessibility information,** check *The Guide* for park programs, services, and facilities that are partially or fully accessible. You can also get *The Grand Canyon National Park Accessibility Guide* at park entrances, Canyon View Center, Yavapai Observation Station, Kolb Studio, Tusayan Museum, and Desert View Information Center. Temporary accessibility permits are available at the park entrances, Canyon View Information Plaza, and Yavapai Observation Station. Wheelchairs are available at no charge for temporary use inside the park. You can usually find one of these wheelchairs at the Canyon View Center. Wheelchair-accessible shuttle buses can be arranged a day in advance by calling the national park (© **928/638-0591**). Accessible tours can also be arranged by contacting any lodge transportation desk or by calling **Grand Canyon National Park Lodges** (© 928/638-2631).

BY BUS   March through November, free shuttle buses operate on four routes within the park. The **Village Route** bus circles through Grand Canyon Village throughout the day with frequent stops at the Canyon View Information Plaza, Market Plaza (site of a general store, bank, laundry, and showers), hotels, campgrounds, restaurants, and other facilities. The **Hermit's Rest Route** bus takes visitors to eight canyon overlooks west of Bright Angel Lodge. The **Kaibab Trail Route** bus, which stops at the Canyon View Information Plaza, Pipe Creek Vista, the South Kaibab trail head, and Yaki Point, provides the only access to Yaki Point, the trail head for the South Kaibab Trail to the bottom of the canyon. The **Canyon View/Mather Point Route** is specifically for visitors who need mobility assistance and shuttles between the Mather Point parking lot and the Canyon View Information Center. There's also a Hiker Express bus to Yaki Point. This bus stops at Bright Angel Lodge and the Back Country Information Office. Hikers needing transportation to or from Yaki Point when the bus is not running can use a taxi (© **928/638-2822**).

Trans Canyon (© **928/638-2820**) offers shuttle-bus service between the South Rim and the North Rim. The vans leave the South Rim at 1:30pm and arrive at the North Rim at 6:30pm. The return trip leaves the North Rim at 7am, arriving back at the South Rim at noon. The fare is $65 one-way and $110 round trip; reservations are required. There is also a shuttle to Marble Canyon.

BY CAR   There are service stations outside the south entrance to the park in Tusayan, at Desert View near the east entrance (this station is seasonal), and east of the park at Cameron. Because of the long distances within the park and to towns outside the park, be sure you have plenty of gas before setting out on a drive. Gas at the canyon is very expensive.

If you want to avoid **parking** headaches, try using the lot in front of the Canyon Village Marketplace (the general store), which is up a side road near Yavapai Lodge and the Canyon View Information Plaza. From this large parking area, a paved hiking trail leads to the historic section of the village in less than 1.5 miles, and most of the route is along the rim. Another option is to park at the Maswik Transportation Center parking lot, which is served by the Village Route shuttle bus.

BY TAXI   There is taxi service available to and from the airport, trail heads, and other destinations (✆ **928/638-2822**). The fare from the airport to Grand Canyon Village is $10 for up to two adults ($5 for each additional person).

FAST FACTS

There's an ATM at the **Bank One** (✆ **928/638-2437**) at Market Plaza, which is near Yavapai Lodge. The bank is open Monday through Thursday from 9am to 5pm and Friday from 9am to 6pm.

The **South Rim Walk-In Clinic** (✆ **928/638-2551**) is on Clinic Drive, off Center Road (the road that runs past the National Park Service ranger office). The clinic is open Monday through Friday from 9am to 6pm and Saturday from 10am to 2pm (may be open later in summer). It provides 24-hour emergency service as well.

The **climate** at the Grand Canyon is dramatically different from that of Phoenix, and between the rim and the canyon floor there's also a pronounced difference. Winter temperatures at the South Rim can be below 0°F (-18°C) at night, with daytime highs in the 20s or 30s (minus single digits to single digits Celsius). Summer temperatures at the rim range from highs in the 80s (20s Celsius) to lows in the 50s (teens Celsius). The North Rim is slightly higher than the South Rim and stays a bit cooler. On the canyon floor, temperatures are considerably higher. In summer, the mercury can reach 120°F (49°C) with lows in the 70s (20s Celsius), while in winter, temperatures are quite pleasant with highs in the 50s (teens Celsius) and lows in the 30s (single digits Celsius).

DESERT VIEW DRIVE

The vast majority of visitors to the Grand Canyon enter through the south entrance, head straight for Grand Canyon Village, and proceed to get caught up in traffic jams. You can avoid much of this congestion and have a much more enjoyable experience if you enter the park through the east entrance. To reach the east entrance from Flagstaff, take U.S. 89 to Ariz. 64. Even before you reach the park, you can stop and take in views of the canyon of the Little Colorado River. These viewpoints are on the Navajo Reservation, and at every stop you'll have opportunities to shop for Native American crafts and souvenirs at the numerous vendors' stalls that can be found at virtually every scenic viewpoint on the Navajo Reservation.

Desert View Drive, the park's only scenic road open to cars, extends for 25 miles from Desert View, which is just inside the park's east entrance, to Grand Canyon Village, the site of all the park's hotels and most of its other commercial establishments. Along Desert View Drive, you'll find not only good viewpoints but also several picnic areas. Much of this drive is through forests, and canyon views are limited, but where there are viewpoints, they are among the best in the park.

Grand Canyon South Rim

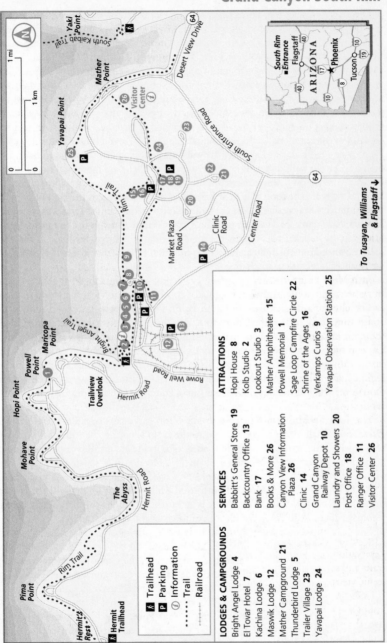

LODGES & CAMPGROUNDS

Bright Angel Lodge **4**
El Tovar Hotel **7**
Kachina Lodge **6**
Maswik Lodge **12**
Mather Campground **21**
Thunderbird Lodge **5**
Trailer Village **23**
Yavapai Lodge **24**

SERVICES

Babbitt's General Store **19**
Backcountry Office **13**
Bank **17**
Books & More **26**
Canyon View Information
  Plaza **26**
Clinic **14**
Grand Canyon
  Railway Depot **10**
Laundry and Showers **20**
Post Office **18**
Ranger Office **11**
Visitor Center **26**

ATTRACTIONS

Hopi House **8**
Kolb Studio **2**
Lookout Studio **3**
Mather Amphitheater **15**
Powell Memorial **1**
Sage Loop Campfire Circle **22**
Shrine of the Ages **16**
Verkamps Curios **9**
Yavapai Observation Station **25**

537

Desert View, with its trading post, general store, snack bar, service station, information center, bookstore, and historic watchtower, is the first stop on this scenic drive. From anywhere at Desert View, the scenery is breathtaking but the very best perspective here is from atop the **Desert View Watchtower.** Architect Mary Elizabeth Jane Colter, who is responsible for much of the park's historic architecture, designed it to resemble the prehistoric towers that dot the Southwestern landscape, but the tower actually dates from 1932. Built as an observation tower and rest stop for tourists, the watchtower incorporates Native American designs and art. The curio shop on the ground floor is a replica of a kiva (sacred ceremonial chamber) and has lots of interesting souvenirs, regional crafts, and books. The tower's second floor features work by Hopi artist Fred Kabotie. Covering the walls are pictographs incorporating traditional designs. On the walls and ceiling of the upper two floors are more traditional images by artist Fred Geary, this time reproductions of petroglyphs from throughout the Southwest. From the roof, which, at 7,522 feet above sea level, is the highest point on the South Rim, it's possible to see the Colorado River, the Painted Desert to the northeast, the San Francisco Peaks to the south, and Marble Canyon to the north. Several black-mirror "reflectoscopes" provide interesting darkened views of some of the most spectacular sections of the canyon. The gift shop offers a pamphlet describing the watchtower in detail.

At **Navajo Point,** the next stop along the rim, the Colorado River and Escalante Butte are both visible, and there's a good view of the Desert View Watchtower. However, I suggest heading straight to **Lipan Point** ★★, where you get what I think is the South Rim's best view of the Colorado River. You can actually see several stretches of the river, including a couple of major rapids. From here you can also view the Grand Canyon supergroup: several strata of rock tilted at an angle to the other layers of rock in the canyon. The red, white, and black rocks of the supergroup are composed of sedimentary rock and layers of lava. One of the park's best-kept secrets, a little-known, though very rugged trail, begins here at Lipan Point (see "Hiking the Canyon," below, for details).

The **Tusayan Museum** (open daily 9am–5pm) is the next stop along Desert View Drive. This small museum is dedicated to the Hopi tribe and the Ancestral Puebloan people who inhabited the region 800 years ago; inside are artfully displayed exhibits on various aspects of Ancestral Puebloan life. Outside is a short, self-guided trail through the ruins of an Ancestral Puebloan village. Free guided tours are available.

Next along the drive is **Moran Point,** from which you can see a bright-red layer of shale in the canyon walls. This point is named for 19th-century landscape painter Thomas Moran, who is known for his paintings of the Grand Canyon.

The next stop, **Grandview Point,** affords a view of Horseshoe Mesa, another interesting feature of the canyon landscape. The mesa was the site of the Last Chance Copper Mine in the early 1890s. Later that same decade, the Grandview Hotel was built and served canyon visitors until its close in 1908. The steep, unmaintained Grandview Trail leads down to Horseshoe Mesa from here. This trail makes a good less-traveled alternative to the South Kaibab Trail, although it is somewhat steeper.

The last stop along Desert View Drive is **Yaki Point,** which is no longer open to private vehicles. The park service would prefer it if you parked your car in Grand Canyon Village and took the Kaibab Trail Route shuttle bus from the Canyon View Information Plaza to Yaki Point. The reality is that people park their cars alongside the main road and walk up the Yaki Point access road. The spectacular view from here encompasses a wide section of the central canyon. The large, flat-topped butte to the northeast is Wotan's Throne, one of the canyon's most readily recognizable features. Yaki Point is the site of the trail head for the South Kaibab Trail and consequently is frequented by hikers headed down to the bottom of the canyon at Phantom Ranch. The South Kaibab Trail is the preferred hiking route down to Phantom Ranch and is a more scenic route than the Bright Angel Trail. If you're planning a day hike into the canyon, this should be your number-one choice. Be sure to bring plenty of water.

GRAND CANYON VILLAGE & VICINITY

Grand Canyon Village is the first stop for the vast majority of the nearly four million people who visit the Grand Canyon every year. Consequently, it is the most crowded area in the park, but it also has the most overlooks and visitor services. Its many historic buildings, while nowhere near as impressive as the canyon itself, add to the popularity of the village, which, if it weren't so crowded all the time, would have a pleasant atmosphere.

For visitors who have entered the park through the south entrance, that unforgettable initial gasp-inducing glimpse of the canyon comes at **Mather Point.** From this overlook, there's a short paved path to the Canyon View Information Plaza, but because you're allowed to park at Mather Point only for a maximum of 1 hour, you'll have to hurry if you want to take in the views and gather some park information.

Continuing west toward the village proper, you next come to **Yavapai Point,** which has the best view from anywhere in the vicinity of Grand Canyon Village. From here you can see the Bright Angel Trail, Indian Gardens, Phantom Ranch, and even the suspension bridge that hikers and mule riders use to cross the Colorado River near Phantom Ranch. Oh yes, and of course you can also see the Colorado River. This viewpoint is a particularly great spot to take sunrise and sunset photos. Here you'll also find the historic **Yavapai Observation Station,** which houses a small museum and has big walls of glass to take in those extraordinary vistas. A paved pathway extends west from Yavapai Point for more than 3 miles to the west side of Grand Canyon Village. This trail also continues 2 miles east to the Pipe Creek Vista.

Continuing west from Yavapai Point, you'll come to a parking lot at park headquarters and a side road that leads to parking at the Market Plaza, which is one of the closest parking lots to the Canyon View Information Plaza.

West of these parking areas is Grand Canyon Village proper, where a paved pathway leads along the rim providing lots of good (though crowded) spots for taking pictures. The village is also the site of such historic buildings as **El Tovar Hotel** and **Bright Angel Lodge,** both of which are worth brief visits to take in the lodge ambience of their lobbies. Inside Bright Angel Lodge, you'll find the **Bright Angel History Room,** which has displays on Mary Elizabeth Jane Colter and the Harvey Girls. Be sure to check out the fireplace, which is designed with all the same geologic layers that appear in the canyon. Adjacent to El Tovar are two historic souvenir and curio shops. **Hopi House Gift Store and Art Gallery,** the first shop in the park, was built in 1905 to resemble a Hopi pueblo and to serve as a place for Hopi artisans to work and sell their crafts. Today, it's full of Hopi and Navajo arts and crafts, including expensive kachina dolls, rugs, jewelry, and pottery. The nearby **Verkamps Curios** originally opened in a tent in 1898, but John Verkamp soon went out of business. The store reopened in 1905 and ever since has been the main place to look for souvenirs and crafts. Just inside the door is a 535-pound meteorite. Both shops are open daily; hours vary seasonally.

To the west of Bright Angel Lodge, two buildings cling precariously to the rim of the canyon. These are the Kolb and Lookout studios, both of which are listed on the National Register of Historic Places. **Kolb Studio** is named for Ellsworth and Emory Kolb, two brothers who set up a photographic studio on the rim of the Grand Canyon in 1904. The construction of this studio generated one of the Grand Canyon's first controversies—over whether buildings should be allowed on the canyon rim. Because the Kolbs had friends in high places, their sprawling studio and movie theater remained. Emory Kolb lived here until his death in 1976, by which time the studio had been listed as a historic building. It now serves as a bookstore, while the auditorium houses special exhibits. **Lookout Studio,** built in 1914 from a design by Mary Elizabeth Jane Colter, was the Fred Harvey Company's answer to the Kolb brothers' studio. Photographs and books about the canyon were sold at the studio, which incorporates architectural styles of the Hopi and the Ancestral Puebloans. The use of native limestone and an uneven roofline allow the studio to blend in with the canyon walls and give it the look of an old ruin. It now houses a souvenir store and two lookout points. Both the Kolb and Lookout studios are open daily; hours vary seasonally.

HERMIT ROAD

Hermit Road leads 8 miles west from Grand Canyon Village to Hermit's Rest; mile for mile, it has the greatest concentration of breathtaking viewpoints in the park. Because it is closed to private vehicles March through November, it is also one of the most pleasant places to do a little canyon viewing or easy hiking during the busiest times of year: no traffic jams, no parking problems, and plenty of free shuttle buses operating along the route. Westbound buses stop at eight overlooks (Trailview, Maricopa Point, Powell Point, Hopi Point, Mohave Point, The Abyss, Pima Point, and Hermit's Rest); eastbound buses stop only at Mohave and Hopi points. From December to February, you can drive your own vehicle along this road, but keep in mind that winters usually mean a lot of snow, and the road can sometimes be closed due to hazardous driving conditions.

Because you probably won't want to stop at every viewpoint along this route, here are some tips to help you get the most out of an excursion along Hermit Road. First of all, keep in mind that the earlier you catch a shuttle bus, the more likely you are to avoid the crowds (buses start 1 hr. before sunrise so photographers can get good shots of the canyon in dawn light). Second, remember that the closer you are to Grand Canyon Village, the larger the crowds will be. So, head out early and get a couple of miles between you and the village before getting off the shuttle bus.

The first two stops are **Trailview Overlook** and **Maricopa Point,** both on the paved section of the Rim Trail and within 1½ miles of the village, thus usually pretty crowded. If you just want to do a short, easy walk on pavement, get out at Maricopa Point and walk back to the village. From either overlook, you have a view of the Bright Angel Trail winding down into the canyon from Grand Canyon Village. The trail, which leads to the bottom of the canyon, crosses the Tonto Plateau about 3,000 feet below the rim. This plateau is the site of Indian Garden, where there's a campground in a grove of cottonwood trees. Because the views from these two overlooks are not significantly different from those in the village, we'd suggest skipping these stops if you've already spent time gazing into the canyon from the village.

Powell Point, the third stop, is the site of a memorial to John Wesley Powell, who, in 1869 with a party of nine men, became the first person to navigate the Colorado River through the Grand Canyon. Visible at Powell Point are the remains of the

Orphan Mine, a copper mine that began operation in 1893. The mine went out of business because transporting the copper to a city where it could be sold was too expensive. Uranium was discovered here in 1954, but in 1966 the mine was shut down, and the land became part of Grand Canyon National Park. Again, we recommend continuing on to the more spectacular vistas that lie ahead.

The next stop is **Hopi Point,** which is one of the three best stops along this route. From here you can see a long section of the Colorado River far below you. Because of the great distance, the river seems to be a tiny, quiet stream, but in reality the section you see is more than 100 yards wide and races through Granite Rapids. Because Hopi Point juts out into the canyon, it is one of the best spots in the park for taking sunrise and sunset photos; shuttle buses operate from 1 hour before sunrise to 1 hour after sunset.

The view is even more spectacular at the next stop, **Mohave Point.** Here you can see the river in two directions. Three rapids are visible from this overlook, and on a quiet day, you can sometimes even hear Hermit Rapids. As with almost all rapids in the canyon, these are formed at the mouth of a side canyon where boulders loosened by storms and carried by flooded streams are deposited in the Colorado River. Don't miss this stop; it's got the best view on Hermit Road!

Next you come to **The Abyss,** the appropriately named 3,000-foot drop created by the Great Mojave Wall. This vertiginous view is one of the most awe-inspiring in the park. The walls of The Abyss are red sandstone that's more resistant to erosion than the softer shale in the layer below. Other layers of erosion-resistant sandstone have formed the freestanding pillars that are visible from here. The largest of these pillars is called the Monument. If you're looking for a good hike along this road, get out here and walk westward to either Pima Point (3 miles distant) or Hermit's Rest (4 miles away).

The **Pima Point** overlook, because it is set back from the road, is another good place to get off the bus. From here, the Rim Trail leads through the forest near the canyon rim, providing good views undisturbed by traffic on Hermit Road. From this overlook, it's also possible to see the remains of Hermit Camp on the Tonto Plateau. Built by the Santa Fe Railroad, Hermit Camp was a popular tourist destination between 1911 and 1930 and provided cabins and tents. Only foundations remain.

The final stop on Hermit Road is at **Hermit's Rest,** which was named for Louis Boucher, a prospector who came to the canyon in the 1890s and was known as the Hermit. The log-and-stone Hermit's Rest building, designed by Mary Elizabeth Jane Colter and built in 1914, is on the National Register of Historic Places and is one of the most fascinating structures in the park. With its snack bar, it makes a great place to linger while you soak up a bit of park history. The steep Hermit Trail, which leads down into the canyon, begins just past Hermit's Rest.

HIKING THE CANYON

No visit to the canyon is complete without journeying below the rim on one of the park's hiking trails. Gazing up at all those thousands of feet of vertical rock walls provides a very different perspective than that from atop the rim. Should you venture far below the rim, you also stand a chance of seeing fossils, old mines, petroglyphs, wildflowers, and wildlife. However, because of the Grand Canyon's popularity, the park's main hiking trails are usually crowded.

That said, there is no better way to see the canyon than on foot (our apologies to the mules), and a hike down into the canyon will likely be the highlight of your visit. The Grand Canyon offers some of the most rugged and strenuous hiking anywhere in the United States, and for this reason anyone attempting even a short walk should be well prepared. Each year, injuries and fatalities are suffered by day hikers who set out without sturdy footgear or without food and adequate amounts of water. Even a 30-minute hike in summer can dehydrate you, and a long hike in the heat can necessitate drinking more than a gallon of water. So, carry and drink at least 2 quarts (2 liters) of water if you go for a day hike during the summer. Don't attempt to hike from the rim to the Colorado River and back in a day; there are plenty of hikers who have tried this and died. Also remember that mules have the right of way.

DAY HIKES

There are no loop trails on the South Rim, but the vastly different scenery in every direction makes out-and-back hikes here as interesting as any loop trail could be. The only problem is that instead of starting out by slogging up a steep mountain, you let gravity assist you in hiking down into the canyon. With little negative reinforcement and few natural turnaround destinations, it is easy to hike so far that the return trip back up the trail becomes an arduous death march. Turn around *before* you become tired. On the canyon rim, the only hiking trail is the Rim Trail, while the Bright Angel, South Kaibab, Grandview, and Hermit trails all head down into the canyon.

For an easy, flat hike, your only option is the **Rim Trail,** which stretches from Pipe Creek Vista east of Grand Canyon Village to Hermit's Rest, 8 miles west of the village. Just over 4.5 miles of this trail are paved, and the portion that passes through Grand Canyon Village is always the most crowded stretch of trail in the park. To the west of the village, after the pavement ends, the Rim Trail leads another 6.7 miles out to Hermit's Rest. For most of this distance, the trail follows Hermit Road, which means you'll have to deal with traffic noise (mostly from shuttle buses). To get the most enjoyment out of a hike along this stretch, I like to head out as early in the morning as possible (to avoid the crowds) and get off at The Abyss shuttle stop. From here it's a 4-mile hike to Hermit's Rest; for more than half of this distance, the trail isn't as close to the road as it is at the Grand Canyon Village end of the route. Plus, Hermit's Rest makes a great place to rest, and from here you can catch a shuttle bus back to the village. Alternatively, you could start hiking from Grand Canyon Village (it's just over 8 miles from the west end of the village to Hermit's Rest) or any of the seven shuttle-bus stops en route, or take the shuttle all the way to Hermit's Rest and then hike back.

The **Bright Angel Trail,** which starts just west of Bright Angel Lodge in Grand Canyon Village, is the most popular trail into the canyon because it starts right where the greatest number of park visitors tend to congregate (near the ice-cream parlor and the hotels). It is also the route used by mule riders headed down into the canyon. Bear in mind that this trail follows a narrow side canyon for several miles down into the Grand Canyon and thus has somewhat limited views. For these reasons, this trail is worth avoiding if you're on foot. On the other hand, it's the only maintained trail into the canyon that has potable water, and there are four destinations along the trail that make good turnaround points. Both 1½ Mile Resthouse (1,131 ft. below the rim) and 3 Mile Resthouse (2,112 ft. below the rim) have water (except in winter, when the water is turned off). Keep in mind that these rest houses take their names from their distance from the rim; if you hike to 3 Mile Resthouse, you still have a 3-mile hike back up. Destinations for longer day hikes include Indian Garden (9 miles round-trip) and Plateau Point (12 miles round-trip), which are both just over 3,000 feet below the rim. There is year-round water at Indian Garden.

The **South Kaibab Trail** ⚜⚜⚜ begins near Yaki Point east of Grand Canyon Village and is the preferred route down to Phantom Ranch. This trail also offers the best views of any of the day hikes into the canyon, so should you have time for only 1 day hike, make it this trail. From the trail head, it's 3 miles round-trip to Cedar Ridge or 6 miles round-trip to Skeleton Point. The hike is very strenuous, and there's no water available along the trail.

If you're looking to escape the crowds and are an experienced mountain or desert hiker with good, sturdy boots, consider the unmaintained **Hermit Trail,** which begins at Hermit's Rest, 8 miles west of Grand Canyon Village at the end of Hermit Road. It's a 5-mile round-trip hike to Santa Maria Spring on a trail that loses almost all of its elevation (1,600–1,700 ft.) in the first 1½ miles. Beyond Santa Maria Spring, the Hermit Trail descends to the Colorado River, but it is a 17-mile hike, one-way, from the trail head. Alternatively, you can do a 7-mile round-trip hike to Dripping Springs. Water from either of these two springs must be treated with a water filter, iodine, or purification tablets, or by boiling for at least 10 minutes, so you're better off just carrying sufficient water for your hike. Hermit Road is closed to private vehicles from March to November, so chances are you'll need to take the free shuttle bus out to the trail head. If you take the first bus of the day, you'll probably have the trail almost all to yourself.

The **Grandview Trail,** which begins at Grandview Point 12 miles east of Grand Canyon Village, is another steep and unmaintained trail that's a good choice for physically fit hikers. The strenuous 6-mile round-trip hike leads down to Horseshoe Mesa, 2,600 feet below the rim-top trail head. There's no water available, so carry at least 2 quarts. Allow at least 7 hours for this rugged hike. Just to give you an idea of how steep this trail is, you'll lose more than 2,000 feet of elevation in the first .75 mile down to Coconino Saddle!

BACKPACKING

Backpacking the Grand Canyon is an unforgettable experience. Although most people are content to simply hike down to Phantom Ranch and back, there are many miles of trails deep in the canyon. Keep in mind, however, that to backpack the canyon, you'll need to do a lot of planning. A **Backcountry Use Permit** is required of all hikers planning to overnight in the canyon, unless you'll be staying at Phantom Ranch in one of the cabins or a dormitory.

Because a limited number of hikers are allowed into the canyon on any given day, it's important to make reservations as soon as it is possible to do so. Reservations are taken in person, by mail, by fax (but not by phone), and online. Contact the **Backcountry Office,** Grand Canyon National Park, P.O. Box 129, Grand Canyon, AZ 86023 (© **928/638-7875** 1–5pm for information; fax 928/638-2125; www.nps.gov/grca). The office begins accepting reservations on the first of every month for the following 5 months. Holiday periods are the most popular—if you want to hike over the Labor Day weekend, be sure you make your reservation on May 1! If you show up without a reservation, go to the Backcountry Information Center (open daily 8am–noon and 1–5pm), adjacent to the Maswik Lodge, and put your name on the waiting list. When applying for a permit, you must specify your exact itinerary, and once in the canyon, you must stick to this itinerary. Backpacking fees include a non-refundable $10 backcountry permit fee and a $5 per person per night backcountry camping fee. American Express, Diners Club, Discover, MasterCard, and Visa are accepted for permit fees. Keep in mind that you'll still have to pay the park entry fee when you arrive at the Grand Canyon.

There are **campgrounds** at Indian Garden, Bright Angel Campground (near Phantom Ranch), and Cottonwood, but hikers are limited to 2 nights per trip at each of these campgrounds (except Nov 15–Feb 28, when 4 nights are allowed at each campground). Other nights can be spent camping at undesignated sites in certain regions of the park.

The *Backcountry Trip Planner* contains information to help you plan your itinerary. It's available through the Backcountry Office (see contact information, above). Maps are available through the **Grand Canyon Association,** P.O. Box 399, Grand Canyon, AZ 86023 (© **800/858-2808** or 928/638-2481; www.grandcanyon.org), and at bookstores and gift shops within the national park, including Canyon View Information Plaza, Kolb Studio, Desert View Information Center, Yavapai Observation Station, Tusayan Museum, and, on the North Rim, at Grand Canyon Lodge.

The best times of year to backpack are spring and fall. In summer, temperatures at the bottom of the canyon are frequently above 100°F (38°C), while in winter, ice and snow at higher elevations make footing on trails precarious (crampons are recommended). Plan to carry at least 2 quarts, and preferably 1 gallon, of water whenever backpacking in the canyon.

The Grand Canyon is an unforgiving landscape, and as such, many people might feel the need of a professional guide while backpacking through this rugged corner of the Southwest. To arrange a guided backpacking trip into the canyon, contact **Discovery Treks,** 6890 E. Sunrise Dr., Suite 120-108, Tucson, AZ 85750 (© **888/256-8731;** www.discoverytreks.com), which offers 2- to 5-day all-inclusive hikes into the canyon with rates ranging from $525 to $1,175 per person. Base camp trips featuring daily day hikes are also available. Another company, **Sky Island Treks** (© **520/622-6966;** www.skyislandtreks.com) leads trips ranging in length from 3 to 13 days. The easier trips stick to well-traveled trails, while the more challenging treks head off into some of the most remote regions of the park. Prices start at $495 for a 3-day trek.

OTHER WAYS OF SEEING THE CANYON
BUS TOURS
If you'd rather leave the driving to someone else and enjoy more of the scenery, opt for a bus or van tour of one or more sections of the park. **Grand Canyon National Park Lodges** (© **928/638-2631**) offers several tours within the park. These can be booked by calling or stopping at one of the transportation desks, which are at Bright Angel, Maswik, and Yavapai lodges (see "Where to Stay," below). Prices range from around $13 for a 1½-hour sunrise tour to around $35 for a combination tour to both Hermit's Rest and Desert View.

MULE RIDES ⚸
Mule rides into the canyon have been popular since the beginning of the 20th century, when the Bright Angel Trail was a toll road. After having a look at the steep drop-offs and narrow path of the Bright Angel Trail, you might decide this isn't exactly the place to trust your life to a mule. Never fear: Wranglers will be quick to reassure you they haven't lost a rider yet. Trips of various lengths and to different destinations are offered. The 1-day trip descends to Plateau Point, where there's a view of the Colorado River 1,300 feet below. This grueling trip requires riders to spend 6 hours in the saddle. Those who want to spend a night down in the canyon can choose an overnight

trip to Phantom Ranch, where cabins and dormitories are available at the only lodge actually in the canyon. From November to March, a 3-day trip to Phantom Ranch is offered; other times of year, you'll ride down 1 day and back up the next. Mule trips range in price from $133 for a 1-day ride to $366 for an overnight ride. Couples get discounts on overnight rides.

Riders must weigh less than 200 pounds fully dressed, stand at least 4 feet 7 inches tall, and speak fluent English. Pregnant women are not allowed on mule trips.

Because these trail rides are very popular (especially in summer), they often book up 6 months or more in advance (reservations are taken up to 23 months in advance). For more information or to make a reservation, contact **Xanterra Parks & Resorts** (© **888/297-2757** or 303/297-2757; www.grandcanyonlodges.com). If at the last minute (5 days or fewer from the day you want to ride) you decide you want to go on a mule trip, contact **Grand Canyon National Park Lodges** at its Arizona phone number (© **928/638-2631**) for the remote possibility that there may be space available. If you arrive at the canyon without a reservation and decide that you'd like to go on a mule ride, stop by the Bright Angel Transportation Desk to get your name put on the next-day's waiting list.

THE GRAND CANYON RAILWAY ★★

In the early 20th century, most visitors to the Grand Canyon arrived by train, and it's still possible to travel to the canyon along the steel rails. The **Grand Canyon Railway** (© **800/843-8724** or 928/773-1976; www.thetrain.com), which runs from Williams to Grand Canyon Village, uses early-20th-century steam engines (Memorial Day weekend to Labor Day weekend) and 1950s-vintage diesel engines (during other months) to pull 1920s passenger cars as well as a dome coach car. Trains depart from the Williams Depot, which is housed in the historic 1908 Fray Marcos Hotel, which also contains a railroad museum, gift shop, and cafe. (Grand Canyon Railway also operates the adjacent Grand Canyon Railway Hotel.) At Grand Canyon Village, the trains use the 1910 log railway terminal in front of El Tovar Hotel.

Passengers have the choice of five classes of service: coach, club, first class, deluxe observation class (upstairs in the dome car), and luxury parlor car. Actors posing as cowboys provide entertainment, including music performances, aboard the train. The round-trip takes 8 hours, including 3¼ hours at the canyon. Fares range from $60 to $155 for adults, $35 to $130 for children 11 to 16, and $25 to $85 for children 2 to 10 (not including tax or the park entry fee).

A BIRD'S-EYE VIEW

Despite controversies over noise and safety (there have been a few crashes over the years), airplane and helicopter flights over the Grand Canyon remain one of the most popular ways to see this natural wonder. Personally, I would rather enjoy the canyon on foot or from a saddle. However, the volume of flights over the canyon each day would indicate that quite a few people don't share my opinion. If you want to join the crowds buzzing the canyon, you'll find several companies operating out of Grand Canyon Airport in Tusayan. Air tours last anywhere from 30 minutes to about 2 hours.

Companies offering tours by small plane include **Air Grand Canyon** (© **800/247-4726** or 928/638-2686; www.airgrandcanyon.com) and **Grand Canyon Airlines** (© **866/235-9422** or 928/638-2359; www.grandcanyonairlines.com). This latter has been offering air tours since 1927 and is the oldest scenic airline at the canyon. Fifty-minute flights cost $89 for adults and $49 to $59 for children.

Helicopter tours are available from **Maverick Airstar Helicopters** (© **866/689-8687** or 928/638-2622; www.airstar.com), **Grand Canyon Helicopters** (© **800/541-4537** or 928/638-2764; www.grandcanyonhelicoptersaz.com), and **Papillon Grand Canyon Helicopters** (© **800/528-2418** or 928/638-2419; www.papillon.com). Rates range from $115 to $145 for a 30-minute flight and from $175 to $205 for a 45- to 55-minute flight. Also, check websites for discounts.

THE GRAND CANYON FIELD INSTITUTE

If you're the active type or would like to turn your visit to the Grand Canyon into more of an educational experience, you may want to consider doing a trip with the **Grand Canyon Field Institute** (© **866/471-4435** or 928/638-2485; www.grandcanyon.org/fieldinstitute). Cosponsored by Grand Canyon National Park and the Grand Canyon Association, the field institute schedules an amazing variety of guided, educational trips, such as challenging backpacking trips through the canyon (some for women only) and programs lasting anywhere from 3 to 10 days. Subjects covered include wilderness studies, geology, natural history, human history, photography, and art.

JEEP TOURS

If you'd like to explore some parts of Grand Canyon National Park that most visitors never see, contact **Grand Canyon Jeep Tours & Safaris** (© **800/320-5337** or 928/638-5337; www.grandcanyonjeeptours.com), which offers three different tours that visit the park as well as the adjacent Kaibab National Forest. One tour stops at a lookout tower that affords an elevated view of the canyon, while another visits an Indian ruin and site of petroglyphs and cave paintings. Prices range from $40 to $94 for adults and $30 to $75 for children 12 and under.

RAFTING THE COLORADO RIVER ★★★

Rafting down the Colorado River as it roars and tumbles through the mile-deep gorge of the Grand Canyon is the adventure of a lifetime. Ever since John Wesley Powell ignored everyone who knew better and proved that it was possible to travel by boat down the tumultuous Colorado, running the big river has become a passion and an obsession with adventurers. Today, anyone from grade-schoolers to grandmothers can join the elite group of people who have made the run. However, be prepared for some of the most furious white water in the world.

Most trips start from Lees Ferry near Page and Lake Powell. It's also possible to start (or finish) a trip at Phantom Ranch, hiking in or out from either the North or South Rim. The main rafting season is April through October, but some companies operate year-round. Rafting trips tend to book up more than a year in advance, and most companies begin taking reservations between March and May for the following year's trips. Expect to pay around $250 per day for your white-water adventure, depending on the length of the trip and the type of boat used.

The following are some of the companies I recommend checking out when you start planning your Grand Canyon rafting adventure:

• **Arizona Raft Adventures,** 4050 E. Huntington Rd., Flagstaff, AZ 86004 (© 800/786-7238; www.azraft.com); 6- to 16-day motor, oar, and paddle trips. Although this is not one of the larger companies operating on the river, it offers lots of different trips, including trips that focus on natural history and geology. They also do trips in paddle rafts that allow you to help navigate and provide the power while shooting the canyon's many rapids. Talk about exciting!

A Shopping Break

Outside the east entrance to the park, the **Cameron Trading Post** (© 800/338-7385 or 928/679-2231; www.camerontradingpost.com), at the crossroads of Cameron where Ariz. 64 branches off U.S. 89, is the best trading post in the state. The original stone trading post, a historic building, now houses a gallery of Indian artifacts, clothing, and jewelry. The main trading post is a more modern building. Don't miss the beautiful terraced gardens in back of the original trading post.

- **Canyoneers,** P.O. Box 2997, Flagstaff, AZ 86003 (© 800/525-0924 or 928/526-0924; www.canyoneers.com); 2- to 6-night motorized-raft trips and 4- to 11-night oar-powered trips, plus several short trips. Way back in 1938, this was the first company to take paying customers down the Colorado, and Canyoneers is still considered one of the top companies on the river.
- **Diamond River Adventures,** P.O. Box 1300, Page, AZ 86040 (© 800/343-3121 or 928/645-8866; www.diamondriver.com); 4- to 8-day motorized-raft trips and 5- to 13-day oar trips. This is the only women-owned and -managed rafting company operating in the Grand Canyon.
- **Grand Canyon Expeditions Company,** P.O. Box O, Kanab, UT 84741 (© 800/544-2691 or 435/644-2691; www.gcex.com); 8-day motorized trips and 14- and 16-day dory trips. No question about it: There's no more exciting way to do the canyon than in a dory! If you've got the time, I highly recommend these dory trips as among the most thrilling adventures in the world.
- **Hatch River Expeditions,** P.O. Box 1200, Vernal, UT 84078 (© 800/433-8966; www.hatchriverexpeditions.com); 4- and 7-day motorized trips. The 4-day trips involve either hiking in to the canyon or out of the canyon. On the 7-day trip, a helicopter lifts you out of the canyon at the end of the trip. This company has been in business since 1929 and claims to be the oldest commercial rafting company in the U.S. With so much experience, you can count on Hatch to provide you with a great trip.
- **Outdoors Unlimited,** 6900 Townsend Winona Rd., Flagstaff, AZ 86004 (© 800/637-7238 or 928/526-4511; www.outdoorsunlimited.com); 5- to 13-day oar and paddle trips. This company has been taking people through the canyon for more than 30 years and usually sends people home very happy.
- **Wilderness River Adventures,** P.O. Box 717, Page, AZ 86040 (© 800/992-8022 or 928/645-3296; www.riveradventures.com); 4- to 8-day motorized-raft trips and 6-, 7-, 12-, and 14-day oar trips. The 4-day trips involve hiking out from Phantom Ranch. This is one of the bigger companies operating on the canyon and it offers a wide variety of trips, which makes it a good one to check with if you're not sure which type of trip you want to do.

For information on 1-day rafting trips at the west end of the Grand Canyon, see "A South Rim Alternative: Havasu Canyon," later in this chapter.

WHERE TO STAY

Hotel rooms both within and just outside the park are in high demand. Make reservations as far in advance as possible, and don't expect to find a room if you head up here in summer without a reservation. There, is, however, one long-shot option. See "Inside the Park," below, for details.

INSIDE THE PARK

All hotels inside the park are operated by **Xanterra Parks & Resorts.** Reservations are taken up to 23 months in advance, beginning on the first of the month. If you want to stay in one of the historic rim cabins at Bright Angel Lodge, reserve at least a year in advance. However, rooms with shared bathrooms at Bright Angel Lodge are often the last in the park to book up, and although they're small and very basic, they're your best bet if you're trying to get a last-minute reservation.

To make reservations at any of the in-park hotels listed below, contact **Grand Canyon National Park Lodges/Xanterra Parks & Resorts,** 6312 S. Fiddlers Green Circle, Suite 600N, Greenwood Village, CO 80111 (© **888/297-2757** or 303/297-2757; www.xanterra.com or www.grandcanyonlodges.com). It is sometimes possible, due to cancellations and no-shows, to get a same-day reservation; it's a long shot, but it happens. Same-day reservations can be made by calling © **928/638-2631.** Xanterra accepts American Express, Discover, MasterCard, and Visa. Children under 16 stay for free in their parent's room.

Expensive

El Tovar Hotel ✦✦   El Tovar Hotel, which first opened its doors in 1905 and was completely renovated in 2005, is the park's premier lodge. Built of local rock and Oregon pine by Hopi craftsmen, it's a rustic yet luxurious mountain lodge that perches on the edge of the canyon (but with views from only a few rooms). The lobby, entered from a veranda set with rustic furniture, has a small fireplace, cathedral ceiling, and log walls on which moose, deer, and antelope heads are displayed. The standard units are rather small, as are the bathrooms. For more legroom, book a deluxe unit. Suites, with private terraces and stunning views, are extremely spacious. The El Tovar Dining Room (see "Where to Dine," below) is the best restaurant in the village. Just off the lobby is a cocktail lounge with a view.

78 units. $130–$185 double; $235–$300 suite. **Amenities:** Restaurant (Continental/Southwestern); lounge; concierge; tour desk; room service. *In room:* TV.

Moderate

Maswik Lodge   Set back ¼ mile or so from the rim, the Maswik Lodge offers spacious rooms and cabins that have been comfortably modernized without the loss of their appealing rustic character. If you don't mind roughing it a bit, the 28 old cabins, which are available only in summer, have lots of character and have benefited tremendously from upgrades a few years ago. These cabins now have high ceilings and ceiling fans and are my top choice away from the rim. If you crave modern appointments, opt for one of the large Maswik North rooms. Second floor rooms have high ceilings and balconies, which makes them the top choices away from the rim.

278 units. $73–$121 double (winter discounts available); $74 cabin. **Amenities:** Cafeteria; lounge; tour desk. *In room:* TV.

Thunderbird & Kachina Lodges   If you want great views, these hotels are your best bets (but only if you can get a room with a view!). These two side-by-side hotels date from the 1960s and, with their dated styling, are a far cry from what you might imagine a national park hotel would look like. They do, however, have a couple of things going for them. They have the biggest windows of any of the four hotels right on the canyon rim, and, after major renovations a couple of years ago, they're the most modern hotels in the park. Try to get a second-story room on the canyon side of either hotel (these rooms at the Kachina Lodge get the nod for having *the* best views). Book early—these two lodges right on the rim are some of the park's most popular accommodations. Just remember, if it's not a view room, you'll be staring at the parking lot.

104 units. $123–$133 double. *In room:* TV, dataport, fridge, coffeemaker, hair dryer, iron.

Yavapai Lodge   Located in several buildings at the east end of Grand Canyon Village (a 1-mile hike from the main section of the village but convenient to the Canyon View Information Plaza), the Yavapai is the largest lodge in the park and thus is where you'll likely wind up if you wait too long to make a reservation. Unfortunately it's also the least-appealing hotel in the national park and far from what you might imagine a national park lodge to be. There are no canyon views, which is why Yavapai is less expensive than the Thunderbird and Kachina lodges. If you must stay here, try for a room in the nicer Yavapai East wing, which is set under shady pines. However, I recommend that you plan ahead and try to stay at one of the lodges right on the rim.

358 units. $93–$100 double; $72–$82 double in winter. **Amenities:** Cafeteria; tour desk. *In room:* TV.

Inexpensive

Bright Angel Lodge & Cabins ✦   Bright Angel Lodge, which began operation in 1896 as a collection of tents and cabins on the edge of the canyon, is the most affordable lodge in the park, and, with its flagstone-floor lobby and huge fireplace, it has a genuine, if crowded, mountain-lodge atmosphere. It offers the greatest variety of accommodations in the park and underwent renovations a few years ago. The best and most popular units are the rim cabins, which should be booked a year in advance for summer. Outside the winter months, other rooms should be booked at least 6 months in advance. Most of the rooms and cabins feature rustic furnishings. The Buckey Suite, the oldest structure on the canyon rim, is arguably the best room in the park, with a canyon view, gas fireplace, and king-size bed. The tour desk, fireplace, museum, and restrooms account for the constant crowds in the lobby.

89 units, 20 with shared bathrooms. $51 double with sink only; $59 double with sink and toilet; $69 double with private bathroom; $84–$240 cabin. **Amenities:** 2 restaurants (American, steakhouse/Southwestern); lounge; ice-cream parlor; tour desk. *In room:* No phone.

Phantom Ranch ✦   Built in 1922, Phantom Ranch is the only lodge at the bottom of the Grand Canyon and has a classic ranch atmosphere. Accommodations are in rustic stone-walled cabins or 10-bed gender-segregated dormitories. Evaporative coolers keep both the cabins and the dorms cool in summer. Make reservations as early as possible, and don't forget to reconfirm. It's also sometimes possible to get a room on the day of departure if there are any last-minute cancellations. To attempt this, you must put your name on the waiting list at the Bright Angel Lodge transportation desk the day before you want to stay at Phantom Ranch.

Family-style meals must be reserved in advance. The menu consists of beef-and-vegetable stew ($21), a vegetarian dinner ($21), and steak ($31). Breakfasts ($18) are hearty, and sack lunches ($10) are available as well. Between meals, the dining hall becomes a canteen selling snacks, drinks, gifts, and necessities. After dinner, it serves as a beer hall. There's a public phone here, and mule-back baggage transfer between Grand Canyon Village and Phantom Ranch can be arranged ($55 each way).

© 928/638-3283 for reconfirmations. 11 cabins, 40 dorm beds. $81 double in cabin; $30 dormitory bed. Mule-trip overnights (with all meals and mule ride included) $366 for 1 person, $652 for 2 people. 2-night trips available Nov–Mar. **Amenities:** Restaurant (American); lounge. *In room:* No phone.

IN TUSAYAN (OUTSIDE THE SOUTH ENTRANCE)

If you can't get a reservation for a room in the park, this is the next closest place to stay. Unfortunately, this area can be very noisy because of the many helicopters and airplanes taking off from the airport. Also, hotels outside the park are very popular with tour groups, which during the busy summer months keep many hotels full. All of the hotels listed here are lined up along U.S. 180/Ariz. 64.

Best Western Grand Canyon Squire Inn ★★ (Kids) If you prefer playing tennis to riding a mule, this may be the place for you. Of all the hotels in Tusayan, this one has the most resortlike feel due to its restaurants, lounges, and extensive recreational amenities. With so much to offer, it almost seems as if the hotel were trying to distract guests from the canyon itself. But even if you don't bowl or play tennis, you'll likely appreciate the large guest rooms with comfortable easy chairs and big windows. In the lobby, which is more Las Vegas glitz than mountain rustic, there are cases filled with old cowboy paraphernalia. Down in the basement there's an impressive Western sculpture, waterfall wall, and even a bowling alley.

Ariz. 64 (P.O. Box 130), Grand Canyon, AZ 86023. (C) 800/622-6966 or 928/638-2681. Fax 928/638-2782. www.grandcanyonsquire.com. 250 units. Mid-Mar to mid-Oct and Christmas holidays $99–$190 double; mid-Oct to mid-Mar $75–$155 double. Children 12 and under stay free in parent's room. AE, DC, DISC, MC, V. **Amenities:** 2 restaurants (Continental, American); 2 lounges; seasonal outdoor pool; 2 tennis courts; exercise room; Jacuzzi; sauna; game room; concierge; tour desk; coin-op laundry; laundry service. *In room:* A/C, TV, dataport, coffeemaker, hair dryer, iron, free local calls.

Grand Hotel ★★ With its mountain lodge–style lobby, this modern hotel lives up to its name, and is your best bet outside the park. There's a flagstone fireplace, log-beam ceiling, and fake ponderosa pine tree trunks holding up the roof. Just off the lobby are a dining room (with evening entertainment ranging from Native American dancers to country-music bands) and a small bar that even has a few saddles for bar stools. Guest rooms are spacious, with a few Western touches, and some have small balconies.

Ariz. 64 (P.O. Box 3319), Grand Canyon, AZ 86023. (C) 888/634-7263 or 928/638-3333. Fax 928/638-3131. www.visitgrandcanyon.com. 120 units. $79–$159 double; $198 suite. Children 17 and under stay free in parent's room. AE, DC, DISC, MC, V. Pets accepted ($10 per night). **Amenities:** Restaurant (American/Southwestern); lounge; indoor pool; Jacuzzi. *In room:* A/C, TV, dataport, coffeemaker, hair dryer.

Holiday Inn Express–Grand Canyon This is one of the newest lodgings in the area and has modern, well-designed—if a bit sterile and characterless—guest rooms. The Holiday Inn Express also manages an adjacent 32-suite property whose rooms have a Western theme. Although these suites are fairly pricey, they're among the nicest accommodations inside or outside the park.

Ariz. 64 (P.O. Box 3245), Grand Canyon, AZ 86023. (C) 888/473-2269 or 928/638-3000. Fax 928/638-0123. www.gcanyon.com/HI. 194 units. $112–$159 double; $152–$250 suite. Rates include continental breakfast. Children under 18 stay free in parent's room. AE, DC, DISC, MC, V. **Amenities:** Indoor pool; Jacuzzi. *In room:* A/C, TV, dataport, hair dryer, iron, high-speed Internet access.

Quality Inn & Suites Canyon Plaza ★ The setting behind the IMAX theater and surrounded by parking lots is none too pretty, but guest rooms are relatively luxurious and the hotel is built around two enclosed skylit courtyards, one of which houses a restaurant and the other a bar and whirlpool. Guest rooms are large and comfortable, with balconies or patios; most also have minibars. The suites contain separate small living rooms, microwaves, and fridges. The hotel is very popular with tour groups.

P.O. Box 520, Grand Canyon, AZ 86023. © 800/228-2673 or 928/638-2673. Fax 928/638-9537. www.grand canyonqualityinn.com. 232 units. Mid-Mar to Oct $130 double, $180 suite; Nov to mid-Mar $80 double, $130 suite. Children 18 and under stay free in parent's room. AE, DC, DISC, MC, V. **Amenities:** Restaurant (American); lounge; outdoor pool; 2 Jacuzzis. *In room:* A/C, TV, dataport, coffeemaker, hair dryer.

Rodeway Inn Red Feather Lodge *Kids* With more than 200 units, this motel is often slow to fill up, so it's a good choice for last-minute bookings. Try to get one of the newer rooms, which are a bit more comfortable than the older ones. The pool here makes this place a good bet for families.

Ariz. 64 (P.O. Box 1460), Grand Canyon, AZ 86023. © 800/424-6423 or 928/638-2414. Fax 928/638-2707. www.red featherlodge.com. 215 units. $69–$149 double. Children under 18 stay free in parent's room. AE, DC, DISC, MC, V. Pets accepted ($50 deposit plus $10 per night). **Amenities:** Restaurant (American); seasonal outdoor pool; exercise room; Jacuzzi. *In room:* A/C, TV, dataport, coffeemaker, hair dryer.

OTHER AREA ACCOMMODATIONS
Cameron Trading Post Motel ★★ *Finds* Located 54 miles north of Flagstaff on U.S. 89 at the junction with the road to the east entrance of the national park, this motel offers some of the most attractive rooms in the vicinity of the Grand Canyon and is part of one of the best trading posts in the state. The motel, adjacent to the historic Cameron Trading Post, is built around the shady oasis of the old trading post's terraced gardens. The garden terraces are built of sandstone, and there's even a picnic table made from a huge slab of stone. Guest rooms feature Southwestern-style furniture and attractive decor. Most have balconies, and some have views of the Little Colorado River (which, however, rarely has much water in it at this point). Don't miss the Navajo tacos in the dining room (the small ones are plenty big enough for a meal).

P.O. Box 339, Cameron, AZ 86020. © 800/338-7385 or 928/679-2231. Fax 928/679-2501. www.camerontrading post.com. 62 units. Feb $49–$69 double; Mar–May $69–$99 double; June to mid-Oct $89–$119 double; mid-Oct to Jan $69–$89 double. Suites $129–$159 year-round. AE, DC, DISC, MC, V. Pets accepted. **Amenities:** Restaurant. *In room:* A/C, TV, coffeemaker.

CAMPING
Inside the Park
On the South Rim, there are two campgrounds and an RV park. **Mather Campground,** in Grand Canyon Village, has more than 300 campsites. Reservations can be made up to 5 months in advance and are highly recommended for stays between April and November (reservations not accepted for other months). Contact the National Park Reservation Service (© 800/365-2267 or 301/722-1257; reservations.nps.gov). Between late spring and early fall, don't even think of coming up here without a reservation; you'll just be setting yourself up for disappointment. If you don't have a reservation, your next best bet is to arrive in the morning, when sites are being vacated. Campsites are $15 per night ($10 per night between December and March; reservations not accepted).

Desert View Campground, with 50 sites, is 26 miles east of Grand Canyon Village and open from mid-May to mid-October only. No reservations are accepted. Campsites are $10 per night.

The **Trailer Village RV park,** with 80 RV sites, is in Grand Canyon Village and charges $25 per night (for two adults) for full hookup. Reservations can be made up to 23 months in advance by contacting **Grand Canyon National Park Lodges/Xanterra Parks & Resorts,** 6312 S. Fiddlers Green Circle, Suite 600N, Greenwood Village, CO 80111 (© 888/297-2757 or 303/297-2757; www.xanterra.com or www.grandcanyonlodges.com). For same-day reservations, call © 928/638-2631.

Outside the Park

Two miles south of Tusayan is the U.S. Forest Service's **Ten-X Campground.** This campground has 70 campsites, is open mid-April through September, and charges $10. It's usually your best bet for finding a site late in the day.

You can also camp just about anywhere within the **Kaibab National Forest,** which borders Grand Canyon National Park, as long as you are more than a quarter mile away from Ariz. 64/U.S. 180. Several dirt roads lead into the forest from the highway, and although you won't find designated campsites or toilets along these roads, you will find spots where others have obviously camped before. This so-called dispersed camping is usually used by campers who have been unable to find sites in campgrounds. Anyone equipped for backpacking could just hike in a bit from any forest road rather than camp right beside the road. One of the most popular roads for this sort of camping is on the west side of the highway between Tusayan and the park's south entrance. For more information, contact the **Tusayan Ranger District,** Kaibab National Forest, P.O. Box 3088, Grand Canyon, AZ 86023 (© **928/638-2443;** www.fs.fed.us/r3/kai).

WHERE TO DINE
INSIDE THE PARK

If you're looking for a quick, inexpensive meal, there are plenty of options. In Grand Canyon Village, choices include **cafeterias** at the Yavapai and Maswik lodges and a **delicatessen** at Canyon Village Marketplace on Market Plaza. The **Bright Angel Fountain,** at the back of the Bright Angel Lodge, serves hot dogs, sandwiches, and ice cream and is always crowded on hot days. My favorite place in the park to grab a quick bite to eat is the **Hermit's Rest Snack Bar,** at the west end of Hermit Road. The stone building that houses this snack bar was designed by Mary Elizabeth Jane Colter, who also designed several other buildings on the South Rim. At Desert View (near the east entrance to the park), there's the **Desert View Trading Snack Bar.** All of these places are open daily for all three meals, and all serve meals for $8 and under.

The Arizona Room SOUTHWESTERN   Because this restaurant has the best view of the three dining establishments right on the South Rim, it is immensely popular. Add to this the fact that the Arizona Room has a menu (pan-seared salmon with melon salsa, baby back ribs with prickly pear or chipotle glaze) almost as creative as that of the El Tovar Dining Room, and you'll understand why there is often a long wait for a table here. To avoid the wait, arrive early, which should assure you of getting a table with a good view out the picture windows. Once the sun goes down, the view is absolutely black, which means you could be dining anywhere—which would defeat the entire purpose. Because this restaurant is open for lunch part of the year, you've got another great option for dining with a billion-dollar view.

At the Bright Angel Lodge. © 928/638-2631. Reservations not accepted. Main courses $8–$12 lunch, $11–$25 dinner. AE, DC, DISC, MC, V. Daily 4:30–10pm (Mar–Oct also open for lunch daily 11:30am–3pm). Closed Jan to mid-Feb.

Bright Angel Coffee Shop AMERICAN   As the least expensive of the three restaurants right on the rim of the canyon, this casual Southwestern-themed coffeehouse in the historic Bright Angel Lodge stays packed throughout the day. Meals are simple and none too memorable, but if you can get one of the few tables near the windows, at least you get something of a view. The menu includes everything from Southwestern favorites such as tacos and fajitas to spaghetti (foods calculated to comfort tired and hungry hikers), but my favorite offerings are the bread bowls full of chili and stew. Wines are available, and service is generally friendly and efficient.

At the Bright Angel Lodge. ℂ 928/638-2631. Reservations not accepted. Main courses $7–$16. AE, DC, DISC, MC, V. Daily 6:30–10:45am and 11:15am–10pm.

El Tovar Dining Room ★★ CONTINENTAL/SOUTHWESTERN   If you're staying at El Tovar, you'll want to have dinner in the hotel's rustic yet elegant dining room. But before making reservations at the most expensive restaurant in the park, be aware that meals can be uneven, and few tables have views of the canyon. With this knowledge in hand, decide for yourself whether you want to splurge on a meal that will definitely be the best food available inside the park, but that might not be as good as you would hope after seeing the prices. The menu leans heavily to the spicy flavors of the Southwest. Plenty of milder, more familiar dishes are offered as well. Service is generally quite good.

At the El Tovar Hotel. ℂ 928/638-2631, ext. 6432. Reservations required for dinner. Main courses $9–$16 lunch, $18–$25 dinner. AE, DC, DISC, MC, V. Daily 6:30–11am, 11:30am–2pm, and 5–10pm.

IN TUSAYAN (OUTSIDE THE SOUTH ENTRANCE)

In addition to the restaurants listed below, you'll also find a steakhouse and a pizza place, as well as familiar chains such as McDonald's, Pizza Hut, and Wendy's.

Canyon Star ★ AMERICAN/MEXICAN   This place aims to compete with the El Tovar and Arizona Room, and serves the most creative Southwestern fare this side of the park boundary, plus you'll have live entertainment while you eat. Try the elk tenderloin or the barbecued buffalo brisket (at lunch, go for the buffalo burger). Evening shows include performances of Native American songs and dances. This place is big, so there usually isn't too long a wait for a table, and even if there is, you can head for the saloon and saddle up a bar stool (some of the stools have saddles instead of seats) while you wait.

At the Grand Hotel, Ariz. 64. ℂ 928/638-3333. Main courses $8–$11 lunch, $13–$25 dinner. AE, DISC, MC, V. Daily 7–10am and 11am–10pm.

Coronado Room ★ CONTINENTAL/SOUTHWESTERN   If you should suddenly be struck with an overpowering desire to have escargot for dinner, don't despair—head for the Best Western Grand Canyon Squire Inn. Now, we're well aware that Best Western and escargot go together about as well as the Eiffel Tower and rattlesnake fritters, but this place really does serve classic Continental fare way out here in the Arizona high country. You'll probably want to stick to the steaks, though (or the wild game such as elk tournedos). You might also want to try a few of the Southwestern appetizers on the menu.

At the Best Western Grand Canyon Squire Inn, Ariz. 64. ℂ 928/638-2681. Reservations recommended. Main courses $16–$25. AE, DC, DISC, MC, V. Daily 5–10pm.

4 A South Rim Alternative: Havasu Canyon ★ ★

Havasu Canyon: 200 miles W of Grand Canyon Village; 70 miles N of Ariz. 66; 155 miles NW of Flagstaff; 115 miles NE of Kingman

With traffic congestion and parking problems becoming the most memorable aspects of many people's trips to the Grand Canyon, you might want to consider an alternative to the South Rim. For most travelers, this means driving around to the North Rim; however, the North Rim is open only from mid-May to late October and itself is not immune to parking problems and traffic congestion.

Another lesser-known alternative is a visit to Havasu Canyon, on the Havasupai Indian Reservation, which entails a 20-mile round-trip hike or horseback ride similar to that from Grand Canyon Village to Phantom Ranch, although with a decidedly different setting at the bottom of the canyon.

ESSENTIALS

GETTING THERE **Havasu Canyon** It isn't possible to drive all the way to Supai village or Havasu Canyon. The nearest road ends 8 miles from Supai at Hualapai Hilltop. This is the trail head for the trail into the canyon and is at the end of Indian Route 18, which runs north from Ariz. 66. The turnoff is 7 miles east of Peach Springs and 31 miles west of Seligman.

The easiest and fastest (and by far the most expensive) way to reach Havasu Canyon is by helicopter from Grand Canyon Airport. Flights are operated by **Papillon Grand Canyon Helicopters** (© 800/528-2418 or 928/638-2419; www.papillon.com). The round-trip air-and-ground day excursion is $505; it's also possible to arrange to stay overnight. Lower rates are available on this company's website.

VISITOR INFORMATION For information on Havasu Canyon, contact the **Havasupai Tourist Enterprises,** P.O. Box 160, Supai, AZ 86435 (© **928/448-2121** or 928/ 448-2141; www.havasupaitribe.com), which handles all campground reservations.

HAVASU CANYON ★★

Havasu Canyon is the canyon of the Havasupai tribe, whose name means "people of the blue-green waters." For centuries, the Havasupai have called this idyllic desert oasis home.

The waterfalls are the main attraction here, and most people are content to go for a dip in the cool waters, sun themselves on the sand, and gaze for hours at the turquoise waters. When you tire of these pursuits, you can hike up the small side canyon to the east of Havasu Falls. Another trail leads along the west rim of Havasu Canyon and can be reached by carefully climbing a steep rocky area near the village cemetery. There's also a trail that leads all the way down to the Colorado River, but this is an overnight hike.

In Supai village, there's a small museum dedicated to the culture of the Havasupai people. Its exhibits and old photos will give you an idea of how little the lives of these people have changed over the years.

The Havasupai entry fee is $20 per person to visit Havasu Canyon, and everyone entering the canyon is required to register at the tourist office in the village of Supai. Because it's a long walk to the campground, be sure you have a confirmed reservation before setting out from Hualapai Hilltop. It's good to make reservations as far in advance as possible, especially for holiday weekends. Although you can make reservations with a credit card, be sure to bring enough cash for your stay in the canyon; there are no ATMs here.

If you plan to hike down into the canyon, start early to avoid the heat of the day. The hike is beautiful, but it's 10 miles to the campground. The steepest part of the trail is the first mile or so from Hualapai Hilltop. After this section, it's relatively flat.

Through **Havasupai Tourist Enterprises** (© **928/448-2121;** www.havasupai tribe.com), you can hire a horse to carry you or your gear down into the canyon from Hualapai Hilltop. Horses cost $75 each way. Many people who hike in decide that it's worth the money to ride out, or at least have their backpacks carried out. Be sure to confirm your horse reservation a day before driving to Hualapai Hilltop. Sometimes no horses are available, and it's a long drive back to the nearest town. There are also pack mules that will carry your gear into and out of the canyon.

If you'd like to hike into Havasu Canyon with a guide, contact **Arizona Outback Adventures,** 16447 N. 91st St., Suite 101, Scottsdale, AZ 85260 (© **866/455-1601** or 480/945-2881; www.azoutbackadventures.com), which leads 3- to 5-day hikes into Havasu Canyon and charges $1,365 to $1,550 per person. **Discovery Treks,** 6890 E. Sunrise Dr., Suite 120-108, Tucson, AZ 85750 (© **888/256-8731;** www.discovery treks.com), offers similar 3-day trips and charges $875 to $1,125 per person.

OTHER AREA ACTIVITIES

If you long to raft the Grand Canyon but have only a couple of free days in your schedule to realize your dream, then you have only a couple of options. Here at the west end of the canyon, it's possible to do a 1-day rafting trip that begins on the Hualapai Indian Reservation. These trips are operated by **Hualapai River Runners,** P.O. Box 538, Peach Springs, AZ 86434 (© **888/255-9550** or 928/769-2419; www. grandcanyonresort.com), a tribal rafting company, and run between mid-March and late October. Expect a mix of white water and flat water (all of it very cold). One-day trips cost $265 per person.

Also in this area, you can visit **Grand Canyon Caverns** (© **928/422-4565;** www. grandcanyoncaverns.com), just outside Peach Springs. The caverns, which are accessed via a 210-foot elevator ride, are open from Memorial Day to October 15, daily from 9am to 5pm, and other months, daily from 10am to 4pm. Admission is $13 for adults, $10 for children 4 to 12. There are also flashlight tours ($15 for adults and $10 for children) and explorers tours ($45).

WHERE TO STAY & DINE
NEAR PEACH SPRINGS

Hualapai Lodge ★ *Finds*   Located in the Hualapai community of Peach Springs, this lodge is by far the most luxurious accommodation anywhere in the region. Guest rooms are spacious and modern, with a few bits of regional decor for character. Most people staying here are in the area to visit or go rafting with Hualapai River Runners or to hike in to Havasu Canyon. The dining room is just about the only place in town to get a meal.

900 Rte. 66 (P.O. Box 538), Peach Springs, AZ 86434-0538. © 888/255-9550 or 928/769-2230. Fax 928/769-2372. www.grandcanyonresort.com. 60 units. Apr–Oct $89–$109 double; Nov–Mar $69–$90 double. Children under 15 stay free in parent's room. AE, DISC, MC, V. **Amenities:** Restaurant (Mexican/Native American/American); outdoor saltwater pool; exercise room; tour desk; coin-op laundry. *In room:* A/C, TV, dataport, coffeemaker, hair dryer.

IN HAVASU CANYON

Havasupai Lodge   Located in Supai village, this lodge is, aside from the campground, the only accommodation in the canyon. The two-story building features standard motel-style rooms that are lacking only TVs and telephones, neither of which are much in demand at this isolated retreat. The only drawback of this comfortable though basic lodge is that it's 2 miles from Havasu Falls and 3 miles from Mooney Falls. The Havasupai Café, across from the general store, serves breakfast, lunch, and dinner. It's a very casual place, and prices are high for what you get because all ingredients must be packed in by horse. Two miles downstream, there is also a campground that charges $10 per person per night. Contact Havasupai Tourist Enterprises (see above) for details.

P.O. Box 160, Supai, AZ 86435. © **928/448-2111** or 928/448-2201. www.havasupaitribe.com. 24 units. $80 double.
MC, V. **Amenities:** Restaurant nearby. *In room:* A/C, no phone.

5 The Grand Canyon North Rim ★★★

42 miles S of Jacob Lake; 216 miles N of Grand Canyon Village (South Rim); 354 miles N of Phoenix; 125 miles W of
Page/Lake Powell

Although the North Rim of the Grand Canyon is only 10 miles from the South Rim
as the crow flies, it's more than 200 miles by road. Because it is such a long drive from
population centers such as Phoenix and Las Vegas, the North Rim is much less
crowded than the South Rim. Additionally, due to heavy snowfall, the North Rim is
open only from mid-May to late October or early November. There are also far fewer
activities or establishments on the North Rim than there are on the South Rim.

The North Rim is on the Kaibab Plateau, which is more than 8,000 feet high on
average and takes its name from the Paiute word for "mountain lying down." The
higher elevation of the North Rim means that instead of the mix of junipers interspersed with ponderosa pines of the South Rim, you'll see dense forests of ponderosa
pines, Douglas firs, and aspens interspersed with large meadows. Consequently, the
North Rim has a much more alpine feel than the South Rim. The 8,000-foot elevation—1,000 feet higher than the South Rim—also means that the North Rim gets
considerably more snow in winter than the South Rim. The highway south from Jacob
Lake is not plowed in winter, when the Grand Canyon Lodge closes down.

ESSENTIALS

GETTING THERE   The North Rim is at the end of Ariz. 67 (the North Rim
Pkwy.), reached from U.S. 89A. **Trans Canyon** (© **928/638-2820**) operates a shuttle between the North Rim and the South Rim of the Grand Canyon during the
months the North Rim is open. The trip takes 5 hours; the fare is $65 one-way and
$110 round trip (reservations required).

FEES   The park entry fee is $20 per car and is good for 1 week. Remember not to
lose the little paper receipt that serves as your admission pass.

VISITOR INFORMATION   For information before leaving home, contact **Grand
Canyon National Park,** P.O. Box 129, Grand Canyon, AZ 86023 (© **928/638-
7888;** www.nps.gov/grca). At the entrance gate, you'll be given a copy of *The Guide*,
a small newspaper with information on park activities. There's also an **information
desk** in the lobby of the Grand Canyon Lodge.

EXPLORING THE PARK

While it's hard to beat the view from a rustic rocking chair on the terrace of the Grand
Canyon Lodge, the best spots for seeing the canyon are Bright Angel Point, Point

---

Tips An Important Note

Visitor facilities at the North Rim are open only from mid-May to mid-October.
From mid-October to November (or until snow closes the road to the North
Rim), the park is open for day use only. The campground may be open after
mid-October, weather permitting.

Imperial, and Cape Royal. **Bright Angel Point** is at the end of a half-mile trail near the Grand Canyon Lodge, and from here you can see and hear Roaring Springs, which is 3,600 feet below the rim and is the North Rim's only water source. You can also see Grand Canyon Village on the South Rim.

At 8,803 feet, **Point Imperial** is the highest point on the North Rim. A short section of the Colorado River can be seen far below, and off to the east the Painted Desert is visible. The Nankoweap Trail leads north from here along the rim of the canyon, and if you're looking to get away from the crowds, try hiking a few miles out along this trail.

Cape Royal is the most spectacular setting on the North Rim, and along the 23-mile road to this viewpoint you'll find several other scenic overlooks. Across the road from the **Walhalla Overlook** are the ruins of an Ancestral Puebloan structure, and just before reaching Cape Royal, you'll come to the **Angel's Window Overlook,** which gives you a breathtaking view of the natural bridge that forms Angel's Window. Once at Cape Royal, you can follow a trail across this natural bridge to a towering promontory overlooking the canyon.

Once you've had your fill of simply taking in the views, you may want to get out and stretch your legs on a trail or two. Quite a few day hikes of varying lengths and difficulty are possible. The shortest is the half-mile paved trail to Bright Angel Point, along which you'll have plenty of company but also plenty of breathtaking views. If you have time for only one hike while you're here, make it down the **North Kaibab Trail.** This trail is 14 miles long and leads down to Phantom Ranch and the Colorado River. To hike the entire trail, you'll need to have a camping permit and be in very good physical condition (it's almost 6,000 ft. to the canyon floor). For a day hike, most people make Roaring Springs their goal. This hike is 9.5 miles round-trip, involves a descent and ascent of 3,000 feet, and takes 6 to 8 hours. You can shorten this hike considerably by turning around at the Supai Tunnel, which is fewer than 1,500 feet below the rim at the 2-mile point. For a relatively easy hike away from the crowds, try the Widforss Point Trail.

If you want to see the canyon from a saddle, contact **Grand Canyon Trail Rides** (© **435/679-8665;** www.canyonrides.com), which offers mule rides varying in length from 1 hour ($30) to a full day ($105).

EN ROUTE TO OR FROM THE NORTH RIM

Between Page and the North Rim of the Grand Canyon, U.S. 89A crosses the Colorado River at **Lees Ferry** in Marble Canyon. Lees Ferry is the starting point for raft trips through the Grand Canyon. This stretch of the river is legendary among anglers for its trophy trout fishing, and when the North Rim closes and the rafting season comes to an end, about the only folks you'll find up here are anglers and hunters. Lees Ferry has a 30-site campground (© **928/355-2319**); reservations are not accepted.

Lees Ferry Anglers (© **800/962-9755** or 928/355-2261; www.leesferry.com), 11 miles west of the bridge at Lees Ferry, is fishing headquarters for the region. Not only does it sell all manner of fly-fishing tackle and offer advice about good spots to try your luck, but it also operates a guide service and rents waders and boats. A guide and boat costs $280 per day for one person or $350 per day for two people.

Along this same stretch of road, you'll find the gravel road that leads to the **Coyote Buttes** ★★★, which are among the most unusual rock formations in Arizona. Basically, these striated conical sandstone hills are petrified sand dunes, which should give you a good idea of why one area of the Coyote Buttes is called The Wave. The buttes are a favorite of photographers. You must have a permit ($5 per person) to visit this area, and only 20 people are allowed to visit each day (with a maximum group size of six people). Reservations must be made 7 months in advance on the first of the month at exactly noon. With the exception of reservations for July and August, all available permits are usually reserved within a few minutes after noon. There's no actual trail to the buttes, so you have to navigate by way of the simple map that you'll be sent when you receive your permit. For more information, contact the **Arizona Strip Interpretive Association/Interagency Visitor Center,** 345 E. Riverside Dr., St. George, UT 84770 (© **435/688-3246;** www.az.blm.gov/asfo/asia.htm).

To learn more about the pioneer history of this remote and sparsely populated region of the state (known as the Arizona Strip), visit **Pipe Spring National Monument** (© **928/643-7105;** www.nps.gov/pisp), which is 45 miles west of Jacob Lake on Ariz. 389 and preserves an early Mormon ranch house that was built in the style of a fort for protection from Indians. This "fort" was also known as Winsor Castle and occasionally housed the wives of polygamists hiding out from the law. In summer, there are living-history demonstrations. The monument is open daily (except New Year's Day, Thanksgiving, and Christmas) from 7am to 5pm June through August, and from 8am to 5pm the rest of the year. Admission is $5 per adult.

WHERE TO STAY
INSIDE THE PARK

Grand Canyon Lodge ★★ Perched right on the canyon rim, this classic mountain lodge is listed on the National Register of Historic Places and is as impressive a lodge as you'll find in any national park. The stone-and-log main building has a soaring ceiling and a viewing room set up with chairs facing a wall of glass, and on either side of this room are flagstone terraces furnished with rustic chairs. Accommodations vary from standard motel units to rustic mountain cabins to comfortable modern cabins. Our favorites are still the little cabins, which, although cramped and paneled with dark wood, capture the feeling of a mountain retreat better than any of the other options. A few units have views of the canyon, but most are tucked back away from the rim. The dining hall has two walls of glass to take in the awesome canyon views.

Xanterra Parks & Resorts, 6312 S. Fiddlers Green Circle, Suite 600N, Greenwood Village, CO 80111. © **888/297-2757** or 303/297-2757, or 928/638-2611 for same-day reservations. Fax 303/297-3175. www.grandcanyonnorthrim.com. 205 units. $93–$124 double. Children 16 and under stay free in parent's room. AE, DISC, MC, V. Closed Oct 15–May 15. **Amenities:** 2 restaurants (American); lounge; tour desk; coin-op laundry.

EN ROUTE TO THE PARK

If you don't have a reservation at the North Rim's Grand Canyon Lodge, you should call the places recommended below to see if you can get a reservation. If so, you can continue on to the North Rim the next morning. Lodges near the canyon fill up early in the day if they aren't already fully booked with reservations made months in advance.

Cliff Dwellers Lodge There isn't much else out this way but this remote lodge, which is affiliated with Lees Ferry Anglers and tends to stay filled up with trout anglers and rafters. The newer, more expensive rooms are standard motel units with combination tub/showers, while the older rooms, in an interesting stone-walled building, have knotty-pine walls but showers only. Despite the rusticity of these latter rooms, they are my favorites in the area. The lodge is close to some spectacular balanced rocks, and it's about 11 miles east to Lees Ferry. The views here are wonderful.

U.S. 89A milepost 547 (H.C. 67, Box 30), Marble Canyon, AZ 86036. © **800/962-9755** or 928/355-2261. Fax 928/355-2271. www.leesferry.com. 21 units. Mar–Nov $60–$70 double, $175 3-bedroom house; Dec–Feb $45 double, $125 3-bedroom house. AE, DISC, MC, V. **Amenities:** Restaurant (American). *In room:* A/C, TV, coffeemaker, no phone.

Lees Ferry Lodge Located at the foot of the Vermilion Cliffs, 3½ miles west of the Colorado River, the Lees Ferry Lodge, built in 1929 of native stone and rough-hewn timber beams, is a small place with simple, rustic accommodations. However, the lodge's restaurant serves as a sort of de facto community center for area residents, and owner Maggie Sacher is usually on hand to answer questions and share stories of life at the foot of the Vermillion Cliffs. Also, the patio seating area in front of the lodge has fabulous views. Boat rentals and fly-fishing guides can be arranged through the lodge, and there's a fly-fishing shop on the premises. The restaurant here has a great, old-fashioned atmosphere. With its rustic character and friendly feel, this is one of my favorite places to stay in the area. Don't miss it.

U.S. 89A (H.C. 67, Box 1), Marble Canyon, AZ 86036. © **800/451-2231** or 928/355-2231. www.leesferrylodge.com. 12 units. $45–$53 double. Children under 5 stay free in parent's room. AE, DISC, MC, V. Pets accepted. **Amenities:** Restaurant (American); game room. *In room:* A/C, coffeemaker, no phone.

Marble Canyon Lodge The Marble Canyon Lodge, built in the 1920s just 4 miles from Lees Ferry, is popular with both rafters and anglers. Accommodations vary considerably in size and age, with some rustic units in old stone buildings and newer motel-style rooms available as well. These latter rooms are the best in the area. You're right at the base of the Vermilion Cliffs here, and the views are great. In addition to the restaurant, there's a general store and fly shop where you can rent a boat or hire a guide.

P.O. Box 6032, Marble Canyon, AZ 86036. © **800/726-1789** or 928/355-2225. Fax 928/355-2227. www.mcg-lees ferry.com. 56 units. $54–$70 double; $72–$86 cottage; $121–$134 apt. Children under 12 stay free in parent's room. AE, DISC, MC, V. Pets accepted. **Amenities:** Restaurant (American). *In room:* A/C, TV, no phone.

CAMPGROUNDS

Located just north of Grand Canyon Lodge, the **North Rim Campground,** with 75 sites and no hookups for RVs, is the only campground at the North Rim. It's open mid-May to mid-October. Reservations can be made up to 5 months in advance by calling the National Park Reservation Service (© **800/365-2267** or 301/722-1257; http://reservations.nps.gov). Campsites cost $15 per night.

There are two nearby campgrounds outside the park in the Kaibab National Forest. They are **DeMotte Park Campground,** which is the closest to the park entrance and has 23 sites, and **Jacob Lake Campground,** which is 30 miles north of the park entrance and has 53 sites. Both charge $12 per night and do not take reservations. They're open May 15 to November 1. You can also camp anywhere in the Kaibab National Forest as long as you're more than a quarter mile from a paved road or water source. So if you can't find a site in a campground, simply pull off the highway in the national forest and park your RV or pitch your tent.

The **Kaibab Camper Village** (© **800/525-0924,** 928/643-7804 in summer, or 928/526-0924 in winter; www.kaibabcampervillage.com) is a privately owned campground in the crossroads of Jacob Lake, 30 miles north of the park entrance. The campground is open from mid-May to mid-October and has around 100 sites. Rates are $13 for tent sites, $27 for RV sites with full hookups. Make reservations well in advance.

WHERE TO DINE
INSIDE THE PARK

Grand Canyon Lodge has a dining room with a splendid view. Because this restaurant is so popular, reservations are required for dinner. More casual choices at the lodge include a cafeteria and a saloon that serves light meals.

OUTSIDE THE PARK

Your only choices for a meal outside the park are the **Kaibab Lodge,** just north of the entrance, and the **Jacob Lake Inn** (© **928/643-7232;** www.jacoblake.com), 45 miles north at the junction with U.S. 89A.

17

Southern Utah's National Parks

For many people, the best part of a Utah vacation is exploring the state's national parks, which offer spectacular red-rock scenery, deep green forests, rivers, historic sites, and numerous opportunities for outdoor recreation.

Although visitation at some national parks has dropped in the past few years, Utah's parks remain popular; Zion National Park broke visitation records in 2004. For those trying to avoid the crowds, try to go in the off season. The parks are busiest in summer, when most children are out of school, so visit at almost any other time. Fall is usually best. Spring is okay, but often windy; and winter can be delightful but chilly.

1 Zion National Park ★★

Early Mormon settler Isaac Behunin is credited with naming his homestead "Little Zion" because it seemed to be a bit of heaven on earth. Today, 150 years later, **Zion National Park** casts a spell over you as you gaze upon its sheer multicolored walls of sandstone, explore its narrow canyons, hunt for hanging gardens of wildflowers, and listen to the roar of the churning, tumbling Virgin River.

Here you'll discover a smorgasbord of experiences, sights, sounds, and even smells, from massive stone sculptures and monuments to lush forests and rushing rivers.

Zion is home to an abundance of wildlife, with mammals ranging from pocket gophers to mountain lions, hundreds of birds (including golden eagles), lizards of all shapes and sizes, and a dozen species of snakes. Mule deer are common, and you may also see foxes, coyotes, ringtails, beaver, porcupines, and plenty of squirrels and bats. Practically every summer visitor sees lizards, often the colorful collared and whiptail varieties, and hears the song of the canyon wren and the call of the piñon jay.

ESSENTIALS

Located in southwest Utah, at elevations ranging from 3,666 feet to 8,726 feet, Zion National Park has several sections: **Zion Canyon,** the main part of the park, where everyone goes, and the less-visited **Kolob Terrace** and **Kolob Canyons** areas.

GETTING THERE **St. George** and **Cedar City** are the closest towns with airport service. From either airport, it's easy to rent a car and drive to Zion. Utah 9 crosses the park, giving the main section of the park two entry gates, south and east. The drive into Zion Canyon from I-15 on the park's western side—following Utah 9 or Utah 17 and Utah 9 to the south entrance at Springdale—is the more popular route.

From the east, a spectacularly scenic 24-mile drive leads from Mt. Carmel on Utah 9, reached from the north or south on U.S. 89. However, be aware that this route into the park drops over 2,500 feet in elevation, passes through the mile-long Zion–Mt. Carmel Tunnel, and winds down six steep switchbacks. The tunnel is too small for two-way traffic that includes vehicles larger than standard passenger cars and pickup trucks. Buses, trucks, and most recreational vehicles must drive down the center of the tunnel, stopping all oncoming traffic. This applies to all vehicles over 7 feet 10 inches wide (including mirrors) or 11 feet 4 inches tall. These vehicles pay a $15 fee, good for two trips through the tunnel in a 7-day period. Contact park offices for details.

Kolob Terrace Road, with viewpoints and trail heads, is north off Utah 9 from the village of Virgin, about 15 miles west of the park's southern entrance. This road is closed in the winter. To reach the Kolob Canyons section, in the park's northwest corner, take the short Kolob Canyons Road off I-15 exit 40.

VISITOR INFORMATION   Contact **Zion National Park,** Utah 9, Springdale, UT 84767-1099 (© 435/772-3256; www.nps.gov/zion). You can order books, maps, and videos from the nonprofit **Zion Natural History Association,** Zion National Park, Springdale, UT 84767 (© 800/635-3959 or 435/772-3265; www.zionpark.org).

The **Zion Canyon Visitor Center & Transportation Hub** (© 435/772-7616), near the south entrance, has outdoor exhibits, sells books and maps, and provides information. The smaller **Kolob Canyons Visitor Center** (© 435/586-9548), in the northwest corner of the park off I-15, provides information, permits, books, and maps. The **Zion Human History Museum** (© 435/772-0168), about 1 mile inside the south entrance, has museum exhibits, park information, and an orientation program, plus a bookstore. Open daily except December 25.

FEES   Entry to the park (for up to 7 days), including unlimited use of the shuttle bus (late Mar to Oct), costs $20 per private vehicle, $10 per individual on foot, bicycle, or motorcycle.

Oversize vehicles pay $15 for use of the Zion–Mt. Carmel Tunnel on the east side of the park (see "Getting There," above).

Backcountry permits, available at either visitor center, are required for all overnight hikes in the park as well as all slot canyon hikes. Permits cost $10 for 1 or 2 people, $15 for 3 to 7, and $20 for 8 to 12.

RANGER PROGRAMS   A variety of free programs and activities are presented, mostly during the summer. Evening programs, which sometimes include a slide show, take place at campground amphitheaters and Zion Lodge. Topics vary but may include the animals or plants of the park, geology of the park, or perhaps some unique feature such as Zion's slot canyons. Rangers give short talks on similar subjects several times daily at the Zion Canyon Visitor Center and at other locations, and lead guided hikes and walks. Schedules are posted throughout the park. Children 6 to 12 can join the Junior Rangers to earn badges and patches.

SEEING THE HIGHLIGHTS

To get the most from your visit, your first stop should be the **Zion Canyon Visitor Center** (see "Visitor Information," above) for the orientation video and exhibits.

Then hop on the free **shuttle bus,** which takes you to the major roadside viewpoints. You'll be able to get off, look at the rock formations, take a short walk, then catch the next shuttle for a ride to the next stop. During the off season (Nov–Mar), you'll use your own vehicle.

We especially recommend stopping at the **Temple of Sinawava** and taking the easy 2-mile round-trip **Riverside Walk,** which follows the Virgin River through a narrow canyon past hanging gardens. Then head back to the lodge (total time: 2–4 hr.). At the lodge, stop by the gift shop and perhaps have lunch in the excellent restaurant.

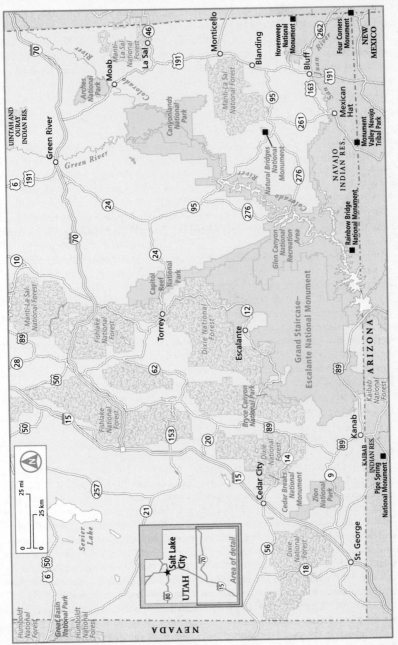

Near the lodge, you'll find the trailhead for the **Emerald Pools.** Especially pleasant on hot days, this hike is discussed below under "Outdoor Pursuits." If you still have time and energy, head back to the south park entrance and stop at **Watchman** (east of Watchman Campground), for the 2-mile, 2-hour round-trip, moderately strenuous hike to a plateau with beautiful views of several rock formations and the town of Springdale.

OUTDOOR PURSUITS

Zion offers a wide variety of hiking trails, ranging from easy half-hour walks on paved paths to grueling overnight hikes over rocky terrain. Hikers with a fear of heights should be especially careful when choosing trails; many include steep drop-offs.

The **Weeping Rock Trail,** among the park's shortest hikes, is a .5-mile round-trip walk from the Zion Canyon Scenic Drive to a rock alcove with a spring and hanging gardens of ferns and wildflowers. Although paved, it's steep and not suitable for wheelchairs.

Another short hike, the **Lower Emerald Pools Trail** ꙮ, is an easy 1-hour walk. If you want to extend your trip to a moderately strenuous 2-hour hike, you can continue along the loop. A .6-mile paved path from the Emerald Pools parking area, suitable for those in wheelchairs with assistance, winds through a forest of oak, maple, fir, and cottonwood to a waterfall, a hanging garden, and the Lower Emerald Pool. From here, a steeper, rocky trail (not appropriate for wheelchairs) continues past cactus, yucca, and juniper another .5 mile to Upper Emerald Pool, with another waterfall. A third pool, just above Lower Emerald Pool, offers impressive reflections of the cliffs. The pools are named for the green color of the water, which is caused by algae.

A particularly scenic hike is the **Hidden Canyon Trail,** a 2-mile moderately strenuous hike that takes about 3 hours. Starting at the Weeping Rock parking area, the trail climbs 800 feet through a narrow water-carved canyon, ending at the canyon's mouth. Those wanting to extend the hike can go another .6 mile to a small natural arch. Hidden Canyon Trail includes long, dizzying drop-offs.

For a strenuous 4-hour, 5-mile hike—one that's definitely not for anyone with even a mild fear of heights—take the **Angel's Landing Trail** ꙮ to a summit that offers spectacular views into Zion Canyon. But be prepared: The final .5 mile follows a narrow, knife-edge trail along a steep ridge, where footing can be slippery even under the best of circumstances. Support chains have been set along parts of the trail.

Hiking **The Narrows** ꙮꙮꙮ is not hiking a trail at all. It involves walking or wading along the bottom of the Virgin River, through a spectacular 1,000-foot-deep chasm that, at a mere 20 feet wide, definitely lives up to its name. Passing fancifully sculptured sandstone arches, hanging gardens, and waterfalls, this moderately strenuous 16-mile one-way hike can take less than a day or several days. The Narrows are subject to flash flooding and can be very treacherous, and park service officials remind hikers that they are responsible for their own safety and should check on current water conditions and weather forecasts. This hike is *not* recommended when rain is forecast. Permits are required for full-day and overnight hikes (check with rangers for details), but are not needed for short day hikes, which you can begin just beyond the end of the 2-mile **Riverside Walk.**

Zion is one of America's few relatively bike-friendly national parks. It permits bikes on the paved **Pa'rus Trail,** which runs several miles along the Virgin River. Bikes are also allowed on the park's established roads, except in the Zion–Mt. Carmel tunnel; from April through October, **Zion Canyon Scenic Drive** north of the Zion–Mt. Carmel Highway is open only to shuttle buses, bicyclists, and hikers, plus tour buses and motorists going to Zion Lodge.

Guided horseback rides in the park are available in warm weather from **Canyon Trail Rides** (© 435/679-8665; www.canyonrides.com), based near Zion Lodge. A 1-hour ride along the Virgin River costs $30, and a half-day ride on the Sand Beach Trail costs $55. Riders must weigh no more than 220 pounds. Children must be at least 7 years old for the 1-hour ride and 10 years old for the half-day ride.

WHERE TO STAY

The only lodging in Zion National Park is Zion Lodge. The other properties listed here are in Springdale, at the park's south entrance.

For additional information on lodging, dining, and area attractions, contact the **Zion Canyon Visitors Bureau,** P.O. Box 331, Springdale, UT 84767 (© **888/518-7070;** www.zionpark.com).

Canyon Ranch Motel   This series of two- and four-unit cottages set back from the highway looks old-fashioned on the outside but provides modern motel rooms inside. Some units have showers only, while others have shower/tub combos. Some units have kitchenettes. Room no. 13, with two queen-size beds, offers great views of the national park's rock formations; views from most other rooms are almost as good. There's a lawn with trees and picnic tables. All rooms are nonsmoking.

668 Zion Park Blvd. (P.O. Box 175), Springdale, UT 84767. © 866/946-6276 or 435/772-3357. www.canyonranch motel.com. 21 units. Apr–Oct $64–$92 double; Nov–Mar $48–$74 double; kitchenettes $10 more year-round. AE, DISC, MC, V. Pets accepted; $10 fee. **Amenities:** Outdoor pool; hot tub. *In room:* A/C, TV, wireless Internet.

Cliffrose Lodge & Gardens ✦   With river frontage and 5 acres of lawns, shade trees, and flower gardens, the Cliffrose offers a beautiful setting just outside the entrance to Zion National Park. The architecture is Southwestern adobe style, with redwood balconies, and the outdoor rock waterfall Jacuzzi is a delight. The modern, well-kept rooms and suites have all the standard motel appointments, plus unusually large bathrooms with combination shower/tubs. Units accommodate two to six; most sleep four.

281 Zion Park Blvd. (P.O. Box 510), Springdale, UT 84767. © 800/243-8824 or 435/772-3234. Fax 435/772-3900. www.cliffroselodge.com. 40 units. Apr–Oct and holidays $119–$179 per unit. Off-season discounts available. AE, DISC, MC, V. **Amenities:** Large heated outdoor pool; Jacuzzi; coin-op laundry. *In room:* A/C, TV/VCR.

Flanigan's Inn ✦✦   A mountain-lodge atmosphere pervades this attractive complex of natural wood and rock, set among trees, lawns, and flowers just outside the entrance to the park. Parts of the inn date from 1947, and all rooms have been renovated. They have Southwestern decor, wood furnishings, and local art. One room has a fireplace; other units have whirlpool tubs. Some units have kitchenettes. A nature trail leads to a hilltop vista, and the inn has an excellent restaurant.

428 Zion Park Blvd. (P.O. Box 100), Springdale, UT 84767. © 800/765-7787 or 435/772-3244. Fax 435/772-3396. www.flanigans.com. 34 units. Mid-Mar to mid-Nov and holidays $99–$119 double; $124–$229 suite. Off-season discounts available. AE, DISC, MC, V. **Amenities:** Restaurant (regional cuisine); heated outdoor pool; outdoor hot tub; full-service spa. *In room:* A/C, TV.

Zion Lodge ✦✦   The motel units and cabins here occupy a splendid location with equally splendid views. Each charming cabin has a private porch, stone (gas-burning) fireplace, two double beds, pine-board walls, and log beams. The comfortable motel rooms have two queen-size beds, a private porch or balcony, and all the usual amenities except TVs. Suites have one king bed, a sitting room, and a wet bar.

Zion National Park, UT. © 435/772-7700. Information and reservations: Xanterra Parks & Resorts, Central Reservations, 6312 S, Fiddlers Green Circle, Ste. 600N, Greenwood Village, CO 80111. © 888/297-2757 or 303/297-2757.

Fax 303/297-3175. www.zionlodge.com. 121 units. Mid-Mar to Nov motel $132 double; cabin $142 double; suite $148 double. Winter discounts and packages available. AE, DISC, MC, V. **Amenities:** Restaurant (see below). *In room:* A/C.

CAMPING

Both of Zion's main **campgrounds** ★★★ have paved roads, well-spaced sites, and lots of trees. Facilities include restrooms with flush toilets but no showers, and a dump station. The fee is $16 per night for basic sites, $18 to $20 per night for sites with electric hookups.

South Campground has 126 sites and no hookups. It's usually open from March through October. Reservations are not accepted, and it often fills by noon in summer. **Watchman Campground** (© **800/365-2267** or http://reservations.nps.gov for reservations) has 168 sites, with electric hookups on two loops. It is open year-round (reservations available spring to early fall only).

Lava Point, with only six sites, is on the Kolob Terrace. It has fire grates, tables, and toilets, but no water, and there's no fee. Vehicles are limited to 19 feet. It's usually open from June through mid-October.

If you can't get a site in the park, or if you prefer hot showers or complete RV hookups, several campgrounds are in the surrounding area. The closest, **Zion Canyon Campground,** 429 Zion Park Blvd., Springdale, UT 84767 (© **435/772-3237;** www.zioncamp.com), is a half mile south of the park entrance. It's open year-round and has 220 sites, many of which are shaded. Although it gets crowded in summer, the campground is clean and well maintained; in addition to the usual showers and RV hookups, you'll find a self-service laundry, dump station, convenience store, and restaurant. Tenters are welcome; rates range from $20 to $28 for two people.

WHERE TO EAT

Red Rock Grill ★★ AMERICAN A mountain-lodge atmosphere prevails here, complete with large windows that face the park's magnificent rock formations. House specialties at dinner include excellent slow-roasted prime rib and the popular wild Alaskan salmon. There are also steaks, several chicken dishes, and vegetarian items such as roasted vegetable tortellini. At lunch, you'll find grilled salmon burgers, beef burgers, sandwiches, and salads; breakfasts offer all the usuals, including a good buffet. Full liquor service is available. For something quick and cheap, Zion Lodge's Castle Dome Café serves burgers, deli sandwiches, hot dogs, pizza, and ice cream on an outdoor patio.

In Zion Lodge, Zion National Park. © 435/772-7760. www.zionlodge.com. Dinner reservations required in summer. Breakfast $3.50–$8.50, lunch $5.95–$7.95, dinner main courses $13–$19. AE, DC, DISC, MC, V. Daily 6:30–10am, 11:30am–3pm, and 5:30–9pm.

Zion Park Gift & Deli ★ *Value* SANDWICHES This is our choice for a top quality deli-style sandwich at an economical price. You can eat at one of the cafe-style tables inside or on the outdoor patio, or carry your sandwich off on a hike. All baked goods are made in-house. In typical deli style, you order at the counter and wait as your meal is prepared with your choice of bread, meats, cheeses, and condiments. Stop here at breakfast for fresh-baked cinnamon rolls, muffins, banana nut bread, and other goodies. Locally made candy, including excellent fudge, and 24 flavors of ice cream and frozen yogurt are also offered. No alcohol is served.

866 Zion Park Blvd., Springdale. © 435/772-3843. $5–$10. AE, DISC, MC, V. Summer Mon–Sat 8am–9pm; reduced hours in winter.

Zion Pizza & Noodle ⭐ *Kids* PIZZA/PASTA   In a former Mormon church with a turquoise steeple, this casual place has small, closely spaced tables. Baked in a slate stone oven, the 12-inch pizzas are our favorites. You can get practically any type you want, including Southwestern burrito pizza and barbecued chicken pizza. You can also design your own with a variety of toppings, from pepperoni to green chiles to pineapple. Options on the noodle side of the menu include pastas such as penne with grilled chicken, broccoli, carrots, fresh cream, and cheese. Calzones and stromboli are available. Beer is served inside and in the delightful year-round beer garden.

868 Zion Park Blvd., Springdale. ⓒ 435/772-3815. www.zionpizzanoodle.com. Reservations not accepted. Entrees $7.95–$14. No credit cards. Summer daily from 4pm; shorter hours in winter.

2 Bryce Canyon National Park ⭐⭐⭐

If you could visit only one national park in your lifetime, we'd send you to **Bryce Canyon.** Here you'll find magic, inspiration, and spectacular beauty. The main draw of the park is the thousands of intricately shaped hoodoos: those silent rock sentinels and congregations gathered in colorful cathedrals, arranged in formations that invite your imagination to run wild.

Hoodoos, geologists tell us, are pinnacles of rock, often oddly shaped, left standing after millions of years of water and wind erosion. But perhaps the truth really lies in a Paiute legend. These American Indians told of a "Legend People" who lived here in the old days and because of their evil ways, were turned to stone by the powerful Coyote. Even today, they remain frozen in time.

Although the colorful hoodoos first grab your attention, it isn't long before you notice the deep amphitheaters that enfold them, with their cliffs, windows, and arches, all in shades of red, brown, orange, yellow, and white. Beyond the rocks are the other faces of the park: three separate life zones, each with its own unique vegetation; and a kingdom of animals, from the busy chipmunks and ground squirrels to the stately mule deer and their archenemy, the mountain lion.

The park is named for Mormon pioneer Ebenezer Bryce, who moved to the area in 1875 with his wife Mary and tried raising cattle. Although they stayed only a few years, Bryce left behind his name and his oft-quoted description of the canyon as "a helluva place to lose a cow."

ESSENTIALS

GETTING THERE   The closest major towns with airports are **St. George** (130 miles southwest on I-15) and **Cedar City** (on I-15 about 80 miles west of the park).

From St. George, travel north on I-15 for 10 miles to exit 16, then head east on Utah 9 for 63 miles to US 89, north 44 miles to Utah 12, and east 13 miles to the park entrance road. The entrance station is 3 miles south of Utah 12. From Cedar City (I-15 exits 57, 59, and 62), follow Utah 14 west 41 miles to its intersection with US 89, and take US 89 north 21 miles to Utah 12, then east 17 miles to the park entrance road.

Utah 12 runs east-west across the park. The bulk of the park, including the visitor center, is accessible from Utah 63, which branches off from Utah 12 and goes south into the main portions of the park. Utah 89 runs north to south, west of the park, and Utah 12 heads east to Tropic.

INFORMATION/VISITOR CENTER   Contact **Bryce Canyon National Park,** P.O. Box 170001, Bryce Canyon, UT 84717 (ⓒ **435/834-5322;** www.nps.gov/brca).

You can order books, maps, and videos from the nonprofit **Bryce Canyon Natural History Association,** P.O. Box 170002, Bryce Canyon, UT 84717 (© **888/362-2642** or 435/834-4600; www.brycecanyon.org).

The **visitor center,** at the north end of the park, has exhibits on the geology and history of the area and a short introductory program. Rangers provide information and backcountry permits. The visitor center is open daily year-round except January 1, Thanksgiving, and December 25.

FEES   Entry to the park (for up to 7 days) costs $20 per vehicle, which includes unlimited use of the park shuttle (when it's operating).

Backcountry camping permits ($5 per trip), available at the visitor center, are required for all overnight trips into the backcountry.

RANGER PROGRAMS   Evening talks, which may include a slide show, take place most nights at campground amphitheaters. Topics vary but may include such subjects as the animals and plants of the park, geology, and the role of humans in the park's early days. Rangers also give half-hour talks on similar subjects several times daily at various locations in the park. They also lead hikes and walks, including a moonlight hike (reservations required) and a wheelchair-accessible 1-hour canyon rim walk. Schedules are posted on bulletin boards at the visitor center, general store, campgrounds, and Bryce Canyon Lodge. During the summer, children under 13 can join the Junior Rangers, participate in a variety of programs, and earn badges and certificates.

SEEING THE HIGHLIGHTS

Because this is our favorite national park, we would be happy to spend our entire vacation here. But if you insist on saving time for the many other fascinating areas in the Southwest, there are ways to see a good deal of Bryce in a short amount of time.

Start at the **visitor center** and watch the short program that explains the area's geology. Then drive the 18-mile (one-way) dead-end **park road,** stopping at viewpoints to gaze down into the canyon. An alternative is to take the free **shuttle,** which will take you to most of the main viewpoints.

Whichever way you choose to get around, make sure you spend at least a little time at **Inspiration Point,** which offers a splendid (and yes, inspirational) view of **Bryce Amphitheater** and its hundreds of statuesque pink, red, orange, and brown hoodoo stone sculptures.

After seeing the canyon from the top down, it's time to get some exercise. Walk at least partway down the **Queen's Garden Trail.** If you can spare 3 hours, hike down the Navajo Loop and return to the rim on the Queen's Garden Trail, as discussed below. An alternative is to take an easy walk along the **Rim Trail,** which provides spectacular views into the canyon. It's especially gorgeous about an hour before sunset.

Bryce Canyon Area Tours & Adventures (© **800/432-5383** or 435/834-5200; www.brycetours.com) offers 1½- to 2-hour tours year-round. They leave from Bryce Canyon Resort next to the shuttle parking area outside the park entrance, at the intersection of the park entrance road and Utah 12. A general tour, stopping at several viewpoints, costs $26 for adults, $12 for children 5 to 15, free for children under 5. Sunset and other specialized tours are also available.

OUTDOOR PURSUITS

One of the things we like best about Bryce Canyon is that you don't have to be an advanced backpacker to really get to know the park. However, all trails below the rim have at least some steep grades, so wear hiking boots with a traction tread and good ankle support to avoid ankle injuries. During the hot summer months, you'll want to hike either early or late in the day, carry plenty of water, and keep in mind that the deeper you go into the canyon, the hotter it gets.

The **Rim Trail,** which does not drop into the canyon but offers splendid views from above, meanders along the rim for over 5 miles. Overlooking Bryce Amphitheater, the trail allows excellent views along most of its length. An easy to moderate walk, it includes a .5-mile section between two overlooks—Sunrise and Sunset—that is suitable for wheelchairs. This trail is a good choice for an after-dinner stroll, when you can watch the changing evening light on the rosy rocks below.

Your best bet for getting down into the canyon and seeing the most with the least amount of sweat is to combine two popular trails—**Navajo Loop** ★★★ and **Queen's Garden.** The total distance is just under 3 miles, with a 521-foot elevation change. Most hikers take 2 to 3 hours to complete the trek. It's best to start at the Navajo Loop trailhead at Sunset Point and leave the canyon on the less-steep Queen's Garden Trail, returning to the rim at Sunrise Point, .5 mile to the north. The Navajo Loop section is fairly strenuous; Queen's Garden is moderate. Along the Navajo Loop you'll pass Thor's Hammer and wonder why it hasn't fallen, then ponder the towering skyscrapers of Wall Street. Turning onto the Queen's Garden Trail, you'll see some of the park's most fanciful formations—including the trail's namesake, majestic Queen Victoria— and Gulliver's Castle.

Those looking for more of a challenge might consider the **Hat Shop Trail,** a strenuous 3.8-mile round-trip with a 900-foot elevation change. Leaving from the Bryce Point Overlook, you'll drop quickly to the Hat Shop, so named because it consists of hard gray "hats" perched on narrow reddish-brown pedestals. Allow 4 hours.

For die-hard hikers who don't mind rough terrain, Bryce has two backcountry trails, usually open in summer only. The **Under-the-Rim Trail** runs for some 23 miles, providing an excellent opportunity to see the park's spectacular scenery. **Riggs Spring Loop Trail,** 8.8 miles long, offers splendid views of the pink cliffs in the southern part of the park. The truly ambitious can combine the two trails for a week-long excursion. Permits are required for all overnight trips.

To see Bryce Canyon the way the early pioneers did, you need to view the landscape from a horse. **Canyon Trail Rides,** P.O. Box 128, Tropic, UT 84776 (© **435/679-8665;** www.canyonrides.com), offers a close-up view of Bryce's spectacular rock formations from the relative comfort of a saddle. The company has a desk inside Bryce Lodge. A 2-hour ride to the canyon floor and back costs $40 per person, and a half-day trip farther into the canyon costs $55 per person. Rides are offered April through November. Riders must be at least 7 years old for the 2-hour trip, at least 10 for the half-day ride, and weigh no more than 220 pounds.

Bryce is beautiful in winter, with the snow creating a perfect white frosting on the red, pink, orange, and brown rock statues. **Cross-country skiers** will find several marked, ungroomed trails (all above the rim), including the Fairyland Trail, which leads 1 mile through a pine and juniper forest to the Fairyland Point Overlook. From here, you can take the 1-mile Forest Trail back to the road, or continue north along the rim for another 1.2 miles to the park boundary. **Snowshoes** may be used above the rim, but not on cross-country ski tracks.

WHERE TO STAY

Room taxes add about 10% to the total cost.

Best Western Ruby's Inn ★★ *(Kids)*   This large Best Western provides most of the beds used by tired park visitors. The lobby is among the busiest places in the area, with an ATM, liquor store, beauty salon, 1-hour film processor, and activities desks where you can book excursions of all sorts, from horseback rides to helicopter tours. Off the lobby are a restaurant, an art gallery, a post office, and a huge general store. Outside are car rentals and two gas stations.

Spread among nine buildings, the modern motel rooms feature wood furnishings, art showing scenes of the area, and shower/tub combos; some have whirlpool tubs. Rooms at the back of the complex are a bit quieter, but you'll have to walk farther to the lobby.

1000 S. Utah 63 (at the entrance to Bryce Canyon), Bryce, UT 84764. (C) **866/866-6616** or 435/834-5341. Fax 435/834-5265. www.rubysinn.com. 368 units. June–Sept $105–$150 double, $166–$176 suite; Oct–May $52–$135 double, $98–$145 suite. AE, DC, DISC, MC, V. Pets accepted. **Amenities:** Restaurant (p. 572); 2 indoor pools; 1 indoor and 1 outdoor Jacuzzi; game room; concierge; multiple activities desks; car-rental desk; courtesy transportation from Bryce Airport; business center; general store; liquor store; salon; 2 coin-op laundries. *In room:* A/C, TV.

Bryce Canyon Lodge ★★★   Location is what you're paying for here, and there's no denying that this is the perfect place to stay while visiting Bryce Canyon. The handsome sandstone and ponderosa pine lodge, opened in 1924, contains a busy lobby, with information desks for horseback riding and other activities, and a well-stocked gift shop.

The lodge suites are luxurious, with ceiling fans and separate sitting rooms. The motel rooms are simple; although the outside of the building looks like a hunting lodge, the guest units are pleasant, modern accommodations, quite spacious, with two queen-size beds and either a balcony or a patio. However, we'd choose the "rustic luxury" of one of the cabins. They're fairly small, with tall ceilings that give a feeling of spaciousness, stone (gas-burning) fireplaces, two double beds, and log beams. It's the right place to stay in a beautiful national park setting like Bryce Canyon. All units are nonsmoking.

Bryce Canyon National Park, UT. (C) **435/834-5361.** Information and reservations: Xanterra Parks & Resorts, Central Reservations, 6312 S, Fiddlers Green Circle, Ste. 600N, Greenwood Village, CO 80111. (C) **888/297-2757** or 303/297-2757. Fax 303/297-3175. www.brycecanyonlodge.com. 114 units (110 in motel rooms and cabins; 3 suites and 1 studio in lodge). $125 motel double; $130 cabin; $110–$140 lodge unit. AE, DISC, MC, V. Closed Nov–Mar. **Amenities:** Restaurant (p. 571); activities desk.

Bryce Point Bed & Breakfast ★   Each room in Lamar and Ethel LeFevre's bed-and-breakfast is named for and decorated in the style of one of the couple's children. For instance, son Les is a firefighter, so the Les and Dela room contains firefighting memorabilia and photos. All units contain queen or king beds and private bathrooms (showers only). The delightful honeymoon cottage is beautifully furnished in country style, with a gas fireplace in the living room, full kitchen, washer/dryer, and king bed in the spacious bedroom.

There's a large enclosed hot tub. The full homemade breakfasts feature selections such as bacon and eggs with pancakes and apple cider syrup. Smoking is not permitted.

61 N. 400 W. (P.O. Box 96), Tropic, UT 84776-0096. (C) **888/200-4211** or 435/679-8629 (voice/fax). www.bryce pointlodging.com. 6 units. $70–$80 double; $90–$120 cottage. Rates include full breakfast. MC, V. **Amenities:** Large enclosed Jacuzzi. *In room:* TV/VCR, dataport, no phone.

Bryce View Lodge *(Value)*   This basic modern American motel gets our vote for the best combination of economy and location. It consists of four two-story buildings, set back from the road and grouped around a large parking lot and attractively landscaped area. The simply decorated rooms are comfortable and quiet. Guests have access to the amenities at Ruby's Inn, across the street.

991 S. Utah 63 (P.O. Box 64002), Bryce, UT 84764. © **888/279-2304** or 435/834-5180. Fax 435/834-5181. www.bryceviewlodge.com. 160 units. Summer $73–$93 double, rest of the year $52–$72 double. AE, DC, DISC, MC, V. Pets accepted. **Amenities:** See Best Western Ruby's Inn, p. 570. In room: A/C, TV.

Foster's (Value)   You'll find quiet, economical lodging at Foster's. A modular unit contains small rooms, each with either one queen or two double beds, decorated with posters showing scenery of the area; bathrooms have showers only. Also on the grounds is a grocery store (open 7am–10pm) with a rather nice bakery.

1150 Utah 12 (P.O. Box 640010), Bryce, UT 84764. © **435/834-5227.** Fax 435/834-5304. www.fostersmotel.com. 52 units. Summer $50 double; winter $35 double. AE, DISC, MC, V. 1½ miles west of the national park access road turnoff. **Amenities:** Restaurant (p. 572). In room: A/C, TV.

CAMPING

Typical of the West's national park campgrounds, the two campgrounds at Bryce offer plenty of trees for a genuine "forest camping" experience, easy access to trails, and limited facilities. **North Campground** ★★ has 107 sites and is open year-round; **Sunset Campground** ★ has 101 sites and is open May through September only. We prefer North Campground because it's closer to the Rim Trail—making it easier to rush over to catch those amazing sunrise and sunset colors—but we would gladly take any site in either campground. They have modern restrooms with running water, but no RV hookups or showers. Reservations are available during the warmer months for North Campground (© **877/444-6777;** www.reserveusa.com). Camping at Sunset Campground is first come, first served; get there early to claim a site. Cost is $10 per night.

Pay showers, a coin-operated laundry, a snack bar, food and camping supplies, and souvenirs are available in the summer at the **General Store** (for information, contact Bryce Canyon Lodge © **435/834-5361**), which is a healthy walk from either campground. The park service operates an RV dump station ($2 fee) in the summer.

Those seeking a commercial campground with hot showers, RV hookups, and all the usual amenities won't do any better than **Ruby's Inn RV Park & Campground** ★★, 1280 S. Utah 63, Bryce, UT 84764 (© **866/866-6616** or 435/834-5301), right outside the park along the park's shuttle-bus route. Many of the 200 sites are shaded and there's an attractive tent area. Facilities include a pool, two coin-op laundries, a game room, horseshoes, barbecue grills, and a store with groceries and RV supplies. Also on the grounds are several camping cabins ($45 double) and tepees ($26 double), which share the campground's bathhouse. Rates for two people are $26 to $29 for RV sites and $18 for tent sites. The campground is open from April through October.

WHERE TO EAT

Bryce Canyon Lodge ★★ AMERICAN   We would come here just for the mountain-lodge atmosphere, with two large stone fireplaces and large windows looking out on the park. But the food's good, too. House specialties at dinner include garlic roasted pork loin with raspberry chipotle glaze, and grilled trout amandine. The menu also offers steaks, chicken, and several vegetarian selections. At lunch, you'll find sandwiches, salads, and other lighter items. Breakfasts offer all the usual American standards and an excellent buffet. The restaurant has full liquor service.

Bryce Canyon National Park. © **435/834-5361.** www.brycecanyonlodge.com. Reservations required for dinner. Main courses $4.95–$10 breakfast and lunch, $13–$22 dinner. AE, DC, DISC, MC, V. Daily 6:30–10:30am, 11am–3:30pm, and 5:30–9:30pm. Closed Nov–Mar.

Cowboy's Buffet & Steak Room STEAK/SEAFOOD   The busiest restaurant in the Bryce Canyon area, this place moves 'em through with buffets at every meal, plus a well-rounded menu and friendly service. The breakfast buffet offers more choices than you'd expect, and at the lunch buffet you'll find country-style ribs, fresh fruit, salads, soups, and vegetables. The dinner buffet features charbroiled rib-eye steak and other meats, pastas, potatoes, and salads. Regular menu dinner entrees include prime rib, steaks, ribs, grilled Utah trout, burgers, and salads. In addition to the large, Western-style dining room, a patio is open in summer. There is full liquor service.

At the Best Western Ruby's Inn, 1000 S. Utah 63, Bryce. © 435/834-5341. www.rubysinn.com. Reservations not accepted. Breakfast and lunch $5.95–$15, dinner main courses and buffets $8.95–$25. AE, DC, DISC, MC, V. Summer daily 6:30am–10pm; winter daily 6:30am–9pm.

Foster's Family Steak House STEAK/SEAFOOD   The simple Western decor here provides the right atmosphere for a family steakhouse. Locally popular for its slow-roasted prime rib and steamed Utah trout, Foster's also offers several steaks (we like the 14-oz. T-bone), sandwiches, a soup of the day, and homemade chili with beans. All of the pastries, pies, and breads are baked on the premises. Bottled beer is available with meals.

At Foster's motel, 1150 Utah 12, about 1½ miles west of the park entrance road. © 435/834-5227. www.fosters motel.com. Breakfast and lunch items $1.75–$6, dinner main courses $9–$20. AE, DISC, MC, V. Mar–Nov daily 7am–10pm; Dec–Feb daily 3–10pm.

3 Capitol Reef National Park ★★★

A wonderful little-known gem, **Capitol Reef National Park** offers loads of that spectacular southern Utah scenery, but with a unique twist and a geologic personality all its own. You'll see the aptly named Hamburger Rocks, sitting atop a white sandstone table; the silent, eerie Temple of the Moon; and the commanding Castle. The colors of Capitol Reef's canyon walls are spectacular, which is why Navajos called this "The Land of the Sleeping Rainbow."

But Capitol Reef is much more than brilliant rocks and barren desert. The Fremont River creates a lush oasis in an otherwise unforgiving land, with cottonwoods and willows along its banks. The area is also rich in history, with thousand-year-old rock art, historic buildings, and other traces of the past.

ESSENTIALS

GETTING THERE   The park straddles Utah 24, which connects with I-70 to the northeast and northwest. Those coming from Bryce Canyon National Park can follow Utah 12 northeast to its intersection with Utah 24, and continue east into Capitol Reef. If you're approaching from the Four Corners area, follow Utah 276 or Utah 95 (or both) north to the intersection with Utah 24, where you'll then go west into the park.

INFORMATION/VISITOR CENTER   Contact **Capitol Reef National Park,** HC 70 Box 15, Torrey, UT 84775-9602 (© **435/425-3791;** www.nps.gov.care).

The **visitor center** is on the park access road at its intersection with Utah 24. It's open daily except December 25 and has exhibits on the area's geology and history. You can get information and backcountry permits, pick up free brochures, and purchase books, maps, and videos.

FEES   Entry to the park (for up to 7 days) costs $5 per vehicle. Free permits, available at the visitor center, are required for all overnight hiking trips into the backcountry.

RANGER PROGRAMS   Rangers present a variety of free programs and activities from spring through fall. Campfire programs take place most evenings at the outdoor amphitheater next to Fruita Campground. Topics vary but may include animals and plants, geology, and human history in and of the area. Rangers also lead hikes and walks and give short talks on history at the pioneer Fruita Schoolhouse and the Mormon homestead. Schedules are posted on bulletin boards at the visitor center and campground. Kids can become Junior Rangers or Junior Geologists; they'll learn to map ancient earthquakes, inspect water bugs, and so on.

SEEING THE HIGHLIGHTS

Start at the **visitor center,** where you will learn about the park's geology and early history. From there, the paved 25-mile round-trip **Scenic Drive** leads south into the park, offering good views of its dramatic canyons and rock formations. Pick up a free copy of the Scenic Drive brochure at the entrance station and set out, stopping at viewpoints to gaze out at the array of colorful cliffs and commanding rocks.

If the weather's dry, drive down the gravel **Capitol Gorge Road** (5 miles round-trip) at the end of the paved Scenic Drive for a look at what many consider the best backcountry scenery in the park. If you're up for a short walk, the relatively flat 2-mile (round-trip) **Capitol Gorge Trail,** which starts at the end of Capitol Gorge Road, takes you to the historic **Pioneer Register,** a rock wall where traveling pioneers "signed in."

HISTORIC SITES

In the park, you'll find evidence of man's presence through the centuries. The **Fremont** people lived along the river as early as A.D. 700, and their petroglyphs (images carved into rock) and pictographs (images painted on rock) are visible on the canyon walls. Prospectors and other travelers passed through **Capitol Gorge** in the late 1800s, leaving their names on a wall of rock that came to be known as the **Pioneer Register.** You can reach it on a 2-mile loop; see p. 574.

Mormon pioneers established the appropriately named community of **Fruita** when they discovered that this was a good spot to grow fruit. The tiny 1896 **Fruita Schoolhouse** served as a church, social hall, and meeting hall, in addition to being a one-room schoolhouse. The school closed in 1941, and it has been restored and furnished with old wood-and-wrought-iron desks, a wood stove, a chalkboard, textbooks, and even the hand bell that used to call students to class. Nearby, the **orchards** planted by the settlers continue to flourish, tended by park workers who invite you to sample the "fruits" of their labors.

The historic **Gifford Farmhouse,** built in 1908, is a typical early-20th-century Utah farmhouse. It offers displays of period objects and often schedules demonstrations of pioneer skills, such as quilting and rug making. Park across the road at the picnic area; a short path leads to the farmhouse.

OUTDOOR PURSUITS

This is the real Wild West; little has changed from the way cowboys, bank robbers, settlers, and gold miners found it in the late 1800s. Among the last areas in the continental United States to be explored, many parts of Capitol Reef National Park are still practically unknown, perfect for those who want to see this rugged country in its natural state. Several local companies offer guide and shuttle services. They include **Hondoo Rivers and Trails,** 90 E. Main St. (P.O. Box 98), Torrey, UT 84775 (ⓒ **800/ 332-2696** or 435/425-3519; www.hondoo.com); and **Wild Hare Expeditions,** 116

W. Main St. (P.O. Box 750194), Torrey, UT 84775 (© **888/304-HARE** or 435/425-3999; www.color-country.net/~thehare).

For those who want to strike out on their own, the park's hiking trails offer panoramic views of colorful cliffs and soaring spires, eerie journeys through desolate steep-walled canyons, and cool oases along the tree-shaded Fremont River. Watch for petroglyphs and other reminders of this area's first inhabitants.

Among the best short hikes is the 2-mile round-trip **Capitol Gorge Trail.** It's easy, mostly level walking along the bottom of a narrow canyon, but looking up at the tall, smooth walls of rock conveys a strong sense of what the pioneers must have seen and felt 100 years ago, when they moved rocks and debris to haul their wagons up this canyon. Starting at the end of the dirt Capitol Gorge Road, the hiking trail leads past the **Pioneer Register,** where prospectors and other early travelers carved their names. The earliest legible signatures were made in 1871 by J. A. Call and "Wal" Bateman.

A more strenuous hike is the 3.5-mile round-trip **Cassidy Arch Trail.** This route offers spectacular views as it climbs steeply from the floor of Grand Wash to high cliffs overlooking the park. From the trail, you'll see Cassidy Arch, a natural stone arch named for outlaw Butch Cassidy, who is believed to have used the Grand Wash as a hideout. The trail is off the Grand Wash dirt road, which branches off the east side of the highway about halfway down the park's Scenic Drive.

As in most national parks, **bikes and four-wheel-drive vehicles** must stay on established roads, but Capitol Reef has several so-called roads—actually little more than dirt trails—that provide exciting opportunities for those using 4×4s or pedal-power. ATVs are not permitted. Both the Grand Wash and Capitol Gorge roads, plus several much longer dirt roads, are open to mountain bikes as well as four-wheel-drive vehicles. Details are available at the visitor center.

WHERE TO STAY

There are no lodging or dining facilities in the park; the town of Torrey, just west of the park entrance, can take care of most needs. Room tax adds 9% to lodging bills.

Capitol Reef Inn & Cafe This older, Western-style motel—small, beautifully landscaped, and well maintained—offers homey, comfortable guest rooms. The furnishings are handmade of solid wood. One unit has a shower/tub combo; the rest have showers only. Facilities include a playground and a lovely desert garden. The book and gift shop offers American Indian crafts, guidebooks, and maps.

360 W. Main St. (Utah 24), Torrey, UT 84775. © 435/425-3271. www.capitolreefinn.com. 10 units. $48 double. AE, DISC, MC, V. Closed Nov–Mar. **Amenities:** Restaurant (p. 575); large hot tub. *In room:* A/C, TV, fridge, coffeemaker.

Sandcreek RV Park & Hostel This hostel consists of one large room in which everyone—both men and women—sleeps, bunkhouse style. The handsome, high-ceilinged log building offers eight single beds, a TV, a microwave, a refrigerator, and a porch with tables and chairs. Hostellers share the bathhouse with campers (see listing below), and linens are available. You'll also find an espresso bar, gift shop, laundry, horseshoe pits, and a natural stone and petrified wood labyrinth that leads to a quiet meditation area.

540 Utah 24, 5 miles west of the park entrance (P.O. Box 750276), Torrey, UT 84775. © 877/425-3578 or 435/425-3577. www.sandcreekrv.com. Hostel $10–$12 per person. MC, V. Closed mid-Oct through Mar.

SkyRidge Inn Bed & Breakfast ★★ This combination B&B and art gallery offers a delightful alternative to the standard motel. Rooms in the three-story Territorial-style inn are distinctively decorated with an eclectic mix of antiques and contemporary art.

Two have private decks with hot tubs; another has a two-person whirlpool tub inside and a private deck.

An impressive fireplace, decorated with over 30 pounds of nails, sits in the gallery and gathering room. The inn sits on 75 acres, with hiking trails and spectacular views. Full breakfasts include homemade granola; fresh-baked coffeecake, muffins, or cinnamon rolls; and a hot entree such as Southwest frittata or pecan griddlecakes. Smoking is not permitted.

950 E. Utah 24 (P.O. Box 750220), Torrey, UT 84775. (C) 800/448-6990 or 435/425-3222. www.skyridgeinn.com. 6 units. Apr–Oct $119–$189 double; Nov–Mar $107–$170 double. Rates include breakfast and evening hors d'oeuvres. AE, MC, V. **Amenities:** Jacuzzi. *In room:* A/C, TV/VCR, CD player, hair dryer.

CAMPING

The 71-site **Fruita Campground,** open year-round, offers modern restrooms, drinking water, picnic tables, fire grills, and an RV dump station, but no showers or RV hookups. It's along the main park road, 1 mile south of the visitor center. Water may be turned off in winter, leaving only pit toilets. Camping costs $10; reservations are not accepted.

The park also has two **primitive campgrounds,** free and open year-round on a first-come, first-served basis. Both have tables, fire grills, and pit toilets, but no water. Check for directions and road conditions before going, because unpaved roads may be impassable in wet weather.

Backcountry camping is permitted in much of the park with a free permit, available at the visitor center. Fires are forbidden in the backcountry.

For a commercial campground with hot showers and RV hookups, we recommend the **Sandcreek RV Park & Hostel,** 540 Utah 24 (P.O. Box 750276), Torrey, UT 84775 ((C) 877/425-3578 or 435/425-3577; www.sandcreekrv.com). Five miles west of the park entrance, this 24-site campground has an open, grassy area, numerous young trees, and great views. Facilities include a large, clean bathhouse; horseshoe pits; a gift shop; an espresso bar; a dump station; and coin-op laundry. The property also has a hostel (see listing above) plus two attractive cabins that share the campground bathhouse ($28 double). Campsite rates are $11 for tents and $16 to $18 for RVs. Open April through mid-October.

WHERE TO EAT

Cafe Diablo ★★ SOUTHWESTERN Looks are deceiving. What appears to be a simple small-town cafe in a converted home is in fact a very fine restaurant, offering innovative beef, pork, chicken, seafood, and vegetarian selections, many created with a Southwestern flair. The menu varies but could include pumpkin seed–crusted local trout served with cilantro-lime sauce and wild-rice pancakes; Utah lamb marinated with sage and rosemary; and artichoke and sun-dried tomato tamales. Pastries and ice creams, all made on the premises, are spectacular. Beer, wine, and cocktails are served.

599 W. Main St., Torrey. (C) 435/425-3070. www.cafediablo.net. Main courses $17–$28. MC, V. Daily 5–10pm. Closed mid-Oct to late Apr.

Capitol Reef Inn & Cafe ★★ *Finds* AMERICAN This local favorite offers fine, fresh, healthy cuisine that's among the best you'll find in Utah. Known for its locally raised trout, the cafe is equally famous for the 10-vegetable salad served with all dinner entrees. Vegetables are grown locally, and several dishes—such as spaghetti and excellent fettuccine primavera—can be ordered vegetarian or with meat or fish. Steaks and chicken are also served. The atmosphere is casual, with comfortable seating,

American Indian crafts, and large windows. The restaurant offers wine, beer, and a limited number of mixed drinks.

360 W. Main St. (435/425-3271. Main courses $4.25-$9 breakfast and lunch, $10–$20 dinner. AE, DISC, MC, V. Daily 7am–9pm. Closed Nov–Mar.

4 Arches & Canyonlands National Parks

Massive sandstone spires and arches that seem to defy gravity, all colored by iron and other minerals in shades of orange, red, and brown, define these two national parks. On opposite sides of the town of Moab, the parks offer numerous opportunities for hiking, mountain biking, and four-wheeling.

No lodging facilities, restaurants, or stores are inside either national park; most visitors stay and eat in Moab. For lodging, camping, and restaurant information for Moab, see "A Base Camp in Moab" (p. 581).

Moab is on U.S. 191, 30 miles south of I-70 (take exit 180 at Crescent Junction) and 53 miles north of Monticello.

ARCHES NATIONAL PARK

Natural stone arches and fantastic rock formations, which look as if they were sculpted by an artist's hand, are the defining features of this park, and they exist in remarkable numbers and variety. Best of all, the formations here seem more accessible and less forbidding than the spires and pinnacles at nearby Canyonlands National Park. Arches is visitor-friendly, with relatively short, well-maintained trails leading to most of the park's major attractions.

Some people think of arches as bridges, but to geologists there's a big difference. Bridges are formed when a river slowly bores through solid rock. The often bizarre and beautiful contours of arches result from the erosive force of rain and snow, which freezes and thaws, dissolving the "glue" that holds sand grains together and chipping away at the stone, until gravity finally pulls a chunk off.

ESSENTIALS

GETTING THERE   From Moab, drive 5 miles north on US 191.

VISITOR INFORMATION   Contact **Arches National Park,** P.O. Box 907, Moab, UT 84532-0907 ((**435/719-2299;** www.nps.gov/arch). **Canyonlands Natural History Association,** 3031 South US 191, Moab, UT 84532 ((**800/840-8978** or 435/259-6003; www.cnha.org), sells books, maps, and videos.

The visitor center, just inside the park entrance gate, provides maps, brochures, and information. It's open daily except December 25.

FEES   Entry to the park (for up to 7 days) costs $10 per vehicle, $5 per motorcycle, bicycle, or pedestrian.

RANGER PROGRAMS   From March through October, rangers lead guided hikes on the Fiery Furnace Trail twice daily (see "Outdoor Pursuits," below), as well as daily nature walks at various park locations. Evening campfire programs (Apr–Oct) cover topics such as rock art, geological processes, and wildlife. A schedule of events is posted at the visitor center. Kids between 6 and 12 can pick up a Junior Ranger booklet at the visitor center. After completing the activities in the booklet and participating in several programs, they'll earn a badge.

SEEING THE HIGHLIGHTS

Arches is the easiest of Utah's national parks to see in a day, if that's all you can spare. An 18-mile (one-way) **scenic drive** offers splendid views of countless natural rock arches and other formations, and several easy hikes reveal additional scenery. Allow 1½ hours for the round-trip drive, adding time for optional hikes. Start by viewing the short program at the **visitor center** to get a feel for what lies ahead. Then drive north along the scenic drive, stopping at viewpoints and for occasional short walks. The scenic drive ends at the often-crowded parking area for the **Devils Garden Trailhead.** From here, you can hike to some of the park's unique arches, including **Landscape Arch,** which is among the longest natural rock spans in the world. From the trailhead parking lot, it's 18 miles back to the visitor center.

OUTDOOR PURSUITS

Most of the hiking trails here are short and relatively easy. Because of the hot summer sun and lack of shade, it's wise to carry water on even the shortest hike.

One easy walk is to **Sand Dune Arch,** a good place to take kids who want to play in the sand. It's only .3 mile (round-trip), but you can add 1.2 miles by continuing to Broken Arch. Sand Dune Arch is hidden among and shaded by rock walls, with a naturally created giant sandbox below the arch. Those continuing to Broken Arch should watch for mule deer and kit foxes along the way. Allow about 30 minutes to Sand Dune Arch and back; to Broken Arch, 1 hour.

From the **Devils Garden Trail,** you can see about 15 to 20 arches on a fairly long, strenuous, and difficult hike, or view some exciting scenery by following only part of the route. We suggest taking at least the easy-to-moderate 1.6-mile round-trip hike to **Landscape Arch** ⭐, a long, thin ribbon of stone that's one of the most beautiful arches in the park. Watch for mule deer along the way, and allow about an hour. Past Landscape Arch, the trail becomes more challenging, but it offers numerous additional views, including panoramas of the curious Double O Arch and a large, dark tower known as Dark Angel. From the section of the trail where Dark Angel is visible, you are 2.5 miles from the trailhead. If you turn back at this point, the round trip will take about 3 hours.

Considered by many to be the park's most scenic hike, the 3-mile round-trip **Delicate Arch Trail** ⭐ is a moderate-to-difficult hike, with slippery slickrock, no shade, and some steep drop-offs along a narrow cliff. Hikers are rewarded with a dramatic and spectacular view of Delicate Arch. Allow 2 to 3 hours.

The **Fiery Furnace Guided Hike** is a difficult and strenuous 2-mile round-trip naturalist-led hike to some of the most colorful formations in the park. Guided hikes venture into this restricted area twice daily from spring through fall, by reservation, and last 2¼ to 3 hours. Cost is $8 for adults, $4 for children 6 to 12.

CAMPING IN THE PARK

At the north end of the park's scenic drive, **Devils Garden Campground** is Arches' only developed camping area. The 52 well-spaced sites nestle among rocks, with plenty of piñon and juniper trees. From March through October, the campground accepts reservations (© 877/444-6777; www.reserveusa.com). In summer, the campground fills early, often by 9am, with people trying to garner the 24 first-come, first-served sites; make reservations or get to the campground early, often by 7:30am. Sites cost $10 per night. There are no showers or RV hookups.

CANYONLANDS NATIONAL PARK

Utah's largest national park is not for the sightseer out for a Sunday afternoon drive. Instead, it rewards those willing to spend time and energy—*lots* of energy—exploring the rugged backcountry. Sliced into districts by the Colorado and Green rivers, this is a land of extremes: vast panoramas, dizzyingly deep canyons, dramatically steep cliffs, broad mesas, and towering spires.

The most accessible part of Canyonlands is the **Island in the Sky District,** in the northern section of the park. A paved road leads to sites such as Grand View Point, which overlooks some 10,000 square miles of rugged wilderness.

The **Needles District,** in the southeast corner, offers only a few viewpoints along the paved road, but it boasts numerous possibilities for hikers, backpackers, and high-clearance 4×4s. Named for its tall red-and-white-striped rock pinnacles, this diverse district is home to impressive arches, including 150-foot-tall Angel Arch, as well as grassy meadows and the confluence of the Green and Colorado rivers.

Most park visitors don't get a close-up view of the **Maze District;** they see it off in the distance. That's because it's practically inaccessible. You'll need a lot of endurance and at least several days to see even a few of its sites, such as the appropriately named Lizard Rock and Beehive Arch.

ESSENTIALS

GETTING THERE   To reach the Island in the Sky Visitor Center, 34 miles west of Moab, take US 191 north to Utah 313, and follow it south into the park. To reach the Needles Visitor Center, 75 miles southwest of Moab, take US 191 south to Utah 211, and follow it west into the park. Getting to the Maze District is a bit more interesting. From I-70 west of Green River, take Utah 24 south. Watch for signs and follow two- and four-wheel-drive dirt roads east into the park.

VISITOR INFORMATION   Contact **Canyonlands National Park,** 2282 SW Resource Blvd., Moab, UT 84532 (© **435/719-2313;** www.nps.gov/cany). Books, very useful maps, and videos are available from the nonprofit **Canyonlands Natural History Association,** 3031 South US 191, Moab, UT 84532 (© **800/840-8978** or 435/259-6003; www.cnha.org).

Island in the Sky Visitor Center, in the northern part of the park, and **Needles Visitor Center,** in the southern section, provide maps, free brochures on hiking trails, and, most important, advice from rangers. We can't overemphasize how brutal the terrain at Canyonlands can be. It's important to know not only your own limitations, but also the limitations of your vehicle and other equipment.

FEES   Entry to the park (for up to 7 days) costs $10 per vehicle, $5 per motorcycle, bicycle, or pedestrian.

Permits, available at visitor centers, are required for all overnight stays except at the established campgrounds. Call © **435/259-4351** for rates and reservations.

RANGER PROGRAMS   On summer evenings at Squaw Flat and Willow Flat campgrounds, rangers offer campfire programs on various aspects of the park. Short morning talks take place in summer at the Island in the Sky Visitor Center and at Grand View Point.

SEEING THE HIGHLIGHTS

Canyonlands is not an easy place to see in a short time. In fact, if your schedule permits only a day or less, we suggest skipping the Needles and Maze districts entirely and going directly to the **Island in the Sky Visitor Center.** After looking at the exhibits, drive to several of the overlooks, stopping along the way for a short hike or two. Make sure you stop at the **Grand View Point Overlook,** at the south end of the paved road. Hiking the **Grand View Trail,** which is especially scenic in the late afternoon, literally gives you the "Grand View" of the park. Allow about 1½ hours for the easy 2-mile walk. We also recommend the **Upheaval Dome Overlook Trail,** which should take about half an hour and will bring you to a mile-wide crater of mysterious origins.

OUTDOOR PURSUITS

Canyonlands has little shade and no reliable water sources, and temperatures soar to 100°F (38°C) in summer. Rangers strongly advise that hikers carry at least a gallon of water per person per day, along with sunscreen, a hat, and all the usual hiking and emergency equipment. If you expect to do serious hiking, try to plan your trip for the spring or fall, when conditions are much more hospitable. Because some trails may be confusing, hikers attempting the longer ones should carry good topographic maps.

In the Island in the Sky District, the **Mesa Arch Trail** provides the casual visitor with an easy .5-mile (round-trip) self-guided nature walk among piñon and juniper trees, cactus, and a plant called Mormon tea, from which Mormon pioneers made a tealike beverage. The loop trail's main scenic attraction is an arch, made of Navajo sandstone, that hangs precariously on the edge of a cliff, framing a spectacular view of nearby mountains. Allow about a half-hour.

An easy 2-mile hike, especially pretty at sunset, is the **Grand View Trail** ✿, which follows the canyon rim from Grand View Point and shows off numerous canyons and rock formations, the Colorado River, and distant mountains. Allow about 1½ hours.

A bit more strenuous is the 5-mile **Neck Spring Trail,** which starts about ½ mile south of the Island in the Sky Visitor Center. Allow 3 to 4 hours for this hike, which follows old paths to two springs. You'll see water troughs, hitching posts, rusty cans, and the ruins of an old cabin. Climb to the top of the rim for a great view of the canyons and the Henry Mountains, some 60 miles away.

In the Needles District, one relatively easy hike is the **Roadside Ruin Trail,** a short (.3-mile), self-guided nature walk that takes about a half-hour round-trip. It leads to a prehistoric granary, probably used by the Anasazi (ancestral Puebloans) some 700 to 1,000 years ago to store corn, nuts, and other foods.

For a bit more of a challenge, try the **Slickrock Foot Trail,** a 2.4-mile loop that leads to several viewpoints and takes 2 or 3 hours. Slickrock—a general term for any bare rock surface—can be slippery, especially when wet. Viewpoints show off the stair-step topography of the area, from its colorful canyons and cliffs to its flat mesas and striped needles.

From **Elephant Hill Trailhead,** you can follow several interconnecting trails into the backcountry. The road to the trailhead is gravel, but it is graded and drivable in most two-wheel-drive passenger cars; those in large vehicles such as motor homes, however, will want to avoid it. The 11-mile round-trip **Elephant Hill–Druid Arch hike** ✦ can be accomplished in 4 to 6 hours and is moderately difficult, with some steep drop-offs and quite a bit of slickrock. But the views are well worth it. You hike through narrow rock canyons, past colorful spires and pinnacles, and on to the huge Druid Arch, which somewhat resembles the stone structures at Stonehenge.

The **Confluence Overlook Trail,** an 11-mile round-trip day or overnight hike, leads to a spectacular bird's-eye view of the confluence of the Green and Colorado rivers and the 1,000-foot-deep gorges they've carved. The hike is moderately difficult, with steep drop-offs and little shade, but it splendidly reveals the many colors of the Needles District, as well as views into the Maze District of the park. Allow 4 to 6 hours.

Unlike most national parks, where all motor vehicles and mountain bikes are restricted to paved roads, Canyonlands has miles of rough four-wheel-drive roads where mechanized transport is king and jacked-up jeeps with oversize tires rule the day. Four-wheelers must stay on designated 4×4 roads, but keep in mind that the term "road" can mean anything from a graded, well-marked, two-lane gravel byway to a pile of loose rocks.

Mountain bikes are also allowed on these roads, but they share space with motor vehicles and occasional hikers and horseback riders. Because some of the four-wheel-drive roads have spots of deep sand—which can turn into quicksand when wet—mountain biking may not be as much fun here as you'd expect.

The best four-wheel-drive adventure in the Island in the Sky District is the **White Rim Road** ✦✦. It winds some 100 miles through the district and affords spectacular views, from broad panoramas of rock and canyon to close-ups of red and orange towers and buttes. A high-clearance 4×4 is necessary. Allow 2 to 3 days for the entire trip. There are primitive campgrounds along the way, but reservations and backcountry permits are needed. Mountain bikers also enjoy this trail, especially when accompanying a four-wheel-drive support vehicle with supplies.

Four-wheel-drive fans going into the Needles District will find one of their ultimate challenges on the **Elephant Hill Jeep Road,** which begins at a well-marked turnoff near Squaw Flat Campground. Although most of the 10-mile trail is only moderately difficult, the stretch over Elephant Hill itself (near the beginning of the drive) can be a nightmare. It has steep, rough slickrock, drifting sand, loose rock, and treacherous ledges. Coming down the hill, you'll reach one switchback that requires you to back to the edge of a steep cliff. This road is also a favorite of mountain bikers, although bikes will have to be walked on some stretches because of the abundance of sand and rocks. The route offers views of numerous rock formations, plus panoramas of steep cliffs and rock "stairs." Allow 8 hours to 3 days. Backcountry permits are needed for overnight trips.

For a spectacular view of the Colorado River, the **Colorado River Overlook Road** in the Needles District can't be beat. This 14-mile round-trip is popular with four-wheelers, backpackers, and mountain bikers. Considered among the park's easiest 4×4 roads, the first part, which is accessible by high-clearance two-wheel-drives, is very easy indeed. But the second half has a few rough and rocky sections that require four-wheel-drive. The road features numerous panoramic vistas and a spectacular 360-degree view of the park and the Colorado River, some 1,000 feet below.

CAMPING IN THE PARK

The park has are two developed campgrounds, both first come, first served. In the Island in the Sky District, **Willow Flat Campground** has 12 sites, picnic tables, fire grates, and vault toilets; camping is $5. In the Needles District, **Squaw Flat Campground** has 26 sites, fire grates, picnic tables, flush toilets, and drinking water; the fee is $10 per night.

A BASE CAMP IN MOAB

Most visitors to Arches and Canyonlands national parks stay in Moab, which offers easy access to both parks, plenty of other opportunities for outdoor recreation, and an abundance of places to sleep and eat. For information, contact the **Moab Area Travel Council,** P.O. Box 550, Moab, UT 84532 (© **800/635-6622** or 435/259-8825; www.discovermoab.com). When you arrive, stop by the **Moab Information Center,** at the corner of Main and Center streets.

WHERE TO STAY

Moab has most of the major medium-priced chains, located on Main Street. Room tax of about 12.25% applies.

Aarchway Inn   Two miles from the entrance to Arches National Park, this well-maintained modern motel has large rooms with great views, decorated in Southwestern style. Photos on the walls depict the area's scenic attractions. Most rooms contain two queen beds, and eight family units also have queen sofa beds. The suites have whirlpool tubs. Facilities include a courtyard with barbecue grills, bike storage, conference rooms, and a gift shop. The entire property is nonsmoking.

1551 N. U.S. 191, Moab, UT 84532. © 800/341-9359 or 435/259-2599. Fax 435/259-2270. www.aarchwayinn.com. 97 units. Mar–Oct $90–$120 double, $135–$175 suite. Off-season discounts available. Rates include continental breakfast. AE, DC, DISC, MC, V. **Amenities:** Large heated outdoor pool; exercise room; indoor Jacuzzi. *In room:* A/C, TV, dataport, fridge, microwave, coffeemaker.

Bowen Motel   This family-owned and -operated motel offers fairly large, comfortable, basic rooms with attractive wallpaper, a king or one or two queen beds, and combination shower/tubs. Refrigerators and microwaves are available. Two family rooms sleep up to six persons each.

169 N. Main St., Moab, UT 84532. © 800/874-5439 or 435/259-7132. Fax 435/259-6641. www.bowenmotel.com. 40 units. $50–$85 double. Off-season discounts available. Rates include continental breakfast. AE, DC, DISC, MC, V. Pets accepted. **Amenities:** Heated outdoor pool. *In room:* A/C, TV.

Red Stone Inn   This centrally located motel is comfortable and quiet. The exterior gives the impression that these are cabins, and the theme continues inside, where colorful posters and maps of area attractions decorate attractive knotty pine walls. Rooms are a bit on the small side, although perfectly adequate and spotlessly maintained. All units have kitchenettes with microwaves, coffeemakers (with coffee supplied), and refrigerators. Three rooms accessible to travelers with disabilities have combination shower/tubs; the rest have showers only. There's a covered picnic area with tables and gas barbecue grills, and a mountain bike work stand and bike wash. Guests have free access to the pool at a motel across the street.

535 S. Main St., Moab, UT 84532. © 800/772-1972 or 435/259-3500. Fax 435/259-2717. www.moabredstone.com. 52 units. Summer $60–$75 double; winter $30–$35 double; prices higher in Sept and during special events. AE, DISC, MC, V. Pets accepted; $5 fee. **Amenities:** Access to heated outdoor pool; indoor hot tub; coin-op laundry. *In room:* A/C, TV, dataport, kitchen.

Sunflower Hill Luxury Inn ★★ This country-style retreat is our choice for a relaxing escape. Located 3 blocks off Main Street on a quiet dead-end road, it offers elegant rooms and lovely outdoor areas. The rooms are individually decorated—for instance, the Summer House Suite boasts a colorful garden-themed mural—and have handmade quilts. Deluxe rooms have jetted tubs and private balconies. The grounds are grassy and shady, with fruit trees and flowers in abundance, plus a swing, picnic table, and barbecue. The substantial breakfast buffet includes homemade breads and fresh-baked pastries, honey-almond granola, fresh fruits, and a hot entree such as a garden vegetable frittata, blueberry pancakes, or asparagus quiche. All units are nonsmoking.

185 N. 300 East, Moab, UT 84532. ⓒ **800/662-2786** or 435/259-2974. Fax 435/259-3065. www.sunflowerhill.com. 12 units. Mar to mid-Nov and holidays $135–$205 double; mid-Nov to Feb $90–$180 double. Rates include full breakfast and evening refreshments. AE, DISC, MC, V. Children under 10 accepted by prior arrangement. **Amenities:** Heated outdoor pool; hot tub; coin-op laundry. *In room:* A/C, TV/VCR, CD player, hairdryer, no phone.

Camping

A number of commercial campgrounds in Moab offer hot showers, RV hookups, and other amenities. Among those we especially like are **Arch View Camp Park,** U.S. 191, at the junction with U.S. 313, 9 miles north of town (P.O. Box 938), Moab, UT 84532 (ⓒ **800/813-6622** or 435/259-7854; www.archviewresort.com). It has more than 70 sites as well as great views into Arches National Park. For two people, tent sites cost $17 and full-hookup RV sites cost $24. Rates for cabins start at $33 for two people. Another good choice, especially for those who want to be downtown, is **Canyonlands Campground & RV Park,** 555 S. Main St., Moab, UT 84532 (ⓒ **800/522-6848** or 435/259-6848; www.canyonlandsrv.com). This quiet, shady campground has 144 sites. For two people, it charges $18 for tent sites, $25 to $27 for RV sites, and $35 for cabins.

WHERE TO EAT

Buck's Grill House ★ AMERICAN WESTERN This popular restaurant is our top choice in Moab for steak. The dining room's subdued Western decor is accented by exposed wood beams and local artwork. The attractive patio, away from the road, has trees and a delightful rock waterfall. Especially good is the grilled 12-ounce New York strip steak, either plain or rubbed with the restaurant's "cowboy" spices. We also recommend buffalo meat loaf, with black onion gravy and mashed potatoes. Southwestern dishes include duck tamale with grilled pineapple salsa. Buck's offers full liquor service and a good wine list, and serves a variety of Utah microbrews.

1393 N. US 191, about 1½ miles north of town. ⓒ **435/259-5201.** Main courses $6.95–$25. DISC, MC, V. Daily 5:30pm–closing.

Eddie McStiff's AMERICAN This bustling, noisy brewpub is half family restaurant and half tavern, with a climate-controlled garden patio as well. You'll find Southwest decor in the dining room, and the tavern looks just as a tavern should—long bar, low light, and lots of wood. The menu includes a good variety of charbroiled meats, excellent pizzas, and a selection of pasta dishes. Specialties include grilled wild Alaskan salmon and slow-smoked barbecued ribs. About a dozen fresh-brewed beers are on tap. Mixed drinks, wine, and beer are sold in the dining room with food only; the tavern sells beer with or without food. (You must be at least 21 to enter the tavern.)

In McStiff's Plaza, 57 S. Main St. (just south of the information center). ⓒ **435/259-2337.** www.eddiemcstiff.com. Main courses $4.75–$18. DISC, MC, V. Mon–Fri 5pm–midnight, Sat–Sun noon–midnight.

Moab Diner *(Kids)* AMERICAN/SOUTHWESTERN   Breakfast—among the best in town—is served all day here. It features all the usual egg dishes, biscuits and gravy, and a spicy breakfast burrito. The decor is definitely diner, but the place does have lots of green plants (real, not plastic). Hamburgers, sandwiches, and salads are the offerings at lunch. For dinner, there's steak, shrimp, and chicken, plus liver and onions. In addition to ice cream, you can get malts and shakes. No alcoholic beverages are served.

189 S. Main St. (2 blocks south of Center St.). © 435/259-4006. Main courses $4.25–$17. MC, V. Daily 6am–10pm. Closed Jan 1, Thanksgiving, and Dec 25.

18

Las Vegas

Las Vegas is a true original; there is nothing like it in America or arguably the world. In other cities, hotels are built near the major attractions. Here, the hotels *are* the major attractions. You can also enjoy great works of art, world-renowned chefs, and rock clubs and arenas that attract major acts. With so many different options available, you don't have to gamble at all!

As if. Vegas is first and foremost a gambling destination. And though the hotels aren't undercharging for everything anymore in an effort to lure you into gambling round the clock, they still do their best to separate you from your cash. The cheap buffets and meal deals still exist, as do some cut-rate rooms, but both are likely to prove the old adage about getting what you pay for. Nevertheless, free drinks are handed to anyone lurking near a slot, and if show tickets aren't in the budget, you won't lack for entertainment. Free lounge shows abound, and the people-watching opportunities alone never pall.

Depending on which areas of the southwest you plan to visit, Las Vegas might make a convenient beginning or ending point to your vacation. Because it's such a popular destination, you can often find bargains on airfare and car-rental rates. And in its own way, Vegas is every bit as amazing as the nearby Grand Canyon and every bit as much a must-see. It's one of the Seven Wonders of the Artificial World. And everyone should experience it at least once—you might find yourself coming back for more.

1 Essentials

GETTING THERE

BY PLANE Almost every major domestic airline, and some international airlines, fly into **McCarran International Airport** (© **702/261-5211;** TDD 702/261-3111; www.mccarran.com), just a few minutes' drive from the southern end of the Strip.

Bell Trans (© **702/739-7990**) runs 20-passenger minibuses daily between the airport and all major Las Vegas hotels and motels all day (7:45am–midnight). The cost is $5 per person each way to Strip and Convention Center area hotels, $6.50 to Downtown or other Off-Strip properties.

Even less expensive are **Citizen's Area Transit (CAT)** buses (© **702/CAT-RIDE**). Bus no. 108 departs from the airport and will take you to the Stratosphere, where you can transfer to the no. 301, which stops close to most Strip and Convention Center area hotels. The no. 109 goes from the airport to the Downtown Transportation Center at Casino Center Boulevard and Stewart Avenue. The fare is $2, 60¢ for seniors and children.

Taxis are also plentiful, and a ride to the Strip costs $12 to $20.

BY CAR The main highway connecting Las Vegas with the rest of the country is I-15 from the northeast (Salt Lake City) and southwest (Los Angeles and San Diego).

Las Vegas

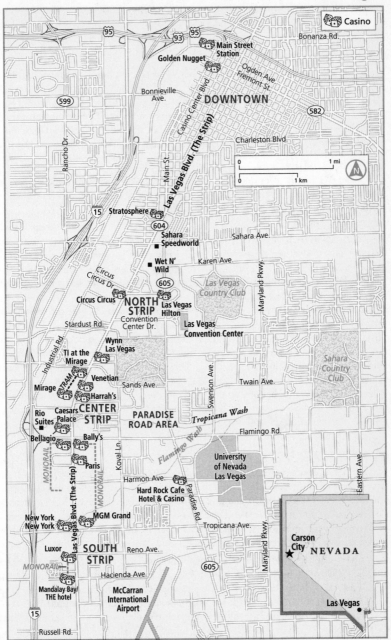

Casino

95

93 95

Main Street
Station

Golden Nugget

Bonanza Rd.

Ogden Ave.
Fremont St.

DOWNTOWN

Bonnieville
Ave.

Casino Center Blvd.

582

599

Charleston Blvd.

Rancho Dr.

Las Vegas Blvd. (The Strip)

Main St.

0   1 mi

0   1 km

N

15   Stratosphere

604

Sahara
Speedworld

Sahara Ave.

Karen Ave.

Wet N'
Wild

Maryland Pkwy.

Circus
Circus Dr.

605

Las Vegas
Country Club

Circus Circus

NORTH
STRIP

Las Vegas
Hilton

Stardust Rd.

Convention
Center Dr.

Las Vegas
Convention Center

Sahara
Country
Club

Industrial Rd.

Wynn
Las Vegas

TI at the
Mirage

TRAM

Venetian

Mirage

Harrah's

Sands Ave.

Swenson Ave.

Twain Ave.

Rio
Suites

Caesars
Palace

CENTER
STRIP

PARADISE
ROAD AREA

Tropicana Wash

Bellagio

MONORAIL

Bally's

Paris

Koval Ln.

Flamingo Wash

Flamingo Rd.

MONORAIL

University
of Nevada
Las Vegas

Eastern Ave.

Harmon Ave.

Hard Rock Cafe
Hotel & Casino

Paradise Rd.

New York
New York

MGM Grand

Tropicana Ave.

Luxor

SOUTH
STRIP

Reno Ave.

Carson
City   NEVADA

MONORAIL

Las Vegas Blvd. (The Strip)

605

Hacienda Ave.

Mandalay Bay/
THE hotel

McCarran
International
Airport

Maryland Pkwy.

Las Vegas

15

Russell Rd.

Lots of folks drive up from Los Angeles, and thanks to the narrow two-lane highway, it can get very crowded on Friday and Sunday afternoons. Other major routes are U.S. 93 from the southeast (Phoenix) and U.S. 95 from the northwest (Reno).

VISITOR INFORMATION

For advance information, call or write the **Las Vegas Convention and Visitors Authority,** 3150 Paradise Rd., Las Vegas, NV 89109 (© **877/VISITLV** or 702/892-0711; www.visitlasvegas.com). Or stop by when you're in town. They're open daily from 8am to 5pm. Another excellent information source is the **Las Vegas Chamber of Commerce,** 3720 Howard Hughes Pkwy., no. 100, Las Vegas, NV 89109 (© **702/735-1616;** www.lvchamber.com). They're open Monday through Friday from 8am to 5pm.

GETTING AROUND

BY CAR   We highly recommend that visitors rent a car. The Strip is too spread out for walking, and public transportation is often ineffective in getting you from Point A to Point B. All the major hotels offer free parking.

BY BUS & TROLLEY   The no. 301 bus operated by **Citizens Area Transit** (© **702/CAT-RIDE**) plies a route between the Downtown Transportation Center (at Casino Center Blvd. and Stewart Ave.) and a few miles beyond the southern end of the Strip. The fare is $2 for adults, 60¢ for seniors (62 and older) and children 5 to 17, and free for those under 5. CAT buses run 24 hours a day and are wheelchair accessible. Exact change is required.

   Las Vegas Strip Trolley (© **702/382-1404**) operates a classic streetcar replica that runs northward from Hacienda Avenue, stopping at all major hotels en route to the Sahara, and then looping back via the Las Vegas Hilton. They do not, however, go to the Stratosphere Tower or Downtown. Trolleys run about every 15 minutes daily between 9:30am and 2am. The fare is $1.75 (free for children under age 5), and exact change is required.

   There are also a number of free transportation services, courtesy of the casinos. A free monorail connects Mandalay Bay with Luxor and Excalibur, another connects Bellagio with the Monte Carlo, still another runs between the MGM and Bally's, and a free tram shuttles between Mirage and TI at the Mirage.

BY MONORAIL

The first leg of a high-tech monorail that will eventually become a citywide mass-transit system opened in 2004. The 4-mile route runs from the MGM Grand at the southern end of The Strip to the Sahara at the northern end, with several stops along the way. These spiffy new trains make the end-to-end run in about 15 minutes, and operate 7 days a week from 8am until midnight. Fares are $3 for a one-way ride but discounts are available for round-trips and multi-ride/day passes.

BY TAXI   Cabs line up in front of all major hotels. They charge $3.20 at the meter drop and 25¢ for each additional ⅛ mile. A taxi from the airport to the Strip will run you $12 to $20, from the airport to Downtown $15 to $20, and between the Strip and Downtown about $10 to $15. Up to five people can ride for the same fare.

   If you want to call a taxi, any of the following companies can provide one: **Desert Cab Company** (© **702/386-9102**), **Whittlesea Blue Cab** (© **702/384-6111**), and **Yellow/Checker Cab/Star Company** (© **702/873-2000**).

FAST FACTS

For physician referrals, call the **Desert Springs Hospital** (② 702/388-4888). Hours are Monday through Friday from 8am to 8pm, and Saturday from 9am to 3pm. Emergency services are available 24 hours a day at **University Medical Center,** 1800 W. Charleston Blvd., at Shadow Lane (② 702/383-2000). **Sunrise Hospital and Medical Center,** 3186 Maryland Pkwy., between Desert Inn Road and Sahara Avenue (② 702/731-8080), also has a 24-hour emergency room. There's a 24-hour **Walgreens** at 3765 Las Vegas Blvd. S. (② 702/739-9638), almost directly across from the Monte Carlo.

The sales tax on meals, goods, and some services is 7%. Clark County hotel room tax is 9%, and in Henderson it's 10%.

2 Where to Stay

If there's one thing Vegas has in spades, it's hotels. Big hotels. The hotels here are the city's biggest tourist attraction, and they pack in the crowds accordingly. A last-minute Vegas vacation can turn into a housing nightmare, so make reservations in advance.

First-time visitors will most likely stay on the Strip, although Downtown is a lot nicer than it used to be, and the rates there are cheaper. The **Las Vegas Convention and Visitors Authority** runs a room reservations hot line (② 877/VISITLV) that can be helpful. **Reservations Plus** (② 800/805-9528) is a free service that finds you a hotel in your price range that meets your specific requirements. They can also arrange packages (including meals, transportation, tours, show tickets, car rentals, and other features).

Vegas does have hotels that eschew the theme scheme. Unlike many of the casino hotels, they are far more likely to cater to kids, making them good choices for families. One of two great selections is the luxurious **Four Seasons** (② 877/632-5000 or 702/632-5000; www.fourseasons.com), inside the Mandalay Bay, although it has its own entrance and facilities. The **Residence Inn by Marriott,** 3225 Paradise Rd., Las Vegas, NV 89109, between Desert Inn Road and Convention Center Drive (② 800/ 331-3131 or 702/796-9300; www.marriott.com), offers clean apartmentlike accommodations with full kitchens and sitting rooms.

All the usual budget chains, including Motel 6, Days Inn, Howard Johnson, Fairfield by Marriott, and Econo Lodge are in Las Vegas.

The following hotels all offer free self- and valet parking.

VERY EXPENSIVE

Bellagio ★★   This $1.6 billion luxury resort is a big, grand, state-of-the-art Vegas hotel. Here you'll find fabulous fountains, classical gardens, an art gallery, and the best collection of restaurants in town. There is even an 8-acre Lake Como stand-in out front, complete with a dazzling choreographed water ballet extravaganza. Rooms are nicely decorated and the roomy bathrooms are even more luxurious. Service is surprisingly good given the size of the place. The pool area is exceptional and the spa is marvelous, if overpriced.

3600 Las Vegas Blvd. S. (at the corner of Flamingo Rd.), Las Vegas, NV 89109. ② 888/987-6667 or 702/693-7111. Fax 702/693-8546. www.bellagio.com. 3,933 units. $139 and up double. Extra person $35. No discount for children. AE, DC, DISC, MC, V. **Amenities:** Casino; showrooms; wedding chapel; 14 restaurants; 6 outdoor pools; fitness center and spa; concierge; tour desk; car-rental desk; business center; 24-hr. room service; in-room massage; laundry service; dry cleaning; nonsmoking rooms; executive-level rooms. *In room:* A/C, TV w/pay movies, dataport, hair dryer, iron/ironing board, safe, high-speed Internet access (for a fee).

Caesars Palace ★★ Caesars is the spectacle that every Vegas hotel should be. A combination of Vegas luxury and a good dose of camp, the hotel is graced by Roman colonnades, marble fountains, and staff members attired in gladiator outfits and togas. But the hotel has a confusing layout, and it takes forever to get anywhere. Accommodations occupy four towers—and by the time you read this, yet another new tower will have been completed, adding 900 more rooms, plus additional restaurants. Art in the rooms keeps to the Greco-Roman theme. The newest rooms are handsome, if not as giggle-inducingly overwhelming as the classic ones, and have floor-to-ceiling windows that offer a hypnotizing panoramic view. You'll likely enjoy a lavish bathroom with marble floor, European fixtures, and oversize marble tubs (about half are whirlpools). The **Garden of the Gods** pool area is a tasteful masterpiece.

3570 Las Vegas Blvd. S. (just north of Flamingo Rd.), Las Vegas, NV 89109. ☎ 877/427-7243 or 702/731-7110. Fax 702/731-6636. www.caesars.com. 2,471 units. From $99 standard double, $109–$500 "run of house deluxe" double; $549–$1,000 suite. Extra person $20. Children under 18 stay free in parent's room. AE, DC, DISC, MC, V. **Amenities:** Casino; wedding chapel; 23 restaurants; 3 outdoor pools; health club and spa; concierge; tour desk; car-rental desk; business center; shopping arcade; 24-hr. room service; laundry service; dry cleaning; nonsmoking rooms; executive-level rooms. In room: A/C, TV w/pay movies, dataport, hair dryer, iron and board, safe, high-speed Internet access (for a fee).

Hard Rock Hotel & Casino ★ The hip flock to the Hard Rock, drawn by the cool 'n' rockin' ambience that pervades the place, from the piano-shaped roulette tables to the "backstage pass" room keys. The new and newly-updated rooms are still a bit too '60s-futuristic hip to come off as posh, but they're certainly less immediately drab than the older versions, and they're more comfortable. Bathrooms are a big step forward— bigger, brighter, shinier. On warm days and nights the Hard Rock's beach-party pool is *the* hangout scene.

4455 Paradise Rd. (at Harmon Ave.), Las Vegas, NV 89109. ☎ 800/473-ROCK (473-7625) or 702/693-5000. Fax 702/693-5588. www.hardrockhotel.com. 657 units. Sun–Thurs $79 and up double; Fri–Sat $145 and up double; from $250 suite. Extra person $35. Children 12 and under stay free in parent's room. AE, DC, MC, V. **Amenities:** Casino; showroom; 6 restaurants; 2 outdoor pools with a lazy-river ride and sandy-beach bottom; small health club and spa; concierge; tour desk; 24-hr. room service; laundry and dry-cleaning service; nonsmoking rooms; executive-level rooms. In room: A/C, TV w/pay movies, dataport, hair dryer, iron/ironing board, high-speed Internet access (for a fee).

Las Vegas Hilton ★ This classy hotel is one of the last of the dying breed of old Vegas hotels, but unlike many of its peers, it's still offering fine accommodations and even a bit more than that. The Hilton's location next to the convention center makes it the preferred choice of business travelers, and its Star Trek attraction—with its own space-themed casino—beams in the leisure crowd. The comfortable rooms, remodeled a few years ago, have bathrooms with large marble tubs; some rooms offer views of an adjacent golf course. A new owner recently took over the Hilton and is doing some minor spiffing up—little remodeling here, some new restaurants there.

3000 Paradise Rd. (at Riviera Blvd.), Las Vegas, NV 89109. ☎ 888/732-7117 or 702/732-5111. Fax 702/732-5805. www.lvhilton.com. 3,174 units. $49 and up double. Extra person $30. Children under 18 stay free in parent's room. AE, DC, DISC, MC, V. **Amenities:** Casino; showrooms; 11 restaurants plus a food court; outdoor pool; golf course adjacent; 6 tennis courts (4 night-lit); health club and spa; Jacuzzi; car-rental desk; business center; shopping arcade; 24-hr. room service; laundry service; dry cleaning; nonsmoking rooms; executive-level rooms. In room: A/C, TV w/pay movies, dataport, hair dryer, iron/ironing board, high-speed Internet access (for a fee).

Paris Las Vegas Casino Resort ★ *Sacre bleu!* The City of Light comes to Sin City in this Strip fantasy hotel. It's theme-run-amok time again, and we are so happy about it. You can stroll down a mini Rue de la Paix, ride an elevator to the top of the Eiffel Tower, stop at an over-priced bakery for a baguette, take your photo by several very nice fountains, and snicker at dubious French signage ("le car rental"). Rooms are disappointingly uninteresting, with furniture that only hints at mock French Regency, and with small but pretty bathrooms that have deep tubs. Try to get a Strip-facing room so you can see the Bellagio's fountains across the street. Overall, not a bad place to stay but a great place to visit.

3655 Las Vegas Blvd. S., Las Vegas, NV 89109. ✆ 888/BONJOUR (266-5687) or 702/946-7000. Fax 702/967-3836. www.parislv.com. 2,916 units. $119–$269 double; $350 and up suites. Extra person $30. Children under 18 stay free in parent's room. AE, DC, DISC, MC. V. **Amenities:** Casino; showrooms; 2 wedding chapels; 11 restaurants; outdoor pool; health club and spa; concierge; tour desk; business center; shopping arcade; 24-hr. room service; laundry service; dry cleaning; nonsmoking rooms; executive-level rooms. *In room:* A/C, TV w/pay movies, dataport, hair dryer, iron/ironing board, safe, high-speed Internet access (for a fee).

The Venetian ★★   The Venetian falls squarely between an outright adult Disneyland experience and the luxury resort sensibility of other Vegas hotels. The hotel impressively re-creates the city of Venice, including the outrageous prices. Rooms are the largest and probably the most handsome in town. They are all "suites," with a good-size bedroom giving way to steps down to a sunken living area, complete with pullout sofa bed. Large bathrooms feature glassed-in showers and deep soaking tubs. A branch of the famous Canyon Ranch Spa is on the premises. Unfortunately the hotel's pool area is disappointing and bland.

The new **Venezia Tower** added over 1,000 more rooms, with the same large and lush footprint and style as the originals. The tower has its own check-in and gestalt—somehow, it comes off even more lush than the original hotel.

3355 Las Vegas Blvd. S., Las Vegas, NV 89109. ✆ 888/2-VENICE (283-6423) or 702/414-1000. Fax 702/414-4805. www.venetian.com. 4,029 units. $125–$399 double. Extra person $35. AE, DC, DISC, MC, V. Kids under 13 stay free in parent's room. **Amenities:** Casino; wedding chapel; showroom; 18 restaurants; 6 outdoor pools; health club and spa; video arcade; concierge; tour desk; car-rental desk; business center; shopping arcade; 24-hr. room service; laundry service; dry cleaning; nonsmoking rooms; executive-level rooms. *In room:* A/C, TV w/pay movies, fax, dataport, fridge, hair dryer, iron/ironing board, safe, high-speed Internet access (for a fee).

Wynn Las Vegas   This is Vegas's newest and perhaps most trumpeted resort, and it came with a $2.7 billion price tag. The result? Something that is at once pretty "wow" and a whole lot "it looks like Bellagio." The hotel has no discernable theme—it's just a classy, mature place to stay. The interior has some superior moments, including considerable use of natural light and a conservatory that runs down the center. A 150-foot tall man-made mountain covered in trees and waterfalls towers out front. The rooms are the hands-down best on the Strip; particularly large, with much-appreciated floor-to-ceiling views and excellent up-to-the-minute bathrooms. The gym is excellent.

3131 Las Vegas Blvd. S. (at the corner of Sands Dr.), Las Vegas, NV 89109. ✆ 888/320-9966 or 702/770-7100. Fax 702/770-1571. www.wynnlasvegas.com. 3,933 units. $249 and up double. Extra person $50; no discount for children. AE, DC, DISC, MC, V. Free self- and valet parking. **Amenities:** Casino; showrooms; 2 wedding chapels; 13 restaurants; 5 outdoor pools; fitness center and spa; concierge; tour desk; car-rental desk; business center; 24-hr. room service; in-room massage; laundry service; dry cleaning; nonsmoking rooms; executive-level rooms. *In room:* A/C, TV w/pay movies, dataport, hair dryer, iron/ironing board, safe, high-speed Internet access (for a fee).

EXPENSIVE

Aladdin Resort & Casino ★   *Note:* The beleaguered and bankrupt Aladdin has been bought by Planet Hollywood, which as of now intends to rename, remodel, and restyle the property. It's a bit of a pity, because the Aladdin is a handsome building both inside and out, with a generic Middle East theme. This is already what a sexy, but distinctly Vegas, hotel ought to be: a little bit of kitsch, a little bit of class, and all of it playful. And we hope that the new owners will concentrate on maintaining and building on these aspects. The rooms are not distinctive, but they are pleasing, and the bathrooms can be quite large, with little Aladdin-lamp-shaped faucets and exotic spice-scented amenities. The pool area is decent but nothing spectacular.

3667 Las Vegas Blvd. S., Las Vegas, NV 89109. ℂ 877/333-WISH (333-9474) or 702/785-5555. Fax 702/785-5558. www.aladdincasino.com. 2,567 units. $99 and up double. Extra person $30; no discount for children. AE, DC, DISC, MC, V. **Amenities:** Casino; performing-arts center; showroom; 19 restaurants; 7 bars/lounges; 2 outdoor pools; health club and spa; Jacuzzi; sauna; concierge; tour desk; car-rental desk; business center; shopping arcade; 24-hr. room service; in-room massage; babysitting; laundry/dry-cleaning service; nonsmoking rooms; executive-level rooms. *In room:* A/C, TV w/pay movies, dataport, hair dryer, iron/ironing board, safe, high-speed Internet access (for a fee).

The Flamingo Las Vegas ✪ A recent renovation has made Bugsy Siegel's "real class joint" better than ever. The Flamingo's exceptional pool area encompasses fishponds, two water slides, five swimming pools, two whirlpools, waterfalls, and a flamingo enclave—plus its spa and tennis courts are a big draw. The guest rooms occupy six towers and sport various styles of decor, most with pretty fabrics and the usual array of room amenities.

3555 Las Vegas Blvd. S. (between Sands Ave. and Flamingo Rd.), Las Vegas, NV 89109. ℂ 800/732-2111 or 702/733-3111. Fax 702/733-3353. www.flamingolv.com. 3,999 units. $79 and up double; $249 and up suite. Extra person $20. Children under 18 stay free in parent's room. Inquire about packages and timeshare suites. AE, DC, DISC, MC, V. **Amenities:** Casino; showrooms; 8 restaurants; 5 outdoor pools; 4 night-lit tennis courts; health club and spa; small video arcade; tour desk; car-rental desk; business center; shopping arcade; 24-hr. room service; in-room massage; babysitting; laundry service; dry cleaning; nonsmoking rooms; executive-level rooms. *In room:* A/C, TV w/pay movies, dataport, hair dryer, iron/ironing board, safe, high-speed Internet access (for a fee).

Golden Nugget ✪✪ You may have seen the Golden Nugget on the short-lived reality show "The Casino," which depicted its new hapless owners learning how to own and run a casino-hotel. You may not be surprised to learn the place recently sold again. There were no plans at press time to indicate the new owners' intents towards their property, but let's hope for the best.

The jewel in Downtown's crown, the Golden Nugget is a luxurious European-style resort featuring gleaming marble and brass and sunny interior spaces. Rooms are decorated in a gold color scheme and feature marble entryways, half-canopy beds, and vanity tables. Suites include a good-size parlor with a wet bar, and his-and-her bathrooms. The presence of a pool, and general overall quality, make this the best hotel Downtown for families.

129 E. Fremont St. (at Casino Center Blvd.), Las Vegas, NV 89101. ℂ 800/634-3454 or 702/385-7111. Fax 702/386-8362. www.goldennugget.com. 1,907 units. $59 and up double; $275 and up suite. Extra person $20. AE, DC, DISC, MC, V. **Amenities:** Casino; showroom; 4 restaurants; outdoor pool; health club and spa; concierge; tour desk; car-rental desk; 24-hr. room service; laundry service; dry cleaning; nonsmoking rooms; executive-level rooms. *In room:* A/C, TV w/pay movies, dataport, hair dryer, iron/ironing board, safe.

Harrah's Las Vegas ✪ Here's another property that is doing its best to keep up with the pace in Vegas, to no great success; it's rather dark, dated, and claustrophobic. Still, there is much to like here, and occasional quite good rates might make the so-so bits worth overlooking. Certainly, they want to be the fun and convivial place we wish more of Vegas were (instead of pretty much catering to high rollers and simply tolerating the rest of us with normal budgets). Guest rooms were recently refurbished, and all are larger than average. Some rooms also contain a kitchen. The hotel's health club is one of the better ones on the Strip, but the pool is underwhelming.

3475 Las Vegas Blvd. S. (between Flamingo and Spring Mountain roads), Las Vegas, NV 89109. ℂ 800/HARRAHS (427-7247) or 702/369-5000. Fax 702/369-5283. www.harrahs.com. 2,700 units. $79 and up standard "deluxe" double, $99 and up standard "superior" double; $199 and up suite. Extra person $20. No discount for children. AE, DC, DISC, MC, V. **Amenities:** Casino; showrooms; 8 restaurants; outdoor pool; health club and spa; concierge; tour desk; car-rental desk; business center; shopping arcade; 24-hr. room service; laundry service; dry cleaning; nonsmoking rooms; executive-level rooms. *In room:* A/C, TV w/pay movies, dataport, hair dryer, iron/ironing board, safe.

Mandalay Bay ★★   It doesn't really evoke Southeast Asia, but the Mandalay Bay actually looks like a resort hotel rather than just a Vegas version of one. You don't have to walk through the casino to get to any of these public areas or the guest room elevators, the pool area is spiffy, and the whole complex is less overwhelming than some of the neighboring behemoths. Rooms are perhaps the finest on the Strip, spacious and subdued in decor. The large bathrooms, stocked with a host of fabulous amenities, are probably the best on the Strip. The hotel's highly touted wave pool can't handle waves of any serious size, but it does offer a nice afternoon's relaxation. There's a topless swimming area as well. See the separate listing below for Mandalay Bay's new THEhotel addition.

3950 Las Vegas Blvd. S. (at Hacienda Ave.), Las Vegas, NV 89119. ℂ 877/632-7000 or 702/632-7000. Fax 702/632-7228. www.mandalaybay.com. 4,427 units. From $99 standard double; from $149 suite; from $149 House of Blues Signature Rooms. Extra person $35. No discount for children. AE, DC, DISC, MC, V. **Amenities:** Casino; 12,000-seat events center; 1,700-seat performing-arts theater; 22 restaurants; 4 outdoor pools; health club and spa; Jacuzzi; sauna; watersports equipment/rental; concierge; tour desk; business center; 24-hr. room service; in-room massage; babysitting; laundry service; dry cleaning; nonsmoking rooms; executive-level rooms. *In room:* A/C, TV w/pay movies, dataport, hair dryer, iron/ironing board, safe, high-speed Internet access (for a fee) in THEhotel suites only.

MGM Grand Hotel/Casino ★★ *Kids*   Set on 114 acres, the massive MGM Grand's theme incorporates various MGM movies. Almost all traces of a failed movement to turn this into a child-friendly venue—including the amusement park and the Wizard of Oz theme—have been wiped out, but the lion habitat and the fabulous pool area make this place popular with families. The Grand Tower rooms are a modern-day homage to 1930s modern—all clean, curvy lines, good wood, and a fun palette of colors (pale pastels or wheaty earth tones), plus black-and-white movie-star glamour photos. They're the best choice in town in their price range. The hip West Wing rooms feature lots of mirrors, frost green glass on bathroom and shower doors, and flat panel TVs.

3799 Las Vegas Blvd. S. (at Tropicana Ave.), Las Vegas, NV 89109. ℂ 800/929-1111 or 702/891-7777. Fax 702/891-1030. www.mgmgrand.com. 5,034 units. $99 and up standard double; $159 and up suite. Extra person $30. Children under 13 stay free in parent's room. AE, DC, DISC, MC, V. **Amenities:** Casino; events arena; showroom; cabaret theater; 2 wedding chapels; 15 restaurants; outdoor pool; fitness center and spa; Jacuzzi; sauna; arcade; concierge; tour desk; car-rental desk; business center; 24-hr. room service; in-room massage; babysitting; laundry service; dry cleaning; nonsmoking rooms; executive-level rooms. *In room:* A/C, TV w/pay movies, dataport, hair dryer, iron/ironing board, safe, high-speed Internet access (for a fee).

The Mirage ★★   From the moment you walk into the Mirage and breathe the faintly tropically perfumed air, you'll just know you are on vacation. The hotel, fronted by waterfalls and tropical foliage, centers on a very "active" volcano that erupts every 15 minutes after dark. Inside, you'll find a verdant rainforest, complete with habitats for Siegfried and Roy's white tigers, and a bunch of Atlantic bottlenose dolphins. The rooms have recently been redone and while the results are not distinctive, they are handsome. The staff is genuinely helpful; any problems that may arise are quickly smoothed out. The pool is one of the nicest in Vegas.

3400 Las Vegas Blvd. S. (between Flamingo Rd. and Sands Ave.), Las Vegas, NV 89109. ℂ 800/627-6667 or 702/791-7111. Fax 702/791-7446. www.mirage.com. 3,044 units. $119 and up double; $249 and up suite. Extra person $30. No discount for children. AE, DC, DISC, MC, V. **Amenities:** Casino; showrooms; 11 restaurants; beautiful outdoor pool; fitness center and spa; concierge; tour desk; car-rental desk; business center; shopping arcade; 24-hr. room service; laundry service; dry cleaning; nonsmoking rooms; executive-level rooms. *In room:* A/C, TV w/pay movies, dataport, hair dryer, iron/ironing board, safe, high-speed Internet access (for a fee).

New York–New York Hotel & Casino ★★ *Kids*   A visit to this spectacular hotel, which looks like the New York City skyline (complete with a roller coaster running through it) is a must. Subtle it isn't. You can gamble in a casino done up as Central Park or play games in the Coney Island arcade. Rooms come in 64 different styles; some are downright tiny and suffocating (just like New York). The original Deco-inspired décor has made way for something they call '40s inspired. We don't see it, but do find it a sophisticated modern color scheme of earth tones and pale pastels, with dark rich wood furniture. Light sleepers should request a room away from the roller coaster. If you're a pool person, go elsewhere—the one here is pretty mediocre.

3790 Las Vegas Blvd. S. (at Tropicana Ave.), Las Vegas, NV 89109. ℂ 800/693-6763 or 702/740-6969. Fax 702/740-6920. www.nynyhotelcasino.com. 2,033 units. $79 and up double. Extra person $30. No discount for children. AE, DC, DISC, MC, V. **Amenities:** Casino; showrooms; 10 restaurants plus a food court; outdoor pool; fitness center and spa; Jacuzzi; sauna; video arcade with carnival midway games; concierge; tour desk; 24-hr. room service; laundry service; dry cleaning; nonsmoking rooms; executive-level rooms. *In room:* A/C, TV w/pay movies, dataport, hair dryer, iron/ironing board, safe, high-speed Internet access (for a fee).

Rio All Suite Hotel & Casino ★   Although it's not on the Strip, the Rio Suites has a carnival atmosphere that packs in the crowds—and the accompanying noise. In addition to its tropically themed resort, the Rio has an immensely popular 41-story tower and Masquerade Village that simulate a European village, complete with shops, restaurants, and a bizarre live-action show in the sky. The "suites" are actually one rather large room with a sofa and coffee table. Rooms feature amenities such as fridges, and floor-to-ceiling windows offer views of the Strip. Note that the hotel actively discourages guests from bringing children.

3700 W. Flamingo Rd. (at I-15), Las Vegas, NV 89103. ℂ 888/752-9746 or 702/777-7777. Fax 702/777-7611. www.playrio.com. 2,582 units. $99 and up double-occupancy suite. Extra person $30. No discount for children. Inquire about golf packages. AE, DC, MC, V. **Amenities:** Casino; showrooms; 13 restaurants plus additional fast-food outlets; 4 outdoor pools; golf course; health club and spa; Jacuzzi; sauna; video arcade; concierge; car-rental desk; business center; shopping arcade; 24-hr. room service; in-room massage; laundry service; dry cleaning; nonsmoking rooms; executive-level rooms. *In room:* A/C, TV w/pay movies, fridge, coffeemaker, hair dryer, iron/ironing board, safe.

THEhotel at Mandalay Bay ★★★   If Prada were a hotel, it would look something like THEhotel. Located in the Mandalay Bay, but with an entirely separate entrance (and an entirely different atmosphere), THEhotel wows you from the start, but not in the usual Vegas marble-gilt-and-chandelier screaming over the top way. Every room is a genuine suite, done in black, tans, and gleaming woods, and an enormous marbled bathroom. All the amenities of Mandalay Bay are just down a long hall. You can use the workout facilities at the gorgeous Bathhouse Spa for only $20. One of the best hotels in Vegas.

3950 Las Vegas Blvd. S., Las Vegas, NV 89119. ℂ 702/632-7777 or 877/632-7000. www.mandalaybay.com. 1,118 units. $189 and up. AE, DC, DISC, MC, V. Free self- and valet parking. **Amenities:** 2 restaurants; bar; access to Mandalay Bay restaurants/pool/casino; health club; spa; tour desk; car rental; business center; sundries shop; 24-hr room service; laundry service. *In room:* A/C, 3 flatscreen plasma TVs, combo printer/fax, wet bar, minibar, hair dryer, iron/ironing board, high-speed Internet access (for a fee), CD/DVD, robes and slippers, scale.

TI at The Mirage ★★   Huh? What happened to Treasure Island? What happened to the pirates? Why, Vegas grew up, that's what. Originally the most modern family-friendly hotel, the former Treasure Island was a blown-up version of Disneyland's Pirates of the Caribbean. But that's all behind them now, and the name change is there to make

sure you understand this is a grown-up, sophisticated resort. What remains, after they stripped the pirate gilt, are well-sized rooms in modified French Regency style that are much nicer than most in their price range. The pool is not that memorable, however.

3300 Las Vegas Blvd. S. (at Spring Mountain Rd.), Las Vegas, NV 89177-0711. ℂ 800/944-7444 or 702/894-7111. Fax 702/894-7446. www.treasureisland.com. 2,891 units. From $69 double; from $109 suite. Extra person $25. No discount for children. Inquire about packages. AE, DC, DISC, MC, V. **Amenities:** Casino; showrooms; 11 restaurants; outdoor pool; health club and spa; very well-equipped game and video arcade; concierge; tour desk; car-rental desk; business center; shopping arcade; 24-hr. room service; laundry service; dry cleaning; nonsmoking rooms; executive-level rooms. *In room:* A/C, TV w/pay movies, fax, dataport, hair dryer, iron and board, safe.

MODERATE

Luxor Las Vegas ★★ (Kids) It would be hard to miss the Luxor's 30-story pyramid, even without the 315,000-watt light beam at the top. The hotel is, despite outward appearances, inviting, classy, and functional. The lobby mixes towering statues of Ramses and animatronic camels with marble and cherrywood in a vaguely Art Deco style. Rooms feature fine Art Deco and Egyptian furnishings and have excellent marble bathrooms, although the recently renovated Pyramid rooms have showers only. Regardless of which room you get, these are some of the few rooms in Las Vegas that stand out.

3900 Las Vegas Blvd. S. (between Reno and Hacienda aves.), Las Vegas, NV 81119. ℂ 888/777-0188 or 702/262-4000. Fax 702/262-4478. www.luxor.com. 4,400 units. Sun–Thurs $59 and up double; Fri–Sat $99 and up double; $149 and up whirlpool suite; $249–$800 other suites. Extra person $25. Children under 12 stay free in parent's room. AE, DC, DISC, MC, V. **Amenities:** Casino; showrooms; 10 restaurants plus a food court; 5 outdoor pools; health club and spa; 18,000-sq.-ft. video arcade; concierge; tour desk; car-rental desk; business center; shopping arcade; 24-hr. room service; dry cleaning; nonsmoking rooms; executive-level rooms. *In room:* A/C, TV w/pay movies, dataport, hair dryer, iron/ironing board, high-speed Internet access (for a fee).

Stratosphere Casino Hotel & Tower ★ (Kids) At 1,149 feet, the Stratosphere is the tallest building west of the Mississippi; it's also in the middle of nowhere on the Strip, which explains the lack of crowds (and lower prices). The panoramic views available from the top of the tower and some amazing thrill rides (see "What to See & Do," below) are the big attractions here. Other perks include a midway area with kiddie-oriented rides and a pool with a view. The smaller-size rooms here are basically motel rooms—really nice motel rooms, but with that level of comfort and style. Ask for a high floor when you reserve to optimize your view.

2000 Las Vegas Blvd. S. (between St. Louis St. and Baltimore Ave.), Las Vegas, NV 89104. ℂ 800/99-TOWER (998-6937) or 702/380-7777. Fax 702/383-5334. www.stratospherehotel.com. 2,500 units. Sun–Thurs $39 and up double; Fri–Sat $59 and up double; $69 and up suite. Extra person $15. Children 12 and under stay free in parent's room. AE, DC, DISC, MC, V. **Amenities:** Casino; showrooms; wedding chapel; 7 restaurants plus several fast-food outlets; large new pool area with great views of the Strip; children's rides and games located at the base of the tower; concierge; tour desk; car-rental desk; shopping arcade; 24-hr. room service; laundry service; dry cleaning; nonsmoking rooms; executive-level rooms. *In room:* A/C, TV w/pay movies, dataport, hair dryer, iron/ironing board, safe.

INEXPENSIVE

Circus Circus Hotel/Casino ★ (Kids) Circus Circus, once the epitome of kitsch, is trying to be taken more seriously. The bright primary colors and garish trims have vanished in favor of subtle, muted tones. Nevertheless, the world's largest permanent circus and indoor theme park are still here, and kids will love it. Tower rooms have newish, just slightly better-than-average furnishings; the Manor section comprises five white three-story buildings out back. These rooms are usually among the least expensive in town, but you get what you pay for. A recent renovation of these rooms added a coat of paint and some new photos on the wall, but not much else. The hotel also has its own RV park.

2880 Las Vegas Blvd. S. (between Circus Circus Dr. and Convention Center Dr.), Las Vegas, NV 89109. ℂ 800/444-CIRC (444-2472), 800/634-3450, or 702/734-0410. Fax 702/734-5897. www.circuscircus.com. 3,744 units. Sun–Thurs $59 and up double; Fri–Sat $79 and up double. Extra person $12. Children under 17 stay free in parent's room. AE, DC, DISC, MC, V. **Amenities:** Casino; circus acts; wedding chapel; 7 restaurants; 2 outdoor pools; midway-style carnival games; video arcade; tour desk; car-rental desk; shopping arcade; 24-hr. room service; laundry service; dry cleaning; nonsmoking rooms; executive-level rooms. *In room:* A/C, TV w/pay movies, hair dryer, safe.

Main Street Station ★★ *Finds*   The Main Street Station, one of the best bargains in the city, is just 2 short blocks away from Fremont Street in Downtown, barely a 3-minute walk. The overall look is turn-of-the-20th-century San Francisco, and the details, from the ornate chandeliers to the wood-paneled lobby, are outstanding. The long and narrow rooms are possibly the largest in Downtown, decorated with simple, vaguely French provincial furniture. The bathrooms are small but well appointed. If you're a light sleeper, request a room on the south side.

200 N. Main St. (between Fremont St. and I-95), Las Vegas, NV 89101. ℂ 800/465-0711 or 702/387-1896. Fax 702/386-4466. www.mainstreetcasino.com. 452 units. $59 and up standard double. AE, DC, DISC, MC, V. **Amenities:** Casino; 3 restaurants; outdoor pool next door at California Hotel; car-rental desk; dry cleaning; nonsmoking rooms. *In room:* A/C, TV w/pay movies.

3 Where to Dine

The dining scene in Las Vegas is a melting pot of midnight steak specials, cheap buffets, and gourmet rooms that rival those found in New York or Los Angeles. One word of warning: You can eat well in Vegas, and you can eat cheaply in Vegas, but it's hard to do both at the same time.

Theme restaurant buffs can chow down at **House of Blues,** in Mandalay Bay, 3950 Las Vegas Blvd. S. (ℂ 702/791-STAR); the **Hard Rock Cafe** at 4475 Paradise Rd., at Harmon Avenue (ℂ 702/632-7607); **ESPN** at 3790 Las Vegas Blvd. S., in New York–New York Hotel & Casino (ℂ 702/ 933-3776); the **Harley Davidson Cafe,** 3725 Las Vegas Blvd. S., at Harmon Avenue (ℂ 702/740-4555); or the **Rainforest Cafe** in the MGM Grand, 3799 Las Vegas Blvd. S. (ℂ 702/891-8580).

For those wanting to sample one of the many hotel buffets, some of the better bets include **Luxor's Pharaoh's Pheast Buffet,** 3900 Las Vegas Blvd. S. (ℂ 702/262-4000); **Mirage Cravings Buffet,** 3400 Las Vegas Blvd. S. (ℂ 702/791-7111); **Rio's Carnival World Buffet,** 3700 W. Flamingo Rd. (ℂ 702/252-7777); **Paris, Le Village Buffet,** 3665 Las Vegas Blvd. S. (ℂ 888/266-5687); **Golden Nugget Buffet,** 129 E. Fremont St. (ℂ 702/385-7111); and **Main Street Station Garden Court,** 200 N. Main St. (ℂ 702/387-1896). The best Sunday brunch buffet in Vegas is **Bally's Sterling Sunday Brunch,** 3645 Las Vegas Blvd. S. (ℂ 702/967-7999).

VERY EXPENSIVE

Aureole ★★★ NOUVELLE AMERICAN   The primary fame of this branch of a New York City fave comes from their gimmicky wine tower, four stories of probably the finest wine collection in Vegas, made even more sensational by the catsuit-clad lovelies who are hoisted on wires to reach bottles requested from the uppermost heights. Lost in this Vegas-show glitz is one of the truly best of the fine dining experiences around. The menu is a three-course prix fixe. Expect marvels like a tender roasted lamb loin and braised shoulder, or a rack of venison accompanied by sweet-potato puree and chestnut crisp. Desserts are playful, including a bittersweet chocolate soufflé with blood-orange sorbet and a Bartlett pear crisp with toasted cinnamon brioche and lemongrass foam.

In Mandalay Bay, 3950 Las Vegas Blvd. S. ✆ 877/632-1766. www.aureolelv.com. Reservations required. Fixed-price dinner $69 or $95 for a tasting menu. AE, DISC, MC, V. Daily 6–10pm.

Commander's Palace ★★ CREOLE This is an offshoot of the famous New Orleans restaurant, so we did expect a lot, and they came through. Service is very good and the food was, if not yet as spectacular as that of their elder cousin's, some of the best we've had in Vegas yet, with not one thing, from appetizer to dessert, that disappointed our palates. Your best bet is probably the $39 three-course Creole favorite, featuring Commander's justly legendary turtle soup with sherry, Louisiana pecan-crusted fish, and signature bread pudding soufflé, three things they do very very well indeed.

In the Desert Passage in the Aladdin hotel, 3663 Las Vegas Blvd. S. ✆ 702/892-8272. www.commanderspalace.com. Reservations suggested. Lunch $16–$20; dinner $28–$39. AE, DISC, MC, V. Mon–Fri 9–11am for breakfast, brunch 11:30am–2pm, dinner 5:30–10pm, Sat–Sun brunch 10:30–2pm, dinner 5:30–10pm.

Picasso ★★★ FRENCH Madrid-born chef Julian Serrano's cooking stands proudly next to the $30 million worth of Picassos that pepper the dining room's walls, making a meal here a truly memorable experience. This may well be the best restaurant in Vegas. The menu changes nightly and is always a choice between a four- or five-course fixed-price dinner or tasting menu. We were bowled over by roasted Maine lobster with a "trio" of corn—kernels, sauce, and flan. Hudson Valley foie gras was crusted in truffles and went down smoothly. The lamb rôti was an outstanding piece of lamb, crusted with truffles—just hope it's on the menu the night you're there. For dessert, a molten chocolate cake leaves any other you may have tried in the dust.

In Bellagio, 3600 Las Vegas Blvd. S. ✆ 702/693-7223. Reservations recommended. Fixed-price 4-course dinner $90, 5-course degustation $100. AE, DC, DISC, MC, V. Wed–Mon 6–9:30pm.

EXPENSIVE

Border Grill ★★★ MEXICAN For our money, here's the best Mexican food in town. This big cheerful space houses a branch of the much lauded L.A. restaurant, conceived and run by the Food Network's "Two Hot Tamales," Mary Sue Milliken and Susan Feniger. This is truly authentic Mexican home cooking. Expect fresh and fabulous food, arranged as brightly on the plates as the decor on the walls. Stay away from the occasionally bland fish and head right toward rich and cheesy dishes like chiles rellenos and chicken *chilaquiles* (a sister to the taco). Don't miss the dense but fluffy Mexican chocolate cream pie.

In Mandalay Bay, 3950 Las Vegas Blvd. S. ✆ 702/632-7403. www.bordergrill.com. Reservations recommended. Main courses $15–$24. AE, DC, DISC, MC, V. Sun–Thurs 11:30am–10:30pm; Fri–Sat 11:30am–11pm.

Bouchon ★★★ BISTRO Thomas Keller made his name with his Napa Valley restaurant The French Laundry, considered by many to be the best restaurant in the United States. Bouchon is a version of his Napa Valley bistro. The menu features humble-sounding dishes that in nearly every case are gold-standard versions of classics. The sweet and supremely fresh Snow Creek oysters seem to melt on contact with your tongue. The pâté is a result of a complex multi-day preparation that produces a rich buttery whip that's worth the $50 price tag. Don't miss the bacon and poached-egg frisee salad, or the cleanly seared salmon over poached leeks. The beef bourguignon and leg of lamb are winners as well. Worth the price if you can afford it.

3355 Las Vegas Blvd. S. ℂ **702/414-6200.** Reservations strongly recommended. Main courses breakfast $8–$21, dinner $21–$33. AE, DC, DISC, MC, V. Daily breakfast 7–10:30am, dinner 5–11pm, Oyster bar open daily 3–11pm, Sat–Sun lunch 11:30am–2:30pm.

Canaletto ✪✪ ITALIAN   Come here for solid, true Italian fare. This place is all the more enjoyable for being perched on the faux St. Mark's Square; in theory, you can pretend you are sitting on the edge of the real thing, a fantasy we don't mind admitting we briefly indulged in. A risotto of porcini, sausage, and white truffle oil was full of strong flavors, while the wood-fired roast chicken was perfectly moist. A properly roasted chicken should be a much-celebrated thing and that alone may be a reason to come here.

In The Venetian Grand Canal Shoppes, 3377 Las Vegas Blvd. S. ℂ **702/733-0070.** Reservations recommended for dinner. Main courses $14–$35. AE, DC, MC, V. Sun–Thurs 11:30am–11pm; Fri–Sat 11:30am–midnight.

Pinot Brasserie ✪✪ BISTRO   Pinot reliably delivers French and American favorites that are thoughtfully conceived and generally delicious. It's an excellent choice if you want a special meal that is neither stratospherically expensive nor too complex. The signature dish, beloved by many, is a roasted chicken accompanied by heaping mounds of garlic fries; but if you wish to get a little more elaborate (and yet rather light), thin slices of smoked salmon with celery rémoulade could be a way to go. Desserts are lovely, and the ice cream is homemade.

In The Venetian, 3355 Las Vegas Blvd. S. ℂ **702/414-8888.** Reservations recommended for dinner. Main courses $14–$18 at lunch, $19–$30 at dinner. AE, DISC, MC, V. Mon–Thu 7–10am, 11:30am–3pm, and 5:30–10pm, Fri 7–10am, 11:30am–3pm, and 5:30–10:30pm, Sat 7am–3pm and 5:30–10:30pm, Sun 7am–3pm and 5:30–10pm.

Rosemary's Restaurant ✪✪✪ AMERICAN   A 15-minute (or so) drive down Sahara is all it takes to eat what the *Vegas-Review Journal* calls the best food in Las Vegas. Rosemary's cuisine covers most regions of the U.S., though Southern influences dominate. Interesting sides include ultra-rich bleu cheese slaw and perfect cornmeal jalapeño hush puppies. A recent visit found the crispy striped bass fighting it out with the pan-seared honey glazed salmon for "best fish dish I've ever had." Desserts, such as lemon icebox pie, are most pleasant. We also recommend trying some of the restaurant's beer suggestions.

8125 W. Sahara. ℂ **702/869-2251.** www.rosemarysrestaurant.com. Reservations strongly suggested. Lunch $12–$16; dinner $18–$29. AE, MC, V. Mon–Fri 11:30am–2:30pm and 5:30–10:30pm.

MODERATE

Grand Wok and Sushi Bar ✪✪ PAN-ASIAN   A pan-Asian restaurant runs the risk of attempting to be a jack of all trades and master of none, but somehow, this MGM eatery pulls it off. We didn't try every cuisine offered (Japanese, Chinese, Korean, Vietnamese, and maybe more!), but a random sampling (including lovely fresh sushi, fat dumplings, and a huge Vietnamese combo soup full of noodles and different kinds of meat) produced really superb food, delicately prepared. Soup portions are most generous—four people could easily split one order and have a nice light and very cheap lunch.

In the MGM Grand, 3799 Las Vegas Blvd. S. ℂ **702/891-7777.** Reservations not accepted. Main courses $9–$15; sushi rolls and pieces $4.50–$12. AE, DC, DISC, MC, V. Restaurant Sun–Thurs 11am–10pm, Fri–Sat 11am–midnight; sushi bar Mon–Thurs 5–10pm, Fri–Sat 11am–midnight, Sun 11am–10pm.

INEXPENSIVE

Capriotti's ✪✪✪ SANDWICHES   It looks like a dump but there's a reason that Capriotti's is one of the fastest growing businesses in town. They roast their own beef and turkeys on the premises and stuff them (or Italian cold cuts, or whatever) into huge sandwiches—the "large" is 20 inches, easily feeding two for under $10 total. And deliciously so; the "Slaw B Joe" (roast beef, coleslaw, and Russian dressing) is fabulous. They even have veggie varieties. We never leave town without a stop here, and you shouldn't, either.

324 W. Sahara Ave. (at Las Vegas Blvd. S.). © 702/474-0229. www.capriottis.com. Most sandwiches under $10. No credit cards. Mon–Fri 10am–5pm; Sat 11am–5pm.

Lotus of Siam ★★★ *Finds* THAI   We don't feel guilty about dragging you out to a strip mall in the east end of Nowhere because here is what critic Jonathan Gold of *Gourmet* magazine called no less than the best Thai restaurant in North America. In addition to all the usual beloved Thai favorites, they have a separate menu featuring lesser-known dishes from Northern Thailand—they don't routinely hand this one out (since most of the customers are there for the $6 lunch buffet). Standouts include the Issan sausage (a grilled sour pork number); and *Sua Rong Hai* ("weeping tiger"), a dish of soft sliced grilled marinated beef. More conventional Thai dishes are also excellent.

953 E. Sahara Ave. #A-5. © 702/735-3033. www.saipinchutima.com. Reservations strongly suggested for dinner. Lunch buffet $5.99; other dishes $3.95–$14. AE, MC, V. Mon–Fri 11:30am–2:30pm and 5:30–9:30pm; Sat–Sun 5:30-10pm.

Monte Carlo Pub & Brewery ★★★ *Kids* *Finds* PUB FARE   Lest you think we are big, fat foodie snobs who can't appreciate a meal unless it comes drenched in truffles and caviar, we hasten to direct you to this lively, working microbrewery and its hearty, not-so-high-falutin' food. There's no romantic atmosphere thanks to the 40 TV sets sprinkled around the room—but no inflated prices. Earning recent raves were the short ribs, in a fine barbecue sauce; the excellent appetizer of chicken fingers and shrimp fried in beer; and the garlic pizza. After 9pm, only pizza is served, and dueling pianos provide dance music and entertainment.

In the Monte Carlo Resort & Casino, 3770 Las Vegas Blvd. S. (between Flamingo Rd. and Tropicana Ave.). © 702/730-7777. Reservations not accepted. Main courses $6–$15. AE, DC, DISC, MC, V. Sun–Thurs 11am–3am; Fri–Sat 11am–4am.

4 What to See & Do

You can't sit at a slot machine forever. (Or maybe you can.) In any event, it shouldn't be too hard to find ways to fill your time between poker hands. Many of the hotels offer free entertainment in the form of light shows, animal-filled parks, and strolling musical performers. Can't-miss shows include the **Bellagio's dancing fountains,** the best free show in town; the **talking statues in Caesars' Forum Shops;** and the **Mirage's exploding "volcano."** Couch potatoes can watch the MGM Grand's 80-foot outdoor video screens, while adventurers head for a roller coaster celebrating that most daredevil of drivers—the New York cabbie. (This last one's not free, but that only heightens the reality of the experience.)

Nevertheless, when you finally tire of Strip-gazing (or your brain shuts down from the overload), there are plenty of other things to see and do in Las Vegas.

Auto Collections at the Imperial Palace ★★   Even if you're not a car person, don't assume you won't be interested in this premier collection of antique, classic, and special-interest vehicles. Check out the graceful lines and handsome sculpture of one of the largest collection of Duesenbergs in the world. The vehicles on display change regularly, but highlights from a recent visit include a 1964 Chaika that belonged to

Soviet leader Nikita Krushchev; FDR's unrestored 1936 V-16 Cadillac; and Al Capone's 1930 V-16 Cadillac.

In the Imperial Palace hotel, 3535 Las Vegas Blvd. S. © **702/794-3174.** www.autocollections.com. Admission $6.95 adults, $3 seniors and children under 12, free for children under 3. Check website for free-admission coupon. Daily 9:30am–9:30pm.

Fremont Street Experience ★★ The Fremont Street Experience in the heart of Downtown Vegas is a 5-block open-air pedestrian mall, a landscaped strip of outdoor cafes, vendor carts, and colorful kiosks purveying food and merchandise. Overhead is a 90-foot-high steel-mesh "celestial vault"; at night, it's the **Sky Parade,** a high-tech light-and-laser show that takes place four times nightly. The canopy also cools the area through a misting system in summer and warms you with radiant heaters in winter. It's a place where you can stroll, eat, or even dance to the music under the lights. The crowd it attracts is more upscale than in years past, and of course, it's a lot less crowded than the hectic Strip.

Fremont St. (between Main St. and Las Vegas Blvd.), Downtown. www.vegasexperience.com. Free admission. Shows nightly every hour on the hour after dark.

King Tut's Tomb & Museum ★ This full-scale reproduction of King Tut-ankhamen's tomb was all handcrafted in Egypt by artisans using historically correct gold leaf and linens, pigments, tools, and ancient methods. It's hardly like seeing the real thing, but if you aren't going to Egypt any time soon, it's a surprisingly enjoyable Vegas fake. A 4-minute introductory film precedes a 15-minute audio tour (available in English, French, Spanish, and Japanese).

In Luxor Las Vegas, 3900 Las Vegas Blvd. S. © **702/262-4000.** Admission $5. Daily 9am–11pm.

Liberace Museum ★★★ *Moments* You can keep your Louvres and Vaticans and Smithsonians; *this* is a museum. Housed in a strip mall, this is a shrine to the glory and excess that was the art project known as Liberace. You've got your costumes (bejeweled), your many cars (bejeweled), your many pianos (bejeweled), and many jewels (also bejeweled). It just shows what can be bought with lots of money and no taste. Unless you have a severely underdeveloped appreciation for camp or take your museum-going very seriously, you shouldn't miss it. The museum is 2½ miles east of the Strip on your right.

1775 E. Tropicana Ave. (at Spencer St.). © **702/798-5595.** www.liberace.org. Admission $13 adults, $8.50 seniors over 64 and students, free for children under 10. Mon–Sat 10am–5pm; Sun noon–4pm. Closed Thanksgiving, Dec 25, and Jan 1.

Madame Tussaud's Celebrity Encounter ★ *Kids* Even if you aren't a fan of wax museums, this one is probably worth a stop. Figures here are state of the art, although some reproductions are considerably better than others. All the waxworks are free-standing, allowing guests to get up close and personal. Go ahead; lay your cheek next to Elvis's or Sinatra's and have your photo taken. The emphasis here is on film, television, music, and sports celebrities. There's also a behind-the-scenes look at the lengthy process involved in creating these figures.

3355 Las Vegas Blvd. S. © **702/862-7800.** www.madametussaudslv.com. Admission $21 adults, $15 seniors and Nevada residents, $9.95 children 6–12, children 5 and under free. Daily 10am–10pm, but hours vary seasonally.

MGM Grand Lion Habitat ★★ *Kids* Hit this attraction at the right time—when the crowds aren't here—and it's one of the best freebies in town. It's a large, multi-level glass enclosure, in which lions frolic throughout the day. In addition to regular viewing spots, you can walk through a glass tunnel and get a worm's eye view of the underside of a lion (provided one is in position); note how very big Kitty's paws are. Multiple lions share show duties, so what you observe is definitely going to depend on who is in residence when you drop by.

In the MGM Grand, 3799 Las Vegas Blvd. S. 𝄐 702/891-7777. Free admission. Daily 11am–10pm.

Secret Garden of Siegfried and Roy & Mirage Dolphin Habitat ★★★ Kids

Get up close and personal with some of the famed duo's white tigers (the one involved in Roy's famous injury is not displayed), lions, and plain old gray elephants, here at this mini-zoo; or better still, watch dolphins frolic in the neighboring Dolphin Habitat. There is nothing quite like the kick you get from seeing a baby dolphin play. Ask the staff to play ball with the dolphins; they toss large beach balls into the pools, and the dolphins hit them out with their noses, leaping out of the water cackling with dolphin glee.

In The Mirage, 3400 Las Vegas Blvd. S. 𝄐 702/791-7111. Admission $12, free for children under 10 if accompanied by an adult. Mon–Fri 11am–5:30pm, Sat–Sun and Major Holidays 10am–5:30pm. Hours subject to change and vary by season.

Speed: The Ride/Las Vegas Cyber Speedway ★★ Kids

This popular stop has three attractions. The first is a remarkable 8-minute virtual-reality ride, **Cyber Speedway,** featuring a three-quarter-size replica of a NASCAR race car. In a separate **3-D motion theater,** you'll don goggles to view a film that puts you right inside another race car for yet another stomach-churning ride. **Speed: The Ride** is a roller coaster that blasts riders out through a hole in the wall by the new NASCAR Cafe, then through a loop, under the sidewalk, through the hotel's marquee, and finally straight up a 250-foot tower. Then you do the whole thing backwards. Not for the faint of heart.

In the Sahara hotel & casino, 2535 Las Vegas Blvd. S. 𝄐 702/737-2111. $15 for 1 ride on each attraction, $20 for all-day pass includes coaster. Stock-car simulator only $10 (you must be at least 48 in. tall to ride), Speed: The Ride (roller coaster) $10 for single ride, $20 for all-day pass includes simulator. Mon–Thurs noon–9pm, Fri noon–10pm, Sat 11am–10pm, Sun 11am–9pm.

Stratosphere Thrill Rides ★★ Kids

Atop the 1,149-foot Stratosphere Tower are two marvelous thrill rides. The **Let It Ride High Roller** (the world's highest roller coaster) was recently revamped to go at even faster speeds as it zooms around a hilly track that is seemingly suspended in midair. Even more fun is the **Big Shot,** a breathtaking free-fall ride that thrusts you 160 feet in the air along a 228-foot spire at the top of the tower, then plummets back down again. Amping up the terror factor is **X-Scream,** a giant teeter-totter-style device that propels you in an open car off the side of the 100-story tower. And now they have the aptly named **Insanity: the Ride,** a spinning whirly-gig of a contraption that straps you into a seat and twirls you around 1,000 feet or so above terra firma. *Note:* The rides are shut down in inclement weather and high winds.

Atop the Stratosphere Casino Hotel & Tower, 2000 Las Vegas Blvd. S. 𝄐 702/380-7777. Admission: Big Shot $8; X-Scream $8; Insanity $8; High Roller $4; plus $9.95 to ascend the Tower (if you dine in the buffet room or Top of the World, there's no charge to go up to the Tower). Multiride and all-day packages also available for varying costs. Sun–Thurs 10am–midnight; Fri–Sat 10am–1am. Hours vary seasonally. Minimum height requirement for both rides is 48 in.

WHERE TO ROLL THE DICE

What? You didn't come to Las Vegas for the Liberace Museum? We are shocked. *Shocked.*

Yes, there are gambling opportunities in Vegas. Let's not kid ourselves; gambling is what Vegas is about. You should casino-hop at least once to marvel (or get dizzy) at the decor/spectacle and the sheer excess of it all. Beyond decoration, there isn't too much difference. All the casinos have slot and video poker machines and offer games such as blackjack, roulette, craps, poker, Pai Gow, keno, and baccarat. If you're a novice, many casinos offer free gambling lessons that include low stakes games, so you won't lose much while you learn.

Some notable places to gamble include the **MGM Grand,** the largest casino (you will get lost); **New York–New York,** where the change carts look like yellow cabs; the light and airy **Mandalay Bay;** the tasteful **Venetian;** the **Las Vegas Hilton,** where the space-themed casino has light beam–activated slots; **Harrah's,** where the "party pits" offer the most fun in town; **Paris–Las Vegas,** where you'll find a kitschy Disneyesque atmosphere; and **Binion's,** where all serious gamblers head, thanks to low minimum bets and the highest betting limits in town.

Downtown, stakes are lower, pretensions are nonexistent, and the clientele are often friendlier. You don't have to be a high roller. You would not believe how much fun you can have with a nickel slot machine. You won't get rich, but neither will most of those guys playing the $5 slots, either.

5 Las Vegas After Dark

Las Vegas is a town that truly comes alive only at night, and you won't lack for things to do. In addition to the free street shows (see "What to See & Do," above), the hotels all have lounges, usually featuring live music, and you haven't truly done Vegas if you don't hit at least one showroom.

For up-to-date listings, call the **Las Vegas Convention and Visitors Authority** (© 877/VISITLV) and ask them to send you a free copy of *Showguide* or *What's On in Las Vegas* (one or both of which will probably be in your hotel room). You can also check out what's playing at **www.visitlasvegas.com**. It's best to plan well ahead if you have your heart set on seeing one of the most popular shows.

THE SHOWS

There are shows all over town, ranging from traditional magic shows to cutting-edge acts. You won't go wrong seeing just about any of **Cirque du Soleil**'s productions—except for Zumanity, which is overrated, they're the best in town. *O,* at the Bellagio (© 888/488-7111), is a breathtaking mix of artistry and acrobatics over a 1½-million-gallon pool; *Mystère,* at TI at the Mirage (© 800/288-7206), is a sophisticated and surreal circus extravaganza; and the newest show, *KÁ,* at the MGM Grand (© 877/ 880-0880) has an actual plot set in a mystical Asian kingdom, with lots of imagery borrowed from magical realist martial arts movies like *Crouching Tiger, Hidden Dragon*. **Celine Dion's** show at Caesar's magnificent theatre is still a hot (and expensive) ticket. This special-effects extravaganza, complete with blooming trees, flying pianos, giant chandeliers, and an enormous LED screen, was directed and produced by Franco Dragone, who previously brought this town *O* and *Mystère*. The **Blue Man Group** at the Venetian is performance art for the masses, but don't let that prevent you

---

Nighttime Is the Right Time

For a great selection of nightlife on the Strip, head for Mandalay Bay; **Aureole, Red Square, rumjungle,** and the **House of Blues** are all popular. You might also check out the incredible nighttime view at the bar atop the **Stratosphere**— nothing beats it.

---

from going and laughing your head off (© **702/414-1000**). And if you want to see a classic Vegas topless revue—oh, why not?—check out *Jubilee!* at Bally's (© **800/237-7469** or 702/739-4567).

Magic fans will love **Lance Burton: Master Magician,** at the Monte Carlo (© **877/386-8224**), whose sleight-of-hand tricks are extraordinary; or you can head for the smart, funny show of **Penn & Teller,** at the Rio (© **888/746-7784**) for magic, juggling, comedy, and some mean stunts.

THE CLUB & BAR SCENE

Most Las Vegas bars and clubs don't even get going until close to midnight. **The Beach,** 365 S. Convention Center Dr., at Paradise Road (© **702/731-1925;** www.beachlv.com), is an immense two-story club that caters to the young and pretty who are looking to party. **Body English,** in the Hard Rock Hotel, 4455 Paradise Rd. (© **702/639-5000**), is what we think a Vegas club should be—an over-the-top clash of Anne Rice and Cher Gothic themed wacky decadence. Expect long lines and a hefty cover charge. **Light,** at the Bellagio, 3600 Las Vegas Blvd. S. (© **702/693-8300**), is a grown-up nightclub that caters to the silver spoon crowd but has a party atmosphere that doesn't feel exclusive.

Country music fans might want to wander on over to the casual **Dylan's,** 4660 Boulder Hwy. (© **702/451-4006**), which offers country music (live and otherwise) and line dancing, with free dance lessons.

Good Times is a quiet neighborhood bar located (for those of you with a taste for subtle irony) in the same complex as the Liberace Museum (1775 E. Tropicana Ave.; © **702/736-9494**). **Gipsy,** at 4605 Paradise Rd. (© **702/731-1919**), is the gay dance club that draws the biggest crowds.

It's still an honor for a comedian to play Vegas, and a number of good comedy clubs are on the Strip. Some good choices are **Comedy Stop,** in the Tropicana, 3801 Las Vegas Blvd. S. (© **800/468-9494**); **The Improv,** at Harrah's, 3475 Las Vegas Blvd. S. (© **800/392-9002**); and **Comedy Club,** at The Riviera, 2901 Las Vegas Blvd. S. (© **800/634-6753**).

Appendix:
The Southwest in Depth

In the Hopi creation myth, the Spider Woman fashioned of clay all the birds and beasts, men and women. With Tawa, the sun god, she sang a song and brought forth life. In the American Southwest, the magic of that story is apparent wherever you turn. A colossal elephant, camel, or medicine man fashioned from stone might dominate the landscape; great canyons cut through the earth's crust, laying bare centuries of rock-layer stories. And human artifacts tell their own stories: spear points left some 9,000 years ago, centuries-old cliff dwellings where the scent of smoke still lingers, and grand missions and fortresses where Catholicism once ruled. It's a land with its own song, one the traveler can't help but be caught up in, stepping to the Spider Woman's ancient rhythm.

1 More Than Desert & Saguaro Cactus

Those who have never visited the American Southwest tend to have some misconceptions. The most common one is that the whole place is a hot desert studded with saguaro cactus. In fact, the Southwest has varied terrain, encompassing all seven of the earth's life zones, from the low Sonoran cactus country, through the higher plateaus studded with piñon and juniper, to the rich forested sections and even high alpine country. And rather than year-round heat, the Southwest has a range of temperatures, including blistering desert climes, midland regions with warm summers and cold winters, and high mountains where the air is always cool and winter brings world-class skiing.

Major landforms traverse the region. The southern Rocky Mountains cut down through central Colorado and northern New Mexico. The Grand Canyon slices across northern Arizona, as do other prominent canyons, which stretch into Utah. Dramatic stone formations carved by weather and erosion stud this region, including those you've likely seen in movies filmed in Monument Valley, as well as others such as Shiprock and

Natural Bridges National Monument. In the south, volcanic mountains called "sky islands" dot the desert, home to abundant wildlife, especially bird populations.

Water is the language of the region, enunciating the fate of what grows and what dies here. Rain is scarce. Rivers are scarcer. The Rio Grande cuts New Mexico nearly in half, barely feeding the towns and cities along its banks. The Colorado River snakes from its namesake state across Utah, Arizona, and Nevada before heading south to the Gulf of California. Over the years it's been heavily dammed, resulting in grand lakes, which supply the desert with electricity and irrigation.

What water there is feeds a remarkable array of plant and animal life. In the Sonoran Desert, the notable saguaro cactus, which can reach 40 feet tall and weigh several tons, stands as a symbol for the entire region. Many other kinds of cactus thrive here as well, as does a range of vegetation, from delicate wildflowers such as the reddish-pink columbine and purple aster to hearty pines such as blue spruce and ponderosa. They help feed and house a broad variety of animal life, from tropical birds such as the elegant trogon to hearty mammals such as pronghorn antelopes, brown bears, and mountain lions. But the desert's most notorious creatures are those that crawl and creep: scorpions, tarantulas, and rattlesnakes. You should avoid these creatures, but don't lose sleep over them—generally, if you leave them alone, they'll do the same to you.

2 How the Southwest Was Won—& Lost

IN THE BEGINNING Archaeologists say that humans first migrated to the Southwest, moving southward from the Bering Land Bridge, around 12,000 B.C. Sites such as Sandia Cave and Folsom—where weapon points were discovered that for the first time clearly established that our prehistoric ancestors hunted now-extinct mammals such as woolly mammoths—are internationally known. When large prey animals died off during the late Ice Age (about 8000 B.C.), people turned to hunting smaller game and gathering wild food.

Stable farming settlements, as evidenced by the remains of domestically grown maize, date from around 3000 B.C. As the nomadic peoples became more sedentary, they built permanent residences, known as pit houses, and made pottery. Cultural differences began to emerge in their choice of architecture and decoration: The Mogollon people, in the southwestern part of modern New Mexico, created brown and red pottery and built large community lodges; the Anasazi (also called ancestral Puebloans), in the Four Corners region, made gray pottery and smaller lodges for extended families. In Arizona, the Sinagua and Hohokam cultures farmed the land, creating extensive irrigation systems.

By about A.D. 700, and perhaps a couple of centuries earlier, the Anasazi had built villages throughout what is now known as the Four Corners region (where New Mexico, Arizona, Utah, and Colorado come together). Chaco Culture National Historic Park and Aztec Ruins National Monument in New Mexico; Mesa Verde National Park in Colorado; and Betatakin, Keet Seel, and Canyon de Chelly in Arizona, among other sites, all exhibit an architectural excellence and skill, and a scientific sensitivity to nature, that marks this as one of America's classic pre-Columbian civilizations.

The sites include condominium-style communities of stone and mud adobe bricks, three and four stories high. The villages incorporated circular spiritual chambers called kivas. The Anasazi also developed the means to irrigate their fields of corn, beans, and squash by controlling the flow of water from area rivers. From Chaco Canyon, they built a complex system of well-engineered roads leading in four directions to other towns or ceremonial centers. Artifacts found during excavation, such as seashells and macaw feathers, indicate they had a far-reaching trade network. The incorporation of solar alignments into some of their architecture has caused modern archaeoastronomers to speculate on the importance of the equinoxes to their religion.

The diminishing of the Anasazi culture, and the emergence of the Pueblo culture in its place, is something of a mystery today. Those who study such things disagree about why the Anasazi left their villages around the 13th century. Some suggest drought or soil exhaustion; others, invasion, epidemic, or social unrest. But by the time the first Spanish explorers arrived in the 1500s, the Anasazi were long gone and the Pueblo culture was well established throughout northern and western New Mexico, from Taos to Zuni, near Gallup. The Hopi had also established their home in northeastern Arizona.

Certain elements of the Anasazi civilization had clearly been kept alive by the Pueblos, including the apartment-like adobe architecture, the creation of rather elaborate pottery, and the use of irrigation or flood farming in their fields. Agriculture, and especially corn, was the economic mainstay.

Each village fiercely guarded its independence. When the Spanish arrived, there were no alliances between villages, even among those with a common language or dialect. No more than a few hundred people lived in any one pueblo, an indication that the natives had learned to keep their population down in order to preserve their soil and other natural resources. But not all was peaceful: They alternately fought and traded with each other, as well as with nomadic Apaches.

THE ARRIVAL OF THE SPANISH

The Spanish controlled the Southwest for 300 years, from the mid–16th to the mid–19th century—longer than the United States has. The Hispanic legacy in language and culture is still strong in the region.

The spark that sent the first European explorers into the region was a fabulous medieval myth that seven Spanish bishops had fled the Moorish invasion of the 8th century, sailed westward to the legendary isle of Antilia, and built themselves seven cities of gold. Hernán Cortés's 1519 discovery and conquest of the Aztecs' treasure-laden capital of Tenochtitlán, now Mexico City, fueled belief in the myth. When a Franciscan friar 20 years later claimed to have sighted, from a distance, "a very beautiful city" in a region known as Cíbola while on a reconnaissance mission for the viceroyalty, the gates were open.

Francisco Vásquez de Coronado, the ambitious young governor of New Spain's western province of Nueva Galicia, was commissioned to lead an expedition to the "seven cities." Several hundred soldiers, accompanied by servants and missionaries, marched overland to Cíbola with him in 1540, along with a support fleet of three ships in the Gulf of California. What they discovered, after 6 hard months on the trail, was a bitter disappointment: Instead of a city of gold, they found a rock-and-mud pueblo at Hawikku, the westernmost of the Zuni towns. The expedition wintered at Tiguex, on the Rio Grande near modern Santa Fe, before proceeding to the Great Plains seeking more treasure at Quivira, in what is now Kansas. The grass houses of the Wichita Indians were all they found.

Coronado returned to New Spain in 1542, admitting failure. Historically, though, his expedition was a great success, contributing the first widespread knowledge of the Southwest and Great Plains, and encountering the Grand Canyon.

By the 1580s, after important silver discoveries in the mountains of Mexico, the Spanish began to wonder if the wealth of the Pueblo country might lie in its land and people rather than its cities. They were convinced that they had been divinely appointed to convert the natives of the New World to Christianity. And so a northward migration began, orchestrated and directed by the royal government. It was a mere trickle in the late 16th century. Juan de Oñate established a capital in 1598 at San Gabriel, near San Juan Pueblo in New Mexico, but a variety of factors led to its failure. Then in 1610, under Don Pedro de Peralta, the migration began in earnest.

It was not dissimilar to America's schoolbook stereotype. Bands of armored conquistadors did troop through the desert, humble robed friars striding by their sides. But most of the pioneers came up the valley of the Rio Grande with oxcarts and mule trains rather than armor, intent on transplanting their Hispanic traditions of government, religion, and material culture to this new world.

RELIGION & REVOLT The 17th century in the Southwest was essentially a missionary era, as Franciscan priests attempted to turn the Indians into model Hispanic peasants. Their churches became the focal point of every pueblo, with Catholic schools a mandatory adjunct. By 1625 there were an estimated 50 churches in the Rio Grande valley, and by 1670, the Franciscans had founded several missions among the Hopi pueblos.

But the Native Americans weren't enthused about doing "God's work"—building new adobe missions, tilling fields for the Spanish, and weaving garments for export to Mexico—so soldiers backed the padres in extracting labor, a system known as *repartimiento*. Simultaneously, the *encomienda* system provided that a yearly tribute in corn and blankets be levied upon each Indian. The Pueblos were willing to take part in Catholic religious ceremonies and proclaim themselves converts. To them, spiritual forces were actively involved in the material world. If establishing harmony with the cosmos meant absorbing Jesus Christ and various saints into their hierarchy of *kachinas* and other spiritual beings, so much the better. But the Spanish friars demanded that they do away with their traditional singing and masked dancing, and with other "pagan practices." When the Pueblo religion was violently crushed and driven literally underground, resentment toward the Spanish grew and festered. In 1680, the Pueblo Revolt erupted.

Popé, a San Juan shaman, catalyzed the revolt. Assisted by other Pueblo leaders, he unified the far-flung Native Americans, who had never confederated before. They pillaged and burned the province's outlying settlements, then turned their attention to Santa Fe, besieging the citizens who had fled to the Palace of the Governors. After 9 days, having reconquered Spain's northernmost American province, they let the refugees retreat south to Mexico.

Popé ordered that the Pueblos return to the lifestyle they had had before the arrival of the Spanish. All Hispanic items, from tools to livestock to fruit trees, were to be destroyed, and the blemish of baptism was to be washed away in the river. But the shaman misjudged the influence of the Spanish upon the Pueblos. They were not the people they had been a century earlier, and they *liked* much of the material culture they had absorbed from the Europeans. What's more, they had no intention of remaining confederated; their independent streak was too strong.

In 1692, led by newly appointed Gov. Don Diego de Vargas, the Spanish recaptured Santa Fe without bloodshed. Popé had died, and without a leader to reunify them, the Pueblos were no match for the Spanish. Vargas pledged not to punish them, but to pardon and convert. Still, when he returned the following year with 70 families to recolonize the city, he used force. And for the next several years, bloody battles persisted throughout the Pueblo country.

By the turn of the 18th century, the Southwest was firmly in Spanish hands. This time, however, the colonists seemed to have learned from some of their errors. They were more tolerant of other religions, and less ruthless in their demands and punishments.

ARRIVAL OF THE ANGLOS In 1739, the first French trade mission entered Santa Fe, welcomed by the citizenry but not by the government. For 24 years, until 1763, a black-market trade thrived between Louisiana and New Mexico. It ended only when France lost its toehold on its North American claims during the French and Indian War against Great Britain.

The Native Americans were more fearsome foes. Apache, Comanche, Ute, and Navajo launched repeated raids against each other and the Rio Grande settlements for most of the 18th century, which led the Spanish and Pueblos to pull closer together for mutual protection. Pueblo and Hispanic militias fought side by side in campaigns against the invaders. But by the 1770s, the attacks had become so savage and destructive that the viceroy in Mexico City created a military jurisdiction in the province, and Gov. Juan Bautista de Anza led a force north to Colorado to defeat the most feared of the Comanche chiefs, Cuerno Verde ("Green Horn"), in 1779. Seven years later, the Comanches and Utes signed a lasting treaty with the Spanish and thereafter helped keep the Apaches in check.

France sold the Louisiana Territory to the young United States in 1803, and the Spanish suddenly had a new intruder to fear. The Lewis and Clark expedition of 1803 went unchallenged, much as the Spanish would have liked to do otherwise. But in 1807, when Lt. Zebulon Pike built a stockade on a Rio Grande tributary in Colorado, he and his troops were taken prisoner by troops from Santa Fe. Pike was transported to the New Mexican capital, where he was interrogated extensively, and then to Chihuahua, Mexico. The report he wrote upon his return was the United States' first inside look at Spain's frontier province.

At first, pioneering American merchants—excited by Pike's observations of the region's economy—were summarily expelled from Santa Fe or jailed, and their goods confiscated. But after Mexico gained independence from Spain in 1821, traders were welcomed. The wagon ruts of the Santa Fe Trail soon extended from Missouri to New Mexico, and from there to Chihuahua. (Later, it became the primary southern highway to California.)

As the merchants hastened to Santa Fe, Anglo-American and French Canadian fur trappers headed into the wilderness. Their commercial hub became Taos, a tiny village near a large pueblo a few days' ride north of Santa Fe. Many married into native or Hispanic families. Perhaps the best known was Kit Carson (1809–1868), a sometime federal agent and sometime scout whose legend is inextricably interwoven with that of the early Southwest.

In 1846, the Mexican War broke out and New Mexico (which included Arizona) became a territory of the United States. There were several causes of the war, including the U.S. annexation of Texas in 1845, disagreement over international boundary, and unpaid claims owed to American citizens by the Mexican government. But foremost was the prevailing U.S. sentiment of "manifest destiny," the belief that the Union should extend "from sea to shining sea." Gen. Stephen Kearny marched south from Colorado; on the plaza in Las Vegas, New Mexico, he announced that he had come to take possession of the area for the United States. His arrival in Santa Fe on August 18, 1846, went unopposed.

An 1847 revolt in Taos resulted in the slaying of the new governor of New Mexico, Charles Bent, but U.S. troops defeated the rebels and executed their leaders. That was the last threat to American sovereignty in the territory. In 1848, the Treaty of Guadalupe Hidalgo officially transferred title of New Mexico, along with Texas, Arizona, and California, to the United States.

Kearny promised that the United States would respect religion and property rights and would safeguard homes and possessions from hostile Indians. His troops behaved with rigid decorum. The United States upheld Spanish policy toward the Pueblos, assuring the survival of their ancestral lands, their traditional culture, and their old religion—which even 3 centuries of Hispanic Catholicism could not do away with.

Meanwhile, on a broad valley of what is now southeastern Nevada, Spanish explorers found a new route to Los Angeles. Named Las Vegas (the meadows), the place had abundant wild grasses and plentiful water. It was also the home to the Paiute Indians. With hopes of teaching the Paiutes to farm, in 1855 Brigham Young assigned 30 Mormon missionaries to build a fort in the valley. It was raided and left in ruins just a few years later, but a precedent was established. By the 1880s, precious minerals had been found, bringing miners to the area. And the land itself proved fertile, attracting farmers. The phenomenon that would one day be Las Vegas had begun.

THE CIVIL WAR   As conflict between the North and South flared east of the Mississippi, the Southwest found itself caught in the debate over slavery. Southerners wanted to expand slavery to the western territories, but abolitionists fought a bitter campaign to prevent that from happening. In 1861, the Confederacy, after seceding from the Union, laid plans to make the region its own as a first step toward capturing the West.

In fact, southern New Mexicans, including those in Tucson (Arizona was still part of the New Mexico Territory), were disenchanted with the attention paid them by Santa Fe and already were threatening to form their own state. So when Confederate Lt. Col. John Baylor captured Fort Fillmore, near Mesilla, and on August 1, 1861, proclaimed all of New Mexico south of the 34th parallel to be the new territory of Arizona, there were few complaints.

The following year, Confederate Gen. Henry Sibley assembled three regiments of 2,600 Texans and moved up the Rio Grande. They defeated Union loyalists in a bloody battle at Valverde, near Socorro; easily took Albuquerque and Santa Fe, which were protected only by small garrisons; and proceeded toward the federal arsenal at Fort Union, 90 miles east of Santa Fe. Sibley planned to replenish his supplies there before continuing north to Colorado, then west to California.

On March 27 and 28, 1862, the Confederates were met head-on in Glorieta Pass, about 16 miles outside of Santa Fe, by regular troops from Fort Union supported by a regiment of Colorado Volunteers. By the second day, the rebels were in control, until a detachment of Coloradoans circled behind the Confederate troops and destroyed their poorly defended supply train. Sibley was forced into a rapid retreat back down the Rio Grande. A few months later, Mesilla was reclaimed for the Union, and the Confederate presence in the New Mexico Territory ended.

THE LAND WARS   The various tribes had not missed the fact that whites were fighting among themselves, and they took advantage of this weakness to step up their raids on border settlements. In 1864, the Navajos, in what is known in tribal history as "The Long Walk," were relocated to the new Bosque Redondo Reservation on the Pecos River at Fort Sumner, in east-central New Mexico. Militia Col. Kit Carson led New Mexico troops in this venture, and was a moderating influence between the Navajos and those who called for their unconditional surrender or extermination. The experiment failed, and within 5 years the Navajos were returned to their homeland, though they were forced to live on a reservation.

Corralling the rogue Apaches in the south presented the territory with its biggest challenge. Led by chiefs Victorio, Nana, and Geronimo, these bands wreaked havoc upon the mining towns. Eventually, they succumbed, and the capture of Geronimo in 1886 was the final chapter in the region's long history of Indian wars.

As the Native American threat decreased, more and more livestock and sheep ranchers established themselves on the vast plains east of the Rio Grande, in the San Juan basin of the northwest, and in the area around present-day Phoenix. Cattle drives up the Pecos Valley, on the Goodnight-Loving Trail, are the stuff of legend; so, too, was Roswell cattle baron John Chisum, whose 80,000 head of beef probably represented the largest herd in America in the late 1870s.

Mining grew as well. Albuquerque blossomed in the wake of a series of major gold strikes in the Madrid Valley, close to ancient turquoise mines. Other gold, silver, and copper discoveries through the 1870s gave birth to boomtowns—infamous for their gambling halls, bordellos, and shootouts in the streets. Tombstone and Bisbee in Arizona, Silver City in New Mexico, and Leadville and Cripple Creek in Colorado remain legendary.

In the late 1870s, the railroads arrived. Now linked by rail to the great markets of America, the region enjoyed an economic boom period. In 1905, the main railway linking southern California with Salt Lake City was completed. Las Vegas, Nevada, became an important refueling point and rest stop on the route.

But ranching invites cattle rustling and range wars, mining beckons feuds and land fraud, and the construction of railroads has often been tied to political corruption and swindles. The Southwest had all of them, especially during the latter part of the 19th century. One of the central figures was William "Billy the Kid" Bonney, a headstrong youth (b. 1858) who became probably the best-known outlaw of the American West. He blazed a trail of bloodshed from Silver City to Lincoln to Fort Sumner, where he was finally killed by Sheriff Pat Garrett in July 1881.

By the turn of the 20th century, most of the violence had been checked. The mineral lodes were drying up, and ranching was taking on increased importance. Economic and social stability were coming.

AGRICULTURE & ATOMS In the late 19th and early 20th century, the southwestern states were officially granted statehood: Nevada in 1864, Colorado in 1876, Utah in 1896, and New Mexico and Arizona in 1912. This was an exciting era for the West. Theodore Roosevelt set aside great tracts of land as national forests and established what is now called the Theodore Roosevelt Dam on the Salt River in Arizona, which enabled large-scale agriculture to take root.

In 1931, the state of Nevada legalized gambling, a decision that forever changed the face of the one-time agricultural and railroad town, Las Vegas.

But the most dramatic development in 20th century occurred during World War II. In 1943, the U.S. government sealed off a tract of land on the Pajarito Plateau, west of Santa Fe, that had been an exclusive boys' school. On this site, in utter secrecy, it built the Los Alamos National Laboratory, otherwise known as Project Y of the Manhattan Engineer District—the "Manhattan Project." Its goal: to split the atom and develop the world's first nuclear weapons.

Under the direction of J. Robert Oppenheimer, later succeeded by Norris E. Bradbury, a team of 30 to 100 scientists and hundreds of support staff lived and worked in almost complete seclusion for 2 years. Their work resulted in the atomic bomb, tested for the first time at the Trinity Site, north of White Sands, on July 16, 1945. The bombings of Hiroshima and Nagasaki, Japan, 3 weeks later, signaled to the world that the nuclear age had arrived.

Despite the rapid integration of the 21st century in many parts of the region, other areas are still resisting the 20th. Many Native Americans, be they Pueblo, Navajo, or Apache, and Hispanic farmers, who till small plots in isolated rural regions, hearken to a time when life had a slower pace.

3 The Southwest Today—from Flamenco to Craps

GROWING PAINS The Southwest is experiencing a reconquest of sorts, as the Anglo population soars, and outside money and values make their way in. The process continues to transform the region's many distinct cultures and their unique ways of life, albeit in a less violent manner than during the Spanish conquest.

Certainly, the new arrivals—many of them from large cities—add a cosmopolitan flavor. The variety of restaurants has greatly improved, as have entertainment options. For their small size, towns such as Taos, Santa Fe, and Flagstaff offer a broad variety of restaurants and cultural events. Santa Fe, Tucson, and Phoenix have developed strong dance and drama scenes, with treats such as flamenco and opera that you'd expect to find in cosmopolitan centers such as New York and Los Angeles. Albuquerque and Tucson have exciting nightlife scenes with a wealth of jazz, rock, country, and alternative music.

Yet many newcomers, attracted by the exotic feel, often bring only a loose appreciation for the area. Some tend to romanticize the lifestyle of other cultures and trivialize their beliefs. Native American symbology, for example, is employed in ever-popular Southwestern decorative motifs; New Age groups appropriate valued rituals, such as sweats (in which believers sit in a very hot, enclosed space to cleanse their spirits). The effects of cultural and economic change are even apparent throughout the countryside, where land is being developed at an alarming rate, often as lots for new million-dollar homes.

Transformation of the local way of life and landscape is also apparent in the stores continually springing up in the area. For some of us, these are a welcome relief from Western clothing stores and provincial dress shops. The downside is that city plazas, which once contained pharmacies and grocery stores frequented by residents, now overflow with T-shirt shops and galleries appealing to tourists. Many locals in these cities now rarely visit their downtown areas except during special events such as fiestas.

Environmental threats are another regional reality. Nuclear-waste issues form part of an ongoing conflict affecting the entire Southwest, and a section of southern New Mexico has been designated a nuclear-waste site. Colorado has its own nuclear waste woes. Cleanup of Rocky Flats nuclear weapons facility has been an ongoing problem.

Still, new ways of thinking have brought positive changes, and many locals have directly benefited from the influx of newcomers and the region's popularity as a tourist destination. Businesses and industries large and small have come to the area. Today, electronics manufacturing, aerospace engineering, and other high-tech industries employ thousands. Local artists and artisans also benefit from growth. Many craftspeople—furniture makers, silversmiths, and weavers—have expanded their businesses. The influx of people has broadened the sensibility of a fairly provincial region. You'll find a level of creativity and tolerance here that you would generally find in very large cities but not in smaller communities.

CULTURAL QUESTIONS Faced with new challenges to their ways of life, both Native Americans and Hispanics are marshaling forces to protect their cultural identities. A prime concern is language. Through the years, many Native Americans have begun to speak more and more English, with their children getting little exposure to their native tongue. To counter the effects, many villages have implemented language classes.

Some of the pueblos have introduced programs to conserve the environment, preserve ancient seed strains, and protect religious rites. Because their religion is tied closely to nature, a loss of natural resources would threaten the entire culture. Outsiders have only limited access to certain rituals, the most notable being the Shalako at Zuni, a popular and elaborate series of year-end ceremonies.

Hispanics, through art and observance of cultural traditions, are also embracing their roots. Throughout the region, murals depicting important historic events, such as the Treaty of Guadalupe Hidalgo of 1848, adorn walls. The Spanish Market in Santa Fe has expanded into a grand celebration of traditional arts, from tin working to santo carving. Public schools have bilingual education programs, allowing young people to embrace their Spanish-speaking roots.

Hispanics are also making their voices heard, insisting on more conscientious development of their neighborhoods and rising to positions of power in government. The region's best example of a prominent Hispanic citizen is Bill Richardson, who was appointed U.S. ambassador to the United Nations and left that post to become energy secretary in President Clinton's cabinet. Now he is New Mexico's governor.

GAMBLING WINS & LOSSES Gambling, a fact of life and source of much-needed revenue for Native American populations across the country, has been a center of controversy in the Southwest for a number of years, and now is well entrenched throughout the region.

Many are concerned about the tone gambling sets in the Southwest, fearing a fate similar to that of Las Vegas, Nevada. Since World War II Las Vegas has expanded rapidly to become a world center for gambling, with attendant problems such as corruption and what some see as lax moral standards.

The Native American casinos aren't as flashy as those in Las Vegas, though they are, for the most part, large and unsightly. The neon-bedecked buildings stand out sorely on some of the region's most picturesque land. Though most residents appreciate the boost that gambling can ultimately bring to the Native American economies, many critics wonder where gambling profits actually go—and if the casinos can possibly be a good thing for the pueblos and tribes.

A number of pueblos and tribes, however, are showing signs of prosperity, and they are using newfound revenues to buy firefighting and medical equipment and to invest in local schools.

4 Art & Architecture

It's all in the light—or at least that's what many artists claim drew them to the Southwest. In truth, the light is only part of the attraction: Nature in this part of the country, with its awe-inspiring thunderheads, endless expanse of blue skies, and rugged desert, is itself a canvas. To record the wonders of earth and sky, early natives imprinted images (in the form of petroglyphs and pictographs) on the sides of caves and on stones, as well as on the sides of pots they shaped from clay dug in the hills.

Today's Native American tribes carry on that legacy, as do the other cultures that have settled here. Life is shaped by the arts. Everywhere you turn, you'll see pottery, paintings, jewelry, and weavings. You're liable to meet an artist whether you're having coffee in a Sedona cafe or walking along Canyon Road in Santa Fe.

The area is full of little villages that maintain their own artistic specialties. Each Indian pueblo has a trademark design, such as **Santa Clara's** and **San Ildefonso's** black pottery and the **Navajo's** geometric emblazoned weavings. Bear in mind that the images often have deep meaning. When purchasing art, you may want to talk to the maker about what the symbols signify.

Hispanic and Native American villagers take their goods to the cities, where for centuries people have bought and traded. Under the portals along plazas, you'll find a variety of works in silver, stone, and pottery for sale. In the cities, you'll find streets lined with galleries, both slick and modest. Trading posts, most notably Arizona's Hubbell Trading Post in Ganado and Cameron Trading Post in Cameron, offer excellent variety and quality. At major markets, such as the **Spanish Market** and **Indian Market** in Santa Fe, some of the top artists from the area sell their works. Smaller shows at the pueblos also attract artists and artisans. The **Northern Pueblo Artists and Craftsman Show,** revolving each July to a different New Mexico pueblo, continues to grow.

Drawn by the beauty of the local landscape and respect for indigenous art, artists from all over have flocked here, particularly during the 20th century. They have established locally important art societies; one of the most notable is the **Taos Society of Artists.** Santa Fe has its own art society, begun in the 1920s by a nucleus of five painters who became known as **Los Cinco Pintores.** Meanwhile, Scottsdale, Tucson, Sedona, Tubac, and Jerome have developed into rich founts for Southwestern and Western art.

The visitor interested in art should exercise some caution, however; there's a lot of schlock out there, targeting the tourist trade. If you persist, you're likely to find much inspiring work as well. The museums and many of the galleries are excellent repositories of local art. Their offerings range from small-town folk art to works by major artists who show internationally.

A RICH ARCHITECTURAL MELTING POT Nowhere else in the United States are you likely to see such extremes of architectural style as in the Southwest. The region's distinctive architecture reflects the diversity of cultures that have left their imprint on the region.

The first people to build in the area were the Anasazi (ancestral Puebloans), who made stone and mud homes at the bottom of canyons and inside caves. **Pueblo-style adobe architecture** evolved and became the basis for traditional homes: sun-dried clay bricks mixed with grass for strength, mud-mortared, and covered with additional protective layers of mud. Roofs are supported by a network of *vigas*—long beams whose ends protrude through the outer facades—and *latillas,* smaller stripped branches layered between the *vigas.* Other adapted Pueblo architectural elements include plastered adobe-brick kiva fireplaces, *bancos* (adobe benches that protrude from walls), and *nichos* (small indentations within a wall that hold religious icons). These adobe homes are characterized by flat roofs and soft, rounded contours.

Spaniards wedded many elements to Pueblo style, such as portals (porches held up with posts, often running the length of a home) and enclosed patios, as well as the simple, dramatic sculptural shapes of Spanish mission arches and bell towers. They also brought elements from the Moorish architecture found in southern Spain: heavy wooden doors and elaborate corbels—carved wooden supports for the vertical posts.

With the opening of the Santa Fe Trail in 1821 and the 1860s gold boom, both of which brought more Anglo settlers, came the next wave of building. New arrivals contributed architectural elements such as neo-Grecian and Victorian influences popular in the middle part of the United States at the time. Distinguishing features of what came to be known as **Territorial-style** architecture can be seen today; they include brick facades and cornices as well as porches, often placed on the second story. You'll also note millwork on doors and wood trim around windows and doorways, double-hung windows, and Victorian bric-a-brac.

Santa Fe Plaza is an excellent example of the convergence of these early architectural styles. On the west side is a Territorial-style balcony, while Pueblo-style vigas and oversize Spanish/Moorish doors mark the Palace of Governors. Outside Tucson, one of the most noted examples of Mission-style architecture still stands at Mission San Xavier del Bac.

In the mid–20th century, architect Frank Lloyd Wright designed several buildings in the Phoenix area, ushering in innovative building concepts. In the desert north of Phoenix, one of his students, Paolo Soleri, built an environmentally sensitive, ideal city called Arcosanti, which is open to the public.

Index

IF YOU BOOK IT, IT SHOULD BE THERE.

Only Travelocity guarantees it will be, or we'll work with our travel partners to make it right, right away. So if you're missing a balcony or anything else you booked, just call us 24/7. 1-888-TRAVELOCITY

travelocit

You'll never roam al